JUVENILE DELINQUENCY

THEORY, PRACTICE AND LAW

SIXTH EDITION

JUVENILE DELINQUENCY

THEORY, PRACTICE AND LAW

SIXTH EDITION

LARRY J. SIEGEL, Ph.D.
University of Massachusetts—Lowell

JOSEPH J. SENNA, M.S.W., J.D.
Northeastern University

WEST PUBLISHING COMPANY

St. Paul   New York   Los Angeles   San Francisco

PHOTO CREDITS

3 A. Ramey/Stock Boston 5 AP Photo/Miami Herald 9 Michael Newman/PhotoEdit 17 AP/Wide World 22 AP Photo/Paula Illingworth 25 AP/Wide World Photos 33 Richard Hutchings/PhotoEdit 38 Mark Richards/PhotoEdit 41 Bob Daemmrich/Stock Boston 49 Deborah Davis/PhotoEdit 54 Michael Dwyer/Stock Boston 87 Peter Vandermark/Stock Boston 91 Michael Newman/PhotoEdit 97 Michelle Bridwell/PhotoEdit 103 David Young-Wolff/PhotoEdit 114 Wide World Photos 137 UPI/Corbis-Bettmann 140 Spencer Grant/Stock Boston 146 Michael Weisbrot and Family/Stock Boston 150 Stock Boston 155 Tony Freeman/PhotoEdit 173 Dorothy Littell/Stock Boston 177 A. Ramey/PhotoEdit 188 Michael Newman/PhotoEdit 191 Tony Freeman/PhotoEdit 195 Reuters/Corbis-Bettman 213 Charles Gatewood/Stock Boston 215 AFP/Corbis-Bettman 216 Hazel Hankin/Stock Boston 219 Michael Newman/PhotoEdit 228 Lionel J-M Delevingne/Stock Boston 234 Steve Starr/Stock Boston 245 Steve Starr/Stock Boston 248 Y. Momatiuk & J. Eastcott/Stock Boston 260 Michael Newman/PhotoEdit 263 Dana White/PhotoEdit 268 Gary Wagner/Stock Boston 275 Jonathan Nourok/PhotoEdit 278 Billy E. Barnes/Stock Boston 280 Bob Kramer/Stock Boston 289 American Humane Society 295 Lou Krasky/AP Wide World 303 Jim Pickerell/Stock Boston 319 Jim West/Impact Visuals 322 Mark Richards/PhotoEdit 336 A. Ramey/Woodfin Camp and Associates 342 A. Ramey/Stock Boston 344 Lonny Sharelson/Impact Visuals 349 Thor Swift/Impact Visuals 359 AP/Wide World Photos 362 David Young-Wolfe/PhotoEdit 364 Elizabeth Crews/Stock Boston 369 AP/Wide World Photos 376 Michael Newman/PhotoEdit 389 Mark Burnett/David R.

(continued following index)

PRODUCTION CREDITS

Cover Image: Gardener, Glen, Clare, Dottie, Bill, and Richard by Alexi Worth. Alexi Worth is an artist living in Brooklyn, N.Y. Image used with permission.

Text Design: Light Source Images, St. Paul

Copyedit: Jan Krygier

Composition: Carlisle Communication

Index: Sandi Schroeder

WEST'S COMMITMENT TO THE ENVIRONMENT

In 1906, West Publishing Company began recycling materials left over from the production of books. This began a tradition of efficient and responsible use of resources. Today, 100% of our legal bound volumes are printed on acid-free, recycled paper consisting of 50% new paper pulp and 50% paper that has undergone a de-inking process. We also use vegetable-based inks to print all of our books. West recycles nearly 27,700,000 pounds of scrap paper annually—the equivalent of 229,300 trees. Since the 1960s, West has devised ways to capture and recycle waste inks, solvents, oils, and vapors created in the printing process. We also recycle plastics of all kinds, wood, glass, corrugated cardboard, and batteries, and have eliminated the use of polystyrene book packaging. We at West are proud of the longevity and the scope of our commitment to the environment.

West pocket parts and advance sheets are printed on recyclable paper and can be collected and recycled with newspapers. Staples do not have to be removed. Bound volumes can be recycled after removing the cover.

Production, Prepress, Printing and Binding by West Publishing Company.

 TEXT IS PRINTED ON 10% POST CONSUMER RECYCLED PAPER

British Library Cataloguing-in-Publication Data. A catalogue record for this book is available from the British Library.

COPYRIGHT © 1981, 1985, 1988, 1991, 1994 By WEST PUBLISHING COMPANY
COPYRIGHT ©1997 By WEST PUBLISHING COMPANY
610 Opperman Drive
P.O. Box 64526
St. Paul, MN 55164-0526

LIBRARY OF CONGRESS CATALOGING-IN-PUBLICATION DATA

Siegel, Larry J.
   Juvenile delinquency : theory, practice, and law / Larry J. Siegel, Joseph J. Senna. — 6th ed.
     p.   cm.
   Includes index.
   ISBN 0-314-09244-7 (alk. paper)
   1. Juvenile delinquency—United States. 2. Juvenile justice. Administration of—United States. I. Senna, Joseph J. II. Title.
HV9104.S53 1997
364.3′6′0973—dc20
                                                 96-25588
                                                  CIP

To my wife Therese J. Libby and my children,
Julie, Andrew, Eric, and Rachel
L.J.S.

To my wife Janet and my children, Christian,
Stephen, Peter, and Joseph
J.J.S.

CONTENTS

6. Social Reaction Theories: Labeling and Conflict   213

9. Peers and Delinquency: Juvenile Gangs and Groups   319

10. Schools and Delinquency — 359

14. Pretrial Procedures 497

15. The Juvenile Trial and Disposition 537

PART SIX
JUVENILE CORRECTIONS   579

16. Juvenile Probation and Community Treatment   581

17. Institutions for Juveniles — **613**

PREFACE

During the past few years the public has given increasing attention to the problem of juvenile delinquency. The media now regularly focuses on youth gangs, violence in schools, and teenage substance abuse. Stories peppered with phrases such as "drive-by shooting" and "the rising tide of gang violence" are standard fare on the nightly news. Politicians, sensing both the fear and frustration of the public, issue regular calls for harsh punishments, including mandatory correctional terms, routine transfer to the adult justice system, and even the death penalty for juveniles, in order to win public support.

Considering the immediacy and importance of the problem of youth crime, it is not surprising that courses on juvenile delinquency have become popular offerings on the nation's college campuses. This text, *Juvenile Delinquency: Theory, Practice, and Law,* is designed to help students understand the nature of juvenile delinquency, its causes and correlates, as well as strategies being used to control or eliminate its occurrence. The text also reviews the legal rules that have been set down to either protect innocent minors or control adolescent misconduct: Can children be required to submit to drug testing in school? Can teachers search suspicious students or use corporal punishment as a method of discipline? Can children testify on closed-circuit TV in child abuse cases? Can a minor be given a death penalty sentence?

Because the study of juvenile delinquency is a dynamic, ever-changing field of scientific inquiry and because the theories, concepts, and processes of this area of study are constantly evolving, we have updated *Juvenile Delinquency: Theory, Practice, and Law* to reflect the changes that have taken place in the study of delinquent behavior during the past few years. Like its predecessors, the sixth edition includes a review of recent legal cases, research studies, and policy initiatives. It provides a groundwork for the study of juvenile delinquency by analyzing and describing the nature and extent of delinquency, the suspected causes of delinquent behavior, and the environmental influences on youthful misbehavior. It covers what most experts believe are the critical issues in juvenile delinquency and analyzes crucial policy issues, including the use of pretrial detention, shock incarceration, mandatory sentencing, and gang control efforts.

GOALS AND OBJECTIVES

Our primary goals in writing this sixth edition remain as they have been for the previous editions:

1. To be as objective as possible, presenting the many diverse views and perspectives that characterize the study of juvenile delinquency and reflect its interdisciplinary nature.
2. To maintain a balance of theory, law, policy, and practice. It is essential that a text on delinquency not solely be a theory book without presenting the juvenile justice system or contain sections on current policies without examining legal issues and cases.
3. To be as thorough and up-to-date as possible. We have attempted to include the most current data and information available.
4. To make the study of delinquency interesting as well as informative. We want to make readers as interested as possible in the study of delinquency so that they will pursue it on an undergraduate or graduate level.

We have tried to provide a test that is both scholarly and informative, comprehensive yet interesting, well organized and objective yet provocative and thought provoking.

ORGANIZATION OF THE TEXT

The sixth edition of *Juvenile Delinquency* has undergone a thorough revision in both content and organization. The text is still divided into six main sections.

Part I examines the concept of delinquency and status offending, the measurement of delinquency, and trends and patterns in the delinquency rate. Chapter 1 has been thoroughly reworked and now contains extensive material on the history of childhood. This material enables the reader to understand how the concept of adolescence evolved over time and how that evolution influenced the development of the juvenile court and the special status of delinquency. Chapter 2 now covers the measurement of delinquent behavior, trends and patterns in teen crime, and the correlates of delinquency, including race, gender, class, and age. The chapter also profiles the chronic offender and contains sections on problem behavior syndrome and turning points in crime.

Part II describes the various theoretical models that have been used to explain the onset of delinquent behavior. Chapter 3 covers recent findings on choice, biological, and psychological theories. Chapter 4 looks at social structural theories, which hold that economic, cultural, and environmental influences control delinquent behavior. Chapter 5 reviews those theories that maintain that improper socialization is the key to understanding delinquent behavior. Chapter 5 also covers the newly emerging integrated theories of delinquency. Chapter 6, which focuses on social reaction theories, has been updated to reflect recent research on labeling and conflict theory.

Part III covers the environmental and individual correlates of delinquency, beginning with Chapter 7, "Gender and Delinquency." This chapter explores the sex-based differences that are thought to account for the gender patterns in the delinquency rate. Also in this section are chapters that cover the influence of families (chapter 8), gangs (chapter 9), schools (chapter 10), and drugs (chapter 11).

Part IV, centering on juvenile justice advocacy, contains material on both the history of juvenile justice and the philosophy and practice of today's juvenile justice system. Chapter 12 covers extensively the emergence of state control over children in need and the development of the juvenile justice system. It also covers the contemporary juvenile justice system, the major stages in the justice process, the role of the federal government in the juvenile justice system, an analysis of the differences between the adult and juvenile justice systems, and extensive coverage of the legal rights of children, including a new time line of constitutional cases.

Part V, focusing on controlling juvenile offenders, contains three chapters on the police and court process. Chapter 13, "Police Work with Juveniles," discusses the role of police in delinquency prevention. It covers legal issues such as major court decisions on school searches and *Miranda* rights of juveniles. It also contains material on race and gender effects on police discretion. Chapter 14, "Pretrial Procedures," contains information on plea bargaining in juvenile court, the use of detention, and transfer to adult jails. It also contains an analysis of the critical factors that influence the waiver decision. Chapter 15, "The Juvenile Trial and Disposition," contains sections on special problems faced by juvenile court judges, such as substance abuse cases and gangs. It reviews the role of the public defender and federal prosecutor in juvenile court and models of sentencing in juvenile court.

Part VI contains two chapters on the juvenile correctional system. Chapter 16 examines community-based treatments, including probation and restitution. Chapter 17 reviews juvenile training schools, emphasizing legal issues such as the right to treatment and innovative programs such as boot camps.

Once again the book closes with a brief overview of significant findings found within the text.

What's New in This Edition

This sixth edition has undergone major structural and organizational changes. This edition contains 17 chapters while previous editions contained 19. We modified the chapter structure because adopters suggested that fewer chapters and a more compact organization might make the book more useful and practical within the time constraints of an academic semester. Therefore, the material on the history of childhood and juvenile justice (which appeared in chapter 13 of the fifth edition) has now been integrated within chapters 1 and 12 of this new edition. The material in chapters 2 and 3 of the previous edition have now been modified and combined within a new chapter 2. In addition to these organizational changes, each chapter has been thoroughly updated. A few of the more important changes and updates are noted below.

- Chapter 1 contains new material on the problems of adolescents in American society, newly created curfew laws, and sections on the history of childhood.
- Chapter 2 reexamines juvenile crime trends and reviews the growing juvenile violence rate. It includes new material on guns and delinquency, the future of juvenile crime, child victimizers, and the pathways to delinquency.
- Chapter 3 now contains material on situational crime control, including the "hot spots" approach. There are new sections on the antisocial personality and extraversion and neuroticism.

- Chapter 4 now contains sections on the possible link between delinquency and poverty, "rage, distrust, and hopelessness," and the effect of gender on anomie. A new "Focus on Delinquency" covers "Crime and the American Dream."
- Chapter 5 now looks at values and delinquency and the concept of "sticky friends." A new "Focus on Delinquency" reviews Project Bootstrap, a treatment program in Madison, Wisconsin.
- Chapter 6 reviews the increasing importance of labeling theory as an explanation of chronic offending. Included are new sections on left realism and peacemaking theory.
- Chapter 7 is now entitled "Gender and Delinquency." It explores gender differences in personality, cognition, and socialization and relates their impact on delinquency. Views of why gender differences in the comission of crime exist are explored in detail.
- Chapter 8 updates material on the family and delinquency. The "Focus on Delinquency" entitled "Juvenile Prostitution" has been updated. The latest data on the nature and extent of child abuse are included as well as research linking child abuse to delinquency.
- Chapter 9 contains the latest data from the National Gang Assessment project, new sections on gang migration, and updated information on the cause of gang formation.
- Chapter 10 reviews recent research on dropping out and delinquency, school climate and delinquency, the latest trends in academic performance, and new programs designed to reduce school-based delinquency.
- Chapter 11 charts the latest trends in teen drug use including the NIDA, ISR, and PRIDE surveys. The drugs–violence link is explored in a new "Focus on Delinquency."
- Chapter 12 is a new chapter which describes the historical development of juvenile justice as well as providing an overview of the contemporary juvenile justice system. It contains a time line of constitutional decisions on juvenile justice as well as charts and tables highlighting the shifting policy orientation of the juvenile justice system. Also presented is review of the Violent Crime Control Act of 1994 and how it affects police work.
- Chapter 13 contains new material on how the police are dealing with violent juvenile crime. A new "Focus on Delinquency" analyzes the *Vernonia v. Acton* decision on suspicionless drug testing of juveniles.
- Chapter 14 updates national detention trends, the deinstitutionalization of status offenders, and waiver. Changing statutory criteria for waiver to the adult court are discussed in some detail.
- Chapter 15 now contains sections on juvenile court jurisdiction, the complex role of the juvenile court prosecutor, and recent data on juvenile court case flow.
- Chapter 16 reviews new information on the success of community treatment programs that challenge the "nothing works" ideology. The latest probation caseload data show that more adolescents are on probation than ever before.
- Chapter 17 reviews the continuing problem of racial disparity in juvenile corrections. The 1995 case of *Alexander v Boyd* helps define the right to treatment in the juvenile justice system. Recent data on juvenile aftercare are analyzed, highlighting the use of risk classification and the importance of juvenile aftercare as a barrier to recidivism.

Learning Tools

The text contains the following features designed to help students learn and comprehend the material:

1. Each chapter begins with an outline.
2. The book contains more than 200 photos, tables, and charts. A foldout time line of juvenile justice history helps students chart the critical incidents in the study of delinquency over the past 200 years.
3. Every chapter contains at least one "**Case in Point**" feature—boxed inserts on intriguing issues concerning juvenile delinquency policy or processes. Within the boxed inserts are critical thinking sections designed to help students conceptualize problems of concern to juvenile delinquency.
4. As in previous editions, "**Focus on Delinquency**" boxed inserts focus attention on topics of special importance and concern. They also include major Supreme Court cases that influence and control the juvenile justice system—for example, *In Re Gault,* which defines the concept of due process for youthful offenders.
5. At the end of each chapter is a list of **key terms** used throughout the chapter. Every effort has been made to include the key terms within the glossary, which concludes the book.
6. Each chapter ends with thought provoking "**Questions for Discussion.**"
7. A glossary lists and defines key terms used in the text.
8. A section called "**American Delinquency**" summarizes some of the text's major findings and conclusions.

Acknowledgments

The preparation of this text would not have been possible without the aid of our colleagues who helped by reviewing the previous edition and gave us important suggestions for improvement. These include Thomas Calhoun, Thomas Segady, Fred Jones, James Larson, Fred Andes, and Mervin White. Earlier reviews were provided by Fred Andes, Robert Agnew, Sarah Boggs, Tom Calhoun, Steven Frazier, Fred Hawley, Tonya Hilligoss, Vincent Hoffman, David Horton, Harold Osborne, Barbara Owen, Ray Paternoster, Joseph Rankin, Thomas Segady, Richard Siebert, Paul Steele, Leslie Sue, Stanley Swart, Pam Tontodonato, Paul Tracy, William Waegel, Bill Wagner, Kim Weaver, Merv White, Michael Wiatrowski.

In addition, important information was provided by the following individuals and institutions: Marty Schwartz; George Knox; G. David Curry; Joan McDermott; Helene Raskin White; Joe Sanborn; Jim Inciardi; Vic Streib; Malcom Klein; Robert Agnew; Eve Buzawa; Chris Marshall; Meda Chesney-Lind; Gerald Hotaling; Marv Zalman; John Laub; Rob Sampson; David Farrington; Larry Sherman; James A. Fox; Jack McDevitt; Alan Lincoln; Lee Ellis; the staff at the Institute for Social Research at the University of Michigan; the National Center for State Courts; the Police Foundation; the Sentencing Project; Kathleen Maguire and the staff of the Hindelang Research Center at State University of New York–Albany; James Byrne of the Criminal Justice Research Center at the University of Massachusetts–Lowell; Kristina Rose and Janet Rosenbaum of the National Criminal Justice Reference Service; Deborah Daro and Karen McCurdy of the National Committee for Prevention of Child Abuse; and Terence Thornberry and the researchers at the Rochester Youth Study, Albany, New York. We extend a special thanks to Dr. Lynn Sametz for providing the time line data.

And, of course, our colleagues at West Publishing did their usual outstanding job of aiding us in the preparation of the text. Mary Schiller, our executive editor, did her usual superb job of guiding us through another edition. Sometimes we don't think we could ever put a book as comprehensive as *Juvenile Delinquency* out without her steady hand at the helm. Paul O'Neill, our production editor on the project, was patient, creative, and understanding, and helped make this a very attractive text. Special thanks to John Tuvey and Stephanie Buss for their innovative marketing and promotional ideas. Michelle Austin designed the striking cover for this text, which features the work of artist Alexi Worth.

PART ONE

THE CONCEPT OF DELINQUENCY

The field of juvenile delinquency has been an important area of study since the turn of the century. Academicians, practitioners, policymakers, and legal scholars have devoted their attention to basic questions about the nature of youth crime: Who commits delinquent acts? How much delinquency occurs each year? Is the rate of delinquent activity increasing or decreasing? How should delinquency be defined? What can we do to prevent delinquency?

Part I reviews these basic questions in detail. Chapter 1 discusses the origins of society's concern for children and the development of the concept of delinquency. It shows how the definition of delinquency has become quite complex. While society has chosen to treat adult and juvenile law violators separately, it has also expanded the definition of youthful misbehaviors eligible for social control; these are referred to as status offenses. Status offenses include such behaviors as truancy, running away, and incorrigibility. Critics suggest that juveniles' noncriminal behavior is probably not a proper area of concern for law enforcement agencies.

Chapter 2 examines the nature and extent of delinquent behavior. It discusses how social scientists gather information on juvenile delinquency and provides an overview of some of the major trends on juvenile crime. Chapter 2 also discusses the factors related to delinquency—race, gender, class, and age—and links them to an important theme in the study of delinquency: the maintenance of a delinquent career over the life course. Why do some kids continually get in trouble with the law, escalate the seriousness of their offenses, and become adult criminals? Why do others desist from delinquent activities? These are the major themes of the newly emerging life course view of delinquency.

CHAPTER ONE

CHILDHOOD AND DELINQUENCY

INTRODUCTION

You might have read about the following incidents in the press:

- On December 11, 1995, Robert Roberson, an ordained Pentecostal minister in Wenatchee, Washington, and his wife, Connie, were found not guilty of child sexual abuse. The two had been charged along with 40 other residents for participating in a molestation ring. Allegations against the Robersons included charges that they had raped their own five-year-old daughter. Twenty-eight residents of Wenatchee and surrounding areas were incarcerated as a result of the investigation, which began after a police detective's 11-year-old foster child told him she had been a victim of the ring.[1]

- On October 11, 1995, a nine-year-old Saint Louis boy upset with an assignment he was given repeatedly struck his teacher, Nedra Morris, in the chest. The 51-year-old Morris suffered a fatal heart attack. The school board president told the media, "We regret that this has happened."[2]

- On November 8, 1995, a gang of four New York youths attacked a 45-year-old man with a box cutter, hacked off his artificial leg, and left him bleeding on the street. The attackers were caught after they slashed another man's face in order to steal 30 cents.[3]

- In November 1995 two Miami teens, Maryling Flores and Christian Davila, committed suicide by jumping into a canal. Maryling's mother had forbidden them from dating, and the pain of separation was too great to bear: "I feel that without him I can't live," she wrote in her suicide note. Maryling was 13 and Christian was 14.[4]

- A Tennessee woman, Jennie Bain Ducker, was sentenced to 18 years in prison for causing the death of her two young children, Devin, 2, and Dustin, 1, by leaving them in a sweltering car outside a motel where she had gone to meet her boyfriend. The 21-year-old Ducker, who has a history of alcohol abuse and depression, will have to serve six years in prison before being eligible for parole.[5]

- On December 15, 1995, Tonya Kline, a 15-year-old girl was ordered by a South Carolina judge to be shackled to her mother, Deborah Harter, for one month. Kline had been ordered into juvenile detention while awaiting disposition on theft charges. The judge, Wayne Creech, ordered the shackling after Harter told him she would do anything to keep her daughter out of detention. Harter attends school with her daughter and sleeps next to her on a couch in her bedroom. State officials are anxious to evaluate this unusual procedure. "It's obviously unusual," one State Supreme Court Justice stated. "The times in which we live are different."[6]

- On January 27, 1996, Nathan Brooks pleaded not guilty by reason of insanity to charges he killed his parents in a satanic ritual. He had stabbed his mother at least 10 times, and shot his father in the head and beheaded him with a hacksaw; police found the head in a punch bowl surrounded by burnt paper.[7]

These cases illustrate the variety of problems faced by American youth. Many grow up in dysfunctional families headed by alcoholic or substance-abusing parents, live in deteriorated neighborhoods, have access to dangerous weapons, are lured by gangs, and are constantly exposed to extremes of poverty and violence. The Children's Defense Fund, a Washington-based nonprofit organization that keeps track of youth issues, has compiled the data contained in Figure 1.1.

Here we can see why the problems adolescents face in modern American society are extreme and growing. However, as the following "Focus on Delinquency" (page 8) shows, youth crime and violence are not uniquely American problems.

Poverty   More than 20 percent of all children, almost 16 million, are living in poverty. More than 6 million, or 26 percent, of all children *under six* are now living below the poverty line (which is about $15,000 a year for a family of four).[8] The Tufts University Center on Hunger, Poverty, and Nutrition Policy estimates

In November 1995 two Miami teens, Maryling Flores and Christian Davila committed suicide by jumping into a canal. Maryling's mother had forbidden them from dating and the pain of separation was too great to bear. This is the letter that Christian left behind. Suicide is now all too common among teens who suffer from depression and despair and who may feel powerless and out of control.

FIGURE 1.1
The state of America's children

Every Day in America ● ● ●

3	children and youths under 25 die from HIV infection.
6	children and youths under 20 commit suicide.
13	children and youths under 20 are homicide victims.
15	children and youths are killed by firearms.
95	babies die.
145	babies are born a very low birthweight (less than 3.25 pounds).
342	children under 18 are arrested for violent crimes.
518	babies are born to mothers who had late or no prenatal care.
790	babies are born at low birthweight (less than 5.5 pounds).
1,407	babies are born to teen mothers.
2,660	babies are born into poverty.
2,833	high school students drop out each school day.
3,086	public school students are corporally punished each school day.
3,398	babies are born to unmarried mothers.
6,042	children under 18 are arrested.
13,076	public school students are suspended each school day.

Source: Children's Defense Fund, The State of America's Children Yearbook, 1995 (Washington, D.C.: Children's Defense Fund, 1996).

that by the year 2012, 20.7 million, or 28 percent, of all minor children will be living in poverty.[9]

Family Problems Divorce strikes about half of all new marriages; many families sacrifice time with each other to afford better housing and lifestyles. Research shows that children in the United States are being polarized into two distinct economic groups: those born into affluent, two-income, married-couple households and those residing in impoverished, single-parent households.[10]

Urban Decay The destructive environment of deteriorated urban areas prevents too many adolescents from leading productive, fulfilling, or happy lives. Many face an early death from random gunfire and drive-by shootings. Many are homeless, living desperate lives on the street where they are at risk of becoming addicted to drugs and acquiring sexually transmitted diseases including AIDS. A recent study of 425 homeless "street kids" in New York City found that 37 percent earn money through prostitution, and almost one-third had contacted an STD during the past six months.[11]

Educational Issues The U.S. educational system, once the envy of the world, now seems to be failing at-risk youth. We are lagging behind other developed nations in such critical areas as science and mathematics achievement. The rate of retention—being held back to repeat a grade—is far higher than it should be in most communities. Retention rates are associated with another major educational problem—dropping out. It is estimated that about 14 percent of all eligible youths do not finish high school[12] (see Figure 1.2).

Although all young people face stress in the education system, the risks are greatest for the poor, members of racial and ethnic minorities, and recent

FIGURE 1.2
High school completion

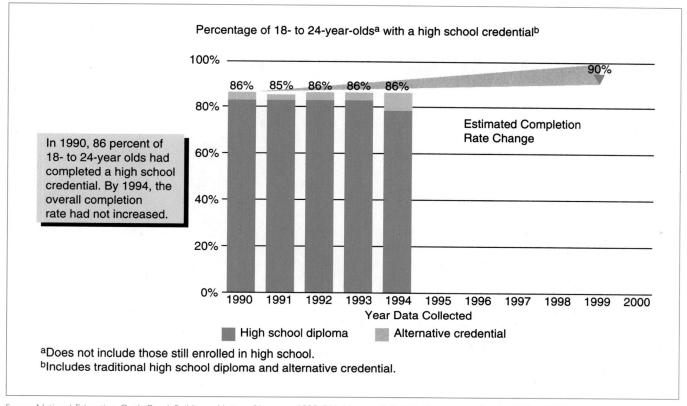

Percentage of 18- to 24-year-olds[a] with a high school credential[b]

In 1990, 86 percent of 18- to 24-year olds had completed a high school credential. By 1994, the overall completion rate had not increased.

Estimated Completion Rate Change

■ High school diploma   ▨ Alternative credential

[a]Does not include those still enrolled in high school.
[b]Includes traditional high school diploma and alternative credential.

Source: National Education Goals Panel, *Building a Nation of Learners,* 1995 (Washington, D.C.: U.S. Government Printing Office, 1995), p. 32.

immigrants. These children usually attend the most underfunded schools, receive inadequate educational opportunities, and have the fewest opportunities to achieve conventional success.

Stress   Measures of teenage stress are also discouraging: The teenage suicide rate has doubled since 1980, teenage drug use is again on the rise, and more than 90 percent of high school students have tried alcohol.[13]

Considering these destructive influences, it should come as no surprise that teenage violence has increased during the past few decades: Rates for homicides involving juvenile offenders are increasing at a much faster pace than for those involving adult offenders.[14]

THE ADOLESCENT DILEMMA

These social and emotional problems have a significant effect on our nation's youth, particularly those transitioning through the tumultuous teenage years. During this period the self, or basic personality, is undergoing a metamorphosis and is vulnerable to a host of external determinants as well as internal physiological changes.[15]

INTERNATIONAL DELINQUENCY

Youth crime, substance abuse, and delinquency are considered major social problems in the United States. Are other nations similarly plagued by juvenile delinquency?

Youth crime is an international problem. For example, juvenile delinquency in the island nation of Singapore is on the rise; the number of arrests of young people more than doubled between 1991 and 1995. Singapore's draconian justice policies became notorious in 1993 when American teen Michael Fay was flogged after being convicted of vandalism. In the aftermath of the Fay case, state legislators in California, Mississippi, and New Hampshire filed bills to adopt corporal punishment as a method of deterring juvenile crime. The recent upswing of delinquency in Singapore suggests that the use of such punitive measures may be an ineffective crime deterrent.

Singapore is not alone among nations experiencing an upsurge in delinquency. James Finckenauer reports that Russia has experienced a significant increase in delinquency; the number of reported acts doubled during the past 10 years. Finckenauer found that teens account for nearly 20 percent of all serious criminal activity in Russia.

Alison Hatch and Curt Griffiths examined the problem of delinquency in Canada. Although Canada has a lower aggregate crime rate than the United States and less per capita violence, it too has its share of problems. Youth crime has been on the rise since 1956. Between 1980 and 1990, the number of youths charged with violent crimes doubled (although the increase in adolescent violence lagged behind that of adults). About one-third of all property crimes are committed by juvenile offenders.

Hatch and Griffiths also identified some of the specific types of youth crime emerging in Canada. They found reports of violent, thrill-seeking behavior (looting, rioting, "wilding") by middle-class youths. Youth gangs are becoming a common feature in larger cities, such as Vancouver and Toronto. Some of these gangs are made up of Canada's burgeoning population of ethnic minorities; for example, Jamaican gangs are involved in the drug trade. Severe economic problems have resulted in the overrepresentation of aboriginal youths (native Canadians such as Inuits in the Arctic region) in crime and substance abuse.

Germany has been racked by well-publicized outbursts of violence against immigrants and minorities by youth gangs of "skinheads." The "skins" are reacting to unemployment and competition for jobs between Germans and immigrants. Some skins are neo-Nazis whose violence is fueled by racial hatred; others are apolitical youths whose violence is motivated by the anger of poverty and ignorance. In addition to these fascist outbursts, juveniles have been involved in about 20 percent of all violent crime in Germany and one-third of all property offenses. Drug abuse is also a common problem. More than 10 percent of German youth have had experience with drugs; Germany has more than 100,000 drug addicts today.

Paul Friday reports that crime in Sweden, a country known for its liberal social welfare programs, is also on the increase. Crime patterns in Sweden seem similar to those in the United States: The majority of offenders are young males, and a few chronic offenders are responsible for a majority of all known offenses. The factors that cause delinquency in Sweden seem similar to those found in the United States—peer influence, alienation, and lack of attachment to society.

These and other studies show that delinquency is not a problem confined to the United States. Finckenauer found that many of the factors that are precursors of youth crime in the United States—alienation, family problems, school failure, substance abuse—may also be contributing to Russian delinquency. The international experience suggests that societies with similar social problems may also share similar rates of delinquency and drug abuse.

Sources: Reuters, "Singapore Says Delinquency Up," *Boston Globe* 17 February 1996, p. 4; James Finckenauer, *Russian Youth, Law, Deviance and the Pursuit of Freedom* (New Brunswick, N.J.: Transaction Books, 1995); Clayton Hartjen, "Legal Change and Juvenile Justice in India" (Paper presented at the American Society of Criminology meeting, Boston, Mass., November 1995); Alison Hatch and Curt Griffiths, "Youth Crime in Canada: Observations for Cross-Cultural Analysis," *International Journal of Comparative and Applied Criminal Justice* 16: 165–79 (1992); Gunther Kaiser, "Juvenile Delinquency in the Federal Republic of Germany," *International Journal of Comparative and Applied Criminal Justice* 16: 185–97 (1992); Marie Douglas, "Auslander Raus! Nazi Raus! An Observation of German Skins and Jugendgangen," *International Journal of Comparative and Applied Criminal Justice* 16: 129–33 (1992); Paul Friday, "Delinquency in Sweden: Current Trends and Theoretical Implications," *International Journal of Comparative and Applied Criminal Justice* 16: 231–44 (1992); Galan Janeksela, "The Significance of Comparative Analysis of Juvenile Delinquency and Juvenile Justice," *International Journal of Comparative and Applied Criminal Justice* 16: 137–47 (1992), on p. 146.

Delinquency is a function of the trials facing many adolescents in modern American society. By the time they reach 15, a significant number of teenagers are approaching adulthood unable to adequately meet the requirements and responsibilities of the workplace, family, and neighborhood. Many suffer from health problems, are educational underachievers, and are already skeptical about their ability to enter the American mainstream.[16]

Adolescence is a time of trial and uncertainty for many youths. They may become extremely vulnerable to emotional turmoil and experience anxiety, humiliation, and mood swings. Adolescents also undergo a period of biological development that proceeds at a far faster pace than at any other time in their lives except infancy. Over a period of a few years, their height, weight, and sexual characteristics change dramatically. The average age at which girls reach puberty today is 12.5 years; 150 years ago, girls matured sexually at age 16. But although they may become biologically mature and capable of having children as early as 14, many youngsters remain emotionally and intellectually immature.[17] Because of this, the problem of teenage pregnancy is a growing concern.

In later adolescence (ages 16 to 18), youths may experience the life crisis that famed psychologist Erik Erikson labeled **ego identity** versus **role diffusion.** Ego identity is formed when youths develop a firm sense of who they are and what they stand for; role diffusion occurs when they experience personal uncertainty, spread themselves too thin, and place themselves at the mercy of leaders who promise to give them a sense of identity they cannot mold for themselves.[18] Psychologists also find that late adolescence is a period dominated by the yearning for independence from parental control.[19] Given this explosive mixture of biological change and desire for autonomy, it should not be surprising that the teenage years are a time of rebelliousness and conflict with authority at home, at school, and in the community.

Problems in the home, the school, and the neighborhood, coupled with health and developmental hazards, have placed a significant portion of American youth

Social and emotional problems have a significant effect on our nation's youth who are going through their tumultuous teen-age years. Adolescence is unquestionably a time of transition. During this period the self, or basic personality, is still undergoing a metamorphosis and is vulnerable to a host of external determinants as well as internal physiological changes. Adolescence is a time of trial and uncertainty for many youths. They may become extremely vulnerable to emotional turmoil and experience anxiety, humiliation, and mood swings. Adolescents also undergo a period of biological development that proceeds at a far faster pace than at any other time in their lives except infancy.

at risk. Although it is impossible to precisely determine the number of **at-risk youth** in the United States, one estimate is that 7 million, or 25 percent of the population under 17, are extremely vulnerable to the negative consequences of criminality, school failure, substance abuse, and early sexuality, while another 7 million can be classified as at "moderate risk."[20]

JUVENILE DELINQUENCY

The problems of youth in modern society have become a major national concern and an important subject for academic study. This text focuses on one area of particular concern: **juvenile delinquency,** or *criminal behavior committed by minors.* The study of juvenile delinquency is important both because of the damage suffered by its victims and the problems faced by its perpetrators. Juveniles who engage in criminal acts are placed under the control of law enforcement, court, and correctional agencies that comprise the **juvenile justice system.** They may be taken into custody by the police, have their cases heard in a juvenile or family court, and be placed in a residential facility that treats troubled children.

More than 2 million youths are now arrested each year for crimes ranging in seriousness from murder to loitering.[21] Although most juvenile law violations are minor, some young offenders are extremely dangerous and violent. More than 500,000 youths belong to street gangs and groups that can put fear into an entire city. Youths involved in multiple serious criminal acts—referred to as lifestyle, repeat, or **chronic delinquent** offenders—are now recognized as a serious social problem. State juvenile authorities must deal with these offenders, along with responding to a range of other social problems, including child abuse and neglect, school crime and vandalism, family crises, and drug abuse.

THE STUDY OF DELINQUENCY

Given the diversity and gravity of these problems, it is essential that the causes and prevention of delinquency be studied in an orderly and scientific manner. It would be difficult, if not impossible, to devise strategies to combat such a complex social phenomenon as juvenile delinquency if its fundamental dimensions were unknown. Is delinquency a function of psychological abnormality? A collective reaction by youths against destructive social conditions? The product of a disturbed home life and disrupted socialization? Does serious delinquent behavior occur only in large urban areas among lower-class youths? Or is it spread throughout the entire social structure? What impact do family life, substance abuse, school experiences, and peer relations have on youth and their law-violating behaviors? We know that most youthful law violators do not go on to become adult criminals (what is known as the **aging-out process**). Yet we do not know why some youths become **chronic career offenders** whose delinquent careers begin early and persist into adulthood. Why does the onset of delinquency begin so early in some children? Why does the severity of their offenses escalate? What factors predict the **persistence,** or continuation, of delinquency, and conversely, what are the factors associated with its **desistance,** or termination? Unless these questions are answered, developing effective prevention and control efforts will be difficult.

The study of delinquency also involves the analysis of the agencies designed to treat youthful offenders who fall into the arms of the law—known collectively as the juvenile justice system. How should police deal with minors who violate the law? What are the legal rights of children? For example, should minors who commit murder receive the death penalty? What kind of correctional programs are most effective with delinquent youths? How effective are educational, community, counseling, and vocational development programs? Is it true, as some critics claim, that most efforts to rehabilitate young offenders are doomed to failure?[22] Should we adopt a punishment or a treatment orientation to combat delinquency, or something in between?

In sum, the scientific study of delinquency requires understanding the nature, extent, and cause of youthful law violations and the methods devised for their control. It also involves the study of important environmental and social issues associated with delinquent behavior, including substance abuse, child abuse and neglect, education, and peer relations. Because of these requirements, this text attempts to provide a comprehensive look at the problem of delinquency by reviewing its nature, extent, cause, and influences and the efforts being made to treat problem youths and prevent the spread of delinquency.

THE DEVELOPMENT OF CHILDHOOD

The fact that children are viewed today as a distinct group with special needs and concerns is, in historical terms, a relatively new concept. It is only for the past 300 years or so that any form of governmental mechanism existed to care for even the most needy children, including those left orphaned and destitute. How did this concept of concern for children develop?

Prior to the seventeenth century, the concept of childhood as we know it today did not exist. Children were not seen as a distinct social group with unique needs and behaviors. In the **paternalistic family** of the time, the father was the final authority on all family matters and exercised complete control over the social, economic, and physical well-being of his wife and children.[23] Children who did not obey were subject to severe physical punishment, even death.

As soon as they were physically capable, children would assume adult roles. Among the working classes, males engaged in peasant farming and/or learning a skilled trade, such as masonry or metalworking; females aided in food preparation or household maintenance.[24] Some peasant youth went into domestic or agricultural service on the great estates or were apprenticed in trades or crafts.[25]

Children of the affluent landholding classes also assumed adult roles at an early age. Girls born into aristocratic families were educated at home and trained to manage an estate's household staff. Because most girls married in their early teens, they were expected to assume the duties of women—supervising servants and ensuring the food supply of the manor—at an early age. A few were taught to read, write, and do sufficient mathematics to handle household accounts.

At age 7 or 8, boys born to landholding families were either sent to a monastery or cathedral school to be trained for a life in the church or selected to be a member of the warrior class and apprenticed as a squire. After apprenticeship ended at age 21, the young nobles entered into the knighthood and returned home to live with their parents. Most remained single because it was widely believed there should only be one married couple residing in a castle. To pass the time and maintain their fighting edge, many entered the tournament circuit, engaging in melees and jousts to win fame and fortune. Upon the death of the father, young nobles assumed their inherited titles, married, and began their own families.

CUSTOM AND PRACTICE

Custom and practice greatly influenced the daily life of children during the Middle Ages. **Primogeniture** required that the oldest surviving male child inherit family lands and titles. He could then distribute them to younger siblings as he saw fit. There was no requirement, however, that portions of the estate be distributed equally, so many youths who received no lands were forced to enter a religious order, become soldiers, or seek wealthy patrons. Primogeniture often caused intense family rivalry that led to blood feuds and tragedy. For example, a mother would die in childbirth, leaving behind an infant who was the sole heir to a family estate and title. If the child's father remarried and produced offspring who had no hope of substantial inheritance, conflicts would arise over the inheritance rights of the firstborn infant and subsequent siblings. Jealousy would create feuds between family members.

Dower The **dower system** mandated that a woman's family bestow money, land, or other wealth on a potential husband or his family in exchange for his marriage to her. Under this agreement, the young woman received a promise of financial assistance, called a **jointure,** from the groom's family. Jointure provided a lifetime income if a wife outlived her mate. The dower system had a significant impact on the role of the women in medieval society and consequently on the role of children. It ensured that marriages would be contracted only within and not across social classes. It gave the woman's father control over whom she married because he could threaten to withhold funds. Females were viewed as economic drains on the family. A father with many daughters and few sons might find himself financially unable to obtain suitable marriages. The youngest girls in many families were forced to enter convents, abandoned, or left at home.

Child Rearing The harshness of medieval life influenced child-rearing practices during the fifteenth and sixteenth centuries. For instance, newborns were almost immediately handed over to **wet nurses,** who fed and cared for them during the first two years of their life. These women often lived away from the family, so parents had little contact with their children. Even the wealthiest families employed wet nurses, because it was considered demeaning for a noblewoman to nurse. **Swaddling,** a common practice, entailed wrapping a newborn entirely in bandages. The bandages prevented any movement and enabled the wet nurse to manage the child easily. This practice was thought to protect the child, but it most likely contributed to high infant mortality rates because the child could not be kept clean.

Discipline Discipline was severe during this period. Young children of all classes, both peasant and wealthy, were subjected to stringent rules and regulations. They were beaten severely for any sign of disobedience or ill temper. Many children of this time would be considered abused if they lived in today's world. The relationship between parent and child was remote. Children were expected to enter the world of adults and to undertake responsibilities early in life, sharing in the work of siblings and parents.

The roots of the impersonal relationship between parent and child can be traced to high mortality rates, which made sentimental and affectionate relationships risky. It would have been foolish for parents to invest emotional effort in relationships that could so easily be terminated by violence, accidents, or disease. Parents often thought that children must be toughened to ensure their survival in a hostile world. Close family relationships were viewed as detrimental to this process. Also, because the oldest male child was viewed as the essential and important element in a family's well-being, younger male and female siblings were considered economic and social liabilities. Children thought to be suffering from disease or retardation were often abandoned to churches, orphanages, or foundling homes.[26]

The Development of Concern for Children

Throughout the seventeenth and eighteenth centuries, a number of developments in England heralded the march toward the recognition of the rights of children. In many instances, these events eventually affected the juvenile legal system as it emerged in America. They include: (1) changes in family style and child care, (2) the English Poor Laws, (3) the apprenticeship movement, and (4) the role of the chancery court.[27]

CHANGES IN FAMILY STRUCTURE

Family structure and the role of children began to change after the seventeenth century as the influence of the great families began to wane. Extended families, which were created over centuries, gave way to the nuclear family structure with which we are familiar today. It became more common for marriage to be based on love and mutual attraction between men and women than on parental consent and paternal dominance. At this time, the concept of childhood as an independent status was developing, and the needs of children were beginning to be understood. But parents still rigidly disciplined their children. Control of a child's actions was considered essential for proper maintenance of the family structure.

To provide more controls over children, grammar and boarding schools were established and began to flourish in many large cities during this time.[28] Their structure and subject matter were quite different from those of today. Children studied grammar, Latin, law, and logic, often beginning at a young age. Teachers in these institutions often ruled by fear, and flogging was their main method of discipline. Students were beaten for academic mistakes as well as moral lapses. Such brutal treatment fell on both the rich and the poor throughout all levels of educational life, including boarding schools and universities. By the mid-eighteenth century, this treatment abated in Europe but it remained in full force in Great Britain. Although this brutal approach to educating children may be difficult to understand now, the child in that society was considered a second-class citizen.

This change in educational practice was prompted in part by the work of such philosophers as Voltaire, Rousseau, and Locke which began to herald a new age for childhood and the family.[29] Their vision produced a period known as the Enlightenment, which stressed a humanistic view of life, freedom, family, reason, and law. The ideal person was sympathetic to others and receptive to new ideas. These new beliefs influenced the lifestyle of the family. The father's authority was tempered, discipline in the home became more relaxed, and the expression of love and affection came to be of deep concern to family members. Upper- and middle-class families began to devote attention to child rearing.

As a result, toward the end of the eighteenth and beginning of the nineteenth centuries, children began to emerge as a readily distinguishable group with independent needs and interests, at least in the wealthier classes. Parents often took greater interest in their upbringing. In addition, serious questions arose over the treatment of children in school. Public outcries led to a decrease in excessive physical discipline. Restrictions were placed on the use of the whip, and in some schools, the imposition of academic assignments or the loss of privileges replaced corporal punishment. Nonetheless, not all customs changed for the better. Girls were still undereducated, parents were still excessively concerned with the moral and religious development of their children, punishment was still primarily physical, and schools continued to mistreat children. Yet the changes in England in this period paved the way for today's family structure of child care.

ENGLISH POOR LAWS

Government action to care of needy children can be traced to the Poor Laws of Great Britain. As early as 1535, the English passed statutes known as **Poor Laws.**[30] These laws allowed for the appointment of overseers to bind out destitute or neglected children as servants. The Poor Laws forced indigent children to serve in the care of families who trained them in agricultural, trade, or domestic services. The Elizabethan Poor Laws of 1601 were a model for dealing with poor children for more than 200 years. These laws created a system of church wardens and overseers who, with the consent of justices of the peace, identified vagrant, delinquent, and neglected children and took measures to put them to work. Often this meant placing them in poorhouses or workhouses or apprenticing them to masters.

THE APPRENTICESHIP MOVEMENT

Apprenticeship in Great Britain existed through almost the entire history of the country.[31] Under this practice, children were placed in the care of adults who trained them to discharge various duties and obtain different skills. Voluntary apprentices were bound out by parents or guardians who wished to secure training for their children. Involuntary apprentices, indigent youth who could not otherwise be cared for, were compelled by the authorities to serve until they were 21 or older. The master–apprentice relationship was similar to the parent–child relationship in that the master had complete responsibility for and authority over the apprentice. If an apprentice was unruly, a complaint could be made and the apprentice could be punished. Incarcerated apprentices were often placed in rooms or workshops apart from other prisoners and were generally treated differently from those charged with a criminal offense. Even at this early stage, the conviction was growing that the criminal law and its enforcement should be applied differently to children.

CHANCERY COURT

The concept of **parens patriae** and the chancery court system also played significant roles in the emerging concern for children.

Chancery courts existed in Great Britain throughout the Middle Ages. They were established primarily to protect property rights, although their authority extended to the welfare of children generally. The major issues in medieval cases that came before the chancery courts concerned guardianship, the uses and control of property, and the arrangement of people and power in relation to the monarchy. Agents of the chancery courts were responsible for controlling and settling problems involving rights to estates and guardianship interests with regard to the hierarchy of families and the state.

Chancery courts were founded on the proposition that children and other incompetents were under the protective control of the king; thus, the Latin phrase *parens patriae* was used referring to the role of the king as the father of his country. As Douglas Besharov states, "The concept apparently was first used by English kings to justify their intervention in the lives of the children of their vassals—children whose position and property were of direct concern to the monarch."[32] In the famous 1827 English case *Wellesley v. Wellesley,* a duke's children were taken away from him in the name and interest of *parens patriae* because of his scandalous behavior.[33] Thus, the concept of *parens patriae* became the theoretical basis for the protective jurisdiction of the chancery courts acting as part of the crown's power.

As time passed, the monarchy used *parens patriae* more and more to justify its intervention in the lives of families and children by its interest in their general welfare. However, as Douglas Rendleman points out, "The idea of parens patriae was actually used to maintain the power of the crown and the structure of control over families known as feudalism."[34]

The chancery courts dealt with the property and custody problems of the wealthier classes. They did not have jurisdiction over children charged with criminal conduct. Juveniles who violated the law were handled within the framework of the regular criminal court system. Nonetheless, the concept of *parens patriae,* which was established with the English chancery court system, grew to refer primarily to the responsibility of the courts and the state to act in the best interests of the child.

CONTROLLING CHILDREN IN AMERICA

While England was using its chancery courts and Poor Laws to deal with children in need, the American colonies were struggling with similar concepts. Initially, the colonies were a haven for poor and unfortunate people looking for religious and economic opportunities denied them in England and Europe. Along with early settlers, many children came not as citizens but as indentured servants, apprentices, or agricultural workers. They were recruited from the various English workhouses, orphanages, prisons, and asylums that housed vagrant and delinquent youths during the sixteenth and seventeenth centuries.[35]

At the same time, the colonies themselves produced illegitimate, neglected, abandoned, and delinquent children. The colonies' initial response to caring for such unfortunate children was to adopt court and Poor Laws systems similar to the English ones. Involuntary apprenticeship, indenture, and binding out of children became integral parts of colonization in America. For example, Poor Laws legislation requiring poor and dependent children to serve apprenticeships was passed in Virginia in 1646 and in Massachusetts and Connecticut in 1673.[36]

The master in colonial America acted as a natural parent, and in certain instances, apprentices would actually become part of the nuclear family structure. If they disobeyed their masters, they would be punished by local tribunals. If masters abused apprentices, courts would assess damages, return the children to the parents, or find them new guardians. Maryland and Virginia developed an orphan's court that supervised the treatment of youth placed with guardians and ensured that they were not mistreated or taken advantage of by their masters. These courts, however, did not supervise children living with their natural parents, leaving intact the parents' right to care for their children.[37]

The apprenticeship system eventually eroded under the pressure of national growth prompted by the War of Independence, the industrial revolution, and the ever-increasing European immigration. It was replaced, after the American Revolution, by the factory system, in which many poor youths sought jobs in mills, mines, and factories and lived in boardinghouses and settlements provided by mill owners.

By the beginning of the nineteenth century, the apprenticeship system could no longer compete with the factory system. Yet the problems of how to deal effectively with growing numbers of dependent youths increased. Early American settlers were firm believers in hard work, strict discipline, and education. These principles were viewed as the only reliable method for spiritual salvation. A child's life was marked by work alongside parents, some schooling, prayer, more work, and further study. The factory system placed burdens on youth which far exceeded existing concepts of hard work. To provide some relief, the Factory Act of the early nineteenth century limited the hours children were permitted to work and the age at which they could begin to work. It also prescribed a minimum amount of schooling to be provided by factory owners.[38]

This act and related statutes were often violated, and conditions of work and school remained troublesome issues well into the twentieth century. Nevertheless, the statutes were a step in the direction of reform.

CONTROLLING CHILDREN

In America, as in England, moral discipline was rigidly enforced. Stubborn child laws were passed that required children to obey their parents.[39] It was not uncommon in the colonies for children who were disobedient or disrespectful to their families to be whipped or otherwise physically chastised. Children were often required to attend public whippings and executions because these events served as important forms of moral instruction. Parents often referred their children to published works and writings on behavior and discipline and expected them to follow their precepts carefully. The early colonists, however, viewed family violence as a sin, and child protection laws were passed as early as 1639 (in New Haven, Connecticut). These laws were generally symbolic and rarely enforced. They expressed the community's commitment to God to oppose sin; offenders usually received lenient sentences.[40]

When it came to child abuse most colonies adopted a protectionist stance, however, few cases of child abuse were actually brought before the courts. The absence of child abuse cases may reflect the nature of life in what were essentially extremely religious households. Children were productive laborers and respected by their parents. In addition, large families provided many siblings and kinfolk who could care for children and relieve stress-producing burdens on parents.[41]

It was once common for child laborers like this 14-year-old girl to work long hours in mills and factories. Conditions such as these existed until the Federal Fair Labor Standards Act of 1938 prohibited children under 16 from working in industries which engaged in interstate commerce. However, exceptions could still be made if employers could show that work did not interfere with schooling, health or well being.

Another view is that children were harshly punished in Early American families, but because the "acceptable" limits of discipline were so high, few parents were charged with assault. Any punishment that fell short of maiming or permanently harming a child was considered within the sphere of parental rights.[42]

The Concept of Delinquency

Considering the rough treatment handed out to children who misbehaved at home or at school, it should come as no surprise that children who actually broke the law and committed seriously criminal acts were dealt with harshly. Before the twentieth century, little distinction was made between adult and juvenile offenders. Although judges considered the age of an offender when deciding punishment, both adults and children were often eligible for the same forms of punishment—prison, corporal punishment, and even the death penalty.[43]

Over the years, this treatment changed, as society became aware of the special needs of children. Beginning in the mid-nineteenth century as immigrant youth poured into America, there was official recognition that children formed a separate group with its own separate needs. Around the nation, in cities such as New York, Boston, and Chicago, groups known as **child savers** were being formed to help needy children. They created community programs to serve needy children and lobbied for a separate legal status for children, which ultimately led to the development of a formal juvenile justice system. (The child saving movement will be discussed more fully in chapter 11.)

DELINQUENCY AND *PARENS PATRIAE*

The current treatment of juvenile delinquents is a by-product of this developing national consciousness. The designation *delinquent* became popular at the onset of the twentieth century when the first separate juvenile courts were instituted. The child savers believed that treating minors and adults equivalently violated the humanitarian ideals of American society. Consequently, the newly emerging juvenile justice system operated under the *parens patriae* philosophy. Minors who engaged in extralegal behavior were viewed as victims of improper care, custody, and treatment at home. Illegal behavior was a sign that the state should step in and take control of the youth before he or she committed a more serious crime. The belief was that the state, through its juvenile authorities, should act in the **best interests of the child.** This means that children should not be punished for their misdeeds but instead should be given the care and custody necessary to remedy and control wayward behavior. Under such a philosophy it makes no sense to find children guilty of specific crimes, such as burglary or petty larceny, because that stigmatizes them and labels them as thieves or burglars. Instead, the catch-all term *juvenile delinquency* should be used as it indicates that the child needs the care, custody, and treatment of the state.

THE LEGAL STATUS OF DELINQUENCY

Although the development of a separate legal status of "juvenile delinquent" is usually credited to the child saving movement of the early twentieth century, the concept that children could be treated differently before the law can actually be traced back much further to its roots in the British legal tradition. Early English jurisprudence held that children under the age of 7 were legally incapable of committing crimes. Children between the ages of 7 and 14 were responsible for their actions, but their age might be used to excuse or reduce their punishment. Our legal system still recognizes that many young people are incapable of making mature judgments and that responsibility for their acts should be limited. Children can intentionally steal cars and know full well that the act is illegal, but they may be incapable of fully understanding the consequences of their behavior and the harm it may cause. Therefore, the law does not punish a youth as it would an adult, and it sees youthful misconduct as evidence of unreasoned or impaired judgment.

Today, the legal status of "juvenile delinquent" refers to a minor child who has been found to have violated the penal code. Most states define "minor child" as an individual who falls under a statutory age limit, most commonly 17 or 18 years of age. Because of their minority status, juveniles are usually kept separate from adults and receive different consideration and treatment under the law. For example, most large police departments employ officers whose sole responsibility is youth crime and delinquency. Every state has some form of separate juvenile court with its own judges, probation department, and other facilities. Terminology is also different: Adults are tried in court; children are adjudicated. Adults are punished; children are treated. If treatment is mandated, children can be sent to secure detention facilities; they cannot normally be committed to adult prisons.

Children also have their own unique legal status. Minors apprehended for a criminal act are usually charged with being a juvenile delinquent regardless of the crime they commit. These charges are usually confidential, trial records are kept secret, and information concerning the name, behavior, and background of delinquent offenders is sealed. Eliminating specific crime categories and maintaining secrecy are efforts to shield children from the stigma of a criminal conviction and to prevent youthful misdeeds from becoming a lifelong burden.

LEGAL RESPONSIBILITY OF YOUTH

The *parens patriae* doctrine places the juvenile delinquent somewhere on the judicial spectrum between criminal and civil law. Criminal laws prohibit activities that are injurious to the well-being of society and threaten the social order, for example, drug use, theft, and rape; they are legal actions brought by state authorities against private citizens. Civil laws, on the other hand, control interpersonal or private activities and are usually initiated by individual citizens. The ownership and transfer of property, contractual relationships, and personal conflicts (torts) are the subjects of the civil law. Also covered under the civil law are provisions for the care and custody of those people who cannot care for themselves—the mentally ill, incompetent, or infirm.

Under *parens patriae,* delinquent acts are not considered criminal violations nor are delinquents considered criminals. Children cannot be found guilty of a crime and punished like adult criminals; the legal action against them is considered more similar (though not identical) to a civil action that determines their "need for treatment." This legal theory recognizes that children who violate the law are in need of the same care and treatment as are law-abiding citizens who cannot care for themselves and require state intervention into their lives.

Although we would like to think that youthful offenders are only taken into state custody for purposes of benign care and treatment, they are in fact also subject to arrest, trial, and incarceration. This has prompted the courts to grant them many of the same legal protections enjoyed by adults accused of criminal offenses. These legal protections include the right to consult an attorney, to be free from self-incrimination, and to be protected from illegal searches and seizures.

Appreciation of the "criminal" nature of the delinquency concept has helped increase the legal rights of minors; however, it has also allowed state authorities to declare that some offenders are "beyond control" and cannot be treated as children. This recognition has prompted the policy of **waiver,** or transferring legal jurisdiction over the most serious and experienced juvenile offenders to the adult court for criminal prosecution. So although the *parens patriae* concept is still applied to children whose law violations are not considered to be serious, the more serious juvenile offenders can be declared "legal adults" and placed outside the jurisdiction of the juvenile court.

STATUS OFFENDERS

A child can also become subject to state authority because of conduct that is illegal only because the child is under age. Such acts are known as **status offenses.** Figure 1.3 illustrates some typical status offenses.

State control over a child's noncriminal behavior is considered consistent with the *parens patriae* philosophy and is used to protect the best interests of the child. Usually, status offenders are put in the hands of the juvenile court when it is determined that their parents are unable or unwilling to care for or control them and that their behavior will eventually hurt themselves and society.

A historical basis exists for status offense statutes. It was common practice early in the nation's history to place disobedient or runaway youths in orphan

FIGURE 1.3
Status offenses

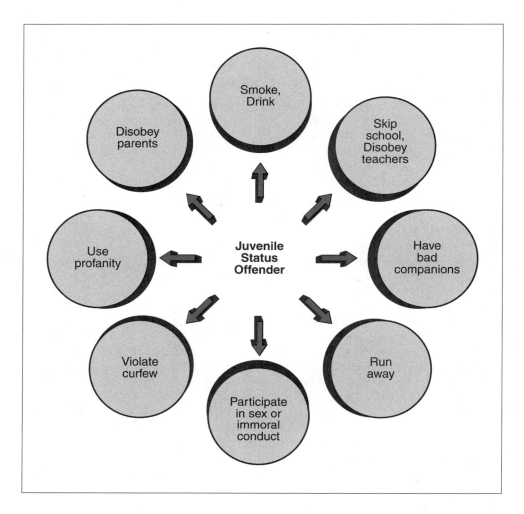

asylums, residential homes, or houses of refuge.[44] When the first juvenile courts were established in Illinois, the Chicago Bar Association described part of their purpose as follows:

> The whole trend and spirit of the [1889 Juvenile Court Act] is that the State, acting through the Juvenile Court, exercises that tender solicitude and care over its neglected, dependent wards that a wise and loving parent would exercise with reference to his own children under similar circumstances.[45]

Until relatively recently, however, almost every state treated status offenders and juvenile delinquents alike, referring to them as either **wayward minors** or **delinquent children.** A trend begun in the 1960s has resulted in the creation of separate status offense categories—children, minors, persons, youths, or juveniles in need of supervision (CHINS, MINS, PINS, YINS, or JINS)—in different states. The purpose of creating separate status offender categories was to shield noncriminal youths from the stigma attached to the label "juvenile delinquent" and to signify that they were troubled youths with special needs and problems (see Table 1.1).

Most states now have separate categories for juvenile conduct that would not be considered criminal if committed by an adult; these sometimes pertain to

TABLE 1.1 Status Offense Laws: Wisconsin and Louisiana

Louisiana	Wisconsin
"Child in need of supervision" means a child who needs care or rehabilitation because: 1. Being subject to compulsory school attendance, he is habitually truant from school or willfully violates the rules of the school; 2. He habitually disobeys the reasonable and lawful demands of his parents, and is ungovernable and beyond their control; 3. He absents himself from his home or usual place of abode without the consent of his parent; 4. He purposefully, intentionally and willfully deceives, or misrepresents the true facts to, any person holding a retail dealer's permit, or his agent, associate, employee or representative, for the purposes of buying or receiving alcoholic beverages or beer, or visiting or loitering in or about any place where such beverages are the principal commodities sold or handled; 5. His occupation, conduct, environment or associations are injurious to his welfare; or 6. He has committed an offense applicable only to children.	The court has exclusive original jurisdiction over a child alleged to be in need of protection or services which can be ordered by the court, and: 1. Who is without a parent or guardian; 2. Who has been abandoned; 3. Who has been the victim of sexual or physical abuse including injury which is self-inflicted or inflicted by another by other than accidental means; 4. Whose parent or guardian signs the petition requesting jurisdiction and states that he or she is unable to care for, control or provide necessary special care or special treatment for the child; 5. Who has been placed for care or adoption in violation of law; 6. Who is habitually truant from school, *after evidence is provided by the school attendance officer that the activities under s. 118.16(5) have been completed;* 7. Who is habitually truant from home and either the child or a parent, *guardian or a relative in whose home the child resides signs* the petition requesting jurisdiction and attests in court that reconciliation efforts have been attempted and have failed; 8. Who is receiving inadequate care during the period of time a parent is missing, incarcerated, hospitalized or institutionalized; 9. Who is at least age 12, signs the petition requesting jurisdiction and attests in court that he or she is in need of special care and treatment which the parent, guardian or legal custodian is unwilling to provide; 10. Whose parent, guardian or legal custodian neglects, refuses or is unable for reasons other than poverty to provide necessary care, food, clothing, medical or dental care or shelter so as to seriously endanger the physical health of the child; 11. Who is suffering emotional damage for which the parent or guardian is unwilling to provide treatment, which is evidenced by one or more of the following characteristics, exhibited to a severe degree: anxiety, depression, withdrawal or outward aggressive behavior; 12. Who, being under 12 years of age, has committed a delinquent act as defined in s.48.12; 13. Who has not been immunized as required by s. 140.05(16) and not exempted under s. 140.05(16)(c); or 14. Who has been determined, under s. 48.30(5)(c), to be not responsible for a delinquent act by reason of mental disease or defect.

Source: LA. Code Juv.Proc.Ann. art. 13 § 12 (West 1979, amended 1987) and Wis.Stat.Ann. § 48.13 (West 1979, amended 1987).

neglected or dependent children as well.[46] Of these states, 11 use the term "child in need of supervision," while the remainder use such terms as "unruly child," "incorrigible child," and "minor in need of supervision." The other jurisdictions either place status offenses within the definition of delinquency, use separate but unlabeled categories, or include them in a general jurisdictional category that establishes the court's control over all children who engage in criminal and specified noncriminal behavior.[47]

Even where there are separate legal categories for delinquents and status offenders, the distinction between them has become blurred. Some noncriminal conduct may be included in the definition of delinquency, and some less serious criminal offenses occasionally may be included within the status offender definition. Also, research shows that there are very few "pure" status offenders who have had no prior involvement in delinquency.[48]

In some states, the juvenile court judge is granted discretion to substitute a status offense for a delinquency charge.[49] Substitution of charges can be used as a bargaining chip to encourage youths originally petitioned to court for delinquency to admit to the charges against them in return for the promise of being included in the less stigmatized status offense category and receiving less punitive treatment.

Separate status offense categories may avoid some of the stigma associated with the delinquency label, but they can have relatively little practical effect on the child's treatment. Youths in either category can be picked up by the police and

On 15 December 1995, Tonya Kline, a 15-year-old girl was ordered by a South Carolina judge to be shackled to her mother, Deborah Harter, for a one month period. Kline had been ordered into juvenile detention while awaiting disposition on theft charges. A judge ordered the shackling after Harter told him she would do anything to keep her daughter out of detention. Should such an extreme measure be used to control status offenders who disobey court orders?

brought to a police station. They can be petitioned to the same juvenile court, where they have a hearing before the same judge and come under the supervision of the probation department, the court clinic, and the treatment staff. At a hearing, status offenders may see little difference between the treatment they receive and the treatment of the delinquent offenders sitting across the room. Although status offenders are usually not detained or incarcerated with delinquents, they can be transferred to secure facilities if they are repeatedly unruly and considered uncontrollable.

AIDING THE STATUS OFFENDER

Efforts have been ongoing to reduce the penalties and stigma borne by status offenders. The federal government's **Office of Juvenile Justice and Delinquency Prevention (OJJDP),** an agency created to identify the needs of youths and fund policy initiatives in the juvenile justice system, has made it a top priority to encourage the removal of status offenders from secure lockups, detention centers, and postdisposition treatment facilities that also house delinquent offenders. Evaluations indicate that this has been a highly successful policy initiative.[50] The number of status offenders who are kept in secure pretrial detention has dropped significantly.

Despite this mandate, juvenile court judges in many states can still detain status offenders in secure lockups if the youths are found in "contempt of court." The act that created the OJJDP was amended in 1987 to allow status offenders to be detained and incarcerated for violations of "valid court orders."[51] Children have been detained for such behaviors as wearing shorts to court, throwing paper on the floor, and, in one Florida case involving a pregnant teenager, not keeping a doctor's appointment.[52] Activists have attempted to outlaw the practice because it puts noncriminal youth in jeopardy; the Florida State Supreme Court forbade the practice in the case of *A.A. v. Rolle* (1992).[53] It remains to be seen whether other jurisdictions will follow suit.

Change in the treatment of status offenders reflects the current attitude toward children who violate the law. On the one hand, there appears to be a national movement to severely sanction youths who commit serious, violent offenses. On the other hand, a great effort has been made to remove nonserious cases, such as those involving status offenders, from the official agencies of justice and to place the offending youths in informal, community-based treatment programs. New York state has experimented with the mandatory diversion or removal of status offenders from the jurisdiction of the juvenile court. Before status offense cases are brought before the juvenile court, they must first be referred to community treatment centers; only those deemed treatment "failures" wind up in juvenile court.[54]

REFORMING STATUS OFFENSE LAWS

For the past two decades national commissions have called for reform of status offense laws. More than 20 years ago, the National Council on Crime and Delinquency, an influential, privately funded think tank, recommended removing status offenders from the juvenile court.[55] In 1976, the federal government's National Advisory Commission on Criminal Justice Standards and Goals, a task force created to develop a national crime policy, opted for the nonjudicial treatment of status offenders: "The only conduct that should warrant family court intervention is conduct that is clearly self-destructive or otherwise harmful to the child."[56] To meet this standard, the commission suggested that the nation's juvenile courts confine themselves to controlling five status offenses: habitual truancy, repeated disregard for parental authority, repeated running away, repeated use of intoxicating beverages, and delinquent acts by youths under the age of 10. The American Bar Association's *National Juvenile Justice Standards Project,* designed to promote significant improvements in the way children are treated by the police and the courts, called for the end of juvenile court jurisdiction over status offenders: "A juvenile's acts of misbehavior, ungovernability or unruliness which do not violate the criminal law should not constitute a ground for asserting juvenile court jurisdiction over the juvenile committing them."[57]

These calls for reform prompted a number of states, including New York, to experiment with replacing juvenile court jurisdiction over most status offenders with community-based treatment programs.[58] A few states, such as Maine, Delaware, Idaho, and Washington, have attempted to eliminate status offense laws and deal with these youth as neglected or dependent children, giving child protective services the primary responsibility for their care. However, juvenile court judges strongly resist removal of status jurisdiction as they believe that reducing their authority over children leads to the "criminalization" of the juvenile court.[59] Legislative changes may be cosmetic because when further efforts to remedy the child's problems through a social welfare approach fail, the case may be referred to the juvenile court for more formal processing.[60]

Those who favor removing status offenders from juvenile court authority charge that their experience with the legal system further stigmatizes these already troubled youths, exposes them to the influence of "true" delinquents, and enmeshes them in a system that cannot really afford to help them.[61] Reformer Ira Schwartz, for one, argues that status offenders "should be removed from the jurisdiction of the courts altogether."[62] Schwartz maintains that status offenders would best be served not by juvenile courts but by dispute resolution and mediation programs designed to strengthen family ties because "status offense cases are often rooted in family problems."[63]

INCREASING SOCIAL CONTROL

Those in favor of retaining the status offense category point to society's responsibility to care for troubled youths. Some have suggested that the failure of the courts to extend social control over wayward youths neglects the rights of concerned parents who are not able to care for and correct their children.[64] Others maintain that the status offense should remain a legal category so that juvenile courts can "force" a youth into receiving treatment.[65] While it is recognized that a court appearance can produce negative "stigma", the taint may be less important than the need for treatment.[66]

Curfew Laws Concern over juvenile misconduct has prompted many state jurisdictions to enact laws that actually expand social control over youth. Beginning in 1990 there has been explosion in the passage of **curfew laws** aimed at restricting the opportunity kids have for "getting in trouble." A recent survey of 77 large American cities found that 59 have such laws and that 26 of these were adopted during the five-year period 1990–1994.[67] More than 125,000 youth are now being arrested for curfew violations each year; in 1985 there were about 63,000 arrests for curfew violations. Designed to deter serious delinquency, curfew laws have created large numbers of new status offenders.

Disciplining Parents   Another approach to controlling status offenders (and delinquents) is to actually punish parents for their children's misconduct. The initial approach was to create laws disciplining parents for "contributing to the delinquency of a minor." The first of these statutes was enacted in Colorado in 1903, and today, forty-two states and the District of Columbia maintain similar laws. As a group, such "contributing" laws allow parents to be sanctioned in juvenile courts for behaviors associated with or suspected of encouraging their child's misbehavior.

In some instances involving delinquent behavior, sanctions mights include having parents pay for damage caused by their children who vandalized a school. All states except New Hampshire have incorporated parental liability laws within their statutes, though most recent legislation places limits on recovery somewhere between the $250 of Vermont and the $15,000 of Texas; the average is $2,500.

Some states now also make parents criminally liable for the illegal acts of their children. Since 1990, there have been more than 18 cases in which parents have been ordered to serve time in jail because their children have been truant from school. Whether such measures are legal and effective remains to be seen. Civil libertarians charge that they violate the constitutional right to due process and seem to be used only against lower-class parents. State laws have been successfully challenged in the lower courts. Criminologists Gilbert Geis and Arnold Binder find little evidence that punishing parents can deter delinquency and conclude that laws sanctioning parents are not only misguided and inadequate but can be described as "nasty and vicious."[68]

Today, all 50 states still retain at least *some* sort of control over status offenders.

ARE THEY REALLY DIFFERENT?

Court jurisdiction over status offenders may be defended if in fact their offending patterns are similar to those of delinquents. Is their current offense only the tip

Anthony Provenzino and his wife Susan enter district court in St. Clair Shores, Michigan on May 6, 1996. They were convicted under Michigan's 2-year-old Parental Responsibility Law for failure to control and supervise their son Alex, a 16-year-old who was involved in drug use and breaking and entering. Should parents face criminal charges for the behavior of their children, even though they may be unaware of their child's illegal activities?

of an antisocial "iceberg," or are they actually noncriminal youths who need only the loving hand of a parental figure interested in their welfare?

A number of studies have attempted to answer this question, but their results are at best inconclusive. Thomas Kelley analyzed the offense patterns of 2,000 juveniles appearing before a large urban court over a five-year period.[69] He found that status offenders have offense careers different from those of delinquents and are less likely to be **recidivists** (repeat offenders). His conclusion: Status offenders are different from juvenile delinquents and deserve different treatment.

In contrast, Charles Thomas employed a sample of youths referred to the juvenile court in Virginia and found that many who appeared on status offense charges had previous experiences as delinquents.[70] Similarly, using a large sample (69,000) of court-processed youths in Utah and Arizona, Howard Snyder found that more than half of all status offenders also had prior delinquency referrals; one-quarter of all delinquents had prior status offense charges.[71] The Thomas and Snyder studies indicate that delinquents and status offenders may be quite similar and deserving of equivalent legal process.

These disparate findings may be explained in part by the fact that there may be different "types" of status offenders, some of whom are similar to delinquents and others who are quite different. In one study, Randall Sheldon, John Horvath, and Sharon Tracy found that status offenders petitioned to court as "runaways" or "unmanageables" were less likely to also experience delinquency charges than status offenders referred to juvenile court for truancy, curfew, or liquor law violations.[72] Similarly, in an evaluation of eight juvenile court programs, Solomon Kobrin and his associates found that status offenders could actually be divided into three groups: (1) first offenders, (2) those with prior status offenses, and (3) those with both a delinquent record and a status offense record.[73] Although first-time offenders typically did not become recidivists, those youths with prior status offense charges were quite likely to progress to more serious delinquent offenses. The fact that many young offenders had mixed delinquent-status offender records indicates that these legal categories are not entirely independent.

The predominant view today is that many status offenders and delinquents share similar social and developmental problems and that consequently both categories should fall under the jurisdiction of the juvenile court. Not surprisingly, research does show that the legal processing of delinquents and status offenders remains quite similar.[74] It is also recognized that some "pure" first-time status offenders are quite different from delinquents and that a juvenile court experience can be harmful to them and escalate the frequency and seriousness of their law-violating behaviors.[75] The removal of these status offenders from the juvenile court is an issue that continues to be debated. The following "Case in Point" explores this question.

THE "DILEMMA" OF DELINQUENCY

The media has highlighted the nation's concerns about delinquency, helping convince the general public that "things are worse than ever." But it is important not to forget that concern about youthful rebellion is not a recent phenomenon. In the 1950s, social commentators were disturbed about the development of a postwar youth culture.[76] The American teenager was viewed as a rebellious troublemaker influenced by cult figures (especially James Dean and Elvis

You have just been appointed by the governor as chairperson of a newly formed group charged with overhauling the state's juvenile justice system.

One primary concern is the treatment of status offenders. Youths charged with being runaways, truants, or incorrigible are petitioned to juvenile court under an existing status offense statute. Those adjudicated as minors in need of supervision are usually placed with the county probation department. In serious cases, they may be removed from the home and placed in foster care or a state or private custodial institution. Recently, a great deal of media attention has focused on the plight of runaway children who live on the streets, take drugs, and engage in prostitution.

At an open hearing, advocates of the current system argue that many families cannot provide the care and control needed to keep kids out of trouble and that it is therefore important for the state to maintain control. They contend that many status offenders have histories of drug and delinquency problems and are little different from those who are arrested on criminal charges. Control by the juvenile court is necessary if such youths are ever to get needed treatment.

Another vocal group argues that it is a mistake for a system that deals with criminal youth to also handle troubled adolescents whose problems usually are the result of child abuse and neglect. They believe that the current statute should be amended to give the state's Department of Social Welfare (DSW) jurisdiction over all noncriminal youths in need of assistance. These opponents of the current law point out that even though status offenders and delinquents are held in separate facilities, those who violate the rules or run away can be transferred to correctional facilities that house criminal youths. Furthermore, the whole process of lawyers, trials, and court proceedings helps convince these troubled youth that they are "bad kids" and social outcasts and not youths who need a helping hand. If necessary, the DSW could place needy children in community mental health clinics or with foster parents; they would, however, be totally removed from the justice system.

Should status offenders be treated differently from juvenile delinquents?

Should distinctions be made between different types of status offenders?

Are status-type problems best handled by social service agencies?

Presley), comic books, movies, and advertising. Teens spoke a separate language ("blast," "drag," "shook up"), had their own dress code (jeans and ducktail haircuts) and listened to the new rock and roll music, which sounded quite alien to their parents, who were part of the "swing generation." Although the delinquency rate was still relatively low, an increase in youth crime between 1950 and 1956 prompted angry public outbursts against a "generation gone sour"; *New York Times* reporter Harrison Salisbury called teens in the '50s the "shook up generation."[77]

These concerns prompted a U.S. Senate subcommittee headed by Estes Kefauver to look into the delinquency problem. Psychologist Frederic Wertham published *The Seduction of the Innocent*, which named comic books with a violent theme as a cause of delinquency; the resulting public outrage forced the comic book industry to adopt a code of standards.[78]

Where We Stand Today Forty years later, many of these problems have not diminished, and some have increased in severity. Many American youths live in neighborhoods where they fear walking to school in the morning and where it is common to begin experimenting with drugs and alcohol at an early age. They live in a country whose leaders tell them to practice sexual abstinence yet also tell them that if they "do it," they should practice "safe sex"; they are bombarded with media campaigns based on the premise that sex sells. The number of teenage pregnancies has increased sharply, and many children born to underage mothers have low birthweights and are extremely vulnerable to health problems. Teenage mothers are more likely to drop out of school and face economic disadvantages that hinder their future.[79] Early sexual experimentation has also increased the proportion of youth who contract a sexually transmitted disease, increasing the threat of AIDS for millions of American youth.[80]

While 1950s youths were reading comic books, 1990s teens are listening to heavy metal rock bands, such an Guns 'N Roses and Metallica, whose songs dwell on Satanism, drug use, and racial hatred. They watch TV shows and movies that rely on graphic scenes of violence as their main theme, including such films as *Seven* and *Silence of the Lambs* which depict brutish acts, such as decapitation and dismemberment.

Finding an appropriate response to juvenile delinquency is a serious concern of the American public. People are concerned about the problems of youths and want to insulate young people from a life of crime and drug abuse. Research suggests that a majority of the American public still favors policies mandating rehabilitation and treatment of known offenders.[81] Evidence also exists that many at-risk youths can be successfully helped with the proper treatment and care.[82]

On the other hand, the general public is wary of teenage hoodlums and gangs and their violent way of life. How can we control their behavior and protect innocent people? Should we embrace a "get tough" policy in which violent teens are locked up or even face the death penalty? Or should we continue to treat delinquents as troubled teens who need a helping hand from a "wise parent?"

This tension pervades every aspect of the legal treatment of youths. For example, the creation of delinquency statutes and an independent juvenile court at the turn of the century is evidence that society recognizes that children are distinctly different from adults and therefore should be treated separately and with more compassion. At the same time, statutes that allow the transfer of delinquents to adult legal jurisdictions show that the legal system is ready and willing to get tough with juveniles. Despite the lip service paid to society's obligation to help at-risk children, prosecutors appear to be exercising their right to waive youths to the adult justice system more frequently today than in the past.[83] Similarly, the Supreme Court has legalized the death penalty for children once they reach age 16.[84] Although the American public is generally in favor of the death penalty, surveys indicate that a substantial majority oppose capital punishment for minors.[85] Still, more than 30 people are on death row for crimes committed during their minority years.

The value conflict in our current response to juvenile delinquency is a potent theme in American jurisprudence.[86] Throughout the country are programs to treat, help, and rehabilitate minor offenders. Existing side by side are efforts to control, incarcerate, and punish youths who violate the law. Some critics have warned that our treatment of juveniles is becoming more and more intrusive and more likely to enmesh them in the justice process, a condition referred to as **widening the net.**[87] In other words, efforts to "help" at risk youth may eventually lead to unattended negative and harmful consequences.

To many experts, our inability to overcome these goal conflicts has resulted in the failure to develop a coherent and effective delinquency control policy. As policy expert Ira Schwartz states,

> The abuses and mistreatment of children that helped give rise to the child-saver movement at the turn of the century and subsequently led to the creation of the juvenile court continue to exist.[88]

Although Schwartz remains optimistic that positive change can be effected, it has been more than nine decades since the first separate juvenile court was created, and conflict still exists over the proper treatment of delinquent youths and their place in modern society. Some commentators, including influential criminologists Travis Hirschi and Michael Gottfredson, have gone as far as suggesting the the juvenile justice system be abolished because (a) youths are just as dangerous as adults and (b) age should not be a factor when considering how to deal with dangerous law violators.[89] Whether their suggestion is taken seriously remains to be seen.

SUMMARY

The study of delinquency is concerned with a number of different issues: the nature and extent of the criminal behavior of youths; the causes of youthful law violations; the legal rights of juveniles; and prevention and treatment techniques.

Studying the problems of young people is especially important when the dynamic nature of adolescence and the stress American youth are under are considered. Drugs, pregnancy, suicide, and social conflict are all taking their toll on today's adolescents.

The concept of a separate status of "childhood" has developed slowly over the centuries. Early family life included such practices as providing a dower and observing primogeniture. Punishment was severe, and children were expected to take on adult roles early in life.

With the start of the seventeenth century came greater recognition of the needs of children. In Great Britain, changes in family structure, the chancery court movement, the Poor Laws, and the apprenticeship programs greatly affected the lives of children. In colonial America, many of the characteristics of English family living were adopted.

In the nineteenth century, neglected, delinquent, and dependent or runaway children were treated no differently from criminal defendants. Children were often charged and convicted of crimes. During this time, however, because of philosophical shifts in the areas of crime and delinquency as well as a change in the emphasis of the concept of *parens patriae*, steps were taken to reduce the responsibility of children under the criminal law in both Great Britain and the United States.

The concept of delinquency was developed in the early twentieth century. Before that, criminal youths and adults were treated in almost the same fashion. A group of reformers, referred to as child savers, helped create a separate delinquency category to insulate juvenile offenders from the influence of adult criminals.

The separate status of juvenile delinquency is still based on the *parens patriae* philosophy, which holds that children have the right to care and custody and that if parents are not capable of providing that care, the state must step in to take control.

Juvenile courts also have jurisdiction over noncriminal, status offenders. Status offenses are illegal only because of the minority status of the offender. They include such misbehavior as truancy, running away, and sexual misconduct. Some experts have called for an end to juvenile court control over status offenders, charging that it merely further stigmatizes already troubled youths. Some research indicates that status offenders are harmed by juvenile court processing. Other studies indicate that status offenders and delinquents are actually quite similar.

Determining treatment of juveniles is an ongoing dilemma in American society. Still uncertain is whether young law violators respond better to harsh punishment or benevolent treatment.

KEY TERMS

ego identity
role diffusion
at-risk youth
juvenile delinquency
juvenile justice system
chronic delinquent
aging-out process
chronic career offenders
persistence
desistance

paternalistic family
primogeniture
dower system
jointure
wet nurses
swaddling
Poor Laws
parens patriae
child savers
best interests of the child

waiver
status offenses
wayward minors
delinquent children
Office of Juvenile Justice and Delinquency
   Prevention (OJJDP)
curfew laws
recidivists
widening the net

QUESTIONS FOR DISCUSSION

1. Is it fair to have a separate legal category for youths? Considering how dangerous young people can be, does it make more sense to group offenders on the basis of what they have done and not their age?
2. At what age are juveniles truly capable of understanding the seriousness of their actions?
3. Is it fair to institutionalize a minor simply for being truant or running away from home? Should the jurisdiction of status offenders be removed from juvenile court and placed with the state department of social services or some other welfare organization?
4. Should delinquency proceedings be secretive? Does the public have the right to know who juvenile criminals are?
5. Can a "get tough" policy help control juvenile misbehavior, or should *parens patriae* remain the standard?
6. Should juveniles who commit felonies such as rape or robbery be treated as adults?

NOTES

1. Reuters, "Couple Cleared of Molesting Children," *Boston Globe* 12 December 1995, p. 28.
2. Reuters, "Did Child's Punch Kill Teacher," *Boston Globe* 12 October 1995, p. 6.
3. Associated Press, "Attackers Steal an Artificial Leg," *Boston Globe* 9 November 1995, p. 17.
4. Associated Press, "8-Th Grade Sweethearts Commit Suicide," *Manchester Union Leader* 9 November 1995, p. D16.
5. Associated Press, "Mother Sentenced in Hot Car Deaths," *Boston Globe* 10 November 1995, p. 20.
6. Associated Press, "Girl, 15, Adapts to Being Tied to Mother," *Boston Globe* 15 December 1995, p. 47.
7. Reuters, "Insanity Is Plea in Parents' Deaths," *Boston Globe* 27 January 1996, p. 80.
8. Jane Knitzer and J. Lawrence Aber, "Young Children in Poverty: Facing the Facts," *American Journal of Orthopsychiatry* 65:174–76 (1995).
9. John Cook and Larry Brown, *Two Americas: Alternative Future for Child Poverty in America* (Medford, Mass.: Tufts University Center on Hunger, Poverty and Nutrition, 1993).
10. David Eggebeen and Daniel Lichter, "Race, Family Structure, and Changing Poverty Among American Children," *American Sociological Review* 56:801–17 (1991).
11. W. Rees Davis and Michael Clatts, "High Risk Youth and the N.Y.C. Street Economy: Policy Implications" (Paper presented at the American Society of Criminology meeting, Boston, Mass., November 1995).
12. Children's Defense Fund, *The State of America's Children, 1991* (Washington, D.C.: Children's Defense Fund, 1991), p. 76.
13. Institute for Social Research Press Release 11 December 1995 (Ann Arbor, Mich.).
14. James Alan Fox, "Teenage Males Are Committing Murder at an Increasing Rate," Press Release 1 November 1992 (College of Criminal Justice, Northeastern University), p. 1.
15. Susan Crimmins and Michael Foley, "The Threshold of Violence in Urban Adolescents" (Paper presented at the

annual meeting of the American Society of Criminology, Reno, Nev., November 1989).

16. Task Force on Education of Young Adolescents, *Turning Points, Preparing American Youth for the 21st Century* (New York: Carnegie Council on Adolescent Development, 1989).

17. Ibid., p. 21.

18. Erik Erikson, *Childhood and Society* (New York: W. H. Norton, 1963).

19. Roger Gould, "Adult Life Stages: Growth Toward Self-Tolerance," *Psychology Today* 8:74–78 (1975).

20. *Turning Points,* p. 27.

21. Federal Bureau of Investigation, *Crimes in the United States, 1994* (Washington, D.C.: U.S. Government Printing Office, 1995), p. 227.

22. John Whitehead and Steven Lab, "A Meta-Analysis of Juvenile Correctional Treatment," *Journal of Research in Crime and Delinquency* 26:276–95 (1989).

23. See Lawrence Stone, *The Family, Sex, and Marriage in England: 1500–1800* (New York: Harper & Row, 1977).

24. This section relies on Jackson Spielvogel, *Western Civilization* (St. Paul, Minn.: West, 1991), pp. 279–86.

25. Ibid., pp. 279–86.

26. See Philipe Aries, *Centuries of Childhood: A Social History of Family Life* (New York: Vintage, 1962).

27. See Douglas R. Rendleman, "Parens Patriae: From Chancery to the Juvenile Court," *South Carolina Law Review* 23:205 (1971).

28. See Stone, *The Family, Sex, and Marriage in England,* and Lawrence Stone, ed., *Schooling and Society: Studies in the History of Education* (Baltimore: Johns Hopkins University Press, 1970).

29. Ibid.

30. See Wiley B. Sanders, *Some Early Beginnings of the Children's Court Movement in England,* National Probation Association Yearbook (New York: National Council on Crime and Delinquency, 1945).

31. Rendleman, "Parens Patriae," p. 205.

32. Douglas Besharov, *Juvenile Justice Advocacy—Practice in a Unique Court* (New York: Practicing Law Institute, 1974), p. 2.

33. *Wellesley v. Wellesley,* 4 Eng. Rep. 1078 (1827).

34. Rendleman, "Parens Patriae," p. 209.

35. See Anthony Platt, "The Rise of the Child Saving Movement: A Study in Social Policy and Correctional Reform," *Annals of the American Academy of Political and Social Science* 381:21–38 (1969).

36. Robert Bremmer, ed., and John Barnard, Hareven Tamara, and Robert Mennel, asst. eds., *Children and Youth in America* (Cambridge, Mass.: Harvard University Press, 1970), p. 64.

37. Elizabeth Pleck, "Criminal Approaches to Family Violence, 1640–1980," in Lloyd Ohlin and Michael Tonry, eds., *Family Violence* (Chicago: University of Chicago Press, 1989), pp. 19–58.

38. Ibid.

39. John R. Sutton, *Stubborn Children: Controlling Delinquency in the United States, 1640–1981* (Berkeley: University of California Press, 1988).

40. Pleck, "Criminal Approaches to Family Violence," p. 29.

41. John Demos, *Past, Present and Personal* (New York: Oxford University Press, 1986), pp. 80–88.

42. Elizabeth Pleck, *Domestic Tyranny: The Making of Social Policy Against Family Violence from Colonial Times to the Present* (New York: Oxford University Press, 1987), pp. 28–30.

43. Graeme Newman, *The Punishment Response* (Philadelphia: J. B. Lippincott, 1978), pp. 53–79; Aries, *Centuries of Childhood* (New York: Knopf, 1962). The history of childhood juvenile justice is discussed in detail in chapter 13.

44. See, generally, David Rothman, *The Discovery of the Asylum* (Boston: Little, Brown, 1971).

45. Reports of the Chicago Bar Association Committee, 1899, cited in Anthony Platt, *The Child Savers* (Chicago: University of Chicago Press, 1969), p. 119.

46. John L. Hutzler, *Juvenile Court Jurisdiction over Children's Conduct: 1982 Comparative Analysis of Juvenile and Family Codes and National Standards* (Pittsburgh: National Center for Juvenile Justice, 1982), p. 2.

47. Ibid.

48. Susan Datesman and Mikel Aickin, "Offense Specialization and Escalation Among Status Offenders," *Journal of Criminal Law and Criminology* 75:1246–75 (1985).

49. Ibid.

50. See, generally, Solomon Kobrin and Malcolm Klein, *National Evaluation of the Deinstitutionalization of Status Offender Programs—Executive Summary* (Los Angeles: Social Science Research Institute, University of Southern California, 1982).

51. 42 U.S.C.A. 5601–5751 (1983 & Supp. 1987).

52. Claudia Wright, "Contempt No Excuse for Locking Up Status Offenders, Says Florida Supreme Court," *Youth Law News* 13:1–3 (1992).

53. *A.A. v. Rolle,* 604 So. 2d 813 (1992).

54. Martin Rouse, "The Diversion of Status Offenders, Criminalization, and the New York Family Court." (Revised version of the paper presented at the American Society of Criminology, Reno, Nev., November 1989).

55. National Council on Crime and Delinquency, "Juvenile Curfews—A Policy Statement," *Crime and Delinquency* 18:132–33 (1972).

56. National Advisory Commission on Criminal Justice Standards and Goals, *Juvenile Justice and Delinquency Prevention* (Washington, D.C.: U.S. Government Printing Office, 1977), p. 311.

57. American Bar Association Joint Commission on Juvenile Justice Standards, *Summary and Analysis* (Cambridge, Mass.: Ballinger, 1977), sect. 1.1.

58. Rouse, "The Diversion of Status Offenders, Criminalization, and the New York Family Court," p. 12.

59. Barry Feld, "Criminalizing the American Juvenile Court," in Michael Tonry, ed., *Crime and Justice, A Review of Research* (Chicago: University of Chicago Press, 1993), p. 232.

60. Marc Miller, "Changing Legal Paradigms in Juvenile Justice," in Peter Greenwood, ed., *The Juvenile Rehabilitation Reader* (Santa Monica, Calif.: Rand Corporation, 1985) p. V.44.

61. Thomas Kelley, "Status Offenders Can Be Different: A Comparative Study of Delinquent Careers," *Crime and Delinquency* 29:365–80 (1983).

62. Ira Schwartz, *(In) Justice for Juveniles: Rethinking the Best Interests of the Child* (Lexington, Mass: Lexington Books, 1989), p. 171.

63. Ibid.

64. Lawrence Martin and Phyllis Snyder, "Jurisdiction over Status Offenses Should Not Be Removed from the Juvenile Court," *Crime and Delinquency* 22:44–47 (1976).

65. Lindsay Arthur, "Status Offenders Need a Court of Last Resort," *Boston University Law Review* 57:631–44 (1977).

66. Ibid.

67. William Ruefle and Kenneth Mike Reynolds, "Curfews and Delinquency in Major American Cities," *Crime and Delinquency* 41:347–363 (1995). Federal Bureau of Investigation, *Crime in the United States, 1994* (Washington, D.C.: United State Government Printing Office, 1995), p. 217.

68. Gilbert Geis and Arnold Binder, "Sins of Their Children: Parental Responsibility for Juvenile Delinquency," *Notre Dame Journal of Law, Ethics, and Public Policy* 5:303–22 (1991); Christi Harlan and Arthur Hayes, "Jailing Parents," *Wall Street Journal,* 18 May 1992, p. B6.

69. Kelley, "Status Offenders Can Be Different."

70. Charles Thomas, "Are Status Offenders Really So Different?" *Crime and Delinquency* 22:438–55 (1976).

71. Howard Snyder, *Court Careers of Juvenile Offenders* (Washington, D.C.: Office of Juvenile Justice and Delinquency Prevention, 1988), p. 65.

72. Randall Shelden, John Horvath, and Sharon Tracy, "Do Status Offenders Get Worse? Some Clarifications on the Question of Escalation," *Crime and Delinquency* 35:202–16 (1989).

73. Solomon Kobrin, Frank Hellum, and John Peterson, "Offense Patterns of Status Offenders," in D. Schichor and D. Kelly, eds., *Critical Issues in Juvenile Delinquency* (Lexington, Mass.: Lexington Books, 1980), pp. 203–35.

74. Chris Marshall, Ineke Marshall, and Charles Thomas, "The Implementation of Formal Procedures in Juvenile Court Processing of Status Offenders," *Journal of Criminal Justice* 11:195–211 (1983).

75. Schwartz, *In Justice for Juveniles,* pp. 378–79.

76. James Gilbert, *A Cycle of Outrage, America's Reaction to the Juvenile Delinquent in the 1950's* (New York: Oxford University Press, 1986).

77. Harrison Salisbury, *The Shook-Up Generation* (New York: Harper, 1958).

78. Frederic Wertham, *Seduction of the Innocent* (Port Washington, N.Y.: Kennikat Press, 1953).

79. *Turning Points,* p. 24.

80. Ibid.

81. Francis Cullen, Sandra Evans Skovron, Joseph Scott, and Velmer Burton, "Public Support for Correctional Treatment: The Tenacity of Rehabilitative Ideology," *Criminal Justice and Behavior* 17:6–18 (1990).

82. Rhena Izzo and Robert Ross, "Meta-Analysis of Rehabilitation Programs for Juvenile Delinquents," *Criminal Justice and Behavior* 17:134–42 (1990).

83. Dean Champion, "Teenage Felons and Waiver Hearing: Some Recent Trends, 1980–1988," *Crime and Delinquency* 35:577–85 (1989).

84. *Stanford v. Kentucky,* and *Wilkins v. Missouri,* 109 S.Ct. 2969 (1989).

85. Sandra Skovron, Joseph Scott, and Francis Cullen, "The Death Penalty for Juveniles: An Assessment of Public Support," *Crime and Delinquency* 35:546–61 (1989).

86. See, generally, Edmund McGarrell, *Juvenile Correctional Reform: Two Decades of Policy and Procedural Change* (Albany, N.Y.: State University of New York Press, 1988); Barry Krisberg, Ira Schwartz, Paul Litsky, and James Austin, "The Watershed of Juvenile Justice Reform," *Crime and Delinquency* 32:5–38 (1986), at 34.

87. Mark Ezell, "Juvenile Arbitration: Net Widening and Other Unintended Consequences," *Journal of Research in Crime and Delinquency* 26:358–77 (1990).

88. Schwartz, *(In) Justice for Juveniles,* p. 17.

89. Travis Hirschi and Michael Gottfredson, "Rethinking the Juvenile Justice System," *Crime and Delinquency* 39:262–71 (1993).

CHAPTER TWO

THE NATURE AND EXTENT OF DELINQUENCY

INTRODUCTION

How common is juvenile delinquency? Who commits delinquent acts, and where are they most likely to occur? Is the juvenile crime rate increasing or decreasing? Are juveniles more likely to become the victims of crime than adults?[1] Without such information it would be impossible to understand the cause of delinquent behaviors and determine effective means to reduce or eliminate their occurrence.

Delinquency experts have devised a variety of data collection methods that they believe can accurately measure the nature and extent of delinquency. This chapter begins with a description of the three most widely used of these data sources: official data, self-report data, and victim data. It also examines the information they provide on juvenile crime rates and trends. These data sources will then be used to provide information on the personal characteristics of adolescent law violators, including their age, gender, race, income, and offending patterns.

MEASURING DELINQUENCY

Delinquency experts have relied on three separate sources of data to measure the nature and extent of crime and delinquency:

- *Official data.* Official data involve the criminal incidents reported to the nation's police departments. This information is collected and disseminated on an annual basis by the **Federal Bureau of Investigation (FBI)** through their Uniform Crime Report (UCR) program.[2] The *UCR* records both the total number of crimes reported to the police for major offense categories, such as murder and rape, and the total number of arrests made for *any crime* that is cleared or solved. Because the age of arrestees is recorded, official data can be used to study trends and patterns in the delinquency rate. Youths with an arrest record are referred to as "official delinquents." Their actions are considered recorded or **official delinquency,** and their behavior becomes part of the "official statistics."
- *Self-report data.* Self-report data are obtained from anonymous surveys or interviews, often conducted in schools, that query adolescents about their participation in illegal acts such as drug abuse and vandalism. Self-report data are aimed at assessing criminal acts that have gone undetected by the police either because victims fail to report crime or because the crime is "victimless" (e.g., drug abuse). They measure the extent of unrecorded juvenile delinquency, the so-called **dark figures of crime.** These data can also be used to compare the personal characteristics (e.g., race and gender) of "official delinquents" with those youths whose criminal activity remains undetected.
- *Victim data.* **Victim surveys** ask those who have experienced crime first-hand to tell about the episode. Victim data would include both crimes reported to the police and crimes that the victim failed to report. They provide important information on where victimization takes place, the likelihood of victimization, and the kinds of personal behaviors and lifestyles that increase the chances of becoming a crime victim. In personal crimes, such as robberies, victims may also be able to identify the age, race, and gender of their assailants. The most widely used victim survey is the federally spon-

sored **National Crime Victimization Survey (NCVS),** an annual survey of thousands of citizens selected from communities across the nation.[3]

Each of these three data sources is discussed in more detail below.

OFFICIAL STATISTICS

The standard source of official crime and delinquency statistics has been the annual effort of the U.S. Justice Department's Federal Bureau of Investigation (FBI) to accumulate information gathered by the nation's police departments on the number of criminal acts reported by citizens and the number of persons arrested each year for criminal and delinquent activity. This effort culminates in the publication of the annual *Uniform Crime Report (UCR),* the best known and most widely used source of national crime and delinquency statistics.

The *UCR* is compiled from statistics sent to the FBI from more than 16,000 police departments serving a majority of the population of the United States. Its major unit of analysis involves the **index crimes,** also known as **Part I offenses:** homicide and non-negligent manslaughter, forcible rape, robbery, aggravated assault, burglary, larceny, arson, and motor vehicle theft (see Table 2.1). A record is compiled by cooperating police agencies every time one of these offenses is reported by a victim or witness. The FBI receives quarterly tallies of these offenses and annually publishes the results. Data are broken down by city, county, standard metropolitan statistical area (SMSA), and geographical divisions of the United States. In addition to these statistics, the *UCR* provides information on the number and characteristics of individuals who have been arrested for these and all other criminal offenses, including vandalism, liquor law violations, and drug trafficking (known as **Part II offenses**). The arrest data include age, sex, and race.

The *UCR* expresses crime data in three ways. First, the number of crimes reported to the police and arrests made are given as raw figures (for example, 23,305 murders occurred in 1994). Second, percent changes in the amount of crime between years are computed (e.g., murder decreased five percent between 1993 and 1994). Finally, crime rates per 100,000 people are computed; that is, when the *UCR* indicates that the murder rate was 9.0 in 1994, it means that about 9 people in every 100,000 fell victim to murder between January 1 and December 31 of 1994. The equation used is:

$$\text{Crime Rate} = \frac{\text{Number of reported crimes}}{\text{Total U.S. population}} \times 100,000 = \text{Rate per } 100,000$$

All three reporting methods will be used in the following discussion, which reviews some of the most significant trends reported by the *UCR.*

CRIME TRENDS IN THE UNITED STATES

Crime continues to be one of the leading social problems in the United States. The crime rate skyrocketed between 1960, when about 3.3 million crimes were reported to police agencies, and 1981, when 13.4 million were reported. Then, after four years of decline (1981 to 1984), the rate went up in 1985 and continued to increase for the remainder of the decade. As the 1990s began, the overall crime rate began to stabilize and decline, dropping about 8 percent between 1990 and 1995.[4] Some large cities, such as New York, reported significant declines in the violence rate (see Figure 2.1).

TABLE 2.1 FBI Index Crimes

The Part I offenses are:

Criminal homicide. a. Murder and nonnegligent manslaughter: the willful (nonnegligent) killing of one human being by another. Deaths caused by negligence, attempts to kill, assaults to kill, suicides, accidental deaths, and justifiable homicides are excluded. Justifiable homicides are limited to: (1) the killing of a felon by a law enforcement officer in the line of duty; and (2) the killing of a felon by a private citizen. b. Manslaughter by negligence: the killing of another person through gross negligence. Traffic fatalities are excluded. While manslaughter by negligence is a Part I crime, it is not included in the Crime Index.

Forcible rape. The carnal knowledge of a female forcibly and against her will. Included are rapes by force and attempts or assaults to rape. Statutory offenses (no force used—victim under age of consent) are excluded.

Robbery. The taking or attempting to take anything of value from the care, custody, or control of a person or persons by force or threat or force of violence and/or by putting the victim in fear.

Aggravated assault. An unlawful attack by one person upon another for the purpose of inflicting severe or aggravated bodily injury. This type of assault usually is accompanied by the use of a weapon or by means likely to produce death or great bodily harm. Simple assaults are excluded.

Burglary. The unlawful entry of a structure to commit a felony or a theft. Attempted forcible entry is included.

Larceny—theft (except motor vehicle theft). The unlawful taking, carrying, leading, or riding away of property from the possession or constructive possession of another. Examples are thefts of bicycles or automobile accessories, shoplifting, pocket-picking, or the stealing of any property or article which is not taken by force and violence or by fraud. Attempted larcenies are included. Embezzlement, "con" games, forgery, worthless checks, etc., are excluded.

Motor vehicle theft. The theft or attempted theft of a motor vehicle. A motor vehicle is self-propelled and runs on the surface and not on rails. Specifically excluded from this category are motorboats, construction equipment, airplanes, and farming equipment.

Arson. Any willful or malicious burning or attempt to burn, with or without intent to defraud, a dwelling, house, public building, motor vehicle or aircraft, personal property of another, etc.

Source: Federal Bureau of Investigation, *Crime in the United States, 1994* (Washington, D.C.: U.S. Government Printing Office, 1995), pp. 380–81.

To some experts, crime rate declines are a sign that crime control efforts are working; to others, it is a result of a diminished teen population. Adolescents are disproportionately involved in crime, so as the number of teens grows in the near future, so too will the crime rate. Even though the crime rate has declined, the FBI estimates that about 14 million serious crimes are still being reported to police annually, a rate of more than 5,000 per 100,000 inhabitants.[5]

MEASURING OFFICIAL DELINQUENCY

Because the *UCR*'s arrest statistics are **disaggregated** (broken down) by suspect's age, they can be used to estimate adolescent participation in the official crime rate. Arrest data must be interpreted with caution, however. First, the number of teenagers arrested does not represent the actual number of youths who have committed delinquent acts but only those caught and officially processed by the police. Some offenders are never counted because they are never caught. Others are

FIGURE 2.1
Crime rate trends, 1960–1995

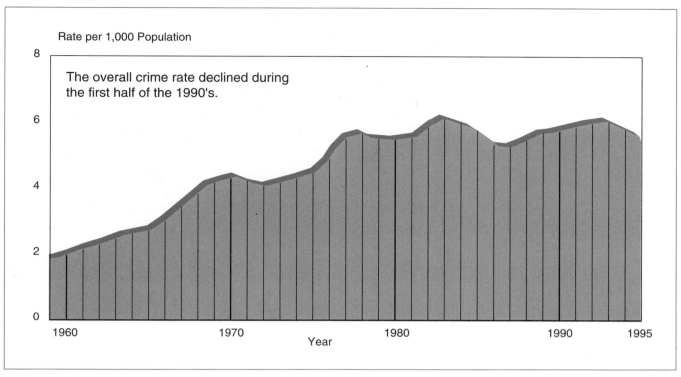

Rate per 1,000 Population

The overall crime rate declined during
the first half of the 1990's.

Source: FBI, UCR, 1994 updated 1995.

counted more than once because multiple arrests of the same individual for different crimes are counted separately in the *UCR*. Consequently, the total number of arrests does not equal the number of people who have been arrested. Put another way, if two million arrests of youths under 18 years of age were made in a given year, we could not be sure if two million individuals had been arrested once or if 500,000 chronic offenders had been arrested four times each. However, as the nature of arrest remains constant over time, increases or decreases in the number and rate of juvenile arrests should give some indication of the trends in juvenile crime.

With these issues in mind, what does the *UCR* tell us about delinquency?

OFFICIAL DELINQUENCY

In 1994 (the last year for which complete data were available), a total of about 14.6 million arrests were made; of these, 2.9 million were for serious Type I crimes and 11.7 million were for less serious Type II crimes.

Jurisdictions that report the age of arrestees to the FBI indicate that about 2.2 million juvenile arrests were made in 1994, constituting 19 percent of all arrests; more than 735,000 juveniles were arrested for the more serious Type I crimes.[6] Juveniles aged 10–17, who encompass less than about one-eighth the U.S. population, are responsible for almost one-third of the serious crime arrests.[7]

In addition to serious crime arrests, about 1.5 million juvenile arrests were made for Part II offenses. Included in this total were 200,000 arrests for running

away from home, 137,000 for disorderly conduct, 131,000 for drug abuse violations, and 105,888 for curfew violations. In all, more than 2.2 million arrests of all kinds in 1994 involved a suspect under age 18.

It comes as no surprise then that crime is a young person's game: Property crime activity peaks at age 16, and the peak age for violent crime arrests is 18. Age-level crime rates continue unabated until age 30, when both the violent and property crime arrest rates begin to decline dramatically. Adolescent participation in the crime rate is underscored by the arrests of very young children for violent crimes. More than 500 youths under 12 years of age were arrested for rape in 1994; of these, 103 were under age 10.

JUVENILE CRIME TRENDS

What are the recent trends in juvenile crime? Juvenile crime has influenced significantly the nation's overall crime statistics. In the 10-year period 1985–1994, the total number of juvenile arrests increased 28 percent; juvenile arrests for violent crime increased 75 percent. During this same period, the number of adult arrests expanded at a much slower pace; total adult arrests increased 19 percent and violent crime arrests increased 48 percent. The teenage juvenile population remained stable during this period (increasing about one percent), so the increase in juvenile crime during this time cannot be explained by a rising adolescent population.

Juvenile crime continued to accelerate despite a decline in the overall crime rate between 1990 and 1994. While adult arrests declined by 2.4 percent, juvenile arrests increased 21 percent. If arrests reflect and represent actual participation in criminal activity, then it is evident that juveniles are increasingly contributing to the nation's crime problem.

Most disturbing are increases in the most serious offense, murder. According to criminologist Alfred Blumstein, beginning in 1985, the number of homicides committed by young people (and their use of handguns to commit them) began to grow at a rapid pace (see Figures 2.2 and 2.3).[8] Juveniles today are better armed and more deadly than ever before. In 1995, juvenile violence rates declined (3%) for the first time in eight years. Is it possible that juvenile crime rates have peaked and now may decline?

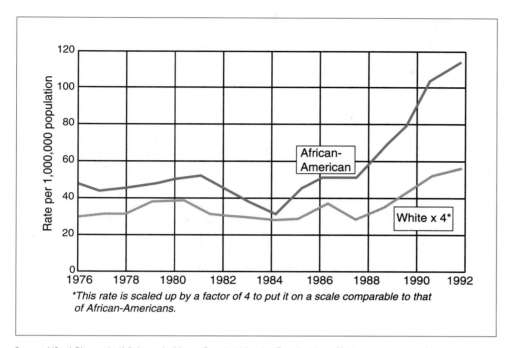

FIGURE 2.2
Homicide arrest rate of 14–17-year-old males

Source: Alfred Blumstein, "Violence by Young People: Why the Deadly Nexus?" *National Institute of Justice Journal,* August 1995, p. 2. The data were generated by Glenn Pierce and James Fox from the FBI's Supplementary Homicide Reports, which are based on reports of individual homicides submitted by the nation's police departments.

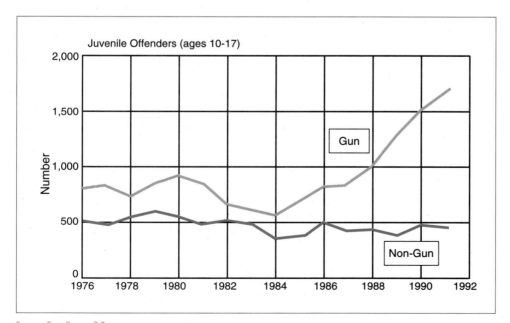

FIGURE 2.3
Number of gun and non-gun homicides

Source: See figure 2.2.

WHAT FACTORS INFLUENCE THE JUVENILE CRIME RATE?

There have been numerous efforts to explain the rapid increase in juvenile crime and violence rates over the past decade. The most important of the suspected influences are discussed briefly below.

HATE AND CONFLICT

American society is marked by deep racial, gender, ethnic, and class conflict. There is little question that numerous acts of teenage aggression are the result of seemingly unmotivated, random street violence. Some of these incidents may find their root cause in hatred or bias. In their analysis of hate-inspired crimes, Jack Levin and Jack McDevitt found that many of the thousands of **hate crimes** committed each year are perpetrated by young people and can be classified into three types:

1. *Thrill-seeking hate crimes.* In the same way that some youths like to get together to "shoot hoops," hate mongers join forces to have fun by bashing minorities or destroying property. Inflicting pain on others gives them a sadistic thrill.
2. *Reactive hate crimes.* Perpetrators of these crimes rationalize criminal behavior as a defensive stand taken against "outsiders" who are threatening their community or way of life. A gang of teens that attacks a new family in the neighborhood because they are the "wrong" race are committing a reactive hate crime.
3. *Mission hate crime.* Some disturbed individuals see it as their "duty" to rid the world of evil. Those on such a mission may seek to eliminate people who threaten their religious beliefs because they belong to a different faith. Others seek to maintain "racial purity" by attacking minorities.[9]

Although it is difficult to determine the influence of hate crime on teen violence, McDevitt estimates that 50,000 hate crimes are committed each year, 70 percent by teens. Adult hate groups actively recruit teens, appealing not only to their hatred of minority groups but to a sense of idealism based on a promise of a return to an "Aryan" system of spirituality, purity, and warriorhood.[10] Whether such groups as the Aryan Nation and Whiter Aryan Resistance can recruit enough young members through the broadcast media and the Internet to increase the overall crime rate remains to be seen.

GUNS

Another important influence on violence rates is the number of weapons in the hands of teens. Between 1985 and 1994, the number of juveniles under 18 arrested on weapons charges rose 103 percent. In 1994, 151 teens per 100,000 were arrested on weapons charges, the highest rate in history. Between 1990 and 1995 alone, the number of youths 18 and under arrested on weapons charges rose 18 percent; in contrast, adult gun arrests remained unchanged.

Adolescents now possess handguns in unprecedented numbers and are using them in violent crimes: 62 percent of the homicides committed by juveniles involve firearms.[11] A recent survey of 4,000 juvenile arrestees in 11 major cities found that 22 percent of them carried guns all or most of the time; far fewer adults carried weapons.[12] Among all age and gender groups, male teens aged 16–19 have by far the highest arrest rate for weapons violations. The topic of youths and guns is addressed in the following "Focus on Delinquency."

GANGS

Another factor that affects teen violence rates may be the explosive growth in teenage gangs. Surveys indicate that there may be more than 500,000 gang members in the United States.[13] A large and growing number of juveniles who kill do so in groups of two or more; multiple-offender killings have doubled since the mid-1980s.[14]

One reason that gang members are so violent is that they commonly possess and carry guns. A recent study of 4,000 arrestees in 11 major cities found that about 7 percent were gang members, and of these, 36 percent stated that they carried a gun all or most of the time.[15] (Gangs are discussed further in chapter 9).

ECONOMIC PROBLEMS

The delinquency rate may be affected by the nation's economic situation. As you may recall from chapter 1, almost 15 million youth now live in poverty, and this figure is expected to increase dramatically over the next 15 years. More children than ever are living in single-parent homes, and they are twice as likely to be living in poverty as those in two-parent homes.[16]

Violence may be a function of urban problems and the economic deterioration in the nation's inner cities.[17] Youths who at one time might have obtained low-skill

Adolescents now possess handguns at an unprecedented rate and use them in violent crimes. A recent survey of 4,000 juvenile arrestees in 11 major cities found that 22 percent of the juvenile carried guns all or most of the time; far fewer adult arrestees carried weapons. These data help explain why juvenile homicide rates are increasing while adult homicide rates are in decline.

IN THE LINE OF FIRE

What is the relationship between guns and youth violence? To explore this issue Joseph Sheley and James Wright conducted a comprehensive analysis of data acquired from 835 male inmates in 6 correctional facilities and 758 male students in 10 inner-city high schools in the United States; the institutions and high schools were located in four states. The urban communities selected for the study have experienced many of the social problems common to urban society, ranging from poverty to drug abuse.

Sheley and Wright found that both the inmates and students experienced what may be described as severe social and family problems. About one-third of the inmates report that they had siblings who had committed serious crime, while 40 percent reported that their siblings had been incarcerated. Many of these youths had family members who owned guns, and almost two-thirds have male family members who routinely carried guns outside the home. The inmates believed that almost all their peers and associates routinely owned and carried guns; gun possession was a normative behavior for these youth. High school youth reported only slightly less exposure to guns and violence. For example, the students said that more than half of their friends owned guns, and 42 percent routinely carried them around outside the home!

Violent victimization experiences were also a common thread that ran through the lives of both juvenile inmates and inner-city high school students. Among the inmates, more than half had been stabbed with a knife, and more than 80 percent had been beaten; one in ten students had been stabbed, and one in three had been beaten up on the way to school.

Sheley and Wright also found a disturbing trend of gun ownership and use among the inmates (86 percent) and students (30 percent). Among both groups, guns owned were high-quality, sophisticated weapons (most commonly, revolvers). These guns were inexpensive and easy to obtain, mostly from friends and family and sometimes from street vendors.

Considering the everyday violence faced by these juveniles, it should come as no surprise that they believed that a handgun afforded them the protection they needed to survive in the urban environment. Indeed, all the evidence collected by Sheley and Wright point to the fact that guns did aid in survival. Guns procured for protection and survival, however, may then be used in the commission of crimes. Threats of legal punishments designed to reduce gun ownership will have little chance of success if juveniles view guns as necessary survival gear in a dangerous urban environment.

Sheley and Wright found a clear connection between gang membership and firearm use. Gang boys engage in a far higher high level of firearm possession than other boys, and members participate in firearm-related activity much more often than nonmembers. Interestingly, the gun–gang association is explained less by the fact that gang boys are involved in the drug trade than it is by the overall dangerousness of the social world inhabited by gang members. When gang boys traverse strange areas, they consider a gun an essential tool for safe passage. These boys have had vast experience with violence and have been the target of violent attacks. Sheley and Wright found that the problems of juvenile violence are not confined to a small group of "bad apples" but are widespread in the impoverished inner city and are spreading outward. Guns are as much a part of these youths' daily routine as a briefcase is for an accountant or a measuring tape is for a carpenter.

Can Guns Be Controlled?

Sheley and Wright concluded that gun control is an almost impossible task. Juveniles want guns and will do what is necessary to obtain them. All 50 states have firearms laws that apply specifically to juveniles; about half explicitly prohibit or restrict a juvenile's possession of a handgun. Some states, such as Massachusetts, California, Georgia, Florida, and Michigan, have toughened penalties for violation of juvenile gun laws. The new legislation in Massachusetts, for example, provides a mandatory minimum six-month sentence for any youth found delinquent on a gun-related charge. At the federal level, the Youth Handgun

Safety Act of 1994 prohibits the possession of handguns by anyone under age 18 and provides criminal penalties of up to 10 years in prison for anyone convicted of providing a handgun to a person under 18.

Toughening existing laws may not help, however, because almost all aspects of illegal gun ownership and use are already heavily penalized. Controlling the supply is equally difficult because so many people own guns that a steady supply of stolen firearms is readily available. In addition, the cost of incarcerating gun possessors is staggering. The Massachusetts law will result in a yearly increase of $5 million in expenditures to house offenders who in the past may have received probation for a first offense.

One possible strategy that is just now being tried is to disrupt gun sales and markets using some of the same tactics that have been directed at illegal drug sales (e.g., having local police take aggressive actions against local dealers, targeting users, and harassing suppliers). Can police patrol programs substantially reduce crime rates? There is growing evidence that directed patrol, narrowly aimed at a particular problem area, may lead to long-term reduction in crime. One such program, known as the Kansas City gun experiment, was directed at restricting the carrying of guns in high-risk places at high-risk times.

Working with academics from the University of Maryland, the Kansas City Police Department focused extra patrols on a "hot spot" high-crime area identified by computer analysis of all gun crimes. A pair of two-officer patrol cars focused exclusively on gun detection from 7 p.m. to 1 a.m. seven days a week; the cars did not respond to any service calls. During the course of the experiment, the officers worked a total of 200 nights (the equivalent of 4,512 officer hours or 2,256 patrol car hours). Of this, 1,218 officer hours were spent on gun patrols, with the remaining hours (70 percent) spent processing arrests and performing other parole-related duties.

Over a 29-week period, the gun patrol officers made thousands of car and pedestrian checks and traffic stops, and made more than 600 arrests. Using frisks and searches, they found 29 guns; an additional 47 weapons were seized by other officers in the experimental area. These seizures increased the total guns found on the beat by 65 percent over the previous 6 months. The ratio of guns seized per direct patrol time was 1 gun per 84 hours.

How did the gun patrol effort affect crime rates? In the target beat in the 29 weeks prior to the gun patrol, 169 gun crimes were committed; only 86 were committed during the gun patrol, a decrease of 49 percent. Drive-by shootings dropped significantly as did homicides. Other crimes not targeted by the experiment showed little overall change. Importantly, none of the seven contiguous beats showed a significant increase in gun crimes, indicating that there was little crime displacement effect. Community surveys conducted before and after the program was initiated indicated that citizens in the target area were less fearful of crime and more satisfied with their neighborhood than residents in adjacent areas. After the extra patrols ended, crime rates returned to their normal levels.

Considering the thousands of guns available in the area, it seems odd that the seizure of 29 additional weapons could have such a dramatic influence on the crime rate. There are three likely explanations for the significant reduction in gun-related crimes. First, it is possible that the weapons seized were taken from high-rate offenders who were among the most likely perpetrators of gun-related crimes. Their "lost opportunity" to commit violent crimes may have resulted in an overall rate decrease. Second, because the gun patrol made more arrests in the area than the norm, it is also possible that some of the most violent criminals were incapacitated long enough to account for a crime rate reduction. Third, as word of the patrol got out, there may have been a general deterrent effect: People contemplating violent crime may have been convinced that the risks of apprehension were unacceptably high.

The Kansas City gun patrol experiment suggests that a modest police patrol effort targeting guns can produce dramatic effects on the crime rate. Whether such efforts should become general police policy remains to be seen. They could increase risks to officer safety, provoke hostile reactions from citizens, and anger people subjected to police searches. These side effects may be acceptable, however, if aggressive police action could significantly reduce the threat of gun violence.

Source: Joseph Sheley and James Wright, *In The Line of Fire: Youth, Guns, and Violence in Urban America* (New York: Aldine de Gruyter, 1995); Lawrence Sherman, James Shaw, and Dennis Rogan, *The Kansas City Gun Experiment* (Washington, D.C.: National Institute of Justice, 1994); "Massachusetts Law Means Jail for Youths with Guns," *New York Times* 17 December 1995, p. 26; Lawrence Greenfeld and Marianne Zawitz, *Weapons Offenses and Offenders* (Washington, D.C.: Bureau of Justice Statistics, 1995).

jobs in factories and shops may find that these legitimate economic opportunities no longer exist. Low-skill manufacturing jobs have been dispersed to overseas plants. Lack of economic opportunity may encourage drug dealing, theft, and violence.[18]

DRUGS

Alfred Blumstein reports that when the increase in teenage violence began in 1985, it was no coincidence that this period also witnessed increases in drug trafficking and arrests for drug crimes.[19]

Teenage substance abusers commit a significant portion of all serious crimes, and inner-city drug abuse problems may in part account for the persistently high violent crime rate.[20] According to Blumstein, groups and gangs involved in the urban drug trade recruit juveniles because they work cheaply, are immune from heavy criminal penalties, and are "daring and willing to take risks."[21] Arming themselves for protection, these drug-dealing juveniles present a menace, which persuades neighborhood adolescents to arm themselves for protection. The result? An "arms race" which produces an increasing spiral of violence (see Chapter 11 for more on drugs, violence and delinquency).

In addition, drug abuse may directly influence teen crime patterns, for example, when alcohol-abusing youths engage in acts of senseless violence. Users may also engage in theft and violence to get money to purchase drugs and support drug habits. Contemporary increases in teenage drug use may portend higher future violence rates.

EMERGING SOCIAL PROBLEMS

The social problems faced by American teens today may be influencing their offending rates. Kathleen Heide, a psychotherapist who specializes in assessing violent youth, finds that a market basket of problems are related to instances of extreme violence:

- child abuse and neglect
- lack of role models
- crisis in leadership
- exposure to violence
- access to guns
- substance abuse
- poverty and lack of resources
- low self-esteem
- inability to deal with strong negative feelings
- boredom and lack of fun activities
- poor judgment and lack of boundaries
- prejudice and intolerance
- feelings that there is nothing left to lose[22]

Violence rates may increase dramatically as more children are subject to these extreme behaviors and emotions and little is done to counteract their negative influence.

WHAT THE FUTURE HOLDS

The number of juveniles will increase by 15 percent, or more than 9 million, between now and 2010; those in the "high-risk" ages—ages 15–17—will increase by more than 3 million, or 31 percent. If the increase in at-risk youth is matched by recent upticks in drug abuse, economic deprivation, and gang recruitment, we should expect significant increases in the delinquency rate and the overall crime rate during the next 15 years. The data presented in Figure 2.4, prepared by criminologist James Alan Fox, predict future delinquency trends in the United States based on population and cultural factors.

PROBLEMS OF OFFICIAL DATA

Using official data to measure delinquency has also been questioned because (a) many victims do not report crime to police, (b) official data only count adolescents who have been "caught," and these youths may be different from those who evade capture, (c) official data may reflect racial and ethnic bias in the arrest process and (d) official data significantly undercount victimless crimes such as drug and alcohol use.

In addition, some police agencies may practice full enforcement, arresting all teens who violate the law, while others may follow a policy of discretion that encourages unofficial handling of juvenile matters through social service agencies. This, too, can influence the arrest data.

Although critics argue that these flaws affect the validity of official data, a growing number believe that the accuracy of official statistics may be improving.[23] After more than 20 years of efforts to increase the sensitivity of police officers to civil rights, arrest statistics may now be less class- and race-biased and, consequently, a more valid indicator of actual participation in delinquent acts.[24]

SELF-REPORTED DELINQUENCY

The validity of official statistics has been debated among juvenile justice experts for some time.[25] In addition to their problematic accuracy, official data have only limited ability to measure particular crime patterns, such as recreational drug use and alcohol abuse. They do not tell us much about the personality, attitudes, and behavior of individual delinquents. Official statistics are useful for the examination of general trends in the relative frequency of delinquent behavior and geographic patterns of youth crime, but they are an inadequate source of individual-level information, such as the personality characteristics of delinquents. In a similar fashion, victimization data are limited to criminal acts in which there is personal contact between victim and offender, rely on the perceptions of people (crime victims) who are under great stress, and can tell us little about the background or characteristics of delinquent offenders. To address these deficiencies, criminologists have sought to develop alternative sources of delinquency statistics, of which the most commonly used are **self-reports** of delinquent behavior.

Self-report studies are designed to obtain information from youthful subjects about their violations of the law. A number of formats have been used: Youths arrested by police are interviewed at the station house; an anonymous survey is simultaneously distributed to every student in a high school; boys in a youth detention center are asked to respond to a survey; youths randomly selected from the population of teenagers are questioned in the privacy of their homes. Self-report studies can be conducted, one to one, between the researcher and the

FIGURE 2.4
Trends in juvenile violence: Future projections
by criminologist James A. Fox

Recent reports of a declining rate of violent crime in cities across the country would seem to be at odds with the growing problem of youth violence. The overall drop in crime hides the grim truth. There are actually two crime trends in America —one for the young, one for the mature—which are moving in opposite directions.

From 1990 to 1994, for example, the overall rate of murder in America changed very slightly, declining a total of four percent. For this same time period, the rate of killing at the hands of adults, age 25 and over declined 18 percent and that for young adults, ages 18-24 rose barely two percent, however, the rate of murder committed by teenagers, ages 14-17 jumped a tragic 22 percent.

The recent surge in youth crime actually occurred while the population of teenagers was on the decline. But this demographic benefit is about to change. As a consequence of the "baby boomerang" (the offspring of the baby boomers), there are now 39 million children in this country who are under the age of ten, more young children than we've had for decades. Millions of them live in poverty. Most do not have full-time parental supervision at home guiding their development and supervising their behavior. Of course, these children will not remain young and impressionable for long; they will reach their high-risk years before too long. As a result, we likely face a future wave of youth violence that will be even worse than that of the past ten years.

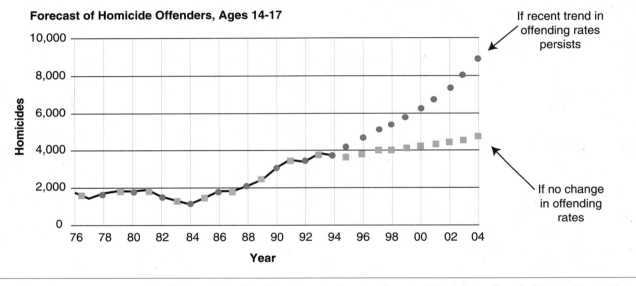

Forecast of Homicide Offenders, Ages 14-17

Source: James Alan Fox, *Trends in Juvenile Violence: A Report to the United States Attorney General on Current and Future Rates of Juvenile Offending* (Boston, Mass.: Northeastern University, 1996).

subject through an interview or a self-administered questionnaire, but more commonly they are done through a mass distribution of anonymous questionnaires.

Although the format can vary, the basic benefits and assumptions of self-report surveys remain constant: They can involve all segments of the population (**cross-sectional data**), including those offenders who have never been arrested and are therefore not part of the official data; they can measure behavior that is rarely detected by police, such as drug abuse; they allow youths to freely describe their illegal activities through the promise of anonymity; and they may measure personality, behavior and attitudes so we can know more about the types of youths who commit delinquent acts.

FIGURE 2.4
(continued)

- From 1985 to 1994, the rate of murder committed by teens, ages 14-17, increased 172 percent. The rate of killing rose sharply for both black and white male teenagers, but not for females.
- Remaining just above one percent of the population, black males ages 14-24 now constitute 17 percent of the victims of homicide and over 30 percent of the perpetrators. Their white counterparts remained about 10 percent of the victims, about 18 percent of the perpetrators, yet declined in proportionate size of the population.
- Guns, and especially handguns, have played a major role in the surge of juvenile murder. Since 1984, the number of juveniles killing with a gun has quadrupled, while the number killing with all other weapons combined has remained virtually constant.
- The largest increase in juvenile homicide involves offenders who are friends and acquaintances of their victims.
- The differential trends by age of offender observed for homicide generalize to other violent offenses. From 1989 to 1994, the arrest rate for violent crimes (murder, rape, robbery and aggravated assault) rose over 46 percent among teenagers, but about 12 percent among adults. In terms of arrest rates per 100,000 population, 14-17 year-olds have now surpassed young adults, ages 18-24.
- By the year 2005, the number of teens, ages 14-17, will increase by 20%, with a larger increase among blacks in this age group (26%).
- Even if the capita rate of teen homicide remains the same, the number of 14-17 year-olds who will commit murder should increase to nearly 5,000 annually because of changing demographics. However, if offending rates continue to rise because of worsening conditions for our nation's youth, the number of teen killings could increase even more.

The challenge for the future, therefore, is how best to deal with youth violence. Without a large-scale effort to educate and support young children and preteens today, we can likely expect a much greater problem of teen violence tomorrow. There is, however, still time to stem the tide, and to avert the coming wave of teen violence. But time is of the essence.

Source: James Alan Fox, *Trends in Juvenile Violence: A Report to the United States Attorney General on Current and Future Rates of Juvenile Offending* (Boston, Mass.: Northeastern University, 1996).

Self-Report Items   Examples of self-report questions appear in Table 2.2. Subjects check the appropriate spaces to indicate how many times they have participated in illegal or deviant behavior. Other formats allow subjects to write in the precise number of times they engaged in each delinquent activity. Note that the sample survey limits the reporting period to the past 12 months, thereby focusing on relatively recent behavior; other surveys can question lifetime involvement.

Surveys measuring self-reported delinquency are also likely to contain items not directly related to delinquent activity (e.g., items requesting information on such diverse topics as subjects' self-image, intelligence, personality, and attitudes toward family, friends, and school; leisure activities; and school activities). Self-report surveys also gather personal information on subjects' family background, social status, race, and sex. Reports of delinquent acts can then be used with this information to create a much more complete picture of delinquent offenders than official statistics can provide.

In sum, criminologists have used self-report studies of delinquency frequently for more than 40 years.[26] They are a valuable source of information on the delinquent activities of youths who have had formal contact with the juvenile justice system and those who have escaped official notice of their delinquent acts; the latter are the "dark figures of crime."

TABLE 2.2 Self-Report Survey Questions

**Please indicate how often in the past 12 months you did each act.
(check the best answer)**

	Never Did Act	One Time	2-5 Times	6-9 Times	10+ Times
Stole something worth less than $50	_____	_____	_____	_____	_____
Stole something worth more than $50	_____	_____	_____	_____	_____
Used cocaine	_____	_____	_____	_____	_____
Been in a fistfight	_____	_____	_____	_____	_____
Carried a weapon such as a gun or knife	_____	_____	_____	_____	_____
Fought someone using a weapon	_____	_____	_____	_____	_____
Stole a car	_____	_____	_____	_____	_____
Used force to steal	_____	_____	_____	_____	_____
(For boys) Forced a girl to have sexual relations against her will	_____	_____	_____	_____	_____

SELF-REPORT DATA

Most self-report studies indicate that the number of juveniles who break the law is far greater than previously believed.[27] In fact, when truancy, alcohol consumption, petty theft, and recreational drug use are included in self-report scales, delinquency appears almost universal.

Self-report studies indicate that the most common juvenile offenses are truancy, drinking alcohol, using a false ID, shoplifting or larceny under fifty dollars, fighting, using marijuana, and damaging the property of others.[28] In chapter 11, self-report data will be used to gauge trends in adolescent drug abuse.

Table 2.3 contains data from what is probably the most complete national survey of juvenile misbehavior, the "Monitoring the Future" survey, which is conducted annually by researchers at the University of Michigan's Institute for Social Research (ISR).[29]

This survey is one of the most methodologically sound and important sources of self-report data because it is conducted nationally on an annual basis and involves a sample of about 3,000 youths.

A number of important conclusions can be drawn from the ISR data. First, a surprising number of these "typical" teenagers reported involvement in serious criminal behavior during the 12 months before the survey: About 13 percent reported hurting someone badly enough so that the victim needed medical care (1 percent said they did this five times or more); about 31 percent reported stealing something worth less than $50 dollars, and another 10 percent stole something worth more than $50; 29 percent reported shoplifting from a store; 14 percent had damaged school property. Yet, of the youths reporting, only 9 percent said they were arrested and taken to a police station.

If the ISR data accurately represent the national distribution of delinquent activities, then the juvenile crime problem is much greater than what the official statistics would have us believe. There are approximately 14 million youths between the ages of 14 and 17. Extrapolating from the ISR findings, this group

Table 2.3 Self-Reported Delinquent Activity during the Past 12 Months—High School Senior Class of 1995

Percent Engaging in Offenses

Crime Category	At Least One Offense	Multiple Offenses
Serious fight	8%	7%
Gang fight	10%	8%
Hurt someone badly	7%	6%
Used a weapon to steal	2%	2%
Stole less than $50	14%	17%
Stole more than $50	4%	6%
Shoplifting	12%	17%
Breaking and entering	11%	13%
Arson	1.5%	1%
Damaged school property	6%	8%

Source: "Monitoring the Future, 1995" (Ann Arbor, Mich.: Institute for Social Research, 1996).

accounts for more than 100% of all theft offenses reported in the *UCR* (7.8 million). More than 3 percent of the students said they used a knife or gun in a robbery. At this rate, high school students commit 1.05 million armed robberies per year. In comparison, the *UCR* tallies about 360,000 armed robberies for all age groups annually.

Although these disturbing statistics show that the delinquency problem is far greater than indicated by the national arrest statistics, self-reports rarely show that the delinquency rate is climbing. Analysis conducted by ISR statisticians indicates that with the exception of assault, patterns of self-reported delinquency have been rather stable since 1975.[30] Property crime rates, most notably shoplifting, may actually be in decline.

When the results of the ISR surveys are compared with various studies conducted over a 20-year period, a uniform pattern emerges: Teenager participation in theft, violence, and damage-related crimes seems to be stable. Although a self-reported crime wave has not occurred, neither has there been any visible reduction in teenage delinquency. Some research efforts indicate that these trends may actually have originated more than 30 years ago, as self-report statistics collected in the late 1970s are little changed from similar data obtained in the 1960s.[31] Although self-report data suggest a stable teenage crime rate, they typically do not include the most serious violent crimes such as murder and rape, which official statistics show are increasing.

VALIDATING SELF-REPORTS

Critics of self-report studies frequently suggest that it is not realistic to expect young people to admit illegal acts candidly. They have nothing to gain, and those taking the greatest risk are the ones with official records. On the other hand, some young people may exaggerate their delinquent acts, forget some of them, or be confused. In addition, many self-reports may not use representative samples, while others contain items that are trivial and not of real interest to police (e.g., "used a false ID").

The most common technique for validating self-reports is to compare the answers that youths give on them with official police records. A typical approach

Most self-report studies indicate that the number of children who break the law is far greater than previously believed. In fact, when petty crimes and status offenses such as truancy, vandalism, and recreational drug abuse are included, delinquency appears almost universal. When self-report studies conducted over a twenty-year period are evaluated, a uniform pattern emerges: teenager participation in theft, violence, and damage-related crimes seems to be stable. Although a self-reported crime wave has not occurred, neither has there been any visible reduction in teenage delinquency.

is to ask youths if they have ever been arrested for or convicted of a delinquent act and then check their official records against their self-reported responses. A number of studies using this method have found a remarkable degree of uniformity between self-reported answers and official records.[32]

Other methods of testing the validity of self-reports are used:

1. The "known group method" compares incarcerated youths with "normal" youths to see whether the former report more delinquency.[33]
2. Peer informants—friends who can verify the honesty of a subject's answers—are used.[34]
3. Subjects are tested twice to see if their answers remain the same (testing across time).
4. Questions are designed to identify those who are lying (e.g., "I have never done anything wrong in my life.").[35]
5. Subjects are asked to take a polygraph to verify their answers.[36]

In general, these efforts have been supportive of self-report techniques.

In what is considered the most thorough analysis of self-report validity, Michael Hindelang, Travis Hirschi, and Joseph Weis made use of data gathered in Seattle and other sites.[37] They concluded that the problems of accuracy in self-reports are "surmountable," that self-reports are more accurate than most criminologists believe, and that self-reports and official statistics are quite compatible. They state that "the method of self-reports does not appear from these studies to be fundamentally flawed. Reliability measures are impressive and the majority of studies produce validity coefficients in the moderate to strong range."[38]

The Hindelang, Hirschi, and Weis findings are supported by studies that indicate that the patterns and trends evident in official delinquency are also contained in self-report data.[39]

Validity Problems Is it possible that the most serious delinquent and drug-abusing adolescents respond to self-reports as candidly as nondelinquents? Recent research by Leonore Simon shows that offenders with the most extensive prior criminality are also the ones most likely to "be poor historians of their own crime commission rates."[40] Stephen Cernkovich, Peggy Giordano, and Meredith Pugh found that self-reports typically exclude the most serious chronic offenders in the teenage population.[41] Institutionalized youth, who are absent from most self-report surveys, are not only more delinquent than the "average kid" in the general youth population but are also considerably more delinquent than the most delinquent youth identified in the typical self-report survey.[42] Their conclusion is that self-reports may be measuring only nonserious, occasional delinquents while ignoring hard-core chronic offenders who may be institutionalized and unavailable for self-reports.

These research studies imply that self-reports are limited because they rarely include the most serious offenders, and that when they do, they may be invalid and unreliable. So although self-reports continue to be used as a standard method of delinquency research, the results obtained must be interpreted with caution.

VICTIMIZATION DATA

The accuracy of official statistics has been the source of much debate. For more than 30 years, critics have charged that official data can lead to a spurious view of delinquency, one dominated by the biases of police.[43] The *UCR* has also been criticized because it only counts those criminal acts reported to police. It ignores those acts that victims failed to report because they believed nothing could be done, were afraid, or did not want to get involved.[44]

Victimization surveys seek to present a more accurate picture of crime in the United States by surveying those affected by it—the victims. The most important of these surveys is a cooperative effort of the Bureau of Justice Statistics of the U.S. Department of Justice and the U.S. Census Bureau, called the National Crime Victimization Survey (NCVS). The NCVS is a massive, annual household survey of victims of criminal behavior in the United States that measures the nature of the crime and the personal characteristics of victims.

The total annual sample size of the NCVS has been about 50,000 households containing about 100,000 individuals. The sample is broken down into sub-samples of 10,000 households (about 20,000 individuals), and each group is interviewed twice a year; for example, people interviewed in January will be recontacted in July. The NCVS has been conducted annually for more than 15 years but was revised recently to increase both the validity and reliability of its estimates.

VICTIMIZATION IN THE UNITED STATES

The National Crime Victimization Survey provides yearly estimates of the total amount of personal-contact crimes (such as assault, rape, and robbery) and household **victimizations** (such as burglary, larceny, and vehicle theft). According to victims' reports, about 44 million crimes occurred in the United States in 1993 (the last year for which data are available), an increase of less than 1 percent from the previous year.[45] This figure includes about 6 million violent crimes, 14 million personal thefts, and 15.8 million household crimes, such as burglary. These crimes take a terrible toll on victims. Considering the monetary value of pain, emotional trauma, disability, and risk of death, the cost is $450 billion, or $1,800 for every person in the United States.[46]

Although at first glance these figures seem overwhelming, victimization rates seem to be stable or declining for most crime categories. Estimates of criminal activity in the United States for the years 1973 to 1993 indicate that the crime rate seems to have peaked in the early 1980s. Similar to the *UCR,* the NCVS shows that crime rates have been essentially stable or in decline during the 1990s.

Many of the differences between the NCVS data and official statistics can be attributed to the fact that many victims do not report their victimizations to police. About 57 percent of violent crimes, 72 percent of personal crimes of theft, and 66 percent of household crimes go unreported.

YOUNG VICTIMS

The National Crime Victimization Survey data indicate that young people are much more likely to be the victims of crime than adults.[47] Although it is common for the media to portray the elderly as particularly vulnerable to violent personal crime, it is actually teenagers who are at greatest risk of victimization. (See Figure 2.5.)

The likelihood of victimization declines with age. Young teens are more than 15 times more likely to be the victim of a personal crime such as robbery than people over age 65. What is both surprising and shocking is that this pattern holds for such serious crimes as rape, aggravated assault, and robbery; juvenile victimization is not just a matter of minor schoolyard assaults.

In addition to these age patterns, NCVS data show that male teenagers had a significantly higher (about 140 per 1,000 versus 96 per 1,000) chance of becoming a victim of violent crime than female teenagers. African-American teens aged 12–15 have a greater chance of becoming a victim of violent crime than white teenagers of the same age, but by age 16 teenagers of both racial groups share an equal victimization risk.

Considering these findings, it is somewhat ironic that, in general, older women are the most likely to have a generalized fear of crime, while teenage males and females are usually found to be the least fearful. Although fear of crime is often difficult to measure, there are some indications that those who are at lowest risk of crime victimization are the most fearful of crime.[48]

THE VICTIMS AND THEIR CRIMINALS

NCVS data can also tell us something about the relationship between victims and offenders. This information is available because victims of violent personal crimes, such as assault and robbery, can identify the age, sex, and race of their attackers.

In general, youths tend to be victimized by their peers: A majority of teens were victimized by other teens, while victims aged 20 and over identified their attackers as being 21 or older. However, people in almost all age groups who were victimized by groups of offenders identified their attackers as teenagers. In general, violent crime victims report that a disproportionate number of their attackers were young, ranging in age from 16 to 25.

FIGURE 2.5
Rate of victimization for y
age groups

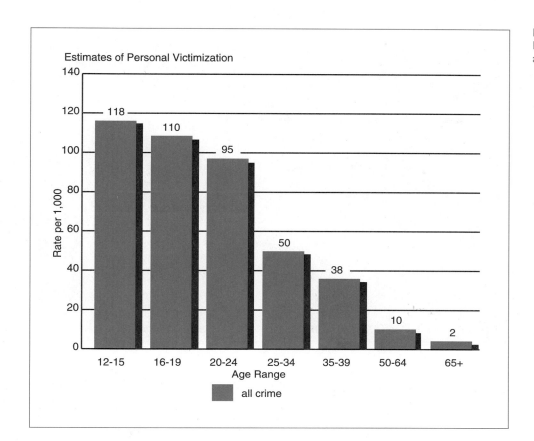

Estimates of Personal Victimization

The NCVS data also tell us that victimization is intraracial: African-American teens tended to be victimized by other African-American teenagers and whites by whites.

Most teens are victimized by people they know or are acquainted with, and their victimization is more likely to occur during the day. In contrast, adults are more often victimized by strangers and at night. One explanation for this pattern is that youths are at greatest risk from their own family and relatives. (Chapter 8 deals with the disturbing issue of child abuse and neglect.)

Another possibility is that many teenage victimizations occur at school. About 13 percent of all crimes of violence take place in school buildings or on school grounds. Teens then tend to be victimized in public places, such as schools and parks, by peers of the same sex, race, and age.

Stranger Attacks   These data belie the fear that children are at great risk of being abducted and harmed by strangers. In fact, research by Gerald Hotaling and David Finkelhor found that the number of children seriously harmed—abducted and murdered—by strangers is less common than had been thought.[49] Each year, there are an average of 52 cases in which it can be verified that a child was abducted and feloniously killed by a stranger. There are typically another 100 cases in which the surrounding circumstances remain unknown except that a child was killed by a stranger, for a total of about 152 stranger homicides a year. The re-

A significant amount of all teenage victimizations occur in public places, such as streets, schools and parks, by peers of the same sex, race, and age. In general, youths tend to be victimized by their peers: a majority of teens were victimized by other teens, while victims aged 20 and over identified their attackers as being 21 or older. However, people in almost all age groups who were victimized by groups of offenders identified their attackers as teenagers.

search indicates that 14- to 17-year-olds account for nearly two out of three victims, a risk nearly seven times greater than that faced by children 9 years old and younger. Girls were twice as likely as boys to be the victims of known stranger homicides, a pattern that contrasts with general homicide rates.

Although stranger victimizations may be less common than once thought, the fact that as many as three children are abducted and killed by strangers every week in the United States is still extremely disturbing. These horrible crimes permanently scar the victims' family and friends and probably take a greater toll on the general public than any other crime.

CHILD VICTIMIZERS

Analysis of the NCVS data indicates that sometime during their lifetime, about 80 percent of the 12-year-olds in the United States will become victims of completed or attempted violent crimes, 99 percent will experience theft, and 40 percent will be injured during the course of the crime.[50] A recent survey of state prison inmates found that youths aged 18 and under were the victims of almost 20 percent of all violent crimes.[51] Figure 2.6 summarizes the findings of this survey.

Although these rates may seem shocking, they may if anything be understated! Recent analysis by L. Edward Wells and Joseph Rankin suggests that compared to other self-report surveys the NCVS seriously *underreports* juvenile victimization. This research indicates that the rate of current and lifetime likelihood of victimization of juveniles may be several times higher than that indicated by the NCVS.[52]

CORRELATES OF DELINQUENCY

The various sources of delinquency data—official records, self-report surveys, victim interviews—tell a great deal about the personal and social factors associated with delinquent behavior. Who are delinquents? What are their personal

FIGURE 2.6
Child victimizers: characteristics of offenders and victims

Characteristics of the offenders

▶ An estimated 18.6% of inmates serving time in State prisons in 1991 for violent crimes, or about 61,000 offenders nationwide, have been convicted of a crime against a victim under age 18.

▶ 1 in 5 violent offenders serving time in a State prison reported having victimized a child.

▶ More than half the violent crimes committed against children involved victims age 12 or younger.

▶ 7 in 10 offenders with child victims reported that they were imprisoned for a rape or sexual assault.

▶ Two-thirds of all prisoners convicted of rape or sexual assault had committed their crime against a child.

▶ All but 3% of offenders who committed violent crimes against children were male.

▶ Violent child-victimizers were substantially more likely than those with adult victims to have been physically or sexually abused when they were children, though the majority of violent offenders regardless of victim age, did not have a history of such abuse.

Characteristics of the victims

▶ 3 in 10 child victimizers reported that they had committed their crimes against multiple victims; they were more likely than those who victimized adults to have had multiple victims.

▶ 3 in 4 victims of violence were female.

▶ For the vast majority of child victimizers in State prison, the victim was someone they knew before the crime:
A third had committed their crime against their own child
About half had a relationship with the victim as a friend, acquaintance, or relative other than offspring

▶ About 1 in 7 reported the victim to have been a stranger to them.

▶ Three-quarters of the violent victimizations of children took place in either the victim's home or the offender's home.

▶ 4 in 10 child victims of violence suffered either forcible rape or another injury.

19% of violent State prison inmates committed their crime against a child; 78% of those convicted of sexual assault had abused a child

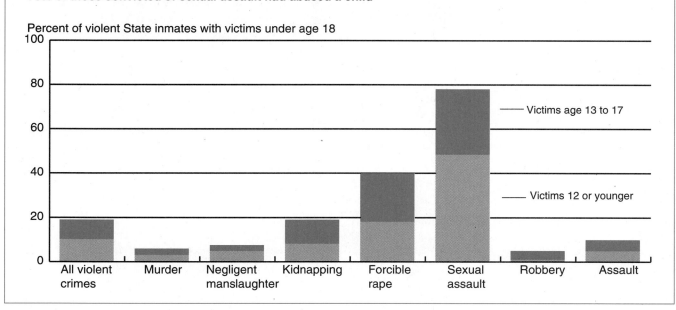

Percent of violent State inmates with victims under age 18

Victims age 13 to 17

Victims 12 or younger

All violent crimes · Murder · Negligent manslaughter · Kidnapping · Forcible rape · Sexual assault · Robbery · Assault

Source: Lawrence Greenfeld, *Child Victimizers: Violent Offenders and Their Victims* (Washington, D.C. Bureau of Justice Statistics, 1996) p. 1.

characteristics: Old? Young? Male? Female? Rich? Poor? What offending patterns are routine? Is delinquency typically a singular act, or is it more likely to be part of a repeated, **chronic** activity that persists over time?

Measurement of the personal traits and social characteristics associated with adolescent misbehavior is essential for the study of delinquency. If, for example, a strong association exists between delinquent behavior and limited social status, then poverty and economic deprivation must be considered in any explanation of the onset of delinquent behavior. If the crime–poverty association is not found, then forces independent of the socioeconomic structure may be responsible for the onset of youthful law violations. It would be fruitless to concentrate delinquency control efforts in such areas as job creation and vocational training if social status were found to be unrelated to delinquent behavior. Similarly, if only a handful of delinquents are responsible for much of all serious crime, then crime control policies might be made more effective by identifying and treating these persistent offenders.

GENDER AND DELINQUENCY

Official arrest statistics, victim data, and self-reports indicate that males are significantly more criminal and delinquent than females. Today, the *UCR* results typically show that the teenage gender ratio for serious violent crime arrests is approximately six to one, and for property crime approximately three to one, in favor of males. Table 2.4 presents a variety of male–female crime ratios. Nonetheless, the number and rate of female arrests have been increasing at a rate faster than that for males. Between 1985 and 1994, the number of arrests of males increased about 25 percent while the number of females arrested increased almost 40 percent. The change in serious violent crime arrests was even more striking: Male rates increased 69 percent and female rates increased 128 percent.

Although males also maintain a significant edge in arrests for most illegal acts, one relationship does contradict this general pattern: Girls are actually more likely than boys to be arrested for being runaways. There are two explanations for this. Girls could simply be more likely than boys to run away from home, or police may view the female runaway as the more serious problem and therefore be more likely to process females through official justice channels. This view may reflect paternalistic attitudes toward troubled girls, regarded by police as likely candidates for "getting in trouble."[53]

These patterns are not unique to the United States. Similar findings have been observed in self-report and official record studies in Great Britain. A Home Office

TABLE 2.4 Gender Differences in Arrest for Representative *UCR* Crimes

Male:Female Ratios

Murder	Robbery	Assault	Burglary	Larceny	Auto	Arson	Runaway
15:1	10:1	4:1	9:1	2:1	5:1	7:1	1:1.3

Source: FBI, *Uniform Crime Reports,* pp. 229–31.

study found that the overall male–female offense ratio was about five to one at ages 10–13 and four to one at ages 14–16. The ratio was much higher for serious crimes; for example, for burglary, it was about seventeen to one.[54]

Self-report data seem to show that the incidence of female delinquency is much higher than previously expected and that, overall, the pattern of delinquency committed by males and females is quite similar; that is, the crimes most males commit are also the ones most females commit.[55] Table 2.5 shows the percentage of males and females interviewed for in the latest ISR survey who admit engaging in delinquent acts during the past 12 months.

Although the ISR survey shows that many females engage in delinquency, most self-reports indicate that males are still more likely than females to be "frequently delinquent," and males are more likely than females to engage in serious felony-type acts.[56] So although self-report studies indicate that female delinquency is more prevalent than reflected in the official statistics and that the content of girls' delinquency is similar to that of boys, the few adolescents who report frequently engaging in serious violent crime are still predominantly male.[57]

A number of factors have been suggested as explanations for the gender differences in the delinquency rate. These include biosocial, sex-role, and socialization differences. Because of their importance, gender differences in the delinquency rate will be discussed in detail in chapter 7.

RACIAL AND ETHNIC PATTERNS IN DELINQUENCY

It thus seems clear that one cannot paint an accurate picture of crime in the United States without relying to some extent on race and ethnicity.[58]

FBI data show that racial minorities are disproportionately represented in arrest statistics. Although African-Americans make up only about 12.5 percent of the population, they account for about 31 percent of all arrests and 36 percent of index crime arrests. There are approximately 38 million white and 7.5 million

TABLE 2.5 Percentage of High School Seniors Who Engaged in Delinquent Acts during the Past 12 Months by Gender

Percent Admitting to at Least One Offense		
Crime Category	Males	Females
Serious fight	18%	11%
Gang fight	23%	14%
Hurt someone badly	20%	5%
Used a weapon to steal	5%	1%
Stole less than $50	40%	23%
Stole more than $50	14%	5%
Shoplifting	36%	24%
Breaking and entering	30%	17%
Arson	4%	1%
Damaged school property	21%	7%

Source: "Monitoring the Future, 1995" (Ann Arbor, Mich.: Institute for Social Research, 1996).

African-American youths aged 5–17, a ratio of about 5:1. Table 2.6 presents the relative involvement of African-American and white juveniles in the arrest data.

African-American youths are arrested for a disproportionate number of serious crimes—murder, rape, robbery, and assault. White youths are arrested for a disproportionate share of arsons. Among Type II crimes, white youth are disproportionately arrested for alcohol-related violations such as driving under the influence, perhaps because they have greater access to automobiles.

SELF-REPORT DIFFERENCES

Official statistics show that minority youths are much more likely than white youths to be arrested for serious criminal behavior and that race is an important predictor of delinquent behavior. To many delinquency experts, this pattern merely reflects racism and discrimination in the juvenile justice system. In other words, African-American youths show up in the official statistics more often because they are more likely to be formally arrested by the police, who, in contrast, will treat white youths informally.

One way to examine this issue is to compare the racial differences in self-reported data with those found in the official delinquency records. Charges of racial discrimination in the arrest process would be supported by an insignificant difference in the levels of delinquency self-reported by different racial groups.

Early efforts by Leroy Gould in Seattle, Harwin Voss in Honolulu, and Ronald Akers in seven midwestern states found that a relationship between race and self-reported delinquency was virtually nonexistent.[59] These research efforts suggested that racial differences in the official crime data may be a function of law enforcement practices; arrest rates may reflect the fact that African-American youths simply have a much greater chance of being arrested and officially processed.[60]

Self-report studies seem to indicate that the delinquent behavior rates of African-American and white teenagers are generally similar and that differences in arrest statistics may indicate a differential selection policy by police.[61] The ISR survey, for example, generally shows that offending differences between African-American and white youths are marginal.[62] However, some experts warn that there are racial differences in the way delinquency is self-reported and that African-American youth may underreport more serious crimes, limiting the ability of self-reports to be a valid indicator of racial differences in the crime rate.[63]

TABLE 2.6 Percentage of Total Juvenile Arrests for Serious Crimes by Race

	Murder	Rape	Robbery	Assault	Burglary	Larceny	Auto theft	Arson
White	38%	55%	36%	55%	74%	70%	56%	80%
Black	59%	43%	62%	43%	24%	27%	41%	18%
Other	3%	2%	2%	2%	3%	3%	3%	2%

*Other includes American Indian, Alaskan Native, Asian, or Pacific Islander.

Source: FBI, UCR, 1994, pp. 229–31.

ARE THE DATA VALID?

Racial patterns in the delinquency rate have long been the subject of considerable controversy. One view is that the disproportionate amount of African-American official delinquency is a result of juvenile justice system bias. According to this view, police are more likely to arrest and courts are more likely to punish minority youths while treating white offenders in a more lenient manner. For example, recent research by Christina Polsenberg and Kenneth Jackson found that minority youth involved in drug offenses are punished more severely than white youths; juvenile court judges may believe that drug offenses are more serious for African-American youths and that white youth are merely "recreational" users.[64] Possession of a prior record, even if it is the product of bias, increases the likelihood that upon subsequent contact, police will formally arrest a suspect rather than release him or her with a warning or take some other "unofficial" action.[65]

Those who challenge this view argue that although some bias in the justice system does exist, there is enough similarity between official and self-report data to conclude that racial differences in the crime rate are real and not solely the result of a racially biased juvenile justice system.[66] In their comprehensive review of race and justice entitled *The Color of Justice,* Samuel Walker, Cassia Spohn, and Miriam DeLone found that African-American youth are arrested at a disproportionately high rate and that for at least some crimes, such as robbery and assault, the evidence is that arrest rate differences are the result of offending rates rather than selection bias or racism on the part of the criminal justice system.[67]

Explaining Racial Patterns A number of attempts have been made to explain racial differences in the official crime data. One view maintains that if in fact the racial differences in the delinquency rate recorded by official data are valid, they are a function of the ecological differences in American society: African-Americans are more likely than whites to be indigent and reside in areas characterized by (1) deteriorated housing; (2) limited or nonexistent legitimate employment and recreational opportunities; (3) anomic behavior patterns; (4) a local criminal tradition that actually predates the current African-American ethnic group in residence; (5) an abnormally high incidence of transient or psychopathological individuals; (6) a disproportionate number of opportunities to engage in criminal behavior or form delinquent subcultures; and (7) poverty being the norm rather than the exception.[68]

Another view is that racial bias has produced a African-American culture that is separate and in opposition to conventional white middle-class values. Located in inner-city ghettos, the African-American subculture has been solidified by unduly harsh economic conditions; there seems little cause for optimism that this will change in the 1990s because most minority youth still see few prospects for economic success.[69] An African-American teenage underclass has developed whose members lack the basic job skills needed to enter the social mainstream: African-Americans are more than three times as likely to be poor as whites; their median income and net worth are much less than those of whites; African-American men are twice as likely to be jobless as white men.[70] The lack of economic opportunity for African-Americans has directly influenced their crime and delinquency rates.[71] In addition, according to Joan McCord and Margaret Ensminger, when African-American males, especially those who lack strong family ties, are directly exposed to racial prejudice, they are more likely to engage in violent behavior.[72]

In sum, official data indicate that African-American youth are arrested for more serious crimes than whites. However, a number of self-report studies conducted by some of the nation's most respected criminologists show that the differences between the races are insignificant and that official differences, therefore, are an artifact of bias in the justice system: Police are more likely to arrest and courts are more likely to convict young African-Americans.[73] If the official data are valid, the participation of African-American youth in serious criminal behavior is generally viewed as a function of their socioeconomic position and the racism they face.

SOCIAL CLASS AND DELINQUENCY

One of the most enduring debates among criminologists is over the relationship between economic status and delinquent behavior. This relationship is a key element of delinquency theory. If delinquency is purely a lower-class phenomenon, then its cause must be rooted in the social forces that are to be found solely in lower-class areas: poverty, unemployment, social disorganization, culture conflict, and alienation.[74] If delinquent behavior is spread throughout the social structure, then its cause must be related to some noneconomic factor: intelligence, personality, socialization, family dysfunction, educational failure, or peer influence.

At first glance, the relationship between class and crime should be clear-cut: Youths who lack wealth or social standing, who live in deteriorated inner-city areas, and who rightfully perceive few legitimate opportunities also should be the ones most likely to use criminal means to achieve their goals. Despite the inherent logic of this observation, available research data do not consistently support this relationship. Many indicators of poverty and economic deprivation do not correlate with delinquency. For example, little, if any, consistent evidence exists that unemployment rates are associated with crime rates.[75] Also, although many lower-class people live conventional and law-abiding lives, a great number of middle-class people are delinquents and criminals.

RESEARCH ON SOCIAL CLASS AND DELINQUENCY

Research on the class–crime relationship has been confusing and contradictory. Those who use official delinquency data persistently find social class to be a significant predictor of delinquency. Juvenile arrest rates are highest in areas that are economically deprived and socially disorganized.[76] Theorists who have based their efforts on official police statistics maintain that those who think delinquency is spread throughout the social classes are just "wishful thinkers"; to many experts, "real" delinquency is a lower-class phenomenon.[77]

However, the first few self-report studies, specifically those conducted by James Short and F. Ivan Nye, did not find a direct relationship between social class and delinquency.[78] They found that socioeconomic class was related to official processing (chances of arrest and incarceration) by police, court, and correctional agencies but not to the actual commission of delinquent acts.

The pioneering work of Nye and Short sparked numerous self-report studies in the 1960s and 1970s, most of which supported their view of a weak or nonexistent relationship between class and delinquency.[79] Some of the most important work was conducted by sociologist Martin Gold. Although in his first few studies Gold found that delinquents were predominantly lower-class youth, his later work with Jay Williams showed no significant self-reported differences among economic classes.[80] The only statistically significant relationship indicated that higher-status white males were more seriously delinquent than other white males!

In the most widely cited research on this issue, Charles Tittle, Wayne Villemez, and Douglas Smith reviewed 35 studies containing 363 separate estimates of the relationship between class and crime.[81] Their conclusion was that little, if any, support exists for the position that delinquency is primarily a lower-class phenomenon. Tittle and his associates argue forcefully that official statistics probably reflect class bias in the way police make arrests. A follow-up study (1991) conducted by Tittle and Robert Meier once again found an insignificant association between delinquency and a variety of social-class measures.[82] These reviews are usually cited by delinquency experts as the strongest refutation of the assertion that lower-class youths are disproportionately delinquent.[83]

In sum, the widespread use of self-reports between 1960 and 1990 uncovered the rather startling fact that poverty was not significantly correlated with delinquency.[84] Most researchers did conclude that lower-class youths were more likely to receive official notice from the justice system. Therefore, they appeared to be overrepresented as official delinquents. Middle-class delinquency, on the other hand, remained hidden.

REASSESSING THE CLASS–DELINQUENCY CONTROVERSY

Those who find fault with Tittle's conclusions usually point to the inclusion of trivial offenses (e.g., using a false ID) in most self-report instruments as the cause of seemingly equal rates of delinquency among social classes. Although middle- and upper-class youths may appear to be as delinquent as those in the lower class, it is because they engage in significant amounts of what are actually status offenses. For example, in one cross-sectional survey of 1,726 youths ages 11–17, Delbert Eliott and Suzanne Ageton found lower-class youths to be much more likely than middle-class youths to engage in serious delinquent acts, such as burglary, assault, robbery, sexual assault, and vandalism.[85] Lower-class youths were much more likely than middle-class youths to have committed "numerous" (more than 200) serious personal and property crimes. Eliott and Ageton found that their self-report data were actually quite similar to official statistics. Other researchers who restrict self-reported behavior to serious "street crimes," such as burglary and robbery, have also shown that class is significantly related to delinquent behavior.[86]

How the concept of "social class" is measured has also been found to significantly influence research findings. While some researchers use "status attainment" variables such parental income and education as measures of social-class affiliation, others use indicators of sustained underclass status, such as years on welfare and unemployment.[87] Margaret Farnworth and her associates found that if class is measured on the basis of parental occupational prestige or status, the association between class and delinquency is insignificant. However, when her subjects were divided into "upperclass" and "underclass" groups based on unemployment and welfare status, a significant social class–delinquency relationship was found.[88]

This recent research suggests that although middle- and upper-class youth may engage in some forms of minor illegal activity, it is members of the underclass who are actually responsible for the majority of serious criminal acts.

Call for Service Data In the future, research on social class and delinquency may use new measures to improve validity. For example, Barbara Warner and Glenn Pierce have used calls for police service by crime victims to measure criminal activity in a neighborhood.[89] Although still considered "official data," calls for service are initiated by crime victims, thereby avoiding the influence of police bias. Using these relatively unbiased measures, Warner and Pierce found that measures of poverty and other ecological variables associated with neighborhood disorganization and decay were in fact related to high crime rates. This research shows that using innovative measures can help clear up the true association between poverty and delinquency.

AGE AND DELINQUENCY

Age is generally agreed to be inversely related to criminality.[90] Official statistics tell us that young people are arrested at a disproportionate rate to their numbers in the population, and victim surveys generate similar findings for crimes in which the age of the assailant can be determined. Youths aged 13–17 collectively make up about 6 percent of the total U.S. population yet account for about 27 percent of the index crime arrests and 16 percent of the arrests for all crimes. In contrast, adults 45 and older, who make up 32 percent of the population, account for only 8 percent of arrests (see Figure 2.7).

Self-report data collected by the Institute for Social Research also indicate that people commit fewer crimes as they mature. The results of a six-year, nationwide survey of high school seniors found that the self-reported rates for such crimes as assault, gang fighting, robbery, stealing, and trespass decline substantially between ages 17 and 23.[91]

Victim data can also be used to evaluate the age–crime relationship. It is possible to derive some estimates of rates of offending by age for the violent personal crimes measured by the National Crime Victimization Survey because victims had the opportunity to view their attackers and estimate their age. In general, when attacked by a group, 48 percent of the time victims identified their attackers as being between 12 and 20; lone attackers were identified as being juveniles about one-third of the time.[92]

AGE–CRIME CONTROVERSY

The relationship between age and crime is highly important to delinquency experts. One of the major criticisms leveled against theories of delinquency causation is that they fail to adequately explain why many youngsters forgo delinquent behavior as they mature, a process referred to as **aging out, desistance,** or **spontaneous remission.** In other words, well-known theories that account for the *start* or onset of delinquency rarely bother to explain why people *stop* committing crime as they mature. This theoretical failure is the subject of considerable academic debate.

One position, championed by respected criminologists Travis Hirschi and Michael Gottfredson, is that the age–crime relationship is a constant: Regardless

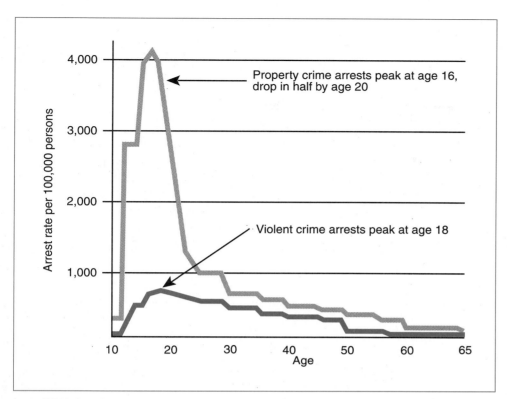

FIGURE 2.7

The relationship between age and serious crime arrests.

Property crime arrests peak at age 16, drop in half by age 20

Violent crime arrests peak at age 18

Arrest rate per 100,000 persons

Age

Source: FBI, *Uniform Crime Reports*, 1994 pp. 178–79.

of race, sex, social class, intelligence, or any other social variable, people commit fewer crimes as they age.[93] In fact, they argue that even the most chronic juvenile offenders will commit fewer crimes as they age.[94]

The Hirschi–Gottfredson concept of age and crime can be best understood through an example. Let's assume that youths who drop out of high school commit more delinquent acts than youths who are committed to their education (see Figure 2.8). According to Hirschi and Gottfredson, members of both groups will commit fewer crimes as they age, but the crime rate of the dropouts will remain relatively higher than the rate of the high school graduates at any given point in their respective life cycles: The observed differences in the respective crime rates of dropouts and graduates, which first appeared in early childhood, will remain constant as they mature. By implication, it would be possible to compare the relative difference in the crime rate of dropouts and graduates (or any other two groups) by measuring their criminal activity at any single point in their lifetime.

Those who oppose the Hirschi–Gottfredson view of the age–crime relationship suggest that although age is an important determinant of crime, other factors directly associated with a person's lifestyle also affect offending rates.[95] For example, David Farrington has shown that crime patterns may evolve over a person's life course. The probability that a person may become a persistent "career criminal" may be influenced by a number of personal and environmental factors.[96] Evidence exists, for example, that the **age of onset** of a delinquent career has an important effect on its length: Those who demonstrate antisocial

FIGURE 2.8

Crime by Age: Dropouts versus Graduates. Although the criminal activity of both groups declines with age, dropouts maintain their position as higher-rate offenders than graduates over the entire life course.

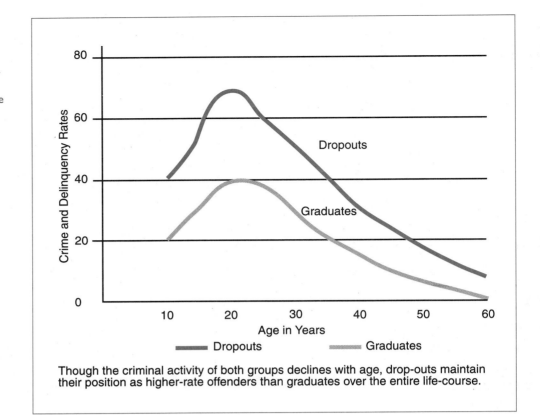

Though the criminal activity of both groups declines with age, drop-outs maintain their position as higher-rate offenders than graduates over the entire life-course.

tendencies at a very early age are more likely to commit more crimes for a longer duration. According to this **"life course"** view, it is important to follow delinquents over their life cycle **(longitudinal studies)** to fully understand the factors that influence offending patterns.[97]

In sum, some criminologists believe that youths who get involved with delinquency at a very early age and who acquire an official record will be the ones most likely to become career criminals; to them, age is a key determinant of delinquency.[98] Those opposed to this view find that the age of onset is irrelevant and that all people commit fewer crimes as they age; the relationship between age and crime is constant.[99]

The true role of the age variable in the production of criminal careers has been the focus of many lively debates in the literature of crime and delinquency.[100] The research evidence indicates that there is a generalized decline in criminal activity as a person matures but that the incidence of some illegal acts, such as substance abuse, fraud, gambling,and drunkenness, may increase.[101] In addition, a small segment of the chronic delinquent population may exist whose criminal behavior remains intact as they reach adulthood.

Why Do People Age Out of Crime?   As youths mature, changing lifestyles may reduce their offending patterns. Alicia Rand's longitudinal study of delinquent males found that youths who got married early, earned a high school diploma, and received vocational training within the armed services were the most likely to desist from crime.[102] People may also go through personality changes. Using a sample of Montreal adolescents, Marc LeBlanc found that self-control increases in adolescence at the same time delinquency rates begin to decline.[103]

Research conducted by Barry Glassner, Margaret Ksander, Bruce Berg, and Bruce Johnson found that aging out of crime might also be linked to a very practical consideration: the fear of punishment. According to Glassner and his associates, youths are well aware that once they reach the age of majority, punishment takes a decidedly more serious turn. They are no longer protected by the kindly arms of the juvenile justice system. As one teenage boy told them,

> When you're a teenager, you're rowdy. Nowadays you aren't rowdy. You know, you want to settle down because you can go to jail now. [When] you are a boy, you can be put into a detention home. But you can go to jail now. Jail ain't no place to go.[104]

Of course, not all juvenile criminals desist as they age; many go on to be chronic offenders as adults. Yet, even people who actively remain in a criminal career will eventually slow down as they age. Crime is too dangerous, physically taxing, and unrewarding, and punishments too harsh and long lasting, to become a long-term way of life for most people.[105]

CHRONIC OFFENDING: CAREERS IN DELINQUENCY

Official and unofficial data sources indicate that although most adolescents age out of crime, a relatively small number of youths who began to violate the law early in their lives (i.e., "early onset") continue at a high rate well into adulthood (i.e.,"persistence").[106] The association between early onset and high-rate persistent offending has been demonstrated in samples drawn from a variety of cultures, time periods, and offender types (e.g., self-reported delinquents, official delinquents).[107]

These high-rate persisters are resistant to change and seem immune from the effects of punishment. Arrest, prosecution, and conviction do little to slow down their offending careers. These so-called "chronic offenders" are responsible for a significant amount of all delinquent and criminal activity.

The Glueck Research   Although interest in chronic, persistent offending is at an all-time high, it is actually not new. In the 1930s, Sheldon Glueck and Eleanor Glueck of Harvard University popularized research on the life cycle of **delinquent careers**.[108] In a series of longitudinal research studies, they followed the careers of known delinquents in order to determine the factors that predicted persistent offending.[109] In their most well known study, *Unraveling Juvenile Delinquency,* they carefully matched a sample of 500 delinquent youths with 500 nondelinquents to ascertain the personal characteristics that predict antisocial behavior.

The Gluecks focused on the early onset of delinquency as a harbinger of a criminal career: "the deeper the roots of childhood maladjustment, the smaller the chance of adult adjustment."[110] They also noted the stability of offending careers: Those who are antisocial early in life are the ones most likely to continue their offending careers into adulthood.

Their research findings convinced them that a number of personal factors present early in life were the most significant predictors of delinquent careers. They identified a variety of social factors related to persistent offending, the most important of which, family relations, included the quality of discipline and emotional ties with parents. The adolescent raised in a large, single-parent family of limited economic means and educational achievement was the one most vulnerable to delinquency.

The Gluecks also evaluated such biological and psychological traits as body type, intelligence, and personality and found that physical and mental factors also played a role in determining behavior. Children with low intelligence, a background of mental disease, and a powerful physique were the ones most likely to become persistent offenders. Although more than 50 years old, the Glueck research is considered a forerunner of current efforts to describe the process of chronic offending and career criminality. The Gluecks' method of giving equal weight to social, biological, and psychological traits corresponds with current thinking on the formation of criminal careers.[111]

THE CHRONIC JUVENILE OFFENDER

Current interest in the delinquent life cycle was also prompted by the "discovery" in the 1970s of the **chronic delinquent offender.** According to this view, a relatively few youthful offenders commit a significant percentage of all serious crimes, and many of these same offenders grow up to become chronic adult criminals who are responsible for a large share of the total adult crime rate.

Chronic offenders can be distinguished from conventional delinquent youths. The latter are youthful law violators who may be apprehended for a single instance of criminal behavior, usually of relatively minor seriousness—shoplifting, joyriding, petty larceny, and so on. The chronic offender begins his or her delinquent career at a relatively young age (under age 10; referred to as "early onset"), has serious and persistent brushes with the law, is building a career in crime, and may be excessively violent and destructive. Moreover, chronic offenders do not age out of crime but continue their law-violating behavior into adulthood.[112] The important conclusion is this: *Early and repeated delinquent activity is the best predictor of future adult criminality.*

A number of important research efforts have set out to chronicle the careers of serious delinquent offenders. The following sections describe these efforts.

DELINQUENCY IN A BIRTH COHORT

The concept of the chronic career offender is most closely associated with the research efforts of Marvin Wolfgang and his associates at the University of Pennsylvania.[113] In 1972, Wolfgang, Robert Figlio, and Thorsten Sellin published a landmark study, *Delinquency in a Birth Cohort,* that has profoundly influenced the very concept of the delinquent offender.

Wolfgang, Figlio, and Sellin used official records to follow through age 18 the delinquent careers of a cohort of 9,945 boys born in Philadelphia in 1945. Data were obtained from police files and school records; socioeconomic status was determined by locating the residence of each member of the cohort and assigning him the median family income for that area.

Findings of the Cohort Study   About one-third of the boys (3,475) had some police contact. The remaining two-thirds (6,470) had none. Those boys with at least one contact with the police during their minority committed a total of 10,214 offenses. Race was found to be the most significant predictor of eventual police contact. Of the 2,902 nonwhite subjects, 1,458 (50.24 percent) had police contact; of the 7,043 white youths, 2,017 (28.64 percent) had police contact. Wolfgang and his associates also noted that minority youths tended to fall in the lower-class category (84.2 percent of nonwhites and 30.8 percent of whites were from lower socioeconomic levels). However, when youths from the same socioeconomic levels were compared, nonwhites still had a higher level of police contact. After further analysis, the researchers were forced to conclude that no single variable predicted juvenile police contact better than race.

Wolfgang found that school-related variables were significantly associated with delinquent behavior. For example, the types of schools youths attended influenced whether they would eventually be picked up by police. A greater proportion of delinquents spent most of their school years in public schools, and fewer delinquents than nondelinquents attended parochial schools. Furthermore, four percent of delinquents, compared with one percent of nondelinquents, attended a public disciplinary institution. Nondelinquents received more education than delinquents (11.24 years completed versus 9.96). Although this relationship was consistent across racial lines, it was equally apparent that nonwhites received significantly less schooling than whites.

Another school-related factor, IQ, also distinguished delinquents from nondelinquents (see chapter 3). The average IQ for nondelinquents was 107.87; for delinquents, it was 100.95. Again, this relationship was consistent across racial lines.

Similarly, school achievement levels were significantly related to delinquent activities: 12.8 percent of nondelinquents were rated "very low" on school achievement; 27.46 percent of delinquents received such negative ratings. Conversely, 19.48 percent of nondelinquents received a "very high" rating, while only 5.63 percent of delinquent youths received that rating. The researchers found major differences in school achievement between the races, with nonwhites doing considerably less well.

CHRONIC OFFENDERS

The most well known discovery of Wolfgang and his associates was that of the so-called chronic offender. The cohort data indicated that 54 percent (1,862) of the sample's delinquent youths were repeat offenders, while the remaining 46 percent (1,613) were one-time offenders. However, the repeaters could be further categorized as nonchronic recidivists and **chronic recidivists.** The former were 1,235 youths who had been arrested more than once but fewer than five times and who made up 35.6 percent of all delinquents. The latter were 627 boys arrested *five times or more* and who accounted for 18 percent of the delinquents and 6 percent of the total sample of 9,945.

It was the chronic offenders (known today as "the chronic 6 percent") who were involved in the most delinquent behavior; they were responsible for 5,305 offenses, or 51.9 percent of all offenses. Even more striking was their involvement in serious criminal acts. Of the entire sample, chronic offenders committed 71 percent of the homicides, 73 percent of the rapes, 82 percent of the robberies, and 69 percent of the aggravated assaults.

Wolfgang and his associates found that arrest and juvenile court experience did little to deter the chronic offenders. In fact, disposition was inversely related to chronic delinquency—the greater the punishment, the more likely they were to engage in repeat delinquent behavior. Strict punishment dispositions also increased the probability that further court action would be taken. Two factors stood out as encouraging recidivism: the seriousness of the original offense and the severity of the disposition. The researchers concluded that the efforts of the juvenile justice system to control or eliminate delinquent behavior may be futile because not only do a greater proportion of those who receive a severe disposition violate the law, but their violations are serious and frequent.

BIRTH COHORT FOLLOW-UP

In a subsequent analysis, Wolfgang and his associates followed a 10 percent sample of the original cohort (974 subjects) through their adulthood to age 30.[114] They divided the sample into three groups: those who had been juvenile offenders only; those who were adult offenders only; and persistent offenders (those who had offenses in both time periods). Those classified as chronic juvenile offenders in the original birth cohort made up 70 percent of the "persistent" group. They had an 80 percent chance of becoming adult offenders and a 50 percent chance of being arrested four or more times as adults. In comparison, subjects with no juvenile arrests had only an 18 percent chance of getting arrested as an adult. The chronic offenders also continued to engage in the most serious crimes. Although they accounted for only 15 percent of the follow-up sample, they were involved in 74 percent of all arrests and 82 percent of all serious crimes, such as homicide, rape, and robbery.

Although persistent delinquency was related to adult criminality, offensive behavior dropped substantially from the juvenile period to the adult period.[115] For example, more than half of the boys arrested twice as juveniles were never arrested as adults. Although desistance was common, those youths who did commit crimes as adults were likely to escalate the seriousness of their offenses.

BIRTH COHORT II

The juveniles who made up Wolfgang's original birth cohort were born in 1945. How have the behavior patterns of youths changed in subsequent years? To answer this question, Wolfgang and his associates Paul Tracy and Robert Figlio conducted a new, larger birth cohort study (Birth Cohort II) of youths born in Philadelphia in 1958 and followed them through age 18.[116] The 1958 cohort was larger than the original, with 27,160 youths, of which 13,160 were males and 14,000 were females.

What did this second cohort study reveal about delinquent behavior? For one thing, the proportion of delinquent youths in the second cohort (1,159 arrests per 1,000 subjects) was larger than that in the 1945 cohort (1,027). However, the overall offending patterns in both cohorts were relatively similar; for example, about one-third of the boys in both samples has at least one police contact before their eighteenth birthday.

The racial differences so apparent in the first cohort were less significant in the second. Although a greater percentage of minority youth (42 percent) than white youth (23 percent) were delinquent, the differences between the two had declined (by 2 percent) since the earlier cohort data were analyzed. The violent crime ratio, which was fifteen to one in the first cohort, had declined to about six to one in the second. In addition, the number of white chronic delinquents increased substantially (by 5 percent), while the number of chronic nonwhite offenders declined (by 2 percent).

Because the second cohort contained female subjects, it allowed for a comparison between male and female delinquency patterns. As might be expected, males were two and a half times more likely to become involved in delinquent behavior than females. In addition, females who did get in trouble with the law were much more likely to be one-time offenders. However, about 7 percent of the delinquent females were classified as chronic recidivists (147 girls).

Of the males in the sample, chronic delinquents (five or more arrests) made up 7.5 percent of the 1958 cohort (compared with 6.3 percent in 1945) and 23 percent of all delinquent offenders (compared with 18 percent in 1945). Chronic male delinquents continued to be responsible for a disproportionate amount of criminal behavior. The 982 chronic male delinquents accounted for 9,240 arrests, or 61 percent of the total. They also committed a disproportionate amount of the most serious crimes: 61 percent of the homicides, 76 percent of the rapes, 73 percent of the robberies, and 65 percent of the aggravated assaults. The chronic female offender was less likely to be involved in serious crime.

It is interesting to note that the 1958 cohort, as a group, was involved in significantly more serious crime than the 1945 group. Subjects in the 1958 cohort committed more serious crimes (455 per 1,000) than the subjects in the first cohort (274 per 1,000); the violent crime ratio between the two samples was three to one.

The 1945 cohort study found that chronic offenders dominate the total juvenile crime rate and continue their law-violating careers as adults. The newer cohort study showed that the chronic delinquent syndrome was being maintained in a group of subjects who were born 13 years later than the original cohort and that, if anything, they were more violent than their older brothers. Finally, the efforts of the justice system seemed to have little preventive effect on the behavior of chronic offenders.

TRACKING THE CHRONIC OFFENDER

Wolfgang's pioneering effort to identify the chronic career offender has been supplemented by a number of other important research studies.[117] Lyle Shannon also used the cohort approach to investigate career delinquency patterns.[118] He employed three cohorts totaling 6,127 youths born in 1942, 1949, and 1955 in Racine, Wisconsin. Shannon also encountered the phenomenon of the chronic career offender who engages in a disproportionate amount of delinquent behavior and later becomes involved in adult criminality. He found that fewer than 25 percent of each cohort's male subjects had five or more nontraffic offenses but accounted for 77 percent to 83 percent of all police contacts in their cohort. Similarly, from 8 percent to 14 percent of the persons in each cohort were responsible for all the serious felony offenses. According to Shannon, if one wished to identify the persons responsible for about 75 percent of the felonies and much of the other crimes—then approximately 5 percent of each cohort— the persons with two or three felony contacts would be the target population. Shannon also found that involvement with the justice system did little to inhibit criminality. Although most youths eventually desisted, a few continued their offending careers as adults even though they had been arrested as teenagers.

A number of other studies have duplicated these findings on chronic offenders. Some have tracked criminal careers by using the records of court-processed youth while others have employed self-report data.[119] Disturbingly, they show that the chronic offender problem may be larger than previously believed. For example, using data from a national youth, Franklyn Dunford and Delbert Elliott were able to identify a **serious career offender type**, whom they defined as a youth committing at least three serious felonies (such as aggravated or sexual assault, gang fighting, car theft, or strong-arm robbery) two or more years in a row. Dunford and Elliott found that only 24 percent of the serious career offenders had ever been arrested, indicating that studies that rely on official data may be underestimating the number of persistent offenders.[120]

THE DEVELOPMENT OF DELINQUENT CAREERS

The "discovery" of the chronic offender has prompted research on the **life cycle of crime**: What causes the onset of delinquency, and what sustains it over the life course? A number of themes are now emerging. One view is that multiple social, personal, and economic factors can influence delinquency and that as these factors change and evolve over time, so too does criminal involvement. In an important paper, Robert Sampson and John Laub describe how delinquency and drug abuse evolve over the **life course**. They found that events and experiences encountered as a child matures influence the direction and frequency of antisocial behavior.[121] For example, delinquents who later manage to find stable work and maintain intact marriages as adults are the ones most likely to desist from crime. In contrast, those who have adverse experiences with the justice system (arrest, incarceration) are stigmatized with negative labels that interfere with family relations and inhibit employment opportunities; these factors heighten criminal liability.[122] A number of factors that encourage delinquency during the life course have been identified, including educational failure and poor family relations. Joan McCord found that fathers who undermine their wives, who are aggressive, and who fight with their families produce children who later become adult offenders.[123]

Dissenting Views   Not all delinquency experts agree with the life-course view. Another theme that has developed is that there is a single underlying criminal propensity **(latent trait)** that is present at birth or soon after. This yet unidentified disposition or trait is established early in life and remains stable over time. The positive association between past and future criminality reflects the presence of this underlying criminogenic trait; what causes crime early in life also is responsible for antisocial behavior in adulthood.[124] The crime-producing trait does not diminish or reduce over the life course. People commit less crime as they age simply because they have fewer criminal opportunities as they mature; the propensity to commit crime remains constant.[125]

Included among the suspected latent traits that produce future criminality are low IQ, impulsive personality, and neuropsychological problems due to problems encountered either in utero, at birth, or soon after.[126]

Proponents of the latent trait view, such as Michael Gottfredson and Travis Hirschi (see chapter 5) and James Q. Wilson and Richard Herrnstein (see chapter 3), believe that criminal tendencies are quite stable over the life course because their underlying cause develops early in life.[127]

Although the life course and latent trait views seem at first irreconcilable, they do have a degree of commonality. Both indicate that crime and delinquency can be viewed as a passage along which people travel, that a criminal career has a beginning and end, and that events and life circumstances influence the journey. In the sections below, some of the most recent research on the factors influencing the onset, maintenance, and termination of a delinquent career are discussed in some detail.

PATHWAYS TO DELINQUENCY

What is the natural history of a delinquent way of life? What causes some youths to begin a delinquent career? Why do some sustain and even escalate their antisocial behavior patterns? In a well known research study Richard Jessor identified a number of factors that lead to what he labels "health/life compromising outcomes." Some of these outcomes are behavioral (e.g., drug use), some biological (e.g., diet, disease), others are environmental, (e.g., poverty) and still others rest on personality traits (e.g., low self-esteem). Each of these factors may act alone or in concert to affect risk-taking behaviors, including delinquency and substance abuse, which eventually lead to a destructive adult lifestyle characterized by low self-esteem, disease, unemployment, and suicide.[128]

Jessor's views coincide with a number of significant research projects being conducted on delinquent lifestyles. Using data taken from a longitudinal cohort study conducted in Pittsburgh (**The Pittsburgh Youth Study**), Rolf Loeber and his associates are now beginning to formulate the **pathways** to crime traveled by at-risk youth.[129] Loeber and his associates found that three paths to a delinquent career can be identified:

1. The authority conflict pathway begins at an early age with stubborn behavior, leading to defiance (doing things one's own way, refusing to do things, disobedience) and then to authority avoidance (staying out late, truancy, and running away). Defiance of parents and authority avoidance lead to more serious offenses, including drug use.
2. The covert pathway begins with minor underhanded behavior (lying, shoplifting) which leads to property damage (setting fires, damaging property) and eventually escalates to more serious forms of delinquency, ranging from joyriding, pickpocketing, larceny, and fencing to writing bad checks, using fake credit cards, car theft, drug dealing, and breaking and entering.
3. The overt pathway consists of an escalation of aggressive acts beginning with aggression (annoying others, bullying) and leading to physical fighting (fighting and gang fighting) followed by violence (attacks on individuals, strong-arming, forced theft).

The Loeber research indicates that each of these paths may lead a youth into a sustained deviant career. Some enter two and even three paths simultaneously: They are stubborn, lie to teachers and parents, are bullies, and commit petty thefts; these adolescents are the ones most likely to become persistent offenders.

The Loeber research is important because it shows that (a) delinquency does in fact escalate as children travel the life course and (b) rather than being unidimensional, antisocial behaviors are varied, allowing offenders to travel more than one path as they shift from delinquent to criminal.

PROBLEM BEHAVIOR SYNDROME (PBS)

The delinquency data seem to suggest that adolescent criminality may be one segment of a general **problem behavior syndrome (PBS),** consisting of unconventional adolescent behavior patterns that are thought to cluster together, such as physical and sexual abuse, smoking and substance abuse, precocious sexual experimentation, pregnancy, school failure, suicide attempts, risk taking and thrill seeking, theft, violence, and mental illness.[130]

There is significant empirical evidence for a PBS. A number of research efforts have found that juveniles who are involved in crime also are likely to engage in a variety of other antisocial behaviors.[131] In fact more than half of all youths with mental or substance abuse problems have been found to suffer from at least one other co-occurring disorder.[132] For example, using data from The Pittsburgh Youth Study, Magda Stouthamer-Loeber and Evelyn Wei found that teenage boys who father children out of wedlock are also are more likely to have had a court appearance, to have dropped out of school, to have been involved in drinking, and to have trafficked in drugs; they are three times more likely to have been involved in car theft and forced entry than nonfathers.[133]

Helene Raskin White's six-year study of more than 400 male and female adolescents identified problem behaviors that clustered together including delinquency, substance abuse, school misconduct and underachievement, precocious sexual behavior, violence (for males only), and suicide and mental health problems (for females only).[134] White found that general problem behaviors were stable: Youths who were having multiple problems at age 15 were also having problems at age 21.

Components of PBS   Table 2.7 lists some of the problem behaviors found by David Farrington to be significantly associated with both self-reported and official delinquency in a cohort of English youth. The breadth of these behaviors supports the existence of a problem behavior syndrome. In an important analysis, Farrington compared his findings with those collected by Rolf Loeber in

TABLE 2.7   Risk Factors for Delinquency and Age at Which They Occur

(a) *Child problem behavior*	Low attainment 11
Troublesome 8–10	High delinquency school 11
Dishonest 10	Frequently truants 12–14
Lies frequently 12–14	Left school 15
Aggressive 12–14	No exams taken by 18
Bullies 14	(f) *Family influences*
(b) *Teenage antisocial behavior*	Poor parental child rearing 8
Heavy drinker 18	Poor parental supervision 8
Heavy smoker 18	Low parent interest in education 8
Drug user 18	Separated from parents 10
Heavy gambler 18	Poor relation with parents 18
High sexual activity 18	(g) *Antisocial influences*
(c) *Physical measures*	Convicted parent 10
Small 8–10	Delinquent sibling 10
Small 18	Sibling behavior problems 8
Tattooed 18	Delinquent friends 14
(d) *Impulsivity*	(h) *Socioeconomic factors*
Lacks concentration/restless 8–10	Low family income 8
High daring 8–10	Low socioeconomic status family 8–10
Lacks concentration/restless 12–14	Poor housing 8–10
High daring 12–14	Large family size 10
High impulsivity 18	Unstable job record 18
(e) *School problems*	Unskilled manual job 18
Low intelligence 8–10	

Source: David Farrington, "Juvenile Delinquency," in J. Coleman, ed., *The School Years* (London: Routledge, 1992), p. 129.

The Pittsburgh Youth Study. He found many areas of commonality. Behaviors that clustered together include family-related problems such as parental conflict, large family size, low income, and a broken home; individual-level factors include poor concentration, hyperactivity, and impulsivity. Comparisons over time (1960s versus 1990s) and place (Pittsburgh versus London) indicate that PBS is not unique to modern American culture.[135]

PBS and Delinquency The interrelationship of these factors is important because they suggest that delinquency may be one of a cluster of antisocial behaviors that either have a common cause or are part of a collective lifestyle. Research shows that at-risk youths may have social and life skill deficits. They have trouble communicating, expressing their feelings, and understanding and being sensitive to the feelings of others. It is possible that adolescents lacking these skills are prey to a variety of problems, ranging from school failure to antisocial acts.[136] Classification of delinquents based on the nature and extent of their problem behaviors may make it easier for correctional personnel to plan effective treatments.[137]

OFFENSE SPECIALIZATION

Most persistent offenders do not seem to specialize in any one type of behavior but, with few exceptions, engage in a variety of delinquent acts and antisocial behaviors as they mature. For example, they cheat on tests, bully kids in the schoolyard, take drugs, commit a burglary, go on to steal a car, and then shoplift from a store.

Recent evidence indicates that over their lifetime, however, some chronic offenders may begin to specialize in particular forms of delinquency.[138] For example, Randall Shelden found that some chronic offenders specialized in serious crimes, while others could be categorized as "chronic nuisance offenders" who were repeatedly referred to court on status- and neglect-type petitions; this latter group "specialized" in running away and truancy.[139]

In another study using a very large sample of about 70,000 court-adjudicated youths in Arizona and Utah, David Farrington, Howard Snyder, and Terrence Finnegan found that about 20 percent of the youths could be considered offense "specialists" who persistently committed one type of offense.[140] The delinquent acts most likely to be the domain of "specialists" included running away from home, liquor violations, incorrigibility, burglary, motor vehicle theft, and drug abuse. Not surprisingly, two of these are status offenses (to which a desperate youth might repeatedly turn for survival), two are criminal offenses that require some degree of skill (burglary and auto theft—two activities that, once proficiency is attained, a youth might repeat), and two involve substance abuse (and therefore might require habitual behavior).[141]

FROM DELINQUENT TO CRIMINAL

Adolescent problem behavior can set processes in motion that eventuate in compromised physical and social well being in the adult years.[142]

Advocates of the life-course view have attempted to chronicle the criminal careers of persistent offenders in order to document the factors that either escalate or reduce delinquent offending.[143] The early data seem to support what is already known about delinquent-criminal career patterns: that early onset predicts later offending; that there is continuity in crime (juvenile offenders are the ones most likely to become adult criminals); and that chronic offenders commit a significant portion of all crimes.[144]

One of the most important of these longitudinal studies, the Cambridge study in delinquent development, followed the offending careers of 411 London boys born in 1953.[145] This longitudinal cohort study, directed since 1982 by David Farrington, is one of the most serious attempts to isolate the factors that predict the continuity of criminal behavior through the life course. The study used self-report data, as well as in-depth interviews and psychological testing. The boys were interviewed 8 times over a period of 24 years, beginning at age 8 and continuing to age 32.

The results of the Cambridge study are quite important because they showed that many of the same patterns found in the United States were repeated in a cross-national sample: the existence of chronic offenders; the continuity of offending; and early onset leading to persistent delinquency.

Continuity of Delinquency Farrington found that the traits present in persistent offenders can be observed as early as age 8. The typical chronic delinquent is a male property offender born into a low-income, large-sized family headed by parents who had criminal records and with delinquent older siblings. The future delinquent receives poor parental supervision, including harsh or erratic punishments; his parents are likely to be in conflict and to separate. He tends to associate with friends who are also delinquents. By age 8, he is already exhibiting antisocial behavior, including dishonesty and aggressiveness. At school, he tends to have low educational achievement and attainment and is restless, troublesome, hyperactive, impulsive, and often truant.

After leaving school at age 18, the persistent delinquent tends to maintain a relatively well paid but low-status job and is likely to have an erratic work history and periods of unemployment. Deviant behavior tends to be versatile, rather than specialized; that is, the typical offender not only commits property offenses, such as theft and burglary, but also engages in violence, vandalism, drug use, excessive drinking, drunk driving, smoking, reckless driving, and sexual promiscuity. He is more likely than nonoffenders to live away from home and have conflict with his parents. The persistent delinquent tends to get tattoos, go out most evenings, and enjoy "hanging out" with groups of friends. He is much more likely than nonoffenders to get involved in fights, to carry weapons, and to use them in violent encounters. The frequency of his offending reaches a peak in his teenage years (about 17 or 18), then declines in his twenties, when he marries or lives with a woman.

By the time he reaches his thirties, the former delinquent is likely to be separated or divorced from his wife and be an absent parent. His employment record remains spotty, and he moves often to rental units, rather than owning his housing. His life is still characterized by evenings out, heavy drinking and substance abuse, and more violent behavior than that of his contemporaries. Because the typical offender provides the same kind of deprived and disrupted family life for his own children that he himself experienced, the social experiences and conditions that produce delinquency are carried on from one generation to the next.

Interestingly, Farrington's sample also contained offenders who have ceased criminal activity, allowing him to study the discontinuity of delinquent offenses: Boys whose background make them vulnerable to delinquency but are able to become nonoffenders tend to be somewhat shy, have few friends (at age 8), have nondeviant parents and siblings, and are rated highly by their mother (at age 10). At-risk youths who manage to attain age 32 without a criminal conviction are not necessarily leading a successful life. They are unlikely to be homeowners and tend to live in dirty home conditions, and have large debts and low-paying jobs. They are the youth most likely to never marry and to be living alone. Youths who experience social isolation at age 8 also experience it at age 32. At-risk youth who one day marry nondeviant women reduce their involvement in criminal activity; marriage to a woman with a criminal record increases criminal involvement.

TURNING POINTS IN CRIME

If there are various pathways to crime and delinquency, are there trails back to conformity? In an important work, *Crime in the Making*, Robert Sampson and John Laub identify the "turning points" in a criminal career.[146] As devotees of the life-course perspective, Sampson and Laub find that the stability of delinquent behavior can be affected by events that occur later in life, even after a chronic delinquent career has been undertaken. Two critical "turning points" are marriage and career. Youths who had significant problems with the law are able to desist from crime as adults if they can become attached to a spouse who supports and sustains them, even when the partner knows they had been in trouble during adolescence. They may encounter employers who are willing to give them a chance despite their record. People who cannot sustain secure marital relations or are failures in the labor market are less likely to desist from crime.

According to Sampson and Laub, these life events help people build relations with individuals and institutions that are life sustaining, a concept they refer to as "social capital." Building this social capital supports conventional behavior and inhibits deviant behavior. For example, a successful marriage creates social capital when it improves a person's stature and feelings of self-worth and encourages others to "take a chance" on the individual. In the same way, having a good career can inhibit crime by creating a stake in conformity; why commit a crime when you are doing well at your job? These relationships are reciprocal: If a person is chosen as an employee, he or she returns the "favor" by doing the best job possible; if the person is chosen as a spouse, he or she blossoms into a devoted partner. Building social capital reduces the likelihood of deviance.

Sampson and Laub's research indicates that events that occur in later adolescence and adulthood do influence the direction of delinquent and criminal careers. Life events can either help terminate or sustain deviant careers. Having established that change is possible, some important questions still need answering: Why do some young people change while others resist? Why do some young people enter strong marriages while others fail? Why are some troubled youths able to conform to the requirements of a job or career while others cannot?

POLICY IMPLICATIONS

The ongoing research efforts to chart the life cycle of crime and delinquency will have a major influence on both theory and policy. Rather than simply asking why juveniles become delinquent or commit antisocial acts, theorists are charting the onset, escalation, frequency, and cessation of delinquent behavior. Some of the theories that rely on a multifactor and/or life-course model will be reviewed in chapters 3 through 7.

Research on delinquent careers has also influenced delinquency control policy. If a relatively few persistent offenders commit a large portion of all delinquent acts and then persist as adult criminals, it follows that steps should be taken to limit their criminal opportunities.[147] One approach is to identify persistent offenders at the beginning stages of their offending careers and provide early intervention and treatment.[148] Identification might be facilitated by research aimed at identifying traits (e.g., impulsive personalities) that can be used to classify high-risk offenders.[149] Because many of these youth suffer from PBS, treatment must be aimed at a garden variety of educational, family, vocational, and psychological problems. Focusing on a single problem such as a lack of employment may be ineffective.[150]

Even the most sophisticated attempts at predicting chronic offending are erroneous more than half the time.[151] Efforts to predict individual cases of chronic offending have proven unreliable.[152] The danger also exists that early identification, arrest, and custody of youth will promote, rather than inhibit, their delinquent careers. For example, Pamela Tontodonato found that youths who have three arrests by age 15 have a greater likelihood of accumulating additional, more serious arrests than those juveniles who accumulate arrests more slowly.[153] Although an intensive law enforcement policy aimed at multiple offenders may have political appeal, it might actually produce a higher overall delinquency rate.

CASE IN POINT

You are a newly appointed judge in the county juvenile court.

A 12-year-old boy, Joseph L., is petitioned to court on a robbery charge. It seems that Joseph, a five-foot-four, 110-pound youngster, used a knife in a schoolyard robbery. You note that this is already his fifth offense. He was arrested at age 9 on a petty larceny, and 6 months later, he was picked up for breaking into a home. At age 10, he was again arrested for a break-in, and at 11, he assaulted and badly beat a younger boy after school. Despite his youth, the boy seems defiant and unafraid when he is found to be a delinquent.

At the sentencing hearing, the prosecutor presents evidence that Joseph has all the character traits of a chronic offender: early onset of delinquency, multiple arrests, increased seriousness of offenses, a history of school failure, low intelligence, siblings who are law violators. The prosecution demands a three-year placement in the state correctional facility for dangerous youth. Defense counsel asks for community supervision. She claims that the state's high-security juvenile facility usually houses much older offenders, many of whom are over 16. Placement will only exacerbate an already serious situation. Considering the boy's tender age, she argues, the case can better be handled by community treatment agencies.

The prosecution counters that chronic offenders will not be impressed with leniency and that community treatment is therefore a waste of time. Although the prosecutor agrees with defense counsel's claim that placement with older delinquents will certainly diminish any chance of future rehabilitation, he believes that this youth has already proven himself beyond control. Society's need for safety outweighs the remote likelihood of rehabilitation, he contends. A period of incarceration is needed in this case to protect the public from a dangerous chronic offender.

Is it fair to place this child with older youth in a high-security treatment center?

Should the needs of society outweigh a child's right to treatment?

Should predictions of future behavior patterns influence the treatment of children?

Despite reservations civil libertarians may have about the concept of the chronic career offender (and the treatment implications), it already has profoundly influenced the daily operations of the juvenile justice system. First, it has strengthened the position of conservative policymakers who call for a "get tough" approach to juvenile delinquency. Although it might seem futile, cruel, and expensive to lock up all juvenile offenders, it makes both economic and practical sense to incarcerate the few chronic offenders who are responsible for most of the crime problem. This view has resulted in the development of tough juvenile sentencing codes, as well as the transfer of serious delinquency cases to the adult court.

The discovery of the chronic offender has significantly shifted juvenile justice philosophy away from a liberal treatment orientation toward a more conservative crime-control model. It may also produce a review of the *parens patriae* doctrine and the jurisdiction of the juvenile court. As Kimberly Kempf suggests, it may make sense to reconstruct the criminal court system so that both petty adult and juvenile cases are handled in one court, chronic adult and juvenile felony cases in another, and status offender cases in a third. The problems of juvenile and adult chronic offenders may be similar enough to warrant the attention of the same judicial authority.[154] The "Case in Point" (page 76) explores some of these issues.

SUMMARY

Official delinquency refers to youths who are arrested by police agencies. What is known about official delinquency comes from the FBI's *Uniform Crime Reports (UCR)*, an annual tally of crimes reported to police by citizens. In addition, the FBI gathers arrest statistics from local police departments. From these, it is possible to determine the number of youths who are arrested each year, along with their age, race, and gender.

About 2 million youths are now being arrested by police annually. A disturbing trend has been an increase in the number of juveniles arrested for violent crimes, especially rape and murder. Although it is not certain why this trend has developed, possible explanations include involvement in gang activity, drug abuse, and participation in hate crimes.

Dissatisfaction with the validity of the *UCR* has prompted criminologists to develop other means of measuring the true amount of delinquent behavior. Self-reports are surveys of youth in which subjects are asked to tell about their misbehavior. Although self-reports indicate that many more crimes are committed than are known to the police, they also show that the delinquency rate is rather stable.

The third method of gathering information on delinquency involves the use of victim surveys. The National Crime Victimization Survey (NCVS) is an annual national survey of the victims of crime conducted by agencies of the federal government. It also indicates that the crime problem is far greater than official statistics indicate. Teenagers seem much more likely to become the victims of crime than people in other age groups.

All three sources of crime statistics agree on one thing, however: Young people commit more crime than adults.

This chapter also reviewed personal and social factors correlated with delinquent behavior. Delinquents are disproportionately male, although female delinquency rates are rising at a faster pace. Minority youth are overrepresented in the delinquency rate, especially for violent crime arrests. Experts are split on the cause of racial differences in the delinquency rate: Some believe they are a function of system bias; others see them as representing actual differences in the delinquency rate. Disagreement also exists over the relationship between class position and delinquency. Some hold that adolescent crime is a lower-class phenomenon, while others see it spread throughout the social structure. Problems in methodology and data collection have obscured the true class–crime relationship. However, official statistics indicate that lower-class youth are responsible for the most serious criminal acts.

Quite a bit of attention has been paid to the age–crime relationship. There is general agreement that delinquency rates decline with age. Some experts believe this phenomenon is universal, while others believe that a small group of offenders persist in crime at a high rate.

The age–crime relationship has spurred research on the nature of delinquency over the life course. One discovery is that of the chronic persistent offender, who begins his or her offending career early in life and persists as an adult. The Gluecks first identified the traits of persistent offenders. Wolfgang and his colleagues identified chronic offenders in a series of cohort studies conducted in Philadelphia. Ongoing research has identified the characteristics of persistent offenders as they mature. There seem to be both personality and social factors that predict long-term offending patterns.

KEY TERMS

official data
self-report data
dark figures of crime
victim data
victim surveys
National Crime Victimization Survey (NCVS)
Federal Bureau of Investigation (FBI)
index crimes
Part I offenses
Part II offenses

disaggregated
hate crimes
cross-sectional data
victimizations
chronic
aging out
desistance
spontaneous remission
age of onset
life course

longitudinal studies
delinquent careers
chronic delinquent offender
chronic recidivists
serious career offender type
life cycle of crime
latent trait
pathways
problem behavior syndrome (PBS)

QUESTIONS FOR DISCUSSION

1. What factors contribute to the aging-out process?
2. Why are males more delinquent than females? Is it a matter of lifestyle, culture, or physical properties?
3. Discuss the racial differences found in the crime rate. What factors account for the differences in the African-American and white crime rates?
4. Discuss the controversy surrounding the role social class plays in delinquency. Do you believe that middle-class youths are as delinquent as lower-class youths?

NOTES

1. Howard Snyder and Melissa Sickmund, *Juvenile Offenders and Victims: A National Report* (Washington, D.C.: National Center for Juvenile Justice, 1995).
2. The most commonly used statistics are the Federal Bureau of Investigation's annual compilation of crime data, referred to as the *Uniform Crime Reports*. The latest volume at the time of this writing is *Crime in the United States: Uniform Crime Reports, 1994* (Washington, D.C.: U.S. Government Printing Office, 1995).
3. Bureau of Justice Statistics, *Criminal Victimization in the United States, 1993* (Washington, D.C.: Bureau of Justice Statistics, 1995).
4. FBI News Release, May 5, 1996.
5. Ibid., p. 5.
6. Federal Bureau of Investigation, *Crime in the United States: Uniform Crime Reports, 1994*, p. 227.
7. All population statistics used in this chapter are from U.S. Bureau of Census, Unpublished data, 1994 (Washington, D.C.: U.S. Department of Census, 1995).
8. Alfred Blumstein, "Violence by Young People: Why the Deadly Nexus," *National Institute of Justice Journal* 229:2–9 (1995).
9. Jack Levin and Jack McDevitt, *Hate Crimes: The Rising Tide of Bigotry and Bloodshed* (New York: Plenum,

1993); personal communication, April 4, 1993, Estimate of hate crimes based on personal communication with Jack McDevitt.

10. Richard Ball and G. David Curry, "The Influence of Adult Extremist Organizations on Juvenile Hate Crime," Paper presented at the American Society of Criminology meeting, Boston, Mass., November 1995.

11. James Alan Fox, *Teenage Males Are Committing Murder at an Increasing Rate* (Boston: Northeastern University, 1992).

12. Scott Decker and Susan Pennell, *Arrestees and Guns: Monitoring the Illegal Firearms Market* (Washington, D.C.: National Institute of Justice, 1995).

13. G. David Curry, Richard Ball, and Scott Decker, "Estimating the National Scope of Gang Crime from Law Enforcement Data," in C. Ronald Huff, ed., *Gangs in America*, 2nd ed. (Newbury Park, Calif.: Sage, 1996).

14. Fox, *Teenage Males Are Committing Murder at an Increasing Rate,* p. 3.

15. Decker and Pennell, *Arrestees and Guns: Monitoring the Illegal Firearms Market.*

16. Snyder and Sickmund, *Juvenile Offenders and Victims: A National Report,* p. 10.

17. National Research Council, *Common Destiny: Blacks and American Society* (Washington, D.C.: National Research Council, 1989).

18. William Julius Wilson, "Studying Inner-City Social Dislocations: The Challenge of Public Agenda Research," *American Sociological Review* 56:1–14 (1991).

19. Blumstein, "Violence by Young People: Why the Deadly Nexus," pp. 2–3.

20. Drug Use Forecasting Update, 1991 (Washington, D.C.: National Institute of Justice, 1992).

21. Blumstein, "Violence by Young People: Why the Deadly Nexus," p. 6.

22. Kathleen Heide, "Why Kids Keep Killing: The Correlates, Causes and Challenges of Juvenile Homicide," Paper presented at the American Society of Criminology meeting, Boston, Mass., November 1995.

23. For the most complete review, see Michael Hindelang, Travis Hirschi, and Joseph Weis, *Measuring Delinquency* (Beverly Hills, Calif.: Sage, 1981).

24. Walter Gove, Michael Hughes, and Michael Geerken, "Are Uniform Crime Reports a Valid Indicator of the Index Crimes? An Affirmative Answer with Minor Qualifications," *Criminology* 23:451–501 (1985); Michael Hindelang, Travis Hirschi, and Joseph Weis, "Correlates of Delinquency: The Illusion of Discrepancy between Self-Report and Official Data," *American Sociological Review* 44:995–1014 (1979).

25. Roger Hood and Richard Sparks, *Key Issues in Criminology* (New York: McGraw-Hill, 1970), p. 72.

26. A pioneering effort of self-report research is A. L. Porterfield's *Youth in Trouble* (Fort Worth, Tex.: Leo Potishman Foundation, 1946). For a review, see Robert Hardt and George Bodine, *Development of Self-Report Instruments in Delinquency Research: A Conference Report* (Syracuse, N.Y.: Syracuse University Youth Development Center, 1965). See also Fred Murphy, Mary Shirley, and Helen Witmer, "The Incidence of Hidden Delinquency," *American Journal of Orthopsychiatry* 16:686–96 (1946).

27. For example, the following studies have noted the great discrepancy between official statistics and self-report studies: Maynard Erickson and LaMar Empey, "Court Records, Undetected Delinquency, and Decision Making," *Journal of Criminal Law, Criminology, and Police Science* 54:456–69 (1963); Martin Gold, "Undetected Delinquent Behavior," *Journal of Research in Crime and Delinquency* 3:27–46 (1966); James Short and F. Ivan Nye, "Extent of Unrecorded Delinquency, Tentative Conclusions," *Journal of Criminal Law, Criminology, and Police Science* 49:296–302 (1958).

28. In addition to the studies listed above, see David Farrington, "Self-Reports of Deviant Behavior: Predictive and Stable?" *Journal of Criminal Law and Criminology* 64:99–110 (1973); Michael Hindelang, "Causes of Delinquency: A Partial Replication and Extension," *Social Problems* 20:471–87 (1973).

29. Jerald Bachman, Lloyd Johnston, and Patrick O'Malley, *Monitoring the Future: Questionnaire Responses from the Nation's High School Seniors, 1995* (Ann Arbor, Mich.: Institute for Social Research, 1996), pp. 102–4.

30. D. Wayne Osgood, Patrick O'Malley, Jerald Bachman, and Lloyd Johnston, "Time Trends and Age Trends in Arrests and Self-Reported Illegal Behavior," *Criminology* 27:389–417 (1989).

31. Rosemary Sarri, "Gender Issues in Juvenile Justice," *Crime and Delinquency* 29:381–97 (1983).

32. Erickson and Empey, "Court Records, Undetected Delinquency, and Decision Making"; H. B. Gibson, Sylvia Morrison, and D. J. West, "The Confession of Known Offenses in Response to a Self-Reported Delinquency Schedule," *British Journal of Criminology* 10:277–80 (1970); John Blackmore, "The Relationship between Self-Reported Delinquency and Official Convictions amongst Adolescent Boys," *British Journal of Criminology* 14:172–76 (1974).

33. Farrington, "Self-Reports of Deviant Behavior: Predictive and Stable?"

34. Gold, "Undetected Delinquent Behavior."

35. Farrington, "Self-Reports of Deviant Behavior: Predictive and Stable?"; F. Ivan Nye and James Short, "Scaling Delinquent Behavior," *American Sociology Review* 22:326–31 (1957).

36. John Clark and Larry Tifft, "Polygraph and Interview Validation of Self-Reported Deviant Behavior," *American Sociological Review* 31:516–23 (1966).

37. Hindelang, Hirschi, and Weis, *Measuring Delinquency.*

38. Ibid., p. 114.

39. Douglas Smith and Laura Davidson, "Interfacing Indicators and Constructs in Criminological Research: A Note on the Comparability of Self-Report and Violence Data for Race and Sex Groups," *Criminology* 24:473–87 (1986); Robert Sampson, "Sex Differences in Self-Reported Delinquency and Official Records: A Multiple Group Structural Modeling Approach," *Journal of Quantitative Criminology* 23:345–68 (1985).

40. Leonore Simon, "Validity and Reliability of Violent Juveniles: A Comparison of Juvenile Self-Reports with Adult Self-Reports Incarcerated in Adult Prisons," Paper presented at the American Society of Criminology meeting, Boston, Mass., November 1995, p. 26.

41. Stephen Cernkovich, Peggy Giordano, and Meredith Pugh, "Chronic Offenders: The Missing Cases in Self-Report Delinquency Research," *Journal of Criminal Law and Criminology* 76:705–32 (1985).

42. Ibid., p. 706.

43. Patrick Jackson, "Assessing the Validity of Official Data on Arson," *Criminology* 26:181–95 (1988); for an early criticism of official data, see Ronald Beattie, "Criminal Statistics in the United States," *Journal of Criminal Law, Criminology, and Police Science* 51:49–53 (1960).

44. Linda Bastian, *Criminal Victimization, 1991* (Washington, D.C.: Bureau of Justice Statistics, 1992).

45. Ibid.

46. Ted Miller, Mark Cohen, and Brian Wiersema, *The Extent and Costs of Crime Victimization: A New Look* (Washington, D.C.: National Institute of Justice, 1995).

47. Joan Johnson, *Criminal Victimization in the United States* (Washington, D.C.: Bureau of Justice Statistics, 1992).

48. Randy LaGrange and Kenneth Ferraro, "Assessing Age and Gender Differences in Perceived Risk and Fear of Crime," *Criminology* 27:697–719 (1989).

49. Gerald Hotaling and David Finkelhor, "Estimating the Number of Stranger Abduction Homicides of Children: A Review of Available Evidence," *Journal of Criminal Justice* 18:385–99 (1990).

50. Herbert Koppel, *Lifetime Likelihood of Victimization* (Washington, D.C.: Bureau of Justice Statistics, Technical Report, 1987).

51. Lawrence Greenfeld, *Child Victimizers: Violent Offenders and Their Victims* (Washington, D.C.: Bureau of Justice Statistics, 1996).

52. L. Edward Wells and Joseph Rankin, "Juvenile Victimization: Convergent Validation of Alternative Measurements," *Journal of Research in Crime and Delinquency* Vol. 32:287–301 (1995): 301–304.

53. For a discussion of sex bias, see Meda Chesney-Lind, "Guilty by Reason of Sex: Young Women and the Criminal Justice System," Paper presented before the American Society of Criminology, Toronto, Canada, 1980.

54. David Farrington, "Juvenile Delinquency," in John Coleman, *The School Years* (London: Routledge, 1992), p. 132.

55. Michael Hindelang, Travis Hirschi, and Joseph Weis, *Measuring Delinquency* (Beverly Hills, Calif.: Sage, 1981); Gary Jensen and Raymond Eve, "Sex Differences in Delinquency: An Examination of Popular Sociological Explanation," *Criminology* 13:427–48 (1976); Michael Hindelang, "Age, Sex, and the Versatility of Delinquent Involvements," *Social Problems* 18:522–35 (1979); James Short and F. Ivan Nye, "Extent of Unrecorded Juvenile Delinquency, Tentative Conclusions," *Journal of Criminal Law, Criminology, and Police Science* 49:296–302 (1958).

56. Rosemary Sarri, "Gender Issues in Juvenile Justice," *Crime and Delinquency* 29:381–97 (1983).

57. For a review, see Meda Chesney-Lind and Randall Shelden, *Girls, Delinquency and Juvenile Justice* (Pacific Grove, Calif.: Brooks/Cole, 1992), pp. 7–14.

58. Samuel Walker, Cassia Spohn, and Miriam DeLone, *The Color of Justice* (Belmont, Calif.: Wadsworth, 1996), p. 229.

59. Leroy Gould, "Who Defines Delinquency? A Comparison of Self-Report and Officially-Reported Indices of Delinquency for Three Racial Groups," *Social Problems* 16:325–36 (1969); Harwin Voss, "Ethnic Differentials in Delinquency in Honolulu," *Journal of Criminal Law, Criminology, and Police Science* 54:322–27 (1963); Ronald Akers, Marvin Krohn, Marcia Radosevich, and Lonn Lanza-Kaduce, "Social Characteristics and Self-Reported Delinquency," in Gary Jensen, ed., *Sociology of Delinquency* (Beverly Hills, Calif.: Sage, 1981), pp. 48–62.

60. David Huizinga and Delbert Elliott, "Juvenile Offenders: Prevalence, Offender Incidence, and Arrest Rates by Race," *Crime and Delinquency* 33:206–23 (1987); Dale Dannefer and Russell Schutt, "Race and Juvenile Justice Processing in Court and Police Agencies," *American Journal of Sociology* 87:1113–32 (1982).

61. Paul Tracy, "Race and Class Differences in Official and Self-Reported Delinquency," in Marvin Wolfgang, Terrence Thornberry, and Robert Figlio, eds., *From Boy to Man, from Delinquency to Crime* (Chicago: University of Chicago Press, 1987), p. 120.

62. Bachman, Johnston, and O'Malley, *Monitoring the Future: Questionnaire Responses from the Nation's High School Seniors, 1995.*

63. Walker, Spohn, and DeLone, *The Color of Justice,* pp. 46–47.

64. Christina Polsenberg and Kenneth Jackson, "Putting Race Into Context: Race, Juvenile Justice Processing and Urbanization," Paper presented at the American Society of Criminology meeting, Boston, Mass., November 1995 (updated version, 1996). For a general review, see Carl Pope and William Feyerherm, "Minority Status and Juvenile Justice Processing (Part I)," *Criminal Justice Abstracts* 22:327–35 (1990); see also Douglas Smith and Jody Klein, "Police Control of Interpersonal Disputes," *Social Problems* 31:468–81 (1984).

65. Donna Bishop and Charles Frazier, "The Influence of Race in Juvenile Justice Processing," *Journal of Research in Crime and Delinquency* 25:242–63 (1989).

66. For a general review, see William Wilbanks, *The Myth of a Racist Criminal Justice System* (Monterey, Calif.: Brooks/Cole, 1987).

67. Walker, Spohn, and DeLone, *The Color of Justice,* pp. 47–48.

68. Daniel Georges-Abeyie, cited in James Byrne and Robert Sampson, *The Social Ecology of Crime* (New York: Springer-Verlag, 1986), p. 99.

69. Tom Joe, "Economic Inequality: The Picture in Black and White," *Crime and Delinquency* 33:287–99 (1987).

70. Troy Duster, "Crime, Youth Unemployment, and the Black Urban Underclass," *Crime and Delinquency* 33:300–16 (1987); Joe, "Economic Inequality: The Picture in Black and White."

71. Duster, "Crime, Youth Unemployment, and the Black Urban Underclass," pp. 301–03.

72. Joan McCord and Margaret Ensminger, "Pathways from Aggressive Childhood to Criminality," Paper presented at the American Society of Criminology meeting, Boston, Mass., November 1995.

73. Carl Pope and William Feyerherm, "Minority Status and Juvenile Processing: An Assessment of the Research Literature," (Paper presented at the American Society of Criminology, Reno, Nev., November 1989).

74. Jefferey Fagan, Elizabeth Piper, and Melinda Moore, "Violent Delinquents and Urban Youths," *Criminology* 24:439–71 (1986).

75. Robert Nash Parker and Allan Horwitz, "Unemployment, Crime, and Imprisonment: A Panel Approach," *Criminology* 24:751–73 (1986).

76. For a general review of these issues, see James Byrne and Robert Sampson, *The Social Ecology of Crime* (New York: Springer-Verlag, 1986).

77. John Braithwaite, "The Myth of Social Class and Criminality Reconsidered," *American Sociological Review* 46:36–57 (1981).

78. James Short and Ivan Nye, "Reported Behavior as a Criterion of Deviant Behavior," *Social Problems* 5:207–13 (1958).

79. Ivan Nye, James Short, and Virgil Olsen, "Socio-economic Status and Delinquent Behavior," *American Journal of Sociology* 63:381–89 (1958); Robert Dentler and Lawrence Monroe, "Social Correlates of Early Adolescent Theft," *American Sociological Review* 26:733–43 (1961); John Clark and Eugene Wenninger, "Socio-economic Class and Areas as Correlates of Illegal Behavior among Juveniles," *American Sociological Review* 27:826–34 (1962); William Arnold, "Continuities in Research: Scaling Delinquent Behavior," *Social Problems* 13:59–66 (1965); LaMar Empey and Maynard Erickson, "Hidden Delinquency and Social Status," *Social Forces* 44:1546–54 (1966); Ronald Akers, "Socio-economic Status and Delinquent Behavior: A Retest," *Journal of Research in Crime and Delinquency* 1:38–46 (1964); Voss, "Ethnic Differentials in Delinquency in Honolulu."

80. Gold, "Undetected Delinquent Behavior," pp. 3:35–41 (1966); Jay Williams and Martin Gold, "From Delinquent Behavior to Official Delinquency," *Social Problems* 20:209–29 (1972).

81. Charles Tittle, Wayne Villemez, and Douglas Smith, "The Myth of Social Class and Criminality: An Empirical Assessment of the Empirical Evidence," *American Sociological Review* 43:643–56 (1978).

82. Charles Tittle and Robert Meier, "Specifying the SES/Delinquency Relationship by Social Characteristics of Contexts," *Journal of Research in Crime and Delinquency* 28:430–55 (1991); idem, "Specifying the SES/Delinquency Relationship," *Criminology* 28:271–99 (1990).

83. For supporting research, see Gary Jensen and Kevin Thompson, "What's Class Got to Do with It? A Further Examination of Power-Control Theory," *American Journal of Sociology* 95:1009–23 (1990); Paul Tracy, "Race and Class Differences in Official and Self-Reported Delinquency," in Marvin Wolfgang, Terrence Thornberry, and Robert Figlio, eds., *From Boy to Man, from Delinquency to Crime* (Chicago: University of Chicago Press, 1987), p. 118.

84. See, for example, David Decker, David Shichor, and Robert O'Brien, *Urban Structure and Victimization* (Lexington, Mass.: Lexington Books, 1982).

85. Delbert Eliott and Suzanne Ageton, "Reconciling Race and Class Differences in Self-Reported and Official Estimates of Delinquency," *American Sociological Review* 45:95–110 (1980). For a similar view, see John Braithwaite, "The Myth of Social Class and Criminality Reconsidered," *American Sociological Review* 46:35–58 (1981).

86. Margaret Farnworth, Terence Thornberry, Marvin Krohn, and Alan Lizotte, *Measurement in the Study of Class and Delinquency: Integrating Theory and Research,* working paper no. 4, rev. (Albany, N.Y.: Rochester Youth Development Survey, 1992), p. 19.

87. Simon Singer and Susyan Jou, "Specifying the SES/Delinquency Relationship by Subjective and Objective Indicators of Parental and Youth Social Status," Paper presented at the annual meeting of the American Society of Criminology, New Orleans, La., November 1992; David Brownfield, "Social Class and Violent Behavior," *Criminology* 24:421–38 (1986).

88. Margaret Farnworth, Terence Thornberry, Marvin Krohn, and Alan Lizotte, "Measurement in the Study of Class and Delinquency: Integrating Theory and Research," *Journal of Research in Crime and Delinquency* 31:32–61 (1994).

89. Barbara Warner and Glenn Pierce, "Reexamining Social Disorganization Theory Using Calls to the Police as a Measure of Crime," *Criminology* 31:493–517 (1993).

90. See, generally, David Farrington, "Age and Crime," in Michael Tonry and Norval Morris, eds., *Crime and Justice, An Annual Review,* vol. 7 (Chicago: University of Chicago Press, 1986), pp. 189–250.

91. Patrick O'Malley, Jerald Bachman, and Lloyd Johnston, "Period, Age and Cohort Effects on Substance Abuse among Young Americans: A Decade of Change, 1976–1986," *American Journal of Public Health* 78:1315–21 (1989); Darrell Steffensmeier, Emilie Allan, Miles Harer, and Cathy Streifel, "Age and the Distribution of Crime," *American Journal of Sociology* 94:803–31 (1989); Alfred Blumstein and Jacqueline Cohen, "Characterizing Criminal Careers," *Science* 237:985–91 (1987).

92. Bureau of Justice Statistics, *Criminal Victimization in the United States, 1993* (Washington, D.C.: Bureau of Justice Statistics, 1995).

93. Travis Hirschi and Michael Gottfredson, "Age and the Explanation of Crime," *American Journal of Sociology* 89:552–84 (1983).

94. Michael Gottfredson and Travis Hirschi, "The True Value of Lambda Would Appear to Be Zero: An Essay on Career Criminals, Criminal Careers, Selective Incapacitation, Cohort Studies, and Related Topics," *Criminology* 24:213–34 (1986); further support for their position can be found in Lawrence Cohen and Kenneth Land, "Age Structure and Crime," *American Sociological Review* 52:170–83 (1987).

95. David Greenberg, "Age, Crime and Social Explanation," *American Journal of Sociology* 91:1–21 (1985).

96. Robert Sampson and John Laub, *Crime in the Making: Pathways and Turning Points through Life* (Cambridge, Mass.: Harvard University Press, 1993).

97. Farrington, "Age and Crime," pp. 236–37.

98. Marvin Wolfgang, Robert Figlio, and Thorsten Sellin, *Delinquency in a Birth Cohort* (Chicago: University of Chicago Press, 1972); Lyle Shannon, *Assessing the Relationship of Adult Criminal Careers to Juvenile Careers: A Summary* (Washington, D.C.: U.S. Department of Justice, 1982); D. J. West and David P. Farrington, *The Delinquent Way of Life* (London: Heinemann, 1977); Donna Hamparian, Richard Schuster, Simon Dinitz, and John Conrad, *The Violent Few* (Lexington, Mass.: Lexington Books, 1978).

99. Rolf Loeber and Howard Snyder, "Rate of Offending in Juvenile Careers: Findings of Constancy and Change in Lambda," *Criminology* 28:97–109 (1990).

100. Travis Hirschi and Michael Gottfredson, "Age and Crime, Logic and Scholarship: Comment on Greenberg," *American Journal of Sociology* 91:22–27 (1985); idem, "All Wise after the Fact," Learning Theory, Again: Reply to Baldwin," *American Journal of Sociology* 90:1330–33 (1985); John Baldwin, "Thrill and Adventure Seeking and the Age Distribution of Crime: Comment on Hirschi and Gottfredson," *American Journal of Sociology* 90:1326–29 (1985).

101. O'Malley, Bachman, and Johnston, "Period, Age, and Cohort Effects on Substance Use among Young Americans."

102. Alicia Rand, "Transitional Life Events and Desistance from Delinquency and Crime," in Marvin Wolfgang, Terence Thornberry, and Robert Figlio, eds., *From Boy to Man, from Delinquency to Crime* (Chicago: University of Chicago Press, 1987), pp. 134–63.

103. Marc Le Blanc, "Late Adolescence Deceleration of Criminal Activity and Development of Self- and Social-Control," *Studies on Crime and Crime Prevention* 2:51–68 (1993).

104. Barry Glassner, Margaret Ksander, Bruce Berg, and Bruce Johnson, "A Note on the Deterrent Effect of Juvenile vs. Adult Jurisdiction," *Social Problems* 31:219–21 (1983), at p. 219.

105. Neal Shover and Carol Thompson, "Age, Differential Expectations, and Crime Desistance," *Criminology* 30:89–104 (1992).

106. D. Wayne Osgood, "The Covariation among Adolescent Problem Behaviors," Paper presented at the annual meeting of the American Society of Criminology, Baltimore, Md., November 1990.

107. Stephen Tibbetts, "Low Birth Weight, Disadvantaged Environment and Early Onset: A Test of Moffitt's Interactional Hypothesis," Paper presented at the American Society of Criminology meeting, Boston, Mass., November 1995.

108. For a review of the Gluecks' careers, see John Laub and Robert Sampson, "The Sutherland–Glueck Debate: On the Sociology of Criminological Knowledge," *American Journal of Sociology* 96:1402–40 (1991).

109. See, for example, Sheldon Glueck and Eleanor Glueck, *500 Criminal Careers* (New York: Knopf, 1930); idem, *One Thousand Juvenile Delinquents* (Cambridge, Mass.: Harvard University Press, 1934); idem, *Unraveling Juvenile Delinquency* (Cambridge, Mass.: Harvard University Press, 1950).

110. Sheldon Glueck and Eleanor Glueck, *Predicting Delinquency and Crime* (Cambridge, Mass.: Harvard University Press, 1967), pp. 82–83.

111. David Rowe and Daniel Flannery, "An Examination of Environmental and Trait Influences on Adolescent Delinquency," *Journal of Research in Crime and Delinquency* 31:374–89 (1994); John Laub and Robert Sampson, "Unraveling Families and Delinquency: A Reanalysis of the Gluecks' Data," *Criminology* 26:355–80 (1988).

112. Arnold Barnett, Alfred Blumstein, and David Farrington, "A Prospective Test of a Criminal Career Model," *Criminology* 27:373–88 (1989).

113. Marvin Wolfgang, Robert Figlio, and Thorsten Sellin, *Delinquency in a Birth Cohort* (Chicago: University of Chicago Press, 1972).

114. Marvin Wolfgang, Terence Thornberry, and Robert Figlio, eds., *From Boy to Man, from Delinquency to*

Crime (Chicago: University of Chicago Press, 1987); Paul Tracy and Robert Figlio, "Chronic Recidivism in the 1958 Birth Cohort," Paper presented at the American Society of Criminology meeting, Toronto, Canada, October 1982, p. 3. This and the next sections lean heavily on this work.

115. Wolfgang, Thornberry & Figlio, *From Boy to Man*, p. 34.

116. Paul Tracy, Marvin Wolfgang, and Robert Figlio, *Delinquency in Two Birth Cohorts, Executive Summary* (Washington, D.C.: U.S. Department of Justice, 1985).

117. See also D. J. West and David P. Farrington, *The Delinquent Way of Life* (London: Heinemann, 1977), p. 15; and Donna Hamparian, Richard Schuster, Simon Dinitz, and John Conrad, *The Violent Few* (Lexington, Mass.: Lexington Books, 1978).

118. Shannon, *Assessing the Relationship of Adult Criminal Careers to Juvenile Careers: A Summary.*

119. Howard Snyder, *Court Careers of Juvenile Offenders* (Washington, D.C.: Office of Juvenile Justice and Delinquency Prevention, 1988).

120. Franklyn Dunford and Delbert Elliott, "Identifying Career Offenders Using Self-Reported Data," *Journal of Research in Crime and Delinquency* 21:57–86 (1984).

121. Robert Sampson and John Laub, "Crime and Deviance in the Life Course," *American Review of Sociology* 18:63–84 (1992).

122. Farnworth, Thornberry, Krohn, and Lizotte, "Measurement in the Study of Class and Delinquency: Integrating Theory and Research."

123. Joan McCord, "Family Relationships, Juvenile Delinquency, and Adult Criminality," *Criminology* 29:397–417 (1991).

124. Daniel Nagin and David Farrington, "The Onset and Persistence of Offending," *Criminology* 30:501–23 (1992).

125. David Rowe and Chester Britt, III, "Developmental Explanations of Delinquent Behavior among Siblings: Common Factor vs. Transmission Mechanisms," *Journal of Quantitative Criminology* 7:315–31 (1991).

126. Terrie Moffitt, "Adolescence-Limited and Life-Course Persistent Antisocial Behavior: A Developmental Taxonomy," *Psychological Review* 100:674–701 (1993).

127. Michael Gottfredson and Travis Hirschi, *A General Theory of Crime* (Stanford, Calif.: Stanford University Press, 1990).

128. Richard Jessor, "Risk Behavior in Adolescence: A Psychosocial Framework for Understanding and Action," in D. E. Rogers and E. Ginzburg, eds., *Adolescents at Risk: Medical and Social Perspectives* (Boulder, Colo.: Westview, 1992).

129. Rolf Loeber, Phen Wung, Kate Keenan, Bruce Giroux, Magda Stouthamer-Loeber, Wemoet Van Kammen, and Barbara Maughan, "Developmental Pathways in Disruptive Child Behavior," *Development and Psychopathology* 5:103–133 (1993).

130. Michael Maxfield and Cathy Spatz Widom, "Childhood Victimization and Patterns of Offending through the Life Cycle: Early Onset and Continuation," Paper presented at the American Society of Criminology meeting, Boston, Mass., November 1995; Richard Jessor, John Donovan, and Francis Costa, *Beyond Adolescence: Problem Behavior and Young Adult Development* (New York: Cambridge University Press, 1991).

131. D. Wayne Osgood, "The Covariation among Adolescent Problem Behaviors," Paper presented at the annual meeting of the American Society of Criminology, Baltimore, Md., November 1990.

132. Paul Greenbaum, Lynn Foster-Johnson, and Amelia Petrila, "Co-Occurring Addictive and Mental Disorders among Adolescents: Prevalence Research and Future Directions," *American Journal of Orthopsychiatry* 66:52–60 (1996).

133. Magda Stouthamer-Loeber and Evelyn Wei, "The Precursors of Young Fatherhood and Its Effect on the Delinquency and Prosocial Careers of Teenage Males," Paper presented at the American Society of Criminology meeting, Boston, Mass., November 1995; for a similar result, see David Rowe, Alexander Vazsonyi, and Aurelio Jose Figueredo, "Mating Effort in Adolescence: Conditional or Alternative Strategy," Paper presented at the American Society of Criminology meeting, Boston, Mass., November 1995.

134. Helene Raskin White, "Early Problem Behavior and Later Drug Problems," *Journal of Research in Crime and Delinquency* 29:412–29 (1992).

135. David Farrington and Rolf Loeber, "Transatlantic Replicability of Risk Factors in the Development of Delinquency," Paper presented at the American Society of Criminology meeting, Boston, Mass., November 1995.

136. For a review, see Tina Mawhorr, "Social Skill Deficits and Juvenile Delinquency: Are Delinquents Really Social Misfits?," Paper presented at the American Society of Criminology meeting, Boston, Mass., November 1995.

137. Richard Dembo, Glenn Turner, James Schmeidler, Camille Chin Sue, Polly Borden, and Darrell Manning, "Development and Evaluation of a Classification of High Risk Youths Entering a Juvenile Assessment Center," *Substance Abuse and Misuse* 31:303–22 (1996).

138. Robert Bursik, "The Dynamics of Specialization in Juvenile Offenses," *Social Forces* 58:851–64 (1980).

139. Randall Shelden, "The Chronic Delinquent: Some Clarifications of a Vague Concept," *Juvenile and Family Court Journal* 40:37–44 (1989).

140. David Farrington, Howard Snyder, and Terence Finnegan, "Specialization in Juvenile Court Careers," *Criminology* 26:461–85 (1988).

141. Ibid.

142. Thomas Dishion and David Andrews, "Preventing Escalation in Problem Behaviors with High-Risk Young Adolescents: Immediate and 1-Year Outcomes," *Journal of Consulting and Clinical Psychology* 63:538–48 (1995).

143. See, for example, the Rochester Youth Development Study, Hindelang Criminal Justice Research Center, 135 Western Avenue, Albany, NY 12222.

144. David Farrington, "The Development of Offending and Antisocial Behavior from Childhood to Adulthood," Paper presented at the Congress on Rethinking Delinquency, University of Minho, Braga, Portugal, July 1992.

145. See, generally, West and Farrington, *The Delinquent Way of Life;* the findings here are reported in Farrington, "The Development of Offending and Antisocial Behavior from Childhood to Adulthood."

146. Sampson and Laub, *Crime in the Making: Pathways and Turning Points through Life.*

147. Kimberly Kempf, "Crime Severity and Criminal Career Progression," *Journal of Criminal Law and Criminology* 79:524–40 (1988).

148. Jeffrey Fagan, "Social and Legal Policy Dimensions of Violent Juvenile Crime," *Criminal Justice and Behavior* 17:93–133 (1990).

149. Peter Greenwood, *Selective Incapacitation* (Santa Monica, Calif.: Rand Corp., 1982).

150. Terence Thornberry, David Huizinga, and Rolf Loeber, "The Prevention of Serious Delinquency and Violence," in James Howell, Barry Krisberg, J. David Hawkins, and John Wilson, eds., *Sourcebook on Serious, Violent, and Chronic Juvenile Offenders* (Thousand Oaks, Calif.: Sage Publications, 1995).

151. Andrew Von Hirsch and Donald Gottfredson, "Selective Incapacitation: Some Queries about Research Design and Equity," *New York University Review of Law and Social Change* 12:11–19 (1984).

152. Scott Decker and Barbara Salert, "Predicting the Career Criminal: An Empirical Test of the Greenwood Scale," *Journal of Criminal Law and Criminology* 77:215–36 (1986).

153. Pamela Tontodonato, "Explaining Rate Changes in Delinquent Arrest Transitions Using Event History Analysis," *Criminology* 26:439–59 (1988).

154. Kimberly Kempf, "Career Criminals in the 1958 Philadelphia Birth Cohort," *Criminal Justice Review* 15:212–35 (1990).

PART TWO

THEORIES OF DELINQUENCY

What causes delinquent behavior? Why do some youths enter a life of crime that persists into their adulthood? Are people products of their environment, or is the likelihood of their becoming a delinquent determined at birth?

Social scientists have speculated on the cause of delinquency for two hundred years. They have organized observed facts about delinquent behavior into complex theoretical models. A theory is a statement that explains the relationship between abstract concepts in a meaningful way. For example, if scientists observe that delinquency rates are usually higher in neighborhoods with high unemployment rates, poor housing, and inadequate schools, they might theorize that environmental conditions influence delinquent behavior. This theory suggest that social conditions can exert a powerful influence on human behavior.

Because the study of delinquency is essentially interdisciplinary, it is not surprising that a variety of theoretical models have been formulated to explain juvenile misbehavior. Each reflects the training and orientation of its creator. Consequently, theories of delinquency reflect many different avenues of inquiry, including biology, psychology, sociology, political science, and economics. Chapter 3 reviews theories that hold that delinquency is essentially an individual factor, caused either by personal choices and decision making or by psychological and biological aspects of human development. Chapters 4, 5, and 6 review sociological theories of delinquency. Chapter 4 reviews those theories that hold that youthful misbehavior is caused by a child's place in the social structure; Chapter 5 covers theories that regard the child's relationships with social institutions and processes as the key to understanding delinquency. Chapter 6 views how delinquents may be the victim of either social labeling or social conflict.

To the student, the variety of delinquency theories is often confusing. Logic dictates that the competing and contradictory theoretical models presented here cannot all be correct. Yet every branch of the social sciences—sociology, psychology, political science, economics—contains competing theoretical models. Why people behave the way they do and how society functions are issues that are far from being settled. So do not lose patience! Recognize that theories of delinquency are attempts to bring together existing knowledge in an attempt to explain the onset and patterns of delinquent behavior. These explanations take on different perspectives because it is possible to view the world and to explain similar facts and data differently. The variation in delinquency theories reflects their creators' interpretations of the world of events.

CHAPTER THREE

FOCUS ON THE INDIVIDUAL: CHOICE AND TRAIT THEORIES

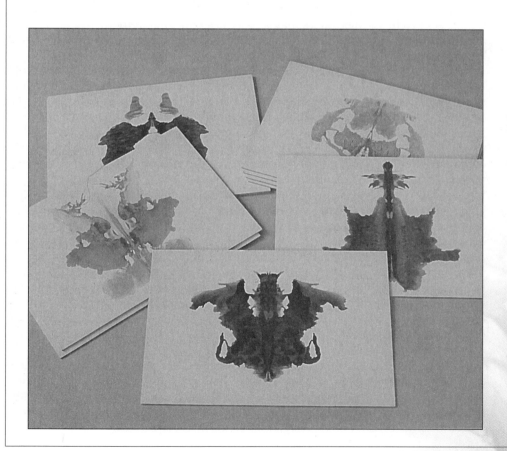

INTRODUCTION

The dynamic center of the whole problem of delinquency and crime will ever be the individual offender.

William Healy

The Individual Delinquent (1915)

If delinquents are a "product of their environment," as some experts suggest, how is it possible that many at-risk youths residing in the most dangerous inner-city neighborhoods live conventional, law-abiding lives? Conversely, why are so many suburban middle-class youth involved in delinquency and substance abuse? Research on persistent offending indicates that relatively few youths in any population become hard-core delinquents.[1] The quality of neighborhood and family life may actually have little impact on individual behavior through the life cycle.[2] To some theorists, the locus of delinquency is rooted in the *individual:* his or her decision-making ability, biological makeup, personality, and psychological profile.

There is more than one explanation of why individuals become crime prone. One position, referred to here generally as **choice theory,** suggests that young offenders engage in antisocial activity because they believe their actions will be beneficial and profitable. Whether they join a gang, steal cars, or sell drugs, their delinquent acts are motivated by the reasoned belief that crime can be a relatively risk-free way to better their personal situation. They have little fear of getting caught or of the consequences of punishment. Some are motivated by fantasies of riches while others may simply enjoy the excitement and short-term gratification produced by criminal acts (e.g., beating up an opponent or "getting high").

All youthful misbehavior, however, cannot be traced to rational choice, profit motive, and criminal entrepreneurship. Some delinquent acts, especially violent ones, seem irrational, selfish, and/or hedonistic. Many forms of delinquency, such as substance abuse and vandalism, appear more impulsive than rational. It is believed that these antisocial behaviors may be inspired by aberrant physical or psychological traits that govern behavioral choices. Although some youths may choose to commit crime simply because they desire conventional luxuries and power, others may be influenced by constitutional abnormalities, such as hyperactivity, low intelligence, biochemical imbalance, or genetic defects. This view of delinquency is referred to here generally as **trait theory** because it links delinquency to biological and psychological traits and environmental conditions that control human development.

Choice and trait theories share common ground because they focus on the individual's mental and behavioral processes. Those who advocate this set of theories recognize that everyone is different—thus everyone reacts to the same set of environmental and social conditions in a unique fashion. Faced with extreme stress and economic hardship, one person will seek employment, borrow money, save for the future, and live a law-abiding life; another will use antisocial or violent behavior to satisfy needs.

This chapter first covers those theoretical models that focus on individual choice. Then it discusses the view that the biological and psychological development of some youngsters makes them violent, aggressive, and antisocial. Finally, it analyzes an attempt to integrate individual choice and trait factors into a singular view of delinquent behavior causation.

CHOICE THEORY

The first formal explanations of crime and delinquency held that human behavior was a matter of choice. Because it was assumed that people had **free will** to choose their behavior, those who violated the law were motivated by personal needs: greed, revenge, survival, hedonism. More than 200 years ago, **utilitarian** philosophers Cesare Beccaria and Jeremy Bentham argued that people weigh the benefits and consequences of their future actions before deciding on a course of behavior.[3] Their writings formed the core of what is today referred to as **classical criminology.**

The classical view of crime and delinquency holds that the decision to violate the law comes after a careful weighing of the benefits and costs of criminal behaviors. Most potential law violators would cease their actions if the potential pain associated with a behavior outweighed its anticipated gain; conversely, law-violating behavior becomes attractive if the future rewards seem far greater than the potential punishment.[4]

According to the classical view, youths who decide to become drug dealers weigh and compare the possible benefits, such as cash to buy cars, clothes, and other luxury items, with the potential penalties, such as arrest followed by a long stay in a juvenile facility. If they believe that drug dealers are rarely caught and even then usually avoid severe punishments, they will more likely choose to become dealers than if they believe that dealers are almost always caught and punished by lengthy prison terms. Put simply, in order to deter or prevent crime, the pain of punishment must outweigh the benefit of illegal gain.[5]

The classical criminologists argued that punishment should be only severe enough to deter a particular offense and that punishments should be graded according to the seriousness of particular crimes: "Let the punishment fit the crime." For example, Beccaria argued that it would be foolish to punish pickpockets and murderers in a similar fashion because this would encourage thieves to kill the victims or witnesses to their crimes.[6] The popularity of the classical approach was in part responsible for the development of the prison as an alternative to physical punishment and the eventual creation of criminal sentences geared to the seriousness of crimes.[7] The classical approach dominated the policy of the U.S. justice system for about 150 years.

By the mid-twentieth century, the concept of the "rational criminal" was challenged by those who believed that crime and delinquency were products of social forces, such as environment and socialization. Breakthroughs in psychology and sociology showed that human behavior was often controlled by outside influences, such as family, school, and peer relations, and that the concept of free will was merely wishful thinking. Mental health professionals argued that delinquents should be treated, not punished, for their misdeeds. Delinquents were viewed as troubled or "sick" individuals who needed **rehabilitation,** rather than punishment; this view was known as the **medical model** of crime.[8] Rather than being punished in prisons for their crimes, youthful (and adult) criminals were offered rehabilitation in secure treatment facilities until they were deemed fit to return to society. Because this position was particularly amenable to the juvenile justice system's *parens patriae* philosophy, the concept of "punishing" delinquents all but disappeared during the twentieth century.[9]

THE RATIONAL DELINQUENT

In the past few years, the view that delinquents *choose* to violate the law has regained prominence as a theoretical approach to the study and control of delinquency. Its reemergence can be traced to a number of trends. Conservatives have viewed efforts to treat known delinquents by treatment, counseling, and other rehabilitation strategies as failures. To some experts, the failure of treatment-oriented programs is a signal that delinquency is not a function of social ills, such as a lack of economic opportunity or family dysfunction. If it were, then educational enrichment, family counseling, job training programs, and the like should be more effective remedies to crime.

The reasoning goes, that if youths "choose" crime, then their behavior can be controlled by the threat of punishments that will "scare" them into choosing conventional over criminal behaviors. Well-known social scientists James Q. Wilson and Richard Herrnstein conclude in their controversial book *Crime and Human Nature* that delinquent behavior is deterrable if offenders experience firsthand the consequences of their behavior:

> That is, a person may become less likely to commit an offense either because he has learned (by experiencing punishment) that certain consequences of that offense are more likely than he had once supposed or because he has come to take more seriously the consequences (again, by having experienced them) that he knew were attached to that behavior.[10]

The rational choice approach has also been supported by the well-publicized resurgence of youth gang activity (see chapter 9 for more on gangs). The emergence of gangs and their involvement in the drug trade strengthens the case for rational choice: These young, well-armed entrepreneurs are seeking to cash in on a lucrative, albeit illegal, "business enterprise." These delinquent youths are constantly processing information to make profitable trading decisions: Will this act turn a profit? Is it good for my career? What are the consequences? How will my competitors react? What do my clients want?[11]

The failure of treatment programs to rehabilitate known delinquents, coupled with a rising teenage gang crime rate, has made it reasonable to view delinquents as individuals who are responsible for their actions and who might respond better to the fear of punishment than to the preventive influence of rehabilitative treatment. Choice theory has reemerged as a force both in the study of the causes of delinquency and as a guide for creating policies to control delinquent behavior.[12] In sum, those who embrace the utility of punishment as a delinquency control mechanism consider the delinquent to be a rational person who is willing and able to consider the consequences of his or her action before making a decision.

THE CONCEPT OF RATIONAL CHOICE

The concept that crime and delinquency are functions of the opportunities presented to motivated offenders has received widespread support from prominent social scientists.[13] Law-violating behavior is viewed as an event that occurs when an offender decides to take the chance of violating the law after considering his or her personal situation (need for money, learning experiences, opportunities for conventional success), values (conscience, moral standards, need for peer approval), and situational factors (how well the target is protected, whether

Choice theory suggests that young offenders engage in antisocial activity because they believe their actions will be beneficial and profitable. Whether they join a gang, steal cars, or sell guns, their delinquent acts are motivated by the reasoned belief that crime can be a relatively risk-free way to make a profit or better their personal situation. They have little fear of getting caught or of the consequences of punishment. Some are motivated by fantasies of riches while others may simply enjoy the excitement and short-term gratification produced by criminal acts.

people are at home, how wealthy the neighborhood is, the likelihood of getting caught, the punishment if apprehended). Accordingly, the decision to commit a specific type of crime and the subsequent entry into a criminal lifestyle is a matter of personal decision making based on a weighing of available information; hence, the term *rational choice*. For example, Felix Padilla observed "rational" delinquency in his study of the activities of contemporary gang boys involved in drug trafficking. Padilla found that gangs are like "employers" who can provide their business associates with security and know-how to conduct "business deals." Gang membership helps juveniles achieve financial success that would otherwise be impossible. As do legitimate business enterprises, some gangs actively recruit new personnel and cut deals with rivals over products and territory.[14]

Conversely, the decision to forgo law-violating behavior may be based on the person's perception that the economic benefits no longer exist or that the probability of successfully committing a crime is less than the probability of being caught and punished. For example, the aging-out process may occur because older offenders desist after realizing that the risks of crime are greater than the potential profit. The solution to crime, therefore, may be the formulation of policies that will cause the potential criminal to choose conventional behaviors over criminal ones.[15]

THE "SEDUCTIONS OF CRIME"

In an important book, sociologist Jack Katz argues that there are **"seductions of crime"** that result from the thrills and benefits provided by delinquent acts.[16] These situational inducements directly precede the commission of a delinquent act and are its driving force: Someone challenges their authority or moral position so they vanquish their opponent with a beating; they want to maximize their pleasure by doing something exciting so they break into and vandalize a school building. Crime becomes pleasurable more for its own sake rather than because it provides some material gain.

According to Katz, choosing to commit a crime satisfies the need to relieve emotional upheavals brought about by moral challenges. Gang boys are rejecting society's expectations that they become conventional adults. They violently defend meaningless turf boundaries and get into brawls in an effort to show their indifference to social expectations. Young killers are choosing to carry on like the avenging gods of mythology, electing to have life or death control over their victims.

Theft crimes bring what Katz calls "sneaky thrills." For many youngsters, shoplifting and theft are attractive because "getting away with it" is a thrilling demonstration of personal competence, especially when the crime is consummated under the eyes of an adult. Getting away with crime is especially thrilling because it shows that the young "thief" can flaunt the moral and legal code with impunity.

Katz finds that the central theme in the choice to commit crime is one of situational inducements for emotional upheaval: humiliation, righteousness, arrogance, ridicule, cynicism, defilement, and vengeance. For example, the assailant interprets the victim's behavior as disrespectful and humiliating, and violence is a way of expressing his or her resulting rage. When the drunk at a party is told to "shut up and go home" because she is disturbing people, she responds, "So, I'm acting like a fool, am I?," goes home and returns with a gun: She must "sacrifice" or injure the body of the victim to maintain her "honor."[17]

A number of research studies have examined Katz's view that situational inducements play an important role in causing adolescents' misbehavior.[18] For example, using a national self-report sample, Bill McCarthy found support for the "seductions of crime" hypothesis. McCarthy's data shows juveniles are most likely to be "seduced" if they neither fear the risk of apprehension nor its social consequences (e.g., losing the respect of their peers); fear of punishment then may help neutralize the attractions of crime.[19]

ROUTINE ACTIVITIES

To some crime experts, the concept of the "motivated offender" is insufficient to explain the cause of crime and delinquency. They argue that illegal behavior is tied not only to the rational and cunning acts of an offender but also to the *opportunity to commit crimes,* controlled in part by both the behavior of potential victims and those who are charged with guarding them (e.g., police officers).[20] Crime may occur not only because criminals decide to break the law but also because victims place themselves at risk and no one is around to protect them![21]

One of the most prominent examples of this view is **routine activities theory,** developed by Lawrence Cohen and Marcus Felson.[22] Cohen and Felson assume that the motivation to commit crime and the supply of offenders are constant.[23] Consequently, the volume and distribution of predatory crime (violent crimes against the person and crimes in which an offender attempts to steal an object directly from its holder) are closely related to the interaction of three variables that reflect the routine activities found in everyday American life: the availability of *suitable targets* (such as homes containing easily salable goods); the absence of *capable guardians* (such as homeowners and their neighbors, friends, and relatives); and the presence of *motivated offenders* (such as unemployed teenagers). If each of these components is present, the likelihood that a predatory crime will take place is greater (see Figure 3.1).

A critical component of the routine activities approach is that it gives equal weight to the role of both the victim and the offender in the crime process. Although Cohen and Felson hold that predatory crime is a matter of rational choice, they also maintain that criminal opportunity is significantly influenced by the victim's lifestyle and behavior. Put another way, the greater the opportunity there is for criminals and victims to interact, the greater the probability of crime; reduce the interaction, and the opportunity for crime will decline.[24]

TESTING THE ROUTINE ACTIVITIES APPROACH

Cohen and Felson have used the routine activities approach to explain the changes in the crime and delinquency rate since 1960. They argue that one reason the juvenile crime rate has increased is that the number of adult caretakers at home during the day (guardians) has decreased because of expanded female participation in the workforce. Because mothers are at work and children are in day care, homes are left unguarded and become more "suitable targets." Similarly, with the growth of suburbia and the decline of the

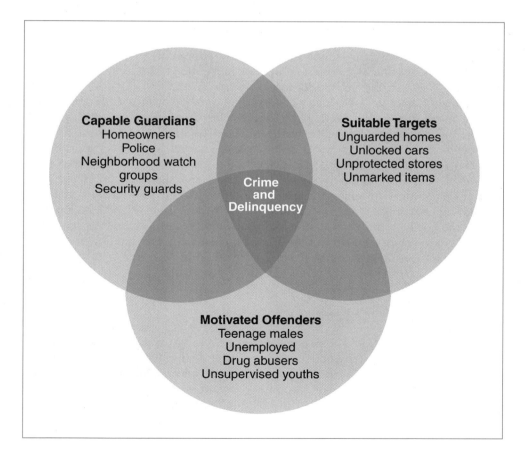

FIGURE 3.1
Routine activities

Capable Guardians
Homeowners
Police
Neighborhood watch
groups
Security guards

Suitable Targets
Unguarded homes
Unlocked cars
Unprotected stores
Unmarked items

Crime
and
Delinquency

Motivated Offenders
Teenage males
Unemployed
Drug abusers
Unsupervised youths

traditional neighborhood, the number of such familiar "guardians" as family, neighbors, and friends has diminished. Research conducted in the United States and other countries has confirmed this hypothesis.[25]

Suitable Targets Routine activities theory suggests that the availability of suitable targets such as easily transportable commodities will increase crime rates. Research has generally supported the fact that the more wealth a home contains, the more likely it will be a crime target.[26] In one study, Cohen and his associates linked burglary rates to color television set purchases, reasoning that the more these high-priced and easily sold goods are available, the more offenders will be "motivated" to steal.[27]

The action of "human targets" also influences delinquent behavior choices. For example, Steven Messner and Kenneth Tardiff studied patterns of urban homicide and found that a person's lifestyle significantly influenced victimization risk: People who tended to stay at home were the ones most likely to be killed by family or friends, while those who went out more often were victimized by strangers.[28] Leslie Kennedy and David Forde found that lower-class young males who have high-risk lifestyles (e.g., frequent bars and walk or drive alone at night) are also the ones most likely to become crime victims.[29]

Motivated Offenders Routine activities theory also links the delinquency rates to social changes that increase the number and motivation of offenders. Robert O'Brien found that delinquency rates will increase if there is a surplus of youths of the same age category all competing for a limited number of jobs and educational opportunities. If during any given period the number of teenagers exceeds the number of available part-time and after-school jobs, the supply of motivated offenders may increase simply because many potential offenders are competing for a limited number of legitimate resources.[30]

In a recent analysis D. Wayne Osgood and his associates substantiated another aspect of routine activities theory: Youths who spend time in "unstructured socializing" with their peers will commit more delinquent acts than those who are more involved in work, school, and studies. Osgood suggests that the link between routine activities and crime is criminal opportunity: Youths who drive around at night with their friends, go to parties, and spend evenings out have greater opportunity to engage in antisocial activities than those who stay home and avoid such high-risk, unstructured behaviors.[31] The Osgood research is important because it shows that not only can the routine activities approach explain broad crime trends but that it can be useful in understanding individual motivations to commit delinquent acts.

PREVENTING DELINQUENCY

If delinquency is a rational choice and a routine activity, then it stands to reason that it can be prevented by convincing potential delinquents that that they will be severely punished for committing delinquent acts and/or by making it so difficult to commit crimes that the potential gain is not worth the risk. Three strategies have evolved from this line of thinking: general deterrence, specific deterrence, and situational crime prevention.

GENERAL DETERRENCE

The **deterrence** concept holds that the choice to commit delinquent acts can be controlled or structured by the threat of punishment. If people fear the power of the law, believing that illegal behavior will result in certain and severe sanctions, they will choose not to commit crimes.[32]

One of the guiding principles of deterrence theory is that the more severe, certain, and swift the punishment, the greater its deterrent effect will be.[33] For example, there will be relatively little deterrent effect, even when a particular crime is punished quite severely, if most people do not believe they will be caught or if the sanctions are slow or delayed in coming, or easily put off.[34] Conversely, even a mild sanction may be sufficient to deter crime if people believe that punishment is certain.

Traditionally, juvenile justice authorities have been reluctant to incorporate deterrence-based punishments on the ground that they interfere with its stated *parens patriae* philosophy. Because, traditionally, children have been punished less severely than adults, the power of the law to deter juvenile crime has been limited. Yet, in recent years, the increase in teenage violence, gang activity, and drug abuse has prompted a reevaluation of deterrence strategies. Juvenile court philosophy has shifted from an emphasis on treatment to concerns with public safety.[35] Police are now more willing to use aggressive tactics, such as gang busting units, to deter membership in drug trafficking gangs; youthful-looking officers have been sent undercover into high schools in order to identify, contact, and arrest student drug dealers.[36]

The courts have also attempted to initiate a deterrence strategy. Juvenile court judges are demonstrating more willingness to waive youths to adult courts; prior record may outweigh need for services in making this decision.[37] Legislators seem willing to pass more restrictive juvenile codes specifying mandatory incarceration sentences in juvenile facilities; the number of incarcerated juveniles continues to increase. Adolescents are not even spared capital punishment: The U.S. Supreme Court has upheld the use of the death penalty for youths over 16.[38] (These changes are discussed further in chapters 12–17).

DETERRING DELINQUENCY?

Can deterrence strategies work? This issue generates considerable debate. A number of studies have contributed data supportive of deterrence concepts. Evidence indicates that the threat of police arrest can deter property crimes.[39] Areas of the country in which punishment is more certain seem to have lower delinquency rates; the more likely people are to perceive that they will be punished for a crime, the less likely they are to engage in that activity.[40]

Although these findings are persuasive, there is actually little conclusive evidence that the threat of apprehension and punishment alone can deter crime.[41] More evidence exists that fear of social disapproval and informal penalties, criticisms, and punishments from parents and friends may actually be greater deterrents to crime than legal punishments.[42]

Deterring Juveniles Deterring juvenile delinquency may also present a greater problem than deterring adult criminality. Although the justice system is taking a harder line on juvenile delinquency, minors are still subject to far more lenient sanctions than adults and by definition are less capable of making mature judgments about their behavior choices. Many younger offenders are unaware of the content of juvenile legal codes, so imposition of a deterrence policy (e.g., mandatory waiver to the adult court for violent crimes), will have little effect on delinquency rates.[43] It seems futile, therefore, to try to deter delinquency through fear of legal punishment.

Research also shows that many juvenile offenders are under the influence of drugs and/or alcohol when they break the law; thus, their decision-making ability may be impaired.[44] Similarly, because juveniles often commit crimes in groups, the deterrent effect of the law may not be able to overcome the influence of peer pressure.

Research by Maynard Erickson and Jack Gibbs suggests that deterrence efforts have little success with delinquent offenders.[45] First, they found that youths do not report being deterred by the threat of a one-year jail sentence any more than they would be by losing spending money or having a 7 p.m. curfew. Second, adults do not seem willing to support a policy of punishment of sufficient severity to deter juvenile crime. Finally, Erickson and Gibbs could not find a clear-cut relationship between perceived certainty of punishment and delinquency rates.

Thus, although on the surface deterrence appears to have benefit as a delinquency control device, there is also reason to believe that it has limited demonstrable effectiveness.

SPECIFIC DETERRENCE

The theory of specific deterrence holds that offenders who are punished severely will not repeat their illegal acts. Juvenile are sent to **secure incarceration** facilities in the belief that their experience will deter future misbehavior.

Specific deterrence is a popular approach to crime control today. The admissions rate to confinement facilities per 100,000 juveniles in the population has increased sharply during the past decade (see chapter 17). Unfortunately, relying on punitive measures may expand rather than reduce future delinquency. Institutions quickly become overcrowded, and nonserious and nonviolent juveniles are packed into swollen facilities with chronic violent offenders. The use of mandatory sentences means that first-time offenders may be treated the same as recidivists. Research has shown that a history of prior arrest, conviction, and punishment is the best predictor of rearrest among young offenders released from correctional institutions. Rather than deter future offending, punishment seems to escalate reoffending.[46]

Why does punishment encourage rather than reduce delinquency? According to some experts, institutionalization cuts youth off from prosocial supports in the community, making them more reliant on deviant peers. Incarceration may also diminish chances for successful future employment, reducing access to legitimate opportunities. Although some researchers have found that punishment may reduce the frequency of future offending, the weight of the evidence suggests that time served has little impact on recidivism.[47] After reviewing relevant literature on the issue, David Altschuler concluded that evidence supporting a specific deterrent effect of incarceration on offenders is altogether lacking.[48] The failure of specific deterrence might help explain why delinquency rates are increasing at the same time that incarceration rates are at an all-time high.

SITUATIONAL CRIME PREVENTION

Situational crime prevention strategies are designed to make it so difficult to commit specific criminal acts that would-be delinquent offenders will be convinced that the risks of crime are greater than the rewards.[49] Rather than deterring or punishing individuals in order to reduce delinquency rates, situational crime reduction strategies typically include limiting the number of motivated offenders; increasing guardianship; and reducing access to suitable targets. Controlling the situation of crime can be accomplished by either (1) increasing the effort needed to commit a crime; (2) increasing the risks to commit a crime; and/or (3) reducing the rewards attached to delinquent acts.

Increasing the effort might involve such **target-hardening techniques** as placing steering locks on cars and putting unbreakable glass on storefronts. Access control can be maintained by locking gates and fencing yards.[50] The facilitators of crime can be controlled by such measures as banning the sale of spray paint to adolescents in an effort to cut down on graffiti or having a photo put on credit cards to reduce their value if stolen.

Increasing the risks of crime might involve such measures as improving surveillance lighting, creating neighborhood watch programs, controlling building entrances and exits, installing burglar alarms and security systems, and increasing the number of private security officers and police patrols.

Reducing the rewards of crime could include strategies such as making car radios removable so they can be taken inside at night, marking property so that it is more difficult to sell when stolen, and having gender-neutral phone listings to discourage obscene phone calls. Tracking systems, such as those made by the LOJACK Corporation, help police locate and return stolen vehicles.

Targeting Hot Spots   In an oft-cited research paper, Lawrence Sherman, Patrick Gartin, and Michael Buerger found that a significant portion of all police

Situational crime prevention strategies are designed to make it so difficult to commit specific criminal acts that would-be delinquent offenders will be convinced that the risks of crime are greater than the rewards. One approach is to remove or control the *facilitators of crime*, by such measures as banning the sale of spray paint to adolescents in an effort to cut down on graffiti.

calls emanate from a relatively few locations: bars, malls, the bus depot, hotels, certain apartment buildings.[51] By implication, concentrating police resources on these **hot spots** could appreciably reduce crime.[52]

One way of structuring situational crime prevention efforts would be to focus on a particular hot spot, an area that is the site of ongoing teenage crime (e.g., a shopping mall, public park, housing project). Directing massive law enforcement efforts in a **crackdown** on crime and delinquency may help reduce city delinquency rates. Lawrence Sherman found that crackdowns work effectively as a short-term crime reduction strategy, but in the long term, their delinquency reduction effect decays once the initial "shock effect" wears off.[53] Crackdowns also may simply displace illegal activity to "safer" areas of the city, where there are fewer police and where there is less chance of apprehension.

CHOICE THEORY IN REVIEW

Regardless of their form, choice theories have at their core a motivated offender who breaks the law because he or she perceives an abundance of benefits and an absence of threat. Increase the threat and reduce the benefits, and the delinquency rate should move ever downward.

This logic is hard to refute. After all, by definition, a person who commits an illegal act but is not *rational* cannot be considered a criminal or delinquent but instead is "not guilty by reason of insanity." Therefore, a criminal, even a juvenile, must be considered rational. Yet several questions remain unanswered by choice theorists. First, why do some people continually choose to break the law even after suffering its consequences, while others are content with living law-abiding yet indigent lives? How can "the good boy in the high crime area" be explained?[54] Similarly, why do affluent youth, such as the Menendez brothers, break the law when they have everything to lose and little to gain?

Choice theorists also have problems explaining seemingly irrational crimes, such as vandalism, arson, and even drug abuse. To say a teenager painted swastikas on a church or synagogue after making a "rational choice" seems inadequate to explain such a destructive, detrimental act.

The relationships observed by rational choice theorists can be explained in other ways. For example, although the high victimization rates in lower-class neighborhoods can be explained by an oversupply of "motivated offenders," they may also be due to other factors, such as social conflict and neighborhood disorganization.[55]

In sum, choice theories are useful in attempting to understand criminal events and victim patterns. However, the question remains: Why are some people "motivated" to commit crime and delinquency while others in similar circumstances remain law-abiding? Why do some people choose crime over legal adherence to the law?

TRAIT THEORIES

A faithful and loyal choice theorist adheres to the belief that some people choose to commit crimes after carefully weighing the benefits of criminal over legal behavior. For example, youths decide to commit a robbery if they believe they will make a good profit, have a good chance of getting away, and, even if caught, stand little chance of being severely punished.

A number of delinquency experts believe that this model is incomplete. They believe it is wrong to infer that all youths choose crime simply because they believe its advantages outweigh its risks. If that was the case, how could senseless and profitless crimes such as vandalism and random violence be explained? These trait theorists argue that human behavioral choices are a function of an individual's mental and/or physical makeup. Most law-abiding youths have personal traits that keep them in the mainstream of conventional society. In contrast, youths who choose to engage in repeated aggressive, antisocial, or conflict-oriented behavior manifest abnormal traits that influence their behavior choices.[56] Uncontrollable, impulsive behavior patterns place some youths at odds with society, and they soon find themselves in trouble with the law. Yes, some experts would say, delinquents may choose their actions, but the decision is a product of all but uncontrollable mental and physical properties and traits.

The view that delinquents are somehow "abnormal" is not a new one. Some of the earliest theories of criminal and delinquent behavior stressed that crime was a product of personal traits and that measurable physical and mental conditions, such as IQ and body build, determined behavior. This view is generally referred to today as **positivism.** Positivists believe that the scientific method can be used to measure the causes of human behavior and that behavior is a function of often uncontrollable factors, such as mental illness.

The source of behavioral control is one significant difference between trait and choice theories: While choice theorists believe that behavior is purely a product of human reasoning, trait theorists believe that behavior is controlled by personal traits.

In the following sections, the history and primary components of trait theory are reviewed.

THE ORIGINS OF TRAIT THEORY

The first attempts to discover why criminal tendencies develop focused on the physical makeup of offenders. Biological traits present at birth were thought to predetermine whether people would live a life of crime.

The originator of this school of thought is generally considered to be the Italian physician Cesare Lombroso (1835–1909).[57] Known as the "father of criminology," Lombroso put his many years of medical research to use in his theory of **criminal atavism.**[58] Lombroso found that delinquents manifest physical anomalies that make them biologically and physiologically similar to our primitive ancestors. These atavistic individuals were viewed as savage throwbacks to an earlier stage of human evolution. Because of this link, the "born criminal" had such physical traits as enormous jaws, strong canines, a flattened nose, and supernumerary teeth (double rows, as in snakes). Lombroso made such statements as "it was easy to understand why the span of the arms in criminals so often exceeds the height, for this is a characteristic of apes, whose forelimbs are used in walking and climbing."[59]

Contemporaries of Lombroso refined the notion of a physical basis of crime. Raffaele Garofalo (1851–1934) shared Lombroso's belief that certain physical characteristics indicate a criminal or delinquent nature.[60] Enrico Ferri (1856–1929), a student of Lombroso, believed it was a combination of biological, social, and organic factors that caused delinquency and crime. Although Ferri accepted the validity of the biological approach to explaining criminal activity, he attempted to interweave physical, anthropological, and social factors into his explanation of the causes of illegal behavior.[61] The English criminologist Charles Goring (1870–1919) challenged the validity of Lombroso's research and claimed instead that delinquent behaviors bore a significant relationship to a condition he referred to as "defective intelligence."[62] Consequently, Goring believed that delinquent behavior was inherited and could therefore best be controlled by regulating the reproduction of families exhibiting such traits as "feeble-mindedness, epilepsy, insanity, and defective social instinct."[63]

Advocates of the inheritance school studied the family trees of criminal and delinquent offenders. They traced the activities of several generations of families believed to have an especially large number of criminal members. The most famous of these studies involved the Jukes and the Kallikaks. Richard Dugdale's *The Jukes: A Study in Crime, Pauperism, Disease, and Heredity* (1875) and Arthur Estabrook's later work *The Jukes in 1915* traced the history of the Jukes, a family responsible for a disproportionate amount of crime.[64]

Advocates of the body-build, or somatotype, school argued that delinquents and criminals manifest distinct physiques that make them susceptible to particular types of delinquent behavior.[65] William H. Sheldon linked body type to delinquency.[66] Mesomorphs have well-developed muscles and an athletic appearance. They are active, aggressive, sometimes violent, and the most likely to become delinquents. Endomorphs have heavy builds and are slow-moving and lethargic. Ectomorphs are tall and thin and less social and more intellectual than the other types.[67]

These early views portrayed delinquent behavior as a function of a single factor or trait, such as body build or defective intelligence. They had a significant impact on early American criminology, which relied heavily on developing a science of "criminal anthropology."[68] Eventually, these views evoked criticism for their unsound methodology and lack of proper scientific controls. Many used captive offender populations and failed to compare experimental subjects with nondelinquents or undetected delinquents.[69] These omissions make it impossible to determine if biological traits produce delinquency. It is equally plausible that police are more likely to arrest, and courts convict, the mentally and physically abnormal. By the middle of the twentieth century, biological theories had fallen out of favor as an explanation of delinquency.

CONTEMPORARY TRAIT THEORY

For most of the twentieth century, delinquency experts scoffed at the notion that a youth's behavior was controlled by physical conditions present at birth. During this period, the majority of delinquency research focused on the social factors, such as poverty and family life, that were believed to be responsible for law-violating behavior. However, a small group of criminologists and penologists kept alive the biological approach. With the publication of Edmond O. Wilson's *Sociobiology: The New Synthesis,* the biological perspective was given a new impetus in the 1980s.[70]

Sociobiology suggests that behavior will adapt to the environment in which it evolved.[71] Most important, creatures of all species are influenced by the innate need to have their genetic material survive and dominate others. Consequently, they do everything in their power to ensure their own survival and that of others who share their gene pool (relatives, ethnic group, etc.). Even when they come to

the aid of others (**reciprocal altruism**), people are motivated by the belief that their actions will be reciprocated and that their gene survival capability will be enhanced. For the aid to occur, the benefit to the recipient must be high, the cost to the helper relatively low, and the chances of their positions being reversed in the future high.

Although sociobiology has been criticized as methodologically unsound and socially dangerous, it has had a tremendous effect on reviving interest in finding a biological basis for crime and delinquency, because if biological (genetic) makeup controls all human behavior, it follows that it should also be responsible for determining whether a person chooses law-violating or conventional behavior.[72]

Environmental Interaction   Trait theory rejects the traditional assumptions that all humans are born with equal potential to learn and achieve (**equipotentiality**) and that thereafter their behavior is controlled by social forces.[73] Although traditional criminologists suggest (either explicitly or implicitly) that all persons are born equal and that parents, schools, neighborhoods, and friends control subsequent development, biosocial theorists argue that no two people (with rare exceptions, such as identical twins) are alike, and therefore each will react to environmental stimuli in a distinct way.

Modern trait theorists assume that a combination of personal traits and the environment produces individual behavior patterns. People with pathological traits such as brain damage, abnormal personality, or a low IQ may have a heightened risk for crime; this risk is elevated by environmental stresses such as poor family life, educational failure, substance abuse, and exposure to delinquent peers. The reverse may also apply: A supportive environment may be strong enough to counteract adverse biological and psychological traits.[74]

It is the interaction between a child's vulnerability caused by physical or mental disorders and his or her environment that produces delinquency. Children born into a disadvantaged environment will not get the social and familial support they need to overcome their disabilities. The relatively small number of youths who suffer both physical and social disabilities and who also lack social supports are the ones who become early onset offenders and persist in a life of crime.[75]

There are actually two branches of trait theory. The first, **biosocial theory** maintains that the development of delinquency is an effect of the interaction of biological traits, such as biochemical and social conditions. The second, **psychological theory,** focuses on such factors as personality, mental illness, and intelligence. Of course, some youths may suffer from a variety of biological and psychological problems.[76]

Today, biosocial theorists seek to explain the onset of antisocial behaviors, such as aggression and violence, from the standpoint of the physical qualities of the offenders.[77] The majority of major research efforts appear to be concentrated in three distinct areas of study: biochemical factors, neurological dysfunction, and genetic influences.

BIOCHEMICAL FACTORS

One area of biosocial research concerns the suspected relationship between antisocial behavior and biochemical makeup.[78] One view is that the body chemistry, influenced and/or controlled by diet, can govern behavior and personality; traits affected by diet are thought to include aggression and depression.[79]

Of particular concern is an unusually high intake of such items as artificial food coloring, milk, and sweets. Some scientists believe that a chronic undersupply or oversupply of vitamins, such as C, B3, and B6, may be related to restlessness and antisocial behavior in youths. Evidence also exists that allergies to foods can influence mood and behavior, resulting in personality swings between hyperactivity and depression.[80]

High intake or excessive exposure to certain common minerals, including magnesium, copper, cadmium, and zinc, has also been linked to aggression.[81] Overexposure to lead, for example, has been traced to learning disabilities, cognitive deficits, lower IQ, and mental dullness, which are considered risk factors for delinquency and violent behavior.[82]

Experimental Evidence   Experimental evidence exists that institutionalized youths have had a long history of poor nutrition, involving diets that were low in protein and high in sugar and other carbohydrates. This evidence suggests a link between food intake, body chemistry, and behavior.[83] Some highly sophisticated experiments show that antisocial youths who are given a diet balanced in nutrients have significantly reduced episodes of antisocial behavior and improved scores on psychological inventories.[84]

In one study, Alexander Schauss compared a sample of incarcerated youths with a nondelinquent control group and found that the most significant factor separating the youths was the extremely high milk intake among the delinquents.[85]

In another study on the influence of diet on such crime-related acts as aggression and hostility, J. Kershner and W. Hawke evaluated the effect that a high-protein, low-carbohydrate, sugarless diet, supplemented by megavitamins, had on children labeled as behavior problems.[86] Kershner and Hawke asked the subjects' parents to evaluate their children on 13 behavior qualities, including hyperactivity, aggression, and attention span. The researchers discovered that the children had significantly improved behavior patterns and that the diet was the most important factor in producing positive change.

In the most oft-cited research on the subject, Stephen Schoenthaler tested 276 incarcerated youths to determine whether a change in the amount of sugar in their diet would have a corresponding influence on their behavior within the institution.[87] Schoenthaler instituted a number of dietary changes: Sweet drinks were replaced with fruit juices; table sugar was replaced with honey; breakfast cereals with high sugar content were eliminated; molasses was substituted for sugar in cooking. Schoenthaler found that these changes produced a significant reduction in disciplinary actions within the institution: The number of assaults, thefts, fighting, and acts of disobedience declined about 45 percent. It is important to note that these results were consistent when such factors as age, previous offense record, and race of the offender were considered.

In another experiment, Schoenthaler and his colleagues found that enriching students' diets in New York City schools was correlated with improved school performance. Gradually eliminating synthetic (artificial) flavors and preservatives (BHA and BHT) and reducing sucrose intake (by limiting ice cream and sweetened cereals) preceded improved scores on national achievement tests. Because school achievement has been consistently linked to delinquent behavior, any improvement in academic performance resulting from dietary changes may help reduce the rate of antisocial activities among the student population.[88]

One area of biosocial research concerns the suspected relationship between antisocial behavior and biochemical makeup. Body chemistry, influenced and/or controlled by diet, may govern behavior and personality; traits affected by diet are thought to include aggression and depression. Can eating junk food be the cause of adolescent violence? If so, what could be done to regulate teen diets?

Dissenting Views   Although this evidence seems persuasive, the relationship between biochemical intake and abnormal behavior is far from settled. Research has been criticized as being both methodologically unsound and also impractical because of the cost of providing dietary supplements for actual and potential delinquents. In addition, a number of controlled experiments have failed to substantiate any real link between the two variables.[89] In one important study, a group of researchers had 25 preschool children and 23 school-age children described as sensitive to sugar follow a different diet for three consecutive three-week periods. One diet was high in sucrose, the second substituted Aspartame (Nutrasweet) for a sweetener, and the third relied on saccharin. Careful measurement of the subjects found little evidence of cognitive or behavioral differences that could be linked to diet. If anything, sugar seemed to have a calming effect on the children.[90]

Reviews of available evidence have uncovered additional evidence to question a diet–delinquency link. The United States, with one of the highest crime and delinquency rates in the world, has a far lower per capita consumption of sugar than other Western nations. Furthermore, adolescents, who usually have the highest crime rate, actually have sugar intakes about one-half that of the general population.[91]

Despite these criticisms, the relationship between diet and delinquency remains unresolved. A careful review of the evidence by Marcel Kinsbourne in *The New England Journal of Medicine* found that although there is little conclusive evidence linking diet and antisocial behavior, it is possible that some foods such as sugar may aggravate existing behavioral or psychological disorders.[92] Further replication and research to study this relationship are certainly warranted.[93]

HORMONAL LEVELS

Hormonal levels are another area of biochemical research. Antisocial behavior allegedly peaks in the teenage years because hormonal activity is at its greatest level during this period. It is argued that increased levels of the male androgen testosterone are responsible for excessive levels of violence among teenage boys. In an impressive review of the literature, Christy Miller Buchanan, Jacquelynne Eccles, and Jill Becker found evidence that hormonal changes are related to mood and behavior, and that adolescents may experience more intense moods, mood swings, anxiety, and restlessness than people at other points in development.[94] These mood and behavior changes have been associated with family conflict and antisocial behavior.

Hormonal sensitivity may begin at the very early stages of life when the fetus can be exposed to abnormally high levels of testosterone while in the uterus. This may trigger a heightened response to the release of testosterone when an adolescent male reaches puberty. As a result, although testosterone levels appear normal, the young male is at risk to overaggressive behavior responses.[95] (Hormonal activity as an explanation of gender differences in the delinquency crime rate is discussed further in chapter 7.)

Neurological Dysfunction

Another focus of biosocial theory is the **neurological,** or brain and nervous system, structure of offenders. Studies measure indicators of system functioning, such as brain waves, heart rate, arousal levels, skin conductance and attention span, cognitive ability, and spatial learning, and compare them to measures of antisocial behavior.

One view is that the neuroendocrine system that controls brain chemistry is the key to understanding violence and aggression. Imbalance in the central nervous system's chemical and hormonal activity has been linked to antisocial behavior and drug abuse.[96]

Another view is that neurological dysfunction, commonly measured with an electroencephalogram (EEG), a CAT scan, or performance indicators (gross motor functions, visual processing, auditory–language functioning), is the key factor in causing aggression and violence. Children who manifest behavior disturbances may have identifiable neurological deficits, such as damage to the hemispheres of the brain.[97] This is sometimes referred to as **minimal brain dysfunction (MBD),** defined as an abnormality in the cerebral or brain structure that causes behavior injurious to a person's lifestyle and social adjustment. Impairment is produced by such factors as low birth weight, brain injury, birth complications, and inherited abnormality.[98] Research indicates that children exhibiting neurological impairment also have an increased risk for a garden variety of developmental problems, such as low IQ scores and cognitive impairment, which have been associated with delinquency.[99]

A number of research efforts have attempted to substantiate a link between neurological impairment and crime. A recent analysis by Stephen Tibbetts found that low birth weight children are also likely to be early onset delinquents; low birth weight is highly correlated with neurological impairment.[100] Clinical analysis of death row inmates found that a significant number had suffered head injuries as children, resulting in damage to their central nervous system and neurological impairment.[101]

Measurement of the brain activity of antisocial youths has revealed impairments that might cause them to experience otherwise unexplainable outbursts of anger, hostility, and aggression.[102] Evidence has been found linking the ability of the brain to process information with schizophrenia, depression, and other mental illnesses.[103] Cross-national studies also support a link between neurological dysfunction and antisocial behavior. Jean Seguin and his associates found that impairment in executive functions (e.g., abstract reasoning, problem-solving skills, motor behavior skills) was related to violent and aggressive behavior in a sample of Montreal youth.[104]

EEG Research A number of research studies have used an electroencephalogram to measure the brain waves and activity of delinquents and then compare them with those of law-abiding adolescents. In what is considered the most significant investigation of EEG abnormality and delinquency, 335 violent delinquents were classified on the basis of their antisocial activities and measured on an EEG.[105] While youths who committed a single violent act had a 12 percent abnormality rate—the same as the general population—the habitually aggressive youths tested at a 57 percent abnormality rate, almost five times higher than the normal rate. Behaviors believed to be highly correlated with abnormal EEG functions include poor impulse control, inadequate social ability, hostility, temper tantrums, destructiveness, and hyperactivity.[106] The following "Focus on Delinquency" takes a look at one such malady often diagnosed in children: Attention Deficit/Hyperactivity Disorder (ADHD).

THE LEARNING DISABILITY–JUVENILE DELINQUENCY LINK

One specific type of MBD that has generated considerable interest is **learning disability (LD),** a term that has been defined by the National Advisory Committee on Handicapped Children:

> Children with special learning disabilities exhibit a disorder in one or more of the basic psychological processes involved in understanding or using spoken or written languages. They may be manifested in disorders of listening, thinking, talking, reading, writing or arithmetic. They include conditions which have been referred to as perceptual handicaps, brain injury, minimal brain dysfunction, dyslexia, developmental aphasia, etc. They do not include learning problems which are due to visual, hearing or motor handicaps, to mental retardation, emotional disturbance, or to environmental disadvantages.[107]

Some learning disabled children have been found to exhibit poor motor coordination (poor hand–eye coordination, trouble climbing stairs, clumsiness, inability to catch a ball, and have improper auditory and vocal responses (do not seem to hear, cannot differentiate sounds and noises).

The relationship between learning disabilities and delinquency has been highlighted by studies showing that arrested and incarcerated youths have a far higher LD rate than do youths in the general population.[108] Although it is estimated that approximately 10 percent of all youths have learning disorders, estimates of LD among adjudicated delinquents range from 26 percent to 73 percent.[109]

Charles Murray, writing in a widely read 1976 federally sponsored study, offered two possible explanations of the link between learning disabilities and delinquency.[110] One view, known as the **susceptibility rationale,** argues that the link is caused by certain side effects of learning disabilities, such as impulsiveness, poor ability to learn from experience, and inability to take social cues. In

ATTENTION DEFICIT/HYPERACTIVITY DISORDER (ADHD)

Many parents have noticed that their children do not pay attention to them—they run around and do things in their own way. Sometimes this inattention is a function of age; in other instances, it is a symptom of a common learning disability referred to as attention-deficit/hyperactive disorder (ADHD), a condition in which a child shows a developmentally inappropriate lack of attention, distractibility, impulsivity, and hyperactivity. Estimates of ADHD in the general population range from 3 percent to 12 percent, but it is much more prevalent in adolescence, where some estimates reach as high as one-third the population. Although the origin of ADHD is still unknown, suspected causes include neurological damage to the frontal lobes of the brain, prenatal stress, and even food additives and chemical allergies. Some experts suggest that the condition might be traced to the neurological effects of abnormal levels of the chemicals dopamine and norepinephrine. ADHD children are most often treated by giving them doses of stimulants, such as Ritalin and Dexedrine, which ironically help these children to control their emotional and behavioral outbursts.

The condition usually results in poor school performance, reflected in high dropout rates, bullying, stubbornness, mental disorder, and a lack of response to discipline—conditions highly correlated with delinquent behavior. A series of research studies now link ADHD to the onset and sustenance of a delinquent career and increased risk for antisocial behavior and substance abuse in adulthood. ADHD children are more likely to be arrested, charged with a felony, and have multiple arrests than non-ADHD youth. There is also evidence that ADHD youth who *also* exhibit early signs of minimal brain dysfunction (MBD) and conduct disorder (e.g., fighting) are the most "at risk" for persistent antisocial behaviors continuing into adulthood.

The various symptoms of ADHD are described in Table A.

TABLE A Symptoms of ADHD
- Lack of attention
- Frequently fails to finish projects
- Does not seem to pay attention
- Does not sustain interest in play activities
- Cannot sustain concentration on schoolwork or related tasks
- Is easily distracted
- Impulsivity
- Frequently acts without thinking
- Often "calls out" in class
- Does not want to wait his or her turn in line or for games
- Shifts from activity to activity
- Cannot organize tasks or work
- Requires constant supervision
- Hyperactivity
- Constantly runs around and climbs on things
- Shows excessive motor activity while asleep
- Cannot sit still; is constantly fidgeting
- Does not remain in his or her seat in class
- Is constantly on the go like a "motor"
- Difficulty regulating emotions
- Difficulty starting a project
- Difficulty staying on track
- Difficulty adjusting to social demands

Source: Harry Wexler, "Attention Deficit Disorder, Drugs and Crime: The Dangerous Mixture," Paper presented at the American Society of Criminology meeting, Boston, Mass., November 1995; Terrie Moffitt and Phil Silva, "Self-Reported Delinquency, Neuropsychological Deficit, and History of Attention Deficit Disorder," *Journal of Abnormal Child Psychology* 16:553–69 (1988); American Psychiatric Association, *Diagnostic and Statistical Manual of the Mental Disorders*, 3rd ed. (Washington, D.C.: American Psychiatric Press, 1987), pp. 50–53.

contrast, the **school failure rationale** assumes that the frustration caused by the LD child's poor school performance leads to a negative self-image and acting-out behavior.

A number of recent research efforts have found that the LD child may not be any more susceptible to delinquent behavior than the non-LD child. Studies indicate that the proposed link between learning disabilities and delinquency may be an artifact of bias in the way the juvenile justice system treats LD youths.[111] For example, when self-reported delinquent behavior of LD and non-LD youth is actually quite similar.[112] Research by Lynn Meltzer and her associates found that although a small number of delinquents had learning disabilities, the majority could not be classified as learning disabled.[113]

These findings can be interpreted as meaning that when LD children get in trouble with the law, they bring with them a record of school problems and low grades and a history of frustrating efforts by agents of the educational system to help them. When information is gleaned from the school personnel at juvenile trials, LD children's poor performance may work against them in the court. Consequently, the view that learning disabilities cause delinquency has been questioned, and the view that LD children are more likely to be arrested and officially labeled delinquent demands further inquiry.

Rethinking the LD–JD Link   Terrie Moffitt recently evaluated the relevant literature on the link between LD and delinquency and concluded that it is a significant correlate of persistent antisocial behavior (conduct disorders).[114] She found that neurological symptoms, such as LD and MBD, correlate highly with factors that create high risk for persistent antisocial behavior: early onset of deviance, hyperactivity, and aggressiveness. Moffitt's review indicates further research is needed on the cause and impact of neurological dysfunction: When do such problems begin? Are they the result of injury during birth? Or of child abuse and neglect?[115] Is there a continuum of learning disabilities, and are the most severely disabled also the most prone to delinquency?[116] Efforts are being made to introduce new technologies in the measurement of brain function and behavior to investigate early detection, prevention, and control of maladapted behaviors.[117]

GENETIC INFLUENCES

Individuals who share genes are alike in personality regardless of how they are reared, whereas rearing environment induces little or no personality resemblance.

David Rowe, *The Limits of Family Influence: Genes, Experiences and Behavior* (1994)[118]

Another area of concern for biosocial theorists is the genetic makeup of delinquents.[119] It has been hypothesized that some youths inherit a genetic configuration that predisposes them to violence and aggression.[120] Biosocial theorists believe that people inherit antisocial behavior characteristics and mental disorders in the same way they inherit genes that control height and eye color.[121]

Early theories of heredity suggested that delinquency-proneness ran in families. However, most families share a similar lifestyle as well as a similar gene pool, making it difficult to determine whether behavior is a function of heredity or environment. Interest in a genetic basis of crime was given new license because of the highly publicized killing of eight Chicago nurses in 1966 by Richard Speck. It was soon reported that Speck possessed an extra male chromosome; instead of the normal 46XY chromosomal structure, his was 47XYY. Although numerous research studies failed to find conclusive proof that males with an extra Y chromosome were disproportionately violent and criminal, interest brought about by the Speck case boosted research on the genetic influences on delinquency. (It was later revealed that Speck's genetic structure was misidentified.)[122]

Biosocial theorists have once again taken up the study of family transmission of delinquent traits. Some recent research shows a significant association in sibling behavior, indicating that brothers and sisters seem to share antisocial lifestyles.[123] However, this is not surprising, as siblings also share the same environment. To establish the influence of environment and genetics independently, criminologists have conducted studies using as samples twins and adopted children.

TWIN STUDIES

One method of studying the genetic basis of delinquency is to compare the behavior of twins with non-twin siblings. If criminality is an inherited trait, identical twins should be quite similar in their behavior because of their common genetic makeup.

Because twins are usually brought up in the same household and share common life experiences, however, any similarity in their delinquent behavior might still be viewed as a function of comparable environmental influences. To guard against this, biosocial theorists have compared the behavior of identical monozygotic (MZ) twins with fraternal dizygotic (DZ) twins; while the former have an identical genetic makeup, the latter share only about 50 percent of their genetic combinations. Research has shown that MZ twins are significantly closer in their personal characteristics, such as intelligence, than are DZ twins.[124] Reviews of twin studies found, that in almost all cases, MZ twins have delinquent and antisocial behavior patterns more similar than those of DZ twins.[125] Karl Christiansen evaluated thousands of Danish twin pairs and found MZ pairs more than twice as likely to be similar as DZ pairs.[126]

Although this research seems to support a connection between genetic makeup and delinquency, there are still issues that need to be addressed. MZ twins are more likely to look alike and to share physical traits than DZ twins, and they are more likely to be treated similarly. Shared behavior patterns may therefore be a function of socialization, not heredity. Critics have also challenged the methodology of these studies and suggest that those that show a conclusive genetic link to behavior use faulty data.[127]

Against this interpretation is research evidence that identical twins reared apart are similar in many traits, including personality, intelligence, and attitudes, as twins who live in the same household.[128] The Minnesota study of twins reared apart found that MZ twins who were separated at birth shared many similarities in personal style and behavior; in contrast, the DZ twins reared apart seldom produce similar behavior patterns.[129] Such findings support a genetic basis of behavior.

ADOPTION STUDIES

Another way to determine whether delinquency is an inherited trait is to compare the behavior of adopted children with that of their biological parents. If the criminal behavior of children is more like that of their biological parents, whom they have never met, than that of their adopted parents, who brought them up, it would indicate that the tendency toward delinquency is inherited, rather than shaped by the environment.

Studies of this kind have generally supported the hypothesis that there is a link between genetics and behavior.[130] David Rowe's comprehensive review finds that adoptees share many of the behavioral and intellectual characteristics of their biological parents despite the social and environmental conditions found in their adoptive homes. Genetic makeup is sufficient to counteract and/or negate even the most extreme environmental conditions (e.g., malnutrition and abuse).[131]

Some of the most influential research in this area has been conducted by Sarnoff Mednick. In one study, Mednick and Bernard Hutchings found that although only 13 percent of the adoptive fathers of a sample of adjudicated delinquent youths had criminal records, 31 percent of their biological fathers had criminal records.[132] Analysis of a control group's background indicated that about 11 percent of the fathers had criminal records. Hutchings and Mednick were forced to conclude that genetics played at least some role in creating delinquent tendencies, because the biological fathers of delinquents were much more likely than biological fathers of noncriminal youths to be criminals themselves.[133]

In addition to a direct link between heredity and delinquency, the literature also shows that behavior traits indirectly linked to delinquency may be at least in part inherited. For example, recent research by Jody Alberts-Corush and her associates shows that the biological parents of adopted hyperactive children are more likely to show symptoms of hyperactivity than are the adoptive parents.[134] In addition, several studies have reported a higher incidence of psychological problems in parents of hyperactive children when compared to control groups. Although all hyperactive children do not become delinquent, the link between this neurological condition and delinquency has been long suspected.

Similarly, there is evidence that intelligence is related to heredity and that low intelligence is a cause of impulsive delinquent acts that are easier to detect and more likely to result in arrest.[135] This connection can create the appearance of a relationship between heredity and delinquency.

Connecting delinquent behavior to heredity is quite controversial because it implies that the cause of delinquency is (a) present at birth, (b) "transmitted" from one generation to the next, and (c) immune to treatment efforts (as genes cannot be altered). Recent evaluations of the gene–crime relationship find that although a relationship can be detected, the better designed research efforts provide less support than earlier and weaker studies.[136] If there is a genetic basis of delinquency, it is likely that genetic factors contribute to certain individual differences that interact with specific social and environmental conditions to bring about antisocial behavior.[137]

PSYCHOLOGICAL THEORIES OF DELINQUENCY

Some experts view the cause of delinquency as essentially psychological.[138] After all, most behaviors labeled delinquent—for example, violence, theft, sexual misconduct—seem to be symptomatic of some underlying psychological problem. Psychologists point out that many delinquent youths have poor home lives; destructive relationships with neighbors, friends, and teachers; and conflicts with authority figures in general. These relationships seem to indicate a disturbed personality structure. Numerous studies of incarcerated youths indicate that the youths' personalities are marked by negative, antisocial behavior characteristics. Because delinquent behavior occurs among youths in every racial, ethnic, and socioeconomic group, psychologists view it as a function of emotional and mental disturbance, rather than as a result of social factors such as racism, poverty, and class conflict.

Considering the presumed relationship between personality disturbance and antisocial behavior, it is not surprising that psychologists have played a prominent role in the study of delinquency. Although many delinquents do not manifest significant psychological problems, enough do to give clinicians a powerful influence on delinquency theory.

Because psychology is a complex and diversified discipline, more than one psychological perspective on crime exists. Three prominent psychological perspectives on delinquency are psychodynamic theory, behavioral theory, and cognitive theory.[139] (See Figure 3.2.)

PSYCHODYNAMIC THEORY

One long-held psychological view of delinquency is based on the pioneering work of the Austrian physician Sigmund Freud (1856–1939).[140] Freud's views are today referred to as **psychodynamic** or **psychoanalytic theory.**

Psychodynamic theory argues that the human personality contains three major components. The *id* is the unrestrained, primitive, pleasure-seeking component with which each child is born. The *ego* develops through the reality of living in the world and helps manage and restrain the id's need for immediate gratification. The *superego* develops through interactions with parents and other significant people and represents the development of conscience and the moral rules that are shared by most adults.

FIGURE 3.2
Psychological perspectives of delinquency

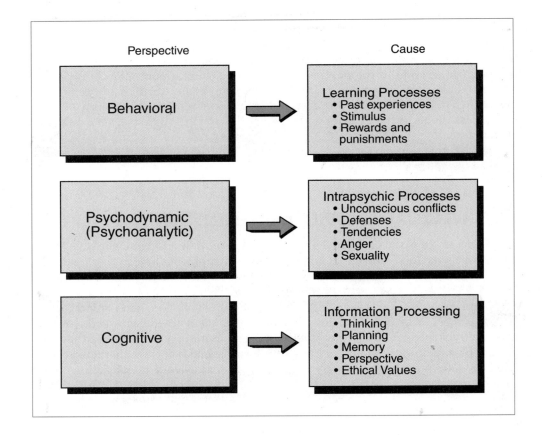

Psychodynamic theory suggests that unconscious motivations for behavior come from the id's compulsion to account for two primal needs—sex and aggression. Human behavior is often marked by symbolic actions that reflect hidden feelings about these needs. For example, stealing a car may reflect a person's unconscious need for shelter and mobility to escape from hostile enemies (aggression) or perhaps an urge to enter a closed, dark, womblike structure that reflects the earliest memories (sex).

All three segments of the personality operate simultaneously. The id dictates needs and desires, the superego counteracts the id by fostering feelings of morality and righteousness, and the ego evaluates the reality of a position between these two extremes. If these components are properly balanced, the individual can lead a normal life. If one aspect of the personality becomes dominant at the expense of the others, however, the individual exhibits neurotic or even psychotic personality traits.

Furthermore, the theory suggests that an imbalance in personality traits caused by a traumatic early childhood can produce a damaged adolescent personality; that is, deep-rooted problems developed early in childhood will cause long-term psychological difficulties. For example, if neglectful parents fail to develop a child's superego adequately, the child's id may become the predominant personality force. Later, the youth may demand immediate gratification, lack compassion and sensitivity for the needs of others, disassociate feelings, act aggressively and impulsively, and demonstrate other psychotic symptoms. Antisocial behavior then may be the result of conflict or trauma occurring early in a child's development, and delinquent activity may become an outlet for violent and antisocial feelings.

Neuroses and Psychosis According to Freud's version of psychodynamic theory, people who experience feelings of mental anguish and are afraid that they are losing control of their personalities are said to be suffering from a form of neurosis and are referred to as neurotics. People who have lost total control and who are dominated by their primitive id are known as psychotics. Their behavior may be marked by bizarre episodes, hallucinations, and inappropriate responses. Psychosis takes many forms, the most common being schizophrenia, a condition marked by illogical thought processes and a lack of insight into behavior. According to the psychoanalytic view, the most serious types of youthful antisocial behavior, such as murder, might be motivated by psychosis, while neurotic feelings would be responsible for less serious delinquent acts and status offenses, such as petty theft and truancy.[141]

Because of changes in psychological thinking, the term *neuroses* is no longer widely used to describe all forms of unconscious conflict. It is now more common to characterize people with more specific types of disorders, including anxiety disorder, mood disorder, and sleep disorder.

THE PSYCHODYNAMIC TRADITION AND DELINQUENCY

A number of psychoanalysts have expanded on Freud's original model to explain the onset of antisocial behaviors. Erik Erickson speculated that many adolescents experience a life crisis in which they feel emotional, impulsive, and uncertain of their role and purpose.[142] To resolve this crisis, most youths achieve a sense of ego identity, a firm sense of who they are and what they stand for.

However, some youths cannot adequately deal with their feelings of role conflict and experience a sense of role diffusion, a sense of uncertainty that makes them susceptible to suggestion and puts them at the mercy of others who might lead them astray. The clash between ego identity and role diffusion is precipitated by an **identity crisis**—a period of inner turmoil during which youths examine inner values and make decisions about life roles. Using Erickson's approach, the behavior of youthful drug abusers might be viewed as an expression of confusion over their place in society, their inability to direct behavior toward useful outlets, and perhaps their dependency on others to offer them solutions to their problems.

Psychoanalysts view youth crime as a result of unresolved conflict between the ego and the superego. Some children, especially those who have been abused or mistreated, may experience unconscious feelings of resentment, fear, and hatred. If this conflict between the ego and the superego cannot be reconciled, the child may regress to a state in which he or she becomes id dominated. This regression may be considered responsible for a great number of mental diseases, from neuroses to psychoses, and in many cases it may be related to criminal behavior.[143]

Psychoanalysts then view delinquents as id-dominated people who suffer from the inability to control impulsive drives. Perhaps because they suffered unhappy experiences in childhood or had families who could not provide proper love and care, delinquents suffer from weak or damaged egos that make them unable to cope with conventional society.[144] In its most extreme form, delinquency may be viewed as a form of psychosis that prevents delinquent youths from appreciating the feelings of their victims or controlling their own impulsive needs for gratification. In a classic work, *Wayward Youth*, psychoanalyst August Aichorn claims that social stress alone could not produce such an emotional state. He identifies **latent delinquents**—youths whose troubled family lives lead them to seek immediate gratification without consideration of right and wrong or the feelings of others.[145]

Others have viewed adolescent antisocial behavior as a consequence of the inability to cope with feelings of oppression. Criminality actually allows youths to strive by producing positive psychic results: helping them to feel free and independent; giving them the possibility of excitement and the chance to use their skills and imagination; providing the promise of positive gain; allowing them to blame others (e.g., the police) for their predicament; and giving them a chance to rationalize their own sense of failure ("If I hadn't gotten into trouble, I could have been a success").[146]

The psychodynamic view is supported by research that shows that a number of serious, violent juvenile offenders suffer from some sort of personality disturbance. James Sorrells's well-known study of juvenile murderers, "Kids Who Kill," found that many homicidal youths could be described as "overtly hostile," "explosive or volatile," "anxious," and "depressed."[147] Likewise, Richard Rosner and his associates found that 75 percent of male adolescents accused of murder could be classified as having some mental illness, including schizophrenia.[148] Abused, depressed, and suicidal children may grow up to vent their feelings in a homicidal rage.[149]

Family Life The psychodynamic approach places heavy emphasis on the family's role in producing a delinquent child. When parents fail to maintain a stable, balanced home life, a child may adapt by turning inward and revamping his or her internal personality components. Antisocial youths frequently come from families in which parents are unable to give love, set consistent limits, and provide the controls that allow children to develop the necessary personal tools to cope with the world within which they live.[150] The exploitive, destructive behavior of a youth may actually be a symbolic call for help. In fact, some psychoanalysts view delinquents' behavior as being motivated by an unconscious urge to be punished. Because these children believe that they are unloved at home, they then see the reason as their own inadequacy—hence, they deserve punishment.

BEHAVIORAL THEORY

Not all psychologists agree that behavior is controlled by unconscious mental processes determined by parental relationships developed early in childhood. Behavioral psychologists argue that a person's personality is learned throughout life during interaction with others. Based primarily on the works of the American psychologist John B. Watson (1878–1958) and popularized by Harvard professor B. F. Skinner (1904–1990), **behaviorism** concerns itself solely with measurable events, not the unobservable psychic phenomena described by psychoanalysts.

Behaviorists suggest that individuals learn by observing how people react to their behavior. Behavior is triggered initially by a stimulus or change in the environment. If a particular behavior is reinforced by some positive reaction or event, that behavior will be continued and eventually learned. However, behaviors that are not reinforced or are punished will be extinguished or become extinct. For example, if children are given a reward (ice cream for dessert) for behaving properly while eating dinner, eventually they will learn to behave properly as a matter of habit. Conversely, if children are punished for some misbehavior, they will eventually learn to associate disapproval with that act and avoid it.

SOCIAL LEARNING THEORY

Not all behaviorists follow the teachings of Watson and Skinner strictly. Some hold that a person's learning and social experiences, coupled with his or her values and expectations, determine behavior. This approach to behavior is known as **social learning theory.** The most widely read social learning theorists are Albert Bandura, Walter Mischel, and Richard Walters.[151] In general, they hold that children will model their behavior according to the reactions they receive from others, either positive or negative; the behavior of those adults with whom they are in close contact, especially parents; and the behavior they view on television and in movies. If children observe aggression, such as an adult slapping or punching someone during an argument, and see that the aggressive behavior is approved or rewarded, they will likely react violently during a similar incident. Eventually, the children will master the techniques of aggression and become more confident that their behavior will bring tangible rewards.[152]

By implication, social learning suggests that children who grow up in homes where violence is a way of life may learn to believe that such behavior is acceptable and rewarding. Even if parents tell children not to be violent and punish them if they are, the children will still model their behavior on the observed parental violence. Thus, children are more likely to heed what parents *do* than what they *say*. Bonnie Carlson found that by middle childhood, some children have already acquired an association between their use of aggression against others and the physical punishment they receive at home. Often their aggressive responses are directed at other family members and siblings. Carlson's conclusion: The family serves as a training ground for violence, with physical punishment playing a prominent role in normalizing the child's use of violence during conflict situations with others.[153]

Bandura has also suggested that adolescent aggression is a result of disrupted dependency relations with parents. This refers to the frustration and anger a child feels when parents provide poor role models and hold back affection and nurturing. He states,

> A child who lacks close dependent ties to his parents can have little opportunity or desire to model himself after them and to internalize their standards of behavior. In the absence of such internalized controls, the child's aggression is likely to be expressed in an immediate, direct and socially unacceptable fashion.[154]

THE MEDIA AND DELINQUENCY

One aspect of social learning theory that has received a great deal of attention is the view that children will model their behavior after characters they observe on TV or see in movies. This is of special concern because the content of both media has been considerably violent for quite some time. Often the violence is of a sexual nature, and some experts fear that there is a link between sexual violence and the viewing of pornography.[155]

Children are particularly susceptible to TV imagery. It is believed that many children consider television images to be real, especially if they are authoritatively presented by an adult (as in a commercial). Of concern is the fact that some children, especially those who are considered "emotionally disturbed," may be unable to distinguish between fantasy and reality when watching TV shows.[156] This is especially important when we consider that systematic viewing of TV begins at 2.5 years of age and continues at a high level during the preschool and early school years; it has been estimated that children ages 2 to 5 watch TV 27.8 hours per week; children 6 to 11, 24.3 hours per week; and teens, 23 hours per week.[157]

A number of research methods have been used to measure the effects of TV viewing on behavior. One method is to expose groups of subjects to violent TV shows in a laboratory setting and then compare their behavior to control groups who viewed nonviolent programming; observations have also been made at playgrounds, athletic fields, and residences. Other experiments require subjects to answer attitude surveys after watching violent TV shows. Still another approach is to use aggregate measures of TV viewing; for example, the number of violent TV shows on the air during a given time period is compared to crime rates during the same period.

TV and Violence Most evaluations of experimental data indicate that watching violence on TV is correlated to aggressive behaviors.[158] Such august bodies as the American Psychological Association and the National Institute of Mental Health support the TV–violence link.[159] In an important review of the literature, Wendy Wood, Frank Wong, and J. Gregory Chachere conclude that violent media

One aspect of social learning theory that has received a great deal of attention is the view that children will model their behavior after characters they observe on TV or see in movies. This is of special concern since the content of both types of media has been considerably violent for quite some time. Popular films starring action heroes such as Arnold Schwarzenegger, shown here in his "Terminator" role, are seen by millions of adolescent males. Should the government prohibit or limit violence on TV? Would that mean censoring the nightly newscast which is often filled with violent images?

has at least a short-term impact on behavior.[160] Subjects who view violent TV shows are likely to commence aggressive behavior almost immediately. This phenomenon is demonstrated by numerous reports of copycat behavior after a particularly violent film or TV show is aired. For example, on November 27, 1995, thieves ignited flammable liquid in a New York City subway token booth, seriously injuring the clerk. Their behavior was virtually identical to a robbery scene in the film *Money Train* (with Wesley Snipes and Woody Harrelson), which had been released a few days before.[161]

RETHINKING THE MEDIA–VIOLENCE LINK

Although the evidence is persuasive, the relationship between TV viewing and violence is still uncertain. A number of critics claim that the evidence simply does not support the claim that TV viewing is related to antisocial behavior.[162] Some critics assert that experimental results are inconclusive and short-lived. Children may react with aggression immediately after viewing violence on TV, but the aggression is quickly extinguished once the viewing ends.[163] Experiments that show that children act aggressively after watching violent TV shows fail to link aggression to actual criminal behaviors, such as rape or assault.

Aggregate data are also inconclusive. Little evidence exists that areas that have the highest levels of violent TV viewing also have rates of violent crime that are above the norm.[164] Millions of children watch violence every night yet fail to become violent criminals. Even if a violent behavior–TV link could be established, it would be difficult to show that antisocial people develop aggressive traits merely from watching TV. It is also possible that already aggressive youths enjoy watching TV shows that conform to and support their behavioral orientation.

COGNITIVE THEORY

One area of psychology that has received increasing recognition in recent years has been **cognitive theory.** Psychologists with a cognitive perspective focus on mental processes, the way people perceive and mentally represent the world around them, and how they solve problems. The pioneers of this school were Wilhelm Wundt (1832–1920), Edward Titchener (1867–1927), and William James (1842–1920). The cognitive perspective contains several subgroups. Gestalt psychology is concerned with perception of the world in whole units, rather than individual pieces. The moral and intellectual development branch is concerned with how adults morally represent and reason about the world. Humanistic psychology stresses self-awareness and "getting in touch with feelings."

MORAL AND INTELLECTUAL DEVELOPMENT THEORY

Of the three branches of cognitive theory mentioned above, the moral and intellectual development branch is perhaps the most important for criminological theory. Jean Piaget (1896–1980), the founder of this approach, hypothesized that people's reasoning processes develop in an orderly fashion, beginning at birth and continuing until they are 12 and older.[165] At first, during the *sensorimotor stage,* children respond to the environment in a simple manner, seeking interesting objects and developing their reflexes. By the fourth and final stage, the *formal operational stage,* they have developed into mature adults who can use logic and abstract thought.

Lawrence Kohlberg applied the concept of moral development to issues in criminology.[166] He suggested that people travel through stages of moral development, during which their decisions and judgments on issues of right and wrong are made for different reasons. It is possible that serious offenders have a moral orientation that differs from that of law-abiding citizens. Kohlberg's stages of development are as follows:

- *Stage 1.* Right is obedience to power and avoidance of punishment.
- *Stage 2.* Right is taking responsibility for oneself, meeting one's own needs, and leaving to others the responsibility for themselves.
- *Stage 3.* Right is being good in the sense of having good motives, having concern for others, and "putting yourself in the other person's shoes."
- *Stage 4.* Right is maintaining the rules of a society and serving the welfare of the group or society.
- *Stage 5.* Right is based on recognized individual rights within a society with agreed-upon rules—a social contract.
- *Stage 6.* Right is an assumed obligation to principles applying to all humankind—principles of justice, equality, and respect for human personality.

Kohlberg classified people according to the stage on this continuum at which their moral development has ceased to grow. In studies conducted by Kohlberg and his associates, criminals were found to be significantly lower in their moral judgment development than noncriminals of the same social background.[167] The majority of noncriminals were classified in stages 3 and 4, while a majority of criminals were in stages 1 and 2. Other research studies involving delinquent youth have found that a significant number were in the first two moral development categories, while nondelinquents were ranked higher.[168] In addition, higher stages of moral reasoning are associated with such behaviors as honesty, generosity, and nonviolence, which are considered incompatible with delinquency.[169]

Moral development theory, then, suggests that people who obey the law simply to avoid punishment or who have outlooks mainly characterized by self-interest are more likely to commit crimes than those who view the law as something that benefits all of society and who honor the rights of others.

INFORMATION PROCESSING

Cognitive theorists who study information processing try to explain antisocial behavior in terms of perception and analysis of data. When people make decisions, they engage in a sequence of cognitive thought processes. They first encode information so that it can be interpreted. They then search for a proper response and decide upon the most appropriate action. Finally, they act on their decision.[170]

According to this cognitive approach, violence-prone adolescents may be using information incorrectly when they make decisions. One reason is that they may be relying on mental "scripts" learned in early childhood that tell them how to interpret events, what to expect, how they should react, and what the outcome of the interaction should be.[171] Hostile children may have learned improper scripts by observing how others react to events; their own parents' aggressive and inappropriate behavior would have considerable impact. Violence becomes a stable behavior because the scripts that emphasize aggressive responses are repeatedly rehearsed as the child matures.

To violence-prone children, people seem more aggressive than they actually are and intend them ill when there is no reason for alarm. As these children mature, they use fewer cues than most people to process information. Some use violence in a calculating fashion as a means of getting what they want; others react in an overly volatile fashion to the slightest provocation. Aggressors are more likely to be vigilant, on edge, or suspicious. They may believe that they are defending themselves, for example, when they attack victims, even though they are misreading the situation.[172]

Cognitive Treatment   Treatment based on information processing acknowledges that people are more likely to respond aggressively to a provocation when thoughts intensify the insult or otherwise stir feelings of anger. Cognitive therapists attempt to teach explosive people to control aggressive impulses by viewing social provocations as problems requiring a solution rather than as insults requiring retaliation. Programs aimed at teaching problem-solving skills may include listening, following instructions, joining in, and using self-control.[173] Some of the most important work in this area has been done by Gerald Patterson and his colleagues at the Oregon Social Learning Center. This kind of treatment program seems to help parents deal effectively with children who have heretofore been disruptive. It stresses the praising of desirable behavior and the punishment of undesirable behavior, such as back talk, with a regimen that includes loss of privileges and short-term isolation in the child's room.[174] (Patterson's techniques are discussed further in chapter 8.)

Personality and Delinquency

Personality can be defined as the reasonably stable patterns of behavior, including thoughts and emotions, that distinguish one person from another.[175] An individual's personality reflects characteristic ways of adapting to life's demands and problems. The way we behave is a function of how our personality enables us to interpret life events and make appropriate behavioral choices.

Can the cause of delinquency be linked to personality? There has been a great deal of research on this subject and an equal amount of controversy and debate over the findings.[176] In their early work, Sheldon Glueck and Eleanor Glueck identified a number of personality traits that characterize delinquents:

- self-assertiveness
- defiance
- impulsiveness
- narcissism
- suspicion
- destructiveness
- sadism
- lack of concern for others

- extroversion
- ambivalence
- feeling unappreciated
- distrust of authority
- poor personal skills
- mental instability
- hostility
- resentment[177]

The Glueck's research is representative of the view that delinquents maintain a distinct personality whose characteristics increase the probability that (a) they will be aggressive and antisocial and (b) their actions will involve them with agents of social control, ranging from teachers to police. A number of personality deficits have been identified in the delinquent population. A common theme is that delinquents are hyperactive, impulsive individuals with short attention spans (attention deficit/hyperactivity disorder), who frequently manifest conduct disorders, anxiety disorders, and depression.[178] These traits make them prone to problems ranging from psychopathology to drug abuse, sexual promiscuity, and violence.[179]

Extraversion and Neuroticism Since the Gluecks' findings were published, other research has attempted to identify personality traits that would increase the chances for a delinquent career.[180] For example, the well-known psychologist Hans Eysenck identified two important personality traits that he associated with antisocial behavior: **extraversion** and **neuroticism.** Extraverts are impulsive individuals who lack the ability to examine their own motives and behaviors; neurotics experience unfounded anxiety, tension, and emotional instability.[181] Youths who lack self-insight and are impulsive and emotionally unstable are likely to interpret events differently than youths who are able to give reasoned judgments to life events. Thus, although the former may act destructively, for example, by taking drugs, the latter will be able to reason that such behavior is ultimately destructive and life threatening.

THE ANTISOCIAL PERSONALITY

It has also been suggested chronic delinquency may result from a personality pattern or syndrome commonly referred to as the **antisocial, psychopathic** or **sociopathic** personality (the terms are used interchangeably). Although no more than three-percent of the male offending population may be classified as sociopathic, it is possible that a large segment of persistent chronic offenders share this trait.[182]

Antisocial (sociopathic) youths exhibit a low level of guilt and anxiety and persistently violate the rights of others. Although they may exhibit superficial charm and above-average intelligence, these traits often mask a disturbed personality that makes them incapable of forming enduring relationships with others and continually involves them in such deviant behaviors as truancy, running away, lying, substance abuse, and impulsivity. They lack the ability to empathize with others. In many cases, the psychopath's home life was filled with frustrations, bitterness, and quarreling from an early age. Consequently, throughout life, the sociopath is unreliable, unstable, demanding, and egocentric. Hervey Cleckley, a leading authority on psychopathy, uses this definition:

> [Psychopaths are] chronically antisocial individuals who are always in trouble, profiting neither from experience nor punishment, and maintaining no real loyalties to any person, group, or code. They are frequently callous and hedonistic, showing marked emotional immaturity, with lack of responsibility, lack of judgment and an ability to rationalize their behavior so that it appears warranted, reasonable and justified.[183]

DEVELOPING AN ANTISOCIAL PERSONALITY

A number of factors have been found to contribute to the development of psychopathic/sociopathic personalities. They include having an emotionally disturbed parent, a lack of love, parental rejection during childhood, and inconsistent discipline.[184] Another view is that psychopathy has its basis in a measurable physical condition: Psychopaths suffer from levels of arousal that are lower than those of the general population. Consequently, psychopathic youths may need greater-than-average stimulation to bring them up to comfortable levels; this view is referred to as **arousal theory.**

Psychologist Linda Mealey accepts both of these positions when she suggests that there are actually two type of sociopaths: primary sociopaths and secondary sociopaths. **Primary sociopaths** have inherited traits that predispose them to antisocial behavior; they have a genotype that predisposes them to become sociopaths. In contrast, **secondary sociopaths** are constitutionally normal but are influenced by negative environmental factors, ranging from poor parenting to racial segregation and social conflict. Mealey suggests that there are two pathways to sociopathic behavior: one that has a genetic basis and one that is environmentally induced.

Sociopathic Behavior   Youths diagnosed as sociopaths are believed to be thrill seekers who engage in violent, destructive behavior. For example, Lewis Yablonsky has described the psychopathic/sociopathic gang boy who engages in violent and destructive sexual escapades to compensate for a fear of responsibility and an inability to maintain interpersonal relationships,[185] and although the research of Helen Raskin White, Erich Labouvie, and Marsha Bates did not directly link delinquency to psychopathy, they did find that delinquents were more likely than nondelinquents to be sensation seekers who desired a hedonistic pursuit of pleasure, an extraverted lifestyle, partying, drinking, and a variety of sexual partners.[186] Psychologists have attempted to treat patients diagnosed as psychopaths with adrenaline, which increases their arousal levels.

THE DELINQUENCY–PERSONALITY LINK

Numerous attempts have been made to show that psychological tests that measure personality can predict the onset of delinquent behavior. The most common of these is the Minnesota Multiphasic Personality Inventory, commonly called the MMPI. Developed by R. Starke Hathaway and J. Charnley McKinley, the MMPI has subscales that purport to measure many different personality traits, including psychopathic deviation (Pd scale), schizophrenia (Sc), and hypomania (overactivity, Ma).[187]

Elio Monachesi and R. Starke Hathaway pioneered the use of the MMPI to predict delinquent behavior.[188] Their early research found that scores on some of the MMPI subscales, especially the Pd scale, predicted delinquency. In one major effort, they administered the MMPI to a sample of ninth-grade boys and girls in Minneapolis and found that Pd scores had a significant relationship to later delinquent involvement.[189] Similar studies have been conducted to classify both criminal and juvenile offenders, as well as substance abusers.[190]

Despite the time and energy put into using MMPI scales to predict delinquency, the results have proved inconclusive. Three surveys of the literature of personality testing, one by Karl Schuessler and Donald Cressey (covering the pre-1950 period), another by Gordon Waldo and Simon Dinitz (covering 1950 to 1965), and a more recent one by David Tennenbaum, found inconclusive evidence that personality traits could indeed predict delinquent involvement.[191]

The personality tests reviewed in these surveys, however, often had methodological flaws, so any negative conclusions must be interpreted with caution.

Some recent research efforts have in fact successfully classified offenders and predicted their behavioral traits on the basis of personality inventory scores.[192] Sufficient evidence exists of an association between some delinquency and personality disturbance to warrant further research on this important yet sensitive issue.

INTELLIGENCE AND DELINQUENCY

Psychologists are concerned with the development of intelligence and its subsequent relationship to behavior. Of particular importance to the study of delinquency is the allegation that there is an inverse relationship between IQ and youthful law violations. It has been charged that youths with low IQs are responsible for a disproportionate share of delinquency.

IQ tests were believed to measure the inborn genetic makeup of individuals, and many criminologists accepted the predisposition of substandard individuals toward delinquency. This view is referred to as the **nature theory** of intelligence. Early criminologists thought that if one could determine which individuals had low IQs, one might be able to identify potential delinquents before they committed socially harmful acts.[193] Because social scientists had a captive group of subjects in training schools and penal institutions, studies began to appear that measured the correlation between IQ and crime by testing adjudicated juvenile delinquents. Delinquent juveniles were believed to be inherently substandard in intelligence and thus naturally inclined to commit more crimes than more intelligent persons. Thus, juvenile delinquents were used as a test group around which numerous theories about intelligence were built.

When the newly developed IQ tests were administered to inmates of prisons and juvenile training schools in the first decades of the twentieth century, the nature (versus nurture) position gained support because a large proportion of the inmates scored low on the tests. Henry Goddard found in his studies in 1920 that many institutionalized persons were what he considered "feeble-minded" and thus concluded that at least half of all juvenile delinquents were mental defectives.[194]

In 1926, William Healy and Augusta Bronner tested a group of delinquents in Chicago and Boston and found that 37 percent were subnormal in intelligence.[195] They concluded that delinquents were five to ten times more likely to be mentally deficient than nondelinquent boys.

These and other early studies were embraced as proof that low IQ scores indicated potentially delinquent children and that a correlation existed between innate low intelligence and deviant behavior.

NURTURE THEORY

The rise of culturally sensitive explanations of human behavior in the 1930s led to the development of the **nurture theory** of intelligence. This view holds that intelligence must be viewed as partly biological but primarily sociological. Nurture theorists discredit the notion that people commit crimes because they have low IQs. Instead, they postulate that environmental stimulation from parents, relatives, social contacts, schools, peer groups, and innumerable others create a child's IQ level and that low IQs result from an environment that also encourages delinquent and criminal behavior.[196] If educational environments could be improved, the result might be both an elevation in IQ scores and a decrease in delinquency.[197]

Studies challenging the assumption that people automatically commit delinquent acts because they have below-average IQs began to appear as early as the 1920s. In 1926 John Slawson studied 1,543 delinquent boys in New York institutions and compared them with a control group of New York City boys.[198] He found that although 80 percent of the delinquents achieved lower scores in abstract verbal intelligence, delinquents were about normal in mechanical aptitude and nonverbal intelligence. These results indicated the possibility of cultural bias in portions of the IQ tests. He also found no relationship between the number of arrests, the types of offenses, and IQ. In 1931, Edwin Sutherland evaluated IQ studies of criminals and delinquents and found evidence disputing the association between intelligence and criminality.[199]

These findings did much to discredit the notion that a strong relationship exists between IQ and criminality, and for many years the IQ–delinquency link was ignored.

IQ AND DELINQUENCY TODAY

A study published 20 years ago by Travis Hirschi and Michael Hindelang revived interest in the association between IQ and delinquency.[200] After conducting a statistical analysis of a number of data sets, Hirschi and Hindelang concluded both that IQ tests are a valid predictor of intelligence and that "the weight of evidence is that IQ is more important than race and social class" for predicting delinquent involvement. They argued that a low IQ increases the likelihood of delinquent behavior through its effect on school performance: Youths with low IQs do poorly in school, and school failure and academic incompetence are highly related to delinquency.

The Hirschi–Hindelang findings have been supported by a number of research efforts.[201] In their widely read *Crime and Human Nature,* James Q. Wilson and Richard Herrnstein concluded that

> there appears to be a clear and consistent link between criminality and low intelligence. That is, taking all offenders as a group, and ignoring differences among kinds of crime, criminals seem, on the average, to be a bit less bright and to have a different set of intellectual strengths and weaknesses than do noncriminals as a group.[202]

Indirect Influence   Those social scientists who conclude that IQ influences delinquent behavior are split on the structure of the associations. Some believe that IQ has an indirect influence on delinquency. For example, when Terrie Moffitt and her associates found a significant relationship between low IQ and delinquency in a Danish cohort, they concluded that children with a low IQ are more likely to engage in delinquent behavior because their poor verbal ability is a handicap in school: Low IQ leads to school failure, and educational underachievement has consistently been associated with delinquency.[203] In a later study, Moffitt, writing with Jennifer White and Phil Silva, found that "high-risk" youths were less likely to become persistent delinquents if they had a relatively high IQ; low IQ increased the probability of a stable delinquent career.[204] The relationship between IQ and delinquency has been found to be consistent after controlling for class, race, and personality traits.[205]

Direct Influence   Some experts believe that IQ may have a direct influence on the onset of delinquent involvement. David Farrington's research on the delinquent life cycle (discussed in chapter 2) suggests that the key linkage between IQ and delinquency is the ability to manipulate abstract concepts. Low intelligence limits adolescents' ability to "foresee the consequences of their offending and to appreciate the feelings of victims."[206] Therefore, youths with limited intelligence are more likely to misinterpret events and gestures, act foolishly, take risks, and engage in harmful behavior.

IQ AND DELINQUENCY RECONSIDERED

The relationship between IQ and delinquency is an extremely controversial issue because it implies there is a condition present at birth that accounts for a child's delinquent behavior throughout the life cycle and that this condition is not easily changed or improved; research shows that measurements of intelligence taken in infancy are a good predictor of later IQ.[207] By implication, if delinquency is not spread evenly through the social structure, neither is intelligence.

Not everyone accepts the IQ–delinquency link. Some research indicates that IQ level has negligible influence on delinquent behavior.[208] IQ research has also been tainted by charges that tests are culturally biased and invalid, making any existing evidence at best inconclusive.[209]

In sum, there is some, albeit inconclusive, evidence that some youths with limited intellectual ability may also be more likely to engage in delinquent behaviors. Many who believe IQ and crime are associated recognize that the linkage is indirect: Intelligence is associated with poor school performance, and it is school failure that causes delinquency.[210] As Wilson and Herrnstein put it, "A child who chronically loses standing in the competition of the classroom may feel justified in settling the score outside, by violence, theft, and other forms of defiant illegality."[211] Because the relationship runs from low IQ to poor school performance to frustration to delinquency, it is important for school officials to recognize the problem and plan programs to help underachievers perform better in school. Educational enrichment programs can help counteract any influence intellectual impairment has on the predilection of young people to commit crime.

CRIME AND HUMAN NATURE

In 1985, James Q. Wilson and Richard Herrnstein published *Crime and Human Nature,* which soon became one of the most talked-about works in criminological literature.[212] This work integrates biosocial factors, such as genetic makeup, IQ, and body build, with the concept of criminal choice theory into a theory of delinquency through the life course that the authors refer to as **crime as choice.**

According to Wilson and Herrnstein, throughout the life course, human behavior is determined by its perceived consequences. Choosing between committing a crime and not committing a crime (referred to as "noncrime") will depend on perception of gains and losses: the larger the ratio of net rewards of crime to the net rewards of noncrime, the greater the tendency to commit the crime.[213]

The rewards for crime come in the form of material gain, sexual gratification, revenge against an enemy, peer approval, and so on; the consequences can include pangs of conscience, revenge of the victim, disapproval of friends and associates, and the possibility of punishment. Noncrime rewards are usually gained in the future: They involve the maintenance of one's self-image, reputation, potential for a happier life, freedom, and so on.

The crime–noncrime choice is influenced by a number of factors, such as the desire to obtain basic rewards—food, clothing, shelter, sex—or learned goals—wealth, power, status. The choice of crime may be influenced by a person's perceived sense of inequity; those who feel cheated by society may turn to crime in order to "catch up."

The crime–noncrime choice is also influenced by biosocial factors present at birth or soon after. These include low intelligence; mesomorphic body type; a criminal father; an impulsive or extraverted personality; and an autonomic nervous system that responds less slowly to stimuli.[214] Wilson and Herrnstein recognize that social factors that develop during the life cycle can also influence behavior. These factors include a turbulent family life, educational underachievement, and membership within a deviant teenage subculture.

According to Wilson and Herrnstein, biological, psychological, and social conditions working in concert can influence thought patterns and eventually individual behavior patterns. The persistence of antisocial behavior through the life course, then, is a function of traits existing at birth and social factors that develop over the life span.

CRITIQUING TRAIT VIEWS

Trait views have been criticized on a number of grounds, including that the research methodology they employ is weak and invalid. Most research efforts use adjudicated or incarcerated offenders. Thus, it is often difficult to determine whether findings represent the delinquent population as a whole or merely those most likely to be arrested and adjudicated by officials of the justice system. For example, in a recent review of heredity studies, Glenn Walters and Thomas White concluded, "Our review leads us to the inevitable conclusion that current genetic research on crime has been poorly designed, ambiguously reported and exceedingly inadequate in addressing the relevant issues."[215]

Some critics also fear that trait theories can be socially and politically damaging. If a significant number of known delinquents come from particular economic, racial, and ethnic groups, is it possible that a corresponding percentage of people in these groups share physical, personality, and mental traits that differ from the norm? If an above-average number of indigent youth become delinquent offenders, can it be assumed that the less affluent are impulsive, greedy, have low IQs, or are genetically inferior? To many social scientists, the implications of these conclusions are unacceptable in light of what is known about race, gender, and class bias.

Critics also suggest that trait theory is limited as a generalized explanation of delinquent behavior because it fails to account for the known patterns of delinquent behavior. Delinquency trends seem to conform to certain patterns linked to social–ecological rather than individual factors—social class, seasonality, population density, and gender roles. Social forces that appear to influence the onset and maintenance of delinquent behavior are not accounted for by explanations of delinquency that focus on the individual. If, as is often the case, the delinquent rate is higher in one neighborhood than another, are we to conclude that youths in high-crime areas are more likely to be watching violent TV shows or eating more sugar-coated cereals than those in low-crime neighborhoods? How can individual traits explain the fact that crime rates vary between cities and between regions?

DEFENDING TRAIT THEORY

> The legitimization of social-psychological, psychiatric, and biosocial approaches to deviant behavior may prove to be an important and productive paradigm shift in the decades ahead.[216]

Theorists who focus on individual traits contend that critics overlook the fact that their research gives equal weight to environmental and social as well as mental and physical factors.[217] Included in the explanation of trait theory is the belief that some people have particular developmental problems that place them at a disadvantage in society, limit their chances of conventional success, and heighten their feelings of anger, frustration, and rage. It also suggests that although the incidence of these personal traits may be spread evenly across the social structure, families in one segment of the population have the financial wherewithal to help ameliorate the problem, while families in another segment lack the economic means and the institutional support needed to help their children. If trait theorists are correct then, delinquency rate differences are a result of differential access to opportunities to either commit crime or receive the care and treatment needed to correct and compensate for developmental problems.

In addition, trait theorists believe that, like it or not, youths are in fact different and may have differing potentials for antisocial acts. For example, gender differences in the violence rate may be explained by the fact that after centuries of aggressive mating behavior, males have become naturally more violent than females.[218] Male aggression may be more a matter of genetic transfer than socialization or cultural patterns.

TRAIT THEORY AND DELINQUENCY PREVENTION

As a group, individual perspectives on delinquency suggest that prevention efforts should be directed at strengthening a youth's home life and personal relationships. Almost all of these theoretical efforts point to the youth's home life as a key factor in delinquent behavior. If parents cannot supply proper nurturing, love, care, discipline, nutrition, and so on, the child cannot develop properly. Whether one believes that delinquency has a biosocial basis, a psychological basis, or a combination of both, it is evident that delinquency prevention efforts should be oriented to reach children early in their development.

It is, therefore, not surprising that county welfare agencies and privately funded treatment centers have offered counseling and other mental health services to families referred by schools, welfare agents, and juvenile court authorities. In some instances, intervention is focused on a particular family problem that has the potential for producing delinquent behavior, for example, alcohol and drug abuse, child abuse, or sexual abuse. In other situations, intervention is more generalized and oriented toward developing the self-image of parents and children or improving discipline in the family.

In addition, individual approaches have been used to prevent court-adjudicated youth from engaging in further criminal activities. This is sometimes referred to as *secondary* or *special prevention*. It has become almost universal for incarcerated and court-adjudicated youths to be given some sort of mental and physical evaluation before they begin their term of correctional treatment. Such rehabilitation methods as psychological counseling and psychotropic medication (involving such drugs as Valium or Ritalin) are often prescribed. In some instances, rehabilitation programs are provided through "drop-in" centers that service youths who are able to remain in their homes; more intensive programs require residential care and treatment. Clearly, agents of the juvenile justice system believe that many delinquent youths and status offenders have psychological or physical problems that their successful intervention can "cure," thus reducing repeat criminal behavior. Faith in this treatment approach suggests widespread agreement among juvenile justice system professionals that the cause of delinquency can be traced to individual pathology; if not, why bother treating them?

While the influence of psychological theory on delinquency prevention has been extensive, programs based on biosocial theory have been dormant for some time. Institutions, however, are beginning to sponsor demonstration projects designed to study the influence of diet on crime and to determine whether regulating the metabolism can affect behavior. Such efforts are relatively new and untested. Similarly, schools are making an effort to help youths with learning disabilities and other developmental problems. Delinquency prevention efforts based on bio-criminological theory are still in their infancy. The following "Case in Point" explores some questions arising out of the biosocial approach.

CASE IN POINT

You are a state legislator who is a member of the subcommittee on juvenile justice. Your committee has been asked to rewrite the state's juvenile code because of public outrage over serious juvenile crime.

At an open hearing, a professor from the local university testifies that she has devised a surefire test to predict violence-prone delinquents. The procedure involves brain scans, DNA testing, and blood analysis. Used with samples of incarcerated adolescents, her procedure has been able to distinguish with 90 percent accuracy between youths with a history of violence and those who are exclusively property offenders. The professor testifies that if each juvenile offender were tested with her procedure, the violence-prone career offender could be easily identified and given special treatment, for example, separated from the general juvenile population or given a longer sentence.

Opponents argue that this type of testing is unconstitutional because it violates the youth's Fifth Amendment right against self-incrimination and can unjustly label nonviolent offenders. They argue that any attempt to base policy on biosocial makeup seems inherently wrong and unfair. Those who favor the professor's approach maintain that it is not uncommon to single out the insane or mentally incompetent for special treatment and that these conditions often have a biological basis. It is better that a few delinquents be unfairly labeled than seriously violent offenders be ignored until it is too late.

Should special laws be created to deal with the "potentially" dangerous offender?

Should offenders be typed on the basis of their biological characteristics?

Is a 10 percent rate of inaccuracy too high to be considered for a basis of prediction? What would you do if the test were 100 percent reliable?

Some questions remain about the effectiveness of individual treatment as a delinquency prevention technique. Little hard evidence exists that clinical treatment alone can prevent delinquency or rehabilitate known delinquents. Critics still point to the failure of the famous Cambridge-Somerville Youth Study as evidence that clinical treatment has little value. In that effort, 325 high-risk predelinquents were given intense counseling and treatment, and their progress was compared with a control group that received no special attention. A well-known evaluation of the project by Joan McCord and William McCord found that the treated youths were more likely to become involved in law violation than the untreated controls.[219] By implication, the danger is that the efforts designed to help youths may actually stigmatize and label them, hindering their efforts to live conventional lives. Critics such as Edwin Schur argue that less is better, that the more we try to help youths, the more likely they will be to see themselves as different, outcasts, troublemakers.[220] Such questions have led to the development of prevention efforts designed to influence the social as well as the psychological world of delinquent and predelinquent youths (see chapters 5 and 6).

SUMMARY

Choice theory holds that people have free will to control their actions. Delinquency is a product of the weighing of the risks of crime against its benefits. If the risk is greater than the gain, people will choose not to commit crime. One way of creating a greater risk is to make sure that the punishments associated with delinquency are severe, certain, and fast.

Choice theorists argue that delinquent behavior can be prevented if youths can be deterred from illegal acts. Consequently, they agree that the punishments for delinquency should be increased. One method is to transfer youths to the criminal courts or to grant the adult justice system original jurisdiction over serious juvenile cases. Similarly, some delinquent experts advocate the use of incapacitation for serious juvenile offenders—for example, using mandatory, long-term sentences for chronic delinquents.

Trait theorists hold that personal and environmental factors dictate behavior choices, that delinquents do not choose to commit crimes freely but are influenced by forces beyond their control.

One of the earliest branches of biosocial theory focused on the biological bases of delinquency. Cesare Lombroso originated the concept of the "born criminal" and linked delinquency to inborn traits. Following his lead were theories based on genetic inheritance and

body build. Although biological theory was in disrepute for many years, it has recently reemerged in importance. Biochemical, neurological, and genetic factors have been linked to aggressiveness and violence in youth. However, because biosocial theory has not been subjected to methodologically sound tests, the results remain problematic.

Another type of individual-level theory has a psychological orientation. Some theorists rely on Freud's psychoanalytic theory and link delinquency to ego development and personality. Others use a behavioral perspective. Social-learning theorists hold that children imitate the adult behavior they observe in daily life or on television. Physiological psychologists study the relationship between physical and mental properties.

Many delinquency prevention efforts are based on psychological theory. Judges commonly order delinquent youths to receive counseling and other mental health care in an attempt to address and remedy psychological issues. Recently, some adjudicated delinquent offenders have been given biochemical therapy. More research needs to be done in order to draw conclusions on this experimental form of treatment. Table 3.1 summarizes the various theories discussed in this chapter.

TABLE 3.1 Choice, Biosocial, and Psychological Theories

Theory	Major Premise	Strengths
Choice Theories		
rational choice	Law-violating behavior is an event that occurs after offenders weigh information on their personal needs and the situational factors involved in the difficulty and risk of committing a crime.	Explains why high-risk youth do not constantly engage in delinquent acts. Relates theory to delinquency control policy. It is not limited by class or other social variables.
routine activities	Crime and delinquency are functions of the presence of motivated offenders, the availability of suitable targets, and the absence of capable guardians.	Can explain fluctuations in crime and delinquency rates. Shows how victim behavior influences criminal choice.
deterrence	People will commit crime and delinquency if they perceive that the benefits outweigh the risks. Crime is a function of the severity, certainty, and speed of punishment.	Shows the relationship between crime and punishment. Suggests a real solution to crime.
Biosocial Theories		
biochemical	Crime, especially violence, is a function of diet, vitamin intake, hormonal imbalance, or food allergies.	Explains irrational violence. Shows how the environment interacts with personal traits to influence behavior.
neurological	Criminals and delinquents often suffer brain impairment, as measured by the EEG. Attention deficit/hyperactive disorder and minimum brain dysfunction are related to antisocial behavior.	Explains irrational violence. Shows how the environment interacts with personal traits to influence behavior.
genetic	Delinquent traits and predispositions are inherited. Criminality of parents can predict the delinquency of children.	Explains why only a small percentage of youth in a high-crime area become chronic offenders.
Psychological Theories		
psychodynamic	The development of the unconscious personality early in childhood influences behavior for the rest of a person's life. Delinquents have weak egos and damaged personalities.	Explains the onset of crime and delinquency. Shows why delinquency and drug abuse cut across class lines.
behavioral	People commit crime when they model their behavior after others they see being rewarded for the same acts. Behavior is enforced by rewards and extinguished by punishment.	Explains the role of others in the crime process. Shows how family life and media can influence delinquency.
cognitive	Individual reasoning processes influence behavior. Reasoning is influenced by the way people perceive their environment and by their moral and intellectual development.	Shows why delinquent behavior patterns change over time as people mature and develop their moral reasoning.
Integrated Theories		
Wilson and Herrnstein's human nature theory	People choose to commit crime when they are biologically and psychologically impaired.	Shows how physical traits interact with social conditions to produce crime. Can account for noncriminal behavior in high-crime areas. Integrates choice and developmental theories.

KEY TERMS

choice theory
trait theory
free will
utilitarian
classical criminology
rehabilitation
medical model
rational choice
"seductions of crime"
routine activities theory
lifestyle
deterrence
secure incarceration
target-hardening techniques
hot spots

crackdown
positivism
criminal atavism
somatotype
reciprocal altruism
equipotentiality
biosocial theory
psychological theory
neurological
minimal brain dysfunction (MBD)
learning disability (LD)
susceptibility rationale
school failure rationale
psychoanalytic theory
psychodynamic theory

identity crisis
latent delinquents
behaviorism
social learning theory
cognitive theory
extraversion
neuroticism
psychopathic
sociopathic
arousal theory
primary sociopaths
secondary sociopaths
nature theory
nurture theory
crime as choice

QUESTIONS FOR DISCUSSION

1. Is there such a thing as the "born criminal"?
2. Is crime psychologically abnormal? Can there be "normal" crimes?
3. Apply psychodynamic theory to such delinquent acts as shoplifting and breaking and entering a house.
4. Can delinquent behavior be deterred by the threat of punishment? If not, how can it be controlled?
5. Should we incapacitate violent juvenile offenders for long periods of time—10 years or more?
6. Does watching violent TV and films encourage youth to be aggressive and antisocial? Do advertisements for beer featuring attractive, scantily dressed young men and women encourage drinking and precocious sex? If not, why bother advertising?
7. Discuss the characteristics of psychopaths. Do you know anyone who fits the description?

NOTES

1. Marvin Wolfgang, Robert Figlio, and Thorsten Sellin, *Delinquency in a Birth Cohort* (Chicago: University of Chicago Press, 1972).
2. Alan Lizotte, Terence Thornberry, Marvin Krohn, Deborah Chard-Wierschem, and David McDowall, "Neighborhood Context and Delinquency: A Longitudinal Analysis," in H. J. Kerner and E. Weitekamp, eds., *Cross-National Longitudinal Research on Human Development and Criminal Behavior* (Dordrecht, The Netherlands: Kluwer Academic Publishers, 1993), pp. 11–15.
3. Jeremy Bentham, *A Fragment on Government and an Introduction to the Principles of Morals and Legislation,* ed. Wilfred Harrison (Oxford: Basil Blackwell, 1967).
4. See, generally, Ernest Van den Haag, *Punishing Criminals* (New York: Basic Books, 1975).
5. See, generally, James Q. Wilson, *Thinking about Crime* (New York: Basic Books, 1975).
6. Cesare Beccaria, *On Crimes and Punishments,* 6th ed., trans. Henry Paolucci (Indianapolis, Ind.: Bobbs-Merrill, 1977), p. 43.
7. F. E. Devine, "Cesare Beccaria and the Theoretical Foundations of Modern Penal Jurisprudence," *New England Journal on Prison Law* 7:8–21 (1982).
8. For an analysis of the rehabilitation philosophy, see Ted Palmer, *Correctional Intervention and Research* (Lexington, Mass.: Lexington Books, 1978).

9. Sanford Fox, "The Reform of Juvenile Justice: The Child's Right to Punishment," *Juvenile Justice* 25:2–9 (1974).

10. James Q. Wilson and Richard Herrnstein, *Crime and Human Nature* (New York: Simon & Schuster, 1985), p. 396.

11. Mary Tuck and David Riley, "The Theory of Reasoned Action: A Decision Theory of Crime," in D. Cornish and R. Clarke, eds., *The Reasoning Criminal* (New York: Springer-Verlag, 1986), pp. 156–69.

12. Wilson, *Thinking about Crime;* Van den Haag, *Punishing Criminals;* Andrew von Hirsch, *Doing Justice: The Choice of Punishments* (New York: Hill & Wang, 1976); Graeme Newman, *Just and Painful* (New York: Macmillan, 1983).

13. See, generally, Derek Cornish and Ronald Clarke, eds., *The Reasoning Criminal* (New York: Springer-Verlag, 1986); see also Philip Cook, "The Demand and Supply of Criminal Opportunities," in Michael Tonry and Norval Morris, eds., *Crime and Justice,* vol. 7 (Chicago: University of Chicago Press, 1986), pp. 1–28; Ronald Clarke and Derek Cornish, "Modeling Offenders' Decisions: A Framework for Research and Policy," in Michael Tonry and Norval Morris, eds., *Crime and Justice,* vol. 6 (Chicago: University of Chicago Press, 1985), pp. 147–87; Morgan Reynolds, *Crime by Choice: An Economic Analysis* (Dallas: Fisher Institute, 1985).

14. Felix Padilla, *The Gang as an American Enterprise* (New Brunswick, N.J.: Rutgers University Press, 1992); Martin Sanchez-Jankowski, *Islands in the Street: Gangs and American Urban Society* (Berkeley: University of California Press, 1991).

15. Travis Hirschi, "Rational Choice and Social Control Theories of Crime," in Derek Cornish and Ronald Clarke, eds., *The Reasoning Criminal* (New York: Springer-Verlag, 1986), p. 114.

16. Jack Katz, *Seductions of Crime* (New York: Basic Books, 1988).

17. Ibid., pp. 12–52.

18. Bill McCarthy and John Hagan, "Mean Streets: The Theoretical Significance of Situational Delinquency among Homeless Youths," *American Journal of Sociology* 3:597–627 (1992).

19. Bill McCarthy, "Not Just 'For the Thrill of It': An Instrumentalist Elaboration of Katz's Explanation of Sneaky Thrill Property Crime," *Criminology* 33:519–39 (1995).

20. Michael Hindelang, Michael Gottfredson, and James Garofalo, *Victims of Personal Crime: An Empirical Foundation for a Theory of Personal Victimization* (Cambridge, Mass.: Ballinger, 1978).

21. James Massey, Marvin Krohn, and Lisa Bonati, "Property Crime and the Routine Activities of Individuals," *Journal of Research in Crime and Delinquency* 26:378–400 (1989).

22. Lawrence Cohen and Marcus Felson, "Social Change and Crime Rate Trends: A Routine Activities Approach," *American Sociological Review* 44:588–608 (1979).

23. For a review, see James LeBeau and Thomas Castellano, "The Routine Activities Approach: An Inventory and Critique," Unpublished review, Center for the Studies of Crime, Delinquency and Corrections, Southern Illinois University–Carbondale, 1987.

24. David Maume, "Inequality and Metropolitan Rape Rates: A Routine Activity Approach," *Justice Quarterly* 6:513–27 (1989).

25. Denise Osborn, Alan Trickett, and Rob Elder, "Area Characteristics and Regional Variates as Determinants of Area Property Crime Levels," *Journal of Quantitative Criminology* 8:265–82 (1992).

26. Massey, Krohn, and Bonati, "Property Crime and the Routine Activities of Individuals," p. 397.

27. Lawrence Cohen, Marcus Felson, and Kenneth Land, "Property Crime Rates in the United States: A Macrodynamic Analysis, 1947–1977, with Ex-Ante Forecasts for the Mid-1980's," *American Journal of Sociology* 86:90–118 (1980).

28. Steven Messner and Kenneth Tardiff, "The Social Ecology of Urban Homicide: An Application of the 'Routine Activities' Approach," *Criminology* 23:241–67 (1985).

29. Leslie Kennedy and David Forde, "Routine Activities and Crime: An Analysis of Victimization in Canada," *Criminology* 28:137–52 (1990).

30. Robert O'Brien, "Relative Cohort Sex and Age-Specific Crime Rates: An Age-Period-Relative-Cohort-Size Model," *Criminology* 27:57–78 (1989).

31. D. Wayne Osgood, Janet Wilson, Patrick O'Malley, Jerald Bachman, and Lloyd Johnston, "Routine Activities and Individual Deviant Behaviors," *American Sociological Review* (in press, 1996).

32. Ernest Van den Haag, "The Criminal Law as a Threat System," *Journal of Criminal Law and Criminology* 73:709–85 (1982).

33. Beccaria, *On Crimes and Punishments.*

34. For the classic analysis on the subject, see Johannes Andenaes, *Punishment and Deterrence* (Ann Arbor: University of Michigan Press, 1974).

35. Gordon Bazemore and Mark Umbreit, "Rethinking the Sanctioning Function in Juvenile Court: Retributive or Restorative Responses to Youth Crime," *Crime and Delinquency* 41:296–316 (1995).

36. Bruce Jacobs, "Anticipatory Undercover Targeting in High Schools," *Journal of Criminal Justice* 22:445–57 (1994).

37. Leona Lee, "Factors Determining Waiver in a Juvenile Court," *Journal of Criminal Justice* 22:329–39 (1994).

38. *Wilkins v. Missouri; Stanford v. Kentucky,* 109 S.Ct. 2969 (1989).

39. Carol Kohfeld and John Sprague, "Demography, Police Behavior, and Deterrence," *Criminology* 28:111–36 (1990).

40. Steven Klepper and Daniel Nagin, "The Deterrent Effect of Perceived Certainty and Severity of Punishment Revisited," *Criminology* 27:721–46 (1989).

41. See, generally, Raymond Paternoster, "The Deterrent Effect of Perceived and Severity of Punishment: A Review of the Evidence and Issues," *Justice Quarterly* 42:173–217 (1987); idem, "Absolute and Restrictive Deterrence in a Panel of Youth: Explaining the Onset, Persistence/Desistance, and Frequency of Delinquent Offending," *Social Problems* 36:289–307 (1989).

42. Donald Green, "Measures of Illegal Behavior in Individual-Level Deterrence Research," *Journal of Research in Crime and Delinquency* 26:253–75 (1989); Charles Tittle, *Sanctions and Social Deviance: The Question of Deterrence* (New York: Praeger, 1980).

43. Eric Jensen and Linda Metsger, "A Test of the Deterrent Effect of Legislative Waiver on Violent Juvenile Crime," *Crime and Delinquency* 40:96–104 (1994).

44. Bureau of Justice Statistics, *Prisoners and Drugs* (Washington, D.C.: U.S. Government Printing Office, 1983); idem, *Prisoners and Alcohol* (Washington, D.C.: U.S. Government Printing Office, 1983).

45. Maynard Erickson and Jack Gibbs, "Punishment, Deterrence, and Juvenile Justice," in D. Shichor and D. Kelly, eds., *Critical Issues in Juvenile Justice* (Lexington, Mass.: Lexington Books, 1980), pp. 183–202.

46. Pamela Lattimore, Christy Visher, Richard Linster, "Predicting Rearrest for Violence among Serious Youthful Offenders," *Criminology* 32:54–83 (1995).

47. Charles Murray and Louis B. Cox, *Beyond Probation* (Beverly Hills, Calif.: Sage, 1979).

48. David Altschuler, "Juveniles and Violence: Is There an Epidemic and What Can be Done," Paper presented at the American Society of Criminology meeting, Boston, Mass., November 1995.

49. Marcus Felson, "Routine Activities and Crime Prevention," in National Council for Crime Prevention, *Studies on Crime and Crime Prevention, Annual Review,* vol. 1 (Stockholm: Scandinavian University Press, 1992), pp. 30–34.

50. Barry Webb, "Steering Column Locks and Motor Vehicle Theft: Evaluations for Three Countries," in Ronald Clarke, ed., *Crime Prevention Studies* (Monsey, N.Y.: Criminal Justice Press, 1994), pp. 71–89.

51. Lawrence Sherman, Patrick Gartin, and Michael Buerger, "Hot Spots of Predatory Crime: Routine Activities and the Criminology of Place," *Criminology* 27:27–55 (1989).

52. For an analysis of hot spots, see James O'Kane, R. Mace Fisher, and Lorraine Green," Mapping Campus Crime," *Security Journal* 5:172–79 (1994); see also Dennis Roncek and Pamela Maier, "Bars, Blocks, and Crimes Revisited: Linking the Theory of Routine Activities to the Empiricism of 'Hot Spots,' " *Criminology* 29:725–53 (1991).

53. Lawrence Sherman, "Police Crackdowns: Initial and Residual Deterrence," in Michael Tonry and Norval Morris, eds., *Crime and Justice, A Review of Research,* vol. 12 (Chicago: University of Chicago Press, 1990), pp. 1–48.

54. Taken from the famous title of an article by Walter Reckless, Simon Dinitz, and Ellen Murray: "The Good Boy in a High Delinquency Area," *Journal of Criminal Law, Criminology, and Police Science* 48:18–26 (1957).

55. Massey, Krohn, and Bonati, "Property Crime and the Routine Activities of Individuals."

56. David Shantz, "Conflict, Aggression, and Peer Status: An Observational Study," *Child Development* 57:1322–1332 (1986).

57. For an excellent review of Lombroso's work, as well as that of other well-known theorists, see Randy Martin, Robert Mutchnick, and W. Timothy Austin, *Criminological Thought, Pioneers Past and Present* (New York: Macmillan, 1990).

58. Marvin Wolfgang, "Cesare Lombroso," in Herman Mannheim, ed., *Pioneers in Criminology* (Montclair, N.J.: Patterson Smith, 1970), pp. 232–71.

59. Gina Lombroso-Ferrero, *Criminal Man According to the Classification of Cesare Lombroso* (1911; reprint, Montclair, N.J.: Patterson Smith, 1972), p. 7.

60. Edwin Driver, "Charles Buckman Goring," in Herman Mannheim,ed., *Pioneers in Criminology* (Montclair, N.J.: Patterson Smith, 1970), pp. 429–42.

61. See, generally, Thorsten Sellin, "Enrico Ferri," in Herman Mannheim, ed., *Pioneers in Criminology* (Montclair, N.J.: Patterson Smith, 1970), pp. 361–84.

62. Driver, "Charles Buckman Goring," pp. 434–35.

63. Ibid., p. 440.

64. Richard Dugdale, *The Jukes* (New York: Putnam, 1910); Arthur Estabrook, *The Jukes in 1915* (Washington, D.C.: Carnegie Institute of Washington, 1916).

65. Ernst Kretschmer, *Physique and Character,* trans. W. J. H. Spratt (London: Kegan Paul, 1925).

66. William Sheldon, *Varieties of Delinquent Youth* (New York: Harper Bros., 1949).

67. For a review of Sheldon's legacy, see C. Peter Herman, "The Shape of Man," *Contemporary Psychology* 37:525–30 (1992).

68. Nicole Hahn Rafter, "Criminal Anthropology in the United States," *Criminology* 30:525–47 (1992).

69. B. R. McCandless, W. S. Persons, and A. Roberts, "Perceived Opportunity, Delinquency, Race, and Body Build among Delinquent Youth," *Journal of Consulting and Clinical Psychology* 38:281–83 (1972).

70. Edmond O. Wilson, *Sociobiology: The New Synthesis* (Cambridge, Mass.: Harvard University Press, 1975).

71. For a general review, see John Archer, "Human Sociobiology: Basic Concepts and Limitations," *Journal of Social Issues* 47:11–26 (1991).

72. Arthur Caplan, *The Sociobiology Debate: Readings on Ethical and Scientific Issues* (New York: Harper & Row, 1978).

73. C. Ray Jeffery, "Criminology as an Interdisciplinary Behavioral Science," *Criminology* 16:149–67 (1978).

74. Ibid., p. 150.

75. Terrie Moffitt, "Adolescence-Limited and Life-Course Persistent Antisocial Behavior: A Developmental Taxonomy," *Psychological Review* 100:674–701 (1993).

76. For a review, see Adrian Raine, *The Psychopathology of Crime: Criminal Behavior as a Clinical Disorder* (New York: Academic Press, 1993).

77. For a thorough review of the biosocial perspective, see Diana Fishbein, "Biological Perspectives in Criminology," *Criminology* 28:27–72 (1990); idem, "Selected Studies on the Biology of Crime," in John Conklin, ed., *New Perspectives in Criminology* (Needham Heights, Mass.: Allyn and Bacon, 1996), 26–38.

78. See, generally, Raine, *The Psychopathology of Crime*; see also Leonard Hippchen, *The Ecologic-Biochemical Approaches to Treatment of Delinquents and Criminals* (New York: Van Nostrand Reinhold, 1978).

79. Paul Marshall, "Allergy and Depression: A Neurochemical Threshold Model of the Relation between the Illnesses," *Psychological Bulletin* 113:23–43 (1993); Elizabeth McNeal and Peter Cimbolic, "Antidepressants and Biochemical Theories of Depression," *Psychological Bulletin* 99:361–74 (1986); for an opposing view, see "Adverse Reactions to Food in Young Children," *Nutrition Reviews* 46:120–21 (1988).

80. Marshall, "Allergy and Depression: A Neurochemical Threshold Model of the Relation between the Illnesses."

81. Raine, *The Psychopathology of Crime,* p. 212.

82. Deborah Denno, "Human Biology and Criminal Responsibility: Free Will or Free Ride?," *University of Pennsylvania Law Review* 137:615–71 (1988).

83. Leonard Hippchen, "Some Possible Biochemical Aspects of Criminal Behavior," *Journal of Behavioral Ecology* 2:1–6 (1981); Sarnoff Mednick and Jan Volavka, "Biology and Crime," in N. Morris and M. Tonry, eds., *Crime and Justice,* vol. 2 (Chicago: University of Chicago Press, 1980), pp. 85–159.

84. Stephen Schoenthaler, "Malnutrition and Maladaptive Behavior: Two Correlational Analyses and a Double-Blind Placebo-Controlled Challenge in Five States," in W. B. Essman, ed., *Nutrients and Brain Function* (New York: Karger, 1987).

85. Alexander Schauss and C. Simonsen, "A Critical Analysis of the Diets of Chronic Juvenile Offenders, Part I," *Journal of Orthomolecular Psychiatry* 8:149–57 (1979).

86. J. Kershner and W. Hawke, "Megavitamins and Learning Disorders: A Controlled Double-Blind Experiment," *Journal of Nutrition* 109:819–26 (1979).

87. Stephen Schoenthaler and Walter Doraz, "Types of Offenses Which Can Be Reduced in an Institutional Setting Using Nutritional Intervention," *International Journal of Biosocial Research* 4:74–84 (1983); idem, "Diet and Crime," *International Journal of Biosocial Research* 4:29–39 (1983).

88. Stephen Schoenthaler, Walter Doraz, and James Wakefield, "The Impact of a Low Food Additive and Sucrose Diet on Academic Performance in 803 New York City Public Schools," *International Journal of Biosocial Research* 8:185–95 (1986).

89. Richard Milich and William Pelham, "Effects of Sugar Ingestion on the Classroom and Playgroup Behavior of Attention Deficit Disordered Boys," *Journal of Counseling and Clinical Psychology* 54:714–18 (1986).

90. Mark Wolraich, Scott Lindgren, Phyllis Stumbo, Lewis Stegink, Mark Appelbaum, and Mary Kiritsy, "Effects of Diets High in Sucrose or Aspartame on the Behavior and Cognitive Performance of Children," *The New England Journal of Medicine* 330:303–06 (1994).

91. Dian Gans, "Sucrose and Unusual Childhood Behavior," *Nutrition Today* 26:8–14 (1991).

92. Marcel Kinsbourne, "Sugar and the Hyperactive Child," *The New England Journal of Medicine* 330:355–56 (1994).

93. Stephen Schoenthaler, "Institutional Nutritional Policies and Criminal Behavior," *Nutrition Today* 24:16–24 (1985), at 24.

94. Christy Miller Buchanan, Jacquelynne Eccles, and Jill Becker, "Are Adolescents the Victims of Raging Hormones? Evidence for Activational Effects of Hormones on Moods and Behavior at Adolescence," *Psychological Bulletin* 111:62–107 (1992).

95. Fishbein, "Selected Studies on the Biology of Crime."

96. Diana Fishbein, David Lozovsky, and Jerome Jaffe, "Impulsivity, Aggression and Neuroendocrine Responses to Serotonergic Stimulation in Substance Abusers," Paper presented at the *American Society of Criminology,* Reno, Nev., November 1989.

97. Kytja Voeller, "Right-Hemisphere Deficit Syndrome in Children," *American Journal of Psychiatry* 143:1004–1009 (1986).

98. Terrie Moffitt, "Adolescence-Limited and Life-Course Persistent Antisocial Behavior: A Developmental Taxonomy," *Psychological Review* 100:674–701 (1993).

99. Leila Beckwith and Arthur Parmelee, "EEG Patterns of Preterm Infants, Home Environment, and Later IQ," *Child Development* 57:777–89 (1986).

100. Stephen Tibbetts, "Low Birth Weight, Disadvantaged Environment and Early Onset: A Test of Moffitt's Interactional Hypothesis," Paper presented at the American Society of Criminology meeting, Boston, Mass.:, November 1995.

101. Dorothy Otnow Lewis, Jonathan Pincus, Marilyn Feldman, Lori Jackson, and Barbara Bard, "Psychiatric, Neurological, and Psychoeducational Characteristics of 15 Death Row Inmates in the United States," *American Journal of Psychiatry* 143:838–45 (1986).

102. See, generally, R. R. Monroe, *Brain Dysfunction in Aggressive Criminals* (Lexington, Mass.: D. C. Heath, 1978).

103. Adrian Raine et al., "Interhemispheric Transfer in Schizophrenics, Depressives and Normals with Schizoid Tendencies," *Journal of Abnormal Psychology* 98:35–41 (1989).

104. Jean Seguin, Robert Pihl, Philip Harden, Richard Tremblay, and Bernard Boulerice, "Cognitive and Neuropsychological Characteristics of Physically Aggressive Boys," *Journal of Abnormal Psychology* 104:614–24 (1995).

105. D. Williams, "Neural Factors Related to Habitual Aggression—Consideration of Differences between Habitual Aggressives and Others Who Have Committed Crimes of Violence," *Brain* 92:503–20 (1969).

106. Charlotte Johnson and William Pelham, "Teacher Ratings Predict Peer Ratings of Aggression at 3-Year Follow-Up in Boys with Attention Deficit Disorder with Hyperactivity," *Journal of Consulting and Clinical Psychology* 54:571–72 (1987).

107. Cited in Charles Post, "The Link between Learning Disabilities and Juvenile Delinquency: Cause, Effect, and 'Present Solutions,'" *Juvenile and Family Court Journal* 31:59 (1981).

108. For a general review, see Concetta Culliver, "Juvenile Delinquency and Learning Disability: Any Link?" Paper presented at the Academy of Criminal Justice Sciences, San Francisco, Calif., April 1988.

109. Joel Zimmerman, William Rich, Ingo Keilitz, and Paul Broder, "Some Observations on the Link between Learning Disabilities and Juvenile Delinquency," *Journal of Criminal Justice* 9:9–17 (1981); J. W. Podboy and W. A. Mallory, "The Diagnosis of Specific Learning Disabilities in a Juvenile Delinquent Population," *Juvenile and Family Court Journal* 30:11–13 (1978).

110. Charles Murray, *The Link between Learning Disabilities and Juvenile Delinquency: A Current Theory and Knowledge* (Washington, D.C.: U.S. Government Printing Office, 1976).

111. Robert Pasternak and Reid Lyon, "Clinical and Empirical Identification of Learning Disabled Juvenile Delinquents," *Journal of Correctional Education* 33:7–13 (1982).

112. Zimmerman et al., "Some Observations on the Link between Learning Disabilities and Juvenile Delinquency."

113. Lynn Meltzer, Bethany Roditi, and Terence Fenton, "Cognitive and Learning Profiles of Delinquent and Learning-Disabled Adolescents," *Adolescence* 21:581–91 (1986).

114. Terrie Moffitt, "The Neuropsychology of Conduct Disorder" (University of Wisconsin–Madison, mimeo, 1992).

115. Elizabeth Kandel and Sarnoff Mednick, "Perinatal Complications Predict Violent Offending," *Criminology* 29:519–30 (1991).

116. James Creechan, "The Masking of Learning Disabilities and Juvenile Delinquency: The Learning Disabilities–Juvenile Delinquency Amplification Model," Paper presented at the annual meeting of the American Society of Criminology, New Orleans, La., November 1992).

117. Diana Fishbein and Robert Thatcher, "New Diagnostic Methods in Criminology: Assessing Organic Sources of Behavioral Disorder," *Journal of Research in Crime and Delinquency* 23:240–67 (1986).

118. David Rowe, *The Limits of Family Influence: Genes, Experiences and Behavior* (New York: Guilford Press, 1995), p. 64.

119. For a review, see Lisabeth Fisher DiLalla and Irving Gottesman, "Biological and Genetic Contributors to Violence—Widom's Untold Tale," *Psychological Bulletin* 109:125–29 (1991).

120. Ibid.

121. L. Erlenmeyer-Kimling, Robert Golden, and Barbara Cornblatt, "A Taxometric Analysis of Cognitive and Neuromotor Variables in Children in Risk for Schizophrenia," *Journal of Abnormal Psychology* 98:203–08 (1989).

122. A. A. Sandberg, G. F. Koeph, T. Ishiara, and T. S. Hauschka, "An XYY Human Male," *Lancet* 262:448–49 (1961); T. R. Sarbin and L. E. Miller, "Demonism Revisited: The XYY Chromosome Anomaly," *Issues in Criminology* 5:195–207 (1970).

123. David Rowe, Joseph Rogers, and Sylvia Meseck-Bushey, "Sibling Delinquency and the Family Environment: Shared and Unshared Influences," *Child Development* 63:59–67 (1992).

124. David Rowe, "Sibling Interaction and Self-Reported Delinquent Behavior: A Study of 265 Twin Pairs," *Criminology* 23:223–40 (1985); Nancy Segal, "Monozygotic and Dizygotic Twins: A Comparative Analysis of Mental Ability Profiles," *Child Development* 56:1051–58 (1985).

125. Mednick and Volavka, "Biology and Crime"; Lee Ellis, "Genetics and Criminal Behavior," *Criminology* 10:43–66 (1982).

126. Karl O. Christiansen, "A Preliminary Study of Criminality among Twins," in S. A. Mednick and Karl O. Christiansen, eds., *The Biosocial Bases of Criminal Behavior* (New York: Gardner Press, 1977).

127. Glenn Walters, "A Meta-Analysis of the Gene–Crime Relationship," *Criminology* 30:595–613 (1992).

128. T. J. Bouchard, D. T. Lykken, D. T. McGue, N. L. Segal, and A. Tellegen, "Sources of Human Psychological Differences: The Minnesota Study of Twins Reared Apart," *Science* 250:223–28 (1990).

129. D. T. Lykken, M. McGue, A. Tellegen, and T. J. Bouchard, Jr., "Emergenesis, Genetic Traits That May Not Run in Families," *American Psychologist* 47:1565–77 (1992).

130. Remi Cadoret, Colleen Cain, and Raymond Crowe, "Evidence for a Gene–Environment Interaction in the Development of Adolescent Antisocial Behavior," *Behavior Genetics* 13:301–10 (1983).

131. Rowe, *The Limits of Family Influence: Genes, Experiences and Behavior,* p. 110.

132. Bernard Hutchings and Sarnoff Mednick, "Criminality in Adoptees and Their Adoptive and Biological Parents: A Pilot Study," in S. A. Mednick and Karl O. Christiansen, eds., *Biosocial Bases of Criminal Behavior* (New York: Gardner Press, 1977).

133. For similar findings, see William Gabrielli and Sarnoff Mednick, "Urban Environment, Genetics, and Crime," *Criminology* 22:645–53 (1984).

134. Jody Alberts-Corush, Philip Firestone, and John Goodman, "Attention and Impulsivity Characteristics of the Biological and Adoptive Parents of Hyperactive and Normal Control Children," *American Journal of Orthopsychiatry* 56:413–23 (1986).

135. Wilson and Herrnstein, *Crime and Human Nature,* p. 131.

136. Walters, "A Meta-Analysis of the Gene–Crime Relationship."

137. Ibid., p. 108.

138. For a thorough review of this issue, see David Brandt and S. Jack Zlotnick, *The Psychology and Treatment of the Youthful Offender* (Springfield, Ill.: Charles C Thomas, 1988).

139. Spencer Rathus, *Psychology* (New York: Holt, Rinehart & Winston, 1996), pp. 11–21.

140. See, generally, Sigmund Freud, *An Outline of Psychoanalysis,* trans. James Strachey (New York: Norton, 1963).

141. Seymour Halleck, *Psychiatry and the Dilemmas of Crime* (Berkeley: University of California Press, 1971).

142. See, generally, Erik Erickson, *Identity, Youth, and Crisis* (New York: Norton, 1968).

143. David Abrahamsen, *Crime and the Human Mind* (New York: Columbia University Press, 1944), p. 137.

144. See, generally, Fritz Redl and Hans Toch, "The Psychoanalytic Perspective," in Hans Toch, ed., *Psychology of Crime and Criminal Justice* (New York: Holt, Rinehart & Winston, 1979), pp. 193–95.

145. August Aichorn, *Wayward Youth* (New York: Viking, 1935).

146. Halleck, *Psychiatry and the Dilemmas of Crime.*

147. James Sorrells, "Kids Who Kill," *Crime and Delinquency* 23:312–20 (1977).

148. Richard Rosner et al., "Adolescents Accused of Murder and Manslaughter: A Five-Year Descriptive Study," *Bulletin of the American Academy of Psychiatry and the Law* 7:342–51 (1979).

149. Milton Rosenbaum and Binni Bennet, "Homicide and Depression," *American Journal of Psychiatry* 143:367–70 (1986).

150. Brandt and Zlotnick, *The Psychology and Treatment of the Youthful Offender,* pp. 72–73.

151. Albert Bandura and Frances Menlove, "Factors Determining Vicarious Extinction of Avoidance Behavior through Symbolic Modeling," *Journal of Personality and Social Psychology* 8:99–108 (1965); Albert Bandura and Richard Walters, *Social Learning and Personality Development* (New York: Holt, Rinehart & Winston, 1963).

152. David Perry, Louise Perry, and Paul Rasmussen, "Cognitive Social Learning Mediators of Aggression," *Child Development* 57:700–11 (1986).

153. Bonnie Carlson, "Children's Beliefs about Punishment," *American Journal of Orthopsychiatry* 56:308–12 (1986).

154. Albert Bandura and Richard Walters, *Adolescent Aggression* (New York: Ronald Press, 1959), p. 32.

155. Edward Donnerstein and Daniel Linz, "The Question of Pornography," *Psychology Today* 20:56–59 (1986).

156. Joyce Sprafkin, Kenneth Gadow, and Monique Dussault, "Reality Perceptions of Television: A Preliminary Comparison of Emotionally Disturbed and Nonhandicapped Children," *American Journal of Orthopsychiatry* 56:147–52 (1986).

157. Daniel Anderson, Elizabeth Pugzles Lorch, Diane Field, Patricia Collins, and John Nathan, "Television Viewing at Home: Age Trends in Visual Attention Time with TV," *Child Development* 57:1024–33 (1986).

158. Lynette Friedrich-Cofer and Aletha Huston, "Television Violence and Aggression: The Debate Continues," *Psychological Bulletin* 100:364–71 (1986).

159. American Psychological Association, *Violence on TV. A Social Issue Release from the Board of Social and Ethical Responsibility for Psychology* (Washington, D.C.: APA, 1985).

160. Wendy Wood, Frank Wong, and J. Gregory Chachere, "Effects of Media Violence on Viewers' Aggression in Unconstrained Social Interaction," *Psychological Bulletin* 109:371–83 (1991).

161. Associated Press, "Hollywood Is Blamed in Token Booth Attack," *Boston Globe,* 28 November 1995, p. 30.

162. Jonathon Freedman, "Television Violence and Aggression: What the Evidence Shows," in S. Oskamp, ed., *Applied Social Psychology Annual: Television as a Social Issue* (Newbury Park, Calif.: Sage, 1988), pp. 144–62.

163. Jonathon Freedman, "Effect of Television Violence on Aggressiveness," *Psychological Bulletin* 96:227–46 (1984); idem, "Television Violence and Aggression: A Rejoinder," *Psychological Bulletin* 100:372–78 (1986).

164. Steven Messner, "Television Violence and Violent Crime: An Aggregate Analysis," *Social Problems* 33:218–35 (1986).

165. See, generally, Jean Piaget, *The Moral Judgement of the Child* (London: Keagan Paul, 1932).

166. Lawrence Kohlberg, *Stages in the Development of Moral Thought and Action* (New York: Holt, Rinehart and Winston, 1969).

167. L. Kohlberg, K. Kauffman, P. Scharf, and J. Hickey, *The Just Community Approach in Corrections: A Manual* (Niantic, Conn.: Connecticut Department of Corrections, 1973).

168. Scott Henggeler, *Delinquency in Adolescence* (Newbury Park, Calif.: Sage, 1989), p. 26.

169. Ibid.

170. K. A. Dodge, "A Social Information Processing Model of Social Competence in Children," in *Minnesota Sympo-*

sium in Child Psychology, vol. 18, ed. M. Perlmutter (Hillsdale, N.J.: Erlbaum, 1986), pp. 77–125.

171. L. Huesman and L. Eron, "Individual Differences and the Trait of Aggression," *European Journal of Personality* 3:95–106 (1989).

172. J. E. Lochman, "Self and Peer Perceptions and Attributional Biases of Aggressive and Nonaggressive Boys in Dyadic Interactions," *Journal of Consulting and Clinical Psychology* 55:404–10 (1987).

173. Ibid., p. 405.

174. See, generally, G. Patterson, J. Reid, and T. Dishion, *Antisocial Boys* (Eugene, Oreg.: Castalia, 1992).

175. See, generally, Walter Mischel, *Introduction to Personality,* 4th ed. (New York: Holt, Rinehart and & Winston, 1986).

176. D. A. Andrews and J. Stephen Wormith, "Personality and Crime: Knowledge and Construction in Criminology," *Justice Quarterly* 6:289–310 (1989); Donald Gibbons, "Comment—Personality and Crime: Non-Issues, Real Issues, and a Theory and Research Agenda," *Justice Quarterly* 6:311–24 (1989).

177. Sheldon Glueck and Eleanor Glueck, *Unraveling Juvenile Delinquency* (Cambridge, Mass.: Harvard University Press, 1950).

178. David Farrington, "Psychobiological Factors in the Explanation and Reduction of Delinquency," *Today's Delinquent* 7:37–51 (1988).

179. Laurie Frost, Terrie Moffitt, and Rob McGee, "Neuropsychological Correlates of Psychopathology in an Unselected Cohort of Young Adolescents," *Journal of Abnormal Psychology* 98:307–13 (1989).

180. See, generally, Hans Eysenck, *Personality and Crime* (London: Routledge and Kegan Paul, 1977).

181. Hans Eysenck and M. W. Eysenck, *Personality and Individual Differences* (New York: Plenum, 1985).

182. Linda Mealey, "The Sociobiology of Sociopathy: An Integrated Evolutionary Model," *Behavioral and Brain Sciences* 18:523–40 (1995).

183. Hervey Cleckley, "Psychopathic States," in S. Aneti, ed., *American Handbook of Psychiatry* (New York: Basic Books, 1959), pp. 567–69.

184. Rathus, *Psychology,* p. 452.

185. Lewis Yablonsky, *The Violent Gang* (Baltimore: Penguin, 1971), pp. 195–205.

186. Helen Raskin White, Erich Labouvie, and Marsha Bates, "The Relationship between Sensation Seeking and Delinquency: A Longitudinal Analysis," *Journal of Research in Crime and Delinquency* 22:197–211 (1985).

187. See, for example, R. Starke Hathaway and Elio Monachesi, "The M.M.P.I. in the Study of Juvenile Delinquents," in A. M. Rose, ed., *Mental Health and Mental Disorder* (London: Routledge, 1956).

188. R. Starke Hathaway and Elio Monachesi, *Analyzing and Predicting Juvenile Delinquency with the M.M.P.I.* (Minneapolis: University of Minnesota Press, 1953).

189. Ibid.

190. Deborah Decker Roman and David Gerbing, "The Mentally Disordered Criminal Offender: A Description Based on Demographic, Clinical and MMPI D," *Journal of Clinical Psychology* 45:983–90 (1989).

191. Karl Schuessler and Donald Cressey, "Personality Characteristics of Criminals," *American Journal of Sociology* 55:476–84 (1950); Gordon Waldo and Simon Dinitz, "Personality Attributes of the Criminal: An Analysis of Research Studies, 1950–1965," *Journal of Research in Crime and Delinquency* 4:185–201 (1967); David Tennenbaum, "Research Studies of Personality and Criminality," *Journal of Criminal Justice* 5:1–19 (1977).

192. Donald Calsyn, Douglass Roszell, and Edmund Chaney, "Validation of MMPI Profile Subtypes among Opioid Addicts Who Are Beginning Methadone Maintenance Treatment," *Journal of Clinical Psychology* 45:991–99 (1989).

193. L. M. Terman, "Research on the Diagnosis of Predelinquent Tendencies," *Journal of Delinquency* 9:124–30 (1925); L. M. Terman, *Measurement of Intelligence* (Boston: Houghton-Mifflin, 1916). For examples, see M. G. Caldwell, "The Intelligence of Delinquent Boys Committed to Wisconsin Industrial School," *Journal of Criminal Law and Criminology* 20:421–28 (1929); and C. Murcheson, *Criminal Intelligence* (Worcester, Mass.: Clark University, 1926), pp. 41–44.

194. Henry Goddard, *Efficiency and Levels of Intelligence* (Princeton, N.J.: Princeton University Press, 1920).

195. William Healy and Augusta Bronner, *Delinquency and Criminals: Their Making and Unmaking* (New York: Macmillan, 1926).

196. Kenneth Eels, *Intelligence and Cultural Differences* (Chicago: University of Chicago Press, 1951), p. 181.

197. Sorel Cahahn and Nora Cohen, "Age versus Schooling Effects on Intelligence Development," *Child Development* 60:1239–49 (1989).

198. John Slawson, *The Delinquent Boys* (Boston: Budget Press, 1926).

199. Edwin Sutherland, "Mental Deficiency and Crime," in Kimball Young, ed., *Social Attitudes* (New York: Henry Holt, 1973), Chap. 15.

200. Travis Hirschi and Michael Hindelang, "Intelligence and Delinquency: A Revisionist Review," *American Sociological Review* 42:471–586 (1977).

201. Terrie Moffitt and Phil Silva, "IQ and Delinquency: A Direct Test of the Differential Detection Hypothesis," *Journal of Abnormal Psychology* 97:1–4 (1988); E. Kandel, S. Mednick, L. Sorenson-Kirkegaard, B. Hutchings, J. Knop, R. Rosenberg, and F. Schulsinger, "IQ as a Protective Factor for Subjects at a High Risk for Antisocial Behavior," *Journal of Consulting and Clinical Psychology* 56:224–26 (1988); Christine Ward and Richard McFall, "Further Validation of the Problem Inventory for

Adolescent Girls: Comparing Caucasian and Black Delinquents and Nondelinquents," *Journal of Consulting and Clinical Psychology* 54:732–33 (1986).

202. Wilson and Herrnstein, *Crime and Human Nature*, p. 148.

203. Terrie Moffitt, William Gabrielli, Sarnoff Mednick, and Fini Schulsinger, "Socioeconomic Status, IQ, and Delinquency," *Journal of Abnormal Psychology* 90:152–56 (1981); for a similar finding, see L. Hubble and M. Groff, "Magnitude and Direction of WISC-R Verbal Performance IQ Discrepancies among Adjudicated Male Delinquents," *Journal of Youth and Adolescence* 10:179–83 (1981).

204. Jennifer White, Terrie Moffitt, and Phil Silva, "A Prospective Replication of the Protective Effects of IQ in Subjects at High Risk for Juvenile Delinquency," *Journal of Consulting and Clinical Psychology* 37:719–24 (1989).

205. Donald Lynam, Terrie Moffitt, and Magda Stouthamer-Loeber, "Explaining the Relations between IQ and Delinquency: Class, Race, Test Motivation, School Failure or Self-Control," *Journal of Abnormal Psychology* 102:11–25, 1993).

206. David Farrington, "Juvenile Delinquency," in John C. Coleman, ed., *The School Years* (London: Routledge, 1992), p. 137.

207. Robert McCall and Michael Carriger, "A Meta-Analysis of Infant Habituation and Recognition Memory Performance as Predictors of Later IQ," *Child Development* 64:57–79 (1993).

208. Scott Menard and Barbara Morse, "A Structuralist Critique of the IQ–Delinquency Hypothesis: Theory and Evidence," *American Journal of Sociology* 89:1347–78 (1984).

209. Ibid.

210. Deborah Denno, "Sociological and Human Developmental Explanations of Crime: Conflict or Consensus," *Criminology* 23:711–41 (1985).

211. Ibid., p. 171.

212. Wilson and Herrnstein, *Crime and Human Nature*.

213. Ibid., p. 44.

214. Ibid., p. 171.

215. Glenn Walters and Thomas White, "Heredity and Crime: Bad Genes or Bad Research," *Justice Quarterly* 27:455–85 (1989), at 478.

216. John Cochran, Peter Wood, and Bruce Arneklev, "Is the Religiosity–Delinquency Relationship Spurious? A Test of Arousal and Social Control Theories," *Journal of Research in Crime and Delinquency* 31:92–113 (1994).

217. Ellis, "Genetics and Criminal Behavior," p. 58.

218. Lee Ellis, "The Evolution of the Nonlegal Equivalent of Aggressive Criminal Behavior," *Aggressive Behavior* 12:57–71 (1986).

219. Joan McCord and William McCord, "A Follow-Up Report on the Cambridge-Somerville Youth Study," *Annals* 322:89–98 (1959).

220. Edwin Schur, *Radical Nonintervention: Rethinking the Delinquency Problem* (Englewood Cliffs, N.J.: Prentice-Hall, 1973).

CHAPTER FOUR

SOCIAL STRUCTURE THEORIES: SOCIAL DISORGANIZATION, STRAIN, AND CULTURAL DEVIANCE

INTRODUCTION

In 1966, sociologist Oscar Lewis coined the phrase **the culture of poverty** to describe the crushing burden faced daily by the large mass of urban poor.[1] The culture of poverty is marked by apathy, cynicism, helplessness, and mistrust of such institutions as police, courts, schools, and government. Mistrust of authority prevents slum dwellers from taking advantage of the few conventional opportunities that are available to them. The result is a permanent American **underclass** whose members have little chance of upward mobility or improvement.

Inner-city neighborhoods experience constant population turnover as their more affluent residents move out to stable suburbs. As cities become **hollowed out**—with a deteriorated inner core surrounded by less devastated but declining suburban communities—delinquency rates spiral upward.[2] Those remaining are forced to live in communities with poorly organized social networks, heterogeneous and alienated populations, and high crime.[3] (See Figure 4.1.) Members of the urban underclass, typically minority group members, are referred to by sociologist William Julius Wilson as **the truly disadvantaged**.[4]

SOCIAL STRATIFICATION

Data gathered from a number of sources support this vision of a racially, socially, and economically **stratified** society. Stratification refers to the unequal distribution of scarce resources. It can also involve different dimensions of human behavior. For example, **economic stratification** refers to the unequal distribution of wealth and income; **political stratification** refers to the unequal ability to gain power or hold office; **prestige stratification** refers to the unequal ability to be well regarded in the community. Family, education, group or religious affiliation, and race all influence the individual's ability to gain a disproportionate share of wealth, power, and prestige.

The United States maintains a stratified society. Although most of us have the financial means to enjoy the fruits of U.S. technology and achievement, about 50 million people live below the poverty line (estimated to be an annual income of about $15,000 for a family of four in 1996). Stratification effects are today becoming sharper. The wealthiest Americans now enjoy a greater share of the economy than ever before: The top 5 percent earn more than half of all income; the poorest Americans, the bottom 20 percent, get less than 5 percent. Since 1967 the top 20 percent of American households have increased their share of the national income by more than $116 billion!

Being Poor   The poor in the United States face many of the same hardships encountered by residents of so-called Third World countries. They are deprived of a standard of living enjoyed by most other citizens. Many, supported by public welfare and private charity throughout their entire lives, have no hope of achieving higher status within conventional society. They attend poor schools, live in substandard housing, and lack good health care. More than half the families are fatherless and husbandless, headed by a female who is the sole breadwinner; many are supported entirely by county welfare and Aid to Families with Dependent Children (AFDC). About 20 percent of white children and 75 percent of African American children are born out of wedlock; about 26 percent

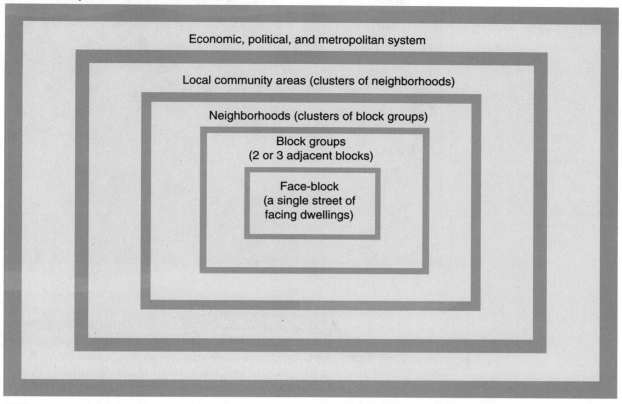

A Community is a Set of Nested Boxes

Economic, political, and metropolitan system

Local community areas (clusters of neighborhoods)

Neighborhoods (clusters of block groups)

Block groups
(2 or 3 adjacent blocks)

Face-block
(a single street of
facing dwellings)

The most basic unit is the face-block, those houses or apartments facing each other across a single street.

Block groups of two or three adjacent city blocks represent a normal zone of adult neighboriness. It is also the area from which children draw their first friends.

Neighborhoods, which are clusters of block groups, traditionally refer to small, socially homogeneous areas defined by interaction patterns and geographic landmarks such as parks, main streets, or railroad tracks.

Local community areas encompass several neighborhoods.

Each community is part of a wider economic, political, and metropolitan system. Looking at the political economy of each place brings into the equation such factors as the distance to good jobs, the availability of public transportation, and the quality of basic services as dictated by citywide political decisions.

Source: Felton Earls and Albert Reiss, Jr., *Breaking the Cycle Predicting and Preventing Violence* (Washington, D.C.: National Institute of Justice, 1994), pp. 10–11.

The poor in the United States face many of the same hardships encountered by residents of so-called third world countries. They are deprived of a standard of living enjoyed by most other citizens. Many, supported by public welfare and private charity throughout their entire lives, have no hope of achieving higher status within conventional society. They attend poor schools, live in substandard housing, and lack good health care. More than half the families are fatherless and husbandless, headed by a female who is the sole breadwinner; many are supported entirely by county welfare and Aid to Families with Dependent Children (AFDC). Here children play in the kitchen in Roxbury section of Boston, one of the cities poorest areas.

of all American families are single-parent households, and 88 percent of these are headed by a woman.[5] Almost 17 million children have been born out of wedlock, half white and the other half minorities; more than 13 million have been born to teenage mothers.[6] Although little empirical evidence exists that living in a single-parent household alone is sufficient to produce delinquent behavior, it seems logical that the problems presented by raising a family in a deteriorated neighborhood are better met by two parents than one.[7]

Child Poverty   Children are especially hard hit by poverty; an estimated 16 million youths live below the poverty line.[8] Children in poor families suffer many social problems including inadequate education and health care. For example, the number of children covered by health insurance is declining and will continue to do so for the foreseeable future.[9] Lack of coverage almost guarantees that they will suffer health problems which will impede their long-term development.

The problems of providing adequate care and discipline to children under these circumstances can be immense. About 7 percent of all U.S. youths under age 13 are **latchkey children,** left unattended after school every day (see Figure 4.2). Many children under 5 are left in the care of strangers and nonfamily members, often in unregulated day care centers.

RACE AND POVERTY

The effects of poverty are most often felt by minority-group members. About 31 percent of African Americans live below the poverty level as compared to 9 percent of white families; African American unemployment rates are typically twice those of white rates. The median income for African American households

FIGURE 4.2
Child care arrangements

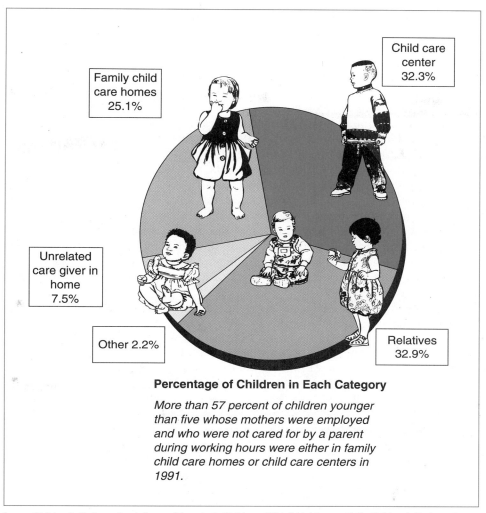

Percentage of Children in Each Category

More than 57 percent of children younger than five whose mothers were employed and who were not cared for by a parent during working hours were either in family child care homes or child care centers in 1991.

Source: Children's Defense Fund, State of America's Children, 1994 (Washington, D.C., Children's Defense Fund, 1995), p. 39.

is about $19,500 as compared to $33,000 for white households. This gap of $13,500 has actually grown over time; the race-based income difference in 1969 was the equivalent of $12,700 in today's dollars.[10] About 26 percent of African American households have no assets while 8 percent are worth more than $100,000; in contrast, only 10% of white households have no assets and 32 percent are worth more than $100,000. One reason for this discrepancy is home ownership rates: 42 percent of African American and 63 percent of white households were owned by a resident.

Although this picture is bleak, there are some positive signs of improvement. The proportion of African Americans falling into the lowest asset category is in decline while the percentage with assets over $100,000 has doubled during the past decade. But in all too many instances, conditions are actually deteriorating: There is increasing inequality in socioeconomic position, greater dependence on social assistance and welfare, and growing numbers of single-parent families.[11]

Social Structure and Delinquency

The picture that emerges is one of destructive social forces affecting all too many adolescents and their families. To some delinquency experts, these unfair and destructive economic and social conditions within the nation's slum areas are the root cause of delinquency. While middle- and upper-class children may engage in minor and occasional delinquent acts—vandalism, use of nonaddictive drugs such as marijuana, petty theft, motor vehicle violations—they refrain from the more serious acts of violence, theft, and gang membership. Middle-class youths are better able to organize their resources in education and in the marketplace. Even those who do engage in delinquent acts are eventually able to *age out* of criminality and become responsible citizens.[12]

Considering their social and economic decay, it comes as no surprise that deteriorated inner-city areas in such cities as New York, Chicago, and Los Angeles are the spawning grounds of youth gangs and groups whose members graduate into adult criminal careers. Is it any wonder, that without hope of earning money and achieving success through legitimate means, many inner-city youths turn to crime as a means of survival, self-esteem, and revenge on a society that has turned its back on them?

Lower-class slum areas are also the scene of the highest crime and victimization rates. Official delinquency rates for such crimes as robbery and larceny are much higher in urban than in suburban and rural areas. Likewise, self-report and official record studies seem to indicate that lower-class youths are the most likely to commit serious delinquent and criminal acts. Nor are these problems unique to the United States: Cross-national data show that countries that spend more on child welfare, providing opportunities for the underprivileged, usually have lower crime rates than those that ignore welfare programs.[13]

This view of delinquency then is essentially structural and cultural. It holds that delinquency is a consequence of the social and economic inequalities built into the social structure. Even those youths who receive the loving support of parents and family members are at risk of crime, delinquency, and arrest over the life course if they suffer from social disadvantage.[14]

Social structure theories tie delinquency rates to socioeconomic conditions and cultural values. Areas that experience high levels of poverty and social disorganization will also have high delinquency rates. Residents view prevailing social values skeptically; they are frustrated by their class position and inability to be part of the "American dream." Structural theories are less concerned with why an individual youth becomes delinquent than why certain ecological areas experience high delinquency rates. The following "Case in Point" explores the question of how to reverse social disorganization.

THE BRANCHES OF SOCIAL STRUCTURE THEORY

The social structure approach has had a long tradition in the study of juvenile delinquency. As Figure 4.3 shows, social structure theories can be classified into three independent yet interrelated subgroups: **social disorganization, strain,** and **cultural deviance** (also called **subcultural theory**).

Social Disorganization Theory Delinquency is a product of the social forces existing in inner-city slum areas. Neighborhoods that lack or have lost the means to control deviance, protect residents, and regulate social conduct are at

You have just been appointed as a presidential advisor on urban problems.

The President informs you that he wants to initiate a demonstration project in a major city that is aimed at showing that government can do something to reduce poverty, crime, and drug abuse.

The area he has chosen for development is a large inner-city neighborhood with more than 100,000 residents. It suffers from disorganized community structure, poverty, and hopelessness. Predatory delinquent gangs run free and terrorize local merchants and citizens. The school system has failed to provide opportunities and educational experiences sufficient to dampen enthusiasm for gang recruitment. Stores, homes, and public buildings are deteriorated and decayed. Commercial enterprise has fled the area, and civil servants are reluctant to enter the neighborhood. There is an uneasy truce between the varied ethnic and racial groups that populate the area. Residents believe little can be done to bring the neighborhood back to life.

You are faced with suggesting an urban redevelopment program that can revitalize the area and eventually bring down the crime rate. You can bring any element of the public and private sector to bear on this rather overwhelming problem, including the military! You can also ask private industry to help in the struggle, promising them tax breaks for their participation.

What programs do you believe could break the cycle of urban poverty?

Would reducing the poverty rate produce a lowered delinquency rate?

Is there a place for private industry in social reorganization?

CASE IN POINT

risk. Within these areas, the unsupervised behavior of juvenile gangs and groups overwhelms the ability of social institutions, such as the family and the school, to maintain order. The result is stable pockets of crime and deviance. Environmental and ecological factors such as substandard housing, low income, unemployment levels, deteriorated housing, substandard schools, broken families, urban

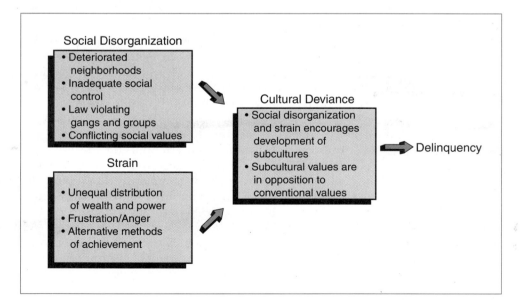

FIGURE 4.3
Branches of social structure theory

density, and overcrowding produce social disorgainzation and are therefore predictive of a high incidence of delinquency.

Strain Theory   Delinquency is linked to the frustration and anger members of the lower class feel when they are locked out of the economic mainstream of society.[15] Emotional strain is the result when desire for middle-class benefits and luxuries cannot be met by the legitimate means available. Anger and frustration create pressure for corrective action, including attacking the sources of frustration or escaping with drugs and alcohol.

Cultural Deviance Theory   According to this view, adolescent residents of disorganized slum areas, perceiving tremendous strain and frustration, become alienated from the values of the dominant culture. The resulting strain and frustration prompts the formation of independent **subcultures** that maintain rules and values in opposition to existing law and custom. Conflict arises when subcultural values and beliefs clash with those of the general culture. Delinquency is not caused then by rebellion against the dominant society but by conformity to the rules of a deviant subculture.

The three branches of structural theory are linked here because each maintains that a person's place in the social structure controls the direction of his or her behavior and that culture, environment, and economy interact to influence behavior. Because each theoretical branch is an important concept of delinquency, they are set out in detail below.

Social Disorganization Theory

The roots of social disorganization theory can be traced to the pioneering research conducted in the famed sociology department at the University of Chicago early in the twentieth century. Chicago's evolution as a city was typical of the transition occurring in many other urban areas as industrialization expanded. Large populations of workers were needed to staff factories and commercial establishments. Waves of Europeans settled in the city to work in the factories and stockyards. The city's wealthy, established citizens were concerned about the moral fabric of society. The belief was widespread that foreign immigrants were crime-prone and morally dissolute. In fact, local groups were created for the very purpose of "saving" the children of poor families from moral decadence. Delinquency was popularly viewed as the property of inferior racial and ethnic groups. (See chapter 11 for a discussion of the child savers.)

Robert Ezra Park (1864–1944), Ernest W. Burgess (1886–1966), Louis Wirth (1897–1952), and their colleagues pioneered research work on the **social ecology** of urban areas. These sociologists focused attention on the influence social institutions have on human behavior. They pioneered the **ecological study** of crime: Law-violating behavior is a function of community level (and not individual-level) social forces operating in an urban environment. They found that the key element of a community is its ability to regulate itself so that common goals (such as living in a crime-free area) can be achieved; this is referred to as **social control**.[16] Those neighborhoods that are incapable of social control because they are racked by disease, crime, mental disorder, and economic failure are the ones most at risk for criminal interactions.

Natural Areas The **Chicago School** researchers found that deteriorated inner-city neighborhoods become **natural areas** for crime. The extraordinarily high level of poverty in these urban neighborhoods causes a breakdown of critical social control institutions, such as the school and the family. According to Wirth, urban areas undergoing rapid growth in population density and diversity experience "segmentalization" of life. People look inward for achievement and shun interpersonal relationships. Interactions among residents in large cities are superficial, fleeting, and exploitive.[17] The resulting social disorganization reduces the ability of social institutions to control behavior, thus causing a high crime rate (see Figure 4.4).

THE AREA STUDIES OF SHAW AND McKAY

The origin of the social disorganization perspective is today most closely associated with the pioneering research conducted in Chicago by sociologists Clifford Shaw and Henry McKay.[18]

In order to explain delinquency within the context of the changing urban ecology Shaw and McKay collected extensive crime data, including the records of almost 25,000 alleged delinquents brought before the Juvenile Court of Cook County from 1900 to 1933. Their ongoing analysis convinced them that the then-popular individual-level explanations of delinquency, which rested on such factors as IQ or body build, were fallacious. It was the ecological conditions of the city itself that caused delinquency. They saw that Chicago had developed into

FIGURE 4.4
Social disorganization theory

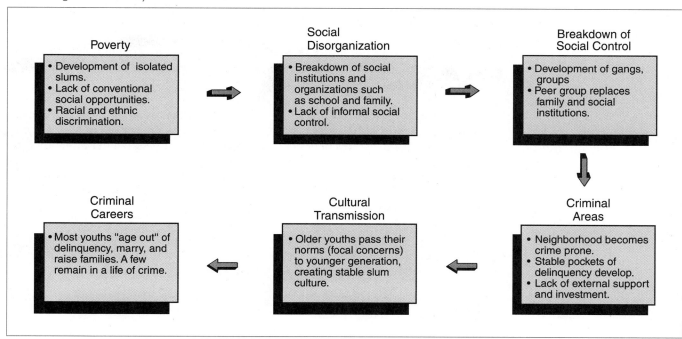

According to social disorganization theory, delinquency is a product of the social forces existing in inner-city slum areas. Within these areas, the unsupervised behavior of juvenile gangs and groups overwhelms the ability of social institutions, such as the family and the school, to maintain order. The result is stable pockets of crime and deviance. Environmental and ecological factors such as substandard housing, low income, high unemployment levels, deteriorated housing, substandard schools, broken families, urban density, and overcrowding, are predictive of a high incidence of delinquency.

distinct neighborhoods, some marked by wealth and luxury, others by over-crowding, poor health and sanitary conditions, and extreme poverty. These slum areas were believed to be the spawning grounds of delinquency.

Shaw and McKay viewed delinquency as a product of **transitional neighborhoods,** ecologically distinct areas that were changing from affluence to decay. Here factories and commercial establishments were interspersed with private residences. In this environment, teenage gangs developed as a means of survival, economic gain, defense, and friendship. Gang youths developed a unique set of cultural values that conflicted with generally accepted social norms and traditions. Gang leaders recruited younger members, passing on delinquent traditions and ensuring survival of the gang from one generation to the next—a process referred to as **cultural transmission.**

Concentric Zones   While mapping crime and delinquency rates in Chicago, Shaw and McKay noted that distinct ecological areas had developed in the city. These comprised a series of concentric zones, each with stable delinquency rates (see Figure 4.5).[19] The areas of heaviest delinquency concentration appeared to be the transitional, inner-city zones, where large portions of foreign-born citizens had recently immigrated. The zones farthest from the city's center were the least prone to delinquency. Analysis of these data indicated a surprisingly stable pattern of delinquent activity in the ecological zones over a 65-year period. Shaw and McKay noted that delinquency rates in these areas were unaffected by population makeup and transition. It seemed that high-risk areas, and not high-risk people, were associated with delinquency rates.

THE CULTURE OF THE SLUM

Shaw and McKay did not restrict their analysis to ecological factors alone. They found a significant correlation between social values and crime rates. Areas with

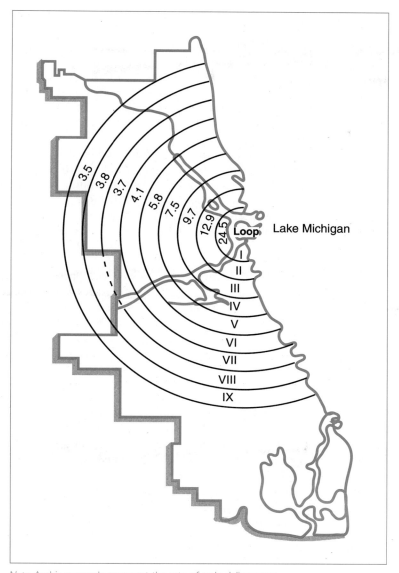

FIGURE 4.5
Shaw and McKay's concentric zones map of Chicago

low delinquency rates were marked by "uniformity, consistency, and universality of conventional values and attitudes."[20] In these low-crime areas, middle-class child-rearing practices prevailed, and residents conformed to the legal code. In contrast, conflicting moral values and powerful attractions to deviant modes of behavior existed in high-crime areas. In disorganized neighborhoods, delinquency provides a means for financially deprived youths to gain prestige, economic achievement, and other satisfactions. Deviant values emerge and become pervasive when the community is neither capable of helping residents realize their legitimate goals nor controlling the behavior of those who embrace illegal activities for personal gain.

Parent-child relationships were seen by Shaw and McKay as having an important influence on the development of social values. In zones with low delinquency rates, parents stressed such values as attending school and church and being involved in community organizations. In high-rate, transitional areas, a diversity of values existed. Some youths were taught to strive for basic middle-class goals; others were exposed to the rackets and illegal activities, such as theft.

Shaw and McKay concluded that, in transitional neighborhoods, deviant and conventional values compete with one another. Adolescents exposed to both value systems are often forced to choose between them and, consequently, may seek out groups that share similar ideas and behavior. Those who choose illegitimate values may find membership in law-violating groups and gangs an essential element of life in slum areas. (See chapter 10's discussion on gang behavior.)

Value Conflict   Because of their deviant values, slum youths often come into conflict with existing middle-class norms, which demand strict obedience to the legal code. Such value conflicts set delinquents and their peer group even further from conventional society. The result is a fuller acceptance of deviant goals and behavior. Shunned by the mainstream, neighborhood street gangs become fixed institutions, recruiting new members and passing on delinquent traditions from one generation to the next.

The quality of social organizations and institutions also varies considerably between high- and low-crime areas. In high-crime areas, conflicting social values neutralize the influence of social control organizations. A close-knit family, which should serve as a buffer against delinquency, exercises little social control in disorganized areas. Families in transitional areas often contain adult members who are themselves profiting from theft, violence, and drug dealing. In these circumstances, family ties can actually encourage delinquency. Even those social control agents with an expressed agenda of crime control and prevention, such as schools and community centers, have only limited impact because they are staffed and funded by outsiders who are not trusted by neighborhood residents.

LEGACY OF SHAW AND McKAY

Most prominent among the many achievements of Shaw and McKay was locating the cause of delinquency within the domain of social ecology. The Shaw-McKay model replaced the view that delinquents were either biologically inferior, intellectually impaired, or psychologically damaged. Their research refuted the assumption that delinquency is a property of any one minority or ethnic group.

Because the basis of their theory was that neighborhood disintegration and slum conditions are the primary causes of delinquent behavior, Shaw and McKay paved the way for the many community action and treatment programs developed in the last half century. Shaw himself was the founder of one very influential community-based treatment program, the Chicago Area Project, which will be discussed later in this chapter.[21]

Another important feature of Shaw and McKay's work was its depiction of delinquent gang membership as a "normal" response to the adverse social conditions in urban slum areas. Gangs provide social and economic advantages that would otherwise be denied youths in these areas. Shaw, McKay, and other Chicago-based theorists, such as Frederick Thrasher, viewed gang members as neither troubled nor depressed.[22] Their illegal behavior was merely a way of generating excitement, social success, and financial gain when all other avenues seemed to be closed.

Shaw and McKay's work has been subject to criticism. Dependence on official statistics is always suspect. For example, high crime rates in the inner city may be a function of police arrest practices. The stable patterns of inner-city delinquency depicted by Shaw and McKay may not actually exist. Social mobility and change in neighborhood composition may in fact influence crime rates.[23] Self-report studies indicate that many middle-class suburban youth commit crimes, a finding that suggests that the cause of delinquency may have little to do with economic deprivation and social disorganization.

These criticisms aside, by introducing a new variable—the ecology of the city—into the study of delinquency, Shaw and McKay set the stage for a whole generation of criminologists to focus on the social influences of delinquent behavior.

THE SOCIAL ECOLOGY OF DELINQUENCY

During mid-century, Shaw and McKay's legacy was continued by area studies conducted by Bernard Lander in Baltimore, David Bordua in Detroit, and Roland Chilton in Indianapolis. As a group, they showed that such ecological conditions as substandard housing, low income, and unrelated people living together predicted a high incidence of delinquency.[24]

The social disorganization view today is still the subject of a great deal of scholarship. Researchers are now using complex statistical models to determine the effects of ecological and social conditions on delinquent crime patterns.[25] A growing body of important studies indicate that the social context of urban areas has significant influence on delinquency rates.[26] This new social ecology of delinquency suggests that social forces operating within depressed urban areas help generate the conditions favorable to drug abuse and delinquency. What are these themes? The sections below describe some of the most significant areas of research.

RELATIVE DEPRIVATION

According to Judith Blau and Peter Blau, a sense of social injustice occurs in communities in which the poor and the wealthy live close to one another. Income inequality causes feelings of **relative deprivation.** The relatively deprived are prone to feelings of anger and hostility, which precede criminal behavior.

The Blaus believe that adolescents residing in poor inner-city areas will experience delinquency-producing status frustration because their neighborhoods are contiguous to some of the most affluent areas in the United States. So, even though deprived teenagers can observe wealth and luxury up close, they have no hope of actually accruing such riches themselves. This condition is felt most acutely by racial and ethnic minorities because they tend to live in low-status areas and in substandard housing.[27]

Research supportive of the Blaus' relative deprivation model has been conducted by a number of criminologists who have linked income inequality to high

A sense of social injustice occurs in communities in which the poor and the wealthy live close to one another. Income inequality causes feelings of relative deprivation. Adolescents residing in a poor inner-city area will experience relative deprivation because their neighborhoods are contiguous to some of the most affluent areas in the United States. So while deprived teenagers can observe wealth and luxury close up, they have no hope of actually achieving riches themselves. This condition is felt most acutely by racial and ethnic minorities because they tend to live in low-status areas and in substandard housing.

delinquency rates.[28] Richard Block found that the variable best able to predict crime rates was the proximity in which poor and wealthy people lived to one another.[29] Inequality seems significantly related to crime rates, especially in areas where residents have high achievement aspirations but few economic opportunities.[30]

These studies indicate that youths living in deteriorated areas of the city that are close to more affluent neighborhoods will be the most likely to resort to such crimes as homicide, robbery, and aggravated assault to express their frustration or achieve monetary gain.

COMMUNITY CHANGE

Some social ecologists contend that, like people, urban areas and neighborhoods have a life cycle in which they undergo significant change: from affluent to impoverished; from impoverished to rehabilitated or **gentrified**; from residential to commercial; from stable to transient. It has been observed that as communities go through these structural changes, levels of social disorder and delinquency likewise change.[31]

An example of this view can be found in Leo Scheurman and Solomon Kobrin's examination of the factors that relate to crime-rate change in urban settings. Scheurman and Kobrin found that communities go through cycles in which neighborhood deterioration precedes increasing rates of crime and delinquency.[32] Communities suffering a rapid increase in antisocial behavior are also the ones most likely to be experiencing rapid increases in the number of single-parent families and unrelated people living together; a change in housing from owner- to renter-occupied units; a loss of semiskilled and unskilled jobs; and a growth in discouraged unemployed workers who are no longer seeking jobs.[33]

The changing racial makeup of communities may also influence crime and delinquency rates. Janet Heitgerd and Robert Bursik found that areas undergoing change in their racial composition will experience corresponding increases in delinquency rates.[34] This phenomenon may reflect community fear of racial conflict: Adults may encourage teens to terrorize the newcomers and commit hate crimes; the result is conflict, violence, and disorder.

WEALTH AND OPPORTUNITY

Although Shaw and McKay did not assume a direct relationship between economic status and criminality, they did imply that areas racked by poverty would also experience social disorganization.

Research has shown that neighborhoods that provide few employment opportunities for youth and adults are the most vulnerable to predatory crime. Unemployment helps destabilize households, and unstable families are the ones most likely to contain children who choose violence and aggression as a means of dealing with limited opportunity.[35]

A lack of employment opportunity also reduces the respect and authority of parents and neighborhood adults, reducing their ability to guide and influence children. Thus the local culture is left to the domination of youth gangs whose members are both feared and respected. Predatory crime increases to levels that cannot easily be controlled by police. Although even the most deteriorated neighborhoods have a surprising degree of familial and kinship strength, the consistent pattern of crime and neighborhood disorganization that follows periods of high unemployment can neutralize an area's inherent social control capability.

Does Delinquency Cause Poverty? It is commonly assumed that poverty causes delinquency. But it is just as likely that the reverse may be true and that delinquency causes poverty.

High-crime rate areas become impoverished because the fear of crime reduces investment and commerce. Middle-class people flee the area in search of safer surroundings; people won't enter the area to shop or do business.[36] The decline in consumer confidence and business activity further reduces employment opportunities, effectively eliminating many area residents from the job market. Periods of sustained criminality and fear sap the neighborhood's economic lifeblood, putting ever greater strain on the area's economic life and encouraging area youth to join gangs for economic survival. A cycle of crime and poverty is introduced which becomes difficult to break or reduce.

Social Embeddedness John Hagan, a noted criminologist, has found that some youths become **embedded** in a delinquent way of life. They have criminal parents, deviant friends, and an ongoing involvement in antisocial behavior. Their lifestyle reduces any chance they may have of gaining steady adult employment, further sustaining their criminal embeddedness.

In contrast, some children in high-crime neighborhoods are fortunate enough to have parents whose connections help them become embedded in conventional society and accumulate social capital. They maintain connections with community leaders, develop political ties, and tap into the local job "network." Their parents' social embeddedness later helps these children to enter the workforce and lead successful lives. If they get in trouble they can use family contacts with agents of the criminal justice system to get off lightly. Even in the most deprived neighborhoods, parents who are socially rather than criminally embedded can help their children avoid delinquent careers.[37]

FEAR

Fear of crime and delinquency is much higher in disorganized neighborhoods than in affluent suburbs.[38] Members of the underclass fear crime and have little confidence that the government can do anything to counter the drug dealers and juvenile gangs that terrorize the neighborhood.[39] People tell others of their personal experiences of being victimized, spreading the word that the neighborhood is getting dangerous and that the chances of future victimization are high.

When fear grips a neighborhood, people do not want to leave their homes at night, so they withdraw from community life; fear has been related to distress, inactivity, and decline in personal health.[40] High levels of fear are also related to deteriorating business conditions, increased population mobility, and the domination of street life by violent gangs and groups.

SOCIAL CONTROLS

Most neighborhood residents share the common goal of living in a crime-free area. Some communities have the power to regulate the behavior of their residents through the influence of such institutions as the family and the school. Other neighborhoods, experiencing social disorganization, find that efforts at social control are weak and attenuated. When community social control efforts are blunted, delinquency rates increase and neighborhood cohesiveness weakens, setting the stage for an endless cycle of community deterioration.

Neighborhoods maintain a variety of agencies and institutions of social control. Some operate on the primary or private level and involve peers, families, and relatives. These sources exert informal control over behavior by either awarding or withholding approval, respect, and admiration. Informal control mechanisms include direct criticism, ridicule, ostracism, desertion, and physical punishment.[41] Communities also use internal networks and local institutions to control delinquency. These include businesses, stores, schools, churches, and voluntary organizations.[42]

Stable neighborhoods are also able to marshal external sources of social control; for example, they can use their political clout to get state and city funding for job programs and economic development; access to these external control sources has been found to mediate delinquency rates.[43] One source of external control may be the ability to increase levels of police services. The presence of police sends a message that the area will not tolerate deviant behavior. Current and potential delinquents may avoid such areas in favor of easier and more appealing "targets."[44]

Neighborhoods that are disorganized cannot mount an effective social control effort. Because the population is transient, interpersonal relationships remain superficial and cannot help reduce deviant behavior. Social institutions, such as schools and churches, cannot work effectively in a climate of alienation and mistrust. In these areas, the absence of political power brokers limits access to external funding and police protection.

Social control is also weakened because unsupervised peer groups and gangs, which flourish in disorganized areas, disrupt the influence of neighborhood control agents.[45] Children surveyed in disorganized areas report that they rarely get involved with conventional social institutions and are therefore vulnerable to involvement with delinquent peer group, interpersonal aggression and delinquency.[46]

RAGE, DISTRUST, AND HOPELESSNESS

Youths in socially disorganized areas experience rage, distrust, and hopelessness. They are socialized in a world where adults maintain a **siege mentality,** believing there are government plots to undermine the neighborhood (e.g., "the AIDS virus was created to kill us off"; "the government brings drugs into the neighborhood to keep people under control").[47] Young people growing up in these areas become very angry, believing no one in power cares about their plight. This "free floating anger" causes adolescents to strike out at the merest hint of provocation.[48]

Michael Greene, a juvenile delinquency expert in New York City, suggests that children living in these conditions become "crusted over"—they do not let people get close to them nor do they give expression to their childhood. They engage in exploitive peer relations and develop a sense of hopelessness. They find that parents and teachers focus on their failures and problems and not their achievements; they are vulnerable to the lure of delinquent gangs and groups.[49]

In sum of these recent attempts to define the influence social ecology has on area delinquency rates support the core social disorganization model: Areas that are deteriorated and disorganized are unable to assemble social forces sufficient to control the behavior of their residents. Rather than dissuade neighborhood youths from joining gangs and committing crime, social forces in these areas encourage and sustain antisocial behavior.

STRAIN THEORY

Strain type theories compose the second type of structural explanation of delinquency rates. The core concept of strain theory is that most people share similar values and aspirations. After all, billions of dollars are spent each year on media advertising to convince people to drive the right car, wear the right clothes, and live in the right neighborhood. Most children attend schools and churches that teach the same of conventional values: honesty, forgiveness, concern, and sexual abstinence. Although societal goals are unvarying, relatively few people have the ability or means to achieve economic and social success. The inability to achieve social goals breeds anger, resentment, and aggression.

All too often, the means for success are stratified by socioeconomic class. In middle- and upper-class communities, feelings of strain are limited because education and prestigious occupations are readily obtainable. In lower-class slum areas, strain occurs because legitimate avenues for success are all but closed to young people. Because legal and socially acceptable means for obtaining success do not exist, individuals may either use deviant methods to achieve their goals or reject socially accepted goals in favor of deviant ones (e.g., abusing drugs or alcohol).

Strain theory (see Figure 4.6) is compatible with social disorganization views because they both link structural variables—poverty, economic opportunity, the availability of goods and services—to crime and delinquency rates; the likelihood of strain is greatest in deteriorated inner-city areas.

FIGURE 4.6
Strain theory

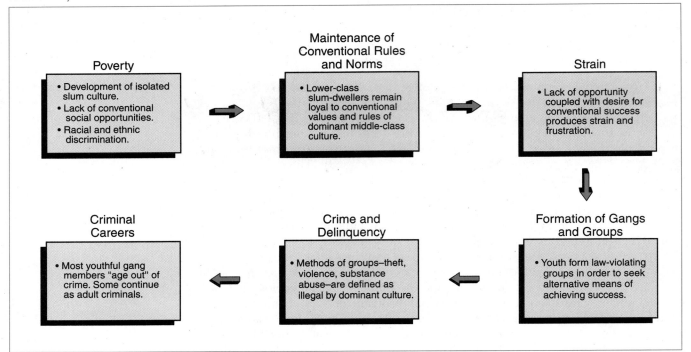

The two models differ in their orientation. Social disorganization theories focus on group processes and how they affect neighborhood delinquency rates. In contrast, strain theories focus on how a sense of alienation, rage, and frustration resulting from economic deprivation and social inequality influences individual offending patterns.

We now turn to the most well known formulation of strain theory, Robert Merton's theory of anomie.

MERTON'S THEORY OF ANOMIE

Strain theories probably owe their popularity to the distinguished U.S. sociologist **Robert Merton**.[50] In 1938, Merton proposed a revised version of the concept of **anomie** that has proven to be one of the most durable theoretical concepts in twentieth-century social thought.[51]

French sociologist Emile Durkheim had first employed the concept of anomie to describe the social malaise that accompanies the breakdown of existing social rules and values brought about by rapid social change.[52] When established norms, customs, and practices are made obsolete, the result is a collective sense of social insecurity and **normlessness.** Anomic conditions arise when the rule of law becomes weakened and powerless to maintain social control. Under these conditions, crime can be considered a "normal" response to existing social conditions.

Merton adapted the concept of anomie to the United State's highly competitive post-industrial society which he believed also produces a sense of alienation and hopelessness. He argued that two elements of modern culture interact to produce

According to Merton, U.S. society is goal-oriented, and wealth and material goods are coveted most of all. Unfortunately, legitimate means to acquiring wealth are stratified across class and status lines. Those with little formal education and few economic resources soon find that they are denied the ability to acquire money and other success symbols legally. Those who are locked out of the legitimate opportunity structure experience a sense of anger, frustration, normlessness and *anomie.*

potentially anomic conditions: culturally defined *goals* of acquiring wealth, success, and power; and socially permissible *means,* such as hard work, education, and thrift. According to Merton, U.S. society is goal oriented, and wealth and material goods are coveted most of all. Unfortunately, legitimate means to acquiring wealth are stratified across class and status lines. Those with little formal education and few economic resources soon find that they are denied the ability to acquire money and other success symbols legally.[53] Because socially mandated success goals are uniform throughout society but access to legitimate means is bound by class and status, those who are locked out of the legitimate opportunity structure experience a sense of anger, frustration, normlessness, and *anomie.* Anomie can lead to the development of criminal or delinquent solutions to the problem of attaining goals, to the rejection of goals, or to the substitution of deviant goals for conventional ones.[54]

SOCIAL ADAPTATIONS

Merton identified five possible modes of adaptation or adjustment an individual can adopt when presented with the various combinations of culturally defined goals and means: conformity, innovation, ritualism, retreatism, and rebellion. Each represents a way of coping with a balance or imbalance of goals and means.

Conformity   Conformity occurs when an individual desires conventional social goals and can attain them legitimately through conventional means; goals and means are in balance. For example, middle-class, college-bound students will obey the law because they recognize that their access to education will provide them with a possibly lucrative career. Conformity is the most common form of adaptation in a stable society.

Innovation Innovation occurs when an individual accepts the goals of society but rejects or is incapable of gaining them through legitimate means. The sense of anomie that develops because of the imbalance between goals and means can be relieved by adopting *innovative* behaviors: stealing cars, selling drugs, committing armed robberies.

Of the five adaptations, innovation is most closely associated with delinquent behavior. The success goal that pervades U.S. culture places such an enormous burden on those lacking economic opportunity that delinquent modes of adaptation are not a surprising result. This condition accounts for the high rate of delinquency in poverty areas, where access to legitimate means is severely limited. The infusion of the success goal in U.S. culture and its effect on crime are discussed in the following "Focus on Delinquency."

Ritualism Ritualism refers to the diminution of the success goals in favor of a strict set of manners and customs that serve no particular purpose. Such practices often exist in religious cults, feudal societies, clubs, college fraternities, and social organizations. Ritualists gain pleasure from traditional ceremonies that have neither a real purpose nor a goal.

Retreatism Retreatism entails a rejection of both the goals and the means of society. Merton suggested that people who adjust in this fashion are "in society but not of it."[55] Included in this category are "psychotics, psychoneurotics, chronic autists, pariahs, outcasts, vagrants, tramps, chronic drunkards, and drug addicts."[56] People who perceive anomie because they have embraced socially acceptable goals but are denied the means to attain them may become retreatists. Because they are morally or otherwise incapable of violence or theft, they attempt to escape their lack of success by withdrawing, either mentally or physically.

Rebellion A rebellious adaptation involves reacting to anomie by substituting an alternative set of goals and means for the accepted ones of society. This adaptation is typical of revolutionaries, who promote radical change in the existing social structure and advocate alternative lifestyles, goals, and beliefs. Revolutionary groups and cults have abounded in the United States, some espousing the violent overthrow of the existing social order and others advocating the use of nonviolent, passive resistance to change society. Rebels may perceive anomie because they feel the government is corrupt or because they want to create alternate opportunities and lifestyles within the existing system.

ANALYZING ANOMIE

Anomie theory is important because it helps explain the dynamic relationship between social and individual sources of criminal behavior. People who lack socially acceptable means of success become frustrated and respond with innovations such as theft or extortion, retreat into drugs or alcohol, or rebel by joining hate, revolutionary, or cultist groups. Considering the extent of economic stratification in U.S. society, anomie predicts that crime and delinquency will prevail in local class culture, which it does.

Although highly influential, a number of questions are left unanswered by anomie theory.

CRIME AND THE AMERICAN DREAM

An important addition to the strain literature has been the publication of *Crime and the American Dream* by Steven Messner and Richard Rosenfeld. Their vision of why crime and delinquency rates in the United States are so high focuses on the function of *cultural* and *institutional* influences in American society.

Messner and Rosenfeld agree with Merton's view that the success goal is pervasive in American culture. They refer to this as the **"American Dream,"** a term that they employ as both a goal and a process. As a goal, the American Dream involves the accumulation of material goods and wealth under conditions of open, individual competition. As a process, it involves the socialization of youth to (a) pursue material success above all else and (b) believe that prosperity is a universally achievable goal in the American culture. Anomic conditions occur because the desire to succeed at any cost drives people apart, weakens the collective sense of community, fosters ambition, and restricts the desirability of other kinds of achievement, such as acquiring a "good name" and respected reputation.

That Americans are conditioned to succeed "at all costs" should come as no surprise because our capitalist system encourages innovation in the pursuit of monetary rewards. Billionaire businesspersons such as Steve Forbes, Ross Perot, Bill Gates, and Donald Trump are considered national heroes whose wealth and lifestyles are universally admired. They become cultural icons and leaders who, many even believe, deserve to be elected President because of their business savvy in accumulating such wealth!

What is distinct about U.S. society, according to Messner and Rosenfeld, and what most likely determines the exceedingly high national crime rate, is that anomic conditions have been allowed to "develop to such an extraordinary degree." Why has this happened? According to Messner and Rosenfeld, it is because institutions that might otherwise control the exaggerated emphasis on financial success have been rendered powerless or obsolete. Social institutions have been undermined for three reasons:

1. Noneconomic functions and roles have been *devalued*. Performance in other institutional settings—the family, school, or community—is assigned a lower priority than the goal of financial success. Human service jobs such as social work and teaching are much less rewarding financially than those of entertainers or athletes. It seems normal and rational in U.S. society to demand that public school teachers take pay cuts or go for years without a raise, and then complain when the owner of a local baseball team allows a slugger to sign with another team rather than pay him $8 million per year.

2. When conflicts emerge, noneconomic roles become subordinate to and must accommodate economic roles. The schedules, routines, and demands of the workplace take priority over those of the home, the school, the community, and other aspects of life. Parents are willing to leave very young children in day care for 10 hours per day or more in order to pursue the careers that can bring them increased levels of luxury.

3. Economic standards and norms penetrate into noneconomic realms. Economic terms become part of the common language: People want you to get to the "bottom line"; spouses view themselves as "partners" who "manage" the household. Business leaders run for public office promising to "run the country like a corporation."

According to Messner and Rosenfeld, the relatively high U.S. delinquency rates can be explained by the interrelationship between culture and institutions. At the cultural level, the dominance of the American Dream mythology ensures that a great many youths will develop wishes and desires for material goods that simply cannot be satisfied by legitimate means. Anomie becomes the norm because no matter how much the typical American has, it's never enough: Adolescents always want the most stylish fashions, the newest music, and the hottest car. As soon as cultural values change, so does their need for material possessions.

At the institutional level, the dominance of economic concerns weakens the informal social control exerted by the family and school. Parents lose their authority when they cannot provide children with economic luxuries. Teachers lose their power when adolescents no longer believe that education will get them what they want.

Cultural and institutional conditions reinforce each other in a neverending loop: Culture determines institutional change and institutional change influences culture.

The Messner–Rosenfeld version of anomie builds upon Merton's views by trying to explain why the success goal has reached such a place of prominence in U.S. culture. The message "to succeed by any means necessary" has become a national icon.

Source: Steven Messner and Richard Rosenfeld, *Crime and the American Dream* (Belmont, Calif.: Wadsworth, 1994).

- Merton did not explain why people choose different adaptations to anomie: Why does one adolescent choose innovation and become a thief while another becomes a "retreatist" and takes drugs?
- The theory also does not adequately explain the "aging-out" phenomenon: Does the fact that crime rates decline with age imply that perceptions of anomie also diminish as people mature? Merton never addresses the dynamics of anomie.
- Anomie theory focuses on behavior of the lower class and is less useful as an explanation of middle-class or white-collar crime. It also does not address gender differences in the crime rate: The assumption would be that if female crime rates are lower, females must also be more likely to embrace conformity. Yet women are less likely to have opportunities for success because of gender discrimination; thus it would seem they would be less likely to conform.
- Critics have also suggested that people actually pursue a number of different life goals and that the economic success goal is merely one among many. Other goals include educational, athletic, and social success and prominence. Achieving these goals is not merely a matter of belonging to a certain social class; other factors, including physical ability, intelligence, personality, and family life, can either hinder or assist in their attainment.[57]

Research on how perceptions of anomie influence delinquent behavior has yielded mixed results. Some research finds that correlations between scales measuring anomie and criminality are lower than expected. However, a number of studies have found an association between perceptions of anomie and deviant behavior. For example, a recent self-report study by Scott Menard found that adolescents who say that it may sometimes be appropriate to employ deviant behaviors in order to achieve social goals (e.g., "In order to gain the respect of your friends, it is sometimes necessary to beat up on other people") were also more likely to commit delinquent acts.[58]

Merton's original formation of anomie, one of the most enduring concepts in the social sciences, has recently been broadened by sociologist Robert Agnew in his General Strain Theory, discussed in some detail below.

GENERAL STRAIN THEORY (GST)

Agnew has broadened Merton's vision of anomie and strain so that it might better explain all forms of delinquent behavior.[59]

According to Agnew, there are actually three sources of strain:

1. *Strain caused by the failure to achieve positively valued goals.* This category of strain includes the disjunction between aspirations and expectations (goals and means); this is what Merton spoke of in his theory of anomie. Such strain will occur when youths aspire for wealth and fame but, because they are poor and undereducated, assume that such goals are impossible to achieve. Also falling within this general category is the strain induced by the disjunction between expectations and actual achievements; for example, when a person compares himself or herself to peers who seem to be doing a lot better financially or socially. A similar form of strain occurs when youths perceive that they are not being treated fairly or that the "playing field" is being tilted against them. Perceptions of inequity may result in many adverse reactions ranging from running away from its source

to lowering the benefits of others through physical attacks or vandalism of their property (e.g., the student who believes he is being "picked on" unfairly by a teacher slashes the tires on his car in revenge).

2. *Strain as the removal of positively valued stimuli from the individual.* Strain may occur because of the actual or anticipated removal or loss of positively valued stimuli.[60] For example, the loss of a girlfriend or boyfriend can produce strain, as can the death of a loved one, moving to a new neighborhood or school, and the divorce or separation of parents. The loss of positive stimuli may lead to delinquency as the adolescent tries to prevent the loss, retrieve what has been lost, obtain substitutes, or seek revenge against those responsible for the loss.

3. *Strain as the presentation of negative stimuli.* Strain may also be caused by negative or noxious stimuli. Included within this category are such pain-inducing social interactions as child abuse and neglect, criminal victimization, physical punishment, family and peer conflict, school failure, and interaction with stressful life events ranging from verbal threats to air pollution. For example, children who are abused at home may take their rage out on younger children at school.

Although these three main sources of strain are independent of each other, they may overlap and be cumulative. For example, insults from a teacher may be viewed as an unfair application of negative stimuli that interferes with academic aspirations and reduces the opportunity to achieve positively valued goals. The greater the intensity and frequency of strain experiences, the greater their impact and the more likely they are to cause delinquency.

Negative Affective States According to Agnew, adolescents engage in delinquency as a result of **negative affective states**—the anger, frustration, disappointment, depression, fear, and other adverse emotions that derive from strain. Of these, *anger* is the key linkage between strain and delinquency.

Each type of strain will increase the likelihood that people will experience anger. Anger increases perceptions of injury and of being wronged. It produces a desire for revenge, energizes individuals to take action, and lowers inhibitions; violence and aggression seem justified if you have been wronged and are righteously angry.

Because it produces these emotions, strain can be considered a predisposing factor for delinquency when it is chronic and repetitive and creates a hostile, suspicious, and aggressive attitude. An individual strain episode may be the situational event, or "trigger," that produces violent or otherwise antisocial behavior. (See Figure 4.7).

COPING WITH STRAIN

Agnew recognizes that not all youths who experience strain become delinquents. Some are able to marshal their emotional, mental, and behavioral resources to cope with the anger and frustration produced by strain. Some defenses are cognitive; individuals may be able to rationalize their frustrating situation: Economic success is "just not that important"; they may be poor but "the next guy is worse off"; and if things didn't work out, then they "got what they deserved."

Others seek behavioral solutions: They run away from adverse conditions or seek revenge against those who caused the strain. Behavioral techniques range

FIGURE 4.7
General Strain Theory (GST)

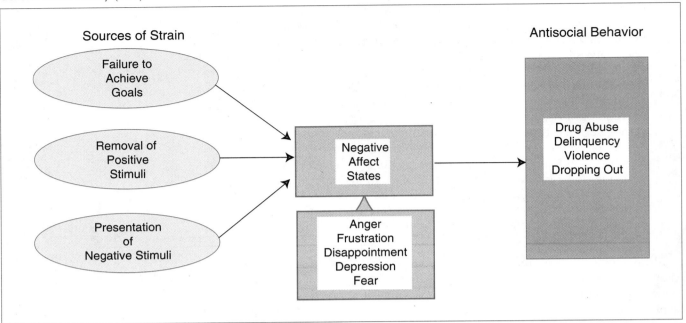

from physical exercise to drug abuse. Some people can cope with strain through legitimate behavior while others fall back on deviant or antisocial coping mechanisms (e.g., taking drugs to cope with emotional pain).

GST acknowledges that the ability to cope with strain is mediated by social and economic capital. The economically deprived are less likely to develop effective coping mechanisms than the affluent. Youths who form associations with delinquent peers are less likely to cope than those who avoid forming relationships with others who reinforce their frustration and anger.

Coping with strain may also be influenced by the *source* of strain. A recent study by Paul Mazerolle and Alex Piquero suggests that when individuals identify a *target* to blame for their problems they are more likely to respond with retaliatory action (e.g., Joe stole my girl away by lying about me so I beat him up!). When individuals internalize blame, delinquent behavior is less likely to occur (e.g., I lost my girlfriend because I was a jerk). Sometimes the source of strain is difficult to pinpoint (e.g., I feel depressed because my parents got divorced); Mazerolle and Piquero find that this type of ambiguous strain is unlikely to produce an aggressive response.[61]

Evaluating GST Agnew's work is quite important because it both clarifies the concept of strain and directs future research agendas. It also adds to the body of literature describing how social and life history events influence offending patterns. Because sources of strain vary over the life course, so too should delinquency rates, and they do.

There is also empirical support for GST. In a recent empirical analysis of his theory using longitudinal survey data, Agnew, with Helene Raskin White, found that adolescents who score high on scales measuring perceptions of strain labeled "life hassles" (e.g., "my classmates do not like me," adults and friends "don't respect my opinions") and "negative life events" (e.g., being victimized by crime, experiencing the death of a close friend, facing serious illness) are also the ones most likely to engage in delinquency.[62]

Independent research efforts have concurred with Agnew's vision of delinquency. Some show that indicators of strain—family breakup, unemployment, moving, feelings of dissatisfaction with friends and school—are positively related to delinquency.[63] Adolescents who report feelings of stress and anger are more likely to interact with delinquent peers and engage in delinquent behaviors.[64] Research shows that in some cases, delinquent behaviors may help to mediate strain: Delinquency is an effective "coping" mechanism that helps relieve feelings of anger and resentment.[65] Strain is reduced by lashing out at others, by stealing, or by vandalizing property.

Gender Issues GST still leaves unanswered a number of questions. For example, as Agnew himself has acknowledged, GST fails to adequately explain gender differences in the delinquency rate. Females experience as much or more strain, frustration, and anger as males, yet their delinquency rate is much lower. Is it possible that there are gender differences in either the perception of strain and/or the ability to cope with its adverse effects? It is possible that even when presented with similar types of strain, males and females respond with a different constellation of negative emotions.[66] Females may be socialized to internalize stress, blaming themselves for their problems; males relieve strain by striking out at others. Clearly more research is needed to understand strain and its influence on behavior.[67]

CULTURAL DEVIANCE/SUBCULTURAL THEORIES

Cultural deviance theories (sometimes called subcultural theory) hold that youth crime is a result of individuals' desire to conform to the cultural values of their immediate environment that are in conflict with those of the greater society. Conformity to the rules, values, and norms of unconventional groups with whom a youth is in close contact results in violation of the rules of conventional society. As Joseph Weis and John Sederstrom interpret cultural deviance, "[D]elinquent behavior is caused by proper socialization within a 'deviant' social group or culture. Juvenile delinquency is merely 'marching to a different drummer.' "[68]

Cultural deviance theories suggest that slum youths violate the law because they adhere to the unique, independent value system existing within lower-class areas. Lower-class values include being tough, never showing fear, living for today, and disrespecting authority. In socially disorganized slums, conventional values such as "honesty," "obedience," and "hard work" make little sense to youths whose only successful adult role models—the neighborhood gun runner, drug dealer, or pimp—earn their living through crime and deviant behaviors (see Figure 4.8).

Cultural deviance/subcultural theory is a link between the concepts of social disorganization and strain theory. Subcultural theorists argue that youths who live in poverty-stricken areas lack the means to achieve conventional success goals. Because they develop feelings of anomie and strain, slum youth create a unique set of cultural values and standards of their own. Instead of aspiring to be "preppies" or "yuppies," lower-class citizens strive to be tough and street-smart,

FIGURE 4.8
Cultural deviance theory

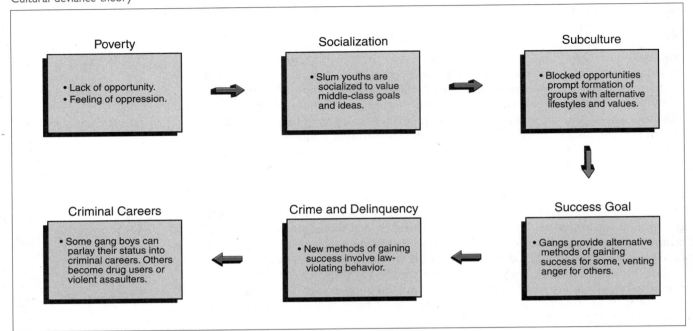

and to have a bad "rep." In other words, feelings of strain and anomie encourage lower-class people to form independent subcultures that provide them with support and nurturance. They may be failures in conventional society, but they are the kings and queens of the neighborhood.

DEVELOPMENT OF SUBCULTURAL THEORY

In 1938, sociologist Thorsten Sellin identified the social factors that promote and sustain independent subcultures.[69] He found that newly arrived immigrant groups brought with them views and beliefs that clashed with the dominant values of U.S. society. For example, some European and Latin cultures demand that males seek violent revenge for perceived slights or insults to female family members. They could not understand it when police arrested them for killing someone who had insulted their daughter or sister. The result was **culture conflict** between agents of the middle class and residents of poverty-stricken areas.

In 1967, Marvin Wolfgang and Franco Ferracuti identified a **subculture of violence** whose norms stressed a potent theme of violence and revenge. Young males living in this urban-based subculture were expected to respond with violence to the slightest provocation.[70]

According to a classic paper by sociologist Walter Miller, slum areas manifest a distinct cultural climate that remains stable over long periods of time.[71] In these areas a unique group of valuelike **focal concerns** dominate life among the lower class. These concerns do not necessarily represent a rebellion against middle-class values; rather, they have evolved specifically to fit conditions in slum areas. The major focal concerns that Miller identifies are trouble, toughness, smartness, excitement, fate, autonomy, belonging, and status: These are described in Table 4.1.

TABLE 4.1 Lower-Class Focal Concerns According to Walter Miller

Trouble. Getting into and staying out of trouble are major concerns of lower-class citizens. Trouble includes such behavior as fighting, drinking, and sexual misconduct. In lower-class communities, people are evaluated in terms of their actual, or potential, involvement in troublemaking activity. Trouble can confer prestige, for example, when a boy gets a reputation for being able to handle himself well in a fight. However, getting into trouble and having to pay the consequences can make a person look foolish and incompetent.

Toughness. Lower-class males refuse to be sentimental or soft and instead value physical strength, fighting ability, and athletic skill. Toughness involves a high tolerance of pain, disdain of fear, fighting skill, and the willingness to accept all manner of hardships without complaint. Lower-class males who cannot meet these standards risk getting a reputation for being weak, inept, and effeminate.

Smartness. Slum boys are proud of their savvy or "street smarts." Smartness means knowing essential urban survival techniques, such as gambling, conning, and outsmarting the law. Youths who fail to attain a reputation for smartness may find themselves held in contempt by their peers, known in the neighborhood as a dupe or a sucker.

Excitement. Fun and excitement can enliven an otherwise drab existence. Gambling, fighting, getting drunk, participating in sexual adventures, and similar risky behaviors are all part of excitement even if they lead to "trouble." In between adventures, kids "chill out" and "be cool." Those who do not seek excitement are weak.

Fate. Getting lucky, finding good fortune, and hitting the jackpot are all tickets out of the slum. Fate means playing the numbers and the horses, and betting on sports.

Autonomy. Lower-class kids desire and value personal freedom and autonomy. Knuckling under to authority figures—police, teachers, and parents—is considered an unacceptable weakness, incompatible with toughness. Autonomy can lead to trouble. Kids who deal with strict or stern teachers by "laying an attitude" on them run the risk of getting left back in school and/or dropping out.

Belonging. Lower-class youths who want to be respected members of the neighborhood join a gang, clique, or youth group.

Status. Lower-class kids want to achieve "status" in their neighborhood by being considered tough, smart, independent, and resourceful. Achieving status allows them to participate in adult activities, such as having sex and drinking. A gang member who achieves status, raises the reputation in the community of the group as a whole.

SUBCULTURAL VALUES TODAY

Although Miller's research was conducted more than 40 years ago, his concepts are still relevant today. Many of the focal concerns he found in the 1950s still hold sway in lower-class culture. Significant numbers of lower-class adolescents are carrying guns today, ready to display their "toughness" if provoked. Substance abuse is on the rise in lower-class areas as youth look for "excitement." "Smartness" leads inner-city kids to devalue formal education and become dropouts; "trouble" means drinking, getting high, and engaging in precocious sex. Gangs and groups in these areas maintain their own language, signs, codes, and moral rules.

As sociologist James Short notes, lower-class youth still consider themselves part of an urban underclass whose members must use their wits to survive ("smartness") or else succumb to poverty, alcoholism, and drug addiction.[72] Exploitation of women abounds in a culture racked by unemployment and limited economic opportunity. Sexual conquest ("trouble") is one of the few areas open to lower-class males for achieving self-respect ("status"). The absence of male authority figures contributes to the fear that marriage will limit freedom ("autonomy"). Peers heap scorn on anyone who allows himself to get "trapped" by a female, fueling the number of single-parent households.

A number of studies of urban gang boys also confirm Miller's view that "street smarts" is an important focal concern, not only to make money but also to achieve self-respect. In his respected study of street gangs, Mercer Sullivan found that success in crime is called "getting paid" or "getting over," which means not only financial reward but achieving a sense of triumph over the grim urban environment.[73]

COHEN'S THEORY OF DELINQUENT SUBCULTURE

Albert Cohen first articulated the theory of delinquent subculture in his 1955 book *Delinquent Boys.*"[74] Cohen's main purpose was to explain the disproportionate amount of official delinquent behavior found in slum neighborhoods. His central position is that delinquent behavior of lower-class youths is actually a protest against the norms and values of the middle-class U.S. culture. Because social conditions make them incapable of achieving success in a legitimate fashion, lower-class youths experience a form of culture conflict that Cohen labels **status frustration.** As a result, many of them join together in teenage gangs and engage in behavior that is nonutilitarian, malicious, and negativistic.[75]

Cohen views delinquents as forming a separate subculture and possessing a value system directly in opposition to that of the larger society. He describes the subculture as one that takes "its norms from the larger culture but turns them upside down. The delinquent's conduct is right, by the standards of his subculture, precisely because it is wrong by the norms of the larger culture."[76]

Causes of Delinquency   According to Cohen, the development of the delinquent subculture is a function of the social and familial conditions children experience as they mature in the ghetto or slum environment. Delinquency is not a product of inherent class inferiority but rather a function of the social and economic limitations suffered by members of the less fortunate groups in U.S. society. The numbing burden of poverty is the real villain in the creation of delinquent careers.[77]

By implication, Cohen suggests that lower-class families are incapable of teaching their offspring proper socialization techniques for entry into the dominant middle-class culture. Lower-class families, permanently cut off from the middle-class way of life, produce children who lack the basic skills necessary to achieve social and economic success in our demanding society. Developmental handicaps produced by a lower-class upbringing include a lack of educational training, poor speech and communication skills, and an inability to delay gratification.[78]

Middle-Class Measuring Rods   One of the more significant handicaps that lower-class children face is the inability to positively impress such authority figures as teachers, employers, or supervisors. Cohen calls the standards these authority figures set **middle-class measuring rods** and maintains that the conflict lower-class youths feel when they fail to meet these standards is a primary cause of delinquency.

Middle-class measuring rods develop because the most important institutions in society—schools, churches, businesses, the military, the justice system, and so on—are dominated by middle-class values. Clients of these institutions (e.g., students, workers, soldiers) are expected to display middle-class values and behaviors, such as verbal skills, ambition, neatness, attention, cleanliness, good manners, and the ability to delay gratification. When lower-class youths cannot meet these criteria, their failures become part of an enduring public record that is consulted whenever they apply for a job, seek educational advancement, or wish to join a social organization. Failure to meet middle-class measuring rods is therefore not an isolated incident that, if not repeated, will be forgotten. It becomes an enduring part of lower-class youths' permanent records that follows them throughout life and helps thwart personal ambitions.

Reactions to Middle-Class Measuring Rods   Cohen's position is that lower-class boys who suffer the rejection of middle-class decision makers are deeply affected by their lack of social recognition.[79] Typically, they may elect to adopt one of three alternative behavior models: the "corner boy" role, the "college boy" role, or the "delinquent boy" role.

The **corner boy** is not delinquent but may engage in some marginal behavior. For example, he is a truant and petty drug user but would never get involved in drug trafficking, in armed robbery, or in other felony crimes. The corner boy spends his time hanging out with his peers, upon whom he depends for support, motivation, and interest. His values, therefore, are those of this group. Eventually the corner boy will marry a local girl and obtain a menial job with few prospects for advancement or success.

The **college boy** embraces the cultural and social values of the middle class. He actively strives to conform to "middle-class measuring rods" in order to move up the social ladder. Ill equipped academically, socially, and linguistically to achieve the rewards of middle-class life, the college boy is fated for frustration and disappointment. Some make it in the middle-class world, but most remain on its margin.

As if sensing that they are headed for eventual disappointment, the **delinquent boy** adopts a set of norms and principles in direct opposition to those of middle-class society.[80] Living for today only, delinquent boys hold a "devil may care" attitude that Cohen calls **short-run hedonism.**

Members of the delinquent subculture are also careful to maintain **group autonomy.** They join gangs and groups that resist control efforts by authority figures. The gang is autonomous, independent, and the focus of "attraction, loyalty, and solidarity."[81]

Although the delinquent boy may be negativistic and malicious, he still may harbor admiration for a few of the norms and values of the larger culture. He may really want to be a success but believes the deck is stacked against him. To deal with this conflict, he resorts to a process Cohen calls **reaction formation**—rejecting outright the conventional goals and values he may desire but knows he can never really achieve.[82] For the delinquent boy, this takes the form of "irrational," "malicious," "unaccountable" hostility toward the norms of respectable middle-class society.[83]

OPPORTUNITY THEORY

In their influential 1960 work, *Delinquency and Opportunity,* Richard Cloward and Lloyd Ohlin added significantly to the knowledge of delinquent subcultures.[84]

Cloward and Ohlin agree with strain theory by suggesting that access to the legitimate means of achieving social goals is stratified by class.[85] However, they maintain that access to *illegitimate* means of achieving social goals is stratified as well. Opportunities for a "successful" criminal career in organized crime and professional theft and drug-dealing gangs are not open to everyone. Both *legitimate and illegitimate* opportunities are closed to youths in the most disorganized inner-city slum areas.

Gang Subcultures A key element in opportunity theory is the assumption that a strong relationship exists between environment and crime. In wealthy or middle-class areas, educational and vocational opportunities abound, and youths can avail themselves of conventional means of getting ahead, such as going to college. However, in low-income areas, legitimate means are more difficult to come by, and therefore, youths must seek illegitimate avenues of success.

Cloward and Ohlin propose that illegitimate avenues of success are also "blocked" for many youths. In fact, they are available only to those growing up in relatively stable areas where adult criminals have developed ongoing criminal enterprises: Accommodations have already been reached, through bribery and corruption, with crooked police and court officials; local businesspersons are willing to buy stolen merchandise with no questions asked; bondsmen are willing to post bail in the case of an unforeseen arrest. Criminal activity—organized crime, drug trafficking, loan sharking, car theft rings, gambling—can provide a stable income and an alternative avenue to legitimate success. Adolescents growing up in the stable slum admire these successful criminals and attach themselves to the gang. By learning the ropes and helping out, they fit right into this *criminal subculture*. At first they may join youth gangs specializing in theft, extortion, and other profitable criminal activities. Later, if they prove their worth, they can become part of the even more profitable adult crime organizations.

Not all youths in the stable slum join criminal gangs. Some remain loyal to the values and rules of conventional society. Others are temperamentally incapable of following either criminal or conventional rules. They take drugs and alcohol and stress playing it cool and being high and strung out. Cloward and Ohlin call their world the *retreatist subculture.*

In those areas where even illegitimate means to success are blocked, youths become members of the *conflict subculture*.[86] They form fighting gangs that defend their turf and engage in extortion and violent crimes. Although the conflict subculture provides little in the way of economic incentives, it allows boys the opportunity for success and ego gratification by enabling them to show their bravery, strength, and fighting prowess.[87]

ANALYZING OPPORTUNITY THEORY

More than 30 years ago Cloward and Ohlin's view of urban delinquency was considered a milestone for guiding delinquency prevention efforts: If kids could be provided with economic opportunities, they would forgo criminal activity and live conventional lives. Social programs of the time were geared to providing these alternatives, but they proved less than successful (see below). Reducing delinquency by providing economic opportunity alone may not be sufficient to reduce delinquency rates.

Research testing the main premises of opportunity theory has also been inconclusive.[88] Recent surveys of gang delinquency have shown that gangs are more pervasive than Cloward and Ohlin imagined, that more than one type of gang (conflict, violent, drug dealing, social) exists in a particular area, and that the commitment of gang boys to one another is less intense than opportunity theory would suggest.[89]

Although these results are discouraging, several other studies appear to support opportunity theory.[90] These studies found that lower-class delinquents report less perception of opportunity than middle-class youth who engage in conventional behavior patterns.[91] Some recent evidence from gang research projects is also supportive of opportunity theory. Studies of gang boys in Detroit by Carl Taylor and Chicago by Felix Padilla suggest that gangs are formed as business enterprises to provide economic opportunity via drug dealing to youths who otherwise would be left out of the economic mainstream.[92] They found evidence that gang boys do in fact share the economic values of the U.S. middle class but lack the opportunity to achieve them through conventional means. Padilla, for example, found that the gang boys he studied certainly know what they are doing violates social norms and laws; they believe that it is really the only course of action readily open.[93] (Gang delinquency is discussed further in chapter 10.)

Social Structure Theory and Delinquency Prevention

Social structure theories suggest that the best method of primary delinquency prevention is local community organization. The effort should be two-pronged. First, deteriorated neighborhoods must be refurbished in order to provide an environment that meets the basic needs of the residents. Second, educational and job opportunities must be created to provide legitimate alternatives to delinquent gangs. In order to achieve these goals, financial support must be made available to needy families to sustain their ability to survive.

Delinquency prevention through community organizations was pioneered in Chicago by Clifford Shaw in the 1930s. In 1933, Shaw initiated the Chicago Area Project, which was designed to produce social change in communities that suffered from high delinquency rates and gang activity. As part of the project, qualified local leaders coordinated social service centers that promoted community solidarity and counteracted social disorganization. More than 20 different projects were developed, featuring discussion groups, counseling services, hobby groups, school-related activities, and recreation. There is still some question of whether these programs had a positive influence on the delinquency rate. Although some evaluations indicated positive results, others showed that the Chicago Area Project efforts did little to reduce juvenile criminality.[94]

In the 1950s, delinquency prevention programs sought to reach out to youths who were unlikely to use settlement houses or community centers. Instead of having troubled youths come to them, **detached street workers** went out into urban slums and created close relationships with juvenile gangs and groups in their own milieu.[95] The most well-known detached street worker program was Boston's Mid-City Project. There, trained social workers sought out and met with youth gangs three to four times a week on the gangs' own turf. Their goal was to modify the organization of the gang and allow gang members a chance to engage in more conventional behaviors. The detached street workers tried to help gang members get jobs and educational opportunities. They acted as go-betweens for gang members with agents of the power structure—lawyers, judges, parole officers, and the like. Despite these efforts, an evaluation of the program by Walter Miller failed to show that it resulted in significant reduction in criminal activity.[96]

The heyday of delinquency prevention programs based on social structure theory was in the 1960s. The approach seemed to jibe politically with the New Frontier policies of the Kennedy administration and the Great Society/War on Poverty approach of the Johnson administration. A great deal of federal money was pumped into delinquency prevention programs using community organization and redevelopment techniques. The most ambitious of these was the New York City-based Mobilization for Youth (MOBY). Funded by more than $50 million, MOBY attempted an integrated approach to community development. Based securely on Cloward and Ohlin's concept of providing opportunities for legitimate success, MOBY organizers attempted to create new employment opportunities in the community, coordinated social services, and sponsored social action groups, such as tenant's committees, legal action services, and voter registration and political action committees. But MOBY died for lack of funding amid serious questions about its utility and use of funds.

The concept of community organization and change to combat delinquency fell into disfavor in the 1970s and 1980s. However, attempts to improve the lives of families to prevent and control delinquency have not ended. One approach has been directed at helping families in need, giving them the resources needed to sustain and improve their lives. If opportunities are available, then families will be better able to control children and remain a primary source of social control.

Another approach has been to help young people develop strategies to resolve conflict peacefully and deal effectively with neighborhood violence. The mass media has been enlisted to discourage violence. Nonetheless, in recent years the focus of delinquency prevention efforts has shifted from the neighborhood reclamation projects of the 1960s to more individualized, family-centered treatments, which will be discussed in chapters 5 and 8.

SUMMARY

Social structure theories hold that delinquent behavior is an adaptation to conditions that predominate in lower-class environments. Social structure theory has three main branches (see Table 4.2). The first, social disorganization, suggests that economically deprived areas lose their ability to control and direct the behavior of their residents. Gangs and groups flourish in these disorganized areas. Deviant values are transmitted from one generation to the next. Shaw and McKay viewed this development principally as a property of youthful street gangs. They found in their study of Chicago that delinquency rates vary widely throughout the city. The probability of adolescents becoming delinquent and getting arrested and later incarcerated depends on whether they live in one of these high-rate areas. Delinquency is a product of the socialization mechanisms within a neighborhood. Unstable neighborhoods have the greatest chance of producing delinquents. More recent ecological theories have expanded on this early research to show how community fear, unemployment, change, and attitudes influence behavior patterns.

The second branch of social structure theory is made up of strain theories. These hold that lower-class youths may actually desire legitimate goals but that their unavailability causes rage, frustration, and substitution of deviant behavior. Robert Merton linked strain to anomie, a condition caused when there is a disjunction between goals and means. In his general strain

TABLE 4.2 Social Structure Theories

Theory	Major Premise	Strengths
Social Disorganization Theories		
social disorganization	The breakdown of informal and formal social control in deteriorated inner-city areas results in the formation of gangs and increasing rates of delinquency.	Accounts for urban crime rates and trends.
relative deprivation	Crime occurs when the wealthy and poor live in close proximity to one another.	Explains high crime rates in deteriorated inner-city areas located near more affluent neighborhoods.
Strain Theories		
anomie	People who adopt the goals of society but lack the means to attain them seek alternatives, such as crime.	Points out how competition for success creates conflict and crime. Suggests that social conditions can account for crime.
general strain theory	Strain has a variety of sources. Strain causes crime in the absence of adequate coping mechanisms.	Identifies the complexities of strain in modern society. Expands on anomie theory. Shows the influences of social events on behavior over the life course. Can explain middle- and upper-class crime.
Cultural Deviance Theories		
subcultural theory	Citizens who obey the street rules of lower-class life (focal concerns) find themselves in conflict with the dominant culture.	Identifies more coherently the elements of lower-class culture that push people into committing street crimes.
Cohen's theory of delinquent subculture	Status frustration of lower-class boys, created by their failure to achieve middle-class success, causes them to join gangs.	Shows how the conditions of lower-class life produce crime. Explains violence and destructive acts. Identifies conflict of lower-class with middle-class.
Cloward and Ohlin's theory of opportunity	Blockage of conventional opportunities causes lower-class youths to join criminal, conflict, or retreatist gangs. Criminal opportunities are limited.	Shows that even illegal opportunities are structured in society. Indicates why people become involved in a particular type of criminal activity.

theory, Robert Agnew identifies two more sources of sources of strain; the removal of positive reinforcements and the addition of negative ones. He shows how strain causes delinquent behavior by creating negative affective states, and the means adolescents employ to cope with strain.

The third branch of structural theory is referred to as cultural deviance or subcultural theory. This theory maintains that the result of social disorganization and strain is the development of independent subcultures that hold values in opposition to mainstream society. Walter Miller argues that almost all lower-class citizens maintain separate value systems, which he calls focal concerns. Albert Cohen identifies a delinquent subculture that is negativistic and destructive. Sociologists Richard Cloward and Lloyd Ohlin take this idea one step further by suggesting that some neighborhoods deny their residents the opportunity for even illegal gain, thereby creating the rise of violence and drug-related subcultures.

The social structure view is still influential today. Modern theorists consider the high level of crime in certain areas to be a function of social disorganization, relative deprivation, and neighborhood transition.

Over the years, a number of delinquency prevention efforts have been based on a social structure approach.

KEY TERMS

culture of poverty
underclass
hollowed out
the truly disadvantaged
stratified
economic stratification
political stratification
prestige stratification
latchkey children
social disorganization
strain
cultural deviance
subcultural theory

subcultures
social ecology
ecological study
social control
Chicago School
natural areas
transitional neighborhoods
cultural transmission
relative deprivation
gentrified
embedded
anomie
negative affective states

culture conflict
subculture of violence
focal concerns
status frustration
middle-class measuring rods
corner boy
college boy
delinquent boy
short-run hedonism
group autonomy
reaction formation
detached street workers

QUESTIONS FOR DISCUSSION

1. Is there a "transitional" area in your town or city?
2. Is it possible that a distinct lower-class culture exists? Do you know anyone who has the focal concerns Miller talks about?
3. Have you ever perceived anomie? What causes anomie? Is there more than one cause of strain?

4. How does poverty cause delinquency?
5. Do middle-class youths become delinquent for the same reasons as lower-class youths?
6. Does "relative deprivation" produce delinquency?

NOTES

1. Oscar Lewis, "The Culture of Poverty," *Scientific American* 215:19–25 (1966).
2. Rodrick Wallace, "Expanding Coupled Shock Fronts of Urban Decay and Criminal Behavior: How U.S. Cities Are Becoming 'Hollowed Out,'" *Journal of Quantitative Criminology* 7:333–55 (1991).
3. Ken Auletta, *The Under Class* (New York: Random House, 1982).
4. William Julius Wilson, *The Truly Disadvantaged* (Chicago: University of Chicago Press, 1987).
5. Children's Defense Fund, *The State of America's Children 1995* (Washington, D.C.: Children's Defense Fund, 1995), p. 28.
6. Ibid., pp. 2–3.
7. James Q. Wilson and Richard Herrnstein, *Crime and Human Nature* (New York: Simon & Schuster, 1985).
8. Ibid., p. 17.
9. Ibid., p. 29.
10. Gretchen Witt and Susan Kalish, "Black Households: How Are They Doing Economically?" *Population Today* 23:3 (1995).
11. Greg Duncan and Willard Rogers, "Has Children's Poverty Become More Persistent?" *American Sociological Review* 56:538–50 (1991).
12. Herman Schwendinger and Julia Siegel Schwendinger, *Adolescent Subcultures and Delinquency* (New York: Prager, 1985).
13. Joanne Savage and Bryan Vila, "Lagged Effects of Nurturance on Crime: A Cross-National Comparison" (Paper presented at the American Society of Criminology meeting, Boston, Mass., November 1995).
14. G. R. Patterson, L. Crosby, and S. Vuchnich, "Predicting Risk for Early Police Arrest," *Journal of Quantitative Criminology* 8:335–53 (1992).
15. Robert Agnew, "Foundation for a General Strain Theory of Crime and Delinquency," *Criminology* 30:47–87 (1992), at 48.
16. Robert Bursik and Harold Grasmick, "The Multiple Layers of Social Disorganization" (Paper presented at the annual meeting of the American Society of Criminology, New Orleans, La., November 1992); Robert Bursik and

Harold Grasmick, "Longitudinal Neighborhood Profiles in Delinquency: The Decomposition of Change," *Journal of Quantitative Criminology* 8:247–56 (1992).

17. Louis Wirth, "Urbanism as a Way of Life," *American Journal of Sociology* 44:1–24 (1938).

18. Clifford R. Shaw and Henry D. McKay, *Juvenile Delinquency and Urban Areas,* rev. ed. (Chicago: University of Chicago Press, 1972).

19. Ibid., p. 52.

20. Ibid., p. 170.

21. Solomon Kobrin, "Chicago Area Project—A Twenty-Five Year Assessment," *Annals of the American Academy of Political and Social Science* 322:20–29 (1950).

22. Frederick Thrasher, *The Gang* (Chicago: University of Chicago Press, 1927).

23. Robert Bursik and James Webb, "Community Change and Patterns of Delinquency," *American Journal of Sociology* 88:24–42 (1982).

24. Bernard Lander, *Towards an Understanding of Juvenile Delinquency* (New York: Columbia University Press, 1954); David Bordua, "Juvenile Delinquency and 'Anomie': An Attempt at Replication," *Social Problems* 6:230–38 (1958); Roland Chilton, "Continuities in Delinquency Area Research: A Comparison of Studies in Baltimore, Detroit, and Indianapolis," *American Sociological Review* 29:71–73 (1964).

25. For a general review, see James Byrne and Robert Sampson, eds., *The Social Ecology of Crime* (New York: Springer-Verlag, 1985).

26. Leo Carroll and Pamela Irving Jackson, "Inequality, Opportunity, and Crime Rates in Central Cities," *Criminology* 21:178–94 (1983).

27. Judith Blau and Peter Blau, "The Cost of Inequality: Metropolitan Structure and Violent Crime," *American Sociological Review* 147:114–29 (1982).

28. Robert Sampson, "Structural Sources of Variation in Race-Age-Specific Rates of Offending Across Major U.S. Cities," *Criminology* 23:647–73 (1985).

29. Richard Block, "Community Environment and Violent Crime," *Criminology* 17:46–57 (1979).

30. Richard Rosenfeld, "Urban Crime Rates: Effects of Inequality, Welfare Dependency, Region and Race," in James Byrne and Robert Sampson, eds., *The Social Ecology of Crime* (New York: Springer-Verlag, 1985), pp. 116–30.

31. Ora Simcha-Fagan and Joseph Schwartz, "Neighborhood and Delinquency: An Assessment of Contextual Effects," *Criminology* 24:667–703 (1986).

32. Leo Scheurman and Solomon Kobrin, "Community Careers in Crime," in Albert Reiss and Michael Tonry, eds., *Communities and Crime* (Chicago: University of Chicago Press, 1986), pp. 67–100.

33. Ibid., p. 96.

34. Janet Heitgerd and Robert Bursik, Jr. "Extracommunity Dynamics and the Ecology of Delinquency," *American Journal of Sociology* 92:775–87 (1987).

35. Richard McGahey, "Economic Conditions, Organization, and Urban Crime," in Albert Reiss and Michael Tonry, eds., *Communities and Crime* (Chicago: University of Chicago Press, 1986), pp. 231–70.

36. Allen Liska and Paul Bellair, "Violent-Crime Rates and Racial Composition: Convergence over Time," *American Journal of Sociology* 101: 578–610 (1995).

37. John Hagan, "The Social Embeddedness of Crime and Unemployment," *Criminology* 31:465–92 (1993).

38. See, generally, Wesley Skogan, "Fear of Crime and Neighborhood Change," in Albert Reiss and Michael Tonry, eds., *Communities and Crime* (Chicago: University of Chicago Press, 1986), pp. 191–232; Stephanie Greenberg, "Fear and Its Relationship to Crime, Neighborhood Deterioration and Informal Social Control," in James Byrne and Robert Sampson, eds., *The Social Ecology of Crime* (New York: Springer-Verlag, 1985), pp. 47–62.

39. Jeffery Will and John McGrath, "Crime, Neighborhood Perceptions, and the Underclass: The Relationship Between Fear of Crime and Class Position," *Journal of Criminal Justice* 23: 163–76 (1995).

40. Catherine Ross, "Fear of Victimization and Health," *Journal of Quantitative Criminology* 9:159–65 (1993).

41. Donald Black, "Social Control as a Dependent Variable," in D. Black, ed., *Toward a General Theory of Social Control* (Orlando, Fla.: Academic Press, 1990).

42. Bursik and Grasmick, "The Multiple Layers of Social Disorganization," pp. 8–10.

43. Robert Bursik, Jr. and Harold Grasmick, "Economic Deprivation and Neighborhood Crime Rates, 1960–1980," *Law and Society* 27:263–84 (1993).

44. Rodney Stark, "Deviant Places: A Theory of the Ecology of Crime," *Criminology* 25:893–911 (1987).

45. Robert Sampson and W. Byron Groves, "Community Structure and Crime: Testing Social Disorganization Theory," *American Journal of Sociology* 94:774–802 (1989).

46. Denise Gottfredson, Richard McNeill, and Gary Gottfredson, "Social Area Influences on Delinquency: A Multilevel Analysis," *Journal of Research in Crime and Delinquency* 28:197–206 (1991).

47. Elijah Anderson, *Streetwise: Race, Class and Change in an Urban Community* (Chicago: University of Chicago Press, 1990), pp. 243–44.

48. Michael Greene, "Chronic Exposure to Violence and Poverty: Interventions that Work for Youth," *Crime and Delinquency* 39:106–24 (1993).

49. Ibid., pp. 110–11.

50. See, for example, Robert Merton, *Social Theory and Social Structure* (Glencoe, Ill.: Free Press, 1957).

51. Robert Merton, "Social Structure and Anomie," *American Sociological Review* 3:672–82 (1938).

52. For samples of his work, see Emile Durkheim, *The Rules of Sociological Method,* 8th ed. (Glencoe, Ill.: Free Press, 1950); idem, *Suicide* (Glencoe, Ill.: Free Press, 1951).

53. Ibid., p. 680.

54. Ibid.

55. Robert Merton, "Social Structure and Anomie," in Marvin Wolfgang, Leonard Savitz, and Norman Johnston, eds., *The Sociology of Crime and Delinquency* (New York: Wiley, 1970), p. 242.

56. Ibid.

57. Robert Agnew, "Goal Achievement and Delinquency," *Sociology and Social Research* 68:435–51 (1984). See also Margaret Farnworth and Michael Leiber, "Strain Theory Revisited: Economic Goals, Educational Means and Delinquency," *American Sociological Review* 54:263–74 (1989).

58. Scott Menard, "A Developmental Test of Mertonian Anomie Theory," *Journal of Research in Crime and Delinquency* 32:136–74 (1995).

59. Agnew, "Foundation for a General Strain Theory of Crime and Delinquency."

60. Ibid., p. 57.

61. Paul Mazerolle and Alex Piquero, "Linking General Strain with Anger: Investigating the Instrumental, Escapist, and Violent Adaptations to Strain" (Paper presented at the American Society of Criminology meeting, Boston, Mass., November 1995).

62. Robert Agnew and Helene Raskin White, "An Empirical Test of General Strain Theory," *Criminology* 30:475–99 (1992).

63. Raymond Paternoster and Paul Mazerolle, "General Strain Theory and Delinquency: A Replication and Extension," *Journal of Research in Crime and Delinquency* 31:235–63 (1994).

64. Teresa Lagrange and Robert Silverman, "Perceived Strain and Delinquency Motivation: An Empirical Evaluation of General Strain Theory" (Paper presented at the American Society of Criminology meeting, Boston, Mass., November 1995).

65. Timothy Brezina, "Adapting to Strain: An Examination of Delinquent Coping Responses," *Criminology* (in press, 1996).

66. Lisa Broidy, "The Role of Gender in General Strain Theory" (Paper presented at the American Society of Criminology meeting, Boston, Mass., November 1995).

67. Robert Agnew, "Gender and Crime: A General Strain Theory Perspective" (Paper presented at the American Society of Criminology meeting, Boston, Mass., November 1995).

68. Joseph Weis and John Sederstrom, *The Prevention of Serious Delinquency: What to Do?* (Washington, D.C.: U.S. Government Printing Office, 1981), p. 30.

69. Thorsten Sellin, *Culture Conflict and Crime,* bulletin no. 41 (New York: Social Science Research Council, 1938).

70. Marvin Wolfgang and Franco Ferracuti, *The Subculture of Violence* (London: Tavistock, 1967).

71. Walter Miller, "Lower Class Culture as a Generating Milieu of Gang Delinquency," *Journal of Social Issues* 14:5–19 (1958).

72. James Short, "Gangs, Neighborhoods and Youth Crime," *Criminal Justice Research Bulletin* 5:1–11 (1990). Sam Houston University, Criminal Justice Research Center, Huntsville, Tex.

73. Mercer Sullivan, "Getting Paid": Youth Crime and Work in the Inner City" (Ithaca, N.Y.: Cornell University Press, 1990).

74. Albert Cohen, *Delinquent Boys* (New York: Free Press, 1955).

75. Ibid., p. 25.

76. Ibid., p. 28.

77. Ibid., pp. 73–74.

78. Ibid., p. 86.

79. Ibid., p. 128.

80. Ibid., p. 30.

81. Ibid., p. 31.

82. Ibid., p. 133.

83. Albert Cohen and James Short, "Research on Delinquent Subcultures," *Journal of Social Issues* 14:20 (1958).

84. Richard Cloward and Lloyd Ohlin, *Delinquency and Opportunity* (New York: Free Press, 1960).

85. See Edwin Sutherland, *Principles of Criminology,* 4th ed. (Philadelphia: J. B. Lippincott, 1947).

86. Clarence Schrag, *Crime and Justice, American Style* (Washington, D.C.: U.S. Government Printing Office, 1971), p. 67.

87. See, for example, Irving Spergel, *Racketville, Slumtown, and Haulburg* (Chicago: University of Chicago Press, 1964).

88. Leon Fannin and Marshall Clinard, "Differences in the Conception of Self as a Male Among Lower- and Middle-Class Delinquents," *Social Problems* 13:205–15 (1965).

89. Jeffery Fagan, "The Social Organization of Drug Use and Drug Dealing Among Urban Gangs," *Criminology* 27:633–69 (1989).

90. Judson Landis and Frank Scarpitti, "Perceptions Regarding Value Orientation and Legitimate Opportunity: Delinquents and Non-Delinquents," *Social Forces* 84:57–61 (1965).

91. James Short, Ramon Rivera, and Ray Tennyson, "Perceived Opportunities, Gang Membership, and Delinquency," *American Sociological Review* 30:56–57 (1965).

92. Carl Taylor, *Dangerous Society* (East Lansing: Michigan State University Press, 1990); Felix Padilla, *The Gang as an American Enterprise* (New Brunswick, N.J.: Rutgers University Press, 1992).

93. Padilla, *The Gang as an American Enterprise,* p. 4.

94. For an intensive look at the Chicago Area Project, see Steven Schlossman and Michael Sedlak, "The Chicago Area Project Revisited," *Crime and Delinquency* 29:398–462 (1983).

95. See New York City Youth Board, *Reaching the Fighting Gang* (New York: New York City Youth Board, 1960).

96. Walter Miller, "The Impact of a 'Total Community' Delinquency Control Project," *Social Problems* 10:168–91 (1962).

CHAPTER FIVE

SOCIAL PROCESS THEORIES: LEARNING, CONTROL, INTEGRATED

INTRODUCTION

Not all sociologists view strain, cultural deviance, and social disorganization as the precursors of youth crime. Residence in an inner-city urban environment alone may be insufficient to cause the onset of individual delinquency.[1] After all, most youths in these areas do not commit serious crimes, and relatively few of those who do go on to become career criminals.[2] More than 14 million youth live in poverty today, and the great majority do not become chronic offenders. Self-report studies also find that many middle-class youths engage in delinquent acts, such as car theft, drug use, and vandalism; this finding suggests that delinquency is spread more evenly throughout society than social structure theorists would have us believe.[3]

It is also accepted that adolescent males commit many more crimes than adolescent females. It is difficult to explain the relatively high male crime rate solely from a structural standpoint because environmental conditions should have an equal impact on members of both sexes. In fact, using a strict interpretation of the social structure perspective, female delinquency rates should actually *be higher* than male rates! Gender discrimination limits the economic opportunities of young females; they should therefore suffer greater amounts of delinquency, producing strain and anger.

If living within the "culture of poverty" alone does not cause delinquency, what does? One important view is that the onset of delinquency can be traced to the quality of a child's **socialization:** the **social process** in which people learn through interaction with significant individuals and institutions what they must know to survive and function in society. The socialization process, directed and influenced by the family, peer group, neighbors, teachers, and other authority figures, has a lifelong influence on a child's self-image, beliefs, values, and behavior.

According to this view, such factors as learning delinquent attitudes from peers, feeling alienated or detached from school, and experiencing conflict in the home help produce antisocial activity. Whether they are rich or poor, improper socialization produces adolescents with a poor self-image who are alienated from conventional social institutions and feel little attachment to a law-abiding lifestyle.

Social process theorists believe little distinction exists in American society between the goal and value orientations of the various social classes. Even youths growing up in the most deteriorated urban areas learn the same values at home, school, and church as upper- and middle-class youths. Although lower-class juveniles face the burden of coping with economic hardships, most are willing to obey legal and moral rules because they enjoy a good home life, supportive friends, and caring teachers. Thus it is adolescents of *any* social class who lack these prerequisites for proper socialization who are at risk to delinquency and drug abuse.

SOCIAL PROCESSES AND DELINQUENCY

Social process theories are grounded in the extensive literature examining the relationship between socialization and delinquent behavior. Numerous research studies have found that as children mature, elements of society with which they have close and intimate contact influence their behavior patterns. The primary influence is the family. When parenting is inadequate, absent, or destructive, a child's normal maturation processes will be interrupted and damaged, and although much debate still occurs over which elements of the parent–child relationship are the most critical, there is little question that family relationships have a significant influence on antisocial behavior.[4] The association between family dysfunction and delinquency is critical when the extent of family breakup, conflict, and abuse is considered. Child protective services agencies receive about three million complaints per year; about 700,000 children are in foster care or some other form of substitute shelter.[5] (Chapter 8 reviews the family's role in delinquency causation.)

The literature linking delinquency to poor school performance, educational disabilities, and inadequate educational facilities is also quite extensive. A youth who feels that teachers do not care, who considers himself or herself to be a hopeless academic failure, who has been left back and who eventually drops out of school is more likely to become involved in a delinquent way of life than an adolescent who is educationally gifted and successful.[6] (Chapter 9 reviews the relationship between schools and delinquency.)

Still another suspected element of deviant socialization are peer-group relations that stress substance abuse, theft, and violence. Youths who form close involvements with peers who engage in antisocial behavior may learn the techniques and attitudes that support delinquency; they may find themselves cut off from more conventional associates and institutions.[7] (Chapter 10 reviews peer relations and delinquency.)

Social process theory then portrays the delinquent youth as someone whose personality and behavior, formed in the crucible of social relationships and societal processes, are at odds with conventional society.

The social process perspective has three main branches (see Figure 5.1). The first, **learning theory,** holds that all aspects of delinquency—both the techniques of crime and the attitudes necessary to support delinquency—are learned through close relationships with others.

The second branch, **social control theory,** views delinquency as a result of weakened commitment to the major institutions of society—family, peers, and school. Because their bond to these institutions of informal social control is severed, some adolescents feel free to exercise antisocial behavior choices.

The main distinction between learning and social control theories lies in their concept of human development and change. Learning theory assumes that people are born "good" and then learn from others to be "bad." It reflects the concerned mother's lament that her formerly well-behaved daughter is "being ruined by her friends" and that her son is "picking up bad habits from his friends." In contrast, social control theory assumes that people are born "bad" and are then socialized by others to be "good." It reflects the belief that a well-behaved child is the product of "a good family upbringing," that children need discipline, and that a delinquent is someone ignored by his or her parents.

Some theorists have tried to reconcile the differences between these views by integrating a wide variety of personal traits and social factors into a unified theoretical model. This third branch of social process theory, referred to as **multifactor** or **integrated** theory, considers the influence of social learning, social control, human traits, and social structure factors in explaining the onset and continuity of a delinquent career. Each of these three branches will be discussed independently below (see Figure 5.1).

FIGURE 5.1
The complex web of social
processes that control adolescent
behavior

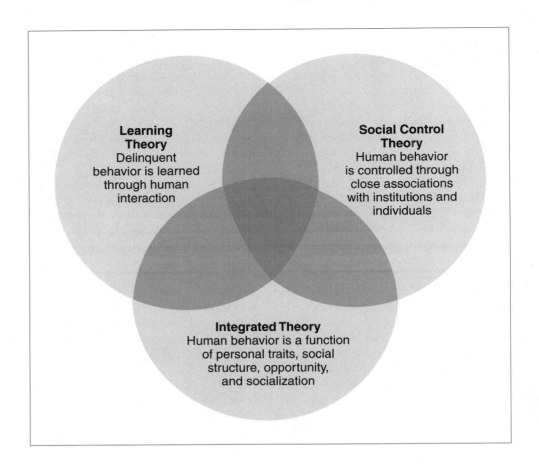

LEARNING THEORY

Learning theory stresses the learning of the attitudes, morals, skills, and behaviors needed to sustain a delinquent career (see Figure 5.2). It suggests that in order to begin a delinquent career, youthful law violators must first *learn* the attitudes, behaviors, and techniques necessary to both commit crimes and then to cope with the emotional turmoil that inevitably results from their behavior. We now turn to descriptions of the most important examples of learning theory.

DIFFERENTIAL ASSOCIATION (DA) THEORY

Edwin Sutherland, long considered the preeminent U.S. criminologist, first formulated the **differential association (DA) theory** in 1939 in his text *Principles of Criminology.*[8] The theory appeared in its final form in 1947. DA was applied then and now to all criminal and delinquent behavior patterns. After Sutherland's death in 1950, his work was continued by his longtime associate Donald Cressey. Cressey was so successful in explaining and popularizing his mentor's efforts that DA remains one of the most enduring explanations of delinquent behavior.

Learning theory stresses that human behavior is learned through group process and social interaction. It suggests that in order to begin a delinquent career, youthful law violators must first *learn* the attitudes, morals, skills behaviors and techniques necessary to both commit crimes and then to cope with the emotional turmoil which is the inevitable consequence of their behavior.

PRINCIPLES OF DIFFERENTIAL ASSOCIATION

The basic principles of differential association are contained in the following statements.[9]

Criminal behavior is learned. This statement differentiates Sutherland's theory from prior attempts to classify delinquent behavior as either an individual trait or a product of the social environment. By suggesting that delinquent and criminal behavior is actually learned, Sutherland implied that it can be classified like any other learned behavior, such as writing, painting, or reading. This statement also reveals Sutherland's allegiance to the psychological aspects of learning.

Criminal behavior is learned in interaction with other persons in a process of communication. Sutherland believed that delinquent behavior is learned actively. An individual does not become a delinquent simply by passively living in a criminogenic environment or being exposed to cultural deviance. Youths participate in the process with other individuals who serve as teachers and guides to delinquent behavior. Delinquency is a group process and cannot appear spontaneously.

The learning of criminal behavior occurs principally within intimate personal groups. Children's contacts with their closest companions—family, friends, and peers—have the greatest influence on their learning of deviant behavior and attitudes. Relationships with these individuals can color and control the interpretation of everyday events, helping youths to overcome social controls and embrace delinquent values and behavior. The intimacy of these associations far outweighs the importance of any other form of communications, for example, movies or television. Even on those rare occasions when violent films seem to provoke mass delinquent episodes, the outbreaks can be more readily explained as a reaction to peer-group pressure than as a reaction to the films themselves.

The learning of criminal behavior includes techniques of committing the crime, which are sometimes very complicated and sometimes very simple, and

FIGURE 5.2
Learning theory of delinquency

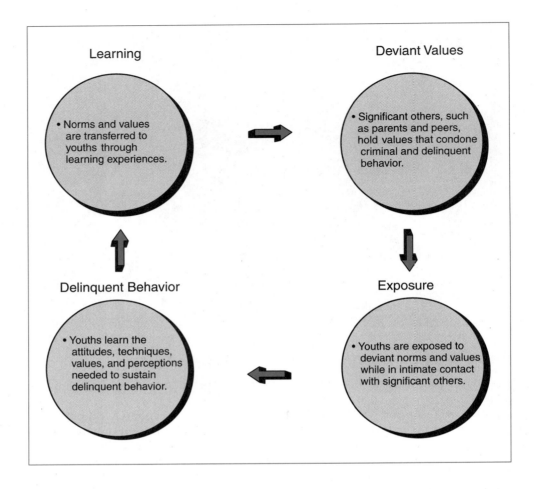

the *specific direction of motives, drives, rationalizations, and attitudes*. Because delinquent behavior is similar to other learned behavior, it follows that the actual techniques of criminality must also be acquired and learned. For example, young delinquents learn from their associates the proper way to pick a lock, shoplift, buy and use guns, and deal drugs. In addition, delinquents must acquire the proper personal attitudes to sustain a delinquent career. The proper way to get high, to smoke a joint, to use a crack pipe are behavior patterns usually acquired from older or more experienced companions.[10] Delinquents must learn how to react properly to their criminal acts—when to defend and/or rationalize their behavior and when to be proud and boastful of their criminal gain; when to show remorse and when to be defiant.

The specific direction of motives and drives is learned from various favorable and unfavorable definitions of the legal codes. Because people's reactions to social rules and laws vary across society, youths constantly come in contact with people who maintain different views on the usefulness of obeying the legal code. Parents and teachers may say one thing, peers another. Juveniles experience what Sutherland calls **culture conflict** when definitions of right and wrong are extremely varied, contradictory, and confusing.

A person becomes delinquent if definitions favorable to violating the law exceed definitions favorable to obeying the law. According to Sutherland's theory, individuals will become delinquent when they are in contact with persons, groups, or events that produce an excess of "definitions toward delinquency" and, concomitantly, when they are isolated from counteracting forces which promote conventional behaviors. A definition *toward* delinquency occurs when a youth is exposed to deviant behaviors (e.g., his parents using alcohol or drugs) or attitudes (e.g., her friends discussing the rewards of a shoplifting spree). A definition *against* delinquency occurs when friends or parents demonstrate their disapproval of crime (see Figure 5.3). Of course, neutral behavior, such as reading a book, also exists. Sutherland and Cressey argue that neutral behavior is important "especially as an occupier of the time of a child so that he is not in contact with criminal behaviors during the time he is so engaged in the neutral behavior."[11]

Differential associations may vary in frequency, duration, priority, or intensity. Whether a child learns to obey the law or to disregard it is influenced by the quality of social interactions. Those of lasting duration will have greater influence than those that are shorter. Frequent contacts have greater effect than rare and haphazard ones. Sutherland did not specify what he meant by *priority,* but Cressey and others have interpreted the term to mean the age of children when they first encounter definitions toward criminality.[12] Contacts made early in life will probably have a greater and more far-reaching influence than those developed later in life. *Intensity* is generally interpreted to mean the importance and

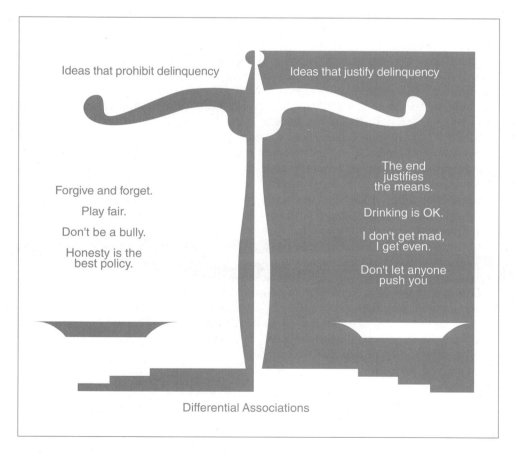

Ideas that prohibit delinquency

Ideas that justify delinquency

Forgive and forget.

Play fair.

Don't be a bully.

Honesty is the best policy.

The end justifies the means.

Drinking is OK.

I don't get mad, I get even.

Don't let anyone push you

Differential Associations

FIGURE 5.3
Differential association theory
Differential association theory assumes that delinquent behavior will occur when the definitions toward delinquency outweigh the definitions against delinquency.

prestige attributed to the individual or groups from whom the definitions are learned. For example, the influence of a father, mother, or trusted friend will far outweigh that of more socially distant figures.

The process of learning criminal behavior by association with criminal and anticriminal patterns involves all the mechanisms involved in any other learning. This statement suggests that the learning of criminal behavior patterns is similar to all other learning experiences and is not a matter of mere imitation.

Although criminal behavior is an explanation of general needs and values, it is not explained by those needs and values as noncriminal behavior is an explanation of the same needs and values. By this principle, Sutherland suggested that the motives for delinquent behavior cannot logically be the same as those for conventional behavior. He ruled out such motives as a desire to accumulate money or social status, a sense of personal frustration, a low self-concept, or any other similar motive as causes of delinquency. They are just as likely to produce such noncriminal behavior as getting a better education or working harder on a job. It is only the learning of deviant norms through contact with an excess of definitions toward criminality that produces delinquent behavior.

TESTING DIFFERENTIAL ASSOCIATION

A number of important research efforts have been devoted to testing the validity of DA. There is evidence that adolescents who maintain close relations with deviant peers will learn delinquent values.[13] Law-violating behavior has been linked to exposure to deviant attitudes.[14] In one classic work, James Short tested a sample of 126 boys and 50 girls incarcerated in state training schools to measure the relationship between frequency, duration, priority, and intensity of interaction with delinquent peers and exposure to crime and delinquency.[15] Short used such measures as the number of friends a youth had who were delinquent, the degree to which a youth associated with criminals, and the intimacy of friendships with delinquents. He found that a consistent relationship existed between delinquent behavior and delinquent associations and that such associations were highly significant for both boys and girls. However, because the study was conducted with institutionalized youths regarded as seriously delinquent, it may not be applicable to the "average" law-violating child.

Some recent research efforts have provided empirical evidence that supports the core concepts of DA. For example, Ross Matsueda and Karen Heimer found evidence that youths who are exposed to deviant definitions are also the ones most likely to become delinquent; this process holds true across racial, age, and class lines.[16] A number of research efforts have found that adolescent substance abusers maintain strong ties to drug-abusing peers and that shared interest in illegal activities brings drug users closer together.[17]

Other research has shown that people are deterred from criminality by the threat of peer and family disapproval.[18] By implication, youths who believe their friends and family hold attitudes in support of deviance will feel free to violate the law; those who believe that their friends and family will condemn their behavior will be deterred from criminal violations.[19]

IS DIFFERENTIAL ASSOCIATION VALID?

Despite these affirmations, not all efforts to verify DA principles have been successful.[20] Designing research to test the assumptions of DA has proven to be a formidable task. It is difficult to conceptualize the principles of the theory, such as a "definition toward delinquency," in a way that lends itself to empirical measurement.[21] Causal ordering is also a problem: Even if delinquent youths have many like-minded friends and report exposure to an excess of prodelinquent definitions, it is difficult to determine whether these associations and definitions *caused* law-violating behavior or were its result. It is possible that the process is one in which youngsters who continually break the law develop a group of like-minded peers who support their behavior, rather than a process in which "innocent" youth are "seduced" into crime by exposure to the deviant attitudes of more delinquent peers.[22]

"Sticky Friends" To remedy this problem, future research may be directed at creating more accurate means with which to test the theory's basic principles.[23] A more valid approach may be to follow a cohort over time to assess the impact of delinquent friends and associations: Does repeated exposure to excess definitions toward deviance escalate deviance through the life course? Some recent research by Mark Warr illustrates the utility of this approach. Warr found that adolescents who acquire delinquent friends are also the ones most likely to eventually engage in delinquent behavior—a finding that supports DA. Warr notes that delinquent friends are "sticky"; once acquired, they are hard to shake. They help lock adolescents into antisocial behavior patterns through the life course. In fact, youths who maintain deviant friendships and close relationships with deviant peers are the ones most likely to continue their offending careers as they mature.[24] Deviant friends help counteract the crime-reducing effects of the aging-out process.[25]

ANALYSIS OF DIFFERENTIAL ASSOCIATION THEORY

Misconceptions about DA theory have tended to produce unwarranted criticism of its principles and meaning.[26] For example, some criminologists claim that the theory is concerned solely with the number of personal contacts and associations a delinquent has with other criminal or delinquent offenders.[27] If this assumption were true, those most likely to become criminals would be police, judges, and correctional authorities because they are constantly associating with criminals. However, Sutherland stressed "excess definitions toward criminality," not mere association with criminals. Thus, although personnel of the juvenile justice system do have extensive associations with criminals, these are more than counterbalanced by their associations with law-abiding citizens.

Another misconception is that definitions toward delinquency are acquired from learning the values of a deviant subculture.[28] Although DA stresses an excess of definitions toward delinquency, it does not specify that they must come solely from lower-class criminal sources. This distinguishes Sutherland's work from social structure theories. Outwardly law-abiding middle-class parents can encourage delinquent behavior by their own drinking, drug use, or family violence, and both middle- and lower-class youth are exposed to media images that express open admiration for violent heroes, such as those played by Arnold Schwarzenegger or Jean-Claude Van Damme. Research by Craig Reinerman and Jeffrey Fagan indicates that the influence of differential associations is not affected by social class, supporting Sutherland's belief that deviant learning can affect middle-class as well as lower-class youth.[29]

There are, however, a number of valid criticisms of Sutherland's work. It fails to explain why one sibling who is exposed to delinquent definitions eventually succumbs to them, while another, living under the same conditions, avoids them.[30] It also fails to account for the origin of delinquent definitions. How did the first "teacher" learn delinquent attitudes and definitions in order to pass them on? Another apparently valid criticism of DA is that it assumes criminal and delinquent acts to be rational and systematic. Thus, it ignores spontaneous and wanton acts of violence and damage that appear to have little utility or purpose, such as the isolated psychopathic killing, which is virtually unsolvable because of the killer's anonymity and lack of delinquent associations.

The most serious criticism of DA theory concerns the vagueness of its terms, which makes it very difficult to test its assumptions. For example, what constitutes an "excess of definitions toward criminality"? How can we determine whether an individual actually has a prodelinquent imbalance of these definitions? It is simplistic to assume that, by definition, all delinquents have experienced a majority of definitions toward delinquency and all nondelinquents, a minority of them. Unless the terms employed in the theory can be defined more precisely, its validity remains a matter of guesswork.

Despite these criticisms, DA theory maintains an important place in the study of delinquent behavior. For one thing, it provides a consistent explanation of *all* types of delinquent and criminal behavior. Unlike the social structure theories discussed previously, it is not limited to the explanation of a single facet of antisocial activity, for example, lower-class gang activity. The theory can also account for the extensive delinquent behavior found even in middle- and upper-class areas, where youths may be exposed to a variety of prodelinquent definitions from such sources as overly opportunistic parents and friends. Finally, the Warr research suggesting that delinquent friends are "sticky" indicates that differential associations might be one of the keys to explaining deviance through the life course.

DIFFERENTIAL REINFORCEMENT (DR) THEORY

A number of attempts have been made to reformulate the concept of differential association, the most important being Ronald Akers's efforts to frame Sutherland's model in a behavioral theory format. He suggests that delinquent behavior, like all behavior, is shaped by the stimuli or reactions of others to that behavior.[31] Extending this idea, social behavior is learned through direct conditioning, or modeling of others' behavior. Likewise, behavior is strengthened through reward or positive reinforcement and weakened by loss of reward (negative punishment) or actual punishment (positive punishment). Youths who receive more rewards than punishments for conforming behavior will be the most likely to remain nondelinquent. This behavioral process is called **differential reinforcement (DR) theory.** Reinforcements, both positive and negative, are usually received in group settings. The most powerful influences are peers and family, but a youth may also be affected by school, social groups, church, and other institutions.

In an empirical analysis of DR, Akers and his associates found that relevant survey items predicted significant amounts of marijuana use (39 percent) and alcohol abuse (32 percent).[32] Other social scientists have confirmed that peer influence and differential reinforcements help shape adolescent behavior.[33] For example, Marvin Krohn and his associates found that DR principles were effective for predicting the maintenance of deviant behaviors, such as cigarette smoking, in a sample of junior and senior high school boys.[34] Krohn found that differential reinforcement of smoking by parents and friends contributed to adolescent misbehavior. Another study using 1,688 adolescent subjects conducted by L. Thomas Winfree and his associates found that DR variables could predict which adolescents were drug users and which ones weren't.[35]

Akers's work has emerged as an important view of the cause of criminal activity. It is one of the few prominent theoretical models that successfully links sociological and psychological variables. In addition, as Akers himself argues, social learning ties in with rational choice theory because they both suggest that people learn the techniques and attitudes necessary to commit crime: Criminal knowledge is gained through experience. After considering the outcome of their past experiences, potential offenders decide which criminal acts will be profitable and which are dangerous and should be avoided.[36] Why do people make rational choices about crime? Because they have learned to balance risks against the potential for criminal gain.

NEUTRALIZATION THEORY

Neutralization theory, sometimes referred to as drift theory, is identified with the writings of David Matza and his associate Gresham Sykes.[37] In furthering Sutherland's views, Sykes and Matza suggest that delinquents hold attitudes and values similar to those of law-abiding citizens but that they learn techniques that enable them to neutralize those values and attitudes temporarily and drift back and forth between legitimate and delinquent behavior. The techniques used by delinquents to weaken the hold of social values are learned through interaction with others.

ELEMENTS OF NEUTRALIZATION THEORY

In his major work, *Delinquency and Drift,* Matza explains neutralization, or drift, theory. He suggests that most individuals spend their lives behaving on a continuum somewhere between total freedom and total restraint. **Drift** is the process by which an individual moves from one extreme of behavior to the other, behaving sometimes in an unconventional, free, or deviant manner and at other times with constraint and sobriety.

The subculture of delinquency, in which criminal behavior is regularly supported, encourages drift in young people. Matza views the subculture as relatively amorphous and without formal rules or values (except those that are bestowed on it by sociologists). He characterizes it as an informal, relatively inarticulate oral tradition. Members of the subculture infer the behavior they are to follow from behavior cues, including slogans and actions, of their comrades.[38]

Writing with Gresham Sykes, Matza subsequently rejects the notion that the subculture of delinquency maintains an independent set of values and attitudes that place the delinquent in direct opposition to the values of the dominant culture. Rather, Matza and Sykes point to the complex pluralistic culture in our society that is both deviant and ethical. Although most youths actually appreciate goal-oriented middle-class values, they may believe that expressing conventional virtues and engaging in accepted behavior would be frowned on by their peers. Therefore, these beliefs remain unconscious or "subterranean" because juveniles are afraid to express them to members of their own group. Juveniles are particularly susceptible to keeping **subterranean values** because peer relations are critical during the adolescent years.[39]

TECHNIQUES OF NEUTRALIZATION

Sykes and Matza suggest that juveniles develop a distinct set of justifications, or neutralization techniques, for their behavior when it violates accepted social norms. These neutralization techniques allow youths to temporarily drift away from the rules of the normative society and participate in deviant behaviors. Sykes and Matza base their theoretical model on the following observations.[40]

First, delinquents sometimes voice a sense of guilt over their illegal acts. If a stable delinquent value system existed in opposition to generally held values and rules, delinquents likely would not exhibit any remorse for their acts, other than regret at being apprehended.

Second, juvenile offenders frequently respect and admire honest, law-abiding persons. "Really honest" persons are often revered, and if for some reason they are accused of misbehavior, the delinquent is quick to defend their integrity. Those admired may include sports figures, clergy, parents, teachers, and neighbors.

Third, delinquents draw a line between those whom they can victimize and those whom they cannot. Members of youths' ethnic groups, churches, or neighborhoods may be off limits as far as crime goes. This practice implies that delinquents are aware of the wrongfulness of their acts. Why else would they limit them?

Finally, delinquents are not immune to the demands of conformity. Most delinquents frequently participate in many of the same social functions as law-abiding youths, for example, school, church, and family activities.

Sykes and Matza argue that these observations substantiate the fact that delinquents operate as part of the normative culture and adhere to its values and standards. How, then, do they account for delinquency? They suggest that delinquency can only occur when accepted social values are "neutralized" through employment of a standard set of rationalizations for illegal behavior. Thus, most youths generally adhere to the rules of society but learn certain techniques to temporarily release themselves from their moral constraints. The most important of these neutralization techniques include the following:[41]

- *Denial of Responsibility.* Delinquents sometimes claim that their unlawful acts were simply not their fault, that they were due to forces beyond their control or were an accident.
- *Denial of Injury.* By denying the wrongfulness of an act, delinquents are able to rationalize their illegal behavior. For example, stealing is viewed as "borrowing," vandalism is considered mischief that got out of hand. Society often agrees with delinquents, labeling their illegal behavior "pranks" and thereby reaffirming that delinquency can be socially acceptable.
- *Denial of a Victim.* Delinquents sometimes rationalize their behavior by maintaining that the victim of crime "had it coming." Thus, vandalism may be directed against a disliked teacher or neighbor, or homosexuals may be beaten up by a gang because the gang finds their behavior offensive.[42] Denying the victim may also take the form of ignoring the rights of an absent or unknown victim, for example, the unseen owner of a department store.
- *Condemnation of the Condemners.* Delinquents view the world as a corrupt place with a dog-eat-dog moral code in which police and judges are on the take, teachers show favoritism, and parents take out their frustrations on

their children. It is ironic and unfair for these authorities to turn around and condemn youthful misconduct. By shifting the blame to others, delinquents are able to repress the feeling that their own acts are wrong.

- *Appeals to Higher Loyalties.* Delinquents argue that they are torn between being loyal to their own peer group while at the same time attempting to abide by the rules of the larger society. The needs of the group take precedence over the rules of society because the demands of the former are immediate and localized.[43]

In sum, the theory of neutralization presupposes a condition in which such statements as "I didn't mean to do it," "I didn't really hurt anybody," "They had it coming to them," "Everybody's picking on me," and "I didn't do it for myself" are used by youths to rationalize violating accepted social norms and values so that they can enter, or drift, into delinquent modes of behavior (see Figure 5.4).

TESTING NEUTRALIZATION

Attempts have been made to verify the assumptions of neutralization theory empirically, but the results have been inconclusive.[44] One area of research has been directed at determining whether there really is a need for adolescent law violators to neutralize moral constraints: If delinquents belong to subcultures that maintain values in opposition to accepted social norms, then there is really no need to neutralize. So far the evidence is mixed. Research studies indicate that delinquents generally approve of social values such as honesty and fairness; others come to the opposite conclusion.[45] Some studies show that delinquent youths approve of criminal behavior such as theft and violence while others find

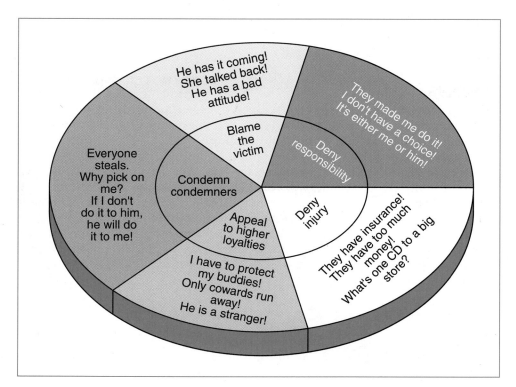

FIGURE 5.4
Techniques of neutralization

evidence that they oppose illegal behavior.[46] In a recent investigation supportive of neutralization, sociologist Robert Agnew found that (a) most adolescents generally voice *disapproval* of deviant behaviors such as violence and (b) neutralizations do in fact enable youths to engage in socially disapproved behavior. The Agnew research is important because it makes use of longitudinal data, enabling him to show that juveniles who at first express neutralizations later go on to engage in violent acts.[47]

ANALYSIS OF NEUTRALIZATION THEORY

The theory of neutralization is a major contribution to the literature of crime and delinquency because it can account for the aging-out process. Neutralization theory implies that youths can forgo criminal behavior when they reach the age of majority because they never really rejected the morality of normative society. Once the needs and pressures of the postteenage world exert themselves—marriage, family, job—delinquents are more likely than ever to drift into legitimate modes of behavior.

Neutralization theory leaves important questions unanswered, however. Do delinquents neutralize law-violating behavior *before* or *after* they commit crimes?[48] If they neutralize their guilt after engaging in illegal activity, then neutralization theory loses its power as an explanation of the *cause* of delinquency and instead becomes a theory describing the *reactions* of juveniles to their misdeeds. Although this question seems critical, criminologist John Hamlin argues that neutralizations should in fact be considered as postdelinquency rationalizations of behavior. He finds they are used only when deviant behavior is detected and condemned by others. It is only when the youth's behavior is viewed as a major threat that the need to neutralize its moral taint occurs. Justifications and excuses neutralize guilt and enable individuals to continue to feel good about themselves.[49]

SOCIAL CONTROL THEORY

Social control theory suggests that many forms of delinquent behavior—using drugs, engaging in sexual acts, skipping school, fighting, getting drunk, and so on—are attractive to almost every teenager. These acts represent the exciting, illicit, adventurous behavior that is glorified on television and in the movies and that serves as the basis for almost all rock music.

Why, then, do most youths obey conventional rules and grow up to be law-abiding adults? For a social control theorist, the answer lies in the strength and direction of their ties with conventional groups, individuals, and institutions. Those who have close relationships with their parents, friends, and teachers and who maintain a positive self-image will be able to resist the lure of deviant behaviors. To not jeopardize their good standing in the community, they refuse to risk detection and punishment for delinquent offenses. On the other hand, youths without these social supports feel free to violate the law; if caught, they have nothing to lose.

SELF-CONCEPT AND DELINQUENCY

Originally, social control theorists speculated that delinquency was a product of weak self-concept and poor self-esteem. Youths who felt good about themselves were able to resist the temptations of the streets; those with a poor self-image were more likely to succumb. As early as 1951, Albert Reiss described how delinquents had weak "ego ideals" and lacked the "personal controls" to produce conforming behavior.[50] In a similar vein, Scott Briar and Irving Piliavin described how delinquents have a weak **commitment to conformity**.[51] They concluded that youths who fear that apprehension for criminal activity will damage their self-image as well as their relationships with others will be most likely to conform to social roles.

CONTAINMENT THEORY

The best-known theoretical model linking the production of delinquent behavior with self-concept is Walter Reckless's **containment theory**.[52] Containment theory contends that society produces a series of pushes and pulls toward delinquency, described below:

1. *Internal Pushes.* Internal pushes involve such personal factors as restlessness, discontent, hostility, rebellion, mental conflict, anxieties, and the need for immediate gratification.
2. *External Pressures.* External pressures are adverse living conditions that influence deviant behavior. They include relative deprivation, poverty, unemployment, insecurity, minority status, limited opportunities, and inequalities.
3. *External Pulls.* External pulls are deviant companions, membership in criminal subcultures or other deviant groups, and such influences as mass media and pornography.

These in turn are counteracted by the following internal and external containments, which help insulate the individual from delinquency.

1. *Inner Containments.* Inner containments consist of the elements of the inner strength of an individual personality—for example, good self-concept, ego strength, high frustration tolerance, goal orientation, and tension-reducing capabilities.
2. *Outer Containments.* Outer containments are the normative constraints that societies and social groups ordinarily use to control their members—for example, a sense of belonging; a consistent moral front; reinforcement of norms, goals, and values; effective supervision; discipline; and a meaningful social role.

Simply put, containment theory suggests that the two containments act as a defense against a person's potential deviation from legal and social norms and work to insulate a youth from the pushes and pulls of criminogenic influences. Of these, a positive self-image is the strongest defense against delinquency.

Reckless and his associates made an extensive effort to validate the principles of containment theory.[53] In a series of studies analyzing containment principles within the school setting, they concluded that the ability of nondelinquents to maintain their conventional "good boy" behavior depends on their holding a positive self-image in the face of environmental pressures toward delinquency.[54]

However, the work of Reckless and his associates has been criticized for a lack of methodological rigor.[55] A series of research studies found little relationship between self-esteem and delinquency, a finding in opposition to the key elements of containment theory. This has led to containment theory being superseded by other social control theories, specifically that of Travis Hirschi.

HIRSCHI'S SOCIAL CONTROL THEORY

Travis Hirschi's version of social control theory, first articulated in his famous book *Causes of Delinquency,* links delinquent behavior to the bond an individual maintains with society. When that bond weakens or breaks, the constraints that society puts on its members are lifted, and an individual may violate the law. Unlike some of the other theoretical models discussed here, Hirschi's social control theory assumes that all individuals are potential delinquents and criminals and that social controls, not moral values, maintain law and order. Without social controls and in the absence of sensitivity to and interest in others, a youth is free to commit criminal acts.[56]

Hirschi speculates that a consistent value system exists and that all people in society are exposed to it equally. Delinquents defy this moral code because their attachment to society is weak. Hirschi views the youthful law violator as someone who rejects social norms and beliefs. The major elements of his argument are (1) there is a "variation in belief in the moral validity of social rules,"[57] (2) this variation is brought about by a weakening of the attachment of the individual to elements of society, and (3) this condition produces delinquent behavior.

Hirschi argues that the **social bond** a person maintains with society is divided into four main elements: attachment, commitment, involvement, and belief (see Figure 5.5).

Attachment   Attachment refers to a person's sensitivity to and interest in others. Psychologists believe that without a sense of attachment, a person becomes a psychopath and loses the ability to relate coherently to the world. The acceptance of social norms and the development of a social conscience depend on attachment to and caring for other human beings. Hirschi views parents,

Hirschi views parents, peers, and schools as the most important social institutions with which a person should maintain ties. Of these, attachment to parents is the most important. Even if a family is shattered by divorce and separation, a child must retain a strong attachment to one or both parents. Without attachment to the family, a child is unlikely to develop feelings of respect for others in authority.

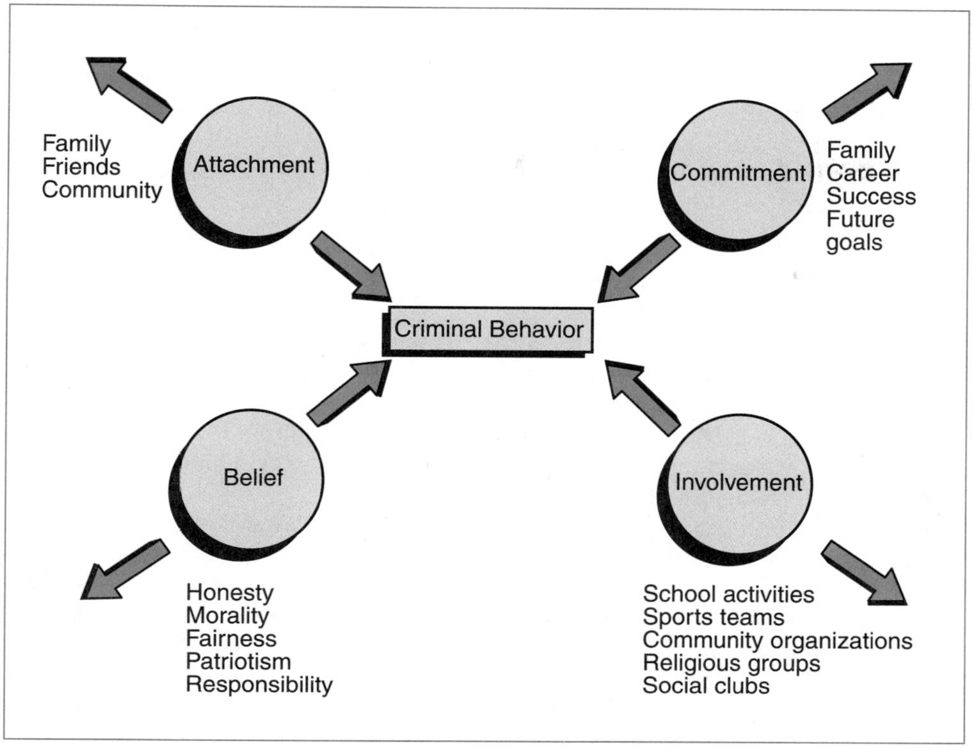

FIGURE 5.5
Elements of the social bond

Family
Friends
Community — Attachment

Commitment — Family
Career
Success
Future
goals

Criminal Behavior

Belief

Honesty
Morality
Fairness
Patriotism
Responsibility

Involvement

School activities
Sports teams
Community organizations
Religious groups
Social clubs

peers, and schools as the most important social institutions with which a person should maintain ties; of these three, attachment to parents is the most important. Even if a family is shattered by divorce and separation, a child must retain a strong attachment to one or both parents. Without attachment to the family, a child is unlikely to develop feelings of respect for others in authority.

Commitment Commitment involves the time, energy, and effort expended in pursuit of conventional lines of action. It embraces such activities as getting an education and saving money for the future. Social control theory holds that if people are committed strongly to enhancing life, property, and reputation, they will be less likely to engage in acts that will jeopardize their standing. Conversely, a lack of commitment to conventional values may foreshadow a condition in which risk-taking behavior, such as delinquency, becomes a reasonable behavior alternative.

Involvement An individual's heavy involvement in conventional activities does not leave time for illegal behavior. Hirschi believes that involvement—in school, recreation, and family—insulates a youth from the potential lure of delinquent behavior that idleness encourages.

Belief People who live in common social settings often share a similar moral doctrine and revere such human values as sharing, protecting the rights of others, and enforcing the legal code. If these beliefs are absent or weakened, individuals are more likely to share in antisocial acts.

Hirschi further suggests that the interrelationship of elements of the social bond influences whether an individual pursues delinquent or conventional activities. For example, boys or girls who feel kinship with and sensitivity toward parents and friends should be more likely to desire and work toward legitimate goals. On the other hand, youths who reject social relationships will probably lack commitment to conventional goals and more likely will be involved in unconventional activities.

EMPIRICAL RESEARCH ON SOCIAL CONTROL THEORY

One of Hirschi's most significant contributions to delinquency research is his impartial verification of the principal hypothesis of social control theory. He administered a complex self-report survey to a sample of more than 4,000 junior and senior high school students in Contra Costa County, California.[58] In a detailed analysis of the data, Hirschi found considerable evidence to support the social control theory model.

Hirschi compared a child's attachment to society ("Would you like to be the kind of person your father is?"; "When you come across things you don't understand, does your mother (father) help you with them?") with his or her deviant behavior. He found that youths who were strongly attached to their parents, even criminal parents, were less likely to participate in delinquent behavior.

Hirschi also found that lack of attachment to the school and to education (e.g., "Do you care what teachers think of you?"; "It is none of the school's business if a student wants to smoke outside the classroom") is a strong predictor of delinquent behavior.

Youths with poor basic academic skills are likely to become detached from school and involved in delinquency. Hirschi traces this important relationship as follows: "The causal chain runs from academic incompetence to poor school performance to disliking of school to rejection of the school's authority to the commission of delinquent acts."[59]

Hirschi also examined the attachment of youths to their friends and other peers, using such questions as "Would you like to be the kind of person your best friends are?" He found that youths who maintain close associations with friends are less likely to commit delinquent acts. Delinquent youths, on the other hand, often maintain weak and distant relationships with their peers. Among Hirschi's most important discoveries are the following:

- Contrary to subcultural theories, the gang rarely recruits "good" boys or influences them to turn "bad."
- Boys who maintain middle-class values are relatively unaffected by the delinquent behavior of their friends, although having delinquent friends was generally related to criminality.
- The idea that delinquents have warm, intimate relationships with one another is a myth.
- "The child with little stake in conformity is susceptible to pro-delinquent influences in his environment; the child with a large stake in conformity is relatively immune to these influences."[60]
- Involvement in school inhibits delinquency. Youths who smoke, drink, date, ride around in cars, and find adolescence "boring" are more prone to delinquency.
- There was little difference in the beliefs of delinquents and nondelinquents; delinquents often respected middle-class attitudes.

Hirschi argues that youths who maintain close associations with friends are less likely to commit delinquent acts. Delinquent youths, on the other hand, often maintain weak and distant relationships with their peers. Delinquents are loners with few intimate friends or trusted companions. Do you agree with Hirschi, or do you believe that delinquents have close ties with members of their gang or clique?

Hirschi's data lend important support to the validity of social control theory. Although the statistical significance of his findings is sometimes less than he expected, his research data are extremely consistent. Only in very rare instances do his findings contradict the theory's most critical assumptions.

CORROBORATING RESEARCH

Hirschi's version of social control theory has been corroborated by research showing that delinquent youth often feel detached from society.[61] Their relationships within the family, peer group, and school often appear strained, indicative of a weakened social bond.[62] For example, Marvin Krohn and his associates found that the quality of the bonds that parents and children have for one another is the key determinant of delinquent behavior. Both self-report and official delinquency are more likely to be present when either party—parent or child—reports a weak level of family attachment.[63]

In his classic replication of social control theory, Michael Hindelang surveyed subjects in the sixth through twelfth grades in a rural New York state school system using many of the same questions found in Hirschi's original survey instrument.[64] With few exceptions, Hindelang's data supported the core concepts of social control theory. The major difference was in the area of attachment to delinquent peers. Hindelang found that close identification with delinquent peers was associated with delinquent activity, while Hirschi's research produced the opposite result; according to Hirschi, any attachment, even to delinquent peers, is beneficial.

Cross-national surveys have also supported the general findings of social control theory.[65] In one study of Canadian youth in Edmonton, Alberta, Teresa Lagrange and Robert Silverman found that perception of parental attachment was the strongest predictor of delinquent or law-abiding behavior. They found that teens who are attached to their parents may develop the social skills that equip them both to maintain harmonious social ties and also to escape life stresses such as school failure.[66]

DISSENTING OPINIONS

More than 70 published attempts have been made to corroborate social control theory by replicating Hirschi's original survey techniques.[67] Although there has been significant empirical support for Hirschi's work, there are also those who question some or all of its elements.

Loners?   Hirschi maintains that delinquents are detached loners whose bonds to family and friends have been broken. Some critics have questioned whether delinquents (1) do in fact have strained relations with family and peers and (2) may in fact be influenced by close relationships with *deviant* peers and family members. A number of research efforts do in fact show that delinquents maintain relationships and are influenced by membership in a deviant peer group.[68] Delinquents may not be "lone wolves" whose only personal relationships are exploitive; their friendship patterns seem quite close to those of conventional youth.[69] In one example, Denise Kandel and Mark Davies found that young male drug abusers maintained even more intimate relations with their peers than nonabusers; illicit drug abuse can be used to predict strong social ties and high levels of intimacy.[70] In another example, a study of dropouts in the Canadian city of Edmonton, Alberta, Leslie Samuelson, Timothy Hartnagel, and Harvey Krahn found that although weak social controls were highly correlated with delinquency, they alone could not explain offending patterns. Equally important was attachment to deviant peers, a group that helped motivate dropouts to commit crime and helped facilitate their delinquent acts.[71]

Deviant Attachments   Hirschi suggests that all attachments, even deviant ones, are beneficial. Critics disagree, suggesting that attachment to deviant others increases delinquent involvements. For example, Gary Jensen and David Brownfield found that drug-abusing adolescents express attachment to parents who use drugs themselves.[72]

All Bond Elements Are Not Equal   Some research efforts also question whether elements of the social bond such as belief or involvement actually influence delinquent behaviors. Hirschi himself found little evidence that delinquents reject conventional values and beliefs. Kimberly Kempf Leonard and Scott Decker's research with younger children found that the concepts of "involvement" and "belief" had relatively little influence over behavior patterns.[73] A recent study by Velmer Burton and his associates found that involvement may even be *positively related* to delinquency. Burton speculates that the more adolescents are involved in behaviors outside the home, the less contact they have with parental supervision and the greater the opportunity they have to commit crime.[74]

Changing Bonds?   Hirschi's theory ignores change in social bonds (e.g., once they are "broken" can they be "repaired?"). Do social bonds change over the life course? Using samples of 12-, 15-, and 18-year-old boys, Randy LaGrange and Helene Raskin White found that age mitigates the relationship between the social bond and delinquency.[75] Mid-teens are more likely to be influenced by their parents and teachers than boys in the other age groups, who are more deeply influenced by their deviant peers. LaGrange and White attribute this finding to the problems of mid-adolescence, when youths have a great need to develop "psychological anchors" to conformity.

Fails to Account for Serious Crimes Some critics charge that social control theory is restricted to only minor acts and cannot explain serious felonies. It may also be age relative, having more explanatory power for certain age groups. Marvin Krohn and James Massey surveyed a sample of 3,065 junior and senior high school students and found that control variables were better able to explain female delinquency than male delinquency and minor delinquency (such as alcohol and marijuana abuse) than more serious delinquent acts. Krohn and Massey conclude that Hirschi's model has utility as an explanation of the onset of delinquency, a period when youthful offenders are both engaging in petty offenses and questioning their commitment and attachment to social institutions.[76]

Does Delinquency Weaken Bonds? The fact that delinquents have weakened bonds is in itself insufficient proof of the validity of social control theory. The weakening of social bonds may be a *result* of delinquent behavior and not its *cause*. It would not be surprising that youths who engage in repeated criminal activity have poor relationships at home and at school. To confirm social control theory, it must be shown that a weakened social bond preceded the delinquent behavior.

Robert Agnew questions the social control theory assumption that a weak bond to society causes delinquency.[77] He suggests an opposing chain of events: Chronic delinquents may find that their bonds to parents, schools, and society are becoming weak and attenuated; in other words, delinquency causes the weakening of social bonds and not vice versa.[78]

In sum, although some research efforts have supported the core concepts of Hirschi's social control theory, other efforts have questioned its explanatory power. However, even its greatest detractors recognize that the theory has been the most influential model of delinquency for the past 25 years.

MULTIFACTOR/INTEGRATED THEORIES

In recent years, delinquency experts have attempted to blend or **integrate** concepts and features of biological, psychological, choice, social structure, and social process theories into a single theoretical model of delinquent career formation. In the sections below, some of the more prominent integrated theories are discussed.

THE GENERAL THEORY OF CRIME (GTC)

In an important work, *A General Theory of Crime,* Travis Hirschi with his colleague Michael Gottfredson has refined and extended his original concepts of social control and social bonds by integrating them with elements of rational choice and psychological theories (discussed in chapter 3).[79]

In their general theory of crime (GTC), Gottfredson and Hirschi argue that to properly understand the nature of crime and delinquency, offenders and their acts must be dealt with as separate issues. *Crimes,* such as robberies or burglaries, are illegal events or deeds that people engage in when they perceive them to be advantageous. For example, burglaries are typically committed by male adolescents seeking cash, liquor, and entertainment; delinquency provides "easy short term gratification."[80] In contrast, *criminals* and *delinquents* are people who maintain a status that maximizes the possibility that they will engage in crimes. Adolescents with delinquent inclinations do not constantly commit crimes; their days are filled with nondelinquent behaviors, such as going to school, parties, concerts, and church. But, given the same set of life circumstances, they have a much higher probability of committing illegal acts than do nondelinquents.

SELF-CONTROL

What, then, causes youths to become excessively delinquency prone? According to the GTC, the explanation for individual differences in the tendency to commit delinquent acts can be found in an adolescent's level of **self-control.** People with limited self-control have **impulsive** personalities. They tend to be insensitive, physical (rather than mental), risk-taking, short-sighted, and nonverbal.[81] They have a "here and now" orientation and refuse to work to achieve distant goals; they lack diligence, tenacity, and persistence in a course of action. Children lacking self-control tend to be adventuresome, active, physical, and self-centered. In adulthood, they have unstable marriages, jobs, and friendships.[82] Criminal acts are attractive to them because they provide easy and immediate gratification, or, as Gottfredson and Hirschi put it, "money without work, sex without courtship, revenge without court delays."[83]

Considering their desire for easy pleasures, it should come as no surprise that people lacking self-control will also engage in risky, exciting, or thrilling behaviors that provide them with immediate and short-term gratification, for example, smoking, drinking, gambling, engaging in illicit sexual activity, or having out-of-wedlock children.[84] (See Figure 5.6.) Because they seek immediate satisfaction, they are more likely to engage in criminal acts, which require stealth, danger, agility, speed, and power, than conventional acts, which demand long-term study and require cognitive and verbal skills.

FIGURE 5.6
Self-control and delinquency

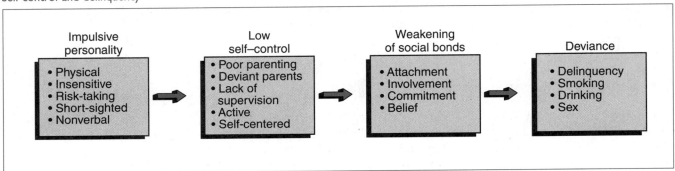

SELF-CONTROL AND SOCIAL BONDS

Gottfredson and Hirschi trace the root cause of poor self-control to inadequate child-rearing practices. Parents who refuse or are unable to monitor a child's behavior, recognize deviant behavior when it occurs, and punish that behavior will produce children who lack self-control. Children who lack self-control are unlikely to be attached to parents, committed to orthodox value and beliefs, and involved in conventional activities. It may be possible that a reciprocal relationship exists between social control and social bonds: An attenuated bond to society further weakens self-control; people with low self-control have difficulty maintaining adequate bonds to society.[85] The causal chain then may flow from an (1) impulsive personality to (2) poor parenting practices to (3) lack of self-control to (4) the withering of social bonds to (5) increased criminal opportunity to (6) amplification of deviance and maintenance of a deviant career throughout the life span.[86]

Gottfredson and Hirschi conclude that the cause of persistent delinquency—the lack of self-control—occurs during the early formative years and then controls behavior throughout the life course.

AN ANALYSIS OF SELF-CONTROL THEORY

Gottfredson and Hirschi's general theory of crime provides answers to many of the questions left open by the original social control model. By separating the concepts of "delinquency" and "delinquents," Gottfredson and Hirschi help explain why some youths who lack self-control can escape criminality: They lack criminal opportunity. Similarly, even those people who have a strong bond to social institutions and maintain self-control may on occasion engage in law-violating behavior: If the opportunity is strong enough, the incentives may overcome self-control. This explains why the so-called "good kid" who has a

According to the General Theory of Crime, individual differences in the tendency to commit delinquent acts are tied to an adolescent's level of **self-control**. People with limited self-control have *impulsive* personalities. They tend to be insensitive, risk-takers, physical (rather than mental), short-sighted, and nonverbal. They have a "here and now" orientation and refuse to work for distant goals; they lack diligence, tenacity, and persistence in a course of action.

strong school record and positive parental relationships can get involved in drugs or vandalism or why the corporate executive with a spotless record gets caught up in business fraud; even successful executives may find their self-control inadequate if the potential for illegal gain runs into the tens of millions.

Gottfredson and Hirschi argue vehemently that life events do not influence the *propensity* to commit crime; the tendency to commit crime is stable. It is criminal opportunities—the occasion to commit crime—that vary significantly over the life course; individual crime rates fluctuate with criminal opportunities.

Testing GTC The GTC is considered an extremely important contribution to the literature of crime and delinquency. A number of research efforts have shown that variables measuring lack of self-control significantly predict criminal behavior.[87] Youths who take drugs and commit crime are in fact impulsive and enjoy engaging in risky behaviors.[88] For example, both male and female drunk drivers have been found to be impulsive individuals who manifest low self-control.[89] Research on violent recidivists indicate that they can be distinguished from other offenders on the basis of their impulsive personality structure.[90] Studies of incarcerated youth show that they enjoy risk-taking behavior and hold values and attitudes that suggest impulsivity.[91] In one recent study, John Gibbs and Dennis Giever found that measures of self-control were able to predict deviant behavior (e.g., cutting class, drinking) among a sample of college students.[92] A similar analysis of self-report data by Giever found that one of the core assumptions of GTC has validity: Parental supervision and management influence both self-control and subsequent deviant behavior.[93]

Cross-national data also have supported the core concepts of GTC. One study of Canadian youth by Marc LeBlanc and his associates found that adolescents with an "ego-centric personality" develop weak social ties and are more likely to engage in delinquency and nonconventional behaviors.[94]

Dissenting Opinion Although the research is generally supportive of the GTC, certain areas need further testing and evaluation. One issue is whether the core principles of the GTC are universal. There is evidence that criminals in other countries do not lack self-control, indicating that the GTC may be culturally limited.[95] Behavior that may be considered imprudent and risky in one culture may be socially acceptable in another and therefore cannot be explained by a "lack of self-control".[96]

Some critics contend that changing life circumstances affect the propensity to commit crime. As you may recall (chapter 2), the life-course view is that as people mature, social influences also evolve: As people go through life, the qualities of their job, marriage, military service, and friendship help sway attitudes and behavior. A number of research studies do in fact show that the propensity to commit crime is not stable and unchanging. Graham Ousey and David Aday, Jr. found that as children mature, peer influence over delinquent behavior choices continues to grow; in contrast, the GTC suggests that the influence of friends should be stable and unchanging.[97] Similarly, Julie Horney and her associates show that changing life circumstances, such as starting and leaving school, abusing substances and then getting straight, and starting or ending personal relationships, all have an influence on the frequency of offending.[98]

Do such changes affect the *propensity* to commit crime or do they merely influence the *opportunity,* as Gottfredson and Hirschi suggest? Continued efforts are needed to test the GTC and establish the validity of its core concepts.

THE SOCIAL DEVELOPMENT MODEL (SDM)

Joseph Weis, J. David Hawkins, and their associates have attempted to integrate some of the most important features of Hirschi's concept of the social bond with aspects of social learning theory (DA and DR).[99] They suggest that social control theory is useful in explaining that children become delinquent because of their inadequate socialization and alienation from important institutional forces, such as the family and the school. Social learning theory contributes the influence of peers and significant others on the learning and assimilation of deviant values and behaviors. Thus, each of these theories can be a useful element of an intergrated theory of delinquency.

According to the **social development model** (SDM), there are a number of personal, psychological, and community-level "risk factors" that make some children susceptible to the development of antisocial behaviors. For example, the quality of community organization influences the child's risk of developing antisocial behavior; social control is less effective when the frontline socializing institutions are weak (as they are in disorganized areas).

Preexisting risk factors are either reinforced or neutralized through socialization. Children are socialized and develop bonds to their family through four processes:

1. perceived opportunities for involvement in activities and interactions with others,
2. the degree of involvement and interaction,
3. the skills to participate in these interactions, and
4. the reinforcement they perceive for their participation.

To create and sustain **prosocial bonds,** the family must not only provide prosocial opportunities but reinforce them by consistent positive feedback. Parental attachment then has the power to affect a child's behavior through the life course, determining both school experiences and personal beliefs and values. For those with strong family relationships, school will be a meaningful experience marked by academic success and commitment to education. Youths in this category are more likely to develop conventional beliefs and values, become committed to conventional activities, and form attachments to conventional others.

Whether or not a child develops antisocial behavior also depends on the quality of his or her attachments to others. Children who remain unattached or develop attachments to deviant others are likely to develop antisocial behavior. Unlike Hirschi's social control theory, which assumes all attachments are beneficial, the SDM suggests that interaction with antisocial peers and adults promotes participation in delinquency and substance abuse over the life course.[100]

As Figure 5.7 shows, the SDM also differs from Hirschi's vision of how the social bond develops. While Hirschi maintains that early family attachments are the key determinate of future behavior, the SDM suggests that involvement in prosocial or antisocial behavior determines the quality of attachments. Those adolescents who perceive opportunities and rewards for antisocial behavior will form deep attachments to deviant peers and become committed to a delinquent way of life. In contrast, those who perceive opportunities for prosocial behavior will take a different path, getting involved in conventional activities and forming attachments to prosocial activities and others.

FIGURE 5.7
The social development model of
antisocial behavior

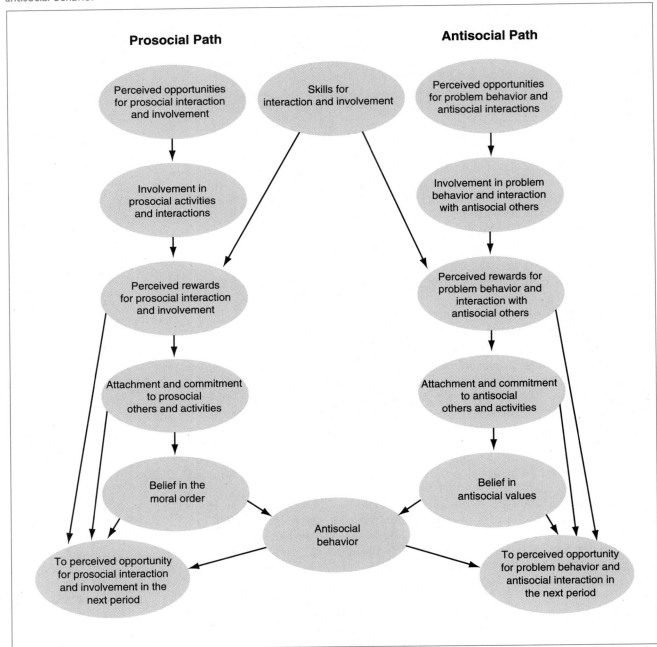

The SDM then holds that commitment and attachment to conventional institutions, activities, and beliefs work to insulate youths from the criminogenic influences of their environment; the prosocial path inhibits deviance by strengthening bonds to prosocial others and activities. Without the proper level of bonding, adolescents can succumb to the influence of deviant others.

Many of the core assumptions of the SDM have been tested empirically, and their validity has been verified.[101] The path predicted by the SDM seems to reflect an accurate picture of the onset and continuation of delinquency and drug abuse. The SDM has also guided treatment interventions to promote the development of strong bonds to family and school, and to help youths use these bonds to resist any opportunity or motivation to take drugs and engage in delinquent behaviors. Preliminary evaluations of one program, the Seattle Social Development Project, indicate that SDM-based interventions can help reduce delinquency and drug abuse.[102]

ELLIOTT'S INTEGRATED THEORY

Another attempt to integrate theories of delinquency has been proposed by Delbert Elliott and his colleagues David Huizinga and Suzanne Ageton.[103] Elliott and his associates discount some aspects of "pure" strain, social control, and learning theory. They contend that strain theory can account for some initial delinquent acts but does not adequately explain why some youths enter into delinquent careers while others, who forgo chronic offending, share similar environmental experiences. Similarly, social control theory cannot explain prolonged delinquent involvement because there is no group support or rewards for this behavior (control theorists, such as Hirschi, portray the delinquent as a loner without close bonds to peers or society). Finally, learning theory is criticized because it portrays the delinquent as a passive actor who simply reacts when confronted with delinquency-producing reinforcements.

Elliott and his colleagues integrate the strongest features of strain, social learning, and social control theories into a single theoretical model (see Figure 5.8). According to this view, adolescents who live in a socially disorganized areas (A), and who are improperly socialized at home (B), face a significant risk of perceiving strain (C); perceptions of strain then lead to weaked bonds with conventional groups, activities, and norms (D). Weak conventional bonds and high levels of perceived strain lead some youths to reject conventional social values (E) and seek out and become bonded to deviant peer groups (F). From these delinquent associations come positive reinforcements for delinquent behaviors; delinquent peers help provide role models for antisocial behavior (G). Attachment to delinquent groups when combined with weak bonding to conventional groups and norms leads to a high level of delinquent behavior and drug abuse.

Elliott and his colleagues have tested their theoretical model with data taken from a national survey of more than 1,000 youths who were interviewed annually over a three-year period. With only a few minor exceptions, the results generally supported their integrated theory: Bonding to a delinquent peer group escalates involvement in criminal activity.[104] Some subjects reported developing strong bonds to delinquent peers even if they did not reject the values of conventional society. Elliott and his associates interpret this finding as suggesting that youths living in disorganized areas may have little choice but to join with law-violating

FIGURE 5.8
Elliott's integrated theory

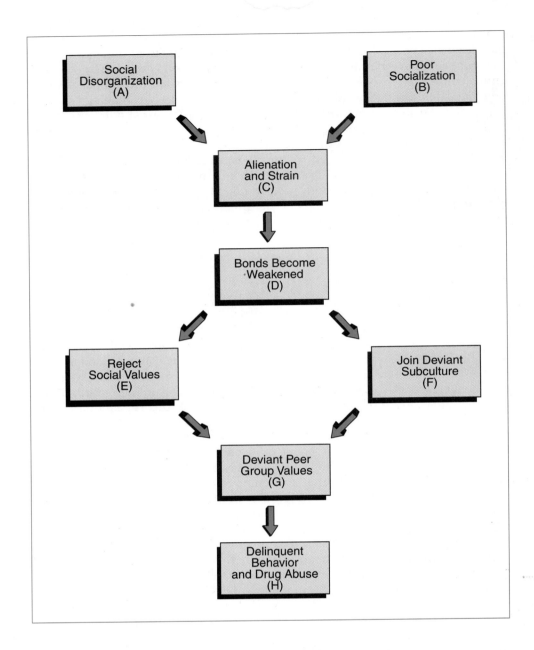

youth groups because conventional groups simply do not exist.[105] They also found that initial experimentation with drugs and delinquency predicted both bonding with a teenage law-violating peer group and involvement in additional delinquency.

The picture Elliott and his colleagues draw of the teenage delinquent is not dissimilar to the one drawn by Weis's social development model: Living in a disorganized neighborhood, feeling hopeless and unable to get ahead, and becoming involved in petty crimes eventually leads to a condition where conventional social values become weak and attenuated. Concern for education, family relations, and the social order is weakened. A deviant peer group becomes

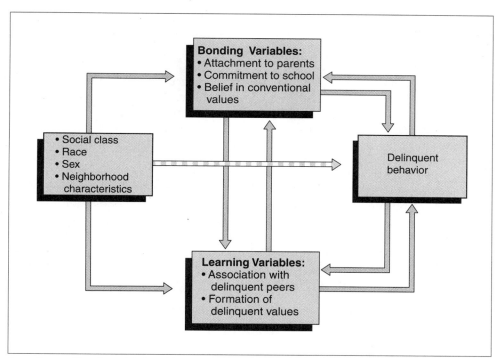

FIGURE 5.9
Overview of the interactional theory of delinquency

Source: Terence Thornberry, Margaret Farnsworth, Alan Lizotte, and Susan Stern, "A Longitudinal Examination of the Causes and Correlates of Delinquency," working paper #1, Rochester Youth Development Study (Albany, N.Y.: Hindelang Criminal Justice Research Center, 1987), p. 11.

an acceptable substitute for law-abiding family and friends, and consequently, the attitudes and skills that support delinquent tendencies are amplified. The results are early experimentation with drugs and delinquency as a way of life.

INTERACTIONAL THEORY

Another important attempt at theory integration is Terence Thornberry's **interactional theory.**[106] (See Figure 5.9.)

Thornberry agrees (with both Weis and Elliott) that the onset of crime can be traced to a deterioration of the social bond during adolescence, marked by a weakened attachment to parents, commitment to school, and belief in conventional values. Thornberry's theory similarly recognizes the influence that risk factors such as lower class status can have on delinquency: Youths growing up in socially disorganized areas are at the greatest risk of having a weakened social bond and subsequently becoming delinquent. The onset of a criminal career is supported by residence in a social setting in which deviant values and attitudes can be learned and reinforced by delinquent peers.

Interactional theory also holds that seriously delinquent youths form belief systems that are consistent with their deviant lifestyles. They seek out the company of other youths who share their interests and who are likely to reinforce their beliefs about the world and support their delinquent behavior. According to interactional theory, then, delinquents seek out a criminal peer group in the same fashion that chess buffs seek out others who share their passion for the game. Deviant peers do not turn "innocent" boys into delinquents. They support and amplify the behavior of youths who have already embraced a delinquent way of life.

Life-Course View Interactional theory addresses developmental concepts (see chapter 2) when it suggests that adolescents pass through different stages of reasoning and sophistication as they mature. Thornberry applies this concept when he suggests that criminality is a developmental process that takes on different meaning and form as a person matures. During early adolescence, attachment to the family is the single most important determinant of whether a youth will adjust to conventional society and be shielded from delinquency. By mid-adolescence, the influence of the family is replaced by the world of friends, school, and youth culture. In adulthood, people's behavioral choices are shaped by their place in conventional society and their own nuclear family. The process is reciprocal: People are shaped by the quality of their social world, and the quality of their social world is influenced by their behavior.

TESTING INTERACTIONAL THEORY

Thornberry's model is being evaluated and tested with a panel of Rochester, New York, youth who are being followed through the cycle of their offending careers; most results seem to support interactional theory. In one analysis, Thornberry and his colleagues examined the influence of peer associations on delinquency and found that they conformed to interactional principles: Associating with delinquent peers leads to increases in delinquency; increased delinquency leads to associations with delinquent peers. As this process unfolds over the life course, antisocial kids will become part of a deviant peer network that will reinforce their behavior; conventional youth will, in turn, be reinforced by their conventional friends.[107] Thornberry and his colleagues have found similar patterns for family and school relations: Delinquency is related to weakened attachments to family and the educational process; delinquent behavior further weakens the strength of the bonds to family and school.[108] Other researchers have supported an interactional relationship between delinquent behavior and moral values (delinquency weakens moral beliefs and weakened beliefs encourage delinquency).[109]

In sum, interactional theory rests on life-course assumptions: Events and relationships that develop during a person's life cycle influence his or her behavior.

Social Process Theories and Delinquency Prevention

The social process theories discussed in this chapter suggest that delinquency is a result of (1) improper socialization, leading to (2) conflict with important social institutions, which leads to (3) deviant forms of behavior. The learning theory branch holds that this process is triggered by values, attitudes, and behaviors learned in close contact with significant others. The social control theory branch points to the youth's weakened relationships with the major deviance-controlling institutions—family, schools, and peers.

By implication, social process theories suggest that delinquency can be prevented by strengthening the relationships between youths and the institutions primarily responsible for their socialization. This objective can be achieved either by strengthening the institutions themselves or by helping the youths better handle preexisting conditions. For example, the neighborhood school might be improved as a delinquency-controlling institution by getting teachers to realize that all students can and should be educated; by expanding preschool education programs; by developing curriculums and educational materials that are relevant to students' lives; by developing teaching methods appropriate to the students; by developing individualized curriculums; and by stressing teacher development. At the same time, school-based delinquency prevention efforts must seek to help the youth who is manifesting problems in school, experiencing school failure, and finding that his or her bond to the educational system has eroded. This implies a need for individual counseling and remedial services for troubled youths. The following "Case in Point" raises some prevention issues that many educators face today.

CASE IN POINT

You have just been appointed the head of curriculum for the local school system. The school board is interested in creating courses that will reduce the incidence of student delinquency and drug abuse. They fear that TV shows, popular music, and films that glorify the use of drugs teach youths that substance abuse and crime are exciting and socially desirable activities. They believe the school must present courses that can counteract the weight of these destructive influences.

You are faced with designing a program that can teach students to "say no" to drugs and crime. One of your advisors suggests that the best approach would be to teach youths about the effects of drugs through media and live presentations in which former users discuss their experiences and problems. She believes that learning about the evils of drugs can counteract the pro-drug influence of commercial TV and rock and roll. In contrast, another advisor argues that the best approach would be a series of workshops that help students develop a bond with their parents and community and learn the value of commitment to conventional behavior and actions. Such workshops would stress techniques of interfamily communications and life skills.

Although both approaches have merit, only one can be chosen to serve as the basis of the new course.

What type of information would you present to the students?

Can students learn not to commit crime and take drugs?

Who could best help students learn not to use drugs or engage in delinquency: Other students? Parents? Teachers? Former users?

Prevention programs must also work to strengthen the internal structure of families in crisis. Because attachment to parents who can provide proper socialization is a cornerstone of all social process theories, it is an essential element of delinquency prevention. This should not mean, however, that all families must conform to a particular lifestyle or pattern. Efforts should be directed at helping the family become a living unit that provides care and support for its members. What should be developed is a family structure that can nurture the positive self-image the child needs to resist the delinquency-promoting forces in his or her environment.

Agents of the juvenile justice system must also recognize that their actions can influence the behavior of youths. For example, if a youth believes that he or she is not being treated fairly by police or court officials, that youth will be likely to seek out peers who share similar views. Consequently, the youth will be likely to experience an excess of definitions toward delinquency as well as a weakening of belief in conventional social rules and values.

Over the years, many local prevention programs have sought to meet goals that coincide with the premise of the social process approach. These efforts replaced, for the most part, the large-scale community development programs based on the social structure theories discussed in chapter 5. Many were demonstration programs that operated for a few years on federal funds; others are ongoing, with funding from state and local governments. Some efforts have been directed at primary prevention (before the onset of delinquency), while others have focused on secondary prevention (treating troubled youths) and tertiary prevention (helping ex-offenders "go straight").

Many primary prevention efforts have been aimed at improving the school experience. For example, the Alternative Learning Project (ALP) in Providence, Rhode Island, helps educationally disillusioned youths develop a learning experience that will encourage positive attachments with their school.[110] It uses such features as a low student–teacher ratio (sixteen to one), individualized programs, emphasis on basic skills, special projects, tutoring, and courses at local colleges. An evaluation of the program indicated that 55 percent of its students go on to college and that absenteeism and dropout rates are greatly reduced. It is unlikely that such results for these youths would have been achieved without the ALP.

Prevention programs have also focused on providing services for youngsters who have been identified as delinquents or pre-delinquents. Such services usually include counseling, job placement, and legal assistance. Their aim is to reach out to troubled youth and provide them with the life skills necessary to function in their often troubling environment. One successful program, Wisconsin's Project Bootstrap, is described in the following "Focus on Delinquency."

In addition to these local efforts, the federal government has sponsored several national delinquency prevention efforts using the principles of social process theory. These include vocational training programs, such as the Job Corps and the Comprehensive Employment Training Act, as well as educational enrichment programs, such as Head Start for preschoolers and Upward Bound for high school students interested in going on to college. Federal budget cutbacks in the past decade have severely restricted these efforts, but local efforts keep the spirit of these programs alive.

SUMMARY

Social process theories explain delinquency as a function of the human interactions that occur daily in society (see Table 5.1.) As a group, they reject the view that delinquents are born criminals or that they are intellectually or psychologically impaired. In a similar vein, social process adherents take a dim view of theoretical models that blame delinquent behavior on the socioeconomic structure of society or on any of its class, racial, or social groupings.

Social process theories often stress the learning of delinquent or nondelinquent behavior. For example, Sutherland's theory of differential association (DA) suggests that delinquency is almost purely a learning process. Similarly, David Matza's neutralization approach describes how youngsters are able to learn techniques that can effectively neutralize the constraints of conventional values.

PROJECT BOOTSTRAP

Project Bootstrap, Inc., which began in Madison, Wisconsin, during the fall of 1987 to meet the needs of at-risk children, is a multifaceted program that integrates the best of current models for educational support, supportive family groups, family mentoring, and alcohol and other drug abuse programs. Project Bootstrap's goal is its namesake, to teach children that with personal initiative they can "haul themselves up from trouble by their bootstraps."

The first goal of the program is to provide a violence-free environment for and improve the school performance of youth experiencing Post Traumatic Stress Disorder (PTSD) due to long-term exposure to inner-city violence. To reach this goal, the program's objectives are to provide (1) in-depth group counseling by a trained clinical psychologist; (2) "hands on" workshops and educational materials that provide alternatives to aggression; (3) speakers on violence, its causes, and its effects; (4) the means through which youth can interact with the Madison Metropolitan Police Department in a positive manner and view the police more favorably; (5) positive family role modeling through a family mentoring program; and (6) a safe surrogate family for youth residing in violent dysfunctional families.

A second goal is to educate at-risk youth about methods for keeping their lives violence-free. To do so, the program provides alternatives-to-aggression support groups for youth of various ages. In addition, field trips to state prisons allow at-risk youth an opportunity to interview prisoners with long-term sentences related to violence.

A third goal of the program is to provide extracurricular educational support designed to increase the number of at-risk students graduating from high school. Objectives to achieve this goal include (1) providing students a safe and nonthreatening environment in which to complete assigned homework; (2) providing students individual tutors to assist students with difficult subjects and concepts; (3) maintaining a progress report system with the Madison School District that is consistent, informative, and timely; (4) developing and maintaining contact with individual school district case managers, counselors, social workers, psychologists, teachers, and administrators; and (5) administering psychological and behavioral tests to help determine the psychological and educational services at-risk students require.

Encouraging parental responsibility for the problems of violent and educationally at-risk youth is also a high priority. This goal is stressed by conducting weekly parent support groups; providing ongoing counseling by a clinical psychologist; developing an interactive relationship among the school district, local law enforcement agencies, county social services, and Project Bootstrap, Inc.; and increasing parental awareness of alcohol and drugs and their effects on children.

Project Bootstrap, Inc., has been very successful. One of the major positive influences the program has had on students is improving their attendance at school. In the 1992-93 school year, for example, attendance improved 78.7 percent, and 82 percent of Project Bootstrap's students remain in school 2 years after completing the program. Problems involving incidents related to student attitude and behavior have improved 72.4 percent. Grade point averages have improved 79 percent. Family- and community-related violence among Project Bootstrap families has decreased 80.6 percent, and 79 percent of Project Bootstrap students are no longer considered immediately at risk.

Source: Office of Juvenile Justice and Delinquency Prevention, *Delinquency Prevention Works* (Washington, D.C.: Office of Juvenile Justice and Delinquency Prevention, 1995), A-29-A-30.

A second branch of social process theory is concerned with the forces of social control. Theorists such as Travis Hirschi view delinquency as a result of the inability of conventional institutions and relationships to restrain the behavior of youths.

Although Hirschi's social control theory does not stress learning per se, it is evident that the weakening of the social bond is a long-term development that involves delinquent youths in an escalating process of antisocial behavior accompanied by a continuous diminution of their attachment to society.

A new approach has been to integrate process concepts with elements taken from other theoretical models. In Gottfredson and Hirschi's general theory of

TABLE 5.1 Social Process Theories

Theory	Major Premise	Strengths
Social Learning Theories		
differential association theory	People learn to commit crime from exposure to antisocial definitions.	Explains onset of criminality. Explains the presence of crime in all elements of social structure. Explains why some people in high-crime areas refrain from criminality. Can apply to adults and juveniles.
differential reinforcement theory	Criminal behavior depends on the person's experiences with rewards for conventional behaviors and punishments for deviant ones. Being rewarded for deviance leads to crime.	Adds learning theory principles to differential association. Links sociological and psychological principles.
neutralization theory	Youths learn ways of neutralizing moral restraints and periodically drift in and out of criminal behavior patterns.	Explains why many delinquents do not become adult criminals. Explains why youthful law violators can participate in conventional behavior.
Social Control Theories		
containment theory	Society produces pushes and pulls toward crime. In some people, they are counteracted by internal and external containments, such as a good self-concept and group cohesiveness.	Brings together psychological and sociological principles. Can explain why some people are able to resist the strongest social pressures to commit crime.
control theory	A person's bond to society prevents him or her from violating social rules. If the bond weakens, the person is free to commit crime.	Explains onset of crime; can apply to both middle- and lower-class crime. Explains its theoretical constructs adequately so they can be measured. Has been empirically tested.
Integrated Theories		
general theory of crime	Youths with impulsive personalities are crime-prone. The likelihood of crime is a function of criminal propensity and criminal opportunity.	Explains the age–crime relationship. Can account for all criminal activities. Identifies criminal opportunity and propensity as independent concepts.
social development theory	Weak social controls produce crime. A person's place in the social structure influences his or her bond to society.	Combines elements of social structural and social process theories. Accounts for variations in the crime rate.
Elliott's integrated theory	Strained and weak social bonds lead youths to associate and learn from deviant peers.	Combines elements of learning, strain, and control theories.
interactional theory	Delinquents go through lifestyle changes during their offending career.	Combines sociological and psychological theories.

crimes (GTC), impulsivity and lack of self-control are blamed for the onset and stability of delinquent behavior. Children who lack self-control may find that their bond to society is weak and attenuated. Weis's social development theory and Elliott's integrated theory contain elements of both social process theory and social structure theory. In general, they hold that youths' place in the social structure, coupled with their interpersonal relationships, creates differential probabilities that they will engage in delinquency. Thornberry adds a life-course component to his interactional theory: The causes of delinquency change as an adolescent passes through the life cycle.

Prevention programs based on social process theories usually prescribe treatment designed to strengthen family ties, improve school performance, or develop a youth's bond to society.

KEY TERMS

socialization

social process

learning theory

social control theory

multifactor theory

integrated theory

differential association (DA) theory

differential reinforcement (DR) theory

drift

subterranean values

social control theory

commitment to conformity

containment theory

integrate

self-control

impulsive

social development model

prosocial bonds

interactional theory

QUESTIONS FOR DISCUSSION

1. Identify the "processes" that produce delinquent behaviors.

2. Have you ever rationalized your deviant acts? What neutralization techniques did you use?

3. Discuss your "inner" and "outer" containments. Does self-esteem really influence behavior?

4. Comment on the statement "Delinquents are made, not born."

5. Of all personal attachments, which are the most important? Why?

6. According to the GTC, stable, unchanging personality traits produce delinquent behaviors. With this in mind, comment on this observation: "People don't change, opportunities do."

NOTES

1. A. Leigh Ingram, "Type of Place, Urbanism, and Delinquency: Further Testing the Determinist Theory," *Journal of Research in Crime and Delinquency* 30:192–212 (1993).

2. Alan Lizotte, Terence Thornberry, Marvin Krohn, Deborah Chard-Wierschem, and David McDowall, "Neighborhood Context and Delinquency: A Longitudinal Analysis," in H. J. Kerner and E. Weitekamp, eds., *Cross-National Longitudinal Research on Human Development and Criminal Behavior* (Dordrecht, The Netherlands: Kluwer Academic Publishers, 1993), pp. 1–11.

3. Walter Reckless, Simon Dinitz, and Ellen Murray, "The Good Boy in a High Delinquency Area," *Journal of Criminal Law, Criminology, and Police Science* 48:18–26 (1957).

4. Lawrence Rosen, "Family and Delinquency: Structure or Function," *Criminology* 23:553–73 (1985).

5. Howard Snyder and Melissa Sickmund, *Juvenile Offenders and Victims: A National Report* (Washington, D.C.: Office of Juvenile Justice and Delinquency Prevention, 1995), pp. 37–40.

6. Kenneth Polk and Walter Schafer, eds., *Schools and Delinquency* (Englewood Cliffs, N.J.: Prentice Hall, 1972).

7. Thomas Berndt, "The Features and Effects of Friendship in Early Adolescence," *Child Development* 53:1447–60 (1982).

8. Edwin Sutherland, *Principles of Criminology* (Philadelphia: J.B. Lippincott, 1939).

9. Edwin Sutherland and Donald Cressey, *Criminology,* 8th ed. (Philadelphia: J.B. Lippincott, 1970), pp. 75–77.

10. Howard Becker, *Outsiders* (New York: Free Press, 1963).

11. Sutherland and Cressey, *Criminology,* pp. 77–79.

12. Ibid.

13. Albert Reiss and A. Lewis Rhodes, "The Distribution of Delinquency in the Social Class Structure," *American Sociological Review* 26:732 (1961).

14. Elton Jackson, Charles Tittle, and Mary Jean Burke, "Offense-Specific Models of the Differential Association Process," *Social Problems* 33:335–56 (1986).

15. James Short, "Differential Association as a Hypothesis: Problems of Empirical Testing," *Social Problems* 8:14–25 (1960).

16. Ross Matsueda and Karen Heimer, "Race, Family Structure and Delinquency: A Test of Differential Association and Control Theories," *American Sociological Review* 52:826–40 (1987).

17. James Orcutt, "Differential Association and Substance Abuse: A Closer Look at Sutherland (With a Little Help from Becker)," *Criminology* 25:341–58 (1987); Denise Kandel, "Friendship Networks, Intimacy, and Illicit Drug Use in Young Adulthood: A Comparison of Two Competing Theories," *Criminology* 29:441–69 (1991); Marvin Krohn and Terence Thornberry, *Rochester Youth Development Study Network Theory: A Model for Understanding Drug Abuse among African-American and Hispanic Youth*, working paper no. 10, (Albany, N.Y.: Hindelang Research Center, 1991).

18. Donald Green, "Measures of Illegal Behavior in Individual-Level Deterrence Research," *Journal of Research in Crime and Delinquency* 26:253–75 (1989).

19. Gerben J. N. Bruinsma, "Differential Association Theory Reconsidered: An Extension and Its Empirical Test," *Journal of Quantitative Criminology* 8:29–46 (1992); Charles Tittle, *Sanctions and Social Deviance: The Question of Deterrence* (New York: Praeger, 1980).

20. Reed Adams, "The Adequacy of Differential Association Theory," *Journal of Research in Crime and Delinquency* 11:1–8 (1974).

21. Jack Gibbs, "The State of Criminological Theory," *Criminology* 25:821–40 (1987).

22. Robert Burgess and Ronald Akers, "A Differential Association-Reinforcement Theory of Criminal Behavior," *Social Problems* 14:128–47 (1966).

23. Ross Matsueda, "The Current State of Differential Association Theory," *Crime and Delinquency* 34:277–306 (1988).

24. Graham Ousey and David Aday, Jr., "The Interaction Hypothesis: A Test Using Social Control Theory and Social Learning Theory," Paper presented at the American Society of Criminology meeting, Boston, Mass., November 1995.

25. Mark Warr, "Age, Peers and Delinquency," *Criminology* 31:17–40 (1993).

26. The most influential critique of differential association is contained in Ruth Kornhauser, *Social Sources of Delinquency* (Chicago: University of Chicago Press, 1978).

27. These misconceptions are derived from Donald Cressey, "Epidemiologies and Individual Conduct: A Case from Criminology," *Pacific Sociological Review* 3:47–58 (1960).

28. Kornhauser, *Social Sources of Delinquency;* in contrast, see Matsueda, "The Current State of Differential Association Theory"; Ronald Akers, "Is Differential Association/ Social Learning Cultural Deviance Theory," *Criminology* 34:229–249(1996).

29. Craig Reinerman and Jeffrey Fagan, "Social Organization and Differential Association: A Research Note from a Longitudinal Study of Violent Juvenile Offenders," *Crime and Delinquency* 34:307–27 (1988).

30. Sue Titus Reed, *Crime and Criminology,* 2nd ed. (New York: Holt, Rinehart & Winston, 1979), p. 234.

31. Robert Burgess and Ronald Akers, "Differential Association—Reinforcement Theory of Criminal Behavior," *Social Problems* 14:128–47 (1968).

32. Ronald Akers, Marvin Krohn, Lonn Lonza-Kaduce, and Marcia Radosevich, "Social Learning and Deviant Behavior: A Specific Test of a General Theory," *American Sociological Review* 44:636–55 (1979).

33. Richard Lawrence, "School Performance, Peers, and Delinquency: Implications for Juvenile Justice," *Juvenile and Family Court Journal* 42:59–69 (1991).

34. Marvin Krohn, William Skinner, James Massey, and Ronald Akers, "Social Learning Theory and Adolescent Cigarette Smoking: A Longitudinal Study," *Social Problems* 32:455–71 (1985).

35. L. Thomas Winfree, Jr., Christine Sellers, and Dennis Clason, "Social Learning and Adolescent Deviance Abstention: Toward Understanding the Reasons for Initiating, Quitting, and Avoiding Drugs," *Journal of Quantitative Criminology* 9:101–23 (1993).

36. John Hamlin, "Misplaced Role of Rational Choice in Neutralization Theory," *Criminology* 26:425–38 (1988).

37. Gresham Sykes and David Matza, "Techniques of Neutralization: A Theory of Delinquency," *American Sociological Review* 22:664–70 (1957); David Matza, *Delinquency and Drift* (New York: Wiley, 1964).

38. Matza, *Delinquency and Drift,* p. 51.

39. David Matza, "Subterranean Traditions of Youth," *Annals* 378:116 (1961).

40. Sykes and Matza, "Techniques of Neutralization," pp. 664–70.

41. Ibid.

42. See, for example, John Kitsuse, "Societal Reaction to Deviant Behavior," *Social Problems* 9:247–56 (1962).

43. For a vivid example of these values, see William F. Whyte, *Street Corner Society* (Chicago: University of Chicago Press, 1955).

44. Ian Shields and George Whitehall, "Neutralization and Delinquency among Teenagers," *Criminal Justice and Behavior* 21:223–35 (1994); Robert A. Ball, "An Empirical Exploration of Neutralization Theory," *Criminologica* 4:22–32 (1966); M. William Minor, "The Neutralization of Criminal Offense," *Criminology* 18:103–20 (1980); Robert Gordon, James Short, Desmond Cartwright, and Fred Strodtbeck, "Values and Gang Delinquency: A Study of Street Corner Groups," *American Journal of Sociology* 69:109–28 (1963).

45. See for example, Larry Siegel, Spencer Rathus, and Carol Ruppert, "Values and Delinquent Youth: An Empirical Reexamination of Theories of Delinquency," *British Journal of Criminology* 13:237–44 (1973).

46. Michael Hindelang, "The Commitment of Delinquents to Their Misdeeds: Do Delinquents Drift?" *Social Problems* 17:500–09 (1970); Robert Regoli and Eric Poole, "The Commitment of Delinquents to Their Misdeeds: A Reexamination," *Journal of Criminal Justice* 6:261–69 (1978).

47. Robert Agnew, "The Techniques of Neutralization and Violence," *Criminology* 32:555–80 (1994).

48. Travis Hirschi, *Causes of Delinquency* (Berkeley: University of California Press, 1969), p. 208.

49. John Hamlin, "Misplaced Role of Rational Choice in Neutralization Theory," *Criminology* 26:425–38 (1988).

50. Albert Reiss, "Delinquency as the Failure of Personal and Social Controls," *American Sociological Review* 16:196–207 (1951).

51. Scott Briar and Irving Piliavin, "Delinquency: Situational Inducements and Commitment to Conformity," *Social Problem* 13:35–45 (1965–66).

52. Walter Reckless, *The Crime Problem* (New York: Appleton-Century Crofts, 1967), pp. 469–83.

53. Among the many research reports by Reckless and his colleagues are Walter Reckless, Simon Dinitz, and Ellen Murray, "The Good Boy in a High Delinquency Area," *Journal of Criminal Law, Criminology, and Police Science* 48:12–26 (1957); idem, "Self-Concept as an Insulator against Delinquency," *American Sociological Review* 21:744–46 (1956); Walter Reckless and Simon Dinitz, "Pioneering with Self-Concept as a Vulnerability Factor in Delinquency," *Journal of Criminal Law, Criminology, and Police Science* 58:515–23 (1967); Walter Reckless, Simon Dinitz, and Barbara Kay, "The Self-Component in Potential Delinquency and Potential Non-Delinquency," *American Sociological Review* 22:566–70 (1957).

54. Reckless, Dinitz, and Kay, "The Self-Component in Potential Delinquency and Potential Non-Delinquency"; Frank Scarpitti, Ellen Murray, Simon Dinitz, and Walter Reckless, "The Good Boy in a High Delinquency Area: Four Years Later," *American Sociological Review* 23:555–58 (1960).

55. Michael Schwartz and Sandra Tangri, "A Note on Self-Concept as an Insulator against Delinquency," *American Sociological Review* 30:922–26 (1965); Clarence Schrag, *Crime and Justice, American Style* (Washington, D.C.: U.S. Government Printing Office, 1971), p. 84.

56. Ibid.

57. Ibid., p. 8.

58. Hirschi's data are examined in his *Causes of Delinquency*.

59. Ibid., p. 132.

60. Ibid., pp. 160–61.

61. Michael Wiatroski, David Griswold, and Mary K. Roberts, "Social Control Theory and Delinquency," *American Sociological Review* 46:525–41 (1981).

62. Patricia Van Voorhis, Francis Cullen, Richard Mathers, and Connie Chenoweth Garner, "The Impact of Family Structure and Quality on Delinquency: A Comparative Assessment of Structural and Functional Factors," *Criminology* 26:235–61 (1988).

63. Marvin Krohn, Susan Stern, Terence Thornberry, and Sung Joon Jang, "The Measurement of Family Process Variables: The Effect of Adolescent and Parent Perceptions of Family Life on Delinquent Behavior," *Journal of Quantitative Criminology* 3:287–315 (1992).

64. Michael Hindelang, "Causes of Delinquency: A Partial Replication and Extension," *Social Problems* 21:471–87 (1973).

65. Josine Junger-Tas, "An Empirical Test of Social Control Theory," *Journal of Quantitative Criminology* 8:18–29 (1992).

66. Teresa Lagrange and Robert Silverman, "Perceived Strain and Delinquency Motivation: An Empirical Evaluation of General Strain Theory," Paper presented at the American Society of Criminology meeting, Boston, Mass., November 1995.

67. For a review of research, see Kimberly Kempf, "The Empirical Status of Hirschi's Control Theory, in Bill Laufer and Freda Adler, eds. *Advances in Criminological Theory* (New Brunswick, N.J.: Transaction Publishers, 1992); pp. 111–138,

68. Richard Lawrence, "Parents, Peers, Schools, and Delinquency," Paper presented at the American Society of Criminology meeting, Boston, Mass., November 1995.

69. Peggy Giordano, Stephen Cernkovich, and M. D. Pugh, "Friendships and Delinquency," *American Journal of Sociology* 91:1170–1202 (1986).

70. Denise Kandel and Mark Davies, "Friendship Networks, Intimacy, and Illicit Drug Use in Young Adulthood: A Comparison of Two Competing Theories," *Criminology* 29:441–67 (1991).

71. Leslie Samuelson, Timothy Hartnagel, and Harvey Krahn, "Crime and Social Control among High School Dropouts," *Journal of Crime and Justice,* 18:129–61 (1990).

72. Gary Jensen and David Brownfield, "Parents and Drugs," *Criminology* 21:543–54 (1983); M. Wiatrowski, D. Griswold, and M. Roberts, "Social Control Theory and Delinquency," *American Sociological Review* 46:525–41 (1981).

73. Kimberly Kempf Leonard and Scott Decker, "The Theory of Social Control: Does It Apply to the Very Young," *Journal of Criminal Justice* 22:89–105 (1994).

74. Velmer Burton, Francis Cullen, T. David Evans, R. Gregory Dunaway, Sesha Kethineni, and Gary Payne, "The Impact of Parental Controls on Delinquency," *Journal of Criminal Justice* 23:111–26 (1995).

75. Randy LaGrange and Helene Raskin White, "Age Differences in Delinquency: A Test of Theory," *Criminology* 23:19–45 (1985).

76. Marvin Krohn and James Massey, "Social Control and Delinquent Behavior: An Examination of the Elements of the Social Bond," *Sociological Quarterly* 21:529–43 (1980).

77. Robert Agnew, "Social Control Theory and Delinquency: A Longitudinal Test," *Criminology* 23:47–61 (1985).

78. For a similar result, see A. E. Liska and M. D Reed, "Ties to Conventional Institutions and Delinquency: Estimating

Reciprocal Effects," *American Sociological Review* 50:547–60 (1985).

79. Michael Gottfredson and Travis Hirschi, *A General Theory of Crime* (Stanford, Calif.: Stanford University Press, 1990).

80. Ibid., p. 27.

81. Ibid., p. 90.

82. Ibid., p. 89.

83. Ibid.

84. Ibid.

85. Michael Polakowski, "Linking Self- and Social Control with Deviance: Illuminating the Structure Underlying a General Theory of Crime and Its Relation to Deviant Activity," *Journal of Quantitative Criminology* 10:41–76 (1994).

86. Bruce Link, Elmer Streuning, Francis Cullen, Patrick Shrout, and Bruce Dohrenwend, "A Modified Labeling Theory Approach to Mental Disorders: An Empirical Assessment," *American Sociological Review* 54:400–23 (1989).

87. Polakowski, "Linking Self- and Social Control with Deviance: Illuminating the Structure Underlying a General Theory of Crime and Its Relation to Deviant Activity," p. 58.

88. David Brownfield and Ann Marie Sorenson, "Self-Control and Juvenile Delinquency: Theoretical Issues and an Empirical Assessment of Selected Elements of a General Theory of Crime, *Deviant Behavior* 14:243–64 (1993); Harold Grasmick, Charles Tittle, Robert Bursik, and Bruce Arneklev, "Testing the Core Empirical Implications of Gottfredson and Hirschi's General Theory of Crime," *Journal of Research in Crime and Delinquency* 30:5–29 (1993); John Cochran, Peter Wood, and Bruce Arneklev, "Is the Religiosity–Delinquency Relationship Spurious? A Test of Arousal and Social Control Theories," *Journal of Research in Crime and Delinquency* 31: 92–123 (1994).

89. Carl Keane, Paul Maxim, and James Teevan, "Drinking and Driving, Self-Control, and Gender: Testing a General Theory of Crime," *Journal of Research in Crime and Delinquency* 30:30–46 (1993).

90. Judith DeJong, Matti Virkkunen, and Marku Linnoila, "Factors Associated with Recidivism in a Criminal Population," *The Journal of Nervous and Mental Disease* 180:543–50 (1992).

91. David Cantor, "Drug Involvement and Offending among Incarcerated Juveniles", Paper presented at the American Society of Criminology meeting, Boston, Mass., November 1995.

92. Jon Gibbs and Dennis Giever, "Self-Control and Its Manifestations among University Students: An Empirical Test of Gottfredson and Hirschi's General Theory," *Justice Quarterly* 12:231–55 (1995).

93. Dennis Giever, "An Empirical Assessment of the Core Elements of Gottfredson and Hirschi's General Theory of Crime," Paper presented at the American Society of Criminology meeting, Boston, Mass., November 1995.

94. Marc LeBlanc, Marc Ouimet, and Richard Tremblay, "An Integrative Control Theory of Delinquent Behavior: A Validation 1976–1985," *Psychiatry* 51:164–76 (1988).

95. Otwin Marenin and Michael Resig, "A General Theory of Crime and Patterns of Crime in Nigeria: An Exploration of Methodological Assumptions," *Journal of Criminal Justice* 23:501–18 (1995).

96. Bruce Arneklev, Harold Grasmick, Charles Tittle, and Robert Bursik, "Low Self-Control and Imprudent Behavior," *Journal of Quantitative Criminology* 9:225–46 (1993).

97. Ousey and Aday, "The Interaction Hypothesis: A Test Using Social Control Theory and Social Learning Theory."

98. Julie Horney, D. Wayne Osgood, and Ineke Haen Marshall, "Criminal Careers in the Short-Term: Intra-Individual Variability in Crime and Its Relations to Local Life Circumstances," *American Sociological Review* 60:655–73 (1995).

99. Joseph Weis and J. David Hawkins, *Reports of the National Juvenile Justice Assessment Centers, Preventing Delinquency* (Washington, D.C.: U.S. Department of Justice, 1981); Joseph Weis and John Sederstrom, *Reports of the National Juvenile Justice Assessment Centers, The Prevention of Serious Delinquency: What to Do* (Washington, D.C.: U.S. Department of Justice, 1981).

100. Julie O'Donnell, J. David Hawkins, and Robert Abbott, "Predicting Serious Delinquency and Substance Use among Aggressive Boys," *Journal of Consulting and Clinical Psychology* 63:529–37 (1995).

101. Ibid., pp. 534–36; Richard Catalano, Rick Kosterman, J. David Hawkins, Michael Newcomb, and Robert Abbott, "Modeling the Etiology of Adolescent Substance Use: A Test of the Social Development Model," *Journal of Drug Issues* (1996).

102. J. David Hawkins, Richard Catalano, Diane Morrison, Julie O'Donnell, Robert Abbott, and L. Edward Day, "The Seattle Social Development Project," in Joan McCord and Richard Tremblay, eds, *The Prevention of Antisocial Behavior in Children* (New York: Guilford, 1992), pp. 139–60.

103. Delbert Elliott, David Huizinga, and Suzanne Ageton, *Explaining Delinquency and Drug Use* (Beverly Hills, Calif.: Sage, 1985).

104. Scott Menard and Delbert Elliott, "Delinquent Bonding, Moral Beliefs, and Illegal Behavior: A Three Wave-Panel Model," *Justice Quarterly* 11:173–88 (1994).

105. Elliott, Huizinga, and Ageton, *Explaining Delinquency and Drug Use,* p. 147.

106. Terence Thornberry, "Towards an Interactional Theory of Delinquency," *Criminology,* 25:863–81 (1987).

107. Terence Thornberry, Alan Lizotte, Marvin Krohn, Margaret Farnworth, and Sung Joon Jang, *Delinquent Peers,*

Beliefs, and Delinquent Behavior: A Longitudinal Test of Interactional Theory, working paper no. 6, rev., Rochester Youth Development Study (Albany, N.Y.: Hindelang Criminal Justice Research Center, 1992).

108. Terence Thornberry, Alan Lizotte, Marvin Krohn, Margaret Farnworth, and Sung Joon Jang, "Testing Interactional Theory: An Examination of Reciprocal Causal Relationships among Family, School and Delinquency," *Journal of Criminal Law and Criminology* 82:3–35 (1991).

109. Menard and Elliott, "Delinquent Bonding, Moral Beliefs and Illegal Behavior," pp. 185–87.

110. J. Wall, J. David Hawkins, D. Lishner, and M. Fraser, *Reports of the National Juvenile Justice Assessment Centers, Juvenile Delinquency Prevention: A Compendium of 36 Program Models* (Washington, D.C.: U.S. Department of Justice, 1981).

CHAPTER SIX

SOCIAL REACTION THEORIES: LABELING AND CONFLICT

INTRODUCTION

The two theoretical models discussed in this chapter, although quite different from one another, share one important characteristic differentiating them from all other theories of delinquency. While other theories portray the youthful offender as a rebel who for one reason or another cannot conform to the rules of society, social reaction theories—labeling and conflict—focus on the role that social and economic institutions play in *producing* delinquent behaviors and how the application of the rule of law in American society influences delinquent behavior. In a sense, the way *society reacts to individuals* and the way *individuals react to society* determine behavior. Social reactions determine which behaviors are considered criminal or conventional; they also determine individual behavior and whether certain individuals will become delinquents or not. These perspectives, therefore, may be considered theories of *social reaction.*

The influence of both of these perspectives on delinquency theory and policy was first felt in the late 1960s and early 1970s. In this period of social ferment, many traditional social institutions began to be questioned and criticized. The role of the government became suspect because of the generally unpopular war in Vietnam and the corruption uncovered in the Nixon administration. Likewise, legal and academic scholars voiced growing suspicions of the juvenile justice system because of its alleged inefficiency and discriminatory practices. Even the educational system was criticized for its failure to provide equal educational opportunities for all.[1]

Considering the climate of those times, it is not surprising that social scientists began to question the role that powerful social institutions played in shaping the direction of the society and influencing the behavior of people living within it. Scholars who were critical of big governmental, educational, corporate, and criminal justice organizations claimed that the efforts of these institutions actually helped produce crime and delinquency. Those holding power were accused of devoting their efforts to controlling the behavior of the lower class in order to protect the interests of the wealthy and powerful.

Some scholars believed that those in power used their influence to control the criminal law for their own benefit.[2] While the illegal behaviors of the have-not members of society were heavily punished, the violations of the upper classes— tax evasion, stock market manipulation, price fixing, political corruption, and so on—often went unprosecuted or were treated as civil violations and thus punishable only with a monetary fine. Critics argued that those in power used their control over social institutions to stigmatize the powerless and brand them as outcasts from society. Even when sincere efforts were made to help the less fortunate, the outcome was to enmesh them further in a deviant or outcast status. For example, educational enrichment efforts, such as the Head Start program, were suspected of helping identify children as intellectually backward and in need of special attention; efforts to provide mental health services branded individuals as "sick" or "crazy." Out of this critical inquiry emerged two potent themes: (1) Concepts of law and justice are applied differently in American society; and (2) those who become involved with the justice system are soon branded deviants or outcasts and launched into a deviant "career."

This type of analysis was soon applied to the study of delinquent behavior. It was alleged that delinquency results from the reactions of politically powerful individuals and groups, especially government social control agencies, to society's less fortunate members. Delinquents are not inherently bad or "evil" kids

In the 1960's, scholars were critical of "big government," claiming that those in power devoted their efforts to controlling the behavior of the lower class and protecting the interests of the wealthy and powerful. Today some right-wing militia groups, equally suspicious of the government, have resorted to violent means to promote their views. The Oklahoma City bombing is the most dramatic illustration of the conflict which is endemic to our complex society. Here suspect Timothy McVeigh is seen in custody of federal authorities.

but are individuals who have had a deviant status conferred on them by those holding economic, political, and social power. A delinquent status results from interpersonal interactions in which youths are made to feel inferior or outcast because of socially unacceptable behavior. These reactions are stratified by class: While lower-class youngsters are arrested, tried, and punished, middle-class youths are sent on their way by a benign, understanding police officer or juvenile court judge.[3] Thus, it is not the quality of the delinquent act itself that is important but the way society and its institutions react to the act. The purpose of social control is to maintain the status quo, ensuring that those in power will stay there.

In this chapter, we will first review labeling theory, which maintains that official reactions to delinquent acts help label youths as criminals, troublemakers, and outcasts and lock them in a cycle of escalating delinquent acts and social sanctions. Then we will turn to conflict theory, which holds that the decision to confer a delinquent label is a product of the capitalist system of economic production and its destructive influence on human behavior.

LABELING THEORY

Labeling theory is less concerned with what causes the onset of an initial delinquent act than with the effect that official handling by police, court, and correctional agencies has on the future of youths who fall into the arms of the law. It is more a theory of delinquent career formation than one that predicts the onset of individual delinquent behaviors.[4]

According to labeling theory, youths may violate the law for a variety of reasons, including but not limited to poor family relationships, neighborhood conflict, peer pressure, psychological and/or biological abnormality, and prodelinquent learning experiences. Regardless of the cause, if a youth's delinquent behavior is detected by law enforcement or school officials, the offender will be given a negative social label that can follow him or her throughout life. These labels include "troublemaker," "juvenile delinquent," "mentally ill," "retarded," "criminal," "junkie," and "thief."

APPLYING LABELS

The way labels are applied and the nature of the labels themselves are likely to have important future consequences for the delinquent. The degree to which youths are perceived as criminals may affect their treatment at home, at work, and at school. Young offenders may find that their parents consider them a detrimental influence on younger brothers and sisters. Their teachers may place them in classes or tracks reserved for students with behavioral problems, thus minimizing their chances of obtaining higher education. The delinquency label may restrict eligibility for employment and negatively affect the attitudes of society in general. Depending on the severity of the label, youthful offenders will be subjected to official sanctions ranging from a mild reprimand to incarceration.

Beyond these immediate results, labeling theory argues that, depending on the visibility of the label and the manner and severity with which it is applied, youths will have an increasing commitment to delinquent careers. As the negative feedback of law enforcement agencies, parents, friends, teachers, and other figures strengthens the commitment, delinquents may begin to reevaluate their identity and come to see themselves as criminals, troublemakers, or "screw-ups." Thus, through a process of identification and sanctioning, reidentification, and increased sanctioning, the identity of young offenders becomes transformed. They are no longer children in trouble; they are *delinquents,* and they accept that label as a personal identity—a process called **self-labeling.**[5] (See Figure 6.1.)

Howard Becker said, "The deviant is one to whom that label has successfully been applied; deviant behavior is behavior that people so label." How would you label the girls in this photo? What do expect their future lives to be like?

FIGURE 6.1
Labeling theory

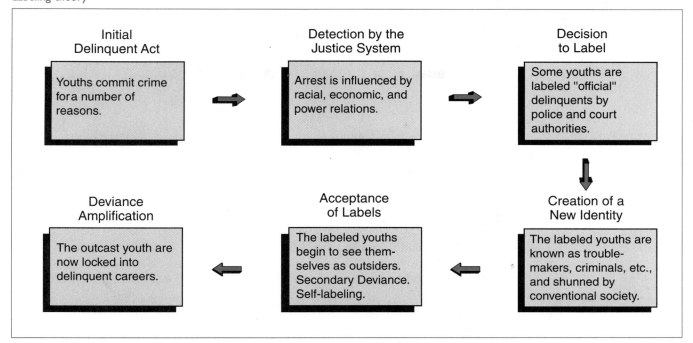

Initial Delinquent Act

Youths commit crime for a number of reasons.

Detection by the Justice System

Arrest is influenced by racial, economic, and power relations.

Decision to Label

Some youths are labeled "official" delinquents by police and court authorities.

Creation of a New Identity

The labeled youths are known as trouble-makers, criminals, etc., and shunned by conventional society.

Acceptance of Labels

The labeled youths begin to see them-selves as outsiders. Secondary Deviance. Self-labeling.

Deviance Amplification

The outcast youth are now locked into delinquent careers.

THE NATURE OF CRIME AND DELINQUENCY

Another important principle of the labeling approach is that the concepts of crime and delinquency are not absolute or permanent but vary according to social norms, customs, and the power structure of society. Those in power control what is considered "right" and "wrong," what is legal and illegal: Acts become outlawed because people in power view them as harmful behaviors.

A number of pioneering labeling theorists helped define the perspective by declaring that deviance is not an absolute concept but one that is relative in both place and time. "Deviance is not a property inherent in certain forms of behavior," argues sociologist Kai Erikson in a classic statement. "It is a property conferred upon those forms by the audiences which directly or indirectly witness them."[6] Later, Edwin Schur suggested that behavior is considered wrong or deviant when it begins to depart from expected social behavior patterns and when it elicits reactions that serve to isolate, treat, correct, or punish individuals engaged in such behavior.[7] So an "eccentric" becomes a "deviant" only when his or her behavior comes to the attention of people or institutions who have the power to control the undesirable behaviors.

In what is probably the most well known statement by a labeling theorist, Howard Becker described how deviance is created by labels:

> Deviance is *not* a quality of the act the person commits, but rather a consequence of the application by others of rules and sanctions to an "offender." The deviant is one to whom that label has successfully been applied; deviant behavior is behavior that people so label.[8]

Becker argues that legal and social rules are created by **moral entrepreneurs,** people who are concerned about social morality and work to control its definition and application. Consequently, who is to be labeled and the forms labeling takes depend on social forces that vary considerably within cultures. Who is in power and how they interpret right and wrong play important roles in defining crime and delinquency. For example, during our own lifetimes, some of us have witnessed the legalization of abortion, the banning of school prayer, and in some states the decriminalization of marijuana. Becker and other labeling theorists help us recognize that our concept of deviance evolves over time.

THE EFFECT OF LABELING

The labeling approach focuses primarily on the social audience's reaction to persons and their behavior and the subsequent effects of that reaction, rather than on the cause of the deviant behavior itself. Furthermore, labeling theorists allege that the treatment of offenders in the labeling process depends far less on their behavior than on the way others view their acts.

People form enduring opinions of others based on brief first impressions.[9] If interactions involve perceptions of deviance, individuals may be assigned negative labels, such as "troublemaker," "nerd," or "fag." People suspected of having these behavior "problems" are carefully scrutinized by those with whom they interact; people are cautious with them, search for signs of deviance, or shun them outright.[10]

Official labels may be applied when deviant behavior runs afoul of socially accepted rules, laws, or conventions. Official or formal labels may include "criminal," "mentally ill," or "dropout." Official labels are often bestowed during ceremonies designed to redefine the deviants' identity and place them apart from the normative social structure, for example, during trials or civil commitment or school disciplinary board hearings.[11] The net effect of this legal and social process is a durable negative label and an accompanying loss of status. The labeled deviant becomes a social outcast who is prevented from enjoying higher education, a well-paying job, and other societal benefits.

We can see an example of this process in stigma-producing ceremonies, such as those that sometimes occur in juvenile courts. Here, young offenders find, perhaps for the first time, that people in authority, in the person of the juvenile court judge, consider them incorrigible outcasts who must be separated from the right-thinking members of society. To reach that decision, the judge relies on the testimony of a parade of witnesses—parents, teachers, police officers, social workers, psychologists—all of whom may testify that the offenders are unfit to be part of conventional society.[12] As the label "juvenile delinquent" is conferred on the offenders, their identity may forever be transformed from boys or girls who have done something bad to "bad" boys or girls.[13]

Self-Fulfilling Prophecy Labeling theorists see these negative labels as creating a self-fulfilling prophecy.[14] If children continually receive negative feedback from parents, teachers, and others whose opinions they value, they will eventually interpret this rejection as accurate and self-defining. Ultimately their behavior will begin to conform to these negative expectations: They become the person others consider them to be. Sociologist Ross Matsueda has found that young people who perceive negative labels from their parents, teachers, and friends begin to appraise themselves in negative terms, for example, "troublemaker." The outcome: a damaged self-image and an increase in antisocial behaviors.[15]

Labeling theorists suggest that labels create a *self-fulfilling prophecy*. If children continually receive negative feedback from parents, teachers, and others whose opinion they value, they will eventually interpret this rejection as accurate and self-defining. In contrast, those receiving positive feedback will conform to these more optimistic expectations. How would the students in this photo be labeled? What do you think their future will hold? Do positive labels have a beneficial long-term influence on people?

Labeling Outcomes   Labeling and stigmatization help create a new, deviant identity. Those exposed to negative social sanctions experience **self-rejection** and a lower self-image. Self-rejecting attitudes ("At times, I think I am no good at all") result in both a weakened commitment to conventional values and behaviors, and the acquisition of motives to deviate from social norms ("Everyone is against me, so why should I obey the rules?").[16]

Facilitating this attitude and value transformation is the bond social outcasts form with similarly labeled peers.[17] It is expected that labeled delinquents will seek out others who are similarly stigmatized because members of conventional society shun and avoid them.[18] Associating with deviant peers helps reinforce preexisting negative evaluations, such as "We were right all along about him—look who his friends are!"

Peers may help the labeled youths "reject their rejector." Teachers are stupid, they are told, cops are dishonest; parents "just don't understand."[19] Group identity enables "outcast youth" to be defiant, to show contempt for the source of the negative labels, to distance themselves from the source of condemnation; these actions help solidify the grip of the negative labels.[20]

PRIMARY AND SECONDARY DEVIANCE

The labeling process was refined by Edwin Lemert in his formulation of primary and secondary deviance.[21]

Lemert argues that deviant acts actually form two distinct classes: primary and secondary. Primary deviants are people who engage in "bad acts" but are not considered "bad people." They are neither labeled as deviant by others nor do they apply self-labels. For example, students who successfully shoplift from the college store, avoiding detection, are not recognized by others as deviant, nor do they recognize themselves as a "thief" or "criminal." Later they may say, "I can't believe I was so stupid and took such a risk." Their act of theft is of little matter to their current and future status; they can go on to graduate without consequence. In this instance, the deviant behavior can be rationalized by the offender as a mistake or slip in an otherwise unblemished life ("Everyone shoplifts once, what's the big deal? I was immature"). Although primary acts may be considered serious, they do not materially affect self-concept.

Although Lemert attaches little importance to primary deviance, he argues that deviations become significant (secondary) when the deviant behavior is repetitive, highly visible, and subject to severe social reaction. The secondary deviant is not someone who has done a bad act; he or she is now considered a "bad person." The college boy who is *caught* shoplifting a book may find himself expelled from school and facing criminal charges. Thereafter he will be watched and suspected, stigmatized and labeled. He may then incorporate this new deviant identity into his own psyche: Maybe he is a "thief"; after all, that's what everyone seems to believe! Had this individual not been caught and labeled, the deviant act would have soon been forgotten, and he would have gone on to graduate and lead a productive life.

Secondary Deviance   All life roles of secondary deviants revolve around the new, albeit damaged, identity they have accepted.[22] Helping them become **resocialized** is the disgrace, punishment, segregation, and social control that typically accompany deviant labels. Self-labeling, combined with social stigmatization, then transforms the person into one who "employs his behavior (deviant) or a role based upon it as a means of defense, attack, or adjustment to the overt and covert problems created by the consequent societal reaction to him."[23]

They may use their damaged identities as a coping mechanism, for example, by joining with others so labeled in a deviant subculture (e.g., a gang or a drug clique). So although the intent of deviant labeling may be to reduce unwanted behavior, the actual effect is to encourage its continuity.

Lemert's model highlights the deviance-producing properties of the labeling process. The model portrays immersion in a deviant identity as a cycle of events (Figure 6.2) in which a deviant act (A) leads to a social reaction (B), to self-conception as a "deviant" (C), to increased, more serious deviant acts (offense escalation) (D), and to greater and more severe social reactions, including legal reprisals (E), until identification with a deviant identity becomes complete (F), a state of events that increases the probability of future deviant acts (**deviance amplification**).[24] Lemert's conceptualization of the labeling process and his description of the primary-secondary deviance dichotomy are major theoretical underpinnings of the labeling approach.

DIFFERENTIAL SOCIAL CONTROL

How does social interaction regulate the process in which labeled adolescents forge a new identity and become secondary deviants? According to Karen Heimer and Ross Matsueda's concept of differential social control, deviant self-evaluations reflect appraisals made by others.[25] Young people who view themselves as delinquents are giving an inner voice to their perceptions of how parents, teachers, peers, and neighbors feel about them. Those who believe that others view them as antisocial or as troublemakers take on roles that reflect this

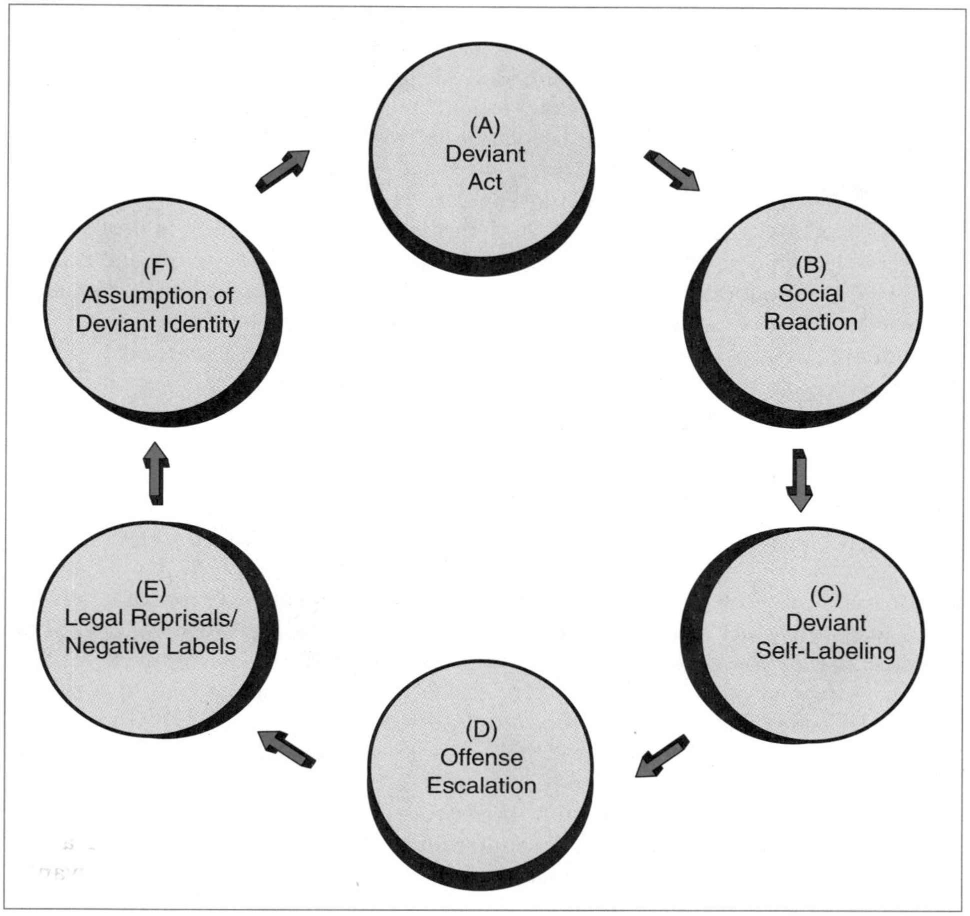

FIGURE 6.2
The cycle of secondary deviance

FIGURE 6.2
The cycle of secondary deviance

assumption; they expect to be suspected and then rejected. Labeled youths may then join up with similarly outcast delinquent peers who facilitate their behavior. Eventually, antisocial behavior becomes habitual and automatic.

Tempering or enhancing the effect of this **reflective role-taking** are informal and institutional *social control* processes. Families, schools, peers, and the social system can either help control young people and dissuade them from crime or encourage and sustain deviance. When these groups are dysfunctional, such as when parents use drugs, they encourage, rather than control, antisocial behavior.

Heimer and Matsueda also argue that **reflected appraisal** has a significant effect on delinquency: Youths who believe that their parents and friends consider them deviants and troublemakers are the ones most likely to engage in delinquency. A "damaged" self-image, influenced and directed by social interaction, controls the content of behavior.[26]

THE JUVENILE JUSTICE PROCESS AND LABELING

Is it possible that the juvenile justice process actually increases the probability that at-risk youths will continue their offending careers? In fact, the justice system has long been suspected of bestowing destructive deviant labels on children who are suspected of being delinquents. In a classic work, Frank Tannenbaum first suggested that social typing, which he called "dramatization of evil," transforms the offender's identity from a doer of evil to an "evil person."[27] Tannenbaum emphasized the role of the juvenile justice system in this scheme: "The entire process of dealing with young delinquents is mischievous insofar as it identifies *him* to *himself* and to the environment as a delinquent person."[28]

Theorists have built upon the work of Tannenbaum, continuing to describe the impact of juvenile justice processing on delinquent labeling and consequent illegal behavior. Delinquents, the argument goes, are in reality the finished products of the juvenile justice "assembly line."[29] Although they enter as children in trouble, they emerge as individuals transformed by decision makers into bearers of criminal histories, which are likely to reinvolve them in criminal activity. Once labeled, the police and other authority figures begin to anticipate that these "troublemakers" will continue their life of crime.[30] Labeled delinquents are assumed to engage in a full range of violence, theft, and drug abuse, although they have not necessarily demonstrated these characteristics by their behavior; they become "perennial suspects."[31] The system designed to reduce delinquency may help produce hardened, stigmatized young criminals.

Degradation Ceremonies According to the labeling perspective, the actions of the juvenile justice system, outwardly aimed at delinquency prevention, actually create the opposite effect by turning the self-perception of a youthful suspect into that of a delinquent.[32] In classic paper, sociologist Harold Garfinkel addressed why this occurs when he described what he called a successful **degradation ceremony,** during which the public identity of an offender is transformed into "something looked on as lower in the social scheme of social types."[33] Garfinkel concludes that this process may be similar in form and function to what is practiced in juvenile court. Going to a juvenile court, being scolded by a judge, having charges read, and being found delinquent after a trial process are all conditions that should produce "successful degradation."

Labeling theory predicts two relationships with regard to juvenile justice processing: (1) The delinquency label will be bestowed upon the powerless members of society in a discriminatory fashion; and (2) the more frequent, prolonged, or decisive the contacts with the juvenile justice system, the more likely it is that an offender will ultimately accept the delinquency label as a personal identity and enter into a life of crime. These two anticipated relationships are discussed below.

DISCRIMINATION IN THE LABELING PROCESS

One of the cornerstones of the labeling perspective is that the likelihood of becoming labeled is skewed along racial and class lines; the burden falls most heavily on the disadvantaged, the poor, and the powerless. Because of stereotypes that portray offenders as young, male, inner-city, minority group members, individuals who belong to such groups are more likely than others to be labeled delinquent.[34]

Much evidence supports the labeling hypothesis. Research shows that police are more likely to arrest and officially process males, minority group members, and those in the lower economic classes than youths who do not share these traits.[35] For example, Carl Pope and William Feyerherm reviewed more than 30 years of research on minorities in the juvenile justice system and found that race, to the disadvantage of minority youths, influences decision making.[36]

Evidence also exists that offenders whose families have economic or political power are likely merely to be given a warning by police officers rather than processed to the juvenile court.[37] In turn, the juvenile court is believed to respond more favorably to youths from middle-class homes than to those from the lower class. Living in a single-parent home has been related to discrimination in the juvenile justice system; under these circumstances, black youths were found to be more at risk than white youths.[38]

Although this evidence is persuasive, some critics dispute the charge that the justice system operates in a distinctly discriminatory fashion.[39] Evidence exists that the factors related to official juvenile justice processing are influenced more by crime-related issues, such as offense seriousness and prior record, than by personal factors, such as racial or economic bias.[40] The factors most closely related to the decision of police to take formal action reflect legal and crime-related variables: prior offense record, association with known delinquents, and involvement in gang violence and drugs. According to this view, regardless of race or class, young people who commit a lot of crime with their friends, use drugs, and get into fights will also get arrested.

THE EFFECTS OF OFFICIAL LABELING

Equally disturbing to labeling theorists is the failure of empirical evidence to consistently confirm that experience with the juvenile justice system produces enduring negative labels. Studies attempting to measure the identity transformation of adolescents at the onset and conclusion of official contact have been contradictory and inconclusive.[41] Some indicate that youths actually feel relief after the conclusion of their juvenile justice experience, rather than shame, stigma, or a diminution of their self-image, as labeling theorists would predict.[42]

A few research efforts have found that although youths who have had experience with the juvenile justice system are the ones most likely to maintain a delinquent self-concept, the relationship between sanctions and labels is far from clear. For example, although Gary Jensen found that youths who experience arrest are the ones most likely to have negative self-images beforehand, there was little evidence that delinquent self-concept increases substantially after police contact.[43]

It is possible then that youths who already maintain a delinquent self-concept are the ones most likely to be arrested and officially processed but that the stigma of an "official label" does little to aggravate an already damaged self-image.[44] Research, then, has not supported a key premise of labeling theory: that juvenile justice processing seems to amplify self-labels.[45] Formal labels bestowed by the juvenile justice system actually had very little impact on a juvenile's self-image: The relationship between sanctions and escalation of delinquent self-image has been found to be very modest.[46]

How can these insignificant labeling effects be explained? Why does juvenile justice processing have little measurable influence on the self-image of court-processed youth? One possibility is that youths who experience arrest and official processing already have such a long and active career as undetected, "secret" deviants that their experience with the juvenile justice system has little effect on their already molded self-concept and identity. Youths involved in antisocial activity from early childhood may consider a juvenile court experience an "occupational hazard"; uncomfortable but not a life-altering event.

It is also possible that significant differences in the manner and type of official processing can influence the direction and impact of the labeling process. Some

You are the planning director for the state department of juvenile justice correctional services.

One of your main concerns is the effect of stigmatization on the criminal offending patterns of delinquent youth. Some of your advisers have suggested that processing youths through the juvenile correctional justice system produces deviant identities that lock them into a criminal way of life. Rather than rehabilitate, the system produces hard-core delinquents who are likely to recidivate. They point to studies that show that an experience with the juvenile justice system has relatively little impact on chronic offenders and, if anything, is associated with escalating the seriousness of their criminal behavior.

Some of the more conservative members of your staff are opposed to making the reduction of stigmatization and labeling a top correctional concern. They remind you that an experience with the juvenile justice system may actually help deter crime. They point to studies that suggest that youths who have been processed through the correctional system are less likely to recidivate than youths who receive lesser punishments, such as community corrections or probation. In addition, they believe that hard-core, violent offenders deserve to be punished; excessive concern for the offender and not their acts ignores the rights of victims and society in general.

These opposing views have left you in a quandary. On the one hand, the system must be sensitive to the adverse effects of stigmatization and labeling. On the other hand, the need for control and deterrence must not be ignored. Despite your dilemma, you must come up with a plan that satisfies both positions.

What types of correctional programs might avoid excessive stigma yet control juvenile offenders?

Should more concern be given to control or to labeling?

young people labeled "delinquents" may be treated punitively while others are offered the benefits of rehabilitation efforts and encouragement by social service agencies. Although the former are damaged by their ordeal, the latter may actually benefit from their experiences. Sociologist Stanley Cohen has written that the quality of treatment by the justice system helps categorize offenders into two distinct groups: One made up of unrepentant and antisocial offenders who are placed in programs that dish out harsh punishments (exclusionary programs) and another that contains more amenable offenders who are placed in programs that continually encourage them to join the mainstream of social life (inclusionary programs). The contrary experiences of members of these two groups may help cancel out the overall stigma generated by juvenile justice processing: While youths in the "excluded" group suffer deeply, those in the "included" group benefit because people have taken a greater interest in them than they have ever experienced before in their lives.[47]

In sum, little hard evidence exists that juvenile justice processing has a deep or lasting effect on a youth's self-image. It may simply be that the effects of early socialization are so overwhelming that by the time a youth is actually labeled by the juvenile justice system the effects are quite insignificant.

EVALUATION OF LABELING THEORY

Although quite influential in the 1970s, labeling theory has declined in importance as a primary theory of delinquency. Four important criticisms of the labeling approach have led to its decline:

1. Labeling theorists failed to explain the onset of the first or primary deviation. Why is it that some people engage in the initial deviant act that leads to their label, while others in the same circumstances stick to conventional behaviors?[48] As criminologist Ronald Akers puts it, "One sometimes gets the impression from reading the literature that people go about minding their own business and then—'wham'—bad society comes along and slaps them with a stigmatized label."[49]

2. According to labeling theory, the overrepresentation of males, minorities, and the poor in the crime rate is a function of discriminatory labeling by social control agents. However, empirical research has failed to consistently show that labels are bestowed in a discriminatory fashion.[50] An analysis of existing research by Charles Tittle and Deborah Curran found that about 40 percent of the research studies indicate a racial effect on juvenile justice decision making and 60 percent do not; about 33 percent of the research studies show a class effect, while 67 percent indicate that class does not influence the labeling process.[51] Although some individual-level discrimination exists, such label-producing actions as arrest, prosecution, and sentencing seem more closely related to the seriousness of the criminal act and the youth's prior record than to personal characteristics. Discrimination in the labeling process is a cornerstone of the theory because it indicates that the manner in which labels are bestowed is the key issue in determining patterns in the crime rate. If people were labeled only because they deserved negative social reactions (that is, they committed serious crimes), then the theory would be invalid because the labeling process would be an effect of crime, rather than its cause.[52]

3. Studies that evaluate the effects of official labeling fail to show it had a deviance amplification effect. Young people undergoing the labeling process were simply not as deeply affected by their experiences as labeling theory predicts.[53]

4. Criminologists found that the labeling concept that "no act is inherently evil or criminal" is naive. This point is driven home by sociologist Charles Wellford, who argues rather conclusively that some crimes, such as rape and homicide, are almost universally sanctioned.[54] He says, "Serious violations of the law are universally understood and *are*, therefore, *in that sense*, intrinsically criminal."[55]

These criticisms led to a decline in labeling theory as an explanation of delinquent behavior. Enthusiasm for the labeling approach also diminished because the general public and academic community seem more concerned with crime control and the best method of curbing delinquent youth than worrying about the stigma such treatment might produce. In one influential work, *Beyond Delinquency*, sociologists Charles Murray and Louis Cox found that youths assigned to a treatment program designed to reduce labels were more likely to later commit delinquent acts than a comparison group who were placed in a traditional and more punitive state training school. The implication was that the deterrent threat of punishment had a greater impact on youths and that the crime-producing influence of negative labels was actually minimal.[56]

LABELING REDUX

Just when it seemed that labeling theory was about to be dropped as an explanation of delinquency it has become the object of renewed interest by the academic community. Criminologists Raymond Paternoster and Leeann Iovanni suggest that the labeling perspective can offer some important insights into delinquent behavior:

1. It identifies the role played by social control agents in the process of delinquency causation. Delinquent behavior cannot be fully understood if the agencies and individuals empowered to control and treat it are ignored.
2. It recognizes that delinquency is not a disease or pathological behavior. It focuses attention on the social interactions and reactions that shape individuals and their behavior.
3. It distinguishes between delinquent acts (primary deviance) and delinquent careers (secondary deviance) and shows that these are separate problems which must be treated differently.[57]

New versions of labeling theory, such as Heimer and Matsueda's differential social control view, are emerging. Research is now being conducted that supports labeling concepts, including cross-national studies that show that official labels lead to social rejection (e.g., estrangement from peers and neighbors) in other cultures.[58]

Labeling Chronic Offenders Labeling theory seems especially relevant today considering what is now known about the life course of chronic offenders: persistence in delinquent activities despite being apprehended by police and punished by the juvenile court. The evidence indicates that labels and sanctions tend to amplify rather than extinguish deviant careers. This view is consistent with the Matsueda research cited earlier which shows that prior delinquency shapes adolescent perceptions of how others view them and also can amplify future misbehavior. In an important research paper, Douglas Smith and Robert Brame found that although labels may not cause adolescents to initiate criminal behaviors, experienced delinquents are *significantly more likely to continue offending if they believe that their parents and peers view them in a negative light.*[59] Labeling then may help sustain delinquency over time.

Until recently, scant attention has been paid to the fact that stigma and negative labels may sustain chronic offending and criminal careers.[60] In fact, the very definition of a chronic offender is a person who has been arrested and therefore labeled multiple times in his or her offending career. Who these youths are and why they begin to acquire a deviant identity are issues addressed by labeling theory. The ability of labeling theory to account for deviance amplification may be of critical value in explaining the criminal career patterns of the chronic offender.

Social Conflict Theory

Unlike traditional theoretical perspectives, which try to explain why an individual violates the law, social conflict theory focuses on the roles social and governmental institutions play in creating and enforcing laws that control behavior and morality. According to this view, society is a constant state of internal conflict. Different groups strive to impose their will on others. Those with money and power succeed in shaping the law to meet their needs and maintain their interests. Those whose behavior cannot conform to the needs of the power elite are defined as delinquents and criminals.

Conflict criminologists then do not view delinquents as rebels who cannot conform to proper social norms, nor do they try to devise innovative ways of controlling youthful misbehavior. Their interests lie in evaluating how the criminal law is used as a mechanism of social control and describing how social, political, and economic power are used to control and shape society (see Figure 6.3).

WHY CRITICAL THINKING EMERGED

It is not accidental that the emergence of conflict theory as an explanation of deviant behavior had its roots in the widespread social and political upheavals of the 1960s,[61] including the Vietnam War, the counterculture movement, and various forms of public protest. Conflict theory flourished within this framework because it provided a theoretical basis to challenge the legitimacy of the government's creation and application of law. Students protesting the war, appalled at the political maneuvering of the Nixon administration, adopted a left-wing ideology. Many pursued graduate study in the social sciences, where they embraced political and social theories critical of the **power elite.** Some then went on to teaching careers where they could continue their left-wing scholarship.

These critical thinkers hurled challenges at the academic world, the center of most theoretical thought in criminology. They claimed that it was archaic, conservative, and out of step with recent changes in society.[62] **Critical criminologists** challenged the fundamental role criminologists play in uncovering the causes of crime and delinquency. At a time of general turmoil in society, they

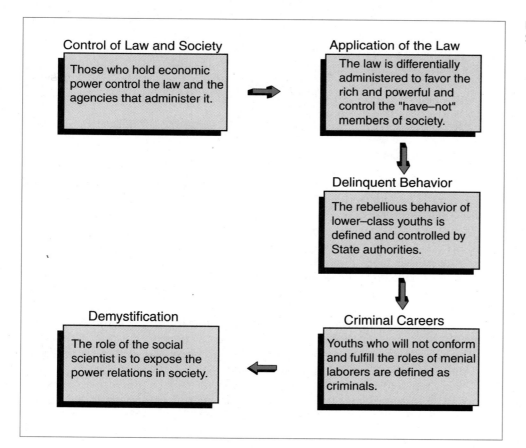

FIGURE 6.3
Social conflict theory

According to the social conflict view, society is a constant state of internal conflict. Different groups strive to impose their will on others. Those with money and power succeed in shaping the law to meet their needs and maintain their interests. Those whose behavior cannot conform to the needs of the power elite are defined as delinquents and criminals.

called for sweeping innovation in academic settings—including changes in the way courses were taught, grading, and tenure. Criminologists were asked to evaluate their own lives and activities to understand their personal role in the crime problem. Was it possible that they were acting as agents of the state, taking money from government agencies to achieve more effective repression of the poor and laboring classes?[63] These social conflict theorists called for rethinking the entire field of law and criminology.[64] From this intellectual ferment emerged a number of branches of social conflict theory.

THE BRANCHES OF SOCIAL CONFLICT THEORY

Several views exist about what produces social conflict. Weberian conflict theorists rely on the belief that conflict between the haves and have-nots of society can occur in any social system. This view relies heavily on the writings of Max Weber (1864–1920), a German economist and social historian who believed that the social and legal systems were controlled by intergroup competition and conflict. Weber argued that there were multiple sources of competition; groups compete not solely for economic dominance but over ethical and religious ideas as well.

Marxist and critical criminologists suggest that the engine that drives human behavior is the economic class conflict inherent in the capitalist system. Law and justice then are not neutral devices that serve the interests of society but are *instruments of power used to protect the power elites' interests.*[65] Crime and delinquency are the natural consequences of the unequal distribution of wealth and power in postindustrial capitalist society.

Despite their significant dogmatic differences, all social conflict theorists agree that those in power define the behavior of the poor as criminal and delinquent while shaping the law to define their own actions as acceptable and appropriate.

Conflict and Labeling The social conflict approach can also be contrasted with the labeling perspective. Social conflict theorists charge that labeling advocates do not go far enough in exposing the crime-producing elements of American culture; that they seem content merely to analyze the behavior of strange and different people. In contrast, social conflict thinkers use historical research and political analysis to understand the social relationships, power relations, and institutional arrangements that produce delinquent and criminal behavior.

To understand the social conflict view better, it is helpful to know some of its philosophical underpinnings, more specifically, the works of Karl Marx.

Marxist Thought

The foundation of social conflict theory can be traced to the political and economic philosophy of Karl Marx (1818–1883).[66]

Marx believed that the character of every civilization is determined by its mode of production—the way its people develop and produce material goods. This concept has two components: (1) productive forces, which include such things as technology, energy sources, and material resources; and (2) productive relations, which are the relationships between the people producing the goods and services. The most important relationship in industrial culture is between the owners of the means of production (the capitalist bourgeoisie) and those who do the actual labor (the proletariat). Throughout history, society has been organized this way—master and slave, lord and serf, and now capitalist and worker.

The political and economic philosophy of the dominant class influences all aspects of life. Consciously or unconsciously, artists, writers, and teachers bend their work to the whims of the capitalist system. Thus, the economic system controls all facets of human life, and consequently, people's lives revolve around the means of production.

Marx held that the laboring class produces goods that exceed wages in value (**surplus value**). The excess value then goes to the capitalists as profit. Although some of this profit is spent on personal luxuries, most is spent on acquiring an ever-expanding capitalist base that relies on advanced technology for efficiency. Thus, capitalists constantly compete with one another to maintain market position. To compete, they must produce goods more efficiently and cheaply, a condition that requires them either to pay workers the lowest possible wages or to replace them with labor-saving machinery. Soon the supply of efficiently made goods outstrips the ability of the laboring classes to purchase them, a condition that precipitates an economic crisis. During this period, weaker enterprises go under and are consequently incorporated into ever-expanding, monopolistic mega-corporations that are strong enough to further exploit the workers. Marx believed, that in the ebb and flow of the business cycle, the capitalist system contains the seeds of its own destruction and that from its ashes would grow a socialist state in which the workers themselves own the means of production.

Although this brief discussion of Marxist thought is only the barest outline of a complex, highly technical topic, it does provide a glimpse of the thought patterns that are the basis of social conflict theory.

ELEMENTS OF SOCIAL CONFLICT THEORY

Based on Marx's theories of economic analysis, the primary goal of social conflict theory is to examine the relationship between the ruling class and the masses, along with the process by which deviance is defined and controlled in capitalist society. By broadening the search for an explanation of deviance to include its defining process, social conflict theorists depart from the narrower focus of earlier positivist models of deviant behavior which viewed crime and delinquency as being a function of individual maladaption.

The most important of these concerns are the nature and purpose of social control. Conflict theorists believe that those in power use the justice system to maintain their relative status while keeping others in a subservient position: Men use their economic power to control and subjugate women; members of the majority group want to stave off economic advancement of minorities; capitalists want to reduce the power of workers to ensure they are willing to accept low wages.

Conflict theory then centers around a view of society in which an elite class uses the criminal law as a means of meeting and controlling threats to its status. The ruling class, then, is a self-interested collective whose primary interest is self-gain.[67]

LAW AND JUSTICE

Social conflict theorists view the criminal law and the criminal justice system as vehicles for controlling the poor, have-not members of society. They help the powerful and rich to impose their particular morality and standards of good behavior on the entire society; protect their property and physical safety from the depredations of the have-nots, even though the cost may be high in terms of the legal rights of those it perceives as a threat; and extend the definition of illegal or criminal behavior to encompass those who might threaten the status quo.[68] The ruling elite draws the lower middle class into this pattern of control, leading it to believe that it also has a stake in maintaining the status quo.[69] According to social conflict theory, the poor may or may not commit more crimes than the rich, but they certainly are arrested and punished more often. The poor are driven to crime because

1. the middle- and upper-class rules and laws have little relationship to the lifestyle of the poor;
2. a natural frustration exists in a society where affluence is well publicized but unattainable to the majority of citizens;
3. a deep-rooted hostility is generated among members of the lower class toward a social order that they are not allowed to shape or participate in.[70]

Conflict theorists contradict the long-held presumption that the American system of law and justice is humane and fair to all citizens. Conflict theory asks us to reevaluate many basic beliefs. For example, that laws protecting private property may actually be designed to preserve the dominance of a ruling elite strikes at the very heart of our moral beliefs that laws are designed to protect *everyone*. For this reason alone, conflict theory has had a profound effect on mid-20th-century criminological thought.

DEMYSTIFICATION

Social conflict theorists consider it essential to demystify law and science. **Demystification** entails a number of different actions. For one thing, radical criminologists charge that an inordinate amount of scientific effort is devoted to unmasking the social conditions of lower-class citizens with the ostensible purpose of improving their lives. Such studies include examinations of lower-class family life, IQs, school performance, and so on. Conflict criminologists argue, however, that these efforts actually serve to keep the lower classes down by "proving" that they are more delinquent and less intelligent and that they have poorer school performance than the middle class. All the while, the tests and instruments used to conduct these studies are biased and inaccurate.[71] Thus, in one sense, demystification entails uncovering the real reasons behind scientific research.

Another aspect of demystification involves identifying the historical development of criminal law. By drawing attention to the "real" reasons such laws as tax codes and statutes prohibiting theft and drug use were created, people will understand the purpose and intent of these laws. If it is found that theft laws, for example, were originally created to maintain the wealth and capital of the rich, then those who violate the law should not perceive themselves as evil, immoral, or wrong but rather as victims of an unjust system.

Demystification also involves identifying hidden power relations in society. For example, radical feminist scholars have focused their attention on how male power (**patriarchy**) is used to control both the economic means of production and the sexuality of women, ensuring continued male dominance. Radical feminists have helped identify the extent of sexual violence and battering, showing that men physically and sexually victimize women in their attempt to maintain control.[72]

Finally, the demystification of capitalist society reveals the controlling nature of the "professional mystique."[73] It is alleged that our society grants inordinate power to professionals to judge and control the population. When teachers, doctors, lawyers, and psychologists judge persons to be "crazy," "stupid," "sick," "unfit," "delinquent," or "criminal," that label creates a social identity. Radical criminologists charge that professionals often suppress and distort the truth, "unmasking" powerless people so that their position of social inferiority is maintained. The system quickly condemns those who speak against it as "subversive," "traitorous," or "mentally ill."

THE CONFLICT CONCEPT OF DELINQUENCY

Conflict theorists view delinquency as a normal response by youth to the social conditions created by capitalist society.[74] In fact, the very creation of a unique legal category, delinquency, is a function of the class consciousness that occurred around the turn of the century.[75] In his book *The Child Savers*, Anthony Platt documents the creation of the delinquency concept and the role played by wealthy child savers in forming the philosophy of the juvenile court. In a later work, Platt claims,

> The child-saving movement tried to do for the criminal justice system what industrialists and corporate leaders were trying to do for the economy—that is, achieve order, stability and control while preserving the existing class system and distribution of wealth.[76]

Thus, the roots of the juvenile delinquency concept can be traced to 19th-century efforts of powerful and wealthy citizens to control the behavior of weak and disenfranchised youths.[77]

Today, critical criminologists still view delinquent behavior as a function of the capitalist system's inherent social and economic inequity. They argue that capitalism accelerates the trend toward replacing human labor with machines so that youths are removed from a useful place in the labor force.[78] This process prolongs their dependency and forces them to be controlled by socialization agencies, such as the family and, most important, the school. These social control agencies prepare youths for placement in the capitalist system by presenting them with behavior models that will help them conform to later job expectations. For example, rewards for good schoolwork correspond to the rewards a factory supervisor uses with subordinate employees. In fact, most schools are set up to reward and nurture youths who show early promise in such areas as self-discipline, achievement, and motivation and who are therefore judged likely to perform well in the capitalist system. Youths who are judged inferior as potential job prospects (Herman and Julia Schwendinger refer to them as "prototypical marginals") become known to the school community as "greasers," "burnouts," and "hoods" and eventually wind up in delinquent roles.[79]

CLASS AND DELINQUENCY

The capitalist system affects youths in each element of the class structure differently. Youths in the lowest classes, who usually live in the most desolated ghetto areas of the nation, form delinquent gangs. These violent gangs serve outcast youths as a means of survival in a system that offers no other reasonable alternative. Other lower-class youths, because of their location in more stable areas, are usually on the fringe of criminal activity.

Conflict theory also acknowledges middle-class delinquency. The alienation of individuals from one another, the never-ending competitive struggle, and the absence of human interest and feeling—all inherent qualities of capitalism—contribute to middle-class delinquency. Because capitalism is such a dehumanizing system, it is not surprising that even middle-class youths turn to drugs, gambling, and illicit sex to find escape and excitement. Thus, conflict theory explains the various forms of delinquent behavior in our society.

According to conflict theorist David Greenberg, adolescents will avoid delinquent activity as long as parents can provide support and funds for rewarding peer relationships.[80] Those youths whose parents' economic positions make this support impossible may turn to delinquent behavior to support their lifestyles. The capitalist system hastens this process because it makes it difficult for teenagers to become part of the job market. Greenberg suggests that adolescent theft then occurs as a response to the disjunction between the desire to participate in social activities with peers and the absence of legitimate sources of funds needed to finance this participation. Greenberg argues that this view helps explain the occurrence of middle-class delinquency. Even though the parents of middle-class youths are more likely to be able to provide them with funds than parents of lower-class youths, the cost of their leisure lifestyle is proportionately greater, so they will be unable to receive the economic support they need. Greenberg views the removal of children from the labor force in 20th-century America as a primary motive behind their law-violating behavior: The increasing level of juvenile crime we are seeing in the United States and in other Western countries, argues Greenberg, originates in the structural position of juveniles in an advanced capitalist economy. As teenagers mature, their vulnerability to peer pressure is reduced if an alternative source of self-esteem and gratification becomes available. If teens can successfully enter the capitalist system, increasing their opportunity to earn money, their crime rates decrease (explaining the aging-out process).

Juvenile Justice   Conflict theorists would suggest that rather than inhibiting delinquent behavior, the juvenile justice system actually may help to create and sustain its occurrence. They claim that the capitalist state fails to control delinquents because it is actually in the state's own best interest to maintain a large number of outcast deviant youths. These youths can then be employed as low-paid marginal workers, willing to work for minimum wage in jobs no one else wants. Thus, labeling by the juvenile justice system fits within the capitalist managers' need to maintain an underclass of cheap labor to be employed in its factories and to buy inferior goods.

EMERGING CONCEPTS OF CONFLICT THEORY

Conflict theory does indeed question the many instances of misguided "official wisdom" that pervade our society, but despite its lofty goals and ideals, critics question its lack of empirical verification.[81] Most research has been by necessity historical and theoretical. Most conflict scholarship and theories lack the specific propositions sociologists require to test them properly.[82]

Criticism of conflict theory has also been directed at its utopianism. To blame the state for all evil seems to ignore the great variety of human differences. Conflict theory also overlooks the fact that a great deal of delinquent behavior is committed by lower-class youths who target their indigent peers. Members of the lower class fear violent local gangs more than they do capitalist profiteers.

To answer its critics, conflict theory has been subdivided, branching off in new directions. One important area is liberal, radical, and Marxist **feminist theory**, which examines the relationship between sex roles, the economic system, and delinquency. (These views will be discussed in chapter 7, Gender and Delinquency.) Two other important views—left realism and peacemaking—are discussed in detail below.

LEFT REALISM

Some radical scholars are now addressing the need for the left to respond to the increasing power of right-wing conservatives. They are troubled by the emergence of a strict "law and order" philosophy, which has as its centerpiece a policy of waiving juveniles to adult court, where they may be punished more severely. At the same time, they find the focus of most left-wing scholarship—the abuse of power by the ruling elite—too narrow. It is wrong, they argue, to ignore the problems of inner-city gang crime and violence, which all too often target indigent people.[83] Those who share these concerns are referred to as **left realists**.[84]

Left realism is most often connected to the writings of British scholars John Lea and Jock Young. In their well-respected 1984 work, *What Is to Be Done about Law and Order?*, they reject the utopian views of "idealistic" Marxists who portray street criminals as revolutionaries.[85] They take the "realistic" approach that street criminals prey on the poor and disenfranchised, thus making them doubly abused, first by the capitalist system and then by members of their own class.

Lea and Young's view of crime causation borrows from conventional sociological theory and closely resembles the relative deprivation approach: Experiencing poverty in the midst of plenty creates discontent; discontent without legitimate opportunity breeds crime. As they put it, "The equation is simple: relative deprivation equals discontent; discontent plus lack of political solution equals crime."[86]

Left realists argue that crime victims in all classes need and deserve protection; crime control reflects community needs. They do not view police and the courts as inherently evil tools of capitalism whose tough tactics alienate the lower classes. These institutions would in fact offer life-saving public services if their use of force could be reduced and their sensitivity to the public increased.[87] Another approach is **preemptive deterrence** in which community organization efforts eliminate or reduce crime before it becomes necessary to employ police forces. If the number of **marginalized** youth (i.e., youth who believe that they are not part of society and have nothing to lose by committing crime) could be reduced, then delinquency rates would decline.[88]

To left realists Martin Schwartz and Walter DeKeseredy, street crime is "real"; the fear of violence among the lower classes has allowed the right wing to seize "law and order" as a political issue.[89] Gangs are not made up of "Robin Hoods," revolutionaries who steal from the rich and give to the poor. Most gang juveniles prey upon members of their own race and class and are happy to keep the proceeds for themselves. According to Schwartz and DeKeseredy, gang kids may be the "ultimate capitalists," hustling their way to obtain the coveted symbols of success.[90]

To left-realists, street crime is "real"; the fear of violence among the lower classes has allowed the right-wing to seize "law and order" as a political issue. Gangs are not made up of *Robin Hoods*," revolutionaries who steal from the rich. Most gang kids prey upon members of their own race and class and are happy to keep the proceeds for themselves. When urban rioting breaks out, it is not multinational corporations who are affected but local businesspeople who are members of the middle class.

Although the implementation of a socialist economy would help eliminate the crime problem, left realists recognize that something must be done in the meantime to control crime under the existing capitalist system. To create crime control policy, left realists welcome not only radical ideas but build upon the work of strain theorists, social ecologists, and other "mainstream" views. Community-based efforts seem to hold the most promise as crime-control techniques.

Left realism has been critiqued by radical thinkers as legitimizing the existing power structure: By supporting the existing definitions of law and justice, it suggests that the "deviant" and not the capitalist system is the root cause of society's problems. Is it not advocating the very institutions that "currently imprison us and our patterns of thought and action"? [91] In rebuttal, a left realist would charge that it is unrealistic to speak of a socialist state lacking a police force or a system of laws and justice, the criminal code does in fact represent public opinion.

PEACEMAKING

According to **peacemakers** such as Richard Quinney, human suffering has risen out of the disunity and separation that characterize postmodern society and that can be eliminated only with the "return of all sentient beings to a condition of wholeness."[92]

Peacemakers hope to promote a peaceful and just society. They draw their inspiration from a variety of religious and philosophical teachings ranging from Quakerism to Zen.

Peacemakers view the efforts of the state to punish and control delinquent youth as crime-encouraging rather than crime-discouraging. If our social, economic, and political systems could be transformed into an engine that eliminates suffering and promotes peace and justice, then crime rates would ultimately decline.

When these views were first articulated in a series of books written by Larry Tifft and Dennis Sullivan more than 15 years ago they actually received little attention.[93] In his book *The Mask of Love* Sullivan recognized the futility of correcting and punishing criminals in the context of our conflict-ridden society:

> The reality we must grasp is that we live in a culture of severed relationships, where every available institution provides a form of banishment but no place or means for people to become connected, to be responsible to and for each other.[94]

This theme of mutual aid rather than coercive punishment as the key to a harmonious society has been adopted by advocates of the peacemaking movement, who are now trying to find humanist solutions to delinquency, drug abuse, and other social problems.[95] Rather than punishment and prison, they advocate such policies as mediation and conflict resolution. Peacemakers would embrace having young offenders meet with their victims in order to understand their problems and perhaps repay them for their loss and suffering. Rather than harsh treatment and punishment, peacemakers advocate reconciliation and restitution.

LABELING, CONFLICT, AND DELINQUENCY PREVENTION

Labeling and social conflict theories have had an important influence on delinquency prevention policy during the past two decades. These theoretical models have drawn attention to the biases in the juvenile justice system and how interacting with the system can actually produce, rather than eliminate, delinquent behavior.

The system of juvenile justice began to become sensitized to the problems of labeling and stigmatization in 1967, when the consequences of a negative label were identified by the President's Commission on Law Enforcement and the Administration of Justice. In its report on juvenile delinquency, the commission stated,

> The affixing of that label [delinquency] can be a momentous occurrence in a youngster's life. Thereafter he may be watched; he may be suspect; his every misstep may be evidence of his delinquent nature. He may be excluded more and more from legitimate activities and opportunities. Soon he may be designed and dealt with as a delinquent and will find it very difficult to move into a law-abiding path even if he can overcome his own belligerent reaction and self-image and seeks to do so.[96]

These sentiments helped set the course for juvenile justice policy. National programs were created to insulate youths from the label-producing processes of the juvenile justice system. Edwin Schur, in his widely read book *Radical Nonintervention,* captured the essence of the social reaction and social conflict approach to delinquency by suggesting that even efforts to treat and rehabilitate delinquents were essentially harmful because they stigmatized youth:

> A great deal of the labeling of delinquents is socially unnecessary and counterproductive. Policies should be adopted, therefore, that accept a greater diversity in youth behavior; special delinquency laws should be exceedingly narrow in scope or else abolished completely, along with preventive efforts that single out specific individuals and programs that employ "compulsory treatment."[97]

Schur argued that the treatment orientation of the juvenile court, directed at dealing with the problems of the "whole" person, merely identified these adolescents as troubled youth who needed state aid.

As the dangers of stigmatization and labeling became known, a massive effort was made on the local, state, and federal levels to limit the interface of youths with the juvenile justice system. One approach was to divert youths from official processing channels at the time of their initial contact with police authorities. The usual practice is to have police refer youths to community treatment facilities and clinics, rather than to the juvenile court.

In a similar vein, youths who have been petitioned to juvenile court are eligible for an additional round of court-based diversion programs. For example, restitution allows juvenile offenders to pay back the victims of their crimes for the damage (or inconvenience) they have caused, instead of receiving an official delinquency label.

If a youth was found delinquent, efforts were made to reduce the stigma by using alternative sanction programs, such as boot camps and intensive probation monitoring. Alternative community-based sanctions substituted for the more heavily intrusive state training schools, a policy known as deinstitutionalization. Whenever possible, anything producing stigma was to be avoided, a philosophy of justice referred to as nonintervention.

The federal government was a prime mover in the effort to divert as many youths from the justice system as possible. The Office of Juvenile Justice and Delinquency Prevention sponsored numerous diversion and restitution programs around the nation. In addition, it made one of its most important priorities the removal of juveniles from adult jails and the discontinuance of housing status offenders and juvenile delinquents together. In sum, these programs were designed to limit, whenever possible, the juvenile's interaction with the formal justice system, to reduce stigmatization, and to make use of informal, nonpunitive treatment modalities.[98]

Although diversion and restitution continue to be widely used, the impetus for the movement seems to have waned. The philosophy of nonintervention has been criticized on several levels. First, it institutionalized a practice that had been carried out informally for years. Police officers and probation officers commonly released children they believed were deserving of a second chance, and only a small percentage of all offenders were continued through the juvenile justice process.[99] Second, many diversion program clients were young and first offenders who had been routinely released informally by the police; hard-core delinquents were not eligible for diversion programs. Consequently, the nonintervention movement actually created a whole new class of juvenile offenders who heretofore might have avoided prolonged contact with juvenile justice agencies; critics referred to this as **widening the net**.[100] Finally, evaluation of existing programs did not indicate that they could reduce the recidivism rate of clients.[101] As a result of these "failures," policy initiatives have now shifted toward greater intervention and more restrictive juvenile justice sanctions. However, many of the nonintervention programs begun in the 1970s still operate today. The following Focus on Delinquency feature describes the Youth at Risk program, which is designed to prevent delinquency, increase self-image, and reduce stigmatization—all concepts that are advocated by social reaction theories.

In the future, it may be possible that some of the idealistic programs suggested by peacemakers will be adopted, especially if the current "get tough on crime" policies prove to be expensive failures. Although it seems idealistic, mutual aid and reconciliation could replace crime control, mandatory sentencing, and the death penalty.

SUMMARY

Social reaction theories view delinquent behavior as a function of the influence that powerful members of society have on less fortunate youths. (See Table 6.1.) Two main branches of the theory are currently popular. Labeling theory views deviant behavior as a product of the deviant labels society imposes on its least powerful citizens. Deviant labels mark people as social outcasts and create barriers between them and the general social order. Eventually, deviant labels transform the offenders' personalities, so that they come to accept their new criminal or delinquent identities as personal ones.

Labeling theorists suggest that delinquent labels lock individuals out of the mainstream of society, thereby ensuring that they will commit future illegal acts to survive. Who is to be labeled and the type of labeling that occurs depend on a youth's position in the social structure. The poor and powerless are much more likely to be labeled than the wealthy and powerful.

Edwin Lemert has defined the difference between primary and secondary deviants. The former are people who cling to a conventional self-image, the latter are people who have accepted the traits implied by deviant labels bestowed on them. Howard Becker has analyzed the different forms that labeling takes with respect to the individual audience's reactions to labeling.

Relatively few studies have empirically validated the labeling perspective. Research efforts aimed at the influence of juvenile justice processing on delinquent youths fail to find that labels produce their expected damaging results. Despite the lack of empirical verification, there has been renewed interest in labeling theory because it helps explain the behavior of chronic offenders.

YOUTH AT RISK

The Youth at Risk (YAR) program was started in 1982 by the Breakthrough Foundation in San Francisco, with original project sites in Oakland and San Jose. Replication in other California cities began in 1983, and the program eventually expanded nationwide. Currently, the most active project sites are Oahu, Philadelphia, Phoenix, and San Jose.

Local YAR programs are set up as not-for-profit corporations and are run for the most part by volunteers. Typically, a local program will hire between one and three staff (which might include an executive director, a manager for the mentor program, and an administrative assistant) to administer the program.

The young people served by the YAR programs are primarily minority urban youth from disadvantaged backgrounds. A typical project site will serve 30–85 youth per year, with an average of about 50. Phoenix and Oahu, the largest programs, will soon have approximately 100 participants per year.

YAR begins with a four- to seven-day residential program in a camp setting. The camp is staffed by local volunteers and a project team from the Breakthrough Foundation, which is contracted by the local program to provide the training. The camp is an intensive experience, with course instruction, guided group discussions, and rigorous physical activities, including a one-day "ropes course." Some lectures are given, but most of the time is spent in large, interactive group discussions.

The instructional sessions focus on the young people's life experience and how it shaped any self-defeating conclusions they have reached about themselves and their futures. The objective is to help the participants reach a "breakthrough," which gives them a different view of their potential. The participants focus next on goals and aspirations and make plans for the upcoming year—for example, getting back into school, giving up violence as a way of resolving conflict, and improving relations with their parents and other family members. These action plans are a major program focus during the subsequent school year.

Back home, each YAR program designs its own follow-up activities. Usually, there are monthly group meetings and community projects, such as cleaning up graffiti or working with younger kids as peer leaders. About half of those who attend the residential program also participate during the school year.

Local volunteers serve as mentors, first as part of the residential program, then during the follow-up year. Each mentor agrees to meet or otherwise be in touch with an assigned participant three times a week. This extensive contact is essential to help the participants keep alive their new way of thinking about themselves until they internalize it. The mentors also direct youth to other people or agencies for specific help they might need (such as literacy training or drug treatment).

Parent involvement is encouraged. The local programs conduct an initial orientation for parents and a second meeting about halfway through the residential program. Typically, about half of the parents attend. Parents are also invited to attend the monthly follow-up meetings with their sons and daughters.

Evaluations of the original 10-day program, all showing positive results, have been conducted of individual programs. It should be noted, however, that the program recently has been cut back to four to seven days in order to reduce costs. These shorter programs have yet to be evaluated formally.

Source: William DeJong, *Preventing Interpersonal Violence Among Youth* (Washington, D.C.: National Institute of Justice, 1994), pp. 76–68.

Social conflict theory holds that the class conflicts present in modern society produce crime and delinquency. The law and legal systems are controlled by those in power, whose aim is to maintain their hold over society. Consequently, their activities are immune, while the deviant behaviors of the lower classes are severely punished. Delinquency occurs when lower-class juveniles rebel against the constraints placed on them by those in power. The role and economic position a youth has in our modern, postindustrial, capitalist society influences his or her delinquent behavior choices.

Labeling and social control theories have had an important effect on delinquency prevention policy. Efforts have been made to eliminate, whenever possible, the stigma of the juvenile justice system. This has meant diverting offenders before trial, limiting detention, and Deinstitutionalization. Peacemakers advocate mediation and restitution rather than punishment for delinquent acts.

TABLE 6.1 Social Reaction Theories

Theory	Major Premise	Strengths
Labeling	Youths are locked into a delinquent career when their behavior is labeled by agents of the justice system and they reorganize their identities around a deviant role.	Explains delinquent careers and the role of social control agents in sustaining deviance.
Conflict	Crime is a function of class conflict. The definition of the law is controlled by people who hold social and political power.	Accounts for class differences in the delinquency rate. Shows how class conflict influences behavior.
Left Realism	Capitalist inequality causes relative deprivation, which results in lower-class discontent and delinquency.	Recognizes that street crime is a lower-class phenomenon that victimizes the lower class.
Peacemaking	Delinquency is a result of the conflict and suffering that characterizes postmodern society.	Suggests humanist policies to reduce delinquency rates such as mediation and conflict resolution.

KEY TERMS

labeling theory
moral entreprenuers
diversion
deinstitutionalization
Howard Becker
self-fulfilling prophecy
primary deviance

secondary deviance
deviance amplification
resocialized
reflective role-taking
reflected appraisal
degradation ceremony
social conflict theory

demystification
surplus value
preemptive deterrence
marginalized
peacemakers
nonintervention
widening the net

QUESTIONS FOR DISCUSSION

1. What are some common labels used in the school setting? How can these hurt youths?
2. Can labels be beneficial to a person? What are some positive effects of labeling?
3. Is it possible to overcome labels? What methods could a person employ to counteract labels?
4. Are there laws that seem to be designed to protect the rich? Is it possible that laws are actually applied fairly?
5. Are there factors in our economy that make Marx's predictions about capitalism obsolete?
6. Discuss examples of the blind obedience we give to professionals, such as doctors, lawyers, and teachers.

NOTES

1. Charles Silberman, *Crises in the Classroom: The Remaking of American Education* (New York: Random House, 1971); idem, "Murder in the Classroom: How the Public Schools Kill Dreams and Mutilate Minds," *Atlantic* 255:82–94 (1970).
2. Richard Quinney, *The Social Reality of Crime* (Boston: Little, Brown, 1970); William Chambliss and Robert Seidman, *Law, Order, and Power* (Reading, Mass.: Addison-Wesley, 1971).
3. These sentiments are contained in some pioneering studies of police discretion, such as Nathan Goldman, *The Differential Selection of Juvenile Offenders for Court Appearance* (New York: National Council on Crime and Delinquency, 1963).

4. For a review of this position, see Anne R. Mahoney, "The Effect of Labeling upon Youths in the Juvenile Justice System: A Review of the Evidence," *Law and Society Review* 8:583–614 (1974). See also David Matza, *Becoming Deviant* (Englewood Cliffs, N.J.: Prentice-Hall, 1974).

5. The self-labeling concept originated in Edwin Lemert, *Social Pathology* (New York: McGraw-Hill, 1951). See also Frank Tannenbaum, *Crime and the Community* (Boston: Ginn, 1936).

6. Kai Erikson, "Notes on the Sociology of Deviance," *Social Problems* 10:307–14 (1962).

7. Edwin Schur, *Labeling Deviant Behavior* (New York: Harper & Row, 1972), p. 21.

8. Howard Becker, *Outsiders: Studies in the Sociology of Deviance* (New York: Macmillan, 1963), p. 9.

9. Nalini Ambady and Robert Rosenthal, "Half a Minute: Predicting Teacher Evaluations from Thin Slices of Nonverbal Behavior and Physical Attractiveness," *Journal of Personality and Social Psychology* 64:431–41 (1993).

10. Monica Harris, Richard Milich, Elizabeth Corbitt, Daniel Hoover, and Marianne Brady, "Self-Fulfilling Effects of Stigmatizing Information on Children's Social Interactions," *Journal of Personality and Social Psychology* 33:41–50 (1992).

11. Harold Garfinkel, "Conditions of Successful Degradation Ceremonies," *American Journal of Sociology* 61:420–24 (1956).

12. M.A. Bortner, *Inside a Juvenile Court: The Tarnished Ideal of Individualized Justice* (New York: University Press, 1982).

13. Edwin Lemert, *Human Deviance, Social Problems, and Social Control* (Englewood Cliffs, N.J.: Prentice-Hall, 1967), p. 15.

14. Charles H. Cooley, *Human Nature and the Social Order* (New York: Scribner, 1902).

15. Ross Matsueda, "Reflected Appraisals, Parental Labeling and Delinquency: Specifying a Symbolic Interactionist Theory," *American Journal of Sociology* 97: 1577–1611 (1992).

16. Howard Kaplan and Hiroshi Fukurai, "Negative Social Sanctions, Self-Rejection, and Drug Use," *Youth and Society* 23 (1992): 275–98.

17. Howard Kaplan, *Toward a General Theory of Deviance: Contributions from Perspectives on Deviance and Criminality* (College Station, Tex.: Texas A&M University, n.d.).

18. Harris et al., "Self-Fulfilling Effects of Stigmatizing Information on Children's Social Interactions," pp. 48–50.

19. Howard Kaplan, *Toward a General Theory of Deviance: Contributions from Perspectives on Deviance and Criminality* (College Station, Tex.: Texas A&M University, n.d.).

20. Howard Kaplan, Robert Johnson, and Carol Bailey, "Deviant Peers and Deviant Behavior: Further Elaboration of a Model," *Social Psychology Quarterly* 30 (1987): 277–84.

21. Lemert, *Social Pathology.*

22. Ibid., p. 73.

23. Ibid., p. 75.

24. Ibid.

25. Karen Heimer and Ross Matsueda, "Role-Taking, Role-Commitment and Delinquency: A Theory of Differential Social Control," *American Sociological Review* (59: 1994), pp. 400–437.

26. Karen Heimer, "Gender, Race, and the Pathways to Delinquency: An Interactionist Explanation," in John Hagan and Ruth Peterson, eds., *Crime and Inequality* (Stanford, Calif.: Stanford University Press, 1995).

27. Tannenbaum, *Crime and the Community.*

28. Ibid., p. 27.

29. Aaron Cicourel, *The Social Organization of Juvenile Justice* (New York: Wiley, 1968).

30. Matza, *Becoming Deviant.*

31. Ibid., p. 78.

32. Stanton Wheeler and Leonard Cottrell, "Juvenile Delinquency: Its Prevention and Control," in Donald Cressey and David Ward, eds., *Delinquency, Crime, and Social Processes* (New York: Harper & Row, 1969), p. 609.

33. Garfinkel, "Conditions of Successful Degradation Ceremonies," p. 424.

34. Ross Matsueda, "Reflected Appraisals: Parental Labeling, and Delinquency: Specifying a Symbolic Interactionist Theory," *American Journal of Sociology* 97:1577–1611 (1992).

35. See, generally, Carl Pope, "Race and Crime Revisited," *Crime and Delinquency* 25:347–57 (1979).

36. Carl Pope and William Feyerherm, "Minority Status and Juvenile Justice Processing," *Criminal Justice Abstracts* 22:327–36 (1990).

37. Nathan Goldman, *The Differential Selection of Juvenile Offenders for Court Appearance* (New York: National Council on Crime and Delinquency, 1963).

38. Carl Pope, "Juvenile Crime and Justice," in Brian Forst, ed., *The Socio-economics of Crime and Justice* (New York: M. E. Sharpe, 1993), pp. 11–26.

39. See, for example, William Wilbanks, *The Myth of a Racist Criminal Justice System* (Monterey, Calif.; Brooks-Cole, 1987).

40. Merry Morash, "Establishment of a Juvenile Police Record," *Criminology* 22:97–111 (1984).

41. Paul Lipsett, "The Juvenile Offender's Perception," *Crime and Delinquency* 14:49 (1968).

42. Eloise Snyder, "The Impact of the Juvenile Court Hearing on the Child," *Crime and Delinquency* 17:180–82 (1971).

43. Gary Jensen, "Labeling and Identity," *Criminology* 18:121–29 (1980).

44. For a similar view, see Suzanne Ageton and Delbert Elliot, "The Effect of Legal Processing on Self-Concept" (Institute of Behavioral Science, University of Colorado, 1973); see also Anne R. Mahoney, "The Effect of Label-

ing upon Youths in the Juvenile Justice System: A Review of the Evidence," *Law and Society Review* 8:583–614 (1974). For an opposing view, see John Hepburn, "The Impact of Police Intervention upon Juvenile Delinquents," *Criminology* 15:235–62 (1977).

45. Richard Anson and Carol Eason, "The Effects of Confinement on Delinquent Self-Image," *Juvenile and Family Court Journal* 37:39–47 (1986); Gerald O'Connor, "The Effect of Detention upon Male Delinquency," *Social Problems* 18:194–97 (1970); David Street, Robert Vintner, and Charles Perrow, *Organization for Treatment* (New York: Free Press, 1966); Jack Foster, Simon Dinitz, and Walter Reckless, "Perception of Stigma Following Public Intervention for Delinquent Behavior," *Social Problems* 20:202 (1972).

46. Charles Thomas and Donna Bishop, "The Effect of Formal and Informal Sanctions on Delinquency: A Longitudinal Comparison of Labeling and Deterrence Theory," *Journal of Criminal Law and Criminology* 75:1222–45 (1984).

47. Stanley Cohen, *Visions of Social Control* (Cambridge, Mass.: Polity Press, 1985).

48. Schur, *Labeling Delinquent Behavior,* p. 14.

49. Ronald Akers, "Problems in the Sociology of Deviance," *Social Forces* 46:463 (1968).

50. Peter Manning, "On Deviance," *Contemporary Sociology* 2:697–99 (1973).

51. Charles Tittle and Debra Curran, "Contingencies for Dispositional Disparities in Juvenile Justice," *Social Forces* 67:23–58 (1988).

52. Charles Wellford, "Labeling Theory and Criminology: An Assessment," *Social Problems* 22:335–347 (1975), at p. 337.

53. David Bordua, "On Deviance," *Annals* 312: 121–23 (1969).

54. Wellford, "Labeling Theory and Criminology."

55. Ibid., p. 337.

56. Charles Murray and Louis Cox, *Beyond Probation* (Beverly Hills, Calif.: Sage, 1979).

57. Raymond Paternoster and Leeann Iovanni, "The Labeling Perspective and Delinquency: An Elaboration of the Theory and an Assessment of the Evidence," *Justice Quarterly* 6:358–94 (1989).

58. Lening Zhang, "The Severity of Official Punishment for Delinquency and Change in Interpersonal Relations in Chinese Society," *Journal of Research in Crime and Delinquency* 31:416–33 (1994); idem, "Peers' Rejection as a Possible Consequence of Official Reaction to Delinquency in Chinese Society," *Criminal Justice and Behavior* 21:387–402 (1994).

59. Douglas Smith and Robert Brame, "On the Initiation and Continuation of Delinquency," *Criminology* 4:607–30 (1994).

60. Charles Tittle, "Two Empirical Regularities (Maybe) in Search of an Explanation: Commentary on the Age/Crime Debate," *Criminology* 26:75–85 (1988).

61. Gresham Sykes, "The Rise of Critical Criminology," *Journal of Criminal Law and Criminology* 65:211–17 (1974).

62. See, for example, Dennis Sullivan, Larry Tifft, and Larry Siegel, "Criminology, Science and Politics," in Emilio Viano, ed., *Criminal Justice Research* (Lexington, Mass.: Lexington Books, 1978), pp. 5–11.

63. Ibid., p. 10.

64. Robert Meier, "The New Criminology: Continuity in Criminological Theory," *Journal of Criminal Law and Criminology* 67 (1977): 461–69 at 463.

65. Walter DeKeseredy and Martin Schwartz, *Contemporary Criminology* (Belmont, Calif.: Wadsworth, 1996), pp. 77.

66. The ideas in this section are taken in part from C. D. Kerning, ed., *Marxism, Communism, and Western Society,* vol. 5 (New York: Herden and Herden, 1972), pp. 342–60.

67. Meier, "The New Criminology," p. 463.

68. Sykes, "The Rise of Critical Criminology," pp. 211–13.

69. Ibid.

70. Ibid.

71. Sullivan, Tifft, and Siegel, "Criminology, Science, and Politics," p. 11

72. See, for example, Kathleen Daly and Meda Chesney-Lind, "Feminism and Criminology," *Justice Quarterly* 5:497–538 (1988); see also K. Daly, *Gender, Crime and Punishment* (New Haven, Conn.: Yale University Press, 1994).

73. Ibid.

74. Robert Gordon, "Capitalism, Class, and Crime in America," *Crime and Delinquency* 19:174 (1973).

75. Richard Quinney, *Class, State and Crime* (New York: Longman, 1977), p. 52.

76. Anthony Platt, "The Triumph of Benevolence: The Origins of the Juvenile Justice System in the United States," in Richard Quinney, ed., *Criminal Justice in America: A Critical Understanding* (Boston: Little, Brown, 1974), p. 367. See also Anthony Platt, *The Child Savers* (Chicago: University of Chicago Press, 1969).

77. Barry Krisberg and James Austin, *Children of Ishmael* (Palo Alto, Calif.: Mayfield, 1978), p. 2.

78. Herman Schwendinger and Julia Schwendinger, "Delinquency and Social Reform: A Radical Perspective," in *Juvenile Justice,* ed. Lamar Empey (Charlottesville: University of Virginia Press, 1979), pp. 246–90.

79. Ibid., p. 252.

80. David Greenberg, "Delinquency and the Age Structure of Crime," in *Crime and Capitalism* (Palo Alto, Calif.: Mayfield, 1981), pp. 118–39.

81. Carl Klockars, "The Contemporary Crises of Marxist Criminology," in James Inciardi, ed., *Radical Criminology: The Coming Crisis* (Beverly Hills, Calif.: Sage, 1980), pp. 92–123.

82. Alan Horowitz, "Marxist Theory of Deviance and Teleology: A Critique of Spitzer," *Social Problems* 24:362 (1977).

83. Anthony Platt, "Criminology in the 1980s: Progressive Alternatives to 'Law and Order,'" *Crime and Social Justice* 21–22: 191–99 (1985).

84. See, generally, Roger Matthews and Jock Young, eds., *Confronting Crime* (London: Sage, 1986); for a thorough review of left realism, see Martin Schwartz and Walter DeKeseredy, "Left Realist Criminology: Strengths, Weaknesses and the Feminist Critique," *Crime, Law and Social Change* 15: 51–72 (1991).

85. John Lea and Jock Young, *What Is to Be Done about Law and Order?* (Harmondsworth, England: Penguin, 1984).

86. Ibid., p. 88.

87. Richard Kinsey, John Lea, and Jock Young, *Losing the Fight against Crime* (London: Blackwell, 1986).

88. DeKeseredy and Schwartz, *Contemporary Criminology*, p. 249.

89. Martin Schwartz and Walter DeKeseredy, "Left Realist Criminology: Strengths, Weaknesses and the Feminist Critique," *Crime, Law and Social Change* 15 (1991): 51–72.

90. Ibid., p. 54.

91. Schwartz and DeKeseredy, "Left Realist Criminology," p. 58.

92. Richard Quinney, "The Way of Peace: On Crime, Suffering, and Service," in Harold Pepinsky and Richard Quinney, eds., *Criminology as Peacemaking* (Bloomington: Indiana University Press, 1991), pp. 8–9.

93. See for example, Larry Tifft and Dennis Sullivan, *The Struggle to Be Human: Crime, Criminology and Anarchism* (Orkney Islands, Over-the-Water-Sanday: Cienfuegos Press, 1979); Dennis Sullivan, *The Mask of Love* (Port Washington, N.Y.: Kennikat Press, 1980).

94. Ibid., p. 141.

95. Pepinsky and Quinney, *Criminology as Peacemaking*.

96. President's Commission on Law Enforcement and the Administration of Justice, *Task Force Report: Juvenile Delinquency and Youth Crime* (Washington, D.C.: Government Printing Office, 1967), p. 43.

97. Edwin Schur, *Radical Nonintervention* (Englewood Cliffs, N.J.: Prentice-Hall, 1973), p. 88.

98. Malcolm Klein, "Deinstitutionalization and Diversion of Juvenile Offenders: A Litany of Impediments," in Norval Morris and Michael Tonry, eds., *Crime and Justice,* vol. 1 (Chicago: University of Chicago Press, 1979).

99. LaMar Empey, "Revolution and Counter Revolution: Current Trends in Juvenile Justice," in David Shichor and Delos Kelly, eds., *Critical Issues in Juvenile Delinquency* (Lexington, Mass.: Lexington Books, 1980), pp. 157–82.

100. James Austin and Barry Krisberg, "The Unmet Promise of Alternatives to Incarceration," *Crime and Delinquency* 28:3–19 (1982).

101. William Selke, "Diversion and Crime Prevention," *Criminology* 20:395–406 (1982).

PART THREE

ENVIRONMENTAL INFLUENCES ON DELINQUENCY

Children's gender relations, their interactions with parents, peers, schools, and substance abuse are all thought to exert a powerful influence on their involvement in delinquent activities. Kids who fail at home, at school, and in the neighborhood are considered prone to sustaining delinquent careers over the life course. Research indicates that chronic, persistent offenders are the ones most likely to experience educational failure, poor home life, and unsatisfactory peer relations.

These social relationships are certainly not simple ones and are subject to different interpretations. For example, there may be little question that educational underachievement is related to delinquency, but significant disagreement exists over the cause and direction of the relationship. A conflict theorist might view children's school failure as a consequence of class conflict and discrimination. A biosocial theorist may view it as a function of learning disabilities or neurological dysfunction. Although both experts conclude that children who do poorly in school are among the most likely to violate the law, their explanations are markedly different.

Beyond their theoretical importance, the family, the school, and the peer group occupy significant positions in daily social life. They can help insulate a child from delinquency or encourage illegal activities. Many delinquency prevention efforts focus on improving family relations, supporting educational achievement, and reducing substance abuse. If the family is believed to be a cause of delinquency, family counseling and therapy may be used to prevent delinquency. Similarly, gang control efforts have been made to counteract the influence of peer group toward delinquency.

Part III contains five chapters devoted to the influences critical social forces have on delinquency. Chapter 7 explores gender relations and their relationship to delinquency. Chapter 8 is devoted to the family. Chapter 9 focuses on the peer group and gangs; Chapter 10 examines the relationship between education and delinquency; and Chapter 11 concerns substance abuse. Among the special topics considered are: child abuse and neglect, school-based crime, gang control efforts, and the relationship between delinquency and drug abuse.

INTRODUCTION

There is little argument that significant gender differences in the delinquency rate exist: Males are much more likely than females to engage in repeat and serious offending. Official statistics show that females are arrested far less often than males and then for relatively minor offenses; correctional data show that about 95 percent of incarcerated inmates are males.

Nor is this relationship a recent occurrence. To early criminologists, the female offender was an aberration who engaged in crimes that usually had a sexual connotation—prostitution, running away (which presumably leads to sexual misadventure), engaging in premarital sex, incorrigibility, and, later, crimes of sexual passion (killing a boyfriend or husband).[1] Delinquency experts often ignored female offenders, assuming either that they rarely violated the law or that, if they did, their illegal acts were status-type offenses. Female delinquency was viewed as moral, emotional, or family related, and such problems were not a concern of traditional criminologists. In fact, the few "true" female delinquents were considered aberrations whose criminal or delinquent activity was a function of their abandoning accepted feminine roles and taking on masculine characteristics, a concept referred to as the **"masculinity hypothesis."**[2]

Because female delinquency was considered unimportant, most early theories of delinquency focused on male misconduct and were tested with samples of male delinquents. Quite often these models did not adequately explain gender differences in the delinquency rate. For example, strain theory (see chapter 4) holds that delinquency results from the failure to achieve socially desirable material goals. Using this logic, females should be more criminal than males because they face *gender discrimination,* a barrier to success unknown to males. Some criminologists take these anomalies as an indication that theoretical explanations of male criminality do not apply to females and that separate explanations for male and female delinquency are required.[3]

CHANGING CONCEPTS OF GENDER

Changing times have brought with them a growing interest in gender and delinquency. Although the female delinquency rate is still much lower than the male rate, it is growing at a faster pace. In addition, there seem to be few gender differences in *crime patterns:* larceny and aggravated assault, the crimes for which most males are arrested for (as measured by the Uniform Crime Reports), are also the ones for which most females are arrested.

Conceptions of gender differences have also been altered. A feminist approach to understanding crime is now firmly established. The stereotype of the female delinquent as a purely sexual deviant is no longer taken seriously.[4] The result has been an increased effort to conduct gender-related research in order to adequately understand and explain differences in male and female offending patterns.

This chapter provides an overview of gender factors in delinquency. It first discusses some of the gender differences in development and offending patterns. It then turns to a more detailed discussion of the explanations of these differences, referred to here as the (1) trait view, (2) socialization view, (3) liberal feminist view, and (4) radical feminist view.

GENDER DIFFERENCES IN DEVELOPMENT

Research on the developmental differences between adolescent males and females is a relatively new area of study. But from the information now available it is possible to see that (a) gender differences in socialization and development do exist and that (b) these differences may in fact have an effect on juvenile offending patterns.[5]

SOCIALIZATION DIFFERENCES

Research shows that there are still many significant differences in the ways females and males are socialized, which affect their development. While males learn to value separation and independence, females are taught that their self-worth depends on their ability to sustain relationships. Girls therefore run the risk of losing themselves in relationships with others while boys may experience a chronic sense of alienation. Yet because so many personal and romantic relationships go sour, females run the risk of feeling alienated and strained because of their failure to achieve relational success.[6]

Girls are socialized to be less aggressive than boys; they are supervised more closely by parents.[7] They learn to respond to provocation by feeling anxious and depressed while boys learn to retaliate.[8] Although females get angry as often as males, many have been taught to blame themselves for harboring such negative feelings. Females are socialized to fear that their anger will harm valued relationships; males are socialized to react with "moral outrage," looking to blame others for their discomfort.[9] Females are much more likely than males to respond to anger with feelings of depression, anxiety, fear, and shame.[10]

Females are more likely than males to be the target of sexual and physical abuse. Female victims have been shown to suffer more seriously from such abuse, sustaining long-term damage to self-image; victims of sexual abuse find it difficult to build autonomy and life skills.

COGNITIVE DIFFERENCES

Measurable cognitive differences also exist between adolescent males and females. Girls have been found to be superior to boys in verbal ability; boys test higher in visual-spatial performance. Girls acquire language sooner, learning to speak earlier and faster with better pronunciation. Girls are far less likely to have reading problems than boys. Boys, on the other hand, do much better on standardized math tests, attributed by some experts to their strategies for approaching math problems. In most cases, cognitive differences are small, narrowing, and usually attributed to cultural expectations. When given training, girls increase visual-spatial skills, making their abilities indistinguishable from those of the boys.

PERSONALITY DIFFERENCES

Girls are often stereotyped as talkative, but research shows that males in many situations spend more time talking than females. While females are more willing to reveal their feelings, males are more likely to introduce new topics and interrupt conversations. Girls are more likely than boys to express concern for

Research shows that girls are more willing to reveal their feelings than boys and more likely to express concern for the well-being of others. They are more concerned about finding the "meaning of life" and less interested in competing for material success. While males learn to value separation and independence, females are taught that their self-worth depends on their ability to sustain relationships with others.

the well-being of others. They are more concerned about finding the "meaning of life" and less interested in competing for material success.[11]

Adolescent females use different knowledge and have different ways of knowing when trying to understand their lives and interactions with others. These gender differences in achieving self-understanding may later affect self-esteem and self-concept. Research shows that as adolescents develop through the life course, males continually raise their self-esteem and self-concept whereas females find their self-confidence lowered.[12]

WHAT CAUSES GENDER DIFFERENCES?

What causes these gender differences to occur? Some experts suggest that the reason may be neurological. Males and females have somewhat different brain organizations: Females are more "left brain" oriented, and males are more "right brain" oriented (the left brain is believed to control language and the right spatial relations). Some point to the hormonal and biochemical differences between the sexes as the key to understanding their behavior.

A third view is that gender differences are a result of the interaction of socialization, learning, and enculturation. Boys and girls may behave differently because they have been exposed to different styles of socialization, different values, and different cultural experiences. It follows then that if members of both sexes were treated evenly and equally exposed to the factors that produce delinquency, their delinquency rates would be equivalent.[13]

Gender Identity   Another explanation of gender differences, referred to as **gender-schema theory,** recognizes the different socialization process of males and females. According to psychologist Sandra Bem, our culture polarizes males and females by forcing them to obey mutually exclusive gender roles or **scripts.** Girls are expected to be "feminine": tender, sympathetic, understanding, and gentle. In contrast, boys are expected to be "masculine": assertive, forceful, competitive, and dominant. Children internalize these scripts and accept gender polarization as normal behavior. Children's self-esteem becomes wrapped up in how closely their behavior conforms to the proper sex role stereotype. When children begin to perceive themselves as either a *boy* or a *girl* (which occurs at about age three) they actively search for information that helps them define their role; they begin to learn what behavior is and is not appropriate for their sex.[14] Girls are expected to behave according to the appropriate "script" and seek approval of their behavior (i.e., Are they acting as a girl should at that age?). In contrast, male "scripts" show that aggressive behavior may be rewarded with peer approval while sensitivity is viewed as nonmasculine.[15]

GENDER DIFFERENCES AND DELINQUENCY

There appears then to be measurable differences in the personality, cognitive ability, and socialization of males and females. These distinctions may explain in part the significant gender differences in delinquency rates. Males seem more aggressive and assertive and less likely to form attachments to others, factors that might increase their participation in crime. Females are more verbally proficient, a skill that may help them deal with conflict without resorting to violence. Females view aggression as a lack of self-control; males view aggression as an appropriate way to gain status and power.[16]

Cognitive and personality differences are magnified when, at an early age, children begin to internalize gender-specific behaviors. Boys unwilling to be tough and aggressive are labeled "sissies" and "crybabies." In contrast, girls are expected to form close bonds with their friends and share feelings. Recent research by Stacey Nofziger finds that one's grasp of his or her gender identity is the most important predictor of intersex differences in the delinquency rate: Members of both sexes who identify with "masculine traits," such as dominance and forcefulness, are more likely to engage in delinquent acts than those who admire "feminine traits," such as affection and compassion. Because boys are more likely to identify with masculine traits, their crime rates are higher. Sex may only affect delinquency, Nofziger concludes, to the extent that females learn to be "feminine" and males "masculine."[17]

GENDER PATTERNS IN DELINQUENCY

Although overall gender differences in the delinquency rate remain significant, over the past decade females have increased their participation in delinquent behaviors at a faster rate than males. For example, between 1990 and 1994 the teenage male arrest rate increased about 19 percent while the teenage female rate increased almost 31 percent.[18] A greater proportion of females are now becoming involved in the most serious offenses, including murder, armed robbery, and aggravated assault.[19] Between 1990 and 1994 female arrests for serious violent crimes increased 48 percent while male arrests increased just 23 percent.

The patterns of male and female criminality also appear to be converging. Self-report data indicate that the rank orderings of male and female delinquency are quite similar: The illegal acts most common for boys—committing petty larceny, using a false ID, and smoking marijuana—are also the most common ones for girls.

FIGURE 7.1
Gender differences in homicide

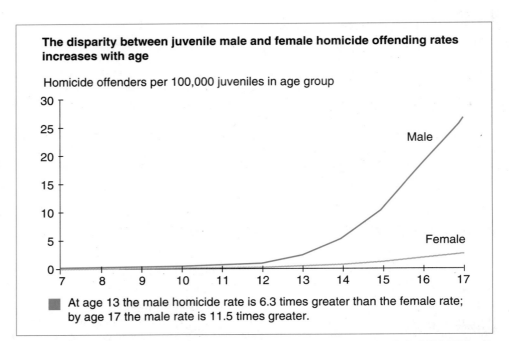

The disparity between juvenile male and female homicide offending rates increases with age

Homicide offenders per 100,000 juveniles in age group

At age 13 the male homicide rate is 6.3 times greater than the female rate; by age 17 the male rate is 11.5 times greater.

Source: Howard Snyder and Melissa Sickmund, *Juvenile Offenders and Victims* (Washington, D.C.: OJJDP, 1995) p. 5.

Violent Behavior

If men were to relinquish the ideal that aggression is a legitimate means of social coercion and a source of status, a range of social problems from schoolyard bullying and domestic violence to terrorism and international conflicts might be brought under control.[20]

Although gender differences in the overall delinquency rate may be converging, there is little question that males continue to be overrepresented in arrests for the most violent crimes. For example, almost all homicide offenders (90 percent) are males.[21] Moreover, while homicide rates increase throughout adolescence, the increase for males is significantly higher than that for females (see Figure 7.1).

There are also gender-related differences in why and how children engage in extreme violence. The typical male juvenile kills a friend or acquaintance with a handgun (67 percent) during an argument. In contrast, the typical female is as likely to kill a family member (41 percent) as a friend or acquaintance (46 percent) and is more likely to use a knife (32 percent) than a male. Both males and females tend to kill males, generally, their brothers, fathers, and friends.

Why do these differences occur and why are girls increasing their involvement in most delinquent activities at a faster pace than boys? There are a number of views on which the remainder of this chapter will focus.

TRAIT VIEWS

There has been a long tradition of tracing the onset of gender differences in the delinquency rate to physical and mental traits that are either uniquely male or female.

HISTORICAL FOUNDATION

The argument that biological and psychological differences in males and females can explain differences in their crime rates is not a new one. The earliest criminologists such as Cesare Lombroso focused their attention on physical characteristics believed to be precursors of crime. Lombroso's concept of the "born criminal" rested upon male-oriented physical and mental traits such as extraordinary strength and agility, lack of emotion, and insensibility to pain. In contrast, female delinquents were viewed as bizarre aberrations. Because the female crime rate was so low and most girls were not delinquents, girls whose behavior deviated from what was considered appropriate for females were believed to be inherently evil or physically maladapted.

The Female Offender With the publication in 1895 of his book *The Female Offender,* Lombroso (with William Ferrero) extended his pioneering work on criminality to include females.[22] Lombroso maintained that women were lower on the evolutionary scale than men, more childlike, less sensitive, and less intelligent.[23] Women who committed crimes (most often prostitution and other sex-related offenses) could be distinguished from "normal" women by physical characteristics—excessive body hair, wrinkles, crow's-feet, and an abnormal cranium, for example.[24] In physical appearance, delinquent females appeared closer both to criminal and noncriminal men than to other women. The *masculinity hypothesis* suggested that delinquent girls have excessive male characteristics.[25]

Lombroso's suggestion that women were lower on the evolutionary scale than men is puzzling because he viewed atavism or primitivism as the key element in producing criminal behavior, yet the crime rate of females is lower than that of males. Lombroso explained this apparent inconsistency by arguing that most girls are restrained from committing delinquent acts by such counterbalancing traits as "piety, maternity, want of passion, sexual coldness, weakness, and undeveloped intelligence."[26] The delinquent female lacks these counterbalancing traits, according to Lombroso, and is therefore "unrestrained in her childlike, unreasoned passions." Lombroso also believed that much female delinquency is masked and hidden.

Lombroso did recognize, however, that there were far fewer female than male delinquents. He suggested that this was a function of the relative homogeneity and uniformity among females; the female "born criminal" was indeed a rare creature. But he also believed that in those cases when a girl did become a delinquent, her behavior might be even more vicious than that of males.[27]

Lombroso's early work on the physical abnormalities of deviant girls portrayed female offenders as suffering from weak egos, abnormal or impulsive personalities, and other psychological problems. Another theme, begun by Lombroso, was that female delinquency was almost always linked to abnormal biological traits.

Lombroso's Influence Lombrosian thought had a significant influence on how the female delinquent was viewed for much of the twentieth century. Delinquency rate differentials were explained in terms of gender-based physical differences. For example, Cyril Burt in 1925 linked female delinquency to menstruation.[28] Similarly, William Healy and Augusta Bronner's research suggested that males' physical superiority enhanced their criminality. Their research showed that about 70 percent of the delinquent girls they studied had abnormal, masculine weight and size characteristics, a finding that supported the "masculinity hypothesis."[29] In a later work (1950), *The Criminality of Women,* Otto Pollak linked the onset of female criminality to the impact of biological conditions: **menstruation, pregnancy,** and **menopause**[30]:

> Thefts, particularly shoplifting, arson, homicide, and resistance against public officials seem to show a significant correlation between the menstruation of the offender and the time of the offense. The turmoil of the onset of menstruation and the puberty of girls appears to express itself in the relatively high frequency of false accusations and—where cultural opportunities permit—of incendiarism. Pregnancy in its turn is a crime-promoting influence with regard to attacks against the life of the fetus and the newborn. The menopause finally seems to bring about a distinct increase in crime, especially in offenses resulting from irritability such as arson, breaches of the peace, perjury, and insults.[31]

Pollak argued that most female delinquency goes unrecorded because the female is the instigator, rather than the perpetrator, of illegal behavior.[32] He suggested that females first use their sexuality to instigate crime and then beguile males in the justice system to obtain deferential treatment. This observation is referred to as the **chivalry hypothesis,** which holds that gender differences in the delinquency rate can be explained by the fact that female criminality is overlooked or forgiven by male agents of the criminal justice system. Those who believe in the chivalry hypothesis point to data that show that although women make up about 20 percent of all arrestees, they account for less than 5 percent of all inmates.

EARLY PSYCHOLOGICAL EXPLANATIONS

As was the case with biology, early psychologists viewed the physical differences between males and females as a basis for their behavior differentials. Sigmund Freud maintained that girls view their lack of a penis as a sign that they have been punished. Boys fear that they also can be punished by having their penis cut off and thus learn to fear women. From this conflict comes **penis envy** and the girl's wish to become a boy. Penis envy often produces an inferiority complex in girls, forcing them to make an effort to compensate for their defect. One way is to identify with their mother and accept a maternal role as wife and child bearer. Also, girls may attempt to compensate for their lack of a penis by becoming narcissistic—dressing well and beautifying themselves.[33]

Freud also claimed that if a young girl does not overcome her penis envy, neurotic episodes may follow:

> If a little girl persists in her first wish—to grow into a boy—in extreme cases she will end as a manifest homosexual, and otherwise she will exhibit markedly masculine traits in the conduct of her later life, will choose a masculine vocation, and so on.[34]

Freud's concept of penis envy has been strongly questioned by more modern psychoanalysts, who scoff at the notion that little girls feel inferior to little boys and charge that Freud's thinking was influenced by the sexist culture in which he lived.[35]

At mid-century, psychodynamic theorists suggested that girls are socialized to be passive and need affection, which helps to explain their low crime rate. However, this personality condition also makes some females susceptible to being manipulated by men, hence, their participation in sex-related crimes, such as prostitution. A girl's wayward behavior, psychoanalysts suggested, was restricted to neurotic theft (kleptomania) and to overt sexual acts, which were a symptom of some unresolved personality maladaption.[36]

FIGURE 7.2
Trait differences in male and female delinquents

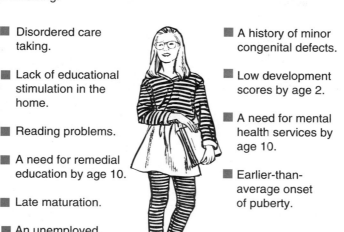

A longitudinal study that followed children born on the Hawaiian island of Kauai in 1955 for 32 years found that the most reliable traits for predicting delinquency in boys included the following:

- Disordered care taking.

- Lack of educational stimulation in the home.

- Reading problems.

- A need for remedial education by age 10.

- Late maturation.

- An unemployed, criminal, or absent father.

In addition, boys appeared to be partic-ularly vulnerable to early childhood learn-ing problems, leading to school failure. A combination of reaching puberty late and lack of a significant male role model also encouraged the persistence of antisocial behavior through adolescence.

In the same longitudinal study, researchers found that delinquent girls then to have the following traits:

- A history of minor congenital defects.

- Low development scores by age 2.

- A need for mental health services by age 10.

- Earlier-than-average onset of puberty.

Researchers hypothesize that birth defects and slow early development could lead to poor self-esteem, while early sexual development may encourage sexual relationships with older males and conflict with parents.

Source: Felton Earls and Albert Reiss, *Breaking the Cycle: Predicting and Preventing Crime* (Washington, D.C.: National Institute of Justice, 1994), pp. 24–25.

According to these early versions of the psychoanalytic approach, gender differences in the delinquency rate can be traced to differences in psychological orientation. Male delinquency reflects aggressive personality traits, while female delinquency reflects their psychosexual development, a function of repressed sexuality, gender conflict, and abnormal socialization.

CONTEMPORARY TRAIT VIEWS

Contemporary biosocial and psychological theorists have continued the tradition of explaining gender differences in delinquency by reason of physical and emotional traits (see Figure 7.2). These more contemporary views recognize that it is the *interaction* of the physical and the psychological with the social environment that produces delinquency.[37]

GUARDIANS OF VIRTUE

The view that female delinquency is sexual in nature and that the great majority of female delinquents' troubles can be linked to their sexual precociousness influenced the treatment of young female offenders in the first juvenile courts. Mary Odem and Steven Schlossman explored this "sexualization" of female delinquency in their study of all girls (n = 220) petitioned to the Los Angeles Juvenile Court in a single year, 1920.

Odem and Schlossman argue that in the first decades of the twentieth century, delinquency "experts" identified young female "sex delinquents" as a major social problem that required a forceful public response. There was concern about a rise in illicit sexual activity among young working-class females. This rise was in part a by-product of newfound freedoms enjoyed by girls after the turn of the century. Young females were getting jobs in stores and offices, where they were more likely to meet eligible young men. Recreation venues now included dance halls, movie theaters, beaches, and amusement parks—areas fraught with opportunities for "sexual experimentation." Civic leaders concerned about immorality mounted a campaign that identified the "sex delinquent" as a moral and sexual threat to American society and advocated a policy of eugenics—sterilization to prevent these inferior individuals from having children.

The juvenile justice system also responded to this "epidemic" of sexuality affecting the Los Angeles lower-class female population. At first, to prevent "moral ruin," female civic leaders and social workers campaigned for special attention to be given to female delinquency. Los Angeles responded by hiring the first female police officers in the nation to deal with girls under arrest and female judges to hear girls' cases in juvenile court. The city also developed a nationally recognized female detention center and a girl's reformatory.

The first female officer in the country was Alice Stebbins Wells, appointed on September 13, 1910. A social worker,

Wells argued that she could better serve her clients if she had full police powers. She and her fellow female officers inspected dance halls, cafes, theaters, and other public places of amusement to ferret out girls who were in danger of moral ruin, sending some home and bringing the incorrigible to the detention center.

Female "referees" were appointed to hear cases involving girls, and female probation officers were assigned to supervise them. The influx of new cases prompted the county to open custodial institutions for girls, including the El Retiro School, which was considered the latest in modern rehabilitative treatment.

When Odem and Schlossman evaluated the juvenile court records of delinquent girls who entered the Los Angeles Juvenile Court in 1920, they found that the majority were petitioned for either suspected sexual activity or behavior that placed them at risk of sexual relations. Despite the limited seriousness of these charges, the majority of girls were detained prior to trial, and while in Juvenile Hall, all were given a compulsory pelvic exam. Girls adjudged sexually delinquent on the basis of the exam were segregated from the merely incorrigible girls to prevent moral corruption. Those testing positive for venereal disease were confined in Juvenile Hall Hospital, usually for one to three months.

After trial, *29 percent* of these female adolescents were committed to custodial institutions—a high price to pay for moral transgressions. Although society was undergoing a sexual revolution, the juvenile court seemed wedded to a philosophy of controlling "immoral" young women, a policy that was to last more than 30 years.

Source: Mary Odem and Steven Schlossman, "Guardians of Virtue: The Juvenile Court and Female Delinquency in Early 20th-Century Los Angeles," *Crime and Delinquency* 37:186–203 (1991).

PRECOCIOUS SEXUALITY

Early theorists linked female sexuality and delinquency to the effects of early or **precocious sexuality.** According to this view, girls who experience an early onset of physical maturity are most likely to engage in antisocial behavior. Sheldon Glueck and Eleanor Glueck found that the 500 delinquent girls in their sample engaged in sexual relations at an early age.[38] In their 1968 work, *Delinquency in Girls,* Cowie, Cowie, and Slater also linked female delinquency to precocious sexuality. Female delinquents were typically promiscuous, considered deviant in a way that required a "more advanced degree of maturation than the (mainly nonsexual) delinquencies of the boys."[39]

Equating female delinquency with sexuality was responsible in part for the view that female delinquency is symptomatic of maladjustment and social isolation.[40] The female delinquent was considered an emotionally disturbed product of a family which failed to provide adequate nurturing. Isolated and alone, the female delinquent substituted sex for love and security. This conclusion had a profound influence on the judicial processing of delinquent girls during much of the twentieth century. The following "Focus on Delinquency" discusses one study that uncovered this "sexualization" of female delinquency.

Although equating female delinquency with sexual activity alone is no longer taken seriously, empirical evidence suggests that girls who reach puberty at an early age are in fact at the highest risk for delinquency.[41] One reason, according to research by Avshalom Caspi, is that "early bloomers" may be more attractive to older adolescent boys and increased contact with this high-risk group places them in jeopardy for antisocial behavior. The delinquency gap between "early" and "late" bloomers narrows when the latter group of girls reach sexual maturity and increase their exposure to boys.[42] The Caspi research is important because it shows how biological and social factors interact to postpone or accelerate delinquent activity, an issue discussed in the following Case in Point.

CASE IN POINT

As the principal of a Northeast junior high school, you get a call from a parent who is disturbed because he has heard a rumor that the student literary digest that the students plan to publish contains a story with a sexual theme. The work is written by a junior high school girl who became pregnant during the year and underwent an abortion. You ask for and receive a copy of the narrative.

The girl's theme is actually a cautionary tale of young love that results in an unwanted pregnancy. The author details her abusive home life, which led her to engage in an intimate relationship with another student; her pregnancy; her conflict with her parents; her decision to abort; and the emotional turmoil that the incident created. She tells students to use contraception if they are sexually active and recommends appropriate types of birth control. There is nothing provocative or sexually explicit in the work.

Some teachers argue that the students should not be allowed to read this material because it has a sexual content from which they must be protected, and that in a sense it encourages students to defy parental authority. Also, some parents may object to a story about precocious sexuality because they fear that it may encourage their children to "experiment." In addition, some believe that such behavior is linked to delinquency and drug abuse. Those who advocate publication believe that students have a right to read about such important issues and decide their own course of action. Censorship would also be a violation of the author's First Amendment rights.

Should you force the story's deletion because its theme is essentially sexually explicit?

HORMONAL DIFFERENCES

As you may recall from chapter 3, some biosocial theorists link antisocial behavior to hormonal influences.[43] The argument is that male sex hormones (**androgens**) account for their more aggressive behavior and that gender-related hormonal differences can also explain the gender gap in delinquency.[44]

Gender differences in the crime rate then may be a function of androgen levels because these hormones cause areas of the brain to become less sensitive to environmental stimuli. This in turn makes males more likely to seek high levels of stimulation and to tolerate more pain in the process,[45] thus making them more likely to commit crimes. Androgens are also linked to brain seizures, which result in greater emotional volatility, especially when the individual is under stress. Some experts believe that androgens affect the brain structure itself (the left hemisphere of the neocortex), effectively reducing sympathetic feelings toward others that help to inhibit the urge to victimize.[46]

A great deal of research has been done on the relationship between hormonal levels and aggression. In general, females who test higher on **testosterone** are more likely to engage in stereotypical male behaviors.[47] Females who have naturally low androgen levels are less aggressive than males, while those who have elevated androgen levels will take on characteristically male traits, including aggression.[48]

Some females are overexposed to male hormones in utero. Females affected this way, according to biosocial theorist Diana Fishbein, may become "constitutionally masculinized" and at risk to delinquency. They may develop abnormal hair growth, large musculature, a low voice, an irregular menstrual cycle, fertility disorders, and hyperaggressiveness; this condition can also develop as a result of steroid use and certain medical disorders.[49] Fishbein has reviewed the literature in this area and finds that after holding constant a variety of factors, including IQ, age, and environment, females exposed to male hormones in utero are more likely to engage in physically aggressive behavior later in life.[50]

PREMENSTRUAL SYNDROME

Early biotheorists suspected that **premenstrual syndrome (PMS)** was a direct cause of the relatively rare instances of female violence and aggression: "For several days prior to and during menstruation, the stereotype has been that 'raging hormones' doom women to irritability and poor judgment—two facets of premenstrual syndrome."[51]

The link between PMS and delinquency was popularized by Katharina Dalton, whose studies of English women led her to conclude that females are more likely to commit suicide and be aggressive and otherwise antisocial before or during menstruation.[52]

Today there is conflicting evidence on the relationship between PMS and female delinquency. Diana Fishbein concludes that there is in fact an association between elevated levels of female aggression and menstruation. Research efforts show that (a) a significant number of incarcerated females committed their crimes during the premenstrual phase, and (b) at least a small percentage of woman appear vulnerable to cyclical hormonal changes which makes them more prone to anxiety and hostility.[53] Nonetheless, the great majority of females who suffer anxiety and hostility prior to and during menstruation do not actually engage in criminal behavior.[54]

Existing research has been criticized on the basis of methodological inadequacy.[55] A valid test of the association must consider its time ordering: It is possible that the psychological and physical stress of antisocial behavior produces early menstruation and not vice versa.[56]

AGGRESSION

Males and females differ with respect to biological vulnerabilities, reflected in consistent findings that males are inherently more likely to aggress.[57]

According to some biosocial theorists, gender differences in the delinquency rate can be explained by inborn differences in **aggression** between males and females.[58] Some psychologists have suggested that these gender-based differences in aggression are present very early in life before socialization can influence behavior. Eleanor Maccoby and Carol Jacklin's influential research found that males were more aggressive in all human societies for which data were available and that gender differences could also be found in subhuman primates. Maccoby and Jacklin linked gender differences to hormonal variations (testosterone) that control behavior.[59]

Not all biosocial theorists view gender differences as merely a matter of hormonal variation. Lee Ellis suggests that gender-based differences in aggression reflect the essential physical dissimilarities in the male and female reproductive systems. Ellis links human behavior to the sociobiological urge to reproduce and maintain the gene pool. He finds that males are naturally more aggressive because they wish to possess and control as many sex partners as possible to increase their chances of producing offspring. Females have learned to control their aggressive impulses because multiple mates do not increase their chances of conception. They instead concentrate their efforts on acquiring things that will help them successfully rear their offspring, such as a reliable mate who will supply material resources.[60]

Female Aggression   The weight of the evidence suggests that males are more aggressive than females. However, evidence also exists that females are more likely to act aggressively under certain circumstances.

1. Males are more likely than females to report physical aggression in their behavior, intentions, and dreams.
2. Females are more likely to feel anxious or guilty about behaving aggressively, and these feelings tend to inhibit aggression.
3. Females behave as aggressively as males when they have the means to do so and believe that their behavior is justified.
4. Females are more likely to empathize with the victim—to put themselves in the victim's place.
5. Sex differences in aggression decrease when the victim is anonymous. Anonymity may prevent females from empathizing with the victim.[61]
6. Females may feel more freedom than males to express anger and aggression in the family setting.[62]

In sum, biosocial theorists find that qualities of male biological traits make males "naturally" more aggressive than females; under some circumstances, however, females may actually be more aggressive than males.

SOCIALIZATION VIEWS

The socialization view is that a child's social development, influenced and controlled by family, peers, teachers, and society, may be the key to understanding delinquent behavior. If a child experiences impairment, trauma, family disruption, and so on, he or she will be more susceptible to delinquent associations and criminality.

Like other theories of delinquency, linking crime rate variations to gender differences in socialization is not new. In a 1928 work, *The Unadjusted Girl,* W. I. Thomas forged a link between socialization, sexuality, and delinquency. He suggested that some impoverished girls who have not been socialized under middle-class family controls become impulsive thrill seekers. According to Thomas, female delinquency is linked to the "wish" for a life of luxury and excitement.[63] Inequities in the social class system condemned poor girls from demoralized families to use sex as a means to gain amusement, adventure, and pretty clothes and other luxuries. Precocious sexuality makes these disadvantaged girls vulnerable to older men who, taking advantage of their naivete, lead them down the path to crime and decadence.[64]

SOCIALIZATION AND DELINQUENCY

Scholars concerned with gender differences in the crime rate attempt to distinguish between the lifestyles of males and females. Girls may be supervised more closely than boys and are expected to stay home more often. If girls behave in a socially disapproved fashion, their parents may be more likely to notice and take action. Adults may be more tolerant of deviant behavior in boys than in girls and expect the former to act tough and take risks.[65] Closer supervision restricts the opportunity for crime and the time available to mingle with delinquent peers. It follows, then, that the adolescent girl who is growing up in a troubled home or one marked by abuse, conflict, or neglect and who lacks parental concern and supervision may have a lifestyle similar to troubled adolescent males and thus be prone to delinquency.

FOCUS ON SOCIALIZATION

At mid-century, a number of writers began to focus on gender-specific socialization patterns as a key determinant of antisocial behavior. This view maintained three assumptions about gender differences in socialization: (1) Families exerted a more powerful influence on girls than boys; (2) girls did not form close same-sex friendships and generally competed with their peers; and (3) girls were primarily sexual offenders. The first assumption was that parents were stricter with girls, whom they perceived as vulnerable and in more need of control, than boys. In some families, adolescent girls rebelled against strict controls, while in others, where parents were absent or unavailable, they turned to the streets for support and companionship. The second assumption was that girls rarely formed close relationships with female peers, whom they viewed as rivals for the few males who would make eligible marriage partners.[66] Instead, girls entered into sexual affairs with older men, who would exploit them, involve them in sexual deviance, and father their illegitimate children.[67] The result was prostitution, petty theft, drug abuse, and marginal lives. Their daughters then would repeat this pattern in a never-ending cycle of despair and exploitation.

Perhaps the best-known work of this type focusing on gender differences as a cause of delinquency is Gisela Konopka's *The Adolescent Girl in Conflict* (1966). More than 30 years ago, Konopka integrated psychoanalytic views with sociological concepts in an effort to explain the onset of deviant behavior in girls.[68]

Konopka suggested that female delinquency has its roots in a girl's feelings of uncertainty and loneliness. During her adolescence, a girl's major emotional need is to be accepted by members of the opposite sex. If normal channels for receiving such approval—family, friends, relatives—are impaired, she may fight isolation by joining a "crowd" or engaging in gratuitous sexual relationships. This behavior eventually leads to "rejection by the community, general experience of having no recognized success . . . and more behavior which increases the feeling of worthlessness."[69]

Konopka identified a number of factors that produce the onset of female delinquent behavior.[70] The onset of puberty in girls is traumatic because of the often cruel way in which it is received by parents and the fear it creates in girls. The social identification process can be dramatic and difficult because of a girl's competitiveness with her mother. In fatherless homes, girls have an especially hard time because "the road to a healthy development toward womanhood through affection for the male and identification with the female simply does not exist."[71] Changing the pattern of females' cultural position can also create problems. Delinquent girls are believed to suffer from a lack of training and education. This locks them into low-paying jobs with little hope for advancement. All of these conditions lead girls to relieve their thwarted ambition through aggressive or destructive behavior. The world presents a hostile environment to some girls; adult authority figures tell them what to do, but no one is there to listen to them.

SUPPORTING VIEWS

At mid-century, a number of experts shared Konopka's emphasis on the family and society as a primary influence on delinquent behavior. Male delinquents were typically portrayed as rebels who, testing their masculinity, espoused "toughness," "excitement," and other lower class values. Males succumbed to the lure of gang delinquency when they perceived few legitimate opportunities available to them. In contrast, female delinquents were portrayed as troubled adolescents, suffering in an inadequate home life, and more often than not, being the victims of sexual and physical abuse. Ruth Morris described delinquent girls as unattractive, poorly groomed youths who reside in homes marked by family tensions or absent parents.[72] In an oft-cited work, *The Delinquent Girl* (1970), Clyde Vedder and Dora Somerville suggested that female delinquency is usually a problem of adjustment to family and social pressure; an estimated 75 percent of institutionalized girls have family problems.[73] They also suggest that girls have serious problems in a male-dominated culture fraught with rigid and sometimes unfair social practices.

Eleanor Glueck and Sheldon Glueck also distinguished between the causes of male and female delinquency. They linked male delinquency to muscular body type; impulsive personality; a hostile, defiant attitude; destructive traits; and a poor home life.[74] Delinquent males had been reared in homes of "little understanding or affection, stability or moral fibre" by parents who were unfit to be role models.[75] In contrast, when they examined the life histories of institutionalized female offenders in their classic work *Five Hundred Delinquent Women*, they found that a significant majority of the subjects had been involved in sexual deviance that began early in their teens.[76] The Gluecks concluded that sexual delinquency and general behavior maladjustment developed simultaneously in girls with unstable home lives.[77]

The adolescent girl who is growing up in a troubled home or one marked by abuse, conflict, or neglect may be prone to delinquency. If a girl grows up in an atmosphere of sexual tension, where hostility exists between her parents or where the parents are absent, she likely will turn to outside sources for affection and support.

Other early efforts linked "rebellious" or sexually precocious behavior to sexual conflicts in the home and incestuous relationships.[78] Broken or disrupted homes were found to predict female delinquency.[79] Females petitioned to juvenile court were more likely than boys to be charged with ungovernable behavior, running way, and sex offenses, and were more likely to reside in a single-parent home.[80] Studies of incarcerated juveniles found that most of the male delinquents were incarcerated for burglary, robbery, and other theft-related offenses, but girls tended to be involved in incorrigibility, sex offenses, and truancy. The conclusion: Boys became delinquent in order to gain status and demonstrate their masculinity by adventurous behavior; girls were delinquent because of hostility toward parents and a consequent need to obtain gratification and attention from others.[81] (See the "Focus on Delinquency" feature in this chapter.)

CONTEMPORARY SOCIALIZATION VIEWS

The view that females are more deeply affected by family disruption and conflict than males has not been abandoned. Investigators continue to support the view that the home life of female delinquents is more dysfunctional than that of male offenders.[82] For example, Meda Chesney-Lind found that a significant amount of female delinquency can be traced to physical and sexual abuse in the home.[83] She writes, "Young women on the run from homes characterized by sexual abuse and parental neglect are forced, by the very statutes designed to protect them, into the life of an escaped convict."[84] (See Table 7.1.)

Joan Moore's analysis of gang girls in east Los Angeles found that many came from troubled homes. Sixty-eight percent of the girls she interviewed were afraid of their fathers, and 55 percent reported fear of their mothers. One girl told Moore about the abuse she received from her mother:

TABLE 7.1 Sexual Abuse and Female Criminality

3 in 10 female inmates in state adult prisons said they had been abused as juveniles
■ 31% of women in prison had been abused before age 18, and 24% after age 18.
■ These women were equally likely to report being sexually as well as physically abused before they entered prison.
■ Females were more likely than male inmates to have been abused in their past (43% vs. 12%).

Source: A. Beck, et al. *Survey of State Prison Inmates, 1991.* (1992).

She would hit me, pinch me, and pull my hair, and then she'd have my brother—the oldest one—get a whip, and whip me, and then I'd have stripes all over my body like a zebra, and I went to school like that.[85]

Many of the girls reported that parents were overly strict and controlling despite the fact that they engaged in drug abuse and criminality themselves. Moore also details accounts of incest and sexual abuse; about 30 percent of the gang girls reported that family members made sexual advances. Considering the restrictions placed on girls and the high incidence of incest, it comes as no surprise that three-quarters reported having run away at least once. Moore concludes;

> Clearly more women than men came from troubled families. They were more likely to have been living with a chronically sick relative, one who died, one who was a heroin addict, or one who was arrested. . . . This seems on the face of it to imply that the gang represents [for girls] . . . a refuge from family problems. . . .[86]

In sum, the socialization approach holds that family interaction and child–parent relations are the key to understanding female delinquency. If a girl grows up in an atmosphere of sexual tension, where hostility exists between her parents or where the parents are absent, she likely will turn to outside sources for affection and support. Unlike boys, girls must follow very narrowly defined behavioral patterns. It is not unusual or unexpected for boys to stay out late at night, drive around with friends, and get involved in other unstructured behaviors linked to delinquency. If, in their reaction to loneliness, frustration, and parental hostility, girls begin to engage in the same "routine" activities as boys (staying out late, drinking, partying and riding around with their friends), they run the risk of being labeled "delinquent."[87]

The socialization approach holds that the psychological pressure of a poor home life is likely to have an even more damaging effect on females than males. Because girls are less likely than boys to have the support of close-knit peer associations, they are more likely to need close parental relationships to retain emotional stability. In fact, girls may become sexually involved with boys to receive support from them, a practice that tends only to magnify their problems.

LIBERAL FEMINIST VIEWS

All of us, despite our differences, are constantly growing and trying to understand each other's oppression, be it as working class women, black or brown women, gay women or middle class women. We are, by struggling, finding new ways of caring about each other, and it is this that gives us hope of having a movement, finally, which will provide for all of our needs.[88]

This statement represents the sentiments of women who are active participants in the feminist movement. Feminist leaders have fought to help women break away from their traditional roles of homemaker and mother and secure for themselves economic, professional, educational, and social advancement. There is little question that the women's movement has revised the way women perceive their roles in society, and it has significantly altered the relationships of women to many important social institutions.

Liberal feminism also has influenced thinking about the nature and extent of delinquency. A number of scholars, including Rita Simon and Freda Adler, have drawn national attention to the changing pattern of female criminality and offered new explanations for the differences between male and female delinquency rates.[89] Their position is that economic conditions and sex role differences are greater influences on delinquency rates than socialization. After all, they believe, improper socialization affects both males and females and therefore cannot be the sole explanation for gender differences in the crime rate.

According to liberal feminists, females are less delinquent than males because their social roles provide them with fewer opportunities to commit crime. As the roles of females become more similar to those of males, however, so too will their crime patterns. Feminist theory implies that female criminality is motivated by the same crime-producing influences as male criminality.

SISTERS IN CRIME

This view was spelled out most clearly more than 20 years ago in Freda Adler's book *Sisters in Crime* (1975), which showed how sex role differences influence crime and delinquency. Adler's major thesis was that by striving for social and economic independence, women have begun to alter social institutions, which had protected males in their traditional positions of power. "The phenomenon of female criminality," she claims, "is but one wave in this rising tide of female assertiveness."[90]

Adler argued that female delinquency patterns and rates would be affected by the changing role of women in society. As females entered new occupations and participated in sports, education, politics, and other "traditional" male endeavors, they would also become involved in crimes that had heretofore been male oriented; delinquency rates would converge. She noted that girls were already becoming increasingly involved in traditionally masculine crimes, such as stealing, gang activity, and fighting.

Adler predicted, that in the future, the women's liberation movement would produce even steeper increases in the rate of female delinquency because it had created an environment in which the social roles of girls and boys converge. Boys, she argued, have traditionally entered puberty ill prepared for the aggression and competition they encounter in the activities of their peer groups. The consequent emotional strain leads them to engage in delinquent activities. Girls, on the other hand, have always maintained traditional, relatively static behavior patterns. These patterns protected them from the pressures of transition into the adult world. However, Adler argued that the modern girl . . . is passing from childhood to adulthood via a new and uncharted course. . . . She is partly pushed and partly impelled into fields previously closed to women. . . . Clearly, the developmental difficulties which encouraged male delinquency in the past are exerting a similar influence on girls.[91]

According to liberal feminists, females are less delinquent than males because their social roles provide them with fewer opportunities to commit crime. As the roles of girls and women become more similar to those of males, so too will their crime patterns. Female criminality is actually motivated by the same crime-producing influences as male criminality.

Adler proclaimed that the changing female role will eventually produce female delinquents and criminals who are quite similar to their male counterparts:

Women are no longer behaving like subhuman primates with only one option. Medical, educational, political and technological advances have freed women from unwantedpregnancies, provided them with male occupational skills, and equalized their strengths with weapons. Is it any wonder that once women were armed with male opportunities, they should strive for status, criminal as well as civil, through established male hierarchical channels.

In the cities . . . young girls are now taking to the streets just as boys have traditionally done. It has now become quite common for adolescent girls to participate in muggings, burglaries, and extortion rings which prey on schoolmates.[92]

SUPPORT FOR LIBERAL FEMINISM

A number of well-known studies supported the feminist view of gender differences in the delinquency rate.[93] The most notable may be Rita Simon's 1975 effort, *The Contemporary Woman and Crime*. Although not specifically devoted to youth crime, Simon's work explains how the consistent increase in female criminality is a function of the changing role of women:

The same factors and conditions that explain women's increased participation in property offenses also serve to explain the slight decline or lack of increase in violent offenses during the same time period. The fact that women have more economic opportunities and more legal rights (divorces and abortions are easier to obtain) and that in recent years they have been developing a rhetoric which legitimizes their newly established socio-legal-economic status seems to lessen the likelihood that they will feel victimized, dependent, and oppressed. The diminishment of such feelings means that they will be less likely to attack their traditional targets: their husbands, lovers, pimps (that is, men with whom they are emotionally involved and dependent upon), and their babies (those recently born and those not yet delivered).[94]

Simon's view has been supported in part by Roy Austin's analysis of the effect the women's liberation and economic emancipation movement has had on the female crime rate.[95] Using 1966 as a jumping-off point (because the National Organization for Women was founded in that year), Austin's research shows that patterns of serious female crime (robbery and auto theft) correlate with indicators of female emancipation (namely, the divorce rate and participation in the labor force). Although, as Austin admits, this research does not conclusively prove that female crime is related to economic and social change, it certainly identifies behavior patterns that support that hypothesis.

In addition to these efforts, a number of self-report studies have supported the liberal feminist view by showing that gender differences in delinquency *patterns* are fading; that is, the delinquent acts committed most (petty larceny) and least often (heroin addiction, armed robbery) by girls are nearly identical to those reported most and least often by boys.[96] Evidence uncovered in numerous self-report studies seems to indicate that the pattern of female delinquency, if not the extent, is now similar to that of male delinquency.[97]

Additional evidence shows that social forces predictive of male delinquency, such as identification with a delinquent peer group, are also associated with female delinquency.[98] Both male and female misconduct, ranging from status offenses to violent crimes, seems now to be motivated by the same social relationships, for example, family structure and function.[99] A study of gang membership by Beth Bjerregaard and Carolyn Smith found that with a few exceptions the factors that motivated males and females to join gangs (e.g. family dysfunction, educational failure, precocious sexuality) are now quite similar.[100]

These studies suggest that as the sex roles of males and females have become more equivalent, their offending patterns also have become more similar. Girls may be joining gangs and committing crimes in order to gain economic advancement and not because they perceive a lack of parental support and affection. Both of these patterns are predicted by liberal feminists.

CRITIQUES OF LIBERAL FEMINISM

Not all delinquency experts believe that changing sex roles actually influence female crime rates. Some argue that the delinquent behavior patterns of girls have remained static and have not been influenced by the women's movement. Females involved in violent crime more often than not have some connection to a male business or intimate partner who influences their behavior. One recent study of women who kill in the course of their involvement in the drug trade found, that rather than act in their own self-interest, they kill on behalf of a man or out of fear of a man.[101]

Others dispute whether overall changes in the female delinquency rate correspond with the feminist movement. For example, in a series of studies Darrell Steffensmeier and his associates conclude that arrest data and juvenile gang studies show little increase in female violence or gang-related acts and that young female offenders do not seem to be catching up with males in terms of violent or serious crimes. Self-report studies show that female participation in most crime patterns has remained stable for the past 10 years, with increases in the areas of drug use and alcohol abuse.[102] In a more recent work, Steffensmeier analyzed data from the period 1960–90 and concluded that the women's movement has not influenced female crime rates.[103]

In sum, the evidence indicates that gender differences in the crime rate have not changed as much as liberal feminist writers had predicted.[104] Consequently, the argument that female crime and delinquency will be elevated by the women's movement has not been given unqualified support.

Is Convergence Possible?   Will the gender differences in the delinquency crime rate eventually disappear as liberal feminists have predicted? Are gender differences permanent and unchanging? Not all experts have abandoned the convergence argument. Criminologist Roy Austin reexamined official and self-report data and claims that a long-term convergence trend is clearly established.[105] In a similar vein, Beth Bjerregaard and Carolyn Smith's study of youth gangs in Rochester, New York, shows that females have increased gang membership and that for both males and females, gang activity is associated with increased levels of crime and drug abuse.[106]

It is possible, as Austin claims, that crime convergence has been delayed by a slower-than-expected change in gender roles; the women's movement has not yet achieved its full impact on social life.[107] One reason is that while expanding their economic role, women have not abandoned their conventional roles as family caretaker and home provider; women today are being forced to cope with added financial and social burdens. If gender roles were truly equivalent, then crime rates may eventually converge; because these changes are now taking place there may be significant changes in female delinquency rates.

RADICAL FEMINIST VIEWS

A number of feminist writers take a more revolutionary view of gender differences in crime. There are a number of scholars who can be categorized as **socialist, radical,** or **Marxist feminists,** who view gender inequality as stemming from the unequal power of men and women in a capitalist society and the exploitation of females by fathers and husbands: Women are considered a "commodity" worth possessing, like land or money.[108] The cause of female delinquency originates with the onset of male supremacy (patriarchy), the subsequent subordination of women, male aggression, and the efforts of men to control females sexually.[109]

Radical feminists focus on the social forces that shape girls' lives and experiences to explain female criminality.[110] They attempt to show how the sexual victimization of girls is often a function of male socialization and that young males learn to be aggressive and exploitive of women. James Messerschmidt, an influential feminist scholar, has formulated complex theoretical models that show how misguided concepts of what is "masculinity" form the inequities built into "patriarchal capitalism." Men dominate business and power in capitalist societies, and males who cannot function well within their parameters are at risk to crime. Women are inherently powerless in such a male-dominated society; their crimes reflect the limitations they have for both legitimate and illegitimate opportunity.[111]

This view is supported by a (1993) national survey conducted by the Center for Research on Women at Wellesley College, which found that 90 percent of adolescent girls are sexually harassed in school, with almost 30 percent reporting having been psychologically pressured to "do something sexual" and 10 percent physically forced to do something sexual.[112]

According to the radical view, exploitation acts as a trigger for delinquent behavior and status offending. When female victims run away and abuse substances, they may be reacting to abuse at home and at school. Their attempts at survival are then labeled deviant or delinquent; victim blaming is not uncommon.[113] Research by Jane Siegel and Linda Meyer Williams shows that a significant number (86 percent) of girls who had been sent to the emergency room to be treated for sexual abuse later reported engaging in physical fighting as a teen or as an adult; many of these abused girls later formed a romantic attachment with an abusive partner. Clearly many girls involved in delinquency, crime, and violence have themselves been the victims of violence in their youth and later as adults.[114]

The Wellesley survey of sexual harassment found that teachers and school officials ignore about 45 percent of the complaints made by female students. Because agents of social control often choose to ignore reports of abuse and harassment, young girls may feel trapped and desperate.

CRIME AND PATRIARCHY

A number of theoretical models have attempted to use a radical or Marxist feminist perspective to explain gender differences in the delinquency rate. For example, in *Capitalism, Patriarchy, and Crime,* James Messerschmidt argues that capitalist society is marked by both patriarchy and class conflict. Capitalists control the labor of workers, while men control women both economically and biologically.[115] This "double marginality" explains why females in a capitalist society commit fewer crimes than males: They are isolated in the family and have fewer opportunities to engage in elite deviance (white-collar and economic crimes); they are also denied access to male-dominated street crimes. Because capitalism renders women powerless, they are forced to commit less serious, nonviolent, and self-destructive crimes, such as abusing drugs. Supporting Messerschmidt's conclusions are the self-report data that show girls report equal rates of substance abuse as males.

POWER-CONTROL THEORY

In one prominent radical feminist work, John Hagan and his associates have speculated that gender differences in the delinquency rate are a function of class differences and economic conditions that in turn influence the structure of family life. Hagan calls his view **power-control theory.**[116]

According to this view, class position influences delinquency by controlling the quality of family life. In paternalistic families, fathers assume the traditional role of breadwinners, while mothers have menial jobs or remain at home. In these homes, mothers are expected to control the behavior of their daughters while granting greater freedom to sons. The parent–daughter relationship can be viewed as a preparation for the "cult of domesticity," which makes daughters' involvement in delinquency unlikely; hence, males exhibit a higher degree of delinquent behavior than their sisters.

On the other hand, in **egalitarian** families—those in which the husband and the wife share similar positions of power at home and in the workplace— daughters gain a kind of freedom that reflects reduced parental control. These families produce daughters whose law-violating behavior mirrors that of their brothers. Ironically, these kind of relationships also occur in female-headed households with absent fathers. Similarly, Hagan and his associates found that when both fathers and mothers hold equally valued managerial positions, the similarity between the rates of their daughters' and sons' delinquency is greatest. By implication, middle-class girls are the most likely to violate the law because they are less closely controlled than their lower-class sisters.

Some of the power-control theory's basic premises, such as the relationship between social class and delinquency, have been challenged. For example, the theory holds that upper-class youths may engage in more petty delinquency than lower-class youths because they are brought up to be "risk takers" who do not fear the consequences of their misdeeds; such relationships may not exist.[117] However, ongoing research by Hagan and his colleagues has tended to support the core relationship between family structure and gender differences in the delinquency rate.[118]

Power-control theory is important because it encourages a new approach to the study of delinquency, one that includes gender differences, class position, and family structure. It also has value as an explanation of the relative increase in female delinquency because it incorporates the effects of the social changes occurring in the feminine role within its explanation of delinquency. With the shift toward single-parent homes brought about by the significant numbers of unwed teenage mothers and the high divorce rate, the patterns Hagan has identified may also undergo change. The decline of the patriarchal family may produce looser family ties on girls, changing sex roles, and increased delinquency.

GENDER AND THE JUVENILE JUSTICE SYSTEM

Not only do gender differences influence the way children commit crimes but they may also have a significant impact on the way they are treated in the juvenile justice system when and if they are apprehended. Several feminist scholars argue that girls are not only the victims of injustice at home but also risk being victimized by agents of the juvenile justice system. In many respects, the treatment they receive today is not too dissimilar from the "sexualization" of female delinquency found by Odem and Schlossman in 1920 Los Angeles (see the "Focus on Delinquency" feature in this chapter). Paternalistic attitudes and the sexual "double standard" increase the likelihood that girls will be referred to juvenile court for status-type offenses and, after adjudication, receive a disposition involving incarceration.

Are girls the "victims" of the juvenile justice system? In her classic 1973 study, Meda Chesney-Lind found that police in Honolulu, Hawaii, were likely to arrest female adolescents for sexual activity that they ignored in male delinquents.[119] Some 74 percent of the females in her sample were charged with sexual activity or incorrigibility; in comparison, only 27 percent of the boys were so charged. Similar to 1920 Los Angeles, the court ordered 70 percent of the females to undergo physical examinations, while requiring only 15 percent of the males to undergo this embarrassing procedure. Girls were also more likely to be sent to a detention facility before trial, and the length of their detention averaged three times that of the boys.

Chesney-Lind concluded that female adolescents have a much narrower range of acceptable behavior than male adolescents. Any sign of misbehavior in girls is seen as a substantial challenge to authority and to the viability of the sexual double standard.

ARE STANDARDS CHANGING?

More than 20 years after the Chesney-Lind research spotlighted the gender "double standard" in juvenile court, distinctions are still being made between male and female offenders. Donna Bishop and Charles Frazier found that girls are

Several feminist scholars argue that girls are not only the victims of injustice at home but also risk being victimized by agents of the juvenile justice system. Paternalistic attitudes and the sexual "double standard" increase the likelihood that girls will be referred to juvenile court for status-type offenses and, after adjudication, receive a disposition involving incarceration.

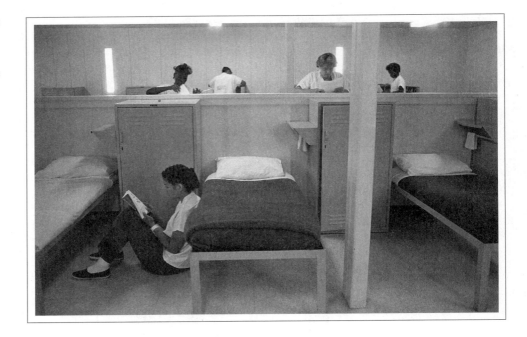

still more likely to be petitioned to court and punished for the status offense of incorrigibility than males; the differences, according to Bishop and Frazier, are "striking and dramatic."[120] Girls are still at a disadvantage if their behavior is viewed as morally incorrect by government officials. Girls who are held in contempt of court for failing to obey a judge's orders are much more likely to be sentenced to six months of incarceration in a secure detention facility than males, a state of affairs that "reflect(s) the continuation of protectionist policies toward female status offenders."[121] The Bishop and Frazier research has been substantiated by other studies showing that girls are much more likely to be sanctioned for status offenses than boys.[122]

Girls may still be subject to harsh punishments if they are considered dangerously immoral. Jill Leslie-Rosenbaum and Meda Chesney-Lind found that girls arrested on status offense charges are more likely than boys to have descriptions of their physical attractiveness placed in case files. There still appears to be an association between male standards of "beauty" and sexual behavior: Judges, social workers, and other criminal justice professionals may look upon attractive girls who engage in sexual behavior more harshly, punishing them while overlooking some of the same behaviors in less attractive girls. In some jurisdictions Rosenbaum and Chesney-Lind found that girls are still being incarcerated for noncriminal status offenses because their behavior does not measure up to (male) decision makers' concepts of proper female behavior.[123]

Although these arguments are persuasive, some recent national data gathered for the federal government by the Pittsburgh-based National Center for Juvenile Justice show that today there is little gender-based difference in state processing of status offenders. Both girls and boys seem to have an equal chance of proceeding to formal adjudication and being sent to out-of-the-home placements for status offenses.[124] This evidence seems to suggest that on a national level the gender bias feared by radical feminists may be in decline.

SUMMARY

The relationship between gender and delinquency has become a topic of considerable interest to criminologists and other experts interested in youth crimes. At one time attention was directed solely at male offenders; the rare female delinquent was considered an oddity. The nature and extent of female delinquent activities have changed, and it appears that girls are now engaging in more frequent and serious illegal activity. Consequently, there is ever-greater interest in gender issues in delinquency.

Sociologists and psychologists now recognize that there are distinct differences in attitude, values, and behavior between boys and girls. Females process information differently from males and have different cognitive and physical strengths. These differences may explain in part gender differences in the delinquency rate.

Attempts to discover the cause of gender differences can be placed in a number of different categories. Early efforts by Cesare Lombroso and his followers place the blame for delinquency on physical differences between males and females. Girls who were delinquent had inherent male characteristics. Later, biosocial theorists viewed a girl's psychological, hormonal, and physical makeup as key to delinquent behavior.

Socialization has also been identified as a cause of delinquency. Males are socialized to be tough and aggressive while females are socialized to be more passive and obedient. The adolescent female offender was portrayed as a troubled girl who lacked love at home and supportive peer relations. She was viewed as a sexual offender whose criminal activities were linked to destructive relationships with men.

More recent views of gender and delinquency incorporate the changes brought about by the women's movement. It is argued that as the social and economic roles of women change, so will their crime patterns. Although a number of research studies support this view, some theorists question its validity. Although the female crime rate has increased and female delinquency patterns now resemble those of male delinquency, the gender gap has not narrowed after more than a decade since the women's rights movement began. Hagan's power-control theory helps us understand why these differences exist and whether change may be forthcoming.

Debate also arises over the treatment girls receive at the hands of the juvenile justice system. Originally, it was thought that police treated girls with chivalry and protected them from the stigma of a delinquency label. Contemporary criminologists charge, however, that girls are actually discriminated against by agents of the justice system.

KEY TERMS

gender-schema theory	chivalry hypothesis	aggression
scripts	penis envy	socialist feminists
masculinity hypothesis	precocious sexuality	radical feminists
menstruation	testosterone	Marxist feminists
pregnancy	premenstrual syndrome (PMS)	power-control theory
menopause	androgens	egalitarian

QUESTIONS FOR DISCUSSION

1. Are girls delinquent for different reasons than boys? Do they have a unique set of problems?
2. Are girls the victims of unfairness at the hands of the justice system, or do they benefit from "chivalry"?
3. Do you believe that as sex roles become more homogenous, female delinquency will become identical to male delinquency in rate and type?
4. Does the sexual double standard still exist?
5. Are lower-class girls more strictly supervised than upper- and middle-class girls? Is control stratified across class lines?

NOTES

1. Cesare Lombroso, *The Female Offender* (New York: Appleton, 1920); W. I. Thomas, *The Unadjusted Girl* (New York: Harper & Row, 1923).
2. Cesare Lombroso and William Ferrero, *The Female Offender* (New York: Philosophical Library, 1895).
3. James Messerschmidt, *Masculinities and Crime* (Lanham, Md.: Rowman and Littlefield, 1993).
4. Rita James Simon, *The Contemporary Woman and Crime* (Washington, D.C.: U.S. Government Printing Office, 1975).
5. This section relies on Spencer Rathus, *Psychology in the New Millennium* (Fort Worth, Tex.: Harcourt Brace College Publishers, 1996); see also Darcy Miller, Catherine Trapani, Kathy Fejes-Mendoza, Carolyn Eggleston, and Donna Dwiggins, "Adolescent Female Offenders: Unique Considerations," *Adolescence* 30:429–35 (1995).
6. Allison Morris, *Women, Crime and Criminal Justice* (Oxford, England: Basil Blackwell, 1987).
7. Dennis Giever, "An Empirical Assessment of the Core Elements of Gottfredson and Hirschi's General Theory of Crime (Paper presented at the American Society of Criminology meeting, Boston, Mass., November 1995).
8. John Mirowsky and Catherine Ross, "Sex Differences in Distress: Real or Artifact?" *American Sociological Review* 60:449–68 (1995).
9. For a review of this issue, see Anne Campbell, *Men, Women and Aggression* (New York: Basic Books, 1993).
10. John Mirowsky and Catherine Ross, "Sex Differences in Distress: Real or Artifact?," pp. 460–65.
11. Ann Beutel and Margaret Mooney Marini, "Gender and Values," *American Sociological Review* 60:436–48 (1995).
12. American Association of University Women, *Shortchanging Girls, Shortchanging America* (Washington, D.C.: American Association of University Women, 1991).
13. David Rowe, Alexander Vazsonyi, and Daniel Flannery, "Sex Differences in Crime: Do Means and Within-Sex Variation Have Similar Causes?," *Journal of Research in Crime and Delinquency* 32:84–100 (1995).
14. Sandra Bem, *The Lenses of Gender* (New Haven, Conn.: Yale University Press, 1993).
15. Walter DeKeseredy and Martin Schwartz, "Male Peer Support and Woman Abuse," *Sociological Spectrum* 13:393–413 (1993).
16. James Messerschmidt, *Masculinities and Crime: Critique and Reconceptualization of Theory* (Lanham, Md.: Rowman and Littlefield, 1993).
17. Stacey Nofziger, "Sex and Gender Identity; A Gendered Look at Delinquency" (Paper presented at the American Society of Criminology meeting, Boston, Mass., November 1995; revised version, January 1996).
18. Federal Bureau of Investigation, *Crime in the United States, 1994* (Washington, D.C.: U.S. Government Printing Office, 1995), p. 224.
19. George Calhoun, Janelle Jurgens, and Fengling Chen, "The Neophyte Female Delinquent: A Review of the Literature," *Adolescence* 28:461–71 (1993).
20. Anne Campbell and Steven Muncer, "Men and the Meaning of Violence," in John Archer, ed., *Male Violence* (London: Routledge, 1995), pp. 332–46, at 346.
21. Howard Snyder and Melissa Sickmund, *Juvenile Offenders and Victims: A National Report* (Washington, D.C.: Office of Juvenile Justice and Delinquency Prevention, 1995), pp. 56–57.
22. Lombroso and Ferrero, *The Female Offender.*
23. Ibid., p. 122.
24. Ibid., pp. 51–52.
25. For a review, see Anne Campbell, *Girl Delinquents* (Oxford, England: Basic Blackwell, 1981), pp. 41–48.
26. Ibid., p. 151.
27. Ibid., pp. 150–52.
28. Cyril Burt, *The Young Delinquent* (New York: Appleton, 1925); see also Warren Middleton, "Is There a Relation between Kleptomania and Female Periodicity in Neurotic Individuals?," *Psychology Clinic,* December 1933, pp. 232–47.
29. William Healy and Augusta Bronner, *Delinquents and Criminals, Their Making and Unmaking* (New York: Macmillan, 1926).
30. Otto Pollak, *The Criminality of Women* (Philadelphia: University of Pennsylvania Press, 1950).
31. Ibid., p. 158.
32. Ibid., p. 10.
33. Sigmund Freud, *An Outline of Psychoanalysis,* trans. James Strachey (New York: Norton, 1949), p. 278.
34. Dorie Klein, "The Etiology of Female Crime: A Review of the Literature," in Freda Adler and Rita Simon, eds., *The Criminology of Deviant Women* (Boston: Houghton Mifflin, 1979), pp. 69–71.
35. Phyliss Chesler, *Women and Madness* (Garden City, N.Y.: Doubleday, 1972); Karen Horney, *Feminine Psychology* (New York: Norton, 1967).
36. Peter Blos, "Preoedipal Factors in the Etiology of Female Delinquency," *Psychoanalytic Studies of the Child* 12:229–42 (1957).
37. See, generally, Ralph Weisheit and Sue Mahan, *Women, Crime and Criminal Justice* (Cincinnati, Ohio: Anderson Publishing, 1988).
38. Sheldon Glueck and Eleanor Glueck, *Five Hundred Delinquent Women* (New York: Knopf, 1934).
39. J. Cowie, V. Cowie, and E. Slater, *Delinquency in Girls* (London: Heinemann, 1968).

40. Anne Campbell, "On the Invisibility of the Female Delinquent Peer Group," *Women and Criminal Justice* 2:41–62 (1990).

41. For a review, see Christy Miller Buchanan, Jacquelynne Eccles, and Jill Becker, "Are Adolescents the Victims of Raging Hormones? Evidence for Activational Effects of Hormones on Moods and Behavior at Adolescence," *Psychological Bulletin* 111:63–107 (1992). (Herein cited as "Raging Hormones.")

42. Avshalom Caspi, Donald Lyman, Terrie Moffitt, and Phil Silva, "Unraveling Girl's Delinquency: Biological, Dispositional, and Contextual Contributions to Adolescent Misbehavior," *Developmental Psychology* (1993).

43. Eleanor Maccoby and Carol Jacklin, *The Psychology of Sex Differences* (Palo Alto, Calif.: Stanford University Press, 1974).

44. Alan Booth and D. Wayne Osgood, "The Influence of Testosterone on Deviance in Adulthood: Assessing and Explaining the Relationship," *Criminology* 31:93–118 (1993).

45. Walter Gove, "The Effect of Age and Gender on Deviant Behavior: A Biopsychosocial Perspective," in A. S. Rossi, ed., *Gender and the Life Course* (New York: Aldine, 1985), pp. 115–44.

46. Lee Ellis, "Evolutionary and Neurochemical Causes of Sex Differences in Victimizing Behavior: Toward a Unified Theory of Criminal Behavior and Social Stratification," *Social Science Information* 28:625–26 (1989).

47. D. H. Baucom, P. K. Besch, and S. Callahan, "Relationship between Testosterone Concentration, Sex Role Identity, and Personality among Females," *Journal of Personality and Social Psychology* 48:1218–26 (1985).

48. Lee Ellis, "Evidence of Neuroandrogenic Etiology of Sex Roles from a Combined Analysis of Human, Nonhuman Primate and Nonprimate Mammalian Studies," *Personality and Individual Differences* 7:519–52 (1986).

49. Diana Fishbein, "The Psychobiology of Female Aggression," *Criminal Justice and Behavior* 19:99–126 (1992).

50. Ibid., p. 122.

51. Spencer Rathus, *Psychology, 3d ed.* (New York: Holt, Rinehart and Winston, 1990), p. 88.

52. See, generally, Katharina Dalton, *The Premenstrual Syndrome* (Springfield, Ill.: Charles C. Thomas, 1971).

53. Diana Fishbein, "Selected Studies on the Biology of Antisocial Behavior," in John Conklin, ed., *New Perspectives in Criminology* (Needham Heights, Mass.: Allyn and Bacon, 1996), pp. 26–38.

54. Fishbein, "Selected Studies on the Biology of Antisocial Behavior"; Karen Paige, "Effects of Oral Contraceptives on Affective Fluctuations Associated with the Menstrual Cycle," *Psychosomatic Medicine* 33:515–37 (1971).

55. B. Harry and C. Balcer, "Menstruation and Crime: A Critical Review of the Literature from the Clinical Criminology Perspective," *Behavioral Sciences and the Law* 5:307–22 (1987).

56. Julie Horney, "Menstrual Cycles and Criminal Responsibility," *Law and Human Nature* 2:25–36 (1978).

57. Ibid., p. 116.

58. Lee Ellis, "The Victimful-Victimless Crime Distinction and Seven Universal Demographic Correlates of Victimful Criminal Behavior," *Personality and Individual Differences* 9:525–48 (1988).

59. Eleanor Maccoby and Carol Jacklin, *The Psychology of Sex Differences* (Stanford, Calif.: Stanford University Press, 1974).

60. Ellis, "Evolutionary and Neurochemical Causes of Sex Differences in Victimizing Behavior," pp. 625–626.

61. Ann Frodi, J. Maccauley, and P. R. Thome, "Are Women Always Less Aggressive Than Men? A Review of the Experimental Literature," *Psychological Bulletin* 84:634–60 (1977).

62. Buchanan, Eccles, and Becker, "Raging Hormones," p. 94.

63. William I. Thomas, *The Unadjusted Girl* (New York: Harper & Row, 1928).

64. Ibid., p. 109.

65. David Farrington, "Juvenile Delinquency," in John Coleman, ed., *The School Years* (London: Routledge, 1992), p. 133.

66. Ruth Morris, "Female Delinquents and Relational Problems," *Social Forces* 43:82–89 (1964).

67. Cowie, Cowie, and Slater, *Delinquency in Girls*, p. 27.

68. Gisela Konopka, *The Adolescent Girl in Conflict* (Englewood Cliffs, N.J.: Prentice-Hall, 1966).

69. Ibid., p. 40.

70. Peter Kratcoski and Lucille Kratcoski, *Juvenile Delinquency* (Englewood Cliffs, N.J.: Prentice-Hall, 1979), pp. 146–47.

71. Konopka, *The Adolescent Girl in Conflict*, p. 50.

72. Ruth Morris, "Female Delinquency and Relational Problems," *Social Forces* 43:82–89 (1964).

73. Clyde Vedder and Dora Somerville, *The Delinquent Girl* (Springfield, Ill.: Charles C. Thomas, 1970).

74. Sheldon Glueck and Eleanor Glueck, *Unraveling Juvenile Delinquency* (Cambridge, Mass.: Harvard University Press, 1950).

75. Ibid., pp. 281–82.

76. Glueck and Glueck, *Five Hundred Delinquent Women*.

77. Ibid., p. 90.

78. Ames Robey, Richard Rosenwal, John Small, and Ruth Lee, "The Runaway Girl: A Reaction to Family Stress," *American Journal of Orthopsychiatry* 34:763–67 (1964).

79. William Wattenberg and Frank Saunders, "Sex Differences among Juvenile Court Offenders," *Sociology and Social Research* 39:24–31 (1954).

80. Don Gibbons and Manzer Griswold, "Sex Differences among Juvenile Court Referrals," *Sociology and Social Research* 42:106–10 (1957).

81. Gordon Barker and William Adams, "Comparison of the Delinquencies of Boys and Girls," *Journal of Criminal Law, Criminology, and Police Science* 53:470–75 (1962).

82. George Calhoun, Janelle Jurgens, and Fengling Chen, "The Neophyte Female Delinquent: A Review of the Literature," *Adolescence* 28:461–71 (1993).

83. Meda Chesney-Lind, "Girls' Crime and Women's Place: Toward a Feminist Model of Female Delinquency" (Paper presented at the American Society of Criminology meeting, Montreal, Canada, November 1987).

84. Ibid., p. 20.

85. Joan Moore, *Going Down to the Barrio: Homeboys and Homegirls in Change* (Philadelphia: Temple University Press, 1991), p. 93.

86. Ibid., p. 101.

87. D. Wayne Osgood, Janet Wilson, Patrick O'Malley, Jerald Bachman, and Lloyd Johnston, "Routine Activities and Individual Deviant Behaviors," *American Sociological Review* (in press, 1996).

88. Deborah Babcox and Madeline Belken, *Liberation: NOW* (New York: Dell, 1971).

89. Simon, *The Contemporary Woman and Crime;* Freda Adler, *Sisters in Crime* (New York: McGraw-Hill, 1975).

90. Adler, *Sisters in Crime.*

91. Ibid., p. 104.

92. Ibid., pp. 10–11.

93. Rita James Simon, "Women and Crime Revisited," *Social Science Quarterly* 56:658–63 (1976).

94. Ibid., pp. 660–61.

95. Roy Austin, "Women's Liberation and Increase in Minor, Major, and Occupational Offenses," *Criminology* 20:407–30 (1982).

96. Michael Hindelang, "Age, Sex, and the Versatility of Delinquency Involvements," *Social Forces* 14:525–34 (1971).

97. Martin Gold, *Delinquent Behavior in an American City* (Belmont, Calif.: Brooks/Cole, 1970), p. 118; John Clark and Edward Haurek, "Age and Sex Roles of Adolescents and Their Involvement in Misconduct: A Reappraisal," *Sociology and Social Research* 50:495–508 (1966); Nancy Wise, "Juvenile Delinquency in Middle-Class Girls," in E. Vaz, ed., *Middle Class Delinquency* (New York: Harper & Row, 1967), pp. 179–88; Gary Jensen and Raymond Eve, "Sex Differences in Delinquency: An Examination of Popular Sociological Explanations," *Criminology* 13:427–48 (1976).

98. Merry Morash, "Gender, Peer Group Experiences, and Seriousness of Delinquency," *Journal of Research in Crime and Delinquency* 23:43–67 (1986).

99. Margaret Farnworth, "Male–Female Differences in Delinquency in Minority-Group Sample," *Journal of Research in Crime and Delinquency* 21:191–212 (1986).

100. Beth Bjerregaard and Carolyn Smith, "Gender Differences in Gang Participation and Delinquency," *Journal of Quantitative Criminology* 9:329–50 (1993).

101. Henry Brownstein, Barry Spunt, Susan Crimmins, and Sandra Langley, "Women Who Kill in Drug Market Situations," *Justice Quarterly* 12:472–98 (1995).

102. Darrell Steffensmeier and Renee Hoffman Steffensmeier, "Trends in Female Delinquency," *Criminology* 18:62–85 (1980). See also idem, "Crime and the Contemporary Woman: An Analysis of Changing Levels of Female Property Crime, 1960–1975," *Social Forces* 57:566–84 (1978); Darrell Steffensmeier and Michael Cobb, "Sex Differences in Urban Arrest Patterns, 1934–1979," *Social Problems* 29:37–49 (1981).

103. Darrell Steffensmeier, "National Trends in Female Arrests, 1960–1990: Assessment and Recommendations for Research," *Journal of Quantitative Criminology* 9:411–37 (1993).

104. Carol Smart, "The New Female Offender: Reality or Myth?" *British Journal of Criminology* 19:50–59 (1979).

105. Roy Austin, "Recent Trends in Official Male and Female Crime Rates: The Convergence Controversy," *Journal of Criminal Justice* 21 (1993):447–66.

106. Beth Bjerregaard and Carolyn Smith, "Gender Differences in Gang Participation, Delinquency, and Substance Abuse," *Journal of Quantitative Criminology* 9 (1993):329–55.

107. Austin, "Recent Trends in Official Male and Female Crime Rates," p. 464.

108. Julia Schwendinger and Herman Schwendinger, *Rape and Inequality* (Beverly Hills, Calif.: Sage, 1983).

109. For a review of feminist theory, see Sally Simpson, "Feminist Theory, Crime and Justice," *Criminology* 27:605–32 (1989).

110. Ibid., p. 611.

111. James Messerschmidt, *Masculinities and Crime: Critique and Reconceptualization of Theory* (Lanham, Md.: Rowmand and Littlefield, 1993).

112. Center for Research on Women, *Secrets in Public: Sexual Harassment in Our Schools* (Wellesley, Mass.: Wellesley College, 1993).

113. Kathleen Daly and Meda Chesney-Lind, "Feminism and Criminology," *Justice Quarterly* 5:497–538 (1988).

114. Jane Siegel and Linda Meyer Williams, "Aggressive Behavior among Women Sexually Abused as Children" (Paper presented at the American Society of Criminology meeting, Phoenix, Ariz., 1993). Revised version.

115. James Messerschmidt, *Capitalism, Patriarchy and Crime* (Totowa, N.J.: Rowman and Littlefield, 1986); for a critique of this work, see Herman Schwendinger and Julia Schwendinger, "The World According to James Messerschmidt," *Social Justice* 15:123–45 (1988).

116. John Hagan, A. R. Gillis, and John Simpson, "The Class Structure and Delinquency: Toward a Power-Control Theory of Common Delinquent Behavior," *American Journal of Sociology* 90:1151–78 (1985); John Hagan, John Simpson, and A. R. Gillis, "Class in the Household: A Power-Control Theory of Gender and Delinquency," *American Journal of Sociology* 92:788–816 (1987).

117. Gary Jensen and Kevin Thompson, "What's Class Got to Do with It? A Further Examination of Power-Control

Theory," *American Journal of Sociology* 95:1009–23 (1990); Kevin Thompson, "Gender and Adolescent Drinking Problems: The Effects of Occupational Structure," *Social Problems* 36:30–44 (1989). For some critical research, see Simon Singer and Murray Levine, "Power Control Theory, Gender and Delinquency: A Partial Replication with Additional Evidence on the Effects of Peers," *Criminology* 26:627–48 (1988).

118. John Hagan, A. R. Gillis, and John Simpson, "Clarifying and Extending Power Control Theory," *American Journal of Sociology* 95:1024–37 (1990).

119. Meda Chesney-Lind, "Judicial Enforcement of the Female Sex Role: The Family Court and the Female Delinquent," *Issues in Criminology* 8:51–59 (1973).

120. Donna Bishop and Charles Frazier, "Gender Bias in Juvenile Justice Processing: Implications of the JJDP Act," *Journal of Criminal Law and Criminology* 82:1162–86 (1992).

121. Ibid., p. 1186.

122. Jean Rhodes and Karla Fischer, "Spanning the Gender Gap: Gender Differences in Delinquency among Inner City Adolescents," *Adolescence* 28:880–89 (1993).

123. Jill Leslie Rosenbaum and Meda Chesney-Lind, "Appearance and Delinquency: A Research Note," *Crime and Delinquency* 40:250–61 (1994).

124. *Juvenile Justice: Minimal Gender Bias Occurred in Processing Noncriminal Juveniles* (Gaithersburg, Md.: General Accounting Office, 1995).

CHAPTER EIGHT

THE FAMILY AND DELINQUENCY

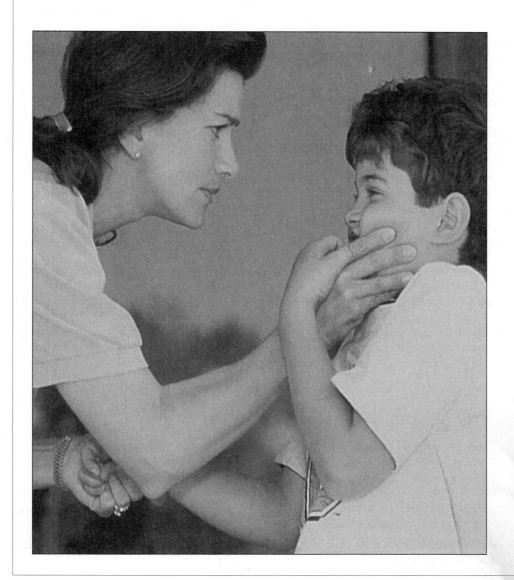

INTRODUCTION

The family is the key social institution for providing the nurturant socialization of young children.[1]

There seems to be little disagreement that family relationships are a pivotal determinant of adolescent behavior through the life course (see Table 8.1). Children growing up in a household characterized by abuse, conflict, and tension, whose parents are absent or separated; and who lack familial love and support will be the ones most likely to engage in violence and delinquency.[2] Conversely, a supportive family life can be very beneficial to children in any social environment or group. Even those children living in so-called "high-crime areas" are better able to resist the temptations of the streets if they receive fair discipline, care, and support from parents who provide them with strong, positive role models.[3] The relationship between family life and delinquency is not unique to American culture; cross-national data support a significant association between family variables and delinquency.[4]

The assumed relationship between delinquency and family life is critical today because the traditional American family is rapidly changing. Extended families, once common because of the economic necessity of sharing housing with many family members, are now for the most part an anachronism. In their place is the isolated nuclear family, described as a "dangerous hot-house of emotions" because of the intensely close contact between parents and children; in these families, problems are unrelieved by contact with other kin living nearby.[5]

The nuclear family is showing signs of breakdown. Much of the parental responsibility for child rearing is delegated to baby-sitters, television, and day care providers. Despite such changes, some families are able to adapt and continue functioning as healthy and caring units, producing well-adjusted children. Others have crumbled under the burden of stress, with severely damaging short- and long-term effects on their children.[6] This is particularly true when child abuse and neglect become part of family life.

Because these domestic issues are so critical for understanding juvenile delinquency, this chapter is devoted to an analysis of the family's role as a delinquency-producing or -inhibiting social institution. The chapter first covers the changing face of the American family. It then reviews how family structure and function influence delinquent behavior. The relationship between child abuse and neglect is then covered in some depth. Finally, programs designed to improve family functioning are briefly reviewed.

THE CHANGING AMERICAN FAMILY

The concept of the American family is changing. The so-called "traditional" family in which there is a male breadwinner and a female homemaker is a thing of the past. No longer can this **paternalistic family** structure, depicted in 1960s television sitcoms like "Father Knows Best" and "Ozzie and Harriet," be considered the norm. Changing sex roles have created a family where women play a much greater role in the economic process than ever before; this social evolution has created a more **egalitarian family** structure in which both spouses contribute to the family's economic and social well-being. More than 70 percent of all mothers of school-age children are now employed, up from 50 percent in 1970 and 40 percent in 1960.[7]

TABLE 8.1   Theoretical Views on the Family and Delinquency

Choice	Parents who do not teach children the consequences of rule-violating behavior will encourage them to be law violators. Parents may promote delinquent behavior choices by encouraging success at any cost; "greed is good."
Biosocial and Psychological	The predisposition to commit crime may be inherited or encouraged by such elements as diet and living conditions. Some delinquency-promoting traits, such as low intelligence and impulsivity, may be inherited. Family interaction influences personality traits that have been associated with delinquent behavior.
Social Structure	The environment children grow up in is controlled by their family's socioeconomic position. The makeup of the family may be controlled by economic conditions. Strain may be produced when families are unable to provide children with the means to achieve socially defined goals.
Social Process	The attachment of children to their family will negate delinquency-promoting inducements in the environment. Children who participate in family activities will be less likely to get involved with deviant peers and groups. Children may learn deviant values from parents. Impulsivity is exacerbated by poor family relations and a lack of discipline.
Social Reaction	Some youths are actually labeled as deviants within their own family and made to feel like outcasts. Socioeconomic class position controls both the family's economic well-being and its child-rearing practices. Lower-class families are paternalistic and tend to control girls more than boys, freeing the latter to engage in delinquency.

Family Makeup   The very makeup and definition of the family are undergoing change. The divorce rate is now about one for every two new marriages. Children of divorce often feel "caught" between their parents, especially in families marked by high levels of hostility and low levels of cooperation. Feeling caught or trapped is related to adjustment problems and later deviant behavior.[8] Children of divorce are more likely to undergo marital breakup as adults, creating a cycle of family dissolution.[9]

People are waiting longer to marry and, when they do marry, are having fewer children. Conversely, single-parent households have become common.[10] In 1970, 12 percent of children lived with one parent; today, that number is about 25 percent. At least half of all children will live part of their childhood with one parent only. More single women than ever are deciding to keep and raise their children; abut 30 percent of all births are to unmarried women. Although the teen birth rate is dropping slightly, more than 500,000 babies are born to teenaged mothers every year, about 200,000 to girls under 18.

The isolated *nuclear family*, has been described as a "dangerous hot-house of emotions" because of the intensely close contact between parents and children; in these families, problems are unrelieved by contact with other kin living nearby. Family stress causes many parents to act destructively toward their children.

Child Care Charged with caring for children is a day care system whose workers are often paid minimum wage. Of special concern are the hundreds of thousands of family day care homes in which a single provider takes care of three to nine children. Several states do not license or monitor these small, private providers. Even in those states that do mandate registration and inspection of day care providers, it is estimated that 90 percent or more of the facilities operate "underground." It is not uncommon for one adult to care for eight infants, an impossible task regardless of training or concern; the development of many children in day care is being compromised.[11]

ECONOMIC STRESS

The American family is also undergoing economic stress. According to the Children's Defense Fund, the vast majority of indigent families are forced to live in hazardous housing, forgo regular health care, weigh paying utility bills against other necessities, cut down on the size of meals or skip some altogether, and place children in substandard child care facilities. Those whose income places them above the poverty line are deprived of government assistance that might help children develop into productive adults. Recent political trends suggest that the social "safety net" is under attack and that poor families can expect less government aid in the coming years.

Will family stress be reduced in the future? As Figure 8.1 shows, the percentage of youth in the population is steadily declining while the percentage of senior citizens is increasing. As people retire, there will be fewer workers to pay social security, medical, and nursing home bills. These costs will put greater economic stress on already burdened American families.

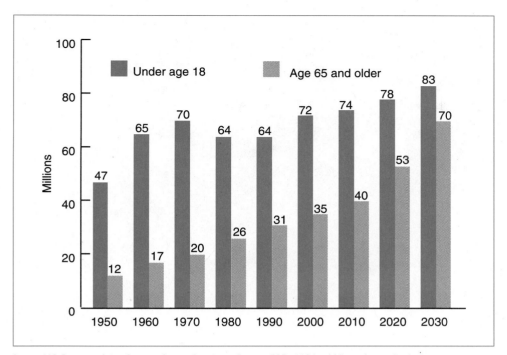

FIGURE 8.1
U.S. Elderly and Child Populations, 1950–2030

Source: U.S. Bureau of the Census, *Current Population Reports* P25–1104: middle series projections.

THE EFFECTS OF STRESS AND CONFLICT

Family stress causes many parents to act destructively toward their children. Abuse and neglect of children have become widespread, serious problems in the United States. Each year, more than one million children are maltreated in a variety of ways, ranging from gross neglect and starvation to overt physical and mental cruelty.[12] Juvenile courts throughout the nation hear approximately 500,000 child neglect and abuse cases annually. As child abuse experts Richard Gelles and Murray Straus put it:

> Parent-to-child violence is so common and so widely approved that one needs few case studies to make the point. In general, the large majority of Americans believes that good parenting requires some physical punishment. . . . Among the thousands of people we have interviewed, it was the absence of physical punishment that was thought to be deviant, not the hitting of children.[13]

Children who are the victims of abuse suffer physical and psychological damage both when the abuse takes place and later in life. Evidence supports a link between the abuse of young children and their subsequent violent and aggressive behavior as juvenile delinquents and status offenders.

THE FAMILY'S INFLUENCE ON DELINQUENCY

It is believed that a destructive and disturbed home environment can have a significant impact on delinquency because the family is the primary unit in which children learn the values, attitudes, and processes that guide their actions throughout their lives.

The effects of a supportive family life can be very beneficial to children in any social environment or group. Even those children living in so-called high-crime areas are better able to resist the temptation of the streets if they receive fair discipline, care, and support from parents who provide them with strong, positive role models.

Four broad categories of family functioning seem to promote delinquent behavior: families disrupted by spousal conflict or breakup; families involved in interpersonal conflict; families that neglect their children's behavior and emotional problems; and families headed by deviant parents who may transmit their behavior to children.[14] (See Figure 8.2.) Each of these factors may also interact to intensify individual effects; for example, drug abusing and deviant parents may be more likely to engage in family conflict, child neglect, and marital breakup. We now take a closer look at these four types of family problems that have been linked to delinquent behavior.

FAMILY BREAKUP: BROKEN HOMES

One of the most enduring controversies in the study of juvenile delinquency is the relationship between a parent being absent from the home and the onset of delinquent behavior. Research indicates that parents whose marriage is secure, who maintain communications and avoid conflict also produce children who are secure and independent.[15] In contrast, children growing up in a home with one or both parents absent due to divorce or separation may be prone to antisocial behavior.

A number of prominent delinquency experts have contended that a **broken home** is a strong determinant of a child's law-violating behavior. The connection seems self-evident as a child is first socialized at home and, from the beginning, learns behaviors, values, and beliefs from parents. Any disjunction in an orderly family structure will, in all likelihood, have a negative impact on the child's life.

The impact of the suspected broken home–delinquency relationship is acute because if current trends continue, fewer than half of all children born today will live continuously through childhood with their own mother and father. Because

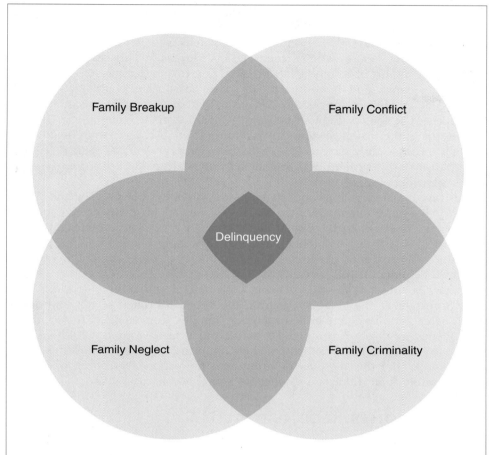

FIGURE 8.2

Family influences on behavior.
Each of these four factors has been
linked to antisocial behavior and
delinquency. Interaction between
these factors may escalate
delinquent activity.

Family Breakup

Family Conflict

Delinquency

Family Neglect

Family Criminality

step-families or so-called **blended families** are less stable than families consisting
of two biological parents, an increasing number of children will experience family
breakup two or even three times during childhood.[16]

A number of clinical studies of youth who have experienced family breakup
indicate they are more likely to demonstrate behavioral problems, inappropriate
conduct, and hyperactivity when compared to children in intact families.[17]
Family breakup is often associated with discord, conflict, hostility, and aggression; children of divorce are suspected of having greater autonomy, lax supervision, weakened attachment, and greater susceptibility to peer pressure.[18]

BROKEN HOME RESEARCH

The relationship between broken homes and delinquency was established in
early research conducted by Ashley Weeks and by Sheldon Glueck and Eleanor
Glueck.[19] Other studies showed that parental absence seemed to affect girls,
white youths, and the affluent more than males, minorities, and the indigent.[20]
But the link was clear: Children growing up in a "broken home" were much more
likely to fall prey to delinquency than those who enjoyed the support of a
two-parent household.

Despite the strong hypothetical case linking broken homes to delinquency, the bulk of empirical research on the matter has been inconclusive. The early studies that established the link between broken homes and delinquency used the records of police, courts, and correctional institutions.[21] This research may be tainted by sampling bias: Youths from broken homes may get arrested, petitioned to juvenile court, and institutionalized more often than youths from intact families, but this does not necessarily mean that they actually engage in more frequent and serious delinquent behavior. Official statistics may reflect the fact that agents of the justice system treat children from disrupted households more formally because they cannot call on parents for support. The juvenile courts' *parens patriae* philosophy calls for official intervention when parental supervision is considered inadequate.

This revisionist view was supported in early works of Clifford Shaw and Henry McKay, who were among the first to provide important evidence that broken homes were not necessarily related to delinquency. They found that the proportion of children living in broken homes in a sample taken from the general population (36 percent) was not significantly different from that found in samples of known delinquents (42 percent).[22]

Numerous subsequent studies, using both official and self-report data, have failed to establish any clear-cut relationship between broken homes and delinquent behavior.[23] Boys and girls from intact families seem as likely to *self-report* delinquency as those whose parents are divorced or separated. Children from broken homes are still more likely to show up in the official statistics. Researchers conclude that the absence of parents has a greater effect on agents of the justice system than it does on the behavior of children.

BROKEN HOMES RECONSIDERED

In a well-known work, Lawrence Rosen and Kathleen Neilson reviewed the literature on the subject and concluded; "The concept of broken homes, no matter how it is defined or measured, has little explanatory power in terms of delinquency."[24] As a result of this and similar scholarship, the focus of research shifted from the broken home to other aspects of the parent–child relationship.

Although researchers have not found a definite relationship between a broken home and delinquency, it may be premature to dismiss the relationship as spurious. A number of recent studies have found that family breakup may have at least an indirect influence on adolescent misbehavior. For example, family structure has been linked to rebellious acts and status offenses such as running away and truancy. Reviewing 50 prior studies on family structure and delinquency, L. Edward Wells and Joseph Rankin found that (a) the prevalence of delinquency is 10 to 15 percent higher in broken homes than in intact homes and (b) the relationship between broken homes and delinquency is strongest for status-type offenses and weakest for serious delinquencies.[25] If broken homes are in fact related to status offenses and not delinquency, the relationship may be caused by weakened parental control and supervision.[26]

Attachment to One Parent Even if a "broken home" delinquency link could be identified, it is possible that children who are strongly attached to a single parent might be insulated from delinquency. Some experts have argued that care givers in single-parent households who maintain high levels of supervision help reduce the likelihood that their children will have police contacts.[27]

However, there are also those who suggest that a single parent, no matter how competent, cannot make up for the absence of a second parent. James Q. Wilson and Richard Herrnstein claim that even if single mothers (or fathers) can make up for the loss of a second parent, it is difficult to do so and the chances of failure are great.[28] In particular, single parents may find it difficult to provide adequate supervision.

These sentiments are supported by research showing that children who are strongly attached to two parents have a lower probability of self-reporting delinquency than those attached to a single parent. Similarly, children who live in single-parent homes who are strongly attached to the custodial parent have a greater chance of committing delinquent acts than children living in intact homes who are strongly attached to both parents.[29]

Educational Encouragement   Although research generally shows little association between family structure and school failure and/or dropout rates, there is also evidence that children who live with single parents receive less encouragement and less help with schoolwork.[30] Children in two-parent households are more likely to want to go on to college than those in single-parent homes.[31] Poor school achievement and limited educational aspirations have been associated with delinquent behavior. Single parents who become involved in their children's education may be able to counteract this effect and help improve their children's school achievement.

Economic Factors   The relationship between broken homes and delinquency may also be mediated by economic factors. The social and economic conditions present in slum areas—poverty, unemployment, alienation—may be the cause of *both* delinquent behaviors and marital breakup.[32] Divorce and separation then can result in the acceleration of economic hardship. White single mothers find that their income declines about 30 percent, to an average of $13,500, after divorce; nonwhite single mothers average $9,000 annually. Many divorced mothers are forced to move to cheaper residences located in deteriorated, disorganized neighborhoods, which places children at risk to delinquency.

FAMILY CONFLICT

Not all unhappy marriages end in divorce. Some continue in an atmosphere of discord and conflict; *intrafamily conflict* is an all too common experience in many American families.[33] The link between parental conflict and delinquency was established almost 40 years ago, when pioneering research by F. Ivan Nye found that a child's perception of his or her parents' marital happiness was a significant predictor of self-reported delinquency.[34]

Contemporary studies have also found that children who grow up in maladapted homes and who witness discord and/or violence later exhibit patterns of emotional disturbance, behavioral problems, and social conflict.[35] There seems to be little difference between the behavioral patterns of children who merely witness intrafamily violence and those who are its victims.[36]

Research has consistently supported the relationship between family conflict, hostility, low warmth and affection, and delinquency.[37] Jill Leslie Rosenbaum found that the family background of incarcerated female delinquents was almost universally dysfunctional; some of the homes were described as "an animal-like environment."[38] Parents of **beyond control** youngsters have been found to be inconsistent setters of rules; to be less likely to praise, encourage, and show interest in their children; and to display high levels of hostile detachment.[39]

Although damaged parent–child relationships are generally associated with delinquency, it is difficult to assess the causal relationship. It is often assumed that preexisting family problems cause delinquency, however, it may also be true that acting-out children put enormous stress on a family.[40] Adolescent misbehavior then may be a precursor of family conflict; dissension and strife lead to more adolescent misconduct, producing an endless cycle of family stress and delinquency.[41]

FAMILY CONFLICT VERSUS BROKEN HOMES

Which is worse, growing up in a home marked by extreme conflict or growing up in a broken home? Should parents stay together "for the sake of the children"? Paul Amato and Bruce Keith reviewed the literature on divorce and family conflict and found, as might be expected, that children in both broken homes and high-conflict intact families were considerably worse off than children in low-conflict intact families.[42] However, children in high-conflict intact families exhibited lower levels of adjustment and well-being than did children in families where parents had divorced; family conflict then may have a more damaging effect on children than divorce. Amato and Keith's other findings include:

- Children growing up in families disrupted by parental death are better adjusted than children of divorce. Parental absence is not a per se cause of antisocial behavior.
- Remarriage did not mitigate the effects of divorce on youth. Children living with a stepparent exhibit (a) as many problems as youths in divorce situations and (b) considerably more problems than do children living with both biological parents.
- Continued contact with the noncustodial parent has little effect on a child's well-being.
- Evidence that the behavior of children of divorce improves over time is inconclusive.
- Postdivorce conflict between parents is related to child maladjustment.

Should parents stay together "for the sake of the children"? Amato and Keith suggest that although divorce is harmful, family conflict may have a more negative impact.

FAMILY NEGLECT

It is believed that children need a warm, close, supportive relationship with their parents in order to thrive. Researchers have found that youths who are neglected by their parents or perceive a lack of family cohesiveness are the ones most likely to engage in delinquent acts and status offenses.[43] Some studies indicate that maternal relations regulate delinquent activity, while others point to the paternal relationship as the key factor.[44] Joan McCord has found that "competent" mothers who are self-confident, nonpunitive, affectionate, and assertive are able to insulate their children from delinquency in even the most deteriorated urban neighborhoods.[45] McCord found that paternal relationships take on greater importance later in the life course. Adolescents best able to avoid delinquent involvement report having unaggressive, nonviolent fathers who hold their wives in high esteem.

A number of independent research studies support the link between the quality of family life and delinquency. Children who feel inhibited with their parents and therefore refuse to discuss important issues with them are more likely to engage in deviant activities and status offenses. Poor child–parent communications have been related to the child running away and subsequently entering the ranks of homeless street kids who get involved in theft and prostitution to survive.[46]

Parent–child relations that are cold and distant have also been linked to the likelihood that the children will have police contacts.[47] Research of the factors distinguishing samples of incarcerated youths from the general population shows that they lack a warm, loving, supportive relationship with their fathers and come from families characterized by minimal paternal involvement with the children.[48] John Laub and Robert Sampson found that measures of the quality of family life, including supervision, attachment to parents, and discipline, are far more important predictors of delinquent or conforming behavior than measures of family structure (such as absent parents, large families, or family income).[49] In addition, David Farrington's analysis of the data from his London-based longitudinal cohort study found that at-risk youths who were able to avoid criminality had supportive mothers who reinforced their sons' favorable self-concept.[50]

DISCIPLINE AND SUPERVISION

One measure of family quality is the ability to use fair and consistent discipline and supervision. Studies using both self-report and official samples show that the parents of delinquent youth tend to be either inconsistent, overly harsh, or extremely lenient in their disciplinary practices.[51]

The link between discipline and deviant behavior is still uncertain. Most Americans still support the use of corporal punishment to discipline children, and attitudes toward physical discipline have changed little in the past 25 years. The use of physical punishment cuts across racial, ethnic, and religious groups. In fact, corporal punishment is actually used more often in families with strong religious orientations because devout parents believe that (a) human nature is sinful and (b) sin deserves punishment.[52]

Good intentions notwithstanding, there is growing evidence of a "violence begetting violence" interaction. Children who are subjected to even minimum amounts of physical punishment may be more likely to use violence themselves in personal interactions. Murray Straus reviewed the concept of discipline in a series of cross-sectional surveys and found a powerful relationship between exposure to physical punishment and later aggression throughout the life course.[53] Physical punishment weakens the bond between parent and child, lowers the child's self-esteem, labels him or her "bad," and undermines his or her faith in justice. It is not surprising, then, that Straus found a high correlation between exposure to physical discipline and street crime.

Evidence also exists that **inconsistent supervision** can promote delinquency. In his early research, F. Ivan Nye found that mothers who threatened discipline but failed to carry it out were more likely to have delinquent children than those who were consistent in their discipline.[54] Contemporary research finds that assaultive boys can be characterized as growing up in homes in which there are poor problem-solving skills and inconsistent discipline.[55]

Youths who believe that their parents care little about their activities and companions are more likely to engage in criminal acts than those who believe that their actions will be closely monitored. For example, Thomas Dishion and his colleagues found that ineffective parental monitoring was associated with attachment to delinquent peers and subsequent involvement in substance abuse in a sample of 206 high-risk youth in Oregon.[56] As might be expected, direct control of children's behavior through close parental supervision has been found to reduce involvement in delinquency and drug abuse.[57] Effective supervision is not merely a matter of the number of parents in the home or the number of children per parent. It more likely reflects style, quality, and intent of parenting than the number of supervisors available.[58]

In sum, significant evidence exists that inconsistent and overly harsh discipline and lax supervision are significant predictors of delinquent behavior.[59]

FAMILY SIZE

Parents may find it hard to control and discipline their children because they have such large families that economic and time resources are spread too thin (resource dilution). Larger families are more likely to produce delinquents than smaller ones, and middle children are more likely to engage in delinquent acts than first- or last-born children.

Some sociologists assume that family size has a direct effect on delinquency, attributing this phenomenon to the stretched resources of the large family and the relatively limited supervision parents can provide for each child. It is also possible that the relationship is indirect, caused by the relationship of family size to some external factor associated with criminality; for example, resource dilution has been linked to educational underachievement, long considered a correlate of delinquency.[60]

Middle children may suffer because they are the most likely to be home when large numbers of siblings are also at home and economic resources are the most stressed.[61] Although family size has not been linked to deviant behavior per se, larger families may run a greater risk of disruption and conflict.[62]

Research now shows that relatively affluent, two-wage-earner families are having fewer children, while indigent, single-parent households are growing larger; children then are at a greater risk today of being both poor and delinquent because indigent families are the ones most likely to have more children![63]

FAMILY CRIMINALITY

A number of studies have found that family criminality and deviance have a powerful influence on delinquent behavior.[64] John Laub and Robert Sampson found that parental deviance disrupts the family's role as an agent of informal social control, increasing the likelihood of chronic offending.[65]

Some of the most important data on parental deviance were gathered by Donald J. West and David P. Farrington as part of the long-term Cambridge Youth Survey. Their cohort data (see chapter 2) indicate that a significant number of delinquent youths have criminal fathers.[66] While 8.4 percent of the sons of noncriminal fathers eventually became chronic offenders, about 37 percent of sons of criminal fathers became multiple offenders.[67] In another important analysis, Farrington found that one type of parental deviance—schoolyard aggression or **bullying**—may be both inter- and intragenerational. Bullies have children who bully others, and these "second-generation bullies" grow up to become the fathers of children who are also bullies, in a never-ending cycle.[68]

The cause of intergenerational deviance is still uncertain. It is possible that environmental, genetic, psychological, or child-rearing factors are responsible for the linkage between generations.

The link might have some biological basis. Research on the sons of alcoholics show that they suffer many neurological impairments related to chronic delinquency.[69] It is possible that either (a) prolonged parental alcoholism causes genetic problems related to developmental impairment or (b) the children of substance-abusing parents are more prone to neurological impairment before, during, or after birth.

The quality of family life may be key: Criminal parents should be the ones *least* likely to have close, intimate relationships with their offspring. Research shows that substance-abusing and/or criminal parents are the ones most likely to use harsh and inconsistent discipline, a factor closely linked to delinquent behavior.[70]

It is also possible that the association is related to the labeling process and family stigma: Social control agents may be quick to fix a delinquent label on the children of known law violators; "the acorn," the reasoning goes, "does not fall far from the tree."[71]

So although there is some agreement that criminal parents produce delinquent offspring, there is by no means certainty about the nature and causal direction of the relationship.[72]

SIBLING INFLUENCES

Most research on the family's influence on delinquency is directed at parental effects. Some evidence exists, however, that deviant siblings may also have an important influence on behavior. In a recent paper, David Rowe and Bill Gulley found that sibling pairs who reported warm, mutual relationships and shared friends were the most likely to behave in a similar fashion. Sibling pairs who maintained a close relationship also had similar rates of drug abuse and delinquency.[73]

A number of interpretations of these data are possible. One is that siblings living in the same environment are influenced by similar social and economic factors. Another possibility is that deviant siblings grow closer because of shared interests. Rowe and Gulley believe that the relationship is due to interpersonal interactions: Older siblings and their peers are admired and imitated by the younger siblings. What seems to be a genetic effect may actually be the result of warm and close sibling interaction.

In sum, what has developed from the research on delinquency and family relationships is a picture of the delinquent's family life that does little to support and much to hinder a growing child's development. The delinquent child grows up in a large family and has parents who may drink, participate in criminal acts, be harsh and inconsistent disciplinarians, be cold and unaffectionate, have marital conflicts, and be poor role models. Thus, the quality of a child's family life seems more important than its structure.

CHILD ABUSE AND NEGLECT

Family violence—particularly violence against children—is a critical priority for criminal justice officials, political leaders and the public we serve.[74]

Concern about the quality of family life has recently increased because of the disturbing reports that many children are physically abused and neglected by their parents and that this harsh treatment has serious consequences for their future behavior. Because of this topic's great importance, the remainder of this chapter is devoted to this issue of child abuse and neglect and its relationship to delinquent behavior.

HISTORICAL FOUNDATION

Parental abuse and neglect is not a modern phenomenon. From infanticide to severe physical beatings for disciplinary purposes, maltreatment of children has occurred throughout history. Some concern for the negative effects of such maltreatment was voiced in the eighteenth century in the United States, but concerted efforts to deal with the problem of endangered children did not begin until 1874.

In that year, residents of a New York City apartment building reported to a public health nurse, Etta Wheeler, that a child in one of the apartments was being abused by her stepmother. The nurse found a young child named Mary Ellen Wilson, who had been repeatedly beaten and was chained to her bed, malnourished from a continuous diet of bread and water. The child was obviously seriously ill, but the police agreed with her parents that the law entitled them to raise Mary Ellen as they saw fit; the New York City Department of Charities claimed it had no custody right over Mary Ellen.

According to legend, Mary Ellen's removal from her parents had to be arranged through the Society for the Prevention of Cruelty to Animals (SPCA) on the ground that she was a member of the animal kingdom, which the SPCA was founded to protect. According to sociologists Richard Gelles and Claire Pedrick Cornell, the truth is less sensational: Mary Ellen's case was heard by a judge because the child needed protection; she eventually was placed in an orphanage.[75]

The case and subsequent jail sentence for Mary Ellen's stepmother received a great deal of press coverage. Not coincidentally, the Society for the Prevention of Cruelty to Children was founded the following year, marking the extension of humane organizations from animals to humans.[76]

THE BATTERED CHILD SYNDROME

In the twentieth century, little legal or medical research into the problems of maltreated children occurred before the work of Dr. C. Henry Kempe of the University of Colorado. In 1962, Kempe reported the results of a survey of medical and law enforcement agencies that indicated that the child abuse rate was much higher than had been thought. He coined a new term, the **battered child syndrome,** which he applied to cases of nonaccidental physical injury to children by their parents or guardians.[77] Kempe's work sparked a flurry of research into the problems of the battered child, and a network of law enforcement, medical, and social service agencies was formed to deal with battered children.[78]

Professionals dealing with such children soon discovered the limitations of Kempe's definition as they came face to face with a wide range of physical and emotional abuse inflicted on children by their parents. As Kempe himself recognized in 1976,

> The term "battered child" has been dropped. . . . When coined 15 years ago, its purpose was to gain the attention of both physicians and the public. We feel, now, that enough

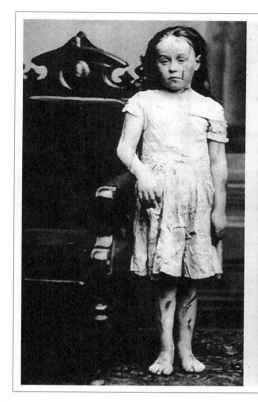

In 1874 Henry Bugh and Etta Angell Wheeler persuaded a New York court to take a child, Mary Ellen, away from her mother on the grounds of child abuse. This is the first recorded case in which a court was used to protect a child. Mary Ellen is shown at age 9 when she appeared in court showing bruises from a whipping and several gashes from a pair of scissors. The other photograph shows her a year later.

progress has been made to move on to a more inclusive phrase—child abuse and neglect. The problem is clearly not just one of *physical* battering. Save for the children who are killed or endure permanent brain damage . . . the most devastating aspect of abuse and neglect is the permanent adverse effects on the developmental process and the child's emotional well-being.[79]

Kempe's pioneering efforts were the first to raise the national consciousness on child abuse.

ABUSE AND NEGLECT DEFINED

The definition of battered children has expanded, and the term **child abuse** is now a generic expression that includes neglect as well as overt physical beating. Specifically, it now describes any physical or emotional trauma to a child for which no reasonable explanation, such as an accident or ordinary disciplinary practices, can be found. Child abuse is generally seen as a pattern of behavior, rather than a single beating or act of neglect. The effects of a pattern of behavior are cumulative; that is, the longer the abuse continues, the more severe the effects on the child.[80]

Although the terms *abuse* and **neglect** are sometimes used interchangeably, they represent different forms of maltreatment. *Neglect* is the more passive term, referring to deprivations that children suffer at the hands of their parents—lack of food, shelter, health care, and love. *Abuse,* on the other hand, is a more overt form of physical aggression against the child, one that often requires medical attention. Yet the distinction between the two terms is often unclear because in many cases both occur simultaneously.

Legally, each state has its own definition of child abuse. Despite the variety of these definitions, they all contain a combination of two or more of the following components:

- Nonaccidental physical injury
- Physical neglect
- Emotional abuse or neglect
- Sexual abuse
- Abandonment[81]

Physical abuse includes throwing, shooting, stabbing, burning, drowning, suffocating, biting, or deliberately disfiguring a child. The greatest number of injuries result from beatings with various kinds of implements and instruments. Some children have been strangled or suffocated with pillows held over their mouths or plastic bags thrown over their heads; a number have been drowned in bathtubs.[82]

Physical neglect results from parents' failure to provide adequate food, shelter, or medical care for their children, as well as failure to protect them from physical danger. **Emotional abuse** or neglect frequently accompanies physical abuse; it is manifested by constant criticism and rejection of the child, who as a result loses self-esteem.[83] **Emotional neglect** includes inadequate nurturing or affection, inattention to a child's emotional development, and lack of concern about maladaptive behavior. **Sexual abuse** refers to the exploitation of children through rape, incest, and molestation by parents, family members, friends, or legal guardians. Finally, **abandonment** refers to the situation in which parents physically leave their children with the intention of completely severing the parent–child relationship.[84]

SEXUAL ABUSE

One aspect of child abuse that has become an issue of growing national concern is sexual abuse. Sexual abuse can vary in content and style. It may range from rewarding a child for sexual behavior that is inappropriate for his or her level of development to using force or the threat of force for the purposes of sex. Sexual abuse can involve children who are well aware of the sexual content of their actions as well as others too young to have any real idea of what their actions mean. It can involve a variety of acts from inappropriate touching and fondling to forcible sexual penetration.

The effects of sexual abuse can be devastating. Abused children suffer disrupted ego development and personality development.[85] Guilt and shame are commonly experienced by survivors, and psychological trauma sometimes continues into adulthood. The ego of the victim may be overwhelmed by rage and horror over the incident.[86] David Finkelhor and Angela Browne of the Family Violence Research Program at the University of New Hampshire have described the aftermath of sexual abuse as involving one of four dynamics:

- **Traumatic sexualization**—the process in which a child's sexual identity is shaped in an inappropriate and dysfunctional way as a result of the abuse episode.
- **Betrayal**—the discovery by abused children that someone whom they trusted and on whom they are dependent caused them harm.

- **Powerlessness**—the process in which the child's will, desires, and sense of competence are negated.
- **Stigmatization**—the negative connotations, such as shame and guilt, that are communicated to children around their experiences and that then become incorporated into their self-image.[87]

The victims of child sexual abuse and their families can experience a number of postabuse traumas. The mothers of abused children experience severe psychological symptoms, including depression and other forms of psychopathology.[88] Traumatic sexualization can lead young victims into such diverse behavior patterns as victimizing their peers, acting in a promiscuous and compulsive fashion, experiencing aversion to sex, or trading sex for affection.[89] Victims commonly suffer frightening hallucinations, nightmares, and periods of profound rage.[90]

The resulting feelings of betrayal correspond to depression, disillusionment, hostility, and anger in some victims; others react with impaired judgment and insecurity, which makes them vulnerable to further abuse.[91] The powerlessness associated with abuse is manifested in fear, anxiety, nightmares, phobias, clinging behavior, hypersensitivity, and lack of coping skills. Research indicates a correlation between the severity of abuse and its long-term effects: The less serious the form of abuse, the more quickly the child can recover.[92] Because they feel shame, guilt and stigmatization, some victims find themselves sexualizing their own children in ways that lead them to sexual or physical abuse. Several studies have found a close association between sexual abuse and adolescent prostitution.[93] (See the following "Focus on Delinquency: Juvenile Prostitution.")

In an important review of 45 studies of the impact of sexual abuse, Kathleen Kendall-Tackett and her associates found that sexually abused children demonstrate symptoms including posttraumatic stress syndrome, precocious sexuality, and poor self-esteem. Children who were frequently abused over long periods of time and who suffered actual penetration of sexual organs were most likely to experience long-term trauma. Kendall-Tackett also found that no single behavior syndrome could be used to identify sexual abuse victims, making diagnosis of the problem at best complex.[94]

THE EXTENT OF CHILD ABUSE: UNREPORTED

How extensive is the incidence of child abuse? It is almost impossible to give an accurate estimate of the extent of child abuse. Many victims are so young that they have not learned to speak or communicate. Some are too embarrassed or afraid to report the abuse. Many incidents occur behind closed doors, and even when other adults witness inappropriate or criminal behavior they may not want to get involved in what they consider a "family matter."

Some of the first and most explosive indications of the severity of the problem came from a widely publicized 1980 national survey conducted by sociologists Richard Gelles, Murray Straus and Suzanne Steinmentz.[95] They estimated that between 1.4 million and 1.9 million children in the United States were annually subject to physical abuse from their parents.

Physical abuse was rarely a one-time act; the average number of assaults per year was 10.5, and the median was 4.5. Gelles and Straus also found that 16 percent of the couples in their sample reported spousal abuse; 50 percent of the

JUVENILE PROSTITUTION

... [Juvenile] prostitutes place themselves at risk the moment they enter the business. They are exploited and victimized by pimps, johns, cops, robbers, muggers, drug addicts, drug dealers, and more. There is a high rate of rape among girl prostitutes as most ply their trade in high-risk crime areas.

One of the most devastating forms of child sexual exploitation is juvenile prostitution. The National Center on Child Abuse and Neglect defines juvenile prostitution as "the use of, or participation by, children under the age of majority in sexual acts with adults or other minors where no force is present." The lack of force may make the relationship between a juvenile prostitute and the customer appear to be an equal economic exchange; however, victims' advocates acknowledge that in reality, the juvenile is a victim, often of an abusive family life, low self-esteem, and a lack of economic alternatives.

How Prevalent Is Juvenile Prostitution?

It is difficult to measure the number of children who are actually involved in prostitution. Estimates from law enforcement officials, social service providers, and researchers have ranged from tens of thousands to 2.4 million children annually. A reasonable estimate is that there are between 100,000 and 300,000 juvenile prostitutes per year. While experts debate the extent of the problem, about 1,200 juveniles are arrested each year for prostitution, some as young as 10 and 11 years old.

Even this estimate indicates a consistent nationwide problem of child sexual exploitation through prostitution. The questions remain: Where do these children come from, and how do they get recruited into prostitution? Youth service professionals suggest several traits or characteristics shared by juvenile prostitutes. Often, these children come from dysfunctional families. Having suffered physical, sexual, or emotional abuse, a majority of child prostitutes are runaways trying to escape their home environment. About 75 percent of juvenile prostitutes are runaways or "throwaways," having been encouraged or forced to leave home by their families.

Research suggests that most of the children who become prostitutes suffer from a negative self-image. Whether by parents, school officials, or peers, these youngsters have been convinced that they have little self-worth. Many of the children "want to be wanted," and the attention of customers and pimps can foster the illusion that these people really care.

---

multichild families reported attacks between siblings; 20 percent of the families reported incidents in which children attacked parents.[96]

Gelles and Strauss conducted a second national survey of family violence in 1985 and found, somewhat surprisingly, that the incidence of very severe violence toward children had declined. They estimated the decline between 1975 and 1985 to be as much as 47 percent.[97] Nonetheless, more than 1 million children were still being subjected to severe violence annually. It is important to note that this second research effort focused exclusively on *two-parent* families; including children from *single-parent* families would have expanded their estimate.[98] Also, if the definition of "severe abuse" used in the survey had included any incident in which a child was hit with an object, such as a stick or a belt, the actual number of child victims would have been closer to *7 million per year.*

Attempts to determine the extent of sexual abuse indicate that perhaps one in ten boys and one in three girls have been the victims of some form of sexual exploitation. An oft-cited survey by Diana Russell found that 16 percent of women reported sexual abuse by a relative and an additional 4.5 percent reported abuse by a father or stepfather.[99] It has been estimated that 30 percent to 75 percent of women in treatment for substance abuse disorders had experienced childhood sexual abuse and rape.[100]

A negative self-image and a lack of marketable skills may force children into prostitution as a means of economic survival. Pimps and other prostitutes may offer food and shelter in exchange for money raised through prostitution. Once the juveniles have entered this lifestyle, they may find it difficult to get out.

Some may suffer more severe forms of mental disorders including schizophrenia, depression, and emotional instability. Of course, these problems may be associated with the dysfunctional family life of juveniles who get involved in prostitution.

Who Are the Pimps?

Recognizing that runaway children are emotionally and financially desperate, pimps exploit these needs for their own personal gain. Almost always men, they will often wait in bus terminals and train stations, offering juveniles traveling alone some companionship and a place to stay. Initially, attention and affection are provided "with no strings attached." Once the juveniles become indebted to him, the pimp "turns them out" in prostitution as a form of repayment.

To increase his profits, a pimp may be a member of an organized ring, sending the juvenile on a circuit that could encompass numerous locations over several states. A booking agent often works as the go-between, organizing the circuit schedule and providing a facade of legitimacy between the pimp and the police. Interestingly, most research disputes the "myth" that pimps kidnap totally innocent children, raping them and turning them out into prostitution. Most youths become pros-titutes by choice, but once in the life, may find themselves subject to the pimp's "control, rules, orders, drugs, violence and manipulation."

What Are the Risks?

Aside from any possible emotional traumas associated with life as a juvenile prostitute, numerous physical risks endanger the child as well. Sexually transmitted diseases, pregnancy, and AIDS are constant dangers. The biological effects of sex at such an early age are not clearly documented but include damage to the vaginal and anal areas. The juveniles rarely seek medical help for fear they may be brought to the attention of authorities.

Along with the risks of disease come the risks of violence, both from pimps and from customers. Although they claim to protect the juveniles, the pimps may allow customers to "rough up" the youths "to teach them a lesson." Some pimps may use cruel and bizarre punishments, such as forcing juveniles to sit on a hot stove, for prostitutes who don't meet their quotas or who cause problems. More common, a pimp controls the juveniles through battering or the threat of violence. Prostitutes are also easy targets for muggers and other criminals. These juveniles are often out late at night with large amounts of cash and are unlikely to report a victimization to the police. Prostitutes are also common targets of serial murderers.

Source: Jennifer Williard, *Juvenile Prostitution* (Washington, D.C.: National Victim Resource Center, 1991); R. Barri Flowers, *Female Crime, Criminals and Cellmates* (Jefferson, N.C.: McFarland, 1995), quotes from pp. 156, 154.

THE EXTENT OF CHILD ABUSE: REPORTED

Not all child abuse and neglect cases are reported to authorities, but those that are take on added importance because they become the focus of state action. A number of national organizations have been collecting data on reported child abuse. Obtaining an accurate estimate of child maltreatment has proven difficult because (a) the methods used to collect data, (b) the data sources, and (c) the definition of child abuse vary considerably between reporting districts.

One important source of reported child abuse and neglect data is the National Committee to Prevent Child Abuse (NCPCA). The committee conducts an annual survey of all 50 states to determine the number and trends of reported child abuse cases.[101] The NCPCA survey indicates that more than 3.1 million cases were reported in 1995 (the last year for which data were available), an increase of 5 percent from the preceding year and up more than 50 percent from 1985. Of the total cases, about 26 percent involved physical abuse, 10 percent sexual abuse, 53 percent neglect, 3 percent emotional maltreatment, and the rest (17 percent) such "other" situations as abandonment and chemical dependency (see Figure 8.3)

The NCPCA survey also found that about one-third of the cases reported were considered **substantiated,** meaning they received some form of child-care services. All told, one million times a year state agencies are called upon to intervene in an abuse case.

The greatest tragedy resulting from child maltreatment is the death of a child. The NCPCA survey estimates that 1,200 children are killed each year as a result of child abuse, a rate of about 2 per 100,000 children. This number has increased by about 50 percent since 1985 when 810 were killed; the rate has increased from 1.3 per 100,000 to 1.8 per 100,000. Young children remain at the highest risk for loss of life: 85 percent of victims were under 5; sadly, 45 percent were 1 year old or younger. Almost half of all child fatalities involved children who had prior or current contact with CPS agencies.

THE CAUSES OF CHILD ABUSE AND NEGLECT

Parental maltreatment of children is a complex problem with neither a single cause nor a single solution. It cuts across racial, ethnic, religious, and socioeconomic lines, affecting the entire spectrum of society. Abusive parents cannot be categorized by sex, age, or educational level. They are persons from all walks of life, with varying cultural and economic backgrounds.

Of all factors associated with child abuse, two are discussed most often: (1) Parents who themselves suffered abuse as children tend to abuse their own children, and (2) isolated and alienated families tend to become abusive. A cyclical pattern of family violence seems to be perpetuated from one generation to the next within families. Evidence indicates that a large number of abused and neglected children grow into adolescence and adulthood with a tendency to engage in violent behavior. The behavior of abusive parents can often be traced to

FIGURE 8.3
Number of child abuse cases reported

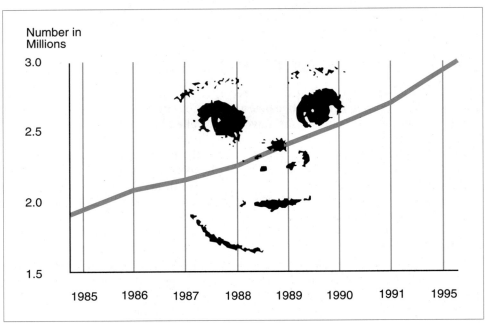

Source: David Wiese and Ching-Tung Lung, *Current Trends in Child Abuse and Fatalities: The Results of the 1995 Annual Fifty-State Survey* (Chicago: National Committee to Prevent Child Abuse, 1996).

Part III Environmental Influences on Delinquency

negative experiences in their own childhood—physical abuse, lack of love, emotional neglect, and incest. These parents become unable to separate their own childhood traumas from their relationships with their children.

Abusive parents often have unrealistic perceptions of the appropriate stages of childhood development. When their children are unable to act "appropriately"— when they cry, throw food, or strike their parents—the parents may react in an abusive manner.[102] For parents such as these, the axiom about not being able to love when you have not known love yourself is painfully borne out in their case histories. They spend their days going around the house, ticking away like unexploded bombs. A fussy baby can be the lighted match.[103]

Parents may also become abusive if they are isolated from friends, neighbors, or relatives who can provide a lifeline in times of crisis:

> Potentially or actually abusing parents are those who live in states of alienation from society, couples who have carried the concept of the shrinking nuclear family to its most extreme form, cut off as they are from ties of kinship and contact with other people in the neighborhood.[104]

Many abusive and neglectful parents describe themselves as highly alienated from their families and lacking close relationships with persons who could provide help and support in stressful situations.[105] The relationship between alienation and abuse may be particularly acute in homes where there has been divorce or separation or in which parents have never actually married: Abusive punishment in single-parent homes has been found to be twice that of two-parent families.[106] Parents who are unable to cope with stressful lifestyles or events— divorce, alcoholism, financial stress, poor housing conditions, recurring mental illness, and drug addiction—are the most at risk.[107]

The number of children killed by their parents has increased by more than 50 percent since 1985. This extreme form of abuse made national headlines in 1994 when Susan Smith, a young South Carolina mother, was accused of killing her two young children. Smith was spared the death penalty after her murder conviction.

In sum, Richard Gelles and Murray Straus describe the abusive parent as

a single parent who was young (under thirty), had been married for less than ten years, had his or her first child before the age of eighteen, and was unemployed or employed part-time. If he or she worked, it would be at a manual labor job . . . women are slightly more likely to abuse their children than men. The reason is rather obvious: Women typically spend more time with children.[108]

SUBSTANCE ABUSE AND CHILD ABUSE

Abusive and neglectful families suffer from severe stress, and it is therefore not surprising that they frequently harbor members who turn to drugs and alcohol. One NCPCA survey found that substance abuse was the cause of child maltreatment most often cited by Child Protection Services (CPS) professionals (63 percent).[109]

Research studies have found a strong association between child abuse and parental alcoholism.[110] In addition, evidence exists of a significant relationship between cocaine and heroin abuse and the neglect and physical abuse of children. In Massachusetts, almost 90 percent of the confirmed cases of abuse and neglect involving a victim under one year in age occurred in families in which one or more members were drug users; about 68 percent of the abused infants were diagnosed as suffering congenital drug addiction.[111]

States are just beginning to respond to women with substance abuse problems who also abuse their children. For example, Illinois employs Project SAFE (Substance Abuse Free Environment) to provide drug- and alcohol-involved women with intensive treatment and training in parenting skills.[112]

SOCIAL CLASS AND ABUSE

Surveys indicate a high rate of reported abuse and neglect cases among lower economic classes. The National Incidence Survey found that children from families earning less than $15,000 per year experienced more abuse and suffered greater injury than children living in more affluent homes.[113] NCPCA surveys have found that more than 40 percent of the families in CPS caseloads either lived in poverty or faced increased financial stress due to unemployment and economic recession.[114] These findings suggest that parental maltreatment of children is predominantly a lower-class problem. Is this conclusion valid?

One view is that the survey statistics are generally accurate and that lower-class parents are in fact more abusive of their children. Low-income families, especially those headed by a single parent, are often subject to greater levels of environmental stress and have fewer resources available to deal with such stress than families with higher incomes.[115] A relationship seems to exist between the burdens of raising a child without adequate economic and social resources and the use of excessive force and discipline. Self-report surveys do in fact show that indigent parents are significantly more likely than affluent parents to condone physical chastisement of children.[116]

Another view is that child abuse rates are so high among the lower class because poor families are more often dealt with by public agencies that automatically report suspected cases to CPS agencies. Higher-income families can afford private treatment, which shields their problems from public view.[117] CPS agents and judges may look differently on abuse cases that involve well-educated suburban dwellers than they do on those involving members of the lower class. Attending physicians may label a child of middle-class parents "accident-prone" under circumstances in which they would judge a lower-class child "abused."[118] Although this view seems plausible, research by Cecil Willis and Richard Wells indicates that police may be less likely to report child abuse by lower-class or minority families because they perceive that violence is more "normal" in these families and that minority children "need" harsher discipline than white children.[119]

Robert Burgess and Patricia Draper offer a third, biosocial explanation for the apparent class differences in child abuse.[120] They find that treatment of children is related to the actual cost to parents of perpetuating their genes through raising offspring. Higher rates of maltreatment in low-income families reflect the stress caused by the burdensome "investment" of resources these parents must make in raising their children. In contrast, middle-class parents devote a smaller percentage of their total resources to raising a family and therefore are less likely to perceive economic and social stress. According to this view, child abuse rates should be highest among lower-class families with large number of children: Few resources must be spread among a large number of gene carriers, limiting the investment in each one's well-being. Burgess and Draper also note that higher abuse rates of emotionally and physically disabled children may occur because these youngsters are "poor prospects for investment that will lead to their successful reproduction as adults."[121]

THE CHILD PROTECTION SYSTEM: PHILOSOPHY AND PRACTICE

For most of the nation's history, courts have operated on the assumption that parents have the right to bring up their children as they see fit. Although child protection agencies have been dealing with the problems of abuse and neglect since the late nineteenth century, recent awareness of child abuse and neglect has prompted judicial authorities to take increasingly bold steps to ensure the safety of children.[122] The age-old assumption that the parent–child relationship is inviolate has been breached. In 1974, Congress passed the Child Abuse Prevention and Treatment Act, which provides funds to states to bolster their services to maltreated children and their parents.[123] This act has been the impetus for all 50 states to improve the legal framework of their child protection systems. Abusive parents are subject to prosecution in criminal courts under the traditional statutes against assault, battery, and homicide. Many states have specific child abuse statutes that make it a felony to injure and abuse children.

State laws specifically prescribe procedures for investigation and prosecution of cases. The legal rights of both parents and children are constitutionally protected. In the cases of *Lassiter v. Department of Social Services* and *Santosky v. Kramer,* the U.S. Supreme Court recognized the child's right to be free from parental abuse and set down guidelines for a termination-of-custody hearing, including the right to legal representation.[124] States provide a *guardian ad litem* for the child (a lawyer appointed by the court to look after the interests of those who do not have the capacity to assert their own rights). States also ensure confidentiality of reporting and mandate professional training and public education programs.[125]

INVESTIGATING AND REPORTING ABUSE

One major problem in enforcing abuse and neglect statutes is that maltreatment of children can easily be hidden from public view. Although state laws require doctors, teachers, and others who deal with children to report suspected abuse and neglect cases to child protection agencies, many maltreated children are out of the law's reach because they are too young for school or because their parents do not take them to a doctor or a hospital. Parents abuse their children in private and, even when confronted, often accuse the child of lying or blame the child's medical problems on accidents of legitimate discipline. Legal and social service agencies must find more effective ways to locate abused and neglected children and to handle such cases once they are found.

All 50 states have statutes requiring that persons suspected of abuse and neglect be reported. Many have gone as far as making failure to report child abuse a criminal offense. Although such statutes are rarely enforced, teachers have been arrested for failing to report abuse or neglect cases.[126]

Once reported to a child protection service agency via a "hotline" or some other source, the case is screened by an intake worker and then turned over to an investigative caseworker; protective service workers will often work with law enforcement officers and other agency personnel. If the caseworker determines that the child is in imminent danger, he or she may immediately remove the child from the home; a court hearing must then be held shortly thereafter to approve the change in custody. Although stories of children abruptly and erroneously taken from their homes abound, it is much more likely that these "gatekeepers" will consider cases unfounded and take no further action; more than 50 percent of all reported cases are so classified.[127] Among the most common reasons for screening out cases is that the reporting party is involved in a child custody case and the screener believes the accusation is a consequence of marital turmoil.[128] As Table 8.2 shows, states vary in the level of evidence needed to substantiate a report of child abuse.

Even when there is compelling evidence of abuse, most social service agencies will try to involve the family in voluntary treatment and counseling without court intervention. Case managers will do periodic follow-ups to determine if treatment plans are being followed. If parents are uncooperative or if the danger to the child is so great that he or she must be removed from the home, then a complaint will be filed in the criminal, family, or juvenile court system.

THE PROCESS OF STATE INTERVENTION

Although procedures vary from state to state, most follow a similar legal process once a social service agency files a court petition alleging abuse or neglect.[129] Parents have the right to counsel in all cases of abuse and neglect, and many states require the court to appoint an attorney for the child as well. The child's attorney, a guardian *ad litem,* often acts as an advocate for the child's welfare as well as provides legal assistance.

When an abuse or neglect petition is prosecuted, an **advisement hearing** is held to notify the parents of the nature of the charges against them. If the parents admit the allegations, the court enters a consent decree, and the case is continued for disposition. Approximately half of all cases are settled by admission at the advisement hearing. If the parents deny the petition, an attorney is appointed for the child, and the case is continued for a pretrial conference.

TABLE 8.2 Evidence Required to Substantiate Child Abuse

States Vary in the Standard of Proof Required to Substantiate Allegations of Child Abuse and Neglect

Level of Evidence to Substantiate a Report			
Case worker's judgment	**Some credible evidence**	**Credible evidence**	**Preponderance of evidence**
Hawaii	Alaska	Alabama	District of Columbia
Mississippi	Arizona	Colorado	Georgia
Ohio	Arkansas	Connecticut	Iowa
Tennessee	California	Florida	Kansas
West Virginia	Idaho	Illinois	New Jersey
Wyoming	Kentucky	Maryland	Oklahoma
	Louisiana	Michigan	Pennsylvania
	Maine	Nebraska	Texas
	Massachusetts	Nevada	Vermont
	Missouri	Rhode Island	Virginia
	Montana	Utah	Washington
	New Hampshire		Wisconsin
	New York		
	North Carolina		
	North Dakota		
	Oregon		
	South Carolina		
	South Dakota		

Higher standards of proof result in slightly lower substantiation rates—

- Where the standard of evidence is the **case worker's judgment** the substantiation rate is 49%.
- Where the standard of evidence is **"some credible evidence"** the substantiation rate is 46%.
- Where the standard of evidence is **"credible evidence"** the substantiation rate is 44%.
- Where the standard of evidence is **"a preponderance of evidence"** the substantiation rate is 43%.

Source: Howard Snyder and Melissa Sickmund, *Juvenile Offenders and Victims* (Washington, D.C.; Office of Juvenile Justice and Delinquency Prevention, 1995), p. 39.

At the **pretrial conference,** the attorney for the social service agency presents an overview of the case and summarizes the evidence. Such matters as admissibility of photos and written reports are settled. The parents' attorney also reviews the facts of the case and reveals the evidence that will be used. At this point in the process, the attorneys can plea bargain; about three-fourths of the cases that go to pretrial conference are settled by a mutually agreed upon "bargain." About 85 out of every 100 petitions filed will be settled at either the advisement hearing or the pretrial conference.

Of the 15 remaining cases, 5 will generally be settled before trial. Usually, no more than 10 cases out of every 100 will actually reach the **trial stage** of the process. These few cases are tried through the regular adversary process, and the allegations of abuse and neglect are almost always readily proved. However, in recent years, some well-publicized trials, including the McMartin Day Care Center case (the longest trial in U.S. history), have resulted in not guilty verdicts. In the McMartin case, as in others, some jurors believed that prosecutors were so anxious to get a conviction that they led young children to believe they were abused even though the physical evidence told another story.

Disposition From the perspective of both the child and the parents, the most crucial part of an abuse or neglect proceeding is the **disposition hearing,** an entirely separate process held after the adjudication. The social service agency presents its case plan, which includes recommendations for returning the child to the parents, any conditions the parents must meet, a visitation plan if the child is to be taken from the parents, and so on. The plan is discussed with the parents, and an agreement is reached by which the parents commit themselves to following the state orders. Between half and two-thirds of all convicted offenders will be required to serve time in incarceration; almost half will be assigned to a form of counseling and treatment. As for the children, some may be placed in temporary state or foster care. Others may be placed in the custody of the state child protective service agency if parental rights are permanently terminated; legal custody can then be assigned to a relative or some other person.

In making their decisions, juvenile or family courts are generally guided by three interests: the role of the parents, protection for the child, and the responsibility of the state. Frequently, these interests conflict. In fact, at times, even the interests of the two parents are at odds. Ideally, the state attempts to

FIGURE 8.4
Process of state intervention in child abuse cases

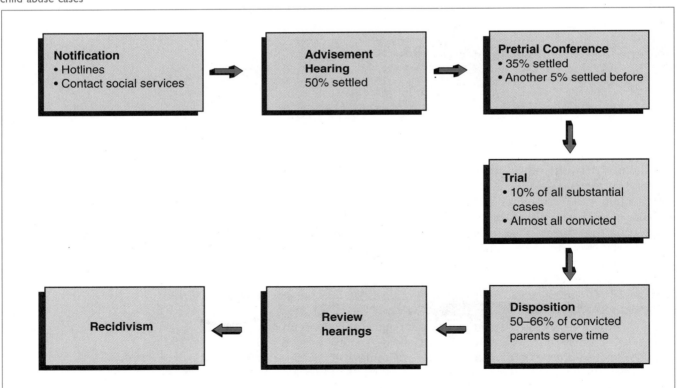

balance the parents' natural right to control their child's upbringing with the child's right to grow into adulthood free from severe physical or emotional harm. This is generally referred to as the **balancing-of-the-interest approach.**

Periodically, **review hearings** are held to determine if the conditions of the case plan are being met. Parents who fail to cooperate are warned that they may lose their parental rights. Most abuse and neglect cases are concluded within a year. Either the parents lose their rights and the child is given a permanent placement, or the child is returned to the parents and the court's jurisdiction ends. This process is summarized in Figure 8.4. The following "Case in Point" explores some questions about state intervention.

CASE IN POINT

You are an investigator with the county's Bureau of Social Services.

A case has been referred to you by the middle school's head guidance counselor. It seems that a young girl, Emily M., has been showing up to school in a dazed and listless condition. She has had a hard time concentrating in class and seems withdrawn and uncommunicative. The 13-year-old has missed more than a normal share of school days and has often been late to class. Last week, she seemed so lethargic that her homeroom teacher sent her to the school nurse. A physical examination revealed that she was malnourished and in poor physical health. She also had evidence of bruising that could only come from a beating. Emily told the nurse that she had been punished by her parents for doing poorly at school and for failing to do her chores at home.

When her parents were called in to school to meet with the principal and head guidance counselor, they claimed that they are members of a religious order that strongly believes that children should be punished severely for their misdeeds. Emily had been placed on a restricted diet as well as beaten with a belt to correct her misbehavior. When the guidance counselor asked them if they would be willing to go into family therapy, they were furious and told her to "mind her own business." It's a sad day, they said, when "God-fearing American citizens cannot bring up their children according to their religious beliefs." The girl is in no immediate danger insofar as her punishment has not been life threatening.

The case is then referred to your office. When you go to see the parents at home, they refuse to make any changes in their behavior and claim they are in the right and you are representative of all that is wrong with society. According to them, the "lax" discipline you want imposed leads to drugs, sex, and other teenage problems.

Should you get a court order removing Emily from her home and requiring the parents to go into counseling?

Should you report the case to the district attorney's office so it can proceed against her parents criminally under the state's Child Protection Act?

Should you take no further action, reasoning that Emily's parents have the right to discipline their child as they see fit?

Should you talk with Emily and see what she wants to happen?

THE ABUSED CHILD IN COURT

One of the most significant problems associated with the prosecution of child abuse and sexual abuse cases is the trauma that a child must go through in a court hearing. Children get confused and frightened and may change their testimony, resulting in the dropping of charges or a mistrial. Much controversy has arisen over the accuracy of children's reports of family violence and sexual abuse, resulting in hung juries in some well-known cases, including the McMartin Day Care case in California.[130] As one expert, Judge Lindsay Arthur of the National Council of Juvenile and Family Court Judges, put it:

> The system may interview the child time and again, each time making her relive the experience, keeping the wound open. It may force her down to court waiting rooms where she sits uncomfortably without even the accoutrements of a dentist's office for hours and then often to be told that the case was continued and to come back next week. She may be put on a witness stand, in a big formal room, with what seems like a thousand eyes staring at her, and a bailiff in full uniform ready to lock her up, and a judge in a black robe towering above her. She may find that the newspapers and television are full of her name and pictures and stories about what happened to her which they obtained from the official records. And this may make her the focus of her classmates with all the brutal teasing that can involve.
>
> The system may also suddenly arrest her father and just as suddenly release him. It may plea bargain away her future hope of rehabilitation without even talking to her, in the name of speedy justice.[131]

State jurisdictions have instituted a number of innovative procedures to minimize the trauma to the child. More than two-thirds have enacted legislation allowing videotaped statements or interviews with child witnesses, taken at a preliminary hearing or at a formal deposition, to be admissible in court. Videotaped testimony spares child witnesses the trauma of testifying in open court. States that allow videotaped testimony usually put some restrictions on its use: Some prohibit the government from calling the child to testify at trial if the videotape is used; some require that the defendant be present during the videotaping; a few specify that the child not be able to see or hear the defendant; some require a finding that the child is "medically unavailable" because of the trauma of the case before videotaping can be used.[132]

More than 30 states now allow a child to testify on closed-circuit television (CCTV). The child is able to view the judge and attorneys, and the courtroom participants are able to observe the child. The standards for CCTV testimony vary widely. Some states, such as New Hampshire, assume that any child witness under age 12 would benefit from not having to appear in court. Others require an independent examination by a mental health professional to determine whether there is a "compelling need" for CCTV testimony.

In addition to innovative methods of testimony, children in sexual abuse cases have been allowed to use anatomically correct dolls to demonstrate happenings that they cannot describe verbally. The Victims of Child Abuse Act of 1990 allows children to use these dolls when testifying in federal courts; at least eight states have passed similar legislation.[133] Similarly, states have relaxed their laws of evidence to allow out-of-court statements by the child to a social worker, teacher, or police officer to be used as evidence (such statements would be otherwise considered **hearsay**). Typically, corroboration is required to support these statements if the child does not also testify.

The prevalence of sexual abuse cases has created new problems for the justice system. All too often accusations are made in conjunction with marital disputes and separation. The fear is growing that children may become unwitting pawns in custody battles; the mere suggestion of sexual abuse is enough to galvanize social service workers and affect the outcome of a bitter divorce action. The juvenile justice system, therefore, must develop techniques that can get at the truth of the matter without creating a lifelong scar on the child's psyche.

LEGAL ISSUES

A number of cases have been brought before the Supreme Court testing the right of children to present evidence at trial using nontraditional methods and settings. Two issues stand out. One is the ability of physicians and mental health professionals to testify about statements made to them by victims of child abuse, especially when the children are incapable of testifying. The second concerns the way children testify in court and the leeway given prosecutors to put them at ease.

Out-of-Court Statements   The use of out-of-court statements has undergone a rapid legal transformation. In *Idaho v. Wright* (1990), the U.S. Supreme Court disallowed the use of statements made to a physician by a child considered incapable of communicating with a jury.[134] The Court ruled that Idaho law was not adequate to guarantee that the child's statements were sufficiently trustworthy and reliable to meet common evidentiary standards. In deciding whether out-of-court statements can be admitted, the Court suggested that judges take into consideration such factors as the child's motives, his or her description of sexual practices, witnesses to the out-of-court statements, and whether the statement was spontaneous in determining the validity of the pretrial admissions.

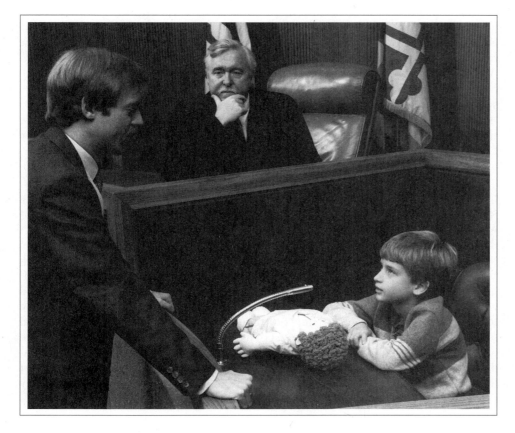

Children in sexual abuse cases have been allowed to use anatomically correct dolls to demonstrate happenings that they cannot describe verbally. The Victims of Child Abuse Act of 1990 allows children to use these dolls when testifying in federal courts; at least eight states have passed similar legislation.

Then, in a 1992 case, *White v. Illinois*, the Court significantly eased the prosecution of child abuse cases by ruling that the state's attorney is required neither to produce young victims at trial nor to demonstrate the reason they were unavailable to serve as witnesses.[135] *White* involved the use as testimony of statements given by the child to the child's baby-sitter and mother, a doctor, a nurse, and a police officer concerning the facts and identity of the alleged assailant in a sexual assault case. The prosecutor twice tried to call the child to testify, but both times the four year old experienced emotional difficulty and could not appear in court. The case outcome then hinged solely on the testimony of the five witnesses who repeated in court the statements made to them by the child.

By allowing the use of hearsay evidence in this case, *White* removes the requirement that prosecutors produce child victims in court. This facilitates the prosecution of child abusers in cases where a court appearance by a victim would prove too disturbing or where the victim is too young to understand the court process.[136] In its decision, the Court noted that statements made to doctors during medical exams or when a victim is upset or excited carry more weight than ones made after careful reflection. The Court ruled that such statements can be admitted during trial because the circumstances in which they were made (for example, during an examination in an emergency room) could not be duplicated simply by having the child testify to them in court.

In-Court Statements Children who are victims of sexual or physical abuse often make poor witnesses because they are traumatized and overwhelmed by court processes. Yet their testimony may be crucial to convict child abusers. In an important 1988 case, *Coy v. Iowa*, the Supreme Court placed limitations on efforts to protect child witnesses in court. During testimony in a sexual assault case, a "one-way" glass screen was set up so that the child victims would not be able to view the defendant (the defendant, however, could view the witnesses as they testified).[137] The Iowa statute that allowed the protective screen assumed that children would be traumatized by their courtroom experience. The U.S. Supreme Court ruled that unless there is a finding that the child witness needs special protection, the Sixth Amendment of the Constitution grants defendants "face-to-face" confrontation with their accusers. *Coy* was viewed as a setback in the prosecution of child abuse cases. In her opinion, Justice Sandra Day O'Connor suggested that if courts found it necessary, it would not be inappropriate to allow children to testify via CCTV or videotape.

Justice O'Connor's views became law in the 1990 landmark case of *Maryland v. Craig*.[138] In this case, a day care operator was convicted of sexually abusing a six-year-old child; one-way CCTV testimony was used during the trial. The decision was overturned in the Maryland Court of Appeals on the grounds that the procedures used were insufficient to show that a trial appearance would be so traumatic that the child could only testify in this manner (via one-way CCTV). On appeal, the U.S. Supreme Court ruled that the Maryland statute that allows CCTV testimony is sufficient because it requires that a determination be made that the child will suffer emotional distress if forced to testify and would not therefore be able to communicate with a jury. The Court stated that before alternatives to in-trial testimony, such as CCTV, could be used, a determination must be made that the child would be traumatized by being forced to testify in the presence of the defendant and that the distress would be more than minimal. In its decision, the Court noted that CCTV could serve as the equivalent of in-court testimony and, properly applied, would not interfere with the defendant's right to confront witnesses.

Taken together, these cases significantly increase the legal tools prosecutors can employ in child abuse cases. They open the door for prosecutions in cases that would have been impossible to pursue before.

DISPOSITION OF ABUSE AND NEGLECT CASES

Just as disagreement is widespread about *when* state intervention into family life is appropriate once an abuse incident is reported, there is also considerable controversy over *what* forms of intervention are helpful. Today, social service agents avoid removing children from the home whenever possible and instead try to employ counseling and support techniques to control abusive relationships. In serious cases, the state may remove children from their parents and place them in shelter care or foster homes. Placement of these children in foster care is intended to be temporary, but it is not uncommon for children to remain in foster care for three years or more. Furthermore, children are likely to be shifted from one temporary home to another during this period, which severely deprives them of much-needed stability. Although some recent research by Cathy Spatz Widom indicates that the effect of out-of-home placements may not be as traumatic as previously believed, those children who were moved around more than three times were twice as likely to get arrested as those children who had more stable foster home placements.[139]

Ultimately, the court has the power to permanently terminate the rights of parents over their children, but because the effects of destroying the family unit are serious and far-reaching, the court does so only in the most severe cases. Judicial hesitancy is illustrated in a recent Virginia appellate case in which grandparents contested a father being awarded custody of his children even though he had a history of alcohol abuse, had already been found to be an unfit parent, and was awaiting appeal of his conviction *for killing the children's mother;* the trial court claimed that he had turned his life around.[140]

In the vast majority of abuse and neglect cases, courts are reluctant to demand the permanent removal of the child. Parents and children are required to participate in treatment programs that seek to rehabilitate the family and prevent a recurrence of the maltreatment. Such programs attempt to alter the psychological, social, and environmental factors that are at the root of the problem. Social casework, mental health services, day care centers, homemaker services, parent effectiveness training, group therapy, and foster grandparent programs are among some of the most frequently used efforts to help children and parents avoid abuse or neglect situations.

Efforts have been ongoing to improve the child protection system and reduce the chances of repeat abuse. Jurisdictions have expedited case processing, instituted court procedures designed not to frighten child witnesses, coordinated investigations between various social service and law enforcement agencies, and assigned an advocate or guardian *ad litem* to support the child in need of protection.

ABUSE, NEGLECT, AND DELINQUENCY

The immediate effects of abuse and neglect are evident—physical injury, malnutrition, emotional depression, death. Less obvious are the suspected effects. Maltreatment of children encourages them to use aggression as a means of solving problems and prevents them from feeling empathy for others. It diminishes their ability to cope with stress and makes them vulnerable to the aggression and violence in the culture. Abused children have fewer positive interactions with peers, are less well liked, and are more likely to have disturbed social interactions.[141]

A significant literature has developed suggesting that abuse and neglect may have a profound effect on behavior in later years. Exposure to excessive physical aggression and emotional chaos in early life provides a foundation for several varieties of violent and antisocial behavior. In fact, sociologists Richard Gelles and Murray Straus state that "with the exception of the police and the military, the family is perhaps the most violent social group, and the home the most violent social setting, in our society."[142] Ray Helfer and C. Henry Kempe contend,

> The effects of child abuse and neglect are cumulative. Once the developmental process of a child is insulted or arrested by bizarre child rearing patterns, the scars remain. One should not be surprised, then, to find that the large majority of delinquent adolescents indicate that they were abused as children.[143]

Aggressive, delinquent behavior is the means by which many abused or neglected children act out their hostility toward their parents. Some join gangs, which furnish a sense of belonging and allow pent-up anger to be expressed in group-approved delinquent acts.

CLINICAL HISTORIES

A considerable body of research examines the clinical histories of known delinquents, typically court-adjudicated or incarcerated youth. A 1975 Philadelphia study found that 82 percent of the juvenile offenders in the sample were abused as children; 43 percent remembered being knocked unconscious by a parent. A research project among 200 juveniles in a detention center in Denver reported that 72 percent remembered being seriously injured by their parents. Statements of 100 of these juveniles, confirmed by their parents or other reliable sources, revealed that 84 percent were significantly abused before the age of 6 and 92 percent were bruised, lacerated, or fractured within one and a half years of their apprehension for delinquency.[144] Likewise, studies of persons convicted of murder reveal "a demonstrable association between homicide and maltreatment in early childhood."[145] Among children who kill or who attempt murder, the most common factor is said to be "the child's tendency to identify himself with aggressive parents, and pattern after their behavior."[146] One study of several cases of murder and murderous assault by juveniles indicated that in all cases "one or both parents had fostered and condoned murderous assault."[147] Adolescent boys who had committed homicide reported being beaten more often by their brothers and sisters.[148]

COHORT STUDIES

Although these findings are persuasive, it is important to note that they use intact samples of delinquent youth; it is possible that child abuse is a reaction to misbehavior and is caused by delinquency and not vice versa. In other words, it is possible that angry parents attack their delinquent and drug-abusing children, and that child abuse is a result of delinquency, not its cause.

One way of solving this methodological dilemma is to follow a cohort of youths who had been reported as victims of child abuse and neglect early in their lives and compare them with a similar cohort of unabused youth. One study conducted by Jose Alfaro in New York found that about half of all children reported to area hospitals as abused children later acquired arrest records. A significant number of boys (21 percent) and girls (29 percent) petitioned to juvenile court had prior histories as abuse cases. Children treated for abuse or neglect were disproportionately involved in violent offenses, including homicide, rape, and assault.[149]

In an important cohort study, Cathy Spatz Widom followed the offending careers of 908 youths reported as abused from 1967 to 1971 and compared them with a control group of 667 unabused youth. Widom found that the abuse and neglect involved a variety of perpetrators, including parents, relatives, strangers, and even grandparents. Twenty-six percent of the abused and neglected sample had juvenile arrests, compared with 17 percent of the comparison group; 29 percent of those who were abused and neglected had adult criminal records, compared with 21 percent of the control group. Widom further found that race, gender, and age also affected the probability that abuse would lead to delinquency: The highest risk group consisted of older, black males who had suffered abuse; about 67 percent of this group went on to become adult criminals. In contrast, only 4 percent of young, white, unabused females became adult offenders.[150] Her conclusion: Being abused or neglected as a child increased the likelihood of arrest as a juvenile by 53 percent, as an adult by 38 percent, and for a violent crime by 38 percent.[151]

Widom also tested the hypothesis that victims of childhood violence resort to violence themselves as they mature. The children in her sample who suffered from physical abuse were the most likely to get arrested for a violent crime; their violent crime arrest rate was double that of the control group. Although this relationship was not unexpected, more surprising was the discovery that *neglected* children maintained significantly higher rates of violence than children in the comparison group. Clearly, family trauma of all kinds influences the likelihood that children will go on to become violent offenders.

Child Victims and Persistent Offending   Widom also interviewed a sample of 500 subjects 20 years after their childhood victimization. Preliminary analysis of this sample indicates that the long-term consequences of childhood victimization continue throughout the life cycle. Potential problems associated with abuse and neglect include mental health concerns, such as depression and suicide attempts; educational problems, including low IQ and poor reading ability; health and safety problems, including substance abuse; and occupational difficulties, including under- and unaggressive employment.

In a more recent analysis of these data, Widom and Michael Maxfield found that by the time they reached age 32 (in 1994), abused children had a higher frequency of adult offending than nonabused children. People who began their offending career as adults were also more likely to be abused as children. Widom and Maxfield conclude that early intervention with at-risk children may be necessary to stop this "cycle of violence."[152]

Sexual Abuse   A recent cohort study by Jane Siegel and Linda Meyer Williams evaluated the long-term effects of sexual abuse on a sample of young males who had been treated as youngsters in a hospital emergency room of a major northeastern city. Siegel and Williams found that the abused youth were nearly twice as likely to suffer an arrest as a matched sample of nonabused children.

The risk was greatest if the abuse took place when the boys were relatively young (under age 7) and the offense was committed by a male. Those who suffered multiple incidents of abuse were at increased risk of criminal involvement.[153] Siegel and Williams have also shown that sexually abused girls share a significant risk of becoming violent over the life course.[154]

Self-Report Studies   Self-report studies also show that child maltreatment increases the likelihood of delinquency. In an important paper, Carolyn Smith and Terence Thornberry, using a group of adolescents in the Rochester, New York, area, were able to show a significant association between self-reported maltreatment and delinquency. The most severely abused youth, whose treatment was serious enough to warrant an official intervention by child protection services, were at the greatest risk for long-term serious delinquency.[155]

THE ABUSE–DELINQUENCY LINK

Such research findings do not necessarily mean that most abused or neglected children eventually become delinquent. Many do not, and many seriously delinquent youths come from what appear to be model homes. Although Widom found that more abused children in her cohort became involved in crime and delinquency than did the unabused, the majority of *both* groups were neither delinquent nor adult offenders. She concludes, "The strength of the cycle of violence may be of less magnitude than some might have expected."[156]

Matthew Zingraff and his associates compared the offending experiences of randomly selected samples of maltreated youth, nonmaltreated poor youth, and general school-age youth taken from a populous county in North Carolina.[157] Controlling for race, age, gender, and family structure, Zingraff found few significant differences between the groups. Although more (14 percent) of the abused youth were arrested than the general school (5 percent) and poverty samples (9 percent), clearly a great majority of abused youth did not get into trouble with the law. Abused adolescents did get involved in significantly more status-type offenses, perhaps indicating that abused kids are more likely to "flee than fight." Their overall conclusion? "Generally, our findings indicate that the risk of delinquency for maltreated children claimed by much of the previous research has been exaggerated."

Although these cohort studies do not support overwhelmingly an abuse–delinquency link, the issue is certainly important enough to sustain further research. The Siegel and Williams research found that more than half of the sexual abuse victims were eventually arrested for crimes; Smith and Thornberry's data indicate that about 45 percent of abused children obtain official records of delinquency.[158] Even if abuse is not a direct cause, it may be a contributing factor in juvenile delinquency. Efforts to combat maltreatment are vital not only to prevent the immediate harms of abuse and neglect but also to reduce the possibility that the victims will settle into patterns of violent, aggressive criminal behavior throughout life.

THE FAMILY AND DELINQUENCY PREVENTION

Because the family is believed to play such an important role in the production of youth crime, it follows that improving family functioning can help prevent delinquency. Counselors commonly work with the families of antisocial youths as part of a court-ordered treatment strategy. Family counseling and therapy are almost mandatory when the child's acting out behavior is suspected to be the result of family-related problems, such as child abuse or neglect,[159] and some jurisdictions have integrated family counseling services into the juvenile court.[160]

EARLY CHILDHOOD INTERVENTION

Another approach to involving the family in delinquency prevention is to attack the problem before it occurs. Early childhood prevention programs have shown indications that they can relieve some of the symptoms associated with chronic delinquency.[161] Among the best known of these is the Syracuse University Family Development Research Program. This program identifies high-risk, indigent women during the latter stages of pregnancy. After the women give birth, paraprofessionals are assigned to work with the mothers, encouraging sound parent–child relationships, providing nutrition information, and helping them to establish relationships with social service agencies. In addition to services for the mother, the program provides four and a half years of quality child care at Syracuse University Children's Center. A 10-year follow-up compared children involved in the Syracuse program with a matched control group and found that those receiving intervention were less likely to be involved in criminal activity, more likely to express positive feelings about themselves, and better able to take an active role in dealing with personal problems. Girls seemed to especially benefit from the program, doing better in school and getting higher teacher evaluations; parents were more likely to express prosocial attitudes.[162]

The Perry Preschool in Michigan has provided disadvantaged students with a two-year program of educational enrichment supplemented with weekly home visits designed to improve child care; children in the program accumulated half the arrests of a matched comparison group and appear better motivated.[163] The highly successful Hawai'i Healthy Start program has helped thousands of families considered at risk to abuse and neglect.[164] Table 8.3 describes some of the features of this program.

Improving Parenting Skills The most widely cited program is the one created at the **Oregon Social Learning Center** (OSLC) by Gerald R. Patterson and his associates.[165] Patterson's long-term research into the lifestyles of antisocial children convinced him that poor parenting skills were associated with antisocial behavior occurring in the home and at school. Family disruption and coercive exchanges between parents and children led to increased family tension, poor academic performance, and negative peer relations. The primary cause of the problem seemed to be that parents did not know how to deal effectively with their children. Sometimes they ignored their children's behavior, at other times, the same childish actions would trigger an explosive rage. Some parents would discipline their children for reasons that had little to do with the children's behavior but rather reflected their own frustrations and conflicts.

Children in turn would react to indifferent parenting in a regular progression from learning to be noncompliant at home to learning to be physically assaultive. Their "coercive" behavior, which included whining, yelling, and temper tantrums, would sometimes be acquired by other family members, exacerbating the already explosive situation. Eventually, family conflict would escalate and flow out of the home into the school and social environment.

TABLE 8.3 An Early Childhood Intervention Program: Hawai'i Healthy Start

The Hawai'i Healthy Start program uses home visitors from the community to provide services to at-risk families. Its goals are to reduce family stress and improve family functioning, improve parenting skills, enhance child health and development, and prevent abuse and neglect.

■ Unlike other similar programs, Hawai'i Healthy Start follows the child from birth (or before) to age 5 with a range of services, and it assists and supports other family members.

■ To ensure systematic enrollment, Healthy Start signs up most families right after delivery of the child, although approximately 10 percent of families are enrolled prenatally.

■ Healthy Start has formal agreements with all hospitals in Hawai'i to enable it to perform postpartum screening through a review of the mother's medical record or a brief in-person interview. Fewer than 1 percent of mothers refuse to be interviewed, 4 to 8 percent later refuse offers of services, and about 7 percent cannot be located after release from the hospital.

■ Paraprofessional home visitors call on families weekly for the first 6 to 12 months. Early in the relationship, the home visitor helps parents develop an Individual Support Plan, specifying the kinds of services they want and need and the means by which to receive them.

■ As part of its oversight, the Maternal Child Health Branch requires completion of a series of Infant/Child Monitoring Questionnaires to identify problems in child development at 4, 12, 20, and 30 months. If these show developmental delays, further assessments are performed and appropriate services are offered.

■ In 1994 a confirmed child care abuse and neglect case cost the Hawai'i family welfare system $25,000 for investigation, related services, and foster care. In contrast, Hawai'i Healthy Start officials estimate an annual average cost of $2,800 per home visitor case.

■ Preliminary evaluation findings indicate that Healthy Start families have lower abuse/neglect rates and their children are developing appropriately for their ages.

Source: Ralph Earle, *Helping to Prevent Child Abuse—and Future Criminal Consequences: Hawai'i Healthy Start* (Washington, DC.: National Institute of Justice, 1995), p. 2.

The OSLC program uses behavior modification techniques to help parents of antisocial children acquire proper care and disciplinary methods. Parents are asked to select several particular behaviors for change. Staff counselors first analyze family dynamics and then work with parents to construct a change program. Parents are asked to closely monitor the particular behaviors and to count the weekly frequency of their occurrence. OSLC personnel teach both social skills to reinforce positive behaviors and constructive disciplinary methods to discourage negative ones. Incentive programs are initiated in which a child can earn points or praise for such desirable behaviors as being cooperative and doing chores. Points can be exchanged for allowance, prizes, or privileges. Parents are also taught effective disciplinary techniques that stress firmness and consistency, rather than "nattering" (low-intensity, nonverbal, or negative verbal behaviors, such as scowling or scolding) or explosive discipline (such as hitting, making humiliating remarks, or screaming). One important technique is the "time out," in which the child is removed for brief isolation in a quiet room. Parents are taught the importance of setting rules and sticking to them. The OSLC has also developed programs especially designed to help high-risk families, such as the Adolescent Transitions Program (ATP), which teaches parents skills to deal with especially troubled adolescents.

The Oregon program is not unique; there are other methods of parent training being used with high-risk youth. For example, Functional Family Therapy (FFT)

is designed to either teach family members new skills they lack or help them to better manage skills they already possess. The program helps teach parents communications skills, provides technical aids to assist in reinforcing functional behavior, and helps institute interpersonal family tasks. Research on Functional Family Therapy finds that it can effectively reduce recidivism of young offenders.[166]

Costs and Effectiveness   Evidence suggests that early intervention in delinquency cases may be the most effective factor in any program's success and that the later the intervention, the more difficult the change process. Psychologist Edward Zigler and his associates found that early and intensive interventions in family functioning can result in significant improvement in parent–child relations and a concomitant reduction in antisocial activities.[167]

The parent training method used by the OSLC may be the most cost-effective method of early intervention.[168] A recent Rand survey found that parent training cost about 1/20th that of a home visit program and that it is more effective in preventing serious crimes. The Rand study estimates that 501 serious crimes could be prevented for every million dollars spent on parent training, a far cheaper solution to the crime problem than the use of long-term incarceration, which would cost about $16,000 to prevent a single crime![169]

FOSTER CARE

More children are being placed in long-term foster family care as an alternative to more secure treatment in the juvenile justice system. Recognizing their growing importance, some programs are focusing on improving the parenting skills of foster families as a method of reducing or preventing delinquency.

One program is the Casey Family Program, which was established to provide planned, long-term family foster care for youth who have no parents or whose parents are unable or unwilling to care for them.[170] Casey's Specialized Family Care (SFC) program operates in Bismarck, North Dakota. Specially recruited, trained, and supported foster families work closely with case managers and social workers. Individual case plans for youth involve a mix of intensive aftercare services and supervision. The foster parents receive intensive training in social control techniques in order to become the primary agents in implementing the treatment plan.

SUMMARY

Family relationships have long been linked to the problem of juvenile delinquency. Early theories viewed the broken home as a cause of youthful misconduct, but research indicates that divorce, separation, or parental death plays a smaller role in influencing delinquent acts than previously thought. Some experts have suggested that broken homes may now have a greater effect than once believed. The quality of family life also has a great influence on a child's behavior. Studies have explored the effect of discipline, parental misconduct, and family harmony on youth crime.

Concern over the relationship between family life and delinquency has been heightened by reports of widespread child abuse and neglect. Cases of abuse and neglect have been found in every level of the economic strata, and it has been estimated that more than one million children are abused each year by their parents.

Two factors are seen as causing child abuse. First, parents who themselves suffered abuse as children tend to abuse their own children. Second, isolated and alienated families tend to become abusive.

Local, state, and federal governments have attempted to alleviate the problem of child abuse. The major issue has been state interference in the family structure. All 50 states have statutes requiring that suspected cases of abuse and neglect be reported.

A number of studies have linked abuse and neglect to juvenile delinquency. They show that a disproportionate number of court-adjudicated youths had been abused or neglected. Although the evidence so far is inconclusive, it suggests that a strong relationship exists between child abuse and neglect and subsequent delinquent behavior.

In order to make it easier to prosecute abusers, the Supreme Court has legalized the use of closed-circuit TV in abuse cases. Most states also allow children to use anatomically correct dolls in testifying in court.

KEY TERMS

paternalistic family
egalitarian family
broken home
blended families
beyond control
resource dissolution
parental deviance
bullying
battered child syndrome
child abuse
neglect

physical abuse
physical neglect
emotional abuse
emotional neglect
sexual abuse
abandonment
traumatic sexualization
betrayal
powerlessness
stigmatization
substantiated

Child Abuse Prevention and Treatment Act
advisement hearing
pretrial conference
trial stage
disposition hearing
balancing-of-the-interest approach
review hearings
hearsay
Oregon Social Learning Center

QUESTIONS FOR DISCUSSION

1. What is the meaning of the terms *child abuse* and *child neglect?*
2. Social agencies, police departments, and health groups all indicate that the incidence of child abuse and neglect is increasing. What is the incidence of such action by parents against children? Are the definitions of *child abuse* and *child neglect* the key elements in determining the volume of child abuse cases in various jurisdictions?
3. What causes parents to abuse their children?
4. What is meant by the term *child protection system?* Do courts act in the best interest of the child when they allow an abused child to remain with the family?
5. Should children be allowed to testify in court via closed-circuit TV? Does this approach prevent defendants in child abuse cases from confronting their accusers?
6. Is corporal punishment ever permissible as a disciplinary method?

NOTES

1. Paul Amato and Bruce Keith, "Parental Divorce and the Well-Being of Children: A Meta-Analysis," *Psychological Bulletin* 110:26–46 (1991).
2. For general reviews of the relationship between families and delinquency, see Alan Jay Lincoln and Murray Straus, *Crime and the Family* (Springfield, Ill.: Charles C. Thomas, 1985); Rolf Loeber and Magda Stouthamer-Loeber, "Family Factors as Correlates and Predictors of Juvenile Conduct Problems and Delinquency," in Michael Tonry and Norval Morris, eds., *Crime and Justice,* vol. 7 (Chicago: University of Chicago Press, 1986), pp. 29–151.

3. Joan McCord, "Family Relationships, Juvenile Delinquency and Adult Criminality," *Criminology* 29:397–417 (1991); Scott Henggeler, ed., *Delinquency and Adolescent Psychopathology: A Family Ecological Systems Approach* (Littleton, Mass.: Wright-PSG, 1982).

4. David Farrington, "Juvenile Delinquency," in John Coleman, ed., *The School Years* (London: Routledge, 1992), pp. 139–40.

5. Ruth Inglis, *Sins of the Fathers: A Study of the Physical and Emotional Abuse of Children* (New York: St. Martin's Press, 1978), p. 131.

6. See Joseph J. Costa and Gordon K. Nelson, *Child Abuse and Neglect: Legislation, Reporting, and Prevention* (Lexington, Mass.: D.C. Heath, 1978), p. xiii.

7. S. E. Shank, "Women and the Labor Market: The Link Grows Stronger," *Monthly Labor Review* 111:3–8 (1988).

8. Christy Buchanan, Eleanor Maccoby, and Sanford Dornbusch, "Caught between Parents: Adolescents' Experience in Divorced Homes," *Child Development* 62:1008–29 (1991).

9. Pamela Webster, Terri Orbuch, and James House, "Effects of Childhood Family Background on Adult Marital Quality and Perceived Stability," *American Journal of Sociology* 101:404–32 (1995).

10. Children's Defense Fund, *The State of America's Children 1995* (Washington, D.C.: Children's Defense Fund, 1995), p. 5.

11. Zigler, "Addressing the Nation's Child Care Crisis, The School of the Twenty-First Century" *American Journal of Orthopsychiatry* 59:484–91, (1989).

12. Ching-Tung Lung and Deborah Daro, *Current Trends in Child Abuse Reporting and Fatalities: The Results of the 1995 Annual Fifty-State Survey* (Chicago: National Committee to Prevent Child Abuse, 1996).

13. Richard Gelles and Murray Straus, *Intimate Violence* (New York: Simon & Schuster, 1988), p. 27.

14. Loeber and Stouthamer-Loeber, "Family Factors," pp. 39–41.

15. Paul Howes and Howard Markman, "Marital Quality and Child Functioning: A Longitudinal Investigation," *Child Development* 60:1044–51 (1989).

16. Barbara Dafoe Whitehead, "Dan Quayle Was Right," *Atlantic Monthly* 271:47–84 (1993).

17. C. Patrick Brady, James Bray, and Linda Zeeb, "Behavior Problems of Clinic Children: Relation to Parental Marital Status, Age, and Sex of Child," *American Journal of Orthopsychiatry* 56:399–412 (1986).

18. Scott Hengeller, *Delinquency in Adolescence* (Newbury Park, Calif.: Sage, 1989), p. 48.

19. Sheldon Glueck and Eleanor Glueck, *Unraveling Juvenile Delinquency* (Cambridge, Mass.: Harvard University Press, 1950); Ashley Weeks, "Predicting Juvenile Delinquency," *American Sociological Review* 8:40–46 (1943).

20. Jackson Toby, "The Differential Impact of Family Disorganization," *American Sociological Review* 22:505–12 (1957); Ruth Morris, "Female Delinquency and Relation Problems," *Social Forces* 43:82–89 (1964); Roland Chilton and Gerald Markle, "Family Disruption, Delinquent Conduct, and the Effects of Sub-classification," *American Sociological Review* 37:93–99 (1972).

21. For a review of these early studies, see Thomas Monahan, "Family Status and the Delinquent Child: A Reappraisal and Some New Findings," *Social Forces* 35:250–58 (1957).

22. Clifford Shaw and Henry McKay, *Report on the Causes of Crime, Social Factors in Juvenile Delinquency*, vol. 2 (Washington, D.C.: U.S. Government Printing Office, 1931), p. 392.

23. John Laub and Robert Sampson, "Unraveling Families and Delinquency: A Reanalysis of the Gluecks' Data," *Criminology* 26:355–80 (1988); Lawrence Rosen, "The Broken Home and Male Delinquency," in M. Wolfgang, L. Savitz, and N. Johnston, eds., *The Sociology of Crime and Delinquency* (New York: Wiley, 1970), pp. 489–95.

24. Lawrence Rosen and Kathleen Neilson, "Broken Homes," in Leonard Savitz and Norman Johnston, eds., *Contemporary Criminology* (New York: Wiley, 1982), pp. 126–35.

25. L. Edward Wells and Joseph Rankin, "Families and Delinquency: A Meta-Analysis of the Impact of Broken Homes," *Social Problems* 38:71–90 (1991).

26. Joseph Rankin, "The Family Context of Delinquency," *Social Problems* 30:466–79 (1983).

27. Loeber and Stouthamer-Loeber, "Family Factors," p. 78.

28. James Q. Wilson and Richard Herrnstein, *Crime and Human Nature* (New York: Simon & Schuster, 1985), p. 249.

29. Joseph Rankin and Roger Kern, "Parental Attachments and Delinquency," *Criminology* 32:495–515 (1994).

30. Marvin Krohn, Terence Thornberry, Lori Collins-Hall, and Alan Lizotte, "School Dropout, Delinquent Behavior, and Drug Use," in Howard Kaplan, ed., *Drugs, Crime and Other Deviant Adaptations: Longitudinal Studies* (New York: Plenum Press, 1995), pp. 163–83.

31. Nan Marie Astone and Sara McLanahan, "Family Structure, Parental Practices and High School Completion," *American Sociological Review* 56:309–20 (1991).

32. Mary Pat Traxler, "The Influence of the Father and Alternative Male Role Models on African-American Boys' Involvement in Antisocial Behavior" (Paper presented at the annual meeting of the American Society of Criminology, New Orleans, La., November 1992).

33. Judith Smetena, "Adolescents' and Parents' Reasoning about Actual Family Conflict," *Child Development* 60:1052–67 (1989).

34. F. Ivan Nye, "Child Adjustment in Broken and Unhappy Unbroken Homes," *Marriage and Family* 19:356–61 (1957); idem, *Family Relationships and Delinquent Behavior* (New York: Wiley, 1958).

35. Michael Hershorn and Alan Rosenbaum, "Children of Marital Violence: A Closer Look at the Unintended Victims," *American Journal of Orthopsychiatry* 55:260–66 (1985).

36. Peter Jaffe, David Wolfe, Susan Wilson, and Lydia Zak, "Similarities in Behavior and Social Maladjustment among Child Victims and Witnesses to Family Violence," *American Journal of Orthopsychiatry* 56:142–46 (1986).

37. Hengeller, *Delinquency in Adolescence,* p. 39.

38. Jill Leslie Rosenbaum, "Family Dysfunction and Female Delinquency," *Crime and Delinquency* 35:31–44 (1989), at 41.

39. Paul Robinson, "Parents of 'Beyond Control' Adolescents," *Adolescence* 13:116–19 (1978).

40. Cindy Hanson, Scott Hennggeler, William Haefele, and J. Douglas Rodick, "Demographic, Individual, and Familial Relationship Correlates of Serious and Repeated Crime among Adolescents and Their Siblings," *Journal of Consulting and Clinical Psychology* 52:528–38 (1984).

41. Hengeller, *Delinquency in Adolescence,* p. 42.

42. Amato and Keith, "Parental Divorce and the Well-Being of Children."

43. Keith Warren and Ray Johnson, "Family Environment, Affect, Ambivalence and Decisions about Unplanned Adolescent Pregnancy," *Adolescence* 24:630–41 (1989).

44. Richard Smith and James Walters, "Delinquent and Non-delinquent Males' Perceptions of Their Fathers," *Adolescence* 13:21–28 (1978).

45. McCord, "Family Relationships, Juvenile Delinquency and Adult Criminality," p. 411.

46. Bill McCarthy and John Hagan, "Mean Streets: The Theoretical Significance of Situational Delinquency among Homeless Youth," *American Journal of Sociology* 98:597–627 (1992).

47. Hanson et al., "Demographic, Individual, and Familial Relationship Correlates of Serious and Repeated Crime among Adolescents and Their Siblings," p. 536.

48. Smith and Walters, "Delinquent and Non-delinquent Males' Perceptions of Their Fathers."

49. Laub and Sampson, "Unraveling Families and Delinquency," p. 375.

50. David Farrington, "The Development of Offending and Antisocial Behavior from Childhood to Adulthood" (Paper presented at the Congress on Rethinking Delinquency, University of Minho, Braga, Portugal, July 1992), p. 9.

51. Gerald Patterson and Magda Stouthamer-Loeber, "The Correlation of Family Management Practices and Delinquency," *Child Development* 55:1299–1307 (1984); Gerald R. Patterson, *A Social Learning Approach: Coercive Family Process,* vol. 3 (Eugene, Ore.: Castalia, 1982).

52. Christopher Ellison and Darren Sherkat, "Conservative Protestantism and Support for Corporal Punishment," *American Sociological Review* 58:131–44 (1993).

53. Murray Straus, "Discipline and Deviance: Physical Punishment of Children and Violence and Other Crime in Adulthood," *Social Problems* 38:101–23 (1991).

54. Nye, *Family Relationships and Delinquent Behavior.*

55. Rolf Loeber and Thomas Dishion, "Boys Who Fight at Home and School: Family Conditions Influencing Cross-Setting Consistency," *Journal of Consulting and Clinical Psychology* 52:759–68 (1984).

56. Thomas Dishion, Deborah Capaldi, Kathleen Spracklen, and Fushong Li, "Peer Ecology of Male Adolescent Drug Use," *Development and Psychopathology* 7:803–24 (1995).

57. Velmer Burton, Francis Cullen, T. David Evans, R. Gregory Dunaway, Sesha Kethineni, and Gary Payne, "The Impact of Parental Controls on Delinquency," *Journal of Criminal Justice* 23:111–26 (1995).

58. Lisa Broidy, "Direct Supervision and Delinquency: Assessing the Adequacy of Structural Proxies," *Journal of Criminal Justice* 23:541–54 (1995).

59. Stephen Cernkovich and Peggy Giordano, "Family Relationships and Delinquency," *Criminology* 25:295–321 (1987).

60. Douglas Downey, "When Bigger Is Not Better: Family Size, Parental Reources, and Children's Educational Performance," *American Sociological Review* 60:746–61 (1995).

61. G. Rahav, "Birth Order and Delinquency," *British Journal of Criminology* 20:385–95 (1980); D. Viles and D. Challinger, "Family Size and Birth Order of Young Offenders," *International Journal of Offender Therapy and Comparative Criminology* 25:60–66 (1981).

62. Linda Waite and Lee Lillard, "Children and Marital Disruption," *American Journal of Sociology* 96:930–53 (1991).

63. David Eggebeen and Daniel Lichter, "Race, Family Structure, and Changing Poverty among American Children," *American Sociological Review* 56:801–17 (1991).

64. For an early review, see Barbara Wooton, *Social Science and Social Pathology* (London: Allen and Unwin, 1959).

65. Laub and Sampson, "Unraveling Families and Delinquency," p. 375.

66. D. J. West and D. P. Farrington, eds., "Who Becomes Delinquent?" in *The Delinquent Way of Life* (London: Heinemann, 1977); D. J. West, *Delinquency, Its Roots, Careers, and Prospects* (Cambridge, Mass.: Harvard University Press, 1982).

67. West, *Delinquency,* p. 114.

68. David Farrington, "Understanding and Preventing Bullying," in Michael Tonry, ed., *Crime and Justice,* vol. 17 (Chicago: University of Chicago Press, 1993), pp. 381–457.

69. Philip Harden and Robert Pihl, "Cognitive Function, Cardiovascular Reactivity, and Behavior in Boys at High Risk for Alcoholism," *Journal of Abnormal Psychology* 104:94–103 (1995).

70. Laub and Sampson, "Unraveling Families and Delinquency," p. 370.

71. D. P. Farrington, Gwen Gundry, and D. J. West, "The Familial Transmission of Criminality," in Alan Lincoln and Murray Straus, eds., *Crime and the Family* (Springfield, Ill.: Charles C. Thomas, 1985) pp. 193–206.

72. See, generally, Wooton, *Social Science and Social Pathology;* H. Wilson, "Juvenile Delinquency, Parental Criminality, and Social Handicaps," *British Journal of Criminology* 15:241–50 (1975).

73. David Rowe and Bill Gulley, "Sibling Effects on Substance Use and Delinquency," *Criminology* 30:217–32 (1992); see also David Rowe, Joseph Rogers, and Sylvia Meseck-Bushey, "Sibling Delinquency and the Family Environment: Shared and Unshared Influences," *Child Development* 63:59–67 (1992).

74. Charles De Witt, director of the National Institute of Justice, quoted in National Institute of Justice, Research in Brief, *The Cycle of Violence* (Washington, D.C.: National Institute of Justice, 1992), p. 1.

75. Richard Gelles and Claire Pedrick Cornell, *Intimate Violence in Families,* 2nd ed. (Newbury Park, Calif.: Sage, 1990), p. 33.

76. Lois Hochhauser, "Child Abuse and the Law: A Mandate for Change," *Harvard Law Journal* 18:200 (1973); see also Douglas J. Besharov, "The Legal Aspects of Reporting Known and Suspected Child Abuse and Neglect," *Villanova Law Review* 23:458 (1978).

77. C. Henry Kempe, C. H. Kempe, F. N. Silverman, B. F. Steele, W. Droegemueller, and H. K. Silver, "The Battered-Child Syndrome," *Journal of the American Medical Association* 181:17–24 (1962).

78. Vincent J. Fontana, "The Maltreated Children of Our Times," *Villanova Law Review* 23:448 (1978).

79. Ray E. Helfer and C. Henry Kempe, eds., *Child Abuse and Neglect: The Family and the Community* (Cambridge, Mass.: Ballinger, 1976), p. xix.

80. Brian G. Fraser, "A Glance at the Past, a Gaze at the Present, a Glimpse at the Future: A Critical Analysis of the Development of Child Abuse Reporting Statutes," *Chicago-Kent Law Review* 54:643 (1977–78).

81. Ibid.

82. Vincent J. Fontana, "To Prevent the Abuse of the Future," *Trial* 10:14 (1974).

83. See, especially, Inglis, *Sins of the Fathers,* chap. 8.

84. Ruth S. Kempe and C. Henry Kempe, *Child Abuse* (Cambridge, Mass.: Harvard University Press, 1978), pp. 6–7.

85. Herman Daldin, "The Fate of the Sexually Abused Child," *Clinical Social Work Journal* 16:20–26 (1988).

86. Gerald Ellenson, "Horror, Rage and Defenses in the Symptoms of Female Sexual Abuse Survivors," *Social Casework: The Journal of Contemporary Social Work* 70:589–96 (1989).

87. David Finkelhor and Angela Browne, "The Traumatic Impact of Child Sexual Abuse: A Conceptualization," *American Journal of Orthopsychiatry* 55:530–41 (1985).

88. Carolyn Moore Newberger, Isabelle Gremy, Christine Waternaux, and Eli Newberger, "Mothers of Sexually Abused Children: Trauma and Repair in Longitudinal Perspective," *American Journal of Orthopsychiatry* 63:92–98 (1993).

89. David Goldston, Dawn Turnquist, and John Knutson, "Presenting Problems of Sexually Abused Girls Receiving Psychiatric Services," *Journal of Abnormal Psychology* 98:314–17 (1989).

90. Ellenson, "Horror, Rage and Defenses in the Symptoms of Female Sexual Abuse Survivors," pp. 589–91.

91. Angela Browne and David Finkelhor, "Impact of Child Sexual Abuse: A Review of the Research," *Psychological Bulletin* 99:66–77 (1986).

92. Judith Herman, Diana Russell, and Karen Trocki, "Long-Term Effects of Incestuous Abuse in Childhood," *American Journal of Psychiatry* 143:1293–96 (1986).

93. Magnus Seng, "Child Sexual Abuse and Adolescent Prostitution: A Comparative Analysis," *Adolescence* 24:665–75 (1989); Dorothy Bracey, *Baby Pros: Preliminary Profiles of Juvenile Prostitutes* (New York: John Jay Press, 1979).

94. Kathleen Kendall-Tackett, Linda Meyer Williams, and David Finkelhor, "Impact of Sexual Abuse on Children: A Review and Synthesis of Recent Empirical Studies," *Psychological Bulletin* 113:164–80 (1993).

95. Murray Straus, Richard Gelles, and Suzanne Steinmentz, *Behind Closed Doors: Violence in the American Family* (Garden City, N.Y.: Anchor Books, 1980); Richard Gelles and Murray Straus, "Violence in the American Family," *Journal of Social Issues* 35:15–39 (1979).

96. Gelles and Straus, "Violence in the American Family," p. 24.

97. Gelles and Straus, *Intimate Violence,* pp. 108–09.

98. Richard Gelles and Murray Straus, *Is Violence Toward Children Increasing? A Comparison of 1975 and 1985 National Survey Rates* (Durham, N.H.: Family Violence Research Program, 1985).

99. Diana Russell, *Sexual Exploitation: Rape, Child Sexual Abuse, and Workplace Harassment* (Beverly Hills, Calif.: Sage, 1984).

100. Maria Root, "Treatment Failures: The Role of Sexual Victimization in Women's Addictive Behavior," *American Journal of Orthopsychiatry* 59:543–49 (1989).

101. Ching-Tung Lung and Deborah Daro, *Current Trends in Child Abuse Reporting and Fatalities: The Results of the 1995 Annual Fifty-State Survey.*

102. Carolyn Webster-Stratton, "Comparison of Abusive and Nonabusive Families with Conduct-Disordered Children," *American Journal of Orthopsychiatry* 55:59–69 (1985); Fontana, "To Prevent the Abuse of the Future," p. 16; Fontana, "The Maltreated Children of Our Times," p. 451; Brandt F. Steele and Carl B. Pollock, "A Psychiatric

Study of Parents Who Abuse Infants and Small Children," in Ray Helfer and C. Henry Kempe, eds., *The Battered Child* (Chicago: University of Chicago Press, 1968), pp. 103–45.

103. Inglis, *Sins of the Fathers,* p. 68.

104. Ibid., p. 53.

105. Brandt F. Steele, "Violence within the Family," in Ray E. Helfer and C. Henry Kempe, eds., *Child Abuse and Neglect: The Family and the Community* (Cambridge, Mass.: Ballinger, 1976), p. 13.

106. William Sack, Robert Mason, and James Higgins, "The Single-Parent Family and Abusive Punishment," *American Journal of Orthopsychiatry* 55:252–59 (1985).

107. Fontana, "The Maltreated Children of Our Times," pp. 450–51. See also Blair Justice and Rita Justice, *The Abusing Family* (New York: Human Sciences Press, 1976); Steele, "Violence within the Family," p. 12; and Nanette Dembitz, "Preventing Youth Crime by Preventing Child Neglect," *American Bar Association Journal* 65:920–23 (1979).

108. Gelles and Straus, *Intimate Violence,* p. 85.

109. Lung and Daro, *Current Trends in Child Abuse,* 1995.

110. Nancy Smyth, Brenda Miller, Paula Janicki, and Pamela Mudar, "Mothers' Protectiveness and Child Abuse: The Impact of Her History of Childhood Sexual Abuse and an Alcohol Diagnosis" (Paper presented at the American Society of Criminology meeting, Boston, Mass., November 1995); Richard Famularo, Karen Stone, Richard Barnum, and Robert Wharton, "Alcoholism and Severe Child Maltreatment," *American Journal of Orthopsychiatry* 56:481–85 (1987).

111. Jordana Hart, "Child Abuse Found Tied to Drug Use," *Boston Globe,* 2 June 1989, p. 23.

112. Deborah Daro and Karen McCurdy, *Current Trends in Child Abuse Reporting and Fatalities: The Results of the 1992 Annual Fifty-State Survey* (Chicago: National Committee for the Prevention of Child Abuse, 1993), 29:19–31.

113. *Study Findings, National Incidence and Prevalence of Child Abuse and Neglect* (Washington, D.C.: Government Printing Office, 1988).

114. Daro & McCurdy, *Current Trends in Child Abuse,* 1992, p. 11.

115. Richard Gelles, "Child Abuse and Violence in Single-Parent Families: Parent Absence and Economic Deprivation," *American Journal of Orthopsychiatry* 59:492–501 (1989).

116. Susan Napier and Mitchell Silverman, "Family Violence as a Function of Occupation Status, Socioeconomic Class, and Other Variables" (Paper presented at the American Society of Criminology meeting, Boston, Mass., November 1995).

117. Karla McPherson and Laura Garcia, "Effects of Social Class and Familiarity on Pediatricians' Responses to Child Abuse," *Child Welfare* 62:387–93 (1983).

118. S. Bittner and E. H. Newberger, "Pediatric Understanding of Child Abuse," *Pediatrics in Review* 7:197–207 (1981); see also E. H. Newberger and P. Bourne, "The Medicalization and Legalization of Child Abuse," *American Journal of Orthopsychiatry* 48:593–607 (1978).

119. Cecil Willis and Richard Wells, "The Police and Child Abuse: An Analysis of Police Decisions to Report Illegal Behavior," *Criminology* 26:695–716 (1988).

120. Robert Burgess and Patricia Draper, "The Explanation of Family Violence," in Ohlin and Tonry, eds. *Family Violence* (Chicago: University of Chicago Press, 1989), pp. 59–117.

121. Ibid., pp. 103–04.

122. Linda Gordon, "Incest and Resistance: Patterns of Father–Daughter Incest, 1880–1930," *Social Problems* 33:253–67 (1986).

123. P.L. 93–247 (1974).

124. *Lassiter v. Department of Social Services,* 452 U.S. 18, 101 S.Ct. 2153 (1981); *Santosky v. Kramer,* 455 U.S. 745, 102 S.Ct. 1388 (1982).

125. For a survey of each state's reporting requirements, abuse and neglect legislation, and available programs and agencies, see Costa and Nelson, *Child Abuse and Neglect.*

126. Martha Brannigan, "Arrests Spark Furor over the Reporting of Suspected Abuse," *Wall Street Journal,* 7 June 1989, p. B8.

127. Debra Whitcomb, *When the Victim Is a Child* (Washington, D.C.: National Institute of Justice, 1992), p. 5.

128. "False Accusations of Abuse Devastating to Families," *Crime Victims Digest* 6 (2):4–5 (1989).

129. Michael S. Wald, "State Intervention on Behalf of 'Neglected Children': A Search for Standards for Placement of Children in Foster Care, and Termination of Parental Rights," *Stanford Law Review* 28:626–706 (1976).

130. For an analysis of the accuracy of children's recollections of abuse, see Candace Kruttschnitt and Maude Dornfeld, "Will They Tell? Assessing Preadolescents' Reports of Family Violence" *Journal of Research in Crime and Delinquency* 29:136–47 (1992).

131. Lindsay Arthur, "Child Sexual Abuse: Improving the System's Response," *Juvenile and Family Court Journal* 37:27–36 (1986).

132. Ibid.

133. Debra Whitcomb, *When the Victim Is a Child,* (Washington, D.C.: National Institute of Justice, 1992), p. 33..

134. *Idaho v. Wright,* 110 S.Ct. 3139 (1990).

135. *White v. Illinois,* 112 S.Ct. 736 (1992).

136. Myrna Raeder, "*White's* Effect on the Right to Confront One's Accuser," *Criminal Justice* Winter 1993, pp. 2–7.

137. *Coy v. Iowa,* 487 U.S. 1012 (1988).

138. *Maryland v. Craig,* 110 S.Ct. 3157 (1990).

139. Cathy Spatz Widom, *The Cycle of Violence* (Washington, D.C.: National Institute of Justice, 1992), p. 1.

140. *Walker v. Fagg,* 400 S.E. 2d 708 (Va. App. 1991).

141. Mary Haskett and Janet Kistner, "Social Interactions and Peer Perceptions of Young Physically Abused Children," *Child Development* 62:679–90 (1991).

142. Richard Gelles and Murray Straus, "Violence in the American Family," *Journal of Social Issues* 35:15 (1979).

143. Helfer and Kempe, *Child Abuse and Neglect,* pp. xvii–xviii.

144. National Center on Child Abuse and Neglect, Department of Health, Education, and Welfare, *1977 Analysis of Child Abuse and Neglect Research* (Washington, D.C.: U.S. Government Printing Office, 1978), p. 29.

145. Steele, "Violence within the Family," p. 22.

146. L. Bender and F. J. Curran, "Children and Adolescents Who Kill," *Journal of Criminal Psychopathology* 1:297 (1940), cited in Steele, "Violence within the Family," p. 21.

147. W. M. Easson and R. M. Steinhilber, "Murderous Aggression by Children and Adolescents," *Archives of General Psychiatry* 4:1–11 (1961), cited in Steele, "Violence within the Family," p. 22. See also J. Duncan and G. Duncan, "Murder in the Family: A Study of Some Homicidal Adolescents," *American Journal of Psychiatry* 127:1498–1502 (1971); C. King, "The Ego and Integration of Violence in Homicidal Youth," *American Journal of Orthopsychiatry* 45:134–45 (1975); and James Sorrells, "Kids Who Kill," *Crime and Delinquency* 23:312–26 (1977).

148. C. H. King, "The Ego and the Integration of Violence in Homicidal Youth," *American Journal of Orthopsychiatry* 45:134–45 (1975).

149. Jose Alfaro, "Report of the Relationship between Child Abuse and Neglect and Later Socially Deviant Behavior," *Exploring the Relationship between Child Abuse and Delinquency,* pp. 175–219.

150. Cathy Spatz Widom, "Child Abuse, Neglect, and Violent Criminal Behavior," *Criminology* 27:251–71 (1989).

151. Widom, *The Cycle of Violence,* p. 1.

152. Michael Maxfield and Cathy Spatz Widom, "Childhood Victimization and Patterns of Offending through the Life Cycle: Early Onset and Continuation" (Paper presented at the American Society of Criminology meeting, Boston, Mass., November 1995).

153. Jane Siegel and Linda Meyer Williams, "Violent Behavior among Men Abused as Children" (Paper presented at the American Society of Criminology meeting, Boston, Mass., November 1995).

154. Jane Siegel and Linda Meyer Williams, "Aggressive Behavior among Women Sexually Abused as Children" (Paper presented at the American Society of Criminology meeting, Phoenix, Ariz., 1993). Revised version.

155. Carolyn Smith and Terence Thornberry "The Relationship between Childhood Maltreatment and Adolescent Involvement in Delinquency," *Criminology* 33:451–77 (1995).

156. Widom, "Child Abuse, Neglect, and Violent Criminal Behavior," p. 267.

157. Matthew Zingraff, "Child Maltreatment and Youthful Problem Behavior," *Criminology* 31:173–202 (1993).

158. Siegel and Williams, "Violent Behavior among Men Abused as Children"; Smith and Thornberry, "The Relationship between Childhood Maltreatment and Adolescent Involvement in Delinquency."

159. Leonard Edwards and Inger Sagatun, "Dealing with Parent and Child in Serious Abuse Cases," *Juvenile and Family Court Journal* 34:9–14 (1983).

160. Susan McPherson, Lance McDonald, and Charles Ryer, "Intensive Counseling with Families of Juvenile Offenders," *Juvenile and Family Court Journal* 34:27–34 (1983).

161. The programs in this section are described in Edward Zigler, Cara Taussig, and Kathryn Black, "Early Childhood Intervention, A Promising Preventative for Juvenile Delinquency," *American Psychologist* 47:997–1006 (1992).

162. Peter Greenwood, Karyn Model, and C. Peter Rydell, *The Cost-Effectiveness of Early Intervention as a Strategy for Reducing Violent Crime* (Santa Monica, Calif.: Rand, 1995).

163. Ibid., p. 7.

164. Ralph Earle, *Helping to Prevent Child Abuse and Future Criminal Consequences: Hawai'i Healthy Start* (Washington, D.C.: National Institute of Justice, 1995).

165. See, generally, Gerald Patterson, "Performance Models for Antisocial Boys," *American Psychologist* 41:432–44 (1986); idem, *Coercive Family Process* (Eugene, Ore.: Castalia, 1982).

166. Donald Gordon, "Functional Family Therapy for Delinquents," in Robert Ross, Daniel Antonowicz, and Gurmeet Dhaliwal, eds., *Going Straight: Effective Delinquency Prevention and Offender Rehabilitation* (Ontario, Canada: Air Training and Publications, 1995), pp. 163–77.

167. Zigler, Taussig, and Black, "Early Childhood Intervention, a Promising Preventative for Juvenile Delinquency," pp. 1000–04.

168. N. A. Wiltz and G. R. Patterson, "An Evaluation of Parent Training Procedures Designed to Alter Inappropriate Aggressive Behavior in Boys," *Behavior Therapy* 5:215–21 (1974).

169. Peter Greenwood, Karyn Model, and C. Peter Rydell, *The Cost-Effectiveness of Early Intervention as a Strategy for Reducing Violent Crime* (Santa Monica, Calif.: Rand, 1995).

170. James Davis, Charley Joyce, Joyce Gerhardt, Peter Pecora, James Traglia, Glen Paddock, Lowell Flemmer, Kent Henderson, and Al Lick, "Implementing Family Foster Care Services with Youth Adjudicated as Delinquent" (Paper presented at the American Society of Criminology meeting, Boston, Mass., November 1995).

CHAPTER NINE

Peers and Delinquency: Juvenile Gangs and Groups

INTRODUCTION

No issues in the study of delinquency are more important today than the effect of peer relations on antisocial behavior and the problems presented by law-violating gangs and groups.[1] Although some gangs are made up of only a few loosely organized neighborhood youths, others have thousands of members who cooperate in highly complex illegal enterprises. A significant portion of all drug distribution in U.S. inner cities is believed to be gang controlled; gang violence accounts for more than 1,000 homicides each year; correctional surveys indicate that about 19 percent of all male and 3 percent of all female inmates are gang members.[2]

Social service and law enforcement groups have made a concerted effort to contain gangs and reduce their criminal activity. Approaches range from introducing treatment-oriented settlement houses to deploying tactical gang control units. The problem of gang control is a difficult one: Gangs flourish in those areas (usually the inner city) where lower-class youths have few conventional opportunities to achieve social and financial success. Although gang members may be subject to arrest, prosecution, and incarceration, a new crop of young recruits is always ready to take the place of their fallen comrades. Those sent to prison find that upon release, their former gangs are only too willing to welcome them back.

This chapter examines the nature and extent of gang and group delinquency. It discusses peer relations and shows how group relations influence delinquent behavior. It then explores the definition, nature, and structure of delinquent gangs. In addition, theories of gang formation, the extent of gang activity, and gang-control efforts are presented.

ADOLESCENT PEER RELATIONS

Psychologists have long recognized that as children mature, their friendship patterns also evolve. Although parents are the primary source of influence and attention in children's early years, between ages 8 and 14, children begin to seek out stable peer groups; both the number and the variety of friendships increase as children go through adolescence. Friends soon begin having a greater influence over decision making than parents.[3] By their early teens, adolescents report it is their friends to whom they turn for emotional support when they are feeling bad and in whom they believe they can confide intimate feelings without worrying about their confidences being betrayed.[4]

As they go through adolescence, children form **cliques,** small groups of friends who share activities and confidences.[5] They also belong to **crowds,** loosely organized groups of children who share interests and activities. While clique members share intimate knowledge of one another, crowds are brought together by mutually shared interest in activities such as sports, religion, and hobbies. Popular youths can be members of a variety of same-sex cliques and crowds, as well as groups containing members of the opposite sex. Both cliques and crowds play important roles in social development. Adolescent self-image is in part formed by perceptions of one's place in the social world—whether he or she is considered an insider or an outcast.[6]

In later adolescence, peer acceptance has a major impact on socialization. Popular youths do well in school and are socially astute. In contrast, youths who are rejected by their peers are more likely to display aggressive behavior and disrupt group activities by bickering or behaving antisocially.[7] Lower-class youths, lacking in educational and vocational opportunities, may place even greater emphasis on friendship than middle-class youths, who can easily replace friends as they change locales and activities (e.g., go off to college).[8]

Peer relations, then, are a significant aspect of maturation. Peers exert a powerful influence on youths and pressure them to conform to group values. Peers guide youths and help them learn to share and cooperate, cope with aggressive impulses, and discuss feelings they would not dare bring up at home. With peers, youths can compare their own experiences and learn that others have similar concerns and problems; they realize that they are not alone.[9]

PEER RELATIONS AND DELINQUENCY

Although experts have long debated the relationship between peer group interaction and delinquency there seems to be little question that adolescents who maintain delinquent friends are more likely to engage in antisocial behavior and drug abuse.[10] Reviews of the research show that delinquent acts tend to be committed in small groups, rather than alone; this process is called **co-offending**.[11] Group process may involve family members as well as peers; brothers are likely to commit offenses with brothers of a similar age.[12]

Mark Warr has found that delinquent groups tend to be small and transitory.[13] Youths often belong to more than one deviant group or clique and develop an extensive network of delinquent associates. Multiple memberships are desirable because delinquent groups tend to "specialize" in different types of delinquent activity: One group may concentrate on shoplifting while another performs home invasions. Warr also found that group roles can vary: An adolescent who assumes a leadership role in one group may be a follower in another.[14]

THE IMPACT OF PEER RELATIONS

Does having antisocial peers cause delinquency, or are delinquents antisocial youths who seek out like-minded companions? Three opposing viewpoints exist on this question. Social control theorists, such as Travis Hirschi, argue that delinquents are as detached from their peers as they are from other elements of society. He maintains that although delinquent youths may acknowledge that they have "friends," their actual personal relationships are cold and exploitative. In an oft-cited work, James Short and Fred Strodtbeck described the importance delinquent youths attach to their peer groups while at the same time observing how delinquents lack the social skills to make their peer relations rewarding or fulfilling.[15] According to this view, antisocial adolescents seek out like-minded peers for criminal associations. If delinquency is committed in groups, it is because "birds of a feather flock together" and not because deviant peers cause otherwise law-abiding youths to commit crimes.

Structural and learning theorists view the delinquency experience as one marked by close peer group support. They link delinquency to the rewards gained by associating with like-minded youth, learning deviant values and behaviors, and being rewarded with peer approval. Youths who maintain friendships with antisocial friends are more likely to become delinquent regardless of their own personality makeup or the type of supervision they receive at home.[16] Even previously law-abiding youths are more likely to get involved in delinquency and substance abuse if they begin to associate with antisocial friends who initiate them into a delinquent career.[17]

A third view is that peers and delinquency are mutually supporting. Antisocial kids join up with like-minded friends; deviant peers sustain and amplify delinquent careers.[18] As adolescents move through the life course, friends will influence their behavior, and their behavior will influence their friends.[19] Mark Warr has found that these antisocial friends help delinquent careers to withstand the aging-out process.[20]

DELINQUENT PEERS

The weight of the empirical evidence indicates that youths who are loyal to delinquent friends, belong to a gang, have "bad" companions, and are otherwise involved with deviant peers are the ones most likely to commit crime.[21] Nonetheless, associating with deviant peers does not necessarily mean that the relationships are close, intimate, and influential. Are delinquents actually close to their peers?

Exploring the quality of delinquent peer relations directly, Peggy Giordano, Stephen Cernkovich, and M. D. Pugh found that both delinquents and nondelinquents actually had similar types of friendship patterns.[22] Delinquent youths reported that their peer relations contained elements of caring and trust and that they could be open and intimate with their friends. Delinquent youths also reported getting more intrinsic rewards from their peers than did nondelinquents. However, there were some differences between the peer relations of delinquents and nondelinquents: The former reported more conflict than the latter with their friends, more feelings of jealousy and competition, and, not unexpectedly, more pronounced feelings of loyalty in the face of trouble. These findings support the view that delinquents' peer group relations play an important part in their lifestyle and stand in contrast to the view that youthful law violators are loners without peer group support.

Youths who are loyal to delinquent friends, belong to a gang, have "bad" companions," and are otherwise involved with deviant peers are the ones most likely to commit crime. Delinquents report having more conflict with their friends than non-delinquents. Delinquents also perceive more feelings of jealousy and competition, and, not unexpectedly, more pronounced feelings of peer loyalty when faced with "trouble."

Part III Environmental Influences on Delinquency

Comparable relationships have been found in studies of peer relations among young drug-involved males.[23] Marvin Krohn and Terence Thornberry, employing data from the Rochester Youth Development cohort study, reached similar conclusions: Alcohol and marijuana users have friendships that are more intimate and varied than those of nonusers.[24]

These findings seem to contradict the social control theory model, which holds that delinquents are loners, and support the cultural deviance view that delinquents form close-knit peer groups and cliques that sustain their behavior. These new data on the peer relations of delinquents seem to suggest that adolescents are influenced by social relationships as they go through the life cycle and that these relationships can influence behavior patterns.

YOUTH GANGS

As youths move through adolescence, they gravitate toward cliques that provide them with support, assurance, protection, and direction. Membership in a clique allows youths to devalue enemies, achieve status, and develop self-assurance. In some instances, the clique provides the social and emotional basis for antisocial activity, including crime and substance abuse, and, in doing so, is transformed into a **gang.**

Although sometimes viewed as a uniquely American phenomenon, youth gangs have also been reported in England, Germany, Italy, New Zealand, Australia, and other countries.[25] Nor are gangs a recent phenomenon. In the 1600s, London was terrorized by organized gangs who called themselves "Hectors," "Bugles," "Dead Boys," and other colorful names. In the seventeenth and eighteenth centuries English gangs wore distinctive belts and pins marked with symbols such as serpents, animals, and stars to identify themselves as members.[26]

Today, the delinquent gang is a topic of considerable interest to many Americans. Such a powerful mystique has grown up around gangs that the mere mention of the word *gang* evokes images of black-jacketed youths roaming the streets at night in groups bearing such colorful names as the Latin Kings, Mafia Crips, the Bounty Hunters, and the Savage Skulls. Films, television shows, novels, and even Broadway musicals, such as *Menace II Society, Boyz N the Hood, New Jack City, Trespass, Fresh, Clockers, Outsiders, West Side Story,* and *Colors* have popularized the youth gang.[27]

Considering the suspected role gangs play in violent crime and drug activity, it is not surprising that they have recently become the target of a great deal of research interest.[28] The secretive, constantly changing nature of juvenile gangs makes them a difficult focus of study. Nonetheless, important attempts have been made to gauge their size, location, makeup, and activities.

WHAT ARE GANGS?

Gangs are groups of youth who collectively engage in delinquent behaviors. Yet a distinction must be made between *group delinquency* and *gang delinquency.* The former consists of a short-lived alliance created to commit a particular crime or engage in a random violent act. In contrast, gang delinquency involves long-lived, complex institutions that have a distinct structure and organization, including identifiable leadership, division of labor (some members are fighters, others are burglars, and still others are deal makers), rules, rituals, and possessions (such as a headquarters and weapons).

Despite Americans' familiarity with gangs, delinquency experts are often at odds over the precise definition of a gang. The term is sometimes used broadly to describe any congregation of youths who have joined together to engage in delinquent acts. However, some police departments, for example, use narrower definitions, designating as gangs only cohesive groups that hold and defend territory, or turf.[29]

Academic experts have also created a variety of definitions to distinguish delinquent gangs from delinquent groups. Some of the core elements generally included in the concept of the gang is that it is an **interstitial group** (a phrase coined by pioneering gang expert Frederick Thrasher to refer to the cracks that form in the fabric of society) and that it maintains standard group processes, such as recruiting new members, setting goals (such as controlling the neighborhood drug trade), assigning roles (appointing someone to negotiate with rivals), and developing status (grooming young members for leadership roles).[30] Table 9.1 provides a series of definitions of teen gangs by leading experts on delinquency.

Although a great deal of divergence exists over the definition of the word *gang*, Malcolm Klein argues that two factors stand out which define the core concept of *youth gang*:

- Members have self-recognition of their gang status, and use special vocabulary, clothing, signs, colors, graffiti and names. Members set themselves apart from the community and are viewed as a separate entity by others. Once they get the label of gang, members eventually accept and take pride in their status.
- There is a commitment to criminal activity, though even the most criminal gang members spend the bulk of their time in non-criminal activities.[31]

NEAR GROUPS AND YOUTH GROUPS

The standard definition of a gang implies that it is a cohesive group that maintains rules and customs and develops ongoing traditions. The media often portray the gang as a "substitute family" for inner-city youth, replacing a torn or dysfunctional nuclear family: Adolescents become members for life.

Not all gang experts share this view. Sociologist Lewis Yablonsky believes that gangs can best be described as **near groups.** According to Yablonsky, human collectives tend to range from highly cohesive, tight-knit organizations to mobs with anonymous members who are motivated by emotions and disturbed leadership. Because youth gangs fall between the two extremes, they can be characterized as near groups. They usually have diffuse role definition, limited cohesion, impermanence, minimal consensus of norms, shifting membership, disturbed leadership, and limited definitions of membership expectations.[32]

In Yablonsky's view, the gang maintains only a small core of totally committed members, who need the gang for satisfaction and other personal reasons. These core members work constantly to keep the momentum of the gang going. On a second level are affiliated youths, who participate in gang activity only when the mood suits them, and on a third level are peripheral members, who participate in a particular situation or fight but usually do not identify with the gang.

The near group model has been supported by the research of James Diego Vigil.[33] Vigil found that boys in Latino **barrio** (neighborhood) gangs could be

TABLE 9.1 Definitions of Teen Gangs

Frederick Thrasher
An interstitial group originally formed spontaneously and then integrated through conflict. It is characterized by the following types of behavior: meeting face to face, milling, movement through space as a unit, conflict, and planning. The result of this collective behavior is the development of tradition, unreflective internal structure, esprit de corps, solidarity, morale, group awareness, and attachment to local territory.

Malcolm Klein
Any denotable adolescent group of youngsters who (a) are generally perceived as a distinct aggregation by others in their neighborhood; (b) recognize themselves as a denotable group (almost invariably with a group name); and (c) have been involved in a sufficient number of delinquent incidents to call forth a consistent negative response from neighborhood residents and/or law enforcement agencies.

Desmond Cartwright
An interstitial and integrated group of persons who meet face to face more or less regularly and whose existence and activities are considered an actual or potential threat to the prevailing social order.

Walter Miller
A self-formed association of peers, bound together by mutual interests, with identifiable leadership, well-developed lines of authority, and other organizational features, who act in concert to achieve a specific purpose or purposes, which generally include the conduct of illegal activity and control over a particular territory, facility, or type of enterprise.

G. David Curry and Irving Spergel
Groups containing law-violating juveniles and adults that are complexly organized, although sometimes diffuse, and sometimes cohesive, with established leadership and membership rules. The gang also engages in a range of crime (but with significantly more violence) within a framework of norms and values in respect to mutual support, conflict relations with other gangs, and a tradition of turf, colors, signs, and symbols. Subgroups of the gang may be deferentially committed to various delinquent or criminal patterns, such as drug trafficking, gang fighting, or burglary.

Source: Frederick Thrasher, *The Gang* (Chicago: University of Chicago Press, 1927), p. 57; Malcolm Klein, *Street Gangs and Street Workers* (Englewood Cliffs, N.J.: Prentice Hall, 1971), p. 13; Desmond Cartwright, Barbara Tomson, and Hersey Schwarts, eds., *Gang Delinquency* (Monterey, Calif.: Brooks/Cole, 1975), pp. 149–50; Walter Miller, "Gangs, Groups, and Serious Youth Crime," in David Schicor and Delos Kelly, eds., *Critical Issues in Juvenile Delinquency* (Lexington, Mass.: Lexington Books, 1980); G. David Curry and Irving Spergel, "Gang Homicide, Delinquency, and Community," *Criminology* 26:382 (1988).

separated into "regular" (inner core), "peripheral" (strong identity but less frequent activity), "temporary" (short-term membership), and "situational" (those who party with the gang but avoid violent confrontations) members. Surveys of Denver gang youth have also found that most adolescents hold membership for only about one year and many began to question the value of ganging after only brief exposure to gang activities.[34]

Sociologist Walter Miller suggests that *law-violating youth group* is a more appropriate term than *gang* to identify collective youth crime.[35] He says, "A law-violating youth group is an association of three or more youths whose members engage recurrently in illegal activities with the cooperation and/or moral support of their companions."[36] Miller recognizes the loose affiliations found in many youth groups. He employs such terms as *cooperation* and *moral support* to convey the idea that collective activities rarely include all group members. Although Miller acknowledges the existence of "formal" delinquent gangs, he recognizes that they represent only one element of collective youth crime, which also includes cliques, networks, bands, corner groups, and so on. In sum, Miller sees the formal street gang, with its committed full-time members, as playing only a small part in the overall problem of collective youth crime.

THE STUDY OF JUVENILE GANGS AND GROUPS

The study of juvenile gangs and groups was prompted by the Chicago School sociologists in the 1920s. Researchers such as Clifford Shaw and Henry McKay were concerned about the nature of the urban environment and how it influenced young people. Delinquency was believed to be a product of unsupervised groups of children of the urban poor and immigrants.

Frederick Thrasher initiated the study of the modern gang in his analysis of more than 1,300 youth groups in Chicago. His report on this effort, *The Gang,* was published in 1927.[37] Thrasher found that the social, economic, and ecological processes that affect the structure of great metropolitan cities create interstitial areas, or cracks, in the normal fabric of society, characterized by weak family controls, poverty, and social disorganization. According to Thrasher, groups of youths develop spontaneously to meet such childhood needs as play, fun, and adventure—activities that sometimes lead to delinquent acts.

The slum area presents many opportunities for conflict between groups of youths and between the groups and adult authority. If this conflict continues, the groups become more solidified, and their activities become primarily illegal. The groups thus develop into gangs, with a name and a structure oriented toward delinquent behavior.

To Thrasher, the gang provides the young, lower-class boy with an opportunity for success. Because adult society does not meet the needs of slum dwellers, the gang steps in by seemingly offering what society fails to provide—excitement, fun, and opportunity. The gang is viewed not as a haven for disturbed youths but rather as an alternative lifestyle for normal boys.

Thrasher's work has influenced significantly the accepted view of the gang. Recent studies of delinquent gang behavior are similar to Thrasher's in their emphasis on the gang as a means for lower-class boys to achieve advancement and opportunity as well as to defend themselves and attack rivals.

GANGS IN THE 1950s AND 1960s

In the 1950s and early 1960s, the threat of gangs and gang violence dominated the public consciousness. Rarely did a week go by without a major city newspaper featuring a story on the violent behavior of gangs and their colorful leaders and names—the Egyptian Kings, the Vice Lords, the Blackstone Rangers. Social service and law enforcement agencies directed major efforts to either rehabilitate or destroy the gangs. Movies, such as *The Wild Ones* and *The Blackboard Jungle,* were made about gangs, and the Broadway musical *West Side Story* romanticized violent gangs.

In his classic 1967 work, *Juvenile Gangs in Context,* Malcolm Klein summarized existing knowledge about gangs.[38] He concluded that gang membership was a way for individual boys to satisfy certain personal needs that were related to the development of youths caught up in the emotional turmoil typical of the period between adolescence and adulthood. This natural inclination to form gangs is reinforced by the perception that the gang represents a substitute for unattainable middle-class rewards. Klein believed that the experience of being a member of a gang would dominate a youngster's perceptions, values, expectations, and behavior, and that the gang was self-reinforcing:

> It is within the gang more than anywhere else that a youngster may find forms of acceptance for delinquent behavior—rewards instead of negative sanctions. And as the gang strives for internal cohesion, the negative sanctions of the "outside world" become interpreted as threats to cohesion, thus providing secondary reinforcement for the values central to the legitimization of gang behavior.[39]

By the mid-1960s, the gang menace seemed to have disappeared. Some experts attribute the decline of gang activity to successful gang-control programs instituted by social service agencies.[40] Others believe that gangs were eliminated because police gang-control units infiltrated gangs, arrested leaders, and constantly harassed members.[41] Gang boys were more likely to be sanctioned by the juvenile justice system and receive more severe sentences than nongang youths.[42] Still others attributed the decline in gang activity to the increase in political awareness that developed during the 1960s. Many gang leaders became involved in the social or political activities of ethnic pride, civil rights, and antiwar groups. In addition, many gang members were drafted. Finally gang activity may have diminished during the 1960s because many gang members became active users of heroin and other drugs, which curtailed their group-related criminal activity.[43]

GANGS RE-EMERGE

Interest in gang activity began anew in the early 1970s. Walter Miller comments on the New York scene:

> All was quiet on the gang front for almost 10 years. Then, suddenly and without advance warning, the gangs reappeared. Bearing such names as Savage Skulls and Black Assassins, they began to form in the South Bronx in the spring of 1971, quickly spread to other parts of the city, and by 1975 comprised 275 police-verified gangs with 11,000 members. These new and mysteriously merging gangs were far more lethal than their predecessors—heavily armed, incited and directed by violence-hardened older men, and directing their lethal activities far more to the victimization of ordinary citizens than to one another.[44]

Gang activity also reemerged in other major cities, including Detroit, El Paso, Los Angeles, and Chicago. Today, the number of gang youths appears, at least in these cities, to be at an all-time high.[45] In addition, such cities as Cleveland, Columbus (Ohio), and Milwaukee, which had not experienced serious gang problems before, saw the development of local gangs.[46] Large urban gangs sent representatives to organize chapters in distant areas or take over existing gangs. For example, Chicago gangs moved into Dade County, Florida, and demanded cooperation and obedience from local gangs. Two major Chicago gangs, the Black Gangster Disciples and their rivals, the Vice Lords, established branches in Milwaukee.[47] Members of Los Angeles's two largest gangs, the Crips and the Bloods, began operations in Midwest cities, forcing local police departments with little experience in gang control to deal with well-organized, established gang activities. Even medium-sized cities saw gangs emerge from local dance and "rap" groups and neighborhood street-corner groups.[48]

The explosion of gang activities in the 1980s was reflected in the renewed media interest in gang activity. Joan Moore reports that the *Los Angeles Times* printed 36 gang-related stories in 1977 and 15 in 1978; by 1988, 69 articles appeared, and in 1989, the number of stories concerning police sweeps, revenge shootings, and murder trials had risen to 267.[49] Clearly, gangs had garnered national attention.

WHY HAS GANG ACTIVITY INCREASED?

Gang activity may have increased because of the involvement of youth gangs in the distribution and sales of illegal drugs.[50] Although early gangs relied on group loyalty and protection of turf to encourage membership, modern gang boys are lured by the quest for drug profits. In some areas, gangs have replaced traditional organized crime families as the dominant suppliers of cocaine and crack. The traditional weapons of gangs—chains, knives, and homemade guns—have been replaced by the "heavy artillery" drug money can buy: Uzi and AK-47 automatic weapons. Felix Padilla studied a Latino gang in Chicago and found that the gang represents "[a] viable and persistent business enterprise within the U.S. economy, with its own culture, logic, and systematic means of transmitting and reinforcing its fundamental business virtues."[51]

Ironically, efforts by the FBI and other federal agencies to crack down on traditional organized crime families in the 1980s have opened the door to more violent youth gangs that control the drug trade on a local level and will not hesitate to use violence to maintain and expand their authority. The division between organized crime and gang crime is becoming increasingly narrow.

Economic Conditions   Although drug trafficking may be an important factor in the increase in gang activity, it is by no means the only one; not all gang boys sell or use drugs, and many dealers are not gang members. Gang activity may also be on the rise because of economic and social dislocation. In her analyses of gangs in postindustrial America, Pamela Irving Jackson found that gang formation is the natural consequence of the evolution from a manufacturing economy with a surplus of relatively high-paying jobs to a low-wage service economy.[52] The American city, which traditionally required a large population base for its manufacturing plants, now faces incredible economic stress as these plants shut down. In this uneasy economic climate, gangs form and flourish while the moderating influences of successful adult role models and stable families decline. From this perspective, the prevalence of youth gangs is a response to the glooming of the American economy and industrial base.

The Family in Crisis   Many commentators link increasing gang membership to the disorganization of the American family (see chapter 8). Gang members often come from families that are torn by parental absence, substance abuse, poverty, and criminality.[53] The gang serves as a substitute family, contributing the support, security, and caring that the "traditional," intact nuclear family is supposed to provide.

Although this argument is compelling, a sizable portion of gang boys come from stable and adequate families, while a significant number of youth from dysfunctional families avoid gang involvement. In some families, one brother or sister is ganged up while another evades gang membership. Thus, although the gang may be a substitute family for some members, it clearly does not have that appeal for all.

CONTEMPORARY GANGS

Thousands of gangs are operating around the country today with hundreds of thousands of members. The gang, however, cannot be viewed as a uniform or homogenous social concept. Gangs vary by activity, makeup, location, leadership style, age, etc. The following sections attempt to describe some of the most salient features of this heterogeneous social phenomenon.

EXTENT OF THE PROBLEM

Estimating the extent of the gang problem today is exceedingly difficult. As noted previously, there are a variety of definitions of gang membership. Definitional diversity means that youths who would be considered gang members in one jurisdiction are ignored in another. For example, some cities have no "gang" problems but are the locale of drug "crews" and "posses," groups with more than a resemblance to gangs. Youths who say they are gang members might belong to an informal group that falls outside generally acceptable definitions of gangs. In addition, gang membership is constantly changing; a continual influx and outflow of members makes creating accurate population estimates extremely problematic.

Despite these difficulties, a number of attempts have been made to inventory gang populations, and all indications show a major increase in gang membership (Table 9.2). Walter Miller conducted two national surveys of gang membership, the first in 1975 and a second in 1982. The first survey indicated gang membership at 55,000; the second survey indicated that gang membership had increased to about 98,000.[54]

In 1992, a research project called the National Assessment of Gang Activity, surveyed police departments in the nation's 79 largest cities and found that 91 percent (72 cities) reported the presence of criminal youth gangs; three other areas reported the presence of drug dealing "posses" and "crews."[55] Data from these cities, along with data collected from 29 smaller cities and 11 county jurisdictions, showed a total of 4,881 gangs with 249,324 members.

A 1994 extension and replication of the National Assessment indicated that nationally there are between 8,625 and 16,643 gangs containing between 378,807 and 555,181 members (the lower range figures are very conservative estimates while the upper range is a statistical estimate derived by using more

TABLE 9.2 Estimates of National Gang Membership Results of National Surveys

Researcher	Year Conducted	Number of Gang Members
Walter Miller	1975	55,000
Walter Miller	1982	98,000
National Gang Assessment	1992	249,324
National Gang Assessment/ Replication	1994	378,807 555,181*
Malcolm Klein	1995	500,000

*Higher number based on more liberal statistical estimating techniques.

liberal statistical estimating techniques).[56] The 1994 survey also estimates that gang members commit between 437,066 and 580,331 serious crimes each year. The 1994 survey then shows that gang activity is significantly higher today than 20 years ago and that gang membership is, if anything, accelerating in the 1990s.[57]

Another survey of "gang cities" conducted throughout the 1990s by Malcolm Klein found that 94 percent of the 189 U.S. cities with populations of 100,000 or more and 800 to 900 of smaller cities with populations of 10,000 to 100,000 have gang problems. Adding these cities would create a total of more than 1,000 gang locations. Although gangs in smaller cities have relatively few members, averaging slightly more than 100, almost half of the larger city gangs report having 500 or more members, including 14 city gangs with more than 4,000 members. Los Angeles alone has more than 1,000 gangs![58] Klein's estimate of 500,000 gang members coincides with the National Assessment's[59] high-range estimate of gang membership.

Still another survey of prosecutors in 192 jurisdictions conducted by Claire Johnson, Barbara Webster, and Edward Connors found that gangs can be found in many smaller cities as well as larger jurisdictions. Table 9.3 shows the type, extent, and activities of gangs in 118 large and 74 small jurisdictions.[60]

In addition to surveys, police departments, and prosecutors' offices, self-report surveys of high school youth estimate that about 13 percent of them may be involved in gangs.[61] Assuming a high school population of 10 million, gang membership might be as high as 1.3 million. Of course, considering definitional ambiguity, this is a very rough estimate; nonetheless, gang membership seems to be expanding rapidly.

TYPES OF GANGS

Gangs are categorized by their activity: Some are devoted to committing violence and protecting their neighborhood boundaries, or turf; others are devoted to theft; some specialize in drug trafficking; others are primarily social groups concerned with recreation, rather than crime.[62]

In their early work, Richard Cloward and Lloyd Ohlin recognized that some gangs specialized in violent behavior; others were **retreatists** whose members actively engaged in substance abuse, and still others were criminal gangs that devoted their energy to crime for profit.[63] Although it has become increasingly difficult to make the criminal-retreatist-conflict distinction because so many gang members are involved in all three behaviors, experts continue to find that on an aggregate level gangs can be characterized according to dominant behavioral activities. For example, Jeffrey Fagan analyzed gang behavior in Chicago, San Diego, and Los Angeles and found that most gangs fall into one of the following four categories:

1. *Social gang.* Involved in few delinquent activities and little drug use other than alcohol and marijuana. Membership is more interested in the social aspects of group behavior.
2. *Party gang.* Concentrates on drug use and sales, while forgoing most delinquent behavior except vandalism. Drug sales are designed to finance members' personal drug use.
3. *Serious delinquent gang.* Engages in serious delinquent behavior while eschewing most drug use. Drugs are used only on social occasions.

TABLE 9.3 Types of Gangs and Their Crimes

Types of Gangs	Gangs in Large Jurisdictions (n=118)				Gangs in Small Jurisdictions (n=74)			
	Operate Here	Commit Violent Crimes	Engage in Drug Trafficking	Use These Types of Drugs	Operate Here	Commit Violent Crimes	Engage in Drug Trafficking	Use These Types of Drugs
Locally based, African-American gangs	83.1%	93.9%	93.9%	98.9% Cocaine 27.2% Heroin 54.3% Marijuana 9.8% Other	60.3%	84.1%	84.1%	97.3% Cocaine 21.6% Heroin 64.9% Marijuana 16.2% Other
Motorcycle gangs	61.9%	71.2%	90.4%	59.1% Cocaine 25.8% Heroin 57.6% Marijuana 72.7% Other	49.3%	61.6%	86.1%	74.2% Cocaine 19.4% Heroin 74.2% Marijuana 51.6% Other
Hispanic gangs	63.6%	97.3%	88.0%	89.4% Cocaine 48.5% Heroin 66.7% Marijuana 24.2% Other	42.5%	83.9%	80.6%	84.0% Cocaine 28.0% Heroin 92.0% Marijuana 20.0% Other
Hate gangs (e.g., KKK, Aryan Nation)	52.5%	74.2%	9.7%	33.3% Cocaine 16.7% Heroin 66.7% Marijuana 33.3% Other	23.3%	58.8%	29.4%	80.0% Cocaine 0.0% Heroin 60.0% Marijuana 20.0% Other
Asian gangs	51.7%	91.8%	45.9%	82.1% Cocaine 64.3% Heroin 32.1% Marijuana 14.3% Other	13.7%	90.0%	40.0%	75.0% Cocaine 50.0% Heroin 0.0% Marijuana 25.0% Other
Gangs based in the Los Angeles area (e.g., Crips, Bloods)	50.0%	89.8%	91.5%	98.1% Cocaine 22.2% Heroin 51.8% Marijuana 13.0% Other	41.1%	76.7%	96.7%	100.0% Cocaine 13.8% Heroin 55.2% Marijuana 20.7% Other
Gangs with origins in the Caribbean (e.g., Jamaican, Dominican Republic)	43.2%	78.4%	100.0%	96.1% Cocaine 3.9% Heroin 7.8% Marijuana 5.9% Other	16.4%	66.7%	100.0%	100.0% Cocaine 25.0% Heroin 66.7% Marijuana 33.3% Other
Other (specify)	28.8%	76.5%	41.0%	78.6% Cocaine 7.1% Heroin 50.0% Marijuana 14.3% Other	34.2%	72.0%	36.0%	88.9% Cocaine 22.2% Heroin 66.7% Marijuana 22.2% Other

Source: Claire Johnson, Barbara Webster, and Edward Connors, *Prosecuting Gangs: A National Assessment* (Washington, D.C.: National Institute of Justice, 1995), p. 4.

4. *Organized gang.* Heavily involved in criminality and drug use and sales. Drug use and sales reflect a systemic relationship with other criminal acts. For example, violent acts are used to establish control over drug sale territories. Highly cohesive and organized, this type of gang is on the verge of becoming a formal criminal organization.[64]

Fagan's findings have been duplicated by other gang observers around the United States. After observing gangs in the Columbus, Ohio, area, C. Ronald Huff found that they could be organized into "hedonistic gangs" (similar to the "party gang"), "instrumental gangs" (similar to the "serious delinquent gang") and "predatory gangs," whose heavy crime and crack use make them similar to the "organized gang" found by Fagan in Chicago and on the West Coast.[65] Carl Taylor adds the **scavenger gang,** a group of impulsive youths who have no common bond beyond surviving in a tough urban environment. These gang members are typically low achievers who prey on any target they encounter. Taylor contrasts the scavenger gang with the **organized/corporate gang,** whose structure and goal orientation make it similar to a Fortune 500 company in its relentless pursuit of profit and market share.[66]

In their recent survey of national gang trends, Cheryl Maxson and Malcolm Klein found that gangs can be organized into groups based on their size, age range, duration of existence, territory, and criminal acts.[67]

- **The Traditional Gang.** In existence for 20 years or more. Contain clear subgroups based on age. Sometimes subgroups are separated by neighborhoods rather than age. Have large age range (members ages are from 10 to 30) and are very large, with hundreds of members. Territorial, with well defined home turf.
- **The Neotraditional Gang.** A newer territorial gang, smaller and newer than the traditional gang, which may evolve into a traditional gang over time.
- **The Compressed Gang.** A smaller gang with less than 50 members, a short history, no subgroups, narrow age range, and less defined territory.
- **The Collective Gang.** A larger group which resembles a "shapeless mass" of adolescent and young adult members that has not developed the distinguishing characteristics of other gangs.
- **The Specialty Gang.** A crime-focused gang which is more criminal than social, and is smaller in size and age range than other gangs. It has a well defined territory which can be based either on territory or the particular form of crime it specializes in, e.g. Drug territories.

By far, the most common is the Compressed gang; the Collective gang is the least common, followed by the Specialty gang. Contrary to public opinion, fewer than half of the Specialty gangs are involved in drug distribution.[68]

These more recent observations seem to validate Cloward and Ohlin's research findings from 30 years ago and show that some but not all gangs are involved in drug activity and some but not all are violent.

LOCATION OF GANGS

The gang problem was traditionally considered an urban, lower-class phenomenon. Two types of urban areas are gang prone. The first is the *transitional neighborhood*, which is marked by rapid population change in which diverse ethnic and racial groups find themselves living side by side and in competition with one another.[69] Intergang conflict and homicide rates are high in these areas, which house the urban "underclass."[70]

The second gang area is the **stable slum,** a neighborhood where population shifts have slowed down, permitting patterns of behavior and traditions to develop over a number of years. Most typical of these areas are the slums in New York and Chicago and the Mexican-American barrios of the Southwest and

California.[71] The stable slum more often contains the large, structured gang clusters that are the most resistant to attempts by law enforcement and social service agencies to modify or disband them.

Shifting Gang Locales   The transitional neighborhood and the stable slum are not the only environments that produce gangs. In recent years, there has been a massive exodus of people from the central city to outlying communities and suburbs. This exodus included not only people from the upper or middle class but lower-income individuals as well. In an ironic twist, once-fashionable outlying neighborhoods in some cities have declined while central city areas are experiencing urban renewal. Inner-city districts of major cities such as New York and Chicago have become enclaves of finance, retail stores, restaurants, and entertainment.[72] Two aspects of this development inhibit gang formation: First, there are few residential areas and thus few adolescent recruits, and second, there is intensive police patrol. As a result, in some areas, such as Miami and Boston, slums or ghettos have shifted from the downtown areas to outer-city, ring-city, or suburban areas—that is, to formerly middle-class areas now in decay. Some midsize cities now contain the type of gangs that only a few years ago were restricted to large metropolitan areas.

Suburban housing projects are also gang prone. Thus, although gangs are still located in areas of urban blight, these areas are often at some distance from their traditional inner-city locations.[73]

MIGRATION

Some of the gangs in smaller cities and towns appear to be "homegrown." For example, in an impressive study, Richard Zevitz and Susan Takata found that gangs of local youth formed in Kenosha, Wisconsin (population: about 80,000) during the mid-'80s. Because these groups copied clothing, insignia, and hand signs of Chicago gangs, authorities leaped to the conclusion that they were recent arrivals from the Chicago area. Zevitz and Takata found, to the contrary, that the Kenosha gangs were formed and populated by local youths.[74]

However, gang migration may also help to account for the national growth in gang activity. A national assessment by Cheryl Maxson, Kristi Woods, and Malcolm Klein found that about 700 U.S. cities had experienced some form of gang migration during the past decade, either short-term (e.g., to sell drugs) or long-term (e.g., to form permanent gangs). Most of the new arrivals were from L.A. gangs, although some came from Chicago, New York, and Detroit. The most common motive for gang members migrating was actually social: Their families had relocated, forcing them to move as well. Others had a specific criminal purpose, such as expanding drug sales and markets. Most of the migrators were African-American or Hispanic males who maintained close ties with members of their original gangs "back home."[75] Although retention of gang identity was important, some migrants joined local gangs, shedding old ties and gaining new affiliations.

Although gang migration remains a serious problem, most cities had local gangs prior to the onset of migration and most likely would have had a gang problem regardless of migration. The number of migrants is relatively small in proportion to the overall gang population, supporting the contention that most gangs are actually "homegrown."

Neighborhood Reactions The presence of gangs in areas unaccustomed to delinquent group activity can have a devastating effect on community life. In his study of Milwaukee gangs, John Hagedorn found neighborhood hostility generated with the formation of the gangs.[76] Milwaukee's gangs had little neighborhood turf affiliation and were formed solely to profit from illegal gain and criminal activity; the gangs formed at the same time minority students were being bused to implement desegregation. Thus, gang recruitment took place on the buses and in schools and not on neighborhood streets. Because of its diffuse nature, these new gangs cut across neighborhoods, rendering local social control ineffective. To make matters worse, residents in the neighborhoods most likely to be plagued by gang violence were "trapped": Residential segregation and a lack of affordable housing prevented many of them from leaving. The result was mixed neighborhoods of struggling working-class and poor families coexisting with drug houses, gangs, and routine violence. Frightened residents had little recourse but to call police when they heard gunshots; neighborhoods became uneasy and unstable.

AGE OF GANG MEMBERS

The ages of gang members range widely, perhaps from as young as 8 to as old as 55.[77]

A recent survey of 3,348 youth, including almost 2,000 gang members, conducted by the National Gang Crime Research Center found that youths first learn about gangs at around age 9, get involved in violence at age 10 or 11, and join their first gang at age 12. Half of the gang boys interviewed had by age 13 (a) fired a pistol, (b) seen someone killed or seriously injured by gang violence, (c) obtained a permanent gang tattoo, and (d) been arrested.[78]

Increasing Ages Gang experts believe that the average age of gang members has been increasing yearly, a phenomenon explained in part by the changing structure of the American economy.[79] Desirable unskilled factory jobs that would entice older boys to leave the gang have been lost. Replacing these legitimate jobs are low-level drug dealing opportunities that require a gang affiliation. William Julius Wilson found that the inability of inner-city males to obtain adequate employment prevents them from attaining adult roles (e.g., they cannot afford to marry and raise families). Criminal records acquired at an early age quickly lock them out of the job market. For many, remaining in a gang into adulthood has become an economic necessity.[80]

In his Milwaukee research, John Hagedorn also found that economic deterioration has had an important impact on the age structure of gang membership. Less than one in five founding members of the youth gangs Hagedorn studied were able to find full-time employment by their mid-twenties; 86 percent had spent considerable time in prison. "Old heads," older members with powerful street reputations were held in high esteem by young gang boys. In the past, ex-members served as a moderating influence, helping steer gang boys into conventional roles and jobs. Today, young adults continue relationships with their old gangs and promote values of hustling, drug use, and sexual promiscuity. As a result, gang affiliations can last indefinitely: It is not unusual to see intergenerational membership with the children and even grandchildren of gang members affiliating with the same gang.[81]

When Hagedorn and his associates interviewed 101 older gang members from 14 Milwaukee area gangs, he found that there are actually four types of adult gang members:

- *Legits* have left the gang and 'hood behind.
- *Dope fiends* are addicted to cocaine and need drug treatment.
- *New Jacks* have given up on the legitimate economy and see nothing wrong in selling cocaine to anyone.
- *Homeboys,* a majority of all adult gang members, work regular jobs, but when they cannot make enough money sell cocaine. They want out of the drug trade and wish to have a "normal" life but believe that ganging is the only way to make ends meet.[82]

GENDER

Of the more than 1,000 gangs included in Thrasher's original survey, only half a dozen of them were female. Females were traditionally involved in gang activities in one of three ways: as auxiliaries, or branches, of male gangs; as part of sexually mixed gangs; and occasionally as autonomous gangs. The first form was the most common. Often, the auxiliaries took on a feminized version of the male gang name, such as the Lady Disciples of The Devil's Disciples.

Thrasher's results may have accurately portrayed female gang membership in the 1920s, but times have changed. Some gang experts, including Joan Moore and Anne Campbell, believe that female gang members are no longer satisfied with being in an auxiliary. Although initial female gang participation may be forged by links to male gang members, once in gangs, girls form close ties with other female members. Peer interactions form the basis for independent female gangs and group criminal activity.[83]

Other research has shown that females may be integrated within existing gangs. For example, Mary Glazier's study of a small-town Pennsylvania gang, "The Hit and Run," found that girls were invited to become gang members because it was considered unacceptable for male members to fight with females who gave them trouble; girl members were given that responsibility.[84]

It is still difficult to determine the precise number of female gangs or the size of their membership. National surveys of gang activity indicate that females commit 5 percent or less of all reported gang crimes and that under 10 percent of gang members are female.[85]

Some local gang surveys, however, indicate that the number of female gang members may be on the rise in some areas of the country.[86] Carl Taylor's analysis of Detroit gangs found that girls were very much involved in gang activity.[87] Also, in an important analysis of Denver youth, Finn-Aage Esbensen and David Huizinga showed that the number of female gang members is higher than previously thought: Approximately 25 percent of the gang members they surveyed were female.[88] Escalating female gang membership then parallels recent increases in female delinquency.

FORMATION

It has long been suggested that gangs form in order to defend their turf from outsiders; thus, gang formation involves a sense of territoriality. Most gang members live in close proximity to one another, and their sense of belonging and loyalty extends only to their small area of the city. At first, a gang may form when members of an ethnic minority newly settled in the neighborhood join together for self-preservation. As the group gains numerical domination over an area, it may view the neighborhood as its territory or turf, which needs to be defended. Defending turf involves fighting rivals who want to make the territory their own.

Local gang surveys indicate that the number of female gang members may be on the rise in some areas of the country. Some indicate that the number of female gang members is higher than previously thought: approximately 25 percent of the gang members they surveyed were female. Escalating female gang membership then parallels recent increases in female delinquency.

Once formed, gangs grow when youths who admire the older gang boys and wish to imitate their lifestyle "apply" and are accepted for membership. Sometimes, the new members will be given a special, diminished identity within the gang that reflects their inexperience and apprenticeship status. Joan Moore and her associates found that once formed, youth cliques (**klikas**) in Hispanic gangs remain together as unique groups with separate names, separate identities, and distinct experiences; they also have more intimate relationships among themselves than among the general gang membership.[89] She likens klikas to a particular class in a university, such as the class of '94, not a separate organization but one that has its own unique experiences.

Moore also found that gangs can expand by including members' kin, even if they do not live in the immediate neighborhood, and rival gang members who wish to join because they admire the gang's way of doing things. Adding outsiders gives the gang the ability to take over new territory. However, it also brings with it new problems, because outsider membership and the grasp for new territory usually result in greater conflicts with rival gangs.

LEADERSHIP

Most experts describe gang leaders as cool characters who have earned their position by demonstrating a variety of abilities—fighting prowess, verbal quickness, athletic distinction, and so on.[90]

Experts emphasize that gang leadership is held by one person and may be restricted to a particular activity, such as fighting, sex, and negotiations. In fact, in some gangs, each age level of the gang has its own leader. Older members may be admired but not necessarily considered leaders by younger members. In his analysis of Los Angeles gangs, Malcolm Klein observed that many gang leaders shrink from taking a leadership role and actively deny leadership. Klein overheard one gang boy claim, "We got no leaders, man. Everybody's a leader, and nobody can talk for nobody else."[91] The most plausible explanation of this ambivalence is the boy's fear that during times of crisis, his decisions will conflict with those of other leaders and he will lose status and face.

COMMUNICATIONS

Gangs today seek recognition both from their rivals and the community as a whole. An enhanced image and reputation depend on a gang's ability to communicate to the rest of the world (see Figure 9.1)

One major source of gang communication is **graffiti.** These wall writings are especially elaborate among Latino gangs, who call their inscriptions *placasos* or *placa,* meaning "sign" or "plaque."[92] Latino gang graffiti will usually contain the writer's street name and the name of the gang. Strength or power is frequently asserted through the use of the term *rifa,* which means "to rule," and *controllo,* indicating that the gang controls the area. Another common inscription is *p/v,* meaning "*por vida,*" this refers to the fact that the gang expects to control the area "for life." The numeral *13,* when used, signifies that the gang is *loco,* or "wild."

Crossed-out graffiti indicates that a territory is being contested by a rival gang, while undisturbed writing indicates that the gang's power has gone unchallenged.

Gangs also communicate by ritualistic argot (speech patterns) and hand signs. Flashing or tossing gang signs in the presence of rivals is often viewed as a direct challenge that can escalate into a verbal or physical confrontation. In Chicago, gangs call this **representing.** Gang boys will proclaim their affiliation ("Latin King Love!" "Stone Killers!") and ask victims "Who do you ride?" or "What do you be about?"; an incorrect response will provoke an attack.[93] False representing can be used to intentionally misinform witnesses and victims; it can be used to expose imposters or neutrals trying to make safe passage through gang-controlled territory.

Still another method of communication is clothing. In some areas, gang members communicate their membership by wearing jackets with the name of their gang embroidered on the back. In Boston neighborhoods, certain articles of clothing, for example, sneakers or sports jackets with a particular team logo, are worn to identify gang membership.[94] In Los Angeles, the two major African-American gangs are the Crips and the Bloods, each with thousands of members. Crips are identified with the color blue and will wear some article of blue clothing—hat, belt, or jacket—to communicate their allegiance; their rivals, the Bloods, identify with the color red.[95] In one famous incident, a Crips member waiting in line to see the gang film *Colors* was shot by a member of the Bloods who, after viewing the film, was apparently upset by the way his gang had been depicted; the victim's blue handkerchief gave away his gang affiliation to his assailant.[96]

Gang boys also commonly tattoo themselves with the name of their gang or a gang sign. This shows permanent loyalty to the gang and warns the community of their membership in a powerful and violent organization.

CRIMINALITY

In the 1600s English gangs broke windows, demolished taverns, assaulted local watchmen, and fought intergang battles (dressed in colored ribbons so members

FIGURE 9.1
Hand signs, and graffiti of street gangs

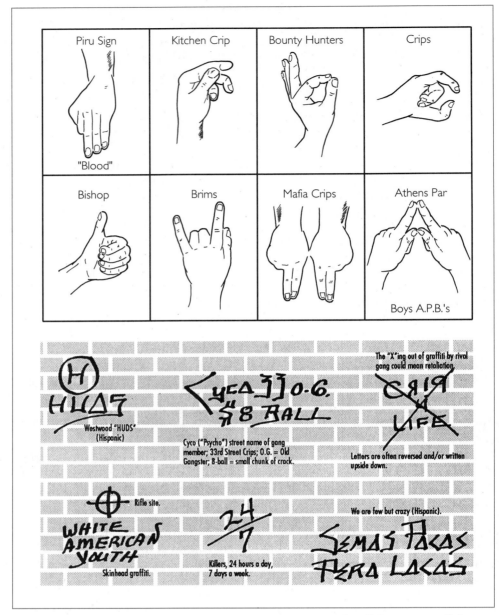

Source: Jerry Kaono, *Operation Safe Streets* (Los Angeles: Los Angeles County Sheriff's Department, n.d.); Sgt. Dallas Riedesel, *Street Gangs*, (Lakewood Police Department, Lakewood, CO) 1992.

could tell who was on their side).[97] Today, gang criminality follows numerous patterns.[98] Some gangs are "eclectic," engaging in a wide range of criminal activity ranging from felony assaults to drug dealing.[99] Other gangs "specialize," for example, drug-oriented gangs concentrate on the sale of marijuana, PCP, cocaine (crack), and amphetamines ("ice"); organized gangs use violence to control a drug territory.

Drug Dealing Although it has become common to associate gangs with drug activity, not all experts agree that gangs are major players in drug trafficking. Research conducted in California by Malcolm Klein, Cheryl Maxson, and Lea Cunningham showed that neighborhoods that suffered a dramatic increase in crack distribution likewise reported an increase in street gang drug involvement. However, gang involvement in the drug trade usually consisted of the distribution of small amounts of drugs at the street level, not significant importation or trafficking. Gang members did not play a major role in drug dealing, nor were their violent episodes a function of drug dealing. The world of crack dealing in Los Angeles belonged to regular drug dealers, not street-gang youth.[100] Mel Wallace also concludes that gang violence in Illinois "has not been drug driven" but is related to many factors, including academic failure and economic decline.[101] Denver gang members, according to Esbensen and Huizinga, are more likely to be involved in drug activity than nongang youth, but there is little evidence that drug sales and distribution are organized activities involving all gang members; fewer than one-third actually sell drugs.[102]

Gang Violence Gang boys are heavily armed and dangerous. Gangs recruit youths who already own guns; new members are likely to increase gun ownership and possession once they join gangs.[103]

Gang members then are ready to retaliate against rival gang boys accused of insults, personal disputes, chance altercations, infringements on territory, or illegal enterprise. Once an insult is perceived or a challenge is offered, the gang's honor cannot be restored until the "debt" is repaid. Police efforts to cool down gang disputes only delay the inevitable revenge—a beating or a drive-by shooting. Random acts of revenge have become so common that physicians now consider the consequences of drive-by shootings as a significant health problem, one that is a major contributor to early morbidity and mortality among adolescents and children in Los Angeles and other major gang cities.[104]

Retaliation is often directed against gang members who step out of line. If subordinates disobey orders, perhaps by using rather than selling drugs, they may be subject to harsh disciplinary action by other gang members. Violence is used to maintain the gang's internal discipline and security.

Another common gang crime is extortion, called "turf tax," which involves forcing people to pay the gang to be protected from dangerous neighborhood youths (presumably themselves). **Prestige crimes,** occur when a gang boy steals or assaults someone, even a police officer, to gain prestige in the gang and neighborhood. These crimes may be part of an initiation right or an effort to establish a special reputation, a position of responsibility, or a leadership role; to prevail in an internal power struggle; or to respond to a challenge from a rival (proving the youth is not a coward).

ETHNIC AND RACIAL COMPOSITION

Most gangs seem to be racially exclusive. Although Lewis Yablonsky found racially mixed violent gangs, the majority of gang observers view gangs as racially homogeneous groups: all white (English, Italian, Irish, and/or Slavic origin), all African-American (African origin), all Hispanic/Latino (Mexican, Puerto Rican, Panamanian, Colombian, and other Spanish-speaking people), or all Asian (Chinese,

Japanese, Korean, Taiwanese, Samoan, and Vietnamese).[105] Most intergang conflict appears to be among groups of the same ethnic and racial background.[106]

The ethnic distribution of gangs corresponds to their geographic location. For example, in Philadelphia and Detroit, the overwhelming number of gang members are African-American. In New York and Los Angeles, Latino gangs predominate, and in San Francisco the small gang population is mostly Asian.[107] Newly emerging immigrant groups are making their presence felt in gangs. Authorities in Buffalo, New York, estimate that 10 percent of their gang population are Jamaicans. Cambodian and Haitian youths are joining gangs in Boston. A significant portion of Honolulu's gangs are Samoans (19 percent) and Filipinos (46 percent).[108]

The National Assessment was able to acquire data on the ethnic distribution of gangs from 26 large cities in the United States. A significant majority of gang boys are African-American (47 percent) and Hispanic (43 percent) followed by Asian (6 percent) and Anglo (4 percent). Although Anglos make up only a small percentage of all gang youth, those jurisdictions (11) that record year-to-year change in the ethnicity of gang populations indicate that their numbers are now growing at a faster rate than other groups. The following "Focus on Delinquency" examines Latino gangs.

African-American Gangs   The first black youth gangs were organized in the early 1920s and specialized in common street crime activities.[109] Because they had few rival organizations in their inner-city locales, they were able to concentrate on committing crimes rather than defending their turf. By the 1930s, however, the expanding number of rival gangs spawned competition, and inner-city gang warfare became commonplace.

In Los Angeles, which is today a hot spot of gang activity, the first black youth gang formed in the 1920s was the Boozies, named after a family that provided a significant portion of its membership. This gang virtually ran the inner city until the 1930s, when rivals began to challenge its criminal monopoly. Over the next 20 years, a number of black gangs, including the Businessmen, Home Street, Slauson, and Neighborhood, emerged and met with varying degrees of criminal success.

In the 1970s, the dominant Crips gang was formed and began to spread over much of Los Angeles. Other neighborhood gangs merged into the Crips or affiliated with it by adding "Crips" to their name (e.g., the Main Street gang became the Main Street Crips). The Crips's dominance has since been challenged by its archrivals, the Bloods. The organization of both of these gangs, whose total membership exceeds 25,000 youths, resembles that of an organized crime family; both are heavily involved in drug trafficking.

In Chicago, The Blackstone Rangers dominated illicit activities for almost 25 years beginning in the 1960s and until the early 1990s, when its leader, Jeff Fort, and many of his associates were indicted and imprisoned.[110] The Rangers, who later evolved into the **El Rukn** gang, worked with "legitimate" businesspeople to import and sell heroin. Earning millions in profits, they established businesses to help them launder drug money. Among their enterprises was a security company, which made it possible for members to bear arms legally. Although many of the convictions were later overturned, the power of El Rukn was ended (Fort remains in a high security prison). The Blackstone Rangers' chief rivals, the Black Gangster Disciples, are now the dominant gang in Chicago.

BARRIO GANGS

According to experts such as Joan Moore and James Diego Vigil, Latino barrio gangs have evolved over time, sustained by continuous waves of poorly educated Mexican immigrants. Each new wave of immigrants settles in existing barrios or creates new ones. There, youngsters subscribe to the *cholo* (marginalized) subculture, with its own set of slang, clothing, style, and values. The *cholo* subculture places a high value on friendship, often imputing family and kinship relationships to peers (by calling them "brother" or "cousin"). Scholastic achievement is devalued and replaced with "partying." Employment is valued only if it requires little effort and brings in enough cash to party. An important aspect of the *cholo* culture is demonstrating *machismo,* or manliness. Barrio youths try to impress their peers and rivals with their ability to drink more than others, their fighting and sexual prowess, and their heart. The *cholo* culture helps these immigrants bridge the gap between the Mexican culture, which they left, and the U.S. culture, into which they have trouble assimilating.

Barrio gangs are not a recent development. Aggressive male youth groups have been a feature of the Mexican community as far back as the nineteenth century. The early barrio gangs were made up of young laborers whose behavior was more oriented around sports and socializing than criminality.

Then in the 1940s, the *pachuco* fad swept through the community; it's advocates wore outlandish outfits (zoot suits) and spoke a unique Spanish-English slang. A well-publicized murder case and some urban disturbances helped brand the *pachucos* as vicious "rat packs." Although most zoot-suiters (who can be compared to members of the heavy metal music culture today) were not gang members or necessarily involved in crime, the press focused attention on them as a major social problem, and a popular stereotype was created. Mexican-American youths became suspect regardless of their actual interest in gangs.

In the 1950s, increasing stigmatization and isolation encouraged the development of deviance. Drug use, which had been quietly tolerated in an earlier generation, was now the target of police crackdowns, and many barrio residents went to prison. Mexican-Americans gained the stereotype of "evil dope dealers," and the early naivete of *cholo* street lifestyle ended.

In the 1960s, the Chicano political movement had an important influence on gangs. First, gangs were romanticized as social bandits in the tradition of earlier Mexican opposition to Anglo authority. Second, gangs (and their adult ex-offender members, the *pintos*) began to be viewed as the fighting branch of the movement that protected the community from the police.

Protecting the community (*la raza*) was an extension of protecting their turf or neighborhood. Youth gangs and their extensions became enmeshed in community affairs, and their problems with the law came to be identified with the problems of the community as a whole.

In the last 10 years, the nature of the Chicano gang has changed significantly. The image of the gang changed within the community, and its purpose was similarly reoriented. A number of reasons exist for this transformation. Publicity about violent Mexican-American prison gangs, such as La Familia, helped create the image that all Chicano gangs were criminally oriented. The *cholo* culture was viewed as a liability of the Chicano movement. When political activism cooled and street demonstrations ended, gang members were not needed as community protectors. The gangs became more closely identified with criminals than with social activists. A new wave of Mexican immigrants rejected the gang culture, and leaders of the existing community requested police protection from the gangs. As gang isolation increased, so too did gang violence and criminality. So from leaders in a sociopolitical movement, gang members became members of an ostracized underclass.

Los Angeles barrio gangs are now being influenced by economic restructuring. The kin-based job-finding networks that helped ease gang boys into conventional society broke down as employers hired the waves of immigrants who flooded into California. Without employment opportunities, young adults hang out with the gang cliques. Their presence empowers the gang and makes it seem more like a family with "older brothers" readily available to guide younger members. Because gang veterans get involved with the affairs of recruits, "street socialization" in the gang becomes more competitive with conventional socialization in the family and the school.

Source: Joan Moore, "Isolation and Stigmatization in the Development of an Underclass: The Case of Chicano Gangs in East Los Angeles," *Social Problems* 33:1–12 (1985); idem, *Homeboys: Gangs, Drugs and Prison in the Barrios of Los Angeles* (Philadelphia: Temple University Press, 1979); James Diego Vigil, *Barrio Gangs: Street Life and Identity in Southern California* (Austin: University of Texas Press, 1988); James Diego Vigil and John Long," Emic and Etic Perspectives on Gang Culture: The Chicano Case," in C. Ronald Huff, ed., *Gangs in America* (Newbury Park, Calif.: Sage, 1990), pp. 55–70; James Diego Vigil, "*Cholos* and Gangs: Culture Change and Street Youth in Los Angeles," in C. Ronald Huff, ed., *Gangs in America* (Newbury Park, Calif.: Sage, 1990), pp. 116–28.

Hispanic gangs are made up of boys whose ethnic ancestry can be traced to one of several Spanish-speaking cultures, such as Puerto Rico and Mexico. They are known for their fierce loyalty to their original or "home" gang; this affiliation is maintained, even if they move to a new neighborhood that contains a rival gang.

African-American gang members, especially those in Los Angeles, have some unique behavioral characteristics. They frequently identify themselves through nicknames, often based on a behavioral trait: "Little .45" might be used by someone whose favorite weapon is a large handgun. Although TV shows portray gangs as wearing distinctive attire, in reality, members usually favor nondescript attire in order to reduce police scrutiny; after all, a routine police search can turn up narcotics or weapons. However, gang boys do frequently use distinctive hairstyles, featuring shaving, cornrows, shaping, and/or braids, that are designed to look like their leaders'. Tattooing is popular, and members often wear colored scarves or "rags" to identify their gang affiliation. In Los Angeles, Crips use blue or black rags, while Bloods normally carry red.

It is also common for African-American gang members to mark their territory with distinctive graffiti. The messages are crude, rather than sophisticated: drawings of guns, dollar signs, proclamations of individual power, and profanity.

Hispanic Gangs   Hispanic gangs are made up of boys whose ethnic ancestry can be traced to one of several Spanish-speaking cultures, such as Puerto Rico and Mexico. They are known for their fierce loyalty to their original or "home" gang; this affiliation is maintained, even if they move to a new neighborhood occupied by a rival gang. Admission to the gang usually involves an initiation ritual in which boys are required to show their fearlessness and prove their *machismo,* or manliness. The most common test requires novices to fight several established members or commit some crime, such as a purse snatching or robbery. The code of conduct associated with membership means never ratting on a brother or even a rival, facing death or prison without betraying their sense of honor.

In some areas, such as Miami, Hispanic gangs are rigidly organized with a fixed leadership hierarchy. However, in southern California, which has the largest concentration of Hispanic youth gangs, leadership is fluid. No youth is "elected" to a post such as president or warlord. During times of crisis, those with particular skills will assume command on a situational basis.[111] For example, one boy will lead in combat, while another will negotiate drug deals.

Hispanic gang boys are known for their distinctive dress codes. Some wear knit, dark-colored watch caps pulled down over the ears with a small roll at the bottom. Others wear a bandanna folded over the forehead and tied in back. Another popular headpiece is the "stingy brim" fedora or a baseball cap with the wearer's nickname and gang affiliation written on the cap's turned-up bill. Members favor tank-style T-shirts or open plaid wool Pendleton shirts, which give them quick access to weapons.

Members also proclaim their affiliations by marking off territory with colorful and intricate graffiti. Hispanic gang graffiti has very stylized lettering, frequently uses three-dimensional designs, and proclaims members' organizational pride and power.

Hispanic gangs have a strong sense of territory or turf, and a great deal of gang violence is directed at warding off any threat to their control. Slights by rivals, including put-downs, stare downs ("mad-dogging"), defacement of gang insignia, and territorial intrusions, can set off a violent and bloody gang confrontation. Newer gangs will carry out this violence with high-powered automatic weapons, a far cry from the zip guns and gravity knives of the past.

Asian Gangs Asian gangs predominate in such cities as New York, Los Angeles, San Francisco, Seattle, and Houston. The earliest gangs, Wah Ching, were formed in the nineteenth century by Chinese youth affiliated with adult crime groups (tongs). In the 1960s, two other gangs—the Joe Boys and Yu Li—formed in San Francisco. They now operate, along with the Wah Ching, in many major U.S. cities. National attention focused on the activities of these Chinese gangs in 1977, when a shootout in the Golden Dragon restaurant in San Francisco left five dead and eleven wounded. On the East Coast, prominent Asian gangs include Flying Dragon, Green Dragon, Ghost Shadows, Fu Ching, So on Leong, Tong So on, and Born to Kill (a Vietnamese gang).[112]

In an important work, Ko-Lin Chin has described the inner workings of Chinese youth gangs today.[113] Chin finds that these gangs have unique qualities, such as their reliance on raising capital from the Chinese community through extortion and then investing this money in legitimate business enterprises. Chinese gangs recruit new members from the pool of disaffected youth who have problems at school and consider themselves among the few educational failures in a culture that prizes academic achievement.

In addition to Chinese gangs, Samoan gangs, primarily the Sons of Samoa, have operated on the West Coast, as have Vietnamese gangs whose influence has been felt in Los Angeles, New York, and Boston. James Diego Vigil and Steve Chong Yun studied Vietnamese gangs and found that their formation can be tied to such external factors as racism, economic problems, and school failure and such internal factors as family stress and failure to achieve the level of success enjoyed by other Asians. Vietnamese gangs are formed when youths feel they need their *ahns,* or brothers, for protection and to achieve a sense of belonging.[114]

Asian gangs tend to victimize members of their own ethnic group. Because of group solidarity and distrust of outside authorities, little is known about their activities.

Anglo Gangs The first American youth gangs were made up of white ethnic youths of European ancestry, especially Irish and Italian immigrants. During the 1950s such ethnic youth gangs commonly competed for dominance with African-American and Hispanic gangs in the nation's largest cities.

Today, the number of organized white gangs is dwindling, although sporadic organized activity is not uncommon, especially in smaller towns.[115] The traditional white gangs have all but disappeared from larger urban areas. Taking their place are derivatives of the English punk and **skinhead** movement of the 1970s. In England, these youths, generally the daughters and sons of lower-class parents, sported wildly dyed hair, often shaved into "mohawks"; military clothes; iron cross earrings; and high-topped military boots. Music was a big part of their lives, and the band that characterized their lifestyle was the punk band the Sex Pistols, led by Johnny Rotten and Sid Vicious. Their creed was anti-establishment, and their anger was directed toward foreigners, whom they believed were taking their jobs.

The punker–skinhead style was brought over to the States by bands that replicated the Sex Pistols's antisocial music, stage presence, and dress; these included the Clash, the Dead Kennedys, and Human Sexual Response. The music, philosophy, and lifestyle of these bands inspired the formation of a variety of white youth gangs. However, unlike their British brothers, American white gang members are often alienated middle-class youths, rather than poor, lower-class youths who are out of society's mainstream. These gang members include "punkers" or "stoners" who dress in the latest heavy metal rock fashions and

Skinhead groups that are devoted to racist, white supremacist activities are being actively recruited by adult hate groups. These teens in Gilroy, California drive around town recruiting new members and distributing pamphlets about white supremacy and the future destruction of American society.

engage in drug- and violence-related activities. Some of these gangs espouse religious beliefs involving the occult and Satanic worship.[116] They engage in satanic rituals and are obsessed with occult themes, suicide, ritual killings, and animal mutilations. Members of these gangs get seriously involved in devil worship, tattoo themselves with occult symbols, and gouge their bodies to draw blood for satanic rituals. There are also skinhead groups that are devoted to racist, white supremacist activities. These youths are being actively recruited by adult hate groups (see chapter 2).

Anglo gangs may be springing up in suburban areas. Members of one such gang, the Spurs Posse of suburban Lakewood, California, made national news in 1993 when they were arrested in connection with a series of rapes committed to gain status in the group. The boys, aged 15 to 18, were accused of victimizing girls as young as 10; the group's members claimed the girls were willing participants.[117] Spurs Posse boys were actually paid to appear on TV tabloid talk shows and brag about their "sexual exploits." The boys were never prosecuted.

WHY DO YOUTHS JOIN GANGS?

Although gangs flourish in lower-class, inner-city areas, gang membership cannot be assumed to be solely a function of lower-class subcultural identity: Many lower-class youths do not join gangs, and middle-class kids are found in suburban skinhead and stoner groups. What are some of the suspected causes of gang delinquency?

ANTHROPOLOGICAL VIEW

Writing about gangs in the 1950s, Herbert Block and Arthur Niederhoffer suggested that gangs appeal to adolescents' deep-seated longing for the tribal group process that sustained and nurtured their ancestors.[118] Block and Niederhoffer found that gang processes and functions are similar to the puberty rites of some tribal cultures; like their ancient counterparts, gang rituals help the child bridge the gap between childhood and adulthood. For example, uniforms, tattoos, and other identifying marks are an integral part of gang culture. Gang initiation ceremonies are similar to activities of young men in Pacific Island cultures. Many gangs put new members through a hazing as an initiation rite to make sure they have "heart," a feature similar to tribal rites. In tribal societies, initiation into a cult is viewed as the death of childhood. By analogy, younger boys in lower-class urban areas yearn for the time when they can join the gang and really start to live. Membership in the adolescent gang "means the youth gives up his life as a child and assumes a new way of life."[119] Gang names are suggestive of "totemic ancestors" because they usually are symbolic (Cobras, Jaguars, and Kings, for example).

Evidence exists that contemporary gangs continue to pass on these traditions through the generations. Surveys have found that more than two-thirds of gang youths have family members who are or were in gangs and that fully two-thirds of the gang youths reported having members in their gang whose parents are also active members. These data indicate that ganging has become a cultural family tradition, to be passed on as a "rite of passage" from one generation to the next.[120] James Diego Vigil has described the rituals of gang initiation, which include physical pummeling to show that the gang boy is brave and ready to leave his matricentric (mother-dominated) household; this process seems reminiscent of tribal initiation rights.[121] For gang members, these rituals become an important part of gang activities. Hand signs and graffiti have a tribal flavor. Gang members adopt nicknames and street identities that reflect personality or physical traits: The more volatile are called "Crazy," "Loco," or "Psycho," while those who wear glasses or read books are dubbed "Professor."[122]

SOCIAL DISORGANIZATION/SOCIOCULTURAL VIEW

Sociologists have commonly viewed the shattering, destructive sociocultural forces in socially disorganized inner-city slum areas as the major cause of gang formation. Thrasher introduced this concept in his pioneering work on gangs, and it is a theme found in the classic studies of Richard Cloward and Lloyd Ohlin and of Albert K. Cohen.[123] Irving Spergel's consummate study *Racketville, Slumtown, and Haulburg* found that Slumtown, the area with the lowest income and the largest population, also had the highest number of violent gangs.[124] According to Spergel, the gang gives lower-class youths a means of attaining a personal reputation and peer group status. Malcolm Klein's oft-cited research of the late '60s and '70s again found that typical gang members came from dysfunctional and destitute families, had family members with criminal histories, and lacked adequate educational and vocational role models.[125]

The social disorganization/sociocultural view retains its prominent position today. Vigil paints a vivid picture of the forces that drive adolescents into gangs in his well-respected work *Barrio Gangs*.[126] Vigil's gang youths are pushed into membership because of poverty and minority status. Those who join gangs are the most marginal youths in the neighborhood, outcasts in their own families. Vigil finds that all barrio dwellers experience at least some forms of psychological, economic, cultural, or social "stressors," which adversely affect their lives. Gang members are usually afflicted with more than one of these stressors, causing them to suffer from "multiple marginality." Barrio youths join gangs seeking a sense of belonging; gangs offer a set of peers with whom friendship and familylike relationships are expected.[127]

Overall, the social disorganization/sociocultural view assumes that gangs are a natural and normal response to the privations of lower-class life and that gangs are a status-generating medium for boys whose aspirations cannot be realized by legitimate means.

Anomie In his recent book on gangs, Irving Spergel suggests that youths are encouraged to join gangs during periods of social, economic, and cultural turmoil—conditions thought to produce anomie-like conditions.[128] For example, gangs formed during the Russian evolution of 1917 and then again during the chaos that followed the crumbling of the Soviet Union in the early 1990s. The rise of right-wing youth gangs in Germany is associated with social and political change brought about by the unification of East and West Germany; skinhead groups have formed in response to immigration from Turkey and North Africa. In the United States, Spergel notes, gangs have formed in areas where rapid population change has resulted in unsettled community norms: "Immigration or emigration, rapidly expanding or contracting populations, and/or the incursion of different racial/ethnic groups or even different segments or generations of the same racial/ethnic populations, can create fragmented communities and gang problems."[129]

PSYCHOLOGICAL VIEW

A minority position on the formation of gangs is that they serve as an outlet for psychologically diseased youths. One proponent of this view is Lewis Yablonsky, whose theory of violent-gang formation holds that violent gangs recruit their members from among the more sociopathic youths living in disorganized slum communities.[130] Yablonsky views the sociopathic youth as one who lacks "social feelings." He "has not been trained to have human feelings or compassion or responsibility for another."[131] Yablonsky supports this contention by pointing to the eccentric, destructive, and hostile sexual attitudes and behavior of gang youths, who are often violent and sadistic. He sums up the sociopathic character traits of gang boys as (1) a defective social conscience marked by limited feelings of guilt for destructive acts against others; (2) limited compassion or empathy for others; (3) behavior dominated by egocentrism and self-seeking goals; and (4) the manipulation of others for immediate self-gratification (e.g., sexually exploitative modes of behavior) without any moral concern or responsibility.

Yablonsky's view is substantiated by cross-cultural studies that have found that gang members suffer from psychological deficits, including impulsivity and poor personality control.[132]

Malcolm Klein's more recent analysis of Los Angeles gangs finds that some street gang members do in fact suffer from psychological and neuropsychological deficits, including low self-concept, social disabilities or deficits, poor impulse control, and limited life skills. Adolescents who display conduct disorders, early onset of antisocial behavior, and violent temperaments are at the greatest risk for later gang membership.[133] Yet, Klein does not consider most gang youths abnormal or pathological. To help them, he believes that psychological therapy is less important than providing gang members with vocational training and educational skills and improving their chances for legitimate opportunities.[134]

RATIONAL CHOICE VIEW

Some youths may join gangs after making the rational choice that gang membership may benefit their law-violating careers and be a source of income. Members of the underclass, who perceive few opportunities in the legitimate economic structure, will turn to gangs as a method of obtaining desired goods and services, either directly through theft and extortion or indirectly through the profits generated by drug dealing and weapon sales. Joining a gang then can be viewed as an "employment decision": The gang can provide its "partners" with the security of knowing they can call on the services of talented "associates" to successfully carry out business ventures. Mercer Sullivan's study of Brooklyn, New York, gangs found that members call success at crime "getting paid," a phrase that imparts an economic edge to gang activity. Gang boys also refer to the rewards of crime as "getting over," which refers to their triumph and pride at "beating the system" and succeeding even though they are way out of the economic mainstream.[135]

According to this view, the gang boy has long been involved in criminal activity and joins the gang as a means of improving his illegal "productivity."[136] Gang membership is *not* a necessary precondition for delinquency; already delinquent youths may join gangs because membership facilitates or enhances their criminal careers.

Felix Padilla found this when he studied the Diamonds, a Latino gang in Chicago.[137] Joining the gang was a decision made after a careful assessment of legitimate economic opportunities. The gang represented a means of achieving aspirations that were otherwise closed off. The Diamonds made collective business decisions; individuals who made their own deals were severely penalized. The gang maintained a distinct organizational structure and carried out other functions similar to those of legitimate enterprises, including personnel recruitment and financing of business ventures with internal and external capital.

The rational choice view is also endorsed by Martin Sanchez-Jankowski in his important book *Islands in the Street*.[138] Sanchez-Jankowski found gangs to be organizations made up of adolescents who maintain a "defiant individualist character." These individuals maintain distinct personality traits: wariness or mistrust of the outside world; self-reliance; isolation from society; good survival instincts; defiance against authority; and a strong belief in the survival of the fittest, that only the strong survive. Youths holding these views and possessing these character traits make a rational decision to join a gang because the gang presents an opportunity to improve the quality of their lives. The gang offers otherwise unobtainable economic and social opportunities, including both support for crime and access to parties, social events, and sexual outlets. Gangs that last the longest and are the most successful are the ones that can offer incentives to these ambitious but destitute youths and control their behaviors. Sanchez-Jankowski's views, important for understanding the economic and social incentives of gang membership, have been supported by independent research data.[139]

The rational choice view holds that gangs provide support for criminal opportunities that might not otherwise be available. Some recent research by Terence Thornberry and his colleagues at the Rochester Youth Development Study support this model. They found that before youths become gang members, their substance abuse and delinquency rates are no higher than those of nongang members. However, once they join the gang, their crime and drug abuse rates increase significantly, only to decrease when they leave the gang. Thornberry concludes that gangs facilitate criminality, rather than provide a haven for youth who are disturbed or already highly delinquent.[140]

Personal Safety　According to Spergel, some adolescents choose to join gangs based on a "rational calculation" to achieve personal safety rather than profit.[141] Youths who are new to a community may believe they will become a target of harassment or attack if they remain "unaffiliated." Motivation may have its roots in interrace or interethnic rivalry: Youths who are white, African-American, Asian, or Hispanic who reside in an area dominated by a different racial or ethnic group may conclude that gang membership is an efficient means of collective protection. Ironically, gang members are more likely to be attacked than nonmembers.

Fun and Support　Some youths join gangs simply to "party" and have fun.[142] They want to hang out with others like themselves and get involved in exciting experiences. Youths can learn the meaning of friendship and loyalty through gang membership. There is evidence that they learn pro-gang attitudes from their peers and that these attitudes direct them to join gangs.[143] Some experts suggest that youths join gangs in an effort to obtain the familylike atmosphere all too often absent from their own homes.

CONTROLLING GANG ACTIVITY

Two basic methods are used to control gang activity: (1) priority targeting by law enforcement and (2) implementation of a variety of social service efforts. Both of these methods will be discussed below.

LAW ENFORCEMENT EFFORTS

In recent years, gang control has often been left to local police departments. Gang control takes three basic forms:

1. The youth service program, in which traditional police personnel, usually from the youth unit, are given responsibility for gang control. No personnel are assigned exclusively or mainly to gang-control work.
2. The gang detail, in which one or more police officers, usually from youth or detective units, are assigned exclusively to gang-control work.
3. The gang unit, established solely to deal with gang problems, to which one or more officers are assigned exclusively to gang-control work.[144]

The National Assessment found that 53 of the 72 police departments surveyed maintained separate gang units. They are involved in such activities as processing of information on youth gangs and gang leaders; prevention efforts, such as mediation programs; enforcement efforts to suppress criminal activity and apprehend those who are believed to have committed crimes; and follow-up investigations directed at apprehending gang members alleged to have committed crimes. About 85 percent of these units provide their personnel with special training in gang control, 73 percent have specific policies directed at dealing with gang boys, and 62 percent enforce special laws designed to control gang activity.[145]

There is evidence that kids learn pro-gang attitudes from their peers and that these attitudes direct them to join gangs. Some experts suggest that kids join gangs in an effort to obtain the family-like atmosphere all too often absent from their own homes. These Hmong gang members in Fresno, California have substituted gang life for their parents' traditional values and customs.

A good example of these units is the Chicago Police Department's 400-plus-officer gang crime section which maintains intelligence on gang problems and trains officers in dealing with gang problems. Through its gang target program, it identifies street gang members and enters their names in a computer bank that is programmed to alert the unit if the youths are picked up or arrested. Some departments also sponsor general prevention programs that can help control gang activities, including school-based lectures, police–school liaisons, information dissemination, recreation programs, and street worker programs that offer counseling, assistance to parents, and community organization, among other services.

Some police departments engage in gang-breaking activities, in which police will focus on the gang leaders and make special efforts to arrest, prosecute, convict, and incarcerate them whenever possible. For example, Los Angeles police conduct intensive anti-gang "sweeps" in which more than 1,000 officers are put on the street to round up and intimidate gang boys. Police say that the sweeps let the gangs know "who the streets belong to" and show neighborhood residents that someone cares.[146] Despite such efforts, the police response to the gang and youth group problem seems fragmented at best; even in Los Angeles, gang membership and violence remain at all-time highs. Few departments have written policies or procedures on how to deal with youths, and many do not provide gang-control training.

Criminologists Mark Moore and Mark A. R. Kleiman suggest that gang sweeps and other traditional police tactics will not work on today's drug gangs. Instead, they argue, gangs should be viewed as organized criminal enterprises and dealt with as traditional organized crime families. They suggest (1) developing informants through criminal prosecutions, payments, and witness protection programs; (2) relying heavily on electronic surveillance and long-term undercover investigations; and (3) using special statutes that create criminal liabilities for conspiracy, extortion, or engaging in criminal enterprises.[147] Of course, such policies are expensive and difficult to implement because they may be needed only against the most sophisticated gangs. However, the gangs that present the greatest threat to urban life may be suitable targets for more intensive police efforts. In addition, as new community-policing strategies are implemented in local neighborhoods (see chapter 13 for more on community policing), it may be possible to garner sufficient local support and information to counteract gang influences.

Gang Resistance Some law enforcement departments conduct in-school programs designed to help youths resist gangs. One is the Gang Resistance Education and Training (GREAT) program, which is similar to the more widely known anti-drug DARE program begun by the Los Angeles Police (see chapter 11 for more on DARE). Originating in Phoenix, Arizona, and now being implemented in other states such as New Mexico and Hawaii, GREAT is a curriculum taught by uniformed police officers to sixth and seventh graders in hourly sessions over an eight-week period. The program emphasizes skill training and information that can help youths resist peer pressure, improve self-esteem, shun violence, and ignore gang influences. A recent evaluation of the program by Dennis Palumbo and Jennifer Ferguson found that GREAT does in fact improve attitudes but that changes are modest and may be ultimately insufficient to persuade adolescents not to join gangs.[148]

SOCIAL SERVICE EFFORTS

In addition to law enforcement activities, a number of social service efforts have attempted to curb gang activity.

Some efforts have involved having social welfare professionals offer direct assistance to at-risk youths. Such social service intervention is actually not new. During the late nineteenth century, social workers of the YMCA worked with youths in Chicago gangs.[149] During the 1950s, at the height of perceived gang activity, the **detached street worker** program was developed in major centers of gang activity.[150] This unique program sent social workers into the community to work with gangs on their own turf. The worker attached himself or herself to a gang, participated in its activities, and tried to get to know its members. The purpose was to act as an advocate of the youths, to provide them with a positive role model, to help orient their activities in a positive direction, and to treat individual problems.

Detached street worker programs are sometimes credited with curbing gang activities in the 1950s and 1960s, although their effectiveness has been challenged on the ground that they helped legitimize delinquent groups by turning them into neighborhood organizations.[151] Some critics believed that the detached street workers helped maintain group solidarity and as a result new members were drawn to the gangs.

In some areas, citywide coordinating groups help orient gang-control efforts. For example, the Chicago Intervention Network operates field offices in various low-income, high-crime areas of the city to provide a variety of services, including neighborhood watches, parent patrols, alternative youth programming, and family support efforts.

Another community approach being implemented in Los Angeles County is the Gang Alternative Prevention Program (GAPP). GAPP is designed to provide intensive supervision of at-risk juveniles who are on probation for relatively minor crimes. Under the program, juveniles receive prevention services before they become entrenched in gangs. GAPP provides such services as (1) individual and group counseling; (2) bicultural and bilingual services to adolescents and their parents; and (3) special programs such as tutoring, parent training, job development, and recreational, educational, and cultural experiences.[152]

Economic Mobilization   Attempts have been made to provide legitimate economic opportunities as an alternative to gang crime. Surveys of gang boys reveal that many might leave gangs if education and vocational opportunities existed.[153] Gang-control efforts were common features of such community programs as the Chicago Area Project and the Mobilization for Youth in New York City, well-known programs that mixed treatment with the provision of economic opportunity.

The era of the massive urban-based opportunity program has ended in the face of budget shortfalls and the deficit economy. Experts such as John Hagedorn have charged that the lack of legitimate economic opportunity for unskilled adolescents creates a powerful incentive for them to become involved in the illegal economy. To reduce the gang problem, hundreds of thousands of high-paying jobs are needed. This solution does not seem practical or probable. As you may recall, the more "embedded" youth become in criminal enterprise, the less likely they are to find meaningful adult work. It is unlikely that gang youth can suddenly be transformed into highly paid professionals. A more reasonable and effective alternative would be to devote a greater degree of available resources to the most deteriorated urban areas, even if it requires pulling funds from groups that have traditionally been recipients of government aid, such as the elderly.[154]

Although social solutions to the gang problem seem elusive, the evidence shows that gang involvement is a socio-ecological phenomenon and must therefore be treated as such. Youths join gangs when they live in deteriorated areas, when their need for economic growth and self-fulfillment cannot be met by existing social institutions, and when gang members are there to recruit them at home or at school.[155] Social causes demand social solutions. Programs that enhance the lives of adolescents at school or in the family are the key to reducing gang delinquency.

SUMMARY

Gangs are a serious problem in many cities, yet little is known about them. Most gang members are males, ages 14 to 21, who live in urban ghetto areas. Ethnic minorities make up the majority of gang members. Gangs can be classified by their structure, behavior, or status. Some are believed to be social groups, others are criminally oriented, and still others are violent.

Gangs developed early in U.S. history and reached their heyday in the 1950s and early 1960s. After a lull of 10 years, gang operations began to increase in the late 1970s. Today an estimated 500,000 youths belong to gangs. Hundreds of thousands of crimes, including drive-by shootings, are believed to be committed annually by gangs. Although most gang members are male, the number of females in gangs is growing at a rate faster than that of males. African-American and Hispanic gangs predominate, but Anglo and Asian gangs are also quite common.

We are still not sure what causes the development of gangs. One view is that they serve as a bridge between adolescence and adulthood in communities where adult control is lacking. Another view suggests that gangs are a product of lower-class social disorganization and serve as an alternative means of advancement for disadvantaged boys. Still another view is that some gangs are havens for psychotic and disturbed youths.

Police departments have tried a number of gang-control techniques, but the efforts have not been well organized. A recent national survey found relatively few training efforts designed to help police officers deal with the gang problem. There are also social service efforts to reduce gang delinquency, including counseling, intensive supervision and economic development programs.

KEY TERMS

cliques
crowds
co-offending
gang
interstitial group
near groups

barrio
retreatists
organized/corporate gang
scavenger gang
stable slum
klikas

graffiti
representing
prestige crimes
detached street worker

QUESTIONS FOR DISCUSSION

1. Do gangs serve a purpose? Differentiate between a gang and a fraternity.

2. Discuss the differences between violent, criminal, and drug-oriented gangs.

3. How do gangs in suburban areas differ from inner-city gangs?
4. Do delinquents have cold and distant relationships with their peers?
5. Can gangs be controlled without changing the economic opportunity structure of society? Are there any truly meaningful alternatives to gangs today for lower-class youths?
6. Can you think of other rituals in society that reflect an affinity or longing for tribal customs? Hint: Have you ever pledged a fraternity or sorority, gone to a wedding, or attended a football game?

NOTES

1. For a general review, see Scott Cummings and Daniel Monti, *Gangs: The Origin and Impact of Contemporary Youth Gangs in the United States* (Albany, N.Y.: State University of New York Press, 1993). This chapter also makes extensive use of George Knox et al., *Gang Prevention and Intervention: Preliminary Results from the 1995 Project Gangpint National Needs Assessment Gang Research Task Force* (National Gang Crime Research Center, 9501 S. King Drive, Chicago, Ill., 1995).
2. George Knox et al. *Preliminary Results of the 1995 Adult Corrections Survey* (Chicago, Ill.: National Gang Research Center, 1995); G. David Curry, Robert J. Fox, Richard Ball, and Daryl Stone, *National Assessment of Law Enforcement Anti-Gang Information Resources, Final Report* (Morgantown, W.V.: National Assessment Survey, 1992), Table 6, pp. 36–37. (Hereinafter cited as *National Assessment.*)
3. Thomas Berndt, "The Features and Effects of Friendships in Early Adolescence," *Child Development* 53:1447–69 (1982).
4. Thomas Berndt and T. B. Perry, "Children's Perceptions of Friendships as Supportive Relationships," *Developmental Psychology* 22:640–48 (1986).
5. Spencer Rathus, *Understanding Child Development* (New York: Holt, Rinehart and Winston, 1988), p. 462.
6. Peggy Giordano, "The Wider Circle of Friends in Adolescence," *American Journal of Sociology* 101:661–97 (1995).
7. Ibid, p. 663.
8. See, generally, Penelope Eckert, *Jocks and Burnouts: Social Categories and Identity in the High School* (New York: Teachers College Press, 1989).
9. Ibid., p. 463.
10. David Cantor, "Drug Involvement and Offending among Incarcerated Juveniles," Paper presented at the American Society of Criminology meeting, Boston, Mass., November 1995.
11. Albert Reiss, "Co-offending and Criminal Careers," in Michael Tonry and Norval Morris, eds., *Crime and Justice*, vol. 10 (Chicago: University of Chicago Press, 1988), pp. 111–121.
12. David Farrington and Donald West, "The Cambridge Study in Delinquent Development: A Long-term Follow-up of 411 London Males," in H. J. Kerner and G. Kaiser, eds., *Criminality: Personality, Behavior, and Life History* (Berlin: Springer-Verlag, 1990), pp. 35–60.
13. Mark Warr, "Organization and Instigation in Delinquent Groups," *Criminology* 34:11–37 (1996).
14. Ibid., pp. 31–33.
15. James Short and Fred Strodtbeck, *Group Process and Gang Delinquency* (Chicago: Aldine, 1965).
16. Kate Keenan, Rolf Loeber, Quanwu Zhang, Magda Stouthamer-Loeber, and Welmoet Van Kammen, "The Influence of Deviant Peers on the Development of Boys' Disruptive and Delinquent Behavior: A Temporal Analysis," *Development and Psychopathology* 7:715–26 (1995).
17. John Cole, Robert Terry, Shari-Miller Johnson, and John Lochman, "Longitudinal Effects of Deviant Peer Groups on Criminal Offending in Late Adolescence," Paper presented at the American Society of Criminology meeting, Boston, Mass., November 1995.
18. Thomas Dishion, Deborah Capaldi, Kathleen Spracklen, and Fuzhong Li, "Peer Ecology of Male Adolescent Drug Use," *Development and Psychopathology* 7:803–24 (1995).
19. Terence Thornberry, Alan Lizotte, Marvin Krohn, Margaret Farnworth, and Sung Joon Jang, "Delinquent Peers, Beliefs, and Delinquent Behavior: A Longitudinal Test of Interactional Theory," working paper no. 6, rev. (Albany, N.Y.: Rochester Youth Development Study, Hindelang Criminal Justice Research Center, 1992), pp. 8–30.
20. Mark Warr, "Age, Peers and Delinquency," *Criminology* 31:17–40 (1993).
21. Cindy Hanson, Scott Henggeler, William Haefele, and J. Douglas Rodick, "Demographic, Individual, and Family Relationship Correlates of Serious Repeated Crime among Adolescents and Their Siblings," *Journal of Consulting and Clinical Psychology* 52:528–38 (1984).
22. Peggy Giordano, Stephen Cernkovich, and M. D. Pugh, "Friendships and Delinquency," *American Journal of Sociology* 91:1170–1202 (1986).
23. Denise Kandel, "Friendship Networks, Intimacy and Illicit Drug Use in Young Adulthood: A Comparison of Two Competing Theories," *Criminology* 29:441–69 (1991).

24. Marvin Krohn and Terence Thornberry, "Network Theory: A Model for Understanding Drug Abuse among African-American and Hispanic Youth," working paper no. 10 (Albany, N.Y.: Rochester Youth Development Study, Hindelang Criminal Justice Research Center, 1991).

25. Irving Spergel, *The Youth Gang Problem: A Community Approach* (New York: Oxford University Press, 1995).

26. Ibid., p. 3.

27. Other well-known movie representations of gangs include *The Wild Ones* and *Hell's Angels on Wheels,* which depicted motorcycle gangs, and *Saturday Night Fever,* which focused on neighborhood street toughs. See also David Dawley, *A Nation of Lords* (Garden City, N.Y.: Anchor, 1973).

28. For a recent review of gang research, see James Howell, "Recent Gang Research: Program and Policy Implications," *Crime and Delinquency* 40:495–515 (1994).

29. Walter Miller, *Violence by Youth Gangs and Youth Groups as a Crime Problem in Major American Cities* (Washington, D.C.: U.S. Government Printing Office, 1975).

30. Ibid., p. 20.

31. Malcolm Klein, *The American Street Gang, Its Nature, Prevalence and Control* (New York: Oxford University Press, 1995), p. 30.

32. Lewis Yablonsky, *The Violent Gang* (Baltimore: Penguin, 1966), p. 109.

33. James Diego Vigil, *Barrio Gangs* (Austin: Texas University Press, 1988), pp. 11–19.

34. Finn-Aage Esbensen and David Huizinga, "Gangs, Drugs and Delinquency in a Survey of Urban Youth", *Criminology* 31:565–87 (1993).

35. Walter Miller, "Gangs, Groups, and Serious Youth Crime," in David Schicor and Delos Kelly, eds., *Critical Issues in Juvenile Delinquency* (Lexington, Mass.: Lexington Books, 1980).

36. Ibid.

37. Frederick Thrasher, *The Gang* (Chicago: University of Chicago Press, 1927).

38. Malcolm Klein, ed., *Juvenile Gangs in Context* (Englewood Cliffs, N.J.: Prentice Hall, 1967), pp. 1–12.

39. Ibid., p. 6.

40. Irving Spergel, *Street Gang Work: Theory and Practice* (Reading, Mass.: Addison-Wesley, 1966).

41. Miller, *Violence by Youth Gangs and Youth Groups as a Crime Problem in Major American Cities,* p. 2.

42. Marjorie Zatz, "Los Cholos: Legal Processing of Chicago Gang Members," *Social Problems* 33:13–30 (1985).

43. Miller, *Violence by Youth Gangs and Youth Groups as a Crime Problem in Major American Cities,* pp. 1–2.

44. Ibid., pp. 1–2.

45. "LA Gang Warfare Called Bloodiest in 5 Years," *Boston Globe,* 18 December 1986, p. A4.

46. John Hagedorn, *People and Folks: Gangs, Crime and the Underclass in a Rustbelt City* (Chicago: Lake View Press, 1988).

47. National School Safety Center, *Gangs in Schools, Breaking Up Is Hard to Do* (Malibu, Calif.: Pepperdine University, 1988), p. 8.

48. C. Ronald Huff, "Youth Gangs and Public Policy," *Crime and Delinquency* 35:524–37 (1989).

49. Joan Moore, *Going Down to the Barrio: Homeboys and Homegirls in Change* (Philadelphia: Temple University Press, 1991), p. 3.

50. Irving Spergel, *Youth Gangs: Problem and Response* (Chicago: University of Chicago, School of Social Service Administration, 1989).

51. Felix Padilla, *The Gang as an American Enterprise* (New Brunswick, N.J.: Rutgers University Press, 1992), p. 3.

52. Pamela Irving Jackson, "Crime, Youth Gangs, and Urban Transition: The Social Dislocations of Postindustrial Economic Development," *Justice Quarterly* 8:379–97 (1991).

53. Joan Moore, *Going Down to the Barrio* (Philadelphia: Temple University Press, 1991), pp. 89–101.

54. Miller, *Violence by Youth Gangs and Youth Groups as a Crime Problem in Major American Cities;* idem, *Crime by Youth Gangs and Groups in the United States* (Washington, D.C.: Office of Juvenile Justice Delinquency Prevention, 1982).

55. See, *National Assessment.*

56. G. David Curry, *Gang Crime and Law Enforcement Record Keeping* (Washington, D.C.: National Institute of Justice, 1994).

57. G. David Curry, Richard Ball, and Scott Decker, "Estimating the National Scope of Gang Crime from Law Enforcement Data," in C. Ronald Huff, ed., *Gangs in America,* 2nd ed. (Newbury Park, Calif.: Sage, 1996).

58. Klein, *The American Street Gang, Its Nature, Prevalence and Control,* pp. 31–35.

59. Ibid., p. 217.

60. Claire Johnson, Barbara Webster, and Edward Connors, *Prosecuting Gangs: A National Assessment* (Washington, D.C.: National Institute of Justice, 1995).

61. PRIDE, Inc. "Teen Drug Use Rises for Fourth Straight Year," Pride, Inc., Atlanta, Ga. November 2, 1995.

62. Jeffrey Fagan, "The Social Organization of Drug Use and Drug Dealing among Urban Gangs," *Criminology* 27:633–69 (1989).

63. Richard Cloward and Lloyd Ohlin, *Delinquency and Opportunity* (New York: Free Press), pp. 1–12.

64. Fagan, "The Social Organization of Drug Use and Drug Dealing among Urban Gangs.", p. 641.

65. Huff, "Youth Gangs and Public Policy," pp. 528–29.

66. Carl Taylor, *Dangerous Society* (East Lansing: Michigan State University Press, 1990).

67. Cheryl Maxson and Malcolm Klein, "Investigating Gang Structures," *Journal of Gang Research* 3:33–42 (1995).

68. Malcolm Klein, personal communication, December 12, 1995.

69. Saul Bernstein, *Youth in the Streets: Work with Alienated Youth Gangs* (New York: Associated Press, 1964).

70. William Julius Wilson, *The Truly Disadvantaged* (Chicago: University of Chicago Press, 1987).

71. Vigil, *Barrio Gangs.*

72. Miller, *Violence by Youth Gangs and Youth Groups as a Crime Problem in Major American Cities,* pp. 17–20.

73. Jerome Needle and W. Vaughan Stapleton, *Reports of the National Juvenile Justice Assessment Centers, Police Handling of Youth Gangs* (Washington, D.C.: Office of Juvenile Justice and Delinquency Prevention, 1983), p. 12.

74. Richard Zevitz and Susan Takata, "Metropolitan Gang Influence and the Emergence of Group Delinquency in a Regional Community," *Journal of Criminal Justice* 20:93–106 (1992).

75. Cheryl Maxson, Kristi Woods, and Malcolm Klein, *Street Gang Migration in the United States: Executive Summary* (Los Angeles: Center for the Study of Crime and Social Control, University of Southern California, 1995).

76. John Hagedorn, "Gangs, Neighborhoods and Public Policy," *Social Problems* 20:529–41 (1991).

77. National School Safety Center, *Gangs in Schools, Breaking Up Is Hard to Do,* p. 7.

78. Knox et al., *Gang Prevention and Intervention,* p. vii.

79. Spergel, *Youth Gangs: Problem and Response,* p. 7; Hagedorn, *People and Folks: Gangs, Crime and the Underclass in a Rustbelt City.*

80. Wilson, *The Truly Disadvantaged.*

81. National Safety Center, *Gangs in Schools, Breaking Up Is Hard to Do,* p. 7.

82. John Hagedorn, Jerome Wonders, Angelo Vega, and Joan Moore, *The Milwaukee Drug Posse Study,* Unpublished leaflet, undated.

83. Moore, *Going Down to the Barrio: Homeboys and Homegirls in Change;* Anne Campbell, *The Girls in the Gang* (Cambridge, Mass.: Basil Blackwood, 1984).

84. Mary Glazier, "Small Town Delinquent Gangs: Origins, Characteristics and Activities," Paper presented at the American Society of Criminology meeting, Boston, Mass., November 1995.

85. Irving Spergel, "Youth Gangs: Continuity and Change," in Michael Tonry and Norval Morris, eds., *Crime and Justice,* vol. 12 (Chicago: University of Chicago Press, 1990), pp. 171–275; Knox et al., *Gang Prevention and Intervention,* p. v.

86. Gary Jensen, "Defiance and Gang Identity: Quantitative Tests of Qualitative Hypothesis," Paper presented at the American Society of Criminology meeting, Boston, Mass., November 1995; Finn Esbensen, Terence Thornberry, and David Huizinga, "Gangs," in David Huizinga, Rolf Loeber, and Terence Thornberry, eds., *Urban Delinquency and Substance Abuse: Technical Report* (Washington, D.C.: Office of Juvenile Justice and Delinquency Prevention, 1991), pp. 1–3.

87. Taylor, *Dangerous Society,* p. 109.

88. Finn-Aage Esbensen and David Huizinga, "Gangs, Drugs and Delinquency in a Survey of Urban Youth," *Criminology* 31:565–87 (1993).

89. Joan Moore, James Diego Vigil, and Robert Garcia, "Residence and Territoriality in Chicano Gangs," *Social Problems* 31:182–94 (1983).

90. William F. Whyte, *Street Corner Society* (Chicago: University of Chicago Press, 1955).

91. Malcolm Klein, "Impressions of Juvenile Gang Members," *Adolescence* 3:59 (1968).

92. Los Angeles County Sheriff's Department, *Street Gangs of Los Angeles County, White Paper* (Los Angeles: LACSD, n.d.), p. 14.

93. LeRoy Martin, *Collecting, Organizing and Reporting Street Gang Crime* (Chicago: Chicago Police Department, 1988).

94. Patricia Wen, "Boston Gangs: A Hard World," *Boston Globe,* 10 May 1988, p. 1.

95. Rick Graves and Ed Allen, *Black Gangs and Narcotics and Black Gangs* (Los Angeles: Los Angeles County Sheriff's Department, n.d.).

96. Associated Press, "California Youth Slain outside Theater Showing *Colors,*" *Boston Globe,* 26 April 1988, p. 6.

97. Spergel, *The Youth Gang Problem: A Community Approach,* p. 3.

98. Joseph Sheley, Joshua Zhang, Charles Brody, and James Wright, "Gang Organization, Gang Criminal Activity, and Individual Gang Members' Criminal Behavior," *Social Science Quarterly* 76:53–68 (1995).

99. Kevin Thompson, David Brownfield, and Ann Marie Sorenson, "Specialization Patterns of Gang and Nongang Offending: A Latent Structure Analysis," Paper presented at the American Society of Criminology meeting, Boston, Mass., November 1995.

100. Malcolm Klein, Cheryl Maxson, and Lea Cunningham, "Crack, Street Gangs and Violence," *Criminology* 4:623–50 (1991).

101. Mel Wallace, "The Gang-Drug Debate Revisited," Paper presented at the annual meeting of the American Society of Criminology, New Orleans, La., November 1992.

102. Esbensen and Huizinga, "Gangs, Drugs, and Delinquency in a Survey of Urban Youth," p. 582.

103. Beth Bjerregaard and Alan Lizotte, "Gun Ownership and Gang Membership," *Journal of Criminal Law and Criminology* 86:37–53 (1995).

104. H. Range Hutson, Deirdre Anglin, and Michale Pratts, Jr., "Adolescents and Children Injured or Killed in Drive-By Shootings in Los Angeles," *The New England Journal of Medicine* 330:324–27 (1994).

105. Miller, *Violence by Youth Gangs and Youth Groups as a Crime Problem in Major American Cities,* pp. 2–26.

106. Malcolm Klein, "Violence in American Juvenile Gangs," in Donald Muvihill, Melvin Tumin, and Lynn Curtis, eds., *Crimes of Violence National Commission on the*

Causes and Prevention of Violence, vol. 13 (Washington, D.C.: U.S. Government Printing Office, 1969), p. 1429.

107. Kevin Cullen, "Gangs Are Seen as Carefully Organized," *Boston Globe,* 7 January 1987, p. 17.

108. *National Assessment,* pp. 60–61.

109. The following description of ethnic gangs leans heavily on the material developed in National School Safety Center, *Gangs in Schools, Breaking Up Is Hard to Do,* pp. 11–23.

110. Spergel, *The Youth Gang Problem: A Community Approach,* pp. 136–37.

111. Los Angeles County Sheriff's Department, *Street Gangs of Los Angeles County, White Paper.*

112. Zheng Wang, Indiana University of Pennsylvania, personnel communication, February 3, 1993.

113. Ko-Lin Chin, *Chinese Subculture and Criminality: Non-traditional Crime Groups in America* (Westport, Conn.: Greenwood Press, 1990).

114. James Diego Vigil and Steve Chong Yun, "Vietnamese Youth Gangs in Southern California," in C. Ronald Huff, ed., *Gangs in America* (Newbury Park, Calif.: Sage, 1990), pp. 146–63.

115. Glazier, "Small Town Delinquent Gangs."

116. For a review, see Lawrence Trostle, *The Stoners, Drugs, Demons and Delinquency* (New York: Garland, 1992).

117. Associated Press, "California Youths Arrested for Gang-Related Rape Game," *Boston Globe,* 20 March 1993, p. 9.

118. Herbert Block and Arthur Niederhoffer, *The Gang: A Study in Adolescent Behavior* (New York: Philosophical Library, 1958).

119. Ibid., p. 113.

120. Knox et al., *Gang Prevention and Intervention,* p. 44.

121. James Diego Vigil, "Group Processes and Street Identity: Adolescent Chicano Gang Members," *Ethos* 16:421–45 (1988).

122. James Diego Vigil and John Long, "Emir and Etic Perspectives on Gang Culture: The Chicano Case," in C. Ronald Huff, ed., *Gangs in America* (Newbury Park, Calif.: Sage, 1990), p. 66.

123. Albert Cohen, *Delinquent Boys* (New York: Free Press, 1955), pp. 1–19.

124. Irving Spergel, *Racketville, Slumtown, and Haulburg: An Exploratory Study of Delinquent Subcultures* (Chicago: University of Chicago Press, 1964).

125. Malcolm Klein, *Street Gangs and Street Workers* (Englewood Cliffs, N.J.: Prentice Hall, 1971), pp. 12–15.

126. Vigil, *Barrio Gangs.*

127. Vigil and Long, "Emir and Etic Perspectives on Gang Culture," p. 61.

128. Spergel, *The Youth Gang Problem: A Community Approach,* pp. 4–5.

129. Ibid.

130. Yablonsky, *The Violent Gang,* p. 237.

131. Ibid., pp. 239–41.

132. Marc Le Blanc and Nadine Lanctot, "Social and Psychological Characteristics of Gang Members According to the Gang Structure and Its Subcultural and Ethnic Making," Paper presented at the American Society of Criminology meeting, Miami, Fla., 1994.

133. Malcolm Klein, *The American Street Gang* (New York: Oxford, 1995).

134. Ibid., p. 163.

135. Mercer Sullivan, *Getting Paid: Youth Crime and Work in the Inner City* (Ithaca, N.Y.: Cornell University Press, 1989), pp. 244–45.

136. Esbensen and Huizinga, "Gangs, Drugs and Delinquency in a Survey of Urban Youth, p. 583," G. David Curry and Irving Spergel, "Gang Involvement and Delinquency among Hispanic and African-American Adolescent Males," *Journal of Research in Crime and Delinquency* 29:273–91 (1992).

137. Padilla, *The Gang as an American Enterprise,* p. 103.

138. Martin Sanchez-Jankowski, *Islands in the Street: Gangs and American Urban Society* (Berkeley: University of California Press, 1991).

139. Gary Jensen, "Defiance and Gang Identity: Quantitative Tests of Qualitative Hypothesis," Paper presented at the American Society of Criminology meeting, Boston, Mass., November 1995.

140. Terence Thornberry, Marvin Krohn, Alan Lizotte, and Deborah Chard-Wierschem, "The Role of Juvenile Gangs in Facilitating Delinquent Behavior," *Journal of Research in Crime and Delinquency* 30:55–87 (1993).

141. Spergel, *The Youth Gang Problem: A Community Approach,* pp. 93–94.

142. Ibid., p. 93.

143. L. Thomas Winfree, Jr., Teresa Vigil Backstrom, and G. Larry Mays, "Social Learning Theory, Self-Reported Delinquency and Youth Gangs, A New Twist on a General Theory of Crime and Delinquency," *Youth and Society* 26:147–77 (1994).

144. Needle and Stapleton, *Reports of the National Juvenile Justice Assessment Centers, Police Handling of Youth Gangs,* p. 19.

145. *National Assessment,* p. 65.

146. Scott Armstrong, "Los Angeles Seeks New Ways to Handle Gangs," *Christian Science Monitor,* 23 April 1988, p. 3.

147. Mark Moore and Mark A. R. Kleiman, *The Police and Drugs* (Washington, D.C.: National Institute of Justice, 1989), p. 8.

148. Dennis Palumbo and Jennifer Ferguson, "Evaluating Gang Resistance Education and Training (GREAT): Is the Impact the Same as the Drug Abuse Resistance Education (DARE)?," *Evaluation Review* 19:597–619 (1995).

149. Barry Krisberg, "Preventing and Controlling Violent Youth Crime: The State of the Art," in Ira Schwartz, ed., *Violent Juvenile Crime* (Minneapolis: University of Min-

nesota, Hubert Humphrey Institute of Public Affairs, n.d.), pp. 5.

150. See, generally, Spergel, *Street Gang Work: Theory and Practice.*

151. For a revisionist view of gang delinquency, see Hedy Bookin-Weiner and Ruth Horowitz, "The End of the Youth Gang," *Criminology* 21:585–602 (1983).

152. Michael Agopian, "Evaluation of the Gang Alternative Prevention Program," Paper presented at the American Society of Criminology meeting, Boston, Mass., November 1995.

153. James Houston, "What Works: The Search for Excellence in Gang Intervention Programs," Paper presented at the American Society of Criminology meeting, Boston, Mass., November 1995.

154. Hagedorn, "Gangs, Neighborhoods and Public Policy."

155. Curry and Spergel, "Gang Involvement and Delinquency among Hispanic and African-American Adolescent Males."

CHAPTER TEN

SCHOOLS AND DELINQUENCY

INTRODUCTION

Many of the underlying problems of delinquency, as well as their prevention and control, are intimately connected with the nature and quality of the school experience.[1]

Because the schools are responsible for educating virtually everyone during most of their formative years and because so much of an adolescent's time is spent in school, some relationship would seem logical between delinquent behavior and what is happening—or not happening—in classrooms throughout the United States. This relationship was pointed out as early as 1939, when a study by the New Jersey Delinquency Commission found that of 2,021 inmates of prisons and correctional institutions in that state, two out of every five had first been committed for **truancy.**[2]

Numerous studies have confirmed that delinquency is related to **academic achievement.** Some find that school-related variables are more important contributing factors to delinquent behavior than the effects of either family or friends.[3] Although there are differences of opinion, most theorists agree that the educational system bears some responsibility for the high rate of juvenile crime (see Table 10.1).

This chapter examines the relationship between the school and delinquency. We first explore how educational achievement and delinquency are related and

TABLE 10.1 Theoretical Views on Schools and Delinquency

View	Educational Impact
Choice	People commit crime because of poor social control. The school can educate youths about the pains of punishment and through disciplinary procedures teach youths that behavior transgressions lead to sanctions. Education can stress moral development.
Biosocial and Psychological	The school can compensate for psychological and biological problems. For example, youths with low IQs or learning disabilities can be put in special classes to ease their frustration and reduce their delinquency-proneness.
Social Structure	The school is a primary cause of delinquency. Middle-class school officials penalize lower-class youths, intensifying their rage, frustration, and anomie.
Social Process	A lack of bond to the school and nonparticipation in educational activities can intensify delinquency-proneness. The school fails to provide sufficient definitions toward conventional behavior to thwart delinquency.
Labeling	Labeling by school officials solidifies negative self-images. The stigma associated with school failure locks youths into a delinquent career pattern.
Conflict	Schools are designated to train lower-class youngsters for menial careers and upper-class youths to be part of the privileged society. Rebellion against these roles promotes delinquency.

what factors in the school experience appear to contribute to delinquent behavior. Next, we turn to delinquency within the school setting itself—vandalism, theft, violence, and so on. Finally, we look at the educational system's attempts to prevent and control delinquency.

THE SCHOOL IN MODERN AMERICAN SOCIETY

The school plays a significant role in shaping the values and norms of American children. In contrast to earlier periods, when formal education was a privilege of the upper classes, the American system of compulsory public education has made schooling a legal obligation for everyone. Today 94 percent of the school-age population attends school, compared with only 7 percent in 1890.[4] In contrast to the earlier, agrarian days of U.S. history, when most adolescents shared in the work of the family and became **socialized** into adulthood as part of the workforce, today's young people, beginning as early as age 3 or 4, spend most of their time in school. The school has become the primary instrument of socialization, the "basic conduit through which the community and adult influences enter into the lives of adolescents."[5]

Because young people spend more time in school, their adolescence is prolonged. As long as students are still economically dependent on their families and have not entered the work world, they are not considered adults, either in their view or that of society. The responsibilities of adulthood come later to modern-day youths than those in earlier generations, and some experts see this prolonged childhood as a factor that contributes to the irresponsible, childish, often irrational behavior of many juveniles who commit delinquent acts.

SOCIALIZATION AND STATUS

Another significant aspect of the educational experience of American youths is that it is overwhelmingly a peer encounter. Most of their activities both during and after school take place with school friends. Young people rely increasingly on peers to serve as role models and consequently become less and less interested in adult role models. The norms and values of the peer culture are often at odds with those of adult society, and a pseudoculture with a distinct social system develops, offering a united front to the adult world. Law-abiding behavior or conventional norms may not be among the values promoted in such an atmosphere. Youth culture may instead admire bravery, defiance, and thrill seeking behavior.

In addition to its role as an instrument of socialization, the school has become a primary determinant of economic and social status in American society. In this highly technological age, education is the key to a job that will mark its holder as "successful." No longer can parents ensure the status of their children through social-class origin alone. Educational achievement has become of equal, if not greater, importance as a determinant of economic success.

Schools, then, are geared toward producing success in the form of academic achievement, which provides the key to profit and position in society. Adolescents derive much of their identity out of what happens to them in school. Virtually all adolescents must participate in the educational system, not only because it is required by law but also because the notion of success is defined in terms of the possession of a technical or professional skill that can be acquired only through formal education.

Children spend their school hours with their peers, and most of their activities after school take place with school friends. Young people rely increasingly on school friends and consequently become less and less interested in adult role models. The norms and values of the peer culture are often at odds with those of adult society, and a pseudoculture with a distinct social system develops, offering a united front to the adult world.

This emphasis on the value of education is fostered by parents, the media, and the schools themselves. Regardless of their social or economic background, most children grow up believing that education is the key to success. Despite their apparent acceptance of the value of education, however, many youths do not meet acceptable standards of school achievement. Whether failure is measured by obtaining low test scores, not being promoted, or dropping out, its incidence continues to be a major social problem of American society. A single school failure for a student often leads to patterns of chronic academic failure. The links between school failure, academic and social aspirations, and delinquency will be explored more fully in the following sections.

EDUCATION IN CRISIS

The critical role schools play in adolescent development is underscored by the problems facing the American education system. Budget cutting has severely reduced educational resources in many communities and curtailed state support for local school systems. Spending in the United States on elementary and secondary education (as a percentage of the gross national product) trails that of other nations. While Sweden spends 7 percent of its gross national product on education, Austria 6 percent, and Japan 4.8 percent, the United States spends 4.1 percent.[6] As a consequence, the United States cannot provide the classroom services routinely available to children in other nations; some Third World nations maintain lower student-teacher ratios than those generally found in the far wealthier United States.[7]

Areas such as reading, math, and science are of particular concern. As of 1995, the National Education Goals Panel, a group set up by the federal and state governments to assess the nation's educational needs, found that fewer than one-third of fourth and eighth graders read at a level that indicated "mastery over challenging subject matter." Reading achievement of 12th graders actually

FIGURE 10.1

Reading Achievement—Grade 4 The National Education Goals Panel has assessed reading achievement and found that many American children do not perform at acceptable performance standards. Wide gaps begin to form as early as fourth grade

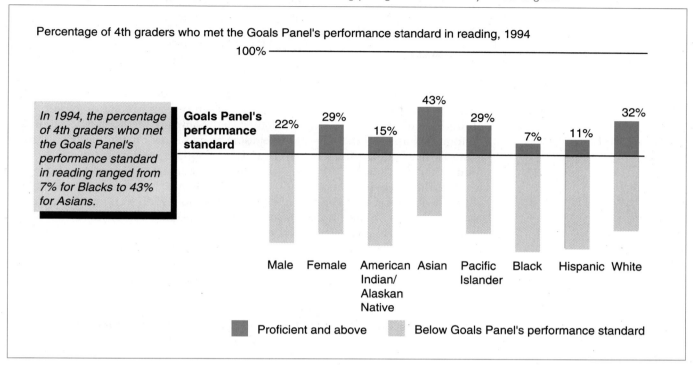

Percentage of 4th graders who met the Goals Panel's performance standard in reading, 1994

In 1994, the percentage of 4th graders who met the Goals Panel's performance standard in reading ranged from 7% for Blacks to 43% for Asians.

Goals Panel's performance standard

Male	Female	American Indian/ Alaskan Native	Asian	Pacific Islander	Black	Hispanic	White
22%	29%	15%	43%	29%	7%	11%	32%

■ Proficient and above   ▨ Below Goals Panel's performance standard

Source: National Education Goals Panel, National Data (Washington, D.C.: U.S. Government Printing Office, 1995), p. 54.

declined between 1992 and 1995; fewer than 20 percent of 12th graders can meet acceptable performance standards in math.[8]

Fewer than one-half of high school seniors demonstrate in-depth knowledge of scientific information or the reasoning ability needed to interpret data in tables and graphs and evaluate and design scientific experiments.[9] By fourth grade, large disparities begin to appear between white and Asian-Pacific Islander children and their African-American and Hispanic peers, with the latter falling rapidly behind; children attending affluent school districts perform better than students in disadvantaged neighborhoods (see Figure 10.1).

A recent six-nation (France, Hungary, Korea, Switzerland, Taiwan, and the United States) comparison of science and math education (e.g., geometry, data analysis, algebra, life science, earth science) achievement found that American students failed to outperform foreign students *in every single area tested*.[10]

One reason American students seem to be lagging in educational achievement is that so many do not read in or out of school. A survey sponsored by the federal government found that 45 percent of fourth graders, 63 percent of eighth graders, and 59 percent of twelfth graders read a total of 10 or fewer pages each day; fewer than half of all students read outside of school; about 30 percent report never reading for fun; and about 22 percent said they either did not have homework assigned or simply did not do it.[11]

The national level of academic performance and resulting educational problems seems critical considering its assumed association with delinquent forms of behavior.

ACADEMIC PERFORMANCE AND DELINQUENCY

The general path toward occupational prestige is education. Thus, when youth are deprived of this avenue of success through poor school performance, there is a greater likelihood of delinquent behavior.[12]

Poor academic performance has been directly linked to delinquent behavior: There is general consensus that students who are chronic underachievers in school are also among the most likely to be delinquent.[13] In fact, researchers commonly find that school failure is a stronger predictor of delinquency than such personal variables as economic class membership, racial or ethnic background, or peer group relations. Studies that compare the academic records of delinquents and nondelinquents, including their scores on standardized tests of basic skills, failure rate, teacher ratings, and other academic measures, have found that delinquents are often academically deficient, a condition that may lead to their leaving school and becoming involved in antisocial activities.[14] Youths who report that they do not like school, do not do well in school, and do not concentrate on their homework are also the ones most likely to self-report delinquent acts.[15] In contrast, at-risk youths, even those with histories of abuse and neglect, who do well in school are often able to avoid delinquent involvement.[16]

CHRONIC OFFENDERS

The academic failure–delinquency association is commonly found among chronic offenders. Lyle Shannon found that youths leaving school without a diploma were significantly more likely to become involved in chronic delinquency than graduates.[17] David Farrington and Donald J. West also found that chronic delinquents were school failures: 33 percent of youths in their sample who felt school was "of little use to them" were recidivists; only 7 percent of those who saw benefits in attending school were repeat offenders.[18] Only 9 percent of the chronic offenders in

Poor academic performance has been directly linked to delinquent behavior; there is general consensus that students who are chronic underachievers in school are also among the most likely to be delinquent. Researchers commonly find that school failure is a stronger predictor of delinquency than such personal variables as economic class membership, racial or ethnic background, or peer group relations.

Wolfgang's Philadelphia cohort graduated from high school, compared with 74 percent of nonoffenders.[19] Chronic offenders also had significantly more disciplinary actions and remedial/disciplinary placements than nonoffenders.[20]

The relationship between school achievement and persistent offending is supported by surveys of prison inmates that indicate that only 40 percent of incarcerated felons had 12 or more years of education, compared with about 80 percent of the general population.[21]

SCHOOL FAILURE AND DELINQUENCY

Although there is general agreement that **school failure** and delinquency are related, some question exists over the nature and direction the relationship takes. One view is that the school experience is a direct cause of delinquent behavior. Children who fail at school soon feel frustrated, angry, and rejected. Believing they will never achieve success through conventional means, they seek out like-minded companions and together engage in antisocial behaviors. Educational failure, beginning early in the life course, evokes negative responses from important people in the child's life, including teachers, parents, and prospective employers. These reactions help solidify feelings of social inadequacy and, in some cases, lead the underachieving student into a pattern of chronic delinquency.

A second view is that school failure leads to psychological and behavioral dysfunction, which are the actual causes of antisocial behavior. For example, academic failure helps reduce self-esteem; studies using a variety of measures of academic competence and self-esteem clearly demonstrate that good students have a better attitude about themselves than do poor students.[22] Reduced self-esteem has also been found to contribute to delinquent behavior.[23] The association then runs from school failure to low self-concept to delinquency. The school failure–delinquency association may be mediated then by efforts to stabilize or improve the self-image of academically challenged children.

A third view is that school failure and delinquency share a common cause; they are all part of the problem behavior syndrome (PBS). It would be therefore erroneous to conclude that school failure precedes antisocial behavior. The research evidence that the association between school failure and delinquency is a function of a PBS includes these aspects:

- Delinquents may have lower IQs than nondelinquents, a factor that might also explain their poor academic achievement.[24]
- Delinquent behavior has also been associated with a turbulent family life, a condition that most likely leads to academic underachievement.
- Delinquency has been associated with low self-control and impulsivity, traits that also may produce school failure.[25]
- The adolescent who both fails at school and engages in delinquency may be experiencing drug use, depression, malnutrition, abuse, and disease, all symptoms of a generally troubled lifestyle.[26]

THE CAUSES OF SCHOOL FAILURE

Although disagreement still exists over the direction the relationship takes, there is little argument that delinquent behavior is linked to a child's educational experiences. A number of factors have been linked to the onset of school failure; the most prominent are discussed in some detail below.

SOCIAL CLASS AND SCHOOL FAILURE

During the 1950s, research by Albert Cohen indicated that delinquency was fundamentally a phenomenon of working-class students who were poorly equipped to function in middle-class schools. Cohen referred to this phenomenon as a failure to live up to "middle-class measuring rods."[27] Jackson Toby reinforced this concept of class-based delinquency, contending that the disadvantages lower-class children have in school (for example, lack of verbal skills, parental education, and motivation) are a direct result of their position in the social structure and implicitly foster their delinquency.[28] These views have been supported by the greater than average retention and dropout rates among lower-class children.

Some theorists contend that the high incidence of failure among lower-class youths is actually fostered by the schools themselves.[29] Children from an impoverished background often find that the school experience can be a frightening one in which constant testing and the threat of failure are clear and ever-present dangers.[30] Research data confirm not only that such children begin school at lower levels of achievement but also that, without help, their performance progressively deteriorates the longer they are in school. If this is true, the school itself becomes an active force in the generation of delinquency insofar as it is linked to failure.[31]

Does Class Really Matter?   Not all experts, however, agree with the social class–school failure–delinquency hypothesis. A number of early research studies found that boys who do poorly in school, regardless of their socioeconomic background, are more likely to be delinquent than those who perform well.[32] There is evidence that affluent students are equally or even more deeply affected by school failure than lower-class students and that middle-class youths who did poorly in school were actually more likely to become delinquent than their lower-class peers.[33]

Arthur Stinchcombe's classic research on rebellion in a high school indicated that upper-class **underachievers** were in fact more prone to be delinquent than lower-class underachievers. Stinchcombe concluded that a lack of consistency between school achievement and occupational goals was a more important contributor to delinquent behavior than social-class position: Youths who wanted to get ahead but lacked the necessary grades were the most prone to rebel. According to Stinchcombe, "[T]he key fact is the future of students, not their origins. Since we know that origins partly determine futures, social class will be an important variable, but in an unusual way."[34]

Academic Pressure   Why might some affluent youth who fail at school be more vulnerable to delinquency than lower-class underachievers? Some research efforts have found that although the pressure to succeed cuts across class lines, there is a significant difference between the degree to which youths think it is important to do well based on parental occupation: Lower-class youth are significantly less likely to indicate that getting good grades or going to college is important.[35] Affluent children, the majority of whom live in intact homes, are generally given more encouragement at home to do well in school and are more likely to be high achievers.[36] School failure may cause more damage to their overinflated expectations while having a lesser effect on lower-class kids who maintain limited educational goals (a finding that jibes with Agnew's General Strain theory, see chapter 5).[37]

TRACKING

> Placement in non-college tracks of the contemporary high school means consignment to an educational oblivion without apparent purpose or meaning.[38]

Most researchers have looked at academic **tracking**—that is, dividing the students into groups according to ability and achievement level—as a contributor to student delinquency.[39] Studies overwhelmingly indicate that, compared with those in college tracks, noncollege preparatory students experience greater academic failure and progressive deterioration of achievement, participate less frequently in extracurricular activities, have an increased tendency to drop out, engage in more frequent misbehavior in school, and commit more delinquent acts. These differences are at least partially caused by assignment to a low academic track, whereby the student is effectively locked out of a chance to achieve educational success.

Some effects of tracking as it relates to delinquency are these:[40]

- *Self-fulfilling prophecy.* Low-track students, from whom little achievement and more misbehavior are expected, tend to live up to these often unspoken assumptions about their behavior, leading to a **self-fulfilling prophecy.**
- *Stigma.* The labeling effect, or **stigma,** of placement in a low track leads to loss of self-esteem, which increases the potential for academic failure and troublemaking both in and out of school.
- *Student subculture.* Students segregated in lower tracks develop a value system that often rewards misbehavior rather than the academic success they feel they can never achieve, through a **student subculture.**
- *Future rewards.* Low-track students are less inclined to conform. Because they see no future rewards for their schooling, they are not concerned with whether their futures are threatened by a record of deviance or low academic achievement.
- *Grading policies.* Low-track students tend to receive lower grades than other students, even for work of equal quality, based on the rationale that students who are not college-bound are "obviously" less bright and do not need good grades to get into college.
- *Teacher effectiveness.* Teachers of high-ability students make more of an effort to teach in an interesting and challenging manner than those who instruct lower-level students.

Some school officials begin stereotyping and tracking students in the lowest grade levels.[41] Educators separate youths into special groups that have innocuous names (e.g., "special enrichment program") but may carry with them the taint of failure and academic incompetence. Junior and senior high school students may be tracked within individual subjects based on their perceived ability. Classes may be labeled in descending order as advanced placement, academically enriched, average, basic, and remedial. As Jeannie Oakes found in her national study of tracking, it is common for students to have all their courses in only one or two tracks.[42]

The effects of negative school labels (e.g., "failure," or "slow" or "special needs") accumulate over time. Thus, a student who fails academically is probably destined to fail again, and over time, the repeated instances of failure can help to produce the career of the "misfit," "delinquent," or "dropout."[43] Consequently, a tracking system keeps certain students from having any hope of achieving academic success, thereby causing a lack of motivation, failure, and rebellion, all of which may foster delinquent behavior.[44]

Another disturbing outcome of tracking is that students are often stigmatized as academically backward if they voluntarily attend a program or institution designed to help underachievers.[45] Teachers consider remedial reading programs to be dumping grounds for youths with a "bad attitude"; consequently, they expect such youths to be disruptive in the classroom.[46]

Oakes, whose landmark study, *Keeping Track,* helped expose the problems associated with tracking, found that

> [t]racking seems to retard the academic progress of many students—those in average and low groups. Tracking seems to foster low self-esteem among these same students and promote school misbehavior and dropping out. Tracking also appears to lower the aspirations of students who are not in the top groups. And perhaps most important, in view of all the above, is that tracking separates students along socioeconomic lines, separating rich from poor, whites from minorities. The end result is that poor and minority children are found far more often than others in the bottom tracks. And once there they are likely to suffer far more negative consequences of schooling than are their more fortunate peers.[47]

School officials who believe tracking is necessary should attempt to create tracks that are flexible, encourage achievement, and allow student mobility within and between them.[48]

ALIENATION

Alienation of students from the educational experience has also been identified as a link between school failure and delinquency. Students who report they neither like school nor care about their teachers' opinions are the ones most likely to exhibit delinquent behaviors.[49] In contrast, students who like school and report greater involvement in school activities also are less likely to engage in delinquent behaviors.[50]

Alienation has been linked to the isolation and impersonality that result from the large size of many modern public schools. Schools are getting larger because smaller school districts have been consolidated into multijurisdictional district schools for most of the twentieth century: In 1900, there were 150,000 school districts; today there are approximately 16,000.[51] Although larger schools are more economical to construct, their climate is often impersonal, and relatively few students can find avenues for meaningful participation. The resulting resentment can breed an environment in which violence and vandalism are likely to occur. Smaller schools offer a more personal environment, in which students can experience more meaningful interaction with the rest of the educational community. Furthermore, teachers and other school personnel have the opportunity in a smaller school to deal with early indications of academic or behavioral problems and thus act to prevent delinquency.

Student Role Students can also be alienated from the traditional student role that continues to operate in the schools. Students are expected to be passive,

Alienation of students from the educational experience has also been identified as a link between school failure and delinquency. Students seem more alienated in larger schools that have an impersonal environment and feature security. Students who report they neither like school nor care about their teachers' opinions are the ones most likely to exhibit delinquent behaviors. Although larger schools are more economical to construct, their climate is often impersonal, and relatively few students can find avenues for meaningful participation. The resulting resentment can breed an environment where violence and vandalism are likely to occur.

docile receivers of knowledge and are seldom encouraged to take responsibility for their own learning. In many schools, students have little voice in decision making. Some of them, therefore, feel excluded from the educational process, and such alienation may at times result in withdrawal from or overt hostility toward the school and all that it represents. Recent research by Patricia Harris Jenkins shows that students who believe that school rules are unfair and unevenly applied will be the ones most likely to engage in school misconduct and commit delinquent acts.[52]

IRRELEVANT CURRICULUM

Still another suspected cause of school failure is students' inability to see the relevance or significance of what they are taught in school. The gap between their education and the real world leads them to believe that the school experience is little more than a waste of time.[53]

Many students, particularly those from low-income families, believe that school has no payoff in terms of their future. Because the legitimate channel appears to be meaningless, "the illegitimate alternative becomes increasingly more attractive and delinquency sometimes results."[54] In his pioneering research, Stinchcombe found that rebelliousness in school was closely linked to the perception that school was irrelevant to future job prospects. He found that students who did not plan to attend college or to use their high school educations directly in their careers were particularly rebellious.[55]

Student perception of middle- and upper-class bias is borne out in the preeminent role of the college preparatory curriculum and the second-class position of vocational and technical programs in many school systems. Furthermore, methods of instruction as well as curriculum materials reflect middle-class mores, language, and customs and have little meaning for the disadvantaged child. Middle-class bias in schools relates not only to class and ethnic background but to intellectual style as well.[56]

For some students, then, school is alien territory—a place where they feel unwelcome either because they lack academic skills or because they are different from the role models that the school holds out to them. Disruption of classes, vandalism, and violence in schools may in part be attempts to obtain enjoyment in otherwise lifeless institutions.[57] For the alienated student, delinquency often appears to be an attractive alternative to the hostile, or at best boring, atmosphere of the school.

Student Subculture   Alienated students attending isolated, impersonal schools that have curriculums irrelevant to their needs will develop support groups that encourage unconventional values. In fact, evidence exists that in many schools, alienated youths form a subculture and work in concert to subvert the educational system. Members of this subculture participate in a higher-than-normal amount of delinquent activity.

The problem, therefore, is not that individual students feel isolated from the educational process but that a loosely structured subculture of youths supporting each other's deviance exists. Individualized treatment efforts will have little effect if they do not take these subcultural influences into account.

Dropping Out

These educational problems all too often translate into **dropping out** of school before completion of high school. More than three million Americans, ages 16–24, have left school permanently without a diploma; of these, more than one million withdrew before completing 10th grade.[58]

The burden of dropping out, with its consequent social costs of lower pay and higher unemployment, falls most heavily on the minority community. Although the African American dropout rate has declined substantially over the past two decades (falling faster than the white dropout rate) minority students still drop out at an unacceptably high rate. About 17 percent of African Americans aged 16–24 are dropouts; the Hispanic dropout rate for this age group is 38 percent.[59]

DROPPING OUT AND DELINQUENCY

It is not unusual to later find dropouts in police files. Studies of adult arrestees find that fewer than half have a 12th-grade education or more,[60] and, as Figure 10.2 shows, a recent 12-city study testing juvenile arrestees for drug use found that those who no longer attended school were much more likely to abuse drugs than those who did attend.[61]

Although it is generally recognized that dropping out of school is fraught with negative social consequences, the impact of dropping out on delinquent behavior has generated much debate. There are two views on this association. *Strain theory* holds that once the pressure and conflict of the school experience end, the probability of continued delinquency among disaffected students should be *reduced*. In contrast, the *control theory* model suggests that any action that weakens or severs ties with conventional society helps establish a youth in a delinquent way of life; dropping out should therefore *increase* delinquent behaviors.

- At 11 to 12 sites, juveniles who no longer attended school tested higher on cocaine abuse than those who attended school.

- Cocaine use was up to 3.7 times higher for those not attending school compared to attendees.

- Marijuana use among those who did not attend school was up to 2.2 times higher than the rate of arrestees who reported attending school.

Source: Drug Use Forecasting: 1994 Annual Report on Adult and Juvenile Arrestees (Washington, D.C.: National Institute of Justice, 1995).

Some early research efforts supported the strain view by finding that delinquent behavior *actually decreases* once a child leaves the school environment. In an oft-cited study of 2,600 male and female students Delbert Elliott and Harwin Voss found that "the rate of delinquency for dropouts increases during the period immediately preceding their leaving school, but once they drop out, both police-recorded and self-admitted delinquency decline rapidly.[62]

Sociologist Daniel Glaser also noted that this phenomenon seems to cut across socioeconomic lines: "In *every* neighborhood and *every* socioeconomic class, most of those who are first arrested *while still in school* are less frequently arrested after they drop out."[63]

These findings have been contradicted by more recently published research supportive of the control theory model. Dropouts have been found to be both more likely to engage in antisocial behavior immediately after leaving school and then persisting in their criminal behavior throughout adulthood.[64]

Marvin Krohn and his associates, using longitudinal data from the Rochester Youth Development Study, provide an alternative view of the dropout–delinquency–drug use association: They found that all three may be part of the *problem behavior syndrome* (see chapter 2). Teens in their study who dropped out also committed crimes, took drugs, and suffered from an abundance of other social problems.[65] Persistent drug abusers were more likely to drop out than nonabusers and, after leaving school, maintained the same level of substance abuse. Problems that began in school *continued after the juvenile left school.* This pattern contradicts both the strain model (which predicts a drop in crime) and control theory (which predicts an increase in crime).

WHY DO YOUNG PEOPLE DROP OUT?

The confusion about the dropout–delinquency association may be explained in part by the fact that young people drop out of school for a variety of reasons. When surveyed, most say they left either because they simply did not like school or wanted to get a job. Others had behavioral problems: They could not get along with teachers, had been expelled, or were under suspension. Almost half of all female dropouts left school because they were pregnant or had already given birth to a child.[66]

Poverty and family dysfunction increases the chances of dropping out among all racial and ethnic groups. One recent study of Canadian youth by Michel Janosz and his associates found that youths at risk to dropping out lived in a single-parent family headed by a parent who was an educational underachiever lacking adequate parenting skills. The Janosz research also showed that poor school performance, indicated by high retention rates and poor grades, was another significant precursor of dropping out.[67]

Being Forced to Drop Out   Some youths have no choice but to drop out. They are pushed out of school because they suffer attention disorders or have poor attendance records. Teachers label them "troublemakers," and school administrators then use suspensions, transfers, and other means to "convince" these unwanted students that leaving school is their only real option. Because minority students often come from circumstances that interfere with their attendance, they are more likely to be labeled as "insubordinate" or "disobedient." Class- and race-based disciplinary practices then may help sustain high dropout rates in the minority community.[68]

Not All Dropouts Are Equal   Research conducted by criminologist G. Roger Jarjoura indicates that the reason a student chooses to drop out of school has a significant impact on his or her future law violations. Those who left school because of problems at home, financial reasons, or poor grades were unlikely to increase their delinquent activity after leaving school. In contrast, those who dropped out in order to get married or because of pregnancy were more likely to increase their violent activities. Those who left school early because they were expelled did not increase their violent activity but were more likely to engage in theft and drug abuse. Leaving school then was not a per se cause of future misconduct. Jarjoura found that juveniles who had a long history of misconduct while in school continued their antisocial behavior after dropping out. Although dropouts engaged in more antisocial activity than graduates, it was the reason they dropped out that influenced their offending patterns.[69]

Dropping Out and School Policy   The focus of this debate has serious implications for educational policy in the United States. Evidence that delinquency rates decline after students leave school has caused some educators and juvenile justice personnel to question the wisdom of compulsory education statutes. Some experts, such as Jackson Toby, argue that forcing unwilling teenagers to stay in school is counterproductive and that truancy and delinquency might be lessened by allowing them instead to assume a productive position in the workforce.[70] For many youths, leaving school can actually have the beneficial effect of escape from a stressful, humiliating situation that offers little promise of any future benefits.

However, if the recent literature proves accurate, dropping out may offer few short- or long-term benefits and therefore must be avoided at all costs. Programs to keep young people in school, to provide them with tutoring, and to create school programs conducive to continued educational achievement may help lower delinquency rates.

DELINQUENCY WITHIN THE SCHOOL

It has become common to view school as a highly dangerous place in which intruders or students victimize teachers and other pupils, vandalize property, and disrupt the educational process.[71] Students who carry weapons to school are a significant cause of concern. Research has shown that students most likely to own guns and bring them to school are the ones who have engaged in other forms of deviant behavior, including drug dealing, assault, and battery.[72]

Urban schools are more prone to delinquency than rural schools, but rural schools are not immune: Principals in rural schools report more student alcohol and tobacco use than those in urban schools; the robbery and theft rate is as high in rural schools as in urban schools.[73]

The federal government's pioneering 1977 study of the school system, *Violent Schools—Safe Schools,* alerted the public to the problem of school-based crime.[74] This survey found that although teenagers spend only 25 percent of their time in school, 40 percent of the robberies and 36 percent of the physical attacks involving this age group occur there.

Since this study was conducted, the level of school crime shows little evidence of waning. As Figure 10.3 shows, surveys of student victimization indicate that

FIGURE 10.3
Student victimization

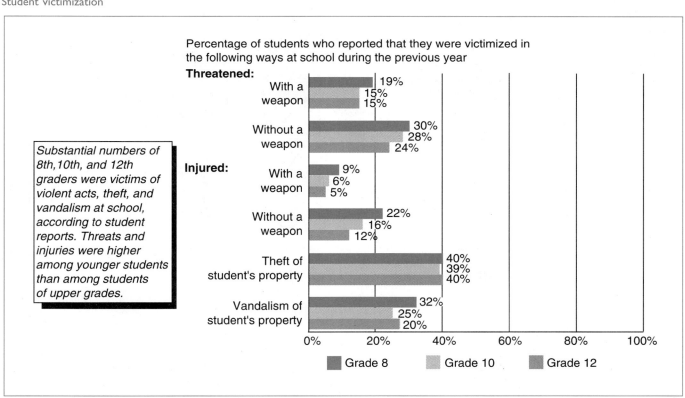

Source: National Education Goals Panel, *National Data* (Washington, D.C.: U.S. Government Printing Office, 1995), p. 144.

FIGURE 10.4
Disruptions in class by students

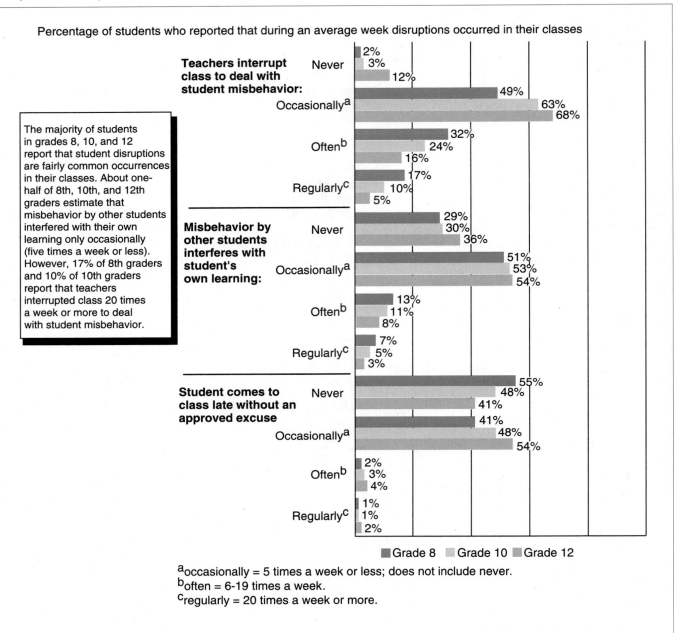

Percentage of students who reported that during an average week disruptions occurred in their classes

The majority of students in grades 8, 10, and 12 report that student disruptions are fairly common occurrences in their classes. About one-half of 8th, 10th, and 12th graders estimate that misbehavior by other students interfered with their own learning only occasionally (five times a week or less). However, 17% of 8th graders and 10% of 10th graders report that teachers interrupted class 20 times a week or more to deal with student misbehavior.

Teachers interrupt class to deal with student misbehavior:
Never — 2% / 3% / 12%
Occasionally[a] — 49% / 63% / 68%
Often[b] — 32% / 24% / 16%
Regularly[c] — 17% / 10% / 5%

Misbehavior by other students interferes with student's own learning:
Never — 29% / 30% / 36%
Occasionally[a] — 51% / 53% / 54%
Often[b] — 13% / 11% / 8%
Regularly[c] — 7% / 5% / 3%

Student comes to class late without an approved excuse
Never — 55% / 48% / 41%
Occasionally[a] — 41% / 48% / 54%
Often[b] — 2% / 3% / 4%
Regularly[c] — 1% / 1% / 2%

■ Grade 8 ■ Grade 10 ■ Grade 12

[a]occasionally = 5 times a week or less; does not include never.
[b]often = 6-19 times a week.
[c]regularly = 20 times a week or more.

Source: National Education Goals Panel, National Data, p. 150.

substantial numbers of 8th-, 10th-, and 12th-grade students are victims of violence, theft, and vandalism each year. About 5 percent of all teachers report being physically attacked, and 13 percent say they were threatened.[75]

Theft and violence are not the only problems being faced by students and teachers. As Figure 10.4 shows, the learning process is constantly being interrupted by students who disrupt classes and compromise the learning experience. Disruption might be expected because so many students abuse substances while in school. More than one-quarter of all students report that it is easy to purchase illegal substances on school grounds; 8 percent of 10th and 12th graders report using alcohol and/or marijuana while at school.[76]

WHO COMMITS SCHOOL CRIME?

Who commits school crime, and what are the factors associated with high crime rates in schools? Gary Gottfredson and Denise Gottfredson reexamined the *Safe School* study data and found that the schools experiencing crime and drug abuse are suffering a condition they refer to as **social disorganization**: a high proportion of students behind grade level in reading; many students from families on welfare; schools located in communities with high unemployment, crime, and poverty; and high divorce rates.[77]

How do schools avoid crime and social conflict? Nancy Weishew and Samuel Peng's analysis of data from the National Education Longitudinal Study found that schools with high achieving and interested students, drug- and alcohol-free environments, positive social climates, strong discipline, and involved parents have fewer behavioral problems within the student body.[78]

Community Influences   A number of researchers have observed that school crime and disruption are functions of the community in which the school is located. In other words, crime in schools does not occur in isolation from crime in the community.[79] In one important analysis, Joan McDermott found that the perpetrators and the victims of school crime cannot be divided into two separate groups.[80] Many young offenders have been victims of delinquency themselves and fear being victimized again. McDermott concludes that school-based violent and theft-related crimes have "survival value": Striking back against another, weaker victim is emotionally satisfying or simply a method of regaining lost possessions or self-respect.

McDermott also found that crime and fear in schools reflect the patterns of antisocial behavior that exist in the surrounding neighborhood. Schools in high-crime areas experience more crime than schools in safer areas; there is less fear in schools in safer neighborhoods than in high-crime ones. Students who report being afraid in school are also more afraid of being in city parks, streets, or subways.

Other research confirms the community influences on school crime. Using data collected from the Boston school system, Daryl Hellman and Susan Beaton found that measures of school disruption such as suspension rates are significantly related to community variables such as family structure: Communities with a high percentage of two-parent families experience fewer school problems. School problems were not related to income level, employment, or the racial composition of the community but were associated with housing quality, population density, and stability.[81]

McDermott's analysis suggests that it may be futile to attempt to eliminate school crime without considering the impact that prevention efforts will have on the community.

REDUCING SCHOOL CRIME

There have been a number of efforts to reduce the amount of crime in schools. Law and order approaches rely on such measures as metal detectors to identify gun-wielding students. Another method to ensure the physical safety of students and school staff is to use mechanical security devices such as surveillance cameras, electronic barriers to keep out intruders, and roving security guards. One program in New York City involves the use of random searches with inexpensive handheld detectors at the start of the school day; students report a greater sense of security and attendance has increased.[82] Some districts have gone so far as infiltrating the student body with youthful undercover detectives. These detectives pose as pupils, attend classes, mingle with students, contact drug dealers, make buys, and arrest campus dealers.[83]

In cities such as Houston, Texas, it is routine to employ armed guards in full uniform during the day. Nor does security end with the conclusion of the school day. In San Diego, an elaborate security system makes use of infrared beams and silent alarms to protect school grounds from vandals and unwelcome visitors.[84] Rather than suspending student violators, some school districts now send them to a separate center for evaluation and counseling so they are kept separate from the law-abiding students.[85]

Critics claim that even though these methods are effective, they reduce staff and student morale. Tighter security, stricter rule enforcement, and fortresslike alterations in a school's physical plant may reduce acts of crime and violence in school only to displace them to the community. Similarly, expelling or suspending troublemakers puts them on the street with nothing to do. Lowering the level of crime in schools may have no real impact on reducing the total amount of crime committed by young people.[86]

Strict Behavioral Controls Some schools have instituted strict controls over student activity, for example, instituting locker searches, preventing students from having lunch off campus, requiring that all visitors report to the school office, and using patrols to monitor drug use. Strict control can be coupled with tight security and increasing penalties and suspensions for fighting, cutting

Some schools have instituted strict controls over student activity, for example, using metal detectors, instituting locker searches, preventing students from having lunch off campus, requiring that all visitors report to the school office, and using patrols to monitor drug use. Strict control can be coupled with tight security, increasing penalties and suspensions for fighting, cutting class, or drinking.

class, or drinking. Unfortunately, although this get-tough policy might impress some students and change the school's climate, there is little evidence that it results in lower school victimization rates.[87] In fact, schools that employ strict controls are also the ones most likely to suffer increases in school-based victimization (most likely because security is aimed at a pre-existing and expanding school crime problem).[88]

Community and Family   As the McDermott research found, controlling school crime is ultimately linked to community and family conditions. When communities experience such changes as increases in unemployment and the number of single-parent households, both school disruption and community crime rates may rise.[89] The school environment can be made safer only if community issues are addressed, for example, by taking steps to keep intruders out of school buildings, putting pressure on local police to develop community safety programs, increasing correctional services, strengthening laws on school safety, and making parents bear greater responsibility for their children's behavior.[90]

Schools must also use community resources in their efforts to control school crime. Most school districts refer problem students to social services outside the school. About 70 percent of public schools provide outside referrals for students with substance abuse problems, while 90 percent offer drug education within the school.[91]

Rather than implementing a strict security/law enforcement policy, it might be more useful to improve school climate and increase educational standards. Programs have been designed to improve the standards of the teaching staff and administrators and the educational climate in the school, increase the relevance of the curriculum, and provide law-related education classes.[92]

THE ROLE OF THE SCHOOL IN DELINQUENCY PREVENTION

For the past two decades, numerous national organizations and political groups have called for reforming the educational system to make it more responsive to the needs of students. Educational leaders now recognize that children undergo enormous pressures while in school that can lead to physical, emotional, and social problems. At one extreme are the pressures to succeed academically and earn admission to a top college; at the other extreme are the crime and substance abuse problems students face on school grounds. It is difficult to talk of achieving academic excellence in a deteriorated school dominated by violence-prone gang members.

A report by the Carnegie Corporation, a leading educational foundation, found that the United States is indeed facing an educational crisis. Student dissatisfaction with school, which begins to increase after elementary school, is accompanied by a growing aversion for teachers and many academic subjects. The rate of student alienation and the social problems that accompany it—absenteeism, dropping out, and substance abuse—all increase as students enter junior high.

Educators have attempted to play a role in delinquency prevention by creating programs that will benefit youths and provide them with opportunities for conventional success in the outside world. Yet change has been slow in coming, and it has only been since the mid-1980s that concern about the educational system, prompted by the findings of the federally funded National Commission on Excellence in Education (in *A Nation at Risk*[93]), focused efforts toward change.

Skepticism exists over whether the American school system, viewed by critics as overly conservative and archaic, can play a significant role in delinquency prevention. Some experts contend that no significant change in the lives of youths is possible by merely changing the schools; the entire social and economic structure of society must be altered if schools are to help students realize their full potential.[94] Others suggest that smaller, alternative schools which create a positive learning environment with low student–teacher ratios, informal classroom structure, and individualized, self-paced learning may be the answer. Although in theory such programs may help promote academic performance and reduce delinquency, evaluations suggest that alternative programs have little effect on delinquency rates.[95]

CASE IN POINT

As principal of a suburban regional high school, you are faced with a growing drug use problem among the student body. There is evidence of dealing on campus, and parents have complained that their kids are bringing home drugs they bought at school. Last week, a 15-year-old overdosed and almost died. At a school board meeting, angry parents charge that this kind of behavior may be OK in the city but not a suburban community to which people come to get away from drugs and delinquency. There is some angry talk that if you can't handle the situation, then a new school principal should be found who can.

The local police offer their solution to combating the drug problem: Institute a tough security policy that makes use of hidden cameras in public areas, such as the parking lot and cafeteria; allow random searches of student lockers and desks; hire a security director who will search students suspected of selling or possessing drugs; turn over to the police all evidence for prosecution; and suspend for the school year students possessing drugs on campus. Some teachers feel these draconian policies are misplaced in a suburban school. They believe that the relatively few offenders should be placed in counseling programs and that, instead of security guards, the school should hire a drug awareness education teacher and teach the students about the dangers of taking drugs.

Should a school drug prevention program stress law enforcement or education?

Is it fair to search student lockers at random?

Are hidden cameras an intrusion of student privacy or a needed security measure?

A danger also exists that the pressure being placed on schools to improve the educational experience of students can produce concomitant pressure on staff members to succeed. For example, there have been recent reports of teachers being prosecuted for encouraging students to cheat on tests by providing them with answer sheets. The pressure to raise student scores on standardized tests was the motive for the faculty cheating.[96]

SCHOOL-BASED PREVENTION PROGRAMS

Education officials have instituted numerous programs to make schools more effective instruments of delinquency prevention.[97] Among the most prevalent strategies are:

- Cognitive—Increase students' awareness about the dangers of drug abuse and delinquency.

- Affective—Improve students' psychological assets and self-image, giving them the resources to resist antisocial behavior.
- Behavioral—Train students in techniques to resist peer pressure.
- Environmental—Establish school management and disciplinary programs that deter crime, such as locker searches.
- Therapeutic—Treat youths who have already manifested problems.[98]

More specific suggestions include creating special classes or schools with individualized educational programs that foster success, rather than failure, for nonadjusting students.[99] Efforts can be made to help students learn to deal constructively with academic failure when it does occur.

More personalized student–teacher relationships have been recommended. This effort to provide young persons with a caring, accepting adult role model will, it is hoped, strengthen the controls against delinquency.

Home–school counselors acting as liaisons between the family and the school might be effective in preventing delinquency. These counselors try to ensure cooperation between the parents and the school and secure needed services—academic, social, and psychological—for troubled students before serious delinquency becomes a problem.

It has been proposed that experiments be undertaken to integrate job training and experience with the usual classroom instruction so that students may see education as a meaningful and relevant prelude to their future careers. Job training programs could emphasize public service, so that students could build a bond with their communities while acquiring useful vocational training.

Table 10.2 illustrates some strategies for increasing the school's ability to prevent delinquency.

Demonstration Projects A number of experimental programs have attempted to prevent or reduce delinquency by manipulating factors in the learning environment. One such project, known as Project PATHE (Positive Action Through Holistic Education) was operated experimentally in four middle and three high schools in South Carolina.[100] Based on control theory, Project PATHE sought to reduce delinquency by raising students' stake in conformity through strengthening their commitment to school, enhancing the opportunities for successful experiences in school, promoting attachment to conforming members of the educational community, and encouraging participation in school activities. By increasing their sense of social competence, belonging, and usefulness, the project sought to promote the development of students in a positive direction. The PATHE program has undergone extensive evaluation by sociologist Denise Gottfredson, who found that the schools in which it was used experienced a moderate reduction in delinquency and school misconduct.[101]

Seattle Social Development Project The Seattle Social Development Project is a similar program, based on the Social Development Theory model discussed in chapter 5. Teachers trained especially for the project were taught classroom management techniques that rewarded appropriate student behavior and minimized disruption. Students were taught to learn cooperatively in small groups, which were given the goal of helping each other master the curriculum. Students were also singled out for cognitive and social skills training, which helped them master problem solving, communication, negotiation, and conflict resolution. Family training classes taught parents how to properly reward and encourage desirable behavior and provide negative consequences for undesirable

TABLE 10.2 School-based Delinquency Prevention Concepts

1. Teacher training programs for parents
2. Policies and practices to ensure that schools and classrooms reflect the best examples of justice and democracy in their organization and operation and in the rules and regulations governing student conduct
3. A guarantee of literacy for elementary school students
4. Special language services for bicultural students
5. Career preparation in schools
6. Effective supportive services in schools
7. Alternative education programs for deviant students
8. Availability of schools for community activities
9. Alternative education programs for students who require them
10. Community education programs
11. Alternatives to the suspension of troublesome students
12. Codes of rights and responsibilities drawn up by all elements of the school community (students, teachers, parents, and administrators)
13. Curriculum reform, especially the use of apprenticeship programs and law-related education
14. Police, school, and community liaison programs
15. Teacher education in appropriate disciplinary techniques and sensitivity to special students
16. Proper training of school security personnel
17. Improved counseling and guidance programs
18. Creation of a more personal atmosphere in schools through architectural design and use of smaller buildings
19. Student and parental involvement in programs to combat violence and vandalism in schools

behavior in a consistent fashion. Other parent training focused on improving children's academic performance while reducing at-risk behaviors such as drug abuse. Evaluations of the Seattle program showed that children in the intervention group enhanced their school commitment and class participation. Girls lowered rates of substance abuse, and boys increased social and schoolwork skills.[102]

Schools may not be able to reduce delinquency single-handedly, but a number of viable alternatives to their current operations could aid a communitywide effort to lessen the problem of juvenile crime. The following "Focus on Delinquency" describes another school-based delinquency control program.

LEGAL RIGHTS WITHIN THE SCHOOL

As educational officials have attempted to restore order within the schools, their actions often have run into opposition from the courts, which are concerned with maintaining the legal rights of minors. The U.S. Supreme Court has sought to balance the civil liberties of students with the school's mandate to provide a reasonable and safe educational environment. In some instances, the Court has sided with students, while in others, the balance has shifted toward the educational establishment. The main issues concerning the rights of children and the schools include compulsory attendance, free speech in school, and school discipline.

COMPULSORY SCHOOL ATTENDANCE

In the United States, compulsory school attendance statutes have been in effect for more than half a century.[103] Children are required by law to attend school

Second Step (Seattle, Washington)

Second Step is a school-based prevention curriculum for elementary school students developed by the Committee for Children, a not-for-profit organization in Seattle. The curriculum has been implemented in a number of cities in both the United States and Canada. Its most widespread use is in the Los Angeles school system, where nearly 350,000 students in grades K–6 receive the program each year.

This research-based program is designed to teach children the "ABCs" of interpersonal relationships, with the ultimate objective of reducing impulsive and aggressive behavior. The curriculum centers on teaching anger management, impulse control, empathy, problem-solving skills, and social skills (such as how to interrupt politely, how to enter a play situation, and how to deal with name-calling).

The Committee sells four Second Step packages: preschool and kindergarten, grades 1–3, grades 4–5, and grades 6–8. The lessons are designed for school teachers and other youth service professionals to present in a classroom or other group setting (such as youth homes, detention centers, YMCAs, and other community centers). All of the materials are developmentally sequenced. Learning objectives and classroom activities are matched to the children's social and academic capabilities.

Each curriculum package is divided into three major units. In the empathy unit, students learn to identify and predict the feelings of others and to provide an appropriate emotional response. In the impulse control unit, students learn problem-solving and communication skills, with a focus on how to handle and solve interpersonal conflict. In the anger management unit, students learn techniques for reducing stress and channeling angry feelings into constructive problem solving.

Customarily presented once or twice a week, the lessons are designed to last 40–50 minutes each. They can be integrated into language arts, social studies, or health education courses. A variety of learning modalities are used so that children are exposed to appropriate role models, have opportunities to practice new skills, and receive reinforcement for prosocial behavior.

The curriculum packages also include audiovisual materials. For example, the grades 6–8 package uses a live action video, entitled "Check It Out," which presents step-by-step modeling of behavioral skills, such as how to make a complaint, deal with peer pressure, and avoid a fight. For grades 2–6, the video "Facing Up" models specific social skills needed to deal with bullying and other types of peer conflict. In the preschool/kindergarten program, hand puppets are used to teach children to "slow down, stop, and think."

Each package has a teacher's guide, which offers a description of each teaching unit, background information, suggestions and resources for handling difficult classroom situations, homework assignments, parent activity sheets, and take-home letters to inform parents about the curriculum. The packages are self-contained and therefore easy to implement. Everything the teacher needs to prepare is there.

Training sessions offered by the Committee for Children focus on curriculum strategies and how to reinforce students' prosocial behavior during regular classes. For example, to reinforce an earlier lesson on sharing, the students might be asked to imagine everything they will be doing that day and then to say which of those activities will provide opportunities for sharing. During the day, the teacher will praise children who share, reminding them in each case of the direct benefits of sharing. As class ends, the students are asked to remember what they did that day and to report which children shared.

Pilot tests of all four curriculums show evidence of gains in both knowledge and behavioral skills. For example, a study of the preschool/kindergarten package showed that, in answering questions about photographs that depicted social situations, children who had been taught the Second Step curriculum were better able to list cues associated with different actors' feelings, to generate solutions to a conflict, to make socially appropriate requests, to demonstrate group entry skills, and to list ways to calm down when angry. An evaluation in Los Angeles also showed strong teacher endorsement for Second Step.

Source: William DeJong, *Preventing Interpersonal Violence Among Youth* (Washington, D.C.: National Institute of Justice, 1994), pp. 65–66.

until a given age, normally 16 or 17.[104] Violations of compulsory attendance laws generally result in complaints that can lead to court action. Often, however, children are truant because of emotional problems or learning disabilities. Many of them might be better off leaving school at an earlier age than the compulsory education law allows. On the other hand, emotionally disturbed and nonconforming children are pushed out of many school systems and thereby deprived of an education. Whether these children have a right to attend school is unclear. Many school systems devote few resources to the difficult student, who may be classified as "bad" or "delinquent."

In 1925, the Supreme Court determined that compulsory education did not necessarily have to be provided by a public school system and that parochial schools could be a reasonable substitute.[105] From that time through the 1970s, the courts upheld the right of the state to make education compulsory. Then, in 1972, in the case of *Wisconsin v. Yoder*, the Supreme Court made an exception to the general compulsory education law by holding that traditional Amish culture was able to give its children the skills that would prepare them for adulthood within Amish society. Thus, the removal of Amish children from school after the completion of the eighth grade was justified.[106] It is not clear, however, whether this decision speaks directly to the issue of compulsory education or whether it is simply another instance of supporting freedom of religion. Therefore, the state's role in requiring school attendance is still unsettled.

FREE SPEECH

Freedom of speech is granted and guaranteed in the First Amendment to the U.S. Constitution. The right has been divided into two major categories as it affects children in schools. The first category involves what is known as *passive speech,* a form of expression not associated with the actual speaking of words. Examples include wearing arm bands or political protest buttons. The most important U.S. Supreme Court decision concerning a student's right to passive speech was in the 1969 case of *Tinker v. Des Moines Independent Community School District*.[107] This case involved the right of students to wear black arm bands to protest the war in Vietnam. Two high school students, ages 16 and 17, were told they would be suspended if they demonstrated their objections to the Vietnam War by wearing black arm bands. They attended school wearing the arm bands and were suspended. According to the Court, in order for the state (in the person of a school official) to justify prohibiting an expression of opinion, it must be able to show that its action was caused by something more than a mere desire to avoid the discomfort and unpleasantness that accompany the expression of an unpopular view. Unless it can be shown that the forbidden conduct will interfere with the discipline required to operate the school, the prohibition cannot be sustained. In *Tinker,* the Court said there was no evidence that the school authorities had reason to believe that the wearing of arm bands would substantially interfere with the work of the school or infringe on the rights of other students.[108]

This decision is significant because it recognizes the child's right to free speech in a public school system. Justice Abe Fortas stated in his majority opinion, "Young people do not shed their constitutional rights at the schoolhouse door."[109] *Tinker* established two things: (1) that a child is entitled to free speech in school under the First Amendment of the U.S. Constitution and (2) that the test used to determine whether the child has gone beyond proper speech is whether he or she materially and substantially interferes with the requirements of appropriate discipline in the operation of the school.

The concept of free speech articulated in *Tinker* was used again in the 1986 case *Bethel School District No. 403 v. Fraser*.[110] This case upheld a school system's right to suspend or otherwise discipline a student who uses obscene or profane language and gestures. Matthew Fraser, a Bethel high school student, used sexual metaphors in making a speech nominating a friend for student office. His statement included these remarks:

I know a man who is firm—he's firm in his pants, he's firm in his shirt, his character is firm—but most . . . of all, his belief in you, the students of Bethel, is firm.

Jeff Kuhlman is a man who takes his point and pounds it in. If necessary, he'll take an issue and nail it to the wall. He doesn't attack things in spurts—he drives hard, pushing and pushing until finally—he succeeds.

Jeff is a man who will go to the very end—even the climax, for each and every one of you.

So vote for Jeff for A.S.B. vice-president—he'll never come between you and the best our high school can be.

The Court found that a school has the right to control lewd and offensive speech that undermines the educational mission. The Court drew a distinction between the sexual content of Fraser's remarks and the political nature of Tinker's arm band. It ruled that the pervasive sexual innuendo of the speech interfered with the school's mission to implant "the shared values of a civilized social order" in the student body.

In a 1988 case, *Hazelwood School District v. Kuhlmeier*, the Court extended the right of school officials to censor "active speech" when it ruled that the principal could censor articles in a student publication.[111] In this case, students had written about their personal experiences with pregnancy and parental divorce. The majority ruled that censorship was justified in this case because school-sponsored publications, activities, and productions were part of the curriculum and therefore designed to impart knowledge. Control over such school-supported activities could be differentiated from the action the Tinkers initiated on their own accord. In a dissent, Justice William J. Brennan accused school officials of favoring "thought control."

SCHOOL DISCIPLINE

Most states have statutes permitting teachers to use corporal punishment to discipline students in public school systems. Under the concept of *in loco parentis*, discipline is one of the assumed parental duties given to the school system. In two decisions, the Supreme Court upheld the school's right to use corporal punishment. In the first case, *Baker v. Owen*, the Court stated,

We hold that the Fourteenth Amendment embraces the right of parents generally to control the means and discipline of their children, but that the state has a countervailing interest in the maintenance of order in the schools . . . sufficient to sustain the right of teachers and school officials must accord to students minimal due process in the course of inflicting such punishment.[112]

In 1977, the Supreme Court again spoke on the issue of corporal punishment in school systems in the case of *Ingraham v. Wright*, which upheld the right of teachers to use corporal punishment.[113] In this case, students James Ingraham and Roosevelt Andrews sustained injuries as a result of a paddling in the Charles Drew Junior High School in Dade County, Florida. The legal problems raised in the case were (1) whether corporal punishment by teachers was a violation in this case of the Eighth Amendment against cruel and unusual punishment and (2) whether the due process clause of the Fourteenth Amendment required that the students receive proper notice and a hearing prior to receiving corporal punishment. The Court held that neither the Eighth Amendment nor the Fourteenth Amendment was violated in this case. Even though Ingraham suffered hematomas on his buttocks as a result of 20 blows with a wooden paddle and Andrews was hurt in the arm, the Supreme Court ruled that such punishment was not a constitutional violation. The Court established the standard that only reasonable discipline is allowed in school systems, but it excepted the degree of punishment administered in this case. The key principle in *Ingraham* is that the reasonableness standard that the Court articulated represents the judicial attitude that the scope of the school's right to discipline a child is by no means more restrictive than the rights of the child's own parents to impose corporal punishment.

Other issues involving the legal rights of students include their due process rights when interrogated, if corporal punishment is to be imposed, and when suspension and expulsion are threatened. When students are questioned by school personnel, no warning as to their legal rights to remain silent or right to counsel need be given. However, when school security guards, on-campus police officials, and public police officers question students, such constitutional warnings are required. In the area of corporal punishment, procedural due process established with the case of *Baker v. Owen* requires that students at least be forewarned about the possibility of corporal punishment as a discipline. In addition, the *Baker* case requires that there be a witness to the administration of corporal punishment and allows the student and the parent to elicit reasons for the punishment.

With regard to suspension and expulsion, the Supreme Court ruled in 1976 in the case of *Goss v. Lopez* that any time a student is to be suspended for up to a period of 10 days, he or she is entitled to a hearing.[114] The hearing would not include a right to counsel or a right to confront or cross-examine witnesses. The Court went on to state in *Goss* that the extent of the procedural due process requirements would be established on a case-by-case basis; that is, each case would represent its own facts and have its own procedural due process elements.

In sum, schools have the right to discipline students, but students are protected from unreasonable, excessive, and arbitrary discipline.

SUMMARY

For several decades, criminologists have attempted to explain the relationship between schools and delinquency. Although no clear causal relationship has been established, research points to many definite links between the delinquent behavior of juveniles and their experiences within the educational system.

Contemporary youths spend much of their time in school because education has become increasingly important as a determinant of social and economic success. Educational institutions are one of the primary instruments of socialization, and it is believed that this role is bound to affect the amount of delinquent behavior by school-age children.

Those who claim a causal link between schools and delinquency cite two major factors in the relationship. The first is academic failure, which arises from a lack of aptitude, labeling, or class conflict and which results in tracking. The second factor is alienation from the educational experience, which is the result of the impersonal nature of schools, the traditionally passive role assigned to students, and students' perception of their education as irrelevant to their future lives.

Student misbehavior, which may have its roots in the school experience itself, ranges from minor infractions of school rules (e.g., smoking and loitering in halls) to serious crimes, such as assault, burglary, arson, drug abuse, and vandalism of school property.

Dissatisfaction with the educational experience frequently sets the stage for more serious forms of delinquency both in and out of school. Some dissatisfied students choose to drop out of school as soon as they reach the legal age, and though some early research has shown a decline in delinquency among those who do drop out, more recent data indicates that drop-outs are more likely to continue offending into adulthood.

School administrators have attempted to eliminate school crime and prevent delinquency. Among the measures taken are security squads, electronic surveillance, and teacher training. Curriculums are being significantly revised to make the school experience more meaningful.

KEY TERMS

truancy	underachievers	student subculture
academic achievement	tracking	alienation
socialized	self-fulfilling prophecy	dropping out
school failure	stigma	social disorganization

QUESTIONS FOR DISCUSSION

1. Was there a delinquency problem in your high school? If so, how was it dealt with?
2. Should disobedient youths be suspended from school? Does this solution hurt or help?
3. What can be done to improve the delinquency prevention capabilities of schools?
4. Is school failure responsible for delinquency, or are delinquents simply school failures?

NOTES

1. U.S. Senate Subcommittee on Delinquency, *Challenge for the Third Century: Education in a Safe Environment* (Washington, D.C.: U.S. Government Printing Office, 1977), p. 1.
2. *Justice and the Child in New Jersey,* report of the New Jersey Juvenile Delinquency Commission (1939), p. 110, cited in Paul H. Hahn, *The Juvenile Offender and the Law* (Cincinnati, Ohio: Anderson, 1978).
3. Delbert S. Elliott and Harwin L. Voss, *Delinquency and the Dropout* (Lexington, Mass.: Lexington Books, 1974), p. 204.
4. U.S. Office of Education, *Digest of Educational Statistics* (Washington, D.C.: U.S. Government Printing Office, 1969), p. 25.
5. Kenneth Polk and Walter E. Schafer, eds., *Schools and Delinquency* (Englewood Cliffs, N.J.: Prentice-Hall, 1972), p. 13.
6. M. Edith Rasell and Laurence Mitchell, *Shortchanging Education: How the U.S. Spends on Grades K–12* (Washington, D.C.: Economic Policy Institute, 1990).
7. Ruth Leger Sivard, *World Military and Social Expenditures 1989* (Washington, D.C.: World Priorities, 1989).

8. National Education Goals Panel, *Data for the National Education Goals Report, Volume 1: National Data* (Washington, D.C.: National Education Goals Panel, 1995), pp. 33–38. Herein cited as *Goals Report*.

9. Lee Jones, Ina Mullis, Senta Raizen, Iris Weiss, and Elizabeth Weston, *The 1990 Science Report Card* (Washington, D.C.: U.S. Government Printing Office, 1992), p. 3.

10. National Education Goals Panel, *Goals Report*, p. 108.

11. Mary Foretsch, *Reading in and out of School* (Washington, D.C.: U.S. Government Printing Office, 1992), pp. 4–5.

12. Simon Singer and Susyan Jou, "Specifying the SES/Delinquency Relationship by Subjective and Objective Indicators of Parental and Youth Social Status" (Paper presented at the annual meeting of the American Society of Criminology, New Orleans, La., November 1992).

13. For reviews, see Bruce Wolford and LaDonna Koebel, "Kentucky Model for Youths at Risk" *Criminal Justice* 9:5–55 (1995); J. David Hawkins, Richard Catalano, Diane Morrison, Julie O'Donnell, Robert Abbott, and L. Edward Day, "The Seattle Social Development Project," in Joan McCord and Richard Tremblay, eds., *The Prevention of Antisocial Behavior in Children* (New York: Guilford, 1992), pp. 139–60.

14. Frank W. Jerse and M. Ebrahim Fakouri, "Juvenile Delinquency and Academic Deficiency," *Contemporary Education* 49:108–09 (1978).

15. Terence Thornberry, Alan Lizotte, Marvin Krohn, Margaret Farnworth, and Sung Joon Jang, "Testing Interactional Theory: An Examination of Reciprocal Causal Relationships among Family, School and Delinquency," *Journal of Criminal Law and Criminology* 82:3–35 (1991).

16. Matthew Zingraff, Jeffrey Leiter, Matthew Johnsen, Kristen Myers, "The Mediating Effect of Good School Performance on the Maltreatment–Delinquency Relationship," *Journal of Research in Crime and Delinquency* 31:62–91 (1994).

17. Lyle Shannon, *Assessing the Relationship of Adult Criminal Careers to Juvenile Careers: A Summary* (Washington, D.C.: U.S. Government Printing Office, 1982).

18. D. J. West and David P. Farrington, *The Delinquent Way of Life* (London: Heinemann, 1977), p. 76.

19. Marvin Wolfgang, Robert Figlio, and Thorsten Sellin, *Delinquency in a Birth Cohort* (Chicago: University of Chicago Press, 1972).

20. Ibid., p. 94.

21. Bureau of Justice Statistics, *Prisons and Prisoners* (Washington, D.C.: U.S. Government Printing Office, 1982), p. 2.

22. Martin Gold, "School Experiences, Self-Esteem, and Delinquent Behavior: A Theory for Alternative Schools," *Crime and Delinquency* 24:274–95 (1978).

23. Ibid.

24. See, generally, James Q. Wilson and Richard Herrnstein, *Crime and Human Nature* (New York: Simon & Schuster, 1985).

25. Michael Gottfredson and Travis Hirschi, *A General Theory of Crime* (Stanford, Calif.: Stanford University Press, 1990); J. D. McKinney, "Longitudinal Research on the Behavioral Characteristics of Children with Learning Disabilities," *Journal of Learning Disabilities* 22:141–50.

26. David Farrington, "The Development of Offending and Antisocial Behavior from Childhood to Adulthood" (Paper presented at the Congress on Rethinking Delinquency, University of Minho, Braga, Portugal, July 1992).

27. Albert K. Cohen, *Delinquent Boys* (New York: Free Press, 1955). See also Kenneth Polk, Dean Frease, and F. Lynn Richmond, "Social Class, School Experience, and Delinquency," *Criminology* 12:84–95 (1974).

28. Jackson Toby, "Orientation to Education as a Factor in the School Maladjustment of Lower-Class Children," *Social Forces* 35:259–66 (1957).

29. William Glaser, *Schools without Failure* (New York: Harper & Row, 1969).

30. Gold, "School Experiences, Self-Esteem, and Delinquent Behavior," p. 292.

31. Ibid., pp. 283–85.

32. Polk, Frease, and Richmond, "Social Class, School Experience, and Delinquency," p. 92.

33. Delos Kelly and Robert Balch, "Social Origins and School Failure," *Pacific Sociological Review* 14:413–30 (1971).

34. Arthur L. Stinchcombe, *Rebellion in a High School* (Chicago: Quadrangle Press, 1964), p. 70.

35. Singer and Jou, "Specifying the SES/Delinquency Relationship by Subjective and Objective Indicators of Parental and Youth Social Status," p. 11.

36. Nan Marie Astone and Sara McLanahan, "Family Structure, Parental Practices and High School Completion," *American Sociological Review* 56:309–20 (1991).

37. Robert Agnew, "Foundation for a General Strain Theory of Crime and Delinquency," *Criminology* 30:47–87 (1992), at 48.

38. Kenneth Polk, "Class, Strain, and Rebellion among Adolescents," in Kenneth Polk and Walter E. Schafer, eds., *Schools and Delinquency* (Englewood Cliffs, N.J.: Prentice-Hall, 1972), p. 34.

39. For an opposing view, see Michael Waitrowski, Stephen Hansell, Charles Massey, and David Wilson, "Curriculum Tracking and Delinquency," *American Sociological Review* 47:151–60 (1982).

40. Based on Walter E. Schafer, Carol Olexa, and Kenneth Polk, "Programmed for Social Class: Tracking in High School," in Kenneth Polk and Walter E. Schafer, eds., *Schools and Delinquency* (Englewood Cliffs, N.J.: Prentice-Hall, 1972), pp. 34–54.

41. Delos Kelly and William Pink, "School Crime and Individual Responsibility: The Perpetuation of a Myth," *Urban Review* 14:47–63 (1982).

42. Jeannie Oakes, *Keeping Track, How Schools Structure Inequality* (New Haven, Conn.: Yale University Press, 1985), p. 48.

43. Ibid., p. 57.

44. Delos Kelly, *Creating School Failure, Youth Crime, and Deviance* (Los Angeles: Trident Shop, 1982), p. 11.

45. Delos Kelly and W. Grove, "Teachers' Nominations and the Production of Academic Misfits," *Education* 101:246–63 (1981).

46. Delos Kelly, "The Role of Teacher's Nominations in the Perpetuation of Deviant Adolescent Careers," *Education* 96:209–17 (1976).

47. Oakes, *Keeping Track*, p. 48.

48. Adam Gamoran, "The Variable Effects of High School Tracking," *American Sociological Review* 57:812–28 (1992).

49. Travis Hirschi, *Causes of Delinquency* (Berkeley, Cal: University of California Press, 1969) pp. 113–24, 132.

50. Richard Lawrence, "Parents, Peers, School and Delinquency," (Paper presented at the American Society of Criminology meeting, Boston, Mass., November 1995).

51. Emil Haller, "High School Size and Student Indiscipline: Another Aspect of the School Consolidation Issue," *Educational Evaluation and Policy Analysis* 14:145–56 (1992).

52. Patricia Harris Jenkins, "School Delinquency and Belief in School Rules" (Paper presented at the annual meeting of the American Society of Criminology, New Orleans, La., November 1992).

53. *Learning into the 21st Century, Report of Forum 5* (Washington, D.C.: White House Conference on Children, 1970).

54. Polk and Schafer, *Schools and Delinquency*, p. 72.

55. Stinchcombe, *Rebellion in a High School*, p. 70; Daniel Glaser, *Crime in Our Changing Society* (New York: Holt, Rinehart & Winston, 1978), pp. 162–63.

56. Polk and Schafer, *Schools and Delinquency*, p. 23.

57. Mihaly Czikszentmihalyi and Reed Larson, "Intrinsic Rewards in School Crime," *Crime and Delinquency* 24:322 (1978).

58. National Center for Educational Statistics, *Dropout Rates in the United States, 1992* (Washington, D.C.: U.S. Department of Education, 1993).

59. National Education Goals Panel, *Goals Report*.

60. *Drug Use Forecasting: 1994 Annual Report on Adult and Juvenile Arrestees* (Washington, D.C.: National Institute of Justice, 1995).

61. Ibid.

62. Eliott and Voss, *Delinquency and the Dropout*.

63. Glaser, *Crime in Our Changing Society*, p. 164.

64. Terence Thornberry, Melanie Moore, and R. L. Christenson, "The Effect of Dropping out of High School on Subsequent Criminal Behavior," *Criminology* 23:3–18 (1985).

65. Marvin Krohn, Terence Thornberry, Lori Collins-Hall, and Alan Lizotte, "School Dropout, Delinquent Behavior, and Drug Use," in Howard Kaplan, ed., *Drugs, Crime and other Deviant Adaptations: Longitudinal Studies* (New York: Plenum Press, 1995), pp. 163–83.

66. Howard Snyder and Melissa Sickmund, *Juvenile Offenders and Victims: A National Report* (Washington, D.C.: Office of Juvenile Justice and Delinquency Prevention, 1995), p. 15.

67. Michel Janosz, Marc LeBlanc, Bernard Boulerice, and Richard Tremblay, *What Information Is Really Needed to Predict School Dropout? A Replication on Two Longitudinal Samples* (University of Montreal, School of Psychoeducation, 1995).

68. Christine Bowditch, "Getting Rid of Troublemakers: High School Disciplinary Procedures and the Production of Dropouts," *Social Problems* 40:493–508(1993).

69. G. Roger Jarjoura, "Does Dropping Out of School Enhance Delinquent Involvement? Results from a Large-Scale National Probability Sample," *Criminology* 31:149–72 (1993).

70. Jackson Toby, *Violence in Schools* (Washington, D.C.: National Institute of Justice, 1983), p. 2.

71. Joan Curclo and Patricia First, *Violence in Schools, How to Proactively Prevent and Defuse It* (Newbury Park, Calif.: Corwin Press, 1993), pp. 6–17.

72. Charles Callahan and Frederick Rivara, "Urban High School Youth and Handguns," *Journal of the American Medical Association* 267:3038–3042 (1992).

73. Wendy Mansfield and Elizabeth Farris, *Public School Principal Survey on Safe, Disciplined and Drug-Free Schools* (Washington, D.C.: U.S. Government Printing Office, 1992), p. 5.

74. National Institute of Education, U.S. Department of Health, Education and Welfare, *Violent Schools—Safe Schools: The Safe Schools Study Report to the Congress*, vol. 1 (Washington, D.C.: U.S. Government Printing Office, 1977).

75. National Education Goals Panel, *Goals Report*, p. 149.

76. National Education Goals Panel, *Goals Report*, pp. 138–39.

77. Gary Gottfredson and Denise Gottfredson, *Victimization in Schools* (New York: Plenum Press, 1985), p. 18.

78. Nancy Weishew and Samuel Peng, "Variables Predicting Students' Problem Behaviors," *Journal of Educational Research* 87:5–17 (1993).

79. James Q. Wilson, "Crime in Society and Schools," in J. M. McPartland and E. L. McDill, eds., *Violence in Schools: Perspective, Programs and Positions* (Lexington, Mass.: D.C. Heath, 1977), p. 48.

80. Joan McDermott, "Crime in the School and in the Community: Offenders, Victims, and Fearful Youth," *Crime and Delinquency* 29:270–83 (1983).

81. Daryl Hellman and Susan Beaton, "The Pattern of Violence in Urban Public Schools: The Influence of School and Community," *Journal of Research in Crime and Delinquency* 23:102–27 (1986).

82. American Academy of Pediatrics Committee on School Health, "Violence in Schools: Current Status and Prevention," in *School Health: Policy and Practice* (Elk Grove Village, Ill.: American Academy of Pediatrics Committee on School Health), pp. 363–80, at 369.

83. Bruce Jacobs, "Anticipatory Undercover Targeting in High Schools,"*Journal of Criminal Justice* 22:445–57 (1994).

84. Kevin Bushweller, "Guards with Guns," *The American School Board Journal* 180:34–36 (1993).

85. Bella English, "Hub Program to Counsel Violent Pupils," *Boston Globe,* 24 February 1987, p. 1.

86. McDermott, "Crime in the School and in the Community," p. 281.

87. Steven Lab and John Whitehead, *The School Environment and School Crime: Causes and Consequences* (Washington, D.C.: National Institute of Justice, 1992).

88. Ibid., p. 5.

89. Hellman and Beaton, "The Pattern of Violence in Urban Public Schools," pp. 122–23.

90. Julius Menacker, Ward Weldon, and Emanuel Hurwitz, "Community Influences on School Crime and Violence," *Urban Education* 25:68–80 (1990).

91. Mansfield and Farris, *Public School Principal Survey on Safe, Disciplined and Drug-Free Schools,* p. iii.

92. Jackie Kimbrough, "School-Based Strategies for Delinquency Prevention," in Peter Greenwood, ed., *The Juvenile Rehabilitation Reader* (Santa Monica, Calif: Rand Corp., 1985), pp. ix, 1–22.

93. National Commission on Excellence in Education, *A Nation at Risk* (Washington, D.C.: U.S. Government Printing Office, 1983).

94. Alexander Liazos, "Schools, Alienation, and Delinquency," *Crime and Delinquency* 24:355–61 (1978).

95. Stephen Cox, William Davidson, and Timothy Bynum, "A Meta-Analytic Assessment of Delinquency-Related Outcomes of Alternative Education Programs," *Crime and Delinquency* 41:219–34 (1995).

96. Gary Putka, "Cheaters in Schools May Not Be Students but Their Teachers," *Wall Street Journal,* 2 November 1989, p. 1.

97. U.S. Senate Subcommittee on Delinquency, *Challenge for the Third Century,* p. 95.

98. William Bukoski, "School-Based Substance Abuse Prevention: A Review of Program Research," *Journal of Children in Contemporary Society* 18:95–116 (1985).

99. See, generally, J. David Hawkins and Denise Lishner, "Schooling and Delinquency," in E. H. Johnson, ed., *Handbook on Crime and Delinquency* (Westport, Conn.: Greenwood Press, 1987).

100. Denise Gottfredson, "An Empirical Test of School-Based Environmental and Individual Interventions to Reduce the Risk of Delinquent Behavior," *Criminology* 24:705–31 (1986).

101. Denise Gottfredson, "Changing School Structures to Benefit High Risk Youth," in Peter Leone, ed., *Understanding Troubled and Troubling Youth* (Newbury Park, Calif.: Sage, 1990), pp. 246–71.

102. Julie O'Donnell, J. David Hawkins, Richard Catalano, Robert Abbott, and L. Edward Day, "Preventing School Failure, Drug Use, and Delinquency among Low-Income Children: Long-Term Intervention in Elementary Schools," *Journal of Orthopsychiatry* 65:87–100 (1995).

103. S. Arons, "Compulsory Education: The Plain People Resist," *Saturday Review* 15:63–69 (1972).

104. Ibid.

105. See *Pierce v. Society of Sisters,* 268 U.S. 610, 45 S.Ct. 571, 69 L.Ed. 1070 (1925).

106. *Wisconsin v. Yoder,* 406 U.S. 205, 92 S.Ct. 1526, 32 L.Ed.2d 15 (1972).

107. *Tinker v. Des Moines Independent Community School District,* 393 U.S. 503, 89 S.Ct. 733 (1969).

108. Ibid.

109. Ibid., p. 741.

110. *Bethel School District No. 403 v. Fraser,* 478 U.S. 675, 106 S.Ct. 3159, 92 L.Ed.2d 549 (1986).

111. *Hazelwood School District v. Kuhlmeier,* 484 U.S. 260, 108 S.Ct. 562, 98 L.Ed.2d 592 (1988).

112. *Baker v. Owen,* 423 U.S. 907, 96 S.Ct. 210, 46 L.Ed.2d 137 (1975).

113. *Ingraham v. Wright,* 430 U.S. 651, 97 S.Ct. 1401 (1977).

114. *Goss v. Lopez,* 419 U.S. 565, 95 S.Ct. 729 (1976).

DRUG USE AND DELINQUENCY

INTRODUCTION

Adolescent **substance abuse** and its association with youth crime and delinquency continue to be vexing problems. Along with major metropolitan areas, such as Los Angeles, New York, and Washington, D.C., almost every town, village, and city in the United States has been forced to confront some type of teenage substance abuse problem. Despite some indications earlier in this decade that drug abuse was in decline, more recent survey evidence now shows that teenagers have resumed their infatuation with substance abuse.

Far too many adolescents are involved with drugs and alcohol. Self-report surveys indicate that more than half of high school seniors have tried drugs and that more than 90 percent use alcohol.[1] Those adolescents who remain at a high risk for drug abuse all too often come from the most impoverished communities and experience a multitude of problems, including school failure and family conflict.[2] Equally troubling is the association between drug use and crime: Drug users commit a significant amount of all crimes, and a significant portion of known criminals are drug abusers.[3] Research indicates that in some cities more than half of all juvenile arrestees test positively for cocaine.[4] Self-report surveys show that drug abusers are more likely to become delinquent than nonabusers.[5] The consistent drug–crime pattern makes teenage substance abuse a key national concern.

This chapter addresses some of the most important issues involving teenage substance abuse. It first reviews the kinds of drugs youths are using and how often they are using them. It then goes into the why of drug abuse: who uses drugs and what are the suspected causes of drug abuse. After describing the association between drug abuse and criminal and delinquent behavior, the chapter concludes with a review of the efforts being made to control the use of drugs in the United States.

SUBSTANCES OF ABUSE

A wide variety of substances generically referred to as "drugs" are sold and used by teenagers. Some are addicting, others are not. Some create hallucinations; others cause a depressive, relaxing stupor; and a few give an immediate, exhilarating uplift. This section will discuss some of the most widely used substances that, because of the danger they present for the user and their association with illegal activity, have been banned from private use.

MARIJUANA AND HASHISH

Commonly called "pot," "grass," and a variety of other names, marijuana is produced from the leaves of *cannabis sativa,* a plant grown throughout the world. **Hashish** (hash) is a concentrated form of cannabis made from unadulterated resin from the female plant. The main active ingredient in marijuana and hashish is tetrahydrocannabinol (THC). THC is a mild hallucinogen that alters sensory impressions.

Marijuana is the drug most commonly used by teenagers. Smoking large amounts of pot or hash can result in drastic distortions in auditory and visual perception, even hallucinations. Small doses produce an early excitement ("high") that gives way to feelings of sedation and drowsiness. Pot use is also related to decreased physical activity, overestimation of time and space, and increased food consumption. When the user is alone, marijuana produces a quiet, dreamy state. In a group, users commonly become giddy and lose perspective.

Although marijuana has not been found to be physically addicting, its long-term effects have been the subject of much debate. During the 1970s, it was reported that smoking pot caused a variety of serious physical and mental problems, including brain damage and mental illness. The dangers of pot and hash may have been significantly overstated; however, use of these drugs does present some health risks, including an increased risk of lung cancer, chronic bronchitis, and other diseases. Marijuana smoking should be avoided by prospective parents: It lowers sperm counts in male users and leads to disrupted ovulation and a greater chance of miscarriage in female users.[6]

COCAINE

Cocaine is a alkaloid derivative of the coca plant first isolated in 1860. When discovered, it was considered a medicinal breakthrough that could relieve fatigue, depression, and various other symptoms, and it quickly became a staple of popular patent medicines. When its addictive qualities and dangerous side effects became apparent, its use was controlled by the Pure Food and Drug Act of 1906.

Cocaine is the most powerful natural stimulant in existence. Its use produces euphoria, laughter, restlessness, and excitement. Overdoses can cause delirium, increased reflexes, violent manic behavior, and possible respiratory failure.

Cocaine can be sniffed, or "snorted," into the nostrils or injected. The immediate feeling of euphoria or rush is short-lived, thus heavy users may snort coke as often as every 10 minutes.

A number of deadly derivatives of cocaine have become popular on the street in recent years. Mixing cocaine and heroin is a highly dangerous practice called "speedballing." **Freebase** is a chemical produced by treating street cocaine with a liquid to remove the hydrochloric acid with which pure cocaine is bonded during manufacture. The freebase is then dissolved in a solvent, usually ether, that crystallizes the purified cocaine. The resulting crystals are crushed and then smoked in a special glass pipe, which provides a high more immediate and powerful than snorting street-strength coke. **Crack,** like freebase, is processed street cocaine. Its manufacture involves using ammonia or baking soda to remove the hydrochlorides and create a crystalline form of cocaine base that can then be smoked. However, unlike freebase, crack is not a pure form of cocaine. It contains remnants of hydrochloride along with additional residue from the baking soda (sodium bicarbonate). In fact, crack gets its name from the fact that the sodium bicarbonate often emits a crackling sound when the substance is smoked.

Also referred to as "rock," "gravel," and "roxanne," crack was introduced and gained popularity on both coasts simultaneously in the mid-1980s. It is relatively inexpensive, can provide a powerful high, and is considered to be highly psychologically addictive.

HEROIN

Narcotic drugs have the ability to produce insensibility to pain and to free the mind of anxiety and emotion. Users experience a rush of euphoria, relief from fear and apprehension, release of tension, and elevation of spirits. After experiencing this uplifting mood for a short period, users become apathetic and drowsy and nod off. Heroin, the most commonly used narcotic in the United States, is produced from opium, a drug derived from the opium poppy flower. Dealers further cut the drug with neutral substances, such as sugar (lactose), so that street heroin is often only one percent to four percent pure.

Heroin is probably the most dangerous commonly used drug. Users rapidly build up a tolerance for it, fueling the need for increased doses to feel the desired effect. Some users will change their method of ingestion to get the required "kick." At first, heroin is usually sniffed or snorted; as tolerance builds, it is "skin popped" (shot into skin, but not into a vein) and then finally injected into a vein or "mainlined."

Through the progressive use of heroin, the user becomes an addict—a person with an overpowering physical and psychological need to continue taking a particular substance or drug by any means possible. If addicts cannot get enough heroin to satisfy their habit, they will suffer withdrawal symptoms. These include irritability, emotional depression, extreme nervousness, pain in the abdomen, and nausea.

ALCOHOL

Alcohol remains the drug of choice for most teenagers. More than 70 percent of high school seniors report using alcohol in the past year, and about 90 percent say they have tried it sometime during their lifetime; by the 12th grade about two-thirds of American youth report that they have "been drunk."[7] More than 20 million Americans are estimated to be problem drinkers, and at least half of these are alcoholics.

The cost of alcohol abuse is quite high. Alcohol may be a factor in nearly half of the murders, suicides, and accidental deaths that occur in the United States.[8]

Long-term alcohol use has been linked with depression and numerous physical ailments ranging from heart disease to cirrhosis of the liver. And while many teens think that drinking stirs their romantic urges, the weight of scientific evidence indicates that alcohol decreases sexual response.

Alcohol-related deaths number 100,000 a year, far more than those related to all other illegal drugs combined. About 1.4 million drivers are arrested each year for driving under the influence, and close to a million more are arrested for other alcohol-related violations.[9] The economic cost of the drinking problem in the United States is equally staggering. An estimated $117 billion is lost each year, including $18 billion from premature deaths, $66 billion in reduced work effort, and $13 billion for treatment.[10]

Considering these problems, why do so many youths drink alcohol to excess? Youths who use alcohol report that it reduces tension, diverts worries, enhances pleasure, improves social skills, and transforms experiences for the better.[11] Although these reactions may follow the limited use of alcohol, alcohol in higher doses acts as a sedative and depressant. Many teens think that drinking stirs their romantic urges; however, the weight of the scientific evidence indicates that alcohol decreases sexual response.[12] Long-term use has been linked with depression and numerous physical ailments ranging from heart disease to cirrhosis of the liver (although there is research linking moderate drinking to a reduction in the probability of heart attack).[13]

ANESTHETICS

Anesthetic drugs are used as nervous system depressants. Local anesthetics block nervous system transmissions; general anesthetics act on the brain to produce a generalized loss of sensation, stupor, or unconsciousness.

The most widely abused anesthetic drug is phencyclidine (PCP), known on the street as "angel dust." PCP can be sprayed on marijuana or other plant leaves and smoked, drunk, or injected. Originally developed as an animal tranquilizer, PCP creates hallucinations and a spaced-out feeling that causes heavy users to engage in extremely violent acts. The effects of PCP can last up to two days; the danger of overdose is extremely high.

INHALANTS

Some substance-abusing youths inhale vapors from lighter fluid, paint thinner, cleaning fluid, and model airplane glue to reach a drowsy, dizzy state sometimes accompanied by hallucinations. Such inhalants produce a short-term sense of excitement and euphoria followed by a period of disorientation, slurred speech, and drowsiness. Amyl nitrate ("poppers") is a commonly used volatile liquid that is inhaled from capsules that are broken.

SEDATIVES/BARBITURATES

Sedatives, the most commonly used drugs of the barbiturate family, depress the central nervous system into a sleeplike condition. On the illegal market, sedatives are called "goofballs" or "downers" or are known by the color of the capsules—"reds" (Seconal), "blue devils" (Amytal), and "rainbows" (Tuinal). Methaqualone (quaaludes, ludes) is a commonly abused sedative.

Doctors can legally prescribe sedatives to patients having difficulty sleeping. Others use them illegally to create feelings of relaxation, sociability, and good humor; overdoses can cause irritability, repellent behavior, and eventual unconsciousness. Barbiturates are probably the major cause of drug-overdose deaths.

TRANQUILIZERS

Tranquilizers relieve uncomfortable emotional feelings by reducing levels of anxiety and promoting relaxation. Legally prescribed tranquilizers, such as Ampazine, Thorazine, Pacatal, and Sparine, were originally designed to control the behavior of people suffering from psychoses, aggressiveness, and agitation. Less powerful tranquilizers, such as Valium, Librium, Miltown, and Equanil, are used to combat anxiety, tension, rapid heart rate, and headaches. The use of increased dosages of illegally obtained tranquilizers can lead to addiction, and withdrawal can be painful and hazardous.

HALLUCINOGENS

Hallucinogens, either natural or synthetic, produce vivid distortions of the senses without greatly disturbing the viewer's consciousness. Some produce hallucinations, and others cause psychotic behavior in otherwise normal people.

One common hallucinogen is mescaline, named after the Mescalero Apaches, who first discovered its potent effect. Mescaline occurs naturally in the peyote, a small cactus that grows in Mexico and the southwestern United States. After initial discomfort, mescaline produces vivid hallucinations in all ranges of colors and geometric patterns, a feeling of depersonalization, and out-of-body sensations.

A second group of hallucinogens are synthetic alkaloid compounds, such as psilocybin. These compounds can be transformed into lysergic acid diethylamide, commonly called LSD. LSD (800 times more potent than mescaline) stimulates cerebral sensory centers to produce visual hallucinations in all ranges of colors, to intensify hearing, and to increase sensitivity. Users often report a scrambling of sensations; they may "hear colors" and "smell music." Users also report feeling euphoric and mentally superior, although to an observer they appear disoriented and confused. Unfortunately, anxiety and panic may occur during the LSD experience, and overdoses can produce psychotic episodes, flashbacks, and even death.

STIMULANTS

Stimulants ("uppers," "speed," "pep pills," "ice") are synthetic drugs that stimulate action in the central nervous system. They produce an intense physical reaction: increased blood pressure, breathing rate, and bodily activity and elevation of mood. One widely used stimulant, amphetamine, produces psychological effects, such as increased confidence, euphoria, fearlessness, talkativeness, impulsive behavior, and loss of appetite.

The commonly used stimulants are Benzedrine ("bennies"), Dexedrine ("dex"), Dexamyl, Bephetamine ("whites"), and Methedrine ("meth," "speed," "crystal meth").

Methedrine is probably the most widely used and most dangerous amphetamine. Some people swallow it; heavy users inject it for a quick rush. Long-term heavy use can result in exhaustion, anxiety, prolonged depression, and hallucinations. A new form of methamphetamine is a crystallized substance with the street name of "ice." Popular on the West Coast and Hawaii, it originated in Asian labs; it is called "batu" by Filipinos, "shaba" by the Japanese, and "hirropon" by Koreans. Smoking this crystal causes weight loss, kidney damage, heart and respiratory problems, and paranoia, symptoms of its better-known competitor, crack.[14]

STEROIDS

Teenagers use highly dangerous anabolic **steroids** to gain muscle bulk and strength for athletics and body building.[15] Black-market sales of these drugs approach $1 billion annually. Although not physically addicting, steroids can become an "obsession" among teens who desire athletic success. Long-term users may spend up to $400 a week on steroids and may support their habit by dealing the drug.

Steroids are dangerous because of the significant health problems associated with their long-term use: liver ailments, tumors, hepatitis, kidney problems, sexual dysfunction, hypertension, and mental problems, such as depression. Steroid use runs in cycles, and other drugs such as Clomid, Teslac, and Halotestin, which carry their own dangerous side effects, are used to curb the need for high dosages. Finally, steroid users often share needles, which puts them at high risk for contracting human immunodeficiency virus (HIV), the virus that causes AIDS.

Drug Use Today

Drug abuse in general has become an alarming social problem in the United States, and the diversity of individual illegal substances has served to make the problem that much more difficult for legal authorities to address.[16] Indicators of cocaine use, such as drug-related deaths, arrests, emergency room overdose admissions, and possession arrests, have all increased faster than for any other drug. Although cocaine use is not widespread, its concentration in large urban areas has contributed to a growing urban crime rate.

Surveys also show that marijuana continues to be the most widely used drug and that synthetic (laboratory-made) drugs have become more popular. Some western states report that methamphetamine ("speed," "crank") use is increasing and that its low cost and high potency have encouraged manufacturers ("cookers") to increase production and distribution efforts. The use of other synthetics, including PCP and LSD, is not widespread nationally but focused in particular areas of the country. For example, California leads the nation in the manufacture of PCP; about two-thirds of all PCP drug labs busted are in California.[17]

Synthetics are popular because labs can be easily hidden in rural areas, and traffickers do not have to worry about border searches or payoffs to foreign growers and intermediaries. Users like synthetics because they are cheap and produce a powerful, long-lasting high that can be greater than that provided by more expensive products, such as cocaine.

Although heroin use has stabilized in most of the country, the United States still has an estimated 500,000 addicts. Heroin abuse seems to be concentrated in a few areas of the country; about one-half of all addicts reportedly reside in New York City.[18]

Despite the concern over these "hard drugs," the most persistent teenage substance abuse problem today is alcohol. Although sometimes teenage alcoholism is considered less of a social problem than other types of substance abuse, it actually produces far more deaths and problems. Teenage alcohol abusers suffer depression, anxiety, and other symptoms of mental distress. It is well established that alcoholism runs in families; thus, today's teenage abusers may be the parents of the next generation of teenage alcoholics.[19]

DRUG USE SURVEYS

A number of attempts have been made to survey teenage drug abuse. Following are descriptions of the three primary sources of data on trends.

1. The federal government sponsors an annual survey conducted by social scientists at University of Michigan's Institute for Social Research. Since 1975, the Michigan research team has conducted a series of annual surveys which now include some 50,000 students from 400 public and private secondary schools.[20] Participants (and the research team reports that students are enthusiastic participants) are queried about their lifetime, monthly, and annual use of 16 commonly abused drugs and substances (including cigarettes and alcohol). Although the early surveys were limited to seniors, they now include 8th and 10th graders. In addition to the annual survey, about 2,400 members of each class surveyed are followed up for 10 years after high school to determine the lifetime incidence of their drug usage.
2. The Parents Resource Institute for Drug Abuse (PRIDE) is an Atlanta-based nonprofit group that conducts annual surveys of more than 200,000 junior and senior high school students in 34 states.
3. The National Household Survey, conducted by the U.S. Department of Health and Human Services, involves the interviewing of approximately 10,000 people in their homes.[21] Data on drug abuse are disaggregated by age so that trends in adolescent substance abuse can be charted.

INSTITUTE FOR SOCIAL RESEARCH (ISR) SURVEY

The Institute for Social Research (ISR) survey is the one most often used to follow the course of teenage substance abuse in the United States. The most recent ISR survey available (1995) indicates that although fewer adolescents are taking drugs today than 20 years ago, there has been a disturbing uptick in drug use during the past few years.

As Figure 11.1, shows, drug use peaked in the late '70s and early '80s and then began a decade-long decline. Then, in 1993 drug use began to increase. Very large increases were recorded in the use of marijuana and hashish. Additional data shows that number of high school seniors smoking pot in the past 30 days rose from about 14 percent in 1991 to 21 percent in 1995, an increase of about 50 percent.

Especially disturbing is the trend for the youngest students, 8th graders aged 13 and 14, who reported an increase in their lifetime, annual, and monthly use of illicit drugs. By 8th grade, more than half the students had drank alcohol, about 1 percent drank on a daily basis and about 15 percent said they had 5 or more drinks in the past 2 weeks. In addition, more than 20 percent reported having used inhalants (see Figure 11.2 on page 398).

Cigarette smoking has also increased in the 1990s. About 19 percent of 8th graders and 28 percent of 10th graders now report smoking during the past 30 days. Among high school seniors, the number who have tried cigarettes during their lifetime has stabilized at about two-thirds. However, the number of seniors who have tried cigarettes in the past month and who smoke every day has been on the increase; more than 20 percent of high school seniors say they now smoke every day.

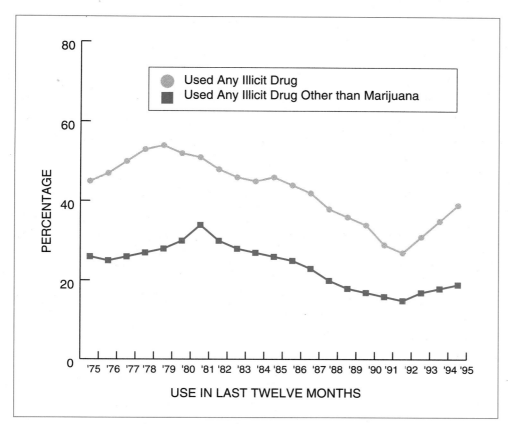

FIGURE 11.1
Trends in annual prevalence of an illicit drug use index for twelfth graders

Source: ISR News Release, December 5, 1995, Ann Arbor, Mich.

PRIDE SURVEY

The most recent PRIDE survey also indicates increases in drug activity, specifically marijuana, hallucinogens, cocaine and inhalants; students also reported increasing their use of cigarettes.

The most recent survey (1995) found that about one-third of high school seniors reported having smoked marijuana in the past year, and about one-fifth smoked monthly.[22] Between 1990 and 1995, the use of marijuana rose more than 100 percent in middle school and 67 percent in high school; during this period high school students increased their use of cocaine by 36 percent. Cigarette usage also reached its highest levels since the 1980s; nearly half of all high school students report smoking during the past year. Although beer drinking reached an all-time high, high school students were less likely to drink wine coolers, possibly because they are no longer being aggressively marketed.

HOUSEHOLD SURVEY

Like the other two surveys, the most recent Household Survey indicates that after more than a decade of decline (1979–1992) drug use is once again increasing among the 12- to 17-year-old group (Figure 11.3 on page 399).

The Household Survey also finds that millions of adolescents have tried drugs and hundreds of thousands are current users. Equally disturbing is the fact that

FIGURE 11.2
Institute of Social Research high school drug survey: Lifetime use of selected drugs by grade, 1995

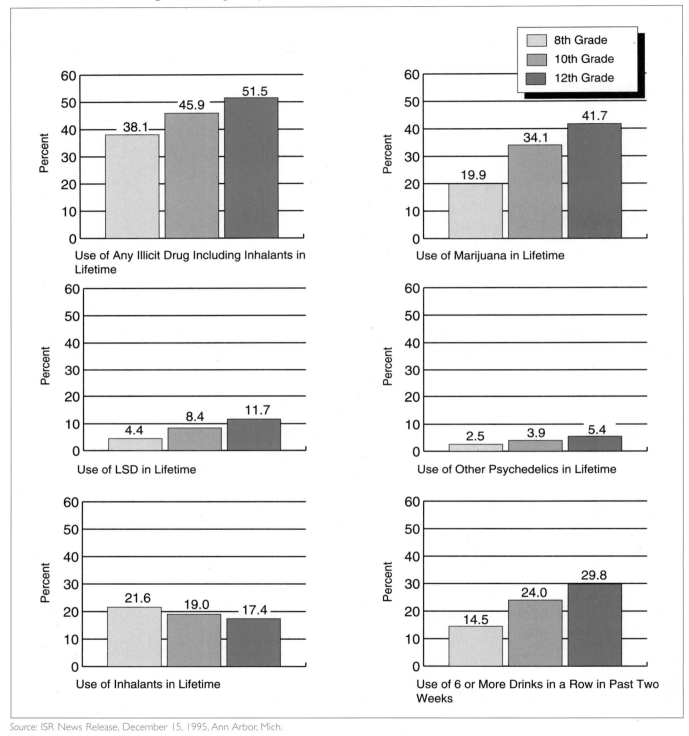

Source: ISR News Release, December 15, 1995, Ann Arbor, Mich.

Part III   Environmental Influences on Delinquency

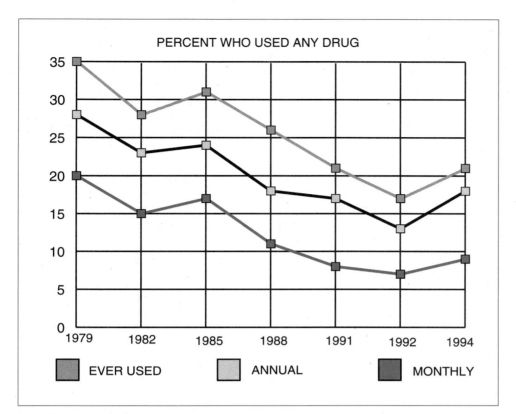

FIGURE 11.3
National Household Survey results: Drug use among adolescents aged 12-17

Source: National Household Survey, 1994.

about 20 percent are alcohol abusers (4 million teenagers), another 11 percent are smokers, and 3 percent (about 600,000 youths) use smokeless tobacco. About 250,000 young Americans (12 to 25) have tried heroin and 5.5 million have used cocaine; of these, 600,000 are current users.

WHY HAS TEENAGE DRUG USE FLUCTUATED?

If the national survey results are valid, teenage drug use has undergone a period of significant change. When drug use declined in the 1980s, one reason may have been changing perceptions about the harmfulness of drugs, such as cocaine and marijuana; as students come to view these drugs as harmful, they tend to use them less. Considering the widespread publicity linking drug use, needle sharing, and the AIDS virus, it comes as no surprise that young people began to see drug taking as more dangerous and risky than in the 1970s. In the 1990s the perceived risk of drugs has been declining. For example, the ISR reports that 79 percent of seniors in 1991 thought they ran a "great risk" if they used marijuana regularly, but by 1995 only 61 percent felt that way.

In addition, during periods when drug use declined youths reported greater disapproval of drug use among their friends. Reducing peer pressure may help account for lower use rates. National ad campaigns to "just say no to drugs" and to stop friends from drinking and driving may have helped reduce peer approval of substance abuse in the 1980's. In the 1990s the number of youths disapproving of drugs has declined (although a majority still disapprove); with lower disapproval has come increased usage.

It also appears that it is becoming easier to obtain drugs, especially for younger adolescents. For example, the ISR survey found that in 1992, 42 percent of 8th graders said it was easy to obtain pot; 3 years later more than half (52 percent) claimed obtaining marijuana was "easy." It should come as no surprise that a cohort of young people who perceive less peer rejection for drug use and who consider drugs risk free and easily available will increase the frequency of their substance abuse.

Today's teens may be less fearful of the dangers of drug abuse and are therefore not deterred from experimentation. The media's anti-drug messages have declined in the 1990s, while at the same time rock and rap bands have frequently placed pro-drug messages in their lyrics. In addition, parents may now be unwilling or reluctant to educate their children about the dangers of substance abuse, because as "baby boomers," they were drug abusers in the 60s and 70s.[23] The PRIDE survey found that only one-third of parents talk to their children about drugs, one-third do not set clear rules, and half of those who do set rules refuse to discipline children when they break them. The PRIDE survey also found that those children who discuss drug use with parents are much less likely to be abusers than those who don't.

ARE THE SURVEY RESULTS ACCURATE?

The results reported in student drug surveys must be interpreted with caution. First, it may be overly optimistic to expect that heavy crack, "ice," and PCP users are going to cooperate with a drug use survey, especially one being conducted by a government agency. Even if willing, they are the ones who are more than likely to be absent from school on the day the survey is administered. They are also likely to be forgetful and give inaccurate accounts of their substance abuse.

Another problem is that the absentee and dropout rate among drug users is so high that it is likely that the most deviant and drug-dependent portion of the adolescent population is omitted from the sample. Research indicates that more than half of all people arrested dropped out of school before the twelfth grade, and more than two-thirds of these arrestees are drug users.[24] Eric Wish has found that the number of juvenile detainees (those arrested and held in a lock-up) who test positively for cocaine is many times higher than that reported for recent use in the ISR survey. For example, about 22 percent of young detainees in Washington, D.C., and 18 percent in Phoenix tested positively for cocaine, a use rate many times higher than that of the general high school population.[25] The inclusion of eighth graders in the ISR sample is one way of getting around the dropout problem. Nonetheless, these surveys, by their design, exclude some of the most drug-prone users.

Although any school-based or home-based survey is tainted by measurement problems such as underreporting, overreporting, and the omission of some high-risk cases, these methodological and measurement problems are consistent over time and therefore do not hinder the *measurement of change* in the national substance abuse rate. That is, prior surveys *also omitted* dropouts and other high-risk youth and been otherwise tainted by over- and under reporting subjects: since the populations being measured are equivalent, any change in the substance abuse rate over time is probably genuine. So although the *validity* of these surveys to precisely measure the actual number of teenage drug abusers may be in doubt, they are more likely *reliable* indicators of trends in substance abuse.

WHY DO TEENAGERS TAKE DRUGS?

To most people, the "why" of teenage drug abuse remains a puzzle: Why do youths engage in an activity that is sure to bring them overwhelming personal problems? Although it is easy to understand the dealers' desire for quick profits, how can we explain the users' disregard for long- and short-term consequences?

SOCIAL DISORGANIZATION

One explanation ties drug abuse to poverty, social disorganization, and a feeling of hopelessness. The involvement in drug use by young minority group members has been tied to such factors as racial prejudice, "devalued identities," low self-esteem, poor socioeconomic status, and the stress of living in the harsh urban environment.[26] The association between drug use, race, and poverty has been linked to the high level of mistrust, negativism, and defiance found in lower socioeconomic areas.[27]

Although social disorganization has long been associated with drug use, the empirical data on the relationship between class and crime has so far been inconclusive. For example, the *National Youth Survey* (NYS), a well-respected longitudinal study of delinquent behavior conducted by Delbert Elliott and his associates, found little if any association between drug use and social class. Although the NYS found that drug use is higher among urban youth, little evidence existed that minority youths or members of the lower class were more likely to abuse drugs than white youths and the more affluent.[28] Research by the Rand Corporation indicates that many drug-dealing youths (about two-thirds) had legitimate jobs at the time they were arrested for drug trafficking.[29] Therefore, it would be difficult to describe drug abusers simply as unemployed dropouts who are trying to escape the reality of a misspent youth.

PEER PRESSURE

Drug use is typically a peer experience. Research shows that adolescent drug abuse is highly correlated with the behavior of "best friends," especially when parental supervision is weak or nonexistent.[30]

Youths living in a deteriorated inner-city slum area, where feelings of alienation and hopelessness run high, often come in contact with established drug users who teach them that drugs can relieve their feelings of personal inadequacy and stress.[31] Perhaps they join with peers to learn the techniques of drug use; their friendships with other drug-dependent youths give them social support for their habit. Data acquired by Terence Thornberry and his associates as part of the Rochester Youth Development study do in fact show that a youth's association with friends who are committed to deviant values increases the probability of drug use.[32] Helene Raskin White's analysis of longitudinal data from a New Jersey cohort of 892 adolescents indicated that adolescent drug use was best predicted by friendships with other drug users.[33]

Peer networks that support drug use may be the most significant influence on long-term substance abuse. Shared feelings and a sense of intimacy lead youths to become fully enmeshed in what has been described as the "drug-use subculture."[34] Research now indicates that drug users do in fact have intimate and warm relationships with substance-abusing peers, which help support their habits and behaviors.[35] The street identity and lifestyle provide users with a clear identity, a role they can fulfill, activities and behaviors they enjoy, and an opportunity for attaining social status among their peers.[36] One of the reasons that it is so difficult to treat hard-core users is that quitting drugs means leaving the "fast life" of the streets.

FAMILY FACTORS

Another explanation is that drug users have a poor family life and a troubled adolescence. Studies have found that the majority of drug users have had an unhappy childhood, punctuated by harsh physical punishment and parental neglect and rejection.[37] The drug abuse–family quality association may involve both racial and gender differences: Females and whites who were abused as children are more likely to have alcohol and drug arrests as adults; abuse was less likely to affect males and African-Americans.[38] It is also common to find substance abusers within large families and with parents who are divorced, separated, or absent.[39]

Social psychologists suggest that drug-abuse patterns may also result from the observation of parental drug use.[40] Youths who learn that drugs provide pleasurable sensations may be the most likely to experiment with illegal substances; a habit may develop if the user experiences lowered anxiety, fear, and tension levels.[41]

James Inciardi, Ruth Horowitz, and Anne Pottieger found a clear pattern of adult involvement in early substance abuse when they studied serious adolescent drug users in Miami. Youths whose drug problems escalated to crack use began their substance abuse careers by experimenting with alcohol at age 7, getting drunk at age 8, having alcohol with an adult present by age 9, and becoming regular drinkers by the time they were 11 years old.[42] Inciardi and his associates found that drinking with an adult present, presumably a parent, was a significant precursor of future substance abuse and delinquency. "Adults," they argue, "who gave children alcohol were also giving them a head start in a delinquent career."[43] Crack-abusing youths do not necessarily come from socially disadvantaged families as much as from families wracked by conflict.

Other family factors associated with teen drug abuse include ineffective discipline skills, including parental conflict over child rearing practices; failure to set rules; and unrealistic demands followed by harsh physical punishments. Low parental attachment, rejection, and excessive family conflict have all been linked to subsequent adolescent substance abuse.[44]

GENETIC FACTORS

The association between parental drug abuse and adolescent behavior may have a genetic basis. Research has shown that the biological children of alcoholics reared by nonalcoholic adoptive parents more often develop alcohol problems than the biological children of the adoptive parents.[45] A number of studies comparing alcoholism among identical (MZ) and fraternal (DZ) twins have found that the degree of concordance (both siblings behaving identically) is twice as high among the MZ groups.[46]

A genetic basis for drug abuse is also supported by recent evidence showing that future substance abuse problems can be predicted by behavior exhibited as early as six years old. The individual traits predicting future abuse occur before and are independent from peer relations and environmental influences.[47]

EMOTIONAL PROBLEMS

Not all drug-abusing youths reside in lower-class slum areas; the problem of middle-class substance abuse is very real. To explain drug abuse across the social structure, some experts have linked it to personality disturbances and emotional problems that can strike young people in any economic class. Psychodynamic explanations of substance abuse suggest that drugs help youths control or express unconscious needs and impulses. Some psychoanalysts believe that adolescents who internalize their problems may use drugs and alcohol as a means to reduce their feelings of inadequacy and insecurity. Introverted people may seek an escape from real or imagined feeling of inferiority or insecurity.[48] Another view is that adolescents who externalize their problems and blame others for their perceived failures are the ones most likely to engage in antisocial behaviors, including substance abuse. Research exists that is supportive of both positions.[49]

Drug abusers are also believed to exhibit psychopathic or sociopathic behavior characteristics, forming what is called an **addiction-prone personality**.[50] Drinking alcohol may reflect a teen's need to remain dependent on an overprotective mother or an effort to reduce the emotional turmoil of adolescence.[51]

Research on the psychological characteristics of narcotics abusers does in fact reveal the presence of a significant degree of personal pathology. Personality testing of known users suggests that a significant percentage suffer from psychotic disorders, including various levels of schizophrenia. Studies have found that addicts suffer personality disorders characterized by a weak ego, a low frustration tolerance, anxiety, and fantasies of omnipotence. Up to half of all drug abusers may also be diagnosed with antisocial personality disorder (ASPD), which is defined as a pervasive pattern of disregard for and violation of the rights of others.[52]

PROBLEM BEHAVIOR SYNDROME

For many adolescents, substance abuse is just one of many problem behaviors that begin early in life and remain throughout the life course.[53] Longitudinal studies show that young people who abuse drugs are maladjusted, alienated, and emotionally distressed, and have many social problems; drug use then seems part of a general problem behavior syndrome or PBS.[54] Having a deviant lifestyle means associating with delinquent peers, living in a family in which parents and siblings abuse drugs, having a low commitment to education, being alienated from the dominant values of society, and engaging in delinquent behaviors at an early age.[55] Research shows that youths who abuse drugs lack commitment to religious values, disdain education, and spend most of their time in peer activities.[56] Those who take drugs do poorly in school, have high dropout rates, and maintain their drug use after they leave school.[57]

RATIONAL CHOICE

Young people may choose to use drugs and alcohol because they want to enjoy their anticipated effects: They want to get high, relax, improve their creativity, escape reality, and increase sexual responsiveness. Research indicates that adolescent alcohol abusers believe that getting high will make them powerful, increase their sexual performance, and facilitate their social behavior; they care little about negative future consequences.[58] Substance abuse, then, may be a function of the rational, albeit mistaken, belief that substance abuse benefits the user.

Patterns of Teenage Drug Use

What are the patterns of teenage drug use? Are all abusers similar, or are there different types of drug involvement? Research indicates that drug-involved youth do take on different roles, lifestyles, and behavior patterns, some of which are described below.[59]

THOSE WHO DISTRIBUTE SMALL AMOUNTS OF DRUGS

Many adolescents who are involved with the use and distribution of small amounts of drugs do not commit any other serious delinquent acts. Most of these petty dealers occasionally sell marijuana, "ice," and PCP to support their own drug use. Their customers are almost always known to them and include friends, relatives, and acquaintances. Deals are arranged over the phone, in school, or at public hangouts and meeting places; however, the actual distribution takes place in more private arenas, such as at home or in cars.

Petty dealers do not consider themselves "seriously" involved in drugs. One girl commented,

> . . . I don't consider it dealing, I'll sell hits of speed to my friends and joints and nickel bags [of marijuana] to my friends, but that's not dealing.

Included in Inciardi, Horowitz, and Pottieger's sample of crack-using adolescents in Miami was Erica, a 16-year-old who modeled, played field hockey, and was a cheerleader. "I'm not really *in* the crack business," she told the investigators. "I just know someone who is and help him out once in a while." When Erica is paid for her services with crack, she may sell it to her friends.[60]

Petty dealers are insulated from the juvenile justice system because their activities rarely result in apprehension and sanction. In fact, few adults notice their activities because they are able to maintain a relatively conventional lifestyle. In several jurisdictions, however, agents of the justice system are cooperating in the development of educational programs to provide nonusers with the skills to resist the "sales pitch" of the petty dealers they meet at school or in the neighborhood.

THOSE WHO FREQUENTLY SELL DRUGS

A small number of adolescents, most often multiple-drug users or heroin or cocaine users, are high-rate dealers who bridge the gap between adult drug distributors and the adolescent user. Although many are daily users, they are not strung-out junkies, and they take part in many normal adolescent activities, such as going to school and socializing with friends.

Frequent dealers often have adults who "front" for them, that is consign them drugs to distribute to friends and acquaintances. They return most of the proceeds to the supplier while keeping a commission for themselves. They may also keep drugs for their personal use, and in fact, some consider their drug dealing as a way of "getting high for free." Winston, aged 17, told Inciardi and his associates,

> I sell the cracks for money and for cracks. The man, he give me this *much*. I sell most of it and I get the rest for me. I like this much. Every day I do this.[61]

Inciardi and his associates found that frequent dealers were also likely to be regular users of crack. About 80 percent of teenagers who dealt crack regularly were daily users.[62]

Frequent dealers are more likely to sell drugs in public and can be seen in known drug hangouts in parks, schools, or other public places. Deals occur irregularly, so the chance of apprehension is not significant, nor is the payoff substantial. A recent survey by Robert MacCoun and Peter Reuter found that drug dealers make about $30 per hour when they are working and clear on average about $2,000 per month. Although these amounts are certainly greater than most dealers could hope to earn in legitimate jobs, they are certainly not enough to afford a steady stream of luxuries; most small-time dealers also hold conventional jobs.[63]

THOSE WHO COMMIT OTHER DELINQUENT ACTS

A more serious type of drug-involved youth is the one who not only uses and distributes multiple substances but also commits both property and violent crimes. Although these youths make up only about 2 percent of the teenage population, they may commit up to 40 percent of the robberies and assaults and about 60 percent of all teenage felony thefts and drug sales. Few gender or racial differences exist among these youths: Girls are as likely as boys to become high-rate, persistent, drug-involved offenders, white youths as likely as African-American youths, middle-class adolescents raised outside the city as likely as lower-class adolescents raised in the city.[64]

In cities, these youths are frequently hired by older dealers to act as street-level drug runners. Each member of a crew of three to twelve boys will handle small quantities of drugs, perhaps three bags of heroin, which are received on consignment and sold on the street; the supplier receives 50 percent to 70 percent of the drug's street value. The crew members also act as lookouts, recruiters, and guards. Although they may be recreational drug users themselves, crew members refrain from using addictive drugs, such as heroin; some major suppliers will only hire "drug-free kids" to make street deals. Between drug sales, the young dealers commit robberies, burglaries, and other thefts. The interrelationship between drug dealing and youth violence is discussed in the "Focus on Delinquency" on pages 406 and 407.

Most youths in the street drug trade have few success skills and either terminate their dealing or become drug dependent. A few, however, develop excellent entrepreneurial skills. Those who are rarely apprehended by police earn the trust of their older contacts and advance in the drug business. They develop their own crews and handle more than a half million dollars a year in

FOCUS ON DELINQUENCY

YOUTH VIOLENCE AND THE ILLICIT DRUG TRADE

Alfred Blumstein and H. John Heinz III have studied the relationship between adolescent involvement in the drug trade and violent crime over time. They note three major "doublings" that have occurred in the recent juvenile crime rate since 1985:

1. homicide rates by youth aged 18 and under;
2. the number of homicides juveniles commit with guns, while there have been no change in non-gun homicides (Figure A); and
3. the arrest rate of non-white juveniles on drug charges, while there has been no growth in the rate for white juveniles (Figure B).

According to Blumstein and Heinz, one explanation for this array of changes involves a process that is driven by the illegal drug markets, which appear to operate in a reasonable equilib-

rium with the demand for drugs despite the massive efforts over the past decade to attack the supply side. That industry understandably recruits juveniles to work in it, partly because they will work more cheaply than adults, partly because they may be less vulnerable to the punishments imposed by the adult criminal justice system, and partly because they tend to be daring and willing to take risks that more mature adults would eschew. The economic plight of many young urban African-American juveniles, many of whom see no other comparably satisfactory route to economic sustenance, makes them particularly amenable to the lure.

These juveniles, as all participants in the illicit drug industry, are very likely to carry guns for self-protection and possibly to help in dispute resolution. Participants in the industry are likely

FIGURE A
Number of gun and non-gun homicides juvenile offenders (10-17)

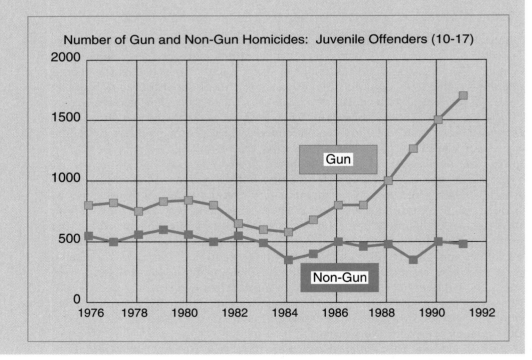

to be carrying a considerable amount of valuable product—money or drugs—and are not likely to be able to call on the police if they are robbed.

Because a reasonably large number of juveniles can be involved in the drug industry in communities where the drug market is active, other teenagers who go to the same school or who walk the same streets are also likely to arm themselves, primarily for their own protection but also because possession of a weapon may become a part of status-seeking in the community. This initiates an escalating process: As more guns appear in the community, that increases the incentive for any single individual to arm himself or herself.

Then, in view of the recklessness and bravado that is often characteristic of teenagers, and their low level of skill in settling disputes other than through the use of physical force many of the fights that would otherwise have taken place can turn into shootings as a result of the presence of the guns. This can be exacerbated by the problems of socialization associated with high levels of poverty, high rates of single-parent households, educational failures, and a widespread sense of economic hopelessness.

By the time people reach the more mature ages beyond the early twenties, it appears that they do develop confidence and are more cautious even if they are armed, and display greater restraint. As an alternative possibility, we may be witnessing a cohort effect, and the current 18-year-olds involved in the higher homicide rates may possibly continue their recklessness. That issue still needs to be watched and explored.

These hypothesized processes are suggested by the national data, and are consistent with them. They can be tested further with city-level data on drugs, guns, and homicides. That would take advantage of the fact that drug markets began to flourish at different times in different cities, early in New York and Los Angeles, later in Washington.

Source: Alfred Blumstein and H. John Heinz III, "Youth Violence, Guns and the Illicit Drug Industry," in Carolyn Block and Richard Block eds., *Trends, Risks, and Interventions in Lethal Violence: Proceedings of the Third Annual Spring Symposium of the Homicide Research Working Group* (Washington, D.C.: National Institute of Justice, 1995), p. 8–11.

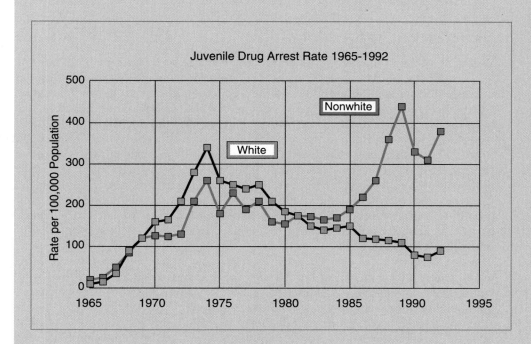

FIGURE B
Juvenile drug arrest rate
1965-1992

Teenage gangs have also emerged as major players in the drug trade. Most prominent are the two largest Los Angeles youth gangs, the Bloods and the Crips. These drug-dealing gangs maintain "rock houses" or "stash houses" where they receive drug shipments arranged by gang members who have the overseas connections and financial backing needed to wholesale drugs. The wholesalers pay the gang for permission to deal in their territory and hire members as a security force.

drug business. Some are able to afford the BMW or Mercedes, jewelry, and expensive clothes that signify success in the drug trade.

DRUG-INVOLVED GANGS

Youths involved in teenage gangs commonly become serious suppliers of narcotics. At one time, primacy in the U.S. drug trade was maintained by traditional organized crime families, which used their control of the Asian heroin market as a principle source of mob income. The monopoly of these families, however, has been broken. Efforts to jail crime bosses, coupled with the popularity and growth of cocaine and synthetic drugs (which are less easily controlled by a single source), have shattered this distribution monopoly. Stepping into the void have been local gangs that have used their drug income to expand their base and power. Prominent among these are biker gangs, such as the Hell's Angels, Outlaws, and Bandidos, which have become active in the manufacture and distribution of synthetics. The Jamaican Posse and Latino gangs control a large part of the East Coast cocaine business, while Chinese gangs now import much of the nation's heroin supply.

Teenage gangs have also emerged as major players in the drug trade. Most prominent are the two largest Los Angeles youth gangs, the Bloods and the Crips, whose total membership is estimated to be more than 20,000 (although actual membership is probably impossible to determine).

In Los Angeles itself, these drug-dealing gangs maintain "rock houses" or "stash houses." The houses receive drug shipments arranged by gang members who have the overseas connections and financial backing needed to wholesale drugs. The wholesalers pay the gang for permission to deal in their territory and hire members as a security force. Lower-echelon gang members help transport the drugs and work the houses, retailing cocaine and other drugs to neighborhood youths. Each member makes a profit for every ounce of "rock" sold. Police estimate that youths who work in "rock houses" will earn $700 and up for a 12-hour shift.[65]

There is still some question as to the extent of the role of gangs in drug dealing. As you may recall, some gang experts now question whether gangs are responsible for as much drug dealing as the media would have us believe. Others show that tightly organized "super" gangs, which traditionally controlled citywide drug dealing, are being phased out and replaced with loosely organized, neighborhood-based groups. The rationale behind this shift is that the turbulent environment of drug dealing is better handled by flexible, informal organizations than rigid, vertically organized gangs with a leader who is far removed from the action.[66]

LOSERS AND BURNOUTS

Some drug-involved youths are losers and burnouts, failures at both dealing and crime. They do not have the savvy to join gangs or groups and instead begin committing unplanned, opportunistic crimes that increase their chances of arrest. In addition, their heavy drug use both increases their risk of apprehension and decreases their value to organized drug distribution networks.

Drug-involved "losers" can earn a living by steering customers to a seller in a "copping" area, touting drug availability for a dealer, or acting as a lookout. However, they are not considered trustworthy or deft enough to handle drugs or money. They may bungle other criminal acts, solidifying their reputation as undesirable:

> Buster is almost always stoned on ludes and beer. He is continually getting caught robbing and is in and out of treatment centers. Once he and another boy robbed [sic] a jewelry store. They smashed the window with a brick and the window fell on them, knocking them both out. The store owner called the cops and an ambulance.[67]

Although these persistent offenders get involved in drugs at a very early age, they receive little attention from the justice system until they have developed an extensive arrest record. By then, they are approaching the end of their minority and will either spontaneously desist or become so deeply entrapped in the drug-crime subculture that little can be done to treat or deter their illegal activities.

PERSISTENT OFFENDERS

Although about two-thirds of substance-abusing youths continue to use drugs after they reach adulthood, about half desist from other criminal activities. Those who persist in both substance abuse and crime as adults maintain the following characteristics:

- They come from poor families.
- Other criminals are members of their families.
- They do poorly in school.
- They started using drugs and committing other delinquent acts at a relatively early age.
- They use multiple types of drugs and commit crimes frequently.
- They have few opportunities in late adolescence to participate in legitimate and rewarding adult activities.[68]

Some evidence exists that these drug-using persisters have low nonverbal IQs and poor physical coordination. Nonetheless, little scientific evidence exists to explain why some drug-abusing youths drop out of crime while others remain active into adulthood.

DRUG USE AND DELINQUENCY

Research has established an association between drug use and delinquency. The connection can take a number of different forms. Crime may be an instrument of the drug trade: Violence erupts when rival drug gangs use their automatic weapons to settle differences and establish territorial monopolies. In New York City, authorities report that crack gangs will burn down their rivals' headquarters, even if people living on the premises are not connected to the drug trade; it is estimated that between 35 percent and 40 percent of New York's homicides are drug related.[69]

The association may be economically motivated. Drug users commit crime in order to pay for their habits. One study conducted in Miami found, that to purchase drugs, 573 narcotics users *annually* committed more than 200,000 crimes, including 6,000 robberies, 6,700 burglaries, and 70,000 larceny offenses; similar research with a sample of 356 addicts accounted for 118,000 crimes annually.[70] If such findings hold true, the nation's estimated half a million heroin addicts may alone be committing more than 100 million crimes each year, and this estimate does not include the criminal activity of cocaine and crack abusers.

Drug users may be more willing to take risks because their inhibitions are lowered by substance abuse. Research indicates that cities with high rates of cocaine abuse are also more likely to experience higher levels of armed robbery; burglary rates are unaffected by cocaine use. It is possible that crack/cocaine users are more willing to engage in a risky armed robbery to get immediate cash than a burglary, which requires more planning and effort.[71]

The Drug–Delinquency Connection   The relationship between drugs and crime is dramatically illustrated by the extent of substance abuse among criminal suspects and those already convicted of crimes. A number of efforts have been made to measure drug use by people immediately arrested for crime. The federal government's *Drug Use Forecasting* (DUF) program tests arrestees in major cities to determine their drug involvement. The results have been startling. In some cities, such as San Diego, New York, and Philadelphia, more than 70 percent of all arrestees, both male and female, test positively for some drug, and this association crosses both gender and racial boundaries.[72]

There is also evidence that incarcerated youth are much more likely to be involved in substance abuse than adolescents in the general population. For example, research by David Cantor on the drug use of incarcerated youth in Washington, D.C., found their drug involvement more than double that of non-incarcerated area youth.[73]

DRUGS AND CHRONIC OFFENDING

It is possible that most delinquents are not actually drug users but that police are just more likely to apprehend muddleheaded substance abusers than clear-thinking abstainers. A second and probably more plausible interpretation of the existing data is that the drug abuse–crime connection is so powerful because many delinquents and criminals are in fact substance abusers. Some recent research by Bruce Johnson and his associates confirms this suspicion. Using data from a nationally drawn self-report survey, these researchers found that fewer than two percent of the youths who responded to the survey (a) report using cocaine or heroin and (b) commit two or more index crimes each year. However, these drug-abusing adolescents accounted for 40 percent to 60 percent of all the index crimes (robbery, theft, drug sales) reported in the sample. Fewer than one-quarter of these hard-core delinquents committed crime solely to support a drug habit. These data suggest that a small core of substance-abusing adolescents commits a significant proportion of all serious crimes. It is also evident that a behavior—drug abuse—that develops in adolescence influences the frequency and extent of delinquent activity through the life course.[74]

The relationship between drug abuse and chronic offending is aptly illustrated by Inciardi, Horowitz, and Pottienger's interviews with crack-involved youth in Miami. The 254 youths in their sample reported committing an astounding 223,439 criminal offenses during the 12 months prior to their interview. It is not surprising, considering that they averaged 879 offenses each, that 87 percent of the sample had been arrested. The greater the involvement in the crack business, the greater the likelihood of committing violent crime. About 74 percent of the hard-core dealers committed robbery, and 17 percent engaged in assault; only 12 percent of the nondealers committed robbery, and only 4 percent engaged in assault.

EXPLAINING DRUG USE AND DELINQUENCY

The general association between delinquency and drug use has been well established in a variety of cultures.[75] It is still far from certain, however, whether (a) drug use *causes* delinquency, (b) delinquent behavior patterns *lead* youths to engage in substance abuse, or (c) both drug abuse and delinquency are *functions* of some other factor that is responsible for both behaviors.[76]

Some of the most sophisticated research on this topic has been conducted by Delbert Elliott and his associates at the Institute of Behavioral Science at the University of Colorado.[77] Using data from the National Youth Survey, a longitudinal study of self-reported delinquency and drug use, Elliott and his colleagues David Huizinga and Scott Menard found a strong association between delinquency and drug use.[78] However, they too found that the direction of the relationship is unclear. As a general rule, drug abuse appears to be a *type* of delinquent behavior and not a *cause* of delinquency. Most youths become involved in delinquent acts before they are initiated into drugs later in their adolescence; it is difficult, therefore, to conclude that drugs cause crime.

According to the Elliott research, both drug use and delinquency seem to reflect a developmental problem. Rather than causing one another, drug use and delinquency seem to be part of a disturbed socialization and lifestyle. The research reveals some important associations between substance abuse and delinquency:

1. Alcohol abuse seems to be a cause of marijuana and drug abuse as (a) most drug users had used alcohol before taking drugs and (b) youths who abstain from alcohol almost never take drugs.
2. Marijuana use is a cause of multiple-drug use: About 95 percent of young people who use more serious drugs, such as crack, started with pot; only 5 percent of serious drug users never smoked pot.
3. Young people who commit felonies started off committing minor delinquent acts. Few (one percent) delinquents report committing felonies only.

The Elliott research has been supported by a number of other studies that also indicate that delinquency and substance abuse are actually part of a general pattern of deviance or problem behavior syndrome. Helene Raskin White, Robert Padina, and Randy LaGrange found that both forms of deviance are related to symptoms of social disturbance, such as association with an antisocial peer group and educational failure.[79] Similar research by Eric Wish also shows a pattern of deviance escalation in which troubled youth start by committing petty crimes and drinking alcohol and then proceed to both harder drugs and more serious crimes. Both their drug abuse and delinquency are part of an urban underclass lifestyle involving limited education, few job and social skills, unstable families, and patterns of law violations.[80]

It is also possible that drug abuse and delinquency have independent causes. White has found that the onset of both delinquency and drug abuse can be traced to the "preferred" deviant behavior of peers: Teenagers whose friends are substance abusers are more likely to abuse substances themselves; adolescents whose peers engage in delinquent behavior are more likely to become delinquents.[81]

By implication, these studies indicate that restricting or reducing substance abuse may have little effect on delinquency rates because drugs are a symptom and not a cause of youthful misbehavior.

DRUG CONTROL STRATEGIES

The United States is in the midst of a well-publicized "war on drugs." Billions are being spent each year to reduce the importation of drugs, deter would-be drug dealers, and treat users. Yet, as most of us know, drug control efforts have been less than successful. Although the overall incidence of drug use has declined, drug use has concentrated in the nation's poorest neighborhoods, with a consequent association between substance abuse and crime.

A number of different drug control strategies have been tried with varying degrees of success. Some are designed to deter drug use by stopping the flow of drugs into the country, apprehending and punishing dealers, and cracking down on street-level drug deals. Another approach is to prevent drug use by educating would-be users and convincing them to "say no to drugs." A third approach is to treat users so they can break free of their addictions. Some of the more important of these efforts are discussed below.

LAW ENFORCEMENT EFFORTS

A variety of law enforcement strategies are aimed both at reducing the supply of drugs and deterring would-be users from drug abuse.

Source Control One approach to drug control is to deter the sale and importation of drugs through the systematic apprehension of large-volume drug dealers, coupled with the enforcement of strict drug laws that carry heavy penalties. This approach is designed to punish known drug dealers and users and deter those who are considering entering into the drug trade.

A major effort has been made to cut off supplies of drugs by destroying overseas crops and arresting members of drug cartels; this approach is known as **source control.** The federal government has been encouraging exporting nations to step up efforts to destroy drug crops and prosecute dealers. Three South American nations—Peru, Bolivia, and Colombia—have agreed to coordinate control efforts with the United States.

However, translating words into deeds is a formidable task. Drug lords are willing and able to fight back through intimidation, violence, and corruption. The United States was forced to invade Panama with 20,000 troops in 1989 to stop its leader, General Manuel Noriega, from trafficking in cocaine.

Adding to control problems is the fact that the drug trade is an important source of revenue for drug-producing countries and destroying it undermines their economy. For example, about 60 percent of the raw coca leaves used to make cocaine for the United States are grown in Peru. The drug trade supports 200,000 Peruvians and brings in more than $3 billion annually. In Bolivia, which supplies 30 percent of the raw cocaine for the U.S. market, 300,000 people are supported with profits from the drug trade; coca is the country's single leading export. About 20 percent of Colombia's overseas exports come from drug cartels, which refine the coca leaves into cocaine before shipping it to the United States.[82] Even if the government of one nation is willing to cooperate in vigorous drug suppression efforts, suppliers in other nations, eager to cash in on the seller's market, would be encouraged to turn more acreage over to coca, poppy, or marijuana production.

Border Control   Law enforcement efforts have also been directed at interdicting drug supplies as they enter the country. Border patrols and military personnel using sophisticated hardware have been involved in massive interdiction efforts; many impressive billion-dollar seizures have been made. It is estimated that between one-quarter and one-third of the annual cocaine supply shipped to the U.S. is seized by drug enforcement agencies. Yet the United States's borders are so vast and unprotected that meaningful interdiction is impossible; between 240 and 340 tons of cocaine and 33 tons of heroin are imported each year with a street value of $38 billion.[83] Even if all importation were ended, homegrown marijuana and lab-made drugs, such as "ice," LSD, and PCP, could become the drugs of choice. Even now, their easy availability and relatively low cost are increasing their popularity among teenagers; they are a $10 billion industry.

Targeting Dealers   Law enforcement agencies have also made a concerted effort to focus on drug trafficking at the national, state, and local levels. Efforts have been made to bust large-scale drug rings. The long-term consequence has been to decentralize drug dealing and encourage teenage gangs to become major suppliers. Ironically, it has proven easier for federal agents to infiltrate and prosecute traditional organized crime groups than to take on drug-dealing youth gangs.

Police can also target, intimidate, and arrest street-level dealers and users in an effort to make drug use so much of a hassle that consumption is cut back and the crime rate reduced. Although some street-level enforcement efforts have had success, others are considered failures. "Drug sweeps" have clogged courts and correctional facilities with petty offenders while proving to be a costly drain on police resources. Such sweeps are also suspected of creating a displacement effect: Stepped-up efforts to curb drug dealing in one area or city may simply encourage dealers to seek out friendlier territory.[84] People arrested, tried, and found guilty of drug-related charges are the fastest growing segment of both the juvenile and adult justice systems. National surveys have found that juvenile court judges are prone to use a "get tough" approach on drug-involved offenders.

They are more likely to be adjudicated, waived to adult court, and receive out-of-home placements than other categories of delinquent offenders, including those who commit violent crimes.[85] Despite these efforts, juvenile drug use continues to grow, indicating that a "get tough" policy is not sufficient to deter or eliminate drug use.

EDUCATION STRATEGIES

Another approach to reducing teenage substance abuse relies on school-based educational programs.

School districts have included drug education programs as a standard part of their curriculum. Drug education now begins in kindergarten and extends through the twelfth grade. More than 80 percent of public school districts do the following within all of their schools: teach students about the causes and effects of alcohol, drug, and tobacco use; teach students to resist peer pressure; and refer students for counseling and treatment outside the educational system.[86] Such educational programs as Project ALERT, based in middle schools in California and Oregon, appear to be successful in training young people to resist recreational drug use and peer pressure to use cigarettes and alcohol.[87]

The most widely known drug education program, **Drug Abuse Resistance Education (DARE),** is an elementary school course designed to give students the skills to resist peer pressure to experiment with tobacco, drugs, and alcohol. It is unique because it employs uniformed police officers to carry the anti-drug message to the students before they enter junior high school. The program focuses on five major areas:

1. Providing accurate information about tobacco, alcohol, and drugs
2. Teaching students techniques to resist peer pressure
3. Teaching students respect for the law and law enforcers
4. Giving students alternatives to drug use
5. Building the self-esteem of students

School districts have included drug education programs as a standard part of their curriculum. Drug education now begins in kindergarten and extends through the twelfth grade. The Students Against Drunk Driving (SADD) program is a national organization dedicated to educating adolescents about the dangers of alcohol use while operating a motor vehicle.

DARE is based on the concept that young people need specific analytical and social skills to resist peer pressure and to say no to drugs. Instructors work with youths to raise their self-esteem, provide them with decision-making tools, and help them identify positive alternatives to substance abuse. Millions of students have already completed the DARE program.[88] More than 40 percent of all school districts incorporate assistance from local law enforcement agencies in their drug-prevention programming.[89] New community policing strategies commonly incorporate the DARE program within their efforts to provide services to local neighborhoods at the grassroots level.[90]

Although DARE is quite popular with both schools and police agencies, a highly sophisticated evaluation of the program by Dennis Rosenbaum and his associates found that it had only a marginal impact on student drug use and attitudes and little overall effect on substance abuse rates.[91] DARE may, however, work better in some settings and with some groups than others.

COMMUNITY STRATEGIES

Another type of drug-control effort relies on the involvement of local community groups. Representatives of various local government agencies, churches, civic organizations, and similar institutions are being brought together to create drug-prevention awareness programs. Their activities often include the creation of drug-free school zones (which encourage police to keep drug dealers away from the areas near schools); Neighborhood Watch Programs, which are geared to spotting and reporting drug dealers; citizen patrols, which frighten dealers away from children in public housing projects; and community centers, which provide an alternative to the street culture.

Community-based programs reach out to high-risk youths, involving them in after-school programs; offering family and individual counseling sessions; delivering clothing, food, and medical care when needed; and encouraging school achievement through tutoring and other services. Community programs also sponsor drug-free activities involving the arts, clubs, and athletics. Evaluations of community programs have shown that they may encourage anti-drug attitudes and help insulate participating youth from an environment that encourages drugs.[92]

TREATMENT STRATEGIES

Several approaches are used to treat known users. Some efforts stem from the perspective that users have low self-esteem; these use various techniques to build up the user's sense of himself or herself. Some make use of traditional psychological counseling while others, such as **multisystemic treatment** (MST) technique, developed by psychologist Scott Henggeler, direct attention to a variety of family, peer, and psychological problems by focusing on problem solving and communication skills.[93] Henggeler has found that adolescent abusers who have gone through MST programs are significantly less likely to recidivate than youths in traditional counseling services.[94]

Another approach has been to involve users in outdoor activities, wilderness training, and after-school community programs.[95]

More intensive efforts use group therapy approaches in which leaders, many of whom have been substance abusers themselves, try to give users the skills and support that can help them reject the social pressure to use drugs. These programs are based on the Alcoholics Anonymous philosophy that users must find within themselves the strength to stay clean and that peer support from those who understand their experiences can be a successful means of achieving a drug-free life.

Residential programs are used with the more heavily involved, and a large network of drug treatment units geared to juveniles has developed. Some are detoxification units that use medical procedures to wean patients from the more addicting drugs. Others are therapeutic communities that attempt to deal with the psychological causes of drug use. Hypnosis, aversion therapy (getting users to associate drugs with unpleasant sensations, such as nausea), counseling, biofeedback, and other techniques are often used.

Little evidence exists that these residential programs, despite their good intentions, can efficiently terminate teenage substance abuse. Many are restricted to families whose health insurance will pay for short-term residential care; when the insurance coverage ends, the teenagers are released, even though their treatment program is not completed. Adolescents do not often enter these programs voluntarily and have little motivation to change.[96] A stay can help stigmatize residents as "druggies" and "addicts" even though they never used hard drugs; while in treatment, they may be introduced to hard-core users with whom they will associate upon release. Evaluations of residential programs show that although abuse is sometimes curtailed during the residential phase of treatment, it resumes once residence terminates and the offender is returned to the community. Even programs that feature intensive aftercare treatment show little evidence of a reversal in substance abuse.[97]

WHAT DOES THE FUTURE HOLD?

The United States appears willing to go to great lengths to fight the drug war. Law enforcement efforts, along with the institution of prevention programs and drug treatment projects, have been stepped up. Yet all drug control strategies are

Opponents of drug legalization argue that it may increase the number of drug exposed children. Here the program director at Hale House, a New York program which cares for children who were born drug exposed, shares a moment with one of her "babies." With proper treatment, drug-exposed babies may be able to eventually be returned to live with their mothers or an extended family member.

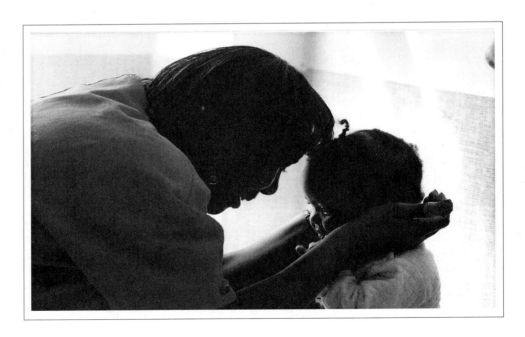

doomed to fail as long as youths want to take drugs and dealers are able to make drug sales a lucrative source of income. Prevention, deterrence, and treatment strategies ignore the core reasons for the drug problem: poverty, hopelessness, boredom, alienation, and family disruption. As the gap between rich and poor widens and the opportunities for legitimate advancement decrease, it should come as no surprise that adolescent drug use continues. It is a sad fact that a smaller percentage of the poor and minority-group members are attending college today than were 10 years ago. The social failures of American society are being translated into teenage substance abuse.

Some commentators have called for the **legalization** of drugs. Although this approach can have the short-term effect of reducing the association between drug use and crime (because, presumably, the cost of drugs would decrease), it may also have grave social consequences. Drug use would most certainly increase, creating an overflow of unproductive, drug-dependent people who must be cared for by the rest of society. The problems of teenage alcoholism should serve as a warning of what can happen when controlled substances are made readily available. However, the implications of drug decriminalization should be further studied: What effect would a policy of partial decriminalization (e.g., legalizing small amounts of marijuana) have on drug use rates? Does a "get tough" policy on drugs help to "widen the net"? Are there alternatives to the criminalization of drugs that could help reduce their use?[98] The Rand Corporation study of drug dealing in Washington, D.C., suggests that law enforcement efforts can have little influence on drug abuse rates as long as dealers can earn more than the minimal salaries they might earn in the legitimate world. Only by improving job prospects and giving young people legitimate future alternatives can hard-core users be made to desist and willingly forgo drug use.[99]

CASE IN POINT

The president has appointed you as the new "Drug Czar" to lead the fight against drugs.

You have $10 billion with which to wage a campaign against drugs. You know that drug use is unacceptably high, especially among poor, inner-city youths; that a great deal of all criminal behavior is drug-related; and that drug-dealing gangs are expanding around the United States.

At an open hearing, drug-control experts express their policy strategies. One group favors putting the money into hiring more law enforcement agents to patrol borders, target large dealers, and make drug raids in the U.S. and abroad. This group calls for such "get tough" measures as the creation of strict drug laws, the mandatory waiver of young drug dealers to the adult court system, and the death penalty for drug-related gang killings.

A second group believes that the best way to deal with drugs is to spend the money on community treatment programs, expand the number of beds in drug detoxification units, and fund research on how to clinically reduce drug dependency.

A third group argues that neither punishment nor treatment can restrict teenage drug use and that the best course is to educate at-risk youths about the dangers of substance abuse and then legalize all drugs but control their distribution. This course of action will help both to reduce crime and violence among drug users and to balance the national debt, as drugs could be heavily taxed.

Should drugs be legalized?

Can law enforcement strategies reduce drug consumption?

Is treatment an effective drug-control technique?

SUMMARY

Drug abuse has been closely linked to juvenile delinquency. Among the most popular drugs are marijuana; cocaine and its derivative, crack; "ice"; LSD; and PCP. However, the most commonly used drug is alcohol, which contributes to almost 100,000 deaths per year.

Self-report surveys indicate that, after years of decline, more teenagers are using drugs today than earlier in the decade. In addition, surveys of arrestees indicate that a significant proportion are current drug users and that many are high school dropouts. The number of drug users may be even higher because surveys of teen abusers may be missing the most delinquent and drug-abusing youths.

A variety of young people use drugs. Some are occasional users who might sell to friends. Others are seriously involved in both drug abuse and delinquency; many of these are gang members. There are also "losers" who filter in and out of the juvenile justice system. A small percentage of teenage users remain involved with drugs into adulthood.

Despite years of research, it is not certain whether drug abuse causes delinquency or delinquency causes drug abuse. Some experts believe that there is a "common cause" for both delinquency and drug abuse, such as alienation, anger, and rage.

Many efforts have been made to control the drug trade. Some attempt to inhibit the importation of drugs from overseas, others are aimed at closing down major drug rings, and a few try to stop street-level dealing. There have also been attempts to treat known users through rehabilitation programs and to reduce juvenile drug use by education efforts. Communities beset by drug problems have mounted grassroots drives to reduce the incidence of drug abuse. So far, these efforts have not been totally successful, and the teenage substance abuse has begun to increase.

KEY TERMS

substance abuse	alcohol	steroids
hashish	anesthetic drugs	addiction-prone personality
marijuana	inhalants	source control
cocaine	sedatives	Drug Abuse Resistance Education (DARE)
freebase	tranquilizers	multisystemic treatment
crack	hallucinogens	legalization
heroin	stimulants	

QUESTIONS FOR DISCUSSION

1. Discuss the differences between the various categories and types of substances of abuse. Is the term *drugs* too broad to have real meaning?
2. Why do you think young people take drugs? Do you know anyone with an addiction-prone personality?
3. What policy might be best used to reduce teenage drug use: Source control? Reliance on treatment? National education efforts? Community-level enforcement?
4. Under what circumstances, if any, might the legalization or decriminalization of drugs be beneficial to society?
5. Do you consider alcohol a drug? Should greater control be placed on the sale of alcohol?
6. Do TV shows and films glorify drug usage and encourage youths to enter the drug trade? Should all images of drinking and smoking be banned from TV? What about advertisements that try to convince young people how much fun it is to drink beer or smoke cigarettes?
7. Why do you think teenage drug use is on the rise? Does the fluctuation of substance abuse rates indicate that social and genetic or personality factors control drug use rates?

NOTES

1. University of Michigan, Institute for Social Research News Release, December 11, 1995.

2. Peter Greenwood, "Substance Abuse Problems among High-Risk Youth and Potential Interventions," *Crime and Delinquency* 38: 444–58 (1992).

3. U.S. Department of Justice, *Drugs and Crime Facts, 1988* (Washington, D.C.: Bureau of Justice Statistics, 1989), pp. 3–4.

4. Thomas Feucht, Richard Stephens, and Michale Walker, "Drug Use among Juvenile Arrestees: A Comparison of Self-Report, Urinalysis and Hair Assay," *Journal of Drug Issues* 24:99–116 (1994).

5. Mary Ellen Macksey-Amiti and Michael Fendrich, "Delinquent Behavior and Inhalant Use among High School Students," Paper presented at the American Society of Criminology meeting, Boston, Mass., November 1995.

6. Dennis Coon, *Introduction to Psychology* (St. Paul, Minn.: West, 1992), p. 178.

7. University of Michigan, Institute for Social Research News Release, pp. 1–3.

8. Special Issue, "Drugs—The American Family in Crisis," *Juvenile and Family Court* 39:45–46 (1988).

9. Federal Bureau of Investigation, *Crime in the United States, 1994* (Washington, D.C.: U.S. Government Printing Office, 1995), p. 221.

10. Robyn Cohen, *Drunk Driving* (Washington, D.C.: Bureau of Justice Statistics, 1992), p. 2.

11. D. J. Rohsenow, "Drinking Habits and Expectancies about Alcohol's Effects for Self versus Others," *Journal of Consulting and Clinical Psychology* 51:752–56 (1983).

12. Spencer Rathus, *Psychology,* 4th ed. (New York: Holt, Rinehart & Winston, 1990), p. 161.

13. William Castelli, cited in G. Kolata, "Study Backs Heart Benefits in Light Drinking," *New York Times,* 3 August 1988, p. A24.

14. Mary Tabor, " 'Ice' in an Island Paradise," *Boston Globe,* 8 December 1989, p. 3.

15. Paul Goldstein, "Anabolic Steroids: An Ethnographic Approach" (Unpublished, Narcotics and Drug Research, Inc., March 1989).

16. Bureau of Justice Assistance, *FY 1988 Report on Drug Control* (Washington, D.C.: U.S. Government Printing Office, 1989).

17. Matt Lait, "California's New Role: Leading PCP Supplier," *Washington Post,* 17 April 1989, p. 1.

18. Ibid., p. 10.

19. Robert Brooner, Donald Templer, Dace Svikis, Chester Schmidt, and Spyros Monopolis, "Dimensions of Alcoholism: A Multivariate Analysis," *Journal of Studies on Alcohol* 51:77–81 (1990).

20. ISR data here are from the press release dated December 11, 1995, University of Michigan News and Information Services, Ann Arbor, Mich.

21. Data in this section come from Department of Health and Human Services, *The Household Survey on Drug Abuse, 1991* (Washington, D.C.: Department of Health and Human Services, 1992).

22. PRIDE, Inc. "Teen Drug Use Rises for Fourth Straight Year," Pride, Inc., Atlanta, Ga., November 2, 1995.

23. Ibid., pp. 6–7.

24. Joyce Ann O'Neil and Eric Wish, *Drug Use Forecasting, Cocaine Use* (Washington, D.C.: U.S. Government Printing Office, 1989), p. 7.

25. Eric Wish, "U.S. Drug Policy in the 1990's: Insights from New Data from Arrestees," *International Journal of the Addictions* 25:1–15 (1990).

26. G. E. Vallant, "Parent–Child Disparity and Drug Addiction," *Journal of Nervous and Mental Disease* 142:534–39 (1966).

27. Charles Winick, "Epidemiology of Narcotics Use," in D. Wilner and G. Kassenbaum, eds., *Narcotics* (New York: McGraw-Hill, 1965), pp. 3–18.

28. Delbert Elliott, David Huizinga, and Scott Menard, *Multiple Problem Youth: Delinquency, Substance Abuse and Mental Health Problems* (New York: Springer-Verlag, 1989).

29. Peter Reuter, Robert MacCoun, and Patrick Murphy, *Money from Crime: A Study of the Economics of Drug Dealing in Washington, D.C.* (Santa Monica, Calif.: Rand, 1990).

30. Thomas Dishion, Deborah Capaldi, Kathleen Spracklen, and Fuzhong Li, "Peer Ecology of Male Adolescent Drug Use," *Development and Psychopathology* 7:803–24 (1995).

31. C. Bowden, "Determinants of Initial Use of Opioids," *Comprehensive Psychiatry* 12:136–40 (1971).

32. Terence Thornberry, Margaret Farnworth, Marvin Krohn, and Alan Lizotte, *Peer Influence and the Initiation to Drug Use* (Albany, N.Y.: Hindelang Criminal Justice Research Center, n.d.).

33. Helene Raskin White, "Marijuana Use and Delinquency: A Test of the 'Independent Cause' Hypothesis," *Journal of Drug Issues* 21:231–56 (1991).

34. R. Cloward and L. Ohlin, *Delinquency and Opportunity: A Theory of Delinquent Gangs* (Glencoe, Ill.: Free Press, 1960).

35. Denise Kandel and Mark Davies, "Friendship Networks, Intimacy and Illicit Drug Use in Young Adulthood: A Comparison of Two Competing Theories," *Criminology* 29:441–71 (1991).

36. James Inciardi, Ruth Horowitz, and Anne Pottieger, *Street Kids, Street Drugs, Street Crime: An Examination*

of Drug Use and Serious Delinquency in Miami (Belmont, Calif: Wadsworth, 1993), p. 43.

37. D. Baer and J. Corrado, "Heroin Addict Relationships with Parents during Childhood and Early Adolescent Years," *Journal of Genetic Psychology* 124:99–103 (1974).

38. Timothy Ireland and Cathy Spatz Widom, *Childhood Victimization and Risk for Alcohol and Drug Arrests* (Washington, D.C.: National Institute of Justice, 1995).

39. S. F. Bucky, "The Relationship between Background and Extent of Heroin Use," *American Journal of Psychiatry* 130:709–10 (1973); I. Chien, D. L. Gerard, R. Lee, and E. Rosenfield, *The Road to H: Narcotics Delinquency and Social Policy* (New York: Basic Books, 1964).

40. J. S. Mio, G. Nanjundappa, D. E. Verlur, and M. D. De-Rios, "Drug Abuse and the Adolescent Sex Offender: A Preliminary Analysis," *Journal of Psychoactive Drugs* 18:65–72 (1986).

41. G. T. Wilson, "Cognitive Studies in Alcoholism," *Journal of Consulting and Clinical Psychology* 55:325–31 (1987).

42. Inciardi, Horowitz, and Pottieger, *Street Kids, Street Drugs, Street Crime,* p. 135.

43. Ibid., p. 136.

44. For a thorough review, see Karol Kumpfer, "Impact of Maternal Characteristics and Parenting Processes on Children of Drug Abusers," Paper presented at the American Society of Criminology meeting, Boston, Mass., November 1995; see also Judith Brook and Li-Jung Tseng, "Influences of Parental Drug Uses, Personality, and Child Rearing on the The Toddler's Anger and Negativity, *Genetic, Social and General Psychology Monographs* 122:107–128 (1996).

45. D. W. Goodwin, "Alcoholism and Genetics," *Archives of General Psychiatry* 42:171–74 (1985).

46. Ibid.

47. Patricia Dobkin, Richard Tremblay, Louise Masse, and Frank Vitaro, "Individual and Peer Characteristics in Predicting Boys' Early Onset of Substance Abuse: A Seven-Year Longitudinal Study," *Child Development* 66:1198–1214 (1995).

48. Ric Steele, Rex Forehand, Lisa Armistead, and Gene Brody, "Predicting Alcohol and Drug Use in Early Adulthood: The Role of Internalizing and Externalizing Behavior Problems in Early Adolescence," *American Journal of Orthopsychiatry* 65:380–87 (1995).

49. Ibid., p. 380–81.

50. Jerome Platt and Christina Platt, *Heroin Addiction* (New York: Wiley, 1976), p. 127.

51. Rathus, *Psychology,* p. 158.

52. Eric Strain, "Antisocial Personality Disorder, Misbehavior and Drug Abuse," *Journal of Nervous and Mental Disease* 163:162–65 (1995).

53. Patricia Dobkin, Richard Tremblay, Louise Masse, and Frank Vitaro, "Individual and Peer Characteristics in Predicting Boys' Early Onset of Substance Abuse: A Seven-Year Longitudinal Study," *Child Development* 66:1198–1214 (1995).

54. Judith Brook, Martin Whiteman, and Patricia Cohen, "Stage of Drug Use, Aggression and Theft/Vandalism," in Howard Kaplan, ed. *Drugs, Crime and Other Deviant Adaptations* (New York: Plenum Press, 1995) pp. 83–96); J. Shedler and J. Block, "Adolescent Drug Use and Psychological Health: A Longitudinal Inquiry," *American Psychologist* 45:612–30 (1990).

55. Greenwood, "Substance Abuse Problems among High-Risk Youth and Potential Interventions," p. 448.

56. John Wallace and Jerald Bachman, "Explaining Racial/Ethnic Differences in Adolescent Drug Use: The Impact of Background and Lifestyle," *Social Problems* 38:333–57 (1991).

57. Marvin Krohn, Terence Thornberry, Lori Collins-Hall, and Alan Lizotte, "School Dropout, Delinquent Behavior, and Drug Use," in Howard Kaplan, ed., *Drugs, Crime and other Deviant Adaptations: Longitudinal Studies* (New York: Plenum Press, 1995), pp. 163–83.

58. B. A. Christiansen, G. T. Smith, P. V. Roehling, and M. S. Goldman, "Using Alcohol Expectancies to Predict Adolescent Drinking Behavior after One Year," *Journal of Counseling and Clinical Psychology* 57:93–99 (1989).

59. The following sections lean heavily on Marcia Chaiken and Bruce Johnson, *Characteristics of Different Types of Drug-Involved Youth* (Washington, D.C.: National Institute of Justice, 1988).

60. Inciardi, Horowitz, and Pottieger, *Street Kids, Street Drugs, Street Crime,* p. 100.

61. Ibid., p. 100.

62. Ibid., p. 101.

63. Robert MacCoun and Peter Reuter, "Are the Wages of Sin $30 an Hour? Economic Aspects of Street-Level Drug Dealing," *Crime and Delinquency* 38:477–91 (1992).

64. Chaiken and Johnson, *Characteristics of Different Types of Drug-Involved Youth,* p. 12.

65. Rick Graves and Ed Allen, *Narcotics and Black Gangs* (Los Angeles: Los Angeles County Sheriff's Department, n.d.)

66. John Hagedorn, "Neighborhoods, Markets, and Gang Drug Organization," *Journal of Research in Crime and Delinquency* 31:264–94 (1994).

67. Ibid., p. 13.

68. Chaiken and Johnson, *Characteristics of Different Types of Drug-Involved Youth,* p. 14.

69. Bureau of Justice Assistance, *FY 1988 Report on Drug Control,* p. 19.

70. James Inciardi, "Heroin Use and Street Crime," *Crime and Delinquency* 25:335–46 (1979); idem, *The War on Drugs* (Palo Alto, Calif.: Mayfield, 1986). W. McGlothlin, M. Anglin, and B. Wilson, "Narcotic Addiction and Crime," *Criminology* 16:293–311 (1978); George Speckart and M. Douglas Anglin, "Narcotics Use and Crime: An Over-

view of Recent Research Advances," *Contemporary Drug Problems,* 13:741–69 (1986); Charles Faupel and Carl Klockars, "Drugs-Crime Connections: Elaborations from the Life Histories of Hard-Core Heroin Addicts," *Social Problems* 34:54–68 (1987).

71. Eric Baumer, "Poverty, Crack and Crime: A Cross-City Analysis," *Journal of Research in Crime and Delinquency* 31:311–27 (1994).

72. National Institute of Justice, *Drug Use Forecasting, 1991 Annual Report* (Washington, D.C.: National Institute of Justice, 1992).

73. David Cantor, "Drug Involvement and Offending of Incarcerated Youth," Paper presented at the American Society of Criminology meeting, Boston, Mass., November 1995.

74. B. D. Hohnson, E. Wish, J. Schmeidler, and D. Huizinga, "Concentration of Delinquent Offending: Serious Drug Involvement and High Delinquency Rates," *Journal of Drug Issues* 21:205–29 (1991).

75. W. David Watts and Lloyd Wright, "The Relationship of Alcohol, Tobacco, Marijuana, and Other Illegal Drug Use to Delinquency among Mexican-American, Black, and White Adolescent Males," *Adolescence* 25:38–54 (1990).

76. For a general review of this issue, see Helene Raskin White, "The Drug Use–Delinquency Connection in Adolescence," in Ralph Weisheit, ed., *Drugs, Crime and Criminal Justice* (Cincinnati, Ohio: Anderson, 1990), pp. 215–56; Speckart and Anglin, "Narcotics Use and Crime"; Faupel and Klockars, "Drugs–Crime Connections."

77. Delbert Elliott, David Huizinga, and Susan Ageton, *Explaining Delinquency and Drug Abuse* (Beverly Hills, Calif.: Sage, 1985).

78. David Huizinga, Scott Menard, and Delbert Elliott, "Delinquency and Drug Use: Temporal and Developmental Patterns," *Justice Quarterly* 6:419–55 (1989).

79. Helene Raskin White, Robert Padina, and Randy LaGrange, "Longitudinal Predictors of Serious Substance Use and Delinquency," *Criminology* 25:715–40 (1987).

80. Wish, "U.S. Drug Policy in the 1990's."

81. White, "Marijuana Use and Delinquency."

82. Drug Enforcement Administration, *National Drug Control Strategy* (Washington, D.C.: U.S. Government Printing Office, 1989).

83. William Rhodes et. al. *What America's Users Spend on Illegal Drugs, 1988–1993* (Cambridge, Mass.: Abt Associates, 1995).

84. Mark Moore, *Drug Trafficking* (Washington, D.C.: National Institute of Justice, 1988).

85. Jeffrey Butts and Melissa Sickmund, *Offenders in Juvenile Court, 1989* (Washington, D.C.: Office of Juvenile Justice and Delinquency Prevention, 1992), p. 1.

86. Ibid.

87. Phyllis Ellickson and Robert Bell, *Prospects for Preventing Drug Use among Young Adolescents* (Santa Monica, Calif.: Rand Corp., 1990).

88. Ibid.

89. Judi Carpenter, *Public School District Survey on Safe, Disciplined and Drug-Free Schools* (Washington, D.C.: U.S. Government Printing Office, 1992), p. 111.

90. David Carter, *Community Policing and D.A.R.E.: A Practitioners Perspective* (Washington, D.C.: Bureau of Justice Assistance, 1995), p. 2.

91. Dennis Rosenbaum, Robert Flwewlling, Susan Bailey, Chris Ringwalt, and Deanna Wilkinson, "Cops in the Classroom: A Longitudinal Evaluation of Drug Abuse Resistance Education (DARE)," *Journal of Research in Crime and Delinquency* 31:3–31 (1994).

92. Wayne Lucan and Steven Gilham, "Impact of a Drug Use Prevention Program: An Empirical Assessment," (Paper presented at the annual meeting of the American Society of Criminology, New Orleans, La., November 1992).

93. Scott Henggeler, *Delinquency and Adolescent Psychopathology: A Family-Ecological Systems Approach* (Littleton, Mass.: Wright-PSG, 1982).

94. Scott Henggeler, "Effects of Multisystemic Therapy on Drug Use and Abuse in Serious Juvenile Offenders: A Progress Report from Two Outcome Studies," *Family Dynamics of Addiction Quarterly* 1:40–51 (1991).

95. Eli Ginzberg, Howard Berliner, and Miriam Ostrow, *Young People at Risk: Is Prevention Possible?* (Boulder, Colo.: Westview Press, 1988), p. 99.

96. Ibid.

97. Miriam Sealock, Denise Gottfredson, and Catherine Gallagher, "Addressing Drug Use and Recidivism in Delinquent Youth: An Examination of Residential and Aftercare Treatment Programs," Paper presented at the American Society of Criminology meeting, Boston, Mass., November 1995.

98. Kathryn Ann Farr, "Revitalizing the Drug Decriminalization Debate," *Crime and Delinquency* 36:223–37 (1990).

99. Reuter, MacCoun, and Murphy, *Money from Crime,* pp. 165–68.

Juvenile Justice Advocacy

Part IV provides a general overview of the juvenile justice system, including its process, history, and legal rules.

Since 1900, juveniles who violate the law have been treated differently from adults. A separate juvenile justice system has been developed that features its own judiciary, rules, and processes.

The separation of juvenile and adult offenders reflects society's concern for the plight of children. Since many experts believe children can be reformed or rehabilitated, it makes sense to treat their law violations more leniently than those of adults. Care, protection, and treatment are the bywords of the juvenile justice system. Of course, to some influential critics, the serious juvenile offender is not deserving of this approach. Consequently, efforts have been made recently to "toughen up" the juvenile system and treat some delinquents much more like adult offenders.

Chapter 12 reviews the history and development of juvenile justice. Emphasis is placed on developments throughout the Nineteenth Century which lead to the establishment of the modern juvenile court system. Chapter 12 also provides an overview of the juvenile justice system and describes its major components, processes, goals, and institutions. It describes the organization of juvenile court, the legal rights of minors and the role of the U.S. Supreme Court in juvenile justice.

Throughout this part, it is stressed that while juveniles are supposed to be treated separately from adults, this division is often blurred by the need to both maintain public order and protect juveniles from the people allegedly trying to help them. The rhetoric of juvenile justice and its reality are often at odds. Today, the emphasis of the juvenile justice system has shifted to controlling violent chronically delinquent youth.

CHAPTER TWELVE

THE HISTORY AND DEVELOPMENT OF JUVENILE JUSTICE

INTRODUCTION

This chapter reviews the history and development of **juvenile justice.** What historical developments led to the first modern juvenile court in Chicago in 1899? What were the origins of the social welfare movement, the state's role in the care and custody of children and the segregation of delinquent children from adult criminal offenders? Efforts to reevaluate the motives of the child savers and other reformists who desired to control the lives of needy children are examined.

This chapter also presents an overview of what juvenile justice means, how it originated, and the various philosophies, processes, organizations, and legal constraints that dominate its operations. The process that takes a youthful offender through a series of steps beginning with arrest and concluding with reentry into society is examined. What happens to young people who violate the law? Do they have legal rights? How are they helped? How are they punished? The answers to these questions explain why the juvenile system exists in its current form.

Included in this chapter is a discussion of the similarities and differences between the adult and juvenile justice systems. The purpose of this discussion is to draw attention to the important principle that children are treated separately in our society. By establishing legislation to segregate delinquent children from adult offenders, society has placed greater importance on the delinquent as a "child" than as a "criminal." Consequently, rehabilitation rather than punishment has traditionally been the goal. Today, with children committing more serious and violent crimes, the juvenile justice system is having greater difficulties finding solutions to handling these offenders.

Today, no single ideology or program dominates the juvenile justice system.[1] A plethora of new and traditional philosophies and models of juvenile justice exist. Are the time-honored considerations related to **parens patriae** and "the best interest of the child" still in place? What is the "justice" model? Are we criminalizing the juvenile justice system?[2]

This chapter's final section reviews the role of the U.S. Supreme Court and federal government in the juvenile justice system. For the first 60 years of the juvenile court's existence, legal rules and procedures were usually nonexistent; the court's operations stressed social service functions. Hearings were informal, there were no attorneys, and the proceedings resembled activities of a social agency as much as a court of law. In the 1960s and 1970s, these procedures changed radically, however, when a series of U.S. Supreme Court decisions brought the juvenile justice system within the scope of the Constitution and fundamentally and permanently changed the face of the nation's juvenile courts.[3] This chapter explains how these decisions have influenced the day-to-day operations of the juvenile justice system, blending social history and the law to present an all-encompassing portrait of the juvenile justice system. Lastly, it deals with the role of the federal government in juvenile justice reform—the key element in funding state juvenile justice and delinquency prevention.

THE DEVELOPMENT OF JUVENILE JUSTICE IN THE NINETEENTH CENTURY

At the start of the nineteenth century, delinquent, neglected, dependent, and runaway children in the United States were treated the same as adult criminal offenders.[4] Like children in England, they were often charged and convicted of crimes, including capital offenses, and received harsh sentences similar to those imposed on adults. The adult criminal code applied to children, and no juvenile court existed.

Throughout the early nineteenth century, various pieces of legislation were introduced to humanize criminal procedures for children. The concept of probation, introduced in Massachusetts in 1841, was geared toward helping young people avoid the trauma of imprisonment.[5] The many books and reports written during this time made the subject of juvenile child care one of intense public interest.

Despite this interest, no special facilities existed for the care of youths in trouble with the law, nor were there separate laws or courts to control their behavior. Youths who committed petty crimes, such as stealing, gambling, or vandalism, were viewed as wayward children or victims of neglect and were placed in community asylums or homes. Youths who were involved in serious crimes were subject to the same punishments as adults—imprisonment, whipping, or death.

Several events led to reforms in the field of child care and nourished the eventual development of the U.S. juvenile justice system: urbanization, the child-saving movement, growing interest in the concept of *parens patriae,* the reform school movement, and the development of Society for the Prevention of Cruelty to Children.

URBANIZATION

Especially during the first half of the nineteenth century, the United States experienced rapid population growth, primarily because of an increase in the birthrate and expanding European immigration. Members of the rural poor and immigrant groups settled in developing urban commercial centers that promised the opportunity for manufacturing jobs. In 1790, 5 percent of the population lived in cities, while 95 percent lived in rural areas. By 1850, the share of the urban population had increased to 15 percent; it jumped to 40 percent in 1900 and 51 percent in 1920.[6] New York almost quadrupled its population in the 30-year stretch between 1825 and 1855: from 166,000 in 1825 to 630,000 in 1855.[7]

Growing urbanization marked the nation's development. The numbers of young people at risk who flooded the cities overwhelmed the existing system of work and training. To accommodate groups of dependent and destitute youths, local jurisdictions developed poorhouses (or almshouses) and workhouses. In these crowded, unhealthy conditions were housed the poor, the insane, the diseased, and vagrant and destitute children.

By the late eighteenth century, many began to question the family's ability to exert social control over their children. Villages developed into urban commercial centers and work began to center around factories, not the home. The children of destitute families left home or were cast loose to make out as best they could; wealthy families could no longer absorb vagrant youth as apprentices or servants.[8] Chronic poverty became an American dilemma, spurring the federal census department to create a new category of underclass citizens labeled "paupers." The affluent began to voice concern over the increase in the number of people in what they considered to be the **dangerous classes.**

Increased urbanization and industrialization also generated the belief that certain segments of the population, namely youths in urban areas and immigrants, were susceptible to the influences of their decayed environment. The belief was held by many that environment, not innate immorality or physical degeneracy, influenced criminal deviance and immorality. The children of these classes were considered a group that might be "saved" by a combination of state and community intervention.[9] Intervention into the lives of these potentially "dangerous classes" to help alleviate their burdens became acceptable for wealthy, civic-minded citizens. Such efforts included shelter care for youths, educational and social activities, and settlement houses.

THE CHILD-SAVING MOVEMENT

The problems generated by large-scale urban growth sparked tremendous interest in the situations of the "new" Americans whose arrival fueled this expansion. In 1817, prominent New Yorkers formed the Society for the Prevention of Pauperism, perhaps the first organized group to focus on the needs of the underclass. Although they concerned themselves with attacking taverns, brothels, and gambling parlors, they also were concerned that the moral training of children of the dangerous classes was falling short of conventional standards. Soon other groups concerned with the general welfare began to form in major urban areas. Their main focus was on extending government control over a whole range of youthful activities that had previously been left to private or family control, including idleness, drinking, vagrancy, and delinquency.

These activists became known as **child savers.** Prominent among them were penologist Enoch Wines; Judge Richard Tuthill; Lucy Flowers, of the Chicago Women's Association; Sara Cooper, of the National Conference of Charities and Corrections; and Sophia Minton, of the New York Committee on Children.[10] They believed that because poor children could become a financial and social burden, they presented a threat to the moral fabric of American society and should be controlled because their behavior could lead to the destruction of the nation's economic system.

Child-saving organizations influenced state legislatures to enact laws giving courts the power to commit children who were runaways, criminal offenders, or out of the control of parents to specialized institutions. The most prominent of the care facilities developed by child savers was the **House of Refuge** in New York, opened in 1825.[11] It was founded on the concept of protecting potential criminal youths by taking them off the streets and reforming them in a family-like environment.

When the House of Refuge opened, the majority of children admitted were status offenders placed there because of vagrancy or neglect. However, the institution was run more like a prison, with work and study schedules, strict discipline, and absolute separation of the sexes. Such a harsh program drove many children to run away, with the result that the House of Refuge was forced to take a more lenient approach. Children were placed in the institution by court order, sometimes over parents' objections. Their length of stay depended on need, age, and skill. Once there, youths were required to do piecework provided by local manufacturers or to work part of the day in the community.

Despite criticism of the program, the concept enjoyed expanding popularity. In 1826, the Boston City Council founded the House of Reformation for juvenile offenders. Similar institutions were opened in Massachusetts and New York in 1847.[12] To these schools, which were both privately and publicly supported, the courts committed children found guilty of criminal violations, as well as those

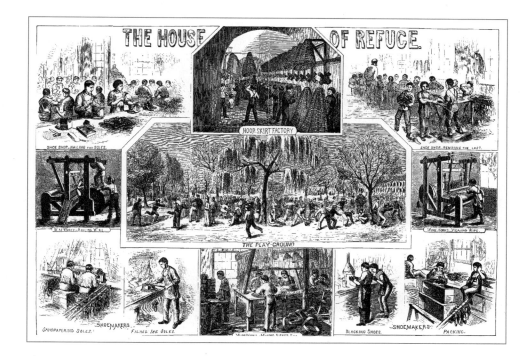

The House of Refuge was one of the earliest juvenile institutions in the United States to offer residents vocational training.

found to be beyond the control of their parents. Because the child savers considered parents of delinquent children to be as guilty as convicted offenders, they sought to have the reform schools establish control over the children. As Robert Mennel states, "By training destitute and delinquent children, and by separating them from their natural parents and adult criminals, refuge managers believed they were preventing poverty and crime."[13]

PARENS PATRIAE AND ITS LEGAL CHALLENGES

The philosophy of *parens patriae* was extended to refuge programs, which were given parental control over a committed child. Robert Mennel summarizes this attitude:

> The doctrine of parens patriae gave refuge managers the best of two worlds, familial and legal: it separated delinquent children from their natural parents and it circumvented the rigor of criminal law by allowing courts to commit children, under loosely worded statutes, to specially created schools instead of jails.[14]

In the course of turning over a child to a refuge, procedures of criminal law did not apply. But this process of institutional control over children in the name of the state and family did not proceed without some significant legal challenges (see Table 12.1). Two of the more critical cases are described below.

EX PARTE CROUSE

In 1838, a man attempted to free his daughter from the Philadelphia House of Refuge, which claimed the right of parental control over her because of unmanageable behavior. The father argued that her commitment without a trial by jury was unconstitutional. In its decision in the case, **Ex Parte Crouse,** the Pennsylvania Supreme Court held that the House of Refuge was specifically planned to reform, restrain, and protect children from depraved parents or their environment.[15]

TABLE 12.1 Notable Early Legal Decisions in Juvenile Justice

Case	Holding
Wellesley v. Wellesley (1827)	In this English case, the children of a duke were removed from his custody by the chancery court in the name of *parens patriae* because of his poor behavior.
Ex Parte Crouse (1838)	In a case involving the commitment of a girl to an institution without a trial, the Pennsylvania Supreme Court held that a child did not require the protection of due process of law and that the House of Refuge could supersede the authority of the parent.
O'Connell v. Turner (1870)	The Illinois Supreme Court declared that a child's vagrancy sentence to a reform school was unconstitutional—the *opposite* result achieved in *Ex Parte Crouse:* The state did not have the authority under *parens patriae* to remove poor children from their parents.
Commonwealth v. Fisher (1905)	The Pennsylvania Supreme Court upheld the constitutionality of the newly enacted Juvenile Court Act to commit a child to the House of Refuge until his or her twenty-first birthday.
Ex Parte Sharpe (1908)	The Idaho Supreme Court upheld the right of the state juvenile court to act in a protective way, by applying the *parens patriae* doctrine concerning the role of juveniles. This decision gave further impetus to the development of the juvenile court movement in the United States.

Crouse, the 12-year-old girl, was classified as a pauper for the purpose of court jurisdiction. The petition, brought by her mother, alleged that she was a poor person and therefore subject to the court. She was then committed to the Philadelphia House of Refuge, even though delinquency laws did not exist and she had committed no violation of the criminal law. Crouse's father objected to the court action and filed a writ of habeus corpus seeking an explanation for her commitment.

The problem in this case was whether the state of Pennsylvania had the right to take custody of Crouse under the guise of helping her, even though she had committed no crime. The Superior Court decided that placing the child in the House of Refuge did not violate here constitutional rights.

The Court concluded that Crouse was being cared for and not punished and therefore could be placed in an institution even without due process of law. The *Crouse* decision established the key legal concept of *parens patriae,* which became the basis of the juvenile court movement. *Crouse* was the first legal challenge to the practice of institutionalizing children who had committed no crime. It gave the state almost complete authority to intervene in the parent–child relationship because of the state's role as *parens patriae.* The court stated:

> The right of parental control is a natural, but not an inalienable one. It is not accepted by the Declaration of Rights out of the subjects of ordinary legislation; and it consequently remains subject to the ordinary legislative power which, if wantonly or inconveniently used, would soon be constitutionally restricted, but the competency of which, as the government is constituted, cannot be doubted.[16]

The *Crouse* decision demonstrated that children could be deprived of the constitutional liberties guaranteed to adults.

The House of Refuge in New York was built in 1824, opened in 1825, and burned in 1838. It housed young boys found to be "juvenile delinquents."

O'CONNELL v. TURNER

Another, more significant case was later decided in favor of the parent and child against the state: *O'Connell v. Turner.*[17] In 1870, Daniel O'Connell was committed to the Chicago Reform School on the ground that he was a vagrant or destitute youth without proper parental care. The parents fought the child's commitment because he had not been convicted of a crime and had been apprehended and confined under a general grant of power to arrest for simple misfortune. The basic legal problem was whether children could be committed to reform schools in the absence of criminal conduct or because of gross misconduct on the part of their parents.

The law was held to be unconstitutional, and on subsequent appeal, the court ordered Daniel O'Connell discharged. As Justice Thornton noted in the case, "The warrant of commitment does not indicate that the arrest was made for a criminal offense. Hence, we conclude that it was made under the general grant of power to arrest and confine for misfortune."[18] The fact that the court in this case distinguished between criminal acts and acts arising from misfortune was significant: All legislation dealing with misfortune cases was subsequently appealed as a direct result of the *O'Connell* decision. Also, as Sanford Fox indicates, the *O'Connell* case changed the course of events in Illinois. The Chicago Reform School closed in 1872, and the case encouraged procedural due process reform for committed youths.[19]

THE DEVELOPMENT OF JUVENILE INSTITUTIONS

Despite the *O'Connell* decision, state intervention in the lives of children continued throughout the latter portion of the nineteenth century and well into the twentieth century. The child savers influenced state and local governments to create institutions, called reform schools, exclusively devoted to the care of vagrant and delinquent youths. State institutions opened in Westboro, Massachusetts, in 1848 and in Rochester, New York, in 1849.[20] Institutional programs began in Ohio in 1850 and in Maine, Rhode Island, and Michigan in 1906.[21] Children lived in congregate conditions and spent their days working in the institution, learning a trade where possible, and receiving some basic education. They were racially and sexually segregated; discipline, often involving whipping and isolation, was harsh; and their physical care was poor. Beverly Smith found that girls admitted to the Western House of Refuge in Rochester, New York, during the 1880s were often labeled as deviant or criminal but were in reality abused, orphaned, and neglected. They too were subject to harsh working conditions, strict discipline, and intensive labor.[22]

While some viewed houses of refuge and reform schools as humanitarian answers to poorhouses and prisons for vagrant, neglected, and delinquent youths, many were opposed to such programs. As an alternative, New York philanthropist Charles Brace helped develop the **Children's Aid Society** in 1853.[23] Brace's formula for dealing with neglected and delinquent youths was to rescue them from the harsh environment of the city and provide them with temporary shelter care. He then sought to place them in private homes throughout the nation. This program was very similar to today's foster home programs. As Fox points out, "The great value to be placed on family life for deviant and crime-prone children was later explicitly set forth in the juvenile court act."[24]

Although the child reformers provided services for children, they could not eliminate juvenile delinquency. Most reform schools were unable to hold youthful law violators and reform them because they lacked both social and financial resources. Large numbers of children needing placement burdened the public coffers supporting such programs. So, although state control over vagrant, delinquent, and neglected children became more widespread after the Civil War, it also became more controversial. As the nation grew, it became evident that private charities and public organizations were unable to care adequately for the growing number of troubled youths.

In 1874, the first **Society for the Prevention of Cruelty to Children** (SPCC) was established in New York; by 1900, there were 300 such societies in the United States.[25] Leaders of the SPCCs were concerned that neglected and abused boys would grow up to join the ranks of the "dangerous classes," becoming lower-class criminals, and that mistreated young girls might become sexually promiscuous women. A growing post-Civil War crime rate and concern about a rapidly shifting and changing population served to swell SPCC membership. In addition, children subjected to cruelty and neglect at home and at school added to the increase in numbers.

SPCC groups influenced state legislatures to pass statutes protecting children from exploitive or neglectful parents, including those who did not provide them with adequate food and clothing or made them beg or work in places where liquor was sold.[26] Criminal penalties were created, and provisions were established for removing children from the home. In some states, such as New York, agents of the SPCC could actually arrest abusive parents; in others, they would inform the police about suspected abuse cases and accompany officers when they made an arrest.[27]

The organization and control of SPCCs varied widely. For example, the New York City SPCC was a city agency supported by municipal funds. It conducted

investigations of delinquent and neglected children for the court and had little to do with the city's other social welfare agencies. In contrast, the Boston SPCC emphasized delinquency prevention and worked closely with social welfare groups; the Philadelphia SPCC emphasized family unity and was involved with other charities.[28]

ESTABLISHMENT OF THE ILLINOIS JUVENILE COURT

Although reform groups continued to lobby for government control over children, the committing of children under the doctrine of *parens patriae* without due process of law began to be questioned. What care was in the best interest of the child? Could the state incarcerate children who had not violated the criminal law? Should children be held in the same facilities that housed adults? These and other questions began to plague reformers and those interested in the plight of children. Institutional deficiencies; the detention of delinquent children in adult jails and prisons; the handling of poor, dependent, ignorant, and noncriminal delinquents without due process by inadequate private child welfare organizations;

and the religious segregation of children all spurred the argument that a juvenile court should be established.

Increasing delinquency rates also hastened the development of a juvenile court. Theodore Ferdinand's analysis of the Boston juvenile court found that in the 1820s and 1830s, very few juveniles were charged with serious offenses. By 1850, juvenile delinquency was the fastest growing component of the local crime problem.[29] Ferdinand concluded that the sizable flow of juvenile cases strengthened the argument that juveniles needed their own special court attuned to their needs.[30]

The child-saving movement culminated in the passage of the **Illinois Juvenile Court Act of 1899** (see Table 12.2). This was a major event in the history of the juvenile justice movement in the United States. Its significance was such that, by 1917, juvenile courts had been established in all but three states.

The principles motivating the Illinois reformers at that time were these:

1. Children, because of their minority status, should not be held as accountable as adult transgressors;
2. The objective of the juvenile justice system is to help the youngster, to treat and rehabilitate rather than punish;
3. Disposition should be predicated on analysis of the youth's special circumstances and needs; and
4. The system should avoid the punitive, adversary, and formalized trappings of the adult criminal process with all its confusing rules of evidence and tightly controlled procedures.

Just what were the ramifications of passage of the Illinois Juvenile Court Act? The traditional interpretation is that the reformers were genuinely motivated to pass legislation that would serve the best interests of the child. U.S. Supreme Court Justice Abe Fortas took this position in the 1967 *In re Gault* case:

> The early reformers were appalled by adult procedures and penalties and by the fact that children could be given long prison sentences and mixed in jails with hardened criminals. They were profoundly convinced that society's duty to the child could not be confined by the concept of justice alone. . . . The child—essentially good, as they saw it—was to be made to feel that he was the object of the state's care and solicitude, not that he was under arrest or on trial. . . . The idea of crime and punishment was to be abandoned. The child was to be treated and rehabilitated and the procedures from apprehension through institutionalization were to be clinical rather than punitive.[31]

The child savers were imbued with a positivistic philosophy and emphasized individual values and judgments about children and their care. Society was to be concerned with where children came from, what their problems were, and how these problems could be handled in the interests of the children and the state.

Interpretations of its intentions and effects differ, but unquestionably, the Illinois Juvenile Court Act established juvenile delinquency as a legal concept and the juvenile court as a judicial forum. The act for the first time distinguished between children who were dependent and neglected and those who were delinquent. Delinquent children were those under the age of 16 who violated the law. The act also established a court specifically for children and an extensive probation program whereby children were to be the responsibility of probation officers. In addition, the legislation allowed children to be committed to institutions and reform programs under the laws and control of the state.

TABLE 12.2 Excerpts from the Illinois Juvenile Court Act of 1899

Section 1. Definitions. This act shall apply only to children under the age of sixteen (16) years not now or hereafter inmates of a State institution, or any training school for boys or industrial school for girls or some institution incorporated under the laws of this State, except as provided in sections twelve (12) and eighteen (18). For the purposes of this act the words *dependent child* and *neglected child* shall mean any child who for any reason is destitute or homeless or abandoned; or dependent upon the public for support; or has not proper parental care or guardianship; or who habitually begs or receives alms; or who is found living in any house of ill fame or with any vicious or disreputable person; or whose home, by reason of neglect, cruelty or depravity on the part of its parents, guardian or other person in whose care it may be, is an unfit place for such a child; and any child under the age of eight (8) years who is found peddling or selling any article or singing or playing any musical instrument upon the streets or giving any public entertainment. The words *delinquent child* shall include any child under the age of 16 years who violates any law of this State or any city or village ordinance. The word *child or children* may mean one or more children, and the word *parent or parents* may be held to mean one or both parents, when consistent with the intent of this act. The word *association* shall include any corporation which includes in its purposes the care or disposition of children coming within the meaning of this act....

Section 3. Juvenile Court. In counties having over 500,000 population the judges of the circuit court shall, at such times as they shall determine, designate one or more of their number whose duty it shall be to hear all cases coming under this act. A special courtroom, to be designated as the juvenile courtroom, shall be provided for the hearing of such cases, and the findings of the court shall be entered in a book or books to be kept for that purpose and known as the "Juvenile Record," and the court may, for convenience, be called the "Juvenile Court."

Section 4. Petition to the Court. Any reputable person, being resident in the county, having knowledge of a child in his county who appears to be either neglected, dependent or delinquent, may file with the clerk of court having jurisdiction in the matter a petition in writing, setting forth the facts, verified by affidavit. It shall be sufficient that the affidavit is upon information and belief....

Section 6. Probation Officers. The court shall have authority to appoint or designate one or more discreet persons of good character to serve as probation officers during the pleasure of the court; said probation officers to receive no compensation from the public treasury. In case a probation officer shall be appointed by any court, it shall be the duty of the clerk of the court, if practicable, to notify the said probation officer in advance when any child is to be brought before the said court; it shall be the duty of the said probation officer to make such investigation as may be required by the court; to be present in court in order to represent the interests of the child when the case is heard; to furnish the court such information and assistance as the judge may require; and to take such charge of any child before and after trial as may be directed by the court.

Section 7. Dependent and Neglected Children. When any child under the age of sixteen (16) years shall be found to be dependent or neglected within the meaning of this act, the court may make an order committing the child to the care of some suitable State institution, or to the care of some reputable citizen of good moral character, or to the care of some training school or an industrial school, as provided by law, or to the care of some association willing to receive it embracing in its objects the purpose of caring or obtaining homes for dependent or neglected children, which association shall have been accredited as hereinafter provided....

Section 9. Disposition of Delinquent Children. In the case of a delinquent child the court may continue the hearing from time to time and may commit the child to the care and guardianship of a probation officer duly appointed by the court and may allow said child to remain in its own home, subject to the visitation of the probation officer; such child to report to the probation officer as often as may be required and subject to be returned to the court for further proceedings, whenever such action may appear to be necessary, or the court may commit the child to the care and guardianship of the probation officer, to be placed in a suitable family home, subject to the friendly supervision of such probation officer, or it may authorize the said probation officer to board out the said child in some suitable family home, in case provision is made by voluntary contribution or otherwise for the payment of the board of such child, until a suitable provision may be made for the child in a home without such payment; or the court may commit the child, if a boy, to a training school for boys, or if a girl, to an industrial school for girls. Or, if the child is found guilty of any criminal offense, and the judge is of the opinion that the best interest requires it, the court may commit the child to any institution within said county incorporated under the laws of this State for the care of delinquent children, or provided by a city for the care of such offenders, or may commit the child, if a boy over the age of ten (10) years, to the State reformatory, or if a girl over the age of ten (10) years, to the State Home for Juvenile Female Offenders. In no case shall a child be committed beyond his or her minority. A child committed to such institution shall be subject to the control of the board of managers thereof, and the said board shall have power to parole such child on such conditions as it may prescribe, and the court shall, on the recommendation of the board, have power to discharge such child from custody whenever in the judgment of the court his or her reformation shall be complete; or the court may commit the child to the care and custody of some association that will receive it, embracing in its objects the care of neglected and dependent children and that has been duly accredited as hereinafter provided....

Section 11. Children under Twelve Years Not to Be Committed to Jail. No court or magistrate shall commit a child under twelve (12) years of age to a jail or police station, but if such child is unable to give bail it may be committed to the care of the sheriff, police officer or probation officer.

Source: Illinois Statute 1899, Section 131.

The most important provisions of the act were these:

- A separate court was established for delinquent, dependent, and neglected children.
- Special legal procedures were to govern the adjudication and disposition of juvenile matters.
- Children were to be separated from adults in courts and in institutional programs.
- Probation programs were to be developed to assist the court in making decisions in the best interests of the state and the child.

WERE THEY REALLY CHILD SAVERS?

Great debate continues over the true aims and objectives of the early child savers. Some historians conclude that they were what they seemed: concerned citizens motivated by humanitarian ideals.[32] Modern scholars, however, have reappraised the child-saving movement. In his groundbreaking book *The Child Savers,* critical thinker Anthony Platt paints a picture of the child savers as representative of the ruling class who were galvanized by the threat of newly arriving immigrants and the urban poor to take action to preserve their way of life.[33] He claims;

> The child savers should not be considered humanists: (1) their reforms did not herald a new system of justice but rather expedited traditional policies which had been informally developed during the nineteenth century; (2) they implicitly assumed that natural dependence of adolescents and created a special court to impose sanctions on premature independents and behavior unbecoming to youth; (3) their attitudes toward delinquent youth were largely paternalistic and romantic but their commands were backed up by force; (4) they promoted correctional programs requiring longer terms of imprisonment, longer hours of labor, and militaristic discipline, and the inculcation of middle class values and lower class skills.[34]

Other critical thinkers followed Platt in finding that child saving was motivated more by self-interest than benevolence.[35] For example, in a recent paper, Randall Shelden and Lynn Osborne traced the early child-saving movement in Memphis, Tennessee, and found that its leaders were a small group of upper-class citizens who desired to control the behavior and lifestyles of another class of citizens: lower-class youth. The outcome was ominous. Most cases petitioned to the juvenile court (which opened in 1910) were for petty crimes, truancy, and other status-type offenses, yet 25 percent of the youths were committed to some form of incarceration; more than 96 percent of the actions with which females were charged were status offenses.[36]

Sanford Fox, a respected legal scholar, has also been critical of the early child-saving reforms. According to Fox, the Illinois Juvenile Court Act restated the belief in the value of coercive prediction; continued nineteenth-century summary trials for children about whom the predictions were to be made; made no improvements in the long-condemned institutional care furnished these same children; codified the view that institutions should, even without badly needed financial help from the legislature, replicate family life; and reinforced the private sectarian interest whose role had long been decried by leading child welfare reformers in the area of juvenile care.[37]

Thus, according to the revisionist approach, the reformers applied the concept of *parens patriae* for their own purposes, including the continuance of middle-

and upper-class values, the control of political systems, and the furtherance of a child labor system consisting of marginal and lower-class skilled workers.

Juvenile Justice in the Early Twentieth Century

Following the passage of the Illinois Juvenile Court Act, similar legislation was enacted throughout the nation. The special courts these laws created maintained jurisdiction over predelinquent (neglected and dependent) and delinquent children. Juvenile court jurisdiction was based primarily on a child's noncriminal actions and status, not strictly on a violation of criminal law. The *parens patriae* philosophy predominated, ushering in a form of personalized justice characterized by a procedural laxity and informality that did not provide juvenile offenders with the full panoply of constitutional protections. The court's process was paternalistic rather than adversarial. Attorneys were not required, and hearsay evidence, inadmissible in criminal trials, was admissible in the adjudication of juvenile offenders. Verdicts were based on a "preponderance of the evidence," instead of "beyond a reasonable doubt," and children were often not granted any right to appeal their convictions. These characteristics allowed the juvenile court to function in a nonlegal manner and to provide various social services to children in need.

The major functions of the juvenile justice system were to prevent juvenile crime and to rehabilitate juvenile offenders. The roles of the two most important actors—the juvenile court judge and the probation staff—were to diagnose the child's condition and prescribe programs to alleviate it. Until 1967, judgments about children's actions and consideration for their constitutional rights were secondary.

By the 1920s, noncriminal behavior in the form of incorrigibility and truancy from school was added to the jurisdiction of many juvenile court systems. Of particular interest was the sexual behavior of young girls, which fell under the jurisdiction of the new courts. Mary Odem and Steven Schlossman have shown how the juvenile court articulated and enforced a strict moral code on working-class girls, not hesitating to incarcerate those who were sexually active.[38] Programs of all kinds—including individualized counseling and institutional care—were used to "cure" juvenile criminality. An entire group of new "experts"—criminologists, sociologists, social workers, probation officers, and psychologists—emerged to deal with delinquency and noncriminal behavior. Much of their effort involved seeking to rehabilitate children brought before the court.

By 1925, juvenile courts existed in virtually every jurisdiction in every state. Although the juvenile court concept expanded rapidly, it cannot be said that each state implemented the philosophy of the court thoroughly. Some jurisdictions established elaborate juvenile court systems, while others passed legislation but provided no services. Some courts had trained juvenile court judges; others had nonlawyers sitting in juvenile cases. Some courts had extensive probation departments; others had untrained probation personnel.[39]

Great diversity also marked juvenile institutions. While some maintained a lenient treatment orientation, others relied on harsh physical punishments, including beatings, straightjacket restraints, immersion in cold water, and solitary confinement in a dark cell with a diet of bread and water.

These conditions were exacerbated by the rapid growth in the juvenile institutional population. Between 1890 and 1920, the number of institutionalized youths jumped 112 percent, a rise that far exceeded the increase in the total number of adolescents in the United States.[40] Despite the juvenile court movement, private institutions were not squeezed out by public institutions; in fact, they grew much faster and larger. John Sutton has carefully reviewed the growth of juvenile institutions during this period. He finds that after 1890, public institutions predominated in areas where people relied on government to solve social problems; private institutions persisted where government authority was weakest. Although professionals deplored the increased institutionalization of youth, the growth was due in part to the successful efforts by reformers to close poorhouses, thereby creating a need for more juvenile institutions to house their displaced populations. In addition, the lack of a coherent national policy on needy children allowed private entrepreneurs to open institutions and fill the void.[41]

REFORMING THE SYSTEM

Concern and reform of this system was slow in coming: After all, why criticize a reform movement designed to treat and not punish? In 1912, the U.S. Children's Bureau was formed as the first federal child welfare agency. By the 1930s, the Bureau began to investigate the state of juvenile institutions and tried to expose some of their more repressive aspects through a series of books and research reports.[42] After World War II, critics, such as Paul Tappan and Francis Allen, began to identify problems in the juvenile justice system, among which were the neglect of procedural rights and the warehousing of youth in dangerous and ineffective institutions. Status offenders commonly were housed with delinquents and given sentences that were more punitive than those given to delinquents.[43]

From its origin, the juvenile court system denied children procedural rights normally available to adult offenders. Due process rights such as representation by counsel, a jury trial, freedom from self-incrimination, and freedom from unreasonable search and seizure were not considered essential for the juvenile court system because the primary purpose of the system was not punishment but rehabilitation. However, the dream of trying to rehabilitate children was not achieved. Individual treatment approaches failed, and delinquency rates soared. In many instances, the courts deprived children of their liberty and treated them unfairly.

Reform efforts, begun in earnest in the 1960s, changed the face of the juvenile justice system. In 1962, New York passed legislation creating a family court system.[44] The new family court was to assume responsibility for all matters involving family life. Its particular emphasis was to be on delinquent, dependent, and neglected children and paternity, adoption, and support proceedings involving parents. In addition, the legislation established a separate classification—person in need of supervision (PINS). This category, covering noncriminal behavior, was the forerunner of such legislative categories as children in need of supervision (CHINS), minors in need of supervisions (MINS), and families in need of supervision (FINS). These labels covered individuals involved in such actions as truancy, running away, and incorrigibility. In using them to establish jurisdiction over children and their families, juvenile courts expanded their roles as social agencies. Because noncriminal children were now involved in the juvenile court system to a greater degree, many juvenile courts had to improve their services as social agencies. Efforts were made to play down the authority of the court as a court of law and to personalize the system of justice for children. These reforms were soon followed by a "due process revolution," which ushered in an era of procedural rights for court-adjudicated youth.

The Contemporary Juvenile Justice System

Today's juvenile system is very much a legal system. The Supreme Court has played a significant, if not monumental, role in the formulation of juvenile law and procedure over the past 25 years. Nevertheless, the courts have neither repudiated the goal of rehabilitating children nor subjected children totally to the procedures and philosophy of the adult criminal justice system.

The **juvenile justice system** exists in all states by statute. Each jurisdiction has a juvenile code and a special court structure to deal with children in trouble. Nationwide, the juvenile justice system consists of thousands of public and private agencies, with a total budget amounting to hundreds of millions of dollars. Most of the nation's 20,000 police agencies have a juvenile component, and more than 3,000 juvenile courts and about an equal number of juvenile correctional facilities exist throughout the nation. There are thousands of juvenile police officers, more than 3,000 juvenile court judges, more than 6,500 juvenile probation officers, and thousands of juvenile correctional employees.[45]

Annually, about 2.2 million juveniles are arrested, more than 1.5 million delinquency cases are petitioned to the courts by police and others, and 500,000 children are placed on formal or informal probation; approximately 98,000 youths are held in secure and nonsecure treatment centers.[46]

These figures do not take into account the large number of children who are referred to community diversion and mental health programs. There are thousands of these programs throughout the nation, and thousands of youth are being held in the community-based institutions that administer them. This multitude of agencies and people dealing with juvenile delinquency and status offenses has led to the development of what professionals in the field view as an incredibly expanded and complex juvenile justice system. The accompanying "Focus on Delinquency" takes a closer look at the nature of this system.

The Juvenile Justice Process

How are children processed by the agencies and organizations of the juvenile justice system?[47] Through what sequential stages do juvenile offenders pass? Most children initially come in contact with the juvenile justice system as a result of a contact with a police officer. When a juvenile commits a serious crime, the police are empowered to make an arrest. Less serious offenses may also require police action, but in these instances, instead of being arrested, the child may be warned, the parents may be called, or a referral may be made to a juvenile social service program. Only about half of all children arrested by the police are actually referred to the juvenile court.

When a police officer takes a child into custody, the child may be brought to the station house lockup and then to a county detention program or intake program prior to a court appearance. At this point, further referral to a social service agency may occur. If the crime is a serious one, the juvenile court prosecutor may initiate a petition against the child. This begins the trial process.

THE JUVENILE JUSTICE SYSTEM—THE KEY PLAYERS, PROGRAMS, AND COSTS

Preventing Delinquency

Under the Juvenile Justice and Delinquency Prevention Act of 1974 (PL. 93-45) the appropriation amendment for 1995–96 grants approximately 140 million dollars for state juvenile justice programs. A portion of these funds are used for exemplary juvenile delinquency prevention programs. In addition, the Violent Crime Control and Law Enforcement Act of 1994 (PL. 103-322) also provides federal funding for juvenile prevention programs.

Hundreds of thousands of children and families are serviced in primary prevention programs targeted at families, schools and the community. Since more than 400,000 children live in foster care, programs such as Permanent Families for Abused and Neglected Children help to prevent delinquency in such children. Court Appointed Special Advocates (CASA) ensure that the courts are familiar with the needs of these children. Schools provide Cities in Schools, law-related education, and peer leadership programs to reduce school violence and prevent students from dropping out. Youth gangs are often served by youth service bureaus, Jobs for Youth, and detached worker programs. Drug prevention programs, such as Drug Abuse Resistance Education (DARE), help kids say no to drugs. Drug-free school zones and citizen's patrols help link youth prevention agencies and organizations.

Juvenile Law Enforcement

Of the 13,000 municipal police agencies, approximately 75 percent provide special programs and services for juvenile offenders. Often police officers concerned with juveniles have a multiplicity of roles and duties. Cost of police services for children is undetermined, but more time is being spent dealing with troubled and violent youths committing serious crimes. Police officers make more than 2.0 million juvenile arrests, of which 600,000 are for serious crimes. The community policing concept is being utilized to decentralize policing and make its services more amenable to juvenile delinquency prevention.

Detention and Pretrial Services

In the United States, there are more than 3,300 jails and about 830 juvenile detention facilities. Many juveniles, upwards of 1,500, are housed in jails on any given day. From 200,000 to 300,000 are being jailed with adults each year. Upwards of 500,000 youths are held in detention facilities each year. Thousands of juveniles receive diversion as an alternative to official procedures. More than 16,000 are tried as adults. The amount of plea bargaining is uncertain because a significant number of juveniles enter guilty pleas admissions in the juvenile court. Forty-eight states and the District of Columbia have waiver proceedings to the criminal court.

After a petition is filed, the child is either released to the custody of his or her parents until the court appearance or detained. When the child appears before the court, the court can decide whether to **waive** the case (transfer it to an adult court) or adjudicate it in juvenile court. If the adjudication or trial declares the child delinquent or in need of supervision, the court initiates a social study of the child's background. After this study, which is called a **predisposition report,** an appropriate disposition leading to a correctional and rehabilitation program is provided. A more detailed analysis of the stages in the juvenile justice process follows (see Figure 12.1 on page 442).

POLICE INVESTIGATION

When a juvenile commits a crime, police agencies have the authority to investigate the incident and then to decide whether to release the child or to

Prosecutors and Public Defenders

Of the 30,000 lawyers in the justice system, including prosecutors and public defenders, only a small percentage work in the juvenile courts. They handle from 500,000 to 600,000 delinquency and status offense cases annually, in addition to thousands of informally handled cases. The public defense system provides the bulk of legal representation to children in the juvenile courts. In some areas, only 50 percent of the children in court receive the assistance of counsel. Cost ranges from 35 dollars to 75 dollars per hour for legal services.

Juvenile Courts

Jurisdiction ordinarily is defined by state statute. There are independent juvenile court systems, family court structures, and juvenile sessions of adult courts. Two factors, age and status, bring children under juvenile court jurisdiction. Judges, juvenile probation officers, court clerks, and juvenile prosecutors control and influence court cases.

In a noted 1967 case, *In re Gault*, the Supreme Court declared that youths have a right to a lawyer and other legal protections. The juvenile courts handle about 1.5 million delinquency cases each year, in addition to about 80,000 status offense cases.

Community Treatment

The most common community disposition employed by the juvenile court is probation. More than 500,000 youths are supervised on juvenile probation. Caseloads range from 60 to 80 per officer. Intensive probation services utilize very small caseloads and intense scrutiny. Statutory restitution programs exist in all 50 states. Residential programs include group homes, boarding schools, foster programs, and rural residences such as farms and camps.

Community programs often cost half as much per child as a secure training school. Recidivism rates tend to be lower generally in the community treatment programs than in large-scale institutional settings.

Juvenile Corrections (Institutional Care)

There are about 1,100 public and 2,000 private juvenile facilities; 98,000 children are held in all types of facilities during a year. Public facilities have a one-day count of 57,000 while 37,000 are confined in private juvenile facilities. The one-day count for African-American youth is twice as high as the rate for Hispanic youth and almost four times as high as the rate for white youth. Average length of stay is about eight months. The budget for juvenile corrections in the states is approximately 2.5 billion dollars annually.

Staff include custody, administrative, and treatment personnel. Institutional placement costs currently are about 25,000 to 40,000 dollars annually per child. States are spending more than 380 million dollars on contracts with private facilities for such specialized services as marine programs and wilderness camps.

Many states indicate a problem with overcrowding. Juveniles in state custody range in age from 11 to 18 years of age. Delinquent offenders constitute nearly 75 percent of all juvenile commitments.

Sources: Howard Snyder and Melissa Sickmund, *Juvenile Offenders and Victims: A National Report* (Washington, D.C.: OJJDP, 1995); Jeffrey Butts et al., *Juvenile Court Statistics, 1992* (Pittsburgh, Pa.: National Center for Juvenile Justice, 1995); also Robert DeComo, et al., *Juveniles Taken into Custody, 1992* (Washington, D.C.: OJJDP, 1995).

detain and refer him or her to the juvenile court. This is often a discretionary decision based not only on the nature of the offense committed but also on the conditions existing at the time of the arrest. Such factors as the type and seriousness of the offense, the child's past contacts with the police, and whether or not the child denies committing the crime determine whether a petition is filed. While juveniles are in the custody of the police, they have basic constitutional rights similar to those of adult offenders. Children are protected against unreasonable search and seizure under the Fourth and Fourteenth Amendments; the Fifth Amendment places limitations on police interrogation procedures.

INTAKE SCREENING

If the police decide to file a petition, the child is referred to juvenile court. The primary issue at this point is whether the child should remain in the community or be placed in a detention facility or shelter home. Also, it is essential to

FIGURE 12.1
The juvenile justice system

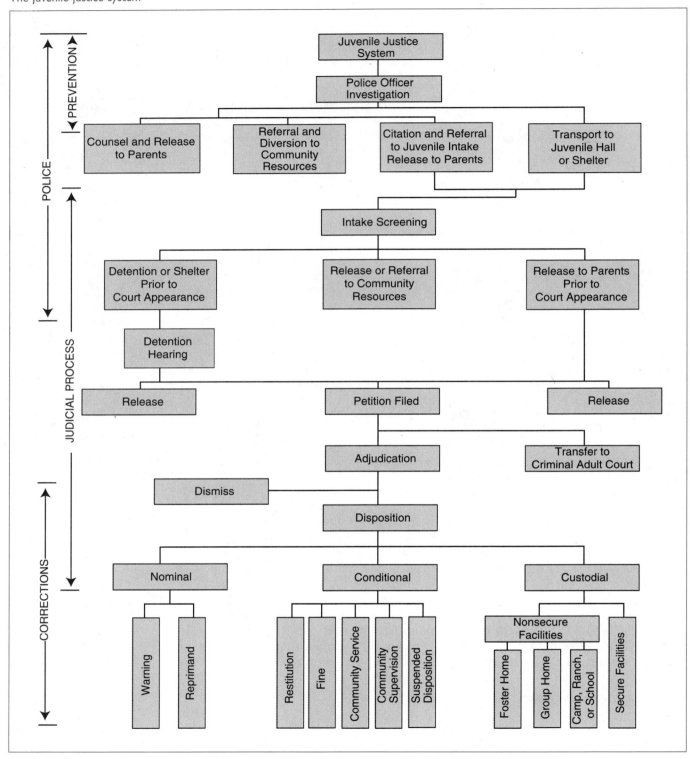

determine whether referral services should be obtained before any further court action. In the past, too many children were routinely taken to court and held in detention facilities to await court appearances. Normally, a **detention hearing** is held to determine whether to remand the child to a shelter or to release the child. At this point, the child has a right to counsel and other procedural safeguards. A child who is not detained is usually released to his or her parent or guardian. Most state juvenile court acts provide for a child to return home to await further court action, except when it is necessary to protect the child, when the child presents a serious danger to the public, or when it is not certain that the child will return to court for further adjudication. In many cases, the police will refer the child to a community service program at intake instead of filing a formal charge.

PRETRIAL PROCEDURES

In most juvenile court jurisdictions, the adjudication process begins with some sort of initial hearing. At this hearing, juvenile court rules of procedure normally require that the juveniles be informed of their right to a trial, that the plea or admission be voluntary, and that they understand the charges and consequences of the plea. The case will often not be further adjudicated if a child admits to the crime at the initial hearing.

In some cases, youths may be detained pending a trial. Many states permit detention or the removal of youths from the home where there is a likelihood of danger to themselves or others. Juveniles who are detained are eligible for bail in a handful of jurisdictions. Plea bargaining may also occur in the juvenile process at any stage of the proceedings.

If the child denies the allegation of delinquency, an **adjudicatory hearing** or trial is scheduled. Under extraordinary circumstances, a juvenile who commits a serious crime may be transferred to an adult court instead of being adjudicated. Today, most jurisdictions have laws providing for such transfers. Whether such a transfer occurs depends on the type of offense, the youth's prior record, the nature of past treatment efforts, the availability of treatment services, and the likelihood that the youth will be rehabilitated in the juvenile court system.

ADJUDICATION

The adjudication is the trial stage of the juvenile court process. If the child does not admit guilt at the initial hearing and is not transferred to an adult court, an adjudication hearing is held to determine the facts of the case. The court hears evidence on the allegations in the delinquency petition. This is a trial on the merits, and rules of evidence similar to those of criminal proceedings generally apply. At this stage of the proceeding, the juvenile offender is entitled to many of the procedural guarantees given adult offenders. These rights include the right to representation by counsel, freedom from self-incrimination, the right to confront and cross-examine witnesses, and, in certain instances, the right to a jury trial. In addition, many states have their own procedures concerning rules of evidence, competence of witnesses, pleadings, and pretrial motions. At the end of the adjudicatory hearing, the court enters a judgment against the juvenile.

The adjudication hearing is the trial stage of the juvenile court process. If the child does not admit to the charges at the initial hearing and is not transferred to an adult court, an adjudication hearing is held to determine the facts of the case. The court hears evidence on the allegations in the delinquency petition. This is a trial on the merits, and rules of evidence similar to criminal proceedings generally apply.

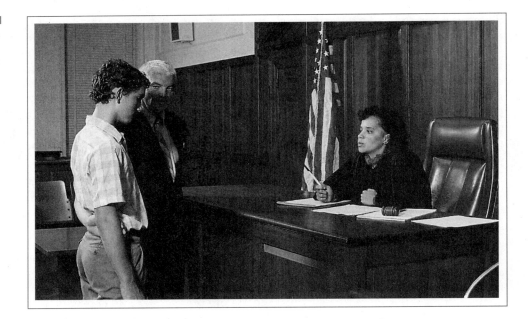

DISPOSITION

If the adjudication process finds the child delinquent, the court must then decide what should be done to treat the child. Most juvenile court acts require a dispositional hearing separate from the adjudication. This is often referred to as a **bifurcated process.** The dispositional hearing is less formal than adjudication. Here, the judge imposes a **disposition** on the juvenile offender in light of the offense, prior record, and family background. The judge has broad discretion and can prescribe a wide range of dispositions—from a simple warning or reprimand to community service or probation to more intense social control measures, such as institutional commitment, including group home, foster care, or secure facility care. In theory, the judge's decision serves the best interests of the child, the family, and the community. Many juvenile statutes require that the judge consider the least restrictive dispositional alternative before imposing any sentence. The disposition is one of the most important stages in the juvenile process because it may be the court's last opportunity to influence the offender's behavior. Disposition is concerned primarily with treating the juvenile and controlling antisocial behavior.

POSTDISPOSITION

Some jurisdictions allow for a program of juvenile aftercare or parole. A youth can be paroled from an institution and placed under the supervision of a parole officer. This means that he or she will complete the period of confinement in the community and receive assistance from the parole officer in the form of counseling, school referral, and vocational training.

In some jurisdictions, adjudication of a delinquency petition can be appealed to a higher court. Such an appeal may involve a review of the statutory basis under which the youth is to receive treatment from the state. Provisions for such appeals vary greatly with each jurisdiction.

Juveniles who are committed to programs of treatment and control have a legal right to treatment. The right to treatment for juveniles requires that states provide suitable rehabilitation programs that include counseling, education, and vocational services. Appellate courts have ruled that if such treatment is not provided, individuals must be released from confinement.

CRIMINAL JUSTICE VERSUS JUVENILE JUSTICE

The components of the adult and juvenile criminal processes are similar. Both include police investigation, arrest, administrative booking, preliminary hearings, bail, plea bargaining and admission of a plea, grand jury indictment, formal arraignment, trial, verdict, sentence, and appeal. However, the juvenile system has a separate, complementary (almost parallel) organizational structure. In many communities, juvenile justice is administered by people who bring special skills to the task. Also, more kinds of facilities and services are available to juveniles than to adults.

The juvenile court, emphasizing individualized treatment, was originally conceived of as a social court, not a formalized court of law. This view met with much criticism over the first 60 years of the twentieth century, resulting in the development of procedures and laws similar to those that protect adult offenders. However, the purpose of the juvenile court continues to be to treat and rehabilitate children, not to punish them. The juvenile justice system was designed not only to prevent juvenile crime and to rehabilitate juvenile offenders but also to provide for abused, neglected, and incorrigible children. In essence, it was to provide services to promote the normal growth and development of all adjudicated children.

One major concern of the juvenile court reform movement was to make certain that the stigma attached to a person who became a convicted criminal offender would not be affixed to young people in juvenile proceedings. Thus, even the language used in the juvenile court differs from that used in the adult criminal court (see Table 12.3 on page 447). Juveniles are not formally indicted for a crime; they have a **petition** filed against them. Secure pretrial holding facilities are called detention centers rather than jails. Similarly, the criminal court trial is called a **hearing** in the juvenile justice system. The "Focus on Delinquency" feature on page 446 compares the two systems.

Legal expert Barry Feld, one of the leading scholars of the juvenile court, believes that over the years the juvenile justice system has taken on more of the characteristics of the adult courts. He refers to this as the "criminalizing" of the juvenile court.[48] Robert Dawson suggests that because the legal differences between the juvenile and criminal systems are narrower than they have ever been, it may be time to abolish the juvenile court and merge it into the larger criminal justice system.[49] During the last 15 years, the juvenile court system has obviously come to resemble more closely the adult court system.

IMPROVING THE JUVENILE JUSTICE SYSTEM

A review of contemporary literature on juvenile justice and delinquency reveals a number of major themes related to what the juvenile justice system should be doing to help youths in trouble and protect society as a whole. Today's experts

SIMILARITIES AND DIFFERENCES BETWEEN JUVENILE AND ADULT JUSTICE SYSTEMS

Since its creation, the juvenile justice system has sought to maintain its independence from the adult justice system. Yet there are a number of similarities that characterize the institutions, processes, and law of the two systems.

Similarities between the Juvenile and Adult Justice Systems

- Police officers, judges, and correctional personnel use discretion in decision making in both the adult and the juvenile systems.
- The right to receive *Miranda* warnings applies to juveniles as well as to adults.
- Juveniles and adults are protected from prejudicial lineups or other identification procedures.
- Similar procedural safeguards protect juveniles and adults when they make an admission of guilt.
- Prosecutors and defense attorneys play equally critical roles in juvenile and adult advocacy.
- Juveniles and adults have the right to counsel at most key stages of the court process.
- Pretrial motions are available in juvenile and criminal court proceedings.
- Negotiations and plea bargain exist for juvenile and adult offenders.
- Juveniles and adults have a right to a hearing and an appeal.
- The standard of evidence in juvenile delinquency adjudications, as in adult criminal trials, is proof beyond a reasonable doubt.
- Juveniles and adults can be placed on probation by the court.
- Both juveniles and adults can be placed in pretrial detention facilities.
- Juveniles and adults can be kept in detention without bail if they are considered dangerous.
- After trial, both can be placed in community treatment programs.

Differences between the Juvenile and Adult Justice Systems

- The primary purpose of juvenile procedures is protection and treatment. With adults, the aim is to punish the guilty.
- Age determines the jurisdiction of the juvenile court. The nature of the offense determines jurisdiction in the adult system.
- Juveniles can be apprehended for acts that would not be criminal if they were committed by an adult (status offenses).
- Juvenile proceedings are not considered criminal; adult proceedings are.
- Juvenile court procedures are generally informal and private. Those of adult courts are more formal and are open to the public.
- Courts cannot release identifying information about a juvenile to the press, but they must release information about an adult.
- Parents are highly involved in the juvenile process but not in the adult process.
- The standard of arrest is more stringent for adults than for juveniles.
- Juveniles are released into parental custody. Adults are generally given the opportunity for bail.
- Juveniles have no constitutional right to a jury trial. Adults have this right. Some state statutes provide juveniles with a jury trial.
- Juveniles can be searched in school without probable cause or a warrant.
- A juvenile's record is generally sealed when the age of majority is reached. The record of an adult is permanent.
- A juvenile court cannot sentence juveniles to county jails or state prisons; these are reserved for adults.
- The U.S. Supreme Court has declared that the Eighth Amendment does not prohibit the death penalty for crimes committed by juveniles ages 16 and 17, but is not a sentence given to children under 16.

TABLE 12.3 Comparison of Terms Used in Adult and Juvenile Justice Systems

	Juvenile Terms	Adult Terms
The Person and the Act	Delinquent child	Criminal
	Delinquent act	Crime
Preadjudicatory Stage	Take into custody	Arrest
	Petition	Indictment
	Agree to a finding	Plead guilty
	Deny the petition	Plead not guilty
	Adjustment	Plea bargain
	Detention facility; child-care shelter	Jail
Adjudicatory Stage	Substitution	Reduction of charges
	Adjudicatory or fact-finding hearing	Trial
	Adjudication	Conviction
Postadjudicatory Stage	Dispositional hearing	Sentencing hearing
	Disposition	Sentence
	Commitment	Incarceration
	Youth development center; treatment center; training school	Prison
	Residential child-care facility	Halfway house
	Aftercare	Parole

seem to be saying that the system can be improved by concerted efforts directed at (1) the prevention of juvenile delinquency, (2) the diversion and removal of problem youths from the juvenile justice system, (3) the incapacitation of serious and violent offenders, (4) fair and just treatment of all youthful offenders, and (5) enhancing the efficiency and effectiveness of the juvenile justice system, particularly the juvenile court. These views represent the shifting philosophies and theoretical models of the juvenile justice system (see Table 12.4 and 12.5).

PREVENTION

Prevention seeks to divert individual youths from antisocial behavior during the early stages of their lives. Building stronger family units, providing counseling in schools, and improving living conditions are all examples of prevention efforts. Prevention also involves developing a comprehensive delinquency plan, collecting data about delinquency in local communities, clarifying delinquency goals, and providing an inventory of community resources and programs. Once these are accomplished, programs of prevention involving health, family, education, employment, recreation, housing, religion, and even the media can play an important role in thwarting juvenile delinquency.

DIVERSION

Even the most conservative critic sees the value of diverting minor offenders from the formal justice process and handling them in a nonpunitive, treatment-oriented fashion. A juvenile can be diverted at any stage of the process. Basically, diversion has focused on certain groups—youths committing minor, noncriminal acts; first offenders; and youths committing minor criminal acts who might be more appropriately handled by social agencies. Diversion programs can be

TABLE 12.4 Shifting Philosophies of Juvenile Justice

Time Frame	Activity
Prior to 1900s	Juveniles treated similar to adult offenders. No distinction by age or capacity to commit criminal acts.
From 1899 to 1950s	Children treated differently, beginning with the Illinois Juvenile Court Act of 1899. By 1925, juvenile court acts are established in virtually every state.
1950s to 1970s	Recognition by experts that the rehabilitation model and the protective nature of *parens patriae* have failed to prevent delinquency.
1960s to 1970s	Introduction of constitutional due process into the juvenile justice system. Punishing children or protecting them under *parens patriae* requires due process of law.
1970s to 1980s	Failure of rehabilitation and due process protections to control delinquency leads to a shift to a crime control and punishment philosophy similar to that of the adult criminal justice system.
1990s	Mixed constitutional protections with some treatment. Uncertain goals and programs; the juvenile justice system relies on punishment and deterrence.

Prevention seeks to divert individual children from antisocial behavior during the early stages of their lives. Building stronger family units, providing counseling in schools and social service agencies, and improving living conditions are all examples of prevention efforts. Prevention also involves developing a comprehensive delinquency plan, collecting data about delinquency in local communities, clarifying delinquency goals, and providing an inventory of community resources and programs.

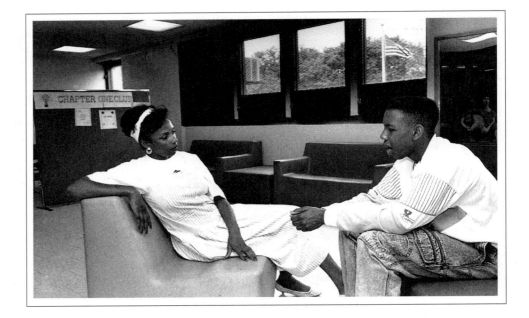

employed by the police, during the intake process or petition filing, and even at adjudication.

The goal of removing noncriminal misbehavior, such as status offenses, from juvenile court jurisdiction also should be seriously considered. In addition, whenever possible, delinquent offenders should be kept separate from adult criminals. School programs, counseling centers, and other activities within the

TABLE 12.5 Theoretical Models of Juvenile Justice

Model	Description	Stage
Rehabilitation	Emphasis on treatment and individual needs of the juvenile; *Parens patriae* philosophy; best interest of child is paramount.	
	Referral to social service; discretion in decision making; police-community prevention programs; arrest and prosecution in most serious cases.	Police
	Use of intake procedures, discretion, and referral; limited use of detention, waiver, and plea bargaining.	Pretrial
	Procedural due process and fairness in a "helping court"; concern about diversion and community treatment.	Adjudication
	Use of indeterminate sentencing; institutional care only as last resort; bifurcated hearing with focus on community alternatives.	Disposition
Justice	Goal is public protection, accountability, and "just deserts"; actions similar to adult criminal justice system; decisions based on nature of offense.	
	Concern about delinquency and serious crimes (as opposed to status offenses); limited discretion; strict application of *Miranda* and search and seizure rules.	Police
	Increased role of prosecutor; full procedural safeguards; fact-finding is important. Plea bargaining acceptable; use of detention and waiver procedure.	Pretrial
	Juvenile guaranteed full procedural due process; admission of guilt allowed with proper rules of procedure; fairness and efficiency are goals of court; use of rules of evidence; procedure similar to that in adult court.	Adjudication
	Decisions based primarily on offense, as opposed to individual's needs; punishment is goal of the juvenile code; determinate sentencing to ensure accountability for behavior.	Disposition
Hybrid	Combines treatment and punishment; goals often in conflict with each other. No consensus on purpose and nature of juvenile justice.	
	Juveniles codes recognize discretion and need for public protection. Arrest, search, and seizure, and *Miranda* rules apply in all cases.	Police
	High priority given to crime-control policy; detention used with required hearing and due process; effort to retain the traditional goal of rehabilitation through diversion and discretion.	Pretrial
	Formal trial; focus on fact-finding and due process; concern for rules of law and procedure at expense of individual interests.	Adjudication
	Stress on sanctions proportionate to seriousness of youth's crime; effort to balance community treatment and public protection; use of wide range of dispositional alternatives.	Disposition

mental health and educational systems might be more appropriate for youths with truancy problems. Those who are incorrigible can be handled in mental health settings.

CONTROLLING VIOLENT OFFENDERS

Research has shown that a small group of youthful offenders may be responsible for a significant amount of serious delinquency and may grow up to be adult offenders. A major national effort is being undertaken to study chronic offenders and develop mechanisms to identify them early in their careers. The juvenile justice system must also develop treatment facilities to deal effectively with the needs of these offenders, including serious drug offenders, while protecting the community from their activities. At first glance, incarceration in secure juvenile facilities may seem to be an inappropriate goal for juvenile justice, but it is actually more humane than the current practice of transferring these youths to the adult system so that they can be held in state prisons.

FAIRNESS

All children processed through the juvenile justice system should be treated fairly and humanely. No distinction should be made between white and minority juvenile offenders or between those in the lower classes and those in the middle and upper classes of society. Nonetheless, research indicates that these distinctions are still being made.[50]

Procedures to ensure due process should exist in all areas of the juvenile justice system. Practices related to investigation, arrest, diversion, detention, arraignment, adjudication, sentencing, and institutionalization must be consistent with our democratic system. Recent U.S. Supreme Court decisions have made it clear that youths charged with delinquent acts and others brought into the juvenile justice system are entitled to virtually all of the due process rights accorded adults.

INCREASING EFFICIENCY AND EFFECTIVENESS

Juvenile justice agencies should be well organized and well managed. The efficient operation of juvenile services requires qualified personnel, adequate organizational structure, sound fiscal management, and the development of successful programs. The general public has for the most part been unenthusiastic about providing money for the care and protection of adolescents in the juvenile justice system. Often, facilities for juveniles are crowded, courts lack personnel, probation services are not sufficiently extensive, and educational and recreational programs are underfinanced and inadequate. Thus, resources must be developed to provide efficient, effective juvenile justice programs. The federal government needs to provide national leadership to encourage the adoption of such programs on the state level.

SIGNIFICANT SUPREME COURT DECISIONS IN JUVENILE LAW

The U.S. Supreme Court has made its mark on the juvenile justice system. Within one decade—1966 to 1975—the Supreme Court handed down five major decisions affecting the equal rights of children within the jurisdiction of the juvenile court. A brief statement regarding each of these cases follow:

Kent v. United States **(1966)** established that procedures concerning waiver (whether the juvenile court would hear a case or waive it to an adult court for trial) must measure up to the essentials of due process of law. A hearing, a right to counsel, and access to social records were required. This case was an important forerunner to the most significant juvenile decision by the Supreme Court, *In re Gault.*[51]

In re Gault **(1967)** held that juveniles at trial faced with incarceration were entitled to many of the rights granted adult offenders. These included counsel, notice of the charges, cross-examination of witnesses, and protection against self-incrimination. *Gault* mandated a more formalized juvenile court system.[52]

In re Winship (1970) ruled that the standard of proof in a delinquency proceeding that could result in a child's commitment must be "proof beyond a reasonable doubt" and not a "preponderance of the evidence." According to the Court, civil labels and good intentions do not obviate the need for criminal due process safeguards in juvenile courts.[53]

McKeiver v. Pennsylvania (1971) held that juveniles were not to be afforded the constitutional right to a jury in a delinquency proceeding. The Court felt that this aspect of the adversarial process was not appropriate for the juvenile justice system.[54]

Breed v. Jones (1975) established that the double jeopardy clause of the Fifth Amendment of the U.S. Constitution extends to juvenile offenders through the Fourteenth Amendment due process clause. Juveniles, henceforth, could not be tried in a juvenile court and then transferred to an adult court for a similar action.[55]

Since 1975, the Supreme Court has decided a number of other important cases dealing with juvenile offenders:

Oklahoma Publishing Co. v. District Court (1977) ruled that a state court could not prohibit the publication of information obtained in an open juvenile proceeding. When photographs were taken and published of an 11-year-old boy suspected of homicide and the local court prohibited further disclosure, the publishing company claimed that the court order was a restraint in violation of the First Amendment. The Supreme Court agreed.[56]

Smith v. Daily Mail Publishing Co. (1979) involved the discovery and subsequent publication of the identity of a juvenile suspect in violation of a state statute prohibiting publication. The Supreme Court declared the statute unconstitutional because it believed the state's interest in protecting the child was not of such magnitude as to justify the use of a criminal statute.[57]

Fare v. Michael C. (1979) held that a child's request to see his probation officer at the time of interrogation did not operate to invoke his Fifth Amendment right to remain silent. According to the Court, the probation officer cannot be expected to offer the type of advice that an accused would expect from an attorney.[58]

Eddings v. Oklahoma (1982) ruled that a defendant's age should be a mitigating factor in deciding whether to apply the death penalty.[59]

Schall v. Martin (1984) upheld a statute allowing for the placement of children in preventive detention before their trial. The Court concluded that it was not unreasonable to detain juveniles for their own protection.[60]

New Jersey v. T.L.O. (1985) determined that the Fourth Amendment applies to school searches. The Court adopted a "reasonable suspicion" standard, as opposed to "probable cause," to evaluate the legality of searches and seizures in a school setting.[61]

Thompson v. Oklahoma (1988) ruled that imposing capital punishment on a juvenile murderer who was 15 years old at the time of the offense violated the Eighth Amendment's constitutional prohibition against cruel and unusual punishment.[62]

Stanford v. Kentucky and *Wilkins v. Missouri* (1989) concluded that the imposition of the death penalty on a juvenile who committed a crime between the ages of 16 and 18 was not unconstitutional and that the Eighth Amendment's cruel and unusual punishment clause did not prohibit capital punishment.[63]

FIGURE 12.2
Time line of major constitutional decisions in juvenile justice

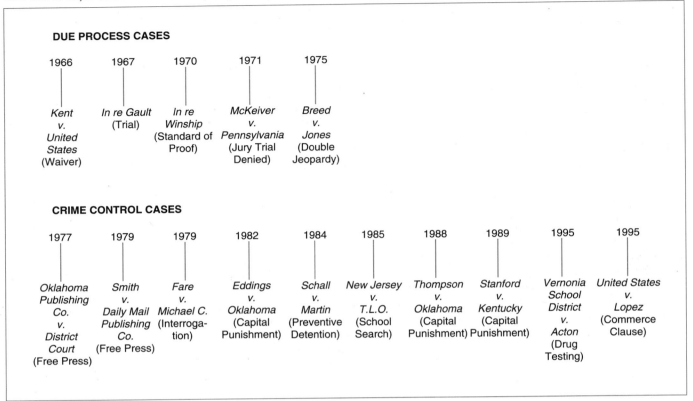

DUE PROCESS CASES

1966	1967	1970	1971	1975
Kent v. United States (Waiver)	In re Gault (Trial)	In re Winship (Standard of Proof)	McKeiver v. Pennsylvania (Jury Trial Denied)	Breed v. Jones (Double Jeopardy)

CRIME CONTROL CASES

1977	1979	1979	1982	1984	1985	1988	1989	1995	1995
Oklahoma Publishing Co. v. District Court (Free Press)	Smith v. Daily Mail Publishing Co. (Free Press)	Fare v. Michael C. (Interroga-tion)	Eddings v. Oklahoma (Capital Punishment)	Schall v. Martin (Preventive Detention)	New Jersey v. T.L.O. (School Search)	Thompson v. Oklahoma (Capital Punishment)	Stanford v. Kentucky (Capital Punishment)	Vernonia School District v. Acton (Drug Testing)	United States v. Lopez (Commerce Clause)

***Vernonia School District v. Acton* (1995)** held that the Fourth Amendment's guarantee against unreasonable searches is not violated by the suspicionless drug testing of all students choosing to participate in interscholastic athletics. The Supreme Court expanded the power of public educators to ensure safe learning environments in schools.[64]

***United States v. Lopez* (1995)** ruled that Congress exceeded its authority under the Commerce Clause when it passed the Gun-Free School Zone Act, which made it a federal crime to possess a firearm within 1,000 feet of a school.[65]

In the hundred or so years that the juvenile court system has been in operation, the Supreme Court has heard very few cases dealing with juvenile delinquency proceedings. The most far-reaching was the *In re Gault* case of 1967, which extended the essentials of due process and fair treatment throughout the juvenile justice system.

Each of the above decisions is discussed in detail in subsequent chapters and is outlined in Figure 12.2.

THE DUE PROCESS REVOLUTION IN REVIEW

Although the *Gault* decision heralded the due process revolution, the movement toward broader procedural protections for juveniles was slowed by a more conservative Supreme Court in the 1970s. Chief Justice Warren Burger believed that the answer to the problems of the juvenile justice system was a return to the informality of the past. This view was operationalized in 1971, for example, in the case of *McKeiver v. Pennsylvania.*[66] The Court expressed its concern that juries in juvenile courts would impinge on the interests of the state and the public in conducting juvenile court proceedings in an efficient, reasonably informal, and flexible manner. What the Court was saying was that a jury trial for juveniles was not essential to a fair and accurate fact-finding process in the juvenile court system.

In the 1980s, the Court continued to limit the expansion of juvenile rights with rulings that recognized the special needs of children. In the *Schall* case, the Court distinguished between adults and juveniles with respect to detaining them before trial, holding that juveniles could be denied bail and held for their own protection and the protection of society.[67] *Schall* was an important case because it dealt with the issue of preventive detention before trial, a process that affects all juvenile court systems. Similarly, in *New Jersey v. T.L.O.,* the Court limited the right of juveniles to be secure from search and seizures. In this case, the Court held that teachers had the right to search students if they violated school rules, even though the students were not suspected of a criminal law violation; adults would be legally immune from this type of search. The *T.L.O.* case concluded that school officials, as representatives of the state, may lawfully conduct searches without a warrant or probable cause.[68]

The future course of constitutional decisions affecting the rights of juveniles while William Rehnquist is chief justice and other conservatives, such as Antonin Scalia, Anthony Kennedy, and Clarence Thomas, are on the bench, is difficult to ascertain. Another unknown is what role Justices Ruth Bader Ginsburg and Stephen Breyer, the newest members of the Supreme Court, appointed by President Clinton in 1993 and 1995 respectively, will play in children's rights issues. Certainly, the thrust of the Supreme Court has been clear over the past decade. Due process and fair treatment must be accorded juveniles throughout the entire juvenile justice process. However, the Court also seems to be saying that the special status of minors gives the state the right to exercise legal controls from which an adult would be exempted. The *McKeiver, Schall,* and *T.L.O.* decisions appear to reflect a shift back to the informality and paternal protection of the juvenile court in preference to further formalizing court proceedings. Whether this trend will continue remains to be seen. However, as Justice Harry A. Blackmun stated in the *McKeiver* case, "If the formalities of the criminal adjudicative process are to be superimposed upon the juvenile court system, there is little need for its separate existence. Perhaps that ultimate disillusionment will come one day, but for the moment we are disinclined to give impetus to it."[69] Considering the makeup and direction of today's Court, we might expect to see Justice Blackmun's prediction one day come true.[70]

Certainly the Court's decisions in the death penalty cases seem to indicate a strong conservative reaction to liberal and ineffective crime-control programs.[71] The *Vernonia* case, extending the school's authority to search students by drug testing, is another example of this philosophy.

Given the more conservative mood of the nation and its legal system, it is unlikely that any liberalization of the legal rights of juveniles will take place in the near future. If anything, the Supreme Court will give states more opportunities to control minors. According to Samuel Davis, a leading expert on juvenile law, the Court will most likely decide juvenile cases individually and apply the theory of due process under the Fourteenth Amendment to establish the child's constitutional rights in the future.[72]

THE JUVENILE JUSTICE AND DELINQUENCY PREVENTION ACT OF 1994—TWENTY YEARS AFTER

History of Federal Juvenile Justice Legislation

Over twenty years have passed since the enactment of the JJDP Act. It was the first major federal law to address juvenile delinquency in a comprehensive manner by providing funds to promote improvements in state and local juvenile justice systems. However, it was not the first federal juvenile delinquency law. In 1912, Congress created the Children's Bureau to improve the operations of America's emerging juvenile court system. Little else happened until the mid-20th century when the Truman Administration convened the National Conference on Children and Youth in 1948 to examine ways to prevent juvenile crime. Although the Conference recommended the Federal government play a greater role in juvenile justice, Congress did nothing.

When juvenile gang activity became a serious state and local problem in the 1960s, the Kennedy Administration worked with Congress to enact the Juvenile Delinquency and Youth Offenses Control Act of 1961. This Act provided funds to states for projects to improve methods of preventing and controlling juvenile crime. The Neighborhood Youth Corps, the Legal Services Corporation and Head Start (an early childhood and education program) evolved from this Federal delinquency initiative. In 1966, President Johnson established the Commission on Law Enforcement and Administration of Justice. The Commission's Task Force on Juvenile Delinquency proposed four major strategies to reduce juvenile crime: (1) decriminalization of status offenses; (2) diversion of youth from the court system into alternative programs; (3) deinstitutionalization by using community homes rather than large training schools; and (4) extending due process rights to juveniles. The Juvenile Delinquency Prevention and Control Act of 1968 was passed to achieve these goals. In the same year, Congress passed the Omnibus Crime Control and Safe Streets Act which involved the U.S. Department of Justice in the juvenile justice system. By this time, numerous federal agencies had become involved with delinquency prevention. A consensus emerged that Federal juvenile justice programs were unfocused and ineffective. Thus, congressional work began on new landmark legislation for the juvenile justice system.

Legislative Reform

By 1974, juvenile delinquency had become a serious nationwide problem. Two themes set the stage for the JJDP Act. First, financial assistance alone was inadequate to combat juvenile crime—comprehensive planning was needed. Secondly, some practices like confining status offenders with delinquents and adult offenders had to be halted. With these considerations, the JJDP Act was passed in 1974. The Act provided Federal funds to divert juveniles from correctional settings into community programs and restitution projects. In particular, Section 223 (a) 12 and 13 of the Act required states to remove status offenders from secure confinement and to separate adults and juvenile offenders as a condition of receiving federal funds. The Act also required that states allocate 75% of the federal funds they received to such community-based programs and promoted the need for small public and private community facilities.

For the time being, these cases affirm the Supreme Court's interest in applying constitutional principles of due process to juvenile justice while maintaining the *parens patriae* philosophy. In so doing, all the states are required to create juvenile court statutes that conform to the dictates of the Court.

In sum, the early cases from *Kent* to *Breed* provided due process protections for children; the latter cases, such as *Schall, T.L.O.,* and *Stanford,* rejected the rehabilitation ideal in favor of a punishment philosophy.[73] With the recentappointments of Clarence Thomas, Ruth Ginsburg, David Souter, and Stephen Breyer, the Supreme Court's views regarding the constitutional rights of juveniles are likely to remain unchanged for years to come.

With congressional support, funding was increased from 25 million in 1974 to 75 million in 1977 and to 100 million by 1980. During this time, status offense cases referred to the juvenile courts decreased, the rate of detention of status offenders decreased, as did the total number of cases referred to the juvenile courts. Unfortunately from 1980 to 1987, the budget of the Office of Juvenile Justice and Delinquency Prevention (administrative arm of the Act) decreased to 66 million dollars because the focus had shifted from delinquency prevention to criminal justice.

The 1988 and 1992 amendments to the JJDP Act reestablished the importance of juvenile delinquency prevention. Congress was concerned about addressing the problems of juvenile gangs, youth development, due process and the overrepresentation of minorities in the juvenile justice system. The new amendments also required the OJJDP to submit to Congress an annual report detailing the number of juveniles in custody, the types of offenses for which they were charged and their race and gender. Funding opportunities became available for states willing to embark on innovative activities, such as improving health services in corrections, removing gender bias from the justice system and creating community correctional alternatives for violent juveniles. Since the Clinton Administration has made crime one of its priorities, the OJJDP budget has increased to 140 million dollars in 1995. After 20 plus years, the Act continues to provide funding for juvenile justice reform.

Accomplishments and Recommendations

Today, virtually all the states are in compliance with the federal mandates for removing status offenders from secure incarceration, as well as separating juveniles from convicted adults, and removing youth from adult jails. From the early 1980s to 1992, the average one-day count of juveniles in adult jails fell from 12,000 to 2,000. In addition, while the percent of violent juvenile crime has increased, the overall rate for juvenile crime has remained stable over the last 5 years. Many states are also working to address the problem of disproportionate minority confinement.

The key question is what does the future hold for the JJDPA? Juvenile crime is a high priority in every state. Deinstitutionalization of status offenders remains a central theme. Expanding community-based programs and services for juveniles as alternatives to institutional care is equally important. It would also be helpful if the federal government extended the mandates of the JJDP Act to cover funding under the Violent Crime Control and Law Enforcement Act of 1994, where funds are also available for juvenile delinquency prevention programs.

In conclusion, a White House Conference on Juvenile Justice is needed to review the nation's juvenile justice system. Such a conference would assess the programs sponsored by JJDP Act and determine which have worked and which have not. Other important issues that need to be examined include: (1) trends of binding juveniles over to adult courts at younger ages; (2) placing continued emphasis on prevention as the most cost-effective way to reduce juvenile crime; (3) reforming secure juvenile correctional facilities and finding institutions where corrections truly works.

The JJDP Act has proven itself to offer tremendous support to states in reforming the juvenile justice system. Today, all the states pursue the Act's goals and objectives. Over two decades, the Act has provided a unique federal-state partnership by assisting states in carrying out their responsibilities in combating juvenile delinquency.

Source: Juvenile Justice and Delinquency Prevention Act of 1974, Pub. L. 93-415; Gordon Raley, "The JJDP Act: A Second Look," Juvenile Justice Journal 2:11-18 (1995).

FEDERAL FUNDING FOR JUVENILE JUSTICE

Since the 1960s, four major efforts have been funded by the government to support the goals of juvenile justice and delinquency reform. First, in 1967, the **President's Commission on Law Enforcement and the Administration of Justice,** a product of the Johnson administration's concern for social welfare, issued its well-thought-out and documented report on juvenile delinquency and its control.[75] Influenced by Cloward and Ohlin's then-popular opportunity theory, the commission suggested that the juvenile justice system must provide underprivileged youths with opportunities for success, including jobs and education. The commission also recognized the need to develop effective law enforcement procedures to control hard-core youthful offenders and at the same time grant them due process of law when they came before the courts.

During the 1960s, the concern was primarily for individual treatment and the rights of juvenile offenders. Child advocates and federal lawmakers were interested in merging the rehabilitation model with due process of law.

The presidential commission report of 1967 acted as a catalyst for the passage of the federal Juvenile Delinquency Prevention and Control (JDP) Act of 1968. This law created a Youth Development and Delinquency Prevention Administration, which concentrated on helping states develop new juvenile justice programs, particularly involving diversion of youth, decriminalization, and "decarceration." In 1968, Congress also passed the Omnibus Safe Streets and Crime Control Act.[76] Title I of this law established the Law Enforcement Assistance Administration (LEAA) to provide federal funds to improve the adult and juvenile justice systems. In 1972, Congress amended the JDP Act of 1968 to allow the LEAA to focus its funding on juvenile justice and delinquency prevention programs. State and local governments were required to develop and adopt comprehensive plans to obtain federal assistance.

Because crime continued to receive much publicity, a second effort called the **National Advisory Commission on Criminal Justice Standards and Goals** was established in 1973 by the Nixon administration.[77] Its report on juvenile justice and delinquency prevention identified such major strategies as (1) preventing delinquent behavior before it occurs; (2) developing diversion activities; (3) establishing dispositional alternatives; (4) providing due process for all juveniles; and (5) controlling the violent and the chronic delinquent.

This commission's recommendations formed the basis for additional legislation, the landmark **Juvenile Justice and Delinquency Prevention Act of 1974.**[78] This important act eliminated the old Youth Development and Delinquency Prevention Administration and replaced it with the Office of Juvenile Justice and Delinquency Prevention (OJJDP) within the LEAA. In 1980, the LEAA was phased out, and the OJJDP became an independent agency in the Department of Justice, Attorney General's Office. The role of the OJJDP was to develop and implement worthwhile programs to prevent and reduce juvenile crimes.

Throughout the 1970s, its two most important goals were (1) removing juveniles from detention in adult jails and (2) eliminating the incarceration together of juvenile and status offenders. During this period, the OJJDP stressed the creation of formal diversion and restitution programs around the United States.

A third effort took place in the 1980s, when the OJJDP shifted its priorities to the identification and control of chronic, violent juvenile offenders. This goal was in line with the Reagan and Bush administrations' more conservative views of justice. The federal government poured millions of dollars into research projects designed to study chronic offenders, predict their behavior, and evaluate programs created to control their activities.

Since 1974, the Juvenile Justice and Delinquency Prevention Act has had a significant impact on juvenile justice policy. It has been an important instrument for removing status offenders from jails and detention centers, as well as providing funds for innovative and effective programs. In 1992, Congress approved the OJJDP reauthorization for another four years.

The latest effort, in 1995, made available further funding for juvenile justice and delinquency prevention through the **Violent Crime Control and Law Enforcement Act of 1994.**[79] Known as the largest piece of crime legislation in the history of America, it was touted by the Clinton administration for providing for

100,000 new police officers and billions of dollars for prisons and prevention programs for both adult and juvenile offenders. (See Focus on Delinquency on page 454—The Juvenile Justice Prevention Act of 1994 which highlights the federal role in juvenile justice legislation.)

SUMMARY

The study of juvenile justice is concerned with juvenile delinquency and antisocial behavior and the agencies involved in their prevention, control, and treatment. The juvenile justice system is also a process consisting of the steps from the initial investigation of a juvenile crime through the appeal of a case. These steps are the police investigation, the intake procedure in the juvenile court, the pretrial procedures used for juvenile offenders, adjudication, disposition, and the postdispositional procedures.

The processing and terminology of the juvenile system can be compared and contrasted with that of the adult criminal justice system. The juvenile court is the heart of the juvenile process. Each jurisdiction organizes its court differently and has varying criteria. The most important factors determining jurisdiction are the age of the offender and the nature of his or her offense.

Over the past three decades, the courts have moved to eliminate the traditional view that a youth brought into the juvenile justice system has no rights. Both the U.S. Supreme Court and the lower courts have granted juveniles procedural safeguards and the protection of due process in the juvenile courts. Major Supreme Court and lower court decisions pertaining to the entire juvenile process have laid down the constitutional requirements for juvenile proceedings.[74] It is important to recognize that in years past, the protec-

tions currently afforded to both adults and children were not available to children.

How the juvenile justice system deals with the adolescent is also determined by cyclical directions of the system and its individual agencies. The following are considered realistic strategies for juvenile justice: (1) delinquency prevention, (2) diversion, (3) incapacitation, (4) fairness and justice for children, and (5) efficiency and effectiveness. Depending on the goals of juvenile justice, certain models or philosophies exist.

Juvenile justice is a very complex system and process whose many strategies are often translated into day-to-day operations and programs. If professionals responsible for the administration of juvenile justice are to make progress in combatting delinquency, they must seek to establish clearly defined goals for the system. In addition, certain key agencies, such as the juvenile court and correctional institutions, must explore how they can deal with youths more comprehensively and effectively.

It is doubtful any real progress in improving the juvenile justice system could be made without significant support from the federal government. By reauthorizing the Juvenile Justice and Delinquency Prevention Act of 1974 and by passing the Violent Crime Control and Law Enforcement Act of 1994, Congress has made a historic effort to address the recent increase in the levels of juvenile crime.

KEY TERMS

Ex Parte Crouse
juvenile justice
parens patriae
juvenile justice system
dangerous classes
child savers
House of Refuge
Children's Aid Society
Society for the Prevention of
    Cruelty to Children

Illinois Juvenile Court Act of
    1899
waive
predisposition report
detention hearing
adjudicatory hearing
bifurcated process
disposition
petition
hearing

models of juvenile justice
status offenders
Kent v. United States (1966)
In re Gault (1967)
In re Winship (1971)
McKeiver v. Pennsylvania (1971)
Breed v. Jones (1975)
Oklahoma Publishing Co. v.
District Court (1977)
Smith v. Daily Mail Publishing

Co. (1979)
Fare v. Michael C. (1979)
Eddings v. Oklahoma (1982)
Schall v. Martin (1984)
New Jersey v. T.L.O. (1985)
Thompson v. Oklahoma (1988)
Stanford v. Kentucky (1989)

Wilkins v. Missouri (1989)
Vernonia School District v. Acton (1995)
United States v. Lopez (1995)
President's Commission on Law
   Enforcement and the
   Administration of Justice

National Advisory Commission on
   Criminal Justice Standards and
   Goals
Juvenile Justice and Delinquency
   Prevention Act of 1994
Violent Crime Control and Law
   Enforcement Act of 1994

QUESTIONS FOR DISCUSSION

1. What factors precipitated the development of the Illinois Juvenile Court Act of 1899?
2. The formal components of the criminal justice system are often considered to be the police, the court, and the correctional agency. How do these components compare with the major areas of the juvenile justice system? Is the operation of justice similar in the juvenile and adult systems?
3. Which philosophy of juvenile justice do you hold? What do you believe is wrong with the other philosophies?
4. Should there be a juvenile justice system, or should juveniles who commit serious crimes be treated as adults and the others be handled by social welfare agencies?
5. The Supreme Court has made a number of major decisions in the area of juvenile justice. What are these decisions? What is their impact on the juvenile justice system?
6. What is the meaning of the term *procedural due process of law*? Explain why and how procedural due process has had an impact on juvenile justice.
7. One of the most significant reforms in dealing with the juvenile offender was the opening of the New York House of Refuge in 1825. What were the social and judicial consequences of this reform on the juvenile justice system?
8. What are the differences between the justice and the rehabilitation models of juvenile justice?
9. What role has the federal government played in the juvenile justice system over the last 20 years?

NOTES

1. See *Report of the Task Force on Juvenile Justice and Delinquency Prevention, Juvenile Justice and Delinquency Prevention* (Washington, D.C.: U.S. Government Printing Office, 1976); for a more current blueprint on reform, see Ira M. Schwartz, ed., *Juvenile Justice and Public Policy—Toward a National Agenda* (New York: Lexington Books, 1992).
2. Martin Forst and Martha Elin Blomquist, "Punishment, Accountability, and the Juvenile Justice System," *Juvenile and Family Court Journal* 43:1 (1992).
3. See, generally, Paul Kfoury, *Children before the Court: Reflections on Legal Issues Affecting Minors* (Boston: Butterworth's Legal Group, 1987); also see Francis Allen, *The Decline of the Rehabilitative Ideal* (New Haven, Conn.: Yale University Press, 1981).
4. Robert M. Mennel, "Origins of the Juvenile Court: Changing Perspectives on the Legal Rights of Juvenile Delinquents," *Crime and Delinquency* 18:68–78 (1972).
5. See, generally, Daniel Glaser, *The Effectiveness of a Prison and Parole System* (Indianapolis, Ind.: Bobbs-Merrill, 1964); and Charles Newman, ed., *Sourcebook on Probation, Parole, and Pardons,* 2nd ed. (Springfield, Ill.: Charles C. Thomas, 1964).
6. Anthony Salerno, "The Child Saving Movement: Altruism or Conspiracy," *Juvenile and Family Court Journal* 42:37 (1991).
7. Ronald Bayer, "The Darker Side of Urban Life: Slums in the City," in Frank Copp and P. C. Dolce, eds., *Cities in Transition: From the Ancient World to Urban America* (Chicago: Nelson Hall, 1974), p. 220.

8. Robert Mennel, "Attitudes and Policies towards Juvenile Delinquency," in Michael Tonry and Norval Morris, eds., *Crime and Justice,* vol. 5, (Chicago: University of Chicago Press, 1983), p. 198.

9. Anthony M. Platt, *The Child Savers: The Invention of Delinquency* (Chicago: University of Chicago Press, 1969).

10. Ibid.

11. Sanford J. Fox, "Juvenile Justice Reform: A Historical Perspective," Stanford Law Review 22: 1187 (1970).

12. Robert S. Pickett, *House of Refuge—Origins of Juvenile Reform in New York State, 1815–1857* (Syracuse, N.Y.: Syracuse University Press, 1969).

13. Mennel, "Origins of the Juvenile Court," pp. 69–70.

14. Ibid., pp. 70–71.

15. 4 Whart. 9 (1839).

16. Ibid., p. 11.

17. *O'Connell v. Turner,* 55 Ill. 280 (1870).

18. Ibid., p. 283.

19. Fox, "Juvenile Justice Reform," p. 1217.

20. U.S. Department of Justice, Juvenile Justice and Delinquency Prevention, *Two Hundred Years of American Criminal Justice: An LEAA Bicentennial Study* (Washington, D.C.: Law Enforcement Assistance Administration, 1976).

21. Ibid., pp. 62–74.

22. Beverly Smith, "Female Admissions and Paroles of the Western House of Refuge in the 1880s, "An Historical Example of Community Corrections," *Journal of Research in Crime and Delinquency* 26:36–66 (1989).

23. Fox, "Juvenile Justice Reform," p. 1229.

24. Ibid., p. 1211.

25. Elizabeth Pleck, "Criminal Approaches to Family Violence, 1640–1980" in Lloyd Ohlin and Michael Tonry, eds., Family Violence (Chicago: University of Chicago Press, 1989), pp. 19–58.

26. Elizabeth Pleck, *Domestic Tyranny: The Making of Social Policy Against Family Violence from Colonial Times to the Present* (New York: Oxford University Press, 1987), p. 28–30.

27. Linda Gordon, *Family Violence and Social Control* (New York: Viking Press, 1988).

28. Kathleen Block and Donna Hale, "Turf Wars in the Progressive Era Juvenile Justice: The Relationship of Private and Public Child Care Agencies," *Crime and Delinquency* 37:225–41 (1991).

29. Theodore Ferdinand, "Juvenile Delinquency or Juvenile Justice: Which Came First?" *Criminology* 27: 79–106 (1989).

30. Ibid., p. 100.

31. *In re Gault,* 387 U.S. 1, 87 S.Ct. 1428, 18 L.Ed. 2d 527 (1967).

32. Salerno, "The Child Saving Movement," p. 37.

33. Platt, *The Child Savers: The Invention of Delinquency.*

34. Ibid., p. 116.

35. Herman Schwendinger and Julia Schwendinger, "Delinquency and the Collective Varieties of Youth," *Crime and Social Justice* 5:7–25 (1976).

36. Randall Shelden and Lynn Osborne, " 'For Their Own Good': Class Interests and the Child Saving Movement in Memphis, Tennessee, 1900–1917," *Criminology* 27:747–67 (1989).

37. Fox, "Juvenile Justice Reform," p. 1229.

38. Mary Odem and Steven Schlossman, "Guardians of Virtue: The Juvenile Court and Female Delinquency in Early 20th-Century Los Angeles," *Crime and Delinquency* 37:186–203 (1991).

39. Katherine Lenroot and Emma Lundberg, *Juvenile Courts at Work,* U.S. Children's Bureau Publication No. 141 (Washington, D.C.: U.S. Government Printing Office, 1925).

40. John Sutton, "Bureaucrats and Entrepreneurs: Institutional Responses to Deviant Children in the United States, 1890–1920," *American Journal of Sociology* 95:1367–1400 (1990).

41. Ibid., p. 1383.

42. Margueritte Rosenthal, "Reforming the Juvenile Correctional Institution: Efforts of the U.S. Children's Bureau in the 1930's," *Journal of Sociology and Social Welfare* 14:47–74 (1987).

43. For an overview of these developments, see Theodore Ferdinand, "History Overtakes the Juvenile Justice System," *Crime and Delinquency* 37:204–24 (1991).

44. N.Y. Fam. Ct. Act, Art. 7, Sec. 712 (Consol. 1962).

45. Kathleen Maguire and Ann Pastore, eds., *Sourcebook of Criminal Justice Statistics, 1994* (Washington, D.C.: U.S. Government Printing Office, 1995).

46. Information in this section comes from a variety of sources, including Maguire and Pastore, *Sourcebook of Criminal Justice Statistics, 1994;* Howard Snyder and Melissa Sickmund, *Juvenile Offenders and Victims: A National Report* (Washington, D.C.: Office of Juvenile Justice and Delinquency Prevention, 1995); *Crime in the United States: Uniform Crime Reports,* 1994 (Washington, D.C.: U.S. Government Printing Office, 1995).

47. For an excellent review of the juvenile process, see Adrienne Volenik, *Checklists for Use in Juvenile Delinquency Proceedings* (Washington, D.C.: American Bar Association, 1985).

48. Barry Feld, "Criminology and the Juvenile Court: A Research Agenda for the 1990s." In Ira M. Schwartz, *Juvenile Justice and Public Policy—Toward a National Agenda* (New York: Lexington Books, 1992), p. 59.

49. Robert O. Dawson, "The Future of Juvenile Justice: Is It Time to Abolish the System?" *Journal of Criminal Law and Criminology* 81:136–55 (1990).

50. Robert Smith, "The Elephant in My Living Room," *Crime and Delinquency* 33:317–24 (1987); "Racial Disparity in California Juvenile Justice System," *Youth Law News: Journal of National Center for Youth Law* 5:10–11 (1992).

51. *In re Gault,* 383 U.S. 541 (1966).
52. *In re Gault,* 387 U.S. 1, 19, 87 S.Ct. 1428 (1967).
53. *In re Winship,* 397 U.S. 358, 90 S.Ct. 1068 (1970).
54. *McKeiver v. Pennsylvania,* 403 U.S. 528, 91 S.Ct. 1976 (1971).
55. *Breed v. Jones,* 421 U.S. 519, 95 S.Ct. 1779 (1975).
56. *Oklahoma Publishing Co. v. District Court,* 430 U.S. 308, 97 S.Ct. 1045, 51 L.Ed. 2d (1977).
57. *Smith v. Daily Mail Publishing Co.,* 443 U.S. 97, 99 S.Ct. 2667, 61 L.Ed. 2d 399 (1979).
58. *Fare v. Michael C.,* 442 U.S. 707, 99 S.Ct. 2560 (1979).
59. *Eddings v. Oklahoma,* 455 U.S. 104, 102 S.Ct. 869, 71 L.Ed. 2d 1 (1982).
60. *Schall v. Martin,* 467 U.S. 253, 104 S.Ct 2403 (1984).
61. *New Jersey v. T.L.O.,* 469 U.S. 325, 105 S.Ct. 733 (1985).
62. *Thompson v. Oklahoma,* 487 U.S. 815, 108 S.Ct. 2687, 101 L.Ed. 2d 702 (1988).
63. *Stanford v. Kentucky,* 492 U.S., 109 S.Ct. 2969 (1989).
64. *Vernonia School District v. Acton,* 115 S.Ct. 2394 (1995).
65. *United States v. Lopez,* 115 S.Ct. 1624 (1995).
66. *McKeiver v. Pennsylvania,* 403 U.S. 528 (1971), at 538.
67. *Schall v. Martin,* 467 U.S. 253 (1984).
68. *New Jersey v. T.L.O.,* 469 U.S. 325 (1985).
69. Ibid., p. 538.
70. For differing views of juvenile justice legal policy, see H. Ted Rubin, *Behind the Black Robe—Juvenile Court Judges and the Court* (Beverly Hills, Calif.: Sage, 1985).
71. Sandra Evans Skouron, Joseph Scott, and Francis Cullen, "The Death Penalty for Juveniles: An Assessment of Public Support," *Crime and Delinquency* 45:562—76 (1989); Dinah Robinson and Stephen Otis, "Patterns of Mitigating Factors in Juvenile Death Penalty Cases," *Criminal Law Bulletin* 28:246–62 (1992); Victor Streib, *The Juvenile Death Penalty Today—A Report* (Cleveland, Ohio: Cleveland Marshall College of Law, 1995).
72. Samuel Davis, *The Rights of Juveniles,* 2d. ed. (update 1994; New York: Clark Boardman, Co. 1984), pp. 7–12.
73. Jay S. Albanese, *Dealing with Delinquency—The Future of Juvenile Justice* (Chicago: Nelson-Hall, 1992), p. 122.
74. Barry Feld, "The Juvenile Court Meets the Principle of the Offense: Legislative Changes in Juvenile Waiver Statutes," *Journal of Criminal Law and Criminology* 78:471 (1987); Joseph Sanborn, Jr., "Constitutional Problems of Juvenile Delinquency Trials," *Judicature* 78:78 (1994).
75. President's Commission on Law Enforcement and the Administration of Justice. *The Challenge of Crime in a Free Society* (Washington, D.C.: U.S. Government Printing Office, 1967).
76. Public Law 90—351, Title I—Omnibus Safe Streets and Crime Control Act of 1968, 90th Congress, June 1968.
77. National Advisory Commission on Criminal Justice Standards and Goals, *A National Strategy to Reduce Crime* (Washington, D.C.: U.S. Government Printing Office, 1973).
78. Juvenile Justice and Delinquency Prevention Act of 1974, Public Law 93—415 (1974). For a critique of this legislation, see Ira Schwartz, *(In) Justice for Juveniles—Rethinking the Best Interests of the Child* (Lexington, Mass.: D.C. Heath, 1989), p. 175.
79. For an extensive summary of the *Violent Crime Control and Law Enforcement Act of 1994,* see *Criminal Law Reporter,* 55:2305–2430 (1994).

PART FIVE

Controlling Juvenile Offenders

Controlling juvenile delinquency is a complex task. While adults who violate the law are subject to clearly defined sanctions, the *parens patriae* philosophy demands that the state always consider the best interests of the child when controlling juvenile behavior. The line between treatment and punishment, however, is often a narrow one. When do the efforts of people truly desiring to help troubled youngsters actually become a crushing burden on them? Is it possible that the doctrine of *parens patriae* goes too far? These are questions that constantly perplex juvenile justice policymakers. Is it possible to create a system in which troubled juveniles are helped using the least restrictive alternatives possible, while at the same time serious juvenile offenders are restrained? Should we be more punitive than we have been, or should we employ even greater compassion and understanding? Or does the answer lie somewhere in between?

Part V contains three chapters devoted to the process and policies used to control juvenile offenders. Chapter 13 deals with police handling of delinquent and status offenders. It contains information on the police role, the organization of police services, and prevention efforts. It explores the power of a police officer to take a child into custody and the rights of the child when arrested and outlines the applicability of *Miranda v. Arizona* to the juvenile process. This chapter also points out how the U.S. Supreme Court has expressly found that juveniles fall within the protection of the Fourth Amendment, and reviews the development of search and seizure in school systems. Chapter 14 is concerned with the important topic of early court processing. It describes such current issues as diversion programs, removal of minor offenders from secure detention facilities, and the transfer of youths to adult courts. The "transfer of jurisdiction" issue, often called waiver, remand, or removal to the criminal court, is a unique and controversial statutory process. The trend is to increase the flow of juvenile cases to adult courts. Chapter 15 discusses the equally important topic of juvenile trial and disposition. It considers the role of the prosecutor, the juvenile court judge, and the defense attorney at adjudication and disposition. Since juveniles, as well as adults, are entitled to fair trials, this chapter concerns itself with a detailed analysis of the landmark constitutional decisions on juvenile justice. Next, it deals with disposition and sentencing—the key element in the juvenile process.

After reading these chapters, the student should have an understanding of how society has attempted to control juvenile offenders, beginning with the prejudicial process and concluding with the disposition.

CHAPTER THIRTEEN

POLICE WORK WITH JUVENILES

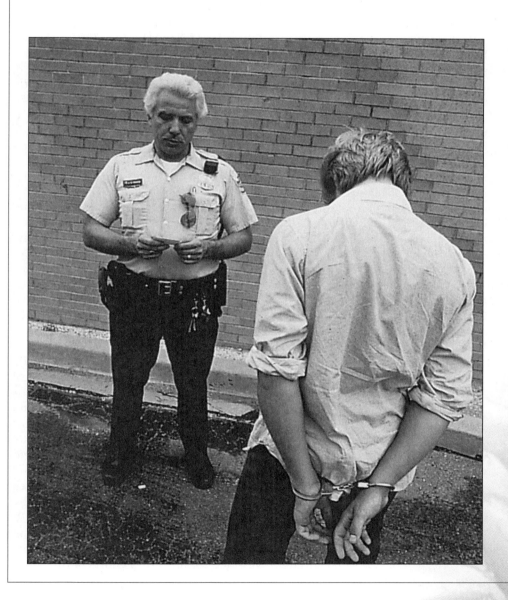

INTRODUCTION

The modern juvenile justice system is the core from which all efforts to control juvenile crime emit. Although other segments of society—the family, the political system, the schools, and religious institutions—play a role, it is with the juvenile justice system that most social control rests. As its law enforcement and social control arm, the police, therefore, becomes the frontline agency that deals with the prevention and control of juvenile delinquency.

In the minds of most citizens, the primary responsibility of the police is to protect the public. From the vast array of films, books, and TV shows that depict the derring-do of police officers in the field, the public has obtained an image of "crime fighters" who "always get their man." Since the tumultuous 1960s, however, the public has become increasingly aware that the reality of police work is quite a bit different from its fictional glorification. When police departments failed to bring the crime rate down despite massive government subsidies, when citizens complained of civil rights violations, and when tales of police corruption became widespread, it was evident that a crisis was imminent in American policing.

During the 1980s and 1990s, a new view of policing emerged around the nation. Rather than foster the view of the police officer as a hell-bent-for-leather crime fighter who only tracks down serious criminals or stops armed robberies in progress, police departments adopted the concept that the police role should be to maintain order in the community, interact with citizens, and be a visible and accessible component of the community. The argument is that police efforts can only be successful if they are conducted in partnership with concerned and active citizens. This movement is referred to as **community policing.**[1]

Interest in the community policing concept does not mean that the crime-control model of law enforcement is history. An ongoing effort is being made to improve the crime-fighting capability of police agencies, and there are some indications that the effort is paying off. Recent research indicates that aggressive, formal action by the police can help reduce the incidence of repeat offending, and technological innovations, such as fingerprint-reading computers, may bring about greater police efficiency.[2] Nonetheless, after 25 years of attempting to improve police effectiveness through a combination of policy and technical advancement, little evidence exists that adding police or improving their skills has had a major impact on their crime-fighting success.[3]

During this era in which experts are rethinking the basic police role, the relationship between police and juvenile offenders has become quite critical. Because police officers represent the authority of the community, even the most casual meeting between a police officer and a young person can have a profound effect on the youth's future. How the youth reacts to this authority figure may depend on the police officer's response to his or her behavior. This more often than not depends on the officer's personal biases and values, as well as his or her role orientation and attitudes toward police work. Working with juvenile offenders may be especially perplexing for police officers because the need to help young people and steer them away from a criminal career may seem to conflict with the traditional police duties of crime prevention and order maintenance. In addition, the police are faced with a nationwide adolescent drug problem, increases in the violent crime arrest rate for teens, and renewed gang activity. While efforts are being made to improve adult crime control efforts of the police, it may also be necessary to increase specialized services for juveniles.

This chapter focuses on police work in juvenile justice and delinquency prevention. It covers the role and responsibilities of the police; the history of policing juveniles; the organization and management of police–juvenile operations; the legal aspects of police work, including custodial interrogation, search and seizure, and lineups; the concept of police discretion; and the relationship between police and community efforts to prevent crime.

THE ROLE OF THE POLICE IN HANDLING JUVENILE OFFENDERS

How do juvenile officers spend their time, and what roles do they perform in the police and criminal justice system? **Juvenile officers** either operate alone as specialists within a police department or as part of the juvenile unit of a police department. Their role is similar to that of officers working with adult offenders—to intervene if the actions of a citizen produce public danger or disorder. Most officers regard the violations of juveniles as nonserious unless they are committed by a chronic troublemaker or involve significant damage to persons or property. Juveniles who misbehave are often ignored or treated informally. Police encounters with juveniles are generally the result of reports made by citizens, and the bulk of such encounters pertain to matters of minor legal consequence.[4]

Of course, police must also deal with serious juvenile offenders whose criminal acts are similar to those of adults, but these are only a small minority of the offender population. Thus, police who deal with delinquency must concentrate on being peacekeepers and crime preventers.[5]

Handling juvenile offenders can produce major **role conflicts** for the police. They may find what they consider their primary duty, **law enforcement**, undercut by the need to aid in the rehabilitation of youthful offenders. A police officer's actions in cases involving adults are usually controlled by the rule of criminal law and his or her own personal judgment, or **discretion**. In contrast, a case involving a juvenile often demands that the officer consider the "best interests of the child" and how the officer's actions will influence the child's future life and well-being. Consequently, police are much more likely to use informal procedures with juvenile offenders than with adults. It is estimated that between 30 percent and 40 percent of all juvenile arrests by police are handled informally within the police department or referred to a community service agency (see Figure 13.1). These informal dispositions are the result of the police officer's discretionary authority, discussed later in this chapter.[6]

Many officers dislike getting involved in juvenile matters, probably because most juvenile crimes are held in low regard by fellow police officers.[7] Juvenile detectives are sometimes referred to as the "Lollipop Squad" or "Diaper Dicks." The field of juvenile law is often referred to as "Kiddie Court." Arresting a 12-year-old girl for shoplifting and bringing her in tears to the police station is not considered the way to win respect from one's peers.

Police intervention in situations involving juveniles can be difficult, frustrating—and emotional. The officer often encounters hostile or belligerent behavior from the juvenile offender, as well as witnesses to the encounter. Overreaction by the officer can result in a major, violent incident. Even if the officer succeeds in quieting or dispersing the crowd of witnesses, the juveniles will probably reappear the next day, often in the same place.[8]

FIGURE 13.1

The police response to juvenile crime. To understand how police deal with juvenile crime, picture a funnel, with the result shown here. For every 500 juveniles taken into custody, a little more than 60 percent are sent to the juvenile court, and almost 33 percent are released.

To understand how police deal with juvenile crime, picture a funnel, with the result shown here. For every 500 juveniles taken into custody, a little more than 60 percent are sent to the juvenile court, and almost 33 percent are released.

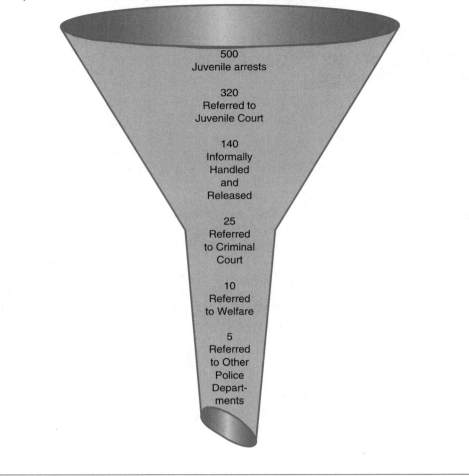

500
Juvenile arrests

320
Referred to
Juvenile Court

140
Informally
Handled
and
Released

25
Referred
to Criminal
Court

10
Referred
to Welfare

5
Referred
to Other
Police
Depart-
ments

Source: Kathleen Maguire and Ann Pastore, eds., *Sourcebook of Criminal Justice Statistics 1994* (Washington, D.C.: U.S. Department of Justice, Bureau of Justice Statistics, 1995); Howard Snyder and Melissa Sickmund, *Juvenile Offenders and Victims: A National Report* (Washington, D.C.: OJJDP, 1995).

Role conflicts are often exacerbated because most police–juvenile encounters involve confrontations brought about by loitering, disturbing the peace, and rowdiness, rather than by serious law violations. Dealing with youth problems brings police officers little job satisfaction. For example, over the last decade, public concern has risen about today's out-of-control youth. Yet, because of legal constraints and family interference, the police are often limited in how they can respond to such status offenders.[9]

What role should the police play in mediating problems with youths—that of hard-line law enforcement or social service-oriented delinquency prevention? The International Association of Chiefs of Police sees the solution as lying somewhere in between: "Most police departments operate juvenile programs that

Handling juvenile offenders can produce major role conflicts for the police. They may find what they consider their primary duty, law enforcement, undercut by the need to aid in the rehabilitation of youthful offenders. A police officer's actions in cases involving adults are usually controlled by the rule of criminal law and his or her own personal judgment, or discretion. Cases involving a juvenile often demand that the officer consider the "best interest of the child" and how the officer's actions will influence the child's future life and well-being.

combine the law enforcement and delinquency prevention roles, and the police should work with the juvenile court to determine a role that is most suitable for the community."[10] In fact, police officers may also act as juvenile prosecutors in some rural courts when attorneys are not available. Thus, the police–juvenile role extends from the on-the-street encounter to the station house to the juvenile court. It seems that for juvenile matters involving minor criminal conduct or incorrigible behavior, the police ordinarily select the "least restrictive alternative" course of action. Such courses include nonintervention, temporary assistance, and referral to community agencies. Violent juvenile crime, on the other hand, requires that the police investigate, arrest, and even detain youths while providing constitutional safeguards similar to those available to adult offenders.

THE POLICE AND VIOLENT JUVENILE CRIME

Violent juvenile offenders are often defined as those juveniles adjudicated delinquent for crimes of homicide, rape, robbery, and aggravated assault. Law enforcement agencies made more than two million arrests of person under age 18 in 1992; nearly six percent were for a violent crime.[11] Table 13.1 illustrates the significant increase in specific violent crimes from 1985 to 1994. This increase in the juvenile arrest rate began in the late 1980s after a decade of relative stability (see Figure 13.2). Some experts predict that if trends continue as they have over the past 10 years, juvenile arrests for violent crime will double by the year 2010 (see chapter 2).[12]

As a result of these dire predictions, police and other justice agencies are experimenting with different methods of dealing with violent youth. Some of the methods have existed for decades, such as placing more officers on the beat. Others use state-of-the-art computer technology to pinpoint the exact locations of violent crimes in order to develop immediate countermeasures.[13] Research

TABLE 13.1 Number of Juveniles Arrested for Violent Crimes (Violent Crime Index)

	1985	1990	1992
Murder	1,195	2,508	3,300
Rape	4,286	4,433	6,300
Robbery	28,680	33,580	45,700
Aggravated Assault	32,800	50,425	74,400

Source: Information taken from previous Uniform Crime Reports—the latest being *Crime in the United States 1994*, Uniform Crime Report (Washington, D.C.: 1995).

FIGURE 13.2
Violent juvenile crime rate
1973–1992

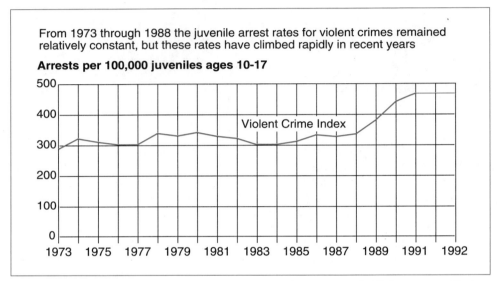

From 1973 through 1988 the juvenile arrest rates for violent crimes remained relatively constant, but these rates have climbed rapidly in recent years

Arrests per 100,000 juveniles ages 10-17

Violent Crime Index

Source: Crime in the United States, 1994. Uniform Crime Reports. (Washington, D.C.: U.S. Department of Justice, 1995).

shows that the following police practices have been used with some degree of success to reduce violent juvenile crime: (1) intensified motorized patrol; (2) field interrogation; (3) foot patrol and neighborhood storefront police stations; (4) citizen contact patrols; and (5) community mobilization, including neighborhood block watch programs and citizen patrols. These strategies address problems of community disorganization and, when combined with other laws and policies, such as restricting the possession of firearms, can be effective deterrents against juvenile violence. Although many of these policing strategies are not new, evidence exists that implementing them as one element of an overall police plan may have an impact on preventing juvenile violence.

In general, one of the most promising police programs dealing with violent juvenile crime involves intensified motorized patrols in marked cars at night in high-crime locations and field interrogations.[14] These tactics indicate that an increased police presence judiciously directed at high-risk times, areas, and persons can deter juvenile violence. Much more research is needed, however, to ensure the long-term effectiveness of this or any other police strategy.

Lastly, one of the key components of any innovative police program dealing with violent juvenile crime is improved communications between the police and the community. This concept, known as community policing, is discussed in more detail at the conclusion of this chapter.

HISTORY OF POLICING JUVENILES

The origin of U.S. police agencies can be traced to early English society.[15] Before the Norman conquest of England, it was up to individuals to aid neighbors and protect each other from thieves and warring groups. This was known as the pledge system. People were entrusted with policing and resolving minor problems. By the thirteenth century, however, the watch system was created to help patrol England's larger communities. This was followed by the establishment of the constable, who was responsible for dealing with more serious crimes. By the seventeenth century, the constable, the justice of the peace, and the night watcher formed the nucleus of the local police system.

When the industrial revolution brought thousands of people from the countryside to work in English urban factories, the need for police protection increased. As a result, the first organized police force was established in London in 1829. The early "bobbies," as they were called, were often corrupt, unsuccessful at stopping crime, and influenced by the wealthy for personal and political gain.[16]

By the mid-nineteenth century, children began to emerge as a distinguishable group. The Poor Laws, the apprenticeship movement, and the restricted family structure, as described in chapter 1, all had an impact on the juvenile legal system. When children violated the law, they were often treated in the same way as adult offenders. But even at this stage, a belief existed that the enforcement of criminal law should be applied differently to children.

Law enforcement in colonial America followed the English model. In the colonies, the local sheriff became the most important police official. By the mid-1800s, formal police departments had formed in such cities as Boston, New York, and Philadelphia. Police work was primitive, officers patrolled on foot, and conflicts often arose between untrained officers and the public.

During the latter portion of the nineteenth century, the problems of how to deal effectively with growing numbers of unemployed, undisciplined, and homeless youths increased; these problems spilled over into the twentieth century. Twentieth-century groups, such as the Wickersham Commission of 1931 and the International Association of Chiefs of Police, became the leading voices for police reform.[17] Their efforts resulted in the creation of specialized police units, known as delinquency control squads.

The most famous police reformer of the 1930s was August Vollmer. As the police chief of Berkeley, California, Vollmer instituted numerous professional reforms, including university training, modern management techniques, prevention programs, and juvenile aid bureaus.[18] These bureaus were generally the first organized special police services for juvenile offenders.

Beginning in the 1960s, police work experienced turmoil, crises, and constant reformation. The U.S. Supreme Court handed down decisions designed to restrict police operations and procedures. Civil unrest produced growing tensions between police and the public. Urban police departments were unable to handle the growing crime rate. With federal funding from the *Law Enforcement Assistance Administration* (LEAA), hundreds of new police programs were developed, police operations were greatly influenced, and police services for children were further enhanced. Even the police role seemed to change from one where the police were simply crime fighters to one in which the police were to have a greater awareness of community issues and crime prevention. This resulted in the emergence of the community policing concept, which is discussed at the end of this chapter.

By the 1980s, most urban police departments recognized that the problem of juvenile delinquency required special attention, although the degree of commitment to this approach varied from one department to another.

The role of the juvenile police officer (one assigned to juvenile work) has taken on added importance, particularly with the increase in violent juvenile and gang-related crime. Today, the majority of the nation's urban law enforcement agencies have specialized juvenile police programs. Typically, such programs involve (1) prevention (e.g., programs involving a police athletic league, Project DARE, and community outreach), and (2) law enforcement work (e.g., juvenile court, school policing, or gang control).[19]

In sum, specialized police work with youths dates back to the first juvenile court in 1899 in Illinois.[20] Although public interest in juvenile delinquency has focused less on police practices than on the juvenile court process itself, law enforcement agents continue to make up the front end of the juvenile justice system. They are the primary referral source for juvenile law violators; they exercise discretion as to whether to arrest a youth; and they often determine whether an arrested youth should be diverted to a community agency or referred to court.

ORGANIZATION OF POLICE SERVICES FOR JUVENILES

The problem of juvenile delinquency and youth crime commonly received little attention from most municipal police departments. Even when juvenile crime was increasing during the 1960s, 1970s, and 1980s, police resources were generally geared to adult offenders. However, the alarming increase in serious juvenile crime in the past few years has made it obvious that the police can no longer neglect youthful antisocial behavior. They need to assign resources to the problem and have the proper organization for coping with it. The theory and practice of police organization have recently undergone many changes, and as a result, police departments are giving greater emphasis to the juvenile function.

The organization of juvenile work depends on the size of the police department, the kind of community in which the department is located, and the amount and quality of resources available in the community. Today, most police agencies recognize that juvenile crime requires special attention.

The police who work with juvenile offenders usually have special skills and talents that go beyond those generally associated with regular police work. In large urban police departments, juvenile services are often established through a special unit. Ordinarily this unit is the responsibility of a command-level police officer. The unit commander assigns officers to deal with juvenile problems throughout the police department's jurisdiction. Police departments with very few officers have little need for an internal division with special functions. Most small departments make one officer responsible for handling juvenile matters for the entire community.

In either large or small departments, it cannot be assumed that only police officers assigned to work with juveniles will be involved in handling juvenile

TABLE 13.2 Law Enforcement Agencies with Specialized Units

Special Units	Type of Agencies	
	Police	Sheriff
Drug Education in Schools	93%	82%
Juvenile Crime	89%	59%
Child Abuse	79%	65%
Missing Children	74%	61%
Gangs	60%	47%
Domestic Violence	45%	40%

Source: Brian Reeves, *State and Local Police Departments and Sheriff Departments,* BJS Bulletin (Washington, D.C.: Bureau of Justice Statistics, 1992).

offenses. When officers on patrol encounter a youngster committing a crime, they are responsible for dealing with the problem initially. However, they generally refer the case to the juvenile unit or the juvenile police officer to follow up. In working with adult offenders, most police officers are concerned primarily with the type of offense the suspect has committed. When working with young people, the juvenile officer is concerned with what to do in cases that cannot be handled with on-the-scene referrals to families or social agencies.[21]

The number of police officers assigned to juvenile work has increased in recent years. The International Association of Chiefs of Police found that approximately 500 departments of the 1,400 surveyed in 1960 had juvenile units. By 1970, the number of police departments with a juvenile specialist had doubled. Today, even relatively small departments have a juvenile specialist[22] and most large law enforcement agencies have entire units specializing in juvenile justice issues. In addition, a large proportion of justice agencies have written policy directives for handling juvenile offenders. Figure 13.3 illustrates the major elements of a police department organization dealing with juvenile offenders; Table 13.2 identifies what proportion of police agencies have certain special juvenile units.

Most juvenile officers are appointed after they have had some general patrol experience. A desire to work with juveniles and a basic understanding of human behavior,[23] along with an aptitude for working with young people,[24] are generally considered essential for the job.

POLICE AND THE RULE OF LAW

While serving as a primary source of referral and diversion of youth from juvenile court, the police are simultaneously required to investigate criminal activity and take juveniles into custody in appropriate cases. Their actions are controlled by statute, constitutional case law, and judicial review. The following methods of police investigation and control in dealing with juvenile offenders are discussed below: (1) the arrest procedure; (2) search and seizure; (3) custodial interrogation; and (4) juvenile lineups.

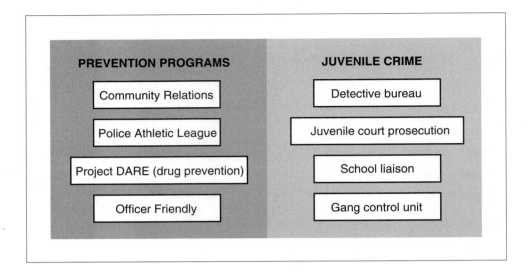

PREVENTION PROGRAMS	JUVENILE CRIME
Community Relations	Detective bureau
Police Athletic League	Juvenile court prosecution
Project DARE (drug prevention)	School liaison
Officer Friendly	Gang control unit

THE ARREST PROCEDURE

Judicial limitations on police discretion in the investigation of offenses involving juveniles are similar to the limitations applied to adult offenders. When a juvenile is apprehended, the police must decide whether to release him or her or make a referral to the juvenile court. Cases involving serious crimes against property or persons are often referred to court. On the other hand, cases involving minor disputes between juveniles, school and neighborhood complaints, petty shoplifting, runaways, and assaults and batteries of minors are often diverted from court action.

Most states require that the law of **arrest** be the same for both adults and juveniles. To make a legal arrest, an officer must have **probable cause** to believe that an offense took place and that the suspect is the guilty party. Probable cause is usually defined as falling somewhere between a mere suspicion and absolute certainty. In misdemeanor cases, the police officer must personally observe the crime to place a suspect in custody. For a felony, the police officer may make the arrest without having observed the crime *if* he or she has probable cause to believe the crime has occurred and the person under arrest has committed it.

The main difference between arrests of adult and arrests of juvenile offenders is the broader latitude police have to control youthful behavior. Police can arrest youths for status offenses, such as truancy, running away, and possession of alcohol; adults would be immune to arrest for such acts. Most existing juvenile codes, for instance, provide broad authority for the police to take juveniles into custody.[25] Such statutes are designed to give the police the authority to act *in loco parentis.* According to Samuel Davis, the broad power granted to police is consistent with the notion that a juvenile is not arrested but "taken into custody," which implies a protective and not a punitive form of detention.[26] Once a juvenile is formally arrested, however, the constitutional safeguards of the Fourth and Fifth Amendments available to adults are applicable to the juvenile as well.

Section 13 of the Uniform Juvenile Court Act, created by the National Conference of Commissioners on Uniform State Laws, is an excellent example of the statutory provisions typically used in state codes regarding juvenile arrest procedures.

Judicial limitations on police discretion in the investigation of offenses involving juveniles are similar to the limitations applied to adult offenders. When they are taken into custody and brought to the station house, juveniles will be searched, fingerprinted and questioned in a fashion not dissimilar from adult offenders.

Section 13. [taking into custody.]

a. A child may be taken into custody:

1. pursuant to an order of the court under this Act;

2. pursuant to the laws of arrest;

3. by a law enforcement officer [or duly authorized officer of the court] if there are reasonable grounds to believe that the child is suffering from illness or injury or is in immediate danger from his surroundings, and that his removal is necessary; or

4. by a law enforcement officer [or duly authorized officer of the court] if there are reasonable grounds to believe that the child has run away from his parents, guardian, or other custodian.

b. The taking of a child into custody is not an arrest, except for the purpose of determining its validity under the constitution of this State or of the United States.[27]

SEARCH AND SEIZURE

Do juveniles have the same constitutional right to be free from unreasonable **search and seizure** as adults? In general, a citizen's privacy is protected by the Constitution's Fourth Amendment, which states;

> The right of the people to be secure in their persons, houses, papers, and effects, against unreasonable searches and seizures, shall not be violated, and no warrants shall issue, but upon probable cause, supported by oaths or affirmation, and particularly describing the place to be searched, and the persons or things to be seized.

Most courts in state jurisdictions have held that the Fourth Amendment ban against unreasonable search and seizure applies to juveniles in delinquency proceedings and that illegally seized evidence is inadmissible in a juvenile trial. To exclude incriminating evidence, a juvenile's attorney makes a pretrial motion to suppress the evidence—the same procedure that is used in the adult criminal process. Virtually all lower court decisions that have considered this issue have conveyed the view that the same standard must apply to juveniles as well as adults. In *State v. Lowry,* the court stated,

> Is it not more outrageous for the police to treat children more harshly than adult offenders, especially when such is violative of due process and fair treatment? Can a court countenance a system, where, as here, an adult may suppress evidence with the usual effect of having the charges dropped for lack of proof, and on the other hand a juvenile can be institutionalized—lose the most sacred possession a human being has, his freedom—for "rehabilitative" purposes because the Fourth Amendment right is unavailable to him?[28]

A full discussion of search and seizure is beyond the scope of this text, but it is important to note that the Supreme Court has ruled that police may stop a suspect and search for and seize evidence without a search warrant under certain circumstances. A person may be searched after a legal arrest but then only in the immediate area of the suspect's control: For example, after an arrest for possession of drugs, the pockets of a suspect's jacket may be searched;[29] an automobile may be searched if there is probable cause to believe a crime has taken place;[30] a suspect's outer garments may be frisked if police are suspicious of his or her activities;[31] and a search may be conducted if a person volunteers for the search.[32] These rules are usually applied to juveniles as well as to adults.

SEARCH AND SEIZURE IN SCHOOLS

One major issue of search and seizure in juvenile law is the right of school officials to search students and their possessions on school grounds and turn over evidence to the police. Searches of students' persons or lockers become necessary when it is believed that students are in the process of violating the law. Drug abuse, theft, assault and battery, and racial conflicts in schools have increased the need to take action against troublemakers. School administrators have questioned students about their illegal activities, conducted searches of students' persons and possessions, and reported suspicious behavior to the police.

In the 1985 landmark decision in *New Jersey v. T.L.O.,* the Supreme Court helped clarify one of the most vexing problems of school searches: whether the Fourth Amendment's prohibition against unreasonable searches and seizures applies to school officials as well as police officers.[33] In this important case, set out in the accompanying "Focus on Delinquency," the Court found that students are in fact constitutionally protected from illegal searches but that school officials are not bound by the same restrictions as law enforcement agents. While police need "probable cause" before they can conduct a search, educators can legally search students when there are reasonable grounds to believe that the students have violated the law or broken school rules. In creating this distinction, the Court recognized the needs of school officials to preserve an environment conducive to education and to secure the safety of their students.

One of the most significant questions left unanswered by *New Jersey v. T.L.O.* is whether teachers and other school officials can search school lockers and desks. Here, the law has been controlled by state decisions, and each jurisdiction may create its own standards. Some allow teachers a free hand in opening lockers and desks.[34] However, not all school districts allow warrantless searches, holding as New Jersey did in *State v. Engerud:*

NEW JERSEY v. T.L.O., 1985

Facts

On March 7, 1980, a teacher at Piscataway High in Middlesex County, New Jersey, discovered two girls smoking in a lavatory. Because this was in violation of school rules, he reported the incident to the principals' office, and the girls were summoned to meet with assistant vice principal Theodore Choplick, who questioned them about their behavior. When one of the girls, T.L.O., claimed she had done nothing wrong, the assistant vice principal demanded to see her purse. When he examined it, he found a pack of cigarettes and also noticed a package of cigarette rolling papers, which are generally associated with the use of marijuana. He then searched the purse thoroughly and found some marijuana, a pipe, s substantial amount of money, a list of students who owed T.L.O. money, and letters implicating her in marijuana dealing. Choplick then informed both T.L.O.'s mother and the police about the evidence he uncovered. Later at the police station, T.L.O. confessed to dealing drugs on campus.

Based on her confession and the evidence recovered from her purse, the state proceeded against T.L.O. in the juvenile court. Her motion to suppress the evidence taken during the school search was rejected by the trial court on the grounds that school officials could search students if they had reasonable cause to believe that the search was necessary to maintain school discipline or enforce school policies; consequently, T.L.O. was found delinquent and sentenced to a year's probation. T.L.O.'s subsequent appeal of the decision was eventually upheld by the New Jersey Supreme Court on the grounds that Choplick's search of T.L.O.'s purse was not justified under the circumstances of the case. The state appealed to the U.S. Supreme Court.

Decision

The Supreme Court held that the prohibitions against illegal search and seizure apply to school as well as law enforcement officials. Teachers are not merely substitute parents but agents of the state who are required to carry out state policy and law. Students do not give up their constitutional rights when they walk on school property. However, school officials also have to maintain an atmosphere that is conducive to learning. A balance must be achieved between a student's right to privacy and the school's need to provide a safe, secure environment. Therefore, the Court ruled that teachers do not need to obtain a warrant before searching a student who is under their authority. In addition, the search need not be based on probable cause to believe that a crime has taken place; rather the legality of the search of a student should depend simply on its reasonableness, considering the scope of the search, the age and sex of the student, and the behavior that prompted it to be made. Of considerable importance is the fact that school searches were found to be justified if a student was suspected of violating the law or of violating school rules. Considering this standard, the search of T.L.O. was found to be justified because the report of her smoking created a reasonable suspicion that she had cigarettes in her purse and the discovery of the rolling papers then gave rise to a reasonable suspicion that she was in possession of marijuana.

Significance of the Case

By giving teachers and other school officials the right to search students if they are suspected of being in violation of school rules, the Court established a significant difference between the due process rights of adults and juveniles. An adult could not be legally searched by an agent of the government under the same circumstances under which T.L.O. was searched. Thus, the *T.L.O.* decision is in keeping with the judicial philosophy espoused in cases such as *Schall v. Martin* and *McKeiver v. Pennsylvania,* which find that juveniles, for their own protection, may be denied certain constitutional safeguards available to adults.

As a practical matter, *New Jersey v. T.L.O.* opens the door for greater security measures being taken on school grounds. It represents the Court's recognition that the nation's educational system is under siege and that educators need greater freedom to maintain school security. Underlying the decision is a recognition of the inherent rights of the mass of law-abiding students to receive an education unimpeded by the disruptive activities of a few troublemakers.

Source: New Jersey v. T.L.O., 105 S.Ct. 733 (1985).

[W]e are satisfied that in the context of this case the student had an expectation of privacy in the contents of his locker. . . . For the four years of high school, the school locker is a home away from home. In it the student stores the kind of personal "effects" protected by the Fourth Amendment.[35]

These and other lower court decisions have helped establish, limit, and define the scope of the school's authority to search lockers and desks.[36]

However, faced with increased crime by students in public schools, particularly illicit drug use, school administrators today are inclined to enforce drug control statutes and administrative rules.[37] Some urban schools are using breathalyzers, drug-sniffing dogs, hidden video cameras, and routine searches of students' pockets, purses, lockers, and cars.[38] In general, courts consider such searches permissible when they are not overly offensive and where there are reasonable grounds to suspect that the student may have violated the law.[39] School administrators are walking a tightrope between the students' constitutional right to privacy and school safety.[40]

Of the 18 reported cases decided by state appellate courts since 1985 that applied the *T.L.O.* standard, the intervention by school officials was upheld in 15.[41] The apparent basis for the opinions was the court's interest in preserving safety in the school system. As Judge White in *T.L.O.* stated,

> Maintaining order in the classroom has never been easy, but in recent years, school disorder has often taken particularly ugly forms: drug use and violent crime in the schools have become major social problems. Annual surveys show over three million crimes occur on school campuses in America.[42]

Faced with this crisis, state courts have not hesitated to lessen the applicability of the Fourth Amendment in a school setting.

In summary, the critical issue with regard to the rights of the student and school searches is the extent of the student's Fourth Amendment protection against unreasonable search and seizure as compared with the extent of the school's authority to conduct searches and the duty of educators to protect other students. Have children lost some of their constitutional rights at the schoolhouse gate as a result of the *T.L.O.* decision? Perhaps. In 1995, the Supreme Court extended the schools' authority to search by legalizing a random drug-testing policy for student athletes. The Supreme Court's recent decision in **Vernonia School District 47J v. Acton** expanded the power of educators to ensure safe learning environments in schools (see the accompanying "Focus on Delinquency" on page 477).[43]

CUSTODIAL INTERROGATION

Parents are usually contacted immediately after a child is taken into custody. In years past, the police often questioned juveniles without their parents or even an attorney present. Any incriminatory statements or confessions that the juveniles made could be used in evidence at trial. However, in 1966, the landmark Supreme Court case **Miranda v. Arizona** placed constitutional limitations on police interrogation procedures used with adult offenders. *Miranda* held that persons in police custody must be told the following:

- They have the right to remain silent.
- Any statements they make can be used against them.
- They have the right to counsel.
- If they cannot afford counsel, it will be furnished at public expense.[44]

VERNONIA SCHOOL DISTRICT 47J v. WAYNE AND JUDY ACTON, GUARDIANS AD LITEM FOR JAMES ACTON, 1995

Facts

In 1989, the Vernonia School District, an Oregon public school system, implemented a suspicionless drug urinalysis program for all students participating in interscholastic athletics. The program was a response to a rise in disciplinary problems that the district believed was related to an increase in drug use among students. When speakers, classes, and even drug-sniffing canines failed to deter student drug use, the school board approved a policy requiring student athletes to submit to random urinalysis as a condition of being allowed to play school sports.

The District's program required testing all interscholastic athletes at the beginning of the season for each athlete's sport. In addition, each week during the sport season, 10 percent of the participants were selected randomly for testing. Those selected for testing provided a urine sample, and adult monitors were present while each randomly selected student produced his or her sample. Males were observed; females were not. Strict procedures were followed to ensure tamper-free samples.

Each urine sample was tested for amphetamines, cocaine, and marijuana. A positive test result triggered a second test. Any student who tested positive could continue participating in sports if the student agreed to take part in a six-week counseling program. Refusal to participate resulted in a student's suspension for the current and following season. A second violation resulted in automatic suspension for two seasons, while a third violation resulted in automatic suspension for three seasons.

This case began when James Acton, a seventh grader, was not permitted to play football when both he and his parents refused to consent to the test. No evidence suggested that James had ever used drugs or that school officials had any reason to suspect him of drug use. The Actons filed suit in federal district court, claiming that the district's program violated the search and seizure protections of the Fourth Amendment and the Oregon Constitution. The district court upheld the schools' testing program, but the Ninth Circuit Court of Appeals reversed the case.

Decision

In a 6–3 decision, the U.S. Supreme Court overturned the Court of Appeals and found that the District's policy did not violate the Fourth and Fourteenth Amendments of the U.S. Constitution. The Court applied a balancing test and weighed the students' privacy interests against the legitimate interests of the district. Applying this test, the Court stated that the privacy rights implicated by the testing program were minimal. In this regard, the Court pointed out that public school students, as minors under compulsory attendance laws, have less Fourth Amendment protection than adults, particularly because they have been committed by their parents to the custody and control of school authorities. In addition, the Court minimized the privacy intrusion by observing that "school sports are not for the bashful and that student athletes routinely showered and changed clothes in front of each other."

With regard to deterrence, the Court stated that the district was responding to an immediate crisis. The Court concluded that deterring drug use by our nation's schoolchildren was "at least as important" as the interests deemed valid by the Court in the nonschool drug testing cases, such as the suspicionless alcohol and drug testing of railroad employees and of Customs Service employees. According to Justice Scalia, "It was self-evident that a drug problem fueled by the role model effect of athletes' drug use is effectively addressed by making sure that athletes do not use drugs." The Court's decision meant that James Acton was required to agree to be tested or forego playing football.

Significance of the Case

As a result of Vernonia, schools may employ safe school programs such as drug testing procedures so long as the policies satisfy the reasonableness test. The landmark decision of New Jersey v. T.L.O., which announced the reasonable suspicion standard, remains in force, and the list of permissible drug programs will likely expand. In other words, this decision should bring forth a spate of suspicionless searches in public schools across the country. Metal detection procedures, the use of drug-sniffing dogs, and random locker searches will be easier to justify. The Vernonia case underscores the importance of eradicating drug use in the nation's school systems. In upholding random, suspicionless drug testing for student athletes, the Supreme Court extended the schools' authority to search one step further, despite court-imposed constitutional safeguards for children. Underlying this decision, like that of New Jersey v. T.L.O., is a recognition that the use of drugs is a serious threat to public safety and to the rights of children to receive a decent and safe education.

Source: Vernonia School District v. Acton 115 S.Ct. 2394 (1995).

These *Miranda* warnings, which secure the adult defendant's Fifth Amendment privilege against self-incrimination, have been made applicable to children taken into custody. The Supreme Court case of *In re Gault* stated that constitutional privileges against self-incrimination are applicable in juvenile cases as well as in adult cases. Because *In re Gault* implies that *Miranda v. Arizona* applies to **custodial interrogation** of juvenile offenders in the pre-judicial stage of the juvenile process, state court jurisdictions apply the requirements of *Miranda* to juvenile proceedings as well. Since the *Gault* decision in 1967, virtually all of the courts that have ruled on the question of the *Miranda* warning have concluded that the warning does apply to the juvenile process.

One difficult problem associated with the custodial interrogation of juveniles has to do with their waiver of *Miranda* rights: Under what circumstances can juveniles knowingly and willingly waive the rights given them by *Miranda v. Arizona* and discuss their actions with the police without benefit of a lawyer? Is it possible for a youngster, acting alone, to be mature enough to appreciate the right to remain silent?

Most courts have concluded that parents or attorneys need not be present for children to effectively waive their rights.[45] In a frequently cited California case, *People v. Lara*, the court said that the question of a child's waiver is to be determined by the **totality of the circumstances doctrine**.[46] This means that the validity of a waiver rests not only on the age of the child but also on a combination of other factors, including the education of the accused; the accused's knowledge of the charge and of the right to remain silent and have an attorney present; whether the youth was allowed to consult with family or friends; whether the interrogation took place before or after charges were filed; the method of interrogation; and whether the accused refused to give statements on prior occasions.[47]

The general rule is that juveniles can waive their rights to protection from self-incrimination but that the validity of this waiver is determined by the circumstances of each case. For example, in *New Hampshire v. Benoit*, a child's custodial statements were considered inadmissible because the child had not been told of the possibility that the statements could be used against him if he were tried as an adult.[48]

In addition, a number of states, recognizing the inability of children to comprehend their legal rights, have demanded by law that a parent or attorney be present when a juvenile is questioned by police; this is referred to as the "interested adult rule."[49]

This doctrine requires that the police explain the *Miranda* warning to the juvenile in the presence of a parent or someone acting *in loco parentis* for the child. Then, the adult must have the opportunity to consult with the child so that the child understands the rights and their significance. Most courts using this rule require that the adult present during the interrogation must be acting in the child's interest and not in any official capacity, as would a youth service employee, court social worker, or probation officer.

In a 1989 Massachusetts case dealing with this problem, the court acted to protect the rights of the juvenile by holding that no other minor, not even a relative, can act as an interested adult. In *Commonwealth v. Guyton*, Guyton's sister, who was three weeks short of her eighteenth birthday, was acting *in loco parentis* for her brother while their mother was away, and the Court ruled that she could not act as an interested adult.[50] On the other hand, some courts have recognized that the interested adult need not be a parent but may be a relative, such as the juvenile's grandfather.[51] Usually, the one exception to the application of the interested adult rule is when the juvenile is over age 14 and the circumstances demonstrate a high degree of intelligence, experience, and knowledge on the part of the juvenile. Only then may the juvenile act alone.

The waiver of *Miranda* rights by a juvenile is probably one of the most controversial legal issues addressed in the state courts. It has also been the subject of federal constitutional review.

Supreme Court Interpretations of *Miranda* to Juvenile Proceedings

In two cases, *Fare v. Michael C.* and *California v. Prysock,* the Supreme Court has attempted to clarify children's rights when they are interrogated by the police. In *Fare v. Michael C.,* the Court ruled that a child's asking to speak to his probation officer was not the equivalent of asking for an attorney; consequently, admissions he made to the police absent legal counsel were held to be admissible in court.[52] (Because of the importance of this case, it is set out in the "Focus on Delinquency" on page 480.) In *California v. Prysock,* the Court was asked to rule on the adequacy of a *Miranda* warning given Randall Prysock, a youthful murder suspect.[53] After reviewing the taped exchange between the police interrogator and the boy, the Court upheld Prysock's conviction when it ruled that even though the *Miranda* warning was given in slightly different language and out of exact context, its meaning was plain and easily understandable, even to a juvenile.

Taken together, *Fare* and *Prysock* make it seem indisputable that juveniles are at least entitled to receive the same *Miranda* rights as adults and ought to be entitled to even greater consideration to ensure that they understand their legal rights.

Miranda v. Arizona is a historic and often symbolic decision that continues to serve to protect the rights of all suspects, adults and children, placed in custody.[54]

JUVENILE LINEUPS

Another important issue arises in the early police processing of juvenile offenders. Should the constitutional safeguards established for adult offenders to protect them during lineups and other police procedures involving suspect identification be applied to juvenile proceedings? In *United States v. Wade,* the Supreme Court held that the accused has a right to have counsel present at postindictment lineup procedures and that pretrial identification is inadmissible when the right to counsel is violated.[55] The Court further clarified this issue in *Kirby v. Illinois,* holding that the defendant's right to counsel at pretrial identification proceedings goes into effect only after the complaint or the indictment has been issued.[56] Based on these decisions, courts have ruled that juveniles also have constitutional protection during lineup and identification procedures. They have a right to counsel at a police lineup once they are charged with a delinquent act, and if this right is violated, the pretrial identification is excluded. For example, in the case of *In re Holley,* a juvenile accused of rape did not have counsel during the lineup identification procedure. In reversing Holley's conviction, the appellate court said the absence of counsel during Holley's lineup precluded a fair trial.[57] State courts have generally followed the mandate of the Supreme Court and applied its holdings to juvenile delinquency proceedings.

Today, almost as much procedural protection is given to children in the juvenile justice courts as to adults brought to the criminal courts. However, the authority of the police to deal with juvenile misconduct under most juvenile codes is ordinarily broader than with adults. Therefore, no aspect of the police

FARE V. MICHAEL C., 1979

Facts

Michael C. was implicated in the murder of Robert Yeager, which occurred during a robbery of Yeager's home. A small truck registered in the name of Michael's mother was identified as having been near the Yeager home at the time of the killing, and a young man answering Michael's description was seen by witnesses near the truck and near the home shortly before Yeager was murdered.

On the basis of this information, the police of Van Nuys, California, arrested Michael at approximately 6:30 p.m. on February 4. He was then 16 years old and on probation to the juvenile court. He had been on probation since the age of 12. Approximately one year earlier, he had served a term in a youth corrections camp under the supervision of the juvenile court. He had a record of several previous offenses, including burglary of guns and purse snatching, stretching back over several years.

When Michael arrived at the Van Nuys station house, two police officers began to interrogate him. No one else was present during the interrogation. The conversation was tape-recorded. One of the officers initiated the interview by informing Michael that he had been brought in for questioning in relation to a murder. The officer fully advised him of his *Miranda* rights. The following exchange then occurred:

Q: Do you understand all of these rights as I have explained them to you?

A: Yeah.

Q: Okay, do you wish to give up your right to remain silent and talk to us about this murder?

A: What murder? I don't know about no murder.

Q: Do you want to give up your right to have an attorney present here while we talk about it?

A: Can I have my probation officer here?

Q: Well, I can't get a hold of your probation officer right now. You have a right to an attorney.

A: How do I know you guys won't pull no police officer in and tell me he's an attorney?

Q: Your probation officer is Mr. Christiansen?

A: Yeah.

Q: Well I'm not going to call Mr. Christiansen tonight. There's a good chance we can talk to him later, but I'm not going to call him right now. If you want to talk to us without an attorney present, you can. If you don't want to, you don't have to. But if you want to say something, you can, and if you don't want to say something, you don't have to. That's your right. You understand that right?

A: Yeah.

Q: Okay, will you talk to us without an attorney present?

A: Yeah, I want to talk to you.

Michael thereupon proceeded to answer questions. He made statements and drew sketches that incriminated him in the Yeager murder.

Largely on the basis of Michael's incriminating statements, probation authorities filed a petition in juvenile court alleging that he had murdered Robert Yeager and that he should be made a ward of the juvenile court.

role is more important than the granting to juvenile officers of a reasonable amount of discretion in the handling of juvenile problems. When should a police officer act to assist a juvenile in need against his or her will? Should a summons be used in lieu of arrest? Under what conditions should a juvenile be taken into protective custody? The following sections describe the factors that influence police discretion and review the policies and programs for its control.

POLICE WORK WITH JUVENILES: DISCRETIONARY JUSTICE

When police officers confront a case involving a juvenile offender, they are forced to use their discretion in choosing an appropriate course of action. Police discretion is defined as selective enforcement of the law by duly authorized

The California Supreme Court reversed the conviction, holding that Michael's request to see his probation officer negated any possible willingness on his part to discuss his case with the police and thereby invoked his Fifth Amendment privilege.

Decision

Michael alleged that statements had been obtained from him in violation of *Miranda* because his request to see his probation officer at the outset of the questioning invoked his Fifth Amendment right to remain silent, just as if he had requested the assistance of an attorney. Accordingly, Michael argued that because the interrogation did not cease until he had a chance to confer with his probation officer, the statements and sketches could not be admitted against him in the juvenile court proceedings.

The Supreme Court reversed and remanded in an opinion by Justice Harry Blackmun. The *Miranda* rule that prior to interrogation the state must warn the accused of the right to an attorney and of the right to remain silent unless an attorney is present "has the virtue of informing police and prosecutors with specificity as to what they may do in conducting custodial interrogation, and of informing courts under what circumstances statements obtained during such interrogation are not admissible," the Court said. In this case, the California court had significantly extended the rule, it continued, and had ignored the basis of the *Miranda* rule, which is the "critical position" lawyers occupy in our legal system. Probation officers frequently are not trained in the law, and moreover they are employees of the state, duty bound to report wrongdoing by the juvenile. "In these circumstances," the Court said, "it cannot be said that the probation officer is able to offer the type of independent advice that an accused would expect from a lawyer retained or assigned to assist him during questioning."

The Court also rejected the contention that the youth's request constituted a request to remain silent. On the basis of the record, his replies show that he "voluntarily and knowingly waived his Fifth Amendment rights."

Significance of the Case

The *Fare v. Michael C.* case applied the "totality of the circumstances" approach to the interrogation of juveniles. The question of whether the accused waived his rights is one of substance, not form. Did the defendant knowingly and voluntarily waive the rights delineated in *Miranda*? The juvenile court was originally correct. The transcript of the interrogation took care to ensure that Michael understood his rights. The police fully explained that he was being questioned in connection with a murder. They informed him of all the rights delineated in *Miranda* and ascertained that he understood them. Nothing indicates that Michael failed to understand what the officers told him. Moreover, after his request to see his probation officer had been denied and after the police officer once more had explained his rights to him, he clearly expressed his willingness to waive his rights and continue the interrogation.

In addition, the Court held that the *Miranda* rule should not be extended to include a juvenile's request to see his or her probation officer. Such a request does not have the same effect as the request to see a lawyer.

Source: *Fare v. Michael C.*, 442 U.S. 23, 99 S.Ct. 2560 (1979).

police agents. Roscoe Pound defined discretion as the authority conferred by law to act in certain conditions or situations in accordance with an official's or agency's own considered conscience or judgment.[58] Discretion operates in the twilight zone between law and morals. According to Kenneth Davis, discretion gives officers a choice from among possible courses of action within the limits on their power.[59] Joseph Goldstein has termed the exercise of police discretion a prime example of **low-visibility decision making** in the criminal justice system.[60] Low-visibility decision making refers to decisions made by public officials in the criminal or juvenile justice systems that the public is not in a position to understand, regulate, or criticize.

Police discretion is probably one of the most controversial and important of all police practices. Discretion exists not only in the police function but also in prosecutorial decision making, judicial judgments, and corrections. Discretion results in the law being applied differently in similar situations. For example, two teenagers are caught in a stolen automobile; one is arrested, the other is released. Two youths are drunk and disorderly; one is sent home, the other is booked and sent to juvenile court. A group of youngsters are involved in a gang fight; only a few are arrested, the others are released.

When police officers confront a case involving a juvenile offender, they are forced to use their personal discretion to choose an appropriate course of action. Police discretion is defined as selective enforcement of the law by duly authorized police agents. Here, officers in Tucson, Arizona grab hold of girls who had been fighting at the El Con Mall. The officers had been in the area due to complaints over gang activity. Should these girls be released with a warning to stay clear of the area or formally arrested and petitioned to juvenile court?

Regardless of what enforcement style they employ, police officers in both the adult and juvenile systems use a high degree of discretion in carrying out their daily tasks. In particular, much discretion is exercised in juvenile work because of the informality that has been built into the system in an attempt to individualize justice. According to Victor Streib, arbitrary discretion is a characteristic of the informal juvenile system.[61] Furthermore, Streib says, police intake officials, prosecutors, judges, and correctional administrators make final, largely unreviewed decisions about children that are almost totally unsupervised in any meaningful way.

The daily procedures of juvenile personnel are not subject to administrative scrutiny or judicial review, except when they clearly violate a youth's constitutional rights. As a result, discretion sometimes deteriorates into discrimination, violence, and other abusive practices on the part of the police. As Herbert Packer has stated, the real danger in discretion is that it allows the law to discriminate against precisely those elements in the population—the poor, the ignorant, the unpopular—who are the least able to draw attention to their plight and to whose sufferings the vast majority of the population is not responsive.[62]

The problem of discretion in juvenile justice is one of extremes. Too little discretion ties the hands of decision makers and provides little flexibility in dealing with individual juvenile offenders. Too much discretion can lead to juvenile injustice. Guidelines and controls are needed to structure the use of discretion.

The first contact a youth usually has with the juvenile justice system is with the police. Studies indicate that a large majority of police decisions at this initial contact involve discretion. Paul Strasburg found that only about 50 percent of all children who come in contact with the police ever get past this initial stage of the juvenile justice process.[63]

In a classic study, Nathan Goldman examined the arrest records for more than 1,000 juveniles from four communities in Pennsylvania to determine what

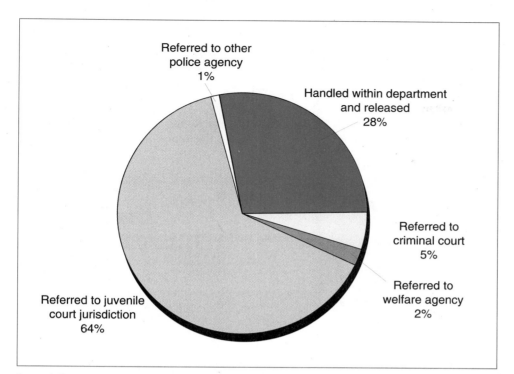

FIGURE 13.4
Police dispositions of juvenile offenders taken into custody

Referred to other
police agency
1%

Handled within department
and released
28%

Referred to
criminal court
5%

Referred to
welfare agency
2%

Referred to juvenile
court jurisdiction
64%

Source: Office of Juvenile Justice and Delinquency Prevention, *Arrests of Youth, 1990* (Washington, D.C.: U.S. Department of Justice, January 1992), p. 5.

factors operated in police referrals of juveniles to the court.[64] He concluded that more than 64 percent of police contacts with juveniles were handled informally without court referral. In another early effort, Irving Piliavin and Scott Briar observed the behavior of 30 officers in the juvenile bureau of a large industrial city. Their study documented further the informality of police discretion in the initial arrest decision.[65] In 1966, Donald Black and Albert Reiss recorded descriptions of 280 encounters between juveniles and the police in an effort to discover discriminatory decision making. They found an unusually low arrest rate.[66] The FBI generally estimates that about one-third of all juvenile arrests involve interdepartmental handling of the case rather than juvenile court referral.[67]

How the police handle juvenile arrests is illustrated in Figure 13.4. Notice that the largest proportion (nearly two-thirds) was referred to the juvenile court system.

These studies indicate that the police use a large amount of discretion in their decisions regarding juvenile offenders. Research generally shows that differential decision making goes on without clear guidance and uniformity. Figure 13.5 illustrates the alternatives in the police–juvenile decision-making process.

ENVIRONMENTAL FACTORS AFFECTING POLICE DISCRETION

How does a juvenile officer decide what to do about a child who is apprehended? As might be expected, the seriousness of the crime, the situation in which it occurred, and the legal record of the juvenile have been found to significantly affect decision making. Police are much more likely to take formal action if the

FIGURE 13.5

Ladder of police–juvenile decision making

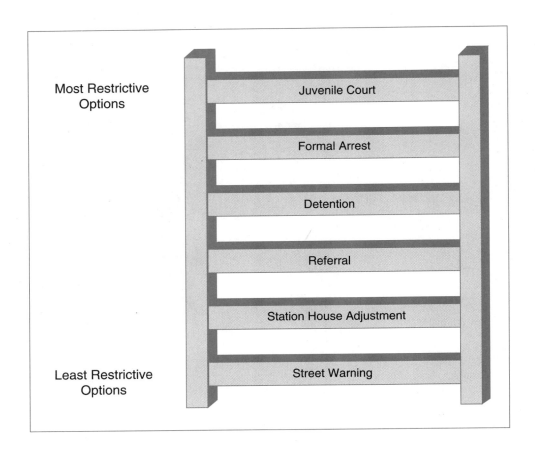

Most Restrictive Options

Juvenile Court

Formal Arrest

Detention

Referral

Station House Adjustment

Least Restrictive Options

Street Warning

crime is serious and has been reported by a victim who is a respected member of the community and if the offender is well known to them.[68] However, these factors are not the only ones that have been found to influence discretion. Some other important influences are discussed below.

The general environment in which the officer works affects the decision. For instance, some officers work in communities that tolerate a fair amount of personal freedom. In liberal environments, the police may be inclined to release juveniles into the community rather than arrest them. Other officers may work in extremely conservative communities that expect a no-nonsense approach to police enforcement. Here, police may be more inclined to arrest a juvenile.

The policies, practices, and customs of the local police department also provide a source of environmental influence. Juvenile officers may be pressured to make more arrests or to refrain from making arrests under certain circumstances. Directives and orders instruct officers to be alert to certain types of violations on the part of juveniles. The chief of police and political officials of a community might initiate policies governing the arrest practices of the juvenile department. For example, local merchants may complain that youths congregating in a shopping center's parking lot are inhibiting business. Police may be called on to make arrests in order to get the point across that loitering will not be tolerated. Under other circumstances, a more informal warning might be given. Similarly, a rash of deaths caused by teenage drunk driving may galvanize the local media to demand police action. The mayor and police chief, sensitive to possible voter dissatisfaction, may therefore demand that formal police action be taken in cases of drunk driving.

Another source of influence is the pressure that individual superiors, such as police supervisors, exert. The sergeant, for example, may initiate formal or informal directives regarding the handling of youths in a given community. Some supervising officers may believe that it is important to curtail disorderly conduct, drinking, or drug use. In addition, certain officers are influenced by the way their peers handle discretionary decision making.

A final environmental factor affecting the performance of officers is their perception of community alternatives to police intervention. Police officers may use arrest because they believe that nothing else can be done and that arrest is the best possible example of good police work. On the other hand, juvenile officers may be apt to refer a large number of juveniles to social service agencies, particularly if they believe that a community has a variety of good resources.

SITUATIONAL FACTORS AFFECTING POLICE DISCRETION

In addition to the environment, a variety of situational factors affect a police officer's decisions. Situational factors are those attached to a particular crime. It is difficult to identify every factor influencing police discretion, but a few stand out as having major significance. Studies show that police officers rely heavily on the demeanor of the juvenile in making decisions. Goldman discovered that community attitudes, political pressures, and the bias of the individual police officer may also influence whether a juvenile offender is arrested, taken into custody, or released.[69] Aaron Cicourel found that the decision to arrest is often based on information regarding the offender's overall demeanor, including dress, attitude, speech, and level of hostility toward the police.[70] Piliavin and Briar found that police perceptions of the attitudes of offenders toward the police, the law, and their own behavior were the most important factors in the decision to process or release an offender.[71]

Most studies conclude that whether the decisions involve juvenile or adult offenders, the following variables are important in the police discretionary process:

- The attitude of the complainant
- The type and seriousness of the offense
- The race and sex of the offender
- The age of the offender
- The attitude of the offender
- The history of the offender's prior contacts with the police
- The perceived willingness of the parents to assist in discipline and in solving the problem (in the case of a child)
- The setting or location in which the incident occurs
- Whether the offender denies the actions or insists on a court hearing (in the case of a child)
- The likelihood that a child can be served by a referral agency in the community

The Impact of Bias on Police Discretion

Do police allow racial, gender, or organizational bias to affect their decisions on whether to arrest youths? A great deal of debate has been generated over this very critical issue. Some experts believe that police decision making is deeply influenced by the offender's personal characteristics, while others maintain that crime-related variables are actually more significant.

RACIAL BIAS

It has long been charged that racially biased police are more likely to act formally with African-American suspects and use their discretion to benefit whites.[72] However, clear-cut proof that police officers act in a generally biased fashion when it comes to racial discrimination has not been established. A number of well-respected studies by Robert Terry, Donald Black, and Albert Reiss and by Richard Lundman found that police are more likely to take offense and demeanor into account than race.[73] Polite, respectful youths were more likely to get the benefit of police discretion, whether they were African-American or white, than youths who displayed a "bad attitude." These findings are supported by T. Edwin Black and Charles Smith's national assessment of juvenile justice processing, which found that there was no difference in the proportion of African-Americans and whites arrested and referred to court, regardless of the nature of the offense.[74] However, it should be noted that Black and Smith found that Hispanics and other racial or ethnic minority groups faced a greater likelihood of court referral than either African-American or white youths.

Some research efforts do show that police discriminate against African-American youths, most notably studies conducted by Terence Thornberry, Dale Dannefer, and Russell Schutt and by Jeffrey Fagan and his associates.[75] However, even research supportive of police discrimination does not indicate that it is overt and unidimensional. For example, Fagan and his associates found that police are more likely to formally process minorities except for crimes of violence, where the pattern is reversed and white offenders are referred to juvenile court at a higher rate.[76]

David Griswold states, "The preponderance, as well as the strength, of the evidence leans toward a view that the police do not discriminate against minorities and that factors other than race weigh most heavily in the police decision-making process."[77]

On the other hand, Donna Bishop and Charles Frazier found that race has a direct effect on decisions made at several processing junctures of the juvenile justice process.[78] Their recent research examines the effect of a juvenile's race in a cohort group of more than 50,000 youths in a large southern city where decisions were made from intake to disposition. According to Bishop and Frazier, African-Americans are more likely to be recommended for formal processing, referred to court, adjudicated delinquent, and given harsher dispositions than comparable whites. In the arrest category, specifically, being African-American increases the probability of formal police action by 11 percent.[79]

One of the most significant recent research efforts on differential processing of minorities is a report from the National Coalition of State Juvenile Justice Advisory Groups.[80] The report points out that minority youth, particularly African-Americans and Hispanics, are overrepresented at various stages of the juvenile justice system. The coalition suggests two possible explanations for this disparity: (1) Differential rates in arrest, incarceration, and even release are the result of a racist system or (2) the differential rates are the result of greater involvement by minorities in juvenile crime.[81] In either case, according to the report, to rectify this imbalance the social structure of society must be altered by improving the educational system, creating more job opportunities, and providing more services for families. The report also recommends that the Office of Juvenile Justice and Delinquency Prevention examine police surveillance and apprehension procedures to determine why minority youths are at a greater risk of being handled differently and to reduce or eliminate any subtle discrimination that may exist in the early stages of the juvenile process.[82]

Another study released in 1992 by the National Council on Crime and Delinquency revealed an equally significant overrepresentation by African-American youths at every point in the California juvenile justice system. Although less than 9 percent of the state youth population, African-Americans accounted for 19 percent of juvenile arrests. The causes for the racial and ethnic disparity included (1) institutional racism, (2) environmental factors, (3) family dysfunction, (4) cultural barriers, and (5) school failure.[83] In sum, we know the following:

1. Some researchers have concluded that the police discriminate against African-American and other minority youths.
2. Some researchers do not find evidence of discrimination.
3. Racial disparity is most often seen at the arrest stage but probably exists at other processing points.
4. The higher arrest rates of minorities are more likely the result of interpersonal, family, community, and organizational differences.
5. Higher arrest rates often result from police discretion with juveniles, street-crime visibility, and high crime rates within a particular group. Such factors, however, may also be linked to a general societal discrimination.
6. In 1995, the Office of Juvenile Justice and Delinquency Prevention reported that the arrest rate of African-American juveniles for property crimes was double that for white juveniles, four times the arrest rate for whites for person-oriented crimes, and five times the arrest rate for whites for drug law violations.[84]

Further research is needed to document what appear to be findings of disproportional arrests of minority juvenile offenders.

GENDER BIAS

Disagreement also exists over police handling of female offenders. Some experts favor the **chivalry or paternalism hypothesis,** which holds that police are more likely to act paternally toward young girls. Others believe that police may be *more* likely to arrest female offenders because their actions violate police officers' cherished stereotypes of the female.

Research by Christy Visher shows that police take race and age into account when arresting females but that these factors are less important for male arrests.[85] Visher finds that chivalry does indeed play a role in female arrests: Younger girls who do not meet police officers' role expectations are more likely to be arrested than their older, more contrite sisters. Meda Chesney-Lind has found that female status offenders may be the victims of police discrimination; she concluded that adolescent girls are often arrested for less serious offenses than adolescent boys.[86] Like police racial bias, disagreement exists over the extent of police gender bias. Merry Morash found that young boys who engage in "typical male delinquent activities are much more likely to develop police records than females;"[87] conversely, Black and Smith's national assessment study found that "the sex of the offender alone appears to have no influence on whether an offender, after being arrested, is referred to the court."[88]

Bishop and Frazier revisited the issue of gender bias in a 1992 study. They found that the historical patterns of gender bias continue: Both female status offenders and male delinquents are differently disadvantaged in the juvenile justice system.[89]

In sum, many of these studies imply the following:

1. Police bias favors females with regard to acts of delinquency.
2. Females seem to be referred to juvenile court for status offenses more often than males.
3. The chivalry or paternalism theory seems to apply where females are less likely than males to be arrested for person- and property-oriented crimes.
4. Some research indicates that males and females receive similar treatment from the police.
5. Evidence exists that the police and most likely the juvenile courts apply a double standard in dealing with male and female juvenile offenders.

To a large degree then, current research findings on police gender bias seem inconclusive. However, there appears to be general agreement that police are unwilling to process females for criminal acts and that they discriminate against them when it comes to arresting them for status offenses.

ORGANIZATIONAL BIAS

Even when police officers are not discriminating on an individual level, the policies used in some departments may result in biased law enforcement practices. Research conducted by a number of police experts, including Douglas Smith, has found that police departments can be characterized by their professionalism and degree of bureaucratization.[90] Departments that are highly bureaucratized and at the same time unprofessional are the ones most likely to be insulated from the communities they serve (Smith labels these departments "militaristic"). According to Smith, isolation can result in the introduction of racial and class bias into the social control process.

The direction of organizational policy may be fueled by the perceptions of police decision makers. A number of experts have found that law enforcement administrators have a stereotyped view of the urban poor as troublemakers who must be kept under control.[91] Consequently, lower-class neighborhoods experience much greater police scrutiny than middle-class areas, and their residents face a proportionately greater chance of arrest and official processing. Merry Morash concludes that youths who fit the "common image"—for example, males, who hang with a tough crowd—significantly increase their chances of being arrested and being officially labeled.[92]

This relationship has been explored in some important recent research. Robert Sampson, using both self-reports and official data, found that teenage residents of neighborhoods with low socioeconomic status had a significantly greater chance of acquiring police records than youths living in higher socioeconomic areas, regardless of the actual crime rates in these areas. Furthermore, Sampson found that this relationship held up after sex, individual income, race, gang membership, and delinquent peers were controlled.[93] Sampson found that when it came time to officially process arrested youth to the juvenile court, the decision was significantly related to the individuals' socioeconomic status.

This research indicates that although police officers may not discriminate on an individual level, departmental policy that focuses attention on lower-class areas may result in class and racial bias in the police processing of delinquent youth.

Considerations of race, economic status, or gender should not determine how the police exercise their authority.[94] Because the police retain a large degree of discretionary power, the ideal goal of nondiscrimination is often difficult to achieve in actual practice. However, policies to limit police discretion can serve to eliminate bias.

LIMITING POLICE DISCRETION

A number of leading organizations have suggested the use of guidelines to limit police discretion. The American Bar Association (ABA) states, "Since individual police officers may make important decisions affecting police operations without direction, with limited accountability and without any uniformity within a department, police discretion should be structured and controlled."[95] The ABA notes further, "There is almost a unanimous opinion that steps must be taken to provide better control and guidance over police discretion in street and station house adjustments of juvenile cases."[96]

One of the leading exponents of police discretion is Kenneth Culp Davis, who has done much to raise the consciousness of criminal justice practitioners about discretionary decision making. Davis recommends controlling administrative discretion through (1) the use of statutorial definition, (2) the development of written policies, and (3) the recording of decisions by criminal justice personnel.[97] Narrowing the scope of juvenile codes, for example, would limit and redefine the broad authority police officers currently have to take youths into custody for criminal and noncriminal behavior. Such practices would provide fair criteria for arrests, adjustment, and police referral of juvenile offenders and would help eliminate largely personal judgments based on the race, attitude, or demeanor of the juvenile. Discretionary decision making in juvenile police work can be better understood by analyzing the "Case in Point" and by examining Figure 13.6.

POLICE WORK AND DELINQUENCY PREVENTION

If the police are to effectively provide services to juveniles while enforcing the law, they need to develop programs and relationships with social service systems. Because the police decide what happens to a juvenile taken into custody, it is essential that they work closely with social service groups on a day-to-day basis. In addition, the police must assume a leadership role in identifying the needs of children in the community and helping the community meet those needs. In helping develop **delinquency prevention** programs, the police must work closely with such organizations as youth service bureaus, the schools, recreational facilities, welfare agencies, and employment programs.[98]

Using **community services** to deal with delinquent and nondelinquent juveniles has many advantages. Such services allow young people to avoid the stigma of being processed by a police agency. They also improve the community's awareness of the need to help youths, and through involvement of local residents, they give a greater recognition to the complexity of the delinquent's problem, thus

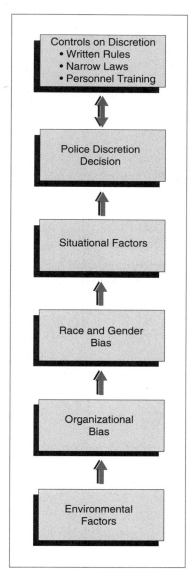

FIGURE 13.6
Discretionary justice with juveniles

CASE IN POINT

Discretionary Decision Making by Police

You are a newly appointed police officer assigned to a juvenile unit of a medium-sized urban police department.

Wayne W. is a 14-year-old white boy who was caught shoplifting with two friends of the same age and sex. Wayne attempted to leave a large department store with a 12-dollar shirt and was apprehended by a police officer in front of the store.

Wayne seemed quite remorseful about the offense. He said several times that he did not know why he did it and that he had not planned to do it. He seemed upset and scared and, while admitting the offense, did not want to go to court.

Wayne had three previous contacts with the police: one for malicious mischief when he destroyed some property, another involving a minor assault of a boy, and a third involving another shoplifting charge. In all three cases, Wayne promised to refrain from ever committing such acts again, and as a result, he was not required to go to court. The other shoplifting offense involved a small baseball worth only three dollars.

Wayne appeared at the police department with his mother because his parents are divorced. She did not seem overly concerned about the case and felt that her son was not really to blame. She argued that he was always getting in trouble and that she was not sure how to control him. She blamed most of his troubles with the law on his being in the wrong crowd.

Store management had left matters in the hands of the police and agreed to support their decision. The other two boys did not steal anything and claimed that they had no idea that Wayne was planning anything when they entered the store. Neither had any criminal record.

Should Wayne be sent to court for trial? What other remedy might be appropriate?

---

developing a sense of public responsibility and support for such programs. Another advantage of using community services is that they make it possible to restrict court referral by the police to cases involving serious crime.

One of the most important institutions playing a role in delinquency prevention is the school. Linking the school with the police is one way to help prevent delinquency. Liaison programs between the police and the schools have been implemented in many communities throughout the United States. Liaison officers from schools and police departments have played a leadership role in developing recreational programs for juveniles. In some instances, they have actually operated such programs. In others, they have encouraged community support for recreational activities, including Little League baseball, athletic clubs, camping outings, and police athletic and scouting programs.

One prominent example of a successful police–community prevention effort is the privately funded **TOP program** in Rochester, New York. TOP stands for Teens on Patrol. Each summer, about 100 youths are hired to patrol the city's parks and recreational areas. The young people help keep the parks "cool" and also learn a lot about police officers; in fact, a number of TOP graduates have gone on to become police officers.[99] **Project DARE** (drug abuse resistance education) is also a well-respected and effective effort by local police departments to prevent teenage drug abuse. DARE programs have been adopted by hundreds of police departments throughout the country. A 1994 study of the DARE program by the National Institute for Justice found that more than half (52 percent) of the school districts nationwide have adopted this program. This study also found that it operates best at increasing students' knowledge about substance abuse and at enhancing social skills.[100]

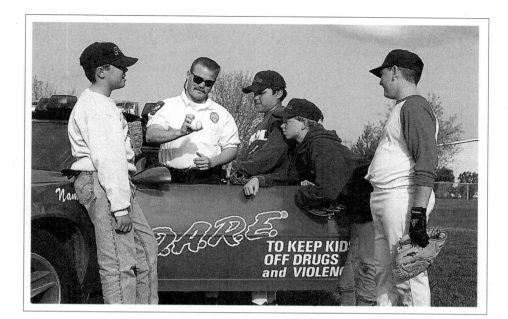

If the police are to effectively provide services to children and enforce the law, they need to develop programs and relationships with social service systems. Then they can play an important role in implementing policies to control and prevent delinquency. The DARE program is a nationally based police-run effort to reduce the incidence of drug abuse among teens.

COMMUNITY POLICING IN THE 1990s

One of the most important changes in American law enforcement is the emergence of the community policing model of crime prevention. This concept is based on the premise that police departments do not make efficient crime-fighting organizations when they operate alone. However, if they gain the trust and assistance of concerned citizens, they can carry out their duties more effectively. Under this model, the main police role should be to increase feelings of community safety and encourage area residents to cooperate with their local police agencies.[101]

Advocates of community policing regard the approach as useful in juvenile justice for a number of reasons:

1. Moving police officers from a position of anonymity in the patrol car to *direct engagement* with a community gives them more immediate *information* about problems unique to a neighborhood and insights into their solutions.
2. Freeing officers from the emergency response system permits them to engage more directly in *proactive crime prevention.*
3. Making operations more visible to the public *increases police accountability to the public.*
4. *Decentralizing* operations allows officers to develop a greater familiarity with the specific workings and needs of various neighborhoods and constituencies in the community and to adapt procedures to accommodate those needs.
5. Encouraging officers to view *citizens as partners* improves relations between police and the public.
6. Moving decision making and discretion downward to patrol officers places more authority in the hands of the people who best know the community's problems and expectations.[102]

The community policing model has been translated into a number of different policy initiatives. It has encouraged police departments around the country to get patrol officers out of patrol cars, where they were viewed as faceless strangers insulated from the community, and into the streets via **foot patrol.** Hundreds of experimental programs have been implemented around the country, and evaluation by the National Neighborhood Foot Patrol Center at Michigan State University indicates they are highly successful.[103]

In addition, the police have encouraged and worked with citizen groups to create neighborhood watch and crime prevention groups. The Police Foundation, a nonprofit organization that conducts research on police issues, has reviewed such efforts in Houston and Newark and found them to be effective methods of increasing citizen cooperation.[104] One of the most well known programs is the Philadelphia block watch program, which cooperates with the police in a number of different delinquency control and victim-aid projects.[105] Another is the innovations neighborhood-oriented policing (INOP) program. The main objectives of the INOP program are to foster community policing initiatives and implement drug reduction efforts at juveniles and adults.[106]

In sum, important efforts have been made by local police departments to involve citizens in the process of delinquency control. Although little clear-cut evidence exists that these efforts can lower crime rates, they seem to be effective methods of improving perceptions of community safety and the quality of community life while involving citizens in the wider juvenile justice network. Under the community policing philosophy, juvenile prevention programs may become more effective crime-control measures. According to Guarino-Ghezzi, innovative police programs that combine reintegration of youth into the community with police surveillance and increased communication are vital components for improving police effectiveness with juveniles.[107]

SUMMARY

As society has become more complex and rates of delinquency and noncriminal behavior have soared, the police have become more important than ever to the juvenile justice system. It is almost always the police officer who has the initial contact with the large number of young people committing antisocial acts, so the importance of the juvenile police officer cannot be overemphasized.

Numerous factors influence the decisions that the police make about juvenile offenders. They include the seriousness of the offense, the harm inflicted on the victim, and the likelihood that the juvenile will break the law again.

The recruitment, selection, and training of juvenile police officers is essential to good police organizations. Police work with young people includes the legal as-

pects of arrest, custodial interrogation, and lineups. Through the *Miranda v. Arizona* decision, the U.S. Supreme Court established a clearly defined procedure for custodial interrogation and police investigations. Such practices are applicable to juvenile suspects. Search and seizure actions, lineups, and other police procedures are also subject to court review. One important issue is police discretion in dealing with juvenile offenders. Discretion is a low-visibility decision made in the administration of adult and juvenile justice. Discretionary decisions are made without guidelines or policy statements from the police administrator. Discretion is essential in providing individualized justice, but such problems as discrimination, unfairness, and bias toward particular groups of juveniles must be controlled.

community policing
juvenile officers
role conflicts
law enforcement
discretion
arrest
probable cause
search and seizure

New Jersey v. T.L.O.
Vernonia School District 47J v.
  Acton
Miranda v. Arizona
custodial interrogation
totality of the circumstances
  doctrine
Fare v. Michael C.

low-visibility decision making
chivalry or paternalism hypothesis
delinquency prevention
community services
TOP program
Project DARE
foot patrol

QUESTIONS FOR DISCUSSION

1. The term *discretion* is often defined as selective decision making by police and others in the juvenile justice system who are faced with alternative modes of action. Discuss some of the factors affecting the discretion of the police when dealing with juvenile offenders.
2. What role should police organizations play in delinquency prevention and control? Is it feasible to expect police departments to provide social services to children and families? How should police departments be better organized to provide for the control of juvenile delinquency?
3. What qualities should a police juvenile officer have? Should a college education be a requirement?
4. In *New Jersey v. T.L.O.*, the Supreme Court held that, although prohibitions against illegal search and seizure apply to school as well as law enforcement officials, teachers do not need to obtain a warrant before searching a student under their authority. As a practical matter, will this decision give rise to overused safety and security measures in our school systems?
5. In light of the traditional and protective role assumed by law enforcement personnel in juvenile justice, is there any reason to have a *Miranda* warning for youths taken into custody?
6. Can the police and community be truly effective in forming a partnership to reduce juvenile delinquency? Discuss the role of the juvenile police officer in preventing and investigating juvenile crime.

NOTES

1. Herman Goldstein, "Toward Community-Oriented Policing: Potential Basic Requirements and Threshold Questions," *Crime and Delinquency* 33:630 (1987).
2. Lawrence Sherman and Richard Berk, "The Specific Deterrent Effects of Arrest for Domestic Assault," *American Sociological Review* 49:261–72 (1984).
3. Craig Uccida and Robert Goldberg, *Police Employment and Expenditure Trends* (Washington, D.C.: Bureau of Government Statistics, 1986).
4. Donald Black and Albert J. Reiss, Jr., "Police Control of Juveniles," *American Sociological Review* 35:63 (1970); Richard Lundman, Richard Sykes, and John Clark, "Police Control of Juveniles: A Replication," *Journal of Research on Crime and Delinquency* 15:74 (1978).
5. American Bar Association, *Standards Relating to Police Handling of Juvenile Problems* (Cambridge, Mass.: Ballinger, 1977), p. 1.
6. FBI, *Uniform Crime Reports 1991* (Washington, D.C.: U.S. Government Printing Office, 1990). More than 40 percent of police–juvenile contacts are referred to juvenile court; see also David Huizinga and Finn Esbensen,

"An Arresting View of Juvenile Justice," *National School Safety Center Journal,* Spring 1992, pp. 13–17.

7. For a discussion of police values and roles, see Michael Brown, *Working the Street: Police Discretion and the Dilemmas of Reform* (New York: Russell Sage, 1981).

8. Samuel Walker, *The Police of America* (New York: McGraw-Hill, 1983), p. 133.

9. Karen A. Joe. "The Dynamics of Running Away, Deinstitutionalization Policies and the Police," *Juvenile Family Court Journal* 46:43–55 (1995).

10. R. Kobetz and B. Borsage, *Juvenile Justice Administration* (Gaithersburg, Md.: IACP, 1973), p. 112.

11. Howard N. Snyder and Melissa Sickmund, *Juvenile Offenders and Victims: A National Report* (Washington, D.C.: Office of Juvenile Justice and Delinquency Prevention, 1995), p. 100.

12. Ibid, p. 111.

13. "Crime—the Lull before the Storm—Teenagers More Violent than Ever," *Newsweek,* 4 December 1995, pp. 40–42.

14. John Wilson and James Howell, "Serious and Violent Juvenile Crime: A Comprehensive Strategy," *Juvenile and Family Court Journal* 45:3–35 (1995); James Howell, ed., *Guide for Implementing Comprehensive Strategy for Serious Violent and Chronic Juvenile Offenders* (Washington, D.C.: OJJDP, 1995).

15. This section relies on such sources as Malcolm Sparrow, Mark Moore, and David Kennedy, *Beyond 911, A New Era for Policing* (New York: Basic Books, 1990); Daniel Devlin, *Police Procedure, Administration, and Organization* (London: Butterworth, 1966); Robert Fogelson, *Big City Police* (Cambridge, Mass., Harvard University Press, 1977); Roger Lane, *Policing the City, Boston 1822–1885* (Cambridge, Mass., Harvard University Press, 1967); Roger Lane, "Urban Police and Crime in Nineteenth–Century America," in Norval Morris and Michael Tonry, eds., *Crime and Justice,* vol. 2 (Chicago: University of Chicago Press, 1980), pp. 1–45; J. J. Tobias, *Crime and Industrial Society in the Nineteenth Century* (New York: Schocken Books, 1967); Samuel Walker, *A Critical History of Police Reform: The Emergence of Professionalism* (Lexington, Mass.: Lexington Books, 1977); idem, *Popular Justice* (New York: Oxford University Press, 1980); President's Commission on Law Enforcement and the Administration of Justice, *Task Force Report: The Police* (Washington, D.C.: U.S. Government Printing Office, 1967), pp. 1–9.

16. See, generally, Walker, *Popular Justice,* p. 61.

17. Law Enforcement Assistance Administration, *Two Hundred Years of American Criminal Justice* (Washington, D.C.: U.S. Government Printing Office, 1976).

18. See August Vollmer, *The Police and Modern Society* (Berkeley: University of California Press, 1936).

19. "Police Departments, 1991 National Survey," *Law Enforcement Technology,* October 1991.

20. See O. W. Wilson, *Police Administration,* 2nd ed. (New York: McGraw-Hill, 1963).

21. National Advisory Commission on Criminal Justice Standards and Goals, *Task Force Report on Juvenile Justice and Delinquency Prevention* (Washington, D.C.: Law Enforcement Assistance Administration, 1976), p. 245.

22. Ibid.

23. National Advisory Commission on Criminal Justice Standards and Goals, *Task Force Report on Juvenile Justice and Delinquency Prevention,* p. 258.

24. American Bar Association, *Standards Relating to Police Handling of Juvenile Problems,* p. 109.

25. Linda Szymanski, *Summary of Juvenile Code Purpose Clauses* (Pittsburgh, Pa.: National Center for Juvenile Justice, 1988); see also, for example, GA Code Ann. 15; Iowa Code Ann. 232.2; Mass. Gen. Laws, ch. 119, 56.

26. Samuel M. Davis, *Rights of Juveniles—The Juvenile Justice System* (New York: Clark-Boardmen, revised June 1989), Sec. 3.3.

27. National Conference of Commissioners on Uniform State Laws, *Uniform Juvenile Court Act* (Chicago: National Conference on Uniform State Laws, 1968), Sec. 13.

28. *State v. Lowry,* 230 A.2d 907 (1967).

29. *Chimel v. Cal.,* 395 U.S. 752, 89 S.Ct. 2034 (1969).

30. *United States v. Ross,* 456 U.S. 798, 102 S.Ct. 2157 (1982).

31. *Terry v. Ohio,* 392 U.S.1, 88 S.Ct. 1868 (1968).

32. *Bumper v. North Carolina,* 391 U.S. 543, 88 S.Ct. 1788 (1968).

33. *New Jersey v. V.T.L.O.,* 469 U.S. 325, 105 S.Ct. 733 (1985).

34. *People v. Overton,* 24 N.Y.2d 522, 301 N.Y.S.2d 479, 249 N.E.2d 366 (1969); Brenda Walts, "*New Jersey v. T.L.O.:* Questions the Court Did Not Answer about School Searches," *Law and Education Journal* 14:421 (1985).

35. *State v. Engerud,* 94 N.J. 331 (1983).

36. *In re Donaldson,* 75 Cal.Rptr. 220 (1969); *People v. Bowers,* 77 Misc.2d 697, 356 N.Y.S.2d 432 (1974); *In re W.,* 29 Cal.App.3d 777, 105 Cal.Rptr. 775 (1973); *Comm. of Pa. v. Dingfelt,* 227 Pa.Supr.380, 323 A.2d 145 (1974).

37. See D. A. Walls, "New Jersey v. T.L.O.: The Fourth Amendment Applied to School Searches," *Oklahoma University Law Review* 11:225–41 (1986); Robert Shepherd, Jr., "Juvenile Justice—Search and Seizures Involving Juveniles," *American Bar Association Journal on Criminal Justice* 5:27–29 (1990).

38. K. A. Bucker, "School Drug Tests: A Fourth Amendment Perspective," *University of Illinois Law Review* 5:275 (1987).

39. J. Hogan and M. Schwartz, "Search and Seizure in the Public Schools," *Case and Comment* 90: 28–32 (1985); M. Meyers, "T.L.O. v. New Jersey— Officially Conducted School Searches and a New Balancing Test," *Juvenile Family Journal* 37:27–37 (1986).

40. For an interesting article suggesting that school officials should not be permitted to search students without suspicion that each student searched has violated the drug or weapons law, see J. Braverman, "Public School Drug Searches," *Fordham Urban Law Journal* 14:629–84 (1986).

41. J. M. Sanchez, "Expelling the Fourth Amendment from American Schools: Students' Rights Six Years after T.L.O.," *Law and Education Journal* 21:381–413 (1992).

42. 469 U.S., at 339; see also National School Safety Center, *School Safety Update* (Malibu, Calif.: Pepperdine University, 1991); U.S. Department of Justice, *School Crime—A National Victimization Survey* (Washington, D.C.: Bureau of Justice Statistics, 1991).

43. *Vernonia School District 47J v. Acton,* 115 S.Ct. 2394 (1995); Bernard James and Jonathan Pyatt, "Supreme Court Extends School's Authority to Search," *National School Safety Center News Journal* 26:29 (1995).

44. *Miranda v. Arizona,* 384 U.S. 436, 86 S.Ct. 1602 (1966).

45. *Commonwealth v. Gaskins,* 471 Pa. 238, 369 A.2d 1285 (1977); *In re E.T.C.,* 141 Vt. 375, 449 A.2d 937 (1982).

46. *People v. Lara,* 67 Cal.2d 365, 62 Cal.Rptr. 586, 432 P.2d 202 (1967).

47. *West v. United States,* 399 F.2d 467 (5th Cir. 1968).

48. *New Hampshire v. Benoit,* 490 A.2d 295 (N.H. 1985).

49. See, for example, *In re E.T.C.,* 141 Vt. 375, 449 A.2d 937 (1982).

50. *Commonwealth v. Guyton,* 405 Mass. 497 (1989).

51. *Commonwealth v. McNeil,* 399 Mass. 71 (1987).

52. *Fare v. Michael C.,* 442 U.S. 23, 99 S.Ct. 2560 (1979).

53. *California v. Prysock,* 453 U.S. 355, 101 S.Ct. 2806 (1981).

54. See, for example, Larry Holtz, "Miranda in a Juvenile Setting—A Child's Right to Silence," *Journal of Criminal Law and Criminology* 79:534–56 (1987).

55. *United States v. Wader,* 388 U.S. 218, 87 S.Ct. 1926 (1967).

56. *Kirby v. Illinois,* 406 U.S. 682, 92 S.Ct. 1877 (1972).

57. *In re Holley,* 107 R.I. 615, 268 A.2d 723 (1970).

58. Roscoe Pound, "Discretion, Dispensation, and Mitigation: The Problem of the Individual Special Case," *New York University Law Review* 35:936 (1960).

59. Kenneth C. Davis, *Discretionary Justice: A Preliminary Inquiry* (Baton Rouge: Louisiana State University Press, 1969); M. Ted Rubin, *Juvenile Justice: Police, Practice and Law* (Santa Monica, Calif.: Goodyear, 1979).

60. Joseph Goldstein, "Police Discretion Not to Invoke the Criminal Process: Low- Visibility Decisions in the Administration of Justice," *Yale Law Journal* 69:544 (1960).

61. Victor Streib, *Juvenile Justice in America* (Port Washington, N.Y.: Kennikat, 1978).

62. Herbert Packer, *The Limits of the Criminal Sanction* (Palo Alto, Calif.: Stanford University Press, 1968).

63. Paul Strasburg, *Violent Delinquents: Report to Ford Foundation from Vera Institute of Justice* (New York: Monarch, 1978), p. 11; Robert Terry, "The Screening of Juvenile Offenders," *Journal of Criminal Law, Criminology, and Police Science* 58:173–81 (1967).

64. Nathan Goldman, *The Differential Selection of Juvenile Offenders for Court Appearance* (Washington, D.C.: National Council on Crime and Delinquency, 1963).

65. Irving Piliavin and Scott Briar, "Police Encounters with Juveniles," *American Journal of Sociology* 70:206–14 (1964); Theodore Ferdinand and Elmer Luchterhand, "Inner-City Youth, the Police, Juvenile Court, and Justice," *Social Problems* 8:510–26 (1970).

66. Black and Reiss, "Police Control of Juveniles"; Richard J. Lundman, "Routine Police Arrest Practices," *Social Problems* 22:127–41 (1974).

67. FBI, *Crime in the U.S.: Uniform Crime Reports, 1989* (Washington, D.C.: U.S. Government Printing Office, 1989), p. 240.

68. Douglas Smith and Christy Visher, "Street-Level Justice: Situational Determinants of Police Arrest Decisions," *Social Problems* 29:167–78 (1981).

69. Goldman, *The Differential Selection of Juvenile Offenders for Court Appearance,* p. 25; Norman Werner and Charles Willie, "Decisions of Juvenile Officers," *American Journal of Sociology* 77:199–214 (1971).

70. Aaron Cicourel, *The Social Organization of Juvenile Justice* (New York: Wiley, 1968).

71. Piliavin and Briar, "Police Encounters with Juveniles," p. 214.

72. Dale Dannefer and Russel Schutt, "Race and Juvenile Justice Processing in Police and Court Agencies," *American Journal of Sociology* 87:1113–32 (1982); Smith and Visher, "Street-Level Justice: Situational Determinants of Police Arrest Decisions."

73. Terry, "The Screening of Juvenile Offenders;" Black and Reiss, "Police Control of Juveniles;" Lundman, "Routine Police Arrest Practices."

74. T. Edwin Black and Charles Smith, *A Preliminary National Assessment of the Numbers and Characteristics of Juveniles Processed in the Juvenile Justice System* (Washington, D.C.: U.S. Government Printing Office, 1980), p. 39.

75. Terence Thornberry, "Race, Socioeconomic Status, and Sentencing in the Juvenile Justice System," *Journal of Criminal Law and Criminology* 70:164–71 (1979); Dannefer and Schutt, "Race and Juvenile Justice Processing in Police and Court Agencies"; Jeffrey Fagan, Ellen Slaughter, and Eliot Hartstane, "Blind Justice? The Impact of Race on the Juvenile Justice Process," *Crime and Delinquency* 33:224–58 (1987).

76. Fagan, Slaughter, and Hartstane, "Blind Justice? The Impact of Race on the Juvenile Justice Process," pp. 237–38.

77. David Griswold, "Police Discrimination: An Elusive Question," *Journal of Police Science and Administration* 6:65–66 (1978).

78. Donna M. Bishop and Charles E. Frazier, "The Influence of Race in Juvenile Justice Processing," *Journal of Research in Crime and Delinquency* 25:242–61 (1988).

79. Ibid., p. 258.

80. National Coalition of State Juvenile Justice Advisory Groups, *A Delicate Balance* (Bethesda, Md.: National Coalition of State Juvenile Justice Advisory Groups, 1989).

81. Ibid., p. 4.

82. Ibid., p. 2. Although not specifically dealing with juveniles, the issue of differential processing for young African-American males is addressed in the following study that found that nearly one of every four African-American men in their twenties is caught up in the criminal justice system: Marc Mauer, *Young Black Men and the Criminal Justice System* (Washington, D.C.: The Sentencing Project, 1990).

83. National Council on Crime and Delinquency, *The Over-Representation of Minority Youth in the California Juvenile Justice System* (San Francisco: NCCD, 1992).

84. Howard Snyder and Melissa Sickmund, *Juvenile Offenders and Victims: A National Report* (Washington, D.C.: Office of Juvenile Justice and Delinquency Prevention, 1995), p. 128.

85. Christy Visher, "Arrest Decisions and Notions of Chivalry," *Criminology* 21:5–28 (1983).

86. Meda Chesney-Lund, "Judicial Enforcement of the Female Sex Role: The Family Court and Female Delinquency Issues," *Criminology* 8:51–71 (1973); idem, "Young Women in the Arms of Law," in L. Bowker, ed., *Women, Crime and the Criminal Justice System,* 2nd ed. (Lexington, Mass.: Lexington Books, 1978).

87. Merry Morash, "Establishment of a Juvenile Record: The Influence of Individual and Peer Group Characteristics," *Criminology* 22:97–112 (1984).

88. Black and Smith, *A Preliminary National Assessment of the Numbers and Characteristics of Juveniles Processed in the Juvenile Justice System,* p. 37.

89. Donna Bishop and Charles Frazier, "Gender Bias in Juvenile Justice Processing: Implications of the JJDP Act," *Journal of Criminal Law and Criminology* 82:1162–86 (1992).

90. Douglas Smith, "The Organizational Context of Legal Control," *Criminology* 22:19–38 (1984).

91. John Irwin, *The Jail: Managing the Underclass in American Society* (Berkeley: University of California Press, 1985).

92. Morash, "Establishment of a Juvenile Record: The Influence of Individual and Peer Group Characteristics."

93. Robert Sampson, "Effects of Socioeconomic Context of Official Reaction to Juvenile Delinquency," *American Sociological Review* 51:876–85 (1986).

94. Institute of Judicial Administration and American Bar Association, Juvenile Justice Standards Project, *Standards Relating to Police Handling of Juvenile Problems* (Cambridge, Mass.: Ballinger, 1977), Standard 2.1.

95. American Bar Association, *Standards of Criminal Justice: Standards Relating to Urban Police Function* (New York: Institute of Judicial Administration, 1972), Standard 4.2, p. 121.

96. Ibid., p. 45.

97. Kenneth C. Davis, *Police Discretion* (St. Paul, Minn.: West, 1975).

98. Sherwood Norman, *The Youth Service Bureau—A Key to Delinquency Prevention* (Hackensack, N.J.: National Council on Crime and Delinquency, 1972), p. 8.

99. Karin Lipson, "Cops and TOPS: A Program for Police and Teens That Works," *Police Chief* 49:45–46 (1982).

100. National Institute for Justice, *The Dare Program: A Review of Prevalence, User Satisfaction and Effectiveness* (Washington, D.C.: U.S. Department of Justice, 1994).

101. For an analysis of this position, see George Kelling and James Q. Wilson, "Broken Windows: The Police and Neighborhood Safety," *Atlantic Monthly* 249:29–38 (1982).

102. U.S. Department of Justice, "Community Policing," *National Institute of Justice Journal,* 225:1–32 (1992).

103. Robert Trojanowicz and Hazel Harden, *The Status of Contemporary Community Policing Programs* (East Lansing: Michigan State University Neighborhood Foot Patrol Center, 1985).

104. Police Foundation, *The Effects of Police Fear Reduction Strategies: A Summary of Findings from Houston and Newark* (Washington, D.C.: Police Foundation, 1986).

105. Peter Finn, "Block Watches Help Crime Victims in Philadelphia," National Institute of Justice Reports, December: 2–10 (1986).

106. James Q. Wilson, "Drugs and Crime," in Michael Tonry and James Q. Wilson, eds., *Crime and Justice—A Review of Research,* vol. 13 (Chicago: University of Chicago Press, 1990).

107. Susan Guarino-Ghezzi, "Reintegrative Police Surveillance of Juvenile Offenders: Forging an Urban Model," *Crime and Delinquency* 40:131–53 (1994).

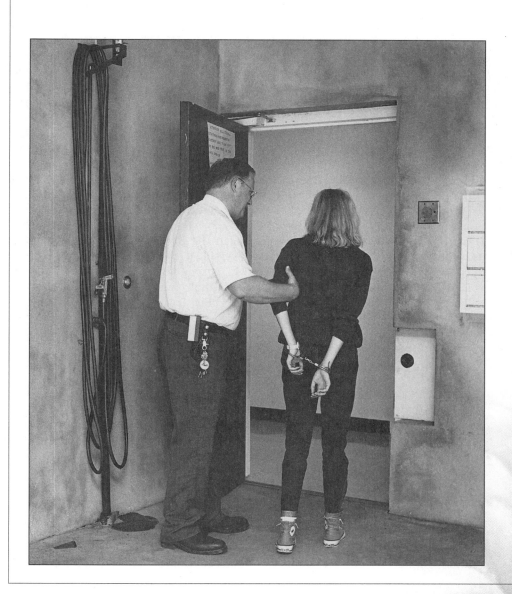

INTRODUCTION

One of the most important stages in the juvenile process is the time between the child's arrest and the adjudicatory hearing. After the juvenile has been taken into police custody, decisions as to the disposition of the case need to be made under police and judicial discretionary authority. By this point, the child has been informed of his or her right to counsel and right to remain silent during questioning. In addition, the child's parents have probably been notified. At this time, the child may be faced with involuntary placement in a detention or shelter care facility. Detention, even if only for a short period, may have a serious effect on the child. For children who are confined unnecessarily, it may contribute to future antisocial and delinquent behavior.

During this period, the child either retains an attorney or is assigned counsel by the court. In addition to detention, the juvenile, the family, and the attorney must also consider diversion, bail, plea bargaining, and, in serious cases, transfer of the child to adult court. The family may seek to work with the police department and the courts to avoid formal judicial proceedings and to get help through a diversion program, or after an interview, the intake probation officer in the court may recommend that no further action be taken against the juvenile. The juvenile might also be supervised by the intake section of the court without a judicial determination.

If the decision is made to file a petition initiating formal judicial action against the juvenile, the child's attorney will seek pretrial release through bail or some other release measure and possibly enter into plea bargaining discussions.

Thus, the period between arrest and adjudication is one of the most critical points in the juvenile justice process. This chapter will examine how the child is handled during this period. First, we will look at the detention system, which takes children out of the community either before their adjudication, disposition, or treatment. Then we will discuss intake in the juvenile court. Intake procedures serve as a means of screening and diverting certain juvenile offenders from juvenile proceedings. Lastly, the chapter will examine bail and plea bargaining for children, diversion, and waiver to adult criminal court. The waiver process is very important because the number of juveniles transferred to adult criminal court has grown substantially in recent years.

THE CONCEPT OF DETENTION

Detention is the temporary care of children by the state in physically restricted facilities pending court disposition or transfer to another agency.[1] Traditional detention facilities for children are designed as secure environments. The approximately 500 secure detention facilities operating around the United States have locked doors, high fences or walls, screens or bars, and other barriers designed to prevent detainees from leaving the facility at will.

Detention facilities of this kind normally handle juveniles at different stages of the juvenile justice process. Some juveniles are kept in detention to await their court hearing. Others have had a trial but have not been sentenced or are awaiting the imposition of their sentence. A third group of children are those whose sentences have been imposed but who are awaiting admittance to a correctional training school. Thus, as the American Bar Association states, "the term 'pre-trial detainee' is inaccurate to describe the many juveniles in detention whose cases have already been adjudicated but whose disposition remains unimplemented."[2]

Other types of residential care programs should be distinguished from detention. **Shelter care,** for example, is the temporary care of children in physically unrestricting facilities. While the secure detention facility is normally used for children who have been charged with delinquent acts, shelter care programs, including receiving homes, group homes, foster care homes, and temporary care facilities, are normally used for dependent and neglected children and status offenders who may be runaways or truants or who are often the victims of sexual and physical abuse.[3]

Regardless of its form, detention should not be viewed as punishment. A juvenile is normally not a sentenced offender when placed in detention. Thus, a detention facility is not to be used as a permanent correctional facility but as a source of temporary care for children who require secure custody.

Most experts in juvenile justice advocate that detention be limited to alleged delinquent offenders who require secure custody for the protection of themselves and others. In the past, however, children who were neglected and dependent, as well as status offenders, were placed in secure detention facilities. To remedy this situation, a national effort has been ongoing to remove status offenders and neglected children from detention facilities that also house juvenile delinquents. In addition, alternatives to detention centers—for example, temporary foster homes, detention boarding homes, and programs of neighborhood supervision— have been developed in numerous jurisdictions. These alternatives enable youths to live in a more homelike setting while the courts dispose of their cases. New types of residential facilities also are being created—some young persons who cannot return home are being held in dormitories and multiple-resident dwellings.[4] Efforts have also been made to improve services in existing secure detention facilities, including reception and diagnosis, community contact involving legal services and family visiting, and counseling, recreational, and educational services.

NATIONAL DETENTION TRENDS

In 1975, about 11,000 youths were housed in detention centers on any given day. Despite 10 years of effort to curb the use of detention, about 15,000 youths were in detention centers on any given day in 1985. There were also about 400,000 admissions to detention facilities during that year.

Since 1988, the number of youth held in short-term detention facilities has *increased* by about 15 percent, to more than 19,000 children on a daily basis. About 560,000 admissions occur each year, of which 296,000 involve delinquency and 20,000 status offenses.[5] In addition, the rise in detention is more common for cases involving males, minorities, and older juveniles (see Tables 14.1 and 14.2).

Juveniles often stay in detention facilities at some point between referral to court and case disposition. In more than 22 percent of delinquency cases (approximately 265,000) in 1992, authorities detained the juvenile prior to disposition. The use of detention in delinquency cases increased about 25 percent from 1988 to 1992, from 237,000 to 296,000. The detention rate in cases involving property offenses increased 24 percent, 58 percent in person-oriented cases, and 14 percent in public order cases.

TABLE 14.1 Detained Delinquency Cases (by Numbers)
Nearly 59,000 more delinquency cases involved detention in 1992 than in 1988—person and property offense cases each accounted for about 45 percent of the overall increase.

Type of Delinquency	1988	1989	1990	1991	1992
Person	46,000	52,700	65,700	66,600	72,500
Property	112,100	118,400	141,400	136,300	139,200
Drugs	27,100	28,200	26,600	22,900	25,300
Public Order	52,000	57,100	63,900	55,700	59,100
TOTAL	237,200	256,400	297,700	281,500	296,100

Source: Jeffrey Butts, et al., *Juvenile Court Statistics—1992* (Pittsburgh, Pa.: National Center for Juvenile Justice, 1995).

TABLE 14.2 Detained Delinquency Cases (by Percentage)
African-American youth made up 31 percent of delinquency cases processed in 1992; they were involved in 39 percent of detained delinquency cases.

Type of Delinquency	White	African-American	Other Races	Total
Person	51%	46%	3%	100%
Property	62%	33%	5%	100%
Drugs	38%	61%	1%	100%
Public Order	64%	33%	3%	100%
TOTAL	57%	39%	4%	100%

Source: Jeffrey Butts, et al., *Juvenile Court Statistics—1992* (Pittsburgh, Pa.: National Center for Juvenile Justice, 1995).

With regard to status offenders, juvenile detention was used in about 8,200 petitioned status offense cases in 1992. The use of detention for such cases declined from 17 percent (12,900 of 77,400 cases) in 1985 to 8 percent (6,500 of 76,700 cases) in 1989, and increased to about 8,000 in 1992[6] (see Tables 14.3 and 14.4). Detention was least likely in truancy cases (2 percent) and most likely in runaway cases (21 percent). Runaways also accounted for the largest group of detained status offenders. Of the estimated 8,000 petitioned status offense cases resulting in detention in 1992, 32 percent involved a youth charged as a runaway.[7]

With regard to the personal characteristics of children admitted to detention, the Office of Juvenile Justice and Delinquency Prevention found that the typical delinquent was male, over 15, and charged with a property crime, while the typical status offender was female, under 16, and a runaway.[8]

These national and local increases and changes are occurring at a time when the overall population of juvenile offenders is decreasing. Experts believe the steady increase in detention use may result from (1) a rise in serious crime by juveniles, (2) a growing link to drug-related crimes, and (3) the involvement of younger children in the juvenile justice system.[9] On the other hand, some things about juvenile detention have not changed: Nearly half of all youths in juvenile

TABLE 14.3 Percent Change in Detained Petitioned Status Offense Cases, 1988–1992

Offense	1988	1992	Percent Change
Status Offense	8,900	8,200	−8%
Runaway	3,400	2,600	−23%
Truancy	700	500	−30%
Ungovernable	2,000	1,000	−49%
Liquor	1,400	1,800	26%
Miscellaneous	1,300	2,200	67%

Source: Jeffrey Butts et al., *Juvenile Court Statistics—1992* (Pittsburgh, Pa.: National Center for Juvenile Justice, 1995).

TABLE 14.4 Offense Profile of Detained Petitioned Status Offense Cases, 1988 and 1992

Offense	1988	1992
Runaway	38%	21%
Truancy	8%	2%
Ungovernable	23%	13%
Liquor	16%	22%
Miscellaneous	15%	27%
TOTAL # of Cases Detained	8,900	8,200

Source: Jeffrey Butts et al., *Juvenile Court Statistics—1992* (Pittsburgh, Pa.: National Center for Juvenile Justice, 1995).

detention are in four states (California, Michigan, Ohio, and Florida); there are great variations among states in the age cutoff for court jurisdiction, which influence detention center custody rates; and there appears to be a serious problem of overrepresentation of minorities in secure detention.[10]

Thus, detention of youth continues to be a major issue in the juvenile justice system, and reducing its use has not been an easy task.

PREADJUDICATION DETENTION

The majority of children taken into custody by the police are released to their parents or guardians. Some are detained overnight in a detention facility until their parents can be notified of the arrest. Police officers normally take a child to a place of detention only after other alternatives have been exhausted. Many juvenile courts in large urban areas have staff members, such as intake probation officers, on duty 24 hours a day to screen detention admissions.

Ordinarily, children who are apprehended for juvenile delinquency are detained if they are inclined to run away while awaiting trial, if it appears that they will commit an offense dangerous to themselves or the community, or if they are violators from other jurisdictions. For example, in an analysis of detention decisions in a single county in Alabama, Belinda McCarthy found that juveniles were indeed being detained because they were a threat to the community,

Detention is the temporary care of children in physically restricted facilities pending court disposition or transfer to another agency. The approximately five hundred traditional detention facilities for children are designed as secure environments with locked doors, high fences or walls, screens or bars, and other obstructions designed to prevent detainees from leaving the facility at will. Here, Reggie, a seventeen year old who was crippled in a stolen car wreck and who just was released from a detention center was re-arrested after a car chase that resulted in him crashing into a methane gasline. When asked why he did it again he replied, "Why should I care, nobody else does." He was driving the car using a crutch to brake and accelerate.

because their own safety was endangered, and because they tended to commit more serious crimes; offender race, class, and gender did not play a role in detention decision making.[11]

However, the criteria used in deciding whether a child should be placed in detention are far from clear; each jurisdiction handles detention decisions differently. In fact, a recent study by Charles Frazier and Donna Bishop employing data on all juveniles processed in a single state over a two-year period failed to uncover any pattern that could help explain how detention decisions were made.[12] Frazier and Bishop concluded that detention decisions were based solely on judicial discretion. Similarly, a recent study of New York state's juvenile offender law in Westchester County, New York, also concluded that detention decisions lack the clearly defined statutory criteria that could result in a reduction in the number of youths admitted to secure detention facilities.[13]

Today, many courts are striving to implement the recommendations of the National Council on Crime and Delinquency (NCCD) and other standard-setting groups that suggest that youth should be detained only if they (1) are likely to commit a new offense, (2) present a danger to themselves or the community, or (3) are likely to run away or fail to appear at subsequent court hearings. David Steinhart's 1994 analysis of the use of NCCD detention criteria in San Francisco describes the developments leading to the decline in admissions in that facility.[14]

RIGHT TO A DETENTION HEARING

A child who is placed in a detention facility or shelter care unit should not be kept there for more than 24 hours. Most jurisdictions require the filing of a formal petition against the child invoking the jurisdiction of the juvenile court within the 24-hour period. To detain a juvenile, there must be clear evidence of probable cause to believe that the child has committed the offense and that he or she will flee the area if not detained. Furthermore, once a child has been detained and a petition filed, the child should not continue in detention without a **detention hearing**.[15] Although the requirements for detention hearings vary considerably among the states, most jurisdictions require that they occur almost immediately after the child's admission to a detention facility and provide the youth with notice and counsel.

The probation department of the juvenile court may help the judge decide whether or not to keep a child in detention. Usually a probation officer in the intake department assists the court in making a decision about the child's release.

In sum, decisions to detain or release juveniles depend on the nature of their actions, whether they are a danger to themselves or others, and whether their parents or lawful guardians can be reached quickly to take them home. If children are to be kept longer than 24 hours, a formal petition must be filed against them and their parents must be notified so that the children can possibly be released in their custody.

DETENTION PROBLEMS

Detention has long been criticized for placing children who have not yet been found to be delinquent in an often harsh environment that is more often than not lacking in any rehabilitative services. As one national survey of detention conditions put it, "The custody was a matter of lock and key, and the instructive experience was more the exception than the rule. . . . Repeatedly, detention emerged as a form of punishment without conviction—and often without crime."[16]

In addition, critics charge that the discretion used when selecting youths for detention often works against the poor and minorities. A study by the Humphrey Institute of Public Affairs found that minority youths are placed in secure detention facilities at a rate three to four times higher than white youths; during the three-year period studied (1979 to 1982) the overrepresentation became increasingly more pronounced.[17] Other researchers also report that differential detention rates are produced by economic, family, and community forces. For example, of almost 2,500 cases taken from the juvenile court records of six New Jersey counties, researchers Russell Schutt and Dale Dannefer found that detention decisions favor protecting some classes of juveniles rather than ensuring them due process.[18] For example, African-American and Hispanic juveniles were quite likely to be detained even if they lived with two parents, but white juveniles were subject to detention only if they lived with one parent. In sum, the cost of detention, overcrowding, poor policy decisions, and overrepresentation by minorities in secure detention facilities are the reasons the system needs reform.

NEW APPROACHES TO DETENTION

Efforts have been ongoing to improve the process and conditions of detention. The Juvenile Detention Committee of the American Correctional Association has developed standards for detention that establish fair and uniform positive expectations for its use. These standards state the following:

> Juvenile detention is the temporary and secure custody of children accused or adjudicated of conduct subject to the jurisdiction of the family/juvenile court who

require a physically restricting environment for their own or the community's protection while pending legal action. Further, juvenile detention should provide and maintain a wide range of helpful services that include, but are not limited to, the following: education, visitation, private communications, counseling, continuous supervision, medical and health care, nutrition, recreation, and reading. To advise the court on the proper course of action required to restore the child to a productive role in the community, detention should also include or provide a system for clinical observation and diagnosis that complements the wide range of helpful services.[19]

Some evidence indicates that preadjudicatory facilities are meeting this goal. The consensus of professional opinion today is that juvenile detention centers should be reserved for those youth who present a clear and substantial threat to the community. As a result, attention is being focused on the development of new approaches to detention care, such as day resource centers, detention alternative programs, and family shelters.[20] In Tennessee and Michigan, for example, nonsecure holdover facilities are being used to service juveniles for a limited period. In Utah, special intake programs are used to screen children to locate more secure housing whenever possible.

In addition, some pretrial detention centers are providing extensive education programs. The Spofford Juvenile Center in the Bronx, New York, is the only pretrial detention center in New York with an educational program approved by the state.[21] The center's instructional program includes a five-and-a-half-hour day, with a curriculum of reading and language arts, math, social studies, science, health and safety education, library skills, physical education, art, and music. Because students remain in detention for varying lengths of time, the curriculum is organized in short modules so that students whose stays are brief can still complete a body of work. The Los Patrinos Juvenile Hall School in Downey, California, also operates with a highly transient population. Yet it has been successful in offering comprehensive instruction in basic academic subjects and technological and functional living skills. It emphasizes helping students to develop positive self-concepts and improved relationships with others.[22] In New Hampshire, young people spend an average of 21 days in the Awaiting Disposition of the Court (ADC) Unit. The unit's on-site educational program employs a nontraditional, holistic learning approach designed to generate student opinions, cultivate discussions, and stimulate responses. The prime curriculum variable is the "Weekly Theme." Several educational themes or modules have been designed both to provide factual information and to promote student discussions on a variety of topics, including U.S. history, basic psychology, and family problems.[23]

Ira Schwartz describes juvenile detention as the underbelly of the juvenile justice system.[24] Because these institutions are often hidden from public scrutiny, many juveniles are confined in antiquated and poorly managed facilities. Schwartz indicates that there is an overreliance on detention and that improvements can result from adequate policy decision making by juvenile justice officials (see the "Focus on Delinquency" feature entitled "Reforming the Juvenile Detention System").

Undoubtedly, juveniles pose special detention problems. But some efforts are being made to improve programs and reduce pretrial detention use, especially in secure settings. Of all the problems associated with detention, however, none is as critical as the issue of placing youths in adult jails.

Reforming the Juvenile Detention System

Juvenile detention facilities hold more children than do any other type of juvenile institution. What are the national trends and issues surrounding juvenile detention? What are the determinants of juvenile detention rates? Are any jurisdictions reducing the use of secure detention? How can we implement changes in detention policy? Ira Schwartz brings together a series of essays to assess today's juvenile detention system and suggests strategies and solutions to deal with the detention crisis.

Schwartz confirmed that on any given day almost 20,000 children are in the detention system and more than 500,000 are admitted every year; there are more than 422 detention facilities or twice the number of training schools. Although national rates declined in the early 1980s, the rate of admission began to rise sharply in the late 1980s. Because the number of juveniles in detention centers has increased, serious overcrowding exists in detention facilities throughout the country.

There has also been a change in the racial composition of detained juvenile offenders. Although there has been a decline in the proportion of white children detained, this has been offset by an increase for African-American males. Overrepresentation of minorities in the juvenile justice system is a major issue, and its causes are being explored by the Office of Juvenile Justice and Delinquency Prevention (OJJDP).

Schwartz and his colleagues point out that there are several important reasons why officials should be concerned about the rising detention rates of children in the juvenile justice system. First, the cost for detention ranges from $70 to $150 per bed, and expenditures for juvenile detention have more than doubled in the last decade to more than 500 million dollars. Second, detention can often have harmful effects on children because of poor institutional conditions and abusive treatment. Third, many children often stay in detention longer than anticipated, thus putting great stress on the available bed space and causing severe overcrowding.

What determines the number of admissions to detention revolves around policy decisions in the juvenile justice system. In a chapter by Terry Martin describing the detention process in Cleveland, Ohio, Martin points that fluctuations in admissions to juvenile detention facilities are driven largely by judicial attitudes regarding who should be confined and not by the rates of serious juvenile violent offenses and property crimes. In a critical article by William Barton, Ira Schwartz, and Franklin Orlando describing detention conditions in Broward County (Ft. Lauderdale), Florida, the authors indicate that dangerous overcrowding was addressed by developing objective intake criteria, increasing the use of release on recognizance, and establishing community-based alternatives. David Steinhart also describes the developments leading to the decline in admissions to detention facilities in San Francisco. Admissions were brought under control through the development, implementation, and monitoring of detention intake screening criteria.

Schwartz and his coauthors not only bring to light the problems and inefficiencies in juvenile detention but suggest an agenda for detention reform. The nine-step program calls for: (1) conducting a comprehensive study of the detention system; (2) adopting objective detention intake criteria; (3) developing 24-hour face-to-face detention intake screening and crisis intervention services; (4) eliminating the practice of committing youth to serve time in detention; (5) creating a detention population management position; (6) developing partnerships between public and private agencies in the delivery of alternative services; (7) enacting legislation that limits the use of detention; (8) creating alternatives to detention and criteria for their use; and (9) developing a mechanism for overseeing and monitoring the detention system.

Although not all experts would agree with Schwartz's entire agenda for reform, there is convincing evidence that detention can be an inappropriate and even degrading experience for many children and requires improvement. At the least it should perform the role for which it was intended—to detain juveniles who are a real risk to the community and who are unlikely to appear in court. The implementation of effective policy changes in the juvenile courts would certainly assist in reducing the size of the detention population and provide secure detention for youths who need it.

Source: Ira Schwartz and William H. Barton, eds., *Reforming Juvenile Detention—No More Hidden Closets* (Columbus: Ohio State University Press, 1994).

DETENTION IN ADULT JAILS

One of the most significant problems with detention is placing youths under 18 in adult jails. This is usually done in rural areas where no other facility exists. Almost all experts in the field of juvenile justice agree that placing children under the age of 18 in any type of jail facility should be prohibited. Juveniles in adult jails can easily be victimized by other inmates, the staff, and themselves.

Juveniles detained in adult jails often live in squalid conditions and are subjected to physical and sexual abuse. A federally sponsored study found that children confined to adult institutions were eight times as likely to commit suicide as those placed in detention centers exclusively for juveniles; they have a 4.5 percent higher rate of suicide than children in the general population.[25] Over the years, jails have been the least progressive of all correctional institutions in the United States. Most jails were constructed in the nineteenth century; few have been substantially improved in the twentieth century, and many are in poor physical condition. Jails throughout the nation are overcrowded, have no rehabilitation programs, provide little or no medical attention, and make no effort to provide adequate plumbing, ventilation, or heating. Many are fire hazards. Courts throughout the nation have ruled that conditions in certain jails make incarceration there a cruel and unusual punishment, a violation of the Eighth and Fourteenth Amendments of the U.S. Constitution. Regardless of the conditions, the argument can be made that jailing juveniles with adults must be viewed as cruel and unusual punishment, considering their status.

Until a few years ago, the placement of juveniles in adult facilities was common. According to a study by the Community Research Center at the University of Illinois, 479,000 juveniles were admitted to adult jails in 1979. Of these, 20 percent were status offenders whose "crimes" included running away or underage drinking. Some 4 percent (more than 19,000 youths) were jailed

One of the most significant problems with detention is placing youngsters under 18 in adult jails. This is usually done in rural areas where no other facility exists. Almost all experts in the field of juvenile justice agree that placing children under the age of 18 in any type of jail facility should be prohibited. Juveniles in adult jails can become the victims of other inmates, of the staff, and of their own hands.

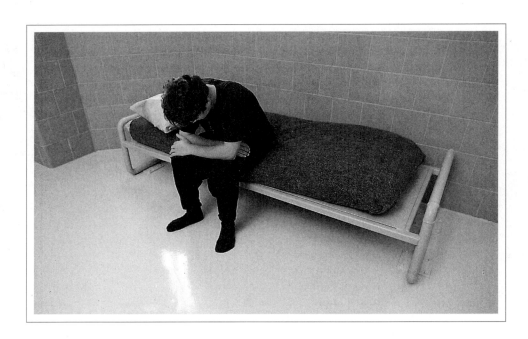

without having committed an offense of any sort; 9 percent were 13 years old or younger.[26] Efforts have been made to change this situation. Some of them are discussed below.

REMOVING YOUTHS FROM ADULT JAILS

The impetus for removing juveniles from adult jails comes from the Office of Juvenile Justice and Delinquency Prevention (OJJDP). In 1989, the Juvenile Justice and Delinquency Prevention Act (JJDPA) of 1974 was amended to require that the states remove all juveniles from adult jails and lockups. The Act states,

> Juveniles alleged to be or found to be delinquent [and status offenders and nonoffenders] shall not be detained or confined in any institution in which they have contact with adult persons incarcerated because they have been convicted of a crime or are awaiting trial on criminal charges or with the part-time or full-time security staff (including management) or direct-care staff of a jail or lockup for adults. . . .[27]

According to federal guidelines, all juveniles in state custody must be separated from adult offenders or the state could lose federal juvenile justice funds. The OJJDP defines separation as the condition in which juvenile detainees have either totally independent facilities or shared facilities that are designed so that juveniles and adults neither have accidental contact nor share programs or treatment staff.[28]

Much debate has arisen over whether the initiative to remove juveniles from adult jails has succeeded. It is still not known how many youths are being held in adult facilities. Some indications are that the numbers have declined significantly from the almost 500,000 a year recorded in 1979. Today, federal agencies estimate that about 1,700 juveniles are being held in adult jails on any given day, and about 53,000 are held in adult jails or lockups sometime during the year; about 30 states (75 percent) are in substantial compliance with federal guidelines. According to a 1990 report of juveniles in custody, the average daily population of juveniles held in adult jails declined nearly 18 percent (from 1,700 to 1,400) between 1980 and 1989.[29]

Such figures may be misleading, however, because they do not include youths held in urban jails for under six hours or in rural ones for under 24 hours, youths transferred to the criminal court, youths in four states that do not cooperate with the federal jail removal initiative, or youths in states that consider anyone over 16 or 17 to be an adult. The Community Research Center in Champaign, Illinois, which monitors the jailing of delinquent youths, believes that a more accurate estimate is that about 200,000 youths are still being jailed with adults each year.[30] Other researchers, on the other hand, still believe that close to half a million youths are detained in adult preadjudicatory facilities (jails or lockups) each year.[31] National trends in juvenile detention rates suggest that the actual number of detainees may have occasionally decreased over the last decade but that the length of time juveniles are held in jails and other secure facilities has increased. On the other hand, the most recent report of the Office of Juvenile Justice and Delinquency Prevention, entitled "Juveniles Taken into Custody— 1992," reveals a 35 percent increase in the number of juveniles in jails based on a one-day census—from 1,736 in 1983 to 2,350 in 1991.[32]

Eliminating the confinement of juveniles in adult institutions continues to be a difficult and ongoing task. In a recent comprehensive study of the jailing of juveniles in Minnesota, Ira Schwartz found that even in a state recognized nationally for juvenile justice reform, the rate of admission of juveniles to adult jails remains unacceptably high.[33] His research also revealed that although the rate of admission was not related to the *seriousness* of the offense, minority youth spent greater amounts of time in jail for the same offenses than white offenders.[34]

In his report, Schwartz suggests that (1) government enact legislation prohibiting the confinement of juveniles in jail; (2) appropriate juvenile detention facilities be established; (3) funds be allocated for such programs; (4) racial disparity in detention be examined; and (5) responsibility for monitoring conditions of confinement be fixed by statutes and court decisions.[35]

There are some promising trends. California, for example, passed legislation ensuring that no minor under juvenile court jurisdiction can be incarcerated in any jail after July 1, 1989.[36] In the landmark federal court case *Hendrickson v. Griggs,* the court found that Iowa had not complied with the juvenile jail removal mandate of the Juvenile Justice and Delinquency Prevention Act and ordered local officials to develop a plan for bringing the state into conformity with the law.[37] As a result, states will face increasing legal pressure to meet jail removal requirements.

Because the actual number of juvenile detainees in adult jails is uncertain, it remains a difficult job to monitor improvement in this area. With federal help, however, some progress appears to have been made in removing juveniles from adult facilities, but thousands each year continue to be held in close contact with adults, and thousands more are held in facilities that, although physically separate, put them in close proximity to adults. To the youths held within their walls, there may appear to be little difference between the juvenile detention facilities and the adult jail.

DEINSTITUTIONALIZATION OF STATUS OFFENDERS

One of the most important juvenile justice policy initiatives of the past two decades has been the removal of status offenders from secure detention facilities that also house delinquents. Along with removing all juveniles from adult jails, the OJJDP has made deinstitutionalization of status offenders a cornerstone of its policy. The Juvenile Justice and Delinquency Prevention Act of 1974 prohibits the secure placement of status offenders in detention facilities.

Removing status offenders from secure detention facilities serves two purposes: (1) it reduces interaction with serious delinquent offenders and (2) it insulates them from the stigma and negative labels associated with being a detainee in a locked facility. **Deinstitutionalization** has its roots in labeling theory, which views the experience of being labeled a delinquent as a primary cause of delinquent careers, and the conflict perspective, which holds that those chosen for sanctions will most likely become social and political outcasts. To counteract the effects of labeling, stigma, and delinquent learning opportunities, nonsecure alternatives—counseling, after-school programs, shelter care, and foster care—have been developed for nondelinquent youths.

The national effort seems to be paying important dividends. About 20 years ago, 3,800 status offenders were in some sort of public secure confinement; in the early 1980s, this number dropped to about 1,000. Since then, the number of status offenders being held in some sort of secure confinement has remained stable or decreased slightly.[38]

More than 15 years ago, the OJJDP funded a national **Deinstitutionalization of Status Offenders (DSO) Project** to demonstrate the feasibility of removing status offenders from secure lockups and to evaluate the effects of deinstitutionalization.[39]

Since their inception, the DSO programs have netted mixed results. One problem was the variant definitions of status offenders held by different agencies. Some agencies limited their programs to "pure" status offenders, who had no record of prior delinquency involvement, while others included "mixed offenders," those with a record of prior delinquency. The evaluation found that the pure status offender was relatively rare; most current status offenders had prior delinquent experiences. Another problem was the "net widening" that resulted with the announcement of the new program. Police became more willing to send youths to the juvenile court rather than handle the cases themselves once they learned of the services available through the new program. Thus, the number of youths processed to court *increased* in a number of cities, impeding the antilabeling, antistigma aspects of the program.

Another problem was uncovered by M. A. Bortner, Mary Sutherland, and Russ Winn, who examined a midwestern community before and after it attempted to deinstitutionalize status offenders. One disappointing finding was that there was very little overall change in the processing of status offenders. Of greater concern was the fact that African-American status offenders were detained more often than whites and that their detention rates actually increased after the DSO effort had been implemented. On a more positive note, the researchers found that after the deinstitutionalization effort was undertaken, the use of formal hearings and severe dispositions for both African-American and white youths dropped substantially.[40]

Anne Schneider has conducted the most comprehensive evaluation of DSO programs on a national level. She found that the DSO programs were successful overall in significantly reducing—but not eliminating—the number of status offenders held in secure detention and the number of status offenders institutionalized after trial. However, the recidivism rate was unaffected by the DSO project, and in some sites, it actually increased; that is, status offenders placed in nonsecure facilities, separate from delinquents, were sometimes more likely to commit repeat offenses than those held in secure detention centers.[41]

This finding suggests that removing status offenders from detention is not a panacea for preventing juvenile crime. However, it was as effective as secure detention. Because shelter care and foster care are much less expensive to maintain than a secure detention facility, deinstitutionalization is at least a more *cost-effective* juvenile justice policy.

For girls, deinstitutionalization may be much less successful. According to Federle and Chesney-Lind, the deinstitutionalization movement of the JJDPA has resulted in girls being removed to mental health and child welfare programs. They conclude that the system appears to be perpetuating the paternalism that has historically characterized juvenile justice for girls.[42]

The debate over the most effective way to handle juvenile status offenders continues, especially when it comes to the concept of deinstitutionalization. Nevertheless, one fact remains clear: Court data show a substantial decline in the use of detention in status offense cases (see Figure 14.1).

FIGURE 14.1
Deinstitutionalization of status
offenders

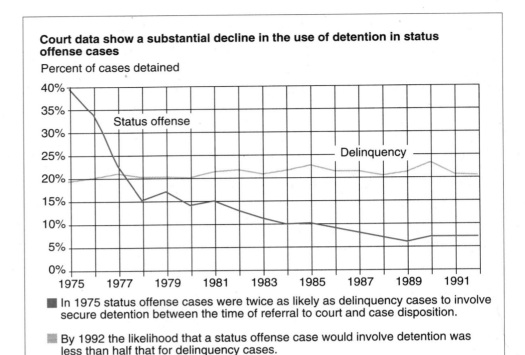

Court data show a substantial decline in the use of detention in status offense cases

Percent of cases detained

- In 1975 status offense cases were twice as likely as delinquency cases to involve secure detention between the time of referral to court and case disposition.

- By 1992 the likelihood that a status offense case would involve detention was less than half that for delinquency cases.

Source: National Center for Juvenile Justice, *Juvenile Court Case Records 1975–1992* (Pittsburgh, Pa.: NCJJ, 1994).

THE INTAKE PROCESS

When the police believe a child needs a court referral, the child becomes involved in the intake division of the court. The term **intake** refers to the screening of cases by the juvenile court system. The child and his or her family are screened by intake officers, who are often probation staff members, to determine whether the child needs the services of the juvenile court. Intake officers may (1) send the youth home with no further action, (2) divert the youth to a social agency, (3) petition him or her to the juvenile court, or (4) file a petition and hold the youth in detention. The intake process reduces demands on limited court resources, screens out cases that are not within the court's jurisdiction, and enables assistance to be obtained from community agencies without court intervention.

Juvenile court intake is now provided for by statute in the majority of states.[43] Also, most of the model acts and standards in juvenile justice suggest the development of juvenile court intake proceedings.[44]

Intake procedures are desirable for the following reasons:

- Filing complaints against children in a court may do more harm than good, because rehabilitation often fails in the juvenile court system.
- Processing children in the juvenile court labels them as delinquent, stigmatizes them, and thus reinforces their antisocial behavior.
- Nonjudicial handling of children gives them and their families an opportunity to work voluntarily with a social service agency.

- Intake screening of children helps conserve already overburdened resources in the juvenile court system.

Intake screening allows juvenile courts to enter into consent decrees with juveniles without filing petitions and without formal adjudication. (The consent decree is basically a court order authorizing disposition of the case without a formal finding of delinquency. It is based on an agreement between the intake department of the court and the juvenile who is the subject of the complaint.[45]

Notwithstanding all of its advantages, intake also has some problems. First, because half of all juveniles who are arrested and brought to court are handled nonjudicially, intake sections are constantly pressured to provide available services for a large group of children. Intake programs also need to be provided 24 hours a day in many urban courts so dispositions can be resolved quickly on the day the child is referred to court. Second, poorly qualified employees in intake are a serious flaw in many court systems.

A third problem is that although almost three-quarters of all state juvenile court systems provide intake and diversion programs, the criteria and procedures for selecting children for such nonjudicial alternatives have not been established. Normally, the intake probation officer undertakes a preliminary investigation to obtain information about the child and the family prior to making a decision. Written guidelines are needed to assist intake personnel in their duties and to alert juveniles and their families to their procedural rights. Some jurisdictions have attempted to provide guidelines for intake decision making. Those guidelines used to determine whether a juvenile case is suitable for adjustment or whether court jurisdiction should be invoked include (1) age of the child; (2) conduct; (3) prior or pending juvenile complaints; (4) the substantial likelihood that the child will cooperate with the adjustment process; and (5) the substantial likelihood that the child is in need of and can receive appropriate services without court intervention.

A number of legal problems are also associated with the intake process. Among them are whether the child has a right to counsel at this stage, whether the child is protected against self-incrimination at intake, and to what degree the child needs to consent to nonjudicial disposition as recommended by the intake probation officer.

Finally, intake dispositions are often determined by the prior juvenile court record, rather than the seriousness of the current offense or the social background of the child. This practice, according to some experts, departs from the court's traditional philosophy of *parens patriae* and does not contribute to the justice or rehabilitation model of today's court. It is important that the juvenile court intake examine its function and make certain its decisions are consistent with its philosophy.[46]

CHANGES IN THE INTAKE PROCESS

Because the intake process is so critical, it has been undergoing changes in various jurisdictions. One important trend in the intake process has been the influence of prosecutors on decision making. Traditionally, the intake process has been controlled by probation personnel whose decisions influenced heavily the presiding juvenile court judge's view of which cases should be handled formally and which should be settled without court action.

This approach to intake, in which probation personnel seek to dispense the least incursive amount of rehabilitative justice, is being replaced in some jurisdictions by a prosecutor who may be more concerned with protecting the public and controlling offenders. Some states, such as Florida, now require that the intake officers get approval from the prosecutor before either accepting or rejecting a delinquency petition. Other states, such as Maryland and California, allow the complaining party to appeal petitions rejected by intake officers to the prosecutor, while in Colorado and Washington prosecutorial screening of cases eliminates any significant probation intake role.[47]

The county's chief legal officer, the district attorney, is now playing a greater role in the juvenile court process. There is evidence of a shift from the rehabilitation model to the due process approach in juvenile justice. As Ted Rubin puts it,

> The prosecutor's authority in the juvenile intake process is likely to develop into a controlling one, stimulated by the prosecutor's public protection image, the increased interest in handling juveniles according to offense and prior record, and diminished confidence in the ideal of rehabilitation.[48]

(A more detailed analysis of the role of the prosecutor is found in chapter 15.)

Diversion

One of the most important alternatives chosen at intake is nonjudicial disposition or, as it is variously called, *nonjudicial adjustment, handling* or *processing, informal disposition, adjustment,* or *diversion.* **Diversion** is the most common term used to refer to the screening out of children from the juvenile court without judicial determination.

Numerous national groups, commentators, lawyers, and criminal justice experts have sought to define the concept of diversion since its inception in the mid-1960s. We suggest that juvenile diversion is the process of placing youths suspected of law-violating behavior into treatment-oriented programs prior to formal trial and disposition in order to minimize their penetration into the justice system and thereby avoid any potential stigma and labeling.

Diversion implies more than simply screening out cases that are trivial or unimportant and for which no additional treatment is needed. Screening involves abandoning efforts to apply any coercive measures to a defendant.[49] In contrast, diversion encourages an individual to participate in some specific program or activity by express or implied threat of further prosecution. Juvenile justice experts define diversion as "the channeling of cases to noncourt institutions in instances where these cases would ordinarily have received an adjudicatory hearing by a court."[50] Whatever definition is used, diversion generally refers to formally acknowledged and organized efforts to process juvenile and adult offenders outside the justice system.[51]

Diversion has become one of the most popular reforms in juvenile justice since it was recommended by the President's Crime Commission in 1967. Arguments for the use of diversion programs contend that

- it keeps the juvenile justice system operating; without it, the system would collapse from voluminous caseloads;
- it is preferable to dealing with the inadequate juvenile justice treatment system;

- it gives legislators and other government leaders the opportunity to reallocate resources to programs that may be more successful in the treatment of juvenile offenders;
- its costs are significantly less than the per capita cost of institutionalization; and
- it helps youths avoid the stigma of being labeled a delinquent, which is believed to be an important factor in developing a delinquent career.[52]

Police-based diversion models include family crisis intervention projects, referral programs, and youth service bureaus. In addition, court-based diversion models have been used extensively for status offenders, minor first offenders, children involved in family disturbances, and children involved in such offenses as shoplifting or minor assault and battery. Court-based diversion programs include intervention projects involving employment, referral for educational programs, and placement of juveniles who are involved with drugs in drug-related programs.[53]

Most court-based diversion programs employ a particular formula for choosing youths for diversion. Such criteria as being a first offender, nonviolent offender, or status offender, and being drug or alcohol dependent are used to select clients. In some programs, youths will be asked to partake of services voluntarily in lieu of a court appearance. In other programs, prosecutors will agree to defer, and then dismiss, a case once a youth has successfully completed a treatment program. Finally, some programs can be initiated by the juvenile court judge after the case has been brought to his or her attention at an initial hearing.[54]

In summary, diversion programs have been created to remove nonserious offenders from the formal justice system, to provide them with nonpunitive treatment services, and to help them avoid the stigma of a delinquent label.

ISSUES IN DIVERSION: WIDENING THE NET

Diversion has been viewed as a promising alternative to official procedures, but over the years its basic premises have been questioned by a number of experts.[55] The most damaging criticism has been that diversion programs, rather than reducing stigma and system penetration, are increasing it by involving children in the juvenile justice system who previously would have been released without official notice. This phenomenon is referred to as **widening the net.** Various studies indicate that police and court personnel are likely to use diversion program services for youths who ordinarily would have been turned loose at the intake or arrest stage.[56] For example, in an analysis of diversion programs in Florida, Charles Frazier and John Cochran found that after controlling for such social and legal variables as race, sex, age, offense severity, and prior record, diverted youths experienced at least as much involvement with the juvenile justice system as did youths who were not selected for diversion.[57] Similarly, after reviewing existing research on the effectiveness of employing diversion with status offenders, Dennis Anderson and Donald Schoen found little evidence that diversion programs have met their stated goals. They conclude that although diversion should not be dismissed as an "unrealistic or harmful fad," neither should it be judged as a "satisfactory approach to juvenile delinquency."[58] Thus, the youths in diversion programs may neither be "saved" from a more serious delinquency label nor freed from significant intrusion in their lives.

Police-based diversion models include family crisis intervention projects, referral programs, and youth service bureaus. In addition, court-based diversion model programs include intervention projects involving employment, referral for educational programs, and placement of juveniles who are involved with drugs in drug-related programs. Most employ counselors to help steer kids out of further trouble with the law.

Why does net widening occur? One explanation is that police and prosecutors find diversion a more attractive alternative to both official processing and outright release—diversion helps them resolve the conflict between doing too much or too little. Second, many local diversion programs receive outside (federal, state, or private) funds. Local officials, worried that they will lose these funds if client quotas are not maintained, beg police and court officials for a few "warm bodies." Police and judges who are reluctant to give up control of offenders they believe need more formal treatment refer youths whom they might have released with a warning in the past. As Sharla Rausch and Charles Logan put it,

> In essence, the diverted population was drawn from a pool of offenders who, prior to the implementation of diversion programs, would probably have been released or left alone. The effect of such a policy has been to expand control over a larger, less seriously involved sector of the juvenile population.[59]

Similarly, Frazier and Cochran found that net widening may result from the fact that diversion staff members often have social service backgrounds: "Most staff believed that the more attention given a youth and the longer the period of time over which the attention was given, the better the prospects for a successful outcome.[60]

Diversion has also been criticized as ineffective and unproductive; that is, youths being diverted make no better adjustment in the community than those who go through official channels. However, not all delinquency experts are critical of diversion. Arnold Binder and Gilbert Geis claim that there are many benefits to diversion that more than balance its negative qualities.[61] They challenge the net-widening concept as being naive: How do we know that diverted youths would have had less interface with the justice system if diversion didn't exist? They suggest that even if juveniles had escaped official labels for their current offense, it may be inevitable that they would eventually fall into the hands of the police and juvenile court. They also point out that the rehabilitative potential of diversion should not be overlooked (see the "Case in Point" for this chapter).

You are the intake worker assigned to the local juvenile court.

Charles is a 13-year-old who was arrested for shoplifting in a department store. He was appearing before the juvenile court for trial and disposition of this, his first delinquency offense. Charles lives with his mother and three younger siblings in a public housing project. His parents are separated, and Charles hasn't seen his father in more than a year. Charles is in the eighth grade, seems bright, but frequently fights in school. The school report indicates that Charles is a sad, lonely child with a hot temper.

The intake worker and defense attorney indicate that Charles wants to remain at home, and both recommend closing the delinquency case. The prosecutor and arresting police officer believe that Charles is an aggressive, acting-out youth whose behavior is unpredictable and who is in need of juvenile court supervision.

Do you believe that Charles would benefit from a diversion program?

How would you assess the juvenile court's role in this type of case?

Although diversion programs are not the panacea their originators believed them to be, at least they offer an alternative to official processing. They can help the justice system devote its energies to more serious offenders while providing counseling and other rehabilitative services to needy youths.

In summary, an examination of the history of diversion indicates that most programs widen the net of the justice system and that their ability to reduce recidivism remains uncertain. According to Mark Ezell, the central theme in the juvenile court movement is the endless search for effective alternatives.[62] Juvenile diversion programs represent one alternative to the traditional process.

THE PETITION

A **complaint** is the report that the police or some other agency makes to the court to initiate the intake process. Once the agency makes a decision in intake that judicial disposition is required, a formal petition is filed. The **petition** is the formal legal complaint that initiates judicial action against a juvenile charged with actions alleging juvenile delinquency or noncriminal behavior. The petition includes such basic information as the name, age, and residence of the child; the parents' names; and the facts alleging the child's delinquency. The police officer, a family member, or a social service agency can bring a petition. If, after being given the right to counsel, the child admits the allegation in the petition, an initial hearing is immediately scheduled for the child to make the admission before the court, and information is gathered to develop a treatment plan.

If the child does not admit to any of the facts in the petition, a date for a scheduled hearing on the petition is set. This hearing, whose purpose is to determine the merits of the petition, is similar to the adult trial. Once a hearing or adjudication date has been set, the probation department, which is the agency providing social services to the court, is normally asked to prepare a social study report. This report, often known as the predisposition report, contains relevant information about the child and recommendation for treatment and service.

When a date has been set for the hearing on the petition, parents or guardians and other persons associated with the petition, such as witnesses, the arresting police officer, and victims, are notified of the hearing. On occasion, the court may issue a summons—a court order requiring the juvenile or others involved in the case to appear for the hearing. The statutes or the juvenile code in a given jurisdiction govern the contents of the petition. Some jurisdictions, for instance, allow for a petition to be filed based on the information and belief of the complainant alone. Others require that the petition be filed under oath or that an affidavit accompany the petition. Some jurisdictions authorize only one official, such as a probation officer or prosecutor, to file the petition. Others allow numerous officials, including family and social service agencies, to set forth facts in the petition.

BAIL FOR CHILDREN

Bail is money or some other security provided to the court to ensure the appearance of a defendant at every subsequent stage of the justice process. Its purpose is to obtain the release from custody of the person charged with the crime. Once the amount of bail is set by the court, the defendant is required to pay a percentage of the entire amount in cash or securities or to pay a professional bail bonding agency to submit a bond as a guarantee for returning to court. If a person is released on bail but fails to appear in court at the stipulated time, the bail deposit is forfeited. The person, if apprehended, is then confined in a detention facility until the court appearance.

With a few exceptions, persons other than those accused of murder are entitled to reasonable bail, as stated in the Eighth Amendment of the U.S. Constitution. There is some controversy today about whether a constitutional right to bail exists or whether the court can impose excessive bail resulting in a person's confinement. In most cases, a defendant has the right to be released on reasonable bail. Many jurisdictions require a bail review hearing by a higher court when a person is detained because he or she is unable to pay an excessive bail. Whether a defendant will appear at the next stage of the juvenile or criminal proceeding is a key issue in determining bail. Bail cannot be used to punish an accused, nor can it be denied or revoked simply at the discretion of the court. Many experts believe that bail is one of the worst aspects of the criminal justice system. It discriminates against the poor. It is costly to the government, which must pay for detention facilities for offenders who are unable to make bail and who could otherwise be in the community. It is dehumanizing to those who must stay in jail because they cannot raise bail. It is even believed that people who await trial in jail have a higher proportion of subsequent convictions than people who are released on bail.

Over the years, few people have come to realize that these same issues apply to the detention of juveniles as well as adults. Juvenile detention prior to adjudication is one of the most serious problems facing the juvenile justice system. Large numbers of juveniles are incarcerated at this critical stage. Poor conditions exist in the detention facilities where they are held, and harmful aftereffects result from the detention process.

Despite these facts, many states refuse juveniles the right to bail. They argue that juvenile proceedings are civil, not criminal, and that detention is rehabilitative, not punitive. In addition, they argue that juveniles do not need a constitutional right to bail because statutory provisions allow children to be released in parental custody. Furthermore, they believe it would be more productive to reduce the number of detention facilities and the children in them than to develop a bail program.

In view of the recognized deficiency of the adult bail system, some experts believe that alternative release programs should be developed within the juvenile justice system. These programs include release on recognizance, release to a third party, and the use of station house summonses or citation programs in lieu of arrest.

Some states do provide bail programs for children. Bail is used only to ensure the presence of the accused at trial; the presumption exists that the accused should be released solely on the basis of being able to make bail. Mark Solar and his colleagues point out that state juvenile bail statutes are divided into three categories: (1) those guaranteeing the right to bail; (2) those that grant the court discretion to give bail; and (3) those that deny a juvenile the right to bail.[63] The consensus generally is that allowing bail for juveniles is in conflict with the *parens patriae* concept and rehabilitation goals of the juvenile justice system.

There is no agreement among jurisdictions, however, on whether a child has the constitutional right to be released on bail. The U.S. Supreme Court has never decided the issue of whether juveniles have a constitutional right to bail. Some courts have stated that bail provisions do not apply to juveniles. Others rely on the Eighth Amendment or on state constitutional provisions or statutes and conclude that juveniles do have a right to bail.

In a bail hearing for a child, the court reviews such factors as the charge, the history of the parents' ability to control the child's behavior, the child's school participation, psychological and psychiatric evaluations, the child's desire to go home, and the parents' interest in continuing to take care of the child while awaiting the trial.

PREVENTIVE DETENTION

An issue closely related to bail is **preventive detention.** This refers to the practice of keeping a person in custody before trial because of his or her suspected danger to the community. Proponents argue that preventive detention can save the victim of crime from any additional trouble from an offender released on bail and also protect potential new victims from harm. Opponents hold that preventive detention statutes deprive offenders of their freedom because guilt has not been proven in the case at hand. It is also unfair, they claim, to punish people for what judicial authorities believe they may do in the future, as it is impossible to predict with any accuracy who will be a danger to the community. Moreover, because judges are able to use unchecked discretion in their detention decisions, an offender could unfairly be deprived of freedom without legal recourse.

Although the Supreme Court has upheld preventive detention of adults, most state jurisdictions allow judges to deny bail to adult offenders only in cases involving murder (capital crimes), when the offenders have jumped bail in the past, or when they have committed another crime while on bail. However, every state allows for preventive detention of juveniles. The reason for this discrepancy hinges on the legal principle that while adults have the right to liberty, juveniles have a right to custody. Therefore, it is not unreasonable to detain youths for their own protection. On June 4, 1984, the Supreme Court dealt with this issue in *Schall v. Martin,* when it upheld the state of New York's preventive detention statute. The Court concluded that there was no indication in the statute that preventive detention was used as punishment.[64] (See the accompanying "Focus on Delinquency.")

SCHALL V. MARTIN

Facts

Gregory Martin was arrested in New York City on December 13, 1977, on charges of robbery, assault, and criminal possession of a weapon. Because he was arrested at 11:30 p.m. and lied about his residence, Martin was kept overnight in detention and brought to juvenile court the next day for an "initial appearance" accompanied by his grandmother. The family court judge, citing possession of a loaded weapon, the false address given to police, and the lateness of the hour the crime occurred (as evidence of a lack of supervision), ordered him detained before trial under section 320.5(3)(6) of the New York State code. Section 320.5 authorizes pretrial detention of an accused juvenile delinquent if "there is a substantial probability that he will not appear in court on the return date or there is a serious risk that he may before the return date commit an act which if committed by an adult would constitute a crime." Later at trial, Martin was found to be a delinquent and sentenced to two years' probation.

While he was in pretrial detention Martin's attorneys filed a habeas corpus petition (demanding his release from custody). Their petition charged that his detention denied him due process rights under the Fifth and Fourteenth Amendments. Their suit was a class action on behalf of all youths subject to preventive detention in New York. The New York appellate courts upheld Martin's claim on the ground that because, at adjudication, most delinquents are released or placed on probation, it was unfair to incarcerate them before trial. The prosecution brought the case to the U.S. Supreme Court for final judgment.

Decision

The Supreme Court upheld the state's right to place juveniles in preventive detention. It held that preventive detention serves the legitimate objective of protecting both the juvenile and society from pretrial crime. Pretrial detention need not be considered punishment merely because the juvenile is eventually released or put on probation. In addition, there are procedural safeguards, such as notice and a hearing, and a statement of facts that must be given to juveniles before they are placed in detention. The Court also found that detention based on prediction of future behavior was not a violation of due process. Many decisions are made in the justice system, such as the decision to sentence or grant parole, that are based in part on a prediction of future behavior, and these have all been accepted by the court as legitimate exercises of state power.

Significance of the Case

Schall v. Martin established the right of juvenile court judges to deny youths pretrial release if they perceive them to be "dangerous." However, the case also established a due process standard for detention hearings that includes notice and a statement of substantial reasons for the detention.

Source: Schall v. Martin, 104 S.Ct. 2403 (1984).

In a recent study of the effect of *Schall,* the American Bar Association concluded that continued refinement of the detention screening process is needed to achieve the twin goals of public safety and protection of juvenile offenders' constitutional rights.[65] Because preventive detention may attach a stigma of guilt to a child presumed innocent, the practice remains a highly controversial one.

THE PLEA AND PLEA BARGAINING

In the adult criminal justice system, the defendant normally enters a plea of guilty or not guilty. More than 90 percent of all adult defendants plead guilty before the trial stage. A large proportion of those pleas involve what is known as plea bargaining. **Plea bargaining** is the exchange of prosecutorial and judicial concessions for guilty pleas.[66] It permits a defendant to plead guilty to a less serious charge in exchange for an agreement by the prosecutor to recommend a reduced sentence to the court.

Few juvenile codes require a guilty or not guilty plea when a petition is filed against a child in juvenile court. In most jurisdictions, an initial hearing is held at which the child either submits to a finding of the facts or denies the petition.[67] If the child admits to the facts, the court determines an appropriate disposition and treatment plan for the child. If the child denies the allegations in the petition, the case normally proceeds to the trial or adjudication stage of the juvenile process. When a child enters no plea, the court imposes a denial of the charges for the child.

A high percentage of juvenile offenders enter guilty pleas or admissions in the juvenile court. How many of these pleas involve plea bargaining between the prosecutor or probation officer and the child's attorney is unknown. In the past, it was believed that plea bargaining was unnecessary in the juvenile justice system because there was little incentive for either the prosecution or the defense to bargain in a system that does not have jury trials, criminal labels, or long sentences. In addition, because the court must dispose of cases in the best interests of the child, plea negotiation seemed unnecessary. Consequently, there has long been a debate among experts over the appropriateness of plea bargaining in the juvenile justice system. The arguments in favor of plea bargaining include lower court costs and efficiency. Others believe that it is an invisible, unfair, unregulated, and unethical process. When used, experts believe the process requires the highest standards of good faith by the prosecutor in the juvenile and adult system.[68]

In recent years, however, growing public concern about violent juvenile crime has spurred attorneys to increasingly seek to negotiate a plea rather than accept the so-called good interests of the court judgment—a judgment that might result in harsher sanctions for their clients. The extension of the adversary process for children has led to an increase in plea bargaining, creating an informal trial process that parallels the adult system. Other factors in the trend toward juvenile plea bargaining include the use of prosecutors rather than probation personnel and police officers in juvenile courts and the ever-increasing caseloads in such courts.

Plea bargaining negotiations generally involve the reduction of a charge, the changing of the proceedings from that of delinquency to a status offense, the elimination of possible waiver proceedings to the criminal court, and agreements between the government and defense regarding dispositional programs for the child. In states where youths are subject to long, mandatory sentences, reduction of the charges may have a significant impact on the outcome of the case, and in states where youths may be waived to the adult court for committing certain serious crimes, a plea reduction may result in the juvenile court maintaining jurisdiction.

Although little clear evidence exists of how much plea bargaining there is in the juvenile justice system, it is apparent that such negotiations do take place and seem to be increasing. In one of the most comprehensive studies of juvenile plea negotiation in juvenile court, Joseph Sanborn found that about 20 percent of the cases processed in Philadelphia resulted in a negotiated plea. Most were for reduced sentences, most typically probation in lieu of incarceration, or if an institutional sentence could not be avoided, assignment to a less restrictive environment. Sanborn found that plea bargaining was a very complex process in juvenile court, depending in large measure on the philosophy of the judge and

PLEADING GUILTY IN JUVENILE COURT

Although the nature and extent of plea bargaining in the adult court system is well documented, plea bargaining in juvenile court has remained a "low visibility" practice. Recent research by Joseph Sanborn sheds more light on the role of plea negotiation in the juvenile justice system.

Sanborn conducted a survey of all 50 states and the District of Columbia to identify legislative and judicial recognition of juvenile plea bargaining. He also observed practices in three juvenile courts and interviewed personnel in order to illustrate the bargaining process.

Sanborn found that 40 states recognize plea negotiations in juvenile court and apply some type of control over the guilty plea process. Twenty-five have formulated rules that control juvenile plea negotiations. Thirteen states have passed legislation that details a judge's obligations when a juvenile pleads guilty; another three states regulate the practice through appellate court ruling. Only 10 states have not addressed the issue of juvenile plea negotiations.

Although most states now address juvenile court pleas, the amount of regulation still varies widely. Most but not all jurisdictions that recognize plea bargaining in juvenile court require judges to remind defendants that they are giving up constitutional rights, warn them of possible sentencing outcomes, determine if the plea was voluntary, and establish if there was a factual basis for the plea.

Sanborn's observation and interview data indicate that there are ecological differences in the way the plea bargaining process is carried out. Urban courts may be more likely to institute formal procedures, while suburban and rural courts are more likely to conduct plea negotiations informally.

Sanborn concludes that as the juvenile court system becomes more formal and punitive, it is essential for juvenile courts to institute more formal and rigorous proceedings in order to ensure that admissions are not later lost on appeal. Fairness dictates that youths, some of whom face long incarceration sentences, understand precisely what they are doing and the implication of pleading guilty for both current and future considerations.

Source: Joseph Sanborn, "Pleading Guilty in Juvenile Court: Minimal Ado about Something Very Important to Young Defendants," *Justice Quarterly* 9:126–50 (1992).

court staff; in general, he found it to be a device that has greater benefit for the defendants than for the court itself.[69] (The accompanying "Focus on Delinquency" takes a closer look at juvenile plea bargaining.)

In summary, the majority of juvenile court cases that are not adjudicated seem to be the result of open admissions rather than actual plea bargaining. Unlike the adult system, where almost 90 percent of all charged offenders are involved in some plea bargaining, there is less plea bargaining in the juvenile court because such common incentives as dropping multiple charges or substituting a misdemeanor for a felony are unlikely. Nonetheless, plea bargaining is firmly entrenched in the juvenile process. Any plea bargain, however, must be entered into voluntarily and knowingly; otherwise, the conviction may be overturned on appeal.

TRANSFER TO THE ADULT COURT

One of the most significant actions that occurs in the early court processing of a juvenile offender is the **transfer** process. Otherwise known as **waiver, bindover,** or **removal,** this process involves transferring a juvenile from the juvenile court to the criminal court. Virtually all state statutes allow for this kind of transfer.

Historically, the American justice system has made a fundamental distinction between children and adults. The juvenile justice system emphasizes rehabilitation, while the criminal justice system emphasizes deterrence, punishment, and social control. Proponents of the transfer process claim that children who commit serious, chronic offenses and who may be hardened offenders should be handled by the criminal court system. In fact, so the argument goes, these children cannot be rehabilitated. Even such well-regarded institutions as the National Council of Juvenile and Family Court Judges have made it their stated policy to favor transfer.[70] The theory is that, unless a waiver policy exists, children may feel immune from "real" punishment.

Opponents suggest that the transfer process is applied to children unfairly and is a halfhearted effort at implementing the treatment philosophy of the juvenile court. Furthermore, some children tried in the adult criminal court may be incarcerated under conditions so extreme that they will be permanently damaged. Another serious disadvantage of transferring a child is the stigma that may be attached to a conviction in the criminal court. Labeling children as adult offenders early in life may seriously impair their future educational, employment, and other opportunities.

In reality, however, some juveniles take advantage of decisions to transfer them to the adult court. Often, although the charge against a child may be considered serious in the juvenile court, the adult criminal court will not find it so; consequently, a child may have a better chance for dismissal of the charges or acquittal after a jury trial.

Today, all states allow juveniles to be tried as adults in criminal courts in one of three ways:

1. *Concurrent jurisdiction.* The prosecutor has the discretion of filing charges for certain offenses in either juvenile or criminal court.
2. *Excluded offenses.* The legislature excludes from juvenile court jurisdiction certain offenses that are either very minor, such as traffic or fishing violations, or very serious, such as murder or rape (offense-based waiver). Statutory exclusion often accounts for the largest number of juveniles tried as adults in criminal court.
3. *Judicial waiver.* The juvenile court waives its jurisdiction and transfers the case to criminal court (this procedure is also known as "binding over" or "certifying" juvenile cases to criminal court). It is the most common transfer provision.

Today, 12 states authorize prosecutors to bring cases in the juvenile or adult criminal court at their discretion; 36 states exclude certain offenses from juvenile court jurisdiction; and 48 states, the District of Columbia, and the federal government have judicial waiver provisions. As indicated, every state has some provision for handling juveniles in adult criminal court.[71]

STATUTORY CRITERIA IN TRANSFER

Statutes set the standards for transfer procedures. Age is of particular importance. Some jurisdictions allow for transfer between the ages of 14 and 17. Others restrict waiver proceedings to mature juveniles and specify particular offenses. In a few jurisdictions, any child can be sentenced to the criminal court system, regardless of age. For example, Massachusetts law states that only juveniles between the ages of 14 and 17 are eligible for transfer and that a child can be transferred only if he or she has (1) previously been committed to the Department of Youth Services and the present offense is punishable by imprisonment or (2) has committed an offense invoking infliction or threat of serious bodily harm.[72] If the above conditions are met, a transfer hearing must be held to determine whether it is in the public interest to transfer the child. The court must consider the seriousness of the alleged offense; the child's family, school, and social history; the general protection of the public; the nature of past treatment efforts for the child; and the likelihood of the child's rehabilitation in the juvenile court.

More than 30 states have amended their waiver policies to automatically exclude certain offenses from juvenile court jurisdiction. For example, Indiana excludes cases involving 16- and 17-year-olds charged with kidnapping, rape, and robbery (if a weapon was used or bodily injury occurred); in Illinois, youths 15 to 16 who are charged with murder, aggravated or sexual assault, or armed robbery with a firearm are automatically sent to criminal court; in Pennsylvania,

One of the most significant actions that occurs in the early court processing of a juvenile offender is the transfer process, which involves transferring a juvenile from the juvenile court to the criminal court. Waivers may even involve very young children who commit serious felony crimes. Here, 14-year-old Eric Smith, left, sits at his trial for the murder of 4-year-old Derrick Robie of the village of Savona, N.Y.

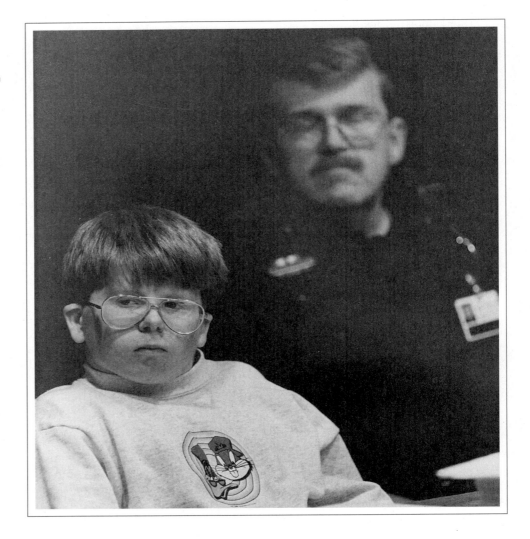

any child accused of murder, regardless of age, is tried before the criminal court.[73] While about half of these jurisdictions automatically exclude serious crimes, such as murder or rape, from the juvenile court; the rest use exclusion to remove minor traffic offenses and public ordinance violations, which are then handled by lower criminal courts. Nonetheless, the trend to exclude serious violent offenses from juvenile court jurisdictions is growing in response to the public demand to get tough on crime. In addition, large numbers of youth (estimated at about 175,000 cases) under 18, are tried as adults where the upper age of juvenile court jurisdiction is 15 or 16.

In a minority of states, statutes allow prosecutors to file particularly serious cases either in the juvenile court or the adult court at their own discretion; this is called **concurrent jurisdiction.**[74] Florida's use of concurrent jurisdiction has increased dramatically since 1981. In 1993 prosecutor transfers accounted for more than 80 percent of the offenders under age 18 who were handled in the Florida criminal courts.[75] Prosecutor discretion appears to be a more effective transfer mechanism than the waiver process.

Thus, the criteria that affect the decision to transfer the child to the criminal court are found in each of the state juvenile court acts. Many states, however, favor keeping children in juvenile court rather than transferring them to criminal court. The ineffectiveness of the criminal justice system is itself an adequate argument for keeping children in juvenile court.

Due Process in Transfer Proceedings

Since 1966, the U.S. Supreme Court and other federal and state courts have attempted to ensure fairness in the waiver process by handing down decisions that spell out the need for due process. Two Supreme Court decisions, *Kent v. United States* (1966) and *Breed v. Jones* (1975), are set out in the accompanying "Focus on Delinquency" because of their significance.[76] The *Kent* case declared a District of Columbia transfer statute unconstitutional and attacked the subsequent conviction of the child by granting him specific due process rights. In *Breed v. Jones,* the Supreme Court declared that the child was granted the protection of the double jeopardy clause of the Fifth Amendment after he was tried as a delinquent in the juvenile court.

Today, as a result of *Kent* and *Breed,* states that have transfer hearings provide specific requirements for transfer proceedings in their juvenile code. For the most part, when a transfer hearing is conducted today, due process of law requires that there be: (1) a legitimate transfer hearing, (2) sufficient notice to the child's family and defense attorney, (3) the right to counsel, and (4) a statement of the reason for the court order regarding transfer. These rights recognize what *Kent v. United States* indicated: namely, that the transfer proceeding is a critically important action in determining the statutory rights of the juvenile offender.

Youths in Adult Court

The issue of waiver is an important one. Waiver is attractive to conservatives because it jibes with the get-tough policy currently popular in the juvenile justice system. Liberals oppose its use because it is in contradistinction to the rehabilitative

KENT V. UNITED STATES AND BREED V. JONES

Kent v. United States: Facts

Morris Kent was arrested at the age of 16 in connection with charges of housebreaking, robbery, and rape. As a juvenile, he was subject to the exclusive jurisdiction of the District of Columbia Juvenile Court. The District of Columbia statute declared that the court could transfer the petitioner "after full investigation" and remit him to trial in the U.S. District Court. Kent admitted his involvement in the offenses and was placed in a receiving home for children. Subsequently, his mother obtained counsel, and they discussed with the social service director the possibility that the juvenile court might waive its jurisdiction. Kent was detained at the receiving home for almost one week. There was no arraignment, no hearing, and no hearing for petitioner's apprehension. Kent's counsel arranged for a psychiatric examination, and a motion requesting a hearing on the waiver was filed. The juvenile court judge did not rule on the motion and entered an order stating, "After full investigation, the court waives its jurisdiction and directs that a trial be held under the regular proceedings of the criminal court." The judge made no finding and gave no reasons for his waiver decision. It appeared that the judge denied motions for a hearing, recommendations for hospitalization for psychiatric observation, requests for access to the social service file, and offers to prove that the petitioner was a fit subject for rehabilitation under the juvenile court.

After the juvenile court waived its jurisdiction, Kent was indicted by the grand jury and was subsequently found guilty of housebreaking and robbery and not guilty by reason of insanity on the charge of rape. Kent was sentenced to serve a period of 30 to 90 years on his conviction.

Decision

The petitioner's lawyer appealed the decision on the basis of the infirmity of the proceedings by which the juvenile court waived its jurisdiction. He further attacked the waiver on statutory and constitutional grounds, stating: "(1) no hearing occurred, (2) no findings were made, (3) no reasons were stated before the waiver, and (4) counsel was denied access to the social service file." The U.S. Supreme Court found that the juvenile court order waiving jurisdiction and remitting the child to trial in the district court was invalid. Its arguments were based on the following:

The theory of the juvenile court act is rooted in social welfare procedures and treatments.

The philosophy of the juvenile court, namely *parens patriae*, is not supposed to allow procedural unfairness.

Waiver proceedings are critically important actions in the juvenile court.

The juvenile court act requiring full investigation in the District of Columbia should be read in the context of constitutional principles relating to due process of law. These principles require at a minimum that the petitioner be entitled to a hearing, access to counsel, access by counsel to social service records, and a statement of the reason for the juvenile court decision.

---

ideal. Some conservative thinkers have argued that the increased use of waiver can help get violent, chronic offenders off the streets. Barry Feld suggests that waiver to adult court should be mandatory for juveniles committing serious, violent crimes.[77] He argues that mandatory waiver would coincide with the currently popular "just deserts" sentencing policy and eliminate potential bias and disparity in judicial decision making. A recent detailed analysis by Feld of legislative changes in juvenile waiver statutes indicates that the nature of the offense, rather than the real needs of the offender, dominates the waiver decision. According to Feld, the waiver of a serious juvenile offender into the adult system on the basis of the offense, rather than an individualized evaluation of the youth's amenability to treatment or dangerousness, is both an indication of and a contributor to the substantive and procedural criminalization of the juvenile court.[78]

Significance of the Case

This case examined for the first time the substantial degree of discretion associated with a transfer proceeding in the District of Columbia. Thus, the Supreme Court significantly limited its holding to the statute involved but justified its reference to constitutional principles relating to due process and the assistance of counsel. In addition, it said that the juvenile court waiver hearings need to measure up to the essentials of due process and fair treatment. Furthermore, in an appendix to its opinion, the Court set up criteria concerning waiver of the jurisdictions. These are:

The seriousness of the alleged offense to the community

Whether the alleged offense was committed in an aggressive, violent, or willful manner

Whether the alleged offense was committed against persons or against property

The prosecutive merit of the complaint

The desirability of trial and disposition

The sophistication and maturity of the juvenile

The record and previous history of the juvenile

Prospects for adequate protection of the public and the likelihood of reasonable rehabilitation

Breed v. Jones: Facts

In 1971, a petition in the juvenile court of California was filed against Jones, who was then 17, alleging that he had committed an offense that, if committed by an adult, would constitute robbery. The petitioner was detained pending a hearing. At the hearing, the juvenile court took testimony, found that the allegations were true, and sustained the petition. The proceedings were continued for a disposition hearing, at which point Jones was found unfit for treatment in the juvenile court. It was ordered that he be prosecuted as an adult offender. At a subsequent preliminary hearing, the petitioner was held for criminal trial, an information was filed against him for robbery,

and he was tried and found guilty. He was committed to the California Youth Authority, over objections that he was being subjected to double jeopardy.

Petitioner Jones sought an appeal in the federal district court on the basis of the double jeopardy argument that jeopardy attaches at the juvenile delinquency proceedings. The writ of habeas corpus was denied.

Decision

The U.S. Supreme Court held that the prosecution of Jones as an adult in the California Superior Court, after an adjudicatory finding in the juvenile court that he had violated a criminal statute and a subsequent finding that he was unfit for treatment as a juvenile, violated the double jeopardy clause of the Fifth Amendment of the U.S. Constitution as applied to the states through the Fourteenth Amendment. Thus, Jones's trial in the California Superior Court for the same offense as that for which he was tried in the juvenile court violated the policy of the double jeopardy clause, even if he never faced the risk of more than one punishment, because double jeopardy refers to the risk or potential risk of trial and conviction, not punishment.

Significance of the Case

The *Breed* case provided answers on several important transfer issues: (1) *Breed* prohibits trying a child in an adult court when there has been a prior adjudicatory juvenile proceeding; (2) probable cause may exist at a transfer hearing, and this does not violate subsequent jeopardy if the child is transferred to the adult court; (3) because the same evidence is often used in both the transfer hearing and subsequent trial in either the juvenile or adult court, a different judge is often required for each hearing.

Sources: *Kent v. United States*, 383 U.S. 541, 86 S.Ct. 1045, 16 L.Ed.2d 84 (1966); *Breed v. Jones*, 421 U.S. 519, 95 S.Ct. 1779 (1975).

Similarly, the trend has been toward giving original jurisdiction for serious juvenile crimes to the adult courts and then giving judges the option of waiving deserving cases back to the juvenile court. Despite these trends toward integrating juveniles into the adult criminal court system, it should be noted that youths cannot be placed in adult correctional facilities until they reach age 16.

Because of the popularity of waiver, the number of youths processed in adult courts by judicial waiver has become significant. In 1992, 1.6 percent of all formally processed delinquency cases were transferred to criminal court. Drug law violation cases were the most likely to be transferred to criminal court (3.1 percent), compared with 2.4 percent of person offense cases, 1.3 percent of

TABLE 14.5   Percent of Petitioned Delinquency Cases Transferred to Criminal Court, 1988 and 1992

Offense	1988	1992
Delinquency	1.2%	1.6%
Person	1.9%	2.4%
Property	1.2%	1.3%
Drugs	1.5%	3.1%
Public Order	0.5%	0.8%

Source: Jeffrey Butts et al., *Juvenile Court Statistics 1992* (Pittsburgh, Pa.: National Center for Juvenile Justice, 1995).

TABLE 14.6   Percent Change in Petitioned Delinquency Cases Transferred to Criminal Court, 1988 and 1992

Offense	Number of Cases 1988	Number of Cases 1992	Percent Change
Delinquency	7,000	11,700	68%
Person	2,000	4,000	101%
Property	3,700	5,200	42%
Drugs	700	1,400	91%
Public Order	500	1,000	90%

Source: Jeffrey Butts et al., *Juvenile Court Statistics 1992* (Pittsburgh, Pa.: National Center for Juvenile Justice, 1995).

property offense cases, and 0.8 percent of petitioned public order offense cases.[79] (See Table 14.5.)

The likelihood of transfer increased from 1.2 percent to 1.6 percent between 1988 and 1992. The greatest change in the use of criminal court transfers was for drug cases, where transfers increased from 1.5 percent to 3.1 percent.

The number of actual cases transferred to criminal court increased 68 percent between 1988 and 1992, from 7,000 to 11,700. The number of transferred person offense cases increased 101 percent. For drug offense and public order offense cases, the number of transfers increased 91 percent and 90 percent respectively. The number of cases in which youth were transferred to criminal court for property offenses increased 42 percent between 1988 and 1992, from 3,700 to 5,200 cases annually.[80] (See Table 14.6.)

Differential increases in juvenile court transfers changed the offense profile of transferred cases between 1988 and 1992. A person offense was the most serious charge in 29 percent of all transferred cases in 1988; by 1992 person offense cases accounted for 34 percent of all transferred cases. Drug offense offenses cases made up 11 percent of transfers to criminal court in 1988 and 12 percent in 1992 (see Table 14.7). No national data are generally available on the number of juvenile cases tried in criminal court under other procedures.[81]

Today, the principal strategy of choice across the nation in attacking serious youth crime, according to most experts, is to place more juveniles in the adult court. This is done by lowering the age of juvenile court jurisdiction, dropping the age for transfer to criminal court, increasing the number of offenses requiring placement in the adult court, and giving the prosecutor more discretion to file juvenile cases in the criminal court.[82]

TABLE 14.7 Offense Profile of Delinquency Cases Transferred to Criminal Court, 1988 and 1992

Offense	1988	1992
Person	29%	34%
Property	53%	45%
Drugs	11%	12%
Public Order	8%	9%
Total # Transferred Cases	7,000	11,700

Source: Jeffrey Butts et al., Juvenile Court Statistics 1992 (Pittsburgh, Pa.: National Center for Juvenile Justice, 1995).

DEBATING THE WAIVER CONCEPT

Despite the increased use of waiver, the efficacy of transferring youths to the adult court has been questioned. One alleged shortcoming is that the actual treatment of delinquents in adult court is quite similar to what they might have received had they remained in the custody of juvenile authorities; therefore, why transfer them? For example, New York's law has been criticized on the grounds that 70 percent of children arraigned in adult courts are waived to juvenile court, wasting both time and money; 40 percent of juveniles tried in adult court are sentenced to probation; and only 3 percent of the juvenile offenders tried in adult court received longer sentences than they could have been given in juvenile court.[83]

Recent studies in two states (Pennsylvania and Oregon) found that in the majority of transferred cases sentenced to incarceration, the length of criminal court sentences did not exceed three years—which is within the range of options typically available to juvenile courts.[84] In other words, incarcerated, transferred juveniles do not always receive longer sentences. McNulty also questions the idea of whether waiver to the Arizona criminal courts is an effective method of dealing with serious juvenile offenders. She points out that there is little evidence to support the idea that adult sentencing of juveniles is consistent, equitable, or effective.[85]

Other critics view transfer as adding undue burdens to youthful offenders. Research conducted by Cary Rudman, Eliot Hartstone, Jeffrey Fagan, and Melinda Moore compared case outcomes of a group of waived violent juvenile offenders with a control group of offenders with similar case characteristics retained in juvenile court. Using data from four jurisdictions, the researchers found that it took two and a half times as long (246 days verses 98 days) to process a waiver case than one that was retained in juvenile court.[86] During most of this added time, the juvenile was held in a detention center. The study also found that waived youths were treated quite harshly by the adult justice system: 90 percent were convicted; all convictions were to the top offense charged, indicating that they engaged in relatively little plea negotiation; 91 percent of convicted youth were incarcerated (73 percent in prison and 18 percent in jail); and youths convicted in adult court received sentences five times longer than those retained in the juvenile court. With regard to the latter issue, youths convicted in adult courts received sentences averaging 247 months for murder and 171 months for rape; in comparison, juvenile courts sentenced offenders to 55 months for murder and 16 months for rape. The research effort concluded that transferring youths to the adult court did indeed fulfill the get-tough role for which it was designed. However, it also found that program services for waived youths were lacking and that delinquencies will eventually come back to haunt

TABLE 14.8 Factors Influencing Waiver from Juvenile Court to Adult Court

OFFENSE	■ Seriousness of offense ■ Person or property offense ■ Violent crime
JUDICIAL POLICY	■ Merit of complaint ■ Feasibility of trial
OFFENDER	■ Maturity of child ■ Record of previous history ■ Amenability for treatment

society when waived youngsters are eventually released from prison without receiving adequate treatment.

The severe sentences given to waived youth have been substantiated by a federally sponsored survey of waiver in 12 urban jurisdictions, including Seattle, Miami, Chicago, and Denver. Of the 344 cases sent to criminal court, 66 percent resulted in a finding of guilt, and 77 percent of the convicted juveniles were sentenced to jail or prison for an average of 6.8 years. These figures indicate that juveniles are receiving somewhat longer prison sentences than adults for comparable crimes.[87]

More serious are the objections raised by M. A. Bortner, whose research led to the conclusion that the transfer decision may be motivated by administrative and political considerations.[88] Bortner studied the records of 214 youths remanded to adult court in a western county. There was little evidence that the waived youths were any more dangerous or unruly than youths treated by the juvenile court. Nor was there any evidence that their transfer enhanced public safety. However, by turning a small portion of their clientele over to the adult court and by portraying these youths as the most dangerous, the juvenile court authorities were able to show that they were concerned for public safety while at the same time keeping control over the vast majority of youths in their jurisdiction and deflecting criticism of their entire juvenile justice operations. Critics see the new methods of dealing with offenders as inefficient, ineffective, and philosophically out of step with the original concept of the juvenile court. Supporters view them as a means of getting the most serious, chronic juvenile offenders off the streets for long periods, while ensuring that rehabilitation plays a lesser role.

Another question raised by critics is whether or not transfers to the adult court are carried out fairly and equitably. One warning sign is the fact that minorities are waived at a rate that is greater than their representation in the population. Jeffery Fagan and his associates have identified the existence of such racial disparity in decision making from apprehension through the commitment stage.[89]

Using **prosecutorial discretion** to determine whether to proceed in the juvenile or the criminal justice system is also a much maligned practice (see Table 14.8 for a listing of the many factors influencing the waiver decision). Although most states require that a waiver decision be made at a judicial hearing, a few jurisdictions allow the prosecutor to determine jurisdiction by filing a complaint in the juvenile or adult court. In still other jurisdictions, where the juvenile court may have no jurisdiction over certain crimes, the prosecutor can in effect control which court hears the case on the basis of the charge filed against the child. Such an approach eliminates the requirement of a waiver hearing but leaves a great deal of discretion in the hands of the prosecutor.[90]

A recent analysis of juvenile waiver by Frank Zimring argues that, despite its faults, waiver is superior to alternative methods for handling the most serious juvenile offenders.[91] The major argument for waiver rests on the premise that the modern juvenile court is still preferable to the criminal justice system, because juveniles are given greater chances for rehabilitation, even though certain cases will always occur in which the minimum criminal penalty is greater than that available to the juvenile court. Nonetheless, it is equally important to keep in mind the possible consequences of transfers: (1) greater risk to juveniles who could be transferred to an adult jail during trial; (2) punishment that is less swift than juvenile processing; (3) lower conviction rates and shorter incarcerations in the adult system; and (4), higher recidivism rates for youths tried in adult courts.

In sum, the trend has been to increase the flow of juvenile cases to adult courts. This policy change can be attributed to the get-tough attitude toward the serious, chronic juvenile offender. A number of important questions have been raised about the fairness and propriety of this method of handling serious juvenile cases. The big question is, what is accomplished by treating juveniles like adults? The following "Case in Point" considers the question of waiver.

CASE IN POINT

You are a newly appointed judge whose jurisdiction embraces criminal cases heard in the lower criminal court.

One week after his twelfth birthday, Dexter G., an honor student with a strict religious education, had his first contact with the justice system.

Dexter was arrested and charged with criminal homicide after he allegedly took his father's rifle, aimed from a third-floor bedroom window, and shot 8-year-old James once in the head as he rode along on his bicycle. James died instantly. Dexter was subsequently released to the custody of his parents.

The law of this jurisdiction requires that all persons charged with murder, regardless of age, stand trial as an adult in criminal court. If convicted of murder, Dexter could be sentenced to life imprisonment without parole. The state's Juvenile Court Act has a waiver provision that permits the criminal court judge to transfer the case to juvenile court if the child is under 17 and if the accused demonstrates that he is amenable to treatment and rehabilitation.

Dexter is a healthy youth with above-average intelligence and no apparent psychological problems. He has shown no emotion or remorse regarding the killing. Psychiatrists who examined Dexter indicate that the boy said he was "playing hunter" when the rifle accidentally discharged.

If you were the judge, would you transfer the case to the juvenile court for jurisdiction?

What criteria would you use in making this decision?

The issue of waiver has become critical in recent years because transfer to the adult court is viewed as an efficient means of dealing with the violent and chronic juvenile offender. The seriousness of the offense plays a significant role in determining juvenile waiver, as do the number and the nature of prior offenses and prior treatment.[92] Waiver is also a refutation of the child's right to be treated in the juvenile justice system.[93] Yet studies of the impact of recent changes in waiver statutes have yielded inconclusive results. Meanwhile, more than half of the legislators responding to a national survey on juvenile crime expect to consider waiver legislation that makes it easier to transfer juveniles into adult courts[94] (see the accompanying "Focus on Delinquency" for the real-life drama regarding transfer to the adult court). Clearly the issue of waiver will continue to be debated for some time to come.

A Tumultuous Real-Life Transfer Hearing: In re Edward O'Brien (1996)

Facts

In July of 1995, Edward O'Brien, a 15-and-a-half-year-old boy, was arraigned and subsequently indicted for murder in Middlesex County, Massachusetts. O'Brien was accused of stabbing and killing a 42-year-old mother of four children in her home.

In accordance with Massachusetts law, a juvenile can be tried as an adult only when a court at a transfer hearing finds him dangerous and incapable of being rehabilitated through treatment. The statute establishes a "rebuttable presumption," the burden of which is on the defendant to prove (1) that he is not dangerous and (2) that he is amenable to treatment. At the transfer hearing in the O'Brien case, the prosecutor and defense called numerous witnesses and presented documentary evidence, including 49 different exhibits, for court review.

The following criteria were considered by the court in determining if O'Brien was to be transferred to the adult court for trial:

(1) Nature and seriousness of the crime—the grand jury retained an indictment charging first-degree murder in a particularly horrendous slaying.

(2) Delinquency record—the defendant had none.

(3) Child's age—at the time of arrest, the defendant was 15 and a half years old and a young man of great physical size for his age.

(4) Family and social history—a review of all this information led the court to describe the defendant's family history as "uneventful" in relation to the crime.

(5) Success or lack thereof of any past treatment—there was no record of any remedial attention given or needed by the defendant.

The juvenile court judge viewed the issue in the following way: "Either this child is capable of growth which will allow him to make free moral decisions when he ponders the enormity of his actions, or he is . . . destined to be forever enveloped in mindless depravity and cannot ever learn the requirements of tolerable human behavior."

Findings

As noted previously, Massachusetts General Laws, Chapter 119, Section 61, requires a two-pronged finding to transfer a child to the criminal court. After applying these factors to the O'Brien case, the court denied transfer and ordered that the defendant be retained and tried within the juvenile justice system. First, the court found that the presumption of dangerousness had not been rebutted by the defendant based on the nature of the crime. Second, the testimony regarding the clinical, social, and legal factors led the court to conclude that the presumption that the defendant is not amenable to treatment had been rebutted.

Significance

If transferred to the adult Superior Court and found guilty, the defendant could be sentenced to life imprisonment. If retained in the juvenile court and found delinquent by reason of murder, he would be sentenced to the State Department of Youth Services until the age of majority and then to state prison for a total confinement of 15 to 20 years.

Immediately after the juvenile court ruling, the district attorney filed an appeal. The governor of Massachusetts called on the state legislature to pass a bill that would automatically try 15- to 17-year-olds as adults when they are accused of committing murder and aggravated rape. Although an automatic transfer statute would satisfy the outcry against violent crime, it would also significantly reduce the effectiveness of the justice system in rehabilitating violent juveniles.

Source: *In re Edward O'Brien,* Commonwealth of Massachusetts, District Court Department of Trial Court, Somerville Division, No. 9510-JV 141 (1996).

SUMMARY

Many important decisions about what happens to a child may occur prior to adjudication. Detention in secure facilities for those charged with juvenile delinquency and involuntary placement in shelter care for those involved in noncriminal behavior place severe limitations on the rights of the child and the parents. There has been a major effort in the past few years to remove juveniles from detention in adult jails and to make sure that status offenders are not placed in secure pretrial detention facilities.

Most statutes ordinarily require a hearing on detention if the initial decision is to keep the child in custody. At a detention hearing, the child has a right to counsel and is generally given other procedural due process safeguards, notably the privilege against self-incrimination and the right to confront and cross-examine witnesses. In addition, most state juvenile court procedures provide criteria to be used in deciding whether to detain a child. These include (1) the need to protect the child, (2) the likelihood that the child presents a serious danger to the public, and (3) the likelihood that the child will return to court for adjudication.

The intake stage is essentially a screening process to decide what action should be taken regarding matters referred to the court. The law enforcement officer is required to make decisions about court action or referral to social agencies. In addition, it is important for law enforcement agencies and the juvenile courts to have sound working relationships. Their objective is the same: to protect the child and the community.

Throughout the early court stage of the juvenile process, the issue of discretion plays a major role. In the last decade, juvenile justice practitioners have made efforts to divert as many children as possible from the juvenile courts and place them in nonsecure treatment programs. Critics charge that diversion programs actually involve more youths in the justice system than would be the case had the programs not been in operation, a concept referred to as widening the net. Moreover, the effectiveness of diversion as a crime-reducing policy has been questioned.

Those who are held for trial are generally released to their parents, on bail, or through other means, such as on recognizance. Because the juvenile justice system, like the adult system, is not able to try every child accused of a crime or a status offense due to personnel limitations, diversion programs seem to hold greater hope for the prevention and control of delinquency. As a result, such subsystems as diversion, statutory intake proceedings, plea bargaining, and other informal adjustments are essential ingredients in the administration of the juvenile justice system.

An issue related to bail is preventive detention, which refers to the right of a judge to deny persons release before trial on the grounds that they may be dangerous to themselves or others. Advocates of preventive detention argue that dangerous juvenile offenders should not be granted bail and pretrial release because they would then have an opportunity to intimidate witnesses and commit further crimes. Opponents retaliate that defendants are "innocent until proven guilty" and therefore should be allowed freedom before trial.

In addition to normal juvenile justice processing, thousands of other youths are transferred to the adult court because of the serious nature of their crimes. This process, known as waiver, is an effort to remove serious offenders from the juvenile process and into the more punitive adult system. Recent research indicates that waived youth are quite likely to receive incarceration sentences.

Prior to the creation of first modern juvenile court in Illinois in 1899, juveniles were tried in adult criminal courts. However even with the development of the juvenile court system, it is recognized that certain crimes require that children be tried as adults. Today, virtually all jurisdictions provide by statute for waiver or transfer of juvenile offenders to the criminal courts. The number of juveniles transferred to criminal court has grown substantially in recent years. More research is needed on the impact of transferring juveniles to the adult justice system.

detention
shelter care
detention hearing
deinstitutionalization
Deinstitutionalization of Status Offenders (DSO)
   Project
intake
diversion

widening the net
complaint
petition
bail
preventive detention
Schall v. Martin
plea bargaining
transfer

waiver
bindover
removal
concurrent jurisdiction
Kent v. United States
Breed v. Jones
prosecutorial discretion

QUESTIONS FOR DISCUSSION

1. Why has the use of jails and detention facilities for children been considered one of the greatest tragedies in the juvenile justice system?

2. Processing juvenile cases in an informal manner—that is, without filing a formal petition—is common in the juvenile court system. Describe some methods of informally handling cases in the juvenile court.

3. The use of diversion programs in the juvenile justice system has become common in an effort to channel cases to noncourt institutions. Discuss the advantages and disadvantages of diversion. Describe diversion programs and their common characteristics.

4. What is the purpose of bail? Do children as well as adults have a constitutional or statutory right to

bail? What factors are considered in the release of a child prior to formal adjudication?

5. Under extraordinary circumstances, once juvenile proceedings have begun, the juvenile court may seek to transfer a juvenile to the adult court. This is often referred to as a transfer proceeding. Is such a proceeding justified? Under what conditions? Does the juvenile court afford the public sufficient protection against serious juvenile offenders?

6. Explain the meaning of preventive detention. Is such a concept in conflict with the fundamental principle of presumption of innocence?

7. Do you think plea bargaining for juvenile offenders is desirable? Why or why not?

NOTES

1. National Council on Crime and Delinquency, *Standards and Guides for the Detention of Children and Youth* (New York: NCCD, 1961), p. 1.; American Correctional Association, *Standards for Juvenile Detention Facilities* (Laurel, Md.: ACA, 1991).

2. American Bar Association, *Standards Relating to Interim Status of Juveniles* (Cambridge, Mass.: Ballinger, 1977), p. 4.

3. National Council on Crime and Delinquency, *Standards and Guides for the Detention of Children and Youth,* p. 12.

4. See Community Research Associations, *Michigan Holdover Network—Short-Term Detention Strategies* (Washington, D.C.: U.S. Department of Justice, 1986).

5. Howard Snyder and Melissa Sickmund, *Juvenile Offenders and Victims—A National Report* (Washington, D.C.: OJJDP, 1995), p. 157; Jeffery Butts et al., *Juvenile Court*

Statistics—1992 (Pittsburgh, Pa.: National Center for Juvenile Justice, 1995), p. 10; Robert DeComo et al., *Juveniles Taken Into Custody—1992* (San Francisco: NCCD, 1995), p. 27.

6. Butts et al., *Juvenile Court Statistics—1992,* p. 32.

7. Ibid., p. 34.

8. Snyder and Sickmund, *Juvenile Offenders and Victims—A National Report,* pp. 143–50.

9. Edward J. Loughran, "How to Stop Our Kids from Going Bad," *Boston Globe,* 11 February 1990, p. 42.

10. Ira M. Schwartz and William H. Barton, eds., *Reforming Juvenile Detention—No More Hidden Closets* (Columbus: Ohio State University Press, 1994), p. 176.

11. Belinda McCarthy, "An Analysis of Detention," *Juvenile and Family Court Journal* 36:49–50 (1985).

12. Charles Frazier and Donna Bishop, "The Pretrial Detention of Juveniles and Its Impact on Case Dispositions,"

Journal of Criminal Law and Criminology 76:1132–52 (1986).

13. L. Rosner, "Juvenile Secure Detention," Journal of Offender Counseling Services and Rehabilitation 12:57–76 (1988).

14. David Steinhart, "Objective Juvenile Detention Criteria: The California Experience," in Ira Schwartz and William Barton, eds., Reforming Juvenile Justice Detention—No More Hidden Closets (Columbus: Ohio State University Press, 1994), p. 47.

15. American Bar Association, Standards Relating to Interim Status of Juveniles, p. 86; Claudia Worrell, "Pretrial Detention of Juveniles: Denial of Equal Protection Marked by the Parens Patriae Doctrine," Yale Law Review 95:174–93 (1985).

16. Edward Wakin, Children without Justice—A Report by the National Council of Jewish Women (New York: National Council of Jewish Women, 1975), p. 43; Ira M. Schwartz, (In) Justice for Juveniles—Rethinking the Best Interests of the Child (Lexington, Mass.: D.C. Heath, 1989), Chap. 3.

17. Hubert H. Humphrey Institute of Public Affairs, The Incarceration of Minority Youth (Minneapolis: Humphrey Institute, 1986); Katherine Hunt Federle and Meda Chesney- Lind, "Special Issues in Juvenile Justice: Gender, Race and Ethnicity," in Ira Schwartz, ed., Juvenile Justice and Public Policy (New York: Lexington Books, 1992), Chap. 9.

18. Russell Schutt and Dale Dannefer, "Detention Decisions in Juvenile Cases: JINS, JDs and Genders," Law and Society Review 22:509–20 (1988).

19. S. Smith and D. Roush, "Defining Juvenile Detention Goals: ACA Committee Takes the Lead," Corrections Today 51:220–21 (1989); See also Earl Dunlap and David Roush, "Juvenile Detention as Process and Place," Juvenile and Family Court Journal 46:1–16 (1995).

20. I. Schwartz, G. Fishman, R. Hatfield, B. A. Krisberg, and Z. Eisikovitz, "Juvenile Detention: The Hidden Closets Revisited," Justice Quarterly 4:219–35 (1987); John Criswell, "Juvenile Detention Resource Centers: Florida's Experience Provides a Model for Nation in Juvenile Detention," Corrections Today 49:22–26 (1987).

21. Learning behind Bars: Selected Educational Programs from Juvenile Jail and Prison Facilities (Laurel, Ind.: Correctional Education Association, 1989), p. 5.

22. Ibid., p. 10.

23. Ibid., p. 13.

24. Schwartz and Barton, eds. Reforming the Juvenile Justice System—No More Hidden Closets, p. 176.

25. Office of Juvenile Justice and Delinquency Prevention News Release, 4 January 1981. According to the national census of 1989, the suicide rate for children in jails is four to six times higher than in public juvenile detention centers.

26. Reported in "Juveniles in Our Nation's Jails," Criminal Justice Newsletter, 14 February 1983, p. 8. These youths could have been held separately from adult offenders, although in the same facility.

27. Juvenile Justice and Delinquency Prevention Act, Sec. 223 (a)(12), 1974, amended 1980.

28. "OJJDP Helps States Remove Juveniles from Jails," Juvenile Justice Bulletin (Washington, D.C.: U.S. Department of Justice, 1990).

29. "Qualities of Best Plans for Rural 'Jail Removal' Described," Criminal Justice Newsletter, 15 April 1987.

30. Community Research Associates, The Jail Removal Initiative: A Summary Report (Champaign, Ill.: Community Research ASS 1987).

31. Charles Frazier, Preadjudicatory Detention—From Juvenile Justice: Policies, Programs and Services (Chicago: Dorsey Press, 1989), pp. 143–68.

32. DeComo et al., Juveniles Taken Into Custody—1992, p. 51.

33. Ira Schwartz, Linda Harris, and Lauri Levi, "The Jailing of Juveniles in Minnesota," Crime and Delinquency 34:131 (1988).

34. See, generally, Ira Schwartz, ed., "Children in Jails," Crime and Delinquency 34:131–228 (1988).

35. Schwartz, Harris, and Levi, "The Jailing of Juveniles in Minnesota," p. 134.

36. David Steinhart, "California Legislation Ends Jailing of Children—the Story of a Policy Reversal," Crime and Delinquency 34:150 (1988).

37. Henry Swanger, "Hendrickson v. Griggs—a Review of Legal and Policy Implications for Juvenile Justice Policymakers," Crime and Delinquency 34:209 (1988); Hendrickson v. Griggs, 672 F.Supp. 1126 (N.D. Iowa 1987).

38. "Assessing the Effects of the Deinstitutionalization of Status Offenders," Juvenile Justice Bulletin (Washington, D.C.: U.S. Department of Justice, 1990), p. 1; Snyder and Sickmund, Juvenile Offenders and Victims—A National Report, p. 147.

39. Solomon Kobrin and Malcolm Klein, National Evaluation of the Deinstitutionalization of Status Offender Programs, Executive Summary (Washington, D.C.: U.S. Department of Justice, 1982); I. Spergel, F. Reamer, and J. Lynch, "Deinstitutionalization of Status Offenders: Individual Outcome and System Effects," Journal of Research in Crime and Delinquency 4:32 (1981).

40. M. A. Bortner, Mary Sutherland, and Russ Winn, "Race and the Impact of Juvenile Institutionalization," Crime and Delinquency 31:35–46 (1985).

41. Anne L. Schneider, The Impact of Deinstitutionalization on Recidivism and Secure Confinement of Status Offenders (Washington, D.C.: U.S. Department of Justice, 1985). For a similar view, see Susan Datesman and Mikel Aickin, "Offense Specialization and Escalation among Status Offenders," Journal of Criminal Law and Criminology 75:1246–75 (1984).

42. Duran Bell and Kevin Lang, "The Intake Dispositions of Juvenile Offenders," Journal of Research in Crime and

Delinquency 22:309–28 (1985); Federle and Chesney-Lind, "Special Issues in Juvenile Justice: Gender, Race and Ethnicity," p. 189.

43. American Bar Association, *Standards Relating to Juvenile Probation Function* (Cambridge, Mass.: Ballinger, 1977), p. 25.

44. National Council on Crime and Delinquency, *Standard Family Court Act* (San Francisco, CA.: NCCD, 1979), p. 12; William Sheridan, *Model Acts for Juvenile and Family Courts,* p. 13; National Conference of Commissioners on Uniform State Laws, *Uniform Juvenile Court Act,* p. 9.

45. American Bar Association, *Standards Relating to Juvenile Probation Function,* p. 53.

46. Leona Lee, "Factors Influencing Intake Disposition in a Juvenile Court," *Juvenile and Family Court Journal* 46:43–62 (1995).

47. Ted Rubin, "The Emerging Prosecutor Dominance of the Juvenile Court Intake Process," *Crime and Delinquency* 26:299–318 (1980).

48. Ibid., p. 318.

49. National Advisory Commission on Criminal Justice Standards and Goals, *Courts* (Washington, D.C.: U.S. Government Printing Office, 1967), p. 20.

50. Paul Nejelski, "Diversion: The Promise and the Danger," *Crime and Delinquency Journal* 22:393–410 (1976); Kenneth Polk, "Juvenile Diversion: A Look at the Record," *Crime and Delinquency* 30:648–59 (1984).

51. President's Commission on Law Enforcement and Administration of Justice, *Task Force Report: Juvenile Delinquency and Youth Crime* (Washington, D.C.: U.S. Government Printing Office, 1967).

52. Ibid.

53. Polk, "Juvenile Diversion: A Look at the Record."

54. See Raymond T. Nimmer, *Diversion—The Search for Alternative Forms of Prosecution* (Chicago: American Bar Foundation, 1974); Mark Ezell, "Juvenile Arbitration: Net-Widening and Other Unintended Consequences," *Journal of Research in Crime and Delinquency* 26:358–77 (1989).

55. Edwin E. Lemert, "Diversion in Juvenile Justice: What Hath Been Wrought," *Journal of Research in Crime and Delinquency* 18:34–46 (1981).

56. Don C. Gibbons and Gerald F. Blake, "Evaluating the Impact of Juvenile Diversion Programs," *Crime and Delinquency Journal* 22:411–19 (1976); Richard J. Lundman, "Will Diversion Reduce Recidivism?" *Crime and Delinquency Journal* 22:428–37 (1976); B. Bullington, J. Sprowls, D. Katkin, and M. Phillips, "A Critique of Diversionary Juvenile Justice," *Crime and Delinquency* 24:59–71 (1978); Thomas Blomberg, "Diversion and Accelerated Social Control," *Journal of Criminal Law and Criminology* 68:274–82 (1977); Sharla Rausch and Charles Logan, "Diversion from Juvenile Court: Panacea or Pandora's Box," in J. Klugel, ed., *Evaluating Juvenile Justice* (Beverly Hills, Calif.: Sage, 1983), pp. 19–30.

57. Charles Frazier and John Cochran, "Official Intervention, Diversion from the Juvenile Justice System, and Dynamics of Human Services Work: Effects of a Reform Goal Based on Labeling Theory," *Crime and Delinquency* 32:157–76 (1986); Charles Frazier and Sara Lee, "Reducing Juvenile Detention Rates or Expanding the Official Control Nets: An Evaluation of a Legislative Reform Effort," *Crime and Delinquency* 38:204–14 (1992).

58. Dennis Anderson and Donald Schoen, "Diversion Programs: Effect of Stigmatization on Juvenile/Status Offenders," *Juvenile and Family Court Journal* 36:13–25 (1985).

59. Rausch and Logan, "Diversion from Juvenile Court," p. 20.

60. Frazier and Cochran, "Official Intervention, Diversion from the Juvenile Justice System, and Dynamics of Human Services Work," p. 171.

61. Arnold Binder and Gilbert Geis, "Ad Populum Argumentation in Criminology: Juvenile Diversion as Rhetoric," *Criminology* 30:309–33 (1984).

62. Mark Ezell, "Juvenile Diversion: The Ongoing Search for Alternatives," in Ira M. Schwartz, ed., *Juvenile Justice and Public Policy* (New York: Lexington Books, 1992), pp. 45–59.

63. Mark Soler, James Bell, Elizabeth Jameson, Carole Shauffer, Alice Shotton, and Loren Warboys, *Representing the Child Client* (New York: Matthew Bender, 1989), Sec. 5.03b.

64. *Schall v. Martin,* 467 U.S. 253, (1984).

65. James Brown, Robert Shepherd, and Andrew Shookhoff, *Preventive Detention after Schall v. Martin* (Washington, D.C.: American Bar Association, 1985); Michael O'Rourke, "Juvenile Justice—Preventive Detention of Juveniles: Have They Held Your Child Today: *Schall v. Martin,*" *Southern Illinois University Law Journal* 4:315–33 (1985).

66. Albert W. Alschuler, "The Prosecutor's Role in Plea Bargaining," *University of Chicago Law Review* 36:50–112 (1968); Joyce Dougherty, "A Comparison of Adult Plea Bargaining and Juvenile Intake," *Federal Probation* (June 1988):72–79.

67. Sanford Fox, *Juvenile Courts in a Nutshell* (St. Paul, Minn.: West, 1985), pp. 154–56.

68. See Darlene Ewing, "Juvenile Plea Bargaining: A Case Study," *American Journal of Criminal Law* 6:167 (1978); Adrienne Volenik, *Checklists for Use in Juvenile Delinquency Proceedings* (Chicago: American Bar Association, 1985); Bruce Green, "Package Plea Bargaining and the Prosecutor's Duty of Good Faith," *Criminal Law Bulletin* 25:507–50 (1989).

69. Joseph Sanborn, "Plea Negotiations in Juvenile Court" (Ph.D. diss., State University of New York at Albany, 1984); Joseph Sanborn, "Philosophical, Legal and Systematic Aspects of Juvenile Court Plea Bargaining," *Crime and Delinquency* 39:509–27 (1993).

70. National Council of Juvenile and Family Court Judges, "The Juvenile Court and Serious Offenders," *Juvenile and Family Court Journal* 35:13 (1984).

71. Melissa Sickmund, *How to Get Juveniles to Criminal Court,* OJJDP Update on Statistics (Washington, D.C.: Bureau of Justice Statistics, 1994); Eric Fritsch and Craig Hemmens, "Juvenile Waiver in the United States 1979–1995—A Comparison and Analysis of State Waiver Statutes," *Juvenile and Family Court Journal* 46:17–36 (1995).

72. Mass.Gen.Laws Ann. ch. C.119, 61.

73. Ind. Code Ann. 31-6-2(d) 1987; Ill.Ann.Stat. Ch. 37 Sec. 805 (1988); Penn. Stat. Ann. Title 42 6355(a)(1982).

74. Joseph White, "The Waiver Decision: A Judicial, Prosecutorial or Legislative Responsibility," *Justice for Children* 2:28–30 (1987).

75. Snyder and Sickmund, *Juvenile Offenders and Victims—A National Report,* p. 156.

76. *Kent v. United States,* 383 U.S. 541, 86 S.Ct. 1045, 16 L.Ed.2d 84 (1966); *Breed v. Jones,* 421 U.S. 519, 95 S.Ct. 1179, 44 L.Ed.2d 346 (1975).

77. Barry Feld, "Delinquent Careers and Criminal Policy," *Criminology* 21:195–212 (1983).

78. Barry Feld, "The Juvenile Court Meets the Principle of the Offense: Legislative Changes in Juvenile Waiver Statutes," *Journal of Criminal Law and Criminology* 78:471–534 (1987); Paul Marcotte, "Criminal Kids," *American Bar Association Journal* 76:60–66 (1990).

79. Butts et. al., *Juvenile Court Statistics—1992,* p. 13.

80. Ibid.

81. Ibid.

82. Robert Shepard, "The Rush to Waive Children to Adult Courts," *American Bar Association Journal of Criminal Justice* 10:39–42 (1995).

83. Richard Allinson and Joan Potter, "Is New York's Tough Juvenile Law a Charade?" *Corrections* 9:40–45 (1983).

84. Snyder and Sickmund, *Juvenile Offenders and Victims—A National Report,* p. 157.

85. Elizabeth McNulty, *The Transfer of Juvenile Offenders to Adult Court: Panacea or Problem?* (Unpublished paper presented at the American Society of Criminology Annual Meeting, Boston, Mass., November 1995).

86. Cary Rudman, Eliot Hartstone, Jeffrey Fagan, and Melinda Moore, "Violent Youth in Adult Court: Process and Punishment," *Crime and Delinquency* 32:75–96 (1986).

87. "Study Finds Strict Handling of Youths Sent to Adult Court," *Criminal Justice Newsletter,* 15 May 1987, pp. 8–10.

88. M. A. Bortner, "Traditional Rhetoric, Organizational Realities: Remand of Juveniles to Adult Court," *Crime and Delinquency* 32:53–73 (1986).

89. Jeffrey Fagan, Martin Forst, and T. Scott Vivona, "Racial Determinants of the Judicial Transfer Decision: Prosecuting Violent Youth in Criminal Court," *Crime and Delinquency* 33:359–86 (1987); J. Fagan, E. Slaughter, and E. Hartstone, "Blind Justice: The Impact of Race on the Juvenile Justice Process," *Crime and Delinquency* 53:224–58 (1987); J. Fagan and E. P. Deschenes, "Determinants of Judicial Waiver Decisions for Violent Juvenile Offenders," *Journal of Criminal Law and Criminology* 81:314–47 (1990).

90. Soler et al., *Representing the Child Client.*

91. Frank Zimring, "Treatment of Hard Cases in American Juvenile Justice: In Defense of the Discretionary Waiver," *Notre Dame Journal of Law, Ethics and Policy* 5:267–80 (1991).

92. F. W. Barnes and R. S. Franz, "Questionably Adult: Determinants and Effects of the Juvenile Waiver Decision," *Justice Quarterly* 6:117–35 (1989).

93. See the interesting case of *Toomey v. Clark,* 876 F.2d 1433 (9th Cir., 1989), where the juvenile court's consideration of criteria involving petitioner's pregnancy in its decision to decline jurisdiction was deemed not to be sex discrimination and a violation of the equal protection clause.

94. National Conference of State Legislators, *State Legislative Priorities, 1995* (Denver: NCSL, 1995), p. 12.

CHAPTER FIFTEEN

THE JUVENILE TRIAL AND DISPOSITION

INTRODUCTION

The development of the juvenile court and the separate process for handling children resulted from reform movements of the nineteenth and early twentieth centuries. The strategic role played by the juvenile court in setting juvenile justice policy has already been described. Throughout its history, the juvenile court has played a major role in helping to care for troubled youths who come before it. In fact, its influence is probably greater than that of the adult court because it is also charged with the care and treatment of offenders and not merely their punishment and control.[1] Therefore, the court and its representatives must consider their actions carefully because a wrong decision can have long-term consequences for young offenders.

Compounding the problem is the magnitude of cases handled by the nation's juvenile courts each year. The latest study (1992) found that the nation's juvenile courts petitioned and formally processed an estimated 743,700 delinquency offense cases and 54,700 status offense cases (see Figures 15.1 and 15.2). This estimate does not take into account the hundreds of thousands of informally handled or nonpetitioned cases adjusted or diverted by the courts. When petitioned and nonpetitioned cases are added together, 1,471,200 delinquency cases and 97,300 status offense cases were processed in 1992. Compared with 1988, delinquency cases increased by more than 26 percent and status offense cases by 18 percent. Thus, the nation's juvenile court system continues to deal with an enormous number of youths who need care, protection, treatment, and control.

This chapter describes the adjudication stage of the juvenile justice process. About 57 percent of all formally processed cases, or 427,000 youths, are adjudicated as delinquent while 56 percent of all petitioned status offense cases,

Judge Benjamin Lindsay presided over juvenile court in Denver, Colorado from 1900 to 1927.

FIGURE 15.1
Juvenile court processing of
delinquency cases, 1992

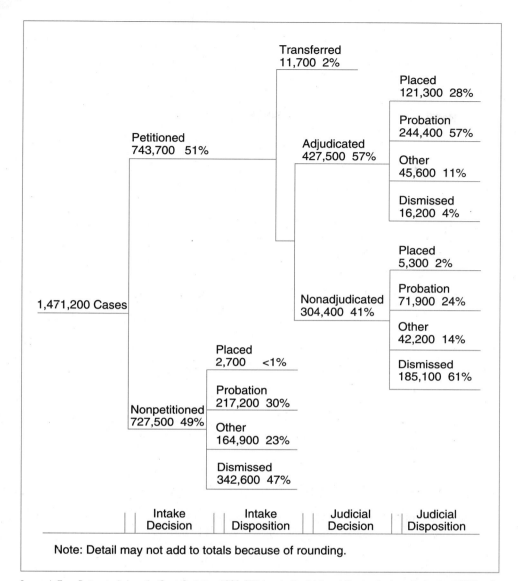

Note: Detail may not add to totals because of rounding.

Source: Jeffrey Butts et al., *Juvenile Court Statistics, 1992* (Pittsburgh, Pa.: National Center for Juvenile Justice, 1995), p. 9.

or 54,700 youths, are involved in adjudication.[2] The term *adjudication* refers to the trial stage of the juvenile court proceedings. This chapter initially explores the operation of the juvenile court and the role of the important legal actors in the trial and disposition—the juvenile court prosecutor, the judge, the defense attorney, and the probation officer. In addition, it looks at the constitutional and due process rights of the child at trial—particularly those rights dealing with counsel and trial by jury—through a detailed analysis of landmark U.S. Supreme Court decisions. Various procedural rules that govern the adjudicatory and dispositional hearings are also reviewed. The chapter concludes with a discussion of dispositional alternatives and trends in sentencing that affect juvenile dispositions.

FIGURE 15.2
Juvenile court processing of
petitioned status offense cases,
1992

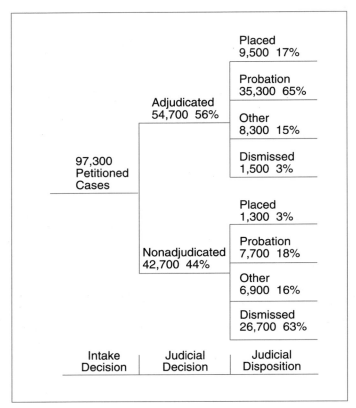

Source: Jeffrey Butts et al., *Juvenile Court Statistics, 1992* (Pittsburgh, Pa.: National Center for Juvenile Justice, 1995), p. 9.

THE JUVENILE COURT AND ITS OPERATION

The **juvenile court** is the centerpiece of the juvenile justice system. It plays a major role in controlling juvenile behavior and delivering social services to children in need. Efforts to control juvenile crime depend largely on how the juvenile court is organized and on what laws apply to those who appear before it (see Figure. 15.3).

Today's juvenile court is a specialized court for children. Its organizational structure varies in each state. A juvenile court can be (1) a special session of a lower court of trial **jurisdiction,** (2) part of a high court of general trial jurisdiction, (3) an independent statewide court, or even (4) part of a broader family court. The juvenile court includes a judge, probation staff, government prosecutors and defense attorneys, and a variety of social service programs. It functions in a sociolegal manner and seeks to promote rehabilitation within a framework of procedural due process. It is concerned with acting in the best interest of the child and in the best interest of public protection, often incompatible goals. At the same time, the juvenile courts are faced with an increasing and changing workload. They handle more than 4,000 delinquency cases each day, which amounts to more than 1.5 million cases each year.

Most juvenile courts in the United States are established as lower courts of limited jurisdiction as part of a district court, city court, or recorder's court and

FIGURE 15.3
Juvenile judicial system

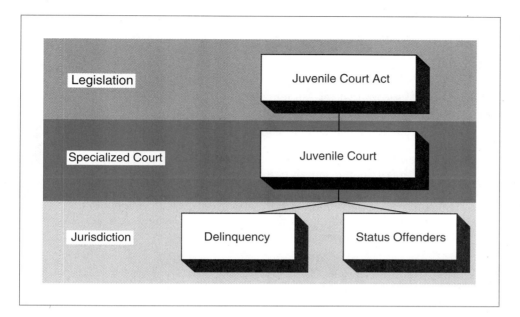

are limited solely to juvenile delinquency matters. Salaries, physical facilities, and even the prestige of the court can all be directly affected by its jurisdictional location. These factors tend to influence the ability of the court to attract competent personnel, including judges, and to obtain necessary resources from the state legislature. It is unclear why juvenile courts have been structured as part of lower trial courts in many states. Quite possibly it was to provide local attention to juvenile matters, as some experts believe that a lower court relates more efficiently and effectively to the concerns of parents and young people in the local community. In addition, legislators may have seen the juvenile court as an inferior court, relegated to the lowest level because of its jurisdiction over children. Massachusetts is an example of a state whose juvenile courts are placed in a special session of lower courts of limited trial jurisdiction. The state allows juvenile sessions to be heard in its district courts, and it has established special juvenile courts in major urban areas.

On the other hand, an increasing number of states—including Alaska, California, Colorado, Florida, Illinois, and Wisconsin—place juvenile matters at the highest court of general trial jurisdiction.[3] Here, juvenile cases are tried in the more prestigious courts of general jurisdiction. States that deal with juvenile matters at the highest trial court level have an integrated organizational structure that results in more efficient and effective court administration. Such courts are also better able to secure the funding they need to improve physical facilities and hire competent judicial and probation personnel.

Some states have *independent juvenile court systems.* Such systems may be referred to as statewide juvenile courts. Separately organized and independent juvenile courts exist in such states as Connecticut and Utah and in parts of other states, such as Georgia and Kansas. New York and Hawaii have also organized their juvenile courts on a statewide basis, although the New York system is called a family court system.[4] The major advantages to the statewide independent system are that it can serve sparsely populated areas within a given jurisdiction, it permits judicial personnel and others to deal exclusively with children's matters, and it can obtain legislative funding better than other court systems. On the other hand, the very benefit of its form—obtaining legislative funding—can also act as a detriment. Separately organized juvenile courts encounter resistance from legislators concerned with duplication of effort and unwilling to provide resources for the control and prevention of juvenile delinquency.

The major disadvantage of implementing a family court structure is that it requires major reorganization of the existing court system by the legislature. The costs are substantial, especially in the first few years of the court's existence. Where family court structures do exist, there are little statistical data to indicate that they have reduced delinquency or improved family programs.

However, it has become apparent to some experts that to treat the related problems of intrafamily crime, divorce, and child neglect in separate courts is to encourage inconsistency in court administration and decision making and to foster ineffective case-flow management. Thus, they believe it would be preferable to deal with juvenile matters in a family court system.

JUVENILE COURT JURISDICTION

Juvenile court jurisdiction is defined by state statutes, constitutional amendments, or state legislation. The New York Family Court, for example, claims its roots from the New York constitution; legislation serves merely to implement the constitutional mandate and specify the details of the court's makeup and operation. More often, juvenile courts are created by the authority of the legislature. Thus, the jurisdiction itself is generally controlled by legislative enactment.

AGE

The states differ over the age that brings children under the original jurisdiction of the juvenile court.[5] Most states (e.g., Alaska, California, Minnesota, and Wyoming) include all children under 18. Others (e.g., Louisiana, Massachusetts, and Michigan) set the upper limit at under 17. Still other states (e.g., North Carolina and Connecticut) have established the juvenile age as under 16 (see Table 15.1).

At one time, some jurisdictions established age ranges that varied according to the sex or geographic location of the juvenile, but statutes employing these distinctions have been held to be in violation of the equal protection clause or due process clause of the Constitution. For example, in the case of *Lamb v. Brown*, an Oklahoma statute that allowed females under the age of 18 the benefits of juvenile court proceedings while limiting the same benefits to males under 16 was held to be unconstitutional.[6]

A few state statutes describe juvenile court jurisdiction in terms of minimum age. Massachusetts, for example, defines a child as a person who is under 17 but over 7 years of age.[7] In most states, court jurisdiction is defined by the common law understanding of the responsibility of children. Under the age of 7, children are deemed incapable of committing crimes. There is a rebuttable presumption that children between the ages of 7 and 14 do not have the capacity for criminal behavior. Over the age of 14, children are believed to be responsible for their actions. Some states believe below a minimum age the child is powerless to act and therefore not accountable for criminal conduct.

TABLE 15.1 The Upper Age of Juvenile Court Jurisdiction
The upper age of juvenile court jurisdiction in delinquency matters is defined by state statute—in most states the upper age is 17.

Oldest Age for Original Juvenile Court Jurisdiction in Delinquency Matters				
15 years old	**16 years old**	**17 years old**		
Connecticut	Georgia	Alabama	Kansas	Ohio
New York	Illinois	Alaska	Kentucky	Oklahoma
North Carolina	Louisiana	Arizona	Maine	Oregon
	Massachusetts	Arkansas	Maryland	Pennsylvania
	Michigan	California	Minnesota	Rhode Island
	Missouri	Colorado	Mississippi	South Dakota
	South Carolina	Delaware	Montana	Tennessee
	Texas	District of	Nebraska	Utah
		Columbia	Nevada	Vermont*
		Florida	New Hampshire	Virginia
		Hawaii	New Jersey	Washington
		Idaho	New Mexico	West Virginia
		Indiana	North Dakota	Wisconsin
		Iowa		Wyoming

- Many states have higher upper age limits for juvenile court jurisdiction in status offense, abuse, neglect, or dependency matters—often through age 20.
- In many states the juvenile court has jurisdiction over young adults who committed offenses while juveniles.
- Several states also have minimum ages for juvenile court jurisdiction in delinquency matters—ranging from age 6 to age 12.
- Many states exclude married or otherwise emancipated juveniles from juvenile court jurisdiction.

*In Vermont the juvenile and criminal courts have concurrent jurisdiction over all 16- and 17-year-olds.

Source: Linda A. Szymanski, *Upper Age of Juvenile Court Jurisdiction Statutes Analysis (1994 Update)* (Pittsburgh, Pa.: National Center for Juvenile Justice, 1995); idem, *Lower Age of Juvenile Court Jurisdiction (1994 Update)*.

THE NATURE OF THE OFFENSE—DELINQUENCY

Juvenile court jurisdiction is also based on the nature of the child's actions. If a child commits a crime, the offense normally falls under the category of juvenile delinquency. Definitions of delinquency vary from state to state, but most are based on the common element of a maximum age as well as on the fact that delinquency is an intentional violation of the criminal law.

In recent years, state legislatures concerned about serious juvenile crime have passed laws automatically excluding serious offenses from the jurisdiction of the juvenile court. For example, Maryland excludes crimes punishable by death or life in prison allegedly committed by juveniles over 14 years of age and robbery committed with a dangerous weapon if the accused is over 16 (however, such cases can be transferred back to juvenile court from the adult court).[8]

Another approach has been to give prosecutors the choice of bringing the case to either juvenile court or adult court. For example, Florida gives the prosecutor the right to decide where to bring a case if a juvenile is accused of committing a crime punishable by death or life in prison or if the juvenile is 16 or over and has committed two prior delinquent offenses.[9] These issues are covered more fully in the Chapter 14 discussion on waiver procedures.

Such trends reflect a "toughening up" of juvenile justice policy—removing young offenders from the jurisdiction of the juvenile court so that they can be tried and punished as adults and eventually sentenced to adult prisons. However, this does not mean that the juvenile court has totally abandoned its rehabilitative ideals. Some states still require that juveniles manifest a "need for treatment" or supervision before they can be declared delinquents or status offenders; committing an illegal act is not enough for the state to take control of a child.[10] So there is still recognition that the juvenile court's mandate is something other than control and punishment.

THE NATURE OF THE OFFENSE—STATUS OFFENDERS

Juvenile courts also have jurisdiction over **status offenders,** children whose offenses are not the type of activities for which adults are normally prosecuted. Some juvenile delinquency statutes still include status offenses within their definition, but most states now have separate PINS and CHINS (persons or children in need of supervision) statutes so that separate proceedings can be held for children who are runaways, unmanageable, truant, or incorrigible.

The position of status offenders within the juvenile justice system remains controversial. One of the most difficult problems with such jurisdiction is the statutes themselves. The descriptions of behavior commonly included in these statutes—for example, "unmanageable," "unruly," and "in danger of leading an idle, dissolute, lewd, or immoral life"—have been challenged in court for being unconstitutionally vague and indefinite. However, the courts that have addressed this issue of vagueness have nonetheless upheld the breadth of the statutes in view of their overall concern for the welfare of the child.[11]

The removal of status offenders from secure lockups with delinquent youths has been one of the more successful justice-related policy initiatives. Almost all states have legally prohibited incarcerating status offenders with delinquents. For example, a West Virginia court prohibited the housing of status offenders in "secure, prison-like facilities which also house children guilty of criminal conduct or needlessly subject status offenders to the degradation and physical abuse of incarceration."[12] However, it is not uncommon for judges to get around these prohibitions by holding status offenders in contempt of court if they refuse to honor judicial decrees; a number of states have permitted these youths to then be held in secure detention facilities.[13]

The status offense category often becomes a catchall for offenders who do not fit anywhere else. If there is not enough evidence to support a finding of delinquency, prosecutors sometimes charge youths with being status offenders on the ground that their behavior endangered their morals, their health, or general welfare.[14] Defense attorneys should welcome the substitution of categories as it means their clients will not be subject to the same degree of confinement and control as they would be if they had been found delinquent.

THE PROSECUTOR IN THE JUVENILE COURT

The **juvenile prosecutor** is the government attorney responsible for representing the interests of the state and bringing the state's case against the accused juvenile. Depending on the level of government and the jurisdiction, the prosecutor can be called a district attorney, a county attorney, a state attorney, or a

United States attorney. He or she is a member of the bar and becomes a public prosecutor through political appointment or popular election.

Ordinarily, the juvenile prosecutor is a staff member of the local prosecuting attorney's office. If the office of the district attorney is in an urban area and of sufficient size, the juvenile prosecutor may work exclusively on juvenile and other family law matters. If the caseload of juvenile offenders is small, the juvenile prosecutor may also have criminal prosecution responsibilities.

For the first 60 years of its existence, the juvenile court did not include a prosecutor as a representative of the state in court proceedings.[15] The concept of advocacy and the adversary process were seen as inconsistent with the philosophy of diagnosis and treatment in the juvenile court system. The court followed a social service helping model with informal and noncriminal proceedings believed to be in the best interest of the child.

As we know, these views changed dramatically with the Supreme Court decisions of **Kent v. United States, In re Gault,** and **In re Winship,** which ushered in an era of greater formality and due process rights for children in the juvenile court system.[16] Today, almost all jurisdictions require by law that a prosecutor be present in the juvenile court.

The prosecutor's role in juvenile court is expanding. A number of states have passed legislation giving prosecutors control over intake and waiver decisions. Some have passed concurrent jurisdiction laws that allow prosecutors to decide in which court to bring serious juvenile cases. In some jurisdictions, it is the prosecutor and not the juvenile court judge who is entrusted with making the critical decision of whether to transfer a case to adult court. Consequently, the role of juvenile court prosecutor has become a critical element in the juvenile justice process.

In the words of the American Bar Association, "An attorney for the state, hereinafter referred to as the juvenile prosecutor, should participate in every proceeding of every stage of every case subject to the jurisdiction of the family court in which the state has an interest."[17] Including a prosecutor in juvenile court balances the respective interests of the state, the defense attorney, the child, and the judge, preserving the independence of each party's functions and responsibilities.

THE LEGAL DUTIES OF THE JUVENILE PROSECUTOR

A prosecutor enforces the law, represents the government, maintains proper standards of ethical conduct as an attorney and court officer, participates in programs and legislation involving legal changes in the juvenile justice system, acts as a spokesperson for the field of law, and takes an active role in the community in preventing delinquency and protecting the rights of juveniles. Of these functions, representing the government while presenting the state's case to the court occurs most frequently. In this regard, the prosecutor has many of the following duties:

- Investigate possible violations of the law
- Cooperate with the police, intake officer, and probation officer in ascertaining the facts alleged in the petition
- Authorize, review, and prepare petitions for court
- Play a role in the initial detention decision
- Represent the case in all pretrial motions, probable cause hearings, and consent decrees

- Represent the state at transfer hearings
- Recommend, if necessary, physical or mental examinations for children brought before the court
- Seek amendments or dismissals of filed petitions if appropriate
- Represent the state at the adjudication of the case
- Represent the state at the disposition of the case
- Enter into plea-bargaining discussions with the defense attorney
- Represent the government on appeal and in habeas corpus proceedings
- Be involved in hearings dealing with violation of probation

The ability either to initiate or to discontinue delinquency or status offense allegations represents the control and power a juvenile prosecutor has over a juvenile. Prosecutors have broad discretion in the exercise of their duties. Because due process rights have been extended to juveniles, the prosecutor's role in the juvenile court has in some ways become similar to the prosecutor's role in the adult court. In the case of *State v. Grayer*, for example, a Nebraska court upheld the validity of the discretionary power of the juvenile prosecutor to decide whether to prosecute the child as a juvenile or as an adult.[18]

Court decisions such as this demonstrate the judicial movement toward developing court procedures for juveniles that are similar to those for adults. However, it is important for the juvenile prosecutor not only to represent the government but also to remain cognizant of the philosophy and purpose of the juvenile court.

THE COMPLEX ROLE OF JUVENILE PROSECUTION

Although it may seem evident that prosecutors are beginning to play an ever-expanding role in juvenile courts, the actual impact of their presence may be open to debate. Research by John Laub and Bruce MacMurray conducted in the juvenile court in Boston indicates that prosecutors may find their roles in controlling juvenile court policies to be rather limited.[19] Laub and MacMurray found that prosecutors are considered "outsiders" whose adversarial ideas are not appreciated by juvenile court social service personnel.

Laub and MacMurray found that juvenile court personnel are not open to the idea of having the prosecutor play an important role in the processing of cases or introducing an adversarial system within its confines. They suggest that the prosecutor has to be perceived as an insider or part of the team before he or she can begin to have an important influence on juvenile court operations.

To define the role of the prosecutor in juvenile court, some states have attempted to draw up general policy guidelines or principles for juvenile prosecution based on the recent *Prosecution Standards* issued by the National District Attorneys Association.[20] In *Prosecution Standard 19.2, Juvenile Delinquency*, the prosecutor is defined as an advocate of the state's interest in juvenile court. The state's interest includes (1) the protection of the community from the danger of harmful conduct by the restraint and rehabilitation of juvenile offenders and (2) the concern shared by all juvenile justice system personnel, as *parens patriae*, with promoting the best interests of the child. The prosecutor also has a duty to seek justice in juvenile court by insisting on fair and lawful procedures. This entails ensuring, for example, that baseless prosecutions are not brought, that all juveniles receive fair and equal treatment, that liberal discovery of the state's case is available to defense counsel, that exculpatory evidence is made available to the defense counsel, and that excessively harsh dispositions are not sought. It also entails overseeing police investigative behavior to ensure its compliance with the law.

Because children are committing more serious crimes today and the courts have granted juveniles constitutional safeguards, the prosecutor is likely to play a more significant role in the juvenile court system than in the past. According to Shine and Price, the prosecutor's involvement will promote a due process model that should result in a fairer, more just system for all parties. But they also point out that prosecutors need more information on such issues as (1) how to identify repeat offenders; (2) how to determine which programs are most effective; (3) how early childhood experiences relate to delinquency; (4) how immigrant groups are absorbed into local populations; and (5) what measures can be used in place of secure placements without reducing public safety.[21]

THE JUVENILE COURT JUDGE

The **judge** is the central character in a court of juvenile or family law. His or her responsibilities are quite varied and have become far more extensive and complex in recent years. Following *Kent* and *Gault,* new legal rulings have probed the basic legal aspects of the juvenile justice system. In addition, juvenile cases are far more complex today and represent issues involving social change, such as truancy, alcoholism, the use of drugs by children, juvenile prostitution, and violent juvenile crime. Such cases involve problems of both public safety and individualized treatment for children.

Juvenile or family court judges perform the following functions:

- Rule on pretrial motions involving such legal issues as arrest, search and seizure, interrogation, and lineup identification
- Make decisions about the continued detention of children prior to trial
- Make decisions about plea-bargaining agreements and the informal adjustment of juvenile cases
- Handle bench and jury trials, rule on the appropriateness of conduct, settle questions of evidence and procedure, and guide the questioning of witnesses
- Assume responsibility for holding dispositional hearings and deciding on the treatment accorded the child
- Handle waiver proceedings
- Handle appeals where allowed by statute and where no prior contact has been made with the case[22]

In addition, judges often have extensive control and influence over other service agencies of the court: probation, the court clerk, the law enforcement officer, and the office of the juvenile prosecutor. Of course, courts differ organizationally and procedurally. Larger courts have more resources to handle the volume of juvenile cases. They may also have unique approaches to handling juvenile problems, including specialized offender caseloads, such as for drug users; diversion programs; and a whole host of special social services. Smaller courts, on the other hand, most likely have little more than a judge, a clerk, and a probation staff.

Juvenile court judges exercise considerable leadership in developing services and solutions to juvenile justice problems. In this role, juvenile court judges must respond to the external pressures the community places on juvenile court resources. In fact, research indicates that juvenile court decision making may be influenced more by the needs of the outside community than by the particular philosophy or views of the presiding judge.[23]

According to Judge Leonard Edwards of the Santa Clara, California, Superior Court, who has extensive experience in juvenile and family law, "The juvenile judge must take action to ensure that the necessary community resources are available so that the children and families which come before the court can be well-served."[24] This may be the most untraditional role for the juvenile court judge, but it may also be the most important.

SELECTION AND QUALIFICATIONS OF JUVENILE COURT JUDGES

A variety of methods are used to select juvenile court judges.[25] Sometimes, the governor simply appoints candidates chosen by a screening board. In some states, judges are chosen in popular partisan elections, while in others, judges run for office without party affiliation. In three states—Connecticut, Virginia, and South Carolina—the state legislature appoints judges. About a dozen states have adopted the **Missouri Plan**, which involves (1) a commission to nominate candidates for the bench; (2) an elected official, usually the governor, to make appointments from the list submitted by the commission; and (3) subsequent nonpartisan and uncontested elections in which incumbent judges run on their records (usually every three years).

In some jurisdictions, juvenile court judges handle family-related cases exclusively. In others, they handle criminal and civil cases as well. Traditionally, juvenile court judges have been relegated to a lower status than other judges, with less prestige, responsibility, and salary. Judges assigned to juvenile courts

The judge is the central character in a court of juvenile or family law. His or her responsibilities are quite varied and have become far more extensive and complex in recent years. Juvenile cases have become quite complex and represent issues involving intricate social problems, such as school failure, alcoholism, juvenile prostitution, and chronic violence. Such cases involve problems of both public safety and individualized treatment for children.

have not ordinarily been chosen from the highest levels of the legal profession. Such groups as the American Judicature Society have noted that the field of juvenile justice has often been shortchanged by the appointment of unqualified judges and staff. In some jurisdictions, particularly major urban areas, juvenile court judges may be of the highest caliber, but many courts throughout the nation continue to function with mediocre judges. As the Advisory Council of Judges of the National Council on Crime and Delinquency states,

> Juvenile court has been brilliantly conceived; its legal and social facets are not antithetical, but the preservation of equilibrium between them, which is the key to their successful fusion, depends upon the legal knowledge, social perspective, and eternal vigilance of *one person, the judge.*[26]

Judge Maurice Cohill, former judge of the Juvenile Court of Allegheny County, Pennsylvania, put it most succinctly when he said, "In terms of sheer human impact, the juvenile court is the most important court in the land."[27]

Inducing the best-trained individuals to accept juvenile court judgeships is a very important goal. Where the juvenile court is part of the highest general court of trial jurisdiction, the problem of securing qualified personnel is not as great. However, if the juvenile court is of limited or specialized jurisdiction and has the authority to try only minor cases, it may attract only poorly trained and poorly qualified personnel. Lawyers and judges who practice in juvenile court receive little respect from their colleagues. The term **kiddie court** is often used to describe juvenile court. The juvenile court has a negative image to overcome, because even though what it does is of great importance to parents, children, and society in general, it has been placed at the lowest level of the judicial hierarchy. One group that has struggled to upgrade the juvenile court judiciary is the **National Council of Juvenile and Family Court Judges.** Located in Reno, Nevada, this organization sponsors research and continuing legal education efforts designed to help judges master their field of expertise. Its research arm, the National Center for Juvenile Justice in Pittsburgh, offers assistance to courts in developing information processing and statute analysis methods; it also provides legal consultation to judicial groups. Some juvenile practitioners have even created their own bar association to support child advocacy programs.

THE DEFENSE ATTORNEY

As the result of a series of Supreme Court decisions, the right of a criminal defendant to have counsel at state trials has become a fundamental part of the criminal justice system.[28] Today, federal and state courts must provide counsel to indigent defendants who face the possibility of incarceration.

The American Bar Association (ABA) has described the responsibility of the legal profession to the juvenile court in Standard 2.3 of its *Standards Relating to Counsel for Private Parties.* The ABA states that legal representation should be provided in all proceedings arising from or related to a delinquency or in-need-of-supervision action—including mental competency, transfer, postdisposition, probation revocation and classification, institutional transfer, and disciplinary or other administrative proceedings related to the treatment process—that may substantially affect the juvenile's custody, status, or course of treatment.[29]

Over the past two decades, the rules and procedures of criminal and juvenile justice administration have become extremely complex. Specialized knowledge is essential for the adversary process to operate effectively. Preparation of a case for juvenile court often involves detailed investigation of a crime, knowledge of court procedures, use of rules of evidence, and skills in trial advocacy. Prosecuting and defense attorneys both must have this expertise, particularly when a child's freedom is at stake. The right to counsel in the juvenile justice system is essential if children are to have a fair chance of presenting their cases in court.

In many respects, the role of **defense attorneys** in the juvenile process is similar to that in the criminal and civil areas. Defense attorneys representing children in the juvenile court play an active and important part in virtually all stages of the proceedings. For example, the defense attorney helps to clarify jurisdictional problems and to decide whether there is sufficient evidence to warrant filing a formal petition at intake. He or she also helps outline the child's position regarding detention hearings and bail and explores the opportunities for informal adjustment of the case. If no adjustment or diversion occurs, the defense attorney represents the child at adjudication, presenting evidence and cross-examining witnesses to see that the child's position is made clear to the court. Defense attorneys also play a critically important role in the dispositional hearing. They present evidence bearing on the treatment decision and help the court formulate alternative plans for the child's care. Finally, defense attorneys pursue any appeals from the trial, represent the child in probation revocation proceedings, and generally protect the child's right to treatment.

In some cases, a **guardian *ad litem*** may be appointed by the court. The guardian *ad litem* is an attorney appointed by the court "to promote and protect the interests of a child involved in a judicial proceeding, through assuring representation of those interests in the courts and throughout the social services and ancillary service systems."[30] The guardian *ad litem,* nominally used in abuse, neglect, and dependency cases, may be appointed in delinquency cases where there is a question of a need for a particular treatment (e.g., placement in a mental health center) and the offender and his or her attorney resist placement. The guardian *ad litem* may advocate for the commitment on the ground that it is in the child's "best interests."[31]

Court Appointed Special Advocates (CASA) programs also advise the juvenile court about child placement. The CASA programs (*casa* is spanish for "home") have demonstrated that volunteers can investigate the needs of children and provide a vital link between the judge, the attorneys, and the child in protecting the juvenile's right to a safe placement.[32]

PUBLIC DEFENDER SERVICES FOR CHILDREN

To satisfy the requirement that indigent children and their families be provided with counsel at the various stages of the juvenile justice process, the federal government and the states have had to expand **public defender** services. Three primary alternatives exist for providing children with legal counsel in the juvenile court today: (1) an all-public defender program, (2) an appointed private counsel system, and (3) a combination system of public defenders and appointed private attorneys.

The public defender program is a statewide program organized by legislation and funded by the state government to provide counsel to children at public expense. This program allows access to the expertise of lawyers who spend a considerable amount of time representing juvenile offenders every day. Defender programs generally provide separate office space for juvenile court personnel as well as support staff, and training programs for new lawyers.

In many rural areas, individual public defender programs are not available, so defense services are offered through appointed private counsel. Private lawyers are assigned to individual juvenile court cases and receive compensation for the time and services they provide to the child and the family. When private attorneys are used in large urban areas, they are generally selected from a list established by the court, and they often operate in conjunction with a public defender program. Weakness of a system of assigned private counsel include assignment to cases for which the lawyers are unqualified, inadequate compensation, and lack of supportive or supervisory services.

Even though public defense services for children have grown in recent years, a major concern is continued provision of quality representation to the child and the family at all stages of the juvenile process. In some jurisdictions today, counsel is available to children during only part of the juvenile proceedings. In other jurisdictions, children are not represented in persons-in-need-of-supervision or neglect cases. Often public defender agencies and the assigned counsel system are understaffed and lack adequate support services. Representation needs to be upgraded in all areas of the juvenile court system.

Although juvenile court practice has not traditionally been viewed by the bar with the same esteem as a lucrative corporate practice or adult trial work, defense attorneys must meet the same high standards for competency and professional responsibility when representing a child in the juvenile justice system.

DO LAWYERS MAKE A DIFFERENCE IN JUVENILE COURT?

A number of studies in the early 1980s found that having an attorney either makes no difference in juvenile cases or actually results in more damaging dispositions for clients.[33] Juveniles represented by an attorney are more likely to receive institutional sentences than those who waive their right to counsel. Although not all research efforts arrive at this conclusion, sufficient evidence exists that at least in some jurisdictions, legal representation may not be in a juvenile's best interest.

One possible reason for this surprising finding is that only the most serious juvenile offenders request counsel, and it is these youths who are most likely to receive an institutional sentence. Another view is that counsel in juvenile court functions in a nonadversarial capacity, furthering the interests of the juvenile court rather than those of the client. Joseph Sanborn found quite a bit of role confusion in the three juvenile courts he studied. He found that some juvenile court personnel believed that the lawyer's role should be one of advocating for the client, while others viewed lawyers as guardians who guide juveniles through the treatment process.[34] Some of those Sanborn interviewed thought that attorneys should fight to prove their clients innocent during the trial stage, but that once delinquency was established, they should revert to the guardian role in order to obtain the best treatment possible for their clients. Thus, in a case in which the judge believes that a child needs placement in a secure facility, the attorney may help convince the client that placement is in his or her best interest rather than use all means to block the incarceration.[35]

THE LACK OF QUALITY IN JUVENILE DEFENSE WORK

The inferior quality of legal counsel in juvenile court has been confirmed by a New York study of juvenile defense work. The study, sponsored by the New York State Bar Association, found significant deficiencies in the quality of legal care given youths by their court-appointed lawyers. In 45 percent of the almost 200 cases studied the representation was considered inadequate, and in another 47 percent it appeared that the lawyer had done little or no preparation on the case.

The study also found that lawyers representing juveniles had little knowledge of the statutes governing juvenile law and were also unfamiliar with social services available to children. There were frequent instances of insensitivity to the client's feelings, particularly in cases involving sexual issues or abuse.[36] Based on such information, improving legal services for indigent juveniles may be a tough goal to achieve.

Sanford Fox claims, "Few of the rights granted children in the juvenile justice system would have much real meaning without an attorney to assert them or to advise the child when it is in his best interests to waive them."[37] What he didn't say is that the counsel must be knowledgeable enough on the law to be able to use it to protect the client's best interests. With the increase in serious crimes by juveniles and harsher sentences, it is more important than ever that appropriate procedural safeguards, such as the right to counsel, are essential elements of the juvenile justice system.

In one of the most comprehensive empirical examinations on right to counsel, Barry Feld analyzed variations in the rates of representation and the impact of counsel on juvenile delinquency and status proceedings in Minnesota in 1986.[38] Feld reported that, overall, only 45.3 percent of juveniles in Minnesota received the assistance of counsel. In counties with high rates of representation, 94.5 percent of juveniles had counsel; in counties with medium rates, 46.8 percent had counsel; and in counties with low rates, only 19.3 percent had counsel.[39] The seriousness of the offense increases the likelihood of representation; many juveniles who commit petty offenses go unrepresented because they waive their right to counsel.

Feld's findings confirm previous research in this area: Youths with lawyers receive more serious sentencing dispositions. Almost twice as many youths were removed from their homes and institutionalized in the high-representation counties as in areas where there is low representation. Feld's study provides support for the existence of "varieties of juvenile justice" and suggests that administrative criteria and sentencing guidelines be used to structure dispositional practices in the juvenile court.[40] Feld acknowledges the punitive nature of today's juvenile court and argues that the state must provide appropriate due process protection in this more formal legalistic system.[41]

Based on research, it appears that a great deal of variation still exists in the extent to which juveniles are represented by counsel at adjudication or dispositional hearings in the juvenile court system.[42] The major reasons for this seem to be that

1. some juveniles are not advised of their right to counsel;
2. some defense attorneys do not appear at the hearing;
3. pleas of guilty are entered without full explanation;
4. juveniles waive their right to counsel, often at the encouragement of parents or some public officer;
5. parents are unwilling to retain an attorney; and
6. public defender services are inadequate.

According to some child advocates, juvenile offenders should have an unwaivable right to counsel. But many judicial personnel agree that providing every juvenile with legal counsel would seriously impede the work of the juvenile court.

In spite of *Gault,* now almost 30 years old, there remain serious questions about the real extent and quality of legal representation. According to Feld, it appears that *Gault's* promise of counsel remains unkept for most juveniles in most states.[43]

The latest research, a 1995 American Bar Association study, confirmed the fact that many juveniles go to court unrepresented or with an overworked lawyer whose caseload makes providing effective help impossible.[44] According to the report, which was based on a survey of hundreds of juvenile court defense lawyers and defendants, the juvenile court is not being empowered to do the job properly. Today, as juvenile offenders face the prospect of much longer sentences, mandatory minimum sentences, and time in adult prisons, the need for quality defense attorneys for juveniles has never been greater. The report also found that many juvenile court defense lawyers work on more than 500 cases in one year, and more than half leave their jobs in under two years. The report's recommendations are these:

1. State legislatures need to provide additional funding for the public defenders of juveniles.
2. State and local bar associations need to encourage more lawyers to provide services free of charge to juvenile court defendants.
3. Public defender offices should ensure that lawyers have manageable caseloads.
4. Congress should mandate additional research by holding hearings to identify the quality and accessibility of lawyers in juvenile courts and to evaluate the protection of children's rights in the juvenile justice system.[45]

ADJUDICATION

At the **adjudication** stage of the juvenile process, a hearing is held to determine the merits of the petition claiming that a child is either a delinquent youth or in need of court supervision. The judge is required to make a finding on the evidence in the case and arrive at a judgment. Adjudication is comparable to an adult trial. Rules of evidence in adult criminal proceedings are generally applicable in juvenile court and the standard of proof used—"beyond a reasonable doubt"—is similar to that used in adult trials. The majority of juvenile cases do not reach the adjudicatory state, but serious delinquency cases based on violations of the criminal law, situations where juveniles deny any guilt, cases of repeat offenders, and cases where juveniles are a threat to themselves or the community often do reach this stage.

Much of the controversy over the adjudication process has centered on whether the proceedings have been handled fairly. State juvenile codes vary with regard to the basic requirements of due process and fairness. Most juvenile courts have bifurcated hearings—that is, separate hearings for adjudication and disposition. At disposition hearings, evidence can be submitted that reflects nonlegal factors, such as the child's home life, relationships, and background. Although there has not been sufficient research on hearing fairness, there are some indications that minorities may be handled with disproportionate harshness at disposition.[46]

Edmund McGarrell's study of juvenile court data for 1985 and 1989 indicated that minority youths are more likely to be referred to and petitioned in court, detained, and placed away from the home after adjudication.[47] McGarrell speculates that this trend may be partially attributed to the increase in minority drug offenders. However, what sometimes seems to be racial or ethnic bias may actually be a result of legal or socially relevant factors, such as the willingness to plea bargain, the seriousness of the crime, school performance, and so on.

Most state juvenile codes provide for specific rules of procedure and a finding at adjudication. These rules require that a written petition be submitted to the court, ensure the right of a child to have an attorney, provide that the adjudication proceedings be recorded, allow the petition to be amended, and provide that a child's plea be accepted. Where the child admits to the facts of the petition, the courts generally seek assurance that the plea is voluntary. If plea bargaining is used, prosecutors, defense counsel, and trial judges take steps to ensure the fairness of such negotiations.

At the end of the adjudication hearing, most juvenile court statutes require the judge to make a factual finding on the legal issues and evidence presented in the child's hearing. In the criminal court, this finding is normally an entrée to reaching a verdict. In the juvenile court, however, the finding itself is the verdict; the case is resolved in one of the following three manners:

1. The juvenile court judge makes a finding of fact that the child or juvenile is not delinquent or in need of supervision.
2. The juvenile court judge makes a finding of fact that the juvenile is delinquent or in need of supervision.
3. The juvenile court judge dismisses the case because of insufficient or faulty evidence.

In some jurisdictions, informal alternatives are used, such as filing the case with no further consequences or continuing the case without a finding. These alternatives involve no determination of delinquency or noncriminal behavior. Because of the philosophy of the juvenile court to emphasize treatment and rehabilitation over punishment, a delinquency finding is not the same thing as a criminal conviction. The disabilities associated with conviction, such as disqualifications for employment, entrance into the military service, or involvement in politics, do not apply in an adjudication of delinquency.

Consequently, there are still some significant differences between adult and juvenile proceedings. For instance, only a small proportion of states entitle juveniles to jury trials, and in almost all jurisdictions, juvenile trials are closed to the public.[48] Because juvenile courts are treating some defendants similarly to adult criminals, an argument can be made that the courts should extend the Sixth Amendment right to a public jury trial to these youths.[49] For the most part, however, state juvenile courts operate without recognizing a juvenile's constitutional right to a public jury trial.

CONSTITUTIONAL RIGHTS AT TRIAL

In addition to mandating state juvenile code requirements, the U.S. Supreme Court has mandated the application of constitutional due process standards to the juvenile trial. Due process is addressed in the Fifth and Fourteenth Amendments to the U.S. Constitution. It refers to the need in our legal system for rules and procedures that protect individual rights. Having the right to due process means that no person can be deprived of life, liberty, or property without such protections as legal counsel, an open and fair hearing, and an opportunity to confront those making accusations against him or her. Due process is intended to guarantee that fundamental fairness is available to every citizen.

For many years, children were deprived of their due process rights because the *parens patriae* philosophy governed their relationship to the juvenile justice system. Such rights as having counsel and confronting one's accusers were deemed unnecessary. After all, why should children need protection from the state when the only issue was their treatment, care, and protection? This view changed in the 1960s when, under the leadership of Chief Justice Earl Warren, the U.S. Supreme Court recognized the problems inherent in the juvenile justice system and began to grant due process rights and procedures to minors. As a result of Supreme Court activism, a child is now entitled to many of the same due process rights as an adult. As Justice Hugo Black stated in the landmark 1967 case *In re Gault,*

> When a person, infant or adult, can be seized by the state, charged and convicted, for violating a state criminal law, and then ordered by the state to be confined for six years, I think the Constitution requires that he be tried in accordance with the guarantees of all the provisions of the Bill of Rights, made applicable to the states by the Fourteenth Amendment. Appellants are entitled to these rights not because fairness, impartiality and orderliness, in short, the essentials of due process, require them, and not because they are the procedural rules which have been fashioned from the generality of due process, but because they are specifically and unequivocably granted by provisions of the Fifth and Sixth Amendments which the Fourteenth Amendment makes applicable to the states.[50]

The Warren Court set forth the role of due process in juvenile justice through major decisions made during the 1960s, beginning with *Kent v. United States,* decided in 1966.[51] In *Kent,* the court held that a transfer proceeding was a critically important stage in the juvenile process and must hold to at least minimal due process and fair treatment standards as required by the Fourteenth Amendment. This case was detailed in chapter 14.

In the landmark case of *In re Gault* (1967), the Supreme Court further articulated the basic requirements of due process that must be satisfied in juvenile court proceedings. It held that in an adjudicatory hearing

- the child must be given adequate notice of the charges;
- the child and the parent must be advised of the right to be represented by counsel;
- the child has a constitutional privilege against self-incrimination; and
- the child has the right of confrontation and sworn testimony of witnesses available for cross-examination.[52]

Because of the importance of the *Gault* case in juvenile court proceedings, it is set out in the following "Focus on Delinquency."

The *Gault* decision reshaped the constitutional and philosophical nature of the juvenile court system. As a result, those working in the system—judges, social workers, attorneys—were faced with the problem of reaffirming the rehabilitative ideal of the juvenile court while ensuring that juveniles received proper procedural due process rights. Prior to the *Gault* decision, only a few states required that juveniles be offered the assistance of counsel. Now, according to Linda Szymanski of the National Center for Juvenile Justice, virtually all states provide counsel in one form or another at various stages of the juvenile proceedings.[53]

IN RE GAULT

Facts

Gerald Gault, 15 years of age, was taken into custody by the sheriff of Gila County, Arizona, because a woman complained that he and another boy had made an obscene telephone call to her. At the time, Gerald was under a six-month probation as a result of being found delinquent for stealing a wallet. As a result of the woman's complaint, Gerald was taken to a children's home. His parents were not informed that he was being taken into custody. His mother appeared in the evening and was told by the superintendent of detention that a hearing would be held in the juvenile court the following day. On the day in question, the police officer who had taken Gerald into custody filed a petition alleging his delinquency. Gerald, his mother, and the police officer appeared before the judge in his chambers. Mrs. Cook, the complainant, was not at the hearing. Gerald was questioned about the telephone calls and was sent back to the detention home and then subsequently released a few days later.

On the day of Gerald's release, Mrs. Gault received a letter indicating that a hearing would be held on Gerald's delinquency a few days later. A hearing was held, and the complainant again was not present. There was no transcript or recording of the proceedings, and the juvenile officer stated that Gerald had admitted making the lewd telephone calls. Neither the boy nor his parents were advised of any right to remain silent, the right to be represented by counsel, or any other constitutional rights. At the conclusion of the hearing, the juvenile court committed Gerald as a juvenile delinquent to the state industrial school in Arizona for the period of his minority.

This meant that, at the age of 15, Gerald was sent to the state school until he reached the age of 21 unless discharged sooner. An adult charged with the same crime would have received a maximum punishment of no more than a fifty-dollar fine or two months in prison.

Decision

Gerald's attorneys filed a writ of habeas corpus, which was denied by the Superior Court of the state of Arizona. That decision was subsequently affirmed by the Arizona Supreme Court. On appeal to the U.S. Supreme Court, Gerald's counsel argued that the juvenile code of Arizona under which Gerald was found delinquent was invalid because it was contrary to the due process clause of the Fourteenth Amendment. In addition, Gerald was denied the following basic due process rights: (1) notice of the charges with regard to their timeliness and specificity, (2) right to counsel, (3) right to confrontation and cross-examination, (4) privilege against self-incrimination, (5) right to a transcript of the trial record, and (6) right to appellate review. In deciding the case, the Supreme Court had to determine whether procedural due process of law within the context of fundamental fairness under the Fourteenth Amendment applied to juvenile delinquency proceedings in which a child is committed to a state industrial school.

The Court, in a far-reaching opinion written by Justice Abe Fortas, agreed that Gerald's constitutional rights had been violated. Notice of charges was an essential ingredient of due process of law, as was the right to counsel, the right to cross-examine and to confront witnesses, and the privilege against self-incrimination. The questions of appellate review and a right to a transcript were not answered by the Court in this case.

Significance of the Case

The *Gault* case established that a child had the procedural due process constitutional rights listed above in delinquency adjudication proceedings where the consequences were that the child could be committed to a state institution. It was confined to rulings at the adjudication stage of the juvenile process.

However, this decision was significant not only because of the procedural reforms it initiated but also because of its far-reaching impact throughout the entire juvenile justice system. *Gault* instilled in juvenile proceedings the development of due process standards at the pretrial, trial, and posttrial stages of the juvenile process. While recognizing the history and development of the juvenile court, it sought to accommodate the motives of rehabilitation and treatment with children's rights. It recognized the principle of fundamental fairness of the law for children as well as for adults. Judged in the context of today's juvenile justice system, *Gault* redefined the relationships between juveniles, their parents, and the state. It remains the single most significant constitutional case in the area of juvenile justice.

Source: *In re Gault*, 387 U.S. 1; 87 S.Ct. 1248 (1967).

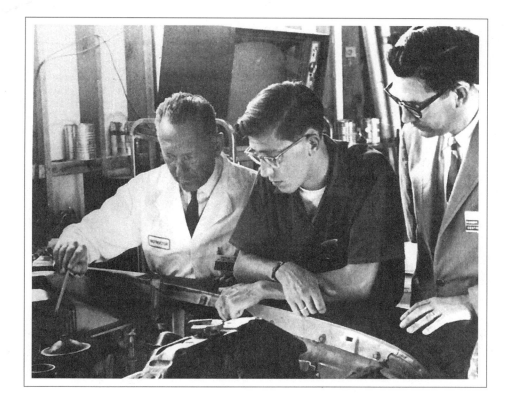

Gerald Gault's (center) successful appeal to the Supreme Court revolutionized the legal rights of young offenders.

Following the *Gault* case, the Supreme Court decided *In re Winship* in 1970. This case considered the issue of the amount of proof required in juvenile delinquency adjudications.[54] Prior to *Winship,* most juvenile courts judged the sufficiency of evidence in juvenile matters by applying a preponderance of the evidence, or clear and convincing evidence, test. In *Winship,* the Court rejected the idea that the juvenile system was a civil system and held that the Fourteenth Amendment due process clause required that delinquency charges in juvenile court be proved beyond a reasonable doubt.

Although the ways in which the traditional juvenile court operates were severely altered by *Kent, Gault,* and *Winship,* the trend toward increased rights for juveniles was somewhat curtailed by the Supreme Court's decision in **McKeiver v. Pennsylvania** (1971). In *McKeiver,* the Court held that trial by jury in a juvenile court's adjudicative stage is not a constitutional requirement.[55] This decision, however, does not prevent states from giving the juvenile a trial by jury as a state constitutional right or by state statute. In the majority of states, a child has no such right. *In re Winship* and *McKeiver v. Pennsylvania,* major decisions signaling the Supreme Court's determination to evaluate the adjudicatory rights of juvenile offenders, are highlighted in a following "Focus on Delinquency."

Once an adjudicatory hearing has been completed, the court is normally required to enter a judgment against the child. This may take the form of declaring the child delinquent, adjudging the child to be a ward of the court, or possibly even suspending judgment so as to avoid the stigma of a juvenile record. After a judgment has been entered in accordance with the appropriate state statute, the

IN RE WINSHIP AND MCKEIVER V. PENNSYLVANIA

In re Winship: Standard of Proof

Following the *Gault* case came *In re Winship*. This case expressly held that a juvenile in a delinquency adjudication must be proven guilty beyond a reasonable doubt.

Facts

Winship, a 12-year-old boy in New York, stole $112 from a woman's pocketbook. The petition that charged Winship with delinquency alleged that this act, if done by an adult, would constitute larceny. Winship was adjudicated a delinquent on the basis of a preponderance of the evidence submitted at the court hearing. During a subsequent dispositional hearing, Winship was ordered placed in a training school in New York state for an initial period of eighteen months, subject to extensions of his commitment until his eighteenth birthday—six years in total. The New York State Supreme Court and the New York Court of Appeals affirmed the lower court decision, sustaining the conviction.

Decision

The problem in the case was whether Section 744(b) of the New York State Family Court Act was constitutional. This section provided that any determination at the conclusion of an adjudicatory hearing must be based on a preponderance of the evidence. The judge decided Winship's guilt on the basis of this standard and not on the basis of proof beyond a reasonable doubt, which is the standard in the adult criminal justice system. The issue in the case was whether proof beyond a reasonable doubt was essential to due process and fair treatment for juveniles charged with an act that would constitute a crime if committed by an adult.

Significance of the Case

Although the standard of proof beyond a reasonable doubt is not stated in the Constitution, the U.S. Supreme Court said that *Gault* had established that due process required the essentials of fair treatment, although it did not require that the adjudication conform to all the requirements of the criminal trial. The Court further said that the due process clause recognized proof beyond a reasonable doubt as being among the essentials of fairness required when a child is charged with a delinquent act. The state of New York argued that juvenile delinquency proceedings were civil in nature, not criminal, and that the preponderance of evidence standard was therefore valid. The U.S. Supreme Court indicated that the standard of proof beyond a reasonable doubt plays a vital role in the American criminal justice system and ensures a greater degree of safety for the presumption of innocence of those accused of a crime.

Thus, the *Winship* case required proof beyond a reasonable doubt as a standard for juvenile adjudication proceedings and eliminated the use of lesser standards such as a preponderance of the evidence, clear and convincing proof, and reasonable proof.

McKeiver v. Pennsylvania: Right to a Jury Trial

One of the most controversial issues in the areas of children's rights at adjudication involves the jury trial. Although the Sixth Amendment guarantees to the adult criminal defendant the

court can begin its determination of possible dispositions for the child. Table 15.2 illustrates the evolution of the juvenile court system in determining judgments.

DISPOSITION

The stage of the juvenile justice process after adjudication is called **disposition**. It is the sentencing step of the juvenile proceedings. At this point, the juvenile court orders treatment for the juvenile to prevent further delinquency. Adrienne Volenik claims that it is here where the original child-saving philosophy of the juvenile court can come into play.[56]

right to a jury trial, the Supreme Court had not seen fit to grant this right to juvenile offenders. In fact, the U.S. Constitution is silent on whether all defendants, including those charged with misdemeanors, have a right to a trial by jury. In the case of *Duncan v. Louisiana*, the Supreme Court held that the Sixth Amendment right to a jury trial applied to all adult defendants accused of serious crimes. However, no mention was made of the juvenile offender. The case of *McKeiver v. Pennsylvania* deals with the right of the juvenile defendant to a jury trial.

Facts

Joseph McKeiver, age 16, was charged with robbery, larceny, and receiving stolen goods, all of which were felonies under Pennsylvania law. McKeiver was subsequently declared delinquent at an adjudication hearing and placed on probation after his request for a jury trial was denied.

In another case, Edward Terry, age 15, was charged with assault and battery on a police officer, misdemeanors under Pennsylvania law. He was declared a juvenile delinquent after an adjudication following a denial of his request for trial by jury.

In an unrelated case in North Carolina, a group of juveniles were charged with willful, riotous, and disorderly conduct, declared delinquent, and placed on probation. Their request for a jury trial was denied.

The Supreme Court heard all three cases together on the single issue of whether a juvenile has a constitutional right to a jury trial in the juvenile court system.

Decision

The court was required to decide whether the due process clause of the Fourteenth Amendment guarantees the right to a jury trial in the adjudication of a juvenile court delinquency case. It answered in the negative, stating that the right to a jury trial guaranteed by the Sixth Amendment and incorporated into the Fourteenth Amendment is not among the constitutional safe guards that the due process clause requires at delinquency adjudication hearings. The Court's reasons were as follows:

- A jury trial is not a necessary component of accurate fact-finding, as are the procedural requirements stated in the *Gault* case.
- Not all the rights constitutionally assured an adult are to be given to a juvenile.
- Insisting on a jury trial for juvenile offenders could fully turn the adjudication into an adversary process.
- Insisting on a jury trial would not remedy the problems associated with the lack of rehabilitation in the juvenile court.
- The preferable approach would be to allow states to experiment and adopt for themselves a jury trial concept in their individual jurisdictions.
- The jury trial, if imposed in the juvenile court, would certainly result in a delay, formality, and the possibility of a public trial, which at this point is not provided in most jurisdictions.

Significance of the Case

The *McKeiver* case temporarily stopped the march toward procedural constitutional due process for juvenile offenders in the juvenile justice system. The majority of the Court believed that juvenile proceedings were different from adult criminal prosecutions. The case also emphasized the fact that, as Justice Blackmun said, jurisdictions are free to adopt their own jury trial position in juvenile proceedings. The Court further noted that the majority of states denied a juvenile the right to a jury trial by statute. Thus, the Court believed that granting the juvenile offender the right to a jury trial would hinder, rather than advance, the system of juvenile justice in the United States.

Source: *In re Winship*, 397 U.S. 358, 90 S.Ct. 1068 (1970); *McKeiver v. Pennsylvania*, 403 U.S. 528, 91 S.Ct. 1976 (1971).

Disposition is the most important phase of juvenile proceedings.[57] In fact, Paul Piersma and his associates describe the disposition as the heart of the juvenile process.[58] Lindsay G. Arthur, who has spent many years working on behalf of the National Council of Juvenile and Family Court Judges, speaks about the importance and the philosophy of disposition:

> A disposition is not simply a sentencing. It is far broader in concept and in application. It should be in the best interest of the child, which in this context means effectively to provide the help necessary to resolve or meet the individual's definable needs, while, at the same time, meeting society's needs for protection.[59]

TABLE 15.2 Six Steps in the Evolution of the Juvenile Court

Step		Description
1. Early U.S. History	_____	Children treated the same as adults
2. Beginning of Twentieth Century	_____	Juvenile Court Act established in Illinois
3. First Half of Twentieth Century	_____	Expansion of juvenile courts and rehabilitation model
4. 1950s and 1960s	_____	Public confidence in treatment eroded
5. In re Gault (1967)	_____	Due process protections introduced
6. 1980s to present	_____	Pendulum moves significantly toward law and order

The dispositional process has not received much attention from the courts. None of the Supreme Court decisions dealing with juvenile justice refers to its significance. Consequently, according to most legal documents, one of the most important issues in the disposition is the lack of proper procedure and due process for the child. In most jurisdictions today, adjudication and disposition hearings are separated, or bifurcated. In addition to a separate dispositional hearing, a child is generally accorded the right to counsel.

The Supreme Court has not ruled on the right to counsel at disposition, but counsel's participation is generally allowed either by state statute or unspoken practice. Defense counsel often represents the child, helps the parents understand the court's decision, and influences the direction of the disposition. Others involved at the dispositional stage include representatives of social service agencies, psychologists, social workers, and probation personnel. The information they have supplied about the child's background often may be disputed at the disposition, and many states now allow cross-examination at this stage of the juvenile process.

Another important issue at the dispositional hearing is the need to obtain information about the child in order to formulate the treatment plan. In determining the type of disposition to be imposed on the child, juvenile court statutes often require the completion of a **predispositional investigation.** Fox describes the needs and purposes of this report:

> Individualized justice is often taken to be the most salient characteristic of juvenile court dispositions. In order to have the disposition conform to this ideal, the juvenile court judge requires information about each particular child. This is usually provided by an investigation, usually performed by a member of the probation staff, and report, known as the social study or disposition report.[60]

The predisposition report in the juvenile court is similar to the presentence report in the adult criminal justice system. Its use at the adjudication may result in prejudicial error against the child and often results in a mistrial. However, social service information is often used at the intake phase of the juvenile process as well as at the disposition. In some jurisdictions, statutes mandate completion of a predisposition report, particularly before a child can be placed in a youth program.

THE PREDISPOSITION REPORT

After the child has admitted to the allegations in the petition or after the allegations have been proved in a juvenile trial, the judge normally orders the probation department to complete a predisposition report. Investigating and evaluating the child prior to juvenile disposition are two of the most important tasks of juvenile probation officers. The predisposition report has a number of purposes:

- It helps the judge decide which disposition is best for the child.
- It aids the juvenile probation officer in developing treatment programs where the child is in need of counseling or community supervision.
- It helps the court develop a body of knowledge about the child that can aid others in treating the child.
- It serves as a source of basic information for systematic research in juvenile justice.

The style and content of predisposition reports vary among jurisdictions and also among juvenile probation officers within the same jurisdiction. The requirements for the use of the report, the sources of dispositional information, the techniques for obtaining it, and the conditions of its distribution vary among jurisdictions and are based on rules of law and procedure.

Some juvenile court probation departments require voluminous reports covering every aspect of the child's life. Other jurisdictions require information about the basic facts of the case and only limited information about the child's background. Individual officers bring their personal styles and educational backgrounds to bear on the development of the report. The probation officer who is a trained social worker, for example, might stress the use of psychological data, while the probation officer who is a lawyer might concentrate on the child's prior record and how dangerous the child is to himself or herself and to the community.

Sources of dispositional data include family members, school officials, and the juvenile. The results of psychological testing, psychiatric evaluations, and intelligence testing may be relevant to the predispositional report. Furthermore, the probation officer might include information about the juvenile's feelings and attitudes concerning his or her case.

Some state statutes make the predisposition report mandatory. Other jurisdictions require the report only when there is a probability that the child will be institutionalized. In Massachusetts, for example, the law reads that "in every case of a delinquent child, a probation officer shall make a report regarding the character of such child, his school record, home surroundings, and previous complaint, if any."[61] Some appellate courts have reversed orders institutionalizing children where the juvenile court did not use a predisposition report in reaching its decision.

Access to predisposition reports is an important legal issue. The Supreme Court ruled in the case of *Kent v. United States* that the child and counsel must be given access to the social service report at transfer proceedings.[62] The National Advisory Commission on Criminal Justice Standards and Goals recommends that no dispositional decision be made on the basis of facts or information in a report not previously disclosed to the defense and prosecuting attorney.[63] According to Robert Shepherd, Jr., of the American Bar Association, this is also an excellent time for the defense attorney to bring to the probation officer's attention any *favorable* information regarding the child.[64]

In the final section of the predisposition report, the probation department recommends a disposition to the presiding judge. This is a very critical aspect of the report as it has been estimated that the court follows more than 90 percent of all probation department recommendations. Thus, it is essential that the purpose of the report, which is to determine the care or treatment plan the child needs, not the child's innocence or guilt, be accomplished.

TYPES OF JUVENILE COURT DISPOSITIONS

Historically, the juvenile court has had broad discretionary power to make dispositional decisions after adjudication. The major categories of dispositional choices are (1) community release, (2) out-of-home placements, (3) fines or restitution, (4) community service, and (5) institutionalization. A more detailed list of the numerous possible dispositions open to the juvenile court judge follows:[65]

- *Informal consent decree.* In minor or first offenses, an informal hearing is held, and the judge will ask the youth and his or her guardian to agree to a treatment program, such as counseling. No formal trial or disposition hearing is held.
- *Probation.* A youth is placed under the control of the county probation department and required to obey a set of probation rules and participate in a treatment program.
- *Home detention.* A child is restricted to his or her home in lieu of a secure placement. Rules include regular school attendance, curfew observance, avoidance of alcohol and drugs, and notification of parents and the youth worker of the child's whereabouts.
- *Court-ordered school attendance.* If truancy was the problem that brought the youth to court, a judge may order mandatory school attendance. Some courts have established court-operated day schools and court-based tutorial programs staffed by community volunteers.
- *Financial restitution.* A judge can order the juvenile offender to make financial restitution to the victim. In most jurisdictions, restitution is part of

A juvenile awaits disposition in his case. Historically, the juvenile court has had broad discretionary power to make dispositional decisions after adjudication. The major categories of dispositional choices include: (1) community release, (2) out-of-home placements, (3) fines or restitution, (4) community service, and (5) institutionalization.

probation (see chapter 16), but in a few states, such as Maryland, restitution can be a sole order.

- *Fines.* Some states allow fines to be levied against juveniles age 16 and over.
- *Community service.* Courts in many jurisdictions require juveniles to spend time in the community working off their debt to society. Community service orders are usually reserved for victimless crimes, such as possession of drugs, or crimes against public order, such as vandalism of school property. Community service orders are usually carried out in such places as schools, hospitals, and nursing homes.
- *Outpatient psychotherapy.* Youths whose behavior is bizarre and disorganized may be required to undergo therapy at a local mental health clinic.
- *Drug and alcohol treatment.* Youths with drug- or alcohol-related problems may be allowed to remain in the community if they agree to undergo drug or alcohol therapy.
- *Commitment to secure treatment.* In the most serious cases, a judge may order an offender admitted into a long-term treatment center, such as a training school, camp, ranch, or group home. These may be either state- or privately run institutions, usually located in remote regions of the state. Training schools provide educational, vocational, and rehabilitation programs in a secure environment (see chapter 17).
- *Commitment to a residential community program.* Youths who commit crimes of a less serious nature but still need to be removed from their homes can be placed in community-based group homes or halfway houses. They attend school or work during the day and live in a controlled, therapeutic environment at night.
- *Foster home placement.* Foster homes are usually used for dependent or neglected children and status offenders. Judges are today placing delinquents with insurmountable problems at home in state-licensed foster care homes.

The authority to order dispositional alternatives generally stems from the juvenile code. Most state statutes allow the juvenile court judge to select whatever disposition is best suited to the child's needs. In addition to the above dispositions, some states go so far as to grant the juvenile court the power to order parents into treatment or suspend a youth's driver's license.

On the other hand, state juvenile codes can limit specifically a judge's discretionary power. For instance, many states prohibit the confining of children in adult institutions.[66] Some states use a minimum age as a criterion for institutional placement, while others limit placement in such facilities to felony offenders only. In certain states, the juvenile court determines commitment in a specific institution, while in others, the youth corrections agency determines where the child will be placed. In other words, there is almost an infinite number of statutory variations to the dispositional process.

Standard 2.1 of the IJA-ABA Juvenile Justice Standards, Standards Relating to Dispositions, articulates the basic policy of seeking the least restrictive alternative in dispositional decision making. In choosing from among statutorily permissible dispositions,

> the court should employ the least restrictive category and duration of disposition that is appropriate to the seriousness of the offense, as modified by the degree of culpability indicated by the circumstances of the particular case, and by the age and prior record of the juvenile.[67]

The imposition of a particular disposition should be accompanied by a statement of the facts supporting the disposition and the reasons for selecting the disposition and rejecting less restrictive alternatives.

Graduated sanction programs for juveniles are another type of dispositional solution being explored by states across the country. Types of graduated sanctions include (1) immediate sanctions for nonviolent offenders; (2) intermediate sanctions, which target repeat minor offenders and first-time serious offenders; and (3) secure care, which is reserved for repeat serious offenders and violent offenders. According to Barry Krisberg and his associates, studies of the best-structured graduated sanction programs reveal that they are often more effective than incarceration.[68] The following "Case in Point" explores the disposition process.

CASE IN POINT

You are a family court judge at a dispositional hearing faced with making a difficult sentencing decision. John M. was arrested at age 16 for robbery and rape. As a juvenile offender, he was subject to the jurisdiction of the juvenile division of the state family court. After a thorough investigation by the police department, the prosecutor formally filed a petition against John for the alleged offenses. Subsequently, John's mother obtained counsel for him. When the prosecutor suggested that the family court might consider transferring the case to the adult court, John admitted his involvement in the offenses and was sent home pending disposition.

At the disposition hearing, the probation officer reported that John was the oldest of three siblings living in a single-parent home. He has had no contact with his father for more than 10 years. Psychological evaluation showed hostility, anger toward females, and great feelings of frustration. His intelligence was below average, and his behavioral and academic records were poor. In addition, John seemed to be involved with a local youth gang, although he denied any formal association with the group. This is John's first formal petition in the family court. Previous contact was limited to an informal complaint for disorderly conduct at age 13, which was dismissed by the court's intake department. John verbalizes superficial remorse for his offenses.

To the prosecutor, John seems to be a youth with poor controls who is likely to commit future crimes. The defense attorney and court staff see the need for program planning to meet John's needs. As the judge, you recognize the seriousness of the crimes committed by John and have at your disposal a wide range of court services that might help in John's rehabilitation. No one can predict or assess John's future behavior and potential dangerousness.

What disposition would you order? (The Family Court Act lists 10 dispositional alternatives for juvenile delinquents: The most severe is commitment to training school; the others are community-level alternatives.)

THE CHILD'S RIGHT TO APPEAL

Juvenile court statutes normally restrict appeals to cases where the juvenile seeks review of a "final order" or a final judgment.[69] Paul Piersma and his associates define a final order as one that ends the litigation between two parties by determining all their rights and disposing of all the issues.[70] The **appellate process** gives the juvenile the opportunity to have the case brought before a reviewing court after it has been heard in the juvenile or family court. Today, the law does not recognize a federal constitutional right of appeal in juvenile or adult criminal cases. In other words, the U.S. Constitution does not require any state to furnish an appeal to a juvenile charged and found to be delinquent in a juvenile or family court. Consequently, appellate review of a juvenile case is a matter of statutory right in each jurisdiction. However, the majority of states do provide juveniles with some method of statutory appeal.

The appeal process was not always part of the juvenile law system. For example, J. Addison Bowman found, that in 1965, few states extended the right of appeal to juveniles.[71] According to the President's Commission on Law Enforcement and Administration of Justice, appellate review was equally limited in 1967:

> By and large, the juvenile court system has operated without appellate surveillance. . . . Two factors contribute substantially to the lack of review. The absence of counsel in the great majority of cases in the first. . . . The other important factor is the general absence of transcripts of juvenile proceedings.[72]

Even in the *Gault* case in 1967, the Supreme Court refused to review the Arizona juvenile code, which provided no appellate review in juvenile matters. It further rejected the right of a juvenile to a transcript.[73]

Today, however, most jurisdictions that provide a child with some form of appeal also provide for counsel and for the securing of a record and transcript, which are crucial to the success of any appeal. Because adult criminal defendants have both a right to counsel at their initial appeal and a right to a stenographic transcript of trial proceedings, it would violate equal protection if juveniles were denied the same rights.

Because juvenile appellate review is a matter of statutory right, each jurisdiction determines for itself what method or scope of review will be used. There are two basic methods of appeal: the direct appeal and the collateral attack. The direct appeal normally involves an appellate court review to determine whether the rulings of law and the judgment of the court based on the evidence presented at the trial were correct. This approach is laid out in Section 59 of the Uniform Juvenile Court Act of the National Conference of Commissioners on Uniform State Laws: "The appeal of the finding should be heard upon the files, records, and minutes or transcripts of the evidence of the juvenile court, giving appreciable weight to the findings of the juvenile court."[74]

A broader review procedure, which is a form of direct review, is the *de novo* review. A **trial *de novo*** is a complete retrial of the original case based on the original petition. All evidence produced at the first trial can be resubmitted, as can additional evidence. The trial *de novo* appeal is limited to only a few jurisdictions in the nation. It is usually encountered when a juvenile is originally tried in a court of very limited jurisdiction and in some administrative proceedings before masters or referees.

The second major area of review involves the collateral attack of a case. The term *collateral* refers to a secondary or indirect method of attacking a final judgment or order of the court. Instead of appealing the original juvenile trial because of errors, prejudice, or lack of evidence, collateral review uses extraordinary legal writs to challenge the lower court position. Two such procedural devices include the **writ of habeas corpus** and the **writ of certiorari.** The habeas corpus writ, known as the "Great Writ," refers to a procedure for determining the validity of a person's custody. In the context of the juvenile court, it is used to challenge the custody of a child in detention or in an institution. The writ of certiorari is an order from a higher to a lower court commanding that the case be brought forward for review. This writ is often the method by which the Supreme

Court exercises its discretionary authority to hear cases regarding constitutional issues. Even though there is no constitutional right to appeal a juvenile case and each jurisdiction provides for appeals differently, juveniles have a far greater opportunity for appellate review today than in years past.

Juvenile Sentencing

For most of the juvenile court's history, disposition was based on the presumed needs of the child. Although such critics as David Rothman and Anthony Platt have challenged the motivations of early reformers in championing rehabilitation, there is little question that the rhetoric of the juvenile court has promoted that ideal.[75] For example, Joseph Goldstein, Anna Freud, and Albert Solnit in their classic work, *Beyond the Best Interest of the Child,* say that placement of children should be based on the **least detrimental alternative** available in order to foster the child's growth and development.[76] This should be the goal whether the children are delinquents or status offenders or are neglected, abandoned, or abused.

Views of juvenile sentencing began changing in the late 1980s and early 1990s. In chapter 14, we discussed the changes in transfer policy that make it easier to waive children to adult court. These changes are evidence of concern about how to handle the chronic juvenile offender. On the other hand, we have also noted a trend to deinstitutionalize status offenders and prohibit their incarceration with delinquent youths. Yet, as we shall see below, many states have imposed requirements for greater determinacy and proportionality so that dispositions are more standardized and more punishment oriented. Some jurisdictions are even suggesting that mandatory sentences of incarceration be used for juveniles convicted of being in possession of a handgun.

DETERMINATE VERSUS INDETERMINATE SENTENCING

Traditionally, states have used the **indeterminate sentence** in juvenile court. In about half of the states, this means having the judge simply place the offender with the state department of juvenile corrections until correctional authorities consider him or her ready to return to society or until the youth reaches his or her legal majority. A preponderance of states, including Missouri, Texas, and West Virginia, consider 18 to be the age of release; others, such as Michigan and Tennessee, peg the termination age at 19; a few, including Kansas, Montana, Ohio, South Carolina, South Dakota, Utah, Virginia, and Wyoming, can retain youths until their twenty-first birthday.[77] In practice, few youths remain in custody for the entire statutory period; juveniles are usually released if their rehabilitation has been judged by the youth corrections department, judge, or parole board to have progressed satisfactorily. This practice is referred to as the **individualized treatment model**—each sentence must be tailored to the individual needs of the child.

Another form of the indeterminate sentence allows judges to specify a maximum term that can be served. For example, in Alabama, Alaska, North Dakota, and Colorado, youths can be sentenced to a maximum of not more than two years in an institution; in Maryland, New Jersey, and Pennsylvania, the maximum sentence is three years.[78] Youths may also be released from incarceration in these jurisdictions if the corrections department considers them to be rehabilitated or they reach the automatic age of termination (usually 18 or 21). In most of the 12 states that stipulate a maximum sentence, the court may extend the sentence depending on the youth's progress in the institutional facility.[79]

A number of states have changed their sentencing policies in an effort to toughen up on juvenile offenders. Some, including Arizona, Georgia, Minnesota, and California, have changed from indeterminate to determinate sentencing in juvenile court. This means sentencing juvenile offenders to a fixed term of years that must be served in its entirety. Virginia and Tennessee have enacted provisions allowing determinate commitments of youth adjudicated for certain serious offenses. Arizona, for example, allows the state juvenile corrections agency to set standards for release by creating statutory guidelines based on offense conditions that are applied during the intake process.[80] California, Colorado, Delaware, Georgia, Connecticut, and Pennsylvania are among the states that have passed laws creating **mandatory sentences** for serious juvenile offenders. For example, Delaware law provides a one-year mandatory sentence for a juvenile who commits any two felony acts during a one-year period; if a previously adjudicated delinquent commits three felonies within a three-year period, he or she receives a mandatory three-year sentence.[81] Juveniles receiving mandatory sentences are usually institutionalized for the full sentence and not eligible for early parole. Pennsylvania passed legislation in 1986 that set up a statewide depository for fingerprints and photographs of dangerous juvenile offenders and youths aged 15 to 17 who are repeat violent offenders.[82] Today, most states have passed fingerprinting statutes for juvenile offenders.[83]

New York's juvenile code gives the adult court original jurisdiction over cases involving 14- and 15-year-olds who commit serious violent felonies and over cases of 13-year-olds who commit murder.[84] If there are mitigating circumstances—for example, if the offender had only a small role in the crime—the adult court judge can waive the case back to the juvenile court. Known as New York's Juvenile Offender Law, this controversial statute reduced the age of criminal responsibility for direct prosecution of youths committing certain offenses in the adult courts and authorized lengthy periods of incarceration. In addition, New York's Designated Felony Act allows the juvenile court judge to sentence youths who commit murder, arson, or kidnapping to a sentence of five years in a juvenile institution.[85] The sentence can be renewed annually until the offender reaches age 21. For less serious felony offenses, the judge can impose a three-year sentence, renewable annually.

Probably the best-known effort to reform sentencing in the juvenile court is the state of Washington's **Juvenile Justice Reform Act of 1977.** This act created a mandatory sentencing policy requiring juveniles ages 8 to 17 who are adjudicated delinquent to be confined in an institution for a minimum time.[86] The legislative intent of the act was to make juveniles accountable for criminal behavior and to provide for punishment commensurate with the (1) age, (2) crime, and (3) prior history of the offender. Washington's tough approach to juvenile sentencing is based on the principle of "proportionality." How much time a youth must spend in confinement is established by the Juvenile Dispositions Standards Commission based on the above three criteria. The introduction of such mandatory sentencing procedures standardizes juvenile dispositions and reduces disparity in the length of sentences, according to advocates of a "get-tough" juvenile justice system. The most popular crime legislation being debated among state legislatures across the country is tougher sentences for juvenile offenders of serious and violent crime.

EVALUATING TOUGH SENTENCING LAWS

Can such changes in juvenile sentencing statutes have positive outcomes for the operation of the juvenile justice system? One reason for optimism has been the rather dramatic changes brought about in the state of Washington by the passage of the Juvenile Justice Reform Act of 1977. Research by Tom Castellano found that within two years of its passage, there was a high degree of compliance with its provisions.[87] The law has moved Washington's juvenile justice system away from informality and disparity toward the procedural regularity found in the adult system.

Castellano concludes that liberals, typically opposed to these types of changes, should be able to cheer the due process rights afforded to offenders, the proportionality that now exists in sentencing, and the fact that under the new code, status offenders no longer can be incarcerated with delinquents. In fact, he disputes the charge that the reform act is a get-tough approach to juvenile justice.

Conservatives can be equally satisfied, that under the new law, serious offenders receive sterner sentences; more than 90 percent of the serious juvenile offenders who come before the court are removed from the community, and many receive sentences ranging from two to four years.

On the other hand, not all statutory changes have had the desired effect. For instance, although New York's Juvenile Offender Law requires that juveniles accused of violent offenses be tried in criminal court and provides serious penalties comparable to those for adults, Simon Singer and David McDowall conclude that the law's aim of deterring juvenile crime has not been achieved.[88] Since the law lowered the age of criminal responsibility and included family court jurisdiction, many youths ended up receiving lighter sentences than they would have in the family court.

At the time it was enacted, the New York law was considered to be among the toughest in the nation pertaining to crimes committed by juveniles ages 13, 14, and 15. Yet, data through 1991 substantiate the findings of Singer and McDowall that indicate that more arrests under the law result in outright dismissal than in any other single disposition.[89]

The growing realization that the juvenile crime rate has stabilized may slow the tide of legislative change in juvenile justice. What is more likely is that states will continue to pass legislation making it easier to transfer youths to the adult court or giving the adult court original jurisdiction over serious cases. Thus, rather than toughening juvenile law for everyone, society may focus on the few more serious cases.

A 1990 survey of all states found that about one-third have a mixture of determinacy and indeterminacy in their sentencing statutes, while only 37 percent maintain the traditional juvenile sentencing model of little or no determinacy.[90] Thus, treatment seems to be a guiding principle in juvenile sentencing, although other purposes are clearly evident and the distinction between the juvenile and adult systems is blurring. The purpose clauses of state juvenile codes are equally divided between those that emphasize treatment, those that stress punishment, and those that seek a balanced approach.[91] As Lloyd Ohlin asks, "Is society willing to sustain the levels of repression and incarceration needed to make more limited incremental gains in crime control?"[92] If states continue to pass legislation to incarcerate some very serious offenders, will juvenile sentencing remain wedded to the *parens patriae* philosophy?

THE FUTURE OF JUVENILE SENTENCING AND SERIOUS CRIME

During the past decade, the treatment-oriented philosophy has taken a back seat to the development of more formal and punitive approaches toward juveniles charged with serious crimes. Although more than half of the states still use indefinite sentencing, the trend for the future continues to point toward more determinate and fixed sentences.

Rita Kramer, author of *At a Tender Age: Violent Youth and Juvenile Justice,* calls for swift and sure sanctions, particularly for violent and repeat offenders. According to Kramer, placing juvenile offenders in a secure institution for a definite period of time should be the response to their acts of violence.[93]

A number of prominent national organizations have also recommended the use of tougher mandatory sentences. For example, the American Bar Association has developed standards that affect the disposition process. Stanley Fisher notes that these standards point to a shift in juvenile court philosophy from the traditional approach of rehabilitation to the concept of just deserts.[94] The standards recommend that juveniles receive determinate or flat sentences without the possibility of parole, rather than the indeterminate sentences that most of them receive now.

The standards further recommend that punishment be classified into three major categories: nominal sanctions, conditional sanctions, and custodial sanctions. *Nominal sanctions* consist of reprimands, warnings, or other minor actions that do not affect the child's personal liberty. *Conditional sanctions* include probation, restitution, and counseling programs. *Custodial sanctions,* which are the most extreme, remove the juvenile from the community into a nonsecure or secure institution.[95] According to the National Conference of State Legislatures, several states have already adapted the minimum/maximum sentencing pattern often used in the adult criminal justice system that forces the offender to serve at least a minimum and up to a maximum amount of their sentence.[96]

In conclusion, the trend today is to increase severely sanctions for juvenile offenders. Juveniles face the prospect of longer sentences, mandatory minimum terms and time in adult jails or prisons, and a host of other new tough juvenile crime statutes. State legislatures have focused on the following priorities in juvenile sentencing:

- *Parental responsibility statutes.* Legislative bodies in Oregon, Illinois, Virginia, and 32 other states have enacted laws holding parents responsible for underaged drinking, graffiti damage, and drunken driving violations. Fines, community service, jail time, and mandatory parenting classes are among the list of punishments being used.[97]
- *Curfew laws.* Curfew laws are becoming commonplace in efforts to reduce delinquency. Seventy-seven percent of major U.S. cities now have curfew ordinances. During the period 1990–95, half of these cities enacted curfew legislation for the first time or updated existing laws. Many cities that have set curfew limits have also gone the exra mile to provide alternative activities for the city's youth (e.g., midnight basketball and other diversionary programs). Unfortunately, there is virtually no existing research that has explored the effects of curfew laws on the level of delinquent behavior.
- *Retributive reforms.* Retributive reforms have led to increased rates of incarceration and longer incarceration terms. The "just deserts" philosophy

is resulting in an expansion of punishment for juvenile offenders. Policymakers are legitimizing the concept of punishment for its own sake, and prosecutors are taking it as a green light to demand more severe punishments with less treatment emphasis, especially for repeat offenders.[98] Perhaps no area of juvenile justice has received more attention of late than that of reforms designed to treat juvenile offenders more like adults. For instance, Alaska, Delaware, Indiana, Louisiana, Minnesota, North Dakota, Oregon, Utah, and West Virginia have added crimes for which juveniles may, or must in some cases, be prosecuted as adults. More than a dozen states have passed laws to treat juvenile court proceedings more like those of adult courts. This includes the fingerprinting and photographing of juvenile defendants.[99]

■ *Firearm bans.* By 1995, 40 states had enacted laws outlawing gun possession by juveniles within a certain distance of a school. Enhanced penalties for crimes involving firearms in school zones, such as mandatory sentences, are being considered by many jurisdictions. Even though the federal Gun Free School Zones Act of 1990 was declared unconstitutional in 1995 on the ground that Congress lacked constitutional power to regulate gun possession because it is a local matter, such laws designed specifically to protect children are being passed at the state level.[100] This trend is illustrated in the accompanying Focus on Delinquency.

THE DEATH PENALTY FOR JUVENILES

The most controversial of all sentences, adult or juvenile, continues to be the death penalty. The execution of minor children has not been uncommon in our nation's history. Victor Streib, a law professor and leading expert on the death penalty for children, claims that about 350 juvenile offenders have been executed since 1642. This represents about 2 percent of the total of more than 18,000 executions carried out since colonial times. As of 1994, 40 persons were on death row for capital crimes committed as juveniles. Given these facts, it is not so shocking that as of 1992, there were 33 people on death row who had committed their crimes as juveniles but were waived to adult court for trial and sentencing. According to Streib, all 33 juvenile offenders on death row are male and had been convicted and sentenced to death for murder.[101]

Of the 37 states that have laws authorizing **capital punishment,** 22 allow it for crimes committed by people under 18. The U.S. Supreme Court had a chance to resolve this issue in the 1982 case of *Eddings v. Oklahoma* but refused to do so.[102] The case involved a 16-year-old boy who killed a highway patrol officer. Although the Court overturned his sentence, it did so on the ground that the trial court had failed to consider his emotional state and troubled childhood when dispensing the death penalty. The Court did not deal with the issue of whether age alone could prohibit a person from being executed. In 1988, however, the Court did prohibit the execution of persons under age 16 in the narrowly interpreted case of *Thompson v. Oklahoma.* Some justices endorsed the idea that a child should be presumed to be less responsible than an adult when he or she commits a criminal homicide. This decision left unanswered the issue of whether the Constitution prohibits the use of the death penalty for juveniles who were 16 or 17 years old when they committed their crimes.[103]

The Supreme Court finally confronted the highly emotional question in 1989 in the cases of **Wilkins v. Missouri** and **Stanford v. Kentucky.**[104] Wilkins was 16

UNITED STATES v. LOPEZ (1995)

Facts

Alfonso Lopez was a twelfth-grade student at a public high school in San Antonio, Texas, when he was charged with violating the Gun-Free School Zones Act of 1990, having been caught carrying a concealed .38 caliber handgun on school grounds. Confronted by school officials Lopez explained that he was to be paid $40 to deliver the gun to "Jason" for use in a gang war.

The Gun-Free School Zones Act made it a federal crime for any individual knowingly to possess a firearm at a place that the individual knows, or has reasonable cause to believe, is a school zone (18 USC Sec. 922 (q)). The Act defined school zone as "in or on the grounds of a public, parochial or private school, or within a distance of 1,000 feet from the grounds of a public, parochial or private school." In passing the Act, Congress relied on its constitutional authority to regulate interstate commerce conferred by the Commerce Clause (U.S. Constitution, Article I, Sec. 8, Cl. 3).

Decision

Lopez was found guilty in the federal district court and sentenced to six months in prison, two years supervised release, and a $50 special fine under the Gun-Free School Zones Act. Lopez defended his case by arguing that Congress exceeded its authority under the Commerce Clause. He appealed to the Fifth Circuit Court of Appeals, which reversed his conviction. The U.S. Supreme Court later affirmed the appellate court decision. The Court said that Congress had exceeded its authority in attempting to regulate a local activity—education—without showing a connection between bringing a firearm onto school grounds and interstate commerce.

Chief Justice William Rehnquist wrote that Congress can regulate only activity that "substantially affects" interstate commerce. He pointed out that possession of a handgun on school grounds was not a commercial activity, and therefore, the criminal statute had nothing to with commerce or any sort of economic enterprise. The Lopez case marked the first time in more than 60 years that the Supreme Court invalidated federal legislation regulating private parties on the basis of the Commerce Clause.

Significance of the Case

The Court's decision allowed Lopez to go free. Looking at the broader picture, the Court rejected the Government's argument that firearm possession on school grounds would lead to violent crime that would be costly to the economy and provide a substantial relationship to interstate commerce. Second, the Court rejected the notion that firearm possession on school grounds, by substantially disrupting the educational process, would reduce the productivity of the workforce and jeopardize the economy. The Court said that to agree to these ideas would convert Congress's power to regulate interstate commerce into a general police power, disrupting the unique relationship between the federal, state, and local governments.

By enforcing limits on the Commerce Clause, the Court moved to slow down the process of federalizing the criminal law. Nevertheless, it is important to keep in mind that this was a close decision (a 5-4 majority). Justice Stephen Breyer, in his dissent, insisted that educational achievement is intimately connected to economic success and that education is itself an enormous economic enterprise. He, therefore, reasoned that Congress had not violated its powers under the Commerce Clause in adopting the Gun-Free School Zones statute. In light of the Breyer dissent and the continuing arguments over whether state criminal offenses should be made violations of federal law, the true significance of the Lopez case and the proper interpretation of the Commerce Clause remain uncertain.

Because gun possession is common for serious juvenile offenders, many states have adopted both statutes prohibiting the possession of handguns by juveniles and gun-free school zone laws. These laws are state laws, thus they are not in conflict with the Lopez decision, which had invalidated an act of Congress under the federal constitution.

Source: 115 S.Ct. 1625 (1995).

when he committed murder; Stanford was 17. The constitutional question raised by these two cases is basically the same as in the *Thompson* case: At what age does the Eighth Amendment ban the death penalty as punishment, no matter what the crime? Critics of the death penalty believed that there was a consensus against executing young people in the United States. Supporters of capital punishment argued that juveniles older than age 16 should be held fully responsible for murder. The Supreme Court concluded that states were free to impose the death penalty for murderers who committed their crimes while age 16 or 17. According to the majority opinion, written by Justice Antonin Scalia, society has not formed a consensus that the execution of such minors constitutes a cruel and unusual punishment in violation of the Eighth Amendment.

Today, the death penalty stands for people who have committed capital crimes while still under the age of majority, and a number of executions of such offenders have already taken place. Of the 137 juvenile death sentences imposed between 1973 and 1995, 9 have been carried out, 40 remain in effect, and 88 have been reversed.[105] (It should be noted, however, that by the time of their execution, the offenders had passed through their teens, as the trial and appeal process consumed many years.)

Those who oppose the death penalty for children, led by Streib, find that it has little deterrent effect on youngsters who are impulsive and do not have a realistic view of the destructiveness of their misdeeds or their consequences. Streib and his associates maintain that the execution of a person who is a child at the time of the crime is cruel and unusual punishment because (1) the condemnation of children makes no measurable contribution to the legitimate goals of punishment, (2) condemning any minor to death violates contemporary standards of decency, (3) the capacity of the young for change, growth, and rehabilitation makes the death penalty particularly harsh and inappropriate, and (4) both legislative attitudes and public opinion reject juvenile executions.[106] Supporters of the death penalty hold that people, regardless of their age, can form criminal intent and therefore should be responsible for their actions. If the death penalty is legal for adults, they argue, then it can also be used for children who commit serious crimes.

CONFIDENTIALITY IN JUVENILE PROCEEDINGS

Along with the rights of juveniles at adjudication and disposition, the issue of **confidentiality** in juvenile proceedings has also received attention in recent years. The debate centers around whether the practice of restricting information in juvenile court proceedings in the interest of protecting the privacy of juveniles is preferable to the current cry for open proceedings that might increase public exposure for juveniles.[107] Confidentiality in the juvenile court deals with two areas: (1) open versus closed hearings and (2) privacy of juvenile records. Considered by many to be a basic tenet of juvenile justice philosophy, the issue of complete confidentiality has become moot in some respects as many legislatures have broadened access to juvenile records.

OPEN VERSUS CLOSED HEARINGS

Generally, juvenile trials are closed to the public and press, and the names of the offenders are kept secret. The Supreme Court has ruled on the issue of privacy in three important decisions. In *Davis v. Alaska,* the Court concluded that any injury resulting from the disclosure of a juvenile's record is outweighed by the right to completely cross-examine an adverse witness.[108] The *Davis* case involved an effort to obtain testimony from a juvenile probationer who was a witness in a criminal trial. After the prosecutor was granted a court order preventing the defense from making any reference to the juvenile's record, the Supreme Court reversed the state court, claiming that a juvenile's interest in confidentiality was secondary to the constitutional right to confront adverse witnesses.

The *Davis* case was a decision of evidentiary significance, whereas the decisions in two subsequent cases, **Oklahoma Publishing Co. v. District Court** and **Smith v. Daily Mail Publishing Co.**, sought to balance juvenile privacy with freedom of the press. In the *Oklahoma* case, the Supreme Court ruled that a state court was not allowed to prohibit the publication of information obtained in an open juvenile proceeding.[109] The case involved an 11-year-old boy suspected of homicide who appeared at a detention hearing and of whom photographs were taken and published in local newspapers. When the local district court prohibited further disclosure, the publishing company claimed that the court order was a restraint in violation of the First Amendment, and the Supreme Court agreed. The *Smith* case involved the discovery and subsequent publication by news reporters of the identity of a juvenile suspect in violation of a state statute prohibiting publication. The Supreme Court, however, declared the statute unconstitutional because it believed that the state's interest in protecting the child's identity was not of such a magnitude as to justify the use of such a statute.[110] Therefore, if newspapers lawfully obtain pictures or names of juveniles, they may publish them. Based on these decisions, it appears that the Supreme Court favors the constitutional rights of the press over the right to privacy of the juvenile offender.

None of the decisions, however, gave the press complete access to juvenile trials. Today, some jurisdictions still bar the press from juvenile proceedings unless they show at a hearing that their presence will not harm the youth. In other words, when states follow a *parens patriae* philosophy, ordinarily the public and press are excluded. However, the court has discretion to permit interested parties to observe the hearings.

PRIVACY OF JUVENILE RECORDS

For most of the twentieth century, juvenile records were kept confidential by case law, or statute. The general rule was that juvenile court records—both legal and social—were considered confidential and thus inaccessible.[111] Today, however, the record itself or information contained in it can be opened by court order in many jurisdictions on the basis of statutory exception. The following groups can ordinarily gain access to juvenile records: (1) law enforcement personnel; (2) the child's attorney; (3) the parents or guardians; (4) military personnel; (5) and public agencies, such as schools, court-related organizations, and correctional institutions.

Many states have enacted laws authorizing a central repository for juvenile arrest records. Some states allow a juvenile adjudication for a criminal act, such as rape, to be used as evidence in a subsequent adult criminal proceeding for the same act to show predisposition or criminal nature.[112] In addition, a juvenile's records may be used during the disposition or sentencing stage of an adult criminal trial in some states.[113] A major problem in dealing with juvenile offenders is the lack of information about serious crimes committed before the age of 18. Knowledge of a defendant's juvenile record may help prosecutors and judges to determine appropriate sentencing for offenders ages 18-24, the age group most likely to be involved in violent crime.

Today, most states recognize the importance of juvenile records in sentencing. Many first-time adult offenders committed numerous crimes as juveniles, and evidence of these crimes may not be available or relevant to sentencing for the adult offenses unless states pass such statutes allowing access. To address this problem, the Department of Justice recently authorized the FBI to accept juvenile records from the states for inclusion in the national criminal records system provided by the National Crime Information Center.[114] States are urged to enact statutes allowing for the consideration of juvenile convictions in adult sentencing. According to such experts as Ira Schwartz, the need for confidentiality to protect juveniles is far less than the need to open up the courts to public scrutiny and accountability.[115] The problem of maintaining confidentiality of juvenile records will become more acute in the future as computerization makes them both more durable and accessible.[116]

In conclusion, virtually every state provides prosecutors and judges access to the juvenile arrest and disposition records of adult offenders. There is a great diversity, however, among the states regarding the provisions for the collection and retention of juvenile records and such information as finger-printing.[117]

SUMMARY

This chapter described two major aspects of the juvenile justice system: adjudication and disposition. Most jurisdictions have a bifurcated juvenile code system that separates the adjudication hearing from the dispositional hearing. Juveniles alleged to be delinquent, as well as children in need of supervision, have virtually all the rights given a criminal defendant at trial—except possibly the right to a trial by jury. In addition, juvenile proceedings are generally closed to the public.

The types of dispositional orders that the juvenile court gives include dismissal, fine, probation, and institutionalization. The use of such dispositions has not curtailed the rising rate of juvenile crime, however. As a result, legislatures and national commissions have begun to take a tougher position with regard to the sentencing of some juvenile offenders. The traditional notion of rehabilitation and treatment as the proper goals for disposition is now being questioned, and some jurisdictions have replaced it with proportionality and determinacy in sentencing procedures. However, many juvenile codes do require that the court consider the "least restrictive" alternative before removing a juvenile from the home.

The predisposition report is the primary informational source for assisting the court in making a judgment about a child's care and treatment.

Once a juvenile is found delinquent or in need of supervision, the juvenile court is empowered through the dispositional process to make fundamental changes in the child's life. In recent years, a number of states have made drastic changes in juvenile sentencing law, moving away from the pure indeterminate sentence and embracing more structured, determinate forms of disposition. If there is any chance for juvenile crime to be reduced in the future, it may well depend on fair, just, and effective disposition. Minnesota took an unusual approach to juvenile crime in 1995. It passed a law allowing judges to hand down double sentences to children found guilty of serious crimes: a juvenile sentence that remains in effect until the defendant turns 21 and a suspended adult sentence that can be reinstated if the juvenile has any further brushes with the law.[118]

Finally, many state statutes require that juvenile hearings be closed and that the privacy of juvenile records be maintained to protect the child from public scrutiny and to provide a greater opportunity for rehabilitation. But this approach may be inconsistent with the public's recent interest in taking a closer look at the juvenile justice system.

KEY TERMS

juvenile court
jurisdiction
status offenders
juvenile prosecutor
In re Gault
In re Winship
judge
Missouri Plan
kiddie court
National Council of Juvenile and
  Family Court Judges
defense attorneys
guardian *ad litem*

Court Appointed Special Advocates
  (CASA)
public defender
adjudication
McKeiver v. Pennsylvania
disposition
predispositional investigation
appellate process
trial *de novo*
writ of habeus corpus
writ of certiorari
least detrimental alternative

indeterminate sentence
individualized treatment model
mandatory sentences
Juvenile Justice Reform Act of 1977
Wilkins v. Missouri
Stanford v. Kentucky
capital punishment
United States v. Lopez
confidentiality
*Oklahoma Publishing Co. v. District
  Court*
Smith v. Daily Mail Publishing Co.

QUESTIONS FOR DISCUSSION

1. Discuss and identify the major participants in the juvenile adjudication process. What are each person's roles and responsibilities in the course of a juvenile trial?

2. The criminal justice system in the United States is based on the adversarial process. Does the same adversary principle apply in the juvenile justice system?

3. Children have certain constitutional rights at adjudication, such as the right to an attorney and the right to confront and cross-examine witnesses. But they do not have the right to a trial by jury. Should juvenile offenders have a constitutional right to a jury trial? Should each state make that determination? Discuss the legal decision that addresses this issue.

4. What is the point of obtaining a predisposition report in the juvenile court? Is it of any value in cases where the child is released to the community? Does it have a significant value in serious juvenile crime cases?

5. The standard of proof in juvenile adjudication is to show that the child is guilty beyond a reasonable doubt. Explain the meaning of this standard of proof in the American judicial system.

6. Should states adopt "get-tough" sentences in juvenile justice or adhere to the individualized treatment model?

7. Do you agree with the principle of imposing the death penalty on juveniles found to have committed certain capital crimes?

NOTES

1. Barry Krisberg, *The Juvenile Court: Reclaiming the Vision* (San Francisco: National Council on Crime and Delinquency, 1988); Edward Humes, *No Matter How Loud I Shout: A Year in the Life of Juvenile Court* (New York: Simon and Schuster, 1995).

2. Howard N. Snyder, Melissa H. Sickmund, Ellen H. Nimick, Terrence A. Finnegan, Dennis P. Sullivan, Rowen S. Poole, and Nancy J. Tierney, *Juvenile Court Statistics, 1989* (Pittsburgh, Pa.: National Center for Juvenile Justice, 1992), pp. 7, 45.

3. National Advisory Commission on Criminal Justice Standards and Goals, *Report of the Task Force on Juvenile Justice and Delinquency Prevention* (Washington, D.C.: U.S. Department of Justice, Law Enforcement Assistance Administration, 1973), p. 277.

4. See N.Y. Fam. Ct. Act 712 (1982).

5. See Samuel Davis, *The Rights of Juveniles,* 2nd ed. (New York: Clark Boardman, 1984, 1992); see also Mark Soler, James Bell, Elizabeth Jameson, Carole Shauffer, Alice Shotton, and Loren Warboys, *Representing the Child Client* (New York: Matthew Bender, 1992).

6. *Lamb v. Brown,* 456 F.2d 18 (1972).

7. Mass. Gen. Laws Ann. Ch. 119, 53 (1979).

8. Md.Cts. & Jud.Proc. Code Ann. 3—804(d)(1)(4) (1980).

9. Fla. Stat. Ann. 39.025(5)(c)(Supp. 1982); Fla. Stat. Ann. 39.04 (2)(E)(4) (Supp. 1981).

10. N.Y. Fam.Ct.Act 73(1)(C) and 732(c) (McKinney Supp. 1979).

11. 359 Mass. 550 (1971); 322 A.2d 58 (1975).

12. State ex rel. *Harris v. Calendine,* 33 S.E.2d 318 (1977).

13. *O. W. v. Bird,* 461 So.2d 967 (Fla.Dist.Ct.App. 1984); *In re Michael G.,* 214 Cal.Rptr. 755 App. Ct. 1 (1985).

14. *In re A,* 130 N.J.Super.Ct. 138, 325 A.2d 837 (1974).

15. U.S. Department of Justice, *Prosecution in the Juvenile Courts* (Washington, D.C.: U.S. Government Printing Office, 1973), p. 9.

16. *Kent v. United States,* 383 U.S. 541, 86 S.Ct. 1045, 16 L.Ed.2d 84 (1966); *In re Gault* 387 U.S. 1, 87 S.Ct. 1428, 18 L.Ed.2d 527 (1967); *In re Winship,* 397 U.S. 358, 90 S.Ct. 1068, 25 L.Ed.2d 368 (1970).

17. American Bar Association, *Standards Relating to Juvenile Prosecution* (Cambridge, Mass.: Ballinger, 1977), p. 13; Robert Shepard, Jr. "The Prosecutor in the Juvenile Court," *ABA Journal on Criminal Justice* 32:36–40 (1968).

18. *State v. Grayer,* 191 Neb. 5231 (1974).

19. John Laub and Bruce MacMurray, "Increasing the Prosecutor's Role in Juvenile Court: Exceptions and Realities" (Unpublished research report, Boston: Northeastern University, 1987).

20. National District Attorneys Association, *Prosecution Standard 19.2, Juvenile Delinquency* (Alexandria, Va.: NDAA, 1992).

21. James Shine and Dwight Price, "Prosecutor & Juvenile Justice: New Roles and Perspectives," in Ira Schwartz, ed., *Juvenile Justice and Public Policy* (New York: Lexington Books, 1992), pp. 101–33.

22. F. Eastman, "Procedures and Due Process," *Juvenile and Family Court Journal* 22 35:36 (1983).

23. Yeheskel Hasenfeld and Paul Cheung, "The Juvenile Court and a People-Processing Organization: A Political Economy Perspective," *American Journal of Sociology* 90:801–24 (1985).

24. Leonard P. Edwards, "The Juvenile Court and the Role of the Juvenile Court Judge," *Juvenile and Family Court Journal* 43:3–45 (1992).

25. Sari Escovitz with Fred Kurland and Nan Gold, *Judicial Selection and Tenure* (Chicago: American Judicature Society, 1974), pp. 3–16.

26. National Council of Juvenile and Family Court Judges, "Juvenile and Family Justice," *Juvenile and Family Court Journal* 3:15 (1992).

27. National Council of Juvenile and Family Court Judges *Annual Report, 1991* (Pittsburgh, Pa.: National Center for Juvenile Justice, 1991).

28. *Powell v. Alabama* 287 U.S. 45, 53 S.Ct. 55, 77, L.Ed.2d 158 (1932); *Gideon v. Wainwright* 372 U.S. 335, 83 S.Ct. 792, 9 L.Ed.2d 799 (1963); *Argersinger v. Hamlin* 407 U.S. 25, 92 S.Ct. 2006, 32 L.Ed.2d 530 (1972).

29. American Bar Association, *Standard Relating to Counsel for Private Parties* (Cambridge, Mass.: Ballinger, 1977).

30. Howard Davidson, "The Guardian ad Litem: An Important Approach to the Protection of Children," *Children Today* 10:23 (1981); Daniel Golden, "Who Guards the Children?" *Boston Globe Magazine,* 27 December 1992, p. 12.

31. Eastman, "Procedures and Due Process," p. 32.

32. Office of Juvenile Justice and Delinquency Prevention, *CASA: Court Appointed Special Advocate for Children,* Juvenile Justice Bulletin (Washington, D.C.: Department of Justice, 1992).

33. S. H. Clarke and G. G. Koch, "Juvenile Court: Therapy or Crime Control and Do Lawyers Make a Difference?" *Law and Society Review* 14:263–308 (1980); David Duffee and Larry Siegel, "The Organization Man: Legal Counsel in Juvenile Court," *Criminal Law Bulletin* 7:544–53 (1971).

34. Joseph Sanborn, "The Defense Attorney's Role in Juvenile Court: Must Justice or Treatment (or Both) Be Compromised?" (Paper presented at the Academy of Criminal Justice Sciences, St. Louis, Mo., March 15–19, 1987), p. 32; Randy Hertz, Martin Guggenheim, and Anthony Amsterdam, *Trial Manual for Defense Attorneys in Juvenile Court* (Chicago: American Law Institute-American Bar Association, 1991).

35. Sanborn, "The Defense Attorney's Role in Juvenile Court," p. 8.

36. Jane Knitzer, *Law Guardians in New York State* (New York: New York State Bar Association, 1985); David Hechler, "Lawyers for Children: No Experience Necessary," *Justice for Children* 1:14–15 (1985).

37. Sanford Fox, *Juvenile Courts* (St. Paul, Minn.: West, 1984), p. 162.

38. Barry C. Feld, "The Right to Counsel in Juvenile Court: An Empirical Study of When Lawyers Appeal and the Difference They Make," *Journal of Criminal Law and Criminology* 79:1187–1346 (1989).

39. Ibid., pp. 1217–18; for concern about the availability of counsel in the adult courts, see also Stephen Bright, Stephen Kinnard, and David Webster, "Keeping Gideon from Being Blown Away," *Criminal Justice Journal of the American Bar Association* 4:10–14 (1990).

40. Feld, "The Right to Counsel in Juvenile Court," p. 1318.

41. Ibid., p. 1346.

42. Steven Clark and Gary Koch, "Juvenile Court: Therapy or Crime Control and Do Lawyers Make a Difference?" *Law and Society Review* 14:263–308 (1980); David Aday, "Court Structure, Defense Attorney Use, and

Juvenile Court Decisions," *Sociological Quarterly* 27:107–19 (1986); James Walter and Susan Ostrander, "An Observational Study of a Juvenile Court," *Juvenile and Family Court Journal* 33:53–69 (1982); Barry Feld, "*In re Gault* Revisited: A Cross-State Comparison of the Right to Counsel in Juvenile Court," *Crime and Delinquency* 34:392–424 (1988).

43. Barry C. Feld, "The Punitive Juvenile Court and the Quality of Procedural Justice: Dysfunctions between Rhetoric and Reality," *Crime and Delinquency* 36:443–65 (1990).

44. American Bar Association, *A Call for Justice—An Assessment of Access to Counsel and Quality of Representation in Delinquency Proceedings* (Washington, D.C.: ABA Juvenile Justice Center, 1995).

45. *The Boston Globe,* "Juveniles Go to Court Unrepresented," 1 January 1996, p. 20.

46. Jeffrey Fagan, Ellen Slaughter, and Eliot Hartstone, "Blind Justice? The Impact of Race on the Juvenile Justice Process," *Criminal Delinquency* 33:224–58 (1987).

47. Edmund McGarrell, "Trends in Racial Disproportionality in Juvenile Court Processing: 1985–1989," *Crime and Delinquency* 39:29–48 (1993).

48. Institute of Judicial Administration, American Bar Association Joint Commission on Juvenile Justice Standards, *Standards Relating to Adjudication* (Cambridge, Mass.: Ballinger, 1980).

49. Joseph B. Sanborn, Jr., "The Right to a Public Jury Trial—A Need for Today's Juvenile Court," *Judicature* 76:230–38 (1993).

50. *In re Gault,* 387 U.S. 1, 87 S.Ct. 1428 (1967), 19.

51. *Kent v. United States,* 383 U.S. 541, 86 S.Ct. 1045 (1966).

52. *In re Gault,* 387 U.S. 1, 91 S.Ct. 1976 (1967).

53. Linda Szymanski, *Juvenile Delinquents' Right to Counsel* (Pittsburgh, Pa.: National Center for Juvenile Justice, 1988).

54. *In re Winship,* 397 U.S. 358, 90 S.Ct. 1068 (1970).

55. *McKeiver v. Pennsylvania,* 403 U.S. 528, 91 S.Ct. 1976 (1971).

56. Adrienne E. Volenik, *Checklist for Use in Juvenile Delinquency Proceedings* (Washington, D.C.: American Bar Association, 1985), p. 42.

57. See, generally, R. T. Powell, "Disposition Concepts," *Juvenile and Family Court Journal* 34:7–18 (1983).

58. Paul Piersma, Jeanette Ganousis, and Prudence Kramer, "The Juvenile Court: Current Problems, Legislative Proposals, and a Model Act," *St. Louis University Law Review* 20:43 (1976); Robert Shepherd, Jr., "Preparing for the Juvenile Disposition," *American Bar Association Criminal Justice Journal* 7:35–36 (1993).

59. Lindsay Arthur, "Status Offenders Need a Court of Last Resort," *Boston University Law Review* 57:63–64 (1977).

60. Sanford Fox, *Juvenile Courts in a Nutshell* (St. Paul, Minn.: West, 1984), p. 221.

61. Mass.Gen.Laws Chap. 119, 57.

62. *Kent v. United States,* 383 U.S. 541, 86 S.Ct. 1045 (1966).

63. National Advisory Commission on Criminal Justice Standards and Goals, *Report of the Task Force on Juvenile Justice and Delinquency Prevention* (Washington, D.C.: U.S. Government Printing Office, 1976), p. 445.

64. See Shepherd, "Preparing for the Juvenile Disposition," p. 36.

65. This section is adapted from Jack Haynes and Eugene Moore, "Particular Dispositions," *Juvenile and Family Court Journal* 34:41–48 (1983); see also Grant Grissom, "Dispositional Authority and the Future of the Juvenile Justice System," *Juvenile and Family Court Journal* 42:25–34 (1991).

66. Criminal Justice Program of National Conference of State Legislatures, *Legal Dispositions and Confinement Policies for Delinquent Youth* (Denver: National Conference of State Legislatures, July 1988), p. 3; American Bar Association Institute of Judicial Administration Standards on Juvenile Justice, *Standards Relating to Dispositions* (Cambridge, Mass.: Ballinger Press, 1977), p. 2.1.

67. Ibid., p. 129.

68. Barry Krisberg, Elliot Currie, and David Onek, "What Works with Juvenile Offenders," *American Bar Association Journal on Criminal Justice,* 10:20–24 (1995).

69. Fox, *Juvenile Courts in a Nutshell,* pp. 254–55.

70. Paul Piersma, Jeanette Ganousis, Adrienne E. Volenik, Harry F. Swanger, and Patricia Connell, *Law and Tactics in Juvenile Cases* (Philadelphia: American Law Institute-American Bar Association, Committee on Continuing Education, 1977), p. 397.

71. J. Addison Bowman, "Appeals from Juvenile Courts," *Crime and Delinquency Journal* 11:63–77 (1965).

72. President's Commission on Law Enforcement and Administration of Justice, Task Force Report, *Juvenile Delinquency and Youth Crime* (Washington, D.C.: U.S. Government Printing Office, 1967), p. 115.

73. *In re Gault,* 387 U.S. 1 87 S.Ct. 1428 (1967).

74. National Conference of Commissioners on Uniform State Laws, *Uniform Juvenile Court Act,* 59 (Philadelphia: American Law Institute, 1968).

75. Anthony Platt, *The Child Savers: The Invention of Delinquency* (Chicago: University of Chicago Press, 1969); David Rothman, *Conscience and Convenience: The Asylum and the Alternative in Progressive America* (Boston: Little, Brown, 1980).

76. Joseph Goldstein, Anna Freud, and Albert Solnit, *Beyond the Best Interests of the Child* (New York: Free Press, 1973).

77. Martin Forst, Bruce Fisher, and Robert Coates, "Indeterminate and Determinate Sentencing of Juvenile Delinquents: A National Survey of Approaches to Commitment and Release Decision Making," *Juvenile and Family Court Journal* 36:1–12 (1985).

78. Ibid., p. 7.

79. Ibid., p. 9.

80. Ibid.

81. Del.Code Ann. Title 10, 937(c) (1977).

82. "Pennsylvania to Build Central Data Base of Juvenile Records," *Criminal Justice Newsletter,* 16 January 1987, p. 1.

83. Neal Miller, State Laws on Prosecutors' and Judges' Use of Juvenile Records National Institute of Justice–Research in Brief (Washington, D.C.: U.S. Dept of Justice, 1995). pp. 2–3.

84. N.Y.Fam.Ct.Act 753 (1978); also see New York State Laws of 1976, Chap. 878.

85. Ibid., 753a (1978).

86. Washington Juvenile Justice Reform Act of 1977, Chap. 291; Wash. Rev.Code Ann. Title 9A, Sec. 1–91 (1977).

87. Thomas Castellano, "The Justice Model in the Juvenile Justice System: Washington State's Experience" (Paper presented at the Academy of Criminal Justice Sciences, St. Louis, Mo., March 15–18, 1987).

88. Simon Singer and David McDowall, "Criminalizing Delinquency: The Deterrent Effects of NYJO Law," *Law and Society Review* 22:Sections 21–37 (1988).

89. New York State Division for Youth, *Research Focus on Youth-Juvenile Offenders,* Vol. 2, No. 1 (1992).

90. Texas Youth Commission, *Juvenile Sentencing in the United States—A Survey* (Austin: Texas Youth Commission, 1991).

91. Linda Szymanski, *Juvenile Code Purpose Clauses* (Pittsburgh, Pa.: National Center for Juvenile Justice), 1991.

92. Lloyd Ohlin, "The Future of Juvenile Justice," *Crime and Delinquency* 29:467 (1983).

93. Rita Kramer, *At a Tender Age: Violent Youth and Juvenile Justice* (New York: Holt, 1988); idem, "Juvenile Justice Is Delinquent," *The Wall Street Journal,* 27 May 1992, p. 34.

94. Stanley Fisher, "The Dispositional Process under the Juvenile Justice Standards Project," *Boston University Law Review* 57:732 (1977).

95. Criminal Justice Program of the National Conference of State Legislatures, *Legal Dispositions and Confinement Policies for Delinquent Youth,* p. 5.

96. *U.S. News and World Report,* "Making Parents Pay—Parental Responsibility," 12 June 1995, p. 42.

97. William Ruefle and Kenneth Reynolds, "Curfews and Delinquency in Major American Cities," *Crime and Delinquency* 41:347–61 (1995); Alexander Marketos, *The Constitutionality of Juvenile Curfews,* Vol. 40, 17–30 (1995).

98. Gordon Bazemore and Mark Umbreit, "Rethinking the Sanctioning Function in Juvenile Court," "Retributive or Restorative Responses to Juvenile Crime," *Crime and Delinquency* 41:296–316 (1995).

99. "Crime and Sentencing State Enactments 1995, and Juvenile Crime and Justice State Enactments, 1995," *National Conference of State Legislatures* (Denver: NCLS, 1995).

100. David Stewart, "Back to the Commerce Clause," *American Bar Association Journal* 81:46–48 (1995).

101. Victor Streib, *Death Penalty for Juveniles* (Bloomington: Indiana University Press, 1987); Paul Reidinger, "The Death Row Kids," *American Bar Association Journal* (April 1989):78; Victor Streib, *The Juvenile Death Penalty Today: Present Death Row Inmates under Juvenile Death Sentences* (Cleveland: Cleveland State University, 25 August 1992).

102. *Eddings v. Oklahoma,* 455 U.S. 104 (1982). 102 S.Ct. 869.

103. Steven Gerstein, "The Constitutionality of Executing Juvenile Offenders, *Thompson v. Oklahoma,*" *Criminal Law Bulletin* 24:91–98 (1988); *Thompson v. Oklahoma,* 108 S.Ct. 2687 (1988).

104. 109 S.Ct. 2969 (1989); for a recent analysis of the *Wilkins* and *Stanford* cases, see the note in "*Stanford v. Kentucky* and *Wilkins v. Missouri*—Juveniles, Capital Crime, and Death Penalty," *Criminal Justice Journal* 11:240–66 (1989).

105. Victor Streib, "The Juvenile Death Penalty Today—A Report," (Cleveland, Ohio: Cleveland Marshall College of Law), 1995.

106. Victor Streib, "Excluding Juveniles from New York's Impendent Death Penalty," *Albany Law Review* 54:625–79 (1990).

107. Paul R. Kfoury, *Children before the Court: Reflection on Legal Issues Affecting Minors* (Boston: Butterworth, 1987), p. 55.

108. *Davis v. Alaska,* 415 U.S. 308 (1974). 94 S.Ct. 1105.

109. *Oklahoma Publishing Co. v. District Court,* 430 U.S. 97 (1977). 97 S.Ct. 1045.

110. *Smith v. Daily Mail Publishing Co.,* 443 U.S. 97 (1977). 99 S.Ct. 2667.

111. Linda Szymanski, *Confidentiality of Juvenile Court Records* (Pittsburgh, Pa.: National Center for Juvenile Justice, 1989).

112. *Houser v. Georgia,* 326 S.E. 2d 513 (1985).

113. *Hayden v. South Carolina,* 322 S.E.2d 14 (1984).

114. "Combatting Violent Crime—Providing for Use of Juvenile Offense Records in Adult Sentencing, *Criminal Law Reporter,* 12 August 1992.

115. Ira M. Schwartz, *(In) Justice for Juveniles: Rethinking the Best Interests of the Child* (Lexington, Mass.: D.C. Heath, 1989), p. 172.

116. See the case of *Alonzo M. v. City Dept. of Probation,* 532 N.E. 2d 1254 (1988), where a New York state statute forbade any reference, even to the family court, of charges that were not proven or were dismissed.

117. *National Institute of Justice Update,* State Laws on Prosecutors' and Judges' Use of Juvenile Records (Washington, D.C.: Office of Justice Programs, 1995).

118. Tommy Sangehompuphen, "Law in Minnesota Lets Judges Give Juveniles Double Sentences," *The Wall Street Journal,* 21 August 1995, p. A12.

PART SIX

JUVENILE CORRECTIONS

Despite efforts to decarcerate as many juveniles as possible, it sometimes becomes necessary to institutionalize youths who need care, custody, and control. A variety of methods have been developed to meet these goals, including community-based and secure treatment programs. Over the years there has been a massive effort to remove non-serious offenders from secure institutions and place them in small, community-based facilities. Yet thousands of youngsters are still sent to secure, prison-like facilities each year.

Children in custody have become an American dilemma. Many incarcerated adult felons report that they were institutionalized as youths. Severe punishment seems to have little deterrent effect on teenagers—if anything, it may prepare them for a life of adult criminality. The juvenile justice system is caught between the futility of punishing juveniles and the public's demand that something be done about serious juvenile crime. Even though the nation seems to be in the midst of a punishment cycle, juvenile justice experts continue to press for judicial fairness, rehabilitation, and innovative programs for juvenile offenders.

The two chapters in Part VI describe the correctional treatment of juveniles in the community and in custody. Both approaches seek "the best interest of the child" and "the protection of the community." Although sometimes contradictory, these two major positions dominate the dispositional process.

Chapter 16 discusses efforts to treat juveniles while they remain in society. The most common community disposition employed by the juvenile court is probation. Theoretically, its goal is to rehabilitate the juvenile offender by treatment, guidance, and supplementary programs while the child remains in the community.

Chapter 17 reviews the history and practices of the juvenile institution and discusses efforts to rehabilitate youths in custody. Most secure institutions are not equipped to provide successful treatment for serious juvenile offenders. They often have limited treatment and educational services, as well as antiquated physical plants. One can understand why the training school is under constant judicial scrutiny.

Both chapters review current data on juvenile programs that provide immediate intervention and appropriate sanctions for delinquent youth. Today, a system of graduated sanctions is the recommended mechanism for obtaining treatment and accountability for delinquent offenders in need of court supervision and placement out of the home.

By reading these chapters you should be able to develop an understanding of how the juvenile justice system deals with children who need treatment and present a danger to themselves and others.

CHAPTER SIXTEEN

JUVENILE PROBATION AND COMMUNITY TREATMENT

INTRODUCTION

After adjudication, the treatment needs of youths found to be either delinquents or status offenders are evaluated by court personnel. Because prevailing juvenile court philosophy demands that young people be subject to the least restrictive disposition alternative possible, the treatment evaluation usually results in a period of community-based corrections.

Community treatment refers to a wide variety of efforts to provide care, protection, and treatment for juveniles in need. These efforts include probation, a variety of treatment services such as social casework, group work, the use of volunteers in probation, as well as **restitution** and other appropriate programs. The term *community treatment* also refers generally to the use of nonsecure and noninstitutional residences, such as foster homes, small group homes, boarding schools or semi-institutional cottage living programs, forestry camps or outdoor camps, and nonresidential programs where youths remain in their own homes and receive counseling, education, family assistance, diagnostic services, case-work services, or vocational training. Parole (aftercare; discussed in chapter 17) is often considered an extension of community treatment. In a broader sense, community treatment includes preventive programs, such as street work with antisocial gangs or early identification and treatment of predelinquents. Such programs are discussed in chapters 9, 10, and 11.

This chapter discusses the concept of community treatment as a dispositional alternative for juveniles who have violated the law and who have been found delinquent by the juvenile court. Their hope for rehabilitation and the hope of society for resolving the problems of juvenile crime lie in the use of community treatment programs. Such programs are generally preferable to training schools because they are smaller, operate in a community setting, and offer creative approaches to treating the juvenile offender. Traditional institutions, on the other hand, are costly to operate and offer limited services.

This chapter begins with a detailed discussion of probation. It examines new and important approaches for providing effective probation services to juvenile offenders. Next, it reviews restitution, which is being used in many jurisdictions to supplement probation supervision. It then traces the development of alternatives to incarceration, including community-based, nonsecure treatment programs. Juvenile court judges generally have considerable latitude regarding the use of the various community-based dispositional alternatives, and this chapter focuses on these programs. Lastly, this chapter reviews studies of the best-structured community-based programs that have proven to be more effective than incarceration.

JUVENILE PROBATION

Although it has many meanings, **probation** usually refers to a legal disposition of nonpunitive type for delinquent youths and those in need of supervision, emphasizing maintenance in the community and treatment without incarceration. Probation is the primary form of community treatment used by the juvenile justice system. The juvenile is placed and maintained in the community under the supervision of a duly authorized officer of the court. The term *probation* also denotes a status or process whereby the juvenile on probation is subject to rules that must be followed and conditions that must be met in order for him or her to remain in the community. Probation often refers to an organizational structure—a probation department (either an independent agency or one attached to a court) that manages, supervises, and treats juveniles and carries out investigations for the court.

Juvenile probation is based on the idea that the juvenile offender is not generally dangerous to the community and has a better chance of being rehabilitated within the community. Advocates of probation and community treatment suggest that the alternative—incarceration—can force juveniles to become further involved in antisocial behavior. Probation provides the child with the opportunity to be closely supervised by trained personnel who can help him or her reestablish forms of acceptable behavior in a community setting.

Probation is a desirable disposition in appropriate cases because (1) it maximizes the liberty of the individual while at the same time vindicating the authority of the law and effectively protecting the public from further violations of law; (2) it promotes the rehabilitation of the offender by maintaining normal community contacts; (3) it avoids the negative and frequently stultifying effects of confinement, which often severely and unnecessarily complicate the reintegration of the offender into the community; and (4) it greatly reduces the financial cost to the public of an effective correctional system.[1]

Because probation is a legal disposition, only a judge can order it. Probation exists in two forms. One is a direct order of probation for such a time and under such conditions as the judge deems proper. The other involves ordering the juvenile to be committed to an institution or department of youth services and then suspending the order and placing him or her on probation. In the majority of jurisdictions, probation is a direct order that is exercised under wide statutory discretion. In particular, the conditions to be followed during the probationary period are subject to the court's discretion.

THE NATURE OF PROBATION

A probation sentence involves a contract between the court and the juvenile. The court promises to hold a period of institutionalization in abeyance; the juvenile promises to adhere to a set of rules or conditions mandated by the court. If the rules are violated, and especially if the juvenile commits another offense, the probation may be revoked. In that case, the contract between the court and the child is terminated, and the original commitment order may be enforced. The rules of probation vary, but they most typically involve such conditions as attending school or work, keeping regular hours, remaining in the jurisdiction, and staying out of trouble.

In the juvenile court, probation is often ordered for an indefinite period of time. Depending on the statutes of the jurisdiction, the seriousness of the offense, and the juvenile's adjustment on probation, youths can remain under the court's supervision until the court no longer has jurisdiction over them, that is, when they reach the age of majority. New York, for example, limits probation to two years for a delinquent and one year for a status offender, extendable under exceptional circumstances. Florida mandates that probation last no longer than could a term of commitment to an institution.[2] State statutes determine if a judge can specify how long a juvenile can be placed under an order of probation.

In most jurisdictions, the status of probation is reviewed regularly to ensure that a juvenile is not kept on probation needlessly. Generally, discretion lies with the probation officer to discharge the youth if he or she is adjusting to the supervision and treatment plan.

As virtually all 50 states have adopted the Uniform Interstate Compact on Juveniles, the supervision of a juvenile probationer can be transferred from one state to another if it is necessary for the youth to move from the original jurisdiction.[3] The compact provides jurisdiction over all nonresident juveniles by allowing for the return of runaways to their home state and for supervision of out-of-state children.

HISTORICAL DEVELOPMENT

Although the major developments in juvenile probation have occurred in the twentieth century, its roots go back much farther. In England, specialized procedures for dealing with youthful offenders can be found as early as 1820, when the magistrates of the Warwickshire quarter sessions adopted the practice of sentencing youthful criminals to prison terms of one day, then releasing them conditionally under the supervision of their parents or masters. This practice was developed further in Middlesex, Birmingham, and London, where probation supervision was first supplied by police officers, then by volunteer philanthropic organizations, and finally by public departments.[4]

In the United States, juvenile probation developed as part of the wave of social reform characterizing the latter half of the nineteenth century. Massachusetts took the first step toward development of a juvenile probation service. Under an act passed in 1869, an agent of the state board of charities was authorized to appear in criminal trials involving juveniles, to find them suitable homes, and to visit them periodically. These services were soon broadened and strengthened, so that by 1890, probation had become a mandatory part of the court structure throughout the state.[5]

Probation was a cornerstone in the development of the juvenile court system. In fact, in some states the early supporters of the juvenile court movement viewed probation legislation as the first step toward achieving the benefits that the new court was intended to provide. The rapid spread of juvenile courts during the first decades of the twentieth century encouraged the further development of probation. The two were closely related, and to a large degree, interdependent institutions sprang from the same dedicated conviction that the young could be rehabilitated and that the public was responsible for protecting them.

By the mid-1960s, juvenile probation had become a major social institution, large, complex, and touching the lives of an enormous number of children in the United States. Today, about 530,000 youths are being supervised on informal and formal (court order) probation; approximately half of those cases are formal probation orders where the juvenile was adjudicated a delinquent or status offender.[6]

With regard to delinquency, adjudicated juveniles were placed on formal probation in 244,000 cases in 1992, or in 57 percent of all adjudicated delinquency cases handled by the juvenile courts. Compared to the period 1988 through 1992, the likelihood of formal probation was unchanged for adjudicated delinquency cases (see Table 16.1).

On the other hand, the number of adjudicated delinquency cases that resulted in a formal probation disposition increased 24 percent between 1988 and 1992 (from about 197,000 to about 245,000 cases; see Table 16.2). The greatest increase involved the number of person offense cases, up to 50 percent, continuing a trend seen in recent years. Property offense cases resulting in probation also increased by 21 percent, while drug law violations cases resulting in formal probation declined by 9 percent.[7]

TABLE 16.1 Percent of Adjudicated Delinquency Cases that Resulted in Formal Probation, 1988 and 1992

Offense	1988	1992
Delinquency	57%	57%
Person	56	55
Property	59	60
Drugs	57	54
Public Order	50	52

Source: Jeffrey Butts et al., *Juvenile Court Statistics 1992* (Pittsburgh, Pa.: National Center for Juvenile Justice, 1995).

TABLE 16.2 Percent Change in Adjudicated Delinquency Cases That Resulted in Formal Probation, 1988–1992

Offense	Number of Cases		Percent Change
	1988	1992	
Delinquency	196,700	244,400	24%
Person	32,400	48,600	50
Property	115,500	140,000	21
Drugs	16,500	15,000	−9
Public Order	32,300	40,700	26

Source: Jeffrey Butts et al., *Juvenile Court Statistics 1992* (Pittsburgh, Pa.: National Center for Juvenile Justice, 1995).

TABLE 16.3 Percent Change in Adjudicated Status Offense Cases that Resulted in Formal Probation, 1988–1992

Offense	Number of Cases		Percent Change
	1988	1992	
Status Offense	31,900	35,300	11%
Runaway	4,200	4,100	−1
Truancy	11,900	14,200	19
Ungovernable	5,600	4,800	−14
Liquor	8,400	9,200	10
Miscellaneous	1,800	2,900	63

Source: Jeffrey Butts, et. al. Juvenile Court Statistics 1992 (Pittsburgh, Pa.: National Center for Juvenile Justice, 1995).

Formal probation was also a significant disposition for status offenders. In 1992 more than 35,000 status offense cases resulted in probation, up 11 percent from 1988 (see Table 16.3). The proportion of cases given probation increased in all offense categories (see Table 16.4). Forty percent of the adjudicated status offense cases that resulted in probation involved truancy as the most serious charge.[8]

Some conclusions can be drawn from this information: (1) For those youth who can be supervised in the community, probation represents an increasingly appropriate disposition; (2) the use of probation allows the juvenile court to

TABLE 16.4 Percent of Adjudicated Status Offense Cases that Resulted in Formal Probation, 1988 and 1992

Offense	1988	1992
Status Offense	59%	65%
Runaway	54	59
Truancy	80	85
Ungovernable	60	66
Liquor	49	56
Miscellaneous	37	41

Source: Jeffrey Butts, et. al. Juvenile Court Statistics 1992 (Pittsburgh, Pa.: National Center for Juvenile Justice, 1995).

tailor a program to the needs and circumstances of each juvenile offender, including those involved in person-oriented offenses; (3) the juvenile justice system continues to have confidence in the rehabilitation model while accommodating demands for legal controls and public protection, even when caseloads may include many more serious offenders than in the past; and (4) probation is often the disposition of choice, particularly for status offenders.

ORGANIZATION AND ADMINISTRATION OF PROBATION

Juvenile probation systems are organized in one of two ways. In the most common form, the juvenile court or a group of courts administers probation services. In the other, an administrative agency such as a state correctional agency, public welfare department, or a combination of such agencies provides probation services to the court. The relationship between the court (especially the judge) and the probation staff, whether it is under the court or in a separate administrative agency, is an extremely close one.

In the typical juvenile probation department, the leadership role of the chief probation officer is central to its effective operation. In addition, large probation departments include one or more assistant chiefs. Each of these middle managers is responsible for one aspect of probation service. One assistant chief might oversee training, while another might supervise and treat special offender groups, and still another might act as liaison with juvenile, police, or community service agencies. The probation officers who investigate and supervise juvenile cases are in direct and personal contact with the supervisory staff.

Each state has its own approach to juvenile probation organization. In some states—Massachusetts, for example—a statewide probation service exists, but actual control over departments is localized within each district court. New York, on the other hand, has in each of its counties a family court with exclusive original jurisdiction over children aged 16 or under; a single department handles probation for the five boroughs of the city of New York. In Maryland, the State Department of Juvenile Services provides probation services to the juvenile courts in each county. Wisconsin's probation program is administered by a county executive department, while in New Jersey, juvenile probation services are managed by judges. Thus, the administration of probation varies from one jurisdiction to another, and there is a considerable lack of uniformity in the roles, organization, and procedures of probation across the states.[9]

The National Center for Juvenile Justice found that, as of 1993, probation services were organized and administered exclusively by the local juvenile court or by the state administrative office of courts in 23 states and the District of Columbia. In another 14 states, probation administration is split between judicial and executive branch departments, while in 10 states, it is handled exclusively at the state level by a state agency. In 2 states, county governments administer probation, and in 3 other states, the responsibility for probation is shared by county and state agencies.[10]

Although it appears that juvenile probation services continue to be predominantly organized under the judiciary, recent legislative activity has been in the direction of transferring those services from the local juvenile court judge to a state court administrative office. Whether juvenile courts or state agencies should administer juvenile probation services is debatable. In years past, the organization of probation services depended primarily on the size of the program and the number of juveniles under its supervision. Today, the judicial–executive controversy is often guided by the amount of money available for these services. Because of this momentum to develop unified court systems, many juvenile court services, including probation, are now being consolidated into state court systems. According to Hurst and Torbet, the transfer of juvenile probation services to state judicial control is consistent with the emerging trend of state funding of courts. Occasionally, local judicial administration of probation has been replaced by state *executive* control.[11]

DUTIES OF JUVENILE PROBATION OFFICERS

The **juvenile probation officer** is responsible for the initial contact with the youth, for continuing to process the case, and for providing services for the juvenile while he or she is under court supervision.

According to the American Bar Association's standards for juvenile justice, juvenile probation officers are involved at four stages of the court process. At intake, they screen complaints by deciding to adjust the matter, refer to an agency for service, or refer to the court for judicial action. During the interim status or predisposition stage, they participate in release or detention decisions. At the postadjudication stage, they assist the court in reaching its dispositional decision. During postdisposition, they supervise juveniles placed on probation.[12]

At intake, the probation staff engages in preliminary discussions with the child and the family to determine whether court intervention is necessary or whether the matter can be better resolved by some form of community service. If the child is placed in a detention facility, the probation officer helps the court decide whether the child should continue to be held or released pending the adjudication and disposition of the case.

The juvenile probation officer exercises tremendous influence over the child and the family by developing a **social investigation report** and submitting it to the court. This report is a clinical diagnosis of the child's problems and of his or her need for court assistance based on the child's social functioning. The report evaluates the child's personality and relationship to family, peers, and community in order to recommend a future treatment plan. Such reports include analyses of children's perceptions of and feelings about their violations, their problems, and their life situations. They should shed light on the value systems that influence behavior. They should also consider the degree of motivation the juveniles have to solve the problems that cause deviant behavior as well as their physical, intellectual, and emotional capacity to change. These reports must examine the influence of family members and other significant persons in producing and possibly solving problems. Neighborhood and peer group determinants of attitudes and behavior also must be analyzed. All of this information must be brought together into a meaningful picture of a complex whole composed of the personality, the problem, and the environmental situation. This relationship must be considered in relation to the various possible alternative dispositions available to the court. Out of this, a constructive treatment plan is developed.

Another important function of the juvenile probation officer is to provide the child with supervision and treatment in the community. The treatment plan is a product of the intake, diagnostic, and investigative aspects of probation. Treatment plans vary. Some juveniles simply report to the probation officer and follow the conditions of probation. In other cases, the probation officer may need to counsel the child and family extensively or, more typically, refer them to other social service agencies, such as local mental health clinics and detoxification centers.

In sum, the juvenile probation officer's role requires a diversity of skills:

- Providing direct counseling and casework services
- Interviewing and collecting social service data
- Making diagnostic recommendations
- Maintaining working relationships with law enforcement agencies
- Using community resources and services
- Using volunteer case aides and probation officers
- Writing predisposition reports
- Working with families of children under supervision
- Providing specialized services, such as group work, behavior modification counseling, or reality therapy counseling
- Supervising specialized caseloads involving children on drugs or children with special psychological or emotional problems
- Making decisions about the revocation of probation and its termination

An important function of the juvenile probation officer is to provide the child with supervision and treatment in the community. The treatment plan is a product of the intake, diagnostic, and investigative aspects of probation. Treatment plans vary. In some cases the probation officer will refer them to other social service agencies, such as a local charitable institution, mental health clinics and detoxification centers where they can receive counseling.

Performance of all these functions requires a high-quality probation staff. Today, juvenile probation officers have legal or social work backgrounds or special counseling skills. Most jurisdictions require juvenile probation officers to have a background in the social sciences and a bachelor's degree. The probation officer's job is not an easy one. High caseloads often make the therapeutic goal difficult to achieve. Overseeing the probationer's compliance with the legal requirements of probation often becomes the short-term goal.

CONDITIONS AND REVOCATION OF JUVENILE PROBATION

Conditions of probation are rules and regulations mandating that a juvenile on probation behave in a particular way. They are important ingredients in the treatment plan devised for the child. Conditions can include restitution or reparation, intensive supervision, intensive probation counseling, participation in a therapeutic program, or participation in an educational or vocational training program. In addition to these specific conditions, state statutes generally allow courts to insist that probationers lead law-abiding lives during the period of probation, that they maintain a residence in a family setting, that they refrain from associating with certain types of people, and that they remain in a particular geographic area unless they have permission to leave.

Probation conditions vary, but they are never supposed to be capricious, cruel, or beyond the capacity of the juvenile to accomplish. Furthermore, conditions of probation should relate to the crime that was committed and to the conduct of the child. The juvenile probation process and the options designed to emphasize individual treatment are illustrated in Figure 16.1.

In recent years, appellate courts have invalidated probation conditions that were harmful and that violated the juvenile's basic due process rights. Restricting a child's movement, insisting on a mandatory program of treatment, ordering indefinite terms of probation, and demanding financial reparation where this is impossible are all grounds for an appellate court review.

If a youth violates the conditions of probation or breaks the law again, the court can **revoke** probation. The juvenile court ordinarily handles a decision to revoke probation upon recommendation of the probation officer. Today, as a result of Supreme Court decisions dealing with the rights of adult probationers, a juvenile is normally entitled to legal representation and a hearing when a violation of probation occurs.[13] This means that juvenile probationers are virtually entitled to the same due process protections as adult probationers.

PROBATION INNOVATIONS

A number of recent innovations have affected or may soon affect probation services for juvenile offenders. Although probation programs have varying rates of recidivism, experts claim they are generally more successful than placement in an institution. As a result, there has been a great deal of experimentation over the years with different probation techniques. Rule enforcement, guidance, and the use of community services remain the common ingredients for delinquency-reducing programs in probation.

FIGURE 16.1
The juvenile probation process

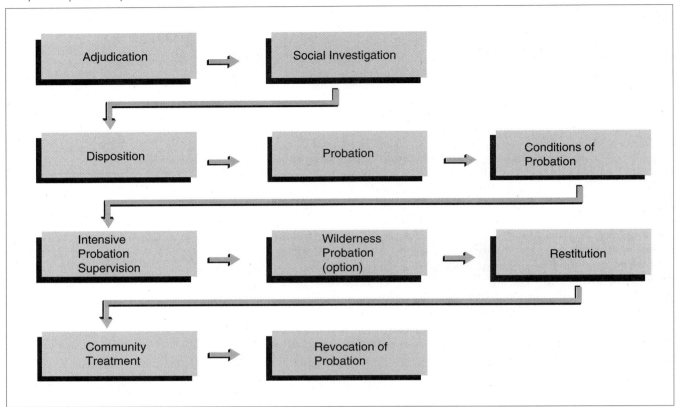

JUVENILE INTENSIVE PROBATION SUPERVISION (JIPS)

One approach that has generated a great deal of enthusiasm is the **juvenile intensive probation supervision (JIPS)** model. This involves treating offenders who would normally have been sent to a secure treatment facility as part of a very small caseload that receives almost daily scrutiny.[14]

Numerous jurisdictions have adopted programs of intensive probation supervision that have proven more successful than limited probation supervision. For example, Georgia, Oregon, and New Jersey have such programs, and the results seem encouraging.[15] The use of intensive probation as a mechanism for removing both children and adults from confinement no doubt will continue to grow. Even if intensive supervision is found to be no more effective in reducing recidivism than more restrictive correctional interventions, its demonstrated cost benefits (it costs about one-third that of confinement) make it an attractive alternative to traditional forms of treatment, such as confinement.[16]

A recent study by Richard Wiebush that examined the 18-month recidivism rate of juvenile felony offenders placed into an intensive probation supervision program showed that the intensive probation supervision was clearly an effective alternative to incarceration.[17] At the same time multifaceted intervention for juvenile probationers (social skills training, counseling, and outdoor adventure programs) may be no more effective than "standard" or "regular" probation services.[18] The need is obvious for continued research to determine what programs with what characteristics work for what types of juvenile offenders.

In sum, the results of certain juvenile intensive probation supervision programs in different jurisdictions indicate that such programs may result in fewer youths reentering the juvenile justice system.[19] Other research, however, shows only marginal benefits. Today, JIPS components can be found in most metropolitan juvenile probation departments in all major regions of the country and are used as a true alternative to incarceration or other forms of out-of-home placement.[20]

Two successful programs—the Wayne County Intensive Probation Program in Detroit, Michigan, and the Lucas County, Ohio, Intensive Supervision Unit—were independently evaluated and found to be as effective as incarceration at less than one-third the cost. The Wayne County Program is highlighted in the accompanying "Focus on Delinquency."[21]

The juvenile justice system, and particularly probation, was founded on the concept of individual rehabilitation. John Augustus, a successful shoemaker and philanthropist, planted the seed of juvenile probation in 1847 when "he bailed nineteen children, from 7 to 15, and reported back to the court in 6 months, whereupon the judge expressed much pleasure at the boys' performance and appearance and remarked that the object of the law had been accomplished."[22] From this early reform effort has evolved the intensive probation supervision programs described above.

USE OF VOLUNTEERS

The use of civilian volunteers to assist probation officers is another practice that has proliferated. For example, the juvenile court of Boulder County, Colorado, has developed an extensive volunteer program of delinquency prevention and treatment.[23] Local volunteers work with juvenile offenders, providing tutoring, group counseling, and job training. The variety of community treatment programs available today allows the court greater flexibility in disposing of juvenile cases.

ELECTRONIC MONITORING

Another program that has been used with adult offenders and is finding its way into the juvenile justice system is **house arrest,** which is often coupled with **electronic monitoring.** This program allows offenders sentenced to probation to remain in the community on the condition that they stay home during specific periods of time—for example, after school or work, on weekends, during evenings. Offenders may be monitored through random phone calls, visits, or, in some jurisdictions, electronic devices. Probationers in an electronic monitoring house arrest program are fitted with a unremovable monitoring device that alerts the probation department's computers if they leave their place of confinement.[24] Although house arrest has not been evaluated extensively in terms of reducing recidivism, its cost, even with active electronic monitoring, is often less than half that of a stay in a detention facility. Two well-known programs, one in Indiana and the other in North Carolina, for instance, appear to operate safely and effectively as alternatives to institutionalization and have become a formal part of probation programming in these jurisdictions.

WAYNE COUNTY INTENSIVE PROBATION PROGRAM

The Wayne County Intensive Probation Program (IPP) in Detroit, Michigan, is administered by the juvenile court and operated by the court probation department and two private, nonprofit agencies under contract with the court. The IPP target population is adjudicated delinquents between ages 12 and 17 who have been committed to the state's Department of Social Services (DSS). The state-funded program was begun in 1983 to reduce the level of delinquency commitments.

Youth referred to the IPP are placed in one of three programs for casework services and supervision: the Probation Department's Intensive Probation Unit (IPU); the In-Home Care Program, operated by Spectrum Human Services, Inc.; or the State Ward Diversion Program, operated by the Comprehensive Youth Training and Community Involvement Program, Inc. (CYTCIP).

The IPU program has the most traditional intensive supervision model of the three programs. It is characterized by low caseloads (a maximum of 10 youths per probation officer) and frequent probation officer contacts and surveillance activities. The IPU operates through a system of four steps, with diminishing levels of supervision as the juvenile demonstrates more responsibility and lawful behavior. Probation officers must have two to three weekly face-to-face contacts with youth during the first phase, and at least one face-to-face contact per week during the subsequent phases. In addition, telephone contacts to check school attendance, curfew adherence, and home behavior are made on a regular basis. Youths remain in the program from 7 to 11 months.

The two private programs have different approaches. The In-Home Care Program employs a family-focused services and treatment approach based on the philosophy that comprehensive family treatment using community resources is needed to alleviate the causes of delinquent behavior. The State Ward Diversion Program is a day treatment program actively involved in several key areas of youths' lives—home, family, school, employment, and community.

The Wayne County Intensive Probation Program was evaluated in 1988. The experimental group consisted of youths assigned to one of the three intensive supervision probation programs; the control group included youth placed in a state institution. Youths were randomly assigned to one of the two groups. The length of the follow-up period was two years.

The overall performances of the experimental and control groups were comparable. Institutionalized youth were slightly less likely to reappear in court than were intensive probation youth; however, this difference disappeared when time at risk in the community was taken into account. The IPP youth committed less serious crimes than the institutional youth, performed better on self-report tests, and were less likely to commit violent crimes measured both by court records and self-report data. It was found that the IPP program was as effective as incarceration at less than one-third the cost. The program saved an estimated $8.8 million over 3 years. The IPP study shows that a variety of program models can be successful in serving high-risk juvenile offenders in the community.

Source: James C. Howell, ed. *Guide for Implementing the Comprehensive Strategy for Serious, Violent and Chronic Juvenile Offenders* (Washington, D.C.: U.S. Department of Justice, OJJDP), 1995.

Joseph B. Vaughn conducted the most recent intensive and descriptive survey of juvenile electronic monitoring in 1989, involving eight programs in five different probation departments.[25] Vaughn found that all the programs adopted electronic monitoring to reduce institutional overcrowdedness and that most agencies reported success in reducing the number of days juveniles spent in detention. In addition, the programs allowed the youths, who would otherwise be detained, to remain in the home and participate in counseling, educational, or vocational activities. Of particular benefit to pretrial detainees was the opportunity to remain in a home environment with supervision. This experience provided the court with a much clearer picture of how the juvenile would eventually perform if given probation. On the other hand, Vaughn found that none of the benefits of the treatment objective in the programs had been empirically validated. The potential for modification in behavior and the duration of any personal changes remain unknown. Overall, the use of electronic monitoring is a new phenomenon, and Vaughn reports that it is too early to assess the impact of such programs on the juvenile justice system.

WILDERNESS PROBATION

Another type of program that seems to be growing in popularity with probation departments is **wilderness probation.** Wilderness probation programs, staffed by probation officers and lay volunteers, are designed to give youngsters a sense of confidence and purpose by involving them in outdoor expeditions.[26] Such programs are used as alternatives to standard dispositions for youths being supervised in the juvenile court. They provide an opportunity for juveniles to confront the difficulties in their lives while achieving positive personal satisfaction. Probation counseling and group therapy are part of this structured program, which is significantly different from a purely recreational field trip. The wilderness program in Douglas County, Nevada, for instance, serves between 30 and 50 youths in three different types of wilderness excursions every month.[27] These programs seem to be proving effective with both probationers and institutionalized youth (see chapter 17 for a discussion of the Outward Bound programs).[28]

BALANCED PROBATION

In recent years, some jurisdictions have turned to a **balanced probation** approach in an effort to enhance the success of probation.[29] Probation systems that integrate community protection, the accountability of the juvenile offender, competency, and individualized attention to the offender incorporate the treatment values of this balanced approach. Some of these juvenile protection programs offer renewed promise for community treatment. The balanced probation approach has been implemented with some success in Deschutes County, Oregon, and Travis County, Texas.[30] These programs are based on the view that juveniles are responsible for their actions and thus incur an obligation whenever they commit an offense. The probation officer establishes a program tailored to the special needs of the offender while helping him or her accept responsibility for his or her own actions. According to Gordon Bazemore, a case can be made for the balanced approach because it specifies a distinctive role and unique objectives for the juvenile probation system.[31]

Although balanced probation programs are still in their infancy and their effectiveness remains to be tested, they have generated immense interest because of their potential for relieving overcrowded correctional facilities and reducing the pain and stigma of incarceration. There seems to be little question that the use of these innovations and probation in general will increase in the years ahead, particularly as the juvenile court is uniquely organized to provide these programs. Not only can the probation officer oversee the individual therapy, but he or she can also make the above-mentioned probation possibilities available to the juvenile offender. Given the $35,000 cost of a year's commitment to a typical residential facility, it should not be a great burden to develop additional innovative probation services.[32]

RESTITUTION

Victim restitution is another widely used method of community treatment. In most jurisdictions, restitution is part of a probationary sentence and is administered by the county probation staff. In some jurisdictions, such as Oklahoma City and Prince George's County, Maryland, independent restitution programs have been set up by local governments, while in others, such as Covington, Louisiana, and Charleston, South Carolina, restitution is administered by a private non-profit organization.[33]

Restitution can take several forms. A juvenile can reimburse the victim of the crime or donate money to a worthy charity or public cause; this is referred to as **monetary restitution.** In other instances, a juvenile can be required to provide some service directly to the victim (**victim service**) or to assist a worthwhile community organization (**community service restitution**).

Requiring youths to reimburse the victims of their crimes is the most widely used method of restitution in the United States. Less widely used but more common in Europe is restitution to a community charity. In the past few years, numerous programs have been set up to enable the juvenile offender to provide service to the victim or to participate in community programs—for example, working in schools for retarded children and fixing up neighborhoods. In some cases, juveniles are required to contribute both money and community service. Other programs emphasize employment and work experience.[34]

Restitution programs can be employed at various stages of the juvenile justice process. They can be part of a diversion program prior to conviction, a method of informal adjustment at intake, or a condition of probation.

Restitution has a number of advantages.[35] It provides the court with alternative sentencing options. It offers direct monetary compensation or service to the victims of a crime. It is rehabilitative, because it gives the juvenile the opportu-

Restitution can take several forms. A child can reimburse the victim of the crime or pay money to a worthy charity or public cause; this is referred to as monetary restitution. In other instances, a juvenile can be required to provide some service directly to the victim (victim service) or to assist a worthwhile community organization (community service restitution). A young offender may find that his restitution order places him in a nursing home. Though such acts can often be beneficial, critics warn that restitution can involve widening the net of social control. Those given restitution orders might only have been placed on probation in the past; instead of an alternative to incarceration, restitution has become an extra burden on some offenders.

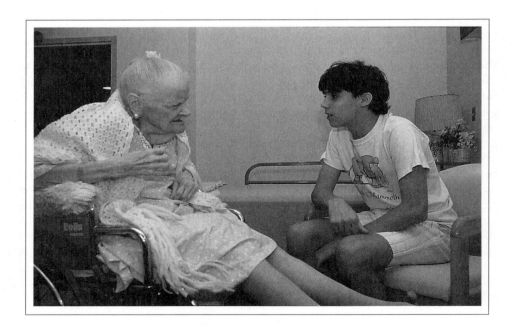

nity to compensate the victim and take a step toward becoming a productive member of society. It also relieves overcrowded juvenile courts, probation caseloads, and detention facilities. Finally, it has the potential for allowing vast savings in the operation of the juvenile justice system. Institutional placement costs currently run about $25,000 to $30,000 annually per child; restitution programs cost far less. Monetary restitution programs in particular may improve the public's attitude toward juvenile justice by offering equity to the victims of crime and ensuring that offenders take responsibility for their actions.

Despite its many advantages, however, some believe that restitution contributes to retribution rather than rehabilitation because it emphasizes justice for the victim and criminal responsibility for illegal acts. There is some concern that restitution creates penalties for juvenile offenders where none existed before.

The use of restitution is increasing around the nation. Many states—among them, Minnesota, Massachusetts, Arizona, and Oklahoma—have developed novel approaches to restitution. Legislation authorizing restitution programs has been passed in virtually all jurisdictions in the United States. In 1977, there were fewer than 15 formal restitution programs around the United States; by 1985, formal programs existed in 400 jurisdictions, and 35 states had statutory provisions that gave courts the authority to order juvenile restitution.[36] Today, all 50 states, as well as the District of Columbia, have statutory restitution programs in one form or another.[37]

A sample statute from the State Juvenile Code of North Carolina indicates the type of statutory language used for restitution programs and the latitude given the juvenile court judge regarding this disposition.

North Carolina Restitution Statute
In the case of any juvenile who is delinquent, the judge may:
(2) Require restitution, full or partial, payable within a twelve-month period to any person who has suffered loss or damage as a result of the offense committed by the juvenile. The judge may determine the amount, terms, and conditions of the restitution. If the juvenile participated with another person or persons, all participants should be jointly and severally responsible for the payment of restitution; however, the judge shall not require the juvenile to make restitution if the juvenile satisfies the court that he does not have, and could not reasonably acquire, the means to make restitution.
(4) Order the juvenile to perform supervised community service consistent with the juvenile's age, skill, and ability, specifying the nature of the work and the number of hours required. The work shall be related to the seriousness of the juvenile's offense and in no event may the obligation to work exceed twelve months.[38]

An example of a successful restitution program is that developed in the Quincy, Massachusetts, district court. The **Alternative Work Sentencing Program (Earn-It)** handles juveniles referred by the court, the county probation department, and the district attorney's office. The program brings together the youth and the victim of the crime in order to develop an equitable work program. Program staff members determine the dollar amount of the victim's loss and place the juvenile in a paying job to earn the money needed to make restitution. Some youths are placed in nonpaying community service jobs to work off requirements specified in court orders. By all indications, Earn-It has been a success. During its first year of operation, in 1975, the program returned $36,000 in restitution payments. Since then more than $100,000 has been returned to victims, the courts, and the community annually.[39]

Although it is difficult to assess the impact of programs like Earn-It on a national level, a federal government evaluation of 85 projects over a two-year period found that they had collected $2,593,581 in monetary restitution and had assigned 355,408 community service hours and 6,052 victim service hours.[40]

DOES RESTITUTION WORK?

How successful is restitution as a treatment alternative for juvenile offenders? Most attempts at evaluation have shown that it is reasonably effective. In an analysis of federally sponsored restitution programs, Peter Schneider and his associates found that about 95 percent of youths who received restitution as a condition of probation successfully completed their orders.[41] Factors that related to success were family income, good school attendance, few prior offenses, minor current offense, and size of restitution order. Schneider found that the youths who received restitution as a sole sanction (without probation) were those originally viewed by juvenile court judges as the better risks, and consequently, they had lower failure and recidivism rates than youths ordered to make restitution after being placed on probation.

In another, more recent, attempt to evaluate restitution, Anne Schneider conducted an in-depth analysis of four programs in Georgia; Oklahoma; Washington, D.C.; and Idaho.[42] She found that the program participants had lower recidivism rates than youths placed in control groups, such as regular probation caseloads. Although Schneider's data indicate that restitution may reduce recidivism, the number of youths who had subsequent involvement in the justice system still seems high. For example, 49 percent of the juveniles in the Clayton County, Georgia, restitution program were petitioned to juvenile court within three years of completing the program, as compared with 60 percent of the probation group; in Washington, D.C., 53 percent of the juveniles ordered to make restitution and 63 percent of the probationers became recidivists.

In sum, the evidence indicates that most restitution orders are successfully completed and that youths who make restitution are less likely to become recidivists (see the following "Focus on Delinquency"). Existing programs meet the important twin goals of retribution and rehabilitation.[43] However, the number of repeat offenses committed by juveniles who made restitution suggests, that by itself, restitution is not the answer to the delinquency problem.

CRITIQUING RESTITUTION

The success of Earn-It and similar programs has encouraged the development of restitution programs in other communities. However, certain problems remain. Offenders often find it difficult to make monetary restitution without securing new or additional employment. This need, charges William Staples, makes restitution seem almost absurd at a time when unemployment rates for youth are "tragically high."[44] Because most members of such programs have been convicted of a crime, many employers are reluctant to hire them. Problems also arise when offenders who need jobs suffer from drinking, drug, or emotional problems. Public and private agencies are likely sites for community service restitution, but their directors are sometimes reluctant to allow delinquent youths access to their organizations.

Thus, even voluntary charitable work can be difficult to obtain. To compensate for this problem, some programs find job opportunities for clients. However, Staples claims that this can cause some youths to view restitution programs as

RESTITUTION IN UTAH

The statewide Utah Juvenile Court operates a structured juvenile restitution program. In the majority of restitution cases, youths make restitution directly in the form of financial payments. Others may be ordered to participate in community service programs to earn money to make restitution. In 1988, financial or community service restitution was used in approximately 30 percent of petitioned cases and 10 percent of nonpetitioned cases.

Under state law, the Utah Juvenile Court may order youths to repair, replace, or make restitution for victims' property and other losses. Probation officers are authorized to develop restitution or community service plans even in cases where youths are not formally brought before the court by petition. In such cases, consent agreements are signed by youths and their parents, and restitution is often paid directly to the victims.

An innovative feature of Utah's approach to juvenile restitution, established by state law in 1979, permits the court to withhold a substantial portion of fines paid by juveniles to underwrite a work restitution fund. The fund allows juveniles otherwise unable to pay restitution to work in community service projects in the private or public sector to earn money to compensate their victims. The juveniles' earnings are paid directly from the fund to the victims.

During the past decade, the use of restitution has increased in Utah. In 1980, court-ordered restitution paid by juveniles and returned to victims was just under $250,000. By 1990, that amount had increased to more than $550,000.

Results

More than 13,000 cases from Utah were studied to assess the association between the use of restitution and subsequent recidivism. Of the probationers ordered to pay restitution, 32 percent became recidivists within a year. In cases involving charges of burglary and theft, which represented the majority of all the cases, significantly fewer youths who were ordered to pay restitution became recidivists than those placed in probation alone. Formal probation cases involving juveniles charged with burglary had a recidivism rate of 31 percent when the disposition included restitution but 38 percent when probation alone was ordered. In the theft cases, the rates were 34 percent recidivism with restitution and 38 percent without it. Restitution combined with probation was consistently associated with lower recidivism rates than probation alone.

Overall, the results of the study suggest that the use of restitution is a significant factor in reducing recidivism among certain juvenile offenders.

Source: Administrative Office of the Courts, *Utah Juvenile Court: Restitution and Community Service Program* (Salt Lake City: Administrative Office of the Courts, 1991); Jeffrey Butts and Howard Snyder, *OJJDP Update on Research, Restitution and Juvenile Recidivism* (Washington, D.C.: U.S. Department of Justice, 1992), p. 4.

employment offices: "Committing a crime can become, for some, the only means of obtaining a job."[45]

Another criticism directed at restitution programs is that they involve **widening the net** of social control. Some critics claim that those given restitution orders would not have received more coercive treatment under any circumstances, and that therefore, instead of an alternative to incarceration, restitution has become an extra burden on some offenders.[46]

Beyond these problems, some juvenile probation officers view restitution programs as a threat to their authority and to the autonomy of their organizations. It is interesting to note that courts believe police officers view restitution more positively than social workers because the police are quick to grasp the retributive nature of restitution.

Another problem restitution programs must deal with is the charge that they foster involuntary servitude. For the most part, the courts have upheld the legality of restitution even though it has a coercive element. Some people believe that restitution is inherently biased against indigent clients because a person who is unable to make restitution payments can have probation revoked and thus face incarceration. To avoid such bias, probation officers should first determine why payment has stopped and then suggest appropriate action for the court to take rather than simply treat nonpayment as a matter of law enforcement.

Finally, restitution orders are subject to the same abuses of discretion as traditional sentencing methods. The restitution orders one delinquent offender receives may be quite different from those given another similarly situated youth. To remedy this situation, a number of jurisdictions have been using restitution guidelines to encourage standardization of orders.

Restitution programs may be an important alternative to incarceration, benefiting the child, the victim, and the juvenile justice system. H. Ted Rubin, a leading juvenile justice expert, even advocates that courts placing juveniles in day-treatment and community-based residential programs also include restitution requirements in their orders and expect that these requirements be fulfilled during placement.[47]

However, all such programs should be evaluated carefully to answer such questions as what type of offenders would be most likely to benefit from restitution, when is monetary restitution more desirable than community service, what is the best point in the juvenile justice process to impose restitution, what is the effect of restitution on the juvenile justice system, and how successful are restitution programs. The evidence does indicate that restitution is inexpensive, avoids stigma, and helps compensate victims of crime.

PRIVATIZATION OF JUVENILE PROBATION

No discussion of innovative juvenile probation programs would be complete without mention of the private sector's role in correctional services.

Juvenile probation is a major component of the juvenile justice system and one that is finding its resources strained by growing caseloads. With juvenile courts placing more than 80 percent of adjudicated delinquents on some form of probation, the agencies that oversee probation represent the most significant area of juvenile corrections. Many juvenile probation programs, however, have been unable to maintain quality and cost-effective services. At the same time, the juvenile justice system is overwhelmed by such problems as drug use, youth gangs, school violence, and serious juvenile crime. To assist the juvenile courts in expanding their efforts and coping with these problems, the Office of Juvenile Justice and Delinquency Prevention (OJJDP) has funded a $1.7 million Private Sector Probation Initiative Program.[48]

Its purpose is to recruit private companies and institutions to offer probation services to selected juveniles. Under this program, a number of jurisdictions contract out probation services to private sources. In the Third Judicial District of Utah, for example, the private–public partnership offers a 90-day intensive supervision program, with a resulting significant reduction in recidivism rates. In Cleveland, Ohio, private-sector court services are provided to status offenders and delinquents at a cost per youth of $80, compared with $1,200 for public-sector probation services. Kenosha County, Wisconsin, contracted for central case management and weekend adventure programs, which has enabled the state to close one of its training schools. San Francisco County was able to retain its status offender services by private contract when budget cuts threatened to eliminate them from the public sector.[49] What these programs demonstrate is that juvenile probation services can be improved by transferring some of the functions and responsibilities to the private sector. In the future, the private sector is expected to offer more juvenile justice services previously performed by government.

Community-Based Programs

To many juvenile justice experts, the institutionalization of even the most serious delinquent youths in a training school, reform school, or industrial institution is a great mistake. A period of confinement in a high-security juvenile institution usually cannot solve the problems that brought a youth into a delinquent way of life, and the experience may actually help to amplify delinquency once the youth returns to the community. Surveys indicate that about 30 percent to 40 percent of adult prison inmates had been juvenile delinquents, and many had been institutionalized as youths. There is little reason to believe that an institutional experience can be beneficial or reduce recidivism.[50]

Because of the problems associated with institutional care, such influential policy-making bodies as the National Council of Juvenile and Family Court Judges, the National Council on Crime and Delinquency, and the American Bar Association have recommended that, whenever possible, treatment of serious offenders be community-based. While recognizing the problems presented by the chronic offender, these groups maintain that adequate security can be maintained in community-based programs.[51] Similar initiatives have been promoted by state governments.[52]

Since the early 1970s, Massachusetts has led the movement to keep juvenile offenders in the community. In the mid-1960s, its Department of Youth Services housed more than 1,000 youngsters in secure training schools. Under Jerome Miller, who became the commissioner of the department in 1969, Massachusetts closed most of its secure juvenile facilities and began a massive deinstitutionalization of juvenile offenders.[53] Today, 27 years after the institutions were closed, the Massachusetts Department of Youth Services operates a community-based correctional system. The vast majority of youths are serviced in nonsecure settings, while the relatively few committed youth are placed in some type of residential setting ranging from group and foster homes to secure facilities and forestry camps.

Initially, many of the early programs suffered from residential isolation and limited services. Over time, however, many of the group homes and unlocked structured residential settings were relocated in residential community environments and became highly successful in addressing the needs of juveniles while presenting little or no security risk to themselves or others.

Roxbury Youthworks, an inner-city program in Boston, is such a private community-based agency controlling juvenile delinquency through a comprehensive range of resources that include (1) evaluation and counseling at a local court clinic; (2) employment and training; (3) detention diversion; and (4) outreach and tracking to help youth reenter the community. Roxbury Youthworks is one of 24 independent programs—both residential and nonresidential—under contract with the state youth services department to provide intensive community supervision for almost 90 percent of all youths under its jurisdiction.[54]

There are other historic examples of jurisdictions that have reduced the need for high-security institutions to treat delinquent offenders. Like Massachusetts,

Vermont moved to a noninstitutional system. It closed the Weeks School—the only training school in the state—in 1979. In 1975, Pennsylvania removed youths from the Camp Hill Penitentiary, which had been used to house the most hard-core juvenile offenders. Three-quarters of the juvenile inmates were returned to programs in their home communities. The remainder were transferred for short periods of time to small, secure institutions, then released. In 1978, Utah established a system of seven community-based programs as an alternative to traditional institutionalization in the state's Youth Development Center. An evaluation comparing the recidivism rates of comparable groups showed higher rates of success for the alternative program.

Today, the deinstitutionalization movement is still alive. Most recently, Maryland closed its Montrose Juvenile Training School, a facility that had been in operation for nearly three-quarters of a century. More than 200 youths were released from the school in less than a year. Many of them should not have been there in the first place as they had not committed serious or violent crimes. Nearly half of the youths were released with services and supervision in their own homes. Most of the others were safely placed in smaller, nonsecure residential programs.[55]

In conclusion, we have seen many states reduce the use of institutionalization in favor of nonsecure facilities and community-based programs.[56] In addition to the above-mentioned jurisdictions, West Virginia, Oklahoma, Oregon, and Louisiana have either closed training schools or reduced the juvenile population in such institutions. Florida changed its system to emphasize community-based services as a result of a formal consent decree arising out of a federal court case. The following "Case in Point" highlights the need for such programs and the difficulty in obtaining services for youths in the juvenile justice system.

CASE IN POINT

You are a juvenile corrections consultant doing a study to determine if dispositional decisions are meeting the needs of youths in juvenile courts.

Jamie B., age 15, was adjudicated a juvenile delinquent. Placed on probation for one charge of shoplifting, he failed to report to the probation officer. Brought into the juvenile court on a second petition, namely being intoxicated and disruptive in public, Jamie admitted to having a substance abuse problem.

At the dispositional stage of the court process, Jamie's attorney asked the court to place him in a drug rehabilitation program. The judge suggested that such services could be obtained in a state training school as other less restrictive dispositional alternatives were not available. Concluding that Jamie's behavior constituted a threat to the community and to his own welfare, the court committed the youth to a state training school for an indeterminate period of time not to exceed two years.

A wide variety of dispositional alternatives are listed in the juvenile code of this jurisdiction. Among these are supervised probation, participation in a supervised day program, placement in a residential or nonresidential treatment program, and commitment to a state training school. The legislative preference for a community-based solution to Jamie's problem is reflected throughout the code. Jamie's lawyer challenges the dispositional decision, claiming that the commitment to a training school without first examining the appropriateness and availability of community-based services was judicial error.

Do you think the commitment order should be vacated and Jamie's case remanded for a new dispositional hearing? Why or why not?

ENCOURAGING COMMUNITY CORRECTIONS

A number of factors have affected the placement of juvenile offenders in nonsecure community-based facilities. At first, reformers, such as Jerome Miller, revealed the futility of exposing youths to the hardships of high-security institutions. Then in 1974, the Juvenile Justice and Delinquency Prevention Act tied the receipt of federal funds for juvenile justice programs to the removal of status offenders from institutions. The "deinstitutionalization of status offenders" mandate in the Act specifies that juveniles not charged with acts that would be crimes for adults shall not be placed in secure correctional facilities. Consequently, many states reformed their juvenile codes to support new community-based treatment programs and to remove status offenders from institutions. Most states now have provisions banning the institutionalization of status offenders with delinquents. In some states, however, *repeat* status offenders may be placed in secure facilities, either public or private, depending on the state. A few states allow status offenders to be institutionalized with delinquents if their behavior is so unruly that the court finds them unamenable to any other kind of treatment.

The second factor fueling the deinstitutionalization movement was an effort to grant children the general right to services and, in particular, the legal **right to treatment.** This concept recognizes the principle that when the juvenile justice system places a child in custody, basic concepts of fairness and humanity suggest that the system supply the child with rehabilitation. The right to treatment (see chapter 17) often meant providing counseling, education, adequate food and medical care, and so on. Consequently, the cost of maintaining youths in secure treatment facilities has skyrocketed. A national survey conducted in 1985 found that the average cost of maintaining one youth for one year was $25,000.[57] In 1987, it was $27,000, and in 1991, the cost was more than $30,000. Future costs may reach $40,000 per bed per year.[58] Considering these costs and the assumed ineffectiveness of institutional treatment, "the least restrictive alternative available" to treat juvenile offenders in many cases means placement in community-based programs.

A word of caution: Although the movement to place juveniles in nonrestrictive, community-based programs continues, *the actual number of incarcerated youths has increased in recent years.* The population of juveniles held in secure public juvenile facilities increased 54 percent from 29,000 in 1977 to more than 53,000 10 years later. Almost 57,000 children are now held in secure public facilities.[59]

Secure institutional programs make up more than one-third of public and private facilities and house more than 50 percent of the total juvenile population, in spite of the emphasis placed on community corrections in the last two decades. Community corrections has supplemented, but not replaced, institutionalization.

Today, most states rely on a sophisticated network of small, secure programs for violent youths coupled with a broad range of highly structured community-based programs for the majority of committed juveniles. Many of the community-based programs are operated by private, nonprofit agencies; secure facilities (discussed in chapter 17) are reserved for only the most serious offenders. At the same time, the incentive is to privatize more of the system and develop a set of smaller, less intensive, and far cheaper alternatives for those children who would not present a significant risk to the community.

RESIDENTIAL COMMUNITY TREATMENT

How are community corrections implemented with delinquent youths? In some cases, adjudicated youths are placed under probation supervision, and the probation department maintains a residential treatment facility. Placement can also be made to the department of social services or juvenile corrections with the direction that the youth be placed in a residential, nonsecure facility.

Residential programs can be divided into four major categories: (1) group homes, including boarding schools and apartment-type settings; (2) foster homes; (3) family group homes; and (4) rural programs.

Group homes are nonsecure, structured residences that provide counseling, education, job training, and family living. They are staffed by a small number of qualified persons, and they generally house 12 to 15 youngsters. The institutional quality of the environment is minimized, and children are given the opportunity to build a close but controlled relationship with the staff. Children reside in the home, attend public schools, and participate in community activities in the area. Over the past two decades, extensive research has been done on group home settings. The following "Focus on Delinquency" illustrates two pioneering community-based residential treatment programs in the field of juvenile corrections that have served as models for many other programs. Unfortunately, these better known programs of the 1970s have not received as much attention today because of limited federal and state funding. Yet, the research on these programs supports the position that they do prevent recidivism and far more cheaply than imprisonment.

Foster care programs typically involve one or two juveniles who live with a family—usually a husband and wife who serve as surrogate parents. The juveniles enter into a close relationship with the foster parents and receive the attention, guidance, and care that they did not receive at home. The quality of the foster home experience depends on the foster parents and their emotional relationship

Most residential programs use group counseling techniques as the major treatment tool. Although group facilities have been used less often than institutional placements in the years past, there is definitely a trend toward developing community-based residential facilities.

Two Examples of Residential Treatment Programs

The Highfields Project

Highfields was a short-term residential, nonsecure program for boys that began in 1950. The youths lived in groups of no more than 20 boys in a large home on an estate in Highfields, New Jersey, for periods of three or four months. They were permitted to leave the grounds under responsible adult supervision. They were also granted furloughs over weekends to visit their families and to retain ties with the community. They also worked 20 to 40 hours a week at a neuropsychiatric clinic. The most important treatment technique was peer pressure exerted through active participation in guided group interaction sessions.

The Highfields project was evaluated by using a controlled group of boys sent to Annandale, a juvenile reform school in the same state. One year after release, Highfields boys had a lower recidivism rate than Annandale boys. The Highfields project was considered as successful as any training school and was much less expensive to operate. However, the validity of the recidivism rates was questioned because of the difficulties associated with matching the control and treatment groups.

The Silverlake Experiment

The Silverlake experiment occurred in Los Angeles County in the mid-1960s. Like Highfields, this program provided a group home experience seeking to create a nondelinquent culture for male youths between the ages of 15 and 18. The participants,

seriously delinquent youths, were placed in a large family residence in a middle-class neighborhood. Some of them attended local high schools, and many returned to their homes on weekends. Only 20 boys at a time lived in the residence. They were responsible for maintaining the residence and for participating in daily group interaction meetings, whose purpose was to implement program goals. The Silverlake program sought to structure a social system with positive norms by discussing the youths' problems and offering alternatives to delinquent behavior.

To evaluate the Silverlake experiment, researchers selected experimental and control groups at random from the youths participating in the program. There was no significant difference in the recidivism rates of the two groups tested, and it was unclear whether one program reduced recidivism more than the other. As both control-group youths and treatment youths lived in the facility, the researchers concluded that the experimental group receiving guided group interaction and the control group were positively affected by the program. Recidivism rates 12 months after release indicated a general reduction in delinquent behavior on the part of participants.

Source: H. Ashley Weeks, *Highfields* (Ann Arbor: University of Michigan Press, 1956); LaMar T. Empey and Stephen Lubeck, *The Silverlake Experiment: Testing Delinquency Theory and Community Intervention* (Chicago: Aldine, 1971).

with the child. Foster care for adjudicated juvenile offenders has not been extensive in the United States. It is most often used for orphans or for children whose parents cannot care for them. Welfare departments generally handle foster placements, and funding of this treatment option has been a problem for the juvenile justice system. However, foster home services for delinquent children and status offenders have expanded as a community treatment approach.

Family group homes combine elements of both foster care and group home placements. Children are placed in a private group home that is run by a single family rather than a professional staff. This model can help troubled youths learn to get along in family-type situations and at the same time help the state avoid the start-up costs and neighborhood opposition often associated with the establishment of a separate public institution. Family group homes can be found in many jurisdictions throughout the United States.

Rural programs include forestry camps, ranches, and farms that provide specific recreational activities or work for juveniles in a rural setting. Individual programs typically handle from 30 to 50 children. Such programs have the disadvantage of isolating children from the community, but reintegration can be achieved if the child's stay is short and if family and friends can visit.

Most residential programs use group counseling techniques as the major treatment tool. Although group facilities have been used less often than institutional placements in years past, there is definitely a trend toward developing community-based residential facilities.

NONRESIDENTIAL COMMUNITY TREATMENT

In **nonresidential programs,** youths remain in their homes or in foster homes and receive counseling, education, employment, diagnostic, and casework services. A counselor or probation officer gives innovative and intensive support to help the child remain at home. Family therapy, educational tutoring, and job placement may all be part of the program.

Nonresidential programs are often associated with the Provo program, begun in 1959 in Utah, and the Essexfields Rehabilitation Project, started in the early 1960s in Essex County, New Jersey.[60] Today, the most well-known approach is **Project New Pride,** which has been replicated in a number of sites around the United States. The accompanying "Focus on Delinquency" (see page 606) describes the Project New Pride program.

CRITICISMS OF THE COMMUNITY TREATMENT APPROACH

Despite its benefits, the community treatment approach has limitations. Public opinion may be against community treatment, especially when it is offered to juvenile offenders who pose a real threat to society. Institutionalization may be the only answer for the violent young offender. Even if the juvenile crime problem abates, society may be unwilling to accept reforms that liberalize policies and practices in the field of juvenile corrections. For example, it is common for neighborhood groups to actively oppose the location of corrections programs in their community. The thought of a center for young drug users being located across the street can send shivers up the spine of many property owners.

Evaluations of recidivism rates do not show conclusively that community treatment is more successful than institutionalization. Some experimental programs indicate that young people can be treated in the community as safely and as effectively as youths placed in an institution. However, commitment to an institution guarantees that the community will be protected against further crime, at least during the time of the juvenile's placement. More research is essential to evaluate the success of community treatment programs.

Much of the early criticism of community treatment was based on poor delivery of services, shabby operation, and haphazard management, follow-up, and planning. In the early 1970s, when Massachusetts deinstitutionalized its juvenile correction system, there was a torrent of reports about the inadequate operation of community treatment programs, based in part on the absence of uniform policies, the existence of different procedures in various programs, and the lack of accountability. The development of needed programs was hampered, and available resources were misplaced. Today's community treatment programs have generally overcome their early deficiencies and operate more efficiently than in the past.

In nonresidential programs, youths remain in their homes or in foster homes and receive counseling, education, employment, diagnostic, and casework services at a community center. A counselor or probation officer gives innovative and intensive support to help the child remain at home. Family therapy, educational tutoring, and job placement may all be part of the program.

It is also possible that deinstitutionalization will result in increased use of pretrial detention for juveniles if judges fear that dangerous children will be treated leniently at adjudication. Also, more children may be transferred to adult courts and subsequently committed to adult prisons. Whether or not this is actually happening has yet to be determined, but law-and-order forces unquestionably are seeking to turn more children over to the adult system.[61]

When all of the issues are considered, community-based programs continue to present the most promising alternative to the poor results of reform schools for the following reasons:

1. Some states have found that residential and nonresidential settings produce comparable or lower recidivism rates.
2. Community-based programs have lower costs and are especially appropriate for large numbers of nonviolent juveniles and those guilty of lesser offenses.
3. Public opinion of community corrections remains positive. In choosing between two approaches—training schools and community-based programs—for all but the most violent or serious juvenile offenders, more than 71 percent of the respondents in a recent public opinion survey indicated they favored a system that relied primarily on community-based services.[62]

As jurisdictions continue to face high rates of violent juvenile crime and ever-increasing costs for juvenile justice services, community-based programs will play an important role in providing rehabilitation of juvenile offenders and ensuring public safety.

RECIDIVISM AND COMMUNITY-BASED PROGRAMS

Has community treatment generally proven successful? Some concrete research efforts have shown this to be true. Lloyd Ohlin and his associates found that

PROJECT NEW PRIDE: AN EXAMPLE OF A NONRESIDENTIAL PROGRAM

One of the most well-known community-based treatment models is Project New Pride. Begun in Denver, Colorado, in 1973, it has been a model for similar programs around the country.

The target group for Project New Pride is serious or violent youthful offenders from 14 to 17 years old. They have at least two prior convictions for serious misdemeanors and/or felonies and are formally charged or convicted of another offense when they are referred to New Pride.

Will any hard-core offenders be accepted into New Pride? The only youths not eligible for participation are those who have committed forcible rape or are diagnosed as severely psychotic; New Pride believes this restriction is necessary in the interest of the safety of the community and of the youths themselves.

The project's specific goals are to work these hard-core offenders back into the mainstream of their communities and to reduce the number of rearrests. Generally, reintegration into the community means reenrolling in school, getting a job, or both.

1. **Schooling.** New Pride youths receive alternative schooling and are then reintegrated into the public school system or directed toward vocational training. Some youths get jobs and pursue a general equivalency diploma (GED). Some of them complete high school in the alternative school (certified by the public school system).

2. **Jobs.** New Pride places specific emphasis on vocational training. The staff recognizes that money is the key to independence for these youths, and the most socially acceptable way to get money is to work for it.

3. **Family.** Not only do the youths benefit from intensive counseling, but their families also have access to counselors. New Pride encourages family members to visit the project facility to observe the daily operations, involve themselves in their child's treatment, and get to know staff.

4. **Community.** New Pride community-based programs are extremely cost-effective when compared with the cost of placing a child in an institution. In Colorado and New Jersey, for example, it costs approximately $28,000 per year to incarcerate a youth; the cost for placing a youth in Denver New Pride or the Juvenile Resource Center in Camden is approximately $4,500.

Program Services

Each participant in New Pride has six months of intensive involvement and a six-month follow-up period, during which the youth slowly reintegrates into the community. During the follow-up period, the youth continues to receive as many services as necessary, such as schooling and job placement, and works closely with counselors.

Source: *Project New Pride* (Washington, D.C.: U.S. Government Printing Office, 1985).

youths in nonsecure placements were less likely to become recidivists than those placed in more secure institutions.[63] However, other reviews of community corrections reached the opposite result. Dennis Romig's national survey of community treatment programs concluded that few were effective in helping youths, and Malcolm Klein's analysis showed that community corrections has many pitfalls.[64] The research on such programs is uneven. Some programs have fairly strong results, but others produce questionable findings.

The dilemmas faced by community treatments are illustrated by the research of the historic **Community Treatment Project (CTP)** of the California Youth Authority. The purpose of the project was to determine whether intensive supervision of juveniles in the community would be more successful than the standard program of institutionalization.[65] The project, established in 1961, served as a model in juvenile justice for more than two decades. The study took children committed from the juvenile courts of Sacramento, Stockton, San Francisco, and Modesto and classified them according to a measure of interpersonal maturity. They were then divided into a control group, treated in a traditional institutional program, and an experimental group, placed in a community institution for eight months. Individual treatment plans were developed for each child in the experimental group. Certain types of youths did especially well; others did not respond to community treatment.

Numerous researchers have examined the data from the Community Treatment Project.[66] On the whole, recidivism rates seemed to be lower for those in community treatment than for those in traditional programs. However, in an important analysis, Paul Lerman showed that the original CTP success was more a function of the way recidivism rates were computed than the actual success of the program. While youths in the CTP were as likely to commit new crimes and get arrested as those in the comparison groups, their control agents were less likely to bring formal action against them. What appeared to be a change in the behavior of clients was actually the result of the change in the behavior of their supervisors. Lerman found that the CTP project was no more effective than traditional institutionalization, nor was it any more cost-effective. Although the track record of community-based corrections is still debatable, many states continue to make a successful transition from large institutions to community-based programs. California, Massachusetts, Utah, and Maryland are examples of states where community-based programs have proven to be at least as effective as traditional correctional programs.

Generally, experts have confirmed the decline of rehabilitation in juvenile justice throughout much of the United States over the past 20 years.[67] But several recent **meta-analysis** studies (studies using an analytic technique that synthesizes results across many programs over time) have refuted the claim that "nothing works" with juvenile offenders and given support to community rehabilitation. Independent studies by Mark Lipsey, Carol Garrett, and Ted Palmer, for instance, have concluded that adjudicated delinquents do respond positively to community treatment.[68] They suggest that rehabilitation is more successful in community rather than institutional settings. According to Krisberg, Currie, and Onek, the most successful community-based programs seem to share at least some of the following characteristics: (1) comprehensive programs dealing with many aspects of youths' lives; (2) intensive programs involving multiple contacts; (3) programs operating outside the formal juvenile justice system; (4) programs building on youths' strengths rather than deficiencies; and (5) programs that adopt a socially grounded approach to understanding a child's situation, rather than a medical–therapeutic approach.[69]

The greatest advantage of community corrections continues to be its cost. A national survey of the costs of treating youths found that the average annual expenditure per child in a training school was $40,000, while a community-based program may cost half as much. Thus, even if community-based correction were only equally successful as secure institutional care, it could still be judged superior on the basis of taxpayer savings alone.[70] **Graduated sanctions,** those that deal with a range of immediate, intermediate, and secure care, are one approach to effective treatment for juvenile offenders.

SUMMARY

Community treatment represents efforts by the juvenile-justice system to keep offenders in the community and spare them the pain and stigma of incarceration in a secure facility. The primary purpose of community treatment is to address the individual needs of juveniles in a home setting, employing any combination of educational, vocational, counseling, or employment services.

The most widely used method of community treatment is probation. Approximately 400,000 youths are currently on probation. They must obey rules given to them by the court and partake in some sort of treatment program. Their behavior in the community is monitored by probation officers. If rules are violated, youths can have their probation revoked and suffer more punitive means of control, such as secure incarceration.

Probation departments have developed restitution programs as a type of community treatment. These involve having the delinquents either reimburse the victims of their crimes or do community service. Although these programs appear successful, critics accuse them of widening the net of social control over young offenders.

Other forms of community treatment are day programs and residential community programs. The former allow youths to live at home while receiving treatment in a nonpunitive, community-based center; the latter require that youths reside in group homes while receiving care and treatment.

Despite criticisms, the cost savings of community treatment, coupled with its benign intentions, are likely to keep these programs growing. They are certainly no worse than secure institutions. Massachusetts, Maryland, Pennsylvania, Florida, and Utah are examples of states that have moved to deinstitutionalization. The research literature clearly shows that community-based graduated sanctions are as effective and sometimes more effective than traditional incarceration for juvenile offenders.

KEY TERMS

community treatment
restitution
probation
juvenile probation officer
social investigation report
conditions of probation
revoke
juvenile intensive probation
  supervision (JIPS)
house arrest

electronic monitoring
wilderness probation
balanced probation
monetary restitution
victim service
community service restitution
Alternative Work Sentencing Program
  (Earn-It)
widening the net
right to treatment

residential programs
group homes
foster care programs
family group homes
rural programs
nonresidential programs
Project New Pride
Community Treatment Project (CTP)
meta-analysis
graduated sanctions

QUESTIONS FOR DISCUSSION

1. Would you want a community treatment program in your neighborhood? Why or why not?
2. Is "widening of the net" a real danger, or are treatment-oriented programs simply a method of helping troubled youths?
3. If a youngster violates the rules of probation, should he or she be placed in a secure institution?
4. Is juvenile restitution fair? Should a poor child have to pay back a wealthy victim, such as a store owner?
5. What are the most important advantages to community treatment for juvenile offenders?
6. What is the purpose of juvenile probation? Identify some conditions of probation and discuss the responsibilities of the juvenile probation officer.

7. Discuss the recent trends in community treatment of juvenile offenders.

8. What programs are successful in helping juvenile offenders?

NOTES

1. American Bar Association, *Standards Relating to Probation,* Standard 1.2 (New York: Institute of Judicial Administration, 1977), p. 10 and *Revised Draft Standards,* 1980; see also Dean J. Champion, *Probation and Parole in the United States* (Columbus, Ohio: Merrill, 1990), Chap. 11.

2. Sanford Fox, *Juvenile Courts* (St. Paul, Minn.: West, 1984), pp. 227–28.

3. Ralph Brendes, "Interstate Supervision of Parole and Probation," in Robert Carter and Leslie Wilkins, eds., *Probation, Parole, and Community Corrections* (New York: Wiley, 1970).

4. George Killinger, Hazel Kerper, and Paul F. Cromwell, Jr., *Probation and Parole in the Criminal Justice System* (St. Paul, Minn.: West, 1976), p. 45.

5. National Advisory Commission on Criminal Justice Standards and Goals, *Corrections* (Washington, D.C.: U.S. Government Printing Office, 1983), p. 75.

6. Jeffrey Butts, Howard N. Snyder, Anne Aughenbaugh, Ellen H. Nimick, Terrence A. Finnegan, Dennis P. Sullivan, Rowen S. Poole, and Nancy J. Tierney, *Juvenile Court Statistics, 1992* (Pittsburgh, Pa.: National Center for Juvenile Justice, 1995); Howard Snyder and Melissa Sickmund, *Juvenile Offenders and Victims: A National Report* (Pittsburgh, Pa.: National Center for Juvenile Justice, 1995), p. 135.

7. Ibid, pp. 15, 16.

8. Ibid, p. 37.

9. Hunter Hurst IV and Patricia McFall Torbet, "Organization and Administration of Juvenile Services: Probation, Aftercare and State Institutions for Delinquent Youth" (Pittsburgh, Pa.: National Center for Juvenile Justice, 1993), p. 10.

10. Ibid, p. 10.

11. Ibid, p. 10.

12. American Bar Association, *Standards Relating to Juvenile Probation Function* (Cambridge, Mass.: Ballinger, 1977), p. 124.

13. *Morrissey v. Brewer,* 408 U.S. 471, 92 S.Ct. 2593, 33 L.Ed.2d 484 (1972); *Gagnon v. Scarpelli,* 411 U.S. 778, 93 S.Ct. 1756, 36 L.Ed.2d 655 (1973).

14. See, generally, James Byrne, "The Control Controversy: A Preliminary Examination of Intensive Probation Supervision Programs in the United States," *Federal Probation* 50:4–16 (1986).

15. For a review of these programs, see James Byrne, ed., *Federal Probation* 50:2 (June 1986); see also Emily Walker, "The Community Intensive Treatment for Youth Program: A Specialized Community-Based Program for High-Risk Youth in Alabama," *Law and Psychology Review* 13:175–99 (1989).

16. Edward Latessa, "The Cost Effectiveness of Intensive Supervision," *Federal Probation* 50:70–74 (1986); John Ott, "Bibliotherapy as a Challenging Condition to the Sentence of Juvenile Probation," *Juvenile and Family Court Journal* 40:63–67 (1989).

17. Richard G. Wiebush, "Juvenile Intensive Supervision: The Impact on Felony Offenders Diverted from Institutional Placement," *Crime and Delinquency* 39:68–89 (1993).

18. H. Preston Elrod and Kevin I. Minor, "Second Wave Evaluation of a Multi-Faceted Intervention for Juvenile Court Probationers," *International Journal of Offender Therapy and Comparative Criminology* 36:249–61 (1992).

19. S. H. Clarke and A. D. Craddock, *Evaluation of North Carolina's Intensive Juvenile Probation Program* (Chapel Hill, N.C.: University of North Carolina Institute of Government, 1987).

20. T. L. Armstrong, *National Survey of Juvenile Intensive Probation Supervision* (Washington, D.C.: Department of Justice, Criminal Justice Abstracts, 1988); National Council on Crime and Delinquency, *Juvenile Intensive Probation Programs—The State of the Art* (San Francisco: NCCD, 1991).

21. Barry Krisberg, Elliot Currie, and David Onek, "What Works with Juvenile Offenders," *Journal of Criminal Justice of American Bar Association* 10:20–52 (1995); William Barton and Jeffrey Butts, *The Metro County Intensive Supervision Experiment* (Ann Arbor, Mich.: Institute for Social Research, 1988).

22. Snyder and Sickmund, *Juvenile Offenders and Victims: A National Report,* p. 70.

23. "Volunteers in Probation," *Newsletter of the National Information Center on Volunteerism.*

24. Richard Ball and J. Robert Lilly, "A Theoretical Examination of Home Incarceration," *Federal Probation* 50:17–25 (1986); Joan Petersilia, "Exploring the Option of House Arrest," *Federal Probation* 50:50–56 (1986); Annesley Schmidt, "Electronic Monitors," *Federal Probation* 50:56–60 (1986); Michael Charles, "The Development of a Juvenile Electronic Monitoring Program," *Federal Probation* 53:3–12 (1989).

25. Joseph B. Vaughn, "A Survey of Juvenile Electronic Monitoring and Home Confinement Programs," *Juvenile and Family Court Journal* 40:1–36 (1989).

26. Robert Callahan, "Wilderness Probation: A Decade Later," *Juvenile and Family Court Journal* 36:31–35 (1985).

27. "Wilderness Programs in Probation," *Juvenile and Family Court Newsletter* vol. 19 (1989), p. 5.

28. Steven Flagg Scott, "Outward Bound: An Adjunct to the Treatment of Juvenile Delinquents: Florida's STEP Program," *New England Journal on Criminal and Civil Confinement* 11:420–37 (1985).

29. Dennis Mahoney, Dennis Romig, and Troy Armstrong, "Juvenile Probation: The Balanced Approach," *Juvenile and Family Court Journal* 39:1–59 (1988).

30. Ibid.; Charles McGee, "Measured Steps toward Clarity and Balance in the Juvenile Justice System," *Juvenile and Family Court Journal* 40:1–24 (1989).

31. Gordon Bazemore, "On Mission Statements and Reform in Juvenile Justice: The Case of the Balanced Approach," *Federal Probation* 61:64–70 (1992).

32. Gordon Bazemore and Mark Umbreit, *Balanced and Restorative Justice* (Washington, D.C.: Office of Juvenile Justice and Delinquency Prevention, 1994).

33. Anne L. Schneider, ed., *Guide to Juvenile Restitution* (Washington, D.C.: Department of Justice, 1985); Anne Schneider and Jean Warner, *National Trends in Juvenile Restitution Programming* (Washington, D.C.: U.S. Government Printing Office, 1989).

34. Gordon Bazemore, "New Concepts and Alternative Practice in Community Supervision of Juvenile Offenders: Rediscovering Work Experience and Competency Development," *Journal of Crime and Justice,* 14:27–45 (1991); Jeffrey Butts and Howard Snyder, *Restitution and Juvenile Recidivism* (Washington, D.C.: Department of Justice, 1992).

35. Anne Newton, "Sentencing to Community Service and Restitution," in *Criminal Justice Abstracts* (Hackensack, N.J.: National Council on Crime and Delinquency, September 1979), pp. 435–68.

36. Anne Schneider, "Restitution and Recidivism Rates of Juvenile Offenders: Results from Four Experimental Studies," *Criminology* 24:533–52 (1986).

37. Linda Szymanski, *Juvenile Restitution Statutes* (Pittsburgh, Pa.: National Center for Juvenile Justice, 1988).

38. N.C. Gen.Laws 7A, 649.

39. Descriptive materials can be obtained from the Earn-It Program, District Court of East Norfolk, Quincy, MA 02169. The Quincy District Court Probation Department was extremely helpful in providing information about this program; see also Jean Warner, Vincent Burke, and Anne L. Schneider, *Directory of Juvenile Restitution Programs* (Washington, D.C.: National Criminal Justice Reference Service, 1987).

40. Peter Schneider, "Research on Restitution: A Guide to Rational Decision Making," in Anne L. Schneider, ed., *Guide to Juvenile Restitution* (Washington, D.C.: Department of Justice, 1985), p. 137.

41. Peter Schneider, William Griffith, and Anne Schneider, *Juvenile Restitution as a Sole Sanction or Condition of Probation: An Empirical Analysis* (Eugene, Ore.: Institute for Policy Analysis, 1980).

42. Anne Schneider, "Restitution and Recidivism Rates of Juvenile Offenders."

43. Burt Galaway, "Restitution as Innovation or Unfilled Promise," *Federal Probation* 52:3–15 (1989).

44. William Staples, "Restitution as a Sanction in Juvenile Court," *Crime and Delinquency* 32:177–85 (1986).

45. Ibid., p. 183.

46. Barry Krisberg and James Austin, "The Unmet Promise of Alternatives to Incarceration," *Crime and Delinquency* 28:374–409 (1982).

47. H. Ted Rubin, "Fulfilling Juvenile Restitution Requirements in Community Correctional Programs," *Federal Probation* 52:32–43 (1988).

48. "Privatizing Juvenile Probation Services: Five Local Experiences," *National Institute of Justice Reports* (Washington, D.C.: Office of Justice Programs, December 1989), p. 10; Yitzhak Bakal and Harvey Lowell, "The Private Sector in Juvenile Corrections," in Ira Schwartz, ed., *Juvenile Justice and Public Policy* (New York: Lexington Books, 1992), p. 196.

49. "Privatizing Juvenile Probation Services," p. 12.

50. Bureau of Justice Statistics, *Report to the Nation on Crime and Justice* (Washington, D.C.: U.S. Government Printing Office, 1988), pp. 44–45; Peter Greenwood, "What Works with Juvenile Offenders: A Synthesis of the Literature and Experience," *Federal Probation* 58:63–67 (1994).

51. National Council of Juvenile and Family Court Judges, "The Juvenile Court and Serious Offenders," *Juvenile and Family Court Journal* 35:16 (Cambridge, Mass.: 1984); American Bar Association, Institute of Judicial Administration, *Standards on Probation,* 1980.

52. Robert Pierce, *Juvenile Justice Reform: State Experiences* (Denver: National Conference of State Legislatures, 1989).

53. Commonwealth of Massachusetts, *Department of Youth Services Annual Report of 1978* (Boston: State Purchasing Agency, 1978); Robert Coates, Alden Miller, and Lloyd Ohlin, *Diversity in a Youth Correctional System* (Cambridge, Mass.: Ballinger Press, 1978); Barry Krisberg, James Austin, and Patricia Steele, *Unlocking Juvenile Corrections* (San Francisco, National Council on Crime and Delinquency, 1989).

54. "Roxbury Agency Offers a Map for Youths at the Crossroads," *Boston Globe,* 18 February 1990, p. 32.

55. Jeffrey Butts, *Youth Corrections in Maryland: The Dawning of a New Era* (Ann Arbor, Mich.: Center for Study of Youth Policy, University of Michigan, 1988).

56. J. Blackmore, M. Brown, and B. Krisberg, *Juvenile Justice Reform—The Bellwether States* (Ann Arbor, Mich.: Center for Study of Youth Policy, University of Michigan, 1988).

57. Bureau of Justice Statistics, *Children in Custody, 1985* (Washington, D.C.: U.S. Government Printing Office, 1986).

58. Bureau of Justice Statistics, *Children in Custody Series, 1975–85 Census of Public and Private Juvenile Detention, Correctional, and Shelter Facilities* (Washington, D.C.: Department of Justice, May 1989), p. 2; Bakal and Lowell, "The Private Sector in Juvenile Corrections," p. 204; James Austin et al., *Juveniles Taken into Custody—1993* (San Francisco, National Council on Crime and Delinquency, 1995).

59. Bureau of Justice Statistics, *Children in Custody Series, 1975–85 Census;* Bureau of Justice Statistics, *Children in Custody, Public Juvenile Facilities, 1987* (Washington, D.C.: Department of Justice, 1989); Office of Juvenile Justice and Delinquency Prevention, *National Juvenile Custody Trends 1978–89* (Washington, D.C.: Department of Justice, 1992).

60. Lamar Empey and Maynard Erickson, *The Provo Experiment* (Lexington, Mass.: D.C. Heath, 1972); Paul Pilnick, Albert Elias, and Neale Clapp, "The Essexfields Concept: A New Approach to the Social Treatment of Juvenile Delinquents," *Journal of Applied Behavioral Sciences* 2:109–21 (1966).

61. Barry Krisberg and Ira Schwartz, "Rethinking Juvenile Justice," *Crime and Delinquency* 29:333–64 (1983); Ira Schwartz, Shenyang Guo, and John Kerbs, "The Impact of Demographic Variables on Public Opinion Regarding Juvenile Justice: Implications for Public Policy," *Crime and Delinquency* 39:5–28 (1993).

62. Ira Schwartz, *Juvenile Justice and Public Policy* (New York: Lexington Books, 1992), p. 217.

63. Lloyd Ohlin, Alden Miller, and Robert Coates, *Juvenile Correctional Reform in Massachusetts* (Washington, D.C.: U.S. Government Printing Office, 1976).

64. Dennis Romig, *Justice for Our Children* (Lexington, Mass.: Lexington Books, 1978); Malcolm Klein, "Deinstitutionalization and Diversion of Juvenile Offenders: A Litany of Impediments," in Norval Morr's and Michael Tonry, eds., *Crime and Justice,* vol. 1 (Chicago: University of Chicago Press, 1979), pp. 145–201.

65. Marguerite Q. Warren, "The Community Treatment Project: History and Prospects," in S. A. Yafsky, ed. *Law Enforcement Science and Technology.* Proceedings of the First National Symposium on Law Enforcement Science and Technology (Washington, D.C.: Thompson, 1967), p. 191.

66. Paul Lerman, "Evaluating the Outcome of Institutions for Delinquents," *Social Work Journal* 13:68–81 (1968); Paul Lerman, *Community Treatment and Social Control* (Chicago: University of Chicago Press, 1975).

67. Dan Macallair, "Reaffirming Rehabilitation in Juvenile Justice," *Youth and Society,* 25:104–23 (1993).

68. Mark W. Lipsey, *Juvenile Delinquency Treatment: A Meta-Analytic Inquiry into the Variability of Effects,* in *Meta-Analysis for Explanation: A Casebook* (San Francisco, CA., Thomas D. Cook et al. eds., Russell Sage Foundation, 1991); Carol Garrett, "Effects of Residential Treatment on Adjudicated Delinquents: A Meta-Analysis," *Crime and Delinquency* 22:287–308 (1985); Ted Palmer, *The Re-Emergence of Correctional Interventions* (Newbury Park, Calif.: Russell Sage Foundation, 1992), p. 69; Barry Krisberg, Elliot Currie, and David Onek, *American Bar Association Journal of Criminal Justice,* vol. 10, p. 51, 1995.

70. S. Lerner, *Good News about Juvenile Justice: The Movement away from Large Institutions and toward Community-Based Services* (Bolinas, Calif.: Ittleson Family Foundation, 1990).

CHAPTER SEVENTEEN

INSTITUTIONS FOR JUVENILES

INTRODUCTION

If, after a dispositionary hearing, the juvenile court judge finds that community treatment is inadequate to deal with the special needs of a delinquent youth, he or she may refer the youth to the state department of youth services for a period of confinement in a state-run treatment center. Another option, where appropriate, is to refer the juvenile to a privately run treatment program that specializes in dealing with a particular social problem (e.g., drug abuse or violent juvenile crime). Such programs are often administered in long-term facilities that hold adjudicated delinquents in environments that limit access to the community.

Today, correctional institutions operated by federal, state, and county governments are generally classified as secure or nonsecure facilities. Secure facilities restrict the movement of residents through staff monitoring, locked entrances and exits, and interior fence controls. Nonsecure institutions, on the other hand, generally do not restrict the movement of the residents and allow much greater freedom of access in and out of the facility.[1]

There has been a general movement in the past 20 years toward using fewer and smaller secure facilities in the belief that these programs allow more freedom and a greater chance of rehabilitating young offenders than do large, bureaucratic institutions. States such as Utah, Vermont, and Massachusetts have for the most part closed their large training schools and now rely on smaller institutions handling fewer than 40 youths. Violent youths and chronic serious offenders are placed in small, high-security treatment units and specialized programs.

This approach enables a diverse network of community-based programs, generally offered by private agencies under contract with the state, to provide specialized individual treatment.[2] One of the most talked about of these private-sector programs is the **Paint Creek Youth Center** (PCYC) in Bainbridge, Ohio. Since its beginning several years ago, the PCYC has been the focus of considerable discussion within the juvenile justice community because it offers an alternative to traditional public correctional services. In a small, open setting, the PCYC combines proven program components, including a highly structured environment, intensive aftercare, low client–staff ratio, job training and work experience, and many other comprehensive services.[3]

The Thomas O'Farrell Youth Center (TOYC), located in Maryland, is another example of effective privatized institutional corrections. It is a 38-bed unlocked, staff-secure residential program for male youth committed to the Maryland Department of Juvenile Services and operated by the North American Family Institute, a nonprofit multiservice agency. Using a philosophy of community dignity and respect for all its members, and exploring the normative treatment model (which emphasizes social rules and expectations), the TOYC has shown a dramatic decline in the number of offenses committed by youth after their institutional experience.[4]

Beyond the secure and nonsecure classifications, there are at least six different categories of juvenile correctional institutions in the United States: (1) detention centers that provide restrictive custody pending adjudication or disposition, (2) shelters that offer nonrestrictive temporary care, (3) reception centers that screen juveniles placed by the courts and assign them to an appropriate facility, (4) training schools or reformatories for adjudicated youths needing a long-term, secure setting, (5) ranch or forestry camps that provide special, long-term residential care in a less restrictive setting, and (6) halfway houses or group homes where juveniles are allowed daily contact with the community.[5] Youth correctional systems often incorporate virtually all of these programs (see Figure 17.1).

In addition to these types of institutions, many states develop a juvenile corrections placement matrix—a blueprint for a broad, comprehensive, risk-based continuum of care. This matrix serves to classify, by level and type of placement, the treatment needed for each youth, taking into account the severity of the current offense and the risk of future recidivism. Using such a matrix, high-risk youth, for example, who are serious or violent offenders would be recommended for secure incarceration. The greatest advantage of the matrix format is that it helps state correctional agencies create a large number of classifications, allowing juvenile offenders to be assigned to different security levels and programs.[6] (See Table 17.1.)

Many experts believe that institutionalizing young offenders generally does more harm than good. It exposes them to prisonlike conditions and to more experienced delinquents without giving them the benefit of constructive treatment programs. In contrast, offenders in the less costly community-based programs often have recidivism rates at least as low as (if not lower than) those

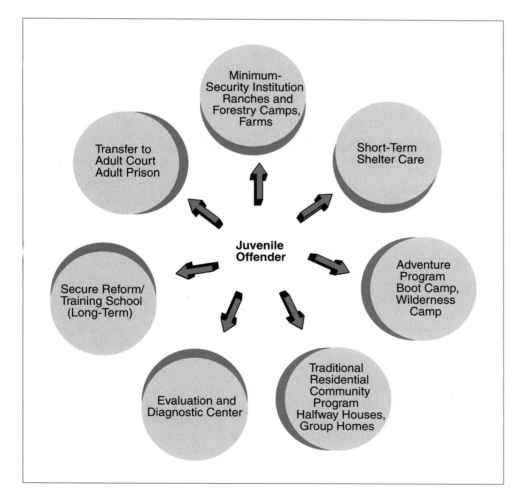

FIGURE 17.1
Institutional options for adjudicated youth

TABLE 17.1 Model Juvenile Corrections Placement Matrix

Seriousness of Offense	Risk Level		
	High Risk	**Medium Risk**	**Low Risk**
Violent Offenses	violent offender program; assaultive sex offender program; secure placement	secure residential program	boot camp; wilderness program
Serious Offenses	secure placement; boot camp	intermediate community program	day treatment; specialized group homes
Less Serious Offenses	short-term (30-day) stay in residential placement; day treatment program of six months; specialized group homes	day treatment; community service	community supervision; mentor program
Minor Offenses	proctor program combining tracking with residential services; community supervision	community supervision	limited supervision; use of volunteers

in institutions. Nonetheless, secure treatment in juvenile corrections is still being used extensively around the country, and the populations of these facilities are continuing to grow.

In this chapter, we analyze the current state of secure juvenile corrections. A brief history of juvenile corrections is presented, and then discussion turns to such issues as the extent of correction, the juvenile client, life in institutions, and treatment issues.

THE HISTORY OF JUVENILE INSTITUTIONS

Until the early 1800s, juvenile offenders as well as neglected and dependent children were confined in adult prisons. Physical conditions in these institutions were horribly punitive and inhumane, a fact that led social reformers to create a separate court system in 1899 and eventually to open correctional facilities solely for juveniles.[7] These early juvenile institutions were industrial schools modeled after adult prisons but designed to protect children from the evil influences in adult facilities. The first was the New York House of Refuge, established in 1825.

Not long after this, states began to establish **reform schools** for juveniles. Massachusetts was the first to open a state reform school—the Lyman School for Boys in Westborough—in 1846. New York opened the State Agricultural and Industrial School in 1849, and Maine opened the Maine Boys' Training School in 1853. By 1900, 36 states had reform schools.[8] Although it is difficult to precisely measure the total population of these institutions, Margaret Werner Cahalan undertook an impressive review of historical corrections statistics in the United States. She found that by 1880, there were approximately 11,468 youths in correctional facilities, a number that more than doubled by 1923 (see Table 17.2).[9] Early reform schools were generally punitive in nature and were based on the concept of rehabilitation (or reform) through hard work and discipline.

In the second half of the nineteenth century, emphasis shifted from the massive industrial schools to the **cottage system.** Juvenile offenders were housed in a compound consisting of small cottages, each of which could accommodate

TABLE 17.2 Youths in Correctional Facilities, 1880–1980

	1880	1890	1904	1910	1923	1980
Number	11,468	14,846	23,034	25,038	27,238	59,414
Per 100,000 population aged 10–20	97	100	126	125	125	136

Source: Margaret Werner Cahalan, *Historical Corrections Statistics in the United States, 1850–1984* (Washington, D.C.: U.S. Department of Justice, 1986), pp. 104–05.

20 to 40 children. A set of cottage parents ran each cottage and attempted to create a homelike atmosphere. It was felt that this setup would be more conducive to rehabilitation than the rigid bureaucratic organization of massive institutions.

The first cottage system was established in Massachusetts in 1855, the second in Ohio in 1858.[10] The system was generally applauded as being a great improvement over the earlier industrial training schools. The general feeling was that by moving away from punishment and toward rehabilitation, diagnosis, and treatment, not only could known offenders be rehabilitated but crime among dependent and unruly children could be prevented.[11]

TWENTIETH-CENTURY DEVELOPMENTS IN THE STRUCTURE OF JUVENILE CORRECTIONS

The early twentieth century witnessed important changes in the structure of juvenile corrections. Because of the influence of World War I, reform schools began to adopt a militaristic style. Living units became barracks; cottage groups became companies; housefathers became captains; and superintendents became majors or colonels. Military-style uniforms became standard.

In addition, the establishment of the first juvenile court in 1899 reflected the expanded use of institutional confinement for delinquent children. As the number of juvenile offenders increased, the forms of juvenile institutions varied to include forestry camps, ranches, and educational and vocational schools. Beginning in the 1930s, for example, camps became a part of the juvenile correctional system. Modeled after the camps run by the Civilian Conservation Corps, the juvenile camps centered on conservation activities, outdoor living, and work as a means of rehabilitation.

Los Angeles County was the first to use camps during this period.[12] Southern California was experiencing problems with transient youths who came to California with no money and then got into trouble with the law. Rather than filling up the jails, the county placed these offenders in conservation camps, paid them small wages, and then released them when they had earned enough money to return home. When the camps proved more rehabilitative than training schools, California established a network of forestry camps in 1935 especially for delinquent boys, and the idea soon spread to other states.[13]

Also during the 1930s, efforts at reforming the juvenile correctional institution were undertaken by the U.S. Children's Bureau, the first federal agency to address juvenile delinquency issues. The bureau conducted studies and projects to determine the effectiveness of the training school concept. Little was learned from these early programs because of limited funding and bureaucratic ineptitude, and the Children's Bureau failed to achieve any significant change in the juvenile correctional field. But such efforts recognized the important role of positive institutional care in delinquency prevention and control.[14]

Another innovation came in the 1940s, with the American Law Institute's Model Youth Correction Authority Act. This act emphasized the use of reception-classification centers. California was the first to try out this new idea, opening the Northern Reception Center and Clinic in Sacramento in 1947. Today, there are many such centers scattered around the United States.

Since the 1970s, the major change in institutionalization has been the effort by the federal government to remove status offenders from institutions housing juvenile delinquents. This initiative also includes removing status offenders from secure pretrial detention centers and removing all juveniles from contact with adults in jails.

This "**decarceration**" policy mandates that courts use the **least restrictive alternative** in providing services for status offenders. This means that a noncriminal child should not be put in a secure facility if a community-based model is available. In addition, the federal government prohibits states from putting status offenders in separate custodial care facilities that are similar in form and function to those used for delinquent offenders. This is to prevent states from merely shifting their institutionalized population around so that one training school houses all delinquents and another houses all status offenders, but actual conditions remain the same.

The decarceration movement has had some dramatic results. At the end of 1977, some 3,376 status offenders were being held in public short- and long-term institutions; by 1985, the number declined to 2,293, and in 1989, the figure stood at 2,245. The latest available data indicate the number has decreased to 1,755, almost another 27 percent.[15] This decline may signify a shift in court policy and judicial decision making; toward encouraging prosecutors to charge youths with delinquency rather than status offenses. Removing status offenders from secure public institutions may mean involving them in privately administered mental health and/or community-based programs. It is difficult to determine whether federal initiatives have resulted in a decline in the custodial population or merely a shift in its whereabouts. One fact is very clear. The Juvenile Justice and Delinquency Prevention Act has encouraged states to prohibit the incarceration of status offenders in secure facilities.

JUVENILE INSTITUTIONS TODAY

There are approximately 1,100 public and 2,200 private juvenile facilities in operation around the United States, holding a one-day count of approximately 98,000 youths.[16] In 1985, there were 1,040 public and 1,996 private juvenile facilities, with 83,402 juveniles in custody. The most recent available data indicate that there are about 1,076 public facilities and 2,032 private facilities with almost 100,000 juvenile offenders in custody on any one day (see Table 17.3). Overall, the number of youth and institutions has increased by about 10 percent in this period, possibly due to a "get tough" policy with juvenile offenders (see Figure 17.2) that has resulted in a growth in institutional programs.

The majority of these institutions are small, nonsecure facilities holding fewer than 20 youths. However, 70 facilities house more than 200 juveniles. Although about 80 percent of the public institutions can be characterized as "closed" and secured, only 20 percent of private institutions are high-security facilities.

	Number of Facilities	%	Number of Annual Juvenile Admissions	%	Number in Custody One-Day Counts	%
Total	**11,651**	**100.0%**	**900,494**	**100.0%**	**99,008**	**100.0%**
Public juvenile facilities	1,076	9.2	683,636	75.9	57,542	58.1
Private juvenile facilities	2,032	17.4	139,813	15.5	36,190	36.6
Adult jails	3,316	28.5	65,263	7.2	1,676	1.7
State and federal adult correctional facilities	1,287	11.0	11,782	1.3	3,600	3.6
Police lockups	3,940	33.8	Unknown	—	Unknown	—

Source: James Austin et al., *Juveniles Taken into Custody: 1993* (Washington, D.C.: OJJDP, 1995).

Public institutions for juveniles can be administered by any number of state agencies: child and youth services; mental health, youth conservation, health, and social services; corrections; and child welfare. Social service departments administer juvenile institutions in 22 states and the District of Columbia, while corrections agencies have this responsibility in 11 states and youth services departments have this responsibility in 13 states. In six jurisdictions, delinquent institutions are administered by a specialized department of family and children's services.[17] Recently, a number of states have created separate youth services organizations and removed juvenile corrections from an existing adult corrections department or mental health agency. Virginia, for instance, created a Department of Youth Services in July 1990, and Arizona's juvenile corrections program became an independent agency after it split from the State Department of Corrections.[18] The institutions in some states fall under a centralized corrections system that covers adults as well as juveniles. Other states operate separate adult and juvenile systems. Maryland has enhanced its juvenile corrections program by creating the Juvenile Services Agency, whose director reports directly to the governor. This agency employs 1,800 workers, oversees an $87 million budget, and serves more than 29,000 juveniles. It operates a secure facility, five youth centers, and four detention centers. These facilities are augmented by contractual residential and nonresidential programs for troubled youths as well as a variety of community-based services.[19]

A diversity of administrative arrangements characterizes the organization of institutional juvenile corrections in the United States today. According to experts, there is a preference for a single statewide department of juvenile corrections.[20] This form of organization seems best able to carry out the courts' dispositions, appropriate monies, and implement effective institutional programs for juveniles.

Overall, the trend is to remove the responsibility for juvenile corrections from adult departments and place it in either a youth services or a family services department. However, the majority of states still place responsibility for the administration of juvenile corrections within social service departments. New Mexico and Wyoming are two states that have created family and children's services departments in recent years.[21]

For the most part, institutional administration—including financial management and program planning—is not an easy task. Unfortunately, it is the quality of administration that often determines the effectiveness of a particular facility.

FIGURE 17.2
Growth in institutional care, 1975 to 1991

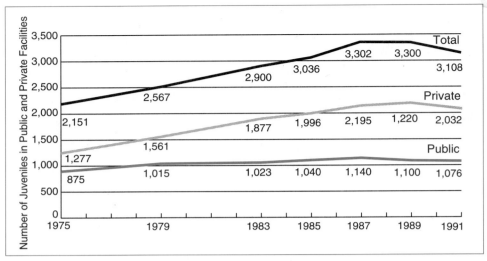

Source: Bureau of Justice Statistics, *Children in Custody 1975–1985* and *Fact Sheet 1987* (Washington, D.C.: U.S. Department of Justice, 1989); Office of Juvenile Justice and Delinquency Prevention, *National Juvenile Custody Trends 1978–1989* (Washington, D.C.: U.S. Department of Justice, 1992); James Austin et. al., *Juveniles Taken into Custody–1993* (Washington, D.C.: OJJDP, 1995).

The physical plants of juvenile institutions across the nation vary tremendously in size and quality. Many of the older training schools are tremendously outdated. Older facilities still tend to place all juvenile offenders in a single building, regardless of the offense. More acceptable structures today include a reception unit with an infirmary, a security unit, and dormitory units or cottages. Planners have concluded that the most effective design for training schools is to have facilities located around a community square. The facilities generally include a dining hall and kitchen area, a storage warehouse, academic and vocational training rooms, a library, an auditorium, a gymnasium, a laundry, maintenance facilities, an administration building, and other basic facilities, such as a commissary, a barber shop, and a beauty shop.

Physical conditions of individual living areas vary widely, depending on the type of facility and the progressiveness of its administration. In the past, most traditional training school conditions were appalling, with juveniles living in unbelievable squalor. Today, most institutions provide youths with toilet and bath facilities, beds, desks, lamps, and tables. New facilities usually provide a single room for each individual.

Most experts recommend that juvenile facilities have indoor and outdoor leisure areas, libraries, academic and vocational education spaces, chapels, facilities where youths can meet with their visitors, a reception and processing room, security fixtures, windows in all sleeping accommodations, and fire safety equipment and procedures. Because institutions for delinquent youth vary in type, it is not necessary that they meet identical physical standards. Security measures used in some closed juvenile institutions, for instance, may not be required in a residential community program.

The physical conditions and architecture of secure facilities for juveniles have come a long way from the training schools of the turn of the century. However, many administrators and state legislators realize that more modernization is

Institutionalized girls are often the "throwaways" of society—those whom nobody wants. Many suffer from inadequate social skills, low self-esteem, and poor home environment. They are often the victims of child and sex abuse and have experienced educational and vocational inequity, and the lack of meaningful treatment options. Although there is a recent movement toward the use of co-ed institutions for juveniles, most girls remain incarcerated in antiquated, single-sex institutions that are usually isolated in rural areas and rarely offer adequate rehabilitative services.

necessary to meet even minimum compliance with national standards for juvenile institutions. Correctional administrators have described conditions as horrendous, and health officials have cited institutions for such violations as pollution by vermin, rodents, and asbestos.[22] Although some positive changes have taken place, there are still enormous problems to overcome.

The majority of juveniles held in long-term facilities are still housed in crowded facilities. Few juveniles are in institutions that meet basic health care criteria. Secure institutions do not take active steps to prevent suicides. Also, juveniles often have only very limited contact with the community during their period of confinement. Such conditions ordinarily make it enormously difficult to rehabilitate juvenile offenders.

Legal efforts, at the heart of more than 20 years of child advocacy, continue to (1) establish procedures to protect the rights of children in institutions; (2) reduce the number of institutionalized juveniles nationwide; and (3) improve the treatment of incarcerated youth, including providing for adequate medical and educational programs.[23]

TRENDS IN JUVENILE CORRECTIONS

There is little question that tremendous variation exists among the states in the use of juvenile correctional facilities. California is by far the leading state in both its use and variety of such facilities. It alone houses almost 20 percent of all residents of public and private institutions.[24] The California incarceration rate for juveniles is more than 525 per 100,000 juveniles in the population. In contrast, Texas has an incarceration rate of about 200 per 100,000. New York, another populous state, has almost 5,000 youths in custody and averages an incarceration rate of 300 per 100,000.[25] In 1991, the national average was 357 juveniles per 100,000 in public custody. The highest rate in public facilities for delinquent acts is in the District of Columbia, an entirely urban population, where the juvenile custody rate is 810 per 100,000 or almost 4 times the national average of 210 per 100,000. These numbers indicate that states address the problems of institutional care in different ways (see Table 17.4).[26]

One major problem facing the juvenile correctional system is overcrowding. Many juvenile institutions contain more residents than they are designed to hold. Overcrowding—and its attendant problems—is one reason that some states, including Idaho, Utah, and Connecticut, have made concerted efforts to close public facilities and house most of their juvenile populations in small, privately run facilities. Colorado, West Virginia, Oregon, Pennsylvania, and North Dakota are also attempting to reduce their secure populations and rely more heavily on community-based programs. This trend is likely to spread to all 50 states.

Changes also occurred in the juvenile institutions of Arizona and Arkansas in the 1990s. The impetus for change in Arizona was a class-action lawsuit brought on behalf of minors confined in the Catalina Mountain Juvenile Institution challenging the inadequate conditions at the institution. In Arkansas, an investigation into abuses at the state's two training schools led to reductions in that state's juvenile correctional population.[27]

Overcrowding has made some states reluctant to increase the number of juvenile residents in their publicly run facilities. Another reason for reluctance is the enormous expense involved. The average cost of housing one resident for one year in 1989 was $27,000. The cost of housing juveniles was among the highest in New York ($54,000), Rhode Island ($78,000), Connecticut ($45,000), Pennsylvania ($44,000), Idaho ($43,100), Oklahoma ($43,000), and Minnesota ($39,100). Costs range from a low of $16,500 to a high of $78,000.[28] Today, the average cost per child in a residential setting is more than $30,000 per year.

In addition, the cost of constructing a 30- to 40-bed secure treatment facility for juvenile offenders can be $6 million or more, or $50,000 to $60,000 per juvenile per year, compared with an operating cost of $5,000 to $10,000 per juvenile per year for most delinquency prevention programs.[29]

PROFILE OF THE INSTITUTIONALIZED JUVENILE

The best source of information on institutionalized youths is the federal government's *Children in Custody* (CIC) census. This survey provides timely information on the number and characteristics of children being held in public and private facilities around the nation. Other excellent references are the Office of

TABLE 17.4 National Trends in Juvenile Corrections—Public and Private

	1979	1989	1991
Juveniles in Custody	71,922	93,945	98,000
Overall Custody Rate per 100,000	251	367	357
Admission Rate per 100,000	2,220	2,974	3,213
Total Expenditures	1,307,684	2,860,818	3,000,000
Total Number of Juvenile Institutions	2,200	3,267	3,200

Source: Office of Juvenile Justice and Delinquency Prevention, *National Juvenile Custody Trends 1978–1989.* (Washington, D.C.: U.S. Department of Justice, 1992); Barbara Allen Hagen, *Public Juvenile Facilities—Children in Custody, 1989* (Washington, D.C.: U.S. Department of Justice, 1991); James Austin et. al., *Juveniles Taken into Custody—1993* (Washington, D.C.: U.S. Department of Justice, 1995).

Juvenile Justice and Delinquency's *Juveniles Taken into Custody Report* and the *Juvenile Court Statistics Report.*

The latest information available indicates that about 98,000 youths were being held in all types of facilities as of 1991 (see Figure 17.3).[30] Of these, approximately 65,000 were long-term institutional commitments, and 33,000 were preadjudication detainees. The census also found that more than 69,000 juveniles were confined for delinquent acts, 8,000 were confined as a result of status offenses, and 18,000 confined as nonoffenders.[31] The public long-term custody population increased 8 percent from 1983 to 1991.

In addition, both secure institutional and open long-term facilities saw increases in their minority populations of approximately 10 percent from 1983 to 1991. Minorities represent more than two-thirds of all residents in public long-term facilities. The state of Washington is one state that has undertaken a variety of programs aimed at eliminating any racial disparities in the juvenile justice system in light of the disproportionate number of minorities in institutional care.

The number of youths in public facilities remained virtually unchanged between 1980 and 1985 (about 50,000) but then increased to 56,723 in 1989 and to more than 57,000 in 1991. Private-sector institutions experienced an increase of approximately 10 percent between 1983 and 1985 (from 31,000 to 34,000), as well as another 10 percent increase from 1985 to 1989 (from 34,000 to 38,000).[32] The latest figure is about 37,000, representing little or no growth in private-sector placement.

The data suggest that despite 25 years of decarceration efforts, the number of incarcerated youths has increased, a trend that reflects the dominance of a conservative, crime control-oriented policy in some states: Nearly half of all juveniles in public training schools in 1991 were in five states (California, New York, Texas, Illinois, and Ohio).

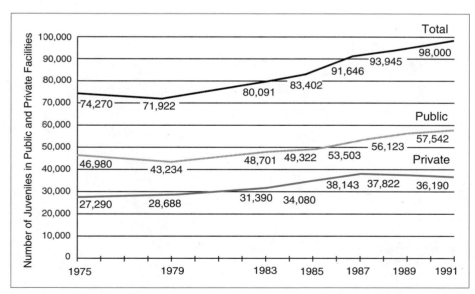

FIGURE 17.3
Rate for incarcerated children, 1985 to 1991

Source: Bureau of Justice Statistics, *Children in Custody 1975–1985* and *Fact Sheet 1987* (Washington, D.C.: U.S. Department of Justice, 1989); Office of Juvenile Justice and Delinquency Prevention, *National Juvenile Custody Trends 1978–1989* (Washington, D.C.: U.S. Department of Justice, 1992); James Austin et. al., *Juveniles Taken into Custody—1993* (Washington, D.C.: U.S. Department of Justice, 1995).

THE HIDDEN JUVENILE CORRECTIONAL SYSTEM

Although the number of institutionalized youths appears to be on the increase, the CIC data may reveal only the tip of the correctional iceberg. For example, the data do not include many of the minors who are incarcerated after they are waived to adult courts or who have their cases tried there because of exclusion statutes. Most states do place underage juveniles convicted of adult charges in youth centers until they reach the age of majority, whereupon they are transferred to an adult facility. In addition, as Ira Schwartz and his colleagues point out, there is a "hidden" system of juvenile control that places wayward youths in private mental hospitals and substance-abuse clinics for behaviors that could easily have brought them a stay in a correctional facility or community-based program.[33]

This "hidden system" is an important community resource for mentally ill children and juvenile substance-abuse offenders. During the past few years, 14 states have made changes in their laws relative to the civil commitment of children. Wyoming, for example, created the State Hospital Juvenile Treatment Program and allowed any adjudicated delinquent or person in need of supervision to be committed to the program. Montana established a Youth Treatment Center for the care of seriously mentally ill children between the ages of 12 and 18, including those who have committed delinquent acts. Michigan and Nebraska have enacted similar comprehensive statutes addressing the placement needs of minors. Other states, such as North Dakota and Missouri, are easing admission procedures for juvenile drug users in order to expand treatment options for them.

These efforts suggest that the number of institutionalized children may be far greater than reported in the CIC surveys. Undoubtedly, private-sector juvenile corrections, in the form of contract services or other institutional support, has become a significant part of the juvenile justice system, particularly for community-based programs.[34]

The "typical" resident is a 15- to 16-year-old white male. However, about one-fifth of all institutionalized juveniles are females. Contrary to popular belief, the great majority of residents were not committed for violent crimes: Most incarcerated youths were property and drug offenders.

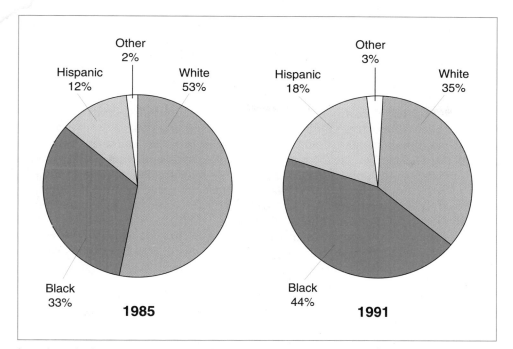

FIGURE 17.4
Public juvenile facilities: one-day counts by race, 1985–1991

Other
2%

Hispanic
12%

White
53%

Black
33%

1985

Other
3%

Hispanic
18%

White
35%

Black
44%

1991

Source: James Austin et. al., *Juveniles Taken into Custody—1993* (Washington, D.C.: U.S. Department of Justice, 1995).

PERSONAL CHARACTERISTICS

The data from the *Children in Custody* report and the OJJDP report of 1995 give some personal background information on children in custody. The "typical" resident described in the report was a 15- to 16-year-old white male who was incarcerated for an average stay of approximately five months in a public facility or six months in a private facility. Almost 80 percent of all the residents in public and private facilities were male and about 20 percent were female.

With regard to racial characteristics, more than 50 percent of all juveniles held in custody were white, 34 percent were African-American, and 12 percent were Hispanic. Racial makeup of the youth differed widely between private and public facilities. More than 63 percent of those in private institutions were white, while more than 54 percent of the juveniles held in public facilities were African-American or Hispanic; only about 34 percent of the juveniles held in private settings were of minority origin. Although the number of white juveniles held in public facilities decreased between 1985 and 1991, the number of African-American and Hispanic juveniles increased by 11 and 6 percent, respectively (see Figure 17.4).

Today, African-American and Hispanic juveniles constitute about 44 percent and 14 percent, respectively, of the juvenile population, while white youths constitute about 43 percent.[35] Because of these changing social patterns, a juvenile in a public facility today is most likely an African-American male between 14 and 17 years of age who is held for a delinquent offense, such as a property crime. On the other hand, a juvenile in a private facility is more likely to be a white male between 14 and 17 years of age who is held for a nondelinquent act, such as running away or truancy.

Although the data shows that a majority of juvenile correctional inmates are white, recent research by Barry Krisberg and his associates found that minority youths are incarcerated at a rate three to four times that of white youths and that this overrepresentation is not a result of differentials in their arrest or crime rates. Of equal importance, minorities are more likely to be confined in secure public facilities rather than in open private facilities that might provide more costly and effective treatment. Minority youths accused of delinquent acts are also less likely than white youths to be diverted from the court system into more lenient, informal sanctions and more likely to receive sentences involving incarceration. Clearly racial disparity in juvenile disposition is a growing problem that demands immediate public scrutiny.[36] Some jurisdictions have initiated their own studies of the extensiveness and causes of racial disproportionality in their own juvenile justice systems.[37] Today, about 60 percent of the juveniles in custody belong to racial or ethnic minorities.

Most juveniles committed to institutions are between 14 and 17 years old. Private facilities tend to house younger youths, while public institutions provide custodial care for older youths, including a small percentage between 18 and 21 years old (see Table 17.5). About 17 percent are 14 or younger. The number of juveniles held in public facilities increased 17 percent in 1985, 5 percent in 1987, and only slightly in 1991. Coupled with a decline in the overall juvenile population, this still means that a greater proportion of the juvenile population apparently is being held in custody.

What do juvenile offenders have to do in order to wind up in a correctional facility? Contrary to popular belief, the great majority of residents are not committed for violent crimes. Most incarcerated youths in the 1980s and early 1990s were property and drug offenders. In fact, the number of delinquents

TABLE 17.5 Demographic Characteristics of Juveniles Held in Public Juvenile Facilities, 1983, 1985, 1987, 1989, and 1991.

	Number of Juveniles				
	1983	1985	1987	1989	1991
Total	**48,701**	**49,322**	**53,503**	**56,123**	**57,542**
Sex					
Male	42,182	42,549	46,012	49,443	51,212
Female	6,519	6,773	7,491	6,680	6,330
Race and ethnicity					
White	27,805	29,969	24,631	22,201	20,139
African-American and Hispanic	23,747	24,820	28,890	33,922	25,318
Other	1,104	1,084	0	0	1,726
Age on census date					
9 years and under	42	60	73	45	0
10–13 years	3,104	3,181	2,675	3,276	3,452
14–17 years	39,571	40,640	42,802	44,894	46,037
18–20 years	4,804	5,409	6,955	7,908	805
21 years and over	86	32	0		

Source: Bureau of Justice Statistics, *Children in Custody 1975–85* and *Fact Sheet 1987* (Washington, D.C.: U.S. Department of Justice, 1989) (data for 1987 computed from *Fact Sheet*); Barbara Allen-Hagen, *Children in Custody—Public Juveniles Facilities, 1989* OJJDP update (Washington, D.C.: U.S. Department of Justice, 1991); James Austin et. al., *Juveniles Taken into Custody— 1993* (Washington, D.C.: U.S. Department of Justice, 1995).

involved in property crimes and nondelinquents committed to public and private institutions—including status offenders and neglected, dependent, and emotionally disturbed youths—was greater than the number of youths committed for violent acts. Thus, the image of the incarcerated delinquent as a violent menace to society is somewhat misleading.

However, the early 1990s did see more violent juvenile crime than any other period in recent history. We know, for instance, that after a decade of relative stability, the juvenile violent crime arrest rate soared between 1990 and 1992 (see chapter 2). The number of juveniles transferred to adult criminal court has also grown substantially in recent years. Some experts believe that juvenile arrests for violent crime will double in the next decade.[38] Although arrest rates are difficult to interpret, they may indicate changes in the offense types taken into custody. "Get tough" laws designed to shift a state's juvenile justice system from a "best interest of the child" model to one that emphasizes public safety will also have an impact on arrest rates. Additional institutional facilities for youths sentenced in adult courts may be needed.

INSTITUTIONAL ADJUSTMENT

More than a decade ago, shocking exposés of the treatment of institutionalized youths focused public attention on the problems of juvenile corrections. Today, some critics believe that the light of public scrutiny has moderated conditions within training schools. There is now greater professionalism among the staff, and staff brutality seems to have diminished. Status offenders and delinquents are for the most part held in separate facilities. Finally, confinement length is shorter, and rehabilitative programming has increased.

Despite such improvements, the everyday life of male inmates still reflects institutional values. Clemens Bartollas, S. J. Miller, and Simon Dinitz identified an inmate value system that in many ways resembles the "inmate social code" found in adult institutions. The general code revolves around the following principles:

> Exploit whomever you can.
> Don't play up to staff.
> Don't rat on your peers.
> Don't give in to others.[39]

In addition to these general rules, the researchers found that there were separate norms for African-American inmates—"exploit whites," "no forcing sex on blacks," "defend your brother"—and for whites—"don't trust anyone," "everybody for himself."

The male inmate code still seems to be in operation. More recent research conducted in five juvenile institutions confirmed the notion that residents formed cohesive groups and adhered to an informal inmate culture in an effort to "do time" gracefully.[40] The more serious the youth's delinquent record and the more secure the institution, the greater the adherence to the inmate social code.

Today, male delinquents are more likely to form allegiances with members of their own racial group and attempt to exploit those outside the group. They also scheme to manipulate staff and take advantage of weaker peers. However, in institutions that are treatment-oriented and where staff–inmate relationships are more intimate, residents are less likely to adhere to a negativistic inmate code.

CULTURE OF THE FEMALE OFFENDER

Females have traditionally been less involved in criminal activities than males. As a consequence, the number of females in institutions has been lower than the number of males. However, the growing involvement of girls in criminal behavior and the feminist movement have drawn more attention to the female juvenile offender. This attention has revealed a double standard of justice. For example, girls are more likely than boys to be incarcerated for status offenses, such as truancy, running away, and sexual misconduct. Institutions for girls are generally more restrictive than those for boys. They have fewer educational and vocational programs and fewer services. They also do a less than adequate job of rehabilitation. It has been suggested that this double standard operates through a chivalrous male justice system that seeks to "protect" young girls from their own sexuality.[41]

Over the years, the number of females held in public institutions has generally declined. This represents the continuation of a long-term trend to remove girls, many of whom are nonserious status offenders, from closed institutions and place them in less restrictive private or community-based facilities. So although a majority of males are today housed in public facilities, most female delinquents reside in private facilities.

In recent years, however, overall admissions of females have increased significantly. For the period 1983 to 1992, the admission of females to public and private juvenile facilities increased by 23 percent. Female admissions to private institutions specifically have risen rapidly, compared with a continuous decline in public institution admissions. Generally, about 39 percent of incarcerated female juveniles are in private facilities, while half that number are in public facilities. (Figure 17.5 compares the rates of growth in female and male admissions from 1979 to 1991.) You will notice, that although steady increases in admissions in public and private facilities exist for males, admissions for females to public facilities increased only until 1987, when they then began to decrease. The in-custody trend for female juvenile offenders is obviously in the area of private facilities.[42]

Institutionalized girls are often runaways seeking to escape intolerable home situations, which can involve abusive or incestuous relationships. Some are pregnant and have no means of support. Many are the "throwaways" of society— those whom nobody wants. Only a few are true delinquents. Recent studies estimate that up to 300,000 female adolescents are involved in prostitution nationwide.[43] This number continues to grow because the number of runaways keeps increasing.

The same double standard that operates to bring a girl into an institution continues to exist once she is in custody. Females tend to be incarcerated for longer terms than most males. In addition, institutional programs for girls tend to be strongly oriented toward the reinforcement of traditional roles for women. Incarcerated females receive training in "womanly arts." How well these programs rehabilitate girls and ready them for life in a quickly changing society is questionable.

Many of the characteristics of juvenile female offenders are similar to those of their male counterparts. These include poor social skills, low self-esteem, and poor home environment. Other problems are more specific to the female juvenile offender, such as sexuality issues, victimization, educational and vocational inequity, and the lack of placement options.

FIGURE 17.5

U.S. public and private juvenile facilities: one-day counts, 1979–1991

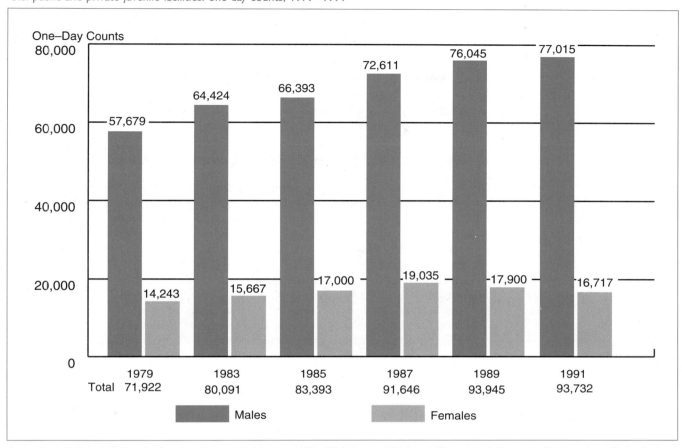

One–Day Counts

	1979	1983	1985	1987	1989	1991
Males	57,679	64,424	66,393	72,611	76,045	77,015
Females	14,243	15,667	17,000	19,035	17,900	16,717
Total	71,922	80,091	83,393	91,646	93,945	93,732

Source: Barry K. Risberg, Robert DeComo, and Norma C. Herrera, *1979–1989 Census of Public and Private Juvenile Detention, Correctional and Shelter Facilities*; U.S. Bureau of the Census population estimates; James Austin et. al., *Juveniles Taken into Custody—1993* (Washington, D.C.: U.S. Department of Justice, 1995).

Although there is a recent movement toward the use of coed institutions for juveniles, most girls remain incarcerated in antiquated, single-sex institutions that are usually isolated in rural areas and rarely offer adequate rehabilitative services. Results of a recent federally sponsored survey of training schools across the nation revealed a definite pattern of inequality in services for boys and girls.[44]

Several factors account for the different treatment of girls. One is sexual stereotyping by administrators, who believe that "girls should be girls" and that teaching them "appropriate" sex roles in prison will help them function effectively in society. These beliefs are often held by the staff as well, many of whom have only a high-school education and hold highly sexist ideas of what is appropriate behavior for adolescent girls. Girls' institutions tend to be smaller than boys' institutions. As a result, they simply do not have the money to offer as many varied programs and services as do the larger male institutions.[45]

In general, it appears that although society is more concerned about protecting girls who act out, it is less concerned about rehabilitating them because the crimes they commit are not serious. These attitudes translate into fewer staff, less modern buildings, and poorer vocational, educational, and recreational programs than those found in boys' institutions. Ilene Bergsmann points out that little time and effort have been devoted to the female offender in the last century. She concludes that differential treatment of females and males in the juvenile justice system begins with the schools, continues with law enforcement, and is perpetuated by the correctional system.[46]

CORRECTIONAL TREATMENT FOR JUVENILES

Nearly all juvenile institutions implement some form of treatment program for youths in custody—counseling on an individual or group basis, vocational and educational training, recreational programs, and religious counseling. In addition, most institutions provide medical and dental health programs of some kind, as well as occasional legal service programs. Generally, the larger the institution, the greater the number of programs and services offered.

The purpose of these various programs is to rehabilitate the youths within the institutions—to reform them into well-adjusted individuals and send them back into the community to be productive citizens. Despite generally good intentions, however, the goal of rehabilitation is rarely attained. National statistics show that a significant number of juvenile offenders commit more crimes after release from incarceration. Whitehead and Lab's 1989 meta-analysis of 50 studies of institutional and community-based programs concluded that correctional treatment has little effect on recidivism.[47]

One of the most common problems in efforts to rehabilitate juveniles is a lack of well-trained staff members to run programs. Budgetary limitations are a primary concern when it comes to planning for institutional programs. It costs a minimum of $27,000 per year to keep a child in an institution—a staggering amount that explains why institutions generally do not employ large professional staffs.

It is also not clear which programs provide the most effective treatment. Some often-cited studies indicate that few of the treatment programs being used in juvenile institutions are effective in preventing future delinquency.

The most glaring problem with treatment programs is that they are not being administered in the way in which they were intended. Although the official goals of many institutions may be treatment and rehabilitation, the actual programs may center around security, control, and punishment. Whether juveniles who respond to a structured setting should be released without knowing if they have been truly rehabilitated is exemplified in the following "Case in Point."

INDIVIDUAL TREATMENT TECHNIQUES— PAST AND PRESENT

One common treatment approach is **individual counseling.** It is estimated that virtually all juvenile institutions use this approach to some extent. This is not surprising as psychological problems such as depression are a real and present problem in juvenile institutions.[48] Individual counseling does not attempt to change a youth's personality. Rather, it attempts to help individuals understand

You are an aftercare worker responsible for evaluating and recommending the release of juveniles from institutional confinement.

William G. was 15 ½ years old when he was committed for 18 months to a secure juvenile institution after being adjudicated delinquent for breaking and entering and larceny. William resided with his aunt and uncle and two cousins. His mother died 3 years ago, and he has had no contact with his father for 10 years. Initial psychological testing indicated that William was a hostile, angry youth with borderline intelligence, poor controls, and no guilt. The psychiatrist believed that William was likely to commit crime in the future. Considering the fact that William was before the juvenile court on two prior occasions (for truancy and drug use), he seemed like a youth out of control.

Recent evaluations of William's institutional progress are in marked contrast to his behavior while living in the community. He has been cooperative and personable and has maintained a positive attitude during his 12 months at the institution. William seems to have benefited from the structural controls and constant monitoring offered in such a setting. On the other hand, he does require special education; because of his poor and inconsistent school record, the public school system is reluctant to take him back.

William is approaching his seventeenth birthday. The prosecutor's office and institutional personnel recommend that William complete his sentence. William's attorney suggests that the youth is ready for some form of residential placement.

How would you decide William's case?

---

and solve their current adjustment problems. The advantage of individual counseling is that institutions can use it superficially with counselors who may not be professionally qualified.

Highly structured counseling, on the other hand, can be based on psychotherapy or psychoanalysis. **Psychotherapy** is an outgrowth of Freudian psychoanalytic techniques and requires extensive analysis of the individual's past childhood experiences. An effective, skilled therapist attempts to help the individual solve conflicts and make a more positive adjustment to society through the altering of negative behavior.

Although individual counseling and psychotherapy are used extensively in institutions and may work well for certain individuals, there is little indication that these treatments are even marginally effective. Fifteen years ago, in a review of ten such programs, Dennis Romig reported that eight had completely negative results.[49]

Another highly used treatment approach for delinquents is **reality therapy.**[50] This approach, developed by William Glasser during the 1970s, emphasizes current, over past, behavior by stressing that offenders are completely responsible for their actions. Glasser believes that a psychoanalytical emphasis on the past may lead children to excuse current and future misbehavior by encouraging them to think of themselves as "sick" and thus unable to change their actions. The success of reality therapy depends greatly on the warmth and concern of the individual counselor. Unfortunately, many institutions rely heavily on this type of therapy because they assume that highly trained professionals are unnecessary to carry it out. Actually, a skilled therapist is essential to the success of this form of treatment. The individual must be knowledgeable about the complexity of personalities and be able to deal with any situation that may come up in the counseling.

The object of reality therapy is to make individuals more responsible people. This end is accomplished by giving them confidence and strength through developing their ability to follow a set of expectations as closely as possible.

Behavior modification, another method of treatment, is used in many institutions.[51] It is based on the theory that all behavior is learned and that current behavior can be shaped through a system of rewards and punishments. This type of program is easily used in an institutional setting that offers points and privileges as rewards for such behaviors as work, study, or the development of skills. It is a reasonably effective technique, especially when a contract is formed with the youth to modify certain behaviors. When youths are aware of what is expected of them, they plan their actions to meet these expectations and then experience the anticipated consequences. In this way, they can be motivated to change. Behavior modification is effective in controlled settings, where a counselor can manipulate the situation, but once the youth is back in the real world, it becomes difficult to use.

In general, effective individual treatment programs are built around the following specific counseling techniques: (1) psychotherapy, (2) reality therapy, and (3) behavior modification. Other less formal approaches include personal growth counseling, substance-abuse treatment, assertiveness training, and self-image and ego development counseling.

GROUP TREATMENT TECHNIQUES

Group therapy is more economical than individual therapy because one therapist can counsel more than one individual at a time. Also, the support of the group is often highly valuable to the individuals in the group, and individuals derive hope from other members of the group who have survived similar experiences. Another advantage of group therapy is that a group can often solve a problem more effectively than an individual.[52]

There are some disadvantages to group therapy. It provides less individualized attention. Everyone is different, and some group members may need more highly individualized treatment. Others may be shy and afraid to speak up in the group and thus fail to receive the benefits of the group experience. Conversely, some individuals may dominate group interaction, making it difficult for the leader to conduct an effective session. Finally, group condemnation may seriously hurt rather than help a participant.

More than any other group treatment technique, group psychotherapy probes into an individual's personality and attempts to restructure it. Relationships in these groups tend to be quite intense. The group is used to facilitate expression of feelings, to solve problems, and to teach members to empathize with one another.

Unfortunately, the components necessary for an effective group psychotherapy session, such as personal interaction, cooperation, and tolerance, are in direct conflict with the antisocial, antagonistic, and exploitive orientation of delinquents. This type of technique can be effective when the members of the group are in attendance voluntarily, but such is not the case with institutionalized delinquents, who are often forced to attend. Consequently, the effectiveness of such programs is questionable.

Guided group interaction (GGI) is a fairly common method of group treatment. It is based on the theory, that through group interactions, a delinquent can begin to realize and solve personal problems. A group leader facilitates interaction among group members, and a group culture develops. Individual members can be mutually supportive and can help develop more acceptable behavior. Guided group interaction was an instrumental factor in the success of programs at Highfields, New Jersey, and Provo, Utah.[53] In the 1980s, a version of GGI called **Positive Peer Culture (PPC)** became popular in juvenile corrections. PPC programs use groups in which peer leaders encourage other youths to conform to conventional behaviors. The rationale for PPC is that if negative peer influence can encourage youths to engage in delinquent behavior, then positive peer influence can help them conform.[54]

Milieu therapy seeks to make all aspects of an inmate's environment a part of his or her treatment and to minimize differences between the custodial staff and the treatment personnel. It also emphasizes peer influence in the formation of constructive values. Milieu therapy attempts to create an environment that encourages meaningful change, increased growth, and satisfactory adjustment. This is often accomplished through peer pressure to conform to group norms.

One early type of milieu therapy based on psychoanalytic theory was developed in Chicago during the late 1940s and early 1950s by Bruno Bettleheim.[55] This therapy attempted to create a conscience, or superego, in delinquent youths by getting them to depend on their therapists to a great extent and then threatening them with the loss of the loving and caring relationship if they failed to control their behavior.

Today, institutional group counseling often focuses on drug and alcohol group counseling, self-esteem development groups, and role-model support sessions. In addition, because considerably more violent juveniles are entering the system than in years past, group sessions serve to deal with appropriate expressions of anger and rage and methods to understand and control such behavior.

EDUCATIONAL, VOCATIONAL, AND RECREATIONAL PROGRAMS

In addition to individual and group treatment programs, most institutions use educational, vocational, and recreational programs designed to teach juveniles skills that will help them adjust more easily when they are released into the community. Educational programs for juveniles are required in long-term facilities because children must go to school until they reach a certain age. Because educational programs are an important part of social development and have therapeutic, as well as instructional, value, they are an essential part of most treatment programs. What takes place through education is related to all other aspects of the institutional program—the work activities, cottage life, recreation, and clinical services.

Educational programs are probably some of the best-staffed programs in training schools, but even at their best, most are inadequate. Training programs must contend with a myriad of problems. Many of the youths coming into these institutions are mentally retarded or have low IQs or learning disabilities. As such, they are educationally disabled and far behind their grade levels in basic academic areas. Most of these youths dislike school and become bored with any type of educational program. Their boredom often leads to acting out and subsequent disciplinary problems.

Ideally, institutions allow the inmates to attend a school in the community or offer programs that lead to a high school diploma or GED certificate. Unfortunately,

Most institutions use vocational and educational treatment programs designed to teach juveniles skills that will help them adjust more easily when they are released into the community. Since educational programs are an important part of social development and have therapeutic value in addition to their instructional values, they are an essential part of most treatment programs.

not all institutions offer these types of programs. Ironically, more secure institutions, because of their large size, are more likely than group homes or day-treatment centers to offer supplemental educational programs, such as remedial reading, physical education, and tutoring. Some more modern educational programs offer computer learning and programmed learning modules.

Vocational training has long been used as a treatment technique for juveniles. Early institutions were even referred to as industrial schools. Today, vocational programs in institutions are varied. Programs offered include auto repair, printing, woodworking, mechanical drawing, food service, cosmetology, secretarial training, and data processing. One obvious problem here is sex-typing. The recent trend has been to allow equal access to all programs offered in institutions that house girls and boys. Sex-typing is more difficult to avoid in single-sex institutions, because funds often cannot be found to offer all types of training.

Vocational programs for youths that include job placement and vocational training, alone, do not positively affect juvenile delinquency. Youths need skills that will give them hope for advancement.

The Ventura School for Female Juvenile Offenders, established under the California Youth Authority, has been a pioneer in the work placement concept. Private industry contracts with the youth authority to establish businesses on the institution's grounds. The businesses hire, train, and pay scale wages for work. Wages are divided into a victim's restitution fund, room and board fees, and forced savings, and a portion is given to the juvenile to purchase canteen items. Trans World Airlines (TWA), for example, has established a ticket reservation center on school grounds. The center handles the overflow phone calls from Los Angeles. Many juveniles have been trained, and a significant number have been employed by TWA or travel agencies upon their release. Ventura also has a program that involves private industry in the manufacture of uniforms at the school, particularly for the petroleum industry. Such skills are often marketable to employers in need of trained workers.[56]

Recreational activity is also an important way to help relieve adolescent aggressions, as evidenced by the many diversionary and delinquency prevention programs that focus on recreation as the primary treatment technique.

In sum, the treatment programs that seem to be most effective for rehabilitating juvenile offenders are those that use a combination of the above-mentioned techniques. Programs that are comprehensive, intensive, built on a juvenile's strengths, and that adopt a socially grounded position have a much greater chance for success. Individual treatment alone often fails to address institutional and community issues. Successful programs typically deal with issues relating to school, peers, work, and community.

Increasingly, the juvenile justice correctional system must address the issue of an increasingly violent juvenile population. How it responds to treatment of the violent offender is of particular interest today.

Treating Chronic and Violent Delinquents

Treating the **chronic juvenile offender** has become a major concern in recent years. Although significant efforts are being made to deinstitutionalize and decarcerate nonserious and status offenders, the question remains what to do with the more serious juvenile delinquents who commit such crimes as rape or robbery. One answer has been to ease waiver rules and standards so that younger children can be transferred to the adult court. A number of states have created concurrent jurisdiction laws, which enable prosecutors to choose whether to bring a case to the adult court or juvenile court.

Another early approach was to incarcerate serious offenders in intensive juvenile treatment programs, where their problems could be dealt with while they were isolated both from society and other juvenile offenders. This policy received impetus from a controversial book by Charles Murray and Louis B. Cox, *Beyond Probation.*[57] Murray and Cox compared chronic delinquents sent to traditional Illinois training school programs with those in an innovative community-based program, the Unified Delinquency Intervention Services. They discovered a **suppression effect**—a reduction in the number of arrests per year of those youths who had been incarcerated. Moreover, the suppression effect for youths sent to training school was higher than for those in less punitive treatment programs. Murray and Cox concluded that the juvenile justice system must choose which policy outcome its programs are aimed at achieving: prevention of delinquency or the care and protection of needy youths. If the former is a proper goal for the juvenile justice system, then institutionalization or the threat of institutionalization is desirable.

Twenty-years ago, Andrew Vachss and Yitzhak Bakal argued that a secure treatment center was necessary to deal with what they called **life-style violent juveniles.**[58] If secure placements were not available, there would be (1) increased use of waiver; (2) a dangerous mixing of offender types within an institutional setting (e.g., nonviolent youths would become exposed to more serious offenders); (3) collapse and failure of alternative programs, because they would become contaminated by chronic offenders; and (4) the continuing problems of a system that returns dangerous juveniles to communities in far more dangerous condition and at the same time continues to incarcerate nondangerous juveniles within its "programs."[59]

There has been a general movement in the past twenty years toward the use of fewer and smaller secure facilities, on the theory that these programs allow more freedom and a greater chance of rehabilitating young offenders than do large bureaucratic institutions. States such as Utah and Vermont have for the most part closed their large training schools and now rely on smaller institutions of less than forty youths. Violent youths and chronic serious offenders are placed in a few small, high-security treatment units. The use of correctional boot camps, which feature intense discipline and physical training, has flourished.

Today, we realize that secure corrections programs should be reserved for only the most serious and violent offenders. Large training schools, in particular, have not proven to be effective in rehabilitating juvenile offenders. Ira Schwartz, a noted expert in juvenile justice, has recommended that all large training schools be closed. Community-based graduated sanctions appear to be as successful as traditional incarceration in reducing recidivism. In the 1970s and 1980s, the claim that few rehabilitative programs worked with juvenile offenders was widely accepted by juvenile justice practitioners. Evidence indicates, however, that many programs, both past and current, have achieved acceptable results, and Dan Macallair points out that a growing number of studies indicate that rehabilitative programs can be effective for juvenile offenders.[60] Exhaustive research by the Office of Juvenile Justice and Delinquency Prevention and other experts also concludes that rehabilitation programs work.[61] A description of some of the more successful correction-based institutional programs is found in the following section.

SPECIALIZED PROGRAMS

Many states have set up specialized programs to deal with the chronic, violent offender. These efforts have been aided and funded by the federal government's **Violent Juvenile Offender (VJO)** program, which tests innovative strategies for reintegrating chronically violent offenders back into the community.[62]

Some offenders pose such a threat to the public that they must be placed in locked, secure, and specialized types of facilities. Youths in these programs also need a wide range of rehabilitation services. Correctional research has shown that the most effective secure programs limit the number of participants and provide them individual services. Large training schools have not been successful in rehabilitating violent juvenile offenders.

The VJO program is an example of secure corrections for violent male offenders. VJO youths are placed in small, secure settings and are gradually reintegrated into the community through community-based programs followed by intensive supervision. The VJO model is based on strengthening the juvenile's ties to positive institutions, providing opportunities for success, and employing a system of rewards and sanctions. Most of the youth in VJO programs have been adjudicated for a major felony. According to Jeffrey Fagan, who conducted in-depth studies of the VJO program, there were fewer and less serious rearrests with VJO youth than with control groups. Fagan concluded that the basic principles of such programs can reduce recidivism among violent juvenile offenders.[63]

Two other programs also merit attention. The Florida Environmental Institute (FEI), also known as "The Last Chance Ranch," targets Florida's most serious juvenile offenders. Located in a remote area of the Florida Everglades, it receives many of its referrals from the adult justice system. (In Florida, a juvenile found guilty as an adult may be returned to the juvenile justice system for treatment.) The FEI philosophy is based on (1) education; (2) therapeutic hard work; (3) a system of rewards; and (4) a strong aftercare component. Although the data on recidivism are unclear for the FEI, studies of traditional training schools often indicate much higher rates—more than 50 percent.[64]

The Capital Offender Program (COP) in Texas is an unusual group treatment program for juveniles committed for homicide.[65] The COP treatment approach focuses on group psychotherapy and seeks to create a sense of personal responsibility and reduce levels of hostility and aggression among the youth in the residential center. Research data suggest that the participants showed a lower rearrest rate and a lower reincarceration rate after participating in the program.

Another approach that seems to show promise is the outdoor education and training programs known collectively as **Outward Bound** programs. Two of these programs are described in the following "Focus on Delinquency."

According to Castellano and Soderstrom, very little is known about the effects of wilderness stress-challenge programs on juvenile recidivism. A study of the Spectrum Wilderness Program in Illinois found that successful completion of the program often resulted in arrest reductions that began immediately and lasted for about one year. Although overall results were mixed, such programs are promising alternatives to traditional juvenile justice placements.[66]

JUVENILE BOOT CAMPS

Correctional **boot camps** are also being developed for juvenile offenders. Boot camps combine the "get tough" elements of adult programs with education, substance abuse treatment, and socialization skills training. The American Correctional Association's Juvenile Project has studied the concept and sees merit in well-run boot camp programs, provided they incorporate the following elements: (1) a focus on concrete feelings and increasing self-esteem, (2) discipline through physical conditioning, and (3) programming in literacy, as well as academic and vocational education.[67]

In theory, a successful boot camp program should rehabilitate juvenile offenders, reduce the number of beds needed in secure institutional programs, and thus reduce the overall cost of care. The Alabama boot camp program for youthful offenders, for instance, estimated considerable savings of one million dollars annually when comparing boot camps with traditional institutional sentences.[68] However, when the issue of recidivism reduction is raised, no one seems convinced that participants in such programs fare any better than those who

JUVENILE REHABILITATION STRATEGIES: WILDERNESS PROGRAMS

Camping or wilderness adventure has usually played a peripheral role in juvenile rehabilitation programs. In the 1930s, the Chicago Area Project developed a summer camping component as part of its delinquency prevention efforts. Many states rotated selected wards from the state training schools through forestry camps, where they worked in fire crews or at maintaining trails. The difference with these newer programs is that the outdoor education component has now assumed a central role. Two well-established and respected programs using these concepts are VisionQuest and the Associated Marine Institutes. Many more use similar techniques.

VisionQuest

VisionQuest, a for-profit contractor with headquarters in Tucson, Arizona, is probably the largest program of its type, with annual commitments in excess of 500 delinquent youths. VisionQuest typically takes youths committed directly by juvenile courts in Pennsylvania, California, and several other states. The length of stay is usually between one year and eighteen months.

To enter the program, each candidate youth must agree to (1) abstain from drugs and sex during his or her commitment, (2) not run away, and (3) complete at least two impact programs, which can include residence in a wilderness camp, cross-country travel on a wagon train, or voyaging on a sailing vessel. In addition to its impact programs, VisionQuest conducts counseling sessions with other family members while a youth is in the program and operates several group homes that facilitate reentry into the community. While they are on the wagon train or in wilderness camp, each youth is assigned to a small group (tepee) of about eight other youths and two junior staff. Each wagon train or wilderness camp consists of about 30 to 45 youths and a similar number of staff. Junior staff members sleep in the tepees with the juveniles and are off duty two days in every seven.

In addition to the wagon trains and sailing programs, VisionQuest is also known for its confrontational style. Committed youths are not allowed to slide by and just "do time." Rather, an individual program is worked out to ensure that each youth is challenged intellectually, physically, and emotionally. When juveniles do not perform up to expectations or begin to "act out," they are "confronted" by one or more senior staff members in an attempt to get them to deal with whatever issues underlie the poor behavior.

Associated Marine Institutes

Associated Marine Institutes (AMI) is the parent agency for a group of nonprofit programs (institutes) located in Florida that use various marine projects as a means of motivating and challenging delinquent youths. Most of AMI's programs are nonresidential, picking up participating youths in the morning and returning them home in the evening, five days a week. During a typical stay of six months in the program, a participating youth will attend remedial classes, learn scuba diving and related safety procedures, study marine biology, and participate in some constructive work project, such as refurbishing an old boat or growing ground cover for some commercial site.

AMI also operates a long-term residential program at Fisheating Creek in south-central Florida. In this program, boys committed by the Dade County Juvenile Court spend six months to a year in an isolated work camp. During the first phase, their living conditions are extremely primitive, and their working conditions are rather hard (digging out stumps to clear an airstrip). Graduation to Phase 2 earns participants the right to sleep in air-conditioned quarters and have better work assignments. The last two phases of the program are spent in one of the nonresidential institutes near their home.

One of the distinctive characteristics of the nonprofit AMI is its heavy reliance on the capitalist spirit. Employee performance is periodically assessed by computerized measures (such as GEDs obtained, program completion rate, or subsequent recidivism rate) applied to all of the youths. End-of-the-year staff bonuses, based on these performance measures, can exceed 10 percent of regular salary. Committed youths can also earn money by participating in various work projects, such as clearing brush, that AMI has contracted to undertake.

Source: Adapted from Peter Greenwood and Franklin Zimring. *One More Chance* (Santa Monica, Calif.: Rand Corp., 1985), pp. 41–42.

serve normal sentences. Corbett and Petersilia do suggest that the research shows that boot camp participants seem less antisocial upon returning to society.[69]

Juvenile corrections agencies also implement shock incarceration programs. These feature high-intensity military discipline and physical training for short periods of time. The expectation is that the offender in such a boot camp will be "shocked" into going straight. These programs are now being used with young adult offenders and juveniles who have been waived to the adult system in Mississippi, Kansas, Florida, Georgia, and other jurisdictions.

There are some experts who believe that juvenile boot camps don't make any sense. They point out that (1) juvenile boot camps cannot save money unless they have hundreds of beds and the stay is limited to three months—conditions that would make the programs pointless; (2) juvenile boot camps are widening the net by including youths who previously would not have been locked up; (3) juvenile boot camps are often limited to shock incarceration and keep costs down by leaving aftercare to overloaded parole officers; and (4) no documentation exists that boot camps decrease delinquency.[70] Margaret Beyer, a psychologist working with delinquents, also points out that boot camps cannot be effective because they violate the basic principles of adolescent behavior: Teenagers want to be treated fairly, reject imposed structure, and respond to encouragement. Beyer believes that juveniles will rebel against the imposed structure, punishment, and unfairness of juvenile boot camps.[71]

In spite of these criticisms, 40 to 50 juvenile boot camps exist in more than 30 states, processing more than 7,500 offenders. They appear to have a place among the array of sentencing options, if for no other reason than to appease lawmakers and the public with the promise of tougher sentences and lower costs.[72] About Face, a boot camp for juvenile drug offenders is highlighted in the "Focus on Delinquency" on page 640.

HOW EFFECTIVE IS TREATMENT?

Without question, the primary justification for incarcerating juvenile offenders is the hope that they will one day be rehabilitated and become productive members of society. If successful rehabilitation were not the ultimate goal of juvenile corrections, the use of residential facilities would be an expensive exercise in futility. In fact, the concept of rehabilitation has been severely criticized by many over the past 20 years. Several reviews of correctional treatment for juveniles (and adults) have concluded that the occasionally successful rehabilitation effort was a rare exception to the general rule of failure; when rehabilitation occurred, it was in special settings with hand-picked offenders. All too often treatment efforts seem misguided and poorly planned, staffed, and funded, and although high hopes may have been held out for a particular treatment modality, those who implement it often fail to take into account the background of their clients, which is frequently marked by emotional trauma and low self-esteem.

Can the treatment of youthful offenders by the juvenile correctional system be written off as a lost cause? Those who support the treatment philosophy believe it is still too early to close the book on rehabilitation and that even partial success is better than none. Although no single program may be able to help all delinquents, and although some hard-core offenders may be immune to all efforts to rehabilitate them, even the most die-hard rehabilitation foe would grant that

ABOUT FACE: A JUVENILE BOOT CAMP PROGRAM

About Face is a boot camp for nonviolent males ages 14 to 17 who were adjudicated of cocaine trafficking. Participants are sentenced to the program by the Memphis juvenile court. About Face participants spend three months in a nonsecure residential facility (the Memphis Naval Air Station, an active military base) followed by six months of aftercare. During two years, a total of 344 youths participated in the program.

About Face's residential program has four main components.

Military training conducted by current and former Navy and Marine personnel. The training includes discipline, drill, physical conditioning, and leadership; however, it intentionally avoids the abusive punitive aspects usually associated with military boot camps.

Counseling based on a cognitive-behavioral model. Youth participate in two hours of group counseling each day and a minimum of one hour of individual counseling per week.

Education using Navy-designed reading and math immersion techniques, computer-assisted learning, and individualized instruction. Youths receive six hours of educational services per day, not including study time.

Spiritual support that includes voluntary attendance at religious services conducted twice a week by members of local African-American churches.

During the About Face aftercare component, youth attend weekly two-hour group counseling sessions and receive continued educational assistance.

An evaluation of the program indicated that the juveniles significantly increased their achievement scores; showed some improvement in psychological testing; and improved their understanding of societal obligations. Recidivism data indicated that almost half of the youth were rearrested during a 20-month period beginning with program entry and concluding with formal discharge. However, later charges were less serious than those incurred in the 12 months preceding entry into the program.

Source: James Howell, ed. *Guide for Implementing the Comprehensive Strategy for Serious, Violent, and Chronic Juvenile Offenders* (Washington, D.C.: U.S. Department of Justice, OJJDP), 1995; About Face, Youth Service USA, 314 South Goodlett Avenue, Memphis, Tennessee.

many programs provide effective treatment to a large number of clients. For example, a national review of delinquency prevention projects by the Rand Corporation in the 1980s found that some innovative programs featuring outdoor work projects have produced dramatic results with even hard-core delinquents,[73] and some studies, including a recent review by Carol Garrett, indicate that the success of juvenile treatment may be greater than previously believed.[74]

Garrett reviewed the findings of 111 methodologically sound juvenile corrections studies conducted between 1960 and 1983. They included programs that stressed psychological counseling, behavior modification, life-skill improvement, or other treatments (e.g., the use of megavitamins). Her conclusion: Institutional treatment can work. Although there was no clear-cut evidence that one particular treatment strategy was most effective, the majority showed change in a positive direction. Garrett does not conclude that successful correctional treatment alone can prevent delinquency, but she does find it has important consequences for the psychological adjustment of offenders and their improved academic achievement.

On the other hand, an analysis of juvenile correctional treatment research between 1975 and 1984 by Steven Lab and John Whitehead indicates that treatment has little impact on recidivism.[75] They report that the state of the evidence concerning correctional treatment presents a vast disparity in opinion regarding whether treatment actually works.

One of the problems with obtaining effective treatment involves adapting programs to the changing character of the juvenile offender population. In response to changes in race, gender, age, and even offenses over the last 20 years, changes must be made in program goals. For example, competency-based education, employment skills, and public service programs may be more relevant today than traditional counseling programs.

Another effort to improve treatment results is by developing valid objective classification systems in juvenile corrections. Susan Guarino-Ghezzi and James Byrne have identified a classification model for structured decision making in this area. Using classifications for risk, treatment, and control, these researchers believe a hierarchy of sanctions could increase accountability and control in juvenile justice policy-making and lead to the development of more effective treatment programs.[76]

Historic literature on the state of treatment in correctional programs, particularly for chronic and violent youths, concluded that many approaches have been tried but little definitive knowledge had resulted from these programs. It is clear, however, that traditional, large training schools are expensive and counterproductive and that more attention should be focused on evaluating different treatment approaches, intensive services, and community-based sanctions, as described in chapter 16. New evidence in the 1990s suggests that some well-developed treatment programs as described above can deter and control delinquent behavior. Education, vocational training, and specific counseling strategies can be effective if they are intensive, relate to program goals, and meet the youth's individual needs.[77]

THE LEGAL RIGHT TO TREATMENT

The primary goal of placing juveniles in institutions is to help them adjust positively to reentry in the community. Therefore, lawyers in the field of juvenile justice claim that children in state-run institutions have a legal **right to treatment.**

The concept of a right to treatment was first introduced to the mental health field in 1960 by Morton Birnbaum.[78] He theorized that individuals who are deprived of their liberty because of a mental illness serious enough to require involuntary commitment are entitled to treatment to correct that condition.

Not until 1966 did any court acknowledge any such right to treatment. That year, in *Rouse v. Cameron,* the District of Columbia Circuit Court of Appeals held that mentally ill individuals were entitled to treatment, an opinion based on interpretation of a District of Columbia statute.[79] Although the court did not expressly acknowledge a constitutional right to treatment, it implied that it could have reached the same decision on constitutional grounds:

> Had appellant been found criminally responsible, he could have been confined a year, at most, however dangerous he might have been. He has been confined four years and the end is not in sight. Since this difference rests only on need for treatment, a failure to supply treatment may raise a question of due process of law. It has also been suggested that failure to supply treatment may violate the equal protection clause. . . . Indefinite confinement without treatment of one who has been found not criminally responsible may be so inhumane as to be "cruel and unusual punishment."[80]

The constitutional right to treatment suggested by the *Rouse* decision was further recognized in 1971 in *Wyatt v. Stickney.*[81] This case was particularly important because it held that involuntary commitment without rehabilitation was a denial of due process of law. There is an "unquestionable . . . constitutional right" for those in noncriminal custody "to receive such individual treatment as will give each of them a realistic opportunity to be cured or to improve his or her mental condition."[82]

Of greater significance, however, is the U.S. Supreme Court's decision in the case of *O'Connor v. Donaldson* in 1975.[83] This case concerned the right to treatment of persons involuntarily committed to mental institutions. The Court concluded that, except where treatment is provided, a state cannot confine persons against their will if they are not dangerous to themselves or to the community. In his concurring opinion, however, Chief Justice Warren Burger rejected the idea that a state has no authority to confine a mentally ill person unless it provides treatment. He also denied that commitment is the *quid pro quo* for treatment.

The right to treatment argument has expanded to include the juvenile justice system. One of the first cases to highlight this issue was *Inmates of the Boys' Training School v. Affleck* in 1972.[84] This case analyzed conditions that allegedly violated juvenile constitutional rights to due process and equal protection and that constituted cruel and unusual punishment. *Affleck* was one of the first cases to describe some of the horrible conditions existing in many of the nation's training schools. The court argued that rehabilitation is the true purpose of the juvenile court and that without that goal, due process guarantees are violated. It condemned such devices as solitary confinement, strip cells, and the lack of educational opportunities and held that juveniles have a statutory right to treatment. The court also established the following minimum standards for all juveniles confined in training schools:

- A room equipped with lighting sufficient for an inmate to read by until 10 p.m.
- Sufficient clothing to meet seasonal needs
- Bedding, including blankets, sheets, pillows, pillow cases, and mattresses, to be changed once a week
- Personal hygiene supplies, including soap, toothpaste, towels, toilet paper, and toothbrush
- A change of undergarments and socks every day
- Minimum writing materials: pen, pencil, paper, and envelopes
- Prescription eyeglasses, if needed
- Equal access to all books, periodicals, and other reading materials located in the training school
- Daily showers
- Daily access to medical facilities, including provision of a 24-hour nursing service
- General correspondence privileges[85]

These minimum requirements were expanded in *Martarella v. Kelly*, which analyzed juvenile treatment facilities and the confinement of persons in need of supervision in New York. The court held that failure to provide these juveniles with adequate treatment violated their right to due process and to be free from cruel and unusual punishment.[86]

In 1974, the case of **Nelson v. Heyne** was heard on appeal in the Seventh Circuit Court of Appeals in Indiana. Because of its significance for the right to treatment issue, the case is outlined in the "Focus on Delinquency" on page 644, titled "*Nelson v. Heyne.*"

In *Morales v. Turman,* the court held that all juveniles confined in training schools in Texas have a constitutional right to treatment. The court established numerous criteria for assessing placement, education skills, delivery of vocational education, medical and psychiatric treatment programs, and daily living conditions.[87]

The *Morales* case marked a historic step in the effort to extend the civil rights of children in institutions. This landmark case challenged conditions and practices in all five juvenile training schools in Texas. *Morales* has had a national impact, establishing benchmark standards for the treatment of detained juveniles, including access to medical and psychiatric care, and meaningful education and appropriate disciplinary treatment.

In a more recent case in New York, *Pena v. New York State Division for Youth,* the court held that the use of isolation, hand restraints, and tranquilizing drugs at Goshen Annex Center was punitive and antitherapeutic and therefore violated the Fourteenth Amendment right to due process and the Eighth Amendment right to protection against cruel and unusual punishment.[88]

CURRENT STATUS OF THE RIGHT TO TREATMENT

Although the U.S. Supreme Court has not yet ruled that juveniles have a constitutional right to treatment, the cases described above have served as a basis for many substantive changes in the juvenile justice system, most notably in the improvement of physical conditions in juvenile institutions and in the judiciary's recognition that it must take a more active role in the juvenile justice system.

The principle theories used by the courts for the right to treatment doctrine include (1) arguments under the due process clause of the Fourteenth Amendment; (2) the use of the Eighth Amendment's prohibition against cruel and unusual punishment; (3) and the application of state statutory or constitutional provisions where rehabilitation is the purpose for which the juvenile offender has been confined.

However, the right to treatment has not been advanced in all instances, and the case law does not totally accept a legal right to treatment for juvenile offenders. For example, in *Ralston v. Robinson,* the Supreme Court rejected a youth's claim that he should continue to be given treatment after he was sentenced to a consecutive term in an adult prison for crimes committed while in a juvenile institution.[89] In reaching its decision, the Court rejected the concept that every juvenile offender, regardless of the circumstances, can benefit from treatment. In the *Ralston* case, the offender's proven dangerousness outweighed the possible effects of rehabilitation.

Similarly, in *Santana v. Callazo,* the influential U.S. First Circuit Court of Appeals rejected a suit brought by residents at the Maricao Juvenile Camp in Puerto Rico on the ground that the administration had failed to provide them with an individualized, comprehensive rehabilitation plan or adequate treatment. The circuit court concluded that it was a legitimate exercise of state authority to incarcerate juveniles solely to protect society from them and that therefore the offender does not have a right to treatment per se. However, courts can evaluate each case individually to determine whether the youth is receiving adequate care.[90]

The *Santana* case also considered the constitutionality of putting juveniles in isolation in detention facilities. After the U.S. Supreme Court denied a writ of

NELSON V. HEYNE

Facts

In a class civil rights action on behalf of juvenile inmates of the Indiana Boys' School, a state institution, a complaint to the district court alleged that defendants' (Robert Heyne, commissioner of corrections; Robert Hardin, director of the Indiana Youth Authority; and Alfred Bennett, superintendent of Indiana Boys' School) practices and policies at the school violated the Eighth and Fourteenth Amendment rights of the juveniles under their care. The alleged practices included the use of corporal punishment, solitary confinement for periods ranging from five to thirty days, intramuscular injections of tranquilizing drugs, and censorship of inmate mail.

The school itself was a medium-security state correctional institution for boys 12 to 18 years of age, where about one-third were noncriminal offenders. The average length of stay at the institution was about six and a half months, and although the school's maximum capacity was under 300 boys, the usual population was about 400. The counseling staff included 20 persons, three of whom were psychologists with undergraduate degrees, and one part-time psychiatrist who spent four hours a week at the institution. The medical staff included one part-time medical physician, one registered nurse, and one licensed practical nurse.

The district court in this case found that it had jurisdiction over the case and thereafter held that the use of corporal punishment and the method of administering tranquilizing drugs by the defendants constituted cruel and unusual punishment in violation of the plaintiffs' Eighth and Fourteenth Amendment rights. In a separate judgment, the court found that the juveniles had a right to an affirmative treatment and that the school had not satisfied the minimal constitutional and statutory standards required. The defendants appealed on January 31, 1974, before the final relief was granted. The Seventh Circuit of the U.S. Court of Appeals granted review.

Decision

In *Nelson v. Heyne*, the circuit court dealt with the issue of a juvenile's constitutional affirmative right to treatment within a closed institution. Specifically, the questions were (1) whether the practices alleged by the defendants were violations of the cruel and unusual punishment clause of the Eighth Amendment and (2) whether defendants had a constitutional right to rehabilitative treatment, and if so, whether the treatment as provided by the school was adequate. The court discussed the practices of corporal punishment in light of the cruel and unusual punishment standard suggested in *Furman v.*

certiorari, the lower court subsequently found that isolation practices can be considered constitutional where they are part of an overall custody and treatment plan for juvenile offenders.[91]

The future of the right to treatment for juveniles is somewhat uncertain. The courts have not gone so far as to order the creation of new programs, nor have they decided what constitutes minimal standards of specific individual treatment. However, federal courts continue to hear on a case-by-case basis complaints that treatment is not up to minimal standards or that inappropriate disciplinary methods are being used. In one such case, *Gary H. v. Hegstrom,* a federal judge ruled that isolation punishments at the McClaren School for Boys in Oregon were excessive and that residents were being denied their right to treatment.[92]

In that case, the circuit court of appeals affirmed the lower court's judgment regarding the existence of unconstitutional conditions at the school and ordered due process hearings prior to confinement in excess of 24 hours and minimum sanitary, health, educational, and medical resources for the residents. But the wholesale adoption of various professional association standards for model

Georgia, 408 U.S. 238, 279 (1971). By that standard, punishment is excessive if it is unnecessary, and it is unnecessary if less severe punishment would serve the same purpose.

Although the court did not find corporal punishment to be cruel and unusual per se, it did find that on the basis of undisputed expert testimony the beatings as applied were unnecessary and therefore excessive, thus violating the Eighth Amendment proscription against cruel and unusual punishment. The court next looked at the school's practice of administering tranquilizing drugs "to control excited behavior" without individual medical authorization and without first trying oral medication. Based on expert testimony at trial that established the possible serious side effects of these drugs, the court rejected the school's assertion that the use of drugs was not punishment. After stressing the need to balance the school's desire to maintain discipline with the child's right to be free from cruel and unusual punishment, the court held that the school's interest in reforming juveniles through the use of drugs in maintaining a rehabilitative atmosphere did not justify the cruel and unusual dangers resulting from poorly supervised administration of tranquilizing drugs.

Turning to the crucial holding by the district court that incarcerated juveniles have an affirmative right to rehabilitative treatment, the Seventh Circuit Court of Appeals noted that the Supreme Court has assumed, although it has not explicitly stated, that the state must provide treatment for incarcerated juveniles. In light of this, the court looked at several recent cases concerning the impact of the *parens patriae* doctrine on this right, most notably the case of *Martarella v. Kelly*, 349 F. Supp. 575 (S.D.N.Y. 1972), in which the court found a clear constitutional right to treatment for juveniles based on the Eighth and Fourteenth Amendments. The appellate court agreed then with the lower court that the juveniles did indeed have a constitutional as well as a statutory right to rehabilitative treatment. Last, the court held that the Quay system of behavior classification used by the school was not treatment. Subsequently the case was remanded to allow the lower court to determine the "minimal standards of care and treatment for juveniles" needed to provide them with their "right to 'individualized' care and treatment."

Significance of the Case

Nelson v. Heyne is the first federal appellate court decision affirming that juveniles have a constitutional as well as a statutory right to treatment. It is also the first to hold that federal judges can require standards by which to judge minimal adherence by institutions to individualized treatment.

Source: *Nelson v. Heyne*, 491 F.2d 353 (7th Cir. 1974).

institutions was not constitutionally mandated. The court also held that it was not appropriate to mandate dispositions that were so costly that other children would be deprived of services. Some experts believe that a case like *Gary H.* will eventually reach the Supreme Court and provide an avenue for a definitive decision on the right to treatment. Thus far, minimum standards of care and treatment have been mandated on a case-by-case basis, with some courts limiting the constitutional protections regarding the right to treatment. In light of the new hard-line approach to juvenile crime, it does not appear that the courts will be persuaded to expand this constitutional theory further.

CHILDREN IN INSTITUTIONS

STRUGGLE FOR BASIC RIGHTS

Several court cases and a large amount of publicity have led a number of federal and state groups to develop standards for the juvenile justice system, including its institutions.[93] The most comprehensive standards are those of the Institute of Judicial Administration–American Bar Association; the American Correctional Association; and the National Council on Crime and Delinquency. These standards provide appropriate guidelines for conditions and practices in juvenile institutions. They call on juvenile corrections administrators to maintain a physically safe and healthy environment for incarcerated youths.

State-sponsored brutality has been for the most part outlawed. Although the use of restraints, solitary confinement, and even medication for unruly residents has not been completely eliminated, the courts have consistently ruled that corporal punishment in any form, other than for one's own protection, is constitutionally unacceptable and violates standards of decency and human dignity.

Disciplinary systems are an important part of any institutional program. Most institutions maintain disciplinary boards that regulate and hear appeals by juvenile inmates. The case of *Wolff v. McDonnell* focused on due process requirements for disciplinary proceedings in adult institutions.[94] Many state court decisions involving children have affirmed the principles in *Wolff v. McDonnell*. To provide the same rights for juveniles, several sets of standards have recommended similar rules and regulations governing juvenile institutional boards, including notice, representation by counsel, and the right to a written record of proceedings and decision.

Isolation or "administrative segregation" is also an issue that has been subject to court review. The leading case, **Lollis v. New York State Department of Social Services,** concluded that confining a female status offender to a small room for a two-week period was unconstitutional.[95] Virtually all courts have generally reached similar conclusions. Juveniles may be confined under such conditions only if they are a serious threat to themselves or others; even then, they should be released as soon as possible.

In the past 20 years there has been considerable litigation over conditions of confinement. Most of it results from the violations of the constitutional rights of the residents. The outcomes of such litigation have become the basis for institutional reform.[96] For a contemporary case on juvenile institutions and the right to treatment, see the "Focus on Delinquency" feature titled *Alexander v. Boyd, and South Carolina Dept. of Juvenile Justice* (1995).

JUVENILE AFTERCARE

Aftercare in the juvenile justice system is the equivalent of parole in the adult criminal justice system. When juveniles are released from an institution through an early-release program or after completing their sentences, they may be placed in an aftercare program of some kind. The belief is that youths who have been institutionalized should not be returned to the community without some form of transitional assistance. Whether individuals who are in aftercare as part of an indeterminate sentence remain in the community or return to the institution for further rehabilitation depends on their actions during the aftercare period.

In a number of jurisdictions, the early release of juveniles resembles the adult parole process. A paroling authority, which may be an independent body or part of the corrections department or some other branch of state services, makes the release decision. Juvenile aftercare authorities, like adult parole officers, review the youth's adjustment within the institution, whether he or she is chemically dependent, what the crime was, and so on.

Some juvenile authorities are even making use of **parole guidelines** first developed with adult parolees. Each youth who enters a secure facility is given a recommended length of confinement that is explained at his or her initial interview with parole authorities. The stay is computed on the basis of the offense record, influenced by aggravating and mitigating factors. The parole authority is not required to follow the recommended sentence but instead uses it

ALEXANDER v. BOYD, AND SOUTH CAROLINA DEPARTMENT OF JUVENILE JUSTICE (1995)

Facts

This case involved juveniles who were temporarily housed at the South Carolina Reception and Evaluation Center, as well as those confined at three long-term institutions. In a class action this group of juveniles claimed that the basic conditions of confinement—food, shelter, sanitation, living space, health care, recreation programs, classification, discipline, and personal safety—were so inadequate that exposure to them constituted a deprivation of their rights secured by the Fourteenth Amendment to the U.S. Constitution.

The Reception and Evaluation Center was the institution designed to receive and evaluate juveniles considered for long-term confinement by the family court. Approximately 2,000 juveniles passed through the institution each year. This institution frequently experienced severe overcrowding.

The three long-term institutions, or training schools, were Willow Lane, John G. Richards, and Birchwood. At the time of trial, the long-term institutions generally housed between 670 and 720 juveniles. The average length of stay was seven months. A brief description of the physical plant and functions of the three campuses follows: Willow Lane housed all of the female juveniles, as well as the less aggressive and younger males. The Willow Lane campus consisted of some 20 structures generally constructed in 1966 and 1972. The campus contained five dormitories, a cafeteria, and educational, medical, and administrative facilities.

John G. Richards housed older male juveniles and contained many of the special program dorms. The campus consisted of five dormitories, a cafeteria, and administrative and recreational facilities. It also contained the "Intake/SPU" unit, which served as a maximum security facility for the Richards and Willow Lane campuses. Birchwood housed the oldest, most aggressive male residents. The Birchwood campus was the newest of the four campuses. Generally constructed in the mid-1970s, the campus contained four dormitories, administrative offices, and voca-

tional and academic educational facilities. It also had an artificially surfaced playing field, a gymnasium, an auditorium, covered picnic shelters, and a baseball diamond.

After a very thorough analysis of the institutions, the District Court found that the following deficiencies represented constitutional and statutory violations of the juveniles' rights:

A. Discipline

The Plaintiffs mounted a variety of attacks against the system of discipline in place at DJJ facilities, which depended primarily on the use of lock-up units and CS gas to punish juveniles for disciplinary infractions. They challenged the procedures by which juveniles were placed in lock-up units and the spartan conditions of the lock-up cells themselves. The Plaintiffs also sought to have the court impose a one-hour limitation on the duration of their stay in lock-up facilities and to have the court prohibit the use of CS gas.

CS gas is a potent form of tear gas used primarily for riot control. The evidence at trial disclosed that, until recently, DJJ agency policy permitted the use of CS gas to "maintain control," as well as to prevent harm or the threat of harm to individuals. CS gas irritates the mucous membranes of those who are exposed to it. Exposure to the gas causes instant pain and spasms in the eyelids, coughing fits, and breathing problems. Documented studies indicate that CS gas can cause damage to the cornea and potential blindness and damage to the skin.

CS gas was applied on a fairly regular basis in the DJJ institutions. The Defendants' own records indicate that gas was used on juveniles more than 180 times in 1993.

The court found that use of CS gas violated the juveniles' constitutional rights under the due process clause of the U.S. Constitution. It caused more anger in the juveniles toward the adults who were supposed to be caring for them. CS gas as a form of punishment taught the victims to inflict pain as a method of controlling others and made the juveniles more volatile.

as a tool in making parole decisions.[97] Whatever approach is used, several primary factors are considered by virtually all jurisdictions when recommending a juvenile for release. They are (1) institutional adjustment, (2) length of stay and general attitude, and (3) likelihood of success in the community.

B. Fire Safety

The Plaintiffs presented testimony on one issue related to fire safety: whether securing the individual cells of the two lock-up units, known as Santee and the SPU unit, with padlocks created an unreasonable risk of harm to the juveniles who were confined in these units.

At DJJ, the greatest risk of harm from fires was from mattress fires. Mattress fires emit insufficient heat to set off the sprinkler system but cause substantial amounts of smoke which can be fatal to the occupants of the units if those juveniles are not removed quickly. In each of the two disciplinary units at DJJ, the 30 individual cells were secured with individual padlocks. In the event of a fire, each cell must be opened by hand, a time-consuming process which constitutes an unreasonable risk of harm to the Plaintiffs housed in these two units. The court concluded that the use of individual padlocks on the cells in the Santee and SPU lock-up units unreasonably infringed upon the Plaintiff's safety interest.

C. Food

At trial, several juveniles, and even the food services director, testified that frequently cockroaches and other foreign matter were present in the food served to the juveniles. The court found that the Defendants had an obligation to provide minimally adequate nourishment to juveniles housed at their institutions, and that food containing cockroaches and other foreign matter fell below what may be deemed minimally adequate.

D. Classification

Classification is the process of separating aggressive juveniles from passive ones and determining appropriate levels of restraint for each juvenile based on the threat the juvenile presents to other juveniles and to the public. The juveniles possess a clearly recognized liberty interest in being free from unreasonable threats to their physical safety. On the other hand, the general public is entitled to reasonable protection from juveniles incarcerated at DJJ.

For these reasons, juveniles in DJJ facilities should be screened and classified, so that the aggressive juveniles are identified and separated from more passive juveniles. Until recently, a rational and minimally adequate system of classification did not exist at DJJ. In response to this litigation, the Defendants have recognized their obligation to establish a minimally adequate classification system.

E. Medical Services

Among the traditionally recognized liberty interests of the Plaintiff class that survive confinement is the right to minimally adequate health care. Testimony at trial disclosed that medical resources for the various DJJ institutions were stretched to the limit. The institutions were forced to rely on only three full-time nurses and a handful of part-time nurses to serve a population totaling almost 900 juveniles. One medical doctor was under contract to visit the facilities once a week for a total of three hours.

At minimum, DJJ should employ a sufficient number of trained medical staff to provide the basic components of a medical system for the institutions. At trial, the Defendants were optimistic that the unconstitutional conditions regarding health care would be cured.

F. Programs

It was apparent from the testimony in this case that programming geared toward correcting the behavior of juveniles was central to the very nature of a juvenile training facility. Every witness who testified in the case asserted that appropriate programming can substantially enhance the juvenile's opportunity to succeed upon release from confinement. Without minimally adequate programming, the agency was simply warehousing the juveniles and ignoring the statutory purpose of their confinement. Based on this evidence, the court found that, under the Constitution, a minimally adequate level of programming was required in order to provide juveniles with a reasonable opportunity to accomplish the purpose of their confinement, to protect the safety of the juveniles and the staff, and to ensure the safety of the community once the juveniles are ultimately released. Minimally adequate program services should be designed to teach juveniles the basic principles that are essential to correcting their conduct. These generally recognized principles include: (1) taking responsibility for the consequences of their actions; (2) learning appropriate ways of responding to others (coping skills); (3) learning to manage their anger; and (4) developing a positive sense of accomplishment.

Risk classifications have also been designed to help parole officers make decisions about which juveniles should receive aftercare services.[98] The risk-based aftercare system uses an empirically derived risk scale to classify youths. Juveniles are identified as most likely or least likely to committ a new offense within a period of release to aftercare supervision.

G. Overcrowding

The defendants conceded in their pleadings that the facilities in this case were overcrowded in a constitutional sense. The court found that a reasonable level of population at DJJ was that level that provided the minimum amount of physical space juveniles need for adequate living conditions and does not unreasonably threaten safety or unreasonably frustrate the purpose of confinement. The plaintiffs argued that the court should order an immediate release of more than 200 juveniles. The court rejected any effort to relieve overcrowding by releasing juveniles back to their communities in an effort to reduce population to the design capacity of the DJJ physical plant constructed in the 1970s. Rather, the court ordered the Defendants to construct additional facilities to house juveniles who are committed to DJJ.

Decision

The District Court found jurisdiction in this case and determined that the due process clause of the Fourteenth Amendment, which encompasses the protections of the Eighth Amendment, was the appropriate standard for reviewing conditions at the institution. The court held that: (1) juveniles had a constitutional right to personal safety; (2) juveniles had a constitutional right to medical services; (3) juveniles had a constitutional right to minimally adequate program services; and (4) juveniles had a constitutional right to relief from institutional overcrowding. Where the purpose of incarcerating juveniles in a state training program was treatment (as in the state of South Carolina), the court concluded that a constitutional right to treatment exists for juveniles and required that the conditions at the institution must relate to that purpose. The State was given the opportunity to correct all the deficiencies. The court was not required to order the release of any juveniles placed in the long-term facilities because of existing conditions.

Significance of the Case

Alexander v. Boyd affirmed that juveniles have constitutional rights when they are placed in institutions. Traditionally, courts that have recognized a constitutional right to rehabilitative treatment for incarcerated juveniles have generally employed two basic theories to divine such a right. The first theory, adopted by the court in *Alexander*, was that due process required that the nature and duration of commitment bear some reasonable relation to the purpose for which the individual was committed. The second theory was known as the quid pro quo, or *mutual compact theory*. Under this approach, courts have held that states were required to rehabilitate incarcerated juveniles as consideration for affording them fewer procedural safeguards than those afforded to adult criminal defendants.

In *Alexander*, the court emphasized that its role in this litigation was to identify standards for treatment and rehabilitation based on the first theory. Once the theory was established, the court determined that constitutional and statutory deficiencies existed at the facilities and ordered that an acceptable plan be developed to correct them.

In sum, this case represents another example in a long line of cases involving the role of the judicial system in remedying constitutional violations in juvenile correctional institutions. It also clearly reestablished that the purpose of the South Carolina juvenile law in confining juveniles was not to punish them but to provide training and services to correct their delinquent behavior. The overriding goal of juvenile rehabilitation was further recognized in this 1995 case.

Source: *Alexander v. Boyd*, 876 F.Supp. 773 (1995).

Armstrong and Altschuler described the critical components of a model aftercare program[99] as follows: (1) preparing youth for progressively increased responsibility in the community; (2) facilitating youth interaction; (3) working with the offender and community support groups; (4) developing new resources; and (5) monitoring the juvenile and the community concerning their ability to deal with each other. As a result of these programs, risk assessment and classification systems have become major case management tools for community supervision.

SUPERVISION

One purpose of aftercare is to provide an individual with some support during the readjustment period following release into the community. The institutionalized minor is likely to have some difficulty making the adjustment. First, the minor's activities have been tightly regimented for some time; once such restraints are removed, the youth may not find it easy to make independent decisions. Second, peers in the institution may have convinced the minor that he or she has been scapegoated by an unforgiving society. Furthermore, the community itself may view the returning minor with a good deal of prejudice; adjustment problems may reinforce a preexisting need to engage in bad habits or deviant behavior.

Juveniles in aftercare programs are supervised by parole caseworkers or counselors whose job is to provide surveillance by maintaining contact with the juvenile, to make sure that a corrections plan is followed, and to show interest and caring in order to help prevent further mistakes by the juvenile. The counselor also keeps the youth informed of available services that may assist in reintegration and counsels the youth and his or her family on the possible root of the original problems related to the delinquency. Unfortunately, aftercare caseworkers, like probation officers, often carry such large caseloads that their jobs are next to impossible to do adequately.

Research has generally questioned the effectiveness of traditional juvenile parole programs (those involving casework and individual or group counseling). In one of the most impressive research efforts on the effectiveness of juvenile parole, Patrick Jackson randomly assigned subjects from the California Youth Authority to either parole or outright discharge.[100] He found that youths under formal parole supervision were actually more likely to become reinvolved in serious offenses than those simply discharged and left on their own. However, there was relatively little difference between the two groups with respect to the chance of being arrested or serving time in another institution. Jackson found that the longer a person was retained on parole, the greater the chance of his or her being rearrested. Thus, Jackson finds that there are few beneficial elements of parole supervision and many potentially harmful side effects.

Despite the less than encouraging results of the Jackson research, there are indications that juvenile aftercare can be very effective if it is combined with innovative treatment efforts. For example, the Violent Juvenile Offender program discussed earlier combined short-term incarceration with intensive follow-up in what appears to be a successful rehabilitative effort. Jeffery Fagan and his colleagues found that highly structured efforts to reintegrate youths into society can have better results than previously thought possible.[101] The Albuquerque (New Mexico) Girls Reintegration Center is an excellent example of a successful community-based program that prepares female juvenile offenders for their eventual release into the community.[102] The program provides participants with positive role models, involvement in community activities, and relevant school and work experience. The Armstrong and Altschuler **Intensive Aftercare Model (IAP)** is important because it offers a balanced, highly structured, comprehensive program of intervention for serious and violent juvenile offenders returning to the community following placement.

Aftercare is a very important stage in the juvenile justice process because few juveniles **age out** of state custody. In 1992, for example, most—upwards of 70 percent—were released to parole or aftercare. Another 10 percent received some other type of conditional release. In some jurisdictions today, the proportion of children released to parole or aftercare is 100 percent.[103] There is almost a total lack of research information about juvenile aftercare, particularly with regard to high-risk juvenile offenders. Yet intensive aftercare services are crucial to the success of residential treatment programs.

AFTERCARE REVOCATION PROCEDURES

A final issue in aftercare for juveniles concerns revocation procedures. Although adult parolees have been entitled to certain procedural rights in revocation proceedings since 1972, the Supreme Court has not yet extended the same rights to juveniles.[104] However, most states have extended these rights to juveniles on their own initiative, as have appellate courts that have considered juvenile aftercare revocation procedures. To avoid revocation, a juvenile parolee must meet the following conditions, among others:

- Adhere to a reasonable curfew set by youth worker or parent
- Refrain from associating with persons whose influence would be detrimental, including but not limited to persons convicted of crimes or persons of a known criminal background
- Attend school in accordance with the law
- Abstain from drugs
- Abstain from alcohol
- Report to the youth worker when required
- Refrain from acts that would be crimes if committed by an adult
- Refrain from operating an automobile without permission of the youth worker or parent
- Refrain from being habitually disobedient and beyond the lawful control of parent or other legal authority
- Refrain from running away from the lawful custody of parent or other lawful authority

Certain procedural safeguards have been set up to ensure that revocation of juvenile parole is handled fairly:

1. The parolee must be notified of the specific conditions of parole.
2. The parolee must receive notice of allegations.
3. The parolee has the right to legal counsel at state expense if necessary.
4. The parolee has the right to confront and cross-examine witnesses.
5. The parolee has the right to introduce documentary evidence and witnesses.
6. The parolee has the right to a hearing before an independent hearing officer who shall be an attorney but not an employee of the revoking agency.

The use of these procedures has led to sound administrative decision making and adequate constitutional safeguards for juveniles in revocation hearings.

SUMMARY

The juvenile institution was developed in the mid-nineteenth century as an alternative to placing youths in adult prisons. Youth institutions evolved over the years from large, closed institutions to today's open, cottage-based education- and rehabilitation-oriented institutions. Most institutions for youths feature libraries and recreational programs and are low-security facilities.

The juvenile institutional population has increased in recent years to more than 90,000 residents, despite efforts to decarcerate status offenders and petty delinquent offenders. Although there has been a shrinking youth population and a stabilization in juvenile arrest rates, there appears to be evidence of higher rolls of incarceration in the future. In addition, increasing numbers of youths are being "hidden" in private mental centers and drug-treatment clinics.

Most institutions maintain intensive treatment programs featuring individual or group therapy. Although a wide variety of techniques are used around the nation, little evidence has been found that any single method is effective in reducing recidivism. Yet the philosophy of treatment and rehabilitation remains an important goal of juvenile practitioners.

The violent offender has come to be recognized as a major social problem. A number of states have set up intensive programs to deal with these hard-core offenders.

The right to treatment is an important issue in juvenile justice. Legal decisions have mandated that a juvenile cannot simply be warehoused in a correctional center but must receive proper care and treatment to aid rehabilitation. What constitutes proper care is still being debated, however, and recent federal court decisions have backed off from holding that every youth can be rehabilitated. Gender is also a factor in equal access to treatment resources: Institutions for females generally have fewer vocational and educational programs than those exclusively for male delinquents.

Most institutions have a standard set of rules and discipline. There have been many exposés of physical brutality in youth institutions, and courts have sought to restrain the use of physical punishment on inmates.

Most juveniles released from institutions are placed on juvenile parole or aftercare. There is limited evidence that this type of community supervision is actually more beneficial than simply releasing youths on their own. Many jurisdictions are experiencing success with community halfway houses and reintegration centers. Some researchers are reaffirming the importance of delinquency prevention, promising new treatment programs, and graduated sanctions in juvenile corrections today.[105]

KEY TERMS

Paint Creek Youth Center
reform schools
cottage system
"decarceration"
least restrictive alternative
individual counseling
psychotherapy
reality therapy
behavior modification
group therapy

guided group interaction (GGI)
Positive Peer Culture (PPC)
milieu therapy
chronic juvenile offender
suppression effect
life-style violent juveniles
Violent Juvenile Offender (VJO)
Outward Bound
boot camps
right to treatment

Nelson v. Heyne
Morales v. Turman
Lollis v. New York State Department of Social Services
aftercare
parole guidelines
Intensive Aftercare Program (IAP)
age-out
Alexander v. Boyd

QUESTIONS FOR DISCUSSION

1. Should status offenders ever be institutionalized with delinquents? Are they really different?
2. What kinds of programs would you implement in a juvenile correctional center?
3. Do you believe that juveniles have a right to treatment? Should all offenders receive psychological counseling? What court decisions give credence to your position?
4. Is the use of physical punishment ever warranted in a juvenile institution? If not, how do you reconcile the fact that the Supreme Court has upheld the use of corporal punishment in public schools?

5. Identify and explain the current problems and issues in juvenile corrections. What possible solutions might you suggest?
6. In light of the extensive use of incarceration for juvenile offenders, do you think the trend toward determinate sentences for serious juvenile crime is desirable? Isn't such an approach in direct conflict with decarceration policy?
7. How should society deal with the chronic juvenile offender? Is incarceration the only practical solution?

8. What is meant by the "legal right" to treatment? Do juveniles have such a right? Discuss the meaning of the cases dealing with this issue.

9. Are boot camps for juveniles a dangerous trend and as ineffective as wholesale incarceration of youth in secure institutions?

NOTES

1. Bureau of Justice Statistics, *Children in Custody 1975–85—Census of Public and Private Juvenile Detention, Correctional and Shelter Facilities* (Washington, D.C.: U.S. Department of Justice, 1989), p. 4.
2. Edward Loughran, "Juvenile Corrections: The Massachusetts Experience," in L. Eddison, ed., *Reinvesting Youth Corrections Resources: A Tale of Three States* (Minneapolis: University of Minnesota, Hubert Humphrey Institute of Public Affairs, 1987), pp. 11–18.
3. Office of Justice Programs, *Private Sector Corrections for Juveniles—Paint Creek Youth Center* (Washington, D.C.: Office of Juvenile Justice and Delinquency Prevention, 1988).
4. For information about this program, contact Director, Thomas O'Farrell Youth Center, Woodstock, MD 21163.
5. Office of Justice Programs, *Children in Custody 1975–85* (Washington, D.C.: U.S. Department of Justice, 1989), p. 4.
6. James Howell, ed., *Guide for Implementing the Comprehensive Strategy for Serious, Violent and Chronic Juvenile Offenders* (Washington, D.C.: OJJDP, 1995).
7. For a detailed description of juvenile delinquency in the 1800s, see J. Hawes, *Children in Urban Society: Juvenile Delinquency in Nineteenth Century America* (New York: Oxford University Press, 1971).
8. D. Jarvis, *Institutional Treatment of the Offender* (New York: McGraw-Hill, 1978), p. 101.
9. Margaret Werner Cahalan, *Historical Corrections Statistics in the United States, 1850–1984* (Washington, D.C.: U.S. Department of Justice, 1986), pp. 104–05.
10. Clemons Bartollas, Stuart J. Miller, and Simon Dinitiz, *Juvenile Victimization: The Institutional Paradox* (New York: Wiley, 1976), p. 6.
11. LaMar T. Empey, *American Delinquency—Its Meaning and Construction* (Homewood, Ill.: Dorsey, 1978), p. 515.
12. Edward Eldefonso and Walter Hartinger, *Control, Treatment, and Rehabilitation of Juvenile Offenders* (Beverly Hills, Calif.: Glencoe, 1976), p. 151.
13. Ibid., p. 152.
14. M. Rosenthal, "Reforming the Justice Correctional Institution: Efforts of U.S. Children's Bureau in the 1930s," *Journal of Sociology and Social Welfare* 14:47–73 (1987).
15. Bureau of Justice Statistics, *Fact Sheet on Children in Custody* (Washington, D.C.: U.S. Department of Justice, 1989); Barbara Allen-Hagen, *Public Juvenile Facilities—Children in Custody, 1989* (Washington, D.C.: Office of Juvenile Justice and Delinquency Prevention, 1991); James Austin et al., *Juveniles Taken into Custody—1993* (Washington, D.C.: OJJDP, 1995).
16. Data in this and the following section come from the federal government's *Children in Custody* series, published biennially by the U.S. Department of Justice's Bureau of Justice Statistics (*Fact Sheet on Children in Custody, 1989*); Austin et al., *Juveniles Taken into Custody—1993*.
17. Hunter Hurst and Patricia Torbet, *Organization and Administration of Juvenile Services: Probation, Aftercare, and State Delinquent Institutions* (Pittsburgh, Pa.: National Center for Juvenile Justice, 1993), p. 4.
18. Ibid.
19. L. Rossi, "Maryland's Juvenile Services Agency: Giving Youths a Chance to Change," *Corrections Today* 51:130 (1989).
20. American Bar Association, Project on Standards for Juvenile Justice, *Standards Relating to Corrections Administration* (Cambridge, Mass.: Ballinger, 1977), Standard 2.1.
21. Hurst and Torbet, *Organization and Administration of Juvenile Services.*
22. Alan Breed and Barry Krisberg, "Is There a Future?" *Corrections Today* 48:14–26 (1986).
23. "My Twenty Years of Child Advocacy," *Youth Law News* 6:3 (1990).
24. Office of Justice Programs, *Children in Custody, 1989* (Washington, D.C.: U.S. Department of Justice, 1991), p. 10; Austin et al; *Juveniles Taken into Custody—1993*, Chapters 1 and 3; Howard Snyder and Melissa Sickmund, *Juvenile Offenders and Victims: A National Report* (Washington, D.C.: OJJDP, 1995), Chapter 7.
25. Ibid, p. 13; Office of Juvenile Justice and Delinquency Prevention, U.S. Department of Justice, *Children in Custody*, Public Juvenile Facilities, 1987. Reported in *Juvenile Justice Bulletin*, October 1988, p. 2; Austin et al; *Juveniles Taken into Custody—1993*, Chapters 1 and 3; Snyder and Sickmund, *Juvenile Offenders and Victims: A National Report*, Chapter 7.
26. Office of Juvenile Justice and Delinquency Prevention, *National Juvenile Custody Trends 1978–89* (Washington, D.C.: Department of Justice, 1992); "Survey on Juvenile Corrections," *Corrections Compendium*, vol.

17, July 1992; Austin et al; *Juveniles Taken into Custody—1993,* Chapters 1 and 3; Snyder and Sickmund, *Juvenile Offenders and Victims: A National Report,* Chapter 7.

27. Breed and Krisberg, "Is There a Future?"; Terry Demchak, "Changes Anticipated in Arizona and Arkansas Juvenile Institutions," *Youth Law News* 10:8–10 (1989).

28. Edward Loughran, "How to Stop Kids from Going Bad," *Boston Globe,* 11 February 1990, p. A21.

29. Bureau of Justice Statistics, *Fact Sheet on Children in Custody,* p. 1.

30. Data from Bureau of Justice Statistics, *Fact Sheet on Children in Custody: Public and Private Juvenile Facilities, 1989* (Washington, D.C.: U.S. Government Printing Office, 1989); Barbara Allen-Hagen, "Children in Custody," *Public Juvenile Facilities, 1989 OJJDP Update* (Washington, D.C.: U.S. Department of Justice, 1991); Austin et al; *Juveniles Taken into Custody—1993,* Chapters 1 and 3; Snyder and Sickmund, *Juvenile Offenders and Victims: A National Report,* Chapter 7.

31. Office of Juvenile Justice and Delinquency Prevention, U.S. Department of Justice, "More Juveniles Held in Public Facilities," *Children in Custody,* (Washington, D.C.: U.S. Department of Justice/Bureau of Justice Statistics, September 1989), p. 2; Austin et al; *Juveniles Taken into Custody—1993,* Chapters 1 and 3; Snyder and Sickmund, *Juvenile Offenders and Victims: A National Report,* Chapter 7.

32. Ibid.; also see David Schichor and Clemens Bartollas, "Comparison of Private and Public Placements" (unpublished paper, California State University, San Bernadino, 1990), which calls for a nationwide effort to evaluate private placements for juvenile offenders.

33. Ira Schwartz, Marilyn Jackson-Beck, and Roger Anderson, "The 'Hidden' System of Juvenile Control," *Crime and Delinquency* 30:371–85 (1984).

34. Rebecca Craig and Andrea Paterson, "State Involuntary Commitment Laws: Beyond Deinstitutionalization," *National Conference of State Legislative Reports* 13:1–10 (1988).

35. Bureau of Justice Statistics, U.S. Department of Justice, "More Juveniles Held in Public Facilities," in *Children in Custody* (Washington, D.C.: U.S. Department of Justice/Bureau of Justice Statistics, September 1989), p. 1; Snyder and Sickmund, *Juvenile Offenders and Victims: A National Report,* (1995), p. 166.

36. Barry Krisberg, Ira Schwartz, G. Fishman, Z. Eisikovits, and E. Gitman, "The Incarceration of Minority Youth," *Crime and Delinquency* 33:173–205 (1987).

37. Craig Fischer, ed. "Washington State Moves to End Juvenile Justice Race Disparity," *Criminal Justice Newsletter* 27:1–8 (1996).

38. "The Young and Violent," *Boston Sunday Globe,* 24 March 1996, p. 81.

39. Bartollas, Miller, and Dinitz, *Juvenile Victimization* Sec. C.

40. Christopher Sieverdes and Clemens Bartollas, "Security Level and Adjustment Patterns in Juvenile Institutions," *Journal of Criminal Justice* 14:135–45 (1986).

41. Several authors have written of this sexual double standard. See E. A. Anderson, "The Chivalrous Treatment of the Female Offender in the Arms of the Criminal Justice System: A Review of the Literature," *Social Problems* 23:350–57 (1976); G. Armstrong, "Females under the Law: Protected but Unequal," *Crime and Delinquency* 23:109–20 (1977); M. Chesney-Lind, "Judicial Enforcement of the Female Sex Role: The Family Court and the Female Delinquent," *Issues in Criminology* 8:51–59 (1973) and "Juvenile Delinquency: The Sexualization of Female Crime," *Psychology Today* 19:43–46 (1974); Allan Conway and Carol Bogdan, "Sexual Delinquency: The Persistence of a Double Standard," *Crime and Delinquency* 23:13–135 (1977); and M. Chesney-Lind, *Girls, Delinquency and the Juvenile Justice System* (San Francisco: Brooks/Cole, 1991).

42. Austin et al., *Juveniles Taken into Custody,* p. 19.

43. Patricia Hersch, "Coming of Age on City Streets," *Psychology Today,* January 1988, p. 28; Daniel Campagna and Donald Puffengerger, *The Sexual Trafficking in Children: An Investigation of the Child Sex Trade* (Dover, Mass.: Auburn House, 1988).

44. "A Look at Juvenile Female Offenders," *Juvenile Corrections and Detention Newsletter* 2:6 (1988).

45. For a historical analysis of a girls' reformatory, see Barbara Brenzel, *Daughters of the State* (Cambridge: MIT Press, 1983).

46. Ilene R. Bergsmann, "The Forgotten Few Juvenile Female Offenders," *Federal Probation* 53:73–79 (1989).

47. For an interesting article highlighting the debate over the effectiveness of correctional treatment, see John Whitehead and Steven Lab, "Meta-Analysis of Juvenile Correctional Treatment," *Journal of Research in Crime and Delinquency* 26:276–95 (1989).

48. Louise Sas and Peter Jaffe, "Understanding Depression in Juvenile Delinquency: Implications for Institutional Admission Policies and Treatment Programs," *Juvenile and Family Court Journal* 37:49–58 (1985–86).

49. Dennis A. Romig, *Justice for Our Children: An Examination of Juvenile Delinquent Rehabilitation Programs* (Lexington, Mass.: Lexington Books, 1978), p. 81.

50. See, generally, William Glasser, "Reality Therapy: A Realistic Approach to the Young Offender," in Robert Schaste and Jo Wallach, eds., *Readings in Delinquency and Treatment* (Los Angeles: Delinquency Prevention Training Project, Youth Studies Center, University of Southern California, 1965); see also Richard Rachin, "Reality Therapy: Helping People Help Themselves," *Crime and Delinquency* 16:143 (1974).

51. Helen A. Klein, "Towards More Effective Behavior Programs for Juvenile Offenders," *Federal Probation*

41:45–50 (1977); Albert Bandura, *Principles of Behavior Modification* (New York: Holt, Rinehart & Winston, 1969); H. A. Klein, "Behavior Modification as Therapeutic Paradox," *American Journal of Orthopsychiatry* 44:353 (1974).

52. J. N. Yong, "Advantages of Group Therapy in Relation to Individual Therapy for Juvenile Delinquents," *Corrective Psychiatry and Journal of Social Therapy* 17:37 (1971).

53. LaMar T. Empey and Steven Lubeck, *The Silverlake Experiment* (Chicago: Aldine, 1971); H. Ashley Weeks, *Youthful Offenders at Highfields* (Ann Arbor, Mich.: University of Michigan Press, 1958); LaMar T. Empey and J. Rabow, "The Provo Experiment in Delinquency Rehabilitation," *American Sociological Review* 26:679 (1961).

54. Larry Brendtero and Arlin Ness, "Perspectives on Peer Group Treatment: The Use and Abuses of Guided Group Interaction/Positive Peer Culture," *Child and Youth Services Review* 4:307–24 (1982).

55. Bruno Bettleheim, *The Empty Fortress* (New York: Free Press, 1967).

56. *California Youth Authority Newsletter,* Ventura School for Juvenile Female Offenders (Ventura, Calif.: California Youth Authority, 1988).

57. Charles Murray and Louis B. Cox, *Beyond Probation* (Beverly Hills, Calif.: Sage, 1979).

58. Andrew Vachss and Yitzhak Bakal, *The Life-Style Violent Juvenile* (Lexington, Mass.: Lexington Books, 1979).

59. Ibid., p. 11.

60. Dan Macallair, "Reaffirming Rehabilitation in Juvenile Justice," *Youth and Society,* 25:104–25 (1993).

61. Barry Krisberg, Elliot Currie, and David Onek, "What Works with Juvenile Offenders," *American Bar Association Journal of Criminal Justice* 10:20–26 (1995).

62. Robert Mathias, Paul DeMuro, and Richard Allinson, eds., *Violent Juvenile Offender* (San Francisco: National Council on Crime and Delinquency, 1984).

63. J. A. Fagan, "Treatment and Reintegration of Violent Juvenile Offenders: Experimental Results," *Justice Quarterly,* 7:233–63 (1990).

64. For a description of the Florida Environmental Institute Program, see Howell *Guide for Implementing the Comprehensive Strategy for Serious, Violent and Chronic Juvenile Offenders.*

65. For a description of the Capital Offender Program, see Howell, *Guide for Implementing the Comprehensive Strategy for Serious, Violent and Chronic Offenders.*

66. Thomas Castellano and Irina Soderstrom, "Therapeutic Wilderness Programs and Juvenile Recidivism: A Program Evaluation," *Journal of Offender Rehabilitation* 17:19–46 (1992); Troy Armstrong, ed., *Intensive Interventions in High Risk Youth: Approaches in Juvenile Probation and Parole* (New York: Willow Tree Press, 1991).

67. William J. Taylor, "Tailoring Boot Camps to Juveniles," *Corrections Today,* July 1992, p. 124.

68. Jerald Burns and Gennaro Vito, "An Impact Analysis of the Alabama Boot Camp Program," *Federal Probation* 59:63–67 (1995).

69. Ronald Corbett and Joan Petersilia, eds., "The Results of a Multisite Study of Boot Camps," *Federal Probation* 58:60–66 (1995).

70. Margaret Beyer, "Juvenile Boot Camps Don't Make Sense," *American Bar Association Journal of Criminal Justice* 10:20–21 (1996).

71. Ibid.

72. Anthony Salerno, "Boot Camps—A Critique and Proposed Alternative," *Journal of Offender Rehabilitation* 20:147–58 (1994).

73. Peter Greenwood and Franklin Zimring, *One More Chance, the Pursuit of Promising Intervention Strategies For Chronic Juvenile Offenders* (Santa Monica, Calif.: Rand Corp., 1985).

74. Carol Garrett, "Effects of Residential Treatment on Adjudicated Delinquents: A Meta-Analysis," *Journal of Research in Crime and Delinquency* 22:287–308 (1985).

75. S. Lab and J. Whitehead, "Analysis of Juvenile Correctional Treatment," *Crime and Delinquency* 34:60–83 (1988).

76. Susan Guarino-Ghezzi and James Byrne, "Developing a Model of Structured Decision Making in Juvenile Corrections: The Mass Experience," *Crime and Delinquency* 35:270–303 (1989).

77. Robert Shepard, Jr., "State Pen or Playpen? Is Prevention 'Pork' or Simply Good Sense," *American Bar Association Journal of Criminal Justice* 10:34–37 (1995).

78. Morton Birnbaum, "The Right to Treatment," *American Bar Association Journal* 46: 499 (1960).

79. *Rouse v. Cameron,* 373 F.2d 451 (D.C.Cir. 1966).

80. Ibid., p. 453.

81. *Wyatt v. Stickney,* 325 F. Supp. 781 (1971); see also Note, "*Wyatt v. Stickney*—A Constitutional Right to Treatment for the Mentally Ill," *University of Pittsburgh Law Review* 34:79–84 (1972).

82. *Wyatt v. Stickney,* 325 F. Supp. 784 (1971).

83. *O'Connor v. Donaldson,* 422 U.S. 563 (1975).

84. *Inmates of the Boys' Training School v. Affleck,* 346 F. Supp. 1354 (D.R.I. 1972).

85. Ibid., p. 1343.

86. *Martarella v. Kelly,* 349 F. Supp. 575 (S.D.N.Y. 1972).

87. *Morales v. Turman,* 383 F. Supp. 53 (E.D. Texas 1974).

88. *Pena v. New York State Division for Youth,* 419 F. Supp. 203 (S.D.N.Y. 1976).

89. *Ralston v. Robinson,* 102 S.Ct. 233 (1981).

90. *Santana v. Collazo,* 714 F.2d 1172 (1st Cir. 1983).

91. *Santana v. Collazo,* 466 U.S. 974 (1984), writ of certiorari denied.

92. *Gary H. v. Hegstrom,* 831 F.2d 1430 (1987); see also David Lambert, "Children in Institutions," *Youth Law News* 8:10–14 (1987).

93. Harry Swanger, Mark Soler, Alice Shotton, James Bell, Elizabeth Jameson, Carole Shauffer, Loren Warboys, Susan Burrell, and Claudia Wright, "Juvenile Institutional Litigation," *Clearinghouse Review* 11:219–21 (1977). Swanger reports that the National Juvenile Law Center in St. Louis has been involved in litigation since 1972 that has sought and obtained reform of such practices as solitary confinement, disciplinary procedures, corporal punishment, forced drugging, and of institutional rules. Examples of the litigation include the following cases: *Nelson v. Heyne*, 355 F. Supp. 451 (N.D. Ind. 1972); *Inmates v. Affleck*, 346 F. Supp. 1354 (D.R.I. 1972); *Morales v. Turman*, 383 F. Supp. 53 (E.D. Tex. 1974). See also Mark Soler, *Representing the Child Client* (New York: Bender & Co., 1988), Release #9, 1993.

94. *Wolff v. McDonnell,* 418 U.S. 539 (1974).

95. *Lollis v. New York State Department of Social Services,* 322 F. Supp. 473 (1970).

96. For extensive analysis of juvenile law, see Samuel Davis, *Rights of Juveniles, the Juvenile Justice System* (New York: Clark Boardman, 1993); Joseph Senna and Larry Siegel, *Juvenile Law—Cases and Comments* (St. Paul, Minn.: West, 1992).

97. Michael Norman, "Discretionary Justice: Decision Making in a State Juvenile Parole Board," *Juvenile and Family Court Journal* 37:19–26 (1985–86).

98. James Maupin, "Risk Classification Systems and the Provisions of Juvenile Aftercare," *Crime and Delinquency* 39:90–105 (1993).

99. T. Armstrong and D. Altschuler, "Recent Developments in Programming of High-Risk Juvenile Parolees," in Albert Roberts, ed., *Critical Issues in Crime and Justice* (San Francisco, Calif.: Sage Publications, 1994).

100. Patrick Jackson, *The Paradox of Control: Parole Supervision of Youthful Offenders* (New York: Praeger, 1983).

101. Jeffrey Fagan, Cary Rudman, and Eliot Hartstone, "Intervening with Violent Juvenile Offenders: A Community Reintegration Model," in Robert Mathias, Paul De-Muro, and Richard Allinson, eds., *Violent Juvenile Offenders* (San Francisco: National Council on Crime and Delinquency, 1984), pp. 207–31.

102. "Girls Reintegration Center—Albuquerque, New Mexico," *Juvenile and Corrections Newsletter* 2:6 (1988).

103. Snyder and Sickmund, *Juvenile Offenders and Victims: A National Report*, p. 177.

104. See *Morrissey v. Brewer,* 408 U.S. 471, 92 S.Ct. 2593, 33 L.Ed.2d 484 (1972). Upon revocation of adult parole, a defendant is entitled to the due process rights of (1) a hearing, (2) written notice of charges, (3) knowledge of evidence against him or her, (4) opportunity to present and cross-examine witnesses, and (5) a written statement of reasons for parole revocation. Most jurisdictions require that these procedures be applied to juveniles.

105. John Wilson and James Howell, "Serious and Violent Juvenile Crime—A Comprehensive Strategy," *Juvenile and Family Court Journal* 45:3–15 (1994); U.S. Department of Justice, Delinquency Prevention Works—A Program Summary (Washington, D.C.: OJJDP, 1995).

CONCLUDING NOTES
AMERICAN DELINQUENCY

We have reviewed in this text the current knowledge of the nature, cause, and correlates of juvenile delinquency and society's efforts to bring about its elimination and control. We have analyzed research programs, theoretical models, governmental policies, and legal cases. Taken in sum, this information presents a rather broad and complex picture of the youth crime problem and the most critical issues confronting the juvenile justice system. Delinquents come from a broad spectrum of society; kids of every race, gender, class, region, family type, and culture are involved in delinquent behaviors. To combat youthful law violations, society has tried a garden variety of intervention and control strategies: tough law enforcement; counseling, treatment and rehabilitation; provision of legal rights; community action; educational programs; family change strategies. Yet, despite decades of intense effort and study, it is still unclear why delinquency occurs and what, if anything, can be done to control its occurrence. One thing is for certain, juvenile crime is one of the most serious domestic problems faced by Americans.

Though uncertainty prevails, it is possible to draw some inferences about youth crime and its control. After reviewing the material contained in this volume, certain conclusions seem self-evident. Some involve social facts; that is, particular empirical relationships and associations have been established that have withstood multiple testing and verification efforts. Other conclusions involve social questions; there are issues that need clarification, and the uncertainty surrounding them has hampered progress in combating delinquency and treating known delinquents.

In sum, we have reviewed some of the most important social facts concerning delinquent behavior and posed some of the critical questions that still remain to be answered.

■ **The statutory concept of juvenile delinquency is in need of review and modification.** Today, the legal definition of a juvenile delinquent is a minor child, usually under the age of 17, who has been found to have violated the criminal law (juvenile code). The concept of juvenile delinquency still occupies a legal position falling somewhere between criminal and civil law; juveniles still enjoy more rights, protections and privileges than adults. Nonetheless, the rising tide of teen violence may eventually put an end to the separate juvenile justice system. If kids are equally or even more violent as adults, why should they be given a special legal status consideration? If the teen violence rate continues to rise, so too may calls for the abolition of a separate juvenile justice system.

■ **The concept of the status offender (PINS, CHINS, and MINS) may be in for revision.** Special treatment for the status offender conforms with the *parens patriae* roots of the juvenile justice system. Granting the state authority to institutionalize non-criminal youth in order "to protect the best interest of the child" cannot be considered an abuse of state authority. While it is likely that the current system of control will remain in place for the near future, it is not beyond the realm of possibility to see the eventual restructuring of the definition of status offenders, with jurisdiction of "pure" non-criminal first offenders turned over to a department of social services, and chronic status offenders and those with prior records of delinquency petitioned to juvenile court as delinquency cases.

■ **Juvenile offenders are becoming more violent.** Official delinquency data suggests that there has been a decade long rise in the juvenile violence rate. At a time when adult violence is in decline, juvenile offenders are committing murder and other serious felony offenses at an increasing pace. Forecasters suggest that an increasing juvenile population portends a near term increase in the overall violence rate.

■ **Easy availability of guns is a significant contributor to teen violence.** Research indicates a close tie between gun use, control of drug markets and teen violence. Unless efforts are made to control the spread of handguns or devise programs to deter handgun use, teen-age murder rates should continue to rise.

■ **The chronic violent juvenile offender is a serious social problem for society and the juvenile justice system.** Official crime data indicates that the juvenile violence rate is at an all-time high. Chronic male delinquent offenders commit a disproportionate amount of violent behavior including a significant amount of the most serious juvenile crimes, such as homicides, rapes, robberies, and aggravated assaults. Many chronic offenders become adult criminals and eventually end up in the criminal court system. How to effectively deal with chronic juvenile offenders and drug users remains a high priority for the juvenile justice system.

Chronic juvenile delinquency has unquestionably become a major concept within the field. The best approach to dealing with chronic offenders remains uncertain, but concern about such offenders has shifted juvenile justice policy toward a punishment-oriented philosophy.

■ **There is still debate about whether the propensity to commit crime changes as people mature.** Delinquency experts are now researching such issues as the onset, escalation, termination and continuation of a delinquent career. There is an on-going debate concerning change in delinquent behavior patterns. One position is that people do not change, conditions and opportunities do. A second view is that real human change is conditioned by life events. If the former position holds true there is little hope of using treatment strategies to change known offenders; a more productive approach would be to limit their criminal opportunities through the use of long-term incarceration. If the latter position is accurate, effective treatment and provision of legitimate opportunities might produce real behavioral changes.

- **Female delinquency has been increasing at a faster pace than male delinquency.** The nature and extent of female delinquent activities changed in the late 1980s, and it now appears that girls are engaging in more frequent and serious illegal activity in the 1990s. While gender differences in the rate of the most serious crimes such as murder still persist, it is possible that further convergence will occur in the near future.

- **There is little question that family environment affects patterns of juvenile behavior.** Family relationships have been linked to the problem of juvenile delinquency by many experts. Broken homes, for instance, are not in and of themselves a cause of delinquency, but some evidence indicates that single-parent households are more inclined to contain children who manifest behavioral problems. Limited resource allocations limit the single-parent's ability to control and supervise children. In addition, there seems to be a strong association in family relationships between child abuse and delinquency. Cases of abuse and neglect have been found in every level of the economic strata, and a number of studies have linked child abuse and neglect to juvenile delinquency. While the evidence is not conclusive, it does suggest that a strong relationship exists between child abuse and subsequent delinquent behavior. This relationship does not bode well for delinquency rates because the extent of reported child abuse is on the increase. Some experts believe a major effort is needed to reestablish parental accountability and responsibility.

- **Juvenile gangs have become a serious and growing problem in many major metropolitan areas throughout the United States.** Ethnic youth gangs, mostly males aged 14 to 21, appear to be increasing in such areas as Los Angeles, Chicago, Boston, and New York. National surveys of gang activity now estimate that there are about 500,000 members in the United States, up sharply over the previous twenty years. One view of gang development is that such groups serve as a bridge between adolescence and adulthood in communities where adult social control is not available. Another view suggests that gangs are a product of lower-class social disorganization and that they serve as an alternative means of economic advancement for poorly motivated and uneducated youth. Today's gangs are more often commercially than culturally oriented, and the profit motive may be behind increasing memberships. It is unlikely that gang control strategies can be successful as long as legitimate economic alternatives are lacking. Look for rapid growth in ganging when the current adolescent population matures and limited job opportunities encourage gang members to prolong their involvement in illegal activities.

- **Many of the underlying problems of youth crime and delinquency are directly related to education.** Numerous empirical studies have confirmed that lack of educational success is an important contributing factor in delinquency; experts generally agree chronic offenders have had a long history of school failure. Dropping out of school is now being associated with long-term antisocial behavior. About ten percent of all victimizations occur on school grounds. School-based crime control projects have not been very successful, and a great deal more effort is needed in this critical area of school-delinquency prevention control.

- **Substance abuse is closely associated with juvenile crime and delinquency.** Self-reported teen substance abuse has increased during the 1990's. Surveys of arrested juveniles indicate sizable numbers of young people are substance abusers. Most efforts in the juvenile justice system to treat young offenders involved with substance abuse seem to be unsuccessful. Traditional prevention efforts and education programs have not had encouraging results.

- **An analysis of the history of juvenile justice over the past 100 years shows how our policy regarding delinquency has gone through cycles of reform.** Many years ago, society primarily focused on the treatment of youth who committed criminal behavior often through no fault of their own. Today, society is concerned with the control of serious juvenile offenders and the development of firm sentencing provisions in the juvenile courts. These cycles represent the shifting philosophies of the juvenile justice system.

- **Today, no single ideology or view dominates the direction, programs, and policies of the juvenile justice system.** Throughout the past decade, numerous competing positions regarding juvenile justice have emerged. As the liberal program of the 1970s has faltered, more restrictive sanctions have been imposed. The "crime control" position seems most formidable today.
  However, there remains a great deal of confusion over what the juvenile justice system does, what it should do, and how it should deal with youthful antisocial behavior. The juvenile justice system operates on the distinctly different yet parallel tracks. On the one hand, significant new funding is available for prevention and treatment strategies. At the same time, states are responding to anxiety about youth crime by devising more punitive measures.

- **Today's problems in the juvenile justice system can often be traced to the uncertainty of its founders, the "child savers."** Such early twentieth-century groups formed the juvenile justice system on the misguided principle of reforming wayward youth and remodeling their behavior. The "best interest of the child" standard has long been the guiding light in juvenile proceedings, calling for the strongest available rehabilitative services. Today's juvenile justice system is often torn between playing the role of social versus crime control agent.

- **In recent years, the juvenile justice system has become more legalistic by virtue of U.S. Supreme Court decisions that have granted children procedural safeguards in various court proceedings.** The case of *In re Gault* of the 1960s motivated state legislators to revamp their juvenile court legal procedures. Today, the Supreme Court is continuing to struggle with making distinctions between the legal rights of adults and minors. Recent Court decisions that allowed children to be searched by teachers and denied their right to a jury trial showed that the Court continues to recognize a legal separation between adult and juvenile offenders. *Vernonia School District v. Acton (1995),* in which the U.S. Supreme Court approved random drug testing of student athletes is the latest example of this distinction. Perhaps the question for the future is whether the Court will find that school authorities have a compelling interest to subject the general school population (other than athletes) to random drug testing.

- **Despite some dramatic distinctions, juveniles have gained many of the legal due process rights adults enjoy.** Among the more significant elements of due process are the right to counsel, evidence efficiency, protection from double jeopardy and self-incrimination, and the right to appeal. The public continues to favor providing juveniles with the same due process and procedural guarantees accorded to adults.

A 1995 report of the American Bar Association on juvenile access to counsel and the quality of legal representation in juvenile court found that the many constitutional protections that adults receive are not actually provided to juvenile offenders. High caseloads, poor pretrial preparation and trial performance, and the lack of dispositional representation are issues where juveniles are being denied due process of law. More resources are needed to implement constitutional procedures so that legal protections are not discarded.

■ **States are increasingly taking legislative action to ensure that juvenile arrest and disposition records are available to prosecutors and judges.** Knowledge of defendants' juvenile records may help determine appropriate sentencing for offenders age 18-24, the age group most likely to be involved in violent crime. Laws that are being passed include: police fingerprinting of juveniles charged with crimes that are felonies if committed by an adult; (2) centralized juvenile arrest and disposition recordholding and dissemination statutes; (3) prosecutor and court access to juvenile disposition records; and (4) limitations on expungement of juvenile records when there are subsequent adult convictions.

■ **The Juvenile Court is the focal point of the contemporary juvenile justice system.** Created at the turn of the century, it was adopted as an innovative solution to the problem of wayward youth. In the first half of the century, these courts (organized by the states) and based on the historic notion of "parens patriae", were committed to the treatment of the child. They functioned without procedures employed in the adult criminal courts. When the system was reviewed by the U.S. Supreme Court in 1966, due process was imposed on the juvenile court system. Thirty years have since passed and numerous reform efforts have been undertaken. But the statement of Judge Abe Fortas "that the child receives the worst of both worlds—neither the protection afforded adults nor the treatment needed for children"—still rings true. Reform efforts have been disappointing.

What are the remedies for the current juvenile court system? Some suggest abolishing the delinquency-status jurisdiction of the courts. This is difficult to do because the organization of the courts is governed by state law. Others want to strengthen the legal rights of juveniles by improving the quality of services of legal counsel. The vast majority of experts believe there is an urgent need to develop meaningful dispositional programs and expand treatment services. Over the last half century, the juvenile court system has been transformed from a rehabilitative to a quasi-criminal court. With limited resources and procedural deficiencies, there is little likelihood of much change in the near future.

■ **The death penalty for children has been upheld by the Supreme Court.** According to the *Wilkins v. Missouri* and *Stanford v. Kentucky* cases in 1989, the Supreme Court concluded that states are free to impose the death penalty for murderers who commit their crimes while age 16 or 17. According to the majority decision written by Justice Antonin Scalia, society has not formed a consensus that such executions are a violation of the cruel and unusual punishment clause of the Eighth Amendment.

■ **One of the most significant changes in American law enforcement has been the emergence of community policing in the field of delinquency prevention.** Community participation and cooperation, citizen crime prevention programs, and education programs such as Project DARE (drug education) have become a mainstay of law enforcement in the 1980s and early 1990s and have had a particularly significant impact on improving perceptions of community safety and the quality of community life in many areas.

The Violent Crime Control and Law Enforcement Act of 1994, described as the largest piece of criminal legislation in the history of the country, and four years in the making, provides major new opportunities for the field of juvenile crime prevention and community policing. Fighting to retain this law's major focus on prevention will be a future goal.

- **The use of detention in the juvenile justice system continues to be a widespread problem.** After almost three decades of work, virtually all jurisdictions have passed laws requiring that status offenders be placed in shelter care programs rather than detention facilities. Another serious problem related to the use of juvenile detention is the need to remove young people from lockups in adult jails. The Office of Juvenile Justice and Delinquency Prevention continues to give millions of dollars in aid to encourage the removal of juveniles from such adult lockups. But eliminating the confinement of children in adult institutions remains an enormously difficult task in the juvenile justice system. Although most delinquency cases do not involve detention, its use is more common for cases involving males, minorities and older juveniles. Juvenile detention is one of the most important elements of the justice system and one of the most difficult to administer. It is experiencing a renewed emphasis on programs linked to short-term confinement.

- **The use of waiver, bind-over, and transfer provisions in juvenile court statutes has been growing.** This trend has led toward a criminalization of the juvenile system. Because there are major differences between the adult and juvenile court systems, transfer to an adult court exposes youths to more serious consequences of their antisocial behavior and is a strong recommendation of those favoring a crime-control model. Waiver of serious offenders is one of the most significant developments in the trend to criminalize the juvenile court. According to the National Conference of State Legislatures, more than half of the states responding to a 1996 survey on juvenile justice reported that they expect to consider legislation that makes it easier to transfer juveniles into adult courts.

- **The role of the attorney in the juvenile justice process requires further research and analysis.** Most attorneys appear to be uncertain whether they should act as adversaries or advocates in the juvenile process. In addition, the role of the juvenile prosecutor has become more significant as a result of new and more serious statutory sentencing provisions, as well as legal standards promulgated by such organizations as the American Bar Association and the National District Attorneys Association.

- **Juvenile sentencing procedures now reflect the desire to create uniformity and limited discretion in the juvenile court, and this trend is likely to continue.** Many states have now developed such programs as mandatory sentences, sentencing guidelines, and limited-discretion sentencing to bring uniformity into the juvenile justice system. As a result of the public's fear about serious juvenile crime, legislators have amended juvenile codes to tighten up juvenile sentencing provisions. Graduated sanctions are the latest type of sentencing solution being explored by states. The most popular piece of juvenile crime legislation in the near future will be tougher sentences for violent and repeat offenders.

■ **In the area of community sentencing, new forms of probation supervision have become commonplace in recent years.** Intensive probation supervision, balanced probation, wilderness probation, and electronic monitoring have become important community-based alternatives over the last few years. Probation continues to be the single most significant intermediate sanction available to the juvenile court system.

■ **Victim restitution is another widely used and programmatic method of community treatment in today's juvenile justice system.** In what is often referred to as monetary restitution; children are required to pay the victims of their crimes or in some instances provide some community service directly to the victim. Restitution provides the court with an important alternative sentencing option and has been instituted by statute in virtually every jurisdiction in the country.

■ **Deinstitutionalization has become an important goal of the juvenile justice system.** The Office of Juvenile Justice and Delinquency Prevention has provided funds to encourage this process. In the early 1980s, the deinstitutionalization movement seemed to be partially successful. Admissions to public juvenile correctional facilities declined in the late 1970s and early 1980s. In addition, the number of status offenders being held within the juvenile justice system was reduced. However, the number of institutionalized children in recent years has increased, and the deinstitutionalization movement has failed to meet all of its optimistic goals.

Nonetheless, the majority of states have achieved compliance with the DSO mandate. Because juvenile crime is a high priority, the challenge to the states will be to retain a focus on prevention despite societal pressures for more punitive approaches. If that can be achieved, then deinstitutionalization will remain a central theme in the juvenile justice system.

■ **The number of incarcerated youths continues to rise.** Today, there are almost 100,000 youths in some type of correctional institution. The juvenile courts seem to be using the most severe of the statutory dispositions, that is, commitment to the juvenile institution, rather than the "least restrictive statutory alternative." In addition, there seems to be a disproportionate number of minority youths incarcerated in youth facilities. The minority incarceration rate is almost four times greater than that for whites and minorities seem to be placed more often in public than in private treatment facilities. The overall organization of the juvenile justice system in the United States is changing. Early on, institutional services for children were provided by the public sector. Today, private facilities and programs service a significant proportion of juvenile admissions. In the next decade, many more juvenile justice systems will most likely adopt privatization of juvenile correctional services.

■ **Despite the growth of alternative treatment programs such as diversion, restitution, and probation, the number of children under secure institutional care has increased, and the success of such programs remains very uncertain.** Nearly all juvenile institutions utilize some form of treatment program for the children in their care. Despite generally positive intentions, the goal of rehabilitation in an institutional setting is very difficult to achieve. Recent studies indicate some programs do work. Those secure programs that emphasize individual attention, reintegrate youths into their homes and communities, and provide intensive aftercare can be successful.

- **The future of the legal right to treatment for juveniles remains uncertain.** The appellate courts have established minimum standards of care and treatment on a case-by-case basis, but it does not appear that the courts can be persuaded today to expand this constitutional theory to mandate that incarcerated children receive adequate treatment. Eventually, this issue must be clarified by the Supreme Court. Reforms in state juvenile institutions often result from class action lawsuits filed on behalf of incarcerated youth such as the recent case of *Alexander v. Boyd* in South Carolina in 1995.

  A serious crisis exists in the U.S. juvenile justice system. How to cope with the needs of large numbers of children in trouble remains one of the most controversial and frustrating issues in our society. The magnitude of the problem is such that over 2 million youths are arrested each year; over 1.5 million delinquency dispositions and 1 million status offense cases are heard in court; and drug abuse is a significant factor in more than 60 percent of all the cases referred to the juvenile courts. Today, the system and the process seem more concerned with crime control and more willing to ignore the rehabilitative ideal. Perhaps the answer lies outside the courtroom in the form of greater job opportunities, improved family relationships, and more effective education. Much needs to be done in delinquency prevention. One fact is also certain: According to many experts, the problem of violent juvenile crime is a national crisis. Developing programs to fight juvenile violence seems to overshadow all other juvenile justice objectives.

- **Federal funding for juvenile delinquency is essential to improving state practices and programs.** The Juvenile Justice and Delinquency Prevention Act of 1974 has had a tremendous impact on America's juvenile justice system. Its mandates to deinstitutionalize status offenders and remove juveniles from adult jails have spurred change for over two decades. The survival of many state programs will likely depend on this federal legislation. Because the Act has contributed to a wide range of improvements, Congress will most likely approve future financial incentives.

- **In 1996, The Coordinating Council on Juvenile Justice and Delinquency Prevention, an independent organization in the executive branch of the federal government, presented its National Juvenile Justice Action Plan.** The Plan is a blueprint for action designed to reduce the impact of juvenile violence and delinquency. It calls upon states and communities to implement the following objectives: (1) provide immediate intervention sanctions and treatment for delinquent juveniles; (2) prosecute serious, violent and chronic juvenile offenders in criminal court; (3) reduce youth involvement with guns, drugs, and gangs; (4) provide educational and employment opportunities for children and youth; (5) break the cycle of violence by dealing with youth victimization, abuse and neglect; (6) strengthen and mobilize communities; (7) support the development of innovative approaches to research and evaluation; and (8) implement an aggressive outreach campaign to combat juvenile violence. This text provides numerous examples of the innovative and effective strategies that are described in the National Juvenile Justice Action Plan.

GLOSSARY

acquittal Release or discharge, especially by verdict of a jury.

action Lawsuit; a proceeding taken in a court of law. Actions are either civil (to enforce a right) or criminal (to punish an offender)

actus reus An illegal act. The actus reus can be an affirmative act, such as taking money or shooting.

addict A person with an overpowering physical and psychological need to continue taking a particular substance or drug by any means possible.

addiction-prone personality The view that the cause of substance abuse can be traced to a personality which has a compulsion for mood altering drugs.

adjudicated Having been the subject of completed criminal or juvenile proceedings and having been convicted or declared a delinquent, a status offender, or a dependent.

adjudication (juvenile) Juvenile court decision, terminating a hearing, that the juvenile is a delinquent, a status offender, or a dependent or that the allegations in the petition are not sustained.

adjudicatory hearing In juvenile proceedings, the fact-finding process wherein the juvenile court determines whether there is sufficient evidence to sustain the allegations in a petition.

adjustment Settlement or bringing to a satisfactory state so that parties are agreed without official intervention of the court.

adversary system Procedure used to determine truth in the adjudication of guilty or innocence, which pits the defense (advocate for the accused) against the prosecution (advocate for the state), with the judge acting as arbiter of the legal rules. Under the adversary system, the burden is on the state to prove the charges beyond a reasonable doubt. This system of having the two parties publicly debate has proved to be the most effective method of achieving the truth regarding a set of circumstances. (Under the accusatory, or inquisitorial, system that is used in continental Europe, the charge is evidence of guilt that the accused must disprove; the judge takes an active part in the proceedings.)

affidavit Written statement of fact, signed and sworn to before a person having authority to administer an oath.

aftercare Supervision given children for a limited period of time after they are released from a training school but still under the control of the school or of the juvenile court.

age of onset Age at which youths begin their delinquent careers. Early onset of delinquency is believed to be linked with chronic offending patterns.

aging out The process in which the individuals reduce the frequency of their offending behavior as they age. Also known as spontaneous remission because people are believed to spontaneously reduce the rate of their criminal behavior as they mature, aging out is thought to occur among all groups of offenders.

aggregate measures Data collected on groups of people rather than individuals. A good example of aggregate data is the Uniform Crime Reports index crimes; though the number of criminal incidents that occur in a given area can be counted, little data is provided on the offenders who commit them or the circumstances in which they occurred. Self-report surveys are usually considered individual-level data, since subjects' responses can be examined on a case-by-case basis.

alienation   Mental condition marked by normlessness and role confusion.

alternative sanctions   That group of sanctions falling between probation and institutionalization; "probation plus." Community-based sanctions, including house arrest and intensive supervision, serve as alternatives to incarceration

androgens   Male sex hormones.

anesthetics   Drugs such as PCP, which are used as nervous system depressants. Local anesthetics block nervous system transmissions; general anesthetics act on the brain to produce a generalized loss of sensation, stupor, or unconsciousness.

anomie   Normlessness that is produced by rapidly shifting moral values. An anomic person has few guides to what is socially acceptable behavior. According to Merton, anomie is a condition that occurs when personal goals cannot be achieved by available means.

antisocial personality   Synonymous with psychopath, the antisocial personality is characterized by lack of normal responses to life situations, the inability to learn from punishment, and violent reactions to nonthreatening events.

appeal   Review of lower court proceedings by a higher court. There is no constitutional right to appeal. However, the "right" to appeal is established by statute in some states and by custom in others. All states set conditions as to type of case or grounds for appeal, which appellate courts may review. An appellate court does not retry the case under review. Rather, the transcript of the lower court case is read by the judges, and the lawyers for the defendant and for the state argue about the merits of the appeal—that is, the legality of lower court proceedings, instead of the original testimony. Appeal is more a process for controlling police, court, and correctional practices than for rescuing innocent defendants. When appellate courts do reverse lower court judgments, it is usually because of "prejudicial error" (deprivation of rights), and the case is remanded for retrial.

appellant   Party who initiates an appeal from one court to another.

appellee   Party in a lawsuit against whom an appeal has been taken.

arousal theory   The view that sociopaths are individuals who need greater than average stimulation to bring them up to comfortable levels of living.

arrest   Taking of a person into the custody of the law, the legal purpose of which is to restrain the accused until he or she can be held accountable for the offense at court proceedings.

The legal requirement for an arrest is probable cause. Arrests for investigation, suspicion, or harassment are improper and of doubtful legality. The police have the responsibility to use only the reasonable physical force necessary to make an arrest. The summons has been used as a substitute for arrest.

arrest warrant   Written court order by a magistrate authorizing and directing that an individual be taken into custody to answer criminal charges.

atavistic   According to Lombroso, the primitive physical characteristics that distinguish born criminals from the general population. Lombrosian theory holds that characteristics of criminals are throwbacks to animals or primitive people.

Augustus, John   Individual credited with pioneering the concept of probation.

authoritarian   Person whose personality revolves around blind obedience to authority.

authority conflict pathway   The path to a criminal career that begins with early stubborn behavior and defiance of parents.

bail   Amount of money that has to be paid as a condition of pretrial release, normally set by a judge at the initial appearance. The purpose of bail is to ensure that people accused of crimes will return for subsequent proceedings. If they are unable to make bail, they are detained in jail.

balancing-of-the-interest approach   In child abuse cases, the efforts of the state to balance the parent's natural right to raise a child with the child's right to grow into adulthood free from physical abuse or emotional harm.

Beccaria   Eighteenth-century Italian philosopher who argued that crime could be controlled by punishments only severe enough to counterbalance the pleasure obtained from them.

behaviorism   Branch of psychology concerned with the study of observable behavior rather than unconscious motives. It focuses on the relationship between particular stimuli and people's responses to them.

beyond a reasonable doubt   Degree of proof required for conviction of a defendant in criminal and juvenile delinquency proceedings. It is less than absolute certainty but more than high probability. If there is doubt based on reason, the accused is entitled to the benefit of that doubt by acquittal.

bifurcated process   The procedure of separating adjudicatory and dispositionary hearing so that different levels of evidence can be heard at each.

biosocial The view that thought and behavior have both biological and social bases.

booking Administrative record of an arrest made in a police station. It involves listing of the offender's name, address, physical description, date of birth, employer, time of arrest and offense and the name of arresting officer. Photographing and fingerprinting of the offender are also part of booking. The Miranda warning is given again (the first time was at the scene of the arrest). In addition, the accused is allowed to make a telephone call.

boot camp A short-term militaristic correctional facility in which inmates undergo intensive physical conditioning and discipline.

burden of proof Duty of proving disputed facts on the trial of a case. The duty commonly lies on the person who asserts the affirmative of an issue and is sometimes said to shift when sufficient evidence is furnished to raise a presumption that what is alleged is true.

bourgeoisie In Marxist theory, the owners of the means of production; the capitalist ruling class.

capital punishment Use of the death penalty to punish transgressors.

career criminal Person who repeatedly violates the law and organizes his or her life-style around criminality. A chronic offender.

case law Law derived from previous court decisions; opposed to statutory law, which is passed by legislatures.

certiorari Literally, "to be informed of, to be made certain in regard to." The name of a writ of review or inquiry.

chancery court Court proceedings created in fifteenth-century England to oversee the lives of high-born minors who were orphaned or otherwise could not care for themselves.

child abuse Any physical, emotional, or sexual trauma to a child for which no reasonable explanation, such as an accident, can be found. Child abuse can also be neglecting to give proper care and attention.

child savers Nineteenth-century reformers who developed programs for troubled youth and influenced legislation creating the juvenile justice system. Today, some critics view them as being more concerned with the control of the poor than with their welfare.

Children's Aid Society Child saving organization which took children from the streets of large cities and placed them with farm families on the prairie.

chivalry hypothesis View that the low female crime and delinquency rates are a reflection of the leniency with which police treat female offenders.

choice theory The school of thought that holds that people will engage in delinquent and criminal behavior after weighing the consequences and benefits of their actions. Delinquent behavior is a rational choice made by a motivated offender who perceives the chances of gain outweigh any perceived punishment or loss.

cholo Latino street youth culture.

chronic delinquent Youth who has been arrested five or more times during his or her minority. This small portion of the offending population are believed to engage in a significant portion of all delinquent behavior.

chronicity State of being a chronic recidivist.

classical theory Theoretical perspective suggesting that (1) people have free will to choose criminal or conventional behaviors; (2) people choose to commit crime for reasons of greed or personal need; (3) crime can be deterred through fear of punishment.

clearance Crime reported to the police that is "solved" by an arrest.

cocaine The most powerful natural stimulant. Its use produces euphoria, laughter, restlessness, and excitement. Overdoses can cause delirium, increased reflexes, violent manic behavior, and possible respiratory failure.

cognitive theory The branch of psychology which studies the perception of reality and the mental processes required to understand the world we live in.

cohort study Study utilizing a sample of people who share a single characteristic, such as place of birth, and whose behavior is followed over a period of time.

commitment Action of a judicial officer ordering that an adjudicated and sentenced adult or adjudicated delinquent or status offender who has been the subject of a juvenile court disposition hearing be admitted to a correctional facility.

common law Basic legal principles that developed in England and became uniform (common) throughout the country. Judges began following previous court decisions (precedent) when new but similar cases arose.

community facility (nonconfinement facility, adult or juvenile) Correctional facility from which residents are regularly permitted to depart, unaccompanied by an official, to use community resources, such as schools or treatment programs, or to seek or hold employment.

community policing Police strategy that emphasizes fear reduction, community organization, and order maintenance, rather than crime fighting.

concurrent sentences Literally, running sentences together. The condition set for serving sentences of imprisonment for multiple charges. When people are convicted of two or more charges, they must be sentenced on each charge. If the sentences are concurrent, they begin the same day and are completed after the longest term has been served. (See also consecutive sentences.)

conduct norms Behaviors that are expected of social group members. If group norms conflict with those of the general culture, members of the group may find themselves described as outcasts or criminals.

conflict theory View that conflict among interest groups, especially those of opposing socioeconomic classes, is the main determinant of human behavior.

consecutive sentences Literally, sentences that follow one another. Upon completion of one sentence, the other term of incarceration begins. (See also concurrent sentences.)

consent decree Decree entered by consent of the parties. Not properly a judicial sentence but in the nature of a solemn contract or agreement of the parties that the decree is a just determination of their rights based on the real facts of the case, if such facts are proved.

containments According to Reckless, internal and external factors and conditions that help insulate youths from delinquency-promoting situations. Most important of the internal containments is a strong self-concept, while external containments include positive support from parents and teachers.

constitutional law Branch of public law of a state that maintains the framework of political and government authorities and functions in accordance with the state's constitution.

conviction Judgment of guilt; verdict by a jury, plea by a defendant, or judgment by a court that the accused is guilty as charged.

co-offending Committing criminal acts in groups. It is believed that a significant number of delinquent acts involve more than one offender.

corner boy According to Cohen, a role in the lower class culture in which young men remain in their birth neighborhood, acquire families and menial jobs and adjust to the demands of their environment.

correctional institution Generic name for long-term adult confinement facilities that are often called prisons, federal or state correctional facilities, or penitentiaries, and for juvenile confinement facilities that are often called training schools, reformatories, boys' ranches, and the like.

correctional institution (juvenile) Confinement facility having custodial authority over delinquents and status offenders committed to confinement after a juvenile disposition hearing.

corrections Generic term that includes all government agencies, facilities, programs, procedures, personnel, and techniques concerned with the investigation, intake, custody, confinement, supervision, or treatment of alleged or adjudicated adult offenders, delinquents, or status offenders.

court Agency of the judicial branch of government authorized or established by statute or constitution and consisting of one or more judicial officers that has the authority to decide on controversies in law and disputed matters of fact brought before it.

crack Processed street cocaine. Its manufacture involves using ammonia or baking soda to remove the hydrochlorides and create a crystalline form of cocaine base which can then be smoked.

crackdown The concentration of police resources on a particular problem area, such as street-level drug dealing, to eradicate or displace criminal activity.

crime Offense against the state; behavior in violation of law for which there is prescribed punishment.

crime control Model of criminal justice that emphasizes the control of dangerous offenders and the protection of society. Its advocates call for harsh punishments as deterrents to crime, such as the death penalty.

criminal justice process Decision-making process from the initial investigation or arrest by police to the eventual release of offenders and their reentry into society; the various sequential criminal justice stages through which offenders pass.

criminal justice standards Models, commentaries, or recommendations for the revision of criminal justice procedures and practices; for example, the American Law Institute's Model Penal Code, the American Bar Association's Standards for Criminal Justice, and the recommendations of the National Advisory Commission on Criminal Justice Standards and Goals.

criminal justice system Group of agencies and organization—police, courts, and corrections—as well as the legislation and appellate courts responsible for the administration of criminal justice and crime control.

criminal law Body of law that defines criminal offenses, prescribes punishments (substantive law), and delineates criminal procedure (procedural law).

criminal sanction Refers to the right of the state to punish people if they violate the rules set down in the criminal code. The punishment is connected to commission of a specific crime.

criminology Study of the causes and treatment of criminal behavior, criminal law, and the administration of criminal justice.

critical criminology Branch of criminology that reviews and analyzes historical and current developments in law and justice in order to expose the interests of the power elite and ruling classes.

cross-sectional data Survey data that involves all age, race, gender, and income segments of the population measured simultaneously. Since people from every age group are represented, age-specific crime rates can be determined. Proponents believe that this is a sufficient substitute for the more expensive longitudinal approach that follows a group of subjects over time in order to measure crime rate changes.

culpable Implication of a wrongful act but one that does not involve malice. It connotes fault rather than guilt.

cultural deviance Condition that exists when obedience to subcultural norms conflicts with the rules and laws of the larger, general culture.

cultural transmission Concept that conduct norms are passed down from one generation to the next so that they become stable within the boundaries of a culture. Cultural transmission guarantees that group life-style and behavior are stable and predictable.

culture conflict Condition brought about when the rules and norms of an individual's subcultural affiliation conflict with the role demands of conventional society.

culture of poverty View that lower-class people form a separate culture with its own values and norms that are in conflict with conventional society; the culture is self-maintaining and ongoing.

dark figures of crime Incidents of crime and delinquency that go undetected by police.

DARE The acronym for Drug Abuse Resistance Education, a school-based anti-drug program initiated by the Los Angeles police and now adopted around the United States.

decarceration A correctional philosophy which stresses the "least restrictive alternative possible" removing as many juveniles from secure detention as possible and making use of community alternatives.

degenerate anomalies According to Lombroso, the primitive physical characteristics that make criminals animalistic and savage.

deinstitutionalization Closing of institutions and moving inmates to community-based programs.

delinquency Juvenile actions or conduct in violation of criminal law and, in some contexts, status offenders.

delinquent Juvenile who has been adjudicated by a judicial officer of a juvenile court as having committed a delinquent act.

delinquent act Act committed by a juvenile for which an adult could be prosecuted in a criminal court. A juvenile who commits such an act can be adjudicated in a juvenile court or prosecuted in a criminal court if the juvenile court transfers jurisdiction.

dependency Legal status of juveniles over whom a juvenile court has assumed jurisdiction because the court has found their care by parents, guardians, or custodians falls short of a legal standard of proper care.

dependents Juveniles over whom a juvenile court has assumed jurisdiction because the court has found their care by parents, guardians, or custodians falls short of a legal standard of proper care.

desistance Phenomenon that relates to the decline in the crime rate as a person matures; synonymous with the aging-out process. Desisters are youths who spontaneously terminate their delinquent careers.

dessert-based sentences Principle of basing sentence length on the seriousness of the criminal act and not the personal characteristics of the defendant or the deterrent impact of the law. Punishment based on what people have done and not on what others may do or what they themselves may do in the future.

detached street workers Program that places social workers in the community in order to reach fighting gangs.

detective Police agent who is assigned to investigate crimes after they have been reported, to gather evidence, and to identify the perpetrator.

detention Temporary care of a child alleged to be delinquent who requires secure custody in physically restricting facilities pending court disposition or execution of a court order.

detention center Government facility that provides temporary care in a physically restricting environment for juveniles in custody pending court disposition.

detention facility (juvenile) Confinement facility having custodial authority over juveniles confined pending and after adjudication.

detention hearing In juvenile proceedings, a hearing by a judicial officer of a juvenile court to determine whether a juvenile is to be detained, to continue to be detained, or to be released while juvenile proceedings are pending in the case.

determinate sentence Involves "fixed" terms of incarceration, such as three years' incarceration. It is felt by many to be too restrictive for rehabilitative purposes; the advantage is that offenders know how much time they have to serve, that is, when they will be released.

deterrence Act of preventing a crime before it occurs by means of the threat of criminal sanctions. Deterrence involves the perception that the pain of apprehension and punishment outweigh any chances of criminal gain or profit.

developmental criminology A branch of criminology that examines change in a criminal career over the life course. Developmental factors include biological, social, and psychological change. Among the topics of developmental criminology are desistance, resistance, escalation, and specialization.

developmental theory View that personal characteristics guide human development and influence and control behavior choices.

differential association Theory positing that criminal behavior is learned when an individual encounters an excess of definitions favoring law violations over those that support conformity to law; also learned in primary groups characterized by intimacy.

discretion Use of personal decision making and choice in carrying out operations in the criminal justice system. For example, police discretion can involve the decision to make an arrest, whole prosecutorial discretion can involve the decision to accept a plea bargain.

disposition For juvenile offenders, the equivalent of sentencing for adult offenders. The theory is that disposition should be more rehabilitative than retributive. Possible dispositions may be dismissal of the case, release of the youth to the custody of his or her parents, placement of the offender on probation, or sending him or her to an institution or state correctional institution.

disposition hearing Hearing in juvenile court conducted after an adjudicatory hearing and subsequent receipt of the report of any predisposition investigation to determine the most appropriate disposition of a juvenile who has been adjudicated a delinquent, a status offender, or a dependent.

dissagregate Analyzing the relationship between two or more independent variables while controlling for the influence of a third dependent variable. For example, looking at the relationship between conviction for murder and the likelihood of a death sentence dissagregated by race would entail separate analysis of the sentencing outcomes of White and African-American convictees.

district attorney County prosecutor who is charged with bringing offenders to justice and enforcing the laws of the state.

diversion Official halting or suspension of formal criminal or juvenile justice proceedings against an alleged offender at any legally prescribed processing point after a recorded justice system entry and the referral of that person to a treatment or care program administered by a nonjudicial public agency or a private agency or the recommendation that the person be released.

dower Middle Ages custom of monetary compensation being given the groom by the bride's family before a marriage could take place.

drift According to Matza, the view that youths move in and out of delinquency and that their life-styles can embrace both conventional and deviant values.

Drug Enforcement Administration (DEA) Federal agency that handles enforcement of federal drug control laws.

due process Basic constitutional principle based on the concept of the primacy of the individual and the complementary concept of limitation on governmental power; a safeguard against arbitrary and unfair state procedures in judicial or administrative proceedings. Embodied in the due process concept are the basic rights of a defendant in criminal proceedings and the requisites for a fair trial. These rights and requirements have been expanded by appellate court decisions and include (1) timely notice of a hearing or trial that informs the accused of the charges against him or her; (2) the opportunity to confront accusers and to present evidence on the accused's own behalf before an impartial jury or judge; (3) the presumption of innocence under which guilt must be proven by legally obtained evidence and the verdict must be supported by the evidence presented; (4) the right of an accused to be warned of constitutional rights at the earliest stage of the criminal process; (5) protection against self-incrimination; (6) assistance of counsel at every critical stage of the criminal process; and (7) the guarantee that an individual will not be tried more than once for the same offense (double jeopardy).

early onset A term that refers to the assumption that a criminal career begins early in life and that people who are deviant at a very young age are the ones most likely to persist in crime.

ecological theory View that the interrelationship between people and their environment influences behavior.

egalitarian family A family structure in which both parents share equal authority and power.

ego identity According to Erikson, ego identity is formed when persons develop a firm sense of who they are and what they stand for.

electroencephalogram (EEG) Device that can record the electronic impulses given off by the brain, commonly called "brain waves."

emancipation Relinquishment of the care, custody, and earnings of a minor child and the renunciation of parental duties.

embedded According to John Hagan, youths who become embedded in a delinquent way of life reduces any chances of future success in the marketplace.

equipotentiality View that all people are equal at birth and are thereafter influenced by their environment.

exclusionary rule Principle that prohibits using evidence illegally obtained in a trial. Based on the Fourth Amendment "right of the people to be secure in their persons, houses, papers, and effects, against unreasonable searches and seizures," the rule is not a bar to prosecution, as legally obtained evidence may be available and may be used in a trial.

extraversion A personality trait marked by impulsivity, and the inability to examine motives and behavior.

family court Court with broad jurisdiction over family matters, such as neglect, delinquency, paternity, support, and noncriminal behavior.

Federal Bureau of Investigation (FBI) Arm of the U.S. Justice Department that investigates violations of federal law, gathers crime statistics, runs a comprehensive crime laboratory, and helps train local law enforcement officers.

felony Criminal offense punishable by death or by incarceration in a state or federal confinement facility for a period whose lower limit is prescribed by statute in a given jurisdiction, typically one year or more.

finding of fact Court's determination of the facts presented as evidence in a case, affirmed by one party and denied by the other.

fine The court-imposed penalty requiring that a convicted person pay a specified sum of money.

focal concerns According to Walter Miller, the value orientations of lower-class cultures whose features include the need for excitement, trouble, smartness, fate, and personal autonomy.

free will View that people are in charge of their own destinies and are free to make personal behavior choices unencumbered by environmental controls.

general deterrence Crime-control policy that depends on the fear of criminal penalties. General deterrence measures, such as long prison sentences for violent crimes, are aimed at convincing the potential law violator that the pains associated with crime outweigh its benefits.

gentrified The process of taking a lower-class area and transforming it into a middle-class enclave through property rehabilitation.

graffiti Inscription or drawing made on a wall or structure. Used by delinquents for gang messages and turf definition.

group home Nonconfining residential facility for adjudicated adults or juveniles or those subject to criminal or juvenile proceedings, intended to reproduce as closely as possible the circumstances of family life and, at minimum, provide access to community activities and resources.

guardian ad litem Court-appointed attorney who protects the interests of a child in cases involving the child's welfare.

habeas corpus Literally, "you have the body." A variety of writs whose objective is to bring a party before a court or judge. The function of the writ is to release the person from unlawful imprisonment.

halfway house Nonconfining residential facility for adjudicated adults or juveniles or for those subject to criminal or juvenile proceedings, intended to provide an alternative to confinement for persons not suitable for probation or in need of a period of readjustment to the community after confinement.

hallucinogens Drugs, either natural or synthetic, that produce vivid distortions of the senses without greatly disturbing the viewer's consciousness. Some produce hallucinations, and others cause psychotic behavior in otherwise normal people. Hashish (hash) is a concentrated form of marijuana made from unadulterated resin from the female plant.

hate crimes Acts of violence or intimidation designed to terrorize or frighten people considered undesirable because of their race, religion, ethnic origin, or sexual orientation.

hearing Presentation of evidence to the juvenile court judge, the judge's consideration of it, and the decision on disposition of the case.

helping professions Occupations such as social work, mental health, and family care that are dedicated to the health and welfare of the needy and indigent.

heroin The most dangerous commonly used drug made from the poppy plant. Users rapidly build a tolerance for it fueling the need for increased doses in order to feel a desired effect.

hot spots of crime According to Sherman, a significant portion of all police calls originate from only a few locations. These hot spots include taverns and housing projects.

impulsivity According to Gottfredson and Hirschi's general theory, the trait that produces criminal behavior. Impulsive people lack self-control.

incarceration Putting a person in prison. The basic purposes of such confinement have been punishment, deterrence, rehabilitation, and integration into the community.

identity crisis Psychological state, identified by Erikson, in which youth face inner turmoil and uncertainty about life roles.

indentured servant Prior to the eighteenth century, a debtor or convicted offender who would work off his or her debt by being assigned a term of servitude to a master who purchased the services from the state.

index crimes Crimes used by the FBI to indicate the incidence of crime in the United States and reported annually in the Uniform Crime Reports. They include murder and nonnegligent manslaughter, robbery, rape, aggravated assault, burglary, larceny, and motor vehicle theft.

indictment Written accusation returned by a grand jury that charges an individual with a specified crime after deter-

mination of probable cause. The prosecutor presents enough evidence to establish probable cause.

indigent Person who is needy and poor or who lacks the means to provide a living.

inhalants Vapors from lighter fluid, paint thinner, cleaning fluid, and model airplane glue sniffed to reach a drowsy, dizzy state sometimes accompanied by hallucinations.

inmate Person in a confinement facility.

innocents Youths who have never been apprehended for a delinquent act.

insanity Unsoundness of mind that prevents one from comprehending the consequences of one's acts or from distinguishing between right and wrong.

instrumental Marxist theory View that capitalist institutions such as the criminal justice system have as their main purpose the control of the poor in order to maintain the hegemony of the wealthy.

intake Process during which a juvenile referral is received and a decision is made to file a petition in juvenile court, to release the juvenile, to place the juvenile under supervision, or to refer the juvenile elsewhere.

intake unit Government agency or unit of an agency that receives juvenile referrals from police, other government agencies, private agencies, or individuals and screens them, resulting in closing of the case, referral to care or supervision, or filing of a petition to juvenile court.

Intensive Aftercare Mode Developed by Armstrong and Altschuler, it offers a balanced, highly structured, comprehensive program of intervention for serious and violent juveniles returning to the community

interactional theory According to Thornberry, interaction with institutions and events during the life course determines criminal behavior patterns. Crimogenic influences evolve over time.

interactionist perspective The view that one's perception of reality is significantly influenced by one's interpretations of the reactions of others to similar events and stimuli.

interrogation Method of accumulating evidence in the form of information or confessions from suspects by police; questioning that has been restricted because of concern about the use of brutal and coercive methods and interest in protecting against self-incrimination.

interstitial   Space that separates things. In criminology, a space or separation in the social fabric. An interstitial area encourages the formation of gangs.

investigation   Inquiry into suspected criminal behavior for the purpose of identifying offenders or gathering further evidence to assist the prosecution of apprehended offenders.

jail   Confinement facility, usually administered by a local law enforcement agency, that is intended for adults but sometimes also contains juveniles. It detains persons pending adjudication and persons committed after adjudication for sentences of a year or less.

judge   Judicial officer who has been elected or appointed to preside over a court of law. The position is created by statute or by constitution, and the officer's decisions in criminal and juvenile cases can be reviewed only by a judge of a higher court.

judgment   Statement of the decision of a court that the defendant is convicted or acquitted of the offense(s) charged.

judicial officer   Any person exercising judicial powers in a court of law.

jurisdiction   Every kind of judicial action; the authority of courts and judicial officers to decide cases.

just deserts   Idea that penalties to be given to convicted offenders should be decided chiefly by reference to the seriousness of the offense and the number and seriousness of prior convictions.

juvenile courts   Courts that have original jurisdiction over persons defined by statute as juveniles and alleged to be delinquents, status offenders, or dependents.

juvenile delinquency   Participation in illegal behavior by a minor who falls under a statutory age limit.

juvenile justice agency   Government agency or subunit thereof whose functions are the investigation, supervision, adjudication, care, or confinement of juveniles whose conduct or condition has brought or could bring them within the jurisdiction of a juvenile court.

Juvenile Justice and Delinquency Prevention Act of 1974   Federal law establishing an office of juvenile justice within the Law Enforcement Assistance Administration to provide funds for the control of juvenile crime.

juvenile justice process   Court proceedings for youths within the "juvenile" age group that differ from the adult criminal process. Under the paternal *(parens patriae)*

philosophy, juvenile procedures are informal and nonadversarial, invoked *for* the juvenile offender rather than *against* him or her; a petition instead of a complaint is filed; courts make findings of involvement or adjudication of delinquency instead of convictions; and juvenile offenders receive dispositions instead of sentences. Recent court decisions *(Kent* and *In re Gault)* have increased the adversarial nature of juvenile court proceedings. However, the philosophy remains one of diminishing the stigma of delinquency and providing for the youth's well-being and rehabilitation, rather than seeking retribution.

juvenile record   Official record containing, at a minimum, summary information pertaining to an identified juvenile concerning juvenile court proceedings and, if applicable, detention and correctional processes.

labeling theory   Theory that views society as creating deviance through a system of social control agencies that designate certain individuals as deviants. The stigmatized individual is made to feel unwanted in the normal social order. Eventually, the individual begins to believe that the label is accurate, assumes it as a personal identity, and enters into a deviant or criminal career.

latchkey children   Children left unsupervised after school by working parents.

latent delinquents   According to Aichorn, youths whose troubled family life leads them to seek immediate gratification without consideration of right and wrong or the feelings of others.

latent trait   A stable feature, characteristic, property, or condition, present at birth or soon after, that makes some people crime–prone over the life course

law   Method for resolving disputes. A rule of action to which people obligate themselves to conform, via their selected representatives and other officials. The principles and procedures of the common law, as distinguished from those of equity.

law enforcement agency   Federal, state, or local criminal justice agency whose principal functions are the prevention, detection, and investigation of crime and the apprehension of alleged offenders.

Law Enforcement Assistance Administration   Unit in the U.S. Department of Justice established by the Omnibus Crime Control and Safe Streets Act of 1968 to administer grants and provide guidance for crime prevention policy and programs.

law enforcement officer   Employee of a law enforcement agency who is an officer sworn to carry out law enforcement duties or a sworn employee of a prosecutorial agency who performs primarily investigative duties. Also called police officer.

law guardian Person with the legal authority and duty of taking care of someone and managing the property and rights of that person, if the person is considered incapable of administering the affairs personally.

learning disabilities Neurological dysfunctions that prevent people from learning up to their potential

left realism A branch of conflict theory that holds that crime is a real social problem experienced by the lower classes. Lower-class concerns about crime must be addressed by radical scholars.

life course perspective A view of delinquency which holds that factors present at birth and events which unfold over a person's life time influence behavior. Life course theory focuses on the onset, escalation, desistance and amplification of delinquent behaviors. Delinquency has both individual and social roots.

lineup Pretrial identification procedure in which a suspect is placed in a group for the purpose of being identified by a witness.

longitudinal study A research design which typically entails repeated measures over time. For example, a cohort may be measured over their life course to determine the risk factors for chronic offending.

mandamus Literally, "we command." A legal, not an equitable, remedy. When issued, it is an inflexible peremptory command to do a particular thing.

mandatory sentence Statutory requirement that a certain penalty shall be set and carried out in all cases on conviction for a specified offense or series of offenses.

manslaughter Voluntary (nonnegligent) killing; intentionally causing the death of another with reasonable provocation.

marijuana (Cannabis sativa) A plant grown throughout the world. The main active ingredient in marijuana is tetrahydrocannabinol or THC, a mild hallucinogen which alters sensory impressions and can cause drastic distortion in auditory and visual perception, even producing hallucinatory effects.

masculinity hypothesis View that women who commit crimes have biological and psychological traits similar to those of men.

medial model View that the justice system should help rehabilitate offenders rather than punish them. Advocates of the medial model liken criminality to a "disease" that can be "cured" through proper treatment.

mens rea Guilty mind; the mental element of a crime or the intent to commit a criminal act.

middle-class measuring rods According to Cohen, the standards with which teachers and other representatives of state authority evaluate lower-class youths. Because they cannot live up to middle-class standards, lower-class youths are bound for failure, which brings on frustration and anger at conventional society.

minor Person who is under the age of legal consent.

Miranda warning Result of two Supreme Court decisions [*Escobedo v. Illinois*, 378 U.S. 478 (1964) and *Miranda v. Arizona*, 384 U.S. 436 (1966)], that require police officers to inform individuals under arrest of their constitutional rights. Although aimed at protecting individuals during in-custody interrogation, the warning must also be given when the investigation shifts from the investigatory stage to the accusatory stage—that is, when suspicion begins to focus on an individual.

misdemeanor Offense punishable by a fine or by incarceration for not more than one year in a county jail. There is no uniform rule; an offense can be a misdemeanor in one jurisdiction and a felony in another.

Model Penal Code Generalized modern codification of that which is considered basic to criminal law, published by the American Law Institute in 1962.

monetary restitution A sanction that requires that adjudicated offenders compensate crime victims by reimbursing them for out-of-pocket losses caused by the crime. Losses can include property damage, lost wages, and medical costs.

moral entrepreneurs Interest groups that attempt to control social life and the legal order in order to promote their own personal set of moral values.

multisystemic treatment Developed by Scott Henggeler to treat adolescent substance abuse, it directs attention to a variety of family, peer and psychological problems by focusing on problem solving and communication skills.

murder Intentionally causing the death of another without reasonable provocation or legal justification, or causing the death of another while committing or attempting to commit another crime.

National Council on Crime and Delinquency
Private national agency that promotes efforts at crime control through research, citizen involvement, and public information efforts.

National Crime Survey Ongoing victimization study conducted jointly by the U.S. Justice Department and the Census Bureau that surveys victims about their experiences with law violation.

negative effective states The anger, depression, disappointment, fear and other adverse emotions that derive from strain.

neurological Pertaining to the brain and central nervous system.

neuroticism A personality trait marked by unfounded anxiety, tension, and emotional instability.

neutralization Ability to overcome social norms and controls. Neutralization theory holds that delinquents adhere to conventional values while "drifting" into periods of illegal behavior. In order to drift, delinquents must first neutralize legal and moral values.

nonjudicial disposition Rendering of a decision in a juvenile case by an authority other than a judge or court of law. Often an informal method used to determine the most appropriate disposition of a juvenile.

nonresidential program Program enabling youths to remain in their homes or foster homes while receiving services.

nonsecure setting Setting in which the emphasis is on the care and treatment of youths without the need to place constraints on them and to worry about the protection of the public.

Office of Juvenile Justice and Delinquency Prevention (OJJDP) Branch of the U.S. Justice Department charged with shaping national juvenile justice policy through the disbursement of federal aid and research funds.

official data Incidents of crime and delinquency that are recorded by police agencies.

official records Data kept by police, courts, and correctional agencies.

parens patriae Power of the state to act in behalf of the child and provide care and protection equivalent to that of a parent.

parole agency Correctional agency that may or may not include a parole authority and whose principal functions are the supervision of adults or juveniles placed on parole.

parole authority Person or correctional agency having the authority to release on parole adults or juveniles committed to confinement facilities, to revoke parole, and to discharge from parole.

parolee Person who has been conditionally released from a correctional institution prior to the expiration of his or her sentence and placed under the supervision of a parole agency.

part I offenses Eight index crimes whose incidence is reported to the FBI by local police.

part II offenses All other crimes other than part I offenses. Arrests for these crimes are reported to the FBI.

paternalism Male domination. A paternalistic family, for instance, is one in which the father is the dominant authority figure.

pathways The view that the path to a delinquent career may have more than one route, beginning with mild misconduct and escalating to serious crimes.

patriarchy Legal or social institution dominated or ruled by a male.

peacemaking A branch of conflict theory that stresses humanism, mediation, and conflict resolution as a means to end crime.

penalty Punishment meted out by law or judicial decision on the commission of a particular offense. It may be death, imprisonment, a fine, or loss of civil privileges.

penis envy According to Freud, girls believe that their lack of a penis is a sign that they have been punished. Their envy of the male's visible sex organ may result in feelings of inferiority and compensation through narcissistic behavior, e.g. being overly concerned with their appearance.

persistence Refers to the offending patterns of youths who continue in a delinquent career despite repeatedly being apprehended and sanctioned by legal authorities.

persisters Those criminals who do not age out of crime; chronic delinquents who continue offending into their adulthood.

person in need of supervision Person usually characterized as ungovernable, incorrigible, truant, and habitually disobedient.

petition Document filed in juvenile court alleging that a juvenile is a delinquent, a status offender, or a dependent and asking that the court assume jurisdiction over the juvenile or that the juvenile be transferred to a criminal court for prosecution as an adult.

petition not sustained Finding by a juvenile court in an adjudicatory hearing that there is insufficient evidence to sustain an allegation that a juvenile is a delinquent, a status offender, or a dependent.

plea-bargaining Discussion between the defense counsel and the prosecution by which the accused agrees to plead guilty for certain considerations. The advantage to the defendant may be in the form of a reduction of the charges, a lenient sentence, or, in the case of multiple charges, dropped charges. The advantage to the prosecution is that a conviction is obtained without the time and expense of lengthy trial proceedings.

police discretion Refers to the ability of police officers to enforce the law selectively. Police officers in the field have great latitude to use their discretion in deciding whether to invoke their arrest powers.

police officer style Refers to the belief that the bulk of police officers can be classified into ideal personality types. Popular style types include: supercops, who desire to enforce only serious crimes, such as robbery and rape; professionals, who use a broad definition of police work; service oriented, who see their job as that of a helping profession; avoiders, who do as little as possible. The actual existence of ideal police officer types has been much debated.

population All people who share a particular personal characteristic, for example, all high school students or all police officers.

positivism Branch of social science that uses the scientific method of the natural sciences and that suggests that human behavior is a product of social, biological, psychological, or economic forces.

power-control According to Hagan, adolescent behavior is controlled by family structure. The power and standing each parent has in the economic structure determines the manner in which they exert control over their families.

precocious sexuality Sexual experimentation in early adolescence.

premenstrual syndrome The stereotype that several days prior to and during menstruation females are beset by irritability and poor judgment as a result of hormonal changes.

presentence report Investigation performed by a probation officer attached to a trial court after the conviction of a defendant. The report contains information about the defendant's background, education, previous employment family, his or her own statement concerning the offense, prior criminal record, interviews with neighbors or acquaintances, and his or her mental and physical condition (i.e., information that would not be made record in the case of a guilty plea or that would be inadmissible as evidence at a trial but could be influential and important at the sentencing stage). After conviction, a judge sets a date for sentencing (usually ten days to two weeks from date of conviction), during which time the presentence report is made. The report is required in felony cases in federal courts; in some states, it is optional at the discretion of the judge, while in others, it is mandatory before convicted offenders can be placed on probation. In the case of juvenile offenders, the presentence report is also known as a social history report.

primary deviance According to Lemert, deviant acts that do not help redefine the self and public image of the offender.

primary sociopaths According to psychologist Linda Mealey, people with an inherited trait which predisposes them to antisocial behavior.

primogeniture Middle Ages practice of allowing only the family's eldest son to inherit lands and titles.

probable cause Reasonable ground to believe the existence of facts that an offense was committed and the accused committed that offense.

probation Sentence entailing the conditional release of a convicted offender into the community under the supervision of the court (in the form of a probation officer) subject to certain conditions for a specific time. The conditions are usually similar to those of parole. (Probation is a sentence, an alternative to incarceration; parole is administrative release from incarceration.) Violation of the conditions of probation may result in revocation of probation.

probation agency Also called probation department. Correctional agency whose principal functions are juvenile intake, the supervision of adults and juveniles placed on probation status, and the investigation of adults and juveniles for the purpose of preparing presentence or predisposition reports to assist the court in determining the proper sentence or juvenile court disposition.

probationer Person required by a court or probation agency to meet certain conditions of behavior; person who may or may not be placed under the supervision of a probation agency.

probation officer Employee of a probation agency whose primary duties include one or more of the probation agency functions.

problem behavior syndrome The belief that delinquency is one of many personal social problems which may also include substance abuse, depression, school failure and anomie.

procedural law Rules that define the operation of criminal proceedings. The methods that must be followed in obtaining warrants, investigating offenses, effecting lawful arrests, using force, conducting trials, introducing evidence, sentencing convicted offenders, and reviewing cases in appellate courts. Substantive law defines criminal offenses; procedural law delineates how the substantive offenses are to be enforced.

prosecutor Representative of the state (executive branch) in criminal proceedings; advocate for the state's case—the charge—in the adversary trial, for example, the attorney general of the United States, U.S. attorneys, attorneys general of the states, district attorneys, and police prosecutors. The prosecutor participates in investigations both before and after arrest, prepares legal documents, participates in obtaining arrest or search warrants, decides whether to charge a suspect and, if so, with which offense. The prosecutor argues the state's case at trial, advises the police, participates in plea negotiations, and makes sentencing recommendations.

prosecutorial agency Federal, state, or local criminal justice agency whose principal function is the prosecution of alleged offenders.

psychoanalytic (psychodynamic) Branch of psychology that holds that the human personality is controlled by unconscious mental processes developed early in childhood.

psychopath Person whose personality is characterized by lack of warmth and affection, inappropriate behavior responses, and an inability to learn from experience. While some psychologists view psychopathy as a result of childhood trauma, others see it as a result of biological abnormality.

psychotic Person who has lost control of his or her thoughts, moods, and feelings.

public defender Lawyer who works in a public agency or under private contractual agreement as defense counsel to indigent defendants.

random sample Sample selected on the basis of chance so that each person in the population has an equal opportunity to be selected.

rationale choice View that crime is a function of a decision-making process in which the potential offender weighs the potential costs and benefits of an illegal acts.

reaction formation According to Cohen, rejecting goals and standards that seem impossible to achieve. Because a boy cannot hope to get into college, for example, he considers higher education a waste of time.

recidivism Repetition of criminal behavior; habitual criminality. Recidivism is measured by (1) criminal acts that resulted in conviction by a court when committed by individuals who are under correctional supervision or who had been released from correctional supervision within the previous three years and (2) technical violations of probation or parole in which a sentencing or paroling authority took action that resulted in an adverse change in the offender's legal status.

referral to intake In juvenile proceedings, a request by the police, parents, or other agency or person that a juvenile intake unit take appropriate action concerning a juvenile alleged to have committed a delinquent act or status offense or to be dependent.

reflected appraisal According to Matsueda and Heimer, a youth's self-evaluation is based on their perceptions of how others evaluate them.

reflective role-taking According to Matsueda and Heimer, youths who view themselves as delinquents are giving an inner-voice to their perceptions how significant others feel about them.

reform school Institution in which efforts are made to improve the conduct of those forcibly detained within. Educational and psychological services are employed to achieve this goal.

rehabilitation Restoring to a condition of constructive activity.

relative deprivation Condition that exists when people of wealth and poverty live in close proximity to one another. Some criminologists attribute crime rate differentials to relative deprivation.

release from detention Authorized exit from detention of a person subject to criminal or juvenile justice proceedings.

release on bail Release by a judicial officer of an accused person who has been taken into custody upon the accused's promise to pay a certain sum of money or property if he or she fails to appear in court as required. The promise may or may not be secured by the deposit of an actual sum of money or property.

release on own recognizance Release, by a judicial officer, of an accused person who has been taken into custody upon the accused's promise to appear in court as required for criminal proceedings.

release (pretrial) Procedure whereby an accused person who has been taken into custody is allowed to be free before and during trial.

residential child-care facility Dwelling other than a detention or shelter care facility that provides living accommodations, care, treatment, and maintenance for children and youths and is licensed to provide such care. Such facilities include foster family homes, group homes, and halfway houses.

residential treatment center Government facility that serves juveniles whose behavior does not necessitate the strict confinement of a training school, often allowing them greater contact with the community.

resource deprivation Effect of growing up under conditions lacking adequate care, custody, and material goods.

responsible Legally accountable for one's actions and obligations.

restitution Restoring of property, or a right, to a person who has been unjustly deprived of it. A writ of restitution is the process by which a successful appellant may recover something of which he or she has been deprived under a prior judgment.

revocation Administrative act performed by a parole authority that removes a person from parole or a judicial order by a court removing a person from parole or probation, in response to a violation on the part of the parolee or probationer.

rights of defendant Powers and privileges that are constitutionally guaranteed to every defendant.

right to counsel Right of the accused to assistance of defense counsel in all criminal prosecutions.

right to treatment Philosophy espoused by many courts that offenders have a statutory right to treatment. A federal constitutional right to treatment has not been established.

role diffusion According to Erikson, role diffusion occurs when youths spread themselves too thin, experience personal uncertainty, and place themselves at the mercy of leaders who promise to give them a sense of identity they cannot develop for themselves.

routine activities View that crime is a "normal" function of the routine activities of modern living. Offenses can be

expected if there is a "motivated offender," and a suitable target that is not protected by capable guardians.

runaway Juvenile who has been adjudicated by a judicial officer of a juvenile court as having committed the status offense of leaving the custody and home of his or her parents, guardians, or custodians without permission and failing to return within a reasonable length of time.

sample Limited number of persons selected for study from a population.

schizophrenia Type of psychosis often marked by bizarre behavior, hallucinations, loss of thought control, and inappropriate emotional responses. There are different types of schizophrenia: catatonic, which characteristically involves impairment of motor activity; paranoid, which is characterized by delusions of persecution; and hebephrenic, which is characterized by immature behavior and giddiness.

school failure rationale The view that frustration causes by the inability of learning disabled children to succeed in school triggers a negative self-image and delinquent behavior.

search and seizure U.S. Constitution protects against any search or seizure engaged in without a lawfully obtained search warrant. A search warrant will be issued if there is probable cause to believe that an offense has been or is being committed.

secondary deviance According to Lemert, deviant acts that redefine the offender's self and public image. Acts become secondary when they form a basis for self-concept, for example, when a drug experimenter becomes an addict.

secondary sociopaths According to psychologist Linda Mealey, people who are constitutionally normal but whose life experiences influence their anti-social behavior. Suspected influences include poor parenting, racial segregation and social conflict.

secure setting Setting that places constraints on youths for care and treatment and for the protection of the public.

security and privacy standards Set of principles and procedures developed to ensue the security and confidentiality of criminal or juvenile record information in order to protect the privacy of the persons identified in such records.

sedatives Most commonly of the barbiturate family. Are able to depress the central nervous system into a sleep like condition.

seductions of crime According to Katz, the view that crime provides thrills and excitement which make it attractive to adolescents. Criminal behavior must be viewed from the perspective of immediate situational inducements which make it attractive.

selective incapacitation Policy of putting suspected chronic offenders behind bars for long periods of time. Advocates suggest that special laws be created to heavily penalize persistent offenders.

self-control theory According to Gottfredson and Hirschi, the view that the cause of delinquent behavior is an impulsive personality. Kids who are impulsive may find that their bond to society is weak and attenuated.

self-fulfilling prophecy Deviant behavior patterns that are a response to an earlier labeling experience. People act in synch with social labels, even if the labels are falsely bestowed.

self-report Research approach that requires subjects to reveal their own participation in delinquent or criminal acts.

sentence Sanction imposed by the court upon a convicted defendant, usually in the form of a fine, incarceration, or probation. Sentencing may be carried out by a judge, jury, or sentencing council (panel of judges), depending on the statutes of the jurisdictions.

sentence, indeterminate Statutory provision for a type of sentence to imprisonment, in which, after the court has determined that the convicted person shall be imprisoned, the exact length of imprisonment and parole supervision is fixed within statutory limits by a parole authority.

sentence, suspended Court decision postponing the pronouncing of sentence upon a convicted person or postponing the execution of a sentence that has been pronounced by the court.

shock probation Sentence that involves a short prison stay to impress the offender with the pains of imprisonment before he or she begins a probationary sentence.

short-run hedonism According to Cohen, the desire of lower-class gang youths to engage in behavior that will give them immediate gratification and excitement but that in the long run will be dysfunctional and negativistic.

situational crime prevention A method of crime prevention that stresses tactics and strategies to eliminate or reduce particular crimes in narrow settings; for example, reducing burglaries in a housing project by increasing lighting and installing security alarms.

skinhead Member of white supremacist gang, identified by a shaved skull and Nazi or Ku Klux Klan markings.

social bond Ties a person has to the institutions and processes of society. According to Hirschi, elements of the social bond include commitment, attachment, involvement, and belief.

social control Ability of social institutions to influence human behavior. Among the primary agencies of formal social control are the school and the justice system.

social disorganization Neighborhood or area marked by culture conflict, lack of cohesiveness, transient population, insufficient social organizations, and anomie.

socialization Process of human development and enculturation. Socialization is influenced by key social processes and institutions.

social learning theory The view that human behavior is modeled through observation of human social interactions, either directly from observing those who are close and intimate contact, or indirectly through the media. Interactions which are rewarded are copied while those which are punished are avoided.

social process Operations of formal and informal social institutions. Elements of the social process include socialization within family and peer groups, the educational process, and the justice system.

social structure Fabric of society. Within the social structure are the various classes, institutions, and groups of society.

sociobiology Branch of science that views human behavior as being motivated by in-bred biological urges and desires. The urge to survive and preserve the species motivates human behavior.

sociopath Person whose personality is characterized by lack of warmth and affection, inappropriate behavior responses, and an inability to learn from experience. Used interchangeably with psychopath and anti-social personality disorder.

somatotyping Categorizing people on the basis of their body build.

specific deterrence Crime-control policy that suggests that punishment should be severe enough to convince previous offenders never to repeat their criminal activity.

spontaneous remission Another term used for the aging-out process.

standard of proof Proof beyond a reasonable doubt—the standard used to convict a person charged with a crime. Many U.S. Supreme Court decisions have made the beyond a reasonable doubt standard a due process and constitutional requirement.

stardom formations According to the Schwendingers, adolescent social networks whose members have distinct dress, grooming, and linguistic behavior

stare decisis "To stand by decided cases." The legal principle by which the decision or holding in an earlier case becomes the standard with which to judge subsequent similar cases.

status offender Juvenile who has been adjudicated by a judicial officer of a juvenile court as having committed a status offense.

status offense Act that is declared by statute to be an offense but only when committed by a juvenile. It can be adjudicated only by a juvenile court.

statutory law Laws created by legislative bodies to meet changing social conditions, public opinion, and custom.

steroids Anabolic steroids are drugs used to gain muscle bulk and strength for athletics and body building.

stigma Social disgrace or condemnation. Stigmatized persons feel they are outsiders or outcasts from society.

stimulants Synthetic drugs that stimulate action in the central nervous system. They produce an intense physical reaction: increased blood pressure, increased breathing rate, increased bodily activity, and elevation of mood. One widely used stimulant, amphetamines, produce psychological effects such as increased confidence, euphoria, fearlessness, talkativeness, impulsive behavior, and loss of appetite.

stop and frisk Practice of police officers who are suspicious of an individual to run their hands lightly over the suspect's outer garments to determine if the person is carrying a concealed weapon. Also called a "patdown" or "threshold inquiry," a stop and frisk is intended to stop short of any activity that could be considered a violation of Fourth Amendment rights.

strain Social psychological condition that is created when a person's social goals cannot be achieved by available legitimate means. Lower-class youths might feel strain because they are denied access to adequate educational opportunities and social support.

stratified Grouped according to social strata or levels. American society is considered stratified on the basis of economic class and wealth.

street crime Illegal acts designed to prey on the public through theft, damage, and violence.

structural Marxist theory View that the law and justice system is designed to maintain the capitalist system and that members of both the owner and worker classes whose behavior threatens the stability of the system will be sanctioned.

subculture Group that is loosely part of the dominant culture that maintains a unique set of values, beliefs, and traditions.

substantive criminal laws Body of specific rules that declare what conduct is criminal and prescribe the punishment to be imposed for such conduct.

subterranean values According to Sykes and Matza, the ability of youthful law violators to repress social norms.

summons Alternative to arrest usually used for petty or traffic offenses; a written order notifying an individual that he or she has been charged with an offense. A summons directs the person to appear in court to answer the charge. It is used primarily in instances of low risk, where the person will not be required to appear at a later date. The summons is advantageous to police officers because it frees them from spending time on arrest and booking procedures; it is advantageous to the accused in that he or she is spared time in jail.

surplus value Marxist view that the laboring classes produce wealth that far exceeds their wages and goes to the capitalist class as profits.

susceptibility rationale The view that the link between learning disabilities and delinquency is caused by side effects of LD: impulsivity, inability to use social cues and poor learning ability.

take into custody Act of the police in securing the physical custody of a child engaged in delinquency. Avoids the stigma of the word *arrest*.

tongs Chinese gangs.

totality of the circumstances Legal doctrine that mandates that a decision maker consider all the issues and circumstances of a case before judging the outcome. For example, before concluding whether a suspect understood his or her *Miranda* warning, a judge must consider the totality of the circumstances under which the warning was given. The suspect's age, intelligence, and competency may be issues that influence his or her understanding and judgment.

tracking Segregating youth in classes based on academic achievement and/or potential. Tracking is believed to be responsible for poor self-image and self-fulfilling prophecy.

training school Correctional institution for juveniles adjudicated to be delinquents or status offenders and committed to confinement by a judicial officer.

tranquilizers Have the ability to relieve uncomfortable emotional feelings by reducing levels of anxiety and promoting relaxation.

transfer hearing Preadjudicatory hearing in juvenile court for the purpose of determining whether juvenile court jurisdiction should be retained or waived over a juvenile alleged to have committed a delinquent act and whether he or she should be transferred to criminal court for prosecution as an adult.

transfer to adult court Decision by a juvenile court resulting from a transfer hearing that jurisdiction over an alleged delinquent will be waived and that he or she should be prosecuted as an adult in a criminal court.

transitional neighborhood Area undergoing a shift in population and structure, usually from middle-class residential to lower-class mixed use.

treatment Rehabilitative method used to effect a change of behavior in an inmate, juvenile delinquent, or status offender. It may be in the form of therapy programs or educational or vocational training.

triads Chinese self-help groups

trial Examination of issues of fact and law in a case or controversy, beginning when the jury has been selected in a jury trial or when the first witness is sworn or the first evidence is introduced in a court trial and concluding when a verdict is reached or the case is dismissed.

type I offenses Another term for index crimes.

type II offenses All crimes other than index and minor traffic offenses. The FBI records annual arrest information for Type II offenses.

UCR Abbreviation for the Federal Bureau of Investigation's uniform crime reporting program.

verdict In criminal proceedings, the decision made by a jury in a jury trial or by a judicial officer in a court trial that a defendant is either guilty or not guilty of the offenses for which he or she has been tried.

victim Person who has suffered death, physical or mental suffering, or loss of property as the result of an actual or attempted criminal offense committed by another person.

victim precipitated Describes a crime in which the victim's behavior was the spark that ignited the subsequent offense, for example, the victim abused the offender verbally or physically.

victim survey Crime-measurement technique that surveys citizens in order to measure their experiences as victims of crime.

waiver Voluntary relinquishment of a known right.

wayward minors Early legal designation for youths who violate the law because of their minority status. Wayward minor statutes have been converted into status offender laws.

widening the net Phenomenon that occurs when programs created to divert youths from the justice system actually involve them more deeply in the official process.

writ of certiorari Order of a superior court requesting that the record of an inferior court (or administrative body) be brought forward for review or inspection.

writ of habeas corpus Judicial order requesting that a person detaining another produce the body of the prisoner and give reasons for his or her capture and detention. Habeas corpus is a legal device used to request that a judicial body review reasons for a person's confinement and the conditions of confinement. Habeas corpus is known as "the great writ."

writ of mandamus Order of a superior court commanding that a lower court or administrative or executive body perform a specific function. It is commonly used to restore rights and privileges lost to a defendant through illegal means.

youthful offender Person adjudicated in criminal court who may be above the statutory age limit for juveniles but who is below a specified upper-age limit for whom special correctional commitments and special record sealing procedures are made available by statute.

youth services bureau Neighborhood youth service agency that coordinates all community services for young people and provides services lacking in the community or neighborhood, especially those designed for the predelinquent or the early delinquent

EXCERPTS FROM THE U.S. CONSTITUTION

AMENDMENT I (1791)

Congress shall make no law respecting an establishment of religion, or prohibiting the free exercise thereof; or abridging the freedom of speech, or of the press; or the right of the people peaceably to assemble, and to petition the government for a redress of grievances.

AMENDMENT II (1791)

A well regulated militia, being necessary to their security of a free state, the right of the people to keep and bear arms, shall not be infringed.

AMENDMENT III (1791)

No soldier shall, in time of peace, be quartered in any house, without the consent of the owner, nor in time of war, but in a manner to be prescribed by law.

AMENDMENT IV (1791)

The right of the people to be secure in their persons, houses, papers, and effects, against unreasonable searches and seizures, shall not be violated, and no warrants shall issue, but upon probable cause, supported by oath or affirmation, and particularly describing the place to be searched, and the persons or things to be seized.

AMENDMENT V (1791)

No person shall be held to answer for a capital, or otherwise infamous, crime unless on a presentment or indictment of a grand jury, except in cases arising in the land or naval forces, or in the militia, when in actual service in time of war or public danger; nor shall any person be subject for the same offense to be twice put in jeopardy of life or limb; nor shall be compelled in any criminal case to be a witness against himself, nor be deprived of life, liberty, or property; without due process of law; nor shall private property be taken for public use without just compensation.

AMENDMENT VI (1791)

In all criminal prosecutions, the accused shall enjoy the right to a speedy and public trial, by an impartial jury of the state and district wherein the crime shall have been committed, which district shall have been previously ascertained by law, and to be informed of the nature and cause of the accusation; to be confronted with the witnesses against him; to have compulsory process for obtaining witnesses in his favor, and to have the assistance of counsel for his defense.

AMENDMENT VII (1791)

In suits at common law, where the value in controversy shall exceed twenty dollars, the right of trial by jury shall be preserved, and no fact tried by a jury shall be otherwise reexamined in any court of the United States, than according to the rules of common law.

AMENDMENT VIII (1791)

Excessive bail shall not be required, nor excessive fines imposed, nor cruel and unusual punishment inflicted.

AMENDMENT IX (1791)

The enumeration in the Constitution of certain rights shall not be construed to deny or disparage others retained by the people.

AMENDMENT X (1791)

The powers not delegated to the United States by the Constitution, nor prohibited by it to the states, are reserved to the states respectively, or to the people.

AMENDMENT XIV (1868)

Section I. All persons born or naturalized in the United States, and subject to the jurisdiction thereof, are citizens of the United States and of the state wherein they reside. No state shall make or enforce any law which abridge the privilege or immunities of citizens of the United States; nor shall any state deprive any person of life, liberty, or property, without due process of law; nor deny to any person within its jurisdiction the equal protection of the laws.

Table of Cases

NAME INDEX

Bell, Duran, 533n.42

Bell, James, 534n.63, 576n.5, 656n.93

Bell, Robert, 421nn.87, 88

Bellair, Paul, 171n.36

Bem, Sandra, 270n.14

Bender, L., 317n.146

Bennet, Binni, 133n.149

Bennett, Alfred, 644

Bentham, Jeremy, 89, 128n.3

Berg, Bruce, 65, 82n.104

Bergsmann, Ilene R., 654n.46

Berk, Richard, 493n.2

Berndt, Thomas, 207n.7, 353nn.3, 4

Bernstein, Saul, 355n.69

Besch, P. K., 271n.47

Besharov, Douglas, 15, 31n.32, 315n.76

Bettleheim, Bruno, 633, 655n.55

Beutel, Ann, 270n.11

Beyer, Margaret, 639, 655nn.70–71

Binder, Arnold, 25, 32n.68, 514, 534n.61

Birnbaum, Morton, 641, 655n.78

Bishop, Donna, 81n.65, 241n.46, 267–268, 273nn.120–121, 486, 488, 496nn.78–79, 89, 502, 532n.12

Bittner, S., 316n.118

Bjerregaard, Beth, 264, 265, 272nn.100, 106, 355n.103

Black, Donald, 171n.41, 483, 488, 493n.4, 495nn.66, 73, 496n.88

Black, Hugo, 555

Black, Kathryn, 317nn.161, 167

Black, T. Edwin, 486, 495n.74

Blackmore, John, 79n.32, 610n.56

Blackmun, Harry A., 453

Blake, Gerald F., 534n.56

Blau, Judith, 149, 171n.27

Blau, Peter, 149, 171n.27

Block, Carolyn, 407n

Block, Herbert, 345, 356nn.118, 119

Block, J., 420n.54

Block, Kathleen, 459n.28

Block, Richard, 150, 171n.29, 407n

Blomberg, Thomas, 534n.56

Blomquist, Martha Elin, 458n.2

Blos, Peter, 270n.36

Blumstein, Alfred, 38, 44, 78n.8, 79nn.19, 21, 82n.112, 407n

Bodine, George, 79n.26

Bogdan, Carol, 654n.41

Bonati, Lisa, 129nn.21, 26, 130n.55

Bookin-Weiner, Hedy, 357n.151

Booth, Alan, 271n.44

Borden, Polly, 83n.137

Bordua, David, 149, 171n.24, 241n.53

Borsage, B., 494n.10

Bortner, M. A., 240n.12, 509, 528, 533n.40, 535n.88

Bouchard, T. J., 132nn.128, 129

Boulerice, Bernard, 132n.104, 387n.67

Bourne, P., 316n.118

Bowden, C., 419n.31

Bowditch, Christine, 387n.68

Bowman, J. Addison, 565, 577n.71

Brady, C. Patrick, 313n.17

Brady, Marianne, 240n.10

Brame, Robert, 226

Brame, Robert, 241n.59

Brandt, David, 133nn.138, 150

Brannigan, Martha, 316n.126

Braverman, J., 495n.40

Bray, James, 313n.17

Breed, Alan, 653n.22, 654n.27

Bremmer, Robert, 31n.36

Brendes, Ralph, 609n.3

Brendtero, Larry, 655n.54

Brenzel, Barbara, 654n.45

Breyer, Stephen, 453, 454, 571

Brezina, Timothy, 172n.65

Briar, Scott, 187, 209n.51, 483, 495nn.65, 71

Bright, Stephen, 576nn.39, 41

Britt, Chester, III, 83n.125

Broder, Paul, 132n.109

Brody, Charles, 355n.98

Brody, Gene, 420nn.48, 49

Broidy, Lisa, 172n.66, 314n.58

Bronner, Augusta, 120, 134n.195, 251, 270n.29

Brook, Judith, 420nn.44, 54

Brooks, Nathan, 4

Brooner, Robert, 419n.19

Brown, James, 534n.65

Brown, Larry, 30n.9

Brown, Michael, 494n.7, 610n.56

Browne, Angela, 290–291, 315nn.87, 91

Brownfield, David, 192, 209n.72, 210n.88, 355n.99

Brownstein, Henry, 272n.101

Bruinsma, Gerben J. N., 208n.19

Buchanan, Christy Miller, 104, 131n.94, 271nn.41, 62, 313n.8

Bucker, K. A., 494n.38

Bucky, S. F., 420n.39

Buerger, Michael, 97, 130n.51

Bukoski, William, 388n.98

Bullington, B., 534n.56

Burger, Warren, 642

Burgess, Ernest W., 144

Burgess, Robert, 208n.22, 208n.31, 297, 316nn.120, 121

Burke, Mary Jean, 207n.14

Burke, Vincent, 610n.39

Burns, Jerald, 655n.68

Burrell, Susan, 656n.93

Bursik, Robert, 83n.138, 151, 170n.16, 171nn.23, 34, 42, 43, 210nn.88, 96

Burt, Cyril, 251, 270n.28

Burton, Velmer, 32n.81, 192, 209n.74, 314n.57

Bushweller, Kevin, 388n.84

Butts, Jeffrey, 421nn.85–86, 532n.5, 597, 609nn.6–8, 610n.55

Bynum, Timothy, 388n.95

Byrne, James, 81n.68, 171nn.25, 38, 609nn.14, 15, 641, 655n.76

C

Cadoret, Remi, 132n.130

Cahahn, Sorel, 134n.197

Cahalan, Margaret Werner, 616, 653n.9

Cain, Colleen, 132n.130

Caldwell, M. G., 134n.193

Calhoun, George, 270n.19, 272n.82

Callahan, Charles, 387n.72

Callahan, Robert, 610n.26

Callahan, S., 271n.47

Calsyn, Donald, 134n.192

Campagna, Daniel, 654n.43

Campbell, Anne, 270nn.9, 20, 25–27, 271n.40, 335

Cantor, David, 210n.91, 353n.10, 421n.73

Capaldi, Deborah, 314n.56, 353n.18, 419n.30

Caplan, Arthur, 130n.72

Carlson, Bonnie, 114, 133n.153

Carpenter, Judi, 421n.89

Carriger, Michael, 135n.207

Carroll, Leo, 171n.26

Carter, David, 421n.90

Carter, Robert, 609n.3

Cartwright, Desmond, 208n.44, 325

Caspi, Avshalom, 255, 271n.42

Castellano, Thomas, 129n.23, 568, 578n.87, 637, 655n.66

Castelli, William, 419n.13

Catalano, Richard, 210nn.101, 102, 388n.102

Cernkovich, Stephen, 51, 80nn.41, 42, 209n.69, 314n.59, 322, 353n.22

Chachere, J. Gregory, 114, 133n.160

Doraz, Walter, 131nn.87, 88
Dornbusch, Sanford, 313n.8
Dornfeld, Maude, 316n.130
Douglas, Marie, 8n
Downey, Douglas, 314n.60
Draper, Patricia, 297, 316nn.120, 121
Driver, Edwin, 130nn.60, 62, 63
Droegemueller, W., 315n.77
Ducker, Jennie Bain, 4
Duffee, David, 576n.33
Dugdale, Richard, 100, 130n.64
Dunaway, R. Gregory, 209n.74, 314n.57
Duncan, Greg, 170n.11
Dunford, Franklyn, 69–70, 83n.120
Dunlap, Earl, 533n.19
Durkheim, Emile, 154, 171–172nn.52–54
Dussault, Monique, 133n.156
Duster, Troy, 81n.70
Dwiggins, Donna, 270n.5

E

Earle, Ralph, 317n.164
Eason, Carol, 241n.45
Easson, W.M., 317n.147
Eastman, F., 576nn.22, 31
Eccles, Jacquelynne, 104, 131n.94, 271nn.41, 62
Eckert, Penelope, 353nn.8–9
Eddison, Leonard P., 653n.2
Edwards, Leonard P., 317n.159, 548, 576n.23
Eels, Kenneth, 134n.196
Eggebeen, David, 30n.10, 314n.63
Eggleston, Carolyn, 270n.5
Eisikovitz, Z., 533n.20, 654n.36
Eldefonso, Edward, 653nn.12–13
Elder, Rob, 129n.25
Elias, Albert, 611n.60
Ellenson, Gerald, 315nn.86, 90
Ellickson, Phyllis, 421nn.87, 88
Elliott, Delbert, 69–70, 80n.60, 83n.120, 199–201, 201, 210nn.103, 104, 211n.109, 240n.44, 385n.3, 387n.62, 401, 411, 419n.28, 421nn.77, 78
Ellis, Lee, 135nn.217, 218, 257, 271nn.46, 48, 58, 60
Ellison, Christopher,, 314n.52
Elrod, H. Preston, 609n.18
Empey, LaMar T., 79nn.27, 32, 242n.99, 603, 611n.60, 653n.11, 655n.53

English, Bella, 388n.85
Ensminger, Margaret, 59, 81n.72
Erickson, Erik, 9, 31n.18, 111–112, 133n.142
Erickson, Maynard, 79nn.27, 32, 96, 130n.45, 611n.60
Erikson, Kai, 217, 240n.6
Erlenmeyer-Kimling, L., 132n.121
Eron, L., 134n.171
Esbensen, Finn-Aage, 335, 354n.34, 355nn.86, 88, 102, 356n.136, 493n.6
Escovitz, Sari, 576n.25
Essman, W. B., 131n.84
Estabrook, Arthur, 100, 130n.64
Evans, T. David, 209n.74, 314n.57
Eve, Raymond, 80n.55, 272n.97
Ewing, Darlene, 534n.68
Eysenck, Hans, 134nn.180, 181
Eysenck, M. W., 134n.181
Ezell, Mark, 32n.87, 515, 534nn.54, 62

F

Fagan, Jeffrey, 84n.148, 172n.89, 208n.29, 330, 332, 354nn.62, 64, 486, 495n.76, 527, 535nn.86, 89, 577n.46, 637, 650, 655n.63, 656n.101
Fakouri, M. Ebrahim, 386n.14
Famularo, Richard, 316n.110
Fannin, Leon, 172n.88
Farnworth, Margaret, 61, 83n.122, 172n.57, 210n.107, 211n.108, 272n.99, 353n.19, 386n.15, 419n.32
Farr, Kathryn Ann, 421n.98
Farrington, David, 63, 72, 73, 74, 79nn.28, 33, 35, 80n.54, 82nn.90, 97, 98, 112, 83nn.117, 124, 135, 140, 141, 84nn.144, 145, 121–122, 134n.178, 135n.206, 271n.65, 285, 286, 313n.4, 314nn.50, 66, 68, 315n.71, 353n.12, 364, 386nn.18, 26
Farris, Elizabeth, 387n.73, 388n.91
Faupel, Charles, 421n.70
Fay, Michael, 8
Federle, Katherine Hunt, 509, 533n.17, 534n.42
Fejes-Mendoza, Kathy, 270n.5
Feld, Barry C., 32n.59, 445, 459n.48, 460n.74, 535nn.77, 78, 552, 576nn.38, 39, 40, 41, 577nn.42, 43
Feldman, Marilyn, 131n.101

Felson, Marcus, 92–93, 129nn.22, 27, 130n.49
Fendrich, Michael, 419n.5
Fenton, Terence, 132n.113
Ferdinand, Theodore, 435, 459nn.29, 30, 43, 495n.65
Ferguson, Jennifer, 350, 356n.148
Ferracuti, Franco, 162, 172n.70
Ferraro, Kenneth, 80n.48
Ferrero, William, 251, 270n.2, 270nn.22–24
Ferri, Enrico, 99–100
Feucht, Thomas, 419n.4
Feyerherm, William, 80n.64, 222, 240n.36
Field, Diane, 133n.157
Figlio, Robert, 66, 68, 80n.61, 82nn.98, 102, 113, 114, 83nn.114, 116, 128n.1, 386nn.19, 20
Figueredo, Aurelio Jose, 83n.133
Finckenauer, James, 8
Finkelhor, David, 53, 80n.49, 290–291, 315nn.87, 91, 94
Finn, Peter, 496n.105
Finnegan, Terrence A., 73, 83nn.140, 141, 575n.2, 609nn.6–8
Firestone, Philip, 133n.134
First, Patricia, 387n.71
Fischer, Craig, 654n.37
Fischer, Karla, 273n.122
Fishbein, Diana, 131nn.77, 95, 96, 132n.117, 256, 271nn.49–50, 53, 54
Fisher, Bruce, 577–578nn.77–80
Fisher, R. Mace, 130n.52
Fisher, Stanley, 569, 578n.94
Fishman, G., 533n.20, 654n.36
Flannery, Daniel, 82n.111, 270n.13
Flemmer, Lowell, 317n.170
Flores, Maryling, 4
Flowers, Lucy, 428
Flwewlling, Robert, 421n.91
Fogelson, Robert, 494n.15
Foley, Michael, 30n.15
Fontana, Vincent J., 315nn.78, 82, 102, 316n.107
Forde, David, 94, 129n.29
Forehand, Rex, 420nn.48, 49
Foretsch, Mary, 386n.11
Forst, Martin, 458n.2, 535n.89, 577–578nn.77–80
Fortas, Abe, 382, 435
Foster, Jack, 241n.45
Foster-Johnson, Lynn, 83n.132
Fox, James Alan, 30n.14, 45, 79nn.11, 14
Fox, Robert J., 353n.2

Levine, Murray, 273n.117
Lewis, Dorothy Otnow, 131n.101
Lewis, Oscar, 138, 170n.1
Liazos, Alexander, 388n.94
Lichter, Daniel, 30n.10, 314n.63
Lick, Al, 317n.170
Li-Jung Tseng, 420n.44
Lillard, Lee, 314n.62
Lilly, J. Robert, 609n.24
Lincoln, Alan, 312n.2, 315n.71
Lindgren, Scott, 131n.90
Lindsay, Benjamin, 538
Link, Bruce, 210n.86
Linnoila, Marku, 210n.90
Linster, Richard, 130n.46
Linz, Daniel, 133n.155
Lippincott, J. B., 207n.8
Lipsett, Paul, 240n.41
Lipsey, Mark, 607, 611n.68
Lipson, Karin, 496n.99
Lishner, Denise, 211n.110, 388n.99
Liska, Allen, 171n.36, 209n.78
Litsky, Paul, 32n.86
Lizotte, Alan, 83n.122, 128n.2, 207n.2,
    210n.107, 211n.108, 313n.30,
    353n.19, 355n.103, 356n.140,
    386n.15, 387n.65, 420n.57
Lochman, John, 134nn.172, 173,
    353n.17
Loeber, Rolf, 71, 72–73, 82n.99,
    83n.129, 84n.150, 135, 353n.16,
    355n.86
Logan, Charles, 514, 534nn.56, 59
Lombroso, Cesare, 99, 251–252,
    270nn.1, 22–24
Lombroso-Ferrero, Gina, 130nn.57, 59
Long, John, 356nn.122, 127
Lonza-Kaduce, Lonn, 208n.32
Lopez, Alfonso, 571
Lorch, Elizabeth Pugzles, 133n.157
Loughran, Edward, 532n.9, 653n.2,
    654n.28
Lowell, Harvey, 610n.48, 611n.58
Lozovsky, David, 131n.96
Lubeck, S., 603, 655n.53
Lucan, Wayne, 421n.92
Luchterhand, Elmer, 495n.65
Lundberg, Emma, 459n.39
Lundman, Richard, 486, 493n.4,
    534n.56
Lykken, D. T., 132nn.128, 129
Lyman, Donald, 135n.205, 271n.
    42
Lynch, J., 533n.39
Lyon, Reid, 132n.111

M

Macallair, Dan, 611n.67, 636, 655n.60
Maccauley, J., 271n.61
Maccoby, Eleanor, 257, 271nn.43, 59,
    313n.8
MacCoun, Robert, 419n.29, 420n.63,
    421n.99
Macksey-Amiti, Mary Ellen, 419n.5
MacMurray, Bruce, 546, 576n.19
Maguire, Kathleen, 459nn.45, 46
Mahan, Sue, 270n.37
Mahoney, Anne R., 240n.4
Mahoney, Dennis, 610n.29
Maier, Pamela, 130n.52
Mallory, W. A., 132n.109
Mannheim, Herman, 130nn.58, 61
Manning, Darrell, 83n.137
Manning, Peter, 241n.50
Mansfield, Wendy, 387n.73, 388n.91
Marcotte, Paul, 535n.78
Marenin, Otwin, 210n.95
Marini, Margaret Mooney, 270n.11
Marketos, Alexander, 578n.97
Markle, Gerald, 313n.20
Markman, Howard, 313n.15
Marshall, Chris, 32n.74
Marshall, Ineke, 32n.74, 210n.98
Marshall, Paul, 131nn.79, 80
Martin, Gregory, 518
Martin, Lawrence, 32n.64
Martin, LeRoy, 355n.93
Martin, Randy, 130n.57
Martin, Terry, 505
Marx, Karl, 229, 230
Mason, Robert, 316n.106
Masse, Louise, 420nn.47, 53
Massey, James, 129nn.21, 26, 130n.55,
    193, 208n.34, 209n.76
Mathias, Robert, 655n.62, 656n.101
Matsueda, Ross, 180, 207n.16,
    208n.23, 218, 220–221, 226,
    240nn.15, 25, 34
Matthews, Roger, 242n.84
Matza, David, 183, 208nn.37, 38, 39,
    40–41, 240nn.4, 30–31
Mauer, Marc, 496n.82
Maughan, Barbara, 83n.129
Maume, David, 129n.24
Maupin, James, 656n.98
Mawhorr, Tina, 83n.136
Maxfield, Michael, 83n.130, 307,
    317n.152
Maxim, Paul, 210n.89
Maxson, Cheryl, 332, 333, 339,
    354n.67, 355n.75

Mazerolle, Paul, 160, 172nn.61, 63
McCall, Robert, 135n.207
McCandless, B. R., 130n.69
McCarthy, Belinda, 501–502, 532n.11
McCarthy, Bill, 92, 129nn.18, 19,
    314n.46
McCord, Joan, 59, 70, 81n.72,
    83n.123, 135n.219, 210n.102, 284–
    285, 313n.3, 314n.45
McCord, William, 135n.219
McCurdy, Karen, 316nn.112, 114
McDermott, Joan, 375, 377, 387n.80,
    388n.86
McDevitt, Jack, 40, 78n.9
McDill, E. L., 387n.79
McDonald, Lance, 317n.160
McDowall, David, 128n.2, 207n.2, 568,
    578n.88
McFall, Richard, 134n.201
McGarrell, Edmund, 32n.86, 553–554,
    577n.47
McGee, Charles, 610n.30
McGee, Rob, 134n.179
McGlothlin, W., 420n.70
McGrath, John, 171n.39
McGue, D. T., 132nn.128, 129
McKay, Henry, 145–147, 148–149,
    171n.18–20, 282, 313n.22, 326
McKeiver, Joseph, 559
McKinley, J. Charnley, 119
McKinney, J. D., 386n.25
McLanahan, Sara, 313n.31, 386n.36
McNeal, Elizabeth, 131n.79
McNeill, Richard, 171n.46
McNulty, Elizabeth, 527, 535n.85
McPartland, J. M., 387n.79
McPherson, Karla, 316n.117
McPherson, Susan, 317n.160
Mealey, Linda, 119, 134n.182
Mednick, Sarnoff, 109, 131n.83,
    132n.115, 132nn.125, 126, 132,
    133n.133, 134n.201, 135n.203
Meier, Robert, 61, 241nn.64, 67
Meltzer, Lynn, 107, 132n.113
Menacker, Julius, 388n.90
Menard, Scott, 135nn.208, 209, 158,
    172n.58, 210n.104, 211n.109, 411,
    419n.28, 421n.78
Menlove, Frances, 133n.151
Mennel, Robert, 31n.36, 429, 458n.4,
    459nn.8, 13, 14
Merton, Robert, 154, 156, 171nn.50,
    51, 172n.55–56
Meseck-Bushey, Sylvia, 132n.123,
    315n.73

Perry, David, 133n.152
Perry, Louise, 133n.152
Perry, T. B., 353n.4
Persons, W. S., 130n.69
Petersilia, Joan, 609n.24, 639, 655n.69
Peterson, John, 32n.73
Peterson, Ruth, 240n.26
Petrila, Amelia, 83n.132
Phen Wung, 83n.129
Phillips, M., 534n.56
Piaget, Jean, 115–116, 133n.165
Pickett, Robert S., 459n.12
Pierce, Glenn, 62
Pierce, Robert, 610n.52
Piersma, Paul, 559, 564, 577nn.58, 70
Pihl, Robert, 132n.104, 314n.69
Piliavin, Irving, 187, 209n.51, 483, 495n.65, 495n.71
Pilnick, Paul, 611n.60
Pincus, Jonathan, 131n.101
Pink, William, 387n.41
Piquero, Alex, 160, 172n.61
Platt, Anthony, 31n.35, 231–232, 241nn.76, 83, 436, 459nn.9, 10, 33, 34, 566, 577n.75
Platt, Christina, 420n.50
Platt, Jerome, 420n.50
Pleck, Elizabeth, 31nn.37, 38, 40, 42, 459nn.25, 26
Podboy, J. W., 132n.109
Polakowski, Michael, 210nn.85, 87
Polk, Kenneth, 207n.6, 385n.5, 386nn.32, 38, 40, 387nn.54, 56, 534n.50, 534n.53
Pollak, Otto, 252, 270nn.30–32
Pollock, Carl B., 315n.102
Polsenberg, Christina, 59, 80n.64
Poole, Eric, 208n.46
Poole, Rowen S., 575n.2, 609nn.6–8
Pope, Carl, 80n.64, 222, 240nn.35, 36, 38
Porterfield, A. L., 79n.26
Post, Charles, 132n.107
Potter, Joan, 535n.83
Pottieger, Anne, 402, 411, 419n.36, 420nn.42, 43, 60, 61, 62
Pound, Roscoe, 481, 495n.58
Powell, R. T., 577n.57
Pratts, Michael, 355n.104
Presley, Elvis, 26–27
Price, Dwight, 547, 576n.21
Provenzino, Anthony, 25
Provenzino, Susan, 25
Pugh, Meredith, 51, 80nn.41, 42, 209n.69, 322, 353n.22

Putka, Gary, 388n.96
Pyatt, Jonathan, 495n.43

Q

Quanwu Zhang, 353n.16
Quinney, Richard, 235, 239n.2, 241n.75, 242nn.92, 95

R

Rabow, J., 655n.53
Rachin, Richard, 654n.50
Radosevich, Marcia, 80n.59, 208n.32
Raeder, Myrna, 316n.136
Rafter, Nicole Hahn, 130n.68
Rahav, G., 314n.61
Raine, Adrian, 131nn.76, 78, 81, 103
Raizen, Senta, 386n.9
Rand, Alicia, 64, 82n.102
Rankin, Joseph, 54, 80n.52, 282, 313nn.25, 26, 29
Rasell, M.Edith, 385n.6
Rasmussen, Paul, 133n.152
Rathus, Spencer, 133n.139, 134n.184, 208n.45, 270n.5, 271n.51, 353n.5, 419n.12, 420n.51
Rausch, Sharla, 514, 534nn.56, 59
Reamer, F., 533n.39
Reckless, Walter, 130n.54, 187, 207n.3, 209nn.52, 53, 54, 241n.45
Redl, Fritz, 133n.144
Reed, M. D., 209n.78
Reed, Sue Titus, 208n.30
Regoli, Robert, 208n.46
Rehnquist, William, 453, 571
Reid, J., 134n.174
Reidinger, Paul, 578n.101
Reinerman, Craig, 181, 208n.29
Reiss, Albert, 171nn.35, 38, 187, 207n.13, 209n.50, 353n.11, 483, 486, 493n.4, 495nn.66, 73
Rendleman, Douglas, 15, 31nn.27, 31, 34
Resig, Michael, 210n.95
Reuter, Peter, 419n.29, 420n.63, 421n.99
Reynolds, Kenneth, 32n.67, 578n.97
Reynolds, Morgan, 129n.13
Rhodes, A. Lewis, 207n.13
Rhodes, Jean, 273n.122
Rhodes, William, 421n.83
Rich, William, 132n.109
Richard, Gelles, 316nn.108, 115
Richards, John G., 647

Riley, David, 129n.11
Ringwalt, Chris, 421n.91
Rivara, Frederick, 387n.72
Rivera, Ramon, 172n.91
Roberson, Connie, 4
Roberson, Robert, 4
Roberts, Albert, 130n.69, 656n.99
Roberts, M., 209n.72
Robey, Ames, 271n.78
Rodick, J. Douglas, 314n.40, 353n.21
Roditi, Bethany, 132n.113
Roehling, P. V., 420n.58
Rogan, Dennis, 43
Rogers, D. E., 83n.128
Rogers, Joseph, 132n.123, 315n.73
Rogers, Willard, 170n.11
Rohsenow, D. J., 419n.11
Roman, Deborah Decker, 134n.190
Romig, Dennis, 610n.29, 611n.64, 631, 654n.49
Roncek, Dennis, 130n.52
Root, Maria, 315n.100
Rosen, Lawrence, 207n.4, 282, 313nn.23, 24
Rosenbaum, Alan, 314n.35
Rosenbaum, Dennis, 415, 421n.91
Rosenbaum, Jill Leslie, 273n.123, 283, 314n.38
Rosenbaum, Milton, 133n.149
Rosenberg, Richard, 134n.201
Rosenfeld, Richard, 157n, 171n.30
Rosenthal, Margueritte, 459n.42, 653n.14
Rosenthal, Robert, 240n.9
Rosenwal, Richard, 271n.78
Rosner, L., 533n.13
Rosner, Richard, 133n.148
Ross, Catherine, 171n.40, 270nn.8, 10
Ross, Robert, 32n.82, 317n.166
Rossi, A. S., 271n.45
Rossi, L., 653n.19
Roszell, Douglass, 134n.192
Rothman, David, 31n.44, 566, 577n.75
Rotten, Johnny, 344
Rouse, Martin, 31nn.54, 58
Roush, David, 533n.19
Rousseau, Voltaire, 13
Rowe, David, 82n.111, 83nn.125, 133, 108–109, 132nn.118, 123, 124, 137, 270n.13, 287, 315n.73
Rubin, Ted, 460n.70, 495n.59, 512, 534n.47, 610n.47
Rudman, Cary, 527, 535n.86, 656n.101
Ruefle, William, 32n.67, 578n.97
Ruppert, Carol, 208n.45

Slawson, John, 121, 134n.198
Small, John, 271n.78
Smart, Carol, 272n.104
Smetena, Judith, 313n.33
Smith, Carolyn, 264, 265, 272n.100, 272n.106, 308, 317n.155
Smith, Charles, 486, 495n.74
Smith, Douglas, 61, 80nn.39, 64, 226, 241n.59, 488, 495nn.68, 72, 496nn.88, 90
Smith, G. T., 420n.58
Smith, Richard, 314nn.44, 48
Smith, Robert, 459n.50
Smith, S., 533n.19
Smyth, Nancy, 316n.110
Snipes, Wesley, 115
Snyder, Eloise, 240n.42
Snyder, Howard, 26, 32n.71, 73, 78n.1, 79n.16, 82n.99, 83nn.119, 140, 141, 207n.5, 270n.21, 459n.46, 494nn.11–12, 496n.84, 532nn.5, 8, 535nn.75, 84, 575n.2, 597, 609nn.6–8, 22, 653nn.24, 25, 654nn.26, 30, 35, 656n.103
Snyder, Phyllis, 32n.64
Soderstrom, Irina, 637, 655n.66
Soler, Mark, 534n.63, 576n.5, 656n.93
Solnit, Albert, 566, 577n.76
Somerville, Dora, 259, 271n.73
Sorenson, Ann Marie, 210n.88, 355n.99
Sorenson-Kirkegaard, L., 134n.201
Sorrells, James, 112, 133n.147, 317n.147
Souter, David, 454
Sparks, Richard, 79n.25
Sparrow, Malcolm, 494n.15
Speck, Richard, 107
Speckart, George, 420n.70
Spergel, Irving, 172n.87, 325, 346, 354nn.25–26, 40, 50, 355nn.79, 85, 97, 356nn.110, 124, 128, 129, 136, 141, 142, 357nn.150, 155, 533n.39
Spielvogel, Jackson, 31nn.24, 25
Spohn, Cassia, 59, 80nn.58, 63, 81n.67
Spracklen, Kathleen, 314n.56, 353n.18, 419n.30
Sprafkin, Joyce, 133n.156
Spraque, John, 129n.39
Spratt, W. J. H., 130n.65
Sprowls, J., 534n.56
Spunt, Barry, 272n.101
Staples, William, 596–597, 610nn.44, 45
Stapleton, W.Vaughan, 355n.73
Stark, Robert, 171n.44

Steele, Brandt F., 315nn.77, 102, 107, 316n.105, 317nn.145, 147
Steele, Patricia, 610n.53
Steele, Ric, 420nn.48, 49
Steffensmeier, Darrell, 272nn.102, 103
Stegink, Lewis, 131n.90
Steinhart, David, 505, 533nn.14, 36
Steinhilber, R.M., 317n.147
Steinmentz, Suzanne, 291, 315n.95
Stephens, Richard, 419n.4
Stern, Susan, 209n.63
Stewart, David, 578n.100
Stinchcombe, Arthur L, 386n.34
Stone, Daryl, 353n.2
Stone, Karen, 316n.110
Stone, Lawrence, 31n.28–29, 31nn. 23, 28
Stouthamer-Loeber, Magda, 72, 83nn.129, 133, 135n.205, 312n.2, 313nn.14, 27, 314n.51, 314n.55, 353n.16
Strachey, James, 133n.140, 270n.33
Strain, Eric, 420n.52
Strasburg, Paul, 495n.63
Straus, Murray, 279, 285, 291–292, 296, 312n.2, 313n.13, 314n.53, 315nn.71, 95, 96, 97, 98, 316n.108, 317n.142
Street, David, 241n.45
Streib, Victor, 482, 495n.61, 570, 578nn.101, 105, 106
Streuning, Elmer, 210n.86
Strodtbeck, Fred, 208n.44, 321, 353n.15
Stumbo, Phyllis, 131n.90
Sue, Camille Chin, 83n.137
Sullivan, Dennis, 235, 241nn.62–63, 71, 242nn.93–94, 575n.2, 609nn.6–8
Sullivan, Mercer, 172n.73, 347, 356n.135
Sung Joon Jang, 209n.63, 210n.107, 211n.108, 353n.19, 386n.15
Sutherland, Edwin, 134n.199, 172n.85, 176, 178–179, 180, 207nn.8, 9, 11–12
Sutherland, Mary, 509, 533n.40
Sutton, John, 31n.39, 459nn.40, 41
Svikis, Dace, 419n.19
Swanger, Harry, 577n.70, 656n.93
Swanger, Henry, 533n.37
Sykes, Gresham, 183, 208nn.37, 40–41, 241nn.61, 68–70
Sykes, Richard, 493n.4
Szymanski, Linda, 494n.25, 555, 577n.53, 578nn.91, 111, 610n.37

Tabor, Mary, 419n.14
Takata, Susan, 333, 355n.74
Tamara, Hareven, 31n.36
Tangri, Sandra, 209n.55–57
Tannenbaum, Frank, 222, 240nn.5, 27–28
Tappan, Paul, 438
Tardiff, Kenneth, 94, 129n.28
Taussig, Cara, 317nn.161, 167
Taylor, Carl, 167, 172n.92, 332, 335, 354n.66, 355n.87
Taylor, William J., 655n.67
Teevan, James, 210n.89
Tellegen, A., 132nn.128, 129
Templer, Donald, 419n.19
Tennenbaum, David, 134n.191
Tennyson, Ray, 172n.91
Terman, L. M., 134n.193
Terry, Edward, 495n.73, 559
Terry, Robert, 353n.17, 486, 495n.63
Thatcher, Robert, 132n.117
Thomas, Charles, 26, 32nn.70, 74, 241n.46
Thomas, Clarence, 453, 454
Thomas, William I., 258, 271nn.63–64
Thome, P. R., 271n.61
Thompson, Carol, 82n.105
Thompson, Kevin, 272n.117, 273n.117, 355n.99
Thornberry, Terence, 80n.61, 82nn.102, 114, 83n.122, 84n.150, 128n.2, 201–202, 207n.2, 208n.17, 209n.63, 210nn.106, 107, 211n.108, 308, 313n.30, 317n.155, 323, 348, 353n.19, 354n.24, 355n.86, 356n.140, 386n.15, 387nn.64, 65, 401, 419n.32, 420n.57, 486, 495n.75
Thrasher, Frederick, 171n.22, 324, 325, 326, 354n.37
Tibbetts, Stephen, 82n.107, 104, 131n.100
Tierney, Nancy J., 575n.2, 609nn.6–8
Tifft, Larry, 79n.36, 235, 241n.71, 242n.93
Titchener, Edward, 115
Tittle, Charles, 61, 207n.14, 210nn.88, 96, 225, 241n.51, 241n.60
Tobias, J. J., 494n.15
Toby, Jackson, 313n.20, 366, 372, 386n.28, 387n.70
Toch, Hans, 133n.144
Tonry, Michael, 31nn.37, 38, 32n.59, 82n.90, 129n.13, 130n.53, 171n.35, 171n.38, 242n.98, 312n.2, 314n.68,

Subject Index

Chronic recidivists, 67
Civilian Conservation Corps, 617
Classical criminology, 89
Cleveland, Ohio, gangs in, 327
Clinical histories on link between
    abuse and delinquency, 306
Cliques, 320
Closed-circuit television (CCTV) in
    child abuse cases, 302, 304
Cobras, 345
Cocaine, 391
Cognitive differences and gender, 247
Cognitive theory, 115
    and information processing, 116–117
    moral and intellectual development
        theory in, 115–116
Cohort studies on link between abuse
    and delinquency, 306–308
Collective gang, 332
College boy, 165
Colorado
    disciplining parents in, 25
    intake process in, 512
    juvenile court operations in, 541
    juvenile sentencing in, 566, 567
    probation system in, 591
    standards of proof for child abuse in,
        299
Columbus, Ohio, gangs in, 327, 332
Commission on Law Enforcement and
    Administration of Justice, 454
Commitment
    in residential community program,
        563
    in securing treatment, 563
    in social control theory, 189
Communications in gangs, 337, 338
Community
    in encouraging corrections, 601
    as factor in controlling school crime,
        377
    social controls in, 152–153
Community-based probation programs,
    599–600
    and recidivism, 605–607
Community change and social ecology,
    150–151
Community influences on school
    crime, 375
Community policing, 464, 491–492
Community services, 563
    in delinquency prevention, 490
    in restitution, 594
Community strategies in drug control,
    415

Community treatment, 441, 582
    criticisms of, 604–607
    nonresidential, 604
    residential, 602–604
Community Treatment Project (CTP)
    of the California Youth Authority,
    606–607
Complaint, 515
Compressed gang, 332
Compulsory school attendance, 380,
    382
Concentric zones, 146
Concurrent jurisdiction, 521, 523
Condemners, condemnation of, 184–
    185
Conditional sanctions, 569
Conditions of probation, 589
Confidentiality in juvenile proceedings,
    572
    open versus closed hearings, 572–
        573
    privacy of records, 573–574
Conflict subculture, 166
Conflict theory
    on delinquency, 231–233
    emerging concepts of, 233
    on juvenile crime, 39–40
    on schools and delinquency, 360
Conformity, 155
Connecticut
    juvenile court operations in, 541,
        542
    juvenile institutions in, 622
    juvenile sentencing in, 567
    standards of proof for child abuse in,
        299
Containment theory, 206
Control theory, 206
    on dropping out, 370
Co-offending, 321
Corner boy, 165
Corporate gang, 332
Correctional training school, 498–499
Correctional treatment for juveniles,
    630–635
Correlates of delinquency, 56
Cottage system, 616–617
Court. See also Adult court; Juvenile
    courts
Court, abused child in, 301–305
Court Appointed Special Advocates
    (CASA) programs, 550
Court-ordered school attendance,
    562
Crack, 391

Crackdown, 98
Crime prevention, situational, 97–98
Crimes
    and the American Dream, 157
    as choice, 122–123
    hate, 39–40
    and human nature, 122–123
    and patriarchy, 266
    prestige, 339
    seductions of, 91–92
    statistics on, 35
    trends in United States, 35–36
Criminal atavism, 99
Criminal behavior, learning, 177–180
Criminal homicide, 36
Criminality
    in family, 286–387
    in gangs, 337–339
Criminal justice versus juvenile justice,
    445
Criminal subculture, 166
Crips, 327, 337, 340, 342
Critical criminologists, 227–228
Cross-sectional data, 47
Crowds, 320
Cultural deviance/subcultural theories,
    144, 161–162
    and delinquency prevention, 167–
        168
    delinquent subculture, 164–165, 169
    development of, 162
    opportunity theory, 165–167, 169
    subcultural theory, 169
    subcultural values today, 163–164
Cultural transmission, 146
Culture conflict, 162, 178
Culture of poverty, 138
Curfew laws, 24, 569
Curriculum, irrelevant, and school fail-
    ure, 369–370
Custodial interrogation, 476, 478–479
Custodial sanctions, 569
Custom and practice, influence on
    children, 12

D

DARE (Drug Abuse Resistance Educa-
    tion), 350, 414–415, 440
Dark figures of crime, 34
Death penalty for juveniles, 28, 95,
    570–572
Decarceration movement, 618
Defense attorney in juvenile court,
    549–553

psychodynamic approach to, 112–113
relationship between delinquency and, 276
role of, in preventing delinquency, 308–311
size of, and discipline, 286
theoretical views on, 277
Family court system, 541
Family criminality, 286–387
Family group homes, 603
Fear and social ecology, 152
Federal Bureau of Investigation (FBI), 34
Federal funding for juvenile justice, 455–457
Female aggression, 257
Female offender, culture of, 628–630
Feminist views
  liberal, 261–265
  Marxist, 233
  radical, 265–267
Fifth Amendment, 523
  and due process, 554–555
Financial restitution, 562–563
Fines, 563
Firearm bans, 570
Florida
  detention in, 501
  intake process in, 512
  juvenile court operations in, 541, 543
  juvenile institutions in, 637, 639
  probation program in, 600
  standards of proof for child abuse in, 299
Florida Environmental Institute, 637
Flying Dragon, 343
Focal concerns, 162
Foot patrol, 492
Forcible rape, 36
Forestry camps, 614, 617
Foster care programs, 602–603
  in preventing delinquency, 311
Foster home placement, 563
Fourteenth Amendment, 506
  and due process, 554–555, 556
Fourth Amendment, 473, 476
Freebase, 391
Free speech, 382–383
Fu Ching, 343
Functional Family Therapy (FFT), 310

G

Gang Alternative Prevention Program (GAPP), 351

Gang delinquency, distinguishing between group delinquency and, 323–324
Gang Resistance Education and Training (GREAT) program, 350
Gangs
  African-American, 340, 342
  age of members, 334–335
  Anglo, 344–345
  Asian, 343
  barrio, 341, 346
  collective, 332
  communications in, 337, 338
  compressed, 332
  controlling activity, 349–352
  corporate, 332
  criminality in, 337–339
  drug-involved, 339, 408–409
  ethnic composition of, 339–340, 342–345
  extent of problem, 329–330
  formation of, 335–336
  gender of members, 335
  guns in, 42, 328
  Hispanic, 342–343
  influence of, on juvenile crime, 41
  international, 323
  and juvenile crime, 91
  leadership of, 336–337
  location of, 332–333
  migration of activity in, 333–334
  neotraditional, 332
  in 1950s and 1960s, 326–327
  organized, 331, 332
  party, 330
  racial composition of, 339–340, 342–345
  and rational choice theory, 90
  reasons for increased activity in, 328
  reasons for joining, 345–348
  scavenger, 332
  serious delinquent, 330
  social, 330
  specialty, 332
  study of, 326–328
  subcultures in, 166
  traditional, 332
  types of, 330–332
  violence in, 339
Gender
  changing concepts of, 246
  and delinquency, 56–57, 249–250
  and development of childhood, 11–12
  differences in development

    cognitive, 247
    personality, 247–248
    reasons for, 248–249
    socialization, 247
  and discrimination, 246
  of gang members, 335
  impact of bias on police discretion, 487–488
  as issue in general strain theory, 161
  in juvenile justice system, 267–268
Gender-schema theory, 248
General deterrence, 95
General strain theory, 158–159, 169
  evaluating, 160–161
General theory of crime, 193–194, 206
  self-control in, 194–196
  testing, 196
Genetic factors in drug use, 402–403
Genetic influences, on juvenile delinquency, 107–108
Gentrification, 150
Georgia
  juvenile court operations in, 541
  juvenile institutions in, 639
  juvenile sentencing in, 567
  standards of proof for child abuse in, 299
Germany, juvenile delinquency in, 8
Gestalt psychology, 115
Ghost Shadows, 343
Graduated sanction programs, 564, 607
Graffiti, 337, 338
Green Dragon, 343
Group autonomy, 165
Group delinquency, distinguishing between gang delinquency and, 323–324
Group homes, 602, 614–615
Group therapy, 632–633
Guardian ad litem, 297, 550
Guided group interaction, 632–633
Guilty, pleading in juvenile court, 520
Gun-Free School Zones Act (1990), 570, 571
Guns
  in gangs, 42, 328
  influence of, on juvenile crime, 40–41, 42–43

H

Halfway houses, 614–615
Hallucinogens, 394
Hard drugs, 395
Hashish, 390–391

Hate, influence of, on juvenile crime, 39–40
Hate crimes, 39–40
Hawaii
    Healthy Start program in, 309, 310
    juvenile court operations in, 541
    standards of proof for child abuse in, 299
Head Start, 204, 454
Hearing
    adjudicatory, 443, 557, 558
    detention, 443, 502–503
    dispositional, 560
Hearsay, 302
Heroin, 391–392, 395
Hidden system of juvenile control, 624
Highlands Project, 603
Hispanic gangs, 342–343
Hispanic juveniles, 624–625
Hollowed out, 138
Home detention, 562
Honolulu, Hawaii
    gangs in, 340
    juvenile justice system in, 267
Hopelessness and social ecology, 153
Hormonal influences in antisocial behavior, 255–256
Hormone levels, in biochemical research, 103–104
Hot spots, targeting, 97–98
House arrest, 591
Household survey on drug use, 397–399
House of Refuge, 428
Houston, Texas, gangs in, 343
Human nature, and crime, 122–123

I

Id, 110, 111, 112
Idaho
    juvenile institutions in, 622
    standards of proof for child abuse in, 299
Identity crisis, 112
Illicit drug trade and youth violence, 406–407
Illinois
    establishment of juvenile court in, 433–437
    juvenile court operations in, 541
    juvenile institutions in, 635
    standards of proof for child abuse in, 299
Illinois Juvenile Court Act (1899), 435

Impulsive personalities, 194
Inconsistent supervision and delinquency, 285–286
In-court statements in child abuse cases, 304–305
Independent juvenile court systems, 541–542
Indeterminate sentence, 566–567
Index crime, 35
Indiana
    electronic monitoring program in, 591
    juvenile sentencing in, 570
Individual counseling, 630–631
Individualized treatment model, 566
Informal consent decree, 562
Informational processing, 116–117
Inhalants, 393
Injury, denial of, 184
In loco parentis, 478
    and school discipline, 383
Inner-city neighborhoods, 138
Innovation, 156
Institute for Social Research (ISR), 62
    survey on substance abuse, 396
    surveys conducted by, 48–49
Institute of Judicial Administration–American Bar Association on institution standards, 645
Intake process, 510–511
    changes in, 511–512
    screening in, 441–443
Integrated theories, 175, 199–201, 206
Intelligence, and delinquency, 120–122
Intensive Aftercare Model (IAP), 650
Interactional theory, 201–202, 206
    testing in, 202
International Association of Chiefs of Police, 471
International delinquency, 8
Interrogation, custodial, 476, 478–479
Interstitial group, 324
Intrafamily conflict, 283
Involvement in social control theory, 189
Iowa, standards of proof for child abuse in, 299

J

Jaguars, 345
Job Corps and the Comprehensive Employment Training Act, 204
Joe Boys, 343
Jointure, 12

Judge in juvenile court, 547–548
    selection and qualifications of, 548–549
Judicial waiver, 521
Justice
    criminal versus juvenile, 445
    discretionary, 480–486
Juvenile aftercare, 646–649
    revocation procedures in, 651
    supervision in, 649–650
Juvenile boot camp program, 637, 639, 640
Juvenile corrections, 441
    categories of, 614–615
    educational programs in, 633–634
    placement matrix, 615
    recreational activity in, 635
    trends in, 621–622
    twentieth-century developments in structure of, 617–618
    vocational training in, 634
Juvenile courts, 441
    defense attorney in, 549–553
    establishment of, in Illinois, 433–437
    judge in, 547–548
        selection and qualifications of, 548–549
    jurisdiction of, 542
        age, 542
        nature of offense
            delinquency, 543–544
            status offenders, 544
    magnitude of cases handled by, 538, 539, 540
    operations of, 540–542
    pleading guilty in, 520
    prosecutor in, 441, 544–545
        complex role of, 546–547
        legal duties of, 545–546
    public defender in, 441
    strategic role played by, 538
    types of dispositions in, 562–564
Juvenile crime
    factors influencing rates, 39–41, 44–45
    role of police in handling violent, 467–469
    trends in, 38–39
Juvenile delinquency
    and academic performance, 364–365
    and age, 62–65
    causes of, 164
    and child abuse and neglect, 305–311

Miltown, 394

Milwaukee, gangs in, 327, 334–335

Minnesota
jailing of juveniles in, 507
juvenile court operations in, 542
juvenile institutions in, 622
juvenile sentencing in, 567, 570
restitution program in, 595

Minnesota Multiphasic Personality Inventory (MMPI), 119

Mission hate crime, 40

Mississippi
juvenile institutions in, 639
standards of proof for child abuse in, 299

Missouri
juvenile institutions in, 624
juvenile sentencing in, 566
standards of proof for child abuse in, 299

Missouri Plan, 548

Mobilization for Youth, 351

Monetary restitution, 594

"Monitoring the Future" Survey, 48

Montana
juvenile institutions in, 624
juvenile sentencing in, 566
standards of proof for child abuse in, 299

Montrose Juvenile Training School, 600

Moral and intellectual development theory, 115–116

Moral entrepreneurs, 217–218

Motor vehicle theft, 36

Multifactor/integrated theories, 175, 193

Multisystemic treatment in drug control, 415

N

National Advisory Commission on Criminal Justice Standards and Goals, 23, 456, 561

National Association of Gang Activity, 329

National Center for Juvenile Justice, 268

National Coalition of State Juvenile Justice Advisory Groups, 486–487

National Commission on Excellence in Education, 377

National Committee to Prevent Child Abuse (NCPCA), 293–294

National Conference of Commissioners on Uniform State Laws, 472
Uniform Juvenile Court Act of, 472–473, 565

National Conference on Children and Youth, 454

National Council of Juvenile and Family Court Judges, 521, 548, 599

National Council on Crime and Delinquency (NCCD), 23, 502, 599

National Crime Victimization Survey (NCVS), 35, 51, 52, 62

National District Attorneys Association, *Prosecution Standards* issued by, 546–547

National Education Goals Panel, 362–363

National Juvenile Justice Standards Project, 24

National Youth Survey (NYS), 401

A Nation at Risk, 377

Natural areas for crime, 145

Near groups, 324–325

Nebraska
juvenile institutions in, 624
standards of proof for child abuse in, 299

Negative affective states, 159

Neglect, family, 284–286

Neighborhood gangs, 324–325, 341, 346

Neighborhoods, transitional, 146

Neighborhood Youth Corps, 454

Neotraditional gang, 332

Neurological dysfunction, 104–105

Neuroses, in psychodynamic theory, 111

Neuroticism, 118

Neutralization theory, 206
analysis of, 186
elements of, 183–184
techniques of, 184–185
testing, 185–186

Nevada, standards of proof for child abuse in, 299

New Hampshire
child testimony in, 302
disciplining parents in, 25
standards of proof for child abuse in, 299

New Jersey
community treatment program in, 604
juvenile sentencing in, 566
standards of proof for child abuse in, 299

New York City
child saver movement in, 17
gang control efforts in, 351
gangs in, 327, 332, 333, 340, 343
homeless children in, 6
school crime reduction program in, 376

New York City-based Mobilization for Youth (MOBY), 168

New York House of Refuge, 616

New York State
child saver movement in, 428, 432
juvenile court operations in, 541, 551
juvenile institutions in, 621, 622
standards of proof for child abuse in, 299

New York State Agricultural and Industrial School, 616

Nominal sanctions, 569

Nonresidential community treatment, 604

Nonsecure institutions, 614

Normlessness, 154–155

North American Family Institute, 614

North Carolina
electronic monitoring program in, 591
juvenile court operations in, 542
restitution program in, 595
standards of proof for child abuse in, 299

North Dakota
juvenile institutions in, 624
juvenile sentencing in, 566, 570
standards of proof for child abuse in, 299

Nuclear family, 276

Nurture theory, 120–121

O

Office of Juvenile Justice and Delinquency Prevention (OJJDP), 23, 236, 487, 505, 507

Official data
in measuring delinquency, 34
problems of, 46

Official delinquency, 34

Official statistics, 35

Ohio
child saver movement in, 428, 432
detention in, 501
juvenile sentencing in, 566
probation system in, 591

standards of proof for child abuse in, 299

Oklahoma
  juvenile institutions in, 622
  probation program in, 600
  restitution program in, 595
  standards of proof for child abuse in, 299

Omnibus Crime Control and Safe Streets Act, 454, 456

Opportunity and wealth, 151–152

Opportunity theory, 165–167, 169
  analyzing, 166–167

Oregon
  juvenile sentencing in, 570
  probation program in, 600
  standards of proof for child abuse in, 299

Oregon Social Learning Center (OSLC), 309–310

Organizational bias, impact of, on police discretion, 488–489

Organized gang, 331, 332

Out-of-court statements in child abuse cases, 303–304

Outpatient psychotherapy, 563

Outward Bound programs, 637

Overcrowding in juvenile correction institutions, 622

P

Pacatal, 394

Paint Creek Youth Center (PCYC), 614

Parens patriae
  and chancery court, 14–15
  and choice theory, 89
  and confidentiality in juvenile proceedings, 573
  and delinquency, 18
  description of, 282, 461
  and due process rights, 555
  and general deterrence, 95
  and intake process, 511
  and juvenile justice system, 426
  and juvenile prosecution, 546
  legal challenges to, 429, 430, 433
  and legal responsibility of youth, 19
  and status offenders, 19

Parental deviance, 286

Parental responsibility statutes, 569

Parent(s). *See also* Families
  child's attachment to one, 25

disciplining, 25

Parents Resource Institute for Drug Abuse (PRIDE), 396, 397

Parent-to-child violence, 279

Parole guidelines, 646–647

Part I offenses, 35, 36

Part II offenses, 35, 37–38

Party gang, 330

Paternalistic family, 11, 276

Pathways, 71

Patriarchy, 231
  and crime, 266

PCP (phencyclidine), 393, 395

Peacemaking, 235

Peer relations
  and delinquency, 321
  and drug use, 401–402
  impact of, 321–322
  and socialization, 320–321

Penis envy, 252

Pennsylvania
  juvenile institutions in, 622
  juvenile sentencing in, 566, 567
  probation program in, 600
  standards of proof for child abuse in, 299

Perry Preschool in Michigan, 309

Persistence, of juvenile delinquency, 10

Persistent offenders and drug use, 409–410

Personality
  and delinquency, 117–118
  link to delinquency, 119–120

Personality differences and gender, 247–248

Petition, 515–516

Phencyclidine (PCP), 393, 395

Philadelphia, gangs in, 340

Physical neglect, 290

Pimps, 293

Pittsburgh Youth Study, 71

Plea, 518–520

Plea bargaining, 518–520

Police. *See also* Law enforcement
  arrest procedures of, 472–473
  role of
    in delinquency prevention, 490
    in handling juvenile offenders, 465–467
    in handling violent juvenile crime, 467–469
    in search and seizure procedures, 473–474
      custodial interrogation, 476, 478–479

in schools, 474–476
services for juveniles, 470–471
work with juveniles
  discretionary justice, 480–486
  history of, 469–470

Police discretion
  environmental factors affecting, 483–485
  impact of bias on, 486–490
  limiting, 489–490
  situational factors affecting, 485

Police investigation in juvenile justice, 440–441

Police juvenile lineups, 479–480

Policing, community, 464, 491–492

Political stratification, 138

Poor Laws, 14, 15, 469

Portrayed female, 335

Positive Peer Culture, 633

Positivism, 99

Postdisposition, in juvenile justice, 444–445

Poverty
  child, 140
  delinquency as cause of, 151
  and race, 140–141
  and social stratification, 138, 140
  statistics on, 5–6

Power-control theory, 266–267

Power elite, 227

Powerlessness, 291
  association with abuse, 291

Preadjudication detention, 501–502

Precocious sexuality, 254–255

Predisposition investigation, 560

Predisposition report, 440, 560–561

Preemptive deterrence, 234

Pregnancy, 252

Premenstrual syndrome, 256

President's Commission on Law Enforcement and Administration of Justice, 236, 455

Prestige crimes, 339

Prestige stratification, 138

Pretrial conference, 299

Pretrial procedures in juvenile justice, 443

Pretrial services, 440

Prevention in juvenile justice, 446

Preventive detention, 517–518

Primary deviance, 219–220

Primary sociopaths, 119

Primogeniture, 12

Privacy of juvenile records, 573–574

Ventura School for Female Juvenile Offenders, 634
Vermont
    disciplining parents in, 25
    juvenile institutions in, 614
    probation program in, 600
    standards of proof for child abuse in, 299
Vice Lords, 326, 327
Victim data in measuring delinquency, 34–35
Victimization, 52
    data on, 51–55
Victims
    denial of, 184
    services for, 594
Victims of Child Abuse Act (1990), 302
Videotaped testimony in child abuse cases, 302
Violence
    gang, 339
    and gender, 250
Violent Crime Control and Law Enforcement Act (1994), 440, 455, 456–457
Violent Juvenile Offender (VJO) program, 636–637
Violent juveniles
    controlling, 449–450
    treating, 635–636

Virginia
    juvenile institutions in, 619
    juvenile sentencing in, 566, 567
    standards of proof for child abuse in, 299
VisionQuest, 638
Vocational training in juvenile correctional institutions, 634
Volunteers in assisting probation officers, 591

W

Waiver, 19, 520
    debating concept of, 527–529
Washington State
    intake process in, 512
    juvenile sentencing in, 567
    standards of proof for child abuse in, 299
Wayne County Intensive Probation (IPP), 592
Wayward minors, 20
Wealth and opportunity, 151–152
West Virginia
    juvenile sentencing in, 566, 570
    probation program in, 600
    standards of proof for child abuse in, 299
Wet nurses, 12

White House Conference on Juvenile Justice, 455
Whiter Aryan Resistance, 40
Wickersham Commission (1931), 469
Widening the net, 28, 237, 513–515, 597
Wilderness probation, 593
Wilderness programs in juvenile rehabilitation strategies, 638
Wisconsin
    juvenile court operations in, 541
    Project Bootstrap in, 204, 205
    standards of proof for child abuse in, 299
Writ of certiorari, 565
Writ of habeas corpus, 565
Wyoming
    juvenile court operations in, 542
    juvenile sentencing in, 566
    standards of proof for child abuse in, 299

Y

Youth at Risk (YAR) program, 238
Youth Development and Delinquency Prevention Administration, 456
Youth gangs, 323–324. See also Gangs
Youths. See Adolescents; Children; Juveniles